Proceedings

25th International Conference on Software Engineering

ICSE 2003

Proceedings

25th International Conference on Software Engineering

ICSE 2003

3–10 May 2003

Portland, Oregon USA

acm

IEEE COMPUTER SOCIETY

IEEE

Los Alamitos, California

Washington • Brussels • Tokyo

IEEE Computer Society Order Number PR01877
ACM Order Number 592030
ISBN 0-7695-1877-X
ISSN 0270-5257

Additional copies may be ordered from:

IEEE Computer Society
Customer Service Center
10662 Los Vaqueros Circle
P.O. Box 3014
Los Alamitos, CA 90720-1314
Tel: + 1-714-821-8380
Fax: + 1-714-821-4641
E-mail: cs.books@computer.org

IEEE Service Center
445 Hoes Lane
P.O. Box 1331
Piscataway, NJ 08855-1331
Tel: + 1-732-981-0060
Fax: + 1-732-981-9667
http://shop.ieee.org/store/
customer-service@ieee.org

IEEE Computer Society
Asia/Pacific Office
Watanabe Bldg., 1-4-2
Minami-Aoyama
Minato-ku, Tokyo 107-0062
JAPAN
Tel: + 81-3-3408-3118
Fax: + 81-3-3408-3553
tokyo.ofc@computer.org

ACM Order Department, P.O. Box 11414, New York, NY 10286-1405
Tel: +1-800-342-6626 (USA and Canada); Tel: +1-212-626-0500 (All other countries); Fax: +1-212-944-1318; acmhelp@acm.org

Editorial production by Anne Jacobs and Frances Titsworth

Cover art production by Joe Daigle/Studio Productions

Printed in the United States of America by Victor Graphics

IEEE COMPUTER SOCIETY

IEEE

ICSE 2003
Table of Contents

Technical Papers

Component Technologies

Testing I

Empirical Studies I

Design Recovery and Documentation

Formal Methods I

Software Design

Testing II

Software Process

Undergraduate Education

Course Delivery and Evaluation

Process and Methodology

Invited Keynote Papers

Invited Paper from the Awardees of the Most Influential Paper from ICSE'15

Invited Papers on the Frontiers of Software Practice

Panel Overviews

Mini-Tutorial

One and Two-day Tutorials

Workshop Overviews

Research Demonstration Summaries

Message from the Chairs

Welcome to the silver anniversary of the International Conference on Software Engineering! Managing the complexity of modern software systems is without question a grand challenge. It is therefore fitting that, inspired by the view of Mount Hood in Portland, Oregon, the theme for this year's meeting is: Scaling New Heights.

ICSE, the premier conference for software engineering, brings together world leaders in software engineering research, practice, and education to present and discuss the most recent advances, trends, and concerns in this ever expanding and critical field. This year's Software Engineering Week, May 3 to 10, 2003, consists of the main ICSE conference and an interesting array of tutorials, workshops, and related events associated or co-located with ICSE.

Keynote talks

Each morning, the ICSE 2003 conference starts with a topical keynote address by an outstanding speaker. On the first morning of the conference, Bertrand Meyer, of ETH Zurich and ISE Santa Barbara, addresses problems of building trusted software components in his keynote, "The Grand Challenge of Trusted Components." Then, on Wednesday, Joanne McGrath Cohoon, an expert on higher education, gender, and technology from the University of Virginia, discusses the declining participation of women in undergraduate and graduate computing and how universities can act to reverse this trend. Finally, Eugene Spafford, of Purdue University, delivers the keynote on Thursday. His very timely talk considers connections between software engineering and information security, illustrating how many of the approaches in information security have a basis in software engineering.

Technical Track

The core of the ICSE program is the set of technical papers, which represent recent and significant advances in software engineering research from contributors around the world. Forty-two technical papers were carefully selected by the program committee from a record number of 324 submissions. The number of technical submissions to ICSE has been steadily rising over the past few years, from 268 in 2001 to 302 in 2003, to the current high. All technical submissions were reviewed by at least three reviewers on the program committee. Expert external reviewers provided extra reviews on many papers. Over 970 reviews were prepared, a heavy burden given that reviews provide constructive criticism to authors of all submissions, whether selected or not. The result is an impressive technical program. Thank you, PC members! Sessions in the technical track are labeled with a "T" in the program.

Experience Track

ICSE has a long tradition of engaging both practitioners and researchers in meaningful dialogue and in the exchange of ideas. The experience report track at ICSE 2003 provides one avenue for facilitating this dialogue. This track includes both traditional experience reports and case studies. This year the community produced a record number of 61 submissions for this track. Of these, 16 were selected for presentation. Sessions in this track are labeled with an "X" in the program.

Education Track

Software engineering education and training can significantly improve the current state of software development and improve industrial practices. The education track at ICSE 2003 provides an international forum for discussing topics related to software engineering education and training, such as curriculum development, innovative methods of course delivery, training programs, collaborative projects with industry, SWEBOK topics, and new software engineering programs. Fifty-two submissions were received for this track, of which 11 were accepted. Sessions in this track are labeled with an "E" in the program.

Awards

Each year at ICSE, the software engineering community honors a few of its members for their significant research and service contributions. This year, ICSE is the forum for the presentation of the SIGSOFT Distinguished Service and Outstanding Research Awards, the IEEE Computer Society Harlan D. Mills award, the newly selected IEEE Fellows, and the Recognition Award from the Journal of Systems and Software.

We also honor the authors of the paper judged to be the Most Influential Paper of ICSE'15 with an award and an invitation to discuss the evolution of this work over the course of the last decade. Unlike typical best paper awards, the program committee evaluates the papers that were accepted in the ICSE ten years previously and honors the authors of the paper that they feel had the most influence on the community. From the perspective of a decade of ensuing research and practice, the program committee revisits the contributions from this previous ICSE. This year the award is being presented to Bashar Nuseibeh, Jeff Kramer, and Anthony Finkelstein for their seminal work on viewpoints.

Frontiers of Software Practice (FoSP)

FoSP talks are invited mini-tutorials that provide an overview of a topic at the frontier of software practice. The FoSP topics were selected based on their interest to a wide range of participants. This year the following speakers give an overview of three frontier topics that software researchers and practitioners grapple with on a daily basis: Clemens Szyperski of Microsoft Corporation, informs us of the state-of-the-art in component technology; Douglas Schmidt of Vanderbilt University and DARPA, discusses patterns, frameworks, and middleware; and Richard Kemmerer of University of California, Santa Barbara, presents the current best practices in CyberSecurity.

Panels and Mini-tutorial

Other highlights of ICSE 2003 include several panels and a special mini tutorial for software engineering researchers. The first panel, "Automotive Software Engineering," is part of a session dedicated to this topic in the experience report track. Leading experts on automotive software development from carmakers, suppliers, and research organizations in the US and Europe will discuss trends and demands for technologies, methods, and tools to develop and integrate software-based car functions. Another timely panel, "Empirical Evaluation: What, Why, When, and How," will encourage a lively debate on methodologies for validating software engineering research. As part of the education track, the third panel, "Undergraduate Software Engineering Degree: Pros and Cons," will debate whether software engineering should be taught as a separate undergraduate program or as part of the undergraduate computer science program. "Modularity in the New Millennium" rounds out the ICSE panels by discussing new and emerging approaches to modularity and separation of concerns. Finally, a special mini-tutorial by Mary Shaw of Carnegie Mellon University will be of particular interest to students and researchers at ICSE as it presents the hallmarks of a good software engineering research paper.

Demonstrations and Posters

Throughout Tuesday, demonstrations will be given of recent research prototypes. During the reception on Wednesday evening, there will be demonstrations as well as poster presentations. Attendees are encouraged to view these presentations and to engage in conversations with the presenters.

Tutorials

Prior to the main ICSE 2003 program, there are 17 tutorials. Topics cover a range of software engineering issues and are presented by recognized leaders in the field. The tutorials were selected from 80 tutorial proposals.

ICSE Workshops

ICSE 2003 is hosting 14 workshops. These workshops provide a small, interactive forum for researchers and practitioners to discuss important and focused topics. Among the workshops are several established workshops (e.g. SELMAS'03, EDSER5, CBSE-6, WOSS'03, STRAW'03) as well as many first- and one-time workshops that focus on a variety of promising techniques and crucial issues in software engineering. These workshops were selected from 30 workshop proposals.

Co-located Workshops and Special Events

This week also includes three special events: the Pioneers Symposium, the New Software Engineering Faculty Symposium, and the Doctoral Symposium. The Pioneers Symposium will bring together early leaders in software engineering to describe their current perspectives on the field. The Doctoral Symposium and New Software Engineering Faculty Symposium are becoming fixtures of ICSE week. In these events, senior and mid-level faculty members volunteer their time to provide guidance and support to graduate students and new faculty members.

This year there are five co-located workshops, the Workshop on Software Configuration Management (SCM-11), the International SPIN Workshop on Model Checking of Software (SPIN 2003), the Workshop on Software Process Simulation Modeling (ProSim 2003), the International Workshop on Program Comprehension (IWPC 2003), and the Summit on Software Engineering Education, happening either before or after the main ICSE program. Finally, this year ICSE is also offering an evening cooperative learning experience on Managing Commitments and Risks: Challenges in Agile Development.

Acknowledgements

Many people devoted a considerable amount of time, energy, and hard work to help organize a program of this magnitude. We would like to thank everyone who served on the organizing committee. Special thanks are in order for Margaret Burnett who did an excellent job on publicity, Gregg Rothermel who kept the web pages up-to-date, and Jo Atlee and Stefan Leue who oversaw the ICSE workshops and co-located events. We thank the program committee members for preparing high quality reviews, doing so on time, and devoting two long days to the program committee meeting. We also thank Holger Hopp (University of Karlsruhe) and Richard van de Stadt (Borbala Conference Services), who kept the submission and reviewing server operating smoothly (and even recovered from a fire), and Mary Kate Rada and Kristine Weiand, from IEEE conference services, and Anne Jacobs and Frances Titsworth, from IEEE publishing, who provided valuable support.

Lori A. Clarke
General Chair

Laurie Dillon
Program Co-Chair

Walter Tichy
Program Chair

Conference Organization

Organizing Committee

General Chair

Lori Clarke
University of Massachusetts, USA
clarke@cs.umass.edu

Program Co-Chairs

Laurie Dillon
Michigan State University, USA
ldillon@cse.msu.edu

Walter Tichy
University of Karlsruhe, Germany
tichy@ira.uka.de

Doctoral Symposium

Dick Hamlet
Portland State University, USA
hamlet@cs.pdx.edu

Mary Lou Soffa
University of Pittsburgh, USA
soffa@cs.pitt.edu

Software Engineering Education and Training

Hossein Saiedian
University of Kansas, USA
saiedian@eecs.ukans.edu

Bruce Weide
The Ohio State University, USA
weide@cis.ohio-state.edu

Experience Reports

Martin Glinz
University of Zurich, Switzerland
glinz@ifi.unizh.ch

Judith A. Stafford
Tufts University, USA
jas@cs.tufts.edu

Research Demonstrations and Posters

Mauro Pezze
Universita' di Milano-Bicocca, Italy
pezze@disco.unimib.it

Bruce Schafer
Oregon University System, USA
schaferb@capital.ous.edu

"Most Influential Paper" Award

Dewayne Perry
University of Texas at Austin, USA
perry@ece.utexas.edu

Treasurer

Phyllis Frankl
Polytechnic University, USA
phyllis@morph.poly.edu

Local Arrangements

Robert Bauer
Rational
rbauer@rational.com

David Garlan
Carnegie Mellon University, USA
garlan@cs.cmu.edu

Tutorials

Dick Fairley
Oregon Graduate Institute of
Science & Technology, USA
dfairley@cse.ogi.edu

Frances Paulisch
Siemens AG, Germany
frances.paulisch@mchp.siemens.de

Newsletter

Hal Hart
TRW, USA
hal.hart@acm.org

Webmaster

Gregg Rothermel
Oregon State University, USA
grother@cs.orst.edu

Frontiers of Software Practice

Betty H.C. Cheng
Michigan State University, USA
chengb@cse.msu.edu

Student Volunteers

David M. Raffo
Portland State University, USA
davidr@sba.pdx.edu

Publicity

Margaret Burnett
Oregon State University, USA
burnett@cs.orst.edu

Panels

Dewayne Perry
University of Texas at Austin, USA
perry@ece.utexas.edu

Workshops & Events

Joanne Atlee
University of Waterloo, Canada
jmatlee@se.uwaterloo.ca

Stefan Leue
Albert-Ludwigs-University Freiburg, Germany
leue@uni-freiburg.de

Industrial Liaisons

James Hook
Oregon Graduate Institute of
Science & Technology, USA
hook@cse.ogi.edu

Vicki Wagers
Oregon Master of Software
Engineering Program
wagersv@omse.org

Program Committee

Program Co-Chairs

Laurie Dillon
Michigan State University, USA
ldillon@cse.msu.edu

Walter Tichy
University of Karlsruhe, Germany
tichy@ira.uka.de

Committee Members

Annie I. Antón
North Carolina State University, USA
aianton@eos.ncsu.edu

George Avrunin
University of Massachusetts at Amherst, USA
avrunin@math.umass.edu

Don Batory
University of Texas at Austin, USA
batory@cs.utexas.edu

Antonia Bertolino
IEI-CNR, Italy
bertolino@iei.pi.cnr.it

Paul C. Clements
CMU Software Engineering Institute, USA
clements@sei.cmu.edu

Prem Devanbu
University of California at Davis, USA
devanbu@cs.ucdavis.edu

Matthew Dwyer
Kansas State University, USA
dwyer@cis.ksu.edu

Steve Easterbrook
University of Toronto, Canada
sme@cs.toronto.edu

Wolfgang Emmerich
University College London, UK
we@acm.org

Jacky Estublier
Grenoble University, France
jacky@imag.fr

Peter H. Feiler
CMU Software Engineering Institute, USA
phf@sei.cmu.edu

Anthony Finkelstein
University College London, UK
a.finkelstein@cs.ucl.ac.uk

Patrice Godefroid
Bell Laboratories, USA
god@bell-labs.com

Mats Heimdahl
University of Minnesota, USA
heimdahl@cs.umn.edu

James D. Herbsleb
Carnegie Mellon University, USA
jherbsleb@acm.org

Ross Jeffery
University of New South Wales, Australia
rossj@cse.unsw.edu.au

Somesh Jha
University of Wisconsin, USA
jha@cs.wisc.edu

Gail Kaiser
Columbia University, USA
kaiser@cs.columbia.edu

Rudolf K. Keller
Zuhlke Engineering AG, Switzerland
keller@iro.umontreal.ca

Richard A. Kemmerer
University of California at Santa Barbara, USA
kemm@cs.ucsb.edu

James Larus
Microsoft Research, USA
larus@microsoft.com

Hausi A. Muller
University of Victoria, Canada
hausi@csr.uvic.ca

Paolo Nesi
University of Florence, Italy
nesi@ingfi1.ing.unifi.it

Adam Porter
University of Maryland, USA
aporter@cs.umd.edu

Alexander Ran
Nokia, USA
alexander.ran@nokia.com

Dieter Rombach
University of Kaiserslautern, Germany
rombach@informatik.uni-kl.de

Barbara G. Ryder
Rutgers University, USA
ryder@cs.rutgers.edu

Kurt Stirewalt
Michigan State University, USA
stire@cse.msu.edu

Tetsuo Tamai
University of Tokyo, Japan
tamai@graco.c.u-tokyo.ac.jp

Frank Tip
IBM T. J. Watson Research Center, USA
tip@watson.ibm.com

Michal Young
University of Oregon, USA
michal@cs.uoregon.edu

Yves Ledru
LSR/IMAG, France
yves.ledru@imag.fr

Gail Murphy
University of British Columbia, Canada
murphy@cs.ubc.ca

Lee J. Osterweil
University of Massachusetts at Amherst, USA
ljo@cs.umass.edu

Lutz Prechelt
abaXX Technology AG, Germany
prechelt@computer.org

Gruia-Catalin Roman
Washington University in St. Louis, USA
roman@cs.wustl.edu

David Rosenblum
University of California at Irvine
and PreCache Inc., USA
drosenblum@precache.com

Gregor Snelting
University of Passau, Germany
snelting@fmi.uni-passau.de

Karsten Schwan
Georgia Institute of Technology, USA
schwan@cc.gatech.edu

Peri Tarr
IBM T. J. Watson Research Center, USA
tarr@us.ibm.com

Axel van Lamsweerde
University of Louvain, Belgium
avl@info.ucl.ac.be

Pamela Zave
AT&T Laboratories Research, USA
pamela@research.att.com

External Reviewers

Thomas A. Alspaugh
Glenn Ammons
Elisa Baniassad
Pierfrancesco Bellini
Michael Benedikt
Jim Benham
Pierre Berlioux
Rastislav Bodik
Robert Bowdidge
Ivan Bruno
Glenn Bruns
Licia Capra
Fu Chen
Yuan Chen
Yunja Choi
Marcus Ciolkowski
Agnès Conte
Davor Cubranic
Pete Danielsen
Benet Devereux
Jurgen Dingel
Greg Eisenhauer
Alessandro Fantechi
Raimund Feldmann
Bernd Freimut
Chen Fu
Ada Gavrilovska
Andrea Giotti
Jean-Francois Girard
Stefania Gnesi
Hans-Gerhard Gross
Roland Groz
William Harrison
Klaus Havelund
Qingfeng He
Jens Heidrich
Chung-hsing Hsu
Daniel Jackson
Stoney Jackson
Sarfraz Khurshid
Kirstin Kohler
Wenqian Liu
Eda Marchetti
Thomas J. Marlowe
Ana Milanova
Nick Mitchell
Juergen Muench
Dirk Muthig
Catherine Oriat
Harold Ossher
Dewayne Perry
Andrea Polini
Sriram K. Rajamani
Sanjai Rayadurgam
Xiaoxia Ren
Martin Robillard
David A. Robinson
Davide Rogai
Rémy Sanlaville
Klaus Schmid
Balasubramanian Seshasayee
Gary Sevitsky
Stephen Siegel
James Skene
Margaret Smith
Marius Bogdan Spinu
John Staudenmayer
Stanley M. Sutton, Jr.
Stefan Tai
Jeffrey M. Thompson
Mike W. Whalen
Patrick Widener
Eric Wohlstadter
Dave Wonnacott
Annie T. T. Ying
Stefanos Zachariadis
Fancong Zeng
Tao Zhang
Dong Zhou

ICSE 2003 Sponsors, Supporters, and Corporate Donors

Sponsoring and Supporting Organizations

IEEE

IEEE Computer Society
Technical Council on
Software Engineering

ACM

ACM SIGSOFT

Corporate Donors

PLATINUM Level

IBM Corporation
IBM Research Division

NORTHROP GRUMMAN
Space Technology

GOLD Level

BMW

NOKIA
CONNECTING PEOPLE

Sun microsystems

BRONZE Level

DAIMLERCHRYSLER

Microsoft Research

Technical Papers

Component Technologies

Pluggable Reflection: Decoupling Meta-Interface and Implementation

David H. Lorenz*
Northeastern University
College of Computer & Information Science
Boston, MA 02115, USA
lorenz@ccs.neu.edu

John Vlissides
IBM T.J. Watson Research Center
P.O. Box 704,
Yorktown Heights, NY 10598, USA
vlis@us.ibm.com

Abstract

Reflection remains a second-class citizen in current programming models, where it's assumed to be imperative and tightly bound to its implementation. In contrast, most object-oriented APIs allow interfaces to vary independently of their implementations. Components take this separation a step further by describing unforeseeable attributes—the key to pluggable third-party components. This paper describes how reflection can benefit from a similar evolutionary path.

1. Introduction

A reflective computation [30, 31, 23] is one that has an accurate representation of itself, and the computation is consistent with its representation. A change to the computation appears in the representation and vice versa. Many object-oriented languages (OOLs) provide a mechanism—*reflection*—that supports reflective computation explicitly. Reflection is a versatile tool, applicable at run-time, compile-time, load-time, and during component assembly.

A tenet of software development in general and object-oriented design in particular is to program to an interface. Doing so allows client and implementation to evolve separately, thereby facilitating code evolution, portability, and testability. Maintaining several native implementations for the same interface also promotes portability, much as multiple back-ends do for a compiler. Swappable implementations can even simplify prototyping and testing, say, by providing a choice of instrumented, optimized, and stubbed out implementations.

Unfortunately, no mainstream OOL extends the benefits of programming to an interface to its reflection facilities.

*Supported in part by the National Science Foundation (NSF) under Grants No. CCR-0098643 and CCR-0204432, and by the Institute for Complex Scientific Software at Northeastern University.

Code that uses reflection is assumed to access the reflective representation—they are one and the same. The result is a situation resembling the one that gave rise to printer drivers. Back then, each application was tailored to work with specific printers. Buying a printer with new or different features required upgrading or replacing the application. Something similar can be said of current applications that use meta-information.

The problem lies in a strong coupling between the reflection interface and its implementation. A debugger, for example, may obtain information about a program being debugged either from a source code repository or through reflection. Debuggers usually work with one information source or the other, not both; changing the source would require substantial rework of the debugger. But that needn't be the case. Reflection is just another application programming interface (API) that can have several implementations.

Consider how a printer driver defines a standard API through which printer and application communicate. Any application that can print may use the printer driver's interface, confident that it will work subsequently with new printers without change. Conversely, a printer needn't be aware of the applications it serves; it can rely on the driver to relay status and problem information to applications. In the same way, decoupling the reflection interface from its implementation affords the novelty of more than one implementation of meta-information. Then third parties, for example, could plug the debugger into either a source code repository or reflection. We call this vision *pluggable reflection.*

The paper demonstrates the potential advantages of pluggability by illustrating two extralingual approaches to pluggable reflection. In the first, clients of reflection are structured as visitors of objects representing a grammar (i.e., an instance of the INTERPRETER pattern [13]). For added flexibility, the second approach implements INTERPRETER dynamically rather than statically using a set of event-based ReflectionBeans components.

Both examples are based on an abstract syntax represen-

0-7695-1877-X/03 $17.00 © 2003 IEEE

tation of reflection. Programming against a grammar as opposed to a physical implementation of reflection is key to retargeting clients of meta-information to different sources. In fact, the INTERPRETER pattern's class hierarchy can mimic Java's reflection facilities precisely enough that clients can use one or the other just by changing import statements.

The ability to retarget tools to different meta-information sources is not only useful but sometimes necessary. In Section 2 we motivate this work by explaining the trade-offs between two meta-information sources. In Section 3 we show the benefits of choosing the most appropriate source, and then in Section 4 the benefits of using both. We describe our experience implementing a javadoc-like tool that can be easily retargeted to various reflective sources. An alternative implementation strategy applies the object-to-component transformation that we present elsewhere [22] to produce JavaBeans from Java's Reflection API.

2. Motivation

The need for pluggable reflection arises as soon as you have more than one source of meta-information. Consider for example the overlap between reflective facilities and source code repositories. Both manage information about classes and their relationships, and both aid in the software development process—they can make changing, tuning, and debugging your program a lot easier.

Yet reflection and repositories have obvious differences that complicate interoperability. Ideally we could ignore such differences, choose either approach, and switch between them freely; the origin of reflective information would be transparent to clients. But in practice, the reflection interface and its implementation are strongly coupled. Again, the code that uses reflective information is the same as the code that accesses the reflective representation.

Suppose you are writing a tool that processes source code, such as a class browser. It requires services found in both the reflection interface and the class repository interface at your disposal (that is, the intersection of those interfaces). You therefore have a choice—you can get class information from either source. Your browser can compile and load classes and then use reflection to reveal their structure, or it can parse the class source, store the information in the repository, and query the repository for the same information (Figure 1).

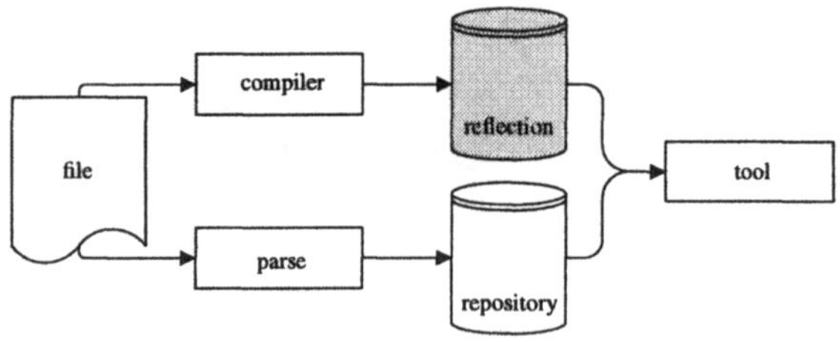

Figure 1. Reflection-repository duality

2.1. Reflection-Repository Trade-offs

Neither approach is adequate in all circumstances. Here are several trade-offs to consider:

- *Completeness.* A reflection-based approach precludes browsing code that is not compilable. Repositories only require the code to be reasonably parsable, and they can make broad assumptions about incomplete portions.
- *Coupling.* Reflection is closely associated with the programming language. As a result, there is tight binding between reflection facilities, client code, and the run-time environment. A repository, in contrast, can be more loosely coupled to its clients. One result is that testing a client apart from the repository is generally easier than testing it apart from the reflection machinery.
- *Semantic mismatch.* A repository may have facilities beyond reflection, such as versioning and concurrency control, that are overkill for simple clients like the class browser, which has no editing or versioning capabilities. The repository doesn't justify its cost for such clients. Conversely, a repository that offers no more than a subset of a language's reflection facilities has limited use in that language.
- *Inconsistency.* Information about a class might be different depending on whether it was obtained from a repository versus reflection. If a program loads a class dynamically, reflection may know about it but not the repository. The repository might provide more accurate information when someone else changes the class.
- *Inflexibility.* If you have a tool designed to use reflection, can you run it without a compiler? If the tool works with files, can you retarget it to use reflection? How easy is it to divorce class-browsing facilities from the mechanisms for extracting and managing source information? The easier all that is, the more flexible and reusable the tool.

Making the meta-information source pluggable makes it easy to choose one approach and change your mind later. It can also offer the best of both worlds.

3. Application

Clearly, the degree of pluggability is determined by the ease with which a tool can be retargeted to either infor-

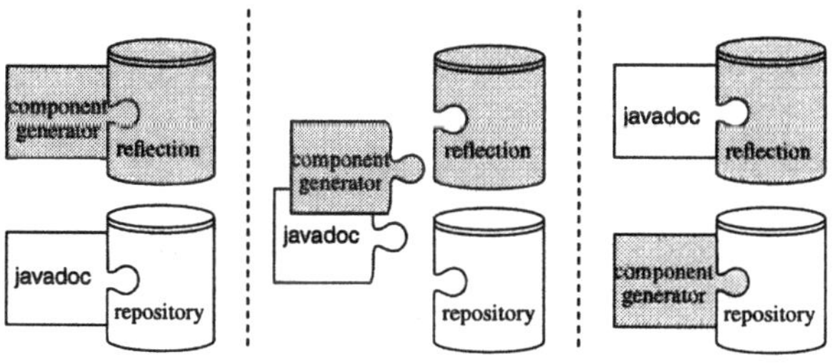

Figure 2. Pluggable reflection

mation source. Conversely, pluggability must cope with changes in the information sources themselves—to a different reflection model, for example, or to a different repository. Figure 2 shows how two tools, each a client of meta-information, can exploit pluggability:

1. Object-to-component generator [22], initially dependent on reflection, is retargeted to use a repository.
2. javadoc [12],[1] normally a repository client, is retargeted to use reflection.

3.1. A Retargetable Component Generator

In previous work, we developed an object-to-component transformation wherein every class in the OO API becomes an event type, and every method becomes a JavaBeans component. A bean can be a transmitter of an event, a receiver of an event, or both. Most beans both receive and transmit and are hence called *transceivers*. There are several kinds of transceiver beans. A bean is considered a *conduit* if it produces only side effects. A complete classification appears elsewhere [22].

We have also prototyped a component generator that performs this transformation automatically [21]. The generator uses reflection to analyze class interfaces (i.e., relying on method signatures only) and then produces a set of components. Later, we wanted to let clients use the generator as a web service [32]. Unfortunately, Java's reflection lacks interfaces, and retargeting required code modifications. Pluggability would let us disconnect a component generator that was designed to work with reflection and plug it into a meta-data repository.

3.2. A Retargetable javadoc

javadoc is a command line tool that reads a `.java` source file and generates HTML documentation from the class declaration and stylized comments. By default, javadoc generates the documentation according to a predefined standard template, subject to limited user options.

[1] `http://java.sun.com/products/jdk/javadoc`

Indeed, early versions gave users little control over its operation. The parse tree was inaccessible, the abstract syntax was not revealed, and altering the tool's processing was not possible.

By JDK 1.2, javadoc had undergone two substantial design changes. First, the internal javadoc representation was exposed in a package called `sun.tools.javadoc`. Second, the format of the documentation became customizable. By running javadoc with the new command-line option `-doclet` *`SomeDocletTool`* (where *`SomeDocletTool`*`.class` is a user-supplied compiled class), the *`SomeDocletTool`* program may use the Doclet API to access the internal representation of the parsed file and to control how the parse tree is processed [28].

For documentation purposes, Sun provides the javadoc-generated HTML files for system classes but generally not their source code. If you don't have the source or the HTML files for a certain class, you cannot re-generate the documentation. Even if you have both the source and the HTML files, there is always uncertainty as to whether the versions you're using are consistent. Unfortunately, javadoc cannot rely on reflection to recover this information despite the functional similarity.

3.2.1. Disparities

The doclet repository that javadoc uses internally resembles reflection in at least two respects:

- The repository is not persistent: its lifetime is limited to that of the hosting javadoc's execution. The repository lives and dies with each such execution, just as reflective information is available only at run-time.
- The Doclet API and the Core Reflection API are nearly isomorphic. The Doclet API classes `ClassDoc`, `MemberDoc`, `FieldDoc`, `ConstructorDoc`, and `MethodDoc` correspond to the Core Reflection API classes `Class`, `Member`, `Field`, `Constructor`, and `Method`. The methods correspond closely as well, although they are distributed a little differently in the two class hierarchies.

Although quite similar, the two APIs are incompatible. The JDK design fails to recognize this similarity, let alone providing the pluggable abstraction and attempting to unify them. As a result, things tend to be more complex than they need to be, and reuse opportunities are forgone. Here are two examples of difficulties in the design, the first seen from its designer's viewpoint and the second from a client's:

1. The Doclet API's design is newer and more complete than the reflection API's. But since no connection between the two was made, the improvements have not and may never make their way into the reflection API.

Class	::=	*name:*String *superclass:*[Class] *interfaces:*Class[] Member[];
Member	::=	Field | Constructor | Method;
Field	::=	*declaringClass:*Class *name:*String *type:*Class;
Constructor	::=	*declaringClass:*Class *name:*String *ParameterTypes:*Class[];
Method	::=	*declaringClass:*Class *name:*String *ReturnType:*Class *ParameterTypes:*Class[];

Figure 3. Grammarized reflection

2. If you already have *SomeReflectionTool* that adheres to the Core Reflection API, you cannot reuse it with javadoc; you must rewrite it as *SomeDocletTool*. The opposite is also true: an existing *SomeDocletTool* cannot be easily applied to reflective information.

   In particular, the `sun.tools.javadoc.doclet.Standard` HTML doclet, which javadoc itself uses by default, cannot be retargeted to `.class` files. Even newly written programs (like your *SomeDocletTool*) cannot use reflection unaltered—a common interface does not exist. There is no way to replace the front-end analyzer. There isn't even a converter in the form of a `ClassDoc` constructor that would translate reflection information into doclets.

Pluggability would let us disconnect javadoc from its repository source, namely doclets, and plug it into reflection.

4 Pluggability

javadoc can be made pluggable. Section 4.1 illustrates such pluggability by using a unified interface as the abstract representation. An alternative abstract representation using generated ReflectionBeans to implement a pluggable reflective javadoc is illustrated in Section 4.2.

4.1. Reconciliation via Abstract Representation

Figure 3 describes a simple abstract grammar for Java's structural reflection akin to similar representations in Smalltalk [14, 7]. Left-hand-side variables are classes; right-hand-side fields are instance variables. In the figure, fields have the general form *label:*type, meaning that the class has an instance variable named *label*. The type of the instance variable can be a primitive type, as in *name:*String, or one of the left-hand-side variables—that is, a reference to another class as in *type:*Class.

A type in square brackets is optional, as in *superclass:*[Class]. That means an instance of Class may have a null superclass. Suffixing a type with "[]" describes a container of values. For example, in *interfaces:*Class[], "interfaces" is the name of an instance variable of type "Array of Class." If the label is missing, we assume the instance variable's name to be the plural of the component type. So Member[] means there is an instance variable named "members" of type "Array of Member."

The grammar describes a subset of reflection syntax. Java's reflection includes information that is not revealed in this grammar, such as modifiers of methods and fields. These were excluded to simplify the exposition. The grammar displayed in Figure 3 is not, however, an ordinary BNF specification. It is an abstract grammar. Information about the concrete syntax of classes, fields, and methods is missing. Hence it is worthless for parsing, but we do not intend to parse class declarations with this grammar.

In sum, this grammar serves as a semantic description of class declarations. An instance of the hierarchy in Figure 3 is better thought of as a typed semantic net than a parse tree. For example, the superclass field of Class is not an instance variable of type String with the name of the superclass. Rather, it is a reference to an instance of type Class that is the superclass itself (if one exists). Another example: Method knows its *declaringClass*—information that requires semantic analysis on top of parsing.

4.1.1. Retargeting legacy reflective code

Applying INTERPRETER to this grammar would yield a precise definition of a class hierarchy, a mirror of `java.lang.reflect`. Legacy code that works with reflection also works with the mirrored repository with trivial code modifications—only import declarations need to be changed. As the name suggests, the mirrored repository is fully compatible with the reflection API. We have also built a tool that parses source files and stores them in this repository. We employ these facilities to demonstrate pluggability's advantages for testing and debugging programs that use reflection.

4.1.2. Writing new retargetable reflective tools

To complete the javadoc example, we describe a prototyped version of javadoc that generates HTML documentation from reflective information, and in Section 4.1.3 we demonstrate its usefulness by comparing its output to the official JDK documentation for the Java Core Reflection API.

We have two alternative approaches to implementing a reflective version of javadoc. The first (re)uses doclets; the

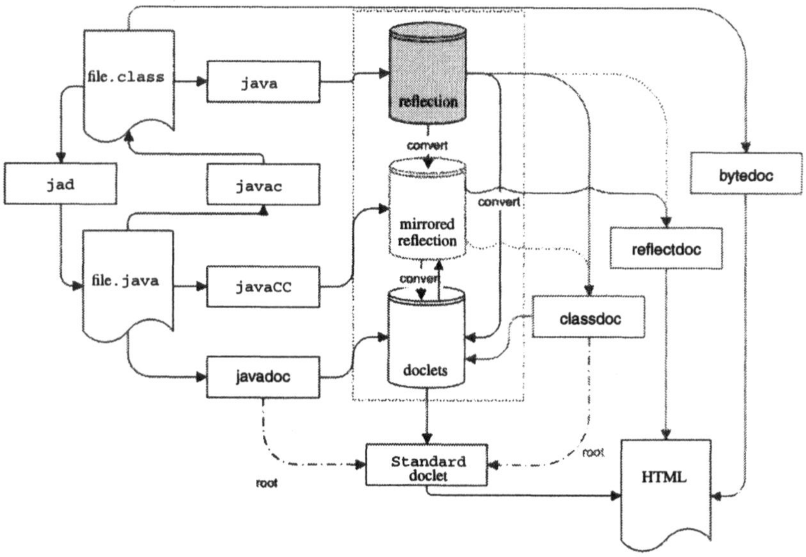

Figure 4. Implementation strategies for a reflective javadoc tool

second does not. The reader is encouraged to use Figure 4 as a guide to the examples in particular and more generally to the difficulties conventional reflection creates and the benefits of pluggability.

Suppose we'd like to make javadoc generate HTML documentation using reflection. One tack is to implement a converter from instances of reflection classes to instances of doclet classes (represented by the downward arrows marked "convert" in the figure). It is possible then to implement a classdoc tool that works much like javadoc except that it documents classes based on reflective information. Unlike javadoc, which works only on `.java` files, classdoc may work on `.class` files, hence its name.

A possible implementation strategy has the tool traversing the reflected information, building a temporary doclet structure, and then passing its root (necessarily of type `sun.tools.javadoc.doclet.Root`) to `Standard.start(Root root)`[2] to generate HTML. Of course, not all doclet information can be constructed from reflective information. Some entries (e.g., comments) must be left empty or assigned default values. This could make the generated documentation look awkward. Avoiding that requires a different implementation approach, one independent of javadoc and the doclet package—a tool that generates the HTML output directly. reflectdoc is such a tool. Yet another implementation strategy would be to develop a bytedoc for parsing the `.class` files directly without using reflection (see Figure 4).

[2]Oddly enough, the JDK `Standard` class neither inherits from `sun.tools.javadoc.Doclet` nor does it implement any interface that would guarantee the existence of a `start` method with the proper signature.

AspectJ, an implementation of AOP for Java, recently provided a javadoc-like tool named ajdoc [19]. Running `ajdoc` *`SomeAspect`*`.java` generates documentation for the aspect *`SomeAspect`*, which includes aspect instance specifications such as `issingleton`, aspectual links to known advisors and advisees, advice summary, and more.

ajdoc is an application that uses this pluggability approach, and it is superior in design to javadoc. Akin to the `-doclet` option of javadoc, which generates output via an alternate doclet, Palm [27] added a `-compiler` option for generating a `RootDoc` instance via an alternate compiler.[3] Thus the user of ajdoc can control both the front-end and the back-end of the compilation. With a supplemental `RootDocMakerImpl` and a minor change to `org.aspectj.tools.ajdoc.Ajdoc.java`, one can build the doclets from `.class` files. For example, running `ajdoc -standard -compiler RootDocMakerImpl java.lang.reflect.Method` would produce documentation for `Method` via reflection. Nevertheless, AspectJ code cannot expect to reflect on aspectual structure but must make do with the underlying object structure. For example, running `ajdoc -compiler RootDocMakerImpl` *`SomeAspect`* generates documentation using reflection, but the result reveals *`SomeAspect`* to be a class, complete with instrumentation details, instead of displaying the aspectual information.

4.1.3. Pluggable reflection's benefits

By applying javadoc to files and reflectdoc to reflection, you can compare the HTML outputs to reveal un-

[3]The option exists but is unsupported in the AspectJ release.

Class java.lang.reflect.Method

```
java.lang.Object
   |
   +----java.lang.reflect.Method
```

---

public final class **Method**
extends Object
implements Member A Method provides information about, and access to, a single method on a class or interface. The reflected method may be a class method or an instance method (including an abstract method).

Figure 5. JDK documentation for `Method`

Class java.lang.reflect.Method

```
java.lang.Object
   |
   +----java.lang.reflect.Method
```

---

public final synchronized **Method**
extends **Object**
implements **Member**

Figure 6. `Method` **documentation obtained via** reflectdoc

expected differences. By applying reflectdoc to system classes, moreover, you may produce documentation that is not included in the standard distribution. For example, Figure 5 is a portion of the JDK 1.2 documentation for `java.lang.reflect.Method`. Figure 6 is the HTML documentation generated by running our reflective version of javadoc, specifically `reflectdoc java.lang.reflect.Method`.

You might appreciate reflectdoc just for presenting reflective information in the familiar format of javadoc. But note the slight differences. Comments appear in Figure 5 but not in Figure 6. The class modifier `synchronized` appears[4] in Figure 6 but not Figure 5. The same is true of URL links, because reflectdoc was run only on `java.lang.reflect.Method`. Future work may include developing activedoc for producing and controlling javadoc's output dynamically.

reflectdoc reveals the following undocumented information about class `Method`:

- Private instance variables: The `Method` class has the variables listed in Figure 7. In the JDK documentation, the Variables section does not exist.

- A private constructor: `Method` has the private default constructor shown in Figure 8.

[4]Bug Id 4109635, fixed in JDK 1.3 [33].

Variable Index

- **clazz**
- **slot**
- **name**
- **returnType**
- **parameterTypes**
- **exceptionTypes**

Figure 7. Variable Index

Constructor Index

- **Method()**

Figure 8. Constructor Index

- A static `copy` method whose signature is shown in Figure 9.

Knowledge of private and undocumented features might not be crucial, but it can offer insight into the software's design. And you never know what you might find unless you look. Judging from the API, one might expect class `Class` to have properties like name, superclass, interfaces, and so forth in its implementation. But one might also expect `Class`'s implementation to be lightweight. reflectdoc reports that class `Class` has no member variables at all,

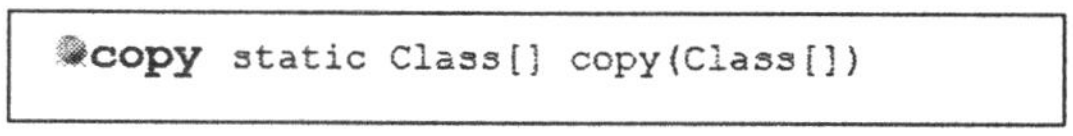

Figure 9. Copy method

thus confirming the latter expectation.

Often, information is deliberately omitted in documentation produced by javadoc (e.g., private members are not displayed), since these are not part of the interface. But whether certain implementation details should be hidden is orthogonal to whether you have access to the information. The `synchronized` modifier bug is an example where even reflective information may be wrong [33].

4.2. Pluggability through Components

The component generator has proven useful for enabling pluggability. So far we've showed pluggability through interface conformity. Now we show an alternative approach to pluggability using components. We demonstrate this again for javadoc by applying the object-to-component transformation and automatic generator to produce ReflectionBeans. The input to the generator is Java's Reflection API; ReflectionBeans are the output.

Using ReflectionBeans instead of the reflection interface makes retargeting much easier. Third-party tools can mix and match with third-party providers of meta-information: simply specify the desired `.jar` file in the tool's classpath. This retargeting requires no source code change or recompilation.

ReflectionBeans act as a facade to the actual source, be it reflection, a repository, or anything else. JavaBeans may seem like overkill here, but they have the added benefit of allowing modest visual programming capabilities.

Figure 10 depicts basic cooperation among ReflectionBeans. VclassTransmitter1 is a transmitter-bean [22]: it translates from the AWT-event world to the class-event world. Specifically, it expects a text event and responds with a corresponding class event. The class event encapsulates the class whose name was received in the class event. Internally, it calls on the reflective operation `Class.forName` to do the job. The button Button1 is connected to the event trigger in VclassTransmitter1.

VclassReceiver1 is a receiver-bean: it works like VclassTransmitter1 but in the opposite direction. On receiving a class event, it fires the name of the class as a text event. Entering a class name in the top text field and pressing the button makes the class name appear in the bottom text field.

This approach is overkill for just propagating a class name, but it illustrates the architecture and its bean-based implementation. A more realistic composition would have nontrivial beans on the communication path between VclassTransmitter1 and VclassReceiver1.

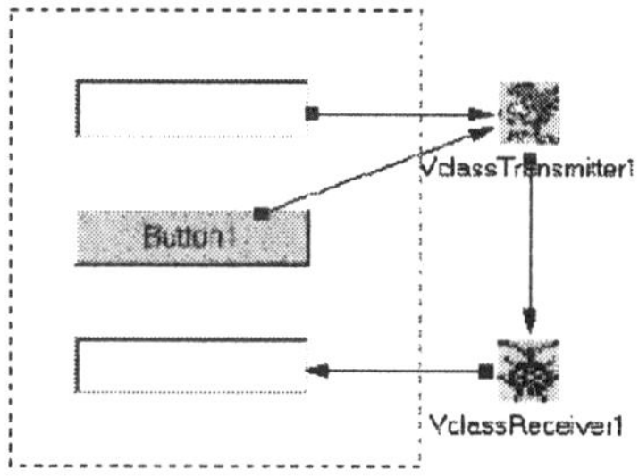

Figure 10. Transmit-Receive

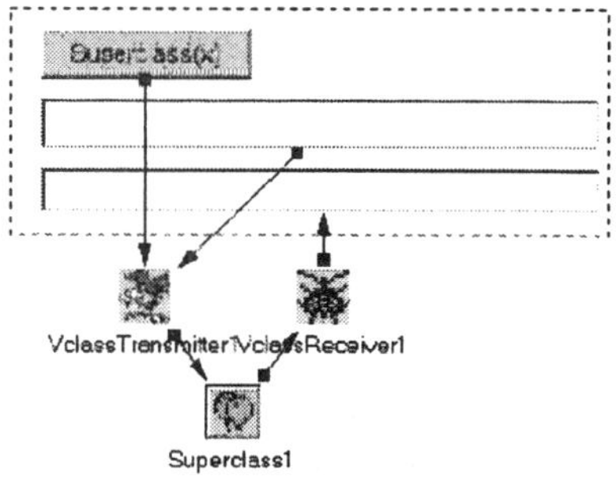

Figure 11. Using the Superclass bean

In Figure 11, a Superclass1 is inserted between those components. Superclass1 is both a class-event receiver and a class-event transmitter. It accepts and fires class events. It does not fire exactly the same event it receives, however; it is a transceiver-bean as opposed to a conduit-bean. Its operation is straightforward. It may use reflection or any other source of meta-information to find the superclass of the incoming class and transmits that superclass as its output. Now if you type a legal class name in the top field and press the button, you would see the name of its superclass in the bottom field.

Although individual beans may be simple, they can perform complex jobs in concert. In Figure 12, pressing the button after entering a class name computes the class' dependents and displays them sequentially in the bottom text field. SuperclassLoop1 composes a Superclass bean and a self-loop. Thus for each input event this composition of beans outputs multiple events, one for each of the superclasses on the path to the `Object` class. InterfacesLoop1 does the same for interfaces.

This example generates all the classes that a given class immediately depends on. When text is entered in the upper field, *TextEvents* are fired to VclassTransmitter1. VclassTransmitter1 reacts by preparing itself to generate and fire a *ClassEvent* containing a class whose name is the string received.[5] The button labeled "Dependences" is connected to the `fire()` method of VclassTransmitter1. When

[5]VclassTransmitter1 can also be customized directly using a bean customizer.

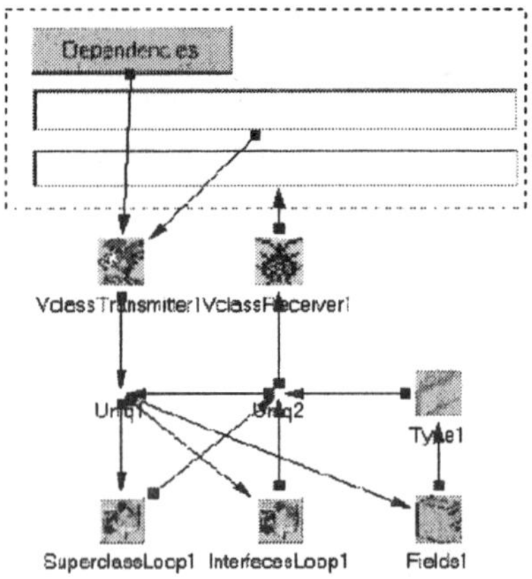

Figure 12. Dependencies

the button is pressed, VclassTransmitter1 transmits the *ClassEvent* if and only if the string is a legal class name.

Once the button is pressed and VclassTransmitter1 fires the *ClassEvent*, it is distributed to Superclass1, Interfaces1, and Fields1. Superclass1 in turn triggers a *ClassEvent* with the superclass of the class. Interfaces1 triggers multiple *ClassEvents*, one for each interface the class implements. Fields1 triggers multiple *FieldEvents*, one for each public field of the class. The *FieldEvents* are received by Type1, which fires a *ClassEvent* corresponding to the field's type. All the *ClassEvents* are subsequently merged and sent, one by one, to VclassReceiver1. Finally, VclassReceiver1 generates a *TextEvent*, and the class names are displayed sequentially.

We applied this approach to javadoc to make its source of reflective information pluggable. Implementing reflectdoc using beans introduces behavioral beans (counters, resetters, etc.) into the datapath to generate HTML rather than just displaying class names. There are in fact two orthogonal datapaths: one governs how reflective information is traversed, the other governs the flow of data. Our original classification [22], which assumed a single datapath, differentiated among several types of transceivers: conduit, converter, transmuter, etc. Implementing reflectdoc requires two datapaths; hence each bean is characterized by a taxonomic tuple, e.g., ⟨transmuter, conduit⟩. To avoid a Cartesian product of bean classifications, we require that any pair of transceivers must include a conduit.[6]

These extensions to our taxonomy are needed to characterize some of the beans that implement javadoc's behavior, for example, regarding event synchronization. Further details are beyond the scope of this paper. The important point is that ReflectionBeans are powerful enough to express real applications.

[6] More generally, given an n-dimensional datapath, all but one dimension must denote a conduit.

5. Related Work

Pluggable reflection would be helpful not only for retargeting javadoc to reflection but also to let new language extensions reason about themselves explicitly. This need is symptomatic of the difficulty in keeping reflection in step with language features. Pluggability could avert this problem. Indeed, pluggable reflection can and should become as standard a facility as garbage collection. In the meantime, the implementation we describe here can help bring reflective facilities to new languages that lack them.

5.1. Mirrors in Self and Smalltalk

The idea of having multiple sources of reflective information is not new. Smith's seminal work [30, 31] explicitly accounts for the possibility of differing kinds of causal connection in reflective systems.

The ANSI Smalltalk standard [15] uses an abstract syntax specification to describe the global components of a Smalltalk program and their relationships. In particular, the work on Mirrors in Self [34], Animorphic Smalltalk [4], and Strongtalk [3] (as well as the `Mirror` interface in JDI) address concerns similar to ours from a programming language perspective [5]. Our extralingual approaches to pluggability should help inform the design and implementation of new reflection mechanisms at the language level.

While we use Java as our testbed, these concepts are valid for other languages. Even in a dynamically typed language such as Smalltalk, the implementation and interface are insufficiently decoupled to achieve pluggability. This becomes apparent when trying to retarget reflective Smalltalk code from a 3-metalevel system (e.g., in Little Smalltalk [6]) to a 5-metalevel system (e.g., in Squeak [17]).

5.2. Intercession

Chiba and Tatsubori [9] extend Java reflection to permit language extensions by re-implementing `java.lang.Class`. They put forth the classes `openjava.mop.OJClass` and `OJMethod` as replacements for `Class` and `Method`. The ability to perform language customization in addition to introspection is achieved using compile-time reflection in their OpenJava compiler [8]. In comparison, we make a point of preserving class names in the mirrored package to ensure that code can run with either the original reflection or the mirrored repository. Instead of creating a dedicated compiler, we can rely on a standard Java compiler. VISITOR [13] furnishes the extended functionality non-invasively.

Javassist [8] supports structural reflection in Java by bytecode manipulation at load-lime without replacing the compiler. Javassist relies on a configuration file and class loading interception. In contrast, we focus on supporting run-time introspection.

5.3. Aspect-Oriented Software Development

Pluggability can be characterized as a separation of concerns—reflective information's use separated from its access. In fact, an attempt to apply VISITOR to effect a form of Aspect-Oriented Programming (AOP) [16] was the genesis of this research. We first characterized implicit invocation combined with VISITOR as an aspect-oriented pattern [20]. Then we developed a taxonomy of JavaBeans [22]. This paper builds on those works.

We introduced two variants of javadoc (classdoc and reflectdoc) that use reflection instead of a repository. More complex tools corroborate the trade-offs and potential benefits of pluggable reflection. Demeter/J [18], for example, is a repository-based tool for adaptive programming (AP). A variant of Demeter/J called DJ uses Java's reflection instead of a repository [29, 26]. Its developers report similar trade-offs in using reflection versus a repository. The effort required to implement DJ underscores the need for pluggability. Ideally, it would have been trivial to retarget Demeter/J; unifying the reflection-repository duality can be viewed as an adaptability problem—the raison d'être of the Demeter system. Demeter achieves structure-shy adaptability through traversal strategies. This may suggest applying a notion similar to the VISITOR approach to achieve better unification in DJ.

5.4. Language Extensions for Components

Jiazzi [24] extends Java with package types as a means for implementing units [11]. One could thus use Jiazzi to define a "blueprint" for the Java reflection package. As with AspectJ, the difficulty in using reflection with Jiazzi stems from its being a language extension.

ArchJava [1, 2] addresses the decoupling of implementation code from architecture. New constructs for ports and connections are introduced to enforce, for example, architectural communication integrity. We aspire to push reflection up to the architectural level, while maintaining "reflective-integrity." Aldrich, et al., mention an archjavadoc tool as future work.

5.5. Visual Programming

Everyone who uses visual programming tools experiences their limitations. Building an application with a JavaBeans builder is no exception. Once the program gets big, the visual description is no longer manageable. Nevertheless, visual programming has undeniable appeal for programming in the small—the kind of programming you do with reflection. Instead of learning the textual syntax of reflection in Java, one can describe a portion of an application visually with only the general understanding of the semantics of reflection JavaBeans. The visualization is however orthogonal to the idea of pluggability.

5.6. Typed Reflection

Reflective code typically uses strings and relies on conventions rather than language mechanisms. Weirich proposes incorporating mechanisms for dynamic type analysis into Java's reflection [35]. In the component approach to pluggability, we assign types to events to achieve typed construction. Typed reflection would make reflective code more concise and safe, but it would not resolve the problem of retargeting a reflective program to another reflective structure or to another language. Unifying the notions of pluggable and typed reflection is a promising tack for further research.

6. Conclusion

People tend to think of reflection as a language feature (and thus coupled to the language) and reflection code as coupled to the language implementation. In this paper, we look at reflection more abstractly as just another interface with the potential for multiple implementations. We consider how to retarget a reflective program to another meta-information source such as a repository, and the benefits of doing so. Indeed, retargetability could even apply across languages: Why couldn't reflectdoc also run on Smalltalk?

To demonstrate reflection as an interface, we took an abstract grammar of a Java class definition and applied the INTERPRETER pattern to it, producing a mirrored class hierarchy with the same interface as reflection. This hierarchy can serve as a class repository by generating a parser that converts source code to instances of the mirrored classes. In particular, visitors written for the INTERPRETER pattern are no different than other clients—they can be retargeted to use reflection as well.

We demonstrated three pluggability approaches:

1. *Legacy clients* of the reflection interface can be retargeted to use the mirrored hierarchy without modification apart from changing import statements.
2. *New clients* that use visitors as building blocks are pluggable at compile-time.
3. For even looser coupling, *third-party clients* may use components as their building blocks, affording full assembly-time pluggability.

The key contribution of this paper lies in staging the problem. In an evolutionary path from conventional to pluggable reflection, mirroring reflection is merely the first step:

a BRIDGE [13] for decoupling users from providers of meta-information. Clients cannot tell the difference between mirrored and genuine reflection. Implicit invocation adds flexibility through looser coupling, allowing third-party composition of reflection information and clients. The Holy Grail, of course, is to give clients uniform access to meta-data sources with disparate and unforeseen semantics.

An obvious limitation of mirroring is that the reflection and repository APIs must be kept in sync. Unfortunately, interfaces invariably evolve. A single interface may go through several versions; parallel interfaces may diverge. How do you reconcile two interfaces that are similar but not identical? Programming to the least common denominator may be unsatisfactory because you cannot exploit the unique advantages of either interface. On the other hand, specialized interfaces make switching implementations difficult, thereby forgoing the benefits of encapsulation, portability, and testability.

Both kinds of interface evolution are found in Java's reflection API. Reflection did not exist in JDK 1.0. Had you wanted to implement a class browser, you would have needed a repository. JDK 1.1 introduced reflection, and you could have migrated your class browser to use it instead. The initial reflection API did not support all class information, however, and so the repository still would have been useful. JDK 1.2 added the ability to access the package that a class belongs to, and it introduced the Doclet API, which can be used instead of a repository. JDK 1.3 added the ability to define proxy classes dynamically, thereby enabling limited behavioral reflection. JDK 1.3 also added the Mirror API, yet another reflective facility as part of the Java Debugging Interface (JDI).

The proliferation of APIs poses a dilemma: How does one design client code that can work with current and future APIs with minimal (ideally zero) change? Printer driver interfaces are a compromise between generic and specialized printing features. Unique or advanced features are typically eschewed to maximize compatibility. As a result, an application that needs a specialized feature must circumvent the printer driver or forgo the feature.

Meanwhile, the role of reflection is expanding. Components in particular rely heavily on reflection, and clients need to understand how so. With increased awareness of reflection comes the need for supporting tools. Traditional tools for source code, such as code beautifiers, metrics and documentation generators, and the like would be most welcome if they worked on reflection. Unfortunately, they rarely do.

Now imagine a world in which reflection is pluggable. Tools can run on source code files, on class repositories, or on reflection without change and without the information sources' a priori knowledge of each other. Different trade-offs among the sources permit the tool to optimize itself to its context.

Testing would come of age in this world. One scenario: A third-party framework comes with a semantic-checking tool for certifying correct customization of the framework. The checker can run on the source code to catch syntax errors. It can also work on class hierarchies to catch semantic errors (such as forgetting to subclass a framework class). And it can run on reflection to check for certain semantic violations that (thanks to the halting problem) can only be discovered at run-time. Moreover, the checker can cache and compare test results, as we did with the javadoc and reflectdoc outputs, to spot inconsistencies. These are some of the benefits we can expect of fully pluggable reflection.

Acknowledgment

We thank Gilad Bracha and the anonymous referees for their valuable comments. Many thanks to Gennady Agranov, Gilad Bracha, Sergei Kojarski, and Jeffrey Palm for helpful discussions on reflection. The reflectdoc tool, the JavaBeans-based retargetable javadoc, and the reflection-based component generator were initially implemented by Predrag Petkovic, and later re-implemented by students in COM3240. Ramanathan Sundaram retargeted the component generator from using reflection to work with meta-information as a web service.

References

[1] J. Aldrich, C. Chambers, and D. Notkin. Component-oriented programming in ArchJava. In D. H. Lorenz and V. C. Sreedhar, editors, *Proceedings of the First OOPSLA Workshop on Language Mechanisms for Programming Software Components*, pages 1–8, Tampa Bay, Florida, Oct. 15 2001. Technical Report NU-CCS-01-06, College of Computer Science, Northeastern University, Boston, MA 02115.

[2] J. Aldrich, C. Chambers, and D. Notkin. ArchJava: Connecting software architecture to implementation. In *Proceedings of the 24th International Conference on Software Engineering*, pages 187–197, Orlando, Florida, May 19-25 2002. ICSE 2002, ACM Press.

[3] L. Bak, G. Bracha, S. Grarup, R. Griesemer, D. Griswold, and U. Hölzle. Mixins in Strongtalk. In A. P. Black, E. Ernst, P. Grogono, and M. Sakkinen, editors, *Proceedings of the Inheritance Workshop at ECOOP 2002*, Málaga, Spain, June 11 2002. ECOOP 2002, University of Jyväsjylä Information Technology Research Institute.

[4] G. Bracha and D. Griswold. Extending smalltalk with mixins. In *OOPSLA Workshop on Extending the Smalltalk Language*, Sept. 1996.

[5] G. Bracha and D. Ungar. Mirrors: Design principles for meta-level facilities of object-oriented programming languages. Unpublished manuscript, 2003.

[6] T. Budd. *A Little Smalltalk*. Addison-Wesley, 1987.

[7] P. J. Caudill and A. Wirfs-Brock. A third generation Smalltalk-80 implementation. In *Proceedings of the 1st Annual Conference on Object-Oriented Programming Systems, Languages, and Applications*, pages 119–130, Portland, Oregon, USA, Sept. 29 - Oct. 2 1986. OOPSLA'86, ACM SIGPLAN Notices 21(11) Nov. 1986.

[8] S. Chiba. Load-time structural reflection in Java. In E. Bertino, editor, *Proceedings of the 14th European Conference on Object-Oriented Programming*, number 1850 in Lecture Notes in Computer Science, pages 313–336, Cannes, France, June 12-16 2000. ECOOP 2000, Springer Verlag.

[9] S. Chiba and M. Tatsubori. Yet another `java.lang.Class`. In *ECOOP'98 Workshop on Reflective Object-Oriented Programming and Systems*, Brussels, Belgium, July 20 1998.

[10] S. Demeyer and J. Bosch, editors. *Object-Oriented Technology. ECOOP'98 Workshop Reader*, number 1543 in Lecture Notes in Computer Science. Workshop Proceedings, Brussels, Belguim, Springer Verlag, July 20-24 1998.

[11] M. Flatt and M. Felleisen. Units: Cool modules for hot languages. In *Proceedings of the conference on programming language design and implementation*, pages 236–248, Montreal, Quebec, Canada, May 1998. PLDI'98, ACM Press.

[12] L. Friendly. The design of distributed hyperlinked programming documentation. In *Proceedings of the International Workshop on Hypermedia Design (IWHD)*, 1995.

[13] E. Gamma, R. Helm, R. Johnson, and J. Vlissides. *Design Patterns: Elements of Reusable Object-Oriented Software*. Professional Computing. Addison-Wesley, 1995.

[14] A. Goldberg and D. Robson. *Smalltalk–80: The Language*. Addison-Wesley, Reading, MA, USA, 1989.

[15] InterNational Committee for Information Technology Standards (formerly NCITS). *Programming Language Smalltalk*, Jan. 1 1998.

[16] G. Kiczales, J. Lamping, A. Mendhekar, C. Maeda, C. Lopes, J.-M. Loingtier, and J. Irwin. Aspect-oriented programming. In M. Akşit and S. Matsuoka, editors, *Proceedings of the 11th European Conference on Object-Oriented Programming*, number 1241 in Lecture Notes in Computer Science, pages 220–242, Jyväskylä, Finland, June 9–13 1997. ECOOP'97, Springer Verlag.

[17] G. Korienek, T. Wrensch, and D. Dechow. *Squeak - A Quick Trip to ObjectLand*. Addison–Wesley Publishing Company, 2001.

[18] K. J. Lieberherr. *Adaptive Object-Oriented Software: The Demeter Method with Propagation Patterns*. PWS Publishing Company, Boston, MA, 1996.

[19] C. V. Lopes and G. Kiczales. Recent developments in AspectJ. In Demeyer and Bosch [10], pages 398–401.

[20] D. H. Lorenz. Visitor Beans: An aspect-oriented pattern. In Demeyer and Bosch [10], pages 431–432.

[21] D. H. Lorenz and J. Vlissides. Automated architectural transformation: Objects to components. Technical Report NU-CCS-00-01, College of Computer Science, Northeastern University, Boston, MA 02115, Apr. 2000. `http://www.ccs.neu.edu/home/-lorenz/papers/reports/NU-CCS-00-01.html`.

[22] D. H. Lorenz and J. Vlissides. Designing components versus objects: A transformational approach. In *Proceedings of the 23rd International Conference on Software Engineering*, pages 253–262, Toronto, Canada, May 12-19 2001. ICSE 2001, IEEE Computer Society.

[23] P. Maes. Concepts and experiments in computational reflection. In OOPSLA'87 [25], pages 147–155.

[24] S. McDirmid, M. Flatt, and W. C. H. Jiazzi. New age components for old-fashioned java. In *Proceedings of the 16th Annual Conference on Object-Oriented Programming Systems, Languages, and Applications*, pages 211–222, Tampa Bay, Florida, Oct. 14-18 2001. OOPSLA'01, ACM SIGPLAN Notices 36(11) Nov. 2001.

[25] OOPSLA'87. *Proceedings of the 2nd Annual Conference on Object-Oriented Programming Systems, Languages, and Applications*, Orlando, Florida, Oct. 4-8 1987. ACM SIGPLAN Notices 22(12) Dec. 1987.

[26] D. Orleans and K. J. Lieberherr. DJ: Dynamic adaptive programming in Java. In A. Yonezawa and S. Matsuoka, editors, *Proceedings of the 3rd International Conference on Metalevel Architectures and Separation of Crosscutting Concerns, Reflection 2001*, number 2192 in Lecture Notes in Computer Science, pages 73–80, Kyoto, Japan, Sept. 25-28 2001. Springer Verlag.

[27] J. Palm. ajdoc. E-mail message, Mon, 18 Mar 2002 21:51:19 -0700 (MST), Mar. 18 2002.

[28] M. Pollack. Code generation using javadoc: Extend javadoc by creating custom doclets. *JavaWorld*, Aug. 2000. `http://www.javaworld.com/javaworld/jw-08-2000/jw-0818-javadoc.html`.

[29] N. Sangal, E. Farrell, K. Lieberherr, and D. H. Lorenz. Interaction schemata: Compiling interactions to code. In *Proceedings of the 30th International Conference on Technology of Object-Oriented Languages and Systems*, pages 268–177, Santa Barbara, CA, Aug. 1-5 2000. TOOLS 30 USA Conference, IEEE Computer Society.

[30] B. C. Smith. *Reflection and Semantics in a Procedural Language*. PhD thesis, MIT LCS TR-272, Jan. 1982.

[31] B. C. Smith. Reflection and semantics in Lisp. In *Proceedings of the 11th ACM SIGPLAN symposium on Principles of programming languages*, pages 23–35, 1984.

[32] R. Sundaram and D. H. Lorenz. Meta-data driven code generator web service. In P. Tarr, A. Finkelstein, B. Hailpern, G. Piccinelli, and J. Stafford, editors, *Proceedings of the OOPSLA 2002 Workshop on Object-Oriented Web Services*, Seattle, Washington, Nov. 5 2002.

[33] A look at the synchronized modifier. *JavaWorld*, June 1999. `http://www.javaworld.com/javaworld/javaqa/1999-06/03-synchronized.html`.

[34] D. Ungar and R. B. Smith. Self: The power of simplicity. In OOPSLA'87 [25], pages 227–242.

[35] S. Weirich. *Programming With Types*. PhD thesis, Cornell University, 2002. Forthcoming.

Component Rank: Relative Significance Rank for Software Component Search

Katsuro Inoue [†], Reishi Yokomori [†], Hikaru Fujiwara[†],
Tetsuo Yamamoto [††], Makoto Matsushita [†] and Shinji Kusumoto [†]
[†] Graduate School of Information Science and Technology, Osaka University
1-3 Machikaneyama, Toyonaka, Osaka 560-8531, Japan
[††] Japan Science and Technology Corporation, 4-1-8, Honmachi,
Kawaguchi, Saitama 332-8531, Japan
{inoue, yokomori, t-yamamt, matusita, kusumoto}@ist.osaka-u.ac.jp

Abstract

Collections of already developed programs are important resources for efficient development of reliable software systems. In this paper, we propose a novel method of ranking software components, called Component Rank, *based on analyzing actual use relations among the components and propagating the significance through the use relations. We have developed a component-rank computation system, and applied it to various Java programs. The result is promising such that non-specific and generic components are ranked high. Using the Component Rank system as a core part, we are currently developing* Software Product Archiving, analyzing, and Retrieving System *named* SPARS.

1. Introduction

Computer systems are becoming core infrastructures of effective and efficient activities of everyday life. Programs involved in computer systems are getting larger and more complex, and a great number of software engineers are engaged in various kinds of software development projects, producing many kinds of programs day by day.

It would be imagined that similar programs have been developed independently in different locations of the world or in different times in the history, without sharing knowledge of other programs. It is considered that well-organized collection of programs or program components will improve productivity of the development and quality of the developed software products.

There are many kinds of software repositories available on the Internet such as Jumbo![13] or ZDNet[25]. These are mostly for software users who want to obtain already developed tools or systems, but not for software developers.

There is also a large software repository called SourceForge[21] where various software development projects are carried out with an open-source development model[20]. In this site, a search feature is provided to find a proper development project, but there is little support to explore program components, libraries, portions of codes, or abstracted algorithms, which are important resources for new development of programs. Reading, understanding, and duplicating well-written software legacies are indispensable activities for contemporary software development. We may want to keep all software legacies in a single repository; however, structuring and keeping consistency of the huge repository would be an impractically complicate and a painful work.

In this paper, we propose a novel method of ranking software components, called *Component Rank*, based on analyzing actual use relations of components and propagating the significance through the use relations.

There have been many researches related on software reusability[6, 9, 17]; however, the significance by actual usage has not been explored yet. The idea behind Component Rank originates from computing fair impact factors (called *influence weights*) of published papers[19]. This approach has been extended to ranking Web documents in the Internet[18].

We will present the Component Rank model for ranking software components, and show a system for computing Component Rank. In this model, a collection of software components is represented as a weighted directed graph whose nodes correspond to the components and edges correspond to the usage relations. Similar components are clustered into one node so that effect of simply duplicated nodes is removed. The nodes in the graph are ranked by their weights which are defined as the elements of the eigenvector of an adjacent matrix for the directed graph.

The Component Rank computation system targets Java

source files containing a class definition as components. This system has been applied to various collections of Java programs, such as JDK, software engineering tools developed by ourselves, business applications and their framework developed by a mid-size software company, and a collection of XML and other tools.

The results show that stable classes frequently invoked or inherited by other classes have generally high ranks. Examples of such classes are for fundamental and standard data structures and for typical exception handers. Non-standard and special classes are listed with low ranks in many cases.

Since this empirical validation of Component Rank is very promising, we are currently developing Software Product Archiving, analyzing, and Retrieving System called *SPARS*, by which software engineers will interactively retrieve software components with various queries.

In Section 2, we will propose Component Rank model. Section 3 will show an implementation of the Component Rank model. The results of applications will be presented in Section 4. Various issues on the model and the implementation will be discussed in Section 5. Finally, we will conclude our discussion with future work in Section 6.

2. Component Rank Model

2.1. Component Graph

Software systems are modeled by a weighted directed graph, called a *Component Graph*. A node in a graph represents a software component, and a directed edge e_{xy} from node x to y represents a *use relation* meaning that component x uses component y.

Here, we do not restrict our discussion to a specific kind of component in the graph. A component may be a source-code module, a link library, or one section of document. The following discussion will hold for any kind of nodes. Also, the use relation is left unspecified here for the extendibility of the model. In Section 4, we will show our concrete implementation for those abstracted nodes and edges, such that the components are Java class files, and that the use relations are the class inheritance, method invocation, and abstract class implementation.

A software system is generally modeled with a component graph that is weakly connected (assuming that there is no redundant component). A set of software systems is also modeled with one component graph. This graph is disconnected if there are no sharing components.

Figure 1 shows a component graph for two software systems X and Y. X consists of 5 components A – E, and Y consists of 4 components F – I. This graph also shows that component C uses both A and B, and D and E use C. Also, H and I use G, and G and F mutually use one another.

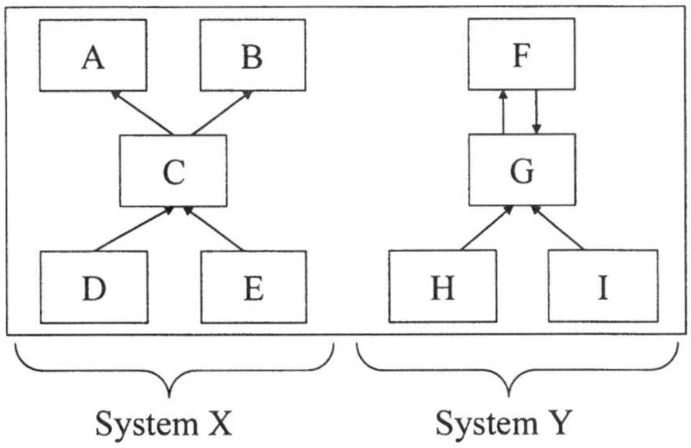

Figure 1. An example of component graph

2.2. Weight of Node

Each node v in component graph G has a non-negative weight value $w(v)$ where $0 \leq w(v) \leq 1$.

Definition 1 (Total Weights of Nodes) *For simplicity of following calculation, we assume that the sum of the weights of all nodes in G is 1, i.e.,*

$$\sum_{v \in G} w(v) = 1$$

Computing the weight for each node under computation policies described below is our objective of this work. The order of the nodes sorted by the weights is called *Component Rank* of the components.

We introduce several definitions to define $w(v)$ for component graph $G = (V, E)$.

Definition 2 (Weight of Edge) *For computation of the weights of nodes, we introduce the weight $w'(e_{ij})$ of an edge $e_{ij} = (v_i, v_j)$, such that*

$$w'(e_{ij}) = d_{ij} \times w(v_i)$$

Figure 2 (a) depicts this definition. Here, d_{ij} is called a *distribution ratio*, where $0 \leq d_{ij} \leq 1$ and the total of d_{ij} for each j is 1. If there is no edge from v_i to v_j, $d_{ij} = 0$. The distribution ratio d_{ij} is used for determining the forwarding weights of v_i to an adjacent node v_j.

Definition 3 (Weight of Node) *The weight of a node v_i is defined as the sum of the weights of all incoming edges e_{ki}, such that*

$$w(v_i) = \sum_{e_{ki} \in \mathrm{IN}(v_i)} w'(e_{ki})$$

Here, $\mathrm{IN}(v_i)$ is the set of the incoming edges of v_i. Figure 2 (b) shows this definition.

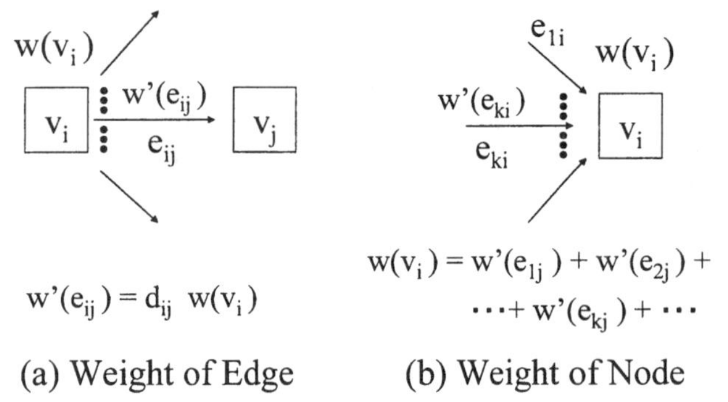

Figure 2. Definition of weights

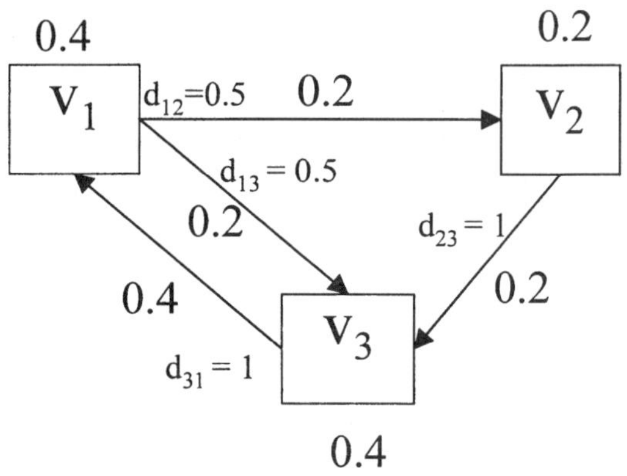

Figure 3. An example of stable weights assigned to nodes and edges

2.3. Computation of Weights

Based on these definitions, we have $n(= |V|)$ simultaneous equations for $w(v_i)$,

$$w(v_i) = \sum_{e_{ki} \in \mathrm{IN}(v_i)} d_{ki} \times w(v_k)$$

Assume that W is a vector of node's weights,

$$W = \begin{pmatrix} w(v_1) \\ w(v_2) \\ \vdots \\ w(v_n) \end{pmatrix}$$

Also, D is a matrix of the distribution ratios,

$$D = \begin{pmatrix} d_{11} & d_{12} & \dots & d_{1n} \\ d_{21} & d_{22} & \dots & d_{2n} \\ \vdots & \vdots & \ddots & \vdots \\ d_{n1} & d_{n2} & \dots & d_{nn} \end{pmatrix}$$

So the simultaneous equations can be rewritten by,

$$W = D^t W \tag{1}$$

where D^t is the transposed matrix of D.

Together with Definition 1, formula (1) can be solved by computing the eigenvector with eigenvalue 1.

Instead of computing the eigenvector, we can also compute the weights of each node by a repeated computation such that, we give initial ad-hoc weights to each node(e.g., $1/n$ to each node), and then propagate them to adjacent nodes through directed edges. The weights are repeatedly recomputed until the all weights become stable.

Figure 3 shows a component graph with computed weights. v_1 has two outgoing edges, and weight 0.4 is evenly divided to two outgoing edges with 0.2 each (i.e., $d_{12} = d_{13} = 0.5$). v_3 has two incoming edges, each with weight 0.2, so that the weight of v_3 is 0.4.

If we assume that the movement of software developer's focus on the target components is represented by a probabilistic state transition, the component graph is a Markov chain model. Thus, computing the weights of the nodes in the graph corresponds to getting a stationary distribution of the chain.

2.4. Convergence of Computation

In the case that a node v_i has no outgoing edge, all distribution ratios d_{ix} become zero. This does not satisfy the requirement of the total sum of the distribution ratio.

Also, if the graph is not strongly connected as shown in Figure 4 (a), the weight of v_1 is repeatedly added to the weight of v_2, causing non-termination in the repeated computation.

In these cases, the eigenvector cannot be solved either. To guarantee the solution of the simultaneous equations, i.e., the termination of repeated computation of the weights, we introduce pseudo use relations between all nodes as shown in Figure 4 (b), and define an amended distribution ratio for each node as follows.

Definition 4 (Amended Distribution Ratio)

$$d'_{ij} = \begin{cases} p \times d_{ij} + (1-p)/n & \textit{if } v_i \textit{ has outgoing edge } e_{ij} \\ 1/n & \textit{if } v_i \textit{ has no outgoing edges} \end{cases}$$

Here $p (0 < p < 1)$ is the ratio between the weight of real use relations and that of pseudo use relations, and we generally employ a fairly large value such as 0.85 as discussed later.

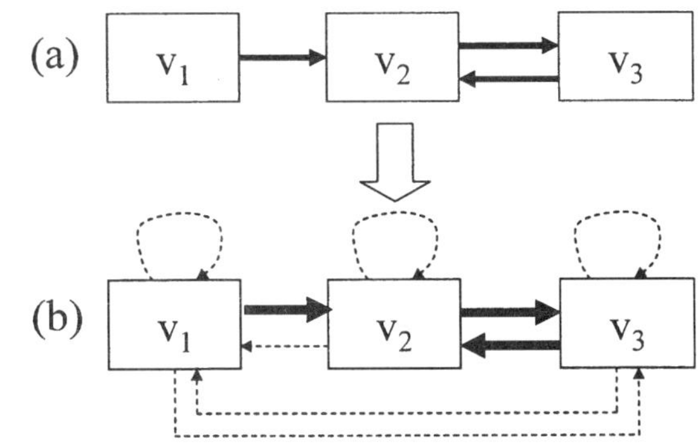

Figure 4. Introduction of pseudo use relation for convergence

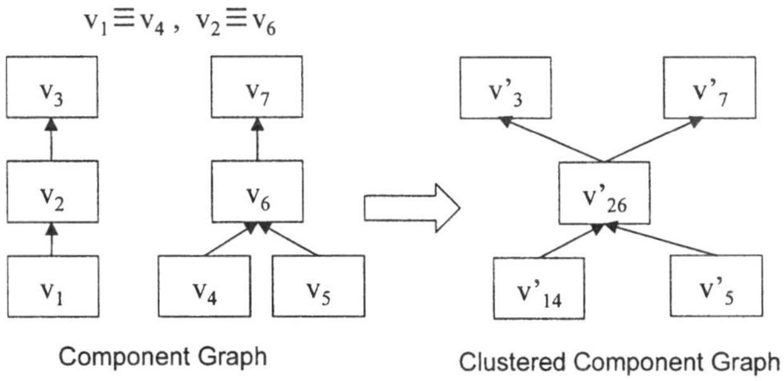

Figure 5. An example of clustered component graph

By using d'_{ij} instead of d_{ij}, we can always compute the weight for a given component graph. This pseudo use relation can be considered as a possible implicit reference of a component to all components (including itself).

2.5. Clustering Components

Software systems are often made by reusing already developed components. Some components are simply copied from previous systems, or some are constructed from those with minor or major modifications.

In the above mentioned method, those reused components are represented as multiple nodes in a component graph, and their weights are computed independently.

We would want to identify the similarity of components and to feed back the similarity information to the computation, in order to obtain more practical weight values.

Assume that we can measure similarity $S(v_1, v_2)$ of any two nodes (components) v_1 and v_2 in a component graph $G = (V, E)$, where $0 \leq S(v_1, v_2) \leq 1$, $S(v, v) = 1$, and $S(v, w) = 0$ if v and w are totally different.

Here, we say that an equivalence relation of v_1 and v_2 exists when $S(v_1, v_2) \geq t$, where t is a criterion of the equivalence. This equivalence relation partitions V into a set of equivalence classes, composing the quotient set V'.

We define the *clustered component graph* $G' = (V', E')$ for G as follows.

Definition 5 (Clustered Component Graph)
$G' = (V', E')$ such that V' is the quotient set of V, and $E' = \{(v'_i, v'_j) | (v_i, v_j) \in E\}$ where v'_i and v'_j are equivalence classes involving v_i and v_j, respectively.

Figure 5 shows an example of a clustered component graph. Two weakly connected subgraphs in the component graph are merged into one weakly connected graph as the clustered component graph. As shown in this example, there are cases such that several independent subgraphs in the component graph are merged into one, and the characteristics of each subgraph can be propagated to other subgraphs.

Using the clustered component graph instead of the component graph, we will compute the weights of each node as the above mentioned approach, including the amendment of the distribution ratio. We simply call *component graph* for *clustered component graph* hereafter, if there is no ambiguity.

3. Component Rank System

3.1. Implementation of Component Rank Model

Based on the Component Rank model discussed in Section 2, we have designed and implemented a system to compute Component Ranks for Java programs. The following features the implementation.

Component: A single Java source file with .java extension is considered as a component. In Java, it is inherently easy to extract components, since each class definition is independently defined as a single file with .java extension. Internal classes are not considered as components here.

Use relation: Class inheritance relation, method invocation, and abstract class implementation are the use relations. Here, we employ only statically detectable ones from the source programs.

Ratio p between real and pseudo use relations: We use p=0.85 which means that the total weight value 0.15 is assigned to the pseudo use relations.

Distribution ratio: The distribution ratios of the real use relations, which go out from one node, are equally

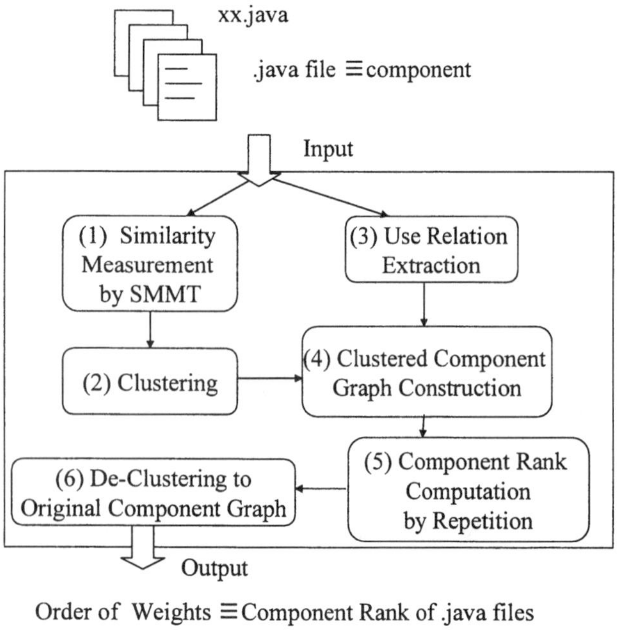

Figure 6. Architecture of the component rank system

the same values. For example, if a node have 5 outgoing edges, the distribution ratio evenly divided for each edge is 0.17. The total of 5 edges is 0.85, and the rest 0.15 is the total of the pseudo use relations, which imaginarily go out to all nodes in the component graph.

Similarity t**:** Similarity metrics for source codes, proposed in [23], is adopted, and its measurement tool SMMT is used. The metrics is based on a combination of a fast code-clone detection by *CCFinder*[14] and a file-difference detection by *diff*[5]. The number of shared source code lines is divided by the number of total lines, producing the similarity value. We employ the similarity criterion $t = 0.80$ here.

3.2. Architecture of the Component Rank System

Figure 6 shows the architecture of our first prototype of the Component Rank system.

(1) The similarity of any two components (files) is computed by SMMT tool, for M input components.

(2) Two components with similarity higher than or equal to t=0.8 are merged into one component. By this clustering, we get $N(\leq M)$ equivalence classes.

(3) The syntax analyzer parses the java source files, and extracts class inheritances, method invocations, and abstract class implementations, as the use relations. The analyzer has been constructed by using Java syntax library ANTLR[1].

(4) The clustered component graph is constructed as a form of N x N amended distribution ratio matrix.

(5) The weights of nodes are computed by propagating initial ad-hoc values through edges until we get the convergence. This method is mostly faster than solving the eigenvector by a math library.

(6) The weighted nodes in the clustered component graph is mapped back to the original components, so that we can see the order of the weight of each component in M, i.e., Component Rank of the Java file, as the output.

The system computes Component Rank fairly efficiently even for a large set of programs. It takes about 7 minutes to compute Component Rank for JDK 1.3.0 (1877 components of totally 575,000 lines.) on a PC workstation (Pentium IV, 2GHz, 2GBytes memory).

4. Experiments

We have applied the Component Rank system to 4 sets of Java programs as follows.

4.1. JDK 1.3.0

All source programs of Java 2 Software Development Kit, Standard Edition 1.3.0[12] (simply referred to JDK 1.3.0 here) are the target of the first application. It is composed of 1877 .java files of totally 575,000 lines of code in Java. These files include the classes which are very important and fundamental ones to develop various Java applications.

Table 1 shows the resulting Component Rank values for each file, listed from the highest rank to the lowest one. The highest one, java.lang.Object class, is the superclass of any class in Java, so that this class is used directly or indirectly by any class, causing it on the top of the ranking.

Other highly ranked classes are also fundamental ones that are possibly invoked or inherited from many other classes. The 3rd class, java.lang.Throwable, is the superclass of any error or exception handlers so that it is used by many classes with error or exception handling.

There are 622 classes with the lowest (1256th) rank. These classes are not used by any other classes at all.

The overall result of Component Rank for JDK 1.3.0 matches to our intuition such that very general and core classes are ranked high, and specific and independent classes are ranked low.

Table 1. Component Rank for JDK 1.3.0

C.Rank	Class Name	Weight
1	java.lang.Object	0.16126
2	java.lang.Class	0.08712
3	java.lang.Throwable	0.05510
4	java.lang.Exception	0.03103
5	java.io.IOException	0.01343
6	java.lang.StringBuffer	0.01214
7	java.lang.SecurityManager	0.01169
8	java.io.InputStream	0.01027
9	java.lang.reflect.Field	0.00948
10	java.lang.reflect.Constructor	0.00936
⋮	⋮	⋮
1256	sunw.util.EventListener	0.00011
1256	⋮	⋮

Table 2. Component Rank for SE tools

C.Rank	Class Name	Weight
1	antlr.Token	0.10727
2	antlr.debug.Event	0.06189
2	antlr.debug.NewLineEvent	0.06189
4	antlr.collections.impl.Vector	0.05434
5	jp.gr.java_conf.keisuken. text.html.HtmlParameter	0.05246
6	jp.gr.java_conf.keisuken. net.server.ServerProperties	0.03699
7	Jama.Matrix	0.01564
8	jp.gr.java_conf.keisuken. util.IntegerArray	0.01390
8	jp.gr.java_conf.keisuken. util.LongArray	0.01390
10	jp.ac.osaka_u.es.ics.iip_lab.metrics. parser.IdentifierInfo	0.01365
⋮	⋮	⋮
418	cktool_new.examples.Main	0.00050

4.2. Collection of SE Tools

We have applied the Component Rank system to a collection of software engineering tools developed in our lab. There are 582 files in total. The following lists their overview.

C-K Metrics Measurement Tool 1: This tool measures C-Kmetrics[4] of Java programs. The package name is cktool, and the tool uses a syntax analyzer ANTLR[1].

C-K Metrics Measurement Tool 2: This is an upgraded tool of above, and is named cktool_new.

Component Rank System: A version of Component Rank system itself is also targeted. It uses library ANTLR, a matrix computation library JAMA[11], and a general utility library Caffe Cappuccino Class Library[3]. The package name is jp.ac.osaka_u.ics. iip_lab.metrics.

Libraries: The source files of above mentioned libraries, ANTLR, JAMA, and Caffe Cappuccino Class Library (the package name is jp.gr.java_conf.keisuken) are included as the target. JDK is excluded here.

Table 2 shows the result of those tools. There are two of the second classes, antlr.debug.Event and antlr,debug.NewLineEvent, having the same weights. These two are merged into a single node in the clustered component graph because of their similarity. Also, two classes of the 8th rank are merged into one.

We have noticed that library classes are generally in higher ranks, and our developed application classes are generally in lower ranks. Also, we knew that many data container classes are ranked high, such as antlr.Token at the first, and antlr.collections.impl.Vector at the 4th rank.

This result also suggests that Component Rank is an indicator of generality and specialty of classes from the view point of usage from other classes.

4.3. Framework and Applications Developed by a Software Company

Daiwa Computer, located in Osaka, Japan, is a software company with about 180 engineers. In that company, various kinds of new technologies in Software Engineering are actively studied and introduced. It holds ISO9001:2000 certificate and CMM Level3 assessment.

In that company, a shared framework for Java applications has been constructed, and various business applications have been developed on this framework.

Using this framework, five Web-based data management applications have been developed. Those applications have similar features but have distinction in their implementation such as databases and their interfaces (SQL, DB2, Oracle, ...).

These five applications and the framework itself are the target of the ranking. They contain 1538 components in total, and these components were clustered into 339 nodes.

The observation we got by this experiment is very similar to the previous two experiments. The classes defined in the framework generally have high ranks. For example, from the first to 10th ranked classes are for the framework. This means that those classes are frequently used by other classes. Also, we knew that classes defining data structures and their containers are highly ranked. The first ranked class is the definition of a record class for database management, which is defined in the framework. These results confirm

Table 3. Search Result Sorted by Component Rank

Order (C.Rank)	Class Name	weight
1(67)	enhydra3.1...dom.Node	0.029110
2(169)	saxon7_0...saxon.om.NodeInfo	0.000969
3(275)	saxon7_0...saxon.pattern.NodeTest	0.000437
4(316)	enhydra3.1...dom.DocumentImpl	0.000368
5(355)	saxon7_0...saxon.pattern.Pattern	0.000324
6(382)	saxon7_0...saxon.Controller	0.000296
7(437)	enhydra3.1...xslt.XSLTEngineImpl	0.000241
8(446)	enhydra3.1...dom.ElementImpl	0.000235
9(500)	saxon7_0...saxon.style.StyleElement	0.000202
10(506)	saxon7_0...saxon.tree.NodeImpl	0.000198
⋮	⋮	⋮
125(4441)	enhydra3.1...FuncID	0.000029
125(4441)	⋮	⋮

our approach, in the sense that core and fundamental components can be easily identified by the rank.

4.4. Searching Components with Component Rank

The rank values computed by our method are generic ones in the sense that any kind of components is ordered in one dimension. We would usually want to search a specific kind of components in which we are interested, and also we may want to sort the found components in the order of their ranks.

To have the first impression of such a search, we have ranked 7171 Java files for text editors *JEDIT* and *jext*, an application server *Enhydra*, an XSLT processor *saxon*, and a Gnutella client *phex* (all these handle XML documents), found in SourceForge[21], in addition to JDK 1.3.0 and the 4 tools shown in Section 4.2.

For these, we searched components with a keyword "getNodetype" by using UNIX tool *grep*, excluding the components having the keyword only in comments. We had 181 matched components, and they are sorted by Component Ranks, as shown in Table 3.

Method "getNodetype" is a method to get the information of the kind of the node in the DOM tree. At the first and second in the sorted order, the definitions of that method appear. Other components use that class. High-ranked components are mainly for the operation of elements and for the analysis of a style sheet, which are fairly generic operations. On the other hand, many low-ranked components are for non-generic and specific purpose ones such as classes for interpreting and performing the contents described by XML.

We would think that this is a very encouraging result, since the high-ranked components are ones which should be directly referred to or should be associated when we build codes related to DOM trees.

5. Discussions

5.1. Weight Computation

In our Component Rank model, the weights of nodes are propagated to other nodes through edges. We would consider another simpler model such that the weight of a node is determined by the number of incoming edges. This alternate model can be easily computed without complex computation for the convergence (or the eigenvector as we do).

However, this alternate model is very fragile to local special references. Consider that a component A is 10 times used by components B1 to B10, and B1 to B10 are not used by any component at all. In the alternate model, the weight of A becomes 10. In the Component Rank model, the weight of A is relatively determined by other components, but A is not ranked high as the alternate model, since the weights of B1 to B10 are relatively low. Thus, we consider that our model is very stable for such local references.

This argument is a similar one such as a comparison of Web search engines between Google and other simple search engines only counting incoming references[18]. The simple engines could easily cheated by intentionally-made local reference links, but Google is resistant to such links.

5.2. Clustering Policy

The clustering similar nodes is an important characteristics of our Component Rank model. If we would model multiple software systems in a component graph without clustering, the graph might be composed of multiple disconnected subgraphs and the weights would be independently computed inside each subgraph, without circulating weights over subgraphs (except for small interaction by the pseudo use relations).

The clustering has an effect that the weights of one software system are propagated to other systems through clustered nodes, resulting in Component Rank as a global ranking in all the software systems.

We have taken a clustering policy such that first similar nodes are clustered then the weight of each node is computed. An alternate policy would be that first we compute the weight of each node in the original component graph, then we cluster the similar nodes by adding similar node's weights as the clustered node's weight.

In our policy, simply copied and used components are not counted repeatedly. Consider a simple case shown in Figure 7 (we do not consider the pseudo use relations for simplicity here). In this case, components A and B are duplicated. In our policy, the result weights for A' and B' are 1/4, while those are 1/3 in the alternate policy. This means that in our policy the existence of simply copied components does not affect the resulting weight. In the alternate policy, if the number of copied components grows, the resulting weights for those components increase.

We believe that it is important not to count simply duplicated components, but to count modified and labored components.

Consider another case shown in Figure 8. In this case, component A is reused, but B is replaced with C. In the result, the weight of A' is 2/5 in our policy, which is higher than 1/3 in the alternate policy. The weight of A' in the alternate policy is 1/3, the same value as the case in Figure 7, even with its structural change.

These examples sharply present that the duplication with modification is properly counted in our policy, but it is not in the alternate policy.

5.3. Similarity Criterion t and Pseudo Use Relation Ratio p

We have investigated different t from 0.10 to 0.90, and knew that the resulting ranks are fairly insensitive to t[24]. There are some components which are clustered with 0.70 or lower, but not with 0.80 or higher. Exception handlers in JDK are examples of those. We thought that such components should be counted separately so we have employed t=0.80 here.

The ratio p between real and pseudo use relations has been explored in detail[7]. We knew that the resulting weight values are affected by p, but that the resulting Component Ranks are insensible to p. The ranks are fairly stable even if we have changed p from 0.75 to 0.95, so we have chosen p=0.85 here.

5.4. Distribution Ratios of Node

In the current implementation of the Component Rank system, we have employed an equal distribution ratios for any outgoing edge from one node. We can consider another policy such that we give some priority to specific outgoing edges which are considered to deserve. At this moment, we do not have a clue to determine the priority, and we think this is a further issue. However, our intuition is that if the component graph becomes huge enough, the priority parameter of distribution ratios would not affect to the result ranks so severely, as we have investigated variations of t and p above.

We have defined the Component Rank model such that the weight of a node is divided and distributed to the outgoing edges so that the total weight of the outgoing edges is the weight of the node (assuming no pseudo edges). We can consider another model where the weight of a node is directly the weights of each edge, without division by the number of the outgoing edges. This model means that nodes with more outgoing edges have higher influence to other nodes totally, than nodes with less outgoing edges. We thought that this is unfair, but we might need a further investigation.

5.5. Scalability

In order to get practically useful results, we need to collect a huge number of source programs. In that sense, the scalability of the system is important. Currently, our Component Rank system works under about 8,000 components due to the limitation of the similarity computation. The current similarity computation is based on a pair-wise execution of *diff*[5] for any two components. This should be changed to a more efficient method such as classification of components by characteristic metrics.

Compared to the similarity computation, the convergence computation is a much lighter process, and we think that it would not limit the scalability.

5.6. Related Works

The Component Rank model proposed here is based on our original intuition, such that, from a huge number of collections of legacy software, we might be able to effectively search software components, pieces of program codes, program patterns, or abstracted algorithms, by using a similar approach as Google[2, 8, 18] for Web pages, together with various program analysis techniques. Google computes the ranks (called *PageRanks*) for HTML documents available in the Internet. The resulting PageRank is practically very useful. A related analyses on the Web links have been discussed in detail in [16].

The Google's approach can be considered as an HTML extension of a method proposed for counting impact of publications, called *influence weight*[19]. The influence weight of a publication is determined by the sum of the weights of incoming references, as the Component Rank model does.

A major distinction of our model from PageRank and the influence weight is that our approach explores similarity between components before the weight computation. This is definitely important for software components. There would be so many copied or slightly modified software components when we simply collect software systems. Without proper handling of those similar components, we could not get reasonable and practical ranks.

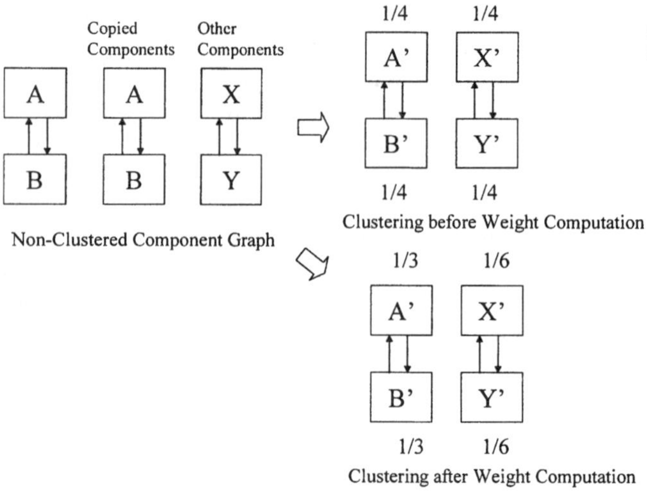

Figure 7. Effect of simple copied components

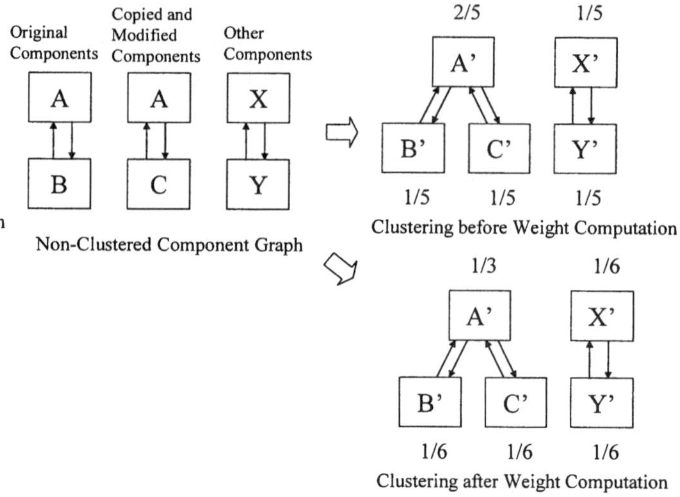

Figure 8. Effect of copied and modified components

Our Component Rank is a true measure of software reuse. There have been many researches on software reusability, and many literatures have been already published[9, 17]. Software reuse is a promising approach to improve the efficiency of software development and the quality of developed software[10, 15].

Many methods to measure reusability of software components have been proposed. Etzkorn's approach[6] is that various static metrics for C++ classes (components), such as cohesion and complexity, are measured and these values are normalized and added. Yamamoto's approach[22] is that class interface information is used to determine reusability. These approaches are based on measuring static properties of components.

Our approach does not measure the property of components, but only uses relation among components. We believe that the overall structure of the components represents much properly the usage history of the component, rather than the metrics of the components. In our model, if a component is repeatedly reused (by not simple copying), the result rank will be higher. However, the property measures are not affected by the repeated reuse.

5.7. SPARS

Using the Component Rank system as a core ranking engine, we are currently developing Software Product Archiving, analyzing, and Retrieving System called *SPARS*. Figure 9 shows SPARS architecture. Various Java source programs are collected, and they are stored in the raw component archive. Those components are ranked by the Component Rank engine and stored as the ranked component archive.

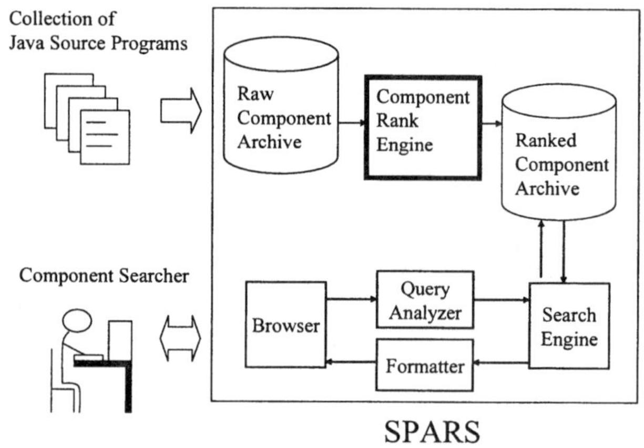

Figure 9. Architecture of SPARS

A component searcher, who is trying to build a software system, will give SPARS queries for some typical definition or typical usage of a class to build, by keywords or portions of source codes. These queries are analyzed and given to the search engine. It retrieves the ranked component archive. The matched results are listed by the ranks, and are returned to the component searcher.

6. Conclusion

We have proposed a novel ranking method of software components, Component Rank, and shown the first implementation of Component Rank. Using the implemented system, various Java programs have been ranked, and the characteristics of Component Rank have been investigated.

Although the results might be still preliminary, we believe that this method is very promising. Using the Component Rank method, we are currently developing a software component retrieval system, SPARS, which will be used in various situations of software development, such as searching, exploring, checking, investigating, reminding or referring to software components, as we use dictionaries and libraries when writing a composition. SPARS might be considered as a Google-like system for software engineers.

There are several further issues. The validity of Component Rank will be explored further.

One approach is to evaluate the rank values directly. However, since we do not know any objective measure inherently correlating to Component Rank, we would use, for a validation, a subjective measure such as questioners to software experts.

Another approach would be to investigate precision and recall of the search results. To do this, we will need to build a proper experimental setting, including correct answers to test queries.

In the Component Rank model, we employed only statical use relations. It is possible to extend to use relations such as method invocation and dynamic class binding. This approach would be more preferable since we can compute the ranks of components without their source codes. Distinction between statical and dynamical ranks is a very intriguing research issue to explore.

We have discussed the Component Rank model only for component retrieval; however, we are planning to apply Component Rank to automatic software architecture composition. There are many literatures for the structuring software architectures from the results of statical analyses of source codes and libraries, or from the results of dynamic analyses of object code execution. We think that those analysis results could be more stabilized by the propagation and convergence computation as the Component Rank model.

Our Component Rank system is currently implemented to accept Java programs only. We will extend to other procedural languages such as C and C++. To do this, we have to define the component and use relation for those languages. Functions and procedure invocations would be practically feasible candidates, but we need further investigation and validation.

Acknowledgments

We express our great thanks to Daiwa Computer Co., Ltd. for the data collection. We also thank Prof. Kumiyo Nakakoji of University of Tokyo / SRA-KTL and Dr. Yunwen Ye of University of Colorado / SRA-KTL for their helpful comments and discussions.

This project is supported by Japan Science and Technology Corporation, Research and Development for Applying Advanced Computational Science and Technology.

References

[1] ANTLR. "http://www.antlr.org/".

[2] S. Brin and L. Page. "The Anatomy of a Large-scale Hypertextual Web Search Engine". *Computer Networks and ISDN Systems*, 30(1-7):107–117, 1998.

[3] Caffe Cappuccino class library. "http://cappuccino.ne.jp /keisuken/java/capp/api/overview-summary.html".

[4] S. Chidamber and C. Kemerer. "A Metrics Suite for Object-Oriented Design". *IEEE Transactions. Software Engineering*, 20(6):476–493, 1994.

[5] Diffutls. "http://www.gnu.org/software/diffutils/".

[6] L. H. Etzkorn, W. E. H. Jr., and C. G. Davis. "Automated Reusability Quality Analysis of OO Legacy Software". *Information and Software Technology*, 43(5):295–308, 2001.

[7] H. Fujiwara. " A New Reusability Metric Based on Reuse Results and Similarity among Programs". Master's thesis, Dept. of Informatics and Mathematical Science, Osaka University, 2002. (In Japanese).

[8] Google. "http://www.google.com".

[9] J. Guo and Luqi. "A Survey of Software Reuse Repositories". In *Proceedings of 7th IEEE International Conference and Workshop on the Engineering of Computer Based Systems*, pages 92–100, Edinburgh, Scotland, April 2000.

[10] S. Isoda. "Experience Report on a Software Reuse Project: Its Structure, Activities, and Statistical Results". In *Proceedings of 14th International Conference on Software Engineering*, pages 320–326, Melbourne, Australia, 1992.

[11] JAMA : A Java Matrix Package. "http://math.nist.gov/ javanumerics/jama/".

[12] Java 2 Software Development Kit, Standard Edition 1.3.0. "http://java.sun.com/j2se/".

[13] JUMBO! "http://www.jumbo.com/".

[14] T. Kamiya, S. Kusumoto, and K. Inoue. "CCFinder: A Multi-Linguistic Token-based Code Clone Detection System for Large Scale Source Code". *IEEE Transactions. Software Engineering*, 28(7):654–670, 2002.

[15] B. Keepence and M. Mannion. "Using Patterns to Model Variability in Product Families". *IEEE Software*, 16(4):102–108, 1999.

[16] J. Kleinberg. "Authoritative Sources in a Hyperlinked Environment". *Journal of the ACM*, 46(5):604–632, 1999.

[17] C. Krueger. "Software Reuse". *ACM Computing Surveys*, 24(2):131–183, 1992.

[18] L. Page, S. Brin, R. Motwani, and T. Winograd. "The PageRank Citation Ranking: Bringing Order to the Web". Technical Report of Stanford Digital Library Technologies Project, 1998." http://www-db.stanford.edu/backrub/ pageranksub.ps".

[19] G. Pinski and F. Narin. "Citation Influence for Journal Aggregates of Scientific Publications: Theory, with Application to the Literature of Physics". *Information Processing and Management*, 12(5):297–312, 1976.

[20] E. S. Raymond. "The Cathedral and the Bazaar". "http://www.tuxedo.org/ esr/writings/cathedral-bazaar/".
[21] SOURCEFORGE.net. "http://sourceforge.net/".
[22] H. Yamamoto, H. Washizaki, and Y. Fukazawa. "The Proposal and Verification of Component Metrics Based on the Reuse Characteristic". In *Workshop of Foundation of Software Engineering (FOSE2001)*, 2001. (In Japanese).
[23] T. Yamamoto, M. Matsusita, T. Kamiya, and K. Inoue. "Measuring Similarity of Large Software Systems Based on Source Code Correspondence". Technical Report of Dept. of ICS, IIP-03-03-02, 2002.
[24] R. Yokomori, H. Fujiwara, T. Yamamoto, M. Matsusita, S. Kusumoto, and K. Inoue. "Proposal of Reusability Evaluation Method Using Relations among Software Components". In *Proceedings of Software Symposium 2002*, pages 216–225, Matsue, Japan, July 2002. (In Japanese).
[25] ZDNet. "http://www.zdnet.com".

The Vienna Component Framework Enabling Composition Across Component Models

Johann Oberleitner Thomas Gschwind Mehdi Jazayeri
Technische Universität Wien
Institut für Informationssysteme
Argentinierstraße 8/E1841
A-1040 Wien, Austria
{joe,tom,jazayeri}@infosys.tuwien.ac.at

Abstract

The Vienna Component Framework (VCF) supports the interoperability and composability of components across different component models, a facility that is lacking in existing component models. The VCF presents a unified component model—implemented by a façade component—to the application programmer. The programmer may write new components by composing components from different component models, accessed through the VCF. The model supports common component features, namely, methods, properties, and events. To support a component model within the VCF, a plugin component is needed that provides access to the component model. The paper presents the VCF's design, implementation issues, and evaluation. Performance measurements of VCF implementations of COM, Enterprise JavaBeans, CORBA distributed objects, and JavaBeans show that the overhead of accessing components through the VCF is negligible for distributed components.

1. Introduction

A primary goal of component-based software engineering is to promote the use of reusable and pre-tested components across projects. As in other engineering disciplines, in which components are well established the reuse of existing parts leads to shorter development cycles, higher quality, increased functionality and hence reduced costs.

In recent years component models such as Enterprise JavaBeans, CORBA objects, and COM+ components have emerged that provide standards for component implementation and component interoperability [12]. Additionally, component models provide services and infrastructure to components such as a meta-information facility, naming and trading services, and transaction monitors. Hence, component developers can use these predefined services and rely on the vendor of a component model implementation to get this support.

The implementation standards define how a component's external interfaces are accessed. These interfaces are the only way to access a component's functionality, such as its operations or its state, from outside the component, hence enforcing the principle of information hiding.

A component model is an indispensable element in a component-based software technology. However, strict standards are also a limiting factor in a component-based software environment. Although all component models define similar features such as methods, properties and events, a standardized way does not exist for implementing a component for a particular model and for porting it to a different component model. Even worse, the significantly easier problem of using a component that is implemented for one component model from a component of another model is only solved for certain pairs of component models.

In an ideal setting, a developer would be able to use the best components available without having to think about the component model they have been implemented for. Such an example could be a stock ticker application that uses a CORBA component for a stock quote service, a JavaBean component that provides an elaborate charting facility and Microsoft's Internet Explorer, a COM component, for displaying current market news.

To solve these composition problems, we have developed the Vienna Component Framework (VCF), a Java based class framework that allows the access of components across different models and the construction of new components in a platform independent way. Two different factors limit the reuse of component source code: the standards that define how a component has to be constructed and the dependency of the component on services provided only by a certain component model. Our framework abstracts both of

0-7695-1877-X/03 $17.00 © 2003 IEEE

these within interfaces. These interfaces build a meta-model for component models. A particular component model is supported by writing a plug-in that queries the component model for its component's meta-information, builds a representation of the component and all of its features and provides the required functionality to access these features. So far, we have implemented plugins for COM, CORBA, Enterprise JavaBeans and JavaBeans demonstrating the extensibility of the framework.

The remainder of the paper is structured as follows. In Section 2 we discuss today's commonly used component models. On the basis of the commonalities and differences of these component models, we discuss the design and overall architecture of VCF in Section 3. Section 4 explains the steps necessary to add support for a new component model and Section 5 focuses on the construction of new components. The evaluation of our approach is shown in Section 6. Related work is described in Section 7. Finally, we draw some conclusions in Section 8.

2. Component Models

To understand how to abstract the features of component models into a uniform framework, one must first analyze the commonalities and differences among currently available component models. Knowledge of these differences and commonalities will help the reader to understand the design and architecture of VCF presented in Section 3.

2.1. COM+

Microsoft's Component Object Model (COM) [8, 17] is used heavily within Microsoft's operating systems. COM components are declared using Microsoft IDL (MIDL) that supports the description of COM component classes and interfaces. Unlike CORBA, interfaces define only methods. Properties are declared using setter and getter methods having special attributes attached to them. MIDL uses its own type system that is based on the C type system including pointers to interfaces. Components are usually implemented with C++ classes or with another COM-capable language. Recent additions to COM have been server-side facilities for load-balancing and transaction monitoring, better known as COM+. However, the client side programming model has remained the same.

Meta-information is provided by type libraries. These libraries can be constructed from the IDL with Microsoft's IDL compiler. To access a component dynamically the so-called `IDispatch` interface can be used. This interface provides a method to create an invocation dynamically.

2.2. CORBA

The Common Object Request Broker Architecture (CORBA) [20, 13] has been defined by the OMG to provide an object infrastructure for interoperability among different hardware and software products. A CORBA object is declared by writing an IDL file that contains the interface definition of the object. This interface takes the definitions of an object's operations and its attributes. The IDL file is compiled by an IDL compiler that generates client stubs and server skeletons for a given language.

The IDL has its own type system which is loosely based on C++. This type system is mapped onto the type system of a given programming language as defined by the corresponding language binding. In case of the Java programming language primitive types are converted to Java types and CORBA object types are converted to client stubs.

CORBA's communication model is based on object invocation where objects may reside locally or remotely. Each request to a CORBA object is processed by the client stub which forwards the request to an Object Request Broker (ORB) that is located on the host of the client. This ORB uses a communication channel to communicate with the ORB on the host of the object's server process. This second ORB forwards the invocation to an appropriate method in the server process.

The OMG has predefined many different services that can be used to enhance the functionality of a CORBA object at development time. A client can use the name service to look up an existing object. Other important services are responsible for transactions, persistence, notification and security. Meta-information for an object is available through an Interface Repository (IR) that provides programmatic access to information about objects. The interface repository usually obtains this information from the IDL files. This information together with Dynamic Interface Invocation (DII) can be used to construct and make dynamic calls at runtime.

2.3. Enterprise JavaBeans

The Enterprise JavaBeans (EJB) [5] component model is an essential part of Sun's J2EE environment and uses the type system of Java. EJBs are components that reside within a container on an application server. The implementation of an EJB consists of Java classes that are deployed in the container. Clients use an enterprise bean's home and remote interface to invoke its methods. The home interface defines methods to create or to look up component instances. The remote interface provides access to a given instance. To interact with an EJB component, the client first obtains a reference to the bean's home interface which the client can use to create a new component instance of the bean or to look up an existing one. Both of these operations return a reference that implements the remote interface.

Enterprise JavaBeans can implement different concepts. Entity beans model business concepts that are represented in database tables. Session beans model a workflow and thus implement a particular task [18]. Usually, they are stateless and have no properties. Message-driven beans are similar to session beans but work in message-oriented middleware settings. They are not considered in this paper.

An EJB application server provides distributed services to their components such as a persistence service, a transaction service, and a security service. These services can be used in a programmatic way and in a descriptive way. Hence, it is not necessary to prepare a component to define transactions and security facilities at compile time since these features can be added by providing a descriptor file when a component is deployed within the application server.

Unlike other component models, EJBs do not support events. Additionally, there is no standardized means to find out at runtime if a component uses a particular service provided by the EJB application server.

2.4. JavaBeans

JavaBeans [11] is a simple component model that relies on the Java programming language. Unlike the other component models presented so far, it only supports components executed locally within the client's virtual machine. A JavaBean is a Java class that has a default constructor and supports the Java serialization mechanism.

JavaBeans support methods, properties and events. These can be defined using the following naming conventions [11]. Publicly accessible methods that have a `get` or a `set` prefix are considered to model property access. The name of the property is deduced from the method's name. A similar approach has been followed for events. All methods that do not fall into properties or eventsets are just methods of the JavaBean. These syntax guidelines, however, can be overridden providing a `BeanInfo` class that specifies which properties, events and methods are accessible from clients.

Since a JavaBean is just a Java class the component model uses Java's type system. An instance of a component is a normal Java object and hence clients access these instances like any other Java object. To query a JavaBean for its meta-information, however, introspection should be used instead of Java's reflection mechanism. Introspection automatically derives the available properties and events on the basis of the above naming conventions and makes use of a `BeanInfo` class if available.

2.5. Comparisons

In the last sections we have shown the characteristics of widely used component models. Of particular interest are the type systems of the different component models. JavaBeans and Enterprise JavaBeans rely on Java's type system, CORBA and COM, however, use their own type systems. CORBA object servers and clients use the type system defined by the OMG's IDL. CORBA's Java language binding provides a mapping to Java types. Unfortunately, a language binding for Sun's Java Virtual Machine does not exist for COM.

All component models provide dynamic invocation. Although the APIs differ considerably, they allow construction of requests dynamically at runtime. Metadata provides information about components and can be used to query the features of component models. The implementation of this metadata interface and the specifics of the information differ among the component models. All of the component models presented above, however, provide enough information to build an internal representation of a component's features.

3. Design

The purpose of the Vienna Component Framework (VCF) is to provide an API that allows for the use of multiple different component models in a uniform way. This enables the use of components implemented for different component models from within a single project without having to deal with the internals of the different component models. This increases the range of components available to software developers.

For the implementation of the VCF, we have chosen to use the Java programming language. The principles of this framework, however, apply equally well to implementations in other object-oriented programming languages.

3.1. Architecture

VCF supports several component models. Each component model is represented by a *plugin*. Support for a new component model can be added by implementing a new component model plugin. Each component model plugin has to provide the functionality to access the features of the corresponding component model. This includes the features for controlling the lifecycle of a component's instance, for making that instance persistent, and for accessing its state and operations.

Component model plugins are not used directly but instead are accessed through a façade component as shown in Figure 1. This allows the integration of new functionality that can be applied to any component model in the façade

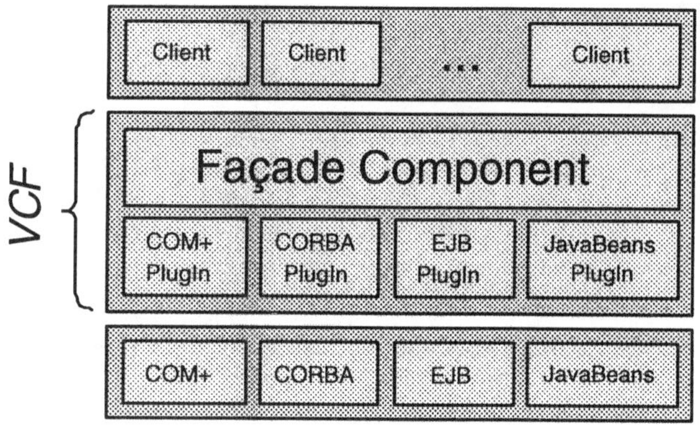

Figure 1. Architecture of the VCF

class without changing the plugins' syntactic or semantic structure [10]. Each instance of a particular component is hosted in an instance of the corresponding plugin class.

3.2. Metadata Interface

One key feature of today's component models is that they provide metadata that allows clients to identify the features that a component provides during run-time. Features identify the different means to interact with a component such as a property that can be changed or an event that may be triggered by the component. Features may statically apply to all instances of a component such as the lifecycle feature, or they may apply to individual instances of a component such as a property.

Since different component models use different features, a component model plugin only has to provide support for those features provided by the underlying component model. VCF provides support for the most commonly used features. A component model plugin, however, may provide support for additional features in case a component model requires a feature not provided natively by VCF.

Currently, VCF provides support for the following features:

Lifecycle provides methods to create and to explicitly destroy instances of a component.

Persistence allows a component instance to be stored on and retrieved from persistent storage.

Method gives access to the methods provided by a component.

Property allows the manipulation of a component's state.

Event allows other components to react to events generated by this component.

All features that are provided by a plugin are returned in a feature container returned by the the plugin's `getFeatures` method. This feature container provides standardized means to add and remove features, and allows queries for a particular feature. These queries range from retrieving all features of an instance to fine-grained queries like searching for all methods that have a particular return type and whose names match a regular expression.

3.3. Component Access

Components may be accessed through the metadata interface or through component stubs created by VCF. The metadata interface allows a component to be queried for its features similar to Java's reflection API. The classes representing the individual features provide methods to access the functionality provided by a feature implementation. Using a component's metadata interface is necessary to interact with components that are loaded during run-time. For instance, this allows application builders to discover, instantiate, and manipulate arbitrary software components. A sample class using VCF's metadata interface is shown in Figure 2.

```
public class Test {
  protected Component anInstance;

  void createComponent (
    ComponentDescription desc) {
    anInstance=Factory.create (desc);
  }
  void accessComponent () {
    IFeatureContainer fc=
        anInstance.getFeatures (
          new PropertyQualifier ("text"));
    IProperty property=fc.firstElement ();
    property.setValue ("new␣Text");
  }
  String retrieveValue () {
    IFeatureContainer fc=
        anInstance.getFeatures (
          new PropertyQualifier ("text"));
    IProperty property=fc.firstElement ();
    return property.getValue ();
  }
}
```

Figure 2. Changing a Property through a Component's Metadata

Using these interfaces has two disadvantages: it is tedious to use for programmers and it imposes a performance overhead since several lines of code are required to access

```
public void printBook(String isbn) {
  // obtain a reference to an instance of the
  // COM library component
  COMLibrary library=new COMLibrary (isbn);

  String[] authors=library.getAuthors ();
  String title=library.getTitle ();
}
```

Figure 3. Sample Code - Interface Access

a feature. Even worse, the access is not statically typed which can lead to programming errors which are hard to find. Hence, to overcome these deficiencies we have provided a facility that generates stub classes providing direct access to the component. A sample method using such a stub is shown in Figure 3.

Although some component models already provide Java interfaces to access their components' features, only methods are accessed in a uniform way. Events and other complicated features are accessed syntactically and semantically in different ways. Our framework maps these different APIs to a single one. If a Java interface exists for a particular component model, the stub classes use these methods to avoid the performance overhead of the metadata interface.

3.4. Typing

Like all of the widely used component models, VCF uses strongly typed components. Different component models, however, use different type systems. Hence, to enable interoperability between these component models, VCF converts between the different type systems used by the different component models.

Type conversion can be effected by simulating the different data types used by the individual component models. While this approach ensures a minimal loss of information, it imposes a huge performance overhead since every operation on a primitive type would have to be simulated by a user-defined type. Additionally, it would require a conversion routine for every type of a component model to the corresponding types of all of the other component models, or otherwise the loss of information would not be minimal.

Due to these problems, we have chosen to convert every type to and from its Java counterpart. This limits the number of conversion routines to two times the number of component models and allows us to encapsulate the conversion routines within the plugin that supports a given component model. Most primitive types such as number values, booleans or character strings can be converted easily across different type systems. Arrays and records that contain no operations can be converted to Java arrays and Java classes respectively. However, we encountered several problems.

Java does not support unsigned data types. Hence, the use of such unsigned data types in COM or CORBA could lead to a loss of precision when converted to the corresponding signed data type in Java such as converting an `unsigned long` to a Java `long`. If such data types are used the full value range is used rarely. However, we made the conversion routines exchangeable at component instantiation time to let VCF users decide which conversion routines shall be used by the plugin.

Another problem is that Java does not support to pass method parameters by reference. Some component models, however, such as COM and CORBA support outgoing parameters and require such parameters. Although Java's call-by-value semantics does not prohibit the modification of object parameters some Java classes do not permit such a modification. To solve this problem we create holder classes automatically for the corresponding Java classes. A similar approach has been taken by CORBA and the Java language binding [20].

Of particular interest with typing issues are types that transport a component's instance pointer or reference. We can distinguish two different occurrences of this. When a reference to an instance is returned to a component's client it has to be converted into a VCF component reference. This is the responsibility of the component model's plugin. Each plugin examines the reference stored in the plugin's component model format, e.g. a COM pointer. If a corresponding VCF component exists already a reference to this component is returned. Otherwise a new VCF component is created, the reference to the native component instance is stored and this instance is analyzed by the plugin.

Passing a component reference to another component is more difficult. When the passed component reference is built for the same component model as the target component the problem can be reduced to extracting the component's reference from the plugin. Other cases are more problematic. In general it is necessary to use a proxy [10] component for the target component model that delegates calls back to the passed component. Currently we have built these proxy only for JavaBeans and EJB. A proxy for COM would need similar mechanisms to the connection point mechanism described in Section 4.4. Similarly a CORBA proxy can be realized by using CORBA's Dynamic Skeleton Interface (DSI) [20].

4. Implementing a Component-Model Plugin

This section discusses the implementation choices for a component model plugin and those that we have made. The description is intended to help the reader understand the work involved in implementing a new component model plugin.

A plugin for a component model consists of one main

plugin class that implements the IComponentPlugIn interface. This class creates the features responsible for lifecycle control and persistence in its constructor. All features that are provided by the plugin are returned in a feature container by the the plugin's getFeatures method. This feature container provides standardized means to add and remove features, and allows queries for a particular feature. These queries range from retrieving all features of an instance to fine-grained queries like searching for all methods that have a particular return type and whose names match a regular expression.

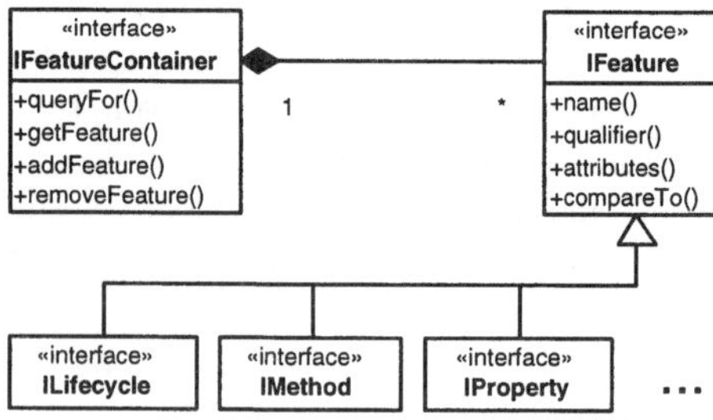

Figure 4. Features

As shown in Figure 4, each type of feature is represented by an interface that extends the IFeature interface. Additionally, each feature contains a qualifier that unambiguously distinguishes instances of a feature from each other and may have custom attributes associated with it. A custom attribute can be used to store information about the feature without modifying its functionality. Clients can query for attributes and change their behavior when they detect the existence of such attributes. For instance, GUI tools could hide a feature from the user if its "user level" attribute has the value "expert."

Unlike CORBA, COM does not provide a language binding for the Java programming language except for Microsoft's Virtual Machine that is no longer supported. Hence, we access COM using Java's Native Interface (JNI), Java's facility to access operating system dependent native code.

4.1. Lifecycle

The lifecycle of a component is controlled with the ILifecycle interface (Figure 5). This interface provides methods to create and destroy components. The create method takes a parameter that is provided by clients to specify which component should be instantiated as well as an additional initialization parameter to initialize the component instance.

Once an instance has been created, each lifecycle feature informs the plugin class to analyze the metadata of the

```
interface ILifecycle extends IFeature {
  void create (InitParameter parameter);
  void destroy ();
}
```

Figure 5. Lifecycle feature

newly created component. During this analysis an instance for each feature implemented by the component is created.

The destroy method invokes the appropriate component model specific mechanisms to destroy a component instance, and invalidates the contained instance reference.

4.2. Methods

The IMethod interface (Figure 6) provides information about a single method of a component. It provides methods to query for the return type and the parameter types of the method. Parameters have methods to set and retrieve their values. The invoke method takes an array of parameters and invokes the method.

```
interface IMethod extends IFeature {
  Object invoke (IParameter[] parameters);
  Class getReturnType ();

  Class[] getParameterTypes ();
  IParameter[] getParameters ();
}
```

Figure 6. Interface for methods

Since all component models support methods, the implementation of IMethod's functionality is straightforward. JavaBeans and Enterprise JavaBeans methods are invoked via Java reflection. CORBA's Interface Repository provides all necessary information to look up a method's name, its return type and its parameter types. Invocations are implemented using CORBA's Dynamic Invocation Interface (DII). COM's type information provides information about COM methods. To invoke a COM component method we use COM's IDispatch interface. To access this interface we access a C++ DLL that is invoked with Java's Native Interface (JNI). Since C++ and Java have different binary representations for data types all types are converted by the plugin at runtime.

4.3. Properties

The state of components that is externally visible can be accessed with the IProperty interface (Figure 7). The methods of this interface are responsible for setting and retrieving a property's value. In addition a method for returning a property's type is available. Another method is used to determine if the property is read-only.

```
interface IProperty extends IFeature{
  void setValue (Object value);
  Object getValue ();
  Class getType ();
  boolean readOnly ();
}
```

Figure 7. Interface for properties

In the case of JavaBeans, certain methods are tagged by syntax conventions to be used as property accessors. Although this is not strictly defined for Enterprise JavaBeans we use the same naming conventions for EJBs too. The access provided by CORBA is different. CORBA interfaces provide attributes that can be used to model properties explicitly. We use the information from the interface repository about these attributes to implement the functionality of the `IProperty` interface. Similar to the implementation of CORBA's method feature the accessor methods are called with DII. COM does not provide attributes as CORBA does. But it uses attributes that mark a method as responsible to get or set a property's value. Hence, we have used these methods to implement properties for COM.

4.4. Eventsets

Eventsets are used to implement callbacks. Component instances send events to their clients leading to the invocation of a method of the client. We followed the design of JavaBeans and used listeners to realize this. As shown in Figure 8 listeners can be added and removed. Additionally, the `IEventset` interface provides methods that return information about listener methods and the type of the listener class. The listener interface has to be implemented by clients and is called by the component instance when a client has to be notified about the occurrence of an event.

```
interface IEventset extends IFeature {
  IMethod[] listenerMethods ();
  Class getListenerClass ();

  void addEventListener (Listener l);
  void removeEventListener (Listener l);
}
```

Figure 8. Interface for eventsets

The implementation of this feature was more challenging than the implementation of methods or properties. First, the mapping is not always as straightforward as in the case of methods. Second, since the client component and the server component change their roles when using callbacks it was necessary to provide a listener class for the client that is compatible with the listener interface specified by the component.

In the case of JavaBeans, the mapping just forwards the calls for registering listeners to the bean instance. Enterprise JavaBeans do not provide events. Although it might be possible to use Java's Message Service (JMS) to simulate events, we do not support this. For CORBA, we use CORBA's event service [23]. An appropriate listener interface is generated and compiled during the first instantiation of a component. COM's analog to an eventset is a connection point [3]. COM components provide connection points that allow clients to subscribe to the events they can emit. Clients may either implement the callback interface or the `IDispatch` interface [17]. This means that it is not necessary to generate a class that implements the outgoing interface but it suffices to implement the invoke method of the `IDispatch` interface [3]. This method takes the id of the target method and all parameters to provide the required functionality. From the type information stored in the type library we create Java interfaces for all outgoing interfaces. If not already created and compiled this interface is created at instantiation time of a component. We have implemented an event sink in C++ that forwards the events with JNI to the appropriate listener classes that are implemented in Java.

4.5. Persistence

Persistence allows clients to store a component's state on, and load it from, persistent storage. We have provided the `IPersist` (Figure 9) interface that provides this functionality. Desktop component models sometimes provide an explicit facility to store an instance data onto persistent storage. Hence, we have encapsulated Java's serialization mechanism and COM's persistence interfaces into `IPersist` to save and restore instance data from a data storage.

Server-side component persistence that stores instances in relational databases such as EJB persistence is implicit and usually transparent to clients. Hence, for these components, we only store enough information to reconstruct the corresponding instance.

```
interface IPersist extends IFeature {
  void load (Storage s);
  void save (Storage s);
}
```

Figure 9. Interface for persistence

4.6. GUI

To provide a uniform GUI representation of components of different component models we have defined a feature interface that returns a `java.awt.Component` object that displays the component's visual representation. In case of JavaBeans this is the bean instance itself. Enterprise Beans and CORBA objects do not provide a GUI at all, hence the interface is not implemented and will not be found by the feature container. COM provides ActiveX controls that are extensively used within Microsoft's operating systems. Java AWT provides means to get operating system handles of its windows. We use this to create an ActiveX host window inside the AWT window. Finally, we put the ActiveX control inside this host window.

4.7. Summary

To implement a new plugin for a component model, the following steps have to be taken. First, the plugin class has to be implemented. This class creates the feature container where it registers all features that can be used to instantiate a component instance, such as the lifecycle feature or the persistence feature. For each type of feature supported by a component model a class that encapsulates the functionality of the feature has to be implemented. This class should implement the VCF interface that corresponds to the type of feature. If necessary, however, a new type of feature can be added just by defining a new feature interface and a qualifier to identify that feature. Once a component has been created, either by the lifecycle feature or by the persistence feature, its metadata can be analyzed. For each entity found in the metadata the appropriate feature class is instantiated and added to the plugin's feature container.

5. Component Construction

The Vienna Component Framework provides a generic programming model to build new components. This programming model allows the programmer to write regular Java classes to build new components. These Java classes and their source code are used to generate source code for any component model supported by a plugin that implements the code generation feature. Hence, the effort necessary to implement components for Enterprise JavaBeans, or CORBA is reduced considerably. We call the classes implemented for our programming model VCF metaclasses since they are the building blocks for new components.

The programming model we use has been influenced by the naming conventions for JavaBeans. These guidelines provide conventions for developers to define properties and eventsets within the Java programming language but without introducing additional language constructs. We have extended these conventions to features not covered by the JavaBeans syntax guidelines such as lifecycle and client-side persistence. In particular, the naming conventions for feature methods consist of its feature name and the features qualifier, for instance the lifecycle destroy method would be named `LifecycleDestroy`. Features that are already available in JavaBeans use those naming conventions.

To support the construction mechanism, we have implemented a special component plugin that enhances the JavaBeans plugin. Its purpose is to parse the meta-information provided by the metaclasses and to parse their source code files. Each feature instance that is created has also some corresponding source code fragments. Hence, we attach these source code fragments to the features as an attribute. Finally, we have an enhanced representation of a component with its features and with the source code fragments that contain the implementation of the features.

Each component model discussed in this paper has its own programming model. During code generation the enhanced representation is used to construct source code for these programming models. All features are processed iteratively. For each feature the source code fragments stored within the attributes are used to generate the required methods, and fields in the created source files.

Since our metaclasses are based on the JavaBeans syntax conventions, the existing class can already be used as a JavaBean. In case of CORBA, we generate the OMG IDL file, and the CORBA object server implementation as Java classes. Java types have to be converted to appropriate CORBA types. In case of Enterprise Beans we generate the home interface, the remote interface, the bean implementation class and the XML deployment descriptor. It is not possible to access recent Java versions from COM components in a straightforward way. Hence, we generate a basic COM component based on C++. The signatures of the methods in the C++ code and in the MS IDL file are generated from the features in the internal representation of the metaclass. Inside the C++ code we make a lookup if a Java VM exists in the current process. If not, we start a virtual machine with means provided by Java's Native Interface. Inside this virtual machine we instantiate an instance of the metaclass and forward all calls to the COM component to these methods. This delegation code also includes the necessary routines to convert between the COM and the Java type system.

Since our framework can be used inside metaclasses it is easily possible to build composite components that contain other components, possibly of different component models. In particular it is possible to encapsulate Enterprise JavaBeans in COM+ components and vice versa.

6. Evaluation

We have evaluated VCF with respect to its genericity and the performance it offers. As we have presented in Section 4, we have already implemented VCF plugins for the COM, CORBA, EJB, and JavaBeans component models. With the implementation of these plugins, we have demonstrated that VCF is generic enough to support the integration of the most commonly used component models. Additionally, we have started the implementation of plugins for X11 applications, SOAP web services [2], and Gnome Bonobo components. Although the implementation of these plugins has not been completed our current results are promising.

To demonstrate VCF's ability to enable composition across multiple different component models, we have implemented the stock ticker application mentioned in Section 1 which combines CORBA, JavaBeans and COM components. Although Java has some support for CORBA we have been able to remove the code necessary for connecting to a CORBA name server and the code responsible for making a connection to a CORBA event channel [13]. Similarly, the access for COM components was as simple as accessing normal Java classes. Using JavaBeans in VCF does not lead to any reduction in code size. Fortunately it does not increase it either. The uniformity across all component models remained the same for all three component models used.

To test the performance provided by VCF, we have implemented a test component for each of the component models currently supported by VCF. These components provide 4 operations.

ping taking no argument and returning nothing.

pong taking a string as argument and returning the same string.

upper taking a string as argument and returning its uppercase representation.

concat taking five strings as argument and returning the concatenation of them.

Our COM server side component using COM+ was running on a Pentium II/300MHz processor with 128MB memory and Windows 2000 and the CORBA and EJB components were running on a Duron/800MHz processor with 256MB memory and Linux 2.4.7. The JavaBean component as well as our clients were running on a Pentium III/550MHz processor with 256MB memory and Windows 2000. For each operation and component model, we have executed three runs with 10000 executions per run. The average of the three executions is shown in Table 1.

For the COM plugin the overhead is about 20%. One reason for this gap is that the native COM implementation

	COM+	CORBA	EJB	JB
ping (native)	6849	12799	33638	0
ping (VCF)	15031 (6970)	13349	33939	30
pong (native)	17495	20560	38165	100
pong (VCF)	21551 (18006)	21301	38586	150
upper (native)	17595	20289	38536	60
upper (VCF)	21631 (18056)	20980	38605	310
concat (native)	35542	31085	42828	130
concat (VCF)	40508 (38072)	32106	43833	581

Table 1. Measured access times (ms)

was implemented using C++ and hence unlike with VCF, COM's types did not have to be converted to Java. After this test, however, we optimized the COM plugin. The performance values of the optimized version are shown in parenthesis.

For CORBA and EJB the performance difference is only about 5%. Unlike for COM the native tests for CORBA and EJB have been implemented using Java explaining the smaller performance overhead compared to our COM evaluation.

As shown in Table 1 using the JavaBeans component with VCF imposes a considerable performance penalty. The overhead is much higher compared to the other component models since JavaBeans are executed within the same application as the client and do not incur the overhead of a remote procedure call. Another reason is that the JavaBean plugin still uses Java's reflection API for the generation of the component's stub classes. Hence, it should be possible to eliminate much of this performance overhead by using native Java calls inside the component stubs.

7. Related Work

The design of VCF has its origin in the generic component model of the Component Workbench, a visual component builder developed by the authors [19]. VCF, however, is more powerful from this former model in many aspects such as the component stubs enabling direct access or the component construction mechanism. Hence, we have built a new release of the Component Workbench that is based on VCF. We are going to integrate all concepts of VCF that are not covered by the original model such as component construction into the Component Workbench. A survey of composition environments can be found in [15].

The Eclipse Platform allows the construction of integrated development environments (IDEs) for different application types such as web sites [6, 7], Java or C++ applications. Eclipse does not provide uniform access across different component models such as VCF. However, Eclipse provides a Standard Widget Toolkit (SWT) [6] that combines a platform independent widget library with platform dependent facilities such as ActiveX controls. We plan to port the Component Workbench to Eclipse in the future.

Interworking specifications support the integration of middleware systems of different kinds [9]. Usually these technologies are restricted to combine two distributed component models such as Interworking between CORBA and COM [9] and are not available for all pairs of component models.

UniFrame [21] is an approach that aims to achieve interoperation of heterogeneous and distributed software components. It provides a metacomponent model that allows the access of various component models, support for the integration and validation of quality of service on an individual component and distributed system level. The UniFrame approach also facilitates the use of generative rules for assembling components out of available choices. One essential part of this approach is the UniFrame Resource Discovery Service (URDS) [24] that provides a solution for the discovery of heterogeneous and distributed software components. URDS has powerful facilities to act as a component trader over the Internet. UniFrame supports Java RMI objects. Efforts have started to integrate other component models [24]. UniFrame, however, does not support the generation of components.

Flexible Packaging [4] defines how a software component's source code has to be structured to defer some decisions about interaction semantics with other components until integration time. Only the essential parts of a component have to be specified early in the design cycle while details can be deferred. Flexible Packaging splits up a component's functionality and its packaging into, respectively, a ware part and a packager part. This separation allows that a component's functionality to be packaged in components that can be used with different architectural styles. Flexible packagers make use of an extension of the C programming language to support the use of typed channels for communication between wares and packagers. This removes the dependencies between packagers and wares and allows the construction of packagers out of description files. While flexible packaging allows the construction of component packages independently of the ware for almost all imaginable component models there is no automatic support for the use of components without writing packaging descriptions. Hence, it is not possible to reuse components where only metadata is available such as VCF's support for component use. On the other hand VCF's component construction is specialized for COTS component models that support common features such as methods and events as described in Section 2.

Jiazzi [16] provides a component infrastructure for Java that enables the construction of large-scale binary components with Java. Jiazzi does not use any core language extensions or language conventions to construct a component. Instead it uses separate source files that describe the visible structure of classes in packages. Jiazzi supports the use of mixins and the open class pattern. However, it supports only the construction of components that conform to the Java class format. Hence, these components can be used from within other Java-based component models but cannot be used as an Enterprise Bean or a CORBA component in their own right.

ArchJava [1] extends the Java programming language with component and connector constructs. These constructs enhance the Java type system and the ArchJava compiler checks if components can be connected by existence of component ports. However, component type checking works on the compiler level. The ArchJava compiler creates true byte code compatible with normal Java virtual machines. But ArchJava ports can only be used with other ArchJava components. Hence, the use of ArchJava with industrial component models is limited.

Unlike VCF, Jiazzi and ArchJava do not provide uniform access to existing component models nor do they provide facilities to generate component code for other component models. On the other hand, it is possible to build VCF plugins for these environments.

Caboom is a product developed by CalKey Technologies [14] for rapid design and development of component-based enterprise applications. It allows the specification of components in UML with OMG's Model Driven Architecture. Caboom is able to generate ready-to-deploy components and whole multi-tier applications for the J2EE, .NET and COM+ platform. Unlike our framework they generate class code for various programming languages not out of one template class but use UML diagrams created by design tools as starting point for code generation. Caboom does not facilitate portable modification of source code after its generation. However, modifications that are applied to the UML diagram are portable to the models.

Our framework supports modification within a component by the use of metaclasses implemented in Java. Although our framework does not support the use of UML diagrams it has the advantage that the template code is a Java class that can be tested and debugged before exporting its functionality to other component models.

8. Conclusions

In this paper, we have presented a framework that enables the composition of software components that have been developed for multiple different component models. From a practitioner's point of view, such a framework allows software developers to choose from a wider range of software components without having to know the details of all the component models available today. They only need to become familiar with a single component framework, giving them more time to focus on the task at hand. From a researcher's vantage point, such a framework provides a basis for the detailed comparison of different component models, both at an implementation level and from a performance point of view. Although component models are conceptually similar, the implementation requirements impose significant differences in their usage, performance, and inherent interoperability. Most research work to date only considers individual component models, rather than cross-model issues.

To evaluate our claims that VCF is able to integrate most of the component models available today, we have implemented plugins for COM, CORBA, Enterprise JavaBeans, and JavaBeans as we have shown in Section 4. Using this infrastructure, we have been able to implement a small application using components that have been implemented for different component models.

We have evaluated the performance of the VCF. As shown in Section 6, VCF imposes only an overhead of—depending on the server-side component model—about 5–20% for server side components compared to accessing the components using their native component models. Additionally, as we have shown with the COM plugin, it should be possible to optimize the generated stubs and subsequently to reduce the performance overhead to about 2–5%.

In future versions, we plan to focus on the optimization of accessing components through VCF and to focus on distributed services such as transactions and security. Furthermore we plan to build additional plugins for web services accessible via SOAP [2] and for classes built for Microsoft's .NET framework [22].

Acknowledgments

We gratefully acknowledge the financial support provided by the European Union as part of the EASYCOMP project (IST-1999-14151) and an IBM University Partnership Award from IBM Research Division, Zurich Research Laboratories. We appreciate the helpful comments and suggestions of Heinz Appoyer, Uwe Zdun and the anonymous reviewers for their helpful comments and suggestions.

References

[1] J. Aldrich, C. Chambers, and D. Notkin. Archjava: Connecting software architecture to implementation. In *Proceedings of the 24th International Conference on Software Engineering*, pages 187–197, 2002.

[2] D. Box et al. *Simple Object Access Protocol (SOAP) 1.1*. W3C, May 2000.

[3] K. Brockschmidt. *Inside OLE*. Microsoft Press, second edition, 1995.

[4] R. DeLine. Avoiding packaging mismatch with flexible packaging. *IEEE Transactions on Software Engineering*, 27(2):124–143, Feb. 2001.

[5] L. G. DeMichiel, L. Ü. Yal cinalp, and S. Krishnan. *Enterprise JavaBeans Specification, Version 2.0*. Sun Microsystems, Apr. 2001. Proposed Final Draft 2.

[6] Eclipse platform technical overview. Technical report, Object Technology International, Inc., 2001. http://www.eclipse.org/whitepaper/eclipse-overview.pdf.

[7] http://www.eclipse.org.

[8] G. Eddon and H. Eddon. *Inside Distributed COM*. Microsoft Press, 1998.

[9] W. Emmerich. *Engineering Distributed Objects*. John Wiley & Sons, 2000.

[10] E. Gamma, R. Helm, R. Johnson, and J. Vlissides. *Design Patterns – Elements of Reusable Object-Oriented Software*. Addison-Wesley, 1995.

[11] G. Hamilton, editor. *JavaBeans*. Sun Microsystems, http://java.sun.com/beans/, July 1997.

[12] G. T. Heineman and W. T. Councill, editors. *Component-Based Software Engineering: Putting the Pieces Together*. Addison-Wesley, 2001.

[13] M. Henning and S. Vinoski. *Advanced CORBA Programming with C++*. Addison Wesley Longman, Inc., 1999.

[14] B. Jadhav. *Caboom White Paper*. Campbell, CA 95008, 2001. http://www.calkey.com.

[15] C. Lüer and A. van der Hoek. Composition environments for deployable software components. Technical Report UCI-ICS-02-18, Department of Information and Computer Science, University of California, Irvine, Aug. 2002.

[16] S. McDirmid, M. Flatt, and W. C. Hsieh. Jiazzi: New-age components for old-fashioned java. In *Proceedings of the 2001 ACM SIGPLAN Conference on Object-Oriented Programming, Systems, Languages & Applications (OOPSLA '01)*, pages 211–222, 2001.

[17] Microsoft Corporation. *The Component Object Model Specification*, 1995.

[18] R. Monson-Haefel. *Enterprise JavaBeans*. O'Reilly & Associates, Inc., first edition, June 1999.

[19] J. Oberleitner and T. Gschwind. Composing distributed components with the component workbench. Technical Report TUV-1841-2002-17, Technische Universität Wien, Jan. 2002. Accepted for publication in the Proceedings of the 3rd Software Engineering and Middleware Workshop.

[20] Object Management Group. *The Common Object Request Broker: Architecture and Specification*, 2.4 edition, 2001.

[21] R. R. Raje, M. Auguston, B. R. Bryant, A. M. Olson, and C. Burt. A unified approach for the integration of distributed heterogeneous software components. In *Proceedings of the Monterey Workshop on Engineering Automation for Software Intensive System Integration*, pages 109–119, 2001.

[22] J. Richter. *Applied Microsoft .NET Framework Programming*. Microsoft Press, 2002.

[23] J. Siegel. *CORBA 3: Fundamentals and Programming*. John Wiley & Sons, Inc., second edition, 2000.

[24] N. N. Siram, R. R. Raje, A. M. Olson, B. R. Bryant, C. C. Burt, and M. Auguston. An architecture for the uniframe resource discovery service. In *Proceedings of the 3rd International Workshop on Software Engineering and Middleware 2002 (SEM 2002)*, pages 22–38, 2002.

Technical Papers

Testing I

Constructing Test Suites for Interaction Testing

Myra B. Cohen
Peter B. Gibbons
Warwick B. Mugridge
Dept. of Computer Science
University of Auckland
Private Bag 92019
Auckland, New Zealand
{myra,peter-g,rick}@cs.auckland.ac.nz

Charles J. Colbourn
Dept of Computer Science and Engineering
Arizona State University
P.O. Box 875406
Tempe, Arizona 85287
charles.colbourn@asu.edu

Abstract

Software system faults are often caused by unexpected interactions among components. Yet the size of a test suite required to test all possible combinations of interactions can be prohibitive in even a moderately sized project. Instead, we may use pairwise or t-way testing to provide a guarantee that all pairs or t-way combinations of components are tested together. This concept draws on methods used in statistical testing for manufacturing and has been extended to software system testing. A covering array, $CA(N; t, k, v)$, is an $N \times k$ array on v symbols such that every $N \times t$ sub-array contains all ordered subsets from v symbols of size t at least once. The properties of these objects, however, do not necessarily satisfy real software testing needs. Instead we examine a less studied object, the mixed level covering array and propose a new object, the variable strength covering array, which provides a more robust environment for software interaction testing. Initial results are presented suggesting that heuristic search techniques are more effective than some of the known greedy methods for finding smaller sized test suites. We present a discussion of an integrated approach for finding covering arrays and discuss how application of these techniques can be used to construct variable strength arrays.

1. Introduction

Many software systems today are built using components. Often, system faults are caused by unexpected interactions among these [28]. For example, suppose we have an Internet-based software system. Our customers may use a variety of browsers. In addition they may be using different operating systems, connection types and printer configurations. In order to completely test this system we want to test our software on all of the possible supported configurations. If we have the system shown in Table 1, we would want to test combinations, such as (Netscape,Windows,LAN,Local) and (Netscape,Windows,LAN,Networked). To test all possible interactions for this system we would need 3^4 or 81 configurations.

Component			
Web Browser	**Operating System**	**Connection Type**	**Printer Config**
Netscape	Windows	LAN	Local
IE	Macintosh	PPP	Networked
Other	Linux	ISDN	Screen

Table 1. Four Components, Each With Three Configurations

This may be reasonable for a small system but the number of necessary tests grows large very quickly. Suppose we had 10 possible components with four possible settings each. We then need 4^{10}=1,048,576 test configurations. One approach used is to guarantee that we test all pairs of interactions or all n-way interactions [2, 5, 17, 12, 23, 27, 29]. In the example shown in Table 1 we can cover all pairs of interactions using only nine different configurations (see Table 2). And in the example of 10 components each with 4 possible settings we can cover all pairs of interactions using at most 25 configurations.

Dalal et al. present empirical results to argue that the testing of all pairwise interactions in a software system finds a large percentage of the existing faults [10]. In further work, Burr et al. provide more empirical results to show that this type of test coverage is effective [3].

If we restrict ourselves to pairwise coverage, we cannot guarantee that we will find faults that occur with three or

0-7695-1877-X/03 $17.00 © 2003 IEEE

Test	Browser	OS	Connection	Printer
1	NetScape	Windows	LAN	Local
2	NetScape	Linux	ISDN	Networked
3	NetScape	Macintosh	PPP	Screen
4	IE	Windows	ISDN	Screen
5	IE	Macintosh	LAN	Networked
6	IE	Linux	PPP	Local
7	Other	Windows	PPP	Networked
8	Other	Linux	LAN	Screen
9	Other	Macintosh	ISDN	Local

Table 2. Test Suite to Cover all Pairs from Table 1

four way interactions. A trade off occurs between the time and cost of testing and the required degree of guaranteed coverage. Williams et al. describe a method to quantify the coverage for a particular interaction level [28]. We can determine how many pairs, or n-way interactions we have covered at each stage when building a test suite. For instance if we have four components, any new test case can contribute at most $\binom{4}{2}$, or 6 new covered pairs. Further, if each component has three configurations, there are a total of $\binom{4}{2}$ 3^2 = 54 possible pairs that must be covered. Therefore any one new test case increases our coverage by at most 11.1% [28]. A similar method is described by Dunietz et al. [12].

It could be assumed that our goal is for 100% coverage at a particular level, such as two or three way coverage. This can be achieved using a minimal number of test cases, with a known combinatorial object, the *covering array*, described below. Dunietz et al. [12] point out that by using such a balanced code, we are also providing higher coverage for stronger interaction levels.

As it is usually too expensive to test all components using three or four way coverage we can benefit from doing this for part of the system. For instance, a particular subset of components may have a higher interaction dependency or a certain combination of components may have more serious effects in the event of a failure. For example, consider a subset of components that control a safety-critical hardware interface. We want to use stronger coverage in that area. However, the rest of our components may be sufficiently tested using pair-wise interaction. We can assign a coverage *strength* requirement to each subset of components as well as to the whole system.

For the safety critical system, we would require that the whole system has 100% coverage for two way interactions, while the safety-critical subset has 100% coverage for three way interactions. The final test suite may, however, have 80% coverage for three way interactions over all components.

In the rest of this paper we examine the combinatorial objects that can be used in component interaction testing. We begin with a description of relevant combinatorial objects and introduce a new model for variable strength interaction testing. We discuss various techniques to build these test suites and present preliminary results using heuristic search techniques. Lastly we discuss how the techniques can be applied and used to build our new model for variable strength interaction.

2. Combinatorial Models

Combinatorial objects are not new to testing. Hedayat et al. [14] discuss the use of orthogonal arrays for statistically designed experiments. These are used across many disciplines including medicine, agriculture and manufacturing [14]. More recently these ideas have been extended to software testing.

2.1. Orthogonal Latin Squares

Mandl proposed using orthogonal Latin squares for testing compilers [17]. A Latin square of order s is an $s \times s$ array with entries from a set S of cardinality s with the condition that for all i in S, i appears exactly once in each row and each column. Two Latin Squares are orthogonal if, when superimposed on each other, the ordered pairs created in each cell cover all s^2 pairs [1, 14].

In this instance, k orthogonal Latin squares of size s are needed to test $k+2$ parameters each with s levels. The cell entries represent $k-2$ elements in each test, and the column and row indices represent the additional 2 parameters.

2.2. Orthogonal Arrays

Brownlie et al. have adapted an engineering concept, called *Robust Testing*, to the task of testing software [2]. They developed the OATs system which uses orthogonal arrays to generate test suites for a software system [2]. k mutually orthogonal Latin squares of order s can be transformed into an orthogonal array $OA_1(s^2; k+2, s, 2)$ [1].

An orthogonal array $OA_\lambda(N; k, v, t)$ is an $N \times k$ array on v symbols such that every $N \times t$ sub-array contains all ordered subsets of size t from v symbols *exactly* λ times [14]. Orthogonal arrays have the property that $\lambda = \frac{N}{v^t}$. Table 2 is an example of an $OA(9; 4, 3, 2)$.

Although the use of orthogonal arrays for testing has been discussed in the literature [2, 27] these may be of less interest in component testing because they could lead to overly large test suites with $\lambda > 1$. For cases of v and k where an orthogonal array with $\lambda = 1$ does exist, clearly this is the optimal test suite. However, there are many values of v and k where an orthogonal array with $\lambda = 1$ does not exist so we must resort to a less restrictive structure; one that requires subsets are instead covered *at least* once as with covering arrays.

2.3. Covering Arrays

A *covering array*, $CA_\lambda(N; t, k, v)$, is an $N \times k$ array on v symbols such that every $N \times t$ sub-array contains all ordered subsets from v symbols of size t *at least* λ times. When $\lambda = 1$ we use the notation $CA(N; t, k, v)$. In such an array, t is called the *strength*, k the *degree* and v the *order*. A covering array is optimal if it contains the minimum possible number of rows. We call the minimum number the *covering array number*, $CAN(t, k, v)$. For example, $CAN(2, 5, 3) = 11$ [4, 21].

Cohen et al. [5, 7] have developed the commercial product, *Automatic Efficient Test Generator* (AETG) to construct covering arrays for software interaction testing. Williams et al. [27] use orthogonal arrays as well as covering arrays to design tests for the interactions of nodes in a network. Stevens et al. [23] suggest creating a knowledge system for the tester that contains the best known covering arrays applicable to testing.

There are often a number of different ways to represent the same combinatorial object. For instance, several other combinatorial objects have been defined with the same effective properties as a covering array. A *strength t transversal cover*, a *qualitatively independent* system and *t-surjective array* [8, 21, 25] are three such objects. In the rest of this document we will use the covering array definition for consistency.

Covering arrays only suit the needs of software testers when all components have the same number of configurations. However, this is often not the case. For instance one component can have four possible configurations and one only two. Indeed, this is a normal occurrence. In addition, constraints can exist for a test suite suggesting that certain value combinations can never occur or that there are aggregate conditions among several fields [10]. Lastly, testers often require that a set of fixed test cases are added to each test suite, regardless of the interaction strength required. These issues cause real testing environments to deviate from covering arrays as defined. In the first case we want to remove these combinations from the tests. In the second case we may need to define aggregate fields or components. In the last case we need to build a test suite on top of already generated test cases. We restrict our subsequent discussion to the first problem, which we feel is the most important deviation from a *fixed level* covering array; however the techniques we discuss could be extended to the others.

Mixed Level Covering Array

0	a	4	d
2	b	6	e
3	c	5	e
2	c	4	d
0	b	5	d
1	a	6	e
1	b	4	d
3	a	6	d
0	c	6	e
2	a	5	e
3	b	4	e
1	c	5	d

Figure 1. $MCA(12; 2, 4^1 3^2 2^1)$

2.4. Mixed Level Covering Arrays

The variation among component levels can be handled with the *mixed level covering array*. Several authors have suggested its use for software testing (see [4, 22, 28]), but few results are known about upper bounds and how to construct these.

A *mixed level* covering array,

$$MCA_\lambda(N; t, k, (v_1 v_2 ... v_k)),$$

is an $N \times k$ array on v symbols, where $v = \sum_{i=1}^{k} v_i$, with the following properties:

1. Each column i $(1 \le i \le k)$ contains only elements from a set S_i of size v_i.

2. The rows of each $N \times t$ subarray cover all t-tuples of values from the t columns at least λ times.

When $\lambda = 1$ we can omit the subscript, representing the array as $MCA(N; t, k, (v_1 v_2 ... v_k))$. We use a shorthand notation to describe mixed covering arrays by combining equal entries in $(v_i : i \le 1 \le k)$. For example three entries each equal to 2 can be written as 2^3. Consider an $MCA(N; t, (w_1^{k_1} w_2^{k_2} ... w_s^{k_s}))$. This can also be written as an $MCA(N; t, k, (v_1 v_2 ... v_k))$ (see Figure 1). In this array we have:

1. $k = \sum_{i=1}^{s} k_i$ and $v = \sum_{i=1}^{s} k_i w_i = \sum_{i=1}^{k} v_i$.

2. Each column i $(1 \le i \le k)$ contains only elements from a set S_i where $|\cup_{i=1}^{k} S_i| = v$.

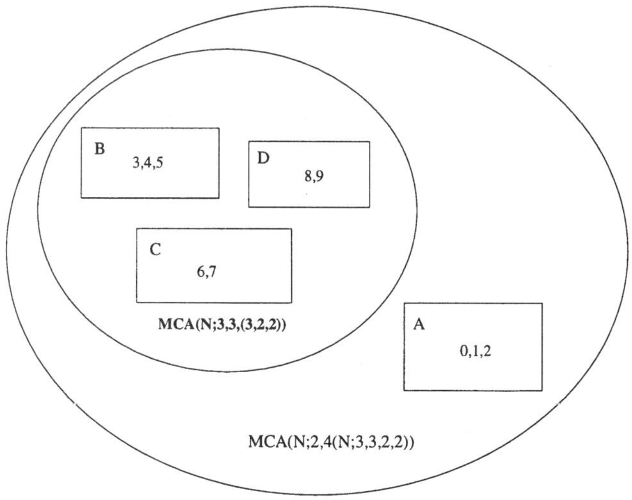

Figure 2. Model of Variable Strength Covering Array.

Component			
A	B	C	D
0	4	7	8
1	3	7	9
2	3	6	8
0	5	6	9
1	4	6	8
2	4	7	9
2	5	7	9
1	5	7	8
0	3	6	9
0	3	7	8
2	4	6	9
1	5	6	8

Table 3. Variable Strength Array for Figure 2

3. The columns are partitioned into s groups $g_1, g_2, ...g_s$ where group g_i contains k_i columns. The first k_1 columns belong to the group g_1, the next k_2 columns belong to group g_2, and so on.
4. If column $r \in g_i$, then $|S_r| = v_i$.

This notation can be used for a fixed-level covering array as well. $CA(N; t, v^k)$ indicates that there are k parameters each containing a set of v symbols. This makes it easier to see that the values from different components can come from different sets.

2.5. Variable Strength Covering Arrays

Being able to guarantee that subsets of components have higher interaction strength is appealing in a real test environment as with the safety-critical example in Section 1. A covering array as it is defined only guarantees a coverage of t-subsets. We may also wish to have coverage of some subsets of size t' for values of $t' > t$. It is for this reason that we present a new model for interaction testing, as illustrated in Figure 2.

Components A and B have three configurations each, while C and D have two (the configurations are labelled $0, 1, 2...9$). The system has a total of 37 interaction pairs, and 60 interaction triples. We require that the subset $\{B, C, D\}$ be covered by 3-way coverage, while the entire system $\{A, B, C, D\}$ is to have 2-way coverage. We therefore require a 100% 2-way coverage and a minimal 3-way coverage of $\frac{12}{60} = 20\%$. As we shall see, the actual 3-way coverage of a test suite may be much higher.

A mixed level covering array to handle 100% of 2-way interactions can be created using only 9 tests. This is shown as the first 9 rows of Table 3. To handle all 3-way interactions, as many as 18 tests are needed. To increase the strength of this array to cover all 3-way interactions of $\{B, C, D\}$, we only need to add 3 more tests. These are the last three rows shown in Table 3. This actually covers $\frac{42}{60} = 70\%$ of the 3-way interactions for our system while covering all of the 3-way interactions for our subset and all 2-way interactions in the whole system.

3. Constructing Covering Arrays

In this section we begin with some known results and present several techniques for finding covering arrays.

3.1. Known Combinatorial Results

There are several types of results known for covering arrays. These include probabilistic bounds that provide a value for the smallest size of N, but do not give us any method for construction. There are constructive results which provide a direct way to create such an object, and finally, there are computational results which are produced as the end product of a search. Of these, the last two are probably the most useful, although knowing the probabilistic bounds helps to guide the search for new constructions. We give a few bounds below, but leave the readers to see Sloane [21] for an excellent survey.

The first known results on covering array numbers are due to Rényi [20] who determined these numbers for the case $t = v = 2$ when N is even. Kleitman and Spencer [16] and Katona [15] independently determined covering array numbers for all N (and $t = v = 2$). They showed that the size of N grows as follows:

$$k = \binom{N-1}{\lceil \frac{N}{2} \rceil}$$

For a large k, this grows logarithmically. In 1990 Gargano, Körner and Vaccaro [13] gave the following probabilistic bound for $t = 2, v > 2$:

$$N = \frac{v}{2} logk(1 + o(1))$$

Östergård [19] showed that $N \leq 11$ for $v = 3, k = 5$, while Sloane [21] mentions that Applegate showed $N = 11$ [21]. More work has been done on these smaller cases. When $t = 3$, the combinatorial research illustrates both the depth of the connection with combinatorial configurations and the difficulties that these pose for software testers. We do not attempt a thorough review here, but instead refer the reader to [4].

3.2. Algebraic Constructions

We give a brief outline of an algebraic construction for a covering array to provide a flavour of constructive techniques. (For a detailed description see [24]). To begin with, we add another condition to our definition of a covering array; the requirement that there are n disjoint rows, i.e. each pair has no t-sets in common.

We begin with $k - 2$ incomplete Mutually Orthogonal Latin Squares (MOLS) of order n that have holes of size $b_1, b_2, ...b_s$. We construct our array by *filling* the holes with covers of order b_i and degree k. We do this by using a set of bijections between the groups of the MOLS and the groups of the $CA(t, k, b_i)$.

Although this provides us with an array with a good known upper bound, this is not always easy to construct. First of all it requires that we find $k - 2$ incomplete MOLS of order n. We may be able to find some of this information in known tables, but in general it is not an easy task (see [9]). Secondly, it is only useful for certain values of n, t, and k.

What is striking from our viewpoint is that, while the more sophisticated constructions yield substantially smaller covering arrays when they can be applied, these same constructions do not apply as generally as we require. In addition, the true challenge facing the software tester is to determine when the construction applies, including what auxiliary ingredients are needed. This overhead limits the applicability of the more complex constructions.

3.3. Heuristic Search Techniques

Computational search techniques to find fixed level covering arrays include standard techniques such as hill climbing and simulated annealing. However, no results have been produced for mixed level arrays using these methods. The only approaches that produce mixed level arrays use greedy methods to find test suites [5, 29, 30]. Initial results shown in Section 5 suggest that combinatorial search techniques have the potential to produce smaller test suites.

There are two problems to address when building covering arrays. One is that we must satisfy the constraint of covering all t-sets of interactions. The other is that we do not know how large our final test suite will be. Test cases can be added incrementally, stopping when the constraints are met, which is the greedy approach. Alternatively we can choose a fixed size array and try to manipulate the space until all constraints are met. This is the method used by the other algorithms.

Other heuristic search techniques for covering arrays have been explored, specifically tabu search and genetic algorithms [22]. We omit them from our discussion here, since Stardom's research indicates that they are not as effective in general as simulated annealing. However, we present one further variant of simulated annealing, the great deluge algorithm (Section 3.7).

3.4. Greedy Algorithms

The AETG system and the Test Case Generator (TCG) [5, 7, 30] use a greedy search technique. Each test suite is built one test at a time, i.e. an $N \times k$ array is built one row at a time. For each subsequent test case to be added, many are created and then the best chosen (see [5, 7, 30]). The greedy portion of these algorithms lies in the step of determining which new symbol to add to each column of each test. This is of course a local optimum.

In each algorithm, information is maintained about which test case interactions are still uncovered and is used as a heuristic to provide a better chance of finding the missing interactions. AETG uses a random approach to finding a pool of test cases. Yu-Wen et al. [30] suggest a deterministic algorithm. The authors begin with a deterministic ordering of the parameters. Another greedy algorithm, the In Parameter-Order (IPO), has the benefit of reusing old test cases when new parameters are added. It does this by expanding in a vertical and horizontal fashion [29].

TCG and IPO have only been tested on pairwise interactions. AETG and TCG seem to be the most effective in finding pairwise interactions, but do not always produce test suites with known covering array numbers.

3.5. Hill Climbing

Hill climbing and simulated annealing are variants of the state space search technique for solving combinatorial optimisation problems. With a general optimisation problem the hope is that the found solution is close to an optimal one.

With many design problems we *know* (from the cost) when we have reached an optimal solution. On the other hand, approximations in these cases are of little value.

An optimisation problem can be specified as a set Σ of feasible solutions (or states) together with a cost $c(S)$ associated with each $S \in \Sigma$. An optimal solution corresponds to a feasible solution with overall (i.e. global) minimum cost. We define, for each $S \in \Sigma$, a set T_S of transformations (or transitions), each of which can be used to change S into another feasible solution S'. The set of solutions that can be reached from S by applying a transformation from T_S is called the neighbourhood $N(S)$ of S.

We start by randomly choosing an initial feasible solution and then generate a randomly chosen transformation of the current feasible solution S. If the transformation results in a feasible solution S' of equal or lower cost, then S' is accepted as the new current feasible solution. If S' is of higher cost, we reject this solution and check another randomly chosen neighbour of the current feasible solution. This allows us to randomly *walk* around Σ, without reducing the goodness of our current solution. Hill climbing has the potential to get stuck in a local minimum (or *freeze*), so stopping heuristics are required. To increase the chance of forming a good solution we repeat the random walk (or *trial*) a number of times, each time beginning with a random initial feasible solution.

In the hill climbing algorithm the current feasible solution is an approximation S to a covering array in which certain t-subsets are not covered. The cost function is based on the number of t-subsets that are not covered, so that a covering array itself will have a cost of zero. A potential transformation is made by selecting one of the k sets belonging to S and then replacing a random point in this k-set by a random point not in the k-set. The number of blocks remains constant throughout the hill climbing trial.

We have used the method described by Stardom [22] to determine our array size. We set loose upper and lower bounds on the size of an optimal array and then use a binary search process to find the smallest sized covering array in this interval. An alternative method is to start with the size of a known test suite and search for a solution. This of course uses less computational resources, but the required test suite size must be known ahead of time. Ideally in a real system this is the method which we would use. For the results in this paper we have used the first method, since we do not yet know what size test suites are obtainable.

Clearly good data structures are required to enable the relative cost of the new feasible solution to be calculated efficiently, and the transition (if accepted) to be made quickly.

3.6. Simulated Annealing

Simulated annealing has been used by Nurmela and Östergård [18], to construct covering designs which have a structure very similar to covering arrays.

Simulated annealing uses the same approach as hill climbing but allows the algorithm, with a controlled probability, to make choices that reduce the quality of the current solution. The idea is to avoid getting stuck in a bad configuration while continuing to make progress. If the transformation results in a feasible solution S' of higher cost, then S' is accepted with probability $e^{-(c(S')-c(S))/K_BT}$, where T is the controlling temperature of the simulation and K_B is a constant. The temperature is lowered in small steps with the system being allowed to approach "equilibrium" at each temperature through a sequence of transitions (or Markov chain) at this temperature. Usually this is done by setting $T := \alpha T$, where α (the *control decrement*) is a real number slightly less than 1. After an appropriate stopping condition is met, the current feasible solution is taken as an approximation to the solution of the problem at hand. Again, we improve our chances of obtaining a good solution by running a number of trials.

Stardom [22] has recently compared simulated annealing with other types of local search, viz. tabu search and genetic algorithms, for finding covering arrays of strength 2. Stardom has reported several new upper bounds (including $CAN(2,16,8) \leq 145$ and $CAN(2,18,11) \leq 225$) using a simulated annealing algorithm. We have improved on some of those bounds using our simulated annealing algorithm. For instance we have found $CAN(2,16,6) \leq 62$. (For a table of known upper bounds for $t = 2$ see [22].)

3.7. Great Deluge Algorithm

One further heuristic search technique is the *great flood* or *great deluge* algorithm [11], and a variant thereof called *threshold accepting*. These follow a strategy similar to simulated annealing but often display more rapid convergence. Instead of using probability to decide on a move when the cost is higher, a worse feasible solution is chosen if the cost is less than the current threshold[1]. As the algorithm progresses, the threshold is reduced moving it closer to zero. Our current research focuses on the application of these algorithms to covering arrays.

3.8. Using an Integrated Approach

Finding the best covering array for a non-trivial problem is difficult. It is possible that a simulated annealing

[1] This threshold value is sometimes referred to as the *water level* which, in a profit maximizing problem, would be rising rather than falling (as is happening in this case).

algorithm, or a greedy method such as AETG, is the best approach, but further comparisons need to be explored.

AETG has been attributed with the best known upper bound of 180 for $CA(2, 20, 10)$. This array does not have a tight bound using an algebraic construction [22]. The AETG patent describes the use of some simple constructions, the merging of smaller test suites and a post processing stage to reduce test cases [6].

In general one would expect the algebraic constructions to use less computational power than the given algorithms. We have not extensively compared the performance of the individual algorithms in this paper, but note that the time to construct test suites is one factor that must be considered and compared when evaluating methods for building these objects. Table 6 gives some sample user CPU times for our versions of three algorithms. Stardom [22] has compared several methods of computational search, but his results are restricted to fixed level arrays and he did not include the TCG or AETG algorithms.

Given the computational efficiency of an algebraic construction, it is the best method to find a covering array when one is known to exist for the given parameters k, t, v. Indeed this idea has been suggested by Stevens et al. [23] who point out that this may not be a simple task. In order to use an algebraic construction we often use smaller objects which must also be constructed. The recursive nature of this makes the existence question alone here quite difficult (see [9]). If we can determine that the smaller objects exist, we first need to build these, and the information on how to do so must be stored somewhere. In addition, we may also need to store many small starter objects, for which space constraints may become a problem. A further issue is that there are many different types of constructions and sometimes multiple ways to arrive at the same object. This perhaps explains why commercial test generators do not yet utilize the best known constructions, but instead search each time from scratch.

By combining several of these techniques we expect to be able to find a large range of arrays that can be expanded or reduced as necessary. We could for instance, begin with a less costly algorithm, such as the TCG and then define a critical point in our test suite where we make a switch to a more computationally expensive algorithm. Another possibility is to simply build a starter test suite deterministically, and then use simulated annealing to reduce its size. An example of this technique is described in [6].

4. Constructing Variable Strength Covering Arrays

Variable strength covering arrays can be viewed as a collection of covering arrays inside of a larger covering array. We could begin by building each individual array separately and then combine these in order to gain the additional coverage needed for the whole system. Or we could begin with a covering array for the whole system and alter it to obtain the higher strength coverage required for the designated component subsets.

Variable Strength Arrays		
Base Array	Subset of Higher Coverage	Test Suite Size
$CA(N; 2, 11, 6)$	$CA(N; 3, 6, 6)$	302
$CA(N; 2, 20, 4)$	$CA(N; 3, 9, 4)$	125
$CA(N; 2, 10, 3)$	$CA(N; 3, 6, 3)$	33
$MCA(N; 2, 5^1 4^4 3^{11} 2^5)$	$MCA(N; 3, 5^1 4^2 3^5)$	80
$MCA(N, 2, 3^5 4^{10} 5^2)$	$MCA(N; 3, 3^2 4^2 5^2)$	100

Table 4. Test Suite Sizes for Variable Strength Arrays Using Simulated Annealing

We outline an ad hoc construction here for the example given in Table 3, and investigate systematic methods for handling variable strength arrays in a subsequent paper. In order to construct the variable strength array we use our AETG algorithm to find a strength two covering array. We then try to remove duplicate pairs in a way that leads to new, uncovered triples. For instance, in the diagram in Table 3 we can see that had the last row of the 2-way coverage been (0,3,6,8) instead of (0,3,6,9), it could have been changed to (0,3,6,9) with the resulting system still providing pairs (0,8), (3,8), (6,8). Thus we could replace the 8 with a 9 without reducing our pair coverage, but covering a new triple. This step could be performed with a simulated annealing algorithm. Lastly we append the missing triples with a random choice of values for the other components.

Another way to approach this is to begin by enumerating all of the interactions for the higher strength subsets. For instance, we could build a mixed level covering array of strength three for components B, C and D and then fill horizontally by adding a column and the symbols needed so that all missing pairs are covered.

Lastly we might simply extend our simulated annealing algorithm to compute the cost as a function of both levels of interaction and build the suite directly in that manner. We are currently working on a program that uses annealing to build these arrays. Table 4 provides some preliminary test suite sizes for variable strength arrays with two different strengths.

The best method for building a variable strength test suite is still open and the discovery of good algorithms and constructions for these is an interesting problem.

5. Computational Results

We have implemented our own versions of the TCG algorithm for pair-wise coverage and the AETG algorithm for t-way coverage. In addition we have implemented both a

	Minimum Test Cases in Test Suite					
	TCG[1]	AETG[1]	Our-TCG	Our-AETG	HC	SA
MCA-1	20	19	18	20	16	15
MCA-2	45	45	42	44	42	42
MCA-3	30	30	25	28	23	21
MCA-4	33	34	32	35	30	30

Table 5. Comparisons for 2-way Coverage

1. Source = Yu-Wen et al.[30]
MCA-1. $MCA(N; 2, 5^1 3^8 2^2)$
MCA-2. $MCA(N; 2, 7^1 6^1 5^1 4^5 3^8 2^3)$
MCA-3. $MCA(N; 2, 5^1 4^4 3^{11} 2^5)$
MCA-4. $MCA(N; 2, 6^1 5^1 4^6 3^8 2^3)$

	CPU User Time in Seconds		
	Our-TCG	Our-AETG	SA
MCA-1	6	58	214
MCA-2	57	489	874
MCA-3	33	368	379
MCA-4	42	376	579
CA-1	1,333	6,001	10,833
CA-2	NA	359	13,495

Table 6. Comparisons of Runtimes

MCA-1. $MCA(N; 2, 5^1 3^8 2^2)$
MCA-2. $MCA(N; 2, 7^1 6^1 5^1 4^5 3^8 2^3)$
MCA-3. $MCA(N; 2, 5^1 4^4 3^{11} 2^5)$
MCA-4. $MCA(N; 2, 6^1 5^1 4^6 3^8 2^3)$
CA-1. $CA(N; 2, 20, 10)$
CA-2. $CA(N; 3, 6, 6)$

hill climbing and simulated annealing program for handling t-way coverage. These algorithms use standard combinatorial techniques to store a t-set as a rank (an integer representation of a subset), which provide a generic way of representing different size sets. The simulated annealing program is based on that of [18]. While our techniques are fully general, we have emphasized the fixed level cases in our reporting so that we can make comparisons with results in the literature. Sample performance results for the TCG, AETG and simulated annealing algorithms are included to give a flavour for the time required to run each of these. All of the programs are written in C++ and run on Linux using an INTEL Pentium IV 1.8 GHZ processor with 512 MB of memory. Variation in the runtimes of these algorithms depends on parameter settings and number of iterations performed.

Although the implementation of our AETG algorithm is as described in the literature [5], it should be acknowledged that the actual commercial product is patented and may include some simple construction techniques as well as post-processing stages. These are not included in our implementation. One additional heuristic has been added in our version of the AETG algorithm, for the case of $t > 2$. In the algorithm described in [5], it is unclear what happens when

	Minimum Test Cases in Test Suite					
	IPO[1]	AETG[1]	Our-TCG	Our-AETG	HC	SA
CA-1	9	9	9	9	9	9
MCA-1	19	15	17	17	16	16
MCA-2	36	41	34	37	30	30
MCA-3	29	28	26	27	21	21
CA-2	66	NA	56	56	47	45
CA-3	218	180	213	198	189	183

Table 7. Comparisons for 2-way Coverage

1. Source = Yu et al.[29]
CA-1. $CA(N; 2, 4, 3)$
MCA-1. $MCA(N; 2, 3^{13})$
MCA-2. $MCA(N; 2, 4^{15} 3^{17} 2^{29})$
MCA-3. $MCA(N; 2, 4^1 3^{39} 2^{35})$
CA-2. $CA(N; 2, 100, 4)$
CA-3. $CA(N; 2, 20, 10)$

choosing a symbol between 2 and $t-1$. The first symbol is always chosen as one of the symbols found in the most uncovered t-sets. We maintain this first step, then continue to choose from a symbol in the same set until we have the first $t-1$ symbols filled in. We then continue to follow the algorithm as stated. Our results for $t=3$ seem to improve on those reported in the literature for the commercial AETG program (see Table 9). Our AETG algorithm runs three hundred times reporting only the smallest array found at the end. All of these iterations were counted as part of the total time reported in Table 6.

For our version of the TCG algorithm, a few minor refinements were applied. The TCG algorithm as described in [30] does not fully describe how ties are handled. We chose to break these randomly in our version of the algorithm. In addition, TCG uses the *least used* symbols as a heuristic when choosing which symbol to include in the test suite. We tightened this definition to count a symbol as being used *only* in the case of it contributing to a new uncovered interaction pair. Our algorithm runs 5,000 times keeping only the best array at the end. All 5,000 iterations were included in the total time reported in Table 6.

The performance results presented for simulated annealing reflect the total time taken to find all arrays through a binary search process. Therefore the numbers reported in Table 6 may be reduced if tighter bounds are used as a starting point.

For all of the algorithms we ran a series of trials, but report only the best test suite obtained (the one with the smallest number of rows). We use the abbreviations *HC* for hill climbing and *SA* for simulated annealing in Tables 5-9. Table 5 compares our results with those reported in [30]. Our TCG and AETG algorithms produce similar results to those reported. In all of the four test suites, however both our hill climbing and simulated annealing algorithms improve significantly on the bounds given by these other algorithms.

	Minimum Test Cases in Test Suite		
	Stardom[1]	Our-AETG	SA
CA-1	65	70	62
CA-2	88	94	87
CA-3	113	120	112
CA-4	116	123	114

Table 8. Comparisons for 2-way Coverage

1. Source = Stardom[22]

CA-1. $CA(N; 2, 16, 6)$
CA-2. $CA(N; 2, 16, 7)$
CA-3. $CA(N; 2, 16, 8)$
CA-4. $CA(N; 2, 17, 8)$

The hill climbing and simulated annealing algorithms both produced similar lower bounds, but in our experimentation we found that quite often the simulated annealing produced these in fewer trials. More experimentation is needed here.

Table 7 compares our results with those reported in [29]. For these examples our algorithms produce arrays at least as small as those produced by the IPO algorithm, although in two cases the reported commercial AETG results are smaller than ours.

Simulated annealing consistently does as well or better than hill climbing, so we report only those results for the next two tables. Table 8 compares results for some fixed level arrays reported in [22]. We have done as well or better than these. Since the results in [22] were obtained from a similar algorithm, we attribute this to the need for better tuning of the parameters of an annealing algorithm. We have not yet fine tuned the cooling schedule which plays a role in the quality of the final results. We plan to do this in the next phase of our investigation.

Lastly, Table 9 compares our results against some known strength-three algebraic constructions reported in [4]. In this case the expectation was that it would be difficult to match the known results in an initial implementation of these algorithms. Here the surprise was that our AETG algorithm found smaller arrays than those reported using the commercial AETG product. This may be due to the additional heuristic added when choosing the first $t-1$ symbols for each test suite. As expected, our simulated annealing algorithm did not perform as well as most of the algebraic constructions. In the case of a $CA(N; 3, 6, 6)$, however, we have found a smaller array using simulated annealing. Further experimentation is needed with a more refined algorithm. Of course, in many cases constructions are not known (or may not exist) such as is true in the last two entries of this table. For these arrays, simulated annealing finds an *optimal* solution. There are very few known constructions for mixed-level covering arrays. Therefore a fixed level array of a larger size would need to be constructed and used in its place. This may require more

	Minimum Test Cases in Test Suite			
	Construction[1]	AETG[1]	Our-AETG	SA
CA-1	33	47	38	33
CA-2	64	105	77	64
CA-3	125	NA	194	152
CA-4	305	343	330	300
CA-5	1331	1508	1473	1426
CA-6	185	229	218	201
MCA-1	NA	NA	114	100
MCA-2	NA	NA	377	360

Table 9. Comparisons for 3-way Coverage

1. Source = Chateauneuf et al.[4]

CA-1. $CA(N; 3, 6, 3)$
CA-2. $CA(N; 3, 6, 4)$
CA-3. $CA(N; 3, 6, 5)$
CA-4. $CA(N; 3, 6, 6)$
CA-5. $CA(N; 3, 6, 10)$
CA-6. $CA(N; 3, 7, 5)$
MCA-1.$MCA(N; 3, 3^2 4^2 5^2)$
MCA-2.$MCA(N; 3, 10^1 6^2 4^3 3^1)$

test cases than a mixed level array found by computational search. Additionally, a real test suite may include special test cases for particular configurations. Once again current constructions do not handle this issue. For this reason, it is interesting to return to the need for an integrated approach, perhaps one that combines algebraic constructions with more sophisticated search methods.

6. Conclusions

We have discussed some of the uses of combinatorial objects in testing interactions among software components, have raised several questions about the types of combinatorial objects that may be useful for the software tester and have suggested some ways to build these objects using known constructions and search techniques.

Preliminary results on hill climbing and simulated annealing for mixed level covering arrays are presented, although more experimentation and tuning of these algorithms is required. In addition, performance measures need to be applied to determine the overall usefulness of each approach.

We have presented a variable strength covering array which handles multiple levels of interactions. These arrays allow us to assign interaction weights to subsets of components. We have provided an ad hoc method to build these but have left the development of formal methods for future work. It is not entirely clear that even variable strength covering arrays will provide the flexibility that is really needed for testing combinatorial systems. We may want to allow some components to be involved in more than one grouping, or perhaps to test individual groupings alone and then to combine these while retaining the original tests.

Lastly, we may think about how this model can be extended to a broader definition of component testing. In this paper we have restricted ourselves to the idea of finding faults when components are tested in combination. We may find we can use this model for quantitative testing, such as determining which combinations cause performance barriers.

Acknowledgments

Research is supported by the Consortium for Embedded and Internetworking Technologies and by ARO grant DAAD 19-1-01-0406.

References

[1] I. Anderson. *Combinatorial Designs and Tournaments.* Oxford University Press, New York, 1997.

[2] R. Brownlie, J. Prowse, and M. S. Padke. Robust testing of AT&T PMX/StarMAIL using OATS. *AT&T Technical Journal*, 71(3):41–7, 1992.

[3] K. Burr and W. Young. Combinatorial test techniques: Table-based automation, test generation and code coverage. In *Proc. of the Intl. Conf. on Software Testing Analysis & Review*, 1998, San Diego.

[4] M. Chateauneuf and D. Kreher. On the state of strength-three covering arrays. *Journal of Combinatorial Designs*, 10(4):217–238, 2002

[5] D. M. Cohen, S. R. Dalal, M. L. Fredman, and G. C. Patton. The AETG system: an approach to testing based on combinatorial design. *IEEE Transactions on Software Engineering*, 23(7):437–44, 1997.

[6] D. M. Cohen, S. R. Dalal, M. L. Fredman, and G. C. Patton. Method and system for automatically generating efficient test cases for systems having interacting elements. *United States Patent*, Number 5,542,043, 1996.

[7] D. M. Cohen, S. R. Dalal, J. Parelius, and G. C. Patton. The combinatorial design approach to automatic test generation. *IEEE Software*, 13(5):83 8, 1996.

[8] D. M. Cohen and M. L. Fredman. New techniques for designing qualitatively independent systems. *Journal of Combinatorial Designs*, 6(6):411–16, 1998.

[9] C. Colbourn and J. Dinitz. Making the MOLS table. In *Computational and Constructive Design Theory*, 1996. (W.D.Wallis, ed.) Kluwer Academic Press, 67-134.

[10] S. R. Dalal, A. J. N. Karunanithi, J. M. L. Leaton, G. C. P. Patton, and B. M. Horowitz. Model-based testing in practice. In *Proc. of the Intl. Conf. on Software Engineering,(ICSE '99)*, 1999, pp. 285-94, New York.

[11] G. Dueck. New optimization heuristics - the great deluge algorithm and the record-to-record travel. *Journal of Computational Physics*, 104:86–92, 1993.

[12] I. S. Dunietz, W. K. Ehrlich, B. D. Szablak, C. L. Mallows, and A. Iannino. Applying design of experiments to software testing. In *Proc. of the Intl. Conf. on Software Engineering, (ICSE '97)*, 1997, pp. 205-215, New York.

[13] L. Gargano, J. Körner, and U. Vaccaro. Capacities: from information theory to extremal set theory. *J. Combin. Theory Ser. A*, 68(2):296–316, 1994.

[14] A. Hedayat, N. Sloane, and J. Stufken. *Orthogonal Arrays.* Springer-Verlag, New York, 1999.

[15] G. Katona. Two applications (for search theory and truth functions) of Sperner type theorems. *Periodica Math.*, 3:19–26, 1973.

[16] D. Kleitman and J. Spencer. Families of k-independent sets. *Discrete Math*, 6:255–262, 1973.

[17] R. Mandl. Orthogonal latin squares: an application of experiment design to compiler testing. *Communications of the ACM*, 28(10):1054–8, 1985.

[18] K. Nurmela and P. R. J. Östergård. Constructing covering designs by simulated annealing. Technical report, Digital Systems Laboratory, Helsinki Univ. of Technology, 1993.

[19] P. R. J. Östergård. Constructions of mixed covering codes. Technical report, Digital Systems Laboratory, Helsinki Univ. of Technology, 1991.

[20] A. Réyni. *Foundations of Probability.* Wiley, New York, 1971.

[21] N. Sloane. Covering arrays and intersecting codes. *Journal of Combinatorial Designs*, 1(1):51–63, 1993.

[22] J. Stardom. Metaheuristics and the search for covering and packing arrays. Master's thesis, Simon Fraser University, 2001.

[23] B. Stevens and E. Mendelsohn. Efficient software testing protocols. In *Proc. of Center for Advanced Studies Conf. (Cascon '98)*, 1998, pp. 270-293, Ontario.

[24] B. Stevens and E. Mendelsohn. New recursive methods for transversal covers. *Journal of Combinatorial Designs*, 7(3):185–203, 1999.

[25] B. Stevens, L. Moura, and E. Mendelsohn. Lower bounds for transversal covers. *Designs Codes and Cryptography*, 15(3):279–299, 1998.

[26] K. C. Tai and L. Yu. A test generation strategy for pairwise testing. *IEEE Transactions on Software Engineering*, 28(1):109-111, 2002.

[27] A. W. Williams and R. L. Probert. A practical strategy for testing pair-wise coverage of network interfaces. In *Proc. Seventh Intl. Symp. on Software Reliability Engineering*, 1996, pp. 246-54.

[28] A. W. Williams and R. L. Probert. A measure for component interaction test coverage. In *Proc. ACS/IEEE Intl. Conf. on Computer Systems and Applications*, 2001, pp. 301-311.

[29] L. Yu and K. C. Tai. In-parameter-order: a test generation strategy for pairwise testing. In *Proc. Third IEEE Intl. High-Assurance Systems Engineering Symp.*, 1998, pp. 254-261.

[30] T. Yu-Wen and W. S. Aldiwan. Automating test case generation for the new generation mission software system. In *Proc. IEEE Aerospace Conf.*, 2000, pp. 431-437.

Improving Web Application Testing with User Session Data

Sebastian Elbaum[†], Srikanth Karre[†], Gregg Rothermel[‡],

[†]Department of Computer Science and Engineering
University of Nebraska - Lincoln
Lincoln, Nebraska
{elbaum,skarre}@cse.unl.edu

[‡]Department of Computer Science
Oregon State University
Corvallis, Oregon
grother@cs.orst.edu

Abstract

Web applications have become critical components of the global information infrastructure, and it is important that they be validated to ensure their reliability. Therefore, many techniques and tools for validating web applications have been created. Only a few of these techniques, however, have addressed problems of testing the functionality of web applications, and those that do have not fully considered the unique attributes of web applications. In this paper we explore the notion that user session data gathered as users operate web applications can be successfully employed in the testing of those applications, particularly as those applications evolve and experience different usage profiles. We report results of an experiment comparing new and existing test generation techniques for web applications, assessing both the adequacy of the generated tests and their ability to detect faults on a point-of-sale web application. Our results show that user session data can produce test suites as effective overall as those produced by existing white-box techniques, but at less expense. Moreover, the classes of faults detected differ somewhat across approaches, suggesting that the techniques may be complimentary.

1. Introduction

Web applications are among the fastest growing classes of software systems in use today. These applications are being used to support a wide range of important activities: business functions such as product sale and distribution, scientific activities such as information sharing and proposal review, and medical activities such as expert-system based diagnoses. Given the importance of such applications, faulty web applications can have far-ranging consequences on businesses, economies, scientific progress, and health. It is important that web applications be reliable, and to help with this, they should be validated.

To address this problem, many types of web application validation techniques have been proposed and many tools have been created. Most of these techniques and tools, however, focus on aspects of validation such as protocol conformance, load testing, broken link detection, and various static analyses, and do not directly address validation of functional requirements. Those tools that do focus on functional requirements primarily provide infrastructure to support capture-replay: recording tester input sequences for use in testing and regression testing.

Recently, a few more formal approaches for testing the functional requirements of web applications have been proposed [11, 17]. In essence, these are "white-box" approaches, building system models from inspection of code, identifying test requirements from those models, and requiring extensive human participation in the generation of test cases to fulfill those requirements. The approaches have shown promise in early empirical studies in terms of support for constructing "adequate" (by some criterion) test suites. However, the approaches also have drawbacks, in part due to differences between web applications and systems developed and operated under more traditional paradigms.

Among these differences, we consider three in particular. First, the usage of web applications can change rapidly. For example, a web site with a popular name that is caught by a search engine can suddenly find itself receiving hundreds of thousands of hits per day rather than just dozens [12]. In such cases, test suites designed with particular user profiles in mind may turn out to be inappropriate.

Second, web applications typically undergo maintenance at a faster rate than other software systems; this maintenance often consists of small incremental changes [9]. To accommodate such changes, testing approaches must be automatable and test suites must be adaptable.

Finally, web applications typically involve complex, multi-tiered, heterogeneous architectures including web servers, application servers, database servers, and clients

0-7695-1877-X/03 $17.00 © 2003 IEEE

acting as interpreters. Testing approaches must be able to handle the various components in this architecture.

Although some recently proposed techniques for testing the functional requirements of web applications [11, 17] partially address this third difference, the first two differences have not yet been addressed. Thus, in this paper, we propose a testing approach that utilizes data captured in user sessions to create test cases. We describe two stand-alone implementations of this approach, and a hybrid implementation that combines the approach with techniques such as the existing white-box approaches just described. We report results of an empirical study comparing these implementations of our approach with two different implementations of an existing approach recently proposed by Ricca and Tonella [17]. Unlike previous studies of web application testing techniques, however, our study assesses the fault detection effectiveness of the approaches.

In the next section we briefly describe the characteristics of the class of web applications that we are considering, and then we review related work on testing these applications. Section 3 describes Ricca and Tonella's technique in greater detail, and then describes our new approach and its implementations. Section 4 presents the design and results of our empirical study of these techniques, and Section 5 summarizes and comments on future work.

2. Background and Related Work

2.1. Web applications

A web site can be differentiated from a web application based on the "ability of a user to affect the state of the business logic on the server" [4]. In other words, requests made of a web application go beyond navigational requests, including some form of data that needs further decomposition and analysis to be served.

Figure 1 shows how a simple web application operates. A user (client) sends a request through a web browser. The web server responds by delivering content to the client. This content generally takes the form of some markup language (e.g., HTML) that is later interpreted by the browser to render a web page at the user site. For example, if a request consists of just a URL (Uniform Resource Locator – a web site address), the server may just fetch a static web page.

Other requests are more complicated and require further infrastructure. For example, in an e-commerce site, a request might include not just a URL, but also data provided by the user. Users provide data primarily through forms consisting of input fields (textboxes, checkboxes, selection lists) rendered in a web page. This information is translated into a set of name-value pairs (input fields' names and their values) and becomes part of the request.

Although the web server receives this request, further elements are needed to process it. First, a group of scripts and

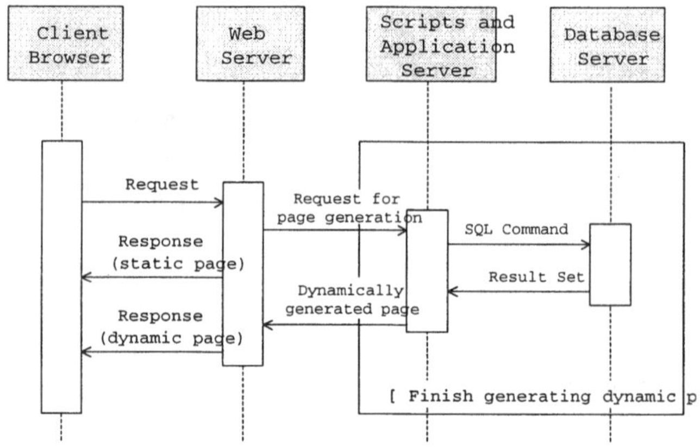

Figure 1. Sequence diagram of a web application.

perhaps an application server may parse the request, query a database server to retrieve information about the item, and then employ further formatting scripts to generate HTML code on the fly to address the user request. This newly generated page, generated at run time and depending on user's input, is called a dynamic web page.

In this context, the application server, database, and scripts collaborate to assemble a response that fits the request. Although in practice requests can be more complex, this example illustrates that there are multiple and varied technical components behind the web server. It is also important to note that scripts such as those just referred to are changed frequently [13], and the technologies supporting them change often, as evident in the frequent appearance of new standards for web protocols (e.g., XML, XSL, SOAP and CCS [10]).

2.2. Related work

The testing of web applications has been led by industry, whose techniques have been oriented primarily toward validation of non-functional requirements. This is evident in the number and variety of existing tools available for the relatively new web application domain. These tools range from markup text language validators and link checkers to various load testing and performance measurement tools.[1]

The variety and quantity of tools for testing functional requirements of web applications, on the other hand, is much more limited. The most common class of functional testing tools provide infrastructure to support the capture and replay of particular user scenarios [16, 18]. Testers execute possible user scenarios, and the tools record events and translate them into a series of scripts that can be replayed later for functional and regression testing. Other classes

[1]A comprehensive list of these tools is available at http://www.softwareqatest.com/qatweb1.html.

of functional testing tools generate test cases by combining some type of web site path exploration algorithm with tester provided inputs [13, 15]. A prototype framework integrating these various features is presented in [19].

Recently, two more formal techniques have been proposed to facilitate testing of functional requirements in web applications. Both techniques employ forms of model-based testing, but can be classified as "white-box" techniques, since they rely on information gathered from the web application code to generate the models on which they base their testing. Liu et al. [11] propose WebTestModel, which considers each web application component as an object and generates test cases based on data flow between those objects. Ricca and Tonella [17] propose a model based on the Unified Modeling Language (UML), to enable web application evolution analysis and test case generation. Both these techniques, in essence, extend traditional path-based test generation and data flow adequacy assessment to the web application domain; the second also builds on the existence of popular UML modelling capabilities.

It is worth noting that the effectiveness of these techniques has been evaluated only in terms of ability to achieve coverage adequacy. We find no reports to date of studies assessing fault detection capabilities of the techniques.

3. Web-Application Testing Techniques

In this section we provide further details about the particular techniques that we have investigated, including existing approaches and user-session based approaches. We first describe our implementations of Ricca and Tonella's approach. This approach is representative of the white-box techniques described in Section 2; it has also shown success in terms of coverage adequacy, and has been presented in detail sufficient to allow its implementation, given a few assumptions. Next, we introduce two new techniques for use in testing functional requirements of web applications. Our techniques are based on data captured in user sessions, and they exploit the availability of user inputs for automatic test case generation. Last, we present one possible integration of these two approaches. Table 1 summarizes the techniques.

Label	Description	Type
WB-1	Simplest Ricca and Tonella implementation [17]	White box
WB-2	WB-1 with boundary values	White box
US-1	Replay captured user sessions	User-session
US-2	Combine interactions from different user sessions	User-session
HYB	Insert user session values into WB-1	Hybrid

Table 1. Web application testing techniques.

3.1. Ricca and Tonella's approach

Conceptually, Ricca and Tonella's [17] approach creates a model in which nodes represent web objects (web pages, forms, frames), and edges represent relationships and interactions among the objects (include, submit, split, link).

For example, Figure 2 shows a model of a component of an application for on-line book purchasing, following the graphical representation used in [17]. The diagram starts at the BookDetail node. This node is dynamically generated in response to a request to browse a particular book. When rendered by the browser, this page contains information about the book and also includes (through edges e1 and e4) two forms: one to add the book to the shopping cart and one to rate the book. Both forms collect user input. If the rating form is submitted (e5), a new BookDetail page is generated with the updated rating for the book. If a valid book quantity is submitted (e2), the shopping cart is updated and a corresponding dynamically generated page is sent to the browser. Otherwise, BookDetail is sent again (e3).

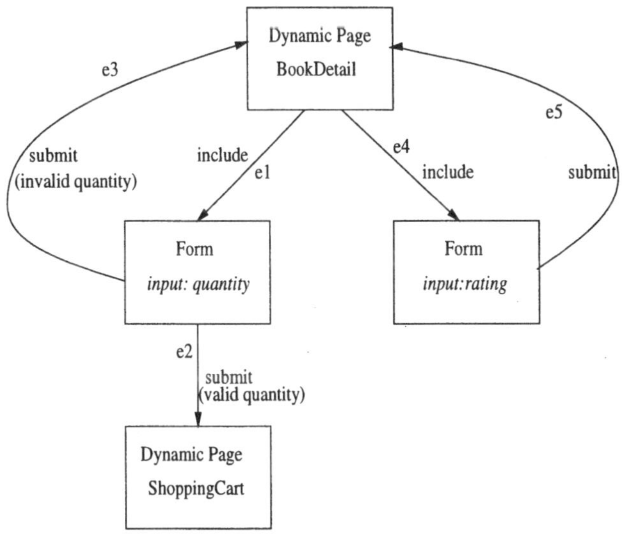

Figure 2. UML model of an e-commerce application.

To generate test requirements and cases, a path expression to match the graph is generated following a procedure similar to the one introduced by Beizer [2]. The path expression corresponding to the example from Figure 2 is $(e1e3) * +(e4e5)*$, where $*$ indicates zero or more occurrences of the immediately preceding edge(s) and $+$ indicates an alternative.

The path expression is used to generate quasi test cases in combination with heuristics to minimize the number of test cases required to satisfy a given criterion. For example, from the path expression for Figure 2, we can derive the sample quasi test cases: $e1e3$, $e1e2$, and $e4e5$. A (human) tester then provides input values so that the tests can be executed. In this approach, then, a test case consists of a sequence of web pages to be visited, together with their corresponding name-value pairs.

We consider two implementations of this approach. Our first implementation, WB-1, attempts to match the methodology presented in [17]. Test cases are generated from the path expression following the suggested procedure, but we were forced to make some assumptions about the implementation where details were not available. Specifically: (1) we tested only independent paths; (2) for search fields that could generate many different pages, we tested using only one input value; and (3) we ignored circular links and textual differences in dynamically generated pages. Once the quasi test cases were generated from the path expression, we filled the forms so that they could be executed.

Our second implementation, WB-2, relaxes some of the assumptions established for WB-1 and incorporates a more elaborate approach for input value selection. In contrast to WB-1, WB-2 uses boundary values as inputs, and utilizes an "each condition/all conditions" strategy to combine them [3]. The test suite consists of test cases in which each variable is set to true once with all the other variables set to false, plus one test case in which all variables are true. The objective of using boundary values and the "each condition/all conditions" strategy was to add formalism to the process of inputting data into the forms, as recommended in one of the examples in [17]. In addition, this technique considers not only differences in links, forms, and frames, but also textual differences when evaluating dynamically generated pages.

3.2. User-session based techniques

One limiting factor in the use of white box web application testing techniques such as Ricca and Tonella's is the cost of finding inputs that exercise the system as desired. Selection of such inputs is slow and must be accomplished manually [17]. User-session based techniques can help with this problem by transparently collecting user interactions and transforming them into test cases. The techniques capture and store the clients' requests in the form of URLs and name-value pairs, and then apply strategies to these to generate test cases.

Because normal web application operation consists of receiving and processing requests, and because a web application runs in just one environment which the organization performing the testing controls, the collection of client request information can be accomplished easily. For example, with minimal configuration changes, the Apache web server can log all received requests [1]. Another slightly more powerful but less transparent alternative that can capture all name-value pairs consists of adding snippets of javascript to the delivered webpages so that all requests invoke a server-side logging script.

As a consequence, user-session based techniques do not require additional infrastructure to collect this data, limiting the impact on web application performance. This is equivalent to having a built-in instrumentation mechanism, an approach well suited to web applications. Another advantage of collecting just the requests is that at that higher abstraction level, some of the complexities introduced by heterogeneous web application architectures are hidden. This lessens the dependencies of user-session based techniques on changes in web application components.

Given the collected URL and name-value pairs, there are many ways in which test cases could be generated. The simplest approach is to sequentially replay individual user sessions. A second approach is to replay a mixture of interactions from several users. A third approach is to replay sessions in parallel so that requests are handled concurrently. A fourth approach is to mix regular user requests with requests that are likely to be problematic (e.g., navigating backward and forward while submitting a form).

A complicating factor for these approaches involves *web application state*. When a specific user request is made of a web application, the outcome of that request may depend on factors not completely captured in URL and name-value pairs alone; for example, an airline reservation request may function differently depending on the pool of available seats. Further, the ability to execute subsequent tests may depend on the system state achieved by preceding tests. The simplest approach of replaying user sessions in their entirety is not affected by application state, provided that initial system state is known and can be instantiated. The use of more complex approaches such as intermixed or parallel replay, however, might often be affected by state.

In such cases, one approach for using user-session data is to periodically take snapshots of the state values (or of a subset of those values) that potentially affect web application response. Associating such snapshots with specific requests, or sequences of requests, increases the likelihood of being able to reproduce portions of user sessions, at the cost of resources and infrastructure.

A second alternative is to ignore state when generating test cases. The resulting test cases may not precisely reproduce the user activity on which they are based, but they may still usefully distribute testing effort relative to one aspect of the users' operational profile (the aspect captured by the operation) in a manner not achieved by white-box testing. From this perspective, the process of using user session data to generate test cases is related to the notion of partitioning the input domain of an application under test in the hopes of being able to effectively sample from the resulting partitions [21]. In this context, the potential usefulness of user-session based testing techniques, like the potential usefulness of white-box testing techniques, need not rest solely on being able to exactly reproduce a particular user session. Rather, that usefulness may reside in using user session data to provide effective partitioning heuristics, together with input data that can be transformed into test cases related to the resulting partitions.

The approaches that we have described for generating test data from user sessions and for addressing the problem of application state each have potential costs and benefits that must be explored. In this paper, we focus on two specific user-session based techniques — a technique that applies entire sessions, and a technique that replays a mixture of sessions — each without incorporating information on state. These techniques are relatively simple, and if they prove effective this would motivate further research on more complex techniques, and further exploration of the tradeoffs among techniques.

Our first technique, US-1, transforms each individual user session into a test case. Given m user sessions, $U_1, U_2, \ldots U_m$, with user session U_i consisting of n requests $r_1, r_2, \ldots r_n$, where each r_i consists of $url[name-value]*$, the test case corresponding to U_i is generated by formatting each of the requests, from r_1 to r_n, into an *http* request that can be sent to a web server. The resulting test suite contains m test cases, one for each user session. (For simplicity, we define a user session as beginning when a request from a new IP address reaches the server and ending when the user leaves the web site or the session times out.)

Our second user-session based technique, US-2, generates new user sessions based on the pool of collected data, creating test cases that contain requests belonging to different users. US-2 is meant to expose error conditions caused by the use of sometimes conflicting data provided by different users. US-2 generates a test case as follows:

- randomly select unused session U_a from session pool;
- copy requests r_1 through r_i, where i is a random number greater than 1 but smaller than n, into the test case;
- randomly select session U_b, where $b \neq a$, and search for any r_j with the same URL as r_i, and if an equivalent request is not found, select another session U_b;
- add all the requests from U_a after r_j to the test case;
- mark U_a "used", and repeat the process until no more unused sessions are available in the pool.

In a sense, US-1 is analogous to a constrained version of a capture-replay tool (e.g, Rational Robot [16]) in which we capture just the URL and name-value pairs that occur throughout a session. In contrast to approaches that capture user events at the client site, however, which can become complicated as the number of users grow, our approach captures just the URL and name-value pairs that are the result of a sequence of the user's events, captured at the server site. This alleviates some of the privacy problems introduced by the more intensive instrumentation used by some capture-replay tools.

Both US-1 and US-2 also have several other potential advantages. First, by utilizing user requests as the base for generating test cases, the techniques are less dependent on the complex and fast changing technology underlying web applications, which is one of the major limitations of white box approaches designed to work with a subset of the available protocols. Second, the level of effort involved in capturing URL and name-value pairs is relatively small as these are already processed by web applications. This is not the case with white box approaches such as Ricca and Tonella's, which require a high degree of tester participation. Third, with these approaches, each user is a potential tester: this implies potential for an economy of scale in which additional users provide more inputs for use in test generation. The potential power of the techniques resides in the number and representativeness of the URL and name-value pairs collected, and the possibility of their use in generating a more powerful test suite (an advantage that must be balanced, however, against the cost of gathering the associated user-session data). Finally, both approaches, unlike traditional capture and replay approaches, automatically capture authentic user interactions for use in deriving test cases, as opposed to interactions created by testers.

We are not proposing, however, to rely solely on users to assess web application quality. Our approach is meant to be applied either in the beta testing phase to generate a baseline test suite based on interactions with friendly customers, or during subsequent maintenance to enhance a test suite that was originally generated by a more traditional method. Further, the approach can help testers monitor and improve test suite quality as the web application evolves, and as its usage proceeds beyond the bounds anticipated in earlier releases and earlier testing.

3.3. Integrating user-session and white box methods

The strengths of structured white-box web application testing techniques such as Ricca and Tonella's might be more successfully leveraged if they can make use of inputs collected during user sessions. This suggests a hybrid testing technique combining techniques presented in the preceding sections with white-box techniques. Such a technique could decrease the cost of input selection, but it remains to be seen whether a user session's value pairs will be effective at detecting faults.

We wished to investigate this question and thus we also implemented a hybrid technique. Conceptually, the integration process matches equivalent user-session sequences with the paths defined by Ricca and Tonella's quasi test cases (quasi because they do not provide values, just target URL paths). Given a quasi test case qt generated by an

WB implementation, qt is translated into a URL sequence $urlSeq_{qt}$. Then, the technique iterates through all collected user sessions to identify those that contain the entire $urlSeq_{qt}$. Once the relevant user sessions have been identified, the name-value pairs corresponding to the matching requests in each session are used to complete the $urlSeq_{qt}$, transforming qt into an executable test case. The process continues until all possible test cases have been generated by combining each WB quasi test case with all user sessions with an equivalent sequence.

4. Empirical Study

4.1. Research questions

RQ1. The first question we address is, how effective are the WB techniques at exposing faults in a web application? Evaluating the effectiveness of the WB techniques will help us assess them, and also provide a baseline against which to compare user-session based techniques.

RQ2. Our second research question concerns the cost-effectiveness of user-session based techniques. We conjecture that test suites generated through these techniques provide a useful combination of effectiveness and efficiency.

RQ3. Last, we want to know what relationship exists between the number of user sessions and the effectiveness of the test suites generated based on those sessions' interactions. Answering this question will help us explore the cost-effectiveness of user-session based test suite generation.

4.2. Variables and metrics

The testing techniques listed in Table 1 constitute our independent variables, and are represented by the labels WB-1, WB-2, US-1, US-2, and HYB.

The dependent variables we wish to capture are coverage and fault detection effectiveness. We use two coverage metrics: percentage of functions covered and percentage of blocks covered in the perl code that generated the dynamic web pages and accessed the databases. Percentage of faults detected constitutes our other measure of effectiveness.

4.3. Experimental setting

4.3.1 E-commerce site

The free and open source on-line bookstore available at gotocode.com constituted the skeleton of our e-commerce application. The e-bookstore functionalities are divided into two groups: customer activities and administration activities. This study concentrates on functionalities that are accessible to the customer, not the administration component. Figure 3 provides a screenshot of the application. Customers can search, browse, register, operate a shopping cart, and purchase books on-line through this site, which operates like other similar popular sites on the web.

Customer functionality is implemented through Perl scripts and modules to handle data and the dynamic generation of HTML pages, Mysql to manage database accesses, a database structure composed of seven tables tracking books, transactions, and other data objects, and Javascript and cookies to provide identification and personalization functionality. An Apache Web Server hosted the application.

We populated the database with information from 100 books (e.g., title, authors, short description, category, price, rating). We adapted the look of the site so that the registration procedure was expedited and logins minimized, which made the navigation process more similar to commercial sites. Last, to capture the information required by the user-session techniques, we modified the scripts generating dynamic web pages. As a result, the generated web pages included additional Javascript code to capture user events and to invoke a logging server-side script.

4.3.2 Fault seeding

We wished to evaluate the performance of web testing techniques with respect to the detection of faults. Such faults were not available with our subject application; thus, to obtain them, we followed a procedure similar to one defined and employed in previous studies of testing techniques [6, 8, 22]. We recruited two graduate students of computer science, each with at least two years of programming experience, and instructed them to insert faults that were as realistic as possible based on their experience. To direct their efforts we gave them a random generator that indicated the approximate location of where a fault was to be seeded, and gave them the following list of fault types to consider:[2]

- Scripting faults. This includes faults associated with variables, such as definitions, deletions, or changes in values, and faults associated with control flow, such as addition of new blocks, redefinitions of execution conditions, removal of blocks, changes in execution order, and addition or removal of function calls.
- Web page faults. This includes addition, deletion, or modification of name-value pairs. Such changes occur in one or more names or values.
- Database query faults. This type of fault consists of the modification of a query expression, which could affect the type of operation, the table to access, fields within the table, or the values of search keys or record values.

[2] These directives are adapted from the fault classification in [14].

Figure 3. Screenshot of e-commerce site used in our experiment.

The graduate students assigned to the task seeded a total of 50 faults. Nine faults were discarded: two were in unused sections of code and the rest had no impact on the application (e.g., the value of a variable was changed after its last usage).

4.3.3 Assignment for participants in study

Once the web application was set up, the challenge was to have users access the site and behave like "typical" users of this type of e-commerce site. Users navigate sites like ours to browse and perhaps purchase books if the material and price are appropriate for their needs and budget. We wished to provide the context and incentive for users to interact with our application under similar circumstances.

To achieve these goals, we instructed our study participants to follow a three step process. First, they completed an on-line form with simple demographic data. This step was required only for the first session of each user. Second, the description of four computer science courses was made available to the participants; the participants needed to select two of those courses. The final step required the participants to access the e-bookstore site to select the most appropriate book(s) for the courses they selected.

To select the most appropriate books, participants had to search and browse until they found those that they considered most appropriate. We provided no definition of appropriateness, so it meant different things to different users, which is supposed to lead to a variety of activities. However, we did provide an incentive so that users took the task completion seriously. The instructions indicated that on completion of the experiment, the five users who selected the most appropriate books for the courses would each receive a ten dollar gift certificate. Further directions specified that, if more than five users selected the most appropriate books, the amount spent would be evaluated, and ties would be broken by considering the time spent on the web site. Again, the objective was to recreate the conditions observed for similar web applications.

4.4. Execution and processing

The US-1, US-2, and HYB techniques required user participation to generate test suites. A list of candidate participants was assembled, containing primarily students from the Department of Computer Science and Engineering at UNL. An email stating participation requirements and incentives was sent to the students on the list. The e-commerce site was then made available to the users for two weeks. Data collected from the user sessions was logged to support subsequent test case generation, which occurred off-line. There were 99 user sessions logged. Fourteen percent of the sessions could not be used because, despite instructions, some users accessed the web site using browsers

Metric	WB-1		WB-2		US-1		US-2		HYB	
	abs	%	abs	%	abs	%	abs	%	abs	%
Test Suite Size	28	–	64	–	85	–	84	–	1089	–
Block Coverage	263	66	306	76	263	66	255	64	260	65
Function Coverage	65	97	66	99	65	97	64	96	65	97
Faults Detected	22	51	25	58	23	53	23	53	23	53

Table 2. Summary data on technique effectiveness.

other than those required. In total, 73 distinct users contributed to the 85 useful sessions. The users had an average age of 24 and 94 percent had on-line buying experience.

After the test suites corresponding to each technique were generated, we ran them on the fault-free web application, which served as an oracle. Then, to measure function and block coverage, the application was instrumented so that a counter would be incremented each time one of those entities was executed. The e-bookstore had a total of 67 functions and 400 blocks. Measuring coverage required a second execution of each test suite.

Last, we evaluated the test suites generated through each technique by activating the seeded faults individually, and determining which faults were revealed by which test cases. Since we had a total of 43 faults, this last step required an equal number of runs of each test suite.

4.5. Results

4.5.1 On technique effectiveness

The results of executing the test suites generated by each of the techniques are presented in Table 2. These results correspond to RQ1 and RQ2, as defined in Section 4.1, and are presented in absolute values and percentages. Overall, WB techniques used the fewest test cases, while the HYB approach employed the greatest number (1089). WB-2 provided the greatest fault detection power with 58% of the faults detected, and the greatest coverage with 76% and 99% of the blocks and functions covered, respectively. Both user-session based techniques performed similarly, not as effectively as WB-2, but slightly better than WB-1. US-2 did not discover more faults than US-1 and the HYB approach did not provide additional fault detection or coverage. This summary, however, fails to reveal some interesting facts about the differences between techniques.

First, although the overall results for fault detection are similar, differences between the approaches are more evident when individual faults are analyzed. A detailed comparison of the most powerful white box and user session based techniques is presented in Table 3. The first row of the table lists the blocks covered, functions covered, and faults detected by WB-2 and US-1. The second and third rows present the same information but focusing on blocks, functions, or faults uniquely associated with one technique and not the other. The fourth row shows the result of executing the tests generated by both techniques.

Technique Combination	Blocks		Functions		Faults	
	abs	%	abs	%	abs	%
$(WB2 \cap US1)$	255	64	65	97	20	47
$(WB2 - US1)$	51	13	1	1	5	12
$(US1 - WB2)$	8	2	0	0	3	7
$(WB2 \cup US1)$	314	79	66	99	28	65

Table 3. Detailed comparison of WB-2 and US-1.

It is evident from the table that the blocks covered by WB-2 and US-1 are not the same: 8 blocks were covered only by US-1, while 51 others were covered only by WB-2. A similar observation can be made about functions covered. Also, 3 of the faults found by US-1 were not found by WB-2, and 5 faults were found only by WB-2. Similar differences occurred with the other techniques. This supports the hypothesis that the distinct approaches we considered are able to find different types of faults. Further, in spite of the unimpressive performance of HYB as we implemented it, the last row row of Table 3 shows that when the test cases of both techniques (representing both approaches) are combined, the resulting coverage and fault detection capabilities are better than for any individual technique.

Second, there are some type of faults that user-session based approaches could rarely capture. Those faults have to do with particular name-value pairs that could not be generated using the forms available through the delivered web pages. For example, when doing a book evaluation in the application, five levels (from 1 to 5 stars) are available through the web site. The only way to construct a request with evaluation values outside that range is to generate the request outside the rendered page. This scenario is rarely originated by regular users, but it could have appeared if the site were detected by search robots that perform that type of request. Again, additional exposure time could have helped accomplish this, but it is more likely that this type of request would be generated by design instead of by user activity. In addition, although we could not identify a certain type of faults that WB techniques are likely to miss, we observed that strategies such as that followed by WB-2 helped lessen the impact of tester input choices on the effectiveness of WB techniques.

4.5.2 On user-sessions versus effectiveness

A detailed analysis of our data revealed that certain techniques could have performed better given some adjustments. WB-2 could have discovered one more fault if the "each condition/all condition" strategy was replaced by a more powerful strategy such as "all variants" [3]. Still, such an approach would require significant additional human participation, and lead to scalability problems.

US-1, on the other hand, could have detected five additional faults, increasing its fault detection effectiveness to 68% (better than the other techniques) if additional exposure was provided through more user sessions. Two of these additional faults were not discovered by WB-2, and required a special combination of input values to be exposed. For example, one fault could have been exposed if a user had attempted to access the shopping cart prior to completing the registration procedure. The three other faults that could have been discovered by US-1, and that were captured by WB-2, required erroneous inputs that did not appear in the collected user sessions. For example, the registration procedure required a password and a confirmation for that password. A fault was exposed when these inputs did not match. WB-2 caught that fault but US-1 did not since no user session exhibited that behavior.

In this study, the effectiveness of user-session based techniques improved as the number of collected sessions increased. Figure 4 shows the relationship between the number of user sessions collected for and employed by US-1, and its effectiveness under the various metrics considered. The x-axis presents the individual sessions from 1 to 85 (corresponding one to one with the test cases generated by US-1), the bars represent the US-1 test case value for the corresponding y-variable, and the line represents the cumulative count of unique faults exposed or blocks and functions covered, as additional sessions exercised the application.

The figure shows that test cases generated from user sessions varied in terms of coverage and fault exposure, and that the cumulative increases in the dependent variables were slower over time. Within the ranges observed, a positive trend in the cumulative counts suggests that user-session based techniques might continue to improve as additional sessions (and potentially additional user behaviors) are collected; however, this trend might also be tempered by the costs of collecting and analyzing additional data, and as the number of detectable faults remaining in the system is reduced. The costs of experimentation constrained our ability to collect further sessions to investigage this; further studies on commercial sites with thousands of sessions per day would provide the opportunity to further analyze such trends.

Using larger numbers of sessions, however, introduces at least one additional challenge in addition to the cost of collecting and managing sessions: the oracle problem [20]. That is, what is the expected output in response to a request, and how do we perform an effective comparison of results to expected results? In a regression testing context, where a web application evolves and produces new versions, this problem can be partially addressed by the procedure we employed in our experiment, where the outputs of one version constitute a baseline against which posterior versions' outputs are compared. This is similar to the solutions provided by capture-replay tools, but at a larger scale.

Still, this scenario presumes that the correctness of results of executing test cases on a baseline can be determined, that initial states can be collected and reused in test execution, and that the execution of thousands of generated test cases can be made affordable. One approach that might help with error detection involves techniques for automatically detecting anomalous behaviors among large sets of executions [5]; these techniques might allow large numbers of generated test cases to be retained usefully.

A second approach involves using existing techniques to reduce test suite size while maintaining coverage by removing redundant test cases from the suite. We briefly explored this second approach, adapting the test suite reduction technique of Harrold et al. [7] and applying it to the test cases generated with US-1. When applied at a functional level, test suite reduction could have reduced test suite size by 98%, with a loss of only three faults (20 were detected). Test suite reduction on block level information reduced the test suite size by 93%, detecting one fewer fault than the complete US-1 original test suite. These results suggest that combining reduction techniques with user-session techniques could be helpful for handling the large number of requests found in commercial e-commerce sites. As defined, however, test suite reduction techniques function only on complete data sets. New techniques will have to be developed to incrementally handle the collection and processing of data as it arrives.

4.6. Threats to validity

This study, like any other, has some limitations. In this section we identify the primary limitations that could have influenced the results and we explain how we tried to control unwanted sources of variation. Some of these limitations are unavoidable consequences of the decision to use controlled experimentation; however, the advantage of control is more certain knowledge of causality.

First, we needed to set up infrastructure to reproduce a web application that resembled as closely as possible those

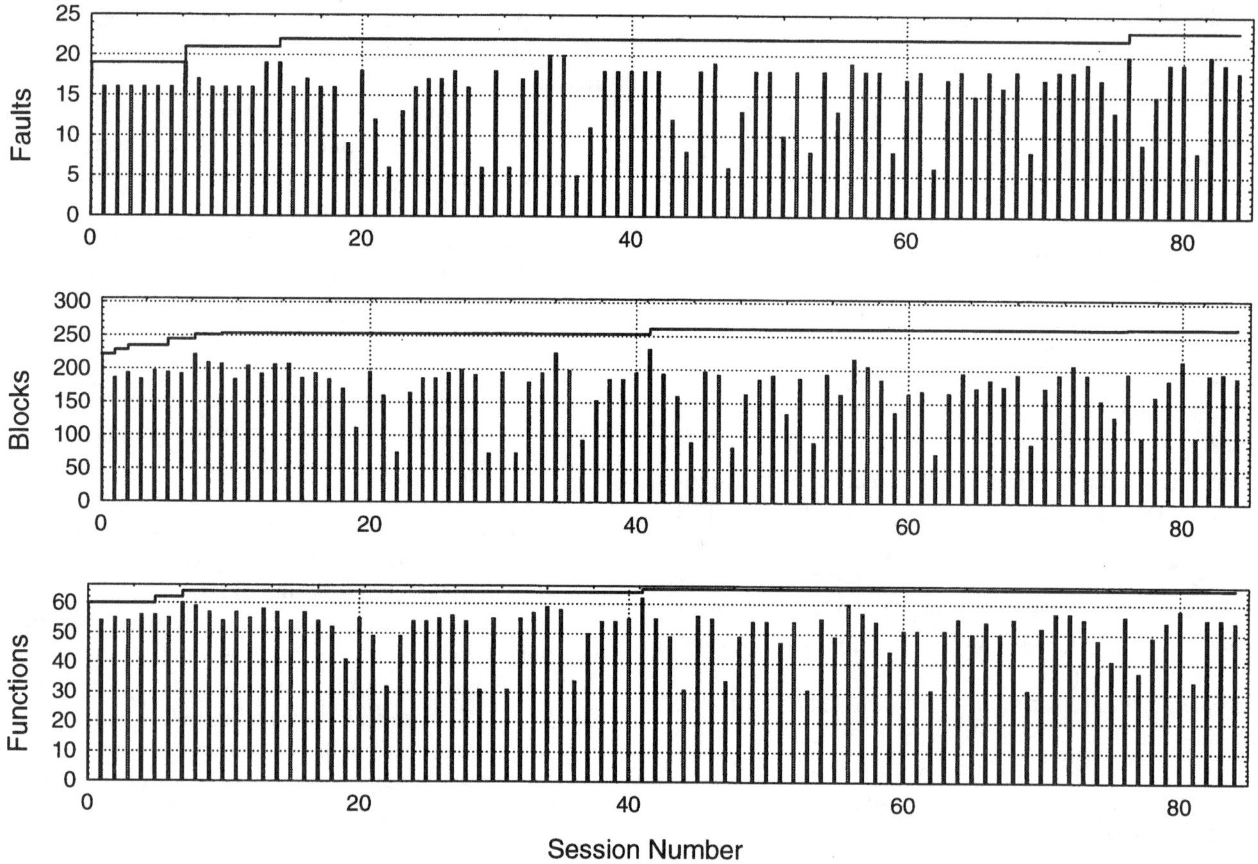

Figure 4. Relationship between the number of user sessions collected and the effectiveness of US-1.

found in the real world. To control for potential threats caused by the lack of representativeness of the web application, we carefully adapted an existing e-commerce application, populating its database, and configuring the site shipping and personalization attributes. In spite of this effort, the resulting web site included just a subset of the technologies used in the field, so our results can be claimed to generalize only to web applications using similar technologies. Additional web applications must be studied to overcome these threats to external validity.

Second, we needed to seed faults in the application so that we could evaluate the testing techniques. Although naturally occurring faults are preferred, obtaining a web application with a large number of known faults was not feasible. As a consequence, we opted for a fault seeding process similar to those commonly used in previous research to measure testing techniques' fault-detection effectiveness. The risk of seeding faults that are not representative of the faults found in web applications is still a threat to external validity. For example, we did not simulate the existence of faults on the client side (e.g., javascript faults).

Third, our user-session based techniques employ user interactions, which implies that we required collection of data from users interacting with the e-commerce site we had set up. User navigation and buying patterns were not our focus, but we wished to reproduce the activities users might perform in this type of site. The instructions for participants included a task and an incentive to make the experience more realistic for a set of potential customers, but are still just an approximation of reality and constitute a threat to external validity because of representativeness, and a threat to internal validity because they could have constituted a nuisance variable that affected the results. Similarly, the input selection that drive the WB techniques is influenced by the testers's ability and intuition for input selection. We diminished the impact of this threat by providing a common strategy for all testers to select their input values.

5. Conclusion

We have presented and quantified a new approach for testing web applications. This new approach differs from existing approaches in that it leverages captured user behavior to generate test cases, leading to a reduction in the amount of required tester intervention. Further, the results of a controlled experiment indicate that this approach's effectiveness is comparable and likely complementary to more formal white box testing approaches.

These results suggest several directions for future work. First, the combination of traditional testing techniques and user-session data would seem to possess a potential that we have not been able to fully exploit. New ways must be found to successfully integrate these approaches. In addition, more complex techniques that consider other factors affecting the approach must be explored; such factors include web application states and concurrent user requests.

Second, the analysis of user-session techniques suggests that using a large number of captured used sessions involves tradeoffs. Additional sessions may provide additional fault detection power, but a larger number of sessions also implies more test preparation and execution time. Techniques for filtering sessions will need to be investigated.

Third, the applicability of the user-session test generation approach will certainly be affected by the efficiency of the data collection process. Further studies are needed to determine under what types of loads this approach is cost-effective. Furthermore, given the observed asymptotic improvement in fault detection, studies will need to consider whether this approach should be applied to all or just a subset of the user-sessions.

Finally, we believe that there are many applications for user-session data that have not been fully explored in the domain of web applications. For example, user-session data could be used to assess the appropriateness of an existing test suite in the face of shifting operational profiles. Through such approaches, we hope to be able to harness the power of user profile data to improve the reliability of this important class of software applications.

Acknowledgments

This work was supported in part by the NSF Information Technology Research program under Awards CCR-0080898 and CCR-0080900 to University of Nebraska, Lincoln and Oregon State University. The e-commerce application was made available by gotocode.com. Madeline Hardojo assisted in the fault seeding process. We especially thank the users who participated in the study, and we thank the reviewers for their helpful comments.

References

[1] Apache-Organization. Apache http server version 2.0 documentation. http://httpd.apache.org/docs-2.0/.

[2] B. Beizer. *Softw. Testing Techniques*. Van Nostrand Reinhold, New York, NY, 1990.

[3] R. Binder. *Testing Object-Oriented Systems*. Addison Wesley, Reading, MA, 2000.

[4] J. Conallen. *Building Web Applications with UML*. Addison-Wesley Publishing Company, Reading, MA, 2000.

[5] W. Dickinson, D. Leon, and A. Podgurski. Finding failures by cluster analysis of execution profiles. In *Proceedings of the International Conference on Software Engineering*, pages 339 – 348, May 2001.

[6] S. Elbaum, A. G. Malishevsky, and G. Rothermel. Test case prioritization: A family of empirical studies. *IEEE Transactions on Software Engineering*, 28(2):159–182, Feb. 2002.

[7] M. Harrold, R. Gupta, and M. Soffa. A methodology for controlling the size of a test suite. *ACM Transactions on Software Engineering and Methodology*, 2(3):270–285, July 1993.

[8] M. Hutchins, H. Foster, T. Goradia, and T. Ostrand. Experiments on the effectiveness of dataflow- and controlflow-based test adequacy criteria. In *Proceedings of the International Conference on Software Engineering*, pages 191–200, May 1994.

[9] E. Kirda, M. Jazayeri, C. Kerer, and M. Schranz. Experiences in Engineering Flexible Web Services. *IEEE Multi-Media*, 8(1):58–65, Jan. 2001.

[10] T. Lee. World wide web consortium. http://www.w3.org/.

[11] C. Liu, D. Kung, P. Hsia, and C. Hsu. Structural testing of web applications. In *Proceedings of the 11th IEEE International Symposium on Software Reliability Engineering*, pages 84–96, Oct. 2000.

[12] S. Manley and M. Seltzer. Web facts and fantasy. In *Proceedings of the 1997 Usenix Symposium on Internet Technologies and Systems*, Monterey, CA, 1997.

[13] B. Michael, F. Juliana, and G. Patrice. Veri-web:automatically testing dynamic web sites. In *Proceedings of 11th International WWW Conference*, Honululu, May 2002.

[14] A. Nikora and J. Munson. Software evolution and the fault process. In *Proceedings of the Twenty Third Annual Software Engineering Workshop, NASA/Goddard Space Flight Center*, 1998.

[15] Parasoft. WebKing. http://www.parasoft.com/jsp/products.

[16] Rational-Corporation. Rational testing robot. http://www.rational.com/products/robot/.

[17] F. Ricca and P. Tonella. Analysis and testing of web applications. In *Proceedings of the International Conference on Software Engineering*, pages 25–34, May 2001.

[18] I. Software Research. eValid. http://www.soft.com/eValid/.

[19] J. Tzay, J. Huang, F. Wang, and W. Chu. Constructing an Object-Oriented Architecture for Web Application Testing. *Journal of Information Science and Engineering* , 18(1):59–84, Jan. 2002.

[20] E. J. Weyuker. On testing non-testable programs. *The Computing Journal*, 15(4):465–470, 1982.

[21] E. J. Weyuker and B. Jeng. Analyzing partition testing strategies. *IEEE Transactions on Software Engineering*, 17(7):703–711, July 1991.

[22] W. Wong, J. Horgan, S. London, and A. Mathur. Effect of test set minimization on fault detection effectiveness. In *Proceedings of the 17th International Conference on Software Engineering*, pages 41–50, Apr. 1995.

Improving Test Suites via Operational Abstraction

Michael Harder Jeff Mellen Michael D. Ernst

MIT Lab for Computer Science
200 Technology Square
Cambridge, MA 02139 USA
{mharder,jeffm,mernst}@lcs.mit.edu

Abstract

This paper presents the operational difference *technique for generating, augmenting, and minimizing test suites. The technique is analogous to structural code coverage techniques, but it operates in the semantic domain of program properties rather than the syntactic domain of program text.*

The operational difference technique automatically selects test cases; it assumes only the existence of a source of test cases. The technique dynamically generates operational abstractions (which describe observed behavior and are syntactically identical to formal specifications) from test suite executions. Test suites can be generated by adding cases until the operational abstraction stops changing. The resulting test suites are as small, and detect as many faults, as suites with 100% branch coverage, and are better at detecting certain common faults.

This paper also presents the area *and* stacking *techniques for comparing test suite generation strategies; these techniques avoid bias due to test suite size.*

1 Introduction

Program specifications play a valuable role in dynamic analyses such as software testing [GG75b, ROT89, CRS96, OL99]. Most previous research on automated specification-based testing has required software testers to provide a formal specification. Furthermore, the research has generally focused on systematic generation of test suites rather than evaluation and comparison of existing test suites. The applicability of previous research is limited by the fact that very few programs are formally specified — most lack even `assert` statements. Additionally, software engineers may desire to improve existing test suites or to use other tools for selecting test cases.

The *operational difference* (OD) technique is a new specification-based test case selection technique that enables augmentation, minimization, and generation of test suites in cooperation with any existing technique for test case generation. It does not require a specification to be provided *a priori*, nor does it require an oracle that indicates whether a particular test case passes or fails. It automatically provides users with an *operational abstraction*. An operational abstraction is syntactically identical to a formal specification, but describes actual behavior, which may or may not be desired behavior. For future testing, the operational abstraction can provide the benefits of an *a priori* specification, such as assisting regression testing by revealing removed functionality and checking test results. The operational abstractions are also useful in their own right.

This research builds on previous testing research, such as structural coverage criteria, but applies it to the semantic domain of program properties rather than the syntactic domain of program text. The key idea behind the operational difference technique is comparison of operational abstractions, which are dynamically generated from program executions. A test case that improves the operational abstraction can be added to a test suite; a test case that does not can be removed, if appropriate. We have implemented the technique and experimentally demonstrated its efficacy in creating test suites with good fault detection.

The remainder of the paper is organized as follows. Section 2 describes how to automatically induce an operational abstraction from a program and a test suite. Section 3 presents the operational difference technique for generating, augmenting, and minimizing test suites. Section 4 details our experimental methodology, and Section 5 reports experiments demonstrating that the operational difference technique compares favorably with other methods. Section 6 provides intuition (and experimental data) for why the technique works. Section 7 summarizes related research, then Section 8 concludes.

2 Generating operational abstractions

An *operational abstraction* is a formal mathematical description of program behavior: it is a collection of logical statements that abstract the program's runtime operation. An operational abstraction is identical in form to a formal specification. However, a formal specification is intended to be written before the code and to express desired behavior.

0-7695-1877-X/03 $17.00 © 2003 IEEE

By contrast, an operational abstraction expresses observed behavior and is induced dynamically from program executions.

Our experiments use the Daikon dynamic invariant detector to generate operational abstractions, but the ideas generalize beyond any particular implementation. Briefly, Daikon discovers likely invariants from program executions by running the program, examining the values that it computes, and detecting patterns and relationships among those values. The detection step uses an efficient generate-and-check algorithm that reports properties that hold over execution of an entire test suite. The output is improved by suppressing invariants that are not statistically justified and by other techniques [ECGN00].[1] Dynamic invariant detection is not affected by the internal structure of the program component being analyzed. In Zhu's terminology [ZHM97], our technique is interface-based, which is a variety of black-box testing.

Generation of operational abstractions from a test suite is unsound: the properties are likely, but not guaranteed, to hold in general. As with other dynamic approaches such as testing and profiling, the accuracy of the inferred invariants depends in part on the quality and completeness of the test cases. When a reported invariant is not universally true for all possible executions, then it indicates a property of the program's context or environment or a deficiency of the test suite. In many cases, a human or an automated tool can examine the output and enhance the test suite, but this paper does not address that issue.

Operational abstractions often match human-written formal specifications [Ern00, ECGN01] or can be proved correct [NE02a, NE02b, NWEG+03]. However, the operational difference technique does not depend on these properties: it generates test suites that detect faults even if the operational abstraction differs from the formal specification that a human might have written, and even if the program is incorrect.

3 Operational difference technique

This section describes the operational difference (OD) technique for generating, augmenting, and minimizing test suites. The OD technique compares the operational abstractions induced by different test suites in order to decide which test suite is superior.

The operational difference technique is automatic, but for test suite generation and augmentation, it assumes the existence of a source of test cases. In other words, the technique selects, but does not generate, test cases — much like other techniques such as those based on code coverage. Test cases may be created by a human, generated at random or from a grammar, generated from a specification, extracted from observed usage, or produced in any other fashion.

procedure OD-GENERATE (**program** P, **int** n)
  testsuite $S \leftarrow \{\}$
  int $i \leftarrow 0$
  while $i < n$ **do**
    testcase $c \leftarrow$ NEWCASE()
    if OPABSTR(P, S) $\neq$ OPABSTR(P, $S \cup \{c\}$) **then**
      $S \leftarrow S \cup \{c\}$
      $i \leftarrow 0$
    else
      $i \leftarrow i + 1$
  return S

Figure 1. Pseudocode implementation of the basic operational difference (OD) test suite generation technique. NEWCASE is a user-specified procedure that generates a candidate test case; our experiments randomly select test cases from a pool. OPABSTR is a procedure that generates an operational abstraction from a program and a test suite; our experiments use the Daikon invariant detector (Section 2).

The basic OD generation technique (Figure 1) starts with an empty test suite and an empty operational abstraction. It repeatedly adds candidate test cases; if they change the operational abstraction, they are retained, under the (possibly incorrect) assumption that an operational abstraction generated from a larger test suite is better. When n candidate cases have been consecutively considered and rejected, the process is complete. The value chosen for n is a tradeoff between the running time of the generation process and the quality of the generated suite; the quality of the test case generation procedure may also influence the best choice for n. We further improve the basic OD generation technique by evaluating several candidate test cases at a time and selecting the case that changes the operational abstraction most, and by minimizing the resulting test suite after generation. The test suite augmentation technique is identical but starts with a non-empty test suite.

The OD test suite minimization technique considers each test case in turn and removes each one whose removal does not change the operational abstraction. Its intuition is that test cases that affect the operational abstraction are more different from one another than test cases that do not affect the operational abstraction. Minimization is similar to generation in that both select a subset of test cases. Minimization differs in that it starts from a suite and removes cases, it considers every case in the suite, and the resulting suite is guaranteed to have the same qualities (such as coverage or operational abstraction) as the original suite. Thus, minimization and generation typically produce quite different suites. Minimization can be useful after generation, because later test cases may subsume earlier ones.

[1]The statistical tests use a user-settable confidence parameter. The results in this paper use the default value, .01. We repeated the experiments with values of .0001 and .99, and the differences were negligible.

Candidate test case	Operational abstraction for abs		Final suite
	Precond.	Postcondition	
5	`x == 5`	`x == orig(x)` `x == return`	√
1	`x >= 1`	`x == orig(x)` `x == return`	√
4	*same*	*same*	

−1	`x >= -1`	`(x >= 1) => (x == return)`
		`(x == -1) => (x == -return)`
		`return >= 1`
			√

−6	*empty*	`(x >= 1) => (x == return)`
		`(x <= -1) => (x == -return)`
		`return >= 1`
			√

−3	*same*	*same*	

0	*same*	`(x >= 0) => (x == return)`
		`(x <= 0) => (x == -return)`
		`return >= 0`
			√

7	*same*	*same*	
−8	*same*	*same*	
3	*same*	*same*	

Figure 2. Example of generating a test suite via the OD-base technique. The candidate test cases are considered in order from top to bottom; a test case is added to the suite if it changes the operational abstraction. The process terminates when $n = 3$ test cases have been consecutively considered and rejected. The final test suite is $\{5, 1, -1, -6, 0\}$. The final operational abstraction has no preconditions and three postconditions. In a postcondition, `orig(x)` stands for the pre-state value of x.

As with many minimization techniques, the OD technique does not guarantee that the minimized suite is the smallest set of cases that can generate the original operational abstraction. Furthermore, there is no guarantee that the removed test case cannot detect a fault. A software engineer might use minimization on test suites of questionable value, such as ones that were randomly generated. Minimization, like test case prioritization, can also be valuable in reducing a test suite. For instance, a large test suite might run every night or every weekend, but developers might run a subset of the suite more frequently.

Statistical tests in the current implementation make the operational abstractions a multiple-entity criterion [JH01]: a single test case may not guarantee that a particular invariant is reported or not reported. This is not a necessary condition of the technique, and we plan to experiment with ways to combine operational abstractions for individual test cases, which will reduce the cost of suite generation.

Figure 2 illustrates how the OD technique with $n = 3$ generates a test suite for the absolute value procedure. The example uses an operational abstraction generator that reports the following properties at procedure entries and exits:

- $var = constant$
- $var \geq constant$
- $var \leq constant$
- $var = \pm var$
- $property \Rightarrow property$

4 Experimental methodology

This section describes the subject programs we used to evaluate the operational difference technique, the measurements we performed, and how we controlled for size when comparing test suite generation strategies.

4.1 Subject programs

Our experiments analyze eight C programs. Each program comes with faulty versions and a pool of test cases. (We discovered additional errors in four of the programs during the course of this research.) Figure 3 lists the subjects.

The first seven programs in Figure 3 were created by Siemens Research [HFGO94], and subsequently modified by Rothermel and Harrold [RH98]. The Siemens researchers generated tests automatically from test specification scripts, then augmented those with manually-constructed white-box tests such that each feasible statement, branch, and def-use pair was covered by at least 30 test cases. The Siemens researchers created faulty versions of the programs by introducing errors they considered realistic. Each faulty version differs from the canonical version by 1 to 5 lines of code. They discarded faulty versions that were detected by more than 350 or fewer than 3 test cases; they considered the discarded faults too easy or too hard to detect. (A test suite detects a fault if the outputs of the faulty and correct versions differ.)

The eighth program, `space`, interprets Array Definition Language inputs. The test pool for `space` contains 13585 cases. 10000 were generated randomly by Vokolos and Frankl [VF98], and the remainder were added by Graves et al. [GHK+01] until every edge in the control flow graph was covered by at least 30 cases. Each time an error was detected during the program's development or later by Graves et al., a new faulty version of the program (containing only that error) was created.

Some of our experiments use test suites generated by randomly selecting cases from the test pool. Other experiments use statement, branch, and def-use coverage suites generated by Rothermel and Harrold [RH98]. These suites were generated by picking tests from the pool at random and adding them to the suite if they added any coverage, until all the coverage conditions were satisfied. There are 1000 test suites for each type of coverage, except that there are no statement or def-use covering suites for `space`.

Threats to validity. Our subject programs are of moderate size; larger programs might have different characteristics. We chose them because they are well-understood from previous research and because we did not have access to other programs with human-generated tests and faulty versions. We suspect that these programs differ from large programs

Program	Program size			Faulty	Test pool			Description
	Procedures	LOC	NCNB	versions	cases	calls	op. abs. size	of program
`print_tokens`	18	703	452	7	4130	619424	97	lexical analyzer
`print_tokens2`	19	549	379	10	4115	723937	173	lexical analyzer
`replace`	21	506	456	30	5542	1149891	252	pattern replacement
`schedule`	18	394	276	9	2650	442179	283	priority scheduler
`schedule2`	16	369	280	9	2710	954468	161	priority scheduler
`tcas`	9	178	136	41	1608	12613	328	altitude separation
`tot_info`	7	556	334	23	1052	13208	156	information measure
`space`	136	9568	6201	34	13585	8714958	2144	ADL interpreter

Figure 3. Subject programs used in experiments. "LOC" is the total lines of code; "NCNB" is the number of non-comment, non-blank lines of code. Test suite size is measured in number of test cases (invocations of the subject program) and number of dynamic non-library procedure calls. Operational abstraction size is the number of invariants generated by the Daikon invariant detector when run over the program and the full test pool.

less than machine-generated tests and faults differ from real ones.

The pool of test cases was generated from test specification scripts, then augmented with code coverage in mind. Thus, the pool may be relatively better for code coverage techniques than for the operational difference technique. The faults were selected based on how many cases detected the fault. This has an undetermined effect, particularly since previous researchers had eliminated the hardest faults, detected by only a few test cases. The small number of faults for certain programs quantized the fault detection ratio to a small number of values, making it harder to correlate with other measures. The combination of few statements—sometimes only 100—and high coverage similarly quantized statement coverage.

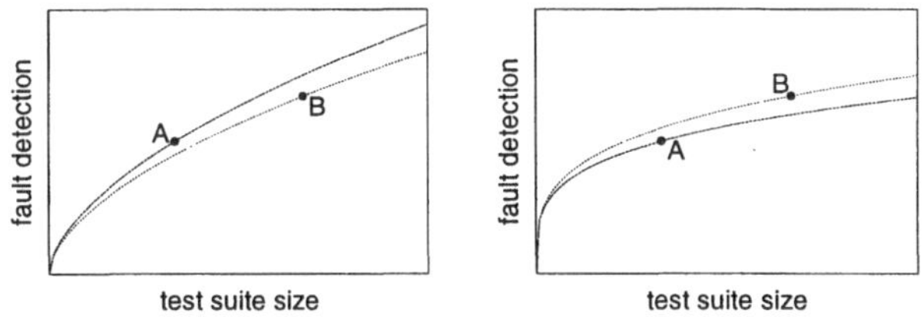

Figure 4. Pitfalls of comparing test suites of different sizes. The labeled points indicate the natural size and fault detection of suites produced by test suite generation techniques A and B. In the two graphs, the natural test suites are identical. The curves show the size and fault detection of "stacked" suites generated by randomly combining or subsetting the natural suites. In the left-hand graph, technique A is superior. In the right-hand graph, technique B is superior.

4.2 Measurement details

This section describes some of the measurements we performed. Others, such as code size, are standard.

Test suite size. We measured test suite size in terms of test cases and procedure calls. Our primary motivation for measuring these quantities is to control for them to avoid conflating them with other effects.

Each test case is an input to the program under test. This is the most readily apparent static measure of size. However, a single case might execute only a few machine instructions or might run for hours.

The number of dynamic non-library procedure calls approximates the runtime required to execute the test suite, which is likely to be more relevant to testers and which has a strong effect on fault detection. We always measured both quantities, but we sometimes present results for only one of them if the other has a similar effect.

Code coverage. For simplicity of presentation, we use the term "code coverage" for any structural code coverage criterion. We measured statement coverage using the GCC `gcov` tool and branch coverage using Bullseye Testing Technology's C-Cover tool. Unreachable code and unrealizable paths in the programs prevent the tools from reporting 100% coverage. We normalized all code coverage measurements by dividing by the number of statements or branches covered by the full set of test cases.

Fault Detection. A test suite detects a fault (actually, detects a faulty version of a program) if the output of the faulty version differs from the output of the correct version, when both are run over the test suite. The fault detection rate of a test suite is the ratio of the number of faulty versions detected to the number of faulty program versions. Section 4.1 describes the faulty versions.

4.3 Comparing test suites via stacking and area

It is misleading to directly compare test suite generation techniques that create suites of different sizes, because test suite size strongly affects fault detection (see Section 6.3).

Comparing test suites using the fault detection to size ratio (also known as "efficiency") is unsatisfactory because the fault-detection-versus-size curve is not a straight line (see Figure 4): doubling size does not double fault detection, and any such curve has points of arbitrarily low efficiency. More seriously, efficiency does not address the question of what technique to use to detect the greatest number of faults for a given test budget (in terms of suite execution time). We propose the *area* technique (described below) to compare test suite generation strategies, rather than simply comparing test suites.

We first observe that even if a test suite generation strategy produces suites of a particular size (call it the natural size), a tester can make suites of arbitrary runtime to fit the testing runtime budget by a process we call *stacking*. If the generated suite is too large, the tester can use a subset of it — if nothing else, a random subset. If the generated suite is too small, the tester can combine suites generated by the technique until they reach the goal size, choosing a subset of the last generated suite. (We assume the test suite generator is not deterministic, so the suites being combined are not identical. For instance, the test suite generator may select test cases, and candidate test cases are presented to it in different orders to create different suites.)

The stacked suites may not be as good as suites directly generated to be of equivalent size. For example, it may be better to generate a suite that covers each statement twice than to stack single-statement-coverage suites to the size of the twice-coverage suites. However, directly generating to an arbitrary size may not be available to testers, and testers may not know which technique to use to create a suite that exactly fits their testing budget. Testers can use stacking with any available test suite generator.

Stacking permits comparison of different test suite generation strategies at arbitrary test suite sizes. Comparing at any particular size might disadvantage one strategy or the other, and different projects have different testing budgets, so it is necessary to compare the techniques at multiple sizes. We sample from fault-detection-versus-size curves induced by stacking, then compare the areas under the curves. This gives an idea of how the techniques are likely to compare at an arbitrary size. More specifically, we create the curves by stacking each test generation strategy to the natural sizes of all the others. In practice, the curves do not cross, so the sense (but not the magnitude) of the comparison could be determined from any single size. The fact that the curves do not cross suggests that stacking tends to preserve the qualities of test suites.

5 Evaluation

This section experimentally evaluates the operational difference (OD) technique for generating, augmenting, and minimizing test suites.

5.1 Test suite generation

We compared test suites generated by the operational difference, statement coverage, branch coverage, def-use coverage, and random selection techniques.

	OD		Statement		Branch		Def-use	
	fault	size	fault	size	fault	size	fault	size
print_tokens	.366	9.3	.409	14.6	.457	16.1	.774	38.6
print_tokens2	.506	6.4	.778	11.7	.738	12.0	.966	35.0
replace	.451	18.1	.347	18.5	.361	18.7	.787	64.9
schedule	.329	10.2	.209	5.8	.442	8.6	.762	23.9
schedule2	.304	13.1	.209	6.9	.242	7.7	.522	25.6
tcas	.547	25.6	.180	5.2	.176	5.8	.163	5.5
tot_info	.719	9.4	.530	6.8	.560	7.4	.704	15.0
Partial average	.460	13.2	.380	9.9	.425	10.9	.670	29.8
space	.795	62.5	–	–	.909	155.2	–	–
Average	**.502**	**19.3**	–	–	**.486**	**28.9**	–	–

Figure 5. Test suites created via automatic generation techniques. "Fault" is the fraction of faults detected. "Size" is the number of test cases in the suite; similar results hold for size measured in terms of number of procedure calls (runtime). All numbers are averaged across 50 suites of each type for each program. Statement and def-use coverage suites were not available for space.

Technique	Ratio
Def-use coverage	1.73
Branch coverage	1.66
Operational difference	1.64
Statement coverage	1.53
Random	1.00

Figure 6. Effectiveness of test suite generation techniques, measured by the area technique of Section 4.3, compared to random selection.

We arbitrarily chose $n = 50$ for the OD technique (Figure 1), meaning the process is terminated when 50 consecutive test cases have been considered without changing the operational abstraction. A different value for n might change generation time or suite quality. The structural coverage suites were generated to achieve perfect coverage; we do not know how many candidate test cases were rejected in a row while generating them.

For each subject program, we generated 50 test suites using the OD technique and measured their average size and fault detection. Figure 5 compares them to other automatically generated suites. These include suites achieving complete statement, branch, and def-use coverage. The "average" line shows that the OD test suites are, on average, 2/3 the size of the branch-covering test suites, but achieve slightly better fault detection (.502 versus .486).

In order to better quantify the differences among the test generation techniques, we employed the area and stacking methodology (Section 4.3) to compare them. We generated operational difference, statement coverage, branch coverage, and def-use coverage suites. Then, we stacked (different) OD, statement, branch, def-use, and random suites to each of their natural sizes, for a total of 20 suites at 4 sizes, describing 5 fault-detection-versus-size curves. We repeated the process 50 times for each program, for a total of approximately 2000 fault detection curves (space had no statement or def-use curves). We summed the area under all of the curves for a given technique, then computed the ratios of the sums. Figure 6 presents the results: def-use performs best, followed by branch and OD (which are nearly indistinguishable), statement, and random.

Constructing structural coverage suites is difficult, tedious, and often impractical. Test cases that covered each structural element at least 30 times were generated by hand (see Section 4.1). By contrast, no special test cases were provided for the OD technique.

5.1.1 Detecting specific faults

The operational difference technique provides about the same fault detection as branch coverage according to the area technique; this is more accurate than simply noting that on average the OD suites are smaller, and have better fault detection, than the branch coverage suites. Additionally, the OD technique is superior for detecting certain types of faults.

We compared the individual fault detection rates for the OD technique and the branch coverage technique. For each fault in each program, we measured the proportion of times the fault was detected by each technique. We then used a nonparametric $P1 = P2$ test to determine if there was a statistically significant difference between the two proportions, at the $p = .05$ level.

There are a total of 163 faults in the 8 programs we examined. The OD technique is better at detecting 65 faults, stacked branch coverage is better at detecting 33 faults, and the difference is not statistically significant for 65 faults.

We wished to determine whether there is a qualitative difference between the faults detected best by the OD technique and the faults detected best by the stacked branch coverage technique. We examined each faulty version by hand to determine whether it changed the control flow graph (CFG) of the program. We treated basic blocks as nodes of the CFG, so adding a statement to a basic block would not change the CFG. Examples of CFG changes include: adding or removing an `if` statement, adding or removing a case from a `switch` statement, and adding or removing a `return` statement. Examples of non-CFG changes include: adding or removing a statement from a basic block, changing a variable name, changing an operator, and modifying the expression in the condition of an `if` statement. If a fault is not a CFG change, it must be a change to the value of an expression in the program. Our results are presented in the following table.

	OD better	Same	Branch better	Total
CFG change	9	11	9	29
Non-CFG change	56	54	24	134
Total	65	65	33	163

The OD technique is better at detecting value (non-CFG) changes. This makes intuitive sense, because our operational abstractions make assertions about the values of variables. The techniques are equally good at detecting CFG changes. (We expected branch coverage to dominate in this case, because it is measured in terms of the CFG.) Finally, in our target programs, the non-CFG change faults outnumber the CFG change faults by a factor of 4.6. The faults were real faults or were created by people who considered them realistic and representative, so the distribution of faults in practice may be similar.

5.2 Test suite augmentation

The operational difference augmentation technique is identical to the generation technique, except the process is started with an existing test suite rather than an empty test suite. We evaluated this technique by staring with branch coverage suites; the following table gives the results of evaluating them using the area technique. (The numbers differ slightly from previous results because we did not compare at the def-use natural size, and because this experiment used the basic rather than the improved OD technique. The raw numbers are available in a technical report [Har02].)

Technique	Ratio
Branch coverage	1.70
Operational difference	1.72
Branch + operational difference	2.16
Random	1.00

As suggested in Section 5.1.1, code coverage and operational coverage techniques are complementary: combining them is more effective than using either in isolation.

5.3 Test suite minimization

For each program, we generated 50 random test suites with 100 cases each. We minimized these by the OD technique and by maintaining branch coverage; this table gives the results, as measured by the area technique.

Technique	Ratio
Branch coverage	1.50
Operational difference	1.21
Random	1.00

Figure 7 shows some additional data: the OD technique results in better fault detection, but also substantially larger test suites, than minimizing while maintaining branch coverage.

6 Why it works

This section explains and justifies the insights that led to the operational difference test suite improvement techniques. Section 6.1 defines operational coverage, which measures the quality of an arbitrary operational abstraction

	Orig		OD-min		Random		Branch-min	
	fault	size	fault	size	fault	size	fault	size
print_tokens	.651	100	.549	48.2	.443	48.2	.314	7.3
print_tokens2	.920	100	.616	14.4	.540	14.4	.740	6.1
replace	.657	100	.443	19.8	.281	19.8	.289	10.5
schedule	.647	100	.449	30.6	.391	30.6	.240	4.8
schedule2	.649	100	.451	39.9	.331	39.9	.231	4.8
tcas	.709	100	.505	26.2	.417	26.2	.177	4.9
tot_info	.887	100	.683	18.0	.539	18.0	.501	5.2
space	.754	100	.736	59.4	.685	59.4	.740	48.0
Average	.734	100	.554	32.1	.453	32.1	.404	11.5

Figure 7. Test suites minimized via automatic techniques. "Fault" is the fraction of faults detected. "Size" is the number of test cases in the suite. All numbers are averaged across 50 suites of each type for each program.

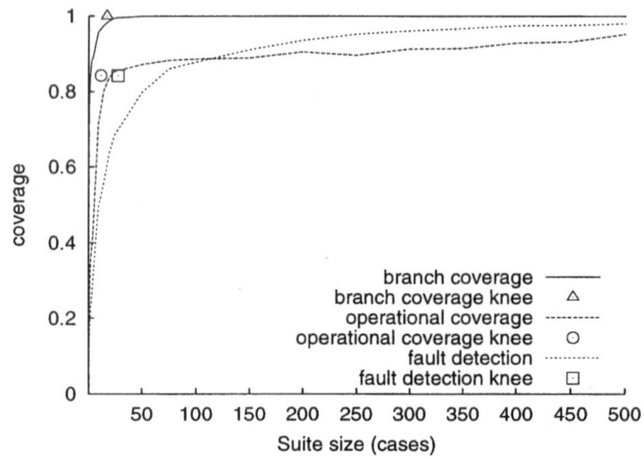

Figure 8. Effect of test suite size (measured in cases) on branch coverage, operational coverage, and fault detection of randomly-generated test suites, for the `replace` program. The other programs have similar graphs, and graphs of fault detection against size in terms of calls are also similar.

against an oracle operational abstraction. Section 6.2 shows that when tests are added at random to a suite, the suite's operational coverage increases rapidly, then levels off at a high value. Section 6.3 shows that operational coverage is correlated with fault detection, even when test suite size and code coverage are held constant.

6.1 Operational coverage

Operational coverage (defined below) measures the difference between an operational abstraction and an oracle or goal specification. Like other coverage measures, operational coverage is a value between 0 and 1 inclusive: 0 for an empty test suite, and 1 for an ideal test suite. It accounts for both false assertions present in, and true assertions missing from, the operational abstraction.

An operational abstraction is a set of assertions about a program, chosen from some grammar. Assume there exists an oracle (goal) operational abstraction G, containing all true assertions in the grammar. We use the oracle only to evaluate and justify the operational difference technique. Application of the OD technique does not require existence of an oracle, though the technique could be extended to take advantage of an oracle when present.

Given a test suite, an operational abstraction OA contains the assertions that are likely true, based on observations made while running the program over the test suite. Define $t = |OA \cap G|$, the number of true assertions in OA. The precision p of OA is the fraction of assertions in OA that are true, so $p = t/|OA|$. The recall r of OA is the fraction of assertions in G that are also in OA, so $r = t/|G|$. Precision and recall are standard measures from information retrieval [Sal68, vR79].

We define the operational coverage c of OA as the weighted average of precision and recall, giving $c = ap + (1-a)r$. For simplicity, we choose $a = .5$, giving $c = (p+r)/2$. For example, suppose the oracle contains 10 assertions, and the operational abstraction contains 12 assertions: 9 true and 3 false. The precision is $9/12$ and the recall is $9/10$, so the operational coverage is $(9/12 + 9/10)/2 = .825$.

Where do the oracles used in Sections 6.2 and 6.3 come from? The oracle is the set of all invariants in Daikon's grammar that are true. This is exactly the operational abstraction Daikon would generate, given a good enough test suite. In the extreme, the (infinitely large) test suite containing all valid inputs to the program would surely be good enough. We did not have such test suites, so we ran Daikon on the full pool of test cases for each program (Figure 3) as an approximation. We believe that the pools are sufficiently large and diverse that adding additional test cases would change the operational abstraction little or not at all.

6.2 Effect of test suite size on fault detection

When tests are added at random to a suite, the operational coverage increases rapidly, then levels off at a high value. In other words, there are two distinct types of test suites. Suites inducing relatively poor operational abstractions are measurably improved by almost any augmentation. Suites inducing good operational abstractions are little affected by augmentation, and the operational abstractions are already so close to ideal that they can never be substantially improved.

Figure 8 plots average branch coverage, operational coverage, and fault detection against suite size for the `replace` program, for 1500 randomly generated test suites of case sizes 1–500. Figure 8 does not plot statement coverage because it lies almost exactly under branch coverage.

Figure 8 also plots the knee of each curve. We computed the knee by finding the size that minimizes the summed mean square error of two lines regressed to the sets of points to its left and right. The knee is the intersection of the pair of lines that fit best. The knee does not necessarily lie on

	cases knee		calls knee	
	cases	coverage	calls	coverage
statement cov.	10	0.96	2971	0.90
operational cov.	15	0.81	3243	0.80
branch cov.	20	0.94	3409	0.87
fault detection	53	0.74	11796	0.73

Figure 9. Table of knee locations, averaged across seven programs. These numbers indicate where plots of statement coverage, operational coverage, fault detection, and branch coverage against time switch from one nearly-linear component to another; they indicate average positions of the knees plotted for one program in Figure 8. The table gives knees using two different metrics for test suite size: number of cases and number of calls.

the curve. Figure 9 gives the average positions of all the knees across all programs. Intuitively, the knee appears at the size that separates low-coverage, easily-improved suites from high-coverage suites that benefit little from the addition of test cases.

The knees are significant for two reasons. First, they indicate roughly what size and coverage users can expect of the generated suites; it is encouraging that they have small sizes and high coverages. More significantly, if the knee was not at a high coverage value, then the slope after the knee would not be very horizontal, and the generation process would take longer to terminate.

6.3 Operational coverage and fault detection

Section 6.2 demonstrated that high absolute levels of operational coverage are achievable. This section shows that increasing the operational coverage (that is, improving the operational abstraction) results in greater fault detection. Section 6.3.1 demonstrates the result for arbitrary test suites, and Section 6.3.2 demonstrates that even when a test suite achieves 100% code coverage, increasing operational coverage improves fault detection.

6.3.1 Random suites

We analyzed 1000 randomly generated test suites for each of the eight programs. The suite sizes, in cases, were uniformly distributed between 1 and the number of cases at the fault detection knee (Section 6.2). We did not consider larger suites, because augmenting a large test suite has little effect.

For each test suite, we calculated its size (in cases and calls), statement coverage, branch coverage, operational coverage, and fault detection. Then, we performed six multiple regressions for each program. These regressions indicate how each predictor affects each result, while holding all other factors constant; for example, it avoids conflating the effect of size and coverage, even though larger suites tend to have more coverage.

Independent variable	Dependent variable		
	op. cov.	stmt. cov.	fault detection
cases	.285	.037	.250
calls	.068	−.005	.337
op. cov.	-	.741	.130
stmt. cov.	.593	-	.167

Independent variable	Dependent variable		
	op. cov.	branch cov.	fault detection
cases	.169	.162	.229
calls	.075	−.005	.337
op. cov.	-	.723	.095
branch cov.	.676	-	.234

Figure 10. Standardized multiple regression coefficients, averaged across eight programs. Standardized coefficients are the coefficients that would be produced if the data analyzed were in standard score form. "Standard score" form means that the variables have been standardized so that each has a mean of zero and a standard deviation of 1. Thus, standardized coefficients reflect the relative importance of the predictor variables. Each column of each table presents the results from a separate multiple regression.

Each column of Figure 10 presents results of one multiple regression. For instance, the upper-left regression uses size and statement coverage as the independent variables, and uses operational coverage as the dependent variable. (We performed two sets of three multiple regressions, rather than one set involving all five variables, because statement coverage and branch coverage are highly correlated; they fail a test of non-collinearity and bias the results. Separating the variables avoids this problem. This means the coefficients for statement and branch coverage cannot be directly compared. There is no significant interaction effect among any other predictor variables at the $p = .10$ level.)

We also computed, but do not show here, raw correlation coefficients. For example, when operational coverage is used to predict fault detection, the coefficient is .340. This means that if operational coverage is increased by 1 percent, and all other predictors are held constant, fault detection increases by .340 percent.

The standardized coefficients in Figure 10 indicate the direction and relative magnitude of correlation between the independent and dependent variables. Test suite runtime is the most important predictor of fault detection, followed by branch coverage, number of cases, statement coverage, and operational coverage.

The important conclusion to draw from this experiment is that operational coverage is a useful predictor of fault detection: test suites with more operational coverage detect faults better. Operational coverage is about as good a predictor of fault detection as statement coverage, but is less good than some other metrics, such as test suite size.

6.3.2 The effect of 100% code coverage

A final experiment further demonstrates the value of operational coverage as a test suite quality metric that is indepen-

Coverage type	Op. cov. coefficient	Mean op. cov.	Mean fault detect	# stat. sig.	# not sig.
statement	.483	.877	.396	5	2
branch	.308	.866	.461	6	2
def-use	.507	.950	.763	2	5

Figure 11. Multiple regression coefficient for operational coverage, when regressed against fault detection. The coefficient for size was not statistically significant for any of the programs, and has been omitted from the table. The coefficient for operational coverage was only statistically significant for some of the programs. The "# stat. sig." column contains this number, and the "# not sig." column contains the number of programs for which the coefficient was not statistically significant. Each value was averaged across all programs for which the operational coverage coefficient was statistically significant.

dent of code coverage metrics.

For each of the subject programs except `space`, we analyzed 1000 suites with statement coverage, 1000 suites with branch coverage, and 1000 suites with def-use coverage. For `space`, we only analyzed 1000 suites with branch coverage. (We obtained the suites from Rothermel and Harrold [RH98]; there were no statement or def-use covering suites for `space`, nor were we able to generate them.) Section 4.1 describes these test suites, and Figure 5 presents their average sizes in cases. The statement and branch coverage suites have about the same number of cases, while the def-use coverage suites are three times as large.

We calculated the size, operational coverage, and fault detection rate of each test suite. For each type of coverage and each program, we performed a multiple regression, with size and operational coverage as the independent variables and fault detection as the dependent variable. We performed 22 multiple regressions in total (7 programs × 3 coverage criteria, plus 1 coverage criterion for `space`). Figure 11 summarizes the results.

The coefficient describes the relationship between operational coverage and fault detection. For example, the coefficient of .48 for statement coverage suites suggests that if the operational coverage of a suite were increased by 1 percent, and all other factors held constant, the fault detection rate would increase by approximately .48 percent.

The mean operational coverage and fault detection indicate how much improvement is possible, since their maximum values are 1.

These results show that, for test suites with branch or statement coverage, increasing operational coverage does increase fault detection. However, for suites with def-use coverage, fault detection is often independent of operational coverage (only 2 programs had statistically significant coefficients). This might be because operational coverage is already near perfect (.95) for those test suites: there is little room for improvement.

Further, these results show that operational coverage is complementary to code coverage for detecting faults. Even when statement or branch coverage is 100%, increasing operational coverage can increase the fault detection of a test suite without increasing test suite size. Stated another way, operational coverage indicates which of otherwise indistinguishable (with respect to code coverage) test suites is best.

6.3.3 Effort to improve test suites

We have demonstrated that both code coverage and operational coverage are correlated to fault detection, and that improving operational coverage tends to detect different faults than improving code coverage does (Section 5.1.1). However, this does not indicate how much relative effort a software tester should invest in improving the two types of coverage. Future work should assess how difficult it is for the programmer to increase operational coverage, relative to the work it takes to achieve a similar gain in statement coverage. Also, the last few percent of code coverage are the hardest to achieve. Is operational coverage similar?

7 Related work

This work complements and extends research in specification-based testing. For the most part, previous research has focused on systematic generation, not evaluation, of test suites, and has required users to provide a specification *a priori*. We relax those constraints, provide new applications, and show how to bring new benefits to specification-based testing.

7.1 Specifications for test suite generation

Goodenough and Gerhart [GG75b, GG75a] suggest that users partition the input domain into equivalence classes and select test data from each class. Specification-based testing was formalized by Richardson et al. [ROT89], who extended implementation-based test generation techniques to formal specification languages. They derive test cases (each of which is a precondition–postcondition pair) from specifications. The test cases can be used as test adequacy metrics. Even this early work emphasizes that specification-based techniques should complement rather than supplement structural techniques, for each is more effective in certain circumstances; our results reinforce this point.

The category-partition method [OB88] calls for writing a series of formal test specifications, then using a test generator tool to produce tests. The formal test specifications consist of direct inputs or environmental properties, plus a list of categories or partitions for each input, derived by hand from a high-level specification. Balcer et al. [BHO89] automate the category-partition method for writing test scripts from which tests can be generated, obeying certain constraints. These specifications describe tests, not the code, and are really declarative programming languages rather than specifications. Although their syntax may be the same, they do not characterize the program, but the tests, and so serve a different purpose than program specifications.

Donat [Don97] distinguishes specifications from test classes and test frames. He gives a procedure for converting the former into each of the latter (a goal proposed in earlier work [TDJ96]), but leaves converting the test frames into test cases to a human or another tool. Dick and Faivre [DF93], building on the work of Bernot et al. [BGM91], use VDM to generate test cases from preconditions, postconditions, and invariants. Meudec [Meu98] also uses a variety of VDM called VDM-SL to generate test sets from a high-level specification of intended behavior. Offutt et al. generate tests from constraints that describe path conditions and erroneous state [Off91] and from SOFL specifications [OL99].

All of this work assumes an *a priori* specification in some form, and most generate both test cases and test suites composed of those test cases. By contrast, the operational difference technique assumes the existence of a test case generator (any of the above could serve), then generates both a test suite and an operational abstraction.

7.2 Specifications for test suite evaluation

Chang and Richardson's structural specification-based testing (SST) technique [CR99] uses formal specifications provided by a test engineer for test selection and test coverage measurement. Their ADLscope tool converts specifications written in ADL [HS94] into a series of checks in the code called coverage condition functions [CRS96]. Once the specification (which is about as large as the original program) is converted into code, statement coverage techniques can be applied directly: run the test suite and count how many of the checks are covered. An uncovered test indicates an aspect of the specification that was inadequately exercised during testing. The technique is validated by discovery of (exhaustively, automatically generated) program mutants.

This work is similar to ours in that both assume a test case generation strategy, then evaluate test suites or test cases for inclusion in a test suite. However, SST requires the existence of an *a priori* specification, whereas the operational difference technique does not, but provides an operational abstraction.

7.3 Related coverage criteria

Several researchers have proposed specification-based notions of coverage that are similar to our definition of operational coverage (Section 6.1). In each case, a test suite is evaluated with respect to a goal specification. The related work extends structural coverage to specifications, computing how much of the specification is covered by execution of the test suite. By contrast, our operational coverage compares two operational abstractions.

Burton [Bur99] uses the term "specification coverage" to refer to coverage of statements in a specification by an execution; this concept was introduced, but not named, by Chang and Richardson [CR99]. Burton further suggests applying boolean operand effectiveness (modified condition/decision coverage or MC/DC) to reified specifications; this coverage criterion requires that each boolean subterm of a branch condition take on each possible value. Other extensions of structural coverage criteria to specification checks are possible [Don97] but have not been evaluated.

Hoffman et al. [HSW99, HS00] present techniques for generating test suites that include tests with (combinations of) extremal values. These suites are said to have boundary value coverage, a variety of data coverage. The Roast tool constructs such suites and supports dependent domains, which can reduce the size of test suites compared to full cross-product domains. Ernst [Ern00] uses the term "value coverage" to refer to covering all of a variable's values (including boundary values); the current research builds on that work.

Hamlet's probable correctness theory [Ham87] calls for uniformly sampling the possible values of all variables. Random testing and operational testing are competitive with or superior to partition testing, debug testing, and other directed testing strategies, at least in terms of delivered reliability [DN84, HT90, FHLS98, FHLS99]. This work makes several reasonable assumptions, such as that testers have good but not perfect intuition and that more than a very small number of tests may be performed. Operational coverage is likely to assist in both operational and random testing, permitting improved test coverage, and better understanding of the test cases, in both situations.

Chang and Richardson's operator coverage [CR99] is not a measure of test suite quality, but concerns the creation of mutant (faulty) versions of programs. Operator coverage is achieved if every operator in the program is changed in some mutant version. The mutants can be used to assess test suite comprehensiveness, in terms of fault detection over the mutants.

Amman and Black [AB01] measure test suite coverage in terms of number of mutant specifications (in the form of CTL formulae) killed. A mutant version of a specification contains a specific small syntactic error, and a test suite is said to kill the mutant if the test suite gives a different result over the faulty version than it does over the correct version. Amman and Black use model checking to check the test cases against the CTL specifications. If every mutant is killed, then every component of the specification is covered, since every component of the specification was mutated.

8 Conclusion

We have presented the operational difference (OD) technique for generating, augmenting, and minimizing test suites. The technique selects test cases by comparing operational abstractions dynamically generated from test suites. An operational abstraction describes observed behavior and is syntactically identical to a formal specification. A test case is considered interesting if its addition or removal changes the operational abstraction. The OD technique is automatic, but (for generation or augmentation) assumes the existence of a test case generator that provides candidate test cases.

The OD generation technique produced test suites that are smaller, and slightly more effective at fault detection, than branch coverage suites. The OD suites are equally good at detecting errors that change the control flow graph and are more effective at detecting non-CFG-changing errors. The two techniques are complementary: combining structural and operational coverage techniques is more effective than using either in isolation.

Two characteristics of our technique for inducing operational abstractions explain the efficacy of the OD technique. First, it is possible to create a high-quality operational abstraction (without knowing precisely how good it is or what the ideal would be) by randomly adding test cases until the operational abstraction stabilizes. Second, improvements in the operational abstraction are correlated with fault detection, even for test suites with 100% code coverage. Thus, even after statement or branch coverage can no longer differentiate among test cases, the OD technique can determine which test cases are most advantageous.

The results do not depend on the generated operational abstraction — which describes actual, not intended, behavior — being close to the formal specification that a human might write (though in practice, they are). Likewise, the results do not depend on the program being correct: the OD technique produces test suites with good fault detection even from buggy programs. (In our experiments, the test programs used to generate the operational abstractions contained errors, and further experiments have confirmed that the OD technique is not hindered by errors in the program from which the operational abstraction is induced.) Finally, there is no need for an oracle that determines whether a test case passes or fails, though subsequent use of the generated test suites might require creation of such an oracle.

The operational difference technique is automatic; it takes as input a test case generator (any test suite or sample inputs will do) but does not require a programmer to provide an *a priori* formal specification. Since such specifications are rare and programmers are loathe to write them (because programmers perceive the cost as too high and the benefit as too low), the OD technique expands the applicability of specification-based testing. The technique has the added benefit of generating a high-quality operational abstraction for the program, which has many benefits in itself; however, users not interested in this benefit never need examine the operational abstraction.

The OD technique is directly analogous to techniques for creating code coverage suites, but it operates over program properties in the semantic domain rather than over source code constructs in the syntactic domain. We believe, and our experiments validate, that operating over (automatically generated) program properties rather than program text holds substantial promise for testing and other software engineering tasks.

Acknowledgments

Benjamin Morse wrote the C/C++ front end to the Daikon system and assisted with data collection. We also thank the other members of the Daikon project, most notably Jeremy Nimmer, for their assistance with our research and tools. Gregg Rothermel provided us the Siemens programs and answered questions. Vibha Sazawal provided statistical consulting. This research was supported by NTT, Raytheon, NSF CAREER grant CCR-0133580, and a gift from Edison Design Group.

References

[AB01] Paul E. Amman and Paul E. Black. A specification-based coverage metric to evaluate test sets. *International Journal of Reliability, Quality and Safety Engineering*, 8(4):275–299, 2001.

[BGM91] Gilles Bernot, Marie Claude Gaudel, and Bruno Marre. Software testing based on formal specifications: a theory and a tool. *IEE Software Engineering Journal*, 6, November 1991.

[BHO89] Marc J. Balcer, William M. Hasling, and Thomas J. Ostrand. Automatic generation of test scripts from formal test specifications. In Richard A. Kemmerer, editor, *Proceedings of the ACM SIGSOFT '89 Third Symposium on Testing, Analysis, and Verification (TAV3)*, pages 210–218, December 1989.

[Bur99] Simon Burton. Towards automated unit testing of statechart implementations. Technical report, Department of Computer Science, University of York, UK, 1999.

[CR99] Juei Chang and Debra J. Richardson. Structural specification-based testing: Automated support and experimental evaluation. In *Proceedings of the 7th European Software Engineering Conference and the 7th ACM SIGSOFT Symposium on the Foundations of Software Engineering*, pages 285–302, September 6–10, 1999.

[CRS96] Juei Chang, Debra J. Richardson, and Sriram Sankar. Structural specification-based testing with ADL. In *Proceedings of the 1996 International Symposium on Software Testing and Analysis (ISSTA)*, pages 62–70, 1996.

[DF93] J. Dick and A. Faivre. Automating the generating and sequencing of test cases from model-based specifications. In *FME '93: Industrial Strength Formal Methods, 5th International Symposium of Formal Methods Europe*, pages 268–284, 1993.

[DN84] Joe W. Duran and Simeon C. Ntafos. An evaluation of random testing. *IEEE Transactions on Software Engineering*, 10(4):438–444, July 1984.

[Don97] Michael R. Donat. Automating formal specification-based testing. In *TAPSOFT '97: Theory and Practice of Software Development, 7th International Joint Conference CAAP/FASE*, pages 833–847. Springer-Verlag, April 1997.

[ECGN00] Michael D. Ernst, Adam Czeisler, William G. Griswold, and David Notkin. Quickly detecting relevant program invariants. In *ICSE 2000, Proceedings of the 22nd International Conference on Software Engineering*, pages 449–458, Limerick, Ireland, June 7–9, 2000.

[ECGN01] Michael D. Ernst, Jake Cockrell, William G. Griswold, and David Notkin. Dynamically discovering likely program invariants to support program evolution. *IEEE Transactions on Software Engineering*, 27(2):1–25, February 2001. A previous version appeared in *ICSE '99, Proceedings of the 21st International Conference on Software Engineering*, pages 213–224, Los Angeles, CA, USA, May 19–21, 1999.

[Ern00] Michael D. Ernst. *Dynamically Discovering Likely Program Invariants*. PhD thesis, University of Washington Department of Computer Science and Engineering, Seattle, Washington, August 2000.

[FHLS98] Phyllis G. Frankl, Richard G. Hamlet, Bev Littlewood, and Lorenzo Strigini. Evaluating testing methods by delivered reliability. *IEEE Transactions on Software Engineering*, 24(8):586–601, August 1998. Special Section: International Conference on Software Engineering (ICSE '97).

[FHLS99] Phyllis Frankl, Dick Hamlet, Bev Littlewood, and Lorenzo Strigini. Correction to: Evaluating testing methods by delivered reliability. *IEEE Transactions on Software Engineering*, 25(2):286, March/April 1999.

[GG75a] John B. Goodenough and Susan L. Gerhart. Correction to "Toward a theory of test data selection". *IEEE Transactions on Software Engineering*, 1(4):425, December 1975.

[GG75b] John B. Goodenough and Susan L. Gerhart. Toward a theory of test data selection. *IEEE Transactions on Software Engineering*, 1(2):156–173, June 1975.

[GHK+01] Todd L. Graves, Mary Jean Harrold, Jung-Min Kim, Adam Porter, and Gregg Rothermel. An empirical study of regression test selection techniques. *ACM Transactions on Software Engineering and Methodology*, 10(2):184–208, April 2001.

[Ham87] Richard G. Hamlet. Probable correctness theory. *Information Processing Letters*, 25(1):17–25, April 20, 1987.

[Har02] Michael Harder. Improving test suites via generated specifications. Technical Report 848, MIT Laboratory for Computer Science, Cambridge, MA, June 4, 2002. Revision of author's Master's thesis.

[HFGO94] Monica Hutchins, Herb Foster, Tarak Goradia, and Thomas Ostrand. Experiments on the effectiveness of dataflow- and controlflow-based test adequacy criteria. In *Proceedings of the 16th International Conference on Software Engineering*, pages 191–200, Sorrento, Italy, May 16–21, 1994.

[HS94] Roger Hayes and Sriram Sankar. Specifying and testing software components using ADL. Technical Report TR-94-23, Sun Microsystems Research, Palo Alto, CA, USA, April 1994.

[HS00] Daniel Hoffman and Paul Strooper. Tools and techniques for Java API testing. In *Proceedings of the 2000 Australian Software Engineering Conference*, pages 235–245, 2000.

[HSW99] Daniel Hoffman, Paul Strooper, and Lee White. Boundary values and automated component testing. *Software Testing, Verification, and Reliability*, 9(1):3–26, March 1999.

[HT90] Dick Hamlet and Ross Taylor. Partition testing does not inspire confidence. *IEEE Transactions on Software Engineering*, 16(12):1402–1411, December 1990.

[JH01] James A. Jones and Mary Jean Harrold. Test-suite reduction and prioritization for modified condition/decision coverage. In *ICSM 2001, Proceedings of the International Conference on Software Maintenance*, pages 92–101, Florence, Italy, November 6–10, 2001.

[Meu98] Christophe Meudec. *Automatic Generation of Software Test Cases From Formal Specifications*. PhD thesis, Queen's University of Belfast, 1998.

[NE02a] Jeremy W. Nimmer and Michael D. Ernst. Automatic generation of program specifications. In *ISSTA 2002, Proceedings of the 2002 International Symposium on Software Testing and Analysis*, pages 232–242, Rome, Italy, July 22–24, 2002.

[NE02b] Jeremy W. Nimmer and Michael D. Ernst. Invariant inference for static checking: An empirical evaluation. In *Proceedings of the ACM SIGSOFT 10th International Symposium on the Foundations of Software Engineering (FSE 2002)*, pages 11–20, Charleston, SC, November 20–22, 2002.

[NWEG+03] Toh Ne Win, Michael D. Ernst, Stephen J. Garland, Dilsun Kırlı, and Nancy Lynch. Using simulated execution in verifying distributed algorithms. In *VMCAI'03, Fourth International Conference on Verification, Model Checking and Abstract Interpretation*, pages 283–297, New York, New York, January 9–11, 2003.

[OB88] T. J. Ostrand and M. J. Balcer. The category-partition method for specifying and generating functional tests. *Communications of the ACM*, 31(6):676–686, June 1988.

[Off91] A. Jefferson Offutt. An integrated automatic test data generation system. *Journal of Systems Integration*, 1(3):391–409, November 1991.

[OL99] A. Jefferson Offutt and Shaoying Liu. Generating test data from SOFL specifications. *The Journal of Systems and Software*, 49(1):49–62, December 1999.

[RH98] Gregg Rothermel and Mary Jean Harrold. Empirical studies of a safe regression test selection technique. *IEEE Transactions on Software Engineering*, 24(6):401–419, June 1998.

[ROT89] Debra J. Richardson, Owen O'Malley, and Cindy Tittle. Approaches to specification-based testing. In Richard A. Kemmerer, editor, *Proceedings of the ACM SIGSOFT '89 Third Symposium on Testing, Analysis, and Verification (TAV3)*, pages 86–96, December 1989.

[Sal68] Gerard Salton. *Automatic Information Organization and Retrieval*. McGraw-Hill, 1968.

[TDJ96] Kalman C. Toth, Michael R. Donat, and Jeffrey J. Joyce. Generating test cases from formal specifications. In *6th Annual Symposium of the International Council on Systems Engineering*, Boston, July 1996.

[VF98] Filippos I. Vokolos and Phyllis G. Frankl. Empirical evaluation of the textual differencing regression testing technique. In *Proceedings of the International Conference on Software Maintenance*, pages 44–53, 1998.

[vR79] C. J. van Rijsbergen. *Information Retrieval*. Butterworths, London, second edition, 1979.

[ZHM97] Hong Zhu, Patrick A. V. Hall, and John H. R. May. Software unit test coverage and adequacy. *ACM Computing Surveys*, 29(4):366–427, December 1997.

Technical Papers

Empirical Studies I

Using Benchmarking to Advance Research: A Challenge to Software Engineering

Susan Elliott Sim
University of Toronto
simsuz@cs.utoronto.ca

Steve Easterbrook
University of Toronto
sme@cs.utoronto.ca

Richard C. Holt
University of Waterloo
holt@uwaterloo.ca

Abstract

Benchmarks have been used in computer science to compare the performance of computer systems, information retrieval algorithms, databases, and many other technologies. The creation and widespread use of a benchmark within a research area is frequently accompanied by rapid technical progress and community building. These observations have led us to formulate a theory of benchmarking within scientific disciplines. Based on this theory, we challenge software engineering research to become more scientific and cohesive by working as a community to define benchmarks. In support of this challenge, we present a case study of the reverse engineering community, where we have successfully used benchmarks to advance the state of research.

1. Introduction

The purpose of this paper is to issue a challenge to software engineering to start defining benchmarks for the key problems in their area. From our experience developing benchmarks and examining other successful benchmarks, we have observed that benchmarking, when embraced by a community, has a strong positive effect on the scientific maturity of a discipline.

Creating a benchmark requires a community to examine their understanding of the field, come to an agreement on what are the key problems, and encapsulate this knowledge in an evaluation. Using the benchmark results in a more rigorous examination of research contributions, and an overall improvement in the tools and techniques being developed. Throughout the benchmarking process, there is greater communication and collaboration among different researchers leading to a stronger consensus on the community's research goals. The technical progress and increased cohesiveness in the community have been viewed as positive side-effects of benchmarking. Instead, we argue that benchmarking should be used to achieve these positive effects.

We initially observed these benefits while building and using a benchmark for program comprehension tools[18, 19]. This experience led us to examine benchmarking more carefully to understand how it has these community effects. We subsequently applied this theory in the development of a second benchmark for fact extractors for the C++ programming language [17].

The critical insight of our theory of benchmarking is this: Within research communities, benchmarks operationalize scientific paradigms, that is, they are a statement of the discipline's research goals and they emerge through a synergistic process of technical knowledge and social consensus proceeding in tandem. The concept of scientific paradigms was first described by Thomas S. Kuhn in the ground-breaking book, *The Structure of Scientific Revolutions* [12]. A scientific paradigm is the dominant view of a science consisting of explicit technical facts and implicit rules of conduct. A benchmark is a succinct statement of both these aspects of a discipline.

By viewing a benchmark as both a technical and a social artefact, we were better able to understand its role with a scientific community. We have developed some guidelines on how to manage the process, thereby making the benefits more accessible. Benchmarking is widely applicable because the technique can be used with a broad range of technology. Some research is more obviously amenable to benchmarking because the performance measures are straightforward, for example, speed or throughput. In software engineering, the performance measures can be quite complex, because our tools and techniques are intended to help with the creation of large software systems.

Benchmarking can be used by any research community that is sufficiently well-established and has a culture of collaboration. Evidence of the former include an existing collection of diverse research results, and an increasing concern in validation of these results. Evidence of the latter includes multi-site research projects, multi-author publications, and standards for reporting, file formats, and the like. From this base, a consensus-based process, led by a small number of key people, can be used to construct a benchmark that is endorsed by the research community.

In this paper, we will argue that benchmarking has a strong positive effect on research, then we will show how these effects can be realised in software engineering. Our arguments about the power of benchmarking are found in the first two sections. Section 2 gives three examples of successful benchmarks from outside of software

0-7695-1877-X/03 $17.00 © 2003 IEEE

engineering. In Section 3, we present our theory of benchmarking. It includes a definition, an account of how it functions within a research community, and an explanation of its effectiveness. The next two sections demonstrate how the theory can be applied. Section 4 presents some practical advice on how to apply the theory and Section 5 illustrates the application of the theory using the fact extractor benchmark. The final section of the paper is a re-statement of the challenge to software engineering, using requirements engineering, model checking, and software evolution as specific examples.

2. Examples of Successful Benchmarks

In this section, we present three benchmarks that were successful in that they advanced a discipline by improving the science and increasing the cohesiveness of the community. Although many publications report on the technical aspects behind the development of various benchmarks, we found relatively few that discuss the social and cultural aspects. The three benchmarks in this section are exceptional in that these non-technical aspects have been discussed in the literature. Nevertheless, we believe that these examples are representative of benchmarking in general, because they are consistent with each other and our own experience.

The three examples are TPC-A™ for database management systems (DBMS), SPEC CPU 2002 for computer systems, and the TREC Ad Hoc Retrieval Task for information retrieval systems.

2.1 TPC-A™

The full name for TPC-A is the Transaction Processing Council (TPC) Benchmark™ A for Online Transaction Processing including a LAN or WAN network[8]. It evolved from the *DebitCredit* test originally published in 1984. This effort was spearheaded by Jim Gray but had so many contributors from industry and academia that the author on the paper was given as "Anon et al." This paper struck a chord in the database community. Researchers began to publish refinements and variants of the test and vendors used the version and interpretation that made their product appear most efficient, further fuelling "benchmarketing" wars. Eventually, a number of representatives from industry and academia formed the TPC for the purpose of standardising and supervising benchmarks for DBMSs. Developing TPC-A™ took over two years and required nearly 1200 person-days of effort contributed by researchers and 35 database vendors who were members of the consortium. The process involved many meetings as well as laboratory work by the members. The TPC-A™ specification is over 40 pages long with 11 different clauses covering issues such as transaction and terminal profiles, scaling rules, response time, and rules for full disclosure.

2.2 SPEC CPU2000

SPEC (Standard Performance Evaluation Corporation) is also a consortium with committees that create a variety of benchmarks. CPU2002 is the one for evaluating computer systems. It supersedes CPU95 and is scheduled to be replaced in 2004. Members of the committees include hardware and software vendors, universities and customers [9]. Requirements, test cases, and votes on benchmark composition are solicited from committee members and the general public through SPEC's web site. The committee uses "benchathons" to refine the benchmark. John Henning explained:

> "The point of a benchathon is to gather as many as possible of the project leaders, platforms, and benchmarks in one place and have them work collectively to resolve technical issues involving multiple stakeholders: At a benchathon, it is common to see employees from different companies looking at the same screen, helping each other" [9, p. 30].

CPU2000 consists of 26 programs (12 with only integer arithmetic and 14 with floating point) to be compiled and run on a computer system.

2.3 TREC Ad Hoc Retrieval Task

TREC (Text Retrieval Conference) is an annual conference on information retrieval sponsored by NIST, and DARPA. Every TREC has included challenges or problems that are open to all participants. One of the two challenges at the first TREC in 1992 was the Ad Hoc Retrieval Task [22]. This task consists of searching a text corpus for articles that match a specific topic. An example of a topic is "What legal actions have resulted from the destruction of Pan Am Flight 103 over Lockerbie, Scotland, on December 21, 1988?" The corpus used in this task originally contained about 740 000 articles and by 1998 had grown to more than twice this size. It consists primarily of news items, such as those from the *Wall Street Journal* and the *Associated Press*. The formatting of the topics has also evolved since the inception of the task.

Members of the community participate in two ways. When the new set of topics is selected and they help in judging the relevance of the articles. They also run their information retrieval systems using the topics and submit the results to the conference organisers. At the conference, organisers and participants unveil and discuss their results.

The Ad Hoc Task was discontinued after 1998 because performance over the previous few years had levelled off. The benchmark was no longer pushing research forward, so the organisers felt that their energy would be better spent on other benchmarks. (By then there were 9 tasks at TREC.) While the Ad Hoc Retrieval Task was by no means solved, researchers had eight years worth of test collections to use in future research.

3. Theory of Benchmarking

Using examples such as those in the previous section and our own experience developing benchmarks, we have formulated a descriptive theory of how benchmarking functions within a scientific research community. A descriptive theory is an explanatory framework to help us better understand the past. We can then use this understanding to guide our use of benchmarking in the future.

This section has four parts, each explaining an aspect of the theory. We begin by giving the scope of theory by describing where the theory does and does not apply. Based on this, we give a definition of what a benchmark is. From there, we examine how a benchmark emerges and is used within a community and why a benchmark is effective for advancing a scientific community.

3.1 Scope

Our theory is concerned primarily with benchmarks that are *created and used by a technical research community*. Benchmarks that are created by a single individual or laboratory and are not used widely tend not to have the same impact on the community and research results. The community of interest may include participants from academia, industry, and government, but they are all primarily interested in scientific research. Benchmarks designed for business or marketing purposes are optimised for different goals, so this theory does not extend to cover those.

3.2 Definition

We use a general definition of benchmark to ensure wide applicability. It applies equally to benchmarking of tools and techniques, as well as other technologies, so we will use these terms interchangeably. We define a benchmark as a test or set of tests used to compare the performance of alternative tools or techniques. A benchmark has three components. A benchmark can be designed by selecting the components hierarchically. However, when a benchmark emerges as part of a community effort, the components can be developed in any order.

Motivating Comparison. This component encompasses two concepts, comparison and motivation. The purpose of a benchmark is to compare, so the comparison that is at the heart of a benchmark must be clearly defined. The motivation aspect refers to the need for the research area, and in turn the benchmark itself and the work on it. Thus, the Motivating Comparison captures both the technical comparison to be made as well as the research agenda that will be furthered by making this comparison.

Task Sample. The tests in the benchmark should be a representative sample of the tasks that the tool or technique is expected to solve in actual practice. Since it is not possible to include the entire population of the problem domain, a selection of tasks acts as surrogates.

Performance Measures. These measurements can be made by a computer or by a human, and can be quantitative or qualitative. Performance is not an innate characteristic of the technology, but is the relationship between the technology and how it is used. As such, performance is a measure of fitness for purpose.

A proto-benchmark is a set of tests that is missing one of these components. The most common proto-benchmarks lack a performance measure and are sometimes called case studies or exemplars. These are typically used to demonstrate the features and capabilities of a new tool or technique, and occasionally used to compare different technologies in an exploratory manner.

3.3 Benchmarks as Paradigms

Benchmarks function within research communities in the same manner as scientific paradigms. Kuhn argued that scientific progress occurs through revolutions, in much the same way that social and political progress occurs. (The conventional view at the time was that science moved in a linear fashion towards a progressively more accurate truth.) The dominant view in a discipline is called a *paradigm* and a revolution is needed to move a discipline from paradigm to another.

A paradigm is the collection of knowledge that is needed to function within a scientific discipline [12]. Within a scientific discipline, the current paradigm captures the community consensus on which problems are worthy of study, and determines what are scientifically acceptable solutions. In this manner, paradigms convey implicit rules for working within the community along with the explicit rules or factual knowledge.

Kuhn's descriptions of paradigms also includes a lifecycle model for a scientific community. A new research field can be characterised as *pre-scientific* if there is not yet consensus on which problems need solving or on what set of research methods are valid approaches to these problems. When a consensus emerges, working within a paradigm constitutes doing *normal science*. A paradigm can become degenerative if little further progress is made. A scientific revolution occurs when the dominant paradigm is displaced by a new one.

A benchmark operationalises a paradigm; it takes an abstract concept and makes it concrete, so it can serve as a guide for action. The motivating comparison and task sample are a statement of the problems that are worth solving. The performance measures show which solutions are held in higher esteem. The benchmark also contains implicit information about how the problem ought to be solved.

Like paradigms, benchmarks emerge though a process of scientific discovery and consensus. Both must progress together for a standard benchmark to emerge, because neither alone is sufficient. For example, a discipline may have the research results necessary to design a good benchmark, but lack the agreement that such an effort ought to be undertaken. This tight relationship between knowledge and consensus means that the existence of a benchmark is indicative of the maturity of a scientific discipline.

3.4 Effectiveness

Using paradigms as a model, an explanation of the success of benchmarks needs to account for both sociological and technical aspects. We will discuss the sociological reasons, before considering the technical reasons.

Sociological Factors. As established in the previous subsection, benchmarks encapsulate paradigms. As concrete problem solutions, they make statements about the valid scientific problems and solutions in the area and the *implicit rules for conducting research.* The presence of a benchmark states that the community believes that contributions ought to be evaluated against clearly defined standards. The benchmark itself promotes the conduct of research that is collaborative, open and public.

Collaboration in benchmarking occurs in two ways. During development, researchers work together to build consensus on what should be in the benchmark. During deployment, the results from different technologies are compared, which requires researchers to look at each other's contributions. Consequently, researchers become more aware of one another's work and ties between researchers with similar interests are strengthened.

Evaluations carried out using benchmarks are, by their nature, open and public. The materials are available for general use, and often so is the technology being tested. It is difficult to hide the flaws of a tool or technique, or to aggrandise its strengths when there is transparency in the test procedures. Moreover, anyone could use the benchmark with the same tools or techniques, and attempt to replicate the results.

These factors together, collaboration, openness, and publicness, result in frank, detailed, and technical communication among researchers. This kind of public evaluation contrasts sharply with the descriptions of tools and techniques that are currently found in software engineering conference or journal publications. A well-written paper is expected to show that the work is a novel and worthy contribution to the field, rather than share advice about how to tackle similar practical problems. Benchmarks are one of the few ways that the dirty details of research, such as debugging techniques, design decisions, and mistakes, are forced out into the open and shared between laboratories.

Technical Factors. The technical reasons for the success of benchmarking lie in its strengths as an empirical method. It has characteristics from both case studies and experiments, and consequently shares features of each of these two well-understood empirical methods. as summarised in Table 1.

Table 1: Comparison of Benchmarking as an Empirical Method to Experiments and Case Studies

Characteristics from Experiments	Characteristics from Case Studies
Features • Use of control factors • Replication • Direct comparison of results	**Features** • Little control over the evaluation setting, (e.g. choice of technology and user subjects) • No tests of statistical significance • Some open-ended questions possible
Advantages • Direct comparison of results	**Advantages** • Method is flexible and robust
Disadvantages • Not suitable for building explanatory theories	**Disadvantages** • Limited control reduces generalisability of results

Like experiments, control of the task sample is used to reduce variability in the results—all tools and techniques are evaluated using the same tasks and experimental materials. However, there is little control over the selection of tools or techniques to be evaluated and the individuals operating them in the evaluation; in this sense, benchmarking is more like a case study because these factors are determined by the situation. Furthermore, tests of statistical significance are not always performed on benchmark results.

Another advantage of benchmarking is that replication is built into the method. Since the materials are designed to be used by in different laboratories, people can perform the evaluation on various tools and techniques, repeatedly, if desired. Also, some benchmarks can be automated, so the computer does the work of executing the tests, gathering the data, and producing the performance measures.

Finally, benchmarking is an accepted and familiar evaluation technique in computer science. They do not usually require additional training or special knowledge to use or understand. Using a benchmark is similar to doing a homework assignment, something most researchers have experienced.

4. Applying the Theory

In the previous section, we presented our theory of how benchmarking functions with scientific research communities. In this section, we examine how the theory can be used to guide practice. Given that benchmarks are indicative of the cohesiveness of a discipline on a technical and sociological level, we hypothesise that benchmarking can be applied proactively to advance the maturity of a scientific community, rather than simply enjoying this maturity as a side-effect. This hypothesis suggests that benchmarking can help whenever a research area needs to become more scientific, needs to codify technical knowledge, or needs to become more cohesive. We will offer evidence that this hypothesis is correct in Section 5.

First, we give some guidance on how to determine whether to begin development of benchmarks in a particular research area. For receptive areas, we describe some principles for the benchmark development and high-level requirements for the end product.

4.1 Preconditions and Caveats

Our theory suggests that there are two conditions that must already exist within a discipline before construction of a benchmark can be fruitfully attempted.

The first precondition is that there must be a minimum level of maturity in the discipline. During the early days, when a research area is becoming established, it is necessary and appropriate to go through a stage where diverse approaches and solutions proliferate. At this time, the bounds of the area are being established and different methods are being applied. This proliferation is desirable, so there will be a variety of tools and techniques to be compared by the benchmark.

Evidence that a community has reached the required level of maturity and is ready to move to a more rigorous scientific basis comes in many forms. Typical symptoms include an increasing concern with validation of research results and with comparison between solutions developed at different laboratories; attempted replication of results; use of proto-benchmarks (or at least attempts to apply solutions to a common set of sample problems), and finally an increasing resistance to accept speculative papers for publication.

This precondition is important because there is a significant cost to developing and maintaining the benchmark, and a danger in committing to a benchmark too early. Walter Tichy writes:

> "Constructing a benchmark is usually intense work, but several laboratories can share the burden. Once defined, a benchmark can be executed repeatedly at moderate cost. In practice, it is necessary to evolve benchmarks to prevent overfitting" [21] (p. 36).

A community must be ready to incur the cost of developing the benchmark, and subsequently maintaining it. Continued evolution of the benchmark is necessary to prevent researchers from making changes to optimise the performance of their contributions on a particular set of tests. Too much effort spent on such optimisations indicates stagnation, suggesting the benchmark should be changed or replaced.

Locking into an inappropriate benchmark too early, using provisional results, can hold back later progress. The advantage of having a benchmark is that the community works together in one direction. However, this commitment means closing off other directions, albeit temporarily. Selection of one paradigm, by definition, excludes others.

The second precondition is that there must be an ethos of collaboration within the community. In other words, there must be a willingness to work together to solve common problems. A past history of collaboration demonstrates the presence of a good working relationship and sets up the expectation that community members take part in such work. This ethos, familiarity, and experience creates a community that is more receptive to the results and therefore more likely to use the benchmark.

If these preconditions are not met, it does not mean benchmarking cannot be employed. Rather, it means that steps to establish these preconditions must first be undertaken. The first precondition can be addressed by time and scientific results. In some situations, it is merely sufficient to wait for a critical mass of sentiment and technology before embarking on the road to a benchmark. In other situations, preliminary research on benchmark components may also be necessary.

The second precondition can be addressed through a series of planned activities, but again, patience is necessary because it takes time to change the ethos of a group. Some ways to build up a collaborative ethos include informal meetings and joint projects between groups, time set aside for discussions at conferences, and workshops where new problems and ideas are explored.

4.2 Process of Benchmark Development

The key principle underlying the benchmark development process is this: scientific knowledge and community consensus progress in lock-step during creation of benchmark. The selected benchmark components must be endorsed by the community.

Choosing the task sample will undoubtedly be controversial. Tichy observed:

> "The most subjective and therefore weakest part of a benchmark test is the benchmark's composition. Everything else, if properly documented, can be checked by the skeptic. Hence, benchmark composition is always hotly debated " [21] (p. 36).

Creating performance measures will be particularly difficult in software engineering. In most cases, no obvious measures are available prior to the benchmarking effort. Although many people associate benchmarking with test of simple one dimensional attributes (such as speed), in fact the measures can address any aspect of fitness for purpose, and hence can be quite complex. A good starting point for identifying suitable measures is existing work on empirical studies in software engineering (see for example [2] [11] [15]).

Since knowledge and agreement must be built up together, a successful benchmark development process needs to have the following attributes.

The effort must be led by a small number of champions. This group keeps the work active and the work often becomes identified with one or two key members of the group. They act primarily as organisers, co-ordinating activities such as opportunities to provide feedback and publication of results.

Design decisions for the benchmark need to be supported by laboratory work. The benchmark should use established research results where possible. In addition, prototypes and small tests may be needed to further understanding or to support decision-making.

The benchmark must be developed by consensus. There must be many opportunities for the general community to participate, to provide feedback, and to endorse the benchmark. Pursuant to Tichy's observation, there must be lots of opportunity to debate. These opportunities can come in a variety of formats. They can be newsgroups or mailing lists for informal discussion. A more formal, written Request for Comment (RFC) procedure could also be used. We have found that face-to-face meetings that occur as part of conferences and seminars are essential.

4.3 Desiderata for Successful Benchmarks

In this section, we present seven requirements or properties of successful benchmarks. These can be used as design goals when creating a benchmark or as dimensions for evaluating an existing one. We took work by Gray [8] and Feather et al. [6], and expanded on them, based on our own observations of successful benchmarks. The first two properties, accessibility and affordability, are primarily concerned with the packaging and delivery of the benchmark. The last five, clarity, relevance, solvability, portability, and scalability, deal with the benchmark problem itself. In the remainder of this subsection, we will describe these properties in detail.

Accessibility. The benchmark needs to be easy to obtain and easy to use. The test materials and results need to be publicly available, so anyone can apply the benchmark to a tool or techniques and compare their results with others. The test and results should easy to use by software engineers with different levels of expertise with empirical studies. Also, if the benchmark is easy to understand, it will be less like to be interpreted incorrectly and will have higher credibility.

Affordability. The cost of using the benchmark must be commensurate with the benefits. The costs commonly involve human resources, as well as software and hardware. Some of these costs can be reduced by automating the benchmark. If the costs are too high or the benefits too low, few people will be likely to use the benchmark. The breakeven point for this relationship will vary according to the maturity of the technology and the status of benchmark results among peers and potential users.

Clarity. The benchmark specification should be clear, self-contained, and as short as possible. This clarity should help ensure that there are no loopholes to be exploited.

Relevance. The task set out in the benchmark must be representative of ones that the system is reasonably expected to handle in a natural (meaning not artificial) setting and the performance measure used must be pertinent to the comparisons being made. This property is as difficult to satisfy as it is important. For some task domains, it is sufficient to use a miniaturisation of a naturally-occurring problem. For others, some ingenuity is required to include enough context to make the problem realistic.

Solvability. It should be possible to complete the task domain sample and to produce a good solution. This feature seems obvious, but is worth stating. A task that is too difficult for all or most tools yields little data to support comparisons. A task that is achievable, but not trivial, provides an opportunity for systems to show their capabilities and their shortcomings.

Portability. The benchmark should be specified at a high enough level of abstraction to ensure that it is portable to different tools or techniques and that it does not bias one technology in favour of others. One implication of this feature is the benchmark may need to implemented more than once for different platforms or for different architectures.

Scalability. The benchmark tasks should scale to work with tools or techniques at different levels of maturity. It should be applicable to research prototypes and commercial products. This property influences the size of task: it should be sufficiently large to showcase the more mature techniques, but not too large to test techniques currently being researched.

5. Case Study: Reverse Engineering

Over the last few years, we have been working to define benchmarks for software reverse engineering tools. During this time we applied and refined the principles described in the previous section.

The first benchmark we developed was for comparing program comprehension tools (i.e. tools that helped programmers understand source code for the purpose of making modifications) [18, 19]. Users of the benchmark had to complete a number of maintenance and documentation tasks on *xfig 3.2.1*, an Open Source drawing program for UNIX.

The second benchmark was CppETS (C++ Extractor Test Suite) [17]. We used a collection of small test programs written primarily in C++ and questions about these programs to evaluate the capabilities of different fact extractors.

Both of these benchmarks were developed in collaboration with other researchers, used by additional researchers and tool developers, and discussed at a workshop or conference. Both benchmarks produced technically interesting results, but a more significant contribution was the deeper understanding of the tools and the research problem that they brought to the community. Since these two benchmarks are similar in terms of their development and impact on the research area, we will describe only CppETS in detail.

5.1 Preconditions in the Reverse Engineering Community

Recall that two preconditions are needed prior to working on a community-based benchmark. These are a minimum level of scientific maturity and a culture of collaborative work. Both of these were present in the reverse engineering community before we began our work.

There was a healthy variety of tools implemented by a number of research groups. Many of these tools had similar features, but used different approaches. It was felt that it would be easier to understand the relative merits of the different tools by applying them to a common software system [1] [3].

The community had a track record of collaboration and discussion. The main conference in the area, Working Conference on Reverse Engineering (WCRE), is organised to maximise discussion time. For example, paper presentations are 20 minutes long instead of the usual 30 minutes and there is a half-hour discussion following three paper presentations. Consequently, there is a culture of public debate and exchange of ideas at conferences. Further evidence of this community's desire to work together can be found in GXL (Graph eXchange Language) [10]. This format for exchanging data between software tools was ratified for use by the community in January, 2001 and has been adopted by over 30 researchers in 8 countries.

5.2 CppETS for C++ Fact Extractors

CppETS is a benchmark for comparing the capabilities of C++ fact extractors. Fact extraction is a fundamental problem in reverse engineering, since all subsequent analysis is affected by the quantity and quality of facts produced. It is a surprisingly difficult problem, particularly for C++, which has led to implementations that use different approaches with varying degrees of success [14]. Consequently, it can be very difficult for a user to select a fact extractor that meets their requirements. We created CppETS to address this need. The design and application of CppETS 1.0 is described in detail elsewhere [17], so we will only describe the salient components here.

Motivating Comparison. To find the most accurate and robust (i.e. resistant to non-standard input) fact extractor for C++.

Task Sample. A collection of test buckets each consisting of small C++ test programs and an associated Question File that asked about different facts that could potentially be extracted from the source code. Teams had to perform an extraction on these test buckets and show that the extractor produced answers to the questions. The solution to a test bucket consisted of the output from the extractor and an Answer File that served as documentation and/or concordance to the output.

Performance Measures. Points were earned for correct answers and completeness of documentation. These points were allocated to Accuracy and Robustness categories.

In terms of the desiderata for benchmarks described above, CppETS fared as follows.

Accessibility. CppETS could be downloaded and used by any interested person. The format for the benchmark was straightforward.

Affordability. It typically took about one person working for two to three days to complete the benchmark. Teams often needed more time because they were developing or repairing their extractors at the same time.

Clarity. The problems set out in the benchmark were clear enough to point out inconsistencies or mis-matches in our collective vocabulary. In some cases the vocabulary could be found in other research areas, such as compilers, they were not in wide use. In other cases, the community was learning to apply the same terms to the same phenomenon. This issue will be discussed further in Section 5.4.

Relevance. The benchmark contained test buckets that tested a variety of C++ language features, as well as buckets that tested common reverse engineering problems, such as missing source code.

Solvability. The test buckets came with varying degrees of difficulty and no tool was expected to be able to earn all available points. It was expected that the extractors would be able to parse, if not correctly analyse, all the test programs in the Accuracy category.

Portability. The test programs were portable to a variety of platforms and compilers. Some of the programs in the Robustness categories did contain compiler extensions, i.e. keywords specific to a compiler, and pre-processor directives with implementation-dependent interpretations. These were included to represent extraction problems found reverse engineering.

Scalability. All of the test buckets in the benchmark were relatively small, which made them easy to understand and score by hand. Without some automated scoring mechanism or an oracle to provide a set of canonical answers, it was difficult to include any test buckets of any significant size. In version 1.1, we included a subset (29 000 lines of code) of the "basesuif" package, which is the core package of Stanford University's SUIF2 compiler system.

5.3 CppETS Development Process

Recall from Section 4.2, that there are three ingredients needed for successful development process. These were champions to lead the process, design decisions that were supported by research, and opportunities for community participation and feedback. All three were present in the development of CppETS.

The benchmark was championed primarily by Susan Elliott Sim. She was joined by Holger Kienle (University of Victoria) for version 1.1. This benchmark built on discussions about C++ fact extraction that were already taking place in the reverse engineering community. Before creating this benchmark, the selection of test buckets was discussed with some researchers who had implemented fact extractors. While developing the benchmark, we used extensive testing in our own laboratories and followed closely two recent papers in the area [4] [7].

To date, we provided two opportunities for the community to participate the development of the benchmark. CppETS 1.0 was discussed at CASCON2001 in November of that year. The following fact extractors participated in this evaluation: Acacia (AT&T, represented by University of Waterloo), cppx (University of Waterloo and Queens), Rigi C++ Extractor (University of Victoria), TkSee/SN (University of Ottawa). CppETS 1.1 was discussed at IWPC (International Workshop on Program Comprehension) in June, 2002. The participants in this workshop were Acacia, cppx, TkSee/SN, and Columbus (University of Szeged and FrontEndART). For both workshops, the benchmark was published in advance and teams submitted their solutions for scoring prior to the workshop. At the workshop, the teams gave presentations on their extractors and how they did on the benchmark. The organisers presented the rankings of the teams and chaired a discussion of the benchmark. At both workshops, the participants and the organisers gained new insights into both their tools and the problem of fact extraction.

The benchmark tasks uncovered errors in all the extractors. Similarly, the teams found mistakes in the benchmark. In both workshops, the fact extractor with the highest score was a surprise to the participants. For the first workshop, the success of TkSee/SN was unexpected because it didn't have a lot of visibility. For the second one, cppx's score was a surprise because it was a significant improvement over the previous workshop.

5.4 Impact of CppETS

According to our theory, a successful benchmark is one that has an impact on the discipline. The full extent of the impact of CppETS will become clear over time, but in the last few months some effects have already appeared.

At the workshops, participants were eager to share their experiences and results. By the end of the day, there was a high level of energy in the room, researchers felt a renewed sense of purpose for their work, and everyone learned a lot. They now have a shared experience of having worked together successfully, which further cements their relationships. These strengthened ties and personal history will make it easier for them to work together in the future. They are looking forward to the next version of CppETS and to co-authoring a paper together.

The benchmark has influenced the development of the fact extractors. CppETS pointed out shortcomings in their tools and raised questions the researchers had not previously considered. The lessons learned from the evaluation will be applied to work on creating a standard schema for C/C++ to be used with GXL.

CppETS has improved both the technical results and the cohesiveness of a community by acting as a vehicle to improve our shared understanding of the problem of fact extraction. The benchmark consists of a series of small extraction problems which made it easy to identify points of disagreement in terminology. Once we were able to establish a common vocabulary for the C++ language features and their analysis, we were able to discuss our conceptualisation of fact extraction more clearly.

An example of this improved understanding relates to identifying the location of a code fragment. Consider the question, "On what line does the definition for function 'average' start?" One possible answer is that it starts on the line containing the function signature, e.g. `int average (int *list)`. Another possible answer is that it starts on the line containing the curly brace that denotes the start of the block containing the function body. An argument can be made for both interpretations, and neither can be said to be more correct until we have some idea how this fact will be used by a subsequent analysis. This problem is further complicated by pre-processor directives and subsequent transformations that occur during the compilation process. These operations may cause a feature in the original source code to move, or disappear entirely.

In order to properly frame an evaluation, we will need to specify a context or downstream analysis for the required facts. In other words, we need to have a task sample that consists of more than just source code. By the same token, fact extractors need to be more clear about what analyses their data models support.

6. The Challenge

We have shown that benchmarking can have a strong positive effect on the scientific maturity of a research community. The benefits of benchmarking include a stronger consensus on the community's research goals, greater collaboration between laboratories, more rigorous examination of research results, and faster technical progress. We believe these benefits can be realised in many areas of software engineering. We conclude the paper by identifying several specific areas of software engineering that we believe are ripe for benchmarking.

6.1 Requirements Engineering

Requirements engineering (RE) has matured as a research community considerably over the past decade, with a series of annual conferences now in their tenth year, and a number of smaller regular workshops. Collaborative links such as the recent European-funded RENOIR network of excellence provide strong evidence of an ethos of collaboration. Hence, the preconditions described in section 4.1 are both met.

In some areas of RE, most notably software specification, proto-benchmarks have been used for years. A recent paper by Feather et al. characterizes these as *exemplars* [6], and identifies the uses, strengths and weaknesses of exemplars for evaluating specification techniques. When used for promoting research comparison and understanding, exemplars have both a motivating comparison and a task sample. However, as Feather et al point out, exemplars lack appropriate evaluation criteria:

> "How can we determine whether the specification language used on one exemplar has appropriate expressiveness, scaleability, evolveability, deductive power, development process efficiency, and so on?"[6, p 423].

This list provides an obvious starting point for defining performance measures. We challenge the RE community to turn some of its exemplars into benchmarks.

6.2 Model Checking

Model checking is an obvious candidate for traditional benchmarking, as speed is an essential property of a model checking algorithm. Several proto-benchmarks have emerged (e.g. the elevator problem used by Plath and Ryan [16]), and nearly all model checking papers include a performance evaluation showing how speed varies, typically with the size of the state space. However, these evaluations have not been standardized in any way.

Moreover, the speed of a particular model checker does not depend in any simple way on the size of the state space. Sreemani and Atlee [20] report that model checkers tend to be sensitive to particular modelling choices, including order of introduction of variables, their types, and the modularity of the system. Reports of the raw performance of model checking engines tends to ignore these factors. Here, a benchmarking effort is clearly needed to develop consensus on appropriate task samples, if we wish to know anything about the relative performance of model checkers in particular applications.

However, there is a less obvious and more interesting application of benchmarking for model checkers that we believe will advance the field more dramatically. One can distinguish between a model checking *engine,* which computes the satisfaction relation for a particular temporal logic, and a model checking *framework*, which includes modelling languages for expressing state machine models, abstraction techniques for reducing large models to a size suitable for fast checking, and tools for translating the models into the input language of the checker engine and for visualizing the results. Recent work on applying model checking to UML models and Statecharts falls into the latter category [13]. Benchmarking here would concentrate less on pure performance, and more on finding out which analysis questions a particular framework can handle. We suspect the impact would be similar to that seen for CppETS.

6.3 Software Evolution

In contrast to the previous two, software evolution is an emerging research community, but they are already pursuing a benchmark. Over the last couple of years, key people in the field have published papers[5] and proposed workshops to draw the community's attention to this problem. This work is motivated by a desire to better understand research results by comparing them using common task samples.

Our advice to this community is to continue pursuing this work, but we feel that it is somewhat early to attain a full-fledged community-based benchmark. We feel that they have not quite attained the first precondition, that is, a sufficient proliferation research results. However, the needed multiplicity of approaches will come with time and so will the consensus and results needed to build a the benchmark. We encourage them to continue with this effort, because it will prepare the community for a benchmark.

The three examples in this section and CppETS illustrate ways that benchmarking can be used in different areas of software engineering. We challenge other areas to start using benchmarking to advance their research. Many branches of software engineering are still in the pre-science stage where there is not yet agreement on a body of knowledge, accepted techniques, or even fundamental problems. Other branches have reached the normal science stage, but are struggling to codify the lasting lessons from research and to have an impact on industrial practice. For areas in both stages, benchmarking will increase the scientific maturity of the area.

A benchmark that has been developed by consensus and is widely accepted provides a beacon for the community. It lights the path for others to follow, shows that there is agreement on what is important, and concentrates attention on a key problem. It is these effects, which emerge out of the benchmarking process, that have a lasting positive impact on a scientific discipline.

Acknowledgements

We would like to thank the following people for their participation in our work with the CppETS benchmark. Mike Godfrey, Jeff Elliott, and Catherine Morton helped with the test cases in version 1.0. Version 1.1 was developed jointly with Holger Kienle. Ian Bull, Rudolf Ferenc, Mike Godfrey, Timothy C. Lethbridge, Andrew Malton, Sergei Marchenko, Volker Riediger, and Andrew Trevors used CppETS and participated in the workshops.

References

[1] M. N. Armstrong and C. Trudeau, "Evaluating Architectural Extractors," presented at Working Conference on Reverse Engineering, Honolulu, HI, pp. 30-39, October 12-14, 1998.

[2] Victor R. Basili, Gianluigi Caldiera, and H. Dieter Rombach, "The Goal Question Metric Approach," in *Encyclopedia of Software Engineering, Two Volume Set*, Gianluigi Caldiera and Dieter H. Rombach, Eds. New York City: John Wiley and Sons, Inc., pp. 528-532, 1994.

[3] Berndt Bellay and Harald Gall, "An Evaluation of Reverse Engineering Tool Capabilities," *Software Maintenance: Research and Practice*, vol. 10, pp. 305-331, 1998.

[4] Ivan T. Bowman, Michael W. Godfrey, and Ric Holt, "Connecting Architecture Reconstruction Frameworks," *Journal of Information and Software Technology*, vol. 42, no. 2, pp. 93-104, 1999.

[5] Serge Demeyer, Tom Mens, and Michel Wermelinger, "Towards a Software Evolution Benchmark," presented at Proceedings of the International Workshop on Principles of Software Evolution, Vienna, Austria, pp. 172-175, 10-11 September 2002.

[6] Martin S. Feather, Stephen Fickas, Anthony Finkelstein, and Axel van Lamsweerde, "Requirements and Specification Exemplars," *Automated Software Engineering*, vol. 4, pp. 419-438, 1997.

[7] Rudolf Ferenc, Susan Elliott Sim, Richard C. Holt, Rainer Koschke, and Tibor Gyimóthy, "Towards a Standard Schema for C/C++," presented at Eighth Working Conference on Reverse Engineering, Stuttgart, Germany, pp. 49-58, 2-5 October 2001.

[8] Jim Gray, "The Benchmark Handbook: For Database and Transaction Processing Systems," San Mateo, CA: Morgan Kaufman Publishers, Inc, 1991.

[9] John L. Henning, "SPEC CPU2000: Measuring CPU Performance in the New Millennium," *IEEE Computer*, pp. 28-35, July, 2000.

[10] Richard C. Holt, Andreas Winter, and Andy Schürr, "GXL: Toward a Standard Exchange Format.," presented at Seventh Working Conference on Reverse Engineering, Brisbane, Queensland, Australia, pp. 162-171, 23-25 November 2000.

[11] Barbara Ann Kitchenham, "Evaluating software engineering methods and tools. Parts 1 to 12.," *ACM SIGSOFT Software Engineering Notes*, vol. 21-23, 1996-1998.

[12] Thomas S. Kuhn, *The Structure of Scientific Revolutions, Third Edition*. Chicago: The University of Chicago Press, 1996.

[13] William E. McUmber and Betty H. C. Cheng, "A Generic Framework for Formalizing UML," presented at Proceedings of the Twenty-third International Conference on Software Engineering, Toronto, Canada, pp. 433-442, 12-19 May 2001.

[14] Gail C. Murphy, David Notkin, William G. Griswold, and Erica S. Lan, "An Empirical Study of Static Call Graph Extractors," *ACM Transactions on Software Engineering and Methodology*, vol. 7, no. 2, pp. 158-191, 1998.

[15] Shari Lawrence Pfleeger, "Experimental Design and Analysis in Software Engineering, Parts 1-6," *ACM SIGSOFT Software Engineering Notes*, vol. 19-20, 1994-1995.

[16] M. Plath and M. Ryan, "SFI: A Feature Integration Tool," in *Advances in Computer Science*, R. Berghammer and Y. Lakhnech, Eds. Heidelberg, Germany: Springer Verlag, pp. 201-216, 1999.

[17] Susan Elliott Sim, Richard C. Holt, and Steve Easterbrook, "On Using a Benchmark to Evaluate C++ Extractors," presented at Tenth International Workshop on Program Comprehension, Paris, France, pp. 114-123, .

[18] Susan Elliott Sim and Margaret-Anne D. Storey, "A Structured Demonstration of Program Comprehension Tools," presented at Seventh Working Conference on Reverse Engineering, Brisbane, Queensland, Australia, pp. 184-193, 23-25 November 2000.

[19] Susan Elliott Sim, Margaret-Anne D. Storey, and Andreas Winter, "A Structured Demonstration of Five Program Comprehension Tools: Lessons Learnt," presented at Seventh Working Conference on Reverse Engineering, Brisbane, Queensland, Australia, pp. 210-212, 23-25 November 2000.

[20] Tirumale Sreemani and Joanne M. Atlee, "Feasibility of Model Checking Software Requirements: A Case Study," presented at Proceedings of COMPAS'96, Gaithersburg, Maryland, pp. 77-88, 17-21 June 1996.

[21] Walter F. Tichy, "Should Computer Scientists Experiment More?" *IEEE Computer*, pp. 32-40, May, 1998.

[22] Ellen M. Voorhees and Donna Harman, "Overview of the Eighth Text REtrieval Conference (TREC-8)," presented at Text REtrieval Conference (TREC-8), Gaithersberg, Maryland, pp. 1-24, November 17-19, 2000.

An Empirical Study of an Informal Knowledge Repository in a Medium-Sized Software Consulting Company

Torgeir Dingsøyr[1], Emil Røyrvik[2]
[1]*SINTEF Telecom and Informatics,* [2]*SINTEF Industrial Management*
{Torgeir.Dingsoyr|Emil.Royrvik}@sintef.no

Abstract

Numerous studies have been conducted on design and architecture of knowledge repositories. This paper addresses the need for looking at practices where knowledge repositories are actually used in concrete work situations. This insight should be used when developing knowledge repositories in the future.

Through methods inspired by ethnography this paper investigates how an unstructured knowledge repository is used for different purposes by software developers and managers in a medium-sized software consulting company. The repository is a part of the company's knowledge management tool suite on the Intranet. We found five distinct ways of using the tool, from solving specific technical problems to getting an overview of competence in the company. We highlight the importance of informal organization and the social integration of the tool in the daily work practices of the company.

1. Introduction

Knowledge Management has attracted a lot of attention in various business domains in the past years, including software engineering [1]. Reasons for the interest in knowledge management are that:

- Software Engineering is knowledge-intensive work; the main asset in software companies is what has been called the "intellectual capital".
- In order to improve software development, the management of knowledge has to be improved as well.

Hanssen et. al. [2] divide between two main strategies for knowledge management:

- Codification - to systematize and store information that represents the knowledge of the company, and make this available for the people in the company.
- Personalization - to support the flow of information in a company by storing information about knowledge sources, like a "yellow pages" of in-house expertise.

Most of the work that has been reported on knowledge management in the software engineering literature (often referred to as work on "experience factory") are from large organizations, such as Daimler Chrysler [3, 4], The NASA Software Engineering Laboratory [5] and Ericsson [6]. See [7] for an overview.

Such organizations can devote a lot of resources on organizational issues such as knowledge management. Many of the software engineering companies have opted for a strategy involving both codification and personalization.

Codification is the strategy that requires the heaviest investment – both in codifying knowledge that exist tacit in people or teams, and also in having an infrastructure for distributing it in the organization.

It is interesting to see how smaller (in this case: medium-size) organizations cope with a codification strategy on scarce resources. In particular, we will examine how a medium-sized software consulting company is using a knowledge repository. But first, we will describe knowledge management tools more in general in the next section.

2. Knowledge management tools

When we talk of tools for knowledge management, we will mean tools that have several users, and are widely available for employees in an organization. This is usually what we can call Intranet tools, that support knowledge management [8] in "at least three ways: 1) Providing compression of time and space among the users. 2) Offering the flexibility to exchange information, and: 3) Supporting information transfer and organizational networking independent of direct contacts between the users" .

There are many dimensions for describing knowledge management tools. Ruggles [9] mentions tools that "generate knowledge", where tools for data mining (to

0-7695-1877-X/03 $17.00 © 2003 IEEE

discover new patterns in data) can be an example. Further, we have "knowledge codification tools" to make knowledge available for others, and "knowledge transfer tools" to decrease problems with time and space when communicating in an organization.

Another dimension is whether the tools are "active" [10] or "passive". By active tools, we mean tools that notify users when it is likely that users require some kind of knowledge. Passive tools require a user to actively seek knowledge without any system support.

We also find another way of categorizing the tools other than the ones mentioned so far, from the book Information Technology for Knowledge Management [11]. The authors divide technology for a "corporate memory" into four parts, shown in Figure 1:

- Knowledge repositories and libraries - tools for handling repositories of knowledge in the form of documents.
- Communities of knowledge workers - tools to support communities of practice in work; like organizing workspaces for communities for online discussions and distributed work.
- Knowledge cartography - tools for mapping and categorizing knowledge, from core competence in a company to individual expertise; what we can refer to as "metaknowledge".
- The flow of knowledge - here we find tools for supporting the interaction between tacit knowledge, explicit knowledge and metaknowledge; that is, that combines the three parts above.

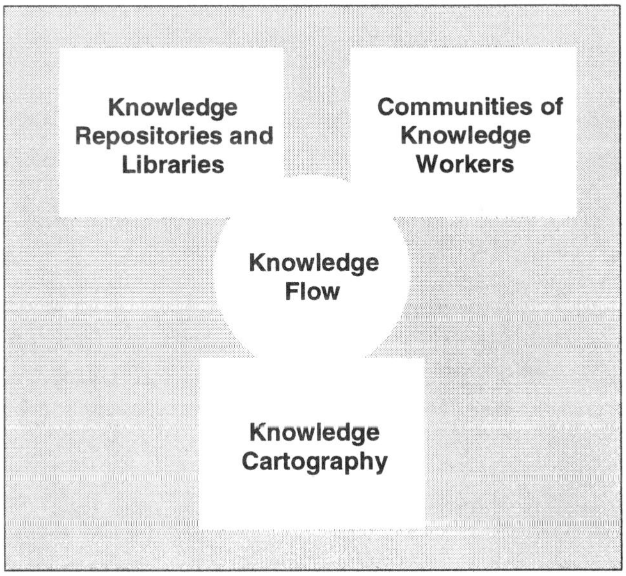

Figure 1. Types of Knowledge Management Tools or Architecture (Borghoff and Pareschi).

Now, we describe knowledge repositories and libraries in more detail.

2.1 Knowledge repositories

Liebowitz and Beckman [12] define knowledge repositories as an "on-line computer-based storehouse of expertise, knowledge, experiences, and documentation about a particular domain of expertise. In creating a knowledge repository, knowledge is collected, summarized, and integrated across sources".

Such repositories are sometimes referred to as "experience bases" or "corporate memories".

The repository can either be filled with knowledge by what van Heijst et. al [13] call "passive collection" – where workers themselves recognize what knowledge has sufficient value to be stored in the repository, or "active collection" – where some people in the organization are scanning communication processes to detect knowledge.

Davenport and Prusak [14] divide between three types of knowledge repositories:

1. *External knowledge repositories* (such as competitive intelligence).
2. *Structured internal knowledge repositories* (such as research reports, product-oriented market material).
3. *Informal internal knowledge repositories* (such as "lessons learned").

There are many examples of informal knowledge repositories from the software engineering literature.

The University of Nebraska-Lincoln has developed a research prototype tool for knowledge management support in software development called BORE [15]: This is a tool which contains information in cases about problem solving experience, and descriptions of resources like tools, projects, people and development methods. These descriptions are used to find relevant solutions when software developers are faced with a new problem.

Another prototype system, is CODE - a general-purpose knowledge management tool which serves as a medium for knowledge capture, transfer and iteration, as well as editing or "packaging" knowledge to make it easily available [16].

The Fraunhofer Institute for Experimental Software Engineering has developed "COIN Experience Factory" – a tool for capturing experience from research projects in software engineering [17].

ICL Finland has developed a knowledge management system, which includes a repository divided in two parts [18]:

- Structured internal knowledge: includes databases for sales and marketing information and employee competence, as well as examples of frequently used

documents, templates, software components, best practice information, and research reports.
- Informal internal knowledge: includes electronic discussion forums, news and "project folders". The project folders contain overviews of the projects, news and important announcements, technical documents and reusable components (for a complete list, refer to the paper cited above).

What kind of knowledge can we expect to find in these repositories? Robert Taylor [19] who has been working in the "information use" field, divides information into seven groups: *Enlightenment* – to use information for ones own amusement, an example can be company-internal news that are not fully relevant to normal work. *Problem understanding* – using information to increase the comprehension of a problem. *Instrumental* – follow guidelines or procedures. *Factual* – use information to determine facts. *Confirmational* – use information to verify other information. *Projective* – make forecasts or scenarios. *Personal or political* – use information to develop relationships.

There has been little work describing how knowledge repositories are used in practice. That is what we aim to do in this paper, and we will be using the classification developed by Taylor in examining the types of usage later.

3. Research method

To obtain the data for the research reported in this article, we used a method inspired by ethnography [20]. For the analysis, we used grounded theory [21]. We observed for 4 weeks at the software consulting company Computas during the autumn 2000. This company was selected because we knew they had been working with knowledge management for a long time and had some interesting tools. We got access to their Intranet systems, and attended all meetings where all the employees were invited as well as meetings in one project. The project was chosen by Computas: a software development project for a public customer. We interviewed eight developers and six managers. Three developers worked in the project we followed, the others had got awards as "knowledge sharers of the month". We interviewed the project leader in the project we followed, as well as two process owners for knowledge-management related processes. We also interviewed two general managers, and three managers who had got a "knowledge sharer of the month" award.

In addition we conducted a so-called Learning History [22] from the development and implementation process of an informal knowledge repository. This entailed interviews and process-meetings with six central contributors.

3.1 Data collection

We used the following data sources:

- Interviews - we used semi-structured interviews with open-ended questions. The interviews were transcribed in full, and in total, we got around 120 pages of transcripts for analysis (also on other knowledge management tools than the knowledge repository). We asked questions like "how do you assess the tools for knowledge management that you have available?", "what knowledge have you found useful from these tools?" and "when do you use the tools?".
- Screenshots - we gathered screenshots from different areas of the knowledge management system.
- Pictures - we took pictures of people in normal work-situations to get a better understanding of the workplace and work processes.
- Logbook - we wrote down observations from everyday life in the company in a logbook, together with memorandums from conversations we had, meetings and presentations we attended.

3.2 Data analysis

How did we organize the analysis of the data that was collected? First, we constructed a database with information from the interviews, documents, and our own logbook observations (using N5, a tool for analysis of qualitative research data). We tagged the information to show what kind of source it came from, and applied a simple categorization of the people that were interviewed: managers, project managers, developers, and people responsible for knowledge management.

We searched in this database for areas of interest, and got the information from the different sources. For example, searching this database for the keyword "skill" would result in 43 occurrences in 10 documents.

After that, we analyzed (and "coded") these chunks of information to find interesting categories that would be usable to build theory later. Would there be any special patterns in what the people were saying? We applied triangulation to see if there were differences between groups of people.

4. The Computas software consulting company

We investigated the usage of a knowledge repository at Computas. Computas is a medium-sized consulting company based in Norway, developing knowledge-based systems for a variety of customers. When it was founded in 1985, it was a spin-off of a larger, more general consulting company, and according to a Norwegian newspaper, "an international staff of specialists will develop expert systems that above all will cover the needs of the demanding oil industry". The newspaper continues: the company shall "offer services in industrial use of knowledge-based expert systems, and software in the field of artificial intelligence".

Since then, the company has grown organically, from just a few employees in the beginning, to around 150 in year 2000. The company has also extended their services and market.

The company's core competence is knowledge management, process-support and implementation of intelligent systems for knowledge-based behavior and knowledge processes.

Important technology for delivering these solutions, are "network and database technology, document management and search, web technology, work process support, coordination technology, artificial intelligence and data mining". The underlying technology for this is Java, Microsoft and SmallTalk technology.

Customers come from three main groups, the public sector, the marine sector and industry. Projects for these customers typically include 3-10 people working for at least half a year, and in some cases for several years. In projects, the participants take on different roles, as "project manager", "technical manager", and "customer contact".

The company is organized around "processes" and "projects". The "process organization" means that they have defined important areas for the company, which has one "process manager", usually with support from a small team. Examples of processes are "Management", "Delivery" and "Support", and also "Knowledge Management". Many employees in the company are responsible for some process issue while working on a project. Most employees have a university degree in Computer Science, and some have a Ph.D. degree, especially in Artificial Intelligence.

The Knowledge Management Process at Computas includes handing out a prize to the "knowledge sharer of the month" in order to promote knowledge management. This prize has been given to people who share their knowledge through Computas's knowledge management tools, or through oral communication.

On first sight, the organization seems very "flat" - with people rotating between different "process manager" positions. But as one employee told us, "of course, there is a hierarchy here as well, it is just not written down any place".

When working in projects, most of the development has traditionally been done "in-house", and not at the customer's site. But it is now getting more frequent that employees work in the customer companies. When we were visiting the company, around 20% of the staff were working somewhere else than in the main company building.

5. The knowledge repository: Well of Experience

Computas has a variety of knowledge management tools available on their Intranet, see [23] for an overview. One of the tools is the unstructured knowledge repository "Well of experience", or WoX. According to Davenport and Prusak's classification it would be an informal internal knowledge repository. It is a small tool for capturing knowledge that would normally be written on yellow stickers, what the company calls "collective yellow stickers". The yellow sticker analogy was in fact a major midwife aid in the initial understanding and practice for getting the system to be used. "Rather than using the post-it note, write your private yellow sticker in the WoX system so others can make use of them". That way the employees always know that there will be some information of use in the system. This way of contributing to the repository is what Heijst et al. describes as a passive collection process.

WoX contains everything from the phone-number to the pizza restaurant on the corner to "how you set up SmallTalk on a special platform". You find information by searching an unstructured database, and can give "credits" to notes that you find useful. Notes with more accumulated credits about an issue show up before notes with less. The tool contains a mechanism to give feedback to the person who wrote the note, and there has been a kind of competition in the company to get the most credits. One developer described this repository as "quite useful - it is simple enough to be used in practice". Another said "you can use WoX as a personal notice board where you can put the same information as you would on a yellow sticker. It's fast to insert notes, and you do not have to worry about where to put it".

When we visited the company, it contained around 600 "experience notes". In 2003, WoX contained around 990 notes and have had about 15,000 searches by 260 users (some customers are also allowed to use the tool in addition to Computas employees). There are 2,300 keywords in the repository.

Employees can search the knowledge repository using a simple search interface available on the company Intranet, see Figure 2. The functionality is simple keyword search, and you can browse the notes and comments on other people's notes that you have contributed, the credits your notes have gotten from others, the latest 10 notes that have been added to the repository, popular keywords as well as the notes with the most credits. In the simple search, you can select if you want to search in the text and subject information of the notes or also in the comments on notes.

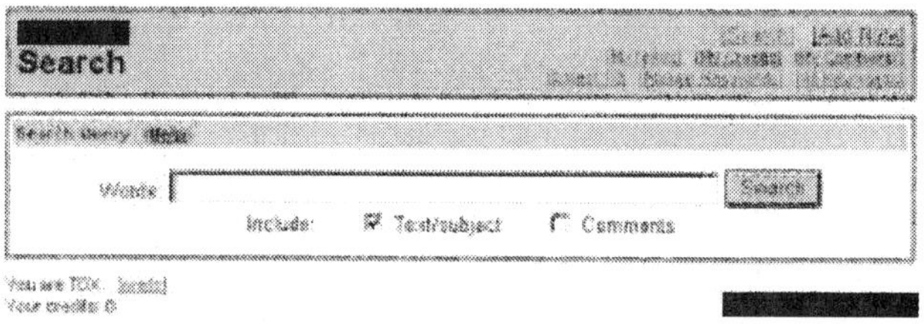

Figure 2. The "Well of experience" (WoX) search interface for the knowledge repository of "experience notes".

Examples of such notes are "how to reduce the size of your profile in Windows NT", "How to remove garbage from an image in SmallTalk", "Technical problems with cookies" and "An implementation of the soundex algorithm in Java". See Figure 3 for a complete example of a note.

Each note contains a subject, a descriptive text, as well as keywords (the one submitting the note defines the keyword, there is no predefined list of keywords), author information and the date it was submitted. When viewing a note, everyone can add a comment to the note, give the note a credit or mail the note as a tip to someone else.

According to one developer "people are very good at submitting notes when they think that something can be useful for others". A manager described it as "a behavioral arena that people use in different ways, that is creating a culture of knowledge sharing, and even creates expectations and lets people experience that others make use of their knowledge". The tool is promoted by posters which can be found on places that people visit a lot, like the one in Figure 4 which was located just outside the staff restaurant.

When we asked people to describe what kind of tools they were using in their work, almost all of the developers mentioned that they were using WoX. All developers but one (seven out of eight) say that they have written experience notes, and all of them have tried to search for experience notes. Among the managers, much fewer were using it actively. Three out of six did not mention WoX when we asked about knowledge management tools in the company.

Are there areas where the tool has been found not to be effective? At least it is not a space devoted to routines and reflection: "WoX is not suitable as an arena for rutinized knowledge and long strings of reasoning." Another critical factor is that "if a tool like WoX shall be useful, the total amount of available information must reach above a critical mass." Hence, the analogy with the yellow stickers. It was vital to get the consultants themselves to put information into the system.

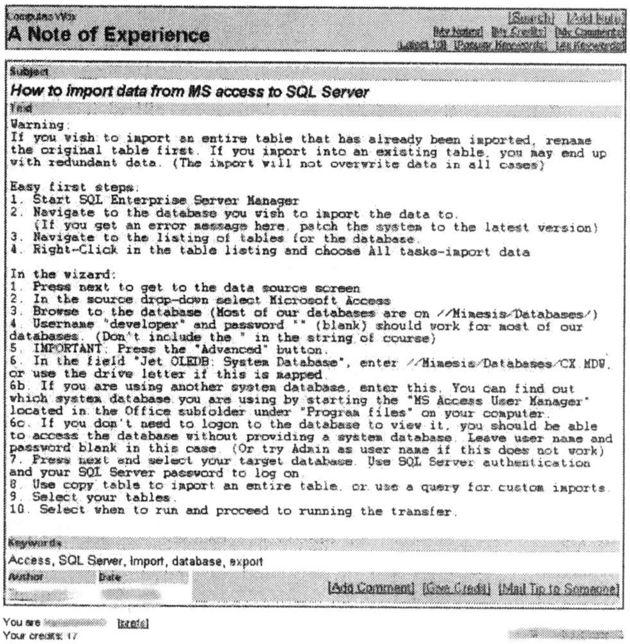

Figure 3. An example experience note.

Summarizing some of the potentials in WoX, one employee said: "New functionality and technical tips are suitable to be mediated by WoX. Also, it is usable for putting bits of programs and reusable components. Put another way, WoX-notes should be little patterns of applied knowledge engineering".

Based on the material from Computas we found five different types of usage of the knowledge repository:

- Solve a specific technical problem.
- Getting an overview of problem areas.
- Avoiding redundancy in having to explain the same solution to several people.
- Improve individual work situation by adjusting technical tools.
- Finding who has a specific competence in the company.

We describe each of these types of usage in more depth:

5.1 Solve a specific technical problem

The most prominent use of this tool seemed to be in "problem solving". As one developer put it "if you run into a problem, then you can use WoX to see if anyone else in the company has had a similar problem", or "when you sit with a problem that you can't solve, or a strange bug, or if you do not understand why the computer does not behave the way it should".

Another developer says: "It happens that I have been searching and have found things in WoX. Then you do not have to search in other places, and maybe spend two or three days".

It is also a good tool for sharing pieces of code, patterns, and reusable components with others.

A problem with the notes that one developer mentioned, is that "the person that writes something has a certain background, and with that background they presume that when they write `first you do this, then that...' - that the others also know what to do". Which is not always the case for complicated matters.

5.2 Getting an overview of problem areas

One said: "if I am stuck and wonder about something, usually I remember that it was written somewhere in WoX in fact, and then I go back and find it". An example is some notes about project-startup that this developer will usually go back to when being in that phase, which happens every 6 months or so. Another developer and another manager also said that they would see almost every day what was new "so I know what is in there, and do not have to search for things".

But people do not write about all types of problems as experience notes. Issues that are more "unofficial knowledge" - as one developer put it: "not things that are unethical, but things that you do that could easily be interpreted wrongly by customers, even though I mean we can stand for it" - that kind of issues you do not find any notes about, and that knowledge is transferred through informal oral communication.

Figure 4. "I've been WoX'ing today, have you?". One of several posters promoting the use of the WoX knowledge repository at Computas.

5.3 Avoiding redundancy

Some would use the WoX system to avoid redundancy in the sense of having to explain the same solution to several people. One developer said: "when the third person comes and asks about the same thing - then you realize that it is about time to document it". He would then later tell people who were asking about the new topic to look it up in WoX. WoX notes can be mailed easily by clicking on "Mail Tip to Someone" when looking at the note.

5.4 Improve individual work situation

Others would improve their individual work situation by adjusting technical tools based on information found in WoX. They would find information on how to improve the tools that they use in their daily work, like Outlook, to make them more easy to use. Another example would be to get to know "how to reduce your profile in Windows NT" - which reduces the booting-time of your operating system quite a bit. A third example of a small improvement is a note on how to burn CDs for customers; which explained how to design covers for the CDs so that they look more professional when delivering a final software product.

5.5 Finding competence

The last major category of types of WoX usage we found in Computas was finding who has a specific competence in the company: "Newbies get a shortcut to discover things that I have spent some time to build up. If they browse WoX a bit, they can find that 'this person knows a lot about low-level Windows-patching' and that 'this person is good at Apache webserver set up'", one developer said. This function of finding and linking "who knows what" is often an underestimated function of knowledge management systems, and in the case of Computas it overlaps with their "Skills-management" system [24]. The WoX notes gives clues to where to search for further knowledge, and may in this way be said to broaden the opportunity structures for knowledge sharing in Computas [25].

6. Discussion

From our interviews with developers and managers at Computas, it seems that the WoX is a tool that is actively used, and is helpful for several purposes, although the knowledge that it contains is unstructured, and the tool was easy to develop.

We note that managers contribute less frequently to the repository than developers. This might be because the kind of knowledge that is useful for developers is easier to codify than knowledge, say on estimation of software projects, or project management.

If we compare the types of usage we found in our interviews with the categories developed by Taylor, we see that "solving a technical problem" and "improving individual work situation" are types of knowledge that we can classify as "instrumental" – something you would look up and follow. "Avoiding redundancy" is also in this category. "Getting an overview of problem areas" is similar to Taylor's "problem understanding". "Finding competence" can be seen as using knowledge as "personal or political".

Why is it that WoX is a popular tool to use at Computas? There were many other tools in the company that were not used as much. WoX had many users and many different types of usage. One reason can be that this tool serves a purpose that other tools in the company do not. It is like a newsgroup on the Internet in one sense, but contains mostly knowledge that is local to the company. Employees have also been encouraged to contribute with experience notes in the tool – through advertisements in the company as in Figure 4, and also through "commercial banners" at the company Intranet. The tool is also easily accessible from the Intranet that most people at Computas use daily. Another reason can be the use of "credits" – that people get feedback on what they have contributed – and are thus motivated to contribute more. A final reason can be the company emphasis on sharing knowledge, that employees who have written many experience notes get a small prize as the "knowledge sharer of the month".

One of the topics discussed in Computas is the organization of the WoX system. Should it be structured or not? For example we found the opinion that too much structure hinders the growth of notes: "We must not construct too many links in WoX. It must not be too formalized. The strength of WoX is that it is organically growing. We have a hierarchy several other places, for example on the [internal] web." On the other hand, utility of the system to some degree means fast access: "WoX is a bit slow, and I miss the opportunity to browse".

"When WoX is so unstructured it is difficult to reuse information. I can see a danger that WoX becomes a kind of Internet (in the negative sense). A huge archive where it is difficult to maneuver and find useful information".

Another discussion in Computas was the explicit integration of WoX with other knowledge management tools, as for instance the Skills Manager. "We have competing mechanisms for knowledge sharing. We have to work more on developing distinct roles for the different electronical mediums we use for sharing knowledge". As an integrated part of dialogues with customers, for example concerning change requests, WoX could also play a part: "WoX could be used as a channel for change request from customers. WoX should be an integral part of development projects with customers and a central part of communication with them. In this way we could have built a pool of experience concerning the establishment of a system for the customer, a pool that both of us could have utilized". WoX would then have stored tips for other users and tips for revisions of the system.

7. Conclusion and further work

We have examined how an informal knowledge repository is used in a medium-sized software consulting company. We found that the well of experience, WoX, is especially appreciated amongst developers and used to a wide degree compared to other similar tools in other companies, even though the company is quite small for a codification strategy. We also found that:

- The Knowledge repository is used for different types of instrumental knowledge, as well as knowledge to increase problem understanding, and to strengthen personal and political ties.

The company plans to develop the tool further.

What can we learn from the usage of the knowledge repository at Computas when developing similar tools in other companies? First of all, we think the emphasis on combining an easy to use technical tool, which does not require rigor in contributing with knowledge (the unstructured nature) and the social incentives for use in the company were fruitful.

We think the emphasis on formal structures, techniques and procedures are generally overrated in the software engineering field, while the power of social aspects are underestimated.

Some main discussion points in the company on how to develop the repository further are:

- There has been a discussion in the company on whether to make the knowledge in the tool more structured. Many have opposed as structure can be found in other tools, and would make the tool harder to use.
- The company has raised a discussion on if it should combine the tool with other tools.

Acknowledgement

We are deeply grateful to all employees we have talked to at Computas for sharing their opinions on experience sharing, and especially Hans Karim Djarraya who has been our main contact person. We would further like to thank Gavin Gaudet and the anonymous reviewers for helpful comments.

We are further grateful to the Research Council of Norway for supporting this work through the projects PROFIT and KUNNE.

References

[1] I. Rus and M. Lindvall, "Knowledge Management in Software Engineering," IEEE Software, no. May/June, pp. 26 - 38, 2002.

[2] M.T. Hansen, N. Nohria, and T. Tierney, "What is your strategy for managing knowledge?," Harvard Business Review, no. 2, vol. 77, pp. 106 - 116, 1999.

[3] K. Schneider, J.P. Von Hunnius, and V.R. Basili, "Experience in Implementing a Learning Software Organization," IEEE Software, no. May/ June, pp. 46 - 49, 2002.

[4] F. Houdek, K. Schneider, and E. Wieser, "Establishing Experience Factories at Daimler-Benz. An Experience Report," Proceedings of the 20th International Conference on Software Engineering, ICSE 20, Kyoto, Japan, 1998.

[5] V.R. Basili, G. Caldiera, F. Mcgarry, R. Pajerski, G. Page, and S. Waligora, "The Software Engineering Laboratory - An operational software experience factory," Proceedings of the 14th International Conference on Software Engineering, ICSE 14, 1992.

[6] C. Johansson, P. Hall, and M. Coquard, ""Talk to Paula and Peter - They Are Experienced" - The Experience Engine in a Nutshell," in Learning Software Organizations : methodology and applications; proceedings from the 11th International Conference on Software Engineering and Knowledge Engineering, SEKE '99, Kaiserslautern, Germany, June 16 -19, 1999., Lecture Notes in Computer Science, vol. 1756, G. Ruhe and F. Bomarius, Eds. Berlin: Springer Verlag, 1999, pp. 171 - 186.

[7] T. Dingsøyr and R. Conradi, "A Survey of Case Studies of the Use of Knowledge Management in Software Engineering," International Journal of Software Engineering and Knowledge Engineering, no. 4, vol. 12, pp. 391 - 414, 2002.

[8] C.P. Ruppel and S.J. Harrington, "Sharing Knowledge Through Intranets: A Study of Organizational Culture and Intranet Implementation," IEEE Transactions on Professional Communication, no. 1, vol. 44, pp. 37 - 52, 2001.

[9] R.L. Ruggles, "Knowledge Management Tools," in Resources for the Knowledge-Based Economy. Boston: Butterworth-Heinemann, 1997.

[10] A. Sørlie, G.J. Coll, E. Dehli, and K. Tangen, "Knowledge Sharing in Distributed Organizations," IJCAI Workshop on Knowledge Management and Organizational Memories, Stockholm, Sweden, 1999.

[11] U.M. Borghoff and R. Pareschi, Information Technology for Knowledge Management. Berlin: Springer Verlag, 1998, ISBN 3 540 63764 8.

[12] J. Liebowitz and T. Beckman, Knowledge Organizations: What Every Manager Should Know. Boca Raion, FL: CRC Press, 1998,

[13] G. Van Heijst, R. Van Der Spek, and E. Kruizinga, "Corporate Memories as a Tool for Knowledge Management," Expert Systems with Applications, no. 1, vol. 13, pp. 41 - 54, 1997.

[14] T.H. Davenport and L. Prusak, Working Knowledge: How Organizations Manage What They Know: Harvard Business School Press, 1998, ISBN 0-87584-655-6.

[15] S. Henniger, "Case-Based Knowledge Management Tools in Software Development," Automated Software Engineering, no. 3, vol. 4, pp. 319-339, 1997.

[16] D. Skuce, "Knowledge management in software design : a tool and a trial," Software Engineering Journal, no. 5, vol. 10, pp. 183-193, 1995.

[17] B. Decker and A. Jedlitschka, "The Integrated Corporate Information Network. iCoIN. A Comprehensive, Web-Based Experience Factory," Proceedings of the Learning Software Organizations Workshop, Kaiserslautern, Germany, 2001.

[18] M. Markkula, "Knowledge Management in Software Engineering Projects," Proceedings of the International conference on Software Engineering and Knowledge Engineering, SEKE'99, Kaiserslautern, Germany, 1999.

[19] R.S. Taylor, "Information Use Environments," Progress in Communication Science, 1991.

[20] D.M. Fetterman, Ethnography: Step by Step, vol. 17: Sage Publications, 1998, ISBN 0-7619-1384-X.

[21] A. Strauss and J. Corbin, Basics of Qualitative Research: Second edition: Sage Publications, 1998, ISBN 0-8039-5939-7.

[22] G. Roth and A. Kleiner, Car Launch: THe human side of managing change. New York: Oxford University press, 1999,

[23] T. Dingsøyr, "Knowledge Management in Medium-Sized Software Consulting Companies," doctoral thesis, Department of Computer and Information Science, Norwegian University of Science and Technology, Trondheim, 2002, pp. 206, ISBN 82-7477-107-9.

[24] T. Dingsøyr and E. Røyrvik, "Skills Management as Knowledge Technology in a Software Consultancy Company," in Proceedings of the Learning Software Organizations Workshop, Lecture Notes in Computer Science, vol. 2176, K.-D. Althoff, R. L. Feldmann, and W. Müller, Eds. Kaiserslautern, Germany: Springer Verlag, 2001, pp. 96-107.

[25] E. Røyrvik and E. Wulff, "Mythmaking and Knowledge Sharing. Living organizational myths and the broadening of opportunity structures for knowledge sharing in a Scandinavian engineering consultant company," Journal of Innovation and Creativity Management, no. 3, vol. 11, 2002.

End-User Software Engineering with Assertions in the Spreadsheet Paradigm

Margaret Burnett, Curtis Cook, Omkar Pendse, Gregg Rothermel, Jay Summet, Chris Wallace
Oregon State University, Corvallis, Oregon, 97331 USA
{burnett, cook, pendse, grother, summet, wallacch}@cs.orst.edu

Abstract

There has been little research on end-user program development beyond the activity of programming. Devising ways to address additional activities related to end-user program development may be critical, however, because research shows that a large proportion of the programs written by end users contain faults. Toward this end, we have been working on ways to provide formal "software engineering" methodologies to end-user programmers. This paper describes an approach we have developed for supporting assertions in end-user software, focusing on the spreadsheet paradigm. We also report the results of a controlled experiment, with 59 end-user subjects, to investigate the usefulness of this approach. Our results show that the end users were able to use the assertions to reason about their spreadsheets, and that doing so was tied to both greater correctness and greater efficiency.

1. Introduction

End-user programming has become a widespread phenomenon. For example, end users create and modify spreadsheets, they author web pages with links and complex formatting specifications, and they create macros and scripts. Although some of these programs are small, one-shot calculations, many are much more serious, affecting significant financial decisions and business transactions. Two recent NSF workshops have determined that end-user programming is in need of serious attention [5]. The reasons are compelling. The number of end-user programmers in the U.S. alone is expected to reach 55 million by 2005, as compared to only 2.75 million professional programmers [5]. Further, evidence abounds of the pervasiveness of errors in the software that end users create [20], with significant economic impact. In one single example, a Texas oil and gas firm lost millions of dollars through spreadsheet errors [19].

To address this problem, we have been researching methods for helping end users create more reliable software. Our approach brings aspects of theoretically sound methodologies, explored previously within the professional software engineering community, into the environments end users use to create software. We term the concept "end-user software engineering"; however, we do not claim or attempt to turn end users into software engineers or ask them learn traditional software engineering methodologies. Instead, the methodologies we employ aim to be not only accessible, but also verifiably productive for end users with little or no formal training in software engineering.

Assertions in the form of preconditions, postconditions, and invariants provide professional programmers with increased ability to maintain and debug software. Assertions provide attractive opportunities for adding rigor to end-user programming for two reasons. First, the use of assertions does not demand an "all or nothing" approach; it is possible to enter one or two assertions and gain some value, without committing to entering a purportedly complete set of assertions. Second, assertions provide a way to make explicit a user's mental model underlying a program, essentially, integrating "specifications" with that program. Such specifications, integrated into end-user programs, could tap into a host of opportunities for harnessing other software engineering methodologies, such as test suite improvement, specification-based test generation, automated test oracle generation, or proofs of program properties.

We have developed an approach for supporting assertions as a critical underpinning of our end-user software engineering work. We have prototyped our approach in the spreadsheet paradigm. Our assertions provide pre- and postcondition Boolean expressions about the results of cell formula execution. The approach supports a variety of relations, as well as composition via logical "and" and "or," in two concrete syntaxes. It is our hope that assertions will enable the user to identify and correct faulty formulas.

In this paper, we first present our approach to integrating assertions into an environment whose goal is to support end user software engineering. We then use this environment to empirically explore the fundamental issues of whether end users can use assertions in the context of an end-user software engineering task, and whether and how their doing so improves the correctness of their programs.

2. Assertions for end users

When creating a spreadsheet, the user has a mental model of how it should operate. One approximation of this model is the formulas they enter, but unfortunately these formulas may contain inconsistencies or faults. These for-

0-7695-1877-X/03 $17.00 © 2003 IEEE

mulas, however, are only one representation of the user's model of the problem and its solution: they contain information on how to generate the desired result, but do not provide ways for the user to communicate other properties. Traditionally, assertions in the form of preconditions, postconditions, and invariants have fulfilled this need for professional programmers, providing a method for making explicit the properties the programmers expect of their program logic, to reason about the integrity of their logic, and to catch exceptions. Our approach attempts to provide these same advantages to end-user programmers.

For professional software developers, the only widely used language that natively supports assertions is Eiffel [15]. To allow programs in other languages to share at least some of the benefits of assertions, methods to add support for assertions to languages such as C, C++ and Awk have been developed (e.g., [2, 29]). Applications of such assertions to software engineering problems have proven promising. For example, there has been research on deriving runtime consistency checks for Ada programs [23, 25]. Rosenblum has shown that these assertions can be effective at detecting runtime errors [22]. However, traditional approaches that employ assertions are aimed at professional programmers, and are not geared toward end users.

2.1 An abstract syntax

As in the above approaches, our assertions are composed of Boolean expressions, and reason about program variables' values (spreadsheet cell values, in the spreadsheet paradigm). Assertions are "owned" by a spreadsheet cell. Cell X's assertion is the postcondition of X's formula. X's postconditions are also preconditions to the formulas of all other cells that reference X in their formulas, either directly or transitively through a network of references.

To illustrate the amount of power we have chosen to support with our assertions, we present them first via an abstract syntax. An *assertion* on cell N is of the form:

(N, {*and-assertions*}), where:
each *and-assertion* is a set of *or-assertions*,
each *or-assertion* is a set of (*unary-relation*, *value-expression*) and (*binary-relation*, *value-expression-pair*) tuples,
each *unary-relation* ∈ {=, <, <=, >, >=},
each *binary-relation* ∈ {to-closed, to-open, to-openleft, to-openright},
each *value-expression* is a valid formula expression in the spreadsheet language,
each *value-expression-pair* is two *value-expressions*.

For example, an assertion denoted using this syntax as (N, {{(to-closed, 10, 20), (= 3)}, {= X2}}) means that N must either be between 10 and 20 or equal to 3; and must also equal the value of cell X2.

This abstract syntax is powerful enough to support a large subset of traditional assertions that reason about values of program variables. We also plan to eventually support inequality ($\neq$) as a unary relation. This operator would be solely for convenience; it would not add power given the relations already present, since $\neq$ can be expressed as an or-assertion composing < with >. This abstract syntax follows CNF (Conjunctive Normal Form): each cell's collection of and-assertions, which in turn compose or-assertions, is intended to evaluate to true, and hence a spreadsheet's assertion is simply an "and" composition of all cells' assertions.

2.2 Concrete syntaxes for end users

The abstract syntax just presented is not likely to be useful to end users. Thus, we have developed two concrete syntaxes corresponding to it: one primarily graphical and one textual. The user can work in either or both as desired.

The graphical concrete syntax, depicted in Figure 1, supports all of the abstract syntax (but in the current prototype implementation, value-expressions have been implemented for only constants). The example is a representation of (output_temp, {{(to-closed, 0, 100)}, {(to-closed, 3.5556, 23.5556)}}). A thick dot is a data point in an ordinal domain; it implements "=". The thick horizontal lines are ranges in the domain, implementing "to-closed" when connected to dots. A range with no lower (upper) bound implements "<=" (">="). It is also possible to halve a dot, which changes from closed ranges to open ranges, "<=" to "<", and so on. Disconnected points and ranges represent the or-assertions. Multiple assertions vertically in the same window represent the and-assertions.

The textual concrete syntax, depicted in Figure 2, is more compact, and supports the same operators as the graphical syntax. Or-assertions are represented with comma separators on the same line (not shown), while and-assertions are represented as assertions stacked up on the

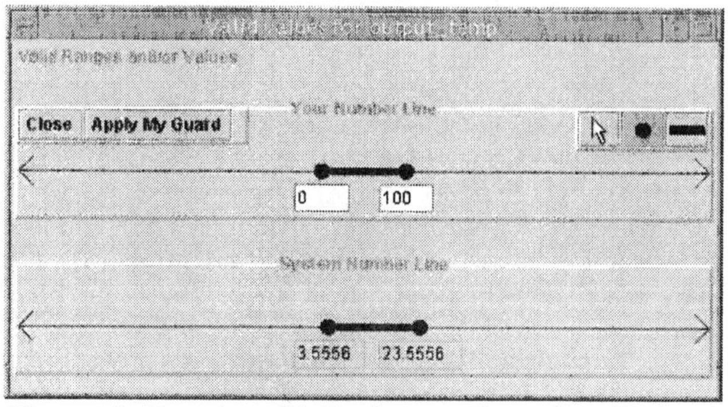

Figure 1: Two (conflicting) assertions "and"ed on the same cell.

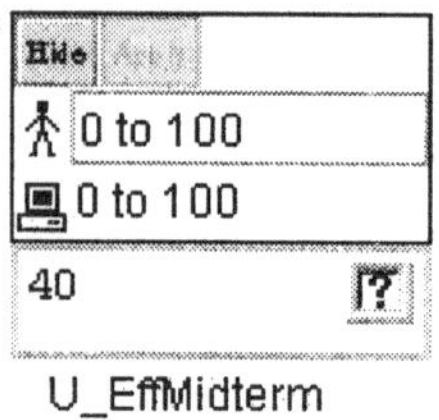

Figure 2: Two assertions in the textual syntax.

same cell, as in Figure 2. There is also an "except" modifier that supports the "open" versions of "to" (e.g., 0 to 10 except 10).

Our system does not use the term "assertion" in communicating with users. Instead, assertions are termed *guards*, so named because they guard the correctness of the cells. The user opens the guard tab above a cell to display the assertion using the textual syntax, or double-clicks the tab to open the graphical window. Although both syntaxes represent assertions as points and ranges, note that points and ranges, with the composition mechanisms just described, are enough to express the entire abstract syntax.

Note that although "and" and "or" are represented, they are not explicit operators in the syntaxes. This is a deliberate choice, and is due to Pane et al.'s research, which showed that end users are not successful at using "and" and "or" explicitly as logical operators [18].

The textual concrete syntax we present here bears some resemblance to recent work on English-like notations for formal specifications. Although assertions and other forms of specification such as property patterns [9] are usually presented using rigorous mathematical notations or finite state automata, there is work on expressing specifications in more accessible notations (e.g., [16, 26]). For example, Propel [26] is a multiple-view approach to properties that includes an English-like representation.

A central difference between that work and ours is that their properties and English-like syntax emphasize sequence. Our assertions have no temporal operators and cannot express sequence. This is appropriate because reasoning about sequence is not a programmer responsibility in declarative paradigms that focus on data definition, such as the spreadsheet paradigm, in which sequence is automatically derived from data dependencies.

2.3 Assertion sources' potential impact

We currently support two sources of assertions. *User assertions* are assertions that the user enters explicitly, one of which appears in Figure 2 next to the stick figure. *System-generated* assertions are assertions resulting from propagating assertions through formulas in the direction of dataflow (using straightforward logic and interval arithmetic), one of which appears in the figure next to the computer icon. (Details of propagation are described in [27].)

Other researchers have developed methods for generating program assertions without requiring programmer input as a source. Daikon [10] generates invariant assertions by extensive examination of a program's behavior over a large test suite. DIDUCE [12] deduces invariant assertions and uses them to check program correctness. DIDUCE has a training phase, in which it considers all behaviors correct and relaxes invariants to encompass them, and then a checking phase, which reports violations to the invariants inferred in the training phase. Raz et al.'s approach to semantic anomaly detection [21] uses off-the-shelf unsupervised learning and statistical techniques, including a variant of Daikon, to infer invariants about incoming data arriving from online data feeds, and their empirical work shows effectiveness. Recent work that can be described as inferring assertions related to correctness of end-user programs involves automatic detection of errors through outlier analysis [17]. This approach is similar in principle to that of Raz et al., but has been developed in the domain of programming-by-demonstration for text processing.

An advantage of these researchers' inferential approaches is that they can relieve the programmer of having to conjure up and explicitly insert assertions. A disadvantage is that these inferences must be "guessed," and some of the guesses can be incorrect. The impact of incorrect guesses on end users' trust and willingness to work with assertions is an issue that requires exploration.

Because of multiple sources of assertions (currently two, potentially more), our approach provides the following three ways for assertions to potentially help users detect faults: (1) there might be multiple assertions on the cell that do not agree, termed an *assertion conflict*, (2) the cell's value might not satisfy the cell's assertion(s), termed a *value violation*, or (3) a system-generated assertion might "look wrong" to the user. When any of these events occur, there may be either a fault in the program (spreadsheet formulas) or an error in the assertions.

2.4 Assertions in an end-user environment

An important difference between our approach to assertions and more traditional approaches is that ours is a component of an integrated set of software engineering features designed particularly for end users. It is not a separate tool, and a user need not use it in an "all or nothing" manner. Instead, the user might enter a few assertions, immediately see their effects on the formulas entered so far, and then apply other forms of validation on other formulas. Feedback about assertions is integrated with the variables (cells) to which they apply. For example, the assertions about cell U_EffMidterm appear at the top of that cell, as already shown in Figure 2. If the two assertions about cell U_EffMidterm were in conflict, their icons would be circled in red. If the cell's value did not satisfy its assertions, the value would be circled.

Microsoft Excel, a popular commercial spreadsheet application, has a data validation feature integrated into the environment that bears a surface-level similarity to the assertions in our environment. Excel, however, does not support propagation of assertions to other cells, does not automatically display assertions, and does not automatically update the display of assertion violations when changes are made. That is, the data validation feature is primarily an optional data entry check that can be invoked from time to time by the user. This is quite different from our approach, because our assertions combine into a network that is the basis of an ever-present reasoning system that gives continuous and up-to-date visual feedback.

In addition to the integration of assertion feedback with the program source code (formulas) and values, in our prototype environment there is also testing feedback integrated in the same fine-grained way via our already incorporated spreadsheet testing methodology known as WYSIWYT ("What You See is What You Test") [11, 24]. WYSIWYT implements a dataflow test adequacy criterion based on definition-use (du) associations, which associate formula subexpressions that define a cell's value (definitions) with references to the cell in other cells' formulas (uses); see [24] for formal definitions. The criterion for complete "testedness" under this methodology is that each executable du-association in the spreadsheet be exercised by test data in such a way that the du-association contributes (directly or indirectly) to the display of a value that is subsequently pronounced correct by the user. Users can convey to the system that a cell's value is correct for the spreadsheet's inputs by checking the checkbox in the corner of the cell. This results in a change of cell border color, which represents the testedness of a cell. Red means untested, purple shades mean partially tested, and blue means fully tested. There is also a "percent tested" indicator at the top of the spreadsheet. These devices are always kept up-to-date. For example, when a formula is modified, the cell border turns red because the cell is untested; borders of cells that reference the modified cell also turn red. Because a principle of our end-user software engineering approach is that assertions be integrated with testing support, the investigation of assertions in this paper is in the context of WYSIWYT.

2.5 Example

We close this section by presenting a simple illustration of our prototype assertion mechanism in the context of the Forms/3 research spreadsheet language [6]. Figure 3(a) shows a portion of a Forms/3 spreadsheet that converts temperatures in degrees Fahrenheit to degrees Celsius. The input_temp cell has a constant value of 200 in its formula and is displaying the same value. There is a user assertion on this cell that limits the value of the cell to between 32 and 212. The formulas of the a, b, and output_temp cells each perform one step in the conversion, first subtracting 32 from the original value, then multiplying by five and finally dividing by nine. The a and b cells have assertions generated by the system (as indicated by the computer icon) which reflect the propagation of the user assertion on the input_temp cell through their formulas. The spreadsheet's creator has told the system that the output_temp cell should range from 0 to 100, and the system has agreed with this range. This agreement was determined by propagating the user assertion on the input_temp cell through the formulas and comparing it with the user assertion on the output_temp cell.

Suppose a user has decided to change the direction of the conversion and make it convert from degrees Celsius to degrees Fahrenheit. A summary follows of the behavior shown by an end user in this situation in a study we conducted early in our design of the approach [28]. The quotes are from a recording of the subject's commentary.

First, the user changed the assertion on input_temp to range from 0 to 100. This caused several red violation ovals to appear, as in Figure 3(b), because the values in input_temp, a, b, and output_temp were now out of range and the assertion on output_temp was now in conflict with the previously specified assertion for that cell. The user decided "that's OK for now," and changed the value in

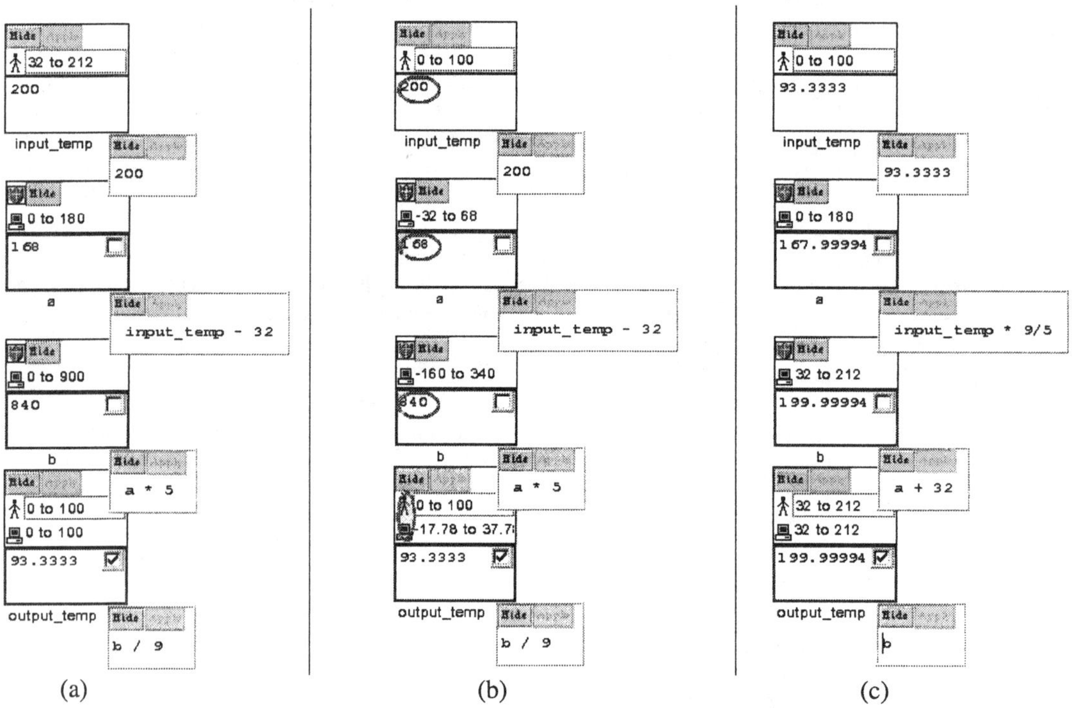

Figure 3: Example at three points in the modification task.

input_temp from 200 to 75 ("something between zero and 100"), and then set the formula in cell a to "input_temp * 9/5" and the formula in cell b to "a + 32".

At this point, the assertion on cell b had a range from 32 to 212. Because the user combined two computation steps in cell a's formula (multiplication and division), the correct value appeared in cell b, but not in output_temp (which still had the formula "b / 9"). The user now chose to deal with the assertion conflict on output_temp, and clicked on the guard icon to view the details in the graphical syntax.

Seeing that the Forms/3 assertion specified 3.5556 to 23.556, the user stated "There's got to be something wrong with the formula" and edited output_temp's formula, making it a reference to cell b. This resulted in the value of output_temp being correct, although a conflict still existed because the previous user assertion remained at 0 to 100. Turning to the graphical syntax window, upon seeing that Forms/3's assertion was the expected 32 to 212, the user changed the user assertion to agree, which removed the final conflict. Finally, the user tested by trying 93.3333, the original output value, to see if it resulted in approximately 200, the original input value. The results were as desired, and the user checked off the cell to notify the system of the decision that the value was correct, as in Figure 3(c).

3. Experiment

Our initial think-aloud study provided early insights into five end users' use and understanding of assertions, but did not statistically evaluate effectiveness. Thus, to investigate empirically whether and how this approach to assertions would increase users' effectiveness at eliminating faults, we conducted a controlled experiment involving 59 subjects to investigate the following research questions:

Will assertions users be more effective debuggers?
Will users understand assertions?
Will assertions help users judge the correctness of their programs (spreadsheets)?

We decided to isolate as much as possible the assertion effects (dependent) variables from that of user choice (whether or not to use assertions), which is also a dependent variable. The effectiveness results could have been confounded if we also required subjects to choose to master assertion entry. By largely eliminating user choice from *this* experiment as a factor, we gained high assurance that assertions would be present in the tasks, which is what enabled us to measure effectiveness and other effects of assertions. In a separate experiment reported elsewhere [31], we investigated user choice to use assertions, which we discuss briefly in Section 5.

3.1 Procedures

The experiment was conducted in a Windows computer lab. The subjects were seated one per computer. Prior to running the experiment, we conducted a four-subject pilot study to test the experimental procedures and materials.

At the beginning of the experiment, the subjects filled out a background questionnaire. The session continued with a 35-minute tutorial to familiarize subjects with the environment, in which they worked on two spreadsheets along with the instructor. Subjects worked in identical end-user software engineering environments, except that the Treatment group (two sessions) had the assertions feature in their environment whereas the Control group (two sessions) did not. To reduce memorization skills as a factor, a quick-reference sheet listing the environment's features was provided to the subjects. The sheet remained with them throughout the experiment, and they were allowed to take notes on it. To ensure that both groups had equal time familiarizing themselves with their environments, we balanced the time spent presenting assertions to the Treatment group by providing additional hands-on practice time to the Control group.

After the tutorial, subjects began their experimental tasks of debugging a grades spreadsheet (20 minutes) and a payroll spreadsheet (15 minutes). The use of two spreadsheets reduced the chances of obscuring the results because of any one spreadsheet's particular characteristics. The tasks necessarily involved time limits, to make sure subjects would work on both spreadsheets, and to remove possible peer influence of some subjects leaving early. The time limits were drawn from times we observed to be required by the pilot study's subjects. The experiment was counterbalanced with respect to problem to prevent learning effects from affecting the results: all subjects worked both problems, but half of each group debugged the problems in the opposite order.

Initially, no assertions were on display for either problem. The Treatment subjects' scenario was that a previous user had devised assertions for some of the cells, which subjects could use by clicking that cell's "see user guard" button. Clicking this button had the same effect as if a helpful user had immediately typed in a user assertion for that cell, but eliminated users having to learn how to enter assertions, or choosing to go to that much trouble. We decided on this procedure instead of having the assertions already present, because the approach is for an interactive environment, in which assertions are likely to be entered and dealt with incrementally. Other than the button, no other assertion editing devices were available. Once an assertion had been entered via the button, it was propagated and displayed as described in Section 2.

At the end of each task, subjects were given a post-task questionnaire which included questions assessing their comprehension and attitudes about the features they had used, and also questions in which they self-rated their performance. Besides the questionnaire responses, data included the subjects' actions, which were electronically captured in transcript files, and their final spreadsheets.

3.2 Subjects

The subjects were non-computer science students who had little or no programming experience. The 59 subjects were randomly divided into two groups: 30 in the Treatment group and 29 in the Control group. Of the 59 subjects, 23 were business students, 22 came from a wide range of sciences (such as psychology, biology, geography, pharmacy, and animal science), and the remaining 14 came from a variety of other non-computer science majors. The average (self-reported) GPA of the Control group was lower than that of the Treatment group but there was no statistically significant difference. Roughly 60% of the subjects had a little programming experience, due to the fact that it is common these days for business and science students to take a high school or college class in programming. Statistical tests on subject data showed no significant differences between the Treatment group and Control group in any of these attributes.

3.3 Problems

The debugging problems were Grades (Figure 4) and Weekly Pay (not shown due to space limitations). Subjects

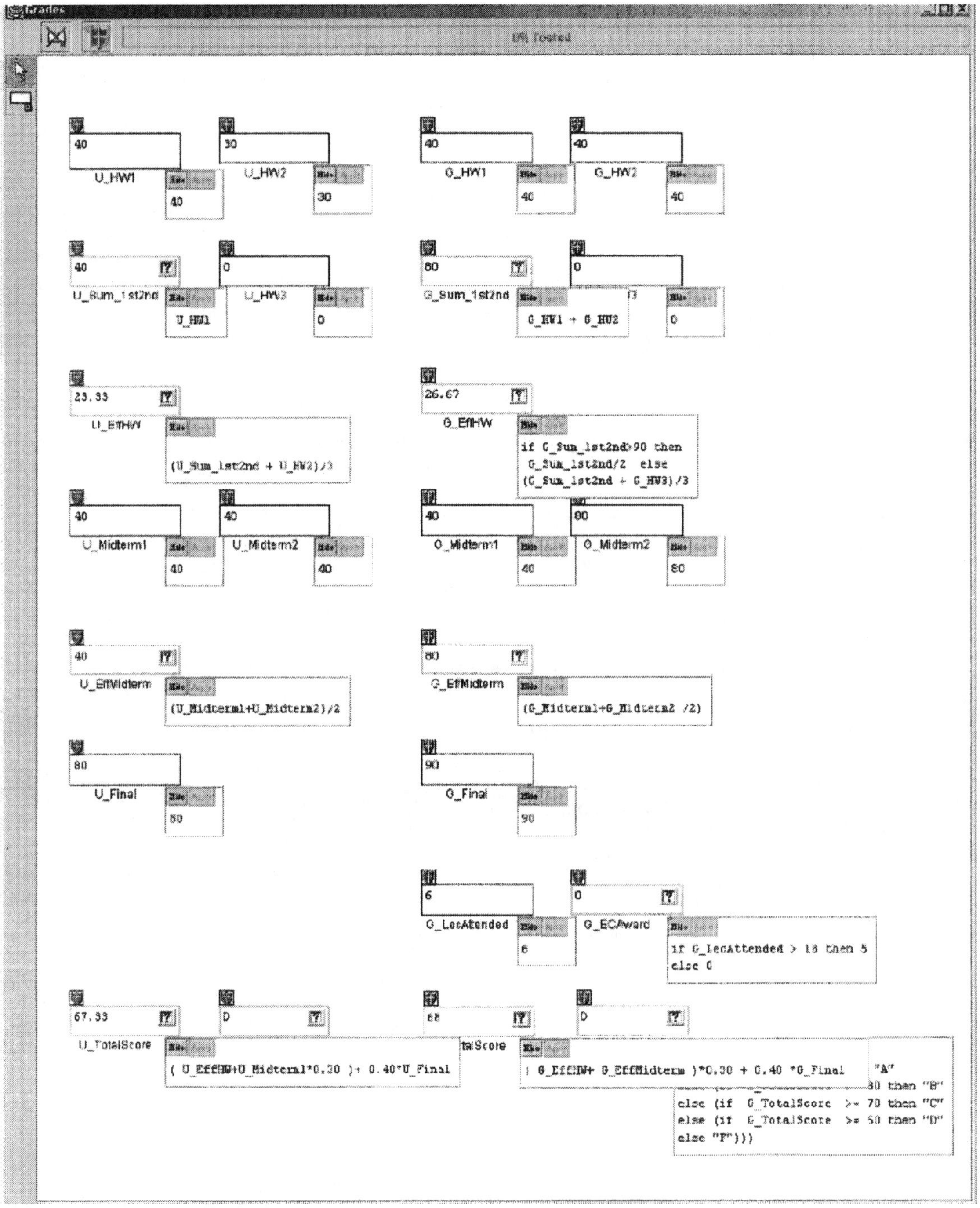

Figure 4: The Grades Spreadsheet.

were given a written description of each spreadsheet. The description explained the functionality of the spreadsheet, and included the ranges of valid values for some of the cells, so that all subjects would have exactly the same information about the spreadsheets, regardless of whether their environment included assertions. The subjects were instructed to "test the spreadsheet thoroughly to ensure that it does not contain errors and works according to the spreadsheet description. Also if you encounter any errors in the spreadsheet, fix them."

The Grades spreadsheet (24 cells) calculates the grades of two students, one graduate and the other undergraduate, with different grading criteria. There are 11 faults in seven cells of this spreadsheet. The Grades spreadsheet was laid out such that it required scrolling, to ensure that *not* all assertions and assertion conflicts would necessarily be visible at any one time. The Weekly Pay spreadsheet (19 cells) calculates the weekly pay and income tax withholding of a salesperson. There are seven faults in five cells of this spreadsheet.

To facilitate comparing the impact of assertions with whatever other mechanisms subjects might use to identify and correct faults, we devised assertions that would expose only some of the faults. To avoid biasing results against the Control group, we included assertions only for cells whose ranges were explicitly stated on the problem description. In choosing which ranges to state, we included all ranges that could be clearly justified without a calculator. Via the button, all Grades cells had user assertions available, which could expose only 8 of the 11 faults. For Weekly Pay, user assertions able to expose 3 of the 7 faults were available.

3.4 Fault types

Allwood [1] classified faults in spreadsheets as mechanical, logical and omission faults, and this scheme is also used in Panko's work [20]. Under Allwood's categorization, mechanical faults were further classified as simple typographical errors or wrong cell references in the cell formulas. Mistakes in reasoning were classified as logical faults. Logical faults in spreadsheets are more difficult than mechanical faults to detect and correct, and omission faults are the most difficult [1]. An omission fault is information that has never been entered into the formulas.

We drew from this research by including faults from each category in each problem. However, the precise distinctions between logical and mechanical are not clear for some types of faults in end-user programming. For example, when computing an average, does dividing by the wrong number mean the subject typed it wrong, or that they are confused about computing averages? In our think-aloud studies we have collected data in which end-user subjects made exactly this error for both of these reasons. Thus, we combined the first two categories into one and then, to be sure coverage of both would be achieved, included several different subtypes under it: incorrect references (which Allwood would classify as mechanical), incorrect constants or an omitted character (could be either logical or mechanical), incorrect operators or application of operators (which Allwood would classify as logical), and an extra subexpression (logical). We also included faults from the third category, omission faults. Table 1 shows a summary of the spreadsheets' faults.

Table 1: Classifications of seeded faults.

	Omission	Logical and Mechanical			
		Ref.	Const. or char.	Oper-ator	Extra subexpr
Grades	2	2	3	3	1
Weekly Pay	1	2	2	2	0

Another classification scheme we have found to be useful in our previous research involves two fault types: reference faults, which are faults of incorrect or missing references, and non-reference faults, which are all other faults. In this study, the omissions and incorrect references are reference faults (7 in total), and the remaining types are non-reference faults (11 in total).

The faults not exposed by assertions were distributed across Table 1's categories, and were also assigned in proportion to the reference/ non-reference categorization.

4. Results

4.1 Debugging effectiveness

4.1.1 Accuracy by subject group. We chose to analyze the act of identifying a fault separately from the act of correcting it. The reason was that there is little information in the literature about end users' abilities to correct a fault even if they have managed to identify it, a gap we hope to help fill. For cells containing exactly one fault, we defined a fault to have been *identified* if the subject changed the formula containing the fault and to have been *corrected* if the changes resulted in a correct formula. When a cell contained two faults, we partitioned the formula into two disjoint subexpressions, one containing each fault. Then if the particular fault's subexpression was changed (or changed correctly), the fault was defined to be identified (or corrected). For example, in cell U_EffHW the original formula in the cell is (U_Sum1st2nd+U_HW2)/3, and the correct formula is (U_Sum1st2nd+U_HW3)/2. The two faults are adding U_HW2 instead of U_HW3 and dividing by 3 instead of 2. The two parts to the formula are the sum and the division. Hence a subject would be credited with identifying (correcting) the fault in the sum if the sum subexpression was changed (changed correctly) and credited with identifying (correcting) the fault in the division if the divisor was changed (changed correctly).

We now state the following (null) hypotheses as statistical vehicles for investigating the accuracy question:

H1: Identify: There will be no difference between the Treatment group's and Control group's number of faults identified.

H2: Correctness: There will be no difference between the Treatment group's and Control group's number of faults corrected.

The faults identified and corrected are summarized in Table 2. A two-factor analysis of variance with repeated measures on the problem (Grades and Weekly Pay) and group (Control and Treatment) showed that the Treatment subjects both identified significantly more faults (F=16.59, df=1, p=.0001) and corrected significantly more faults (F=11.74, df=1, p=.0011) than did the Control subjects. Thus, hypotheses H1 and H2 must both be rejected.

Both the Treatment and Control subjects corrected nearly equal percentages of the faults they identified (Table 3). That is, when they found the faults, they generally succeeded at correcting them. In fact, in the Grades problem the percents corrected once identified were exactly the same for subjects with assertions as for those without assertions, and the difference was very small in the Weekly Pay problem. This suggests that the assertion advantages in *identifying* faults were enough to produce the eventual advantages in correcting them.

4.1.2 Accuracy by fault type. Did assertions especially help with any particular type of faults? Fisher's Exact Test showed that the Treatment group identified significantly more instances on seven of the 18 faults, but they were not all of the same type. In fact, these faults covered four of the five types of faults we seeded (recall Table 1): three were operator or operator application faults, two were incorrect constants, one was an omission, and one was an incorrect reference. Thus, according to Allwood's classification scheme, assertions contributed to effectiveness across a wide range of faults.

Considering instead the reference/non-reference classification of faults reveals an interesting attribute of assertions' effectiveness: subjects in the Treatment group were significantly more effective at identifying and correcting non-reference faults in both problems (Grades corrected: F=9.67, df=1, p=.0029; Weekly Pay corrected: F=8.26, df=1, p=.0057). There was also significance for reference faults on one of the problems (Grades corrected: F=4.67, df=1, p=.0348; Weekly Pay corrected: F=3.72, df=1, p=.0506). In contrast to this, previous empirical work regarding the effectiveness of the WYSIWYT testing methodology (which is based on a dataflow adequacy criterion) on detecting faults has revealed that WYSIWYT's advantage has been primarily in identifying and correcting reference faults [7].

Table 2: Mean number of faults identified and corrected.

	Identified	Corrected
Grades (11 faults)		
Control	5.69	4.83
Treatment	8.07	6.83
Weekly Pay (7 faults)		
Control	4.97	4.59
Treatment	5.90	5.70

Table 3: Percent of identified faults that were eventually corrected.

	Grades	Weekly Pay
Control (n=29)	84.8%	92.4%
Treatment (n=30)	84.8%	96.6%

Since both groups' subjects had WYSIWYT available to them, which is strong on reference faults, it is not surprising that the reference fault improvement brought by assertions was significant on only one problem. The more interesting result is that assertions helped so significantly with non-reference faults, suggesting that the addition of assertions into the environment fills a need not met effectively by the dataflow testing methodology alone.

4.1.3 Debugging speed

H3: Speed: There will be no difference between the Treatment group's and Control group's speed in correcting the faults.

We partitioned the task time into 5-minute blocks—the first 5 minutes, second 5 minutes, and so on—and counted the number of faults that had been corrected by the end of each partition. Since subjects had more time on Grades than on Weekly Pay, there are four partitions for Grades and three for Weekly Pay. As Figure 5 shows, the Treatment subjects identified and corrected faults faster in each of the 5-minute blocks. The Treatment subjects' advantage began very early. The correctness differences were significant for the Weekly Pay problem at the 5-minute mark (identified F=3.70, df=1, p=.0595; corrected F=4.19, df=1, p=.0453), and the subjects were significantly more effective at identifying and correcting faults during the first 5 minutes for the Grades problem (identified F=13.04, df=1, p=.0006; corrected F=15.67, df=1, p=.0002). Thus, H3 is rejected.

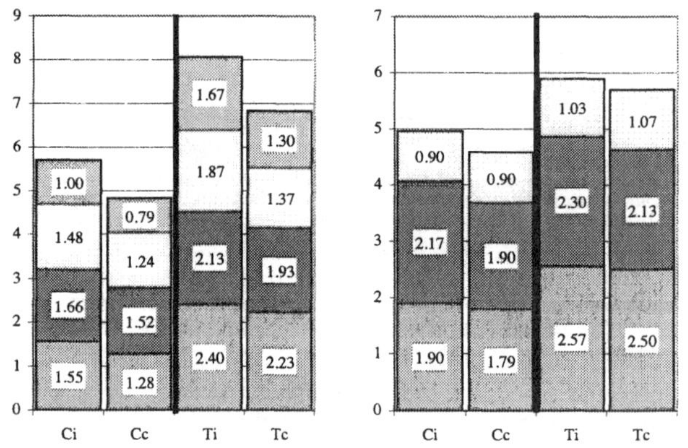

Figure 5: Average faults identified by each group (Ci, Ti) and corrected (Cc, Tc). Each block covers 5 minutes (first 5-minute period at the bottom, etc.), and the data value in it is the number of faults identified/corrected during that time period. Left graph: Grades. Right graph: Weekly Pay.

4.2 Did the users understand assertions?

Assertions had significant positive impacts on subjects' abilities to remove the faults, but to what extent did they understand what the assertions meant? At least some understanding is important, because research in on-line trust has shown that users must believe they understand the system's reasoning, at least roughly, in order to trust its results enough to use them effectively [4, 8].

To help assess the subjects' understanding, we asked several questions about the meanings of the different devices in the context of a two-cell example spreadsheet. The results, which are summarized in Table 4, imply that the Treatment subjects understood the meaning of the assertion features reasonably well. The first four questions were multiple choice. The last question, in which the subjects were required to fill in the result of propagating cellA's assertion (0 to 5) through cellB's formula (cellA + 10), was the most difficult for them, but 53% answered it correctly (10 to 15). An additional 23% answered "0 to 15." The fact that this additional 23% were correct on the upper limit seems to indicate that they had a rough, but imperfect, idea of how propagation worked.

One strong indicator that the subjects believed their understanding was "good enough" for reliance upon assertions can be found in their ratings. Subjects rated the helpfulness of three assertion features and also two testing features. Treatment subjects rated the assertion conflicts the most helpful of all the features. On a scale of 1 to 5 (not helpful to very helpful), their ratings for the assertion conflicts averaged 4.4 (median 5). See Table 5.

Table 4: Percentage of correct responses given by Treatment subjects. (Correct responses are shown in parentheses.)

Question	% correct
What does the red oval on cellA mean? (The value is outside the valid range.)	93%
What does the little stick figure in the cellA guard mean? (The user supplied the guard.)	83%
Why is there a stick figure and a computer on cellB's guard? (The guard was supplied by both Forms/3 and by the user.)	87%
What does the red oval on the cellB guard mean? (The user and Forms/3 disagree on the valid range(s) for this cell.)	63%
Given the formula in cellB and the guard on cellA, what do you think Forms/3 says are the valid range(s) for cellB? (10 to 15)	53%

Table 5: Subjects' helpfulness ratings.

	Assertion conflicts	"Tested" border colors	System-generated assertions	User assertions	% tested
Control	N/A	4.2	N/A	N/A	2.9
Treatment	4.4	4.3	4.2	4.0	3.6

4.3 Judging correctness

After the subjects had completed the experimental tasks, we asked them to what extent they believed they had managed to identify and to correct all the faults. In the practice of software development, it is often this question that the developer uses to decide whether the software is ready to use. For this reason, helping users make reasonable judgments in answer to this question can be important in preventing software from going into use prematurely.

The questionnaire asked them to rate on a 1 ("not confident") to 5 ("very confident") scale, for each problem, how confident they were that they had identified and corrected all the faults. The issue relevant to the effectiveness of assertions is to what extent these self-ratings were correlated with correctness. To this end, we compared self-ratings to actual performance.

H4: Self ratings of correctness: There will be no difference between Control versus Treatment subjects' self-ratings as predictors of correctness (number of faults in the spreadsheets at the end of the experiment).

Regression analysis is the appropriate test for a predictive question of this type. The results for correcting the faults are shown in Table 6; the results for identifying the faults (not shown) are similar. The regression coefficient is the slope of the least squares fitting of the ratings against the faults that were corrected. As the table shows, the Treatment group gave self-ratings that were statistically significant predictors of actual performance, with regression coefficients that were significantly different from zero for both problems. (This was true also for identifying the faults.) The Control group's self-ratings, on the other hand, were ineffective as predictors, and their regression coefficients were not significantly different from zero. In fact, for one problem, the regression coefficient is slightly negative, indicating that the Control group's predictions had a slight tendency to be the *opposite* of their actual performance. Clearly, H4 is rejected.

This result is important. It is a well known and robust result from behavioral science that humans are overconfident about the work they do, and that this tendency is extremely resilient. In the spreadsheet literature this tendency has become known as overconfidence. Such overconfidence has been widely reported in many spreadsheet studies (surveyed in [20]), in the Forms/3 environment [30], and in studies of software professionals [14].

Table 6: Self-ratings as correctness predictors.

	Regression coeff.	t	df	Significance
Grades				
Control	0.168	1.434	27	p = .1645
Treatment	0.210	2.188	28	p = .0375
Weekly Pay				
Control	-0.038	-0.261	27	p = .7963
Treatment	0.477	2.165	28	p = .0394

Although overconfidence of spreadsheet accuracy has previously been reduced to some extent by the WYSIWYT testing methodology, the reductions have not been sufficient to correlate in a statistically significant way with accuracy [13]. The improved level of judgment associated with assertions thus fills a gap in end-user programming, which could prevent some of their software from going into production use too early.

5. Motivating users to enter assertions

We have explained that we designed our experiment to isolate effectiveness of assertions when they were present, and thus while subjects had a choice as to whether and which assertions were present, they did not have to actually enter them.

To address the issue of motivating users to author their own assertions, in parallel with this experiment we began devising an approach for gently inviting end users to enter and use assertions. Our approach attempts to first arouse users' curiosity and then to encourage them to follow through, using a strategy comprised of an intertwined collection of surprises, explanations, and rewards. If the users become curious about assertions, they can obtain on-line explanations about how to go about entering assertions. The details of this strategy and how we have prototyped it are given in [31].

Using this strategy, in a follow-up experiment, we focused specifically on the question of whether users will author their own assertions via the concrete syntaxes of Section 2. In the follow-up experiment, assertions were not explained or even mentioned in the tutorial. Even more important, no pre-written assertions were provided to them. Instead, the tutorial instructed users to explore the environment in any way they wished, and gave them time to practice doing so. The follow-up experiment is reported in [31]. To briefly summarize its results, in their work on the same problems as for the experiment reported here, 15 of the 16 subjects (94%) did choose to author their own assertions, and once they entered one they entered more, averaging 18 assertions per subject. Further, 95% of the assertions they entered were correct.

6. Threats to validity

We attempted to address threats to internal validity for this study by randomly distributing subjects among the groups and statistically checking the distribution for significant differences, by including two problems and counterbalancing them, by distributing the seeded faults among a variety of fault types, by equalizing training time, and by selecting problems from familiar domains.

As in most controlled experiments, however, threats to external validity are more difficult to address given the need to control all other factors. For example, the spreadsheets used may seem rather simple, but most subjects did not achieve 100% correctness of their formulas, indicating that the spreadsheets were not too simple for the amount of time given. Also, although the prototype and experiment included only constants as assertion operands, we do not view this as a threat to validity, because the assertions are fairly powerful even with this restriction. However, the faults we used to seed the spreadsheets may not have been representative of formula faults in real-world spreadsheets.

The fact that the experiment included explicit time limits is a threat to external validity. Explicit time limits were necessary to eliminate the internal threat of subjects stopping only because other subjects were finishing and leaving. In the real world, the amount of time available for debugging is constrained by time pressures, but explicit time limits do not ideally simulate these time pressures.

The short tutorial prior to the experiment included an informal explanation of how system-generated assertions are created through propagation, but no such explanation would be likely in the real world. We have begun to address this concern with our surprise-explain-reward strategy (Section 5), which now includes the essential information about assertions in a network of context-sensitive explanations [3, 31]. The subjects in the follow-up experiment seemed to understand assertions enough to use them effectively, but further empirical work after the explanation system is more mature is required.

The current experiment did not ask users to author their own assertions. Although the follow-up experiment addresses that issue, in neither experiment did the users write their own spreadsheets "from scratch." This approach was necessary for fair quantitative comparisons of spreadsheet errors, and it is consistent with the real-world situation in which the user inherits a spreadsheet from a co-worker. However, the results of this experiment may not generalize to spreadsheets a user creates alone.

7. Conclusion

We have presented an approach for supporting assertions in end-user software, focusing on the spreadsheet paradigm. Our assertions provide expressions about the results of cell executions—that is, postconditions on the executing cell and also preconditions to cells further downstream. Assertions can be generated by the user or the system. The concrete syntaxes by which assertions are represented look to users like simple points and ranges, but these syntaxes are sufficient to express an entire abstract assertion syntax of substantial power.

To evaluate our approach empirically, we conducted a controlled experiment with 59 end-user subjects. The most important results were:

- Assertions did indeed help end users debug more effectively and more efficiently.
- The effectiveness boost applied across a wide range of fault types. Moreover, assertions were extremely effective with non-reference faults, a class that had not been amenable to detection by our dataflow testing methodology for end users.

- Assertions clearly combated the well established tendency of end users toward overconfidence, by significantly improving their ability to judge whether they had done enough to ensure the correctness of their spreadsheets.

Perhaps the most surprising result of all is that end users not only understood assertions, they actually liked them. They rated assertion conflicts as being more helpful than any other feature, and in a follow-up experiment, if subjects discovered assertions, they chose to enter quite a few of them. The facts that they understood and liked assertions are critical outcomes because of their importance in determining whether end users will ultimately use assertions in the real world.

Acknowledgments

We thank the members of the Visual Programming Research Group at Oregon State University for their feedback and help. This work was supported in part by NSF under award ITR-0082265.

References

[1] Allwood, C. Error detection processes in statistical problem solving. *Cognitive Science* 8(4), 1984, 413-437.

[2] Auguston, M., Banerjee, S., Mamnani, M., Nabi, G., Reinfelds, J., Sarkans, U., and Strnad, I. A debugger and assertion checker for the Awk programming language. *Int. Conf. Soft. Eng.*, 1996.

[3] Beckwith, L., Burnett, M., and Cook, C. Reasoning about many-to-many requirement relationships in spreadsheets, *IEEE Symp. Human-Centric Lang. Environ.* Arlington, VA, Sept. 2002, 149-157

[4] Belkin, N. Helping people find what they don't know, *Comm. ACM* 41(8), Aug. 2000, 58-61

[5] Boehm, B. and Basili,, V. Gaining intellectual control of software development, *Computer* 33(5), May 2000, 27-33.

[6] Burnett, M., Atwood, J., Djang, R., Gottfried, H., Reichwein, J., and Yang, S. Forms/3: a first-order visual language to explore the boundaries of the spreadsheet paradigm, *J. Functional Programming*, Mar. 2001, 155-206.

[7] Cook, C., Rothermel, K., Burnett, M., Adams, T., Rothermel, G., Sheretov, A., Cort, F., and Reichwein, J. Does a visual "testedness" methodology aid debugging? TR #99-60-07, Oregon State Univ., rev. March 2001.

[8] Corritore, C., Kracher, B., and Wiedenbeck, S. Trust in the online environment, *HCI International, Vol. 1*, New Orleans, LA, Aug. 2001, 1548-1552.

[9] Dwyer, M., Avrunin, G., and Corbett, J. Patterns in property specifications for finite-state verification, *Int. Conf. Soft. Eng.*, Los Angeles, CA, May 1999, 411-420.

[10] Ernst, M., Cockrell, J., Griswold, W., and Notkin, D. Dynamically discovering likely program invariants to support program evolution, *Int. Conf. Soft. Eng.*, Los Angeles, CA, May 1999, 213-224.

[11] Fisher, M., Cao, M., Rothermel, G., Cook, C., and Burnett, M. Automated test case generation for spreadsheets, *Int. Conf. Soft. Eng.*, Orlando, FL, May 2002, 141-151.

[12] Hangal, S. and Lam, M. Tracking down software bugs using automatic anomaly detection, *Int. Conf. Soft. Eng.*, Orlando, FL, May 2002, 291-301.

[13] Krishna, V., Cook, C., Keller, D., Cantrell, J., Wallace, C., Burnett, M., and Rothermel, G. Incorporating incremental validation and impact analysis into spreadsheet maintenance: an empirical study, *IEEE Int. Conf. Soft. Maintenance*, Florence, Italy, Nov. 2001, 72-81.

[14] Leventhal, L., Teasley, B., and Rohlman, D. Analyses of factors related to positive test bias in software testing. *Int. J. Human-Computer Studies* 41, 1994, 717-749.

[15] Meyer, B. Applying "Design by Contract," *Computer* 25(10), October 1992, 40-51.

[16] Michael, J., Ong, V., and Rowe, N. Natural-language processing support for developing policy-governed software systems, *Int. Conf. Technology for Object-Oriented Languages and Systems*, Santa Barbara, CA, 2001.

[17] Miller, R. and Myers, B. Outlier finding: focusing user attention on possible errors, *ACM Symp. User Interface Software and Technology,* Nov. 2001.

[18] Pane, J., Ratanamahatan, C., and Myers, B. Studying the language and structure in non-programmers' solutions to programming problems. *Int. J. Human-Computer Studies* 54(2), Feb. 2001, 237-264.

[19] Panko, R. Finding spreadsheet errors: most spreadsheet models have design flaws that may lead to long-term miscalculation, *Information Week*, May 1995, 100-100.

[20] Panko, R. What we know about spreadsheet errors. *J. End User Computing*, Spring 1998, 15-21.

[21] Raz, O., Koopman, P., and Shaw, M. Semantic anomaly detection in online data sources, *Int. Conf. Soft. Eng.*, Orlando, FL, May 2002, 302-312.

[22] Rosenblum, D. A practical approach to programming with assertions, *IEEE Trans. Soft. Eng.*, Jan. 1995, 19-31.

[23] Rosenblum, D., Sankar, S. and Luckham, D. Concurrent runtime checking of Annotated Ada programs, *Conf. Foundations Soft. Technology and Theoretical Comp. Science (LNCS 241).* NY, Springer-Verlag, Dec. 1986, 10-35.

[24] Rothermel, G., Burnett, M., Li, L., DuPuis, C., Sheretov, A. A methodology for testing spreadsheets, *ACM Trans. Soft. Eng. and Methodology*, Jan. 2001, 110-147.

[25] Sankar, S., Mandal, M. Concurrent runtime monitoring of formally specified programs, *Computer*, Mar. 1993, 32-41.

[26] Smith, R., Avrunin, G., Clarke, L., and Osterweil, L. Propel: an approach supporting property elucidation, *Int. Conf. Soft. Eng.*, Orlando, FL, May 2002, 11-21.

[27] Summet, J. and Burnett, M. End-user assertions: propagating their implications, TR 02-60-04, Oregon State Univ., 2002.

[28] Wallace, C., Cook, C., Summet, J., and Burnett, M. Assertions in end-user software engineering: a think-aloud study (Tech Note), *IEEE Symp. Human-Centric Lang. Environ.*, Arlington, VA, Sept. 2002, 63-65.

[29] Welch, D., String, S. An exception-based assertion mechanism for C++. *J. Obj. Oriented Prog.* 11(4), 1998, 50-60.

[30] Wilcox, E., Atwood, J., Burnett, M., Cadiz, J., and Cook, C. Does continuous visual feedback aid debugging in direct-manipulation programming systems? *ACM Conf. Human Factors in Computing Systems,* Mar. 1997, 258-265.

[31] Wilson, A., Burnett, M., Beckwith, L., Granatir, O., Casburn, L., Cook, C., Durham, M. and Rothermel, G. Harnessing curiosity to increase correctness in end-user programming, *ACM Conf. Human Factors in Computing Systems*, Ft. Lauderdale, FL, Apr. 2003 (to appear).

Technical Papers

Design Recovery and Documentation

On the Uniformity of Software Evolution Patterns

Evelyn J. Barry
Mays Business School
Texas A&M University
*ebarry@cgsb.tamu.edu****

Chris F. Kemerer
Katz Graduate
School of Business
University of Pittsburgh

Sandra A. Slaughter
Graduate School of
Industrial Administration
Carnegie Mellon University

Abstract

Preparations for Y2K reminded the software engineering community of the extent to which long-lived software systems are embedded in our daily environments. As systems are maintained and enhanced throughout their lifecycles they appear to follow generalized behaviors described by the laws of software evolution. Within this context, however, there is some question of how and why systems may evolve differently. The objective of this work is to answer the question: ***do systems follow a set of identifiable evolutionary patterns?*** *In this paper we use software volatility to describe the lifecycle evolution of a portfolio of 23 software systems. We show by example that a vector of software volatility levels can represent lifecycle behavior of a software system. We further demonstrate that the portfolio's 23 software volatility vectors can be grouped into four distinguishable patterns. Thus, we show by example that there are different patterns of system lifecycle behavior, i.e. software evolution.*

1. Introduction

Software engineers are well aware of the many legacy systems in production today. Even though the world didn't collapse under the threat of the Y2K bug, the adaptation of millions of lines of code emphasized the extent to which long-lived software systems are embedded in our daily business, educational and personal environments. Legacy systems often actively serve organizations far longer than the system designers and programmers who created them [1].

In point of fact, a truly successful system will continually be modified and enhanced [1]. Software lifecycle maintenance[1] is a forward-focused activity used to prolong the productive lifespan of a software system [1]. As much as 90% of lifecycle system costs are spent on software modifications after initial system implementation [2]. Therefore it is imperative that we understand the lifetime system transformations taking place. Such incremental modifications of software systems are often referred to collectively as *software evolution*. Formally, software evolution is defined as "...the dynamic behavior of programming systems as they are maintained and enhanced over their life times" [3].

Researchers have recognized the importance of software evolution for over three decades. Based on a series of empirical observations and analytical studies Lehman and colleagues have developed eight laws of software evolution. These laws describe the incremental transformations experienced by software systems during their lifecycles [4] [5]. A number of empirical studies have provided further support for these characteristics of aging software systems' behaviors. [3] [5] [6] [7] [8] [9] [10] [11, 12],[13].

The laws of software evolution describe general characteristics of the lifecycle transformations software systems experience. Within this context, however, there is some question of how and why systems may evolve differently [11]. Some systems are modified and stay productive for decades [14] while others are replaced in less than five years. Some systems require few changes and others need to be changed almost continuously. In earlier empirical studies of software evolution we have observed differences in patterns of software modifications suggesting that all systems do not follow identical patterns of software evolution [11]. Thus, while all software systems evolve, it is not clear how and why systems evolve in the way they do.

Our main objective in this work is to determine if distinct patterns of lifecycle software volatility can be identified, that is, ***do systems follow a set of identifiable evolutionary patterns?*** We use a series of mapping techniques and factor analysis to illustrate more than one pattern of software evolution.

Our empirical data are based on a 20-year log of lifecycle software maintenance for a large retailer [15]. In the next section we delineate a step-by-step methodology to map the lifecycle patterns of software evolution. These mapping techniques simplify measures of software volatility while retaining characteristic system behavior. Sequential phase analysis and factor analysis identify distinct patterns of software evolution. In the final section of this paper we discuss

[1] We include all software system modifications for corrective, adaptive and enhancement purposes as lifecycle maintenance.

0-7695-1877-X/03 $17.00 © 2003 IEEE

contributions and implications of this work, and its significance to both researchers and practitioners. This work contributes to the set of methodologies we can use for describing, analyzing and comparing software evolution. By combining these techniques with cluster analyses we can detect similarities in lifecycle behaviors across systems.

2. Methodology

In this section we demonstrate a progression of mapping techniques used to describe lifecycle software evolution patterns. Through an inductive process we gradually smooth and simplify longitudinal data until an ordinal vector of software volatility levels represents system's lifecycle volatility. The 23 vectors of software system lifecycle volatility can then be analyzed for similarities in lifecycle behaviors across systems. We now proceed to build software system lifecycle volatility vectors. Our analysis is illustrated throughout by using actual lifecycle software maintenance events for systems in the retailer's application portfolio.

2.1 Determining Software Volatility Dimensions

Recognizing *software volatility*, i.e. software change, as a multi-dimensional phenomenon, we describe software volatility with (1) *amplitude,* (2) *periodicity* and (3) *dispersion* [16, 17][2].

Amplitude measures the change in software system size. To allow comparison of different sized systems we normalize change in system size by the total system size.

Periodicity measures the mean time since software modification. For each program in a system we identify all software modifications completed during that time period and calculate the time since software modification (TSM) for each individual modification to the program. Software modifications are aggregated for the system and time period. The Mean time since software modification ($MTSM_{st}$) is calculated for each time period (t) in each system's (s) lifecycle. Periodicity is defined as MTSM normalized by system age at time period t. Periodicity suggests the frequency with which systems are changed.

Dispersion measures the variance of the TSM for system s and implemented during time period t. Just as periodicity is normalized by system age, dispersion is normalized by system age squared at time t. A low dispersion suggests that all programs in a system are changed on the same schedule. A high dispersion indicates a wide disparity in TSM making it difficult for software managers to determine how many programs will need to be changed at time t.

We start by calculating amplitude, periodicity and dispersion for each month in each system's lifecycle. This yields an unbalanced panel of 3201 system-month observations. If no activity occurs during a system-month observation, amplitude=0, periodicity=1, and dispersion=0, by definition. We illustrate these software volatility measures for systems 2 and 7 from our portfolio, and graph the results. (See Figures 1 and 2.)

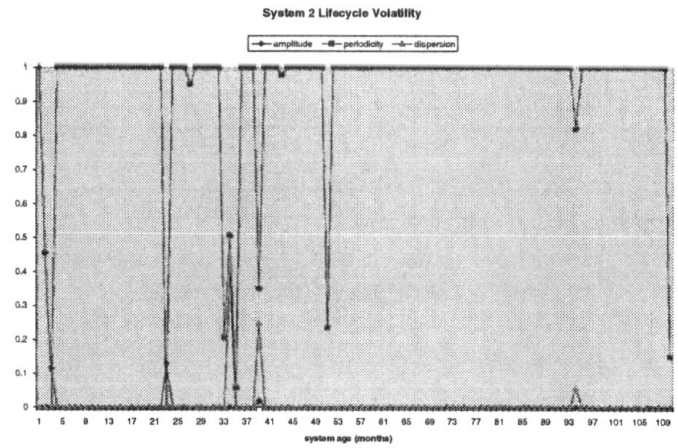

Figure 1: System 2 lifecycle volatility time series

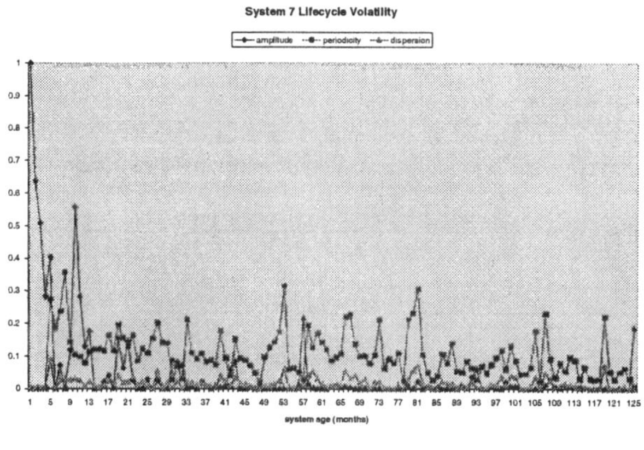

Figure 2: System 7 lifecycle volatility time series

Each of these graphs represents three time series of lifecycle volatility, i.e. amplitude, periodicity and dispersion. However, with this level of detail it is difficult to discern patterns. The same calculations and detailed graphs were prepared for each of the remaining 21 software systems in our portfolio. No two systems display exactly the same volatility. The search for patterns in lifecycle software volatility may be obscured by 20 years of monthly calculations of the three dimensions of software volatility.

[2] For a more formal explanation of each of these measures see the appendix.

2.2 Classifying Software Volatility Dimensions

In order to help discern potential patterns in the data, we combine the three dimensions into a one-dimensional volatility classification for each of the system-month observations in our dataset. Each calculation of amplitude is marked as above average (= 1) or below average (= 0) amplitude.[3] The same procedure marks long (=1) or short (= 0) periodicity, and high (=1) or low (= 0) dispersion. These binary indicators are combined to create eight triples signifying eight classifications of software volatility (A-H). (See Table 1.)

Table 1: Classifications of software volatility

Volatility Class	Amp.	Per.	Dev.	Description
A	Low	Long	Low	Least volatile: occasional small modifications occurring in a well-behaved pattern
B	Low	Long	High	Occasional small modifications with wide variance of behavior among system programs
C	Low	Short	Low	Constant small modifications occurring in a well-behaved pattern
D	Low	Short	High	Constant small modifications with wide variance of behavior among system programs
E	High	Long	Low	Occasional large modifications occurring in a well-behaved pattern
F	High	Long	High	Occasional large modifications with wide variance of behavior among system programs
G	High	Short	Low	Constant large modifications occurring in a well-behaved pattern
H	High	Short	High	Most volatile: constant large modifications with wide variance of behavior among system programs

Volatility class A represents the volatility measure triple (low, long, low). Below average amplitude indicates either that there are no software modifications, or that all the modifications affect small amounts of code. Longer than average periodicity indicates that programs are being modified infrequently. Low dispersion indicates that any programs being modified are all being changed at the same time with the same time interval since previous modification. We conclude that volatility class A has very few, if any, software modifications. At the other extreme, volatility class G has high amplitude, short periodicity and low dispersion. This indicates that (1) software modification size is relatively large, (2) modifications occur frequently, and (3) the time since previous modification is consistent among the programs being changed. Volatility class G is the nightmare that software managers dread. All system programs require large modifications at each time internal.

The application portfolio contains the full lifecycle (maximum of 22 years) for each of the 23 application systems being analyzed, for a total of 3201 system-month observations. The number of occurrences for each volatility classification in our data set is listed in Table 2. There are very few occurrences of volatility classifications B, E, and F. Over half of the volatility occurrences are A or C, indicating smaller than average sizes and long periods between modifications. This indicates that the software portfolio, as a whole, is fairly stable.

Table 2: Frequency of volatility classes in Software portfolio lifecycle

Volatility class	No. of Occurrences	Percentage of TOTAL
A	1398	43.67
B	12	0.37
C	973	30.40
D	448	14.00
E	1	0.03
F	1	0.03
G	281	8.78
H	87	2.72
TOTAL	3201	100.00

2.3 Describing Lifecycle Vectors of Software Volatility Classifications

A vector of volatility classifications can now be built to describe the lifecycle software volatility for each application system. Each element in the (N x 1) vector represents the software volatility classification for one month, i.e. N = number of months in system lifecycle. Software system 2 has a lifecycle of 110 months. Thus, its lifecycle volatility class vector has 110 elements. Each element represents the volatility class for that month. In the same manner, we use system 7's recorded software volatility to create a (125x1) vector of lifecycle volatility classifications.

The elements in each vector describe a chronological pattern of the software system's evolution. We use these lifecycle volatility vectors to complete our longitudinal analysis.

[3] Average amplitude, average periodicity and average dispersion are calculated as the mean values of amplitude, periodicity and dispersion for the unbalanced panel dataset of 3201 system-month observations.

2.4 Identifying Phases of Lifecycle Software Volatility Using Phasic Analysis

There are two predominant methods for longitudinal analysis; time series analysis and phasic analysis [18]. Time series analysis is not appropriate given our use of nominal scale volatility classifications. Thus, we adopt a non-parametric sequential (phasic) analysis technique. This technique been applied in a wide variety of contexts, including the study of information system development processes [19]

Phasic analysis is based on three assumptions. First, events being analyzed can be assembled into groups of more than one occurrence. Second, events or activities cohere into larger events or patterns. Third, the structure of these events or patterns is the result of dynamics driving changes in behavior from one phase to the next [18]. In our use of this technique we look for phases of software volatility. We consider each month's volatility classification as a discrete event and use phasic analysis to identify consecutive months with similar lifecycle volatility classifications.

We use *Winphaser* as our phase sequence analyzer. Winphaser software was written by Michael Holmes, as adapted from [18]. Winphaser identifies phases of length *n* when it detects *n* consecutive like values. For sequences where no predominant classification can be identified Winphaser labels the phase as *pending* (*p*). The phase length parameter, *n*, gives Winphaser enough flexibility to allow its use in a variety of contexts. By changing the phase length researchers can simplify resulting sequential phase patterns. Smaller phase length parameters reduce the number of pending phases, but the resulting increased number of phases reduces our ability to see patterns or iterations of identified activities. However, longer phases provide a coarser description of behavioral patterns and may prevent a more meaningful description of volatility processes. We used bracketing to determine that a phase length equal to three (n=3) was the best tradeoff between these two extremes. Winphaser produced lifecycle phase maps for each of the 23 application systems in our software portfolio.

Winphaser uses Goodman and Kruskal's gamma, γ, to calculate the precedence scores of identified phases [20, 21]. The frequency of each phase is also reported in the gamma map. We used phase frequencies to calculate each phase type's proportion of total lifecycle phases. The precedence scores indicate the prevalent order of phase type occurrence. For example, suppose a system has two phase types reported, *a* and *c*. The frequencies for these phase types are 72 and 8, respectively. The precedence is reported as type *a* followed by type *c*. From this information we build a 10x1 volatility vector as follows (*a,a,a,a,a,a,a,a,a,c*), i.e. phase *a* followed by *c* in a 9:1 ratio.[4]

We use the gamma maps from Winphaser to create 23 (10x1) volatility patterns.

2.5 Converting a Nominal Scale of Volatility Classes to an Ordinal Scale of Volatility Levels

Volatility vectors using the nominal volatility classifications *A-H* and *P* (*pending*) are constructed for each of the application systems in our software portfolio. To further analyze the lifecycle volatility classifications listed in Table 1 we order the nominal volatility classifications according to level of volatility (low to high). There are so few occurrences of volatility classifications *B, E* and *F* in our data that phasic analysis failed to identify any phases of type *B, E* or *F*. Therefore, we order the remaining software volatility classifications (*A,C,D,G,H*). Based on the descriptions for each volatility class, we compare the level of volatility described by each triplet in Table 1. The remaining five volatility classes in order by level of volatility are (*A,D,C,H,G*). Phases labeled *pending*, volatility class *P*, occur when there is no single volatility class to identify three sequential entries. We insert volatility class *P* into the sequence to transition between classes with low amplitude and high amplitude. The ordering of volatility classes is shown in Table 3.

Table 3: Ordering of volatility classifications

Nominal scale	A	D	C	P	H	G
Order	1	2	3	4	5	6

2.6 Grouping Systems with Similar Lifecycle Volatility Vectors

Lifecycle volatility vectors are constructed using the ordered volatility classifications. We now have a set of lifecycle vectors describing the volatility patterns for each system. The ordered volatility vectors have volatility levels ranging 1 to 6, and each element of the vector represents 10% of the phases in the system's lifecycle. The volatility vectors can be used to compare and group systems with similar patterns of behavior. The volatility vectors represent phase sequences that may occur iteratively throughout a system's productive life span. A *base system* was selected from each group to display the main pattern of behavior for the group. Groups 1-4 are numbered in order by overall volatility, lowest to highest.

[4] We are normalizing all vectors and using pro rata share for each volatility class. This helps us compare patterns of system behavior across systems of different ages.

We used several non-parametric analyses to verify our specification of volatility vector groups. We confirmed our selection by calculating the difference of each cluster member system from the representative base member system. We calculate the distance from one vector to another as the difference between each element in one vector from the corresponding element in another vector. The sum of the differences can be used as a measure of the distance (or similarity) between two vectors.

A volatility vector for a completely stable system would be a 10x1 volatility vector of (1,1,1,1,1,1,1,1,1,1). The volatility vector for system 2 is (1, 1, 1, 1, 1, 1, 1, 1, 1, 6). The distance between these vectors can be calculated as the sum of the differences of each pair of corresponding elements[5]. The distance between system 2 and complete stability is (0+0+0+0+0+0+0+0+0+5) = 5. The volatility vector for system 7 is (5, 4, 2, 2, 2, 2, 2, 3, 3, 3). The distance between the system 7 and complete stability is (4+3+1+1+1+1+1+2+2+2) = 18. With this method we can see that system 7 is more volatile than system 2. In Table 4 we list each of the 23 systems with its ordinal volatility vector and its distance from a vector for a completely stable system. We visually arranged the volatility vectors in four groups by their similarities. Group numbers are assigned in order by overall volatility. We selected representative system vectors as base systems for each group are indicated by an asterisk, '*'.

2.7 Using Cluster Analysis to Confirm Groupings of Lifecycle Volatility Vectors

To further verify our selection of these groups we created a file of 23 records, each containing the lifecycle volatility vector found in Table 4. To confirm our manual arrangement of each of the four groups we applied hierarchical cluster analysis using linkage between group clusters[6] with interval squared Euclidean distance measures (SPSS V10.1). Our visual grouping of the volatility patterns aligns with the grouping yielded by the hierarchical cluster analysis. Obtaining the same results by two different methodologies provides support for the strength of the groupings.

[5] In this calculation to make the analysis tractable the ordinal scale of volatility 1-6 is assumed to serve as an interval scale as well.

[6] Average linkage between group clusters maximizes the distance between 2 clusters where distance is the average of distances of all pairs of cases where one member of the pair is from one of the clusters.

Table 4: System volatility vectors by group number

Pattern Group	Sys-tem #	Ordered Volatility Vector										Distance to stability
1	23*	1	1	1	1	1	1	1	1	1	1	0
1	19	1	1	1	1	1	1	1	1	1	1	0
1	14	4	1	1	1	1	1	1	1	1	1	3
1	2	1	1	1	1	1	1	1	1	1	6	5
1	16	1	1	1	1	1	1	1	1	1	4	3
2	13*	1	1	1	1	1	1	6	3	3	3	11
2	17	1	1	1	1	1	1	6	3	3	3	11
2	9	1	1	1	1	1	3	3	3	2	2	8
2	15	1	1	1	1	1	4	3	3	3	3	11
2	21	1	1	1	1	1	1	4	4	4	4	12
2	18	1	1	1	1	1	4	4	3	3	3	12
3	12*	1	1	1	4	4	3	3	3	3	3	16
3	1	1	4	4	4	2	2	2	2	3	3	17
3	5	1	6	3	3	3	4	2	2	2	2	18
3	8	1	1	6	3	3	3	3	3	3	3	19
3	6	2	2	2	3	3	3	3	3	3	3	17
3	20	2	4	4	4	4	3	3	3	3	3	23
3	3	1	1	1	6	4	3	3	3	3	2	17
4	7*	5	4	2	2	2	2	2	3	3	3	18
4	10	5	4	2	2	2	2	2	3	3	3	18
4	4	4	4	1	1	1	1	1	1	3	3	10
4	22	6	4	4	4	4	2	2	3	3	3	25
4	11	6	2	4	4	4	4	3	3	3	3	26

3. Discussion

Our objective in this research was to determine whether all software systems traverse the same lifecycle evolution pattern or whether there are distinctly different patterns among software systems. We used lifecycle volatility as representative of the dynamic behavior of software systems, i.e. software evolution.

We find that systems do not all follow the same volatility pattern, and that there are distinct pattern groups of lifecycle volatility. Using a progression of mapping techniques we simplified the three-dimensional time series of software volatility to an Nx1 vector of software volatility classifications. The end result of these mappings displays a volatility pattern of software system behavior. We prepared volatility patterns for each of the 23 application systems in our software portfolio.

We found four distinct groups of volatility patterns for the systems in our software portfolio. Each group is represented by a base system. Group 1 contains those systems whose volatility is relatively low, i.e., the systems are stable, for at least 90% of the time. The pattern for group 2 is stable for the first 50-60% of the pattern followed by higher volatility in 40-50% of the pattern cycle. Group 3 volatility patterns are stable for a relatively short time, i.e. low volatility for the first 10% of the cycle. This brief level of stability is followed by higher volatility for the remaining cycle pattern. Group 4 volatility patterns start with high volatility, and volatility remains relatively high for the entire cycle pattern.

Our analysis of lifecycle software volatility uses a three-dimensional measure of software volatility: amplitude, periodicity and dispersion. We add a fourth dimension, time, by analyzing lifecycle software system volatility. Our choice of mapping techniques allowed us to transform and simplify a 4-dimensional phenomenon into a 2-dimensional one. This process clarified the views of 23 software system behaviors and allowed us to perceive similarities of behaviors among the systems in our software portfolio.

Our software portfolio generated a set of four distinct volatility patterns. Depending on the age of a system the pattern may represent a full lifecycle from implementation to present, or the same pattern may occur repeatedly in a system's lifecycle.

Two systems may have identical volatility patterns but different lifecycle volatility. For example, systems 7 and 10 have identical lifecycle volatility patterns but dissimilar volatility time series. Lifecycle volatility time series graphs for systems 7 and 10 are displayed as figures 2 and 3, respectively. When you compare the lifecycle volatility time series graphs (Figures 2 and 3) you see how difficult it is to recognize similarities in the behaviors of these systems. By smoothing the data and applying an ordinal scale we can recognize that systems 7 and 10 have the same proportion of low volatility observations indicated by longer than average periodicity. The volatility vector (pattern) for system 7 is identical to that for system 10. (See Table 4.) The smoothing effect of assigning volatility classes eliminated some of the fog and helped identify similarities of behavior.

By using the ordinal scale of software volatility (Table 3), we can plot lifecycle volatility from the phase maps of systems 7 and 10. (See Figures 4 and 5.) Even though systems have identical volatility patterns, there are differences in their lifecycle volatility. One system is much older than the other and exhibits more iterations of the volatility pattern. If managers know the pattern of behavior for a given system they may be able to improve their prediction of resources needed for future lifecycle maintenance support of that system.

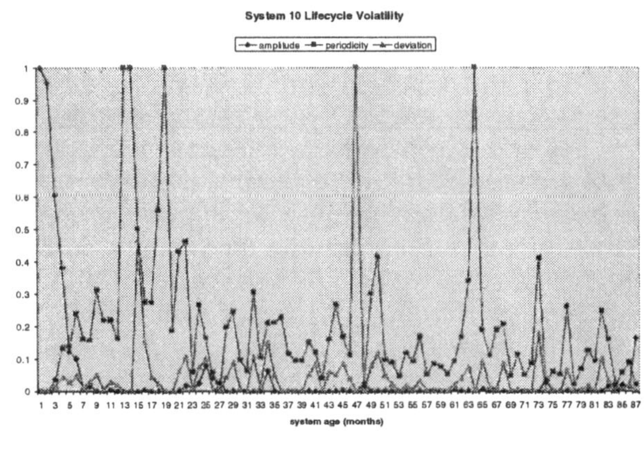

Figure 3: System 10 lifecycle volatility

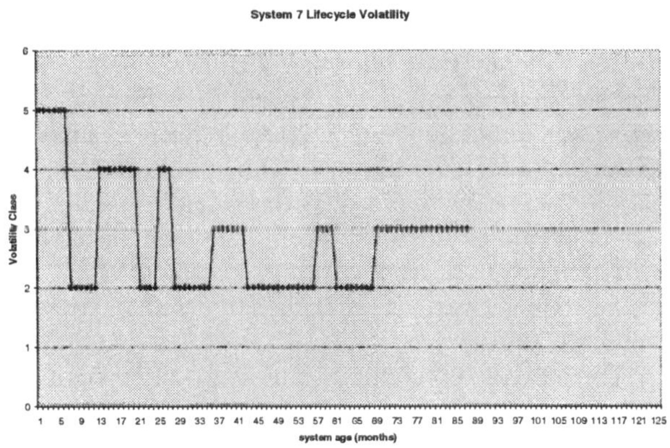

Figure 4: System 7 lifecycle volatility (ordinal scale)

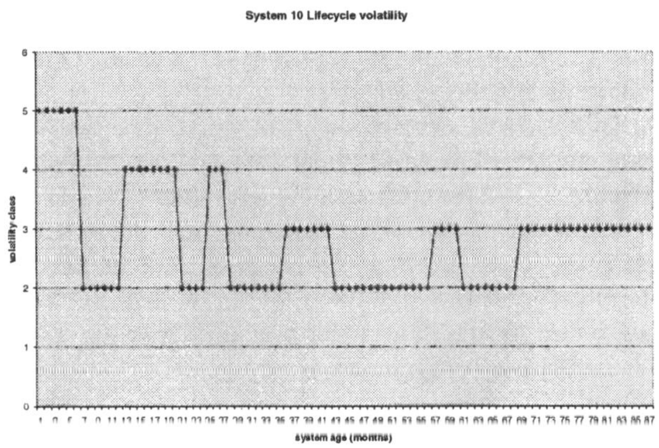

Figure 5: System 10 lifecycle volatility (ordinal scale)

4. Contributions and Implications

Software evolution has been researched for over three decades. While we recognize the many universal elements of software evolution we still observe a wide variety of system behaviors over time. In this work we measure this dynamic behavior as software volatility.

Software volatility is a complex phenomenon. We use a three-dimensional measure of volatility to capture the amplitude (size), periodicity (frequency) and dispersion (consistency) of software system change. We add another dimension, time, by calculating software volatility for each time period (e.g. each month) in a software system's lifecycle. Using a series of mapping techniques we converted the three-dimensional measures of software volatility to a nominal classification (A-H) describing volatility in more general terms. A chronological Nx1 vector was created for each system. The vector had N entries, one for each time period (month) in the system's lifecycle. The vector was processed using phase sequence analysis software tool (*Winphaser*). The resulting gamma analysis allowed us to create a 10x1 volatility vector for each software system showing the sequence and proportion of each type volatility experienced by the system. These vectors were then ordered by overall level of volatility.

The individual volatility patterns for the systems in our software portfolio were grouped for similarity by visually identifying four distinct groups of volatility patterns. As a robustness check we used hierarchical clustering, and found the same four clusters of volatility patterns across the system portfolio.

This work contributes to the set of methodologies we can use for describing, analyzing and comparing the evolution of individual software systems. By combining these techniques with cluster analyses we can detect similarities in system behaviors.

This method enables us to distinguish at least 4 main groups of volatility patterns in our software portfolio. Even though there are universal characteristics of software evolution, there are distinct differences in system lifecycle behavior patterns. From the laws of software evolution we know that software change is inevitable. From our previous work we know how to measure it. From this work we can describe and distinguish differences in software volatility patterns among systems.

The volatility pattern groups provide a separate and distinct classification of software systems. Now we need to determine what these pattern groups can tell us about other similarities among systems. Do certain pattern groups serve particular types of users? We ranked the groups from 1 to 4 by their overall level of volatility. Does it necessarily follow that group 1 will have lower lifecycle costs than groups 2, 3 and 4? Is it true that group 4 will be the most expensive? What do we know *a priori* about a system that will help us to gauge full lifetime costs of a software system being considered for purchase? Can we use pattern group as a factor in the repair/replace decision? Future research can draw upon the results presented here to answer these questions and many others. This analysis has added another perspective of software volatility and improved our general understanding of software evolution and its effect on lifecycle software maintenance outcomes.

5. Appendix

5.1 Amplitude

Amplitude measures the size of software modifications. Nearly two decades ago researchers began measuring software size. Amplitude can be measured as the sum of the size of all modifications made to a software system during time period *t*.

$$Amplitude = [\sum_{all\ modifications} size(modification_i)]_t \,/\, [total\ system\ size]_t$$

We can use any of the measurement units for measuring modification size. Division of the sum of modification sizes by the total size of the system creates a bounded scale invariant measure. Amplitude is an aggregate measure calculated for each system-month observations.[16]

5.2 Periodicity

Periodicity calculation starts with measurement of time between software modifications, TSM_t, for any program modified during time period *t*. We use all software system modifications regardless of their purpose, e.g. corrective, adaptive or enhancement. Time between software modification, TSM, is the elapsed time since the previous modification.

TSM_{jt} = *TSM for change event j in time period t.*[7]

Mean time between software modification, $MTSM_t$, is the mean TSM_j for a system during time period *t*. [8]

$$MTSM_t = (1/N_t)\ \Sigma\sum_{j=1}^{N_t} TSM_j$$

Where N_t = total number of change events for the system during time period t.

[7] Note: i = 0 is the point in time when the software system is initially implemented. Thus, at any time i is equal to the system age.

[8] A change event is a recorded software modification or program creation.

Periodicity$_t$ is MTSM$_t$ normalized by system age at time *t*, i.e.

$Periodicity_t = MTSM_t / t$. [16]

5.3 Dispersion

Dispersion describes how far system behavior varies from the pattern defined by amplitude and periodicity. By definition, dispersion will vary over a software system's lifecycle, but not within each time period *t*. TSM$_{jt}$ will vary within each time period. We could use variance of the TSM$_{jt}$, variance (TSM$_{jt}$), as our measure of dispersion if it were bounded and scale invariant. Scale invariance can be obtained by calculating the variance of normalized TSM$_{jt}$, i.e. NTSM$_{jt}$ = (TSM$_{jt}$)/t. We refer to the normalized variance as Dispersion$_t$.

$Dispersion_t = variance(NTSM_t) = variance(TSM_{jt}/t) = (1/t^2)[variance(TSM_{jt})]$ [16]

6. References

[1] E. B. Swanson and E. Dans, "System Life Expectancy and the Maintenance Effort: Exploring Their Equilibration," *MIS Quarterly*, vol. 24, pp. 277-297, 2000.

[2] K. H. Bennett, "Software Evolution: past, present and future," *Information and Software Technology*, vol. 39, pp. 673-680, 1996.

[3] L. A. Belady and M. M. Lehman, "A Model of Large Program Development," *IBM Systems Journal*, vol. 3, pp. 225-252, 1976.

[4] M. M. Lehman and L. A. Belady, *Program Evolution: Processes of Software Change*. London: Academic Press, 1985.

[5] M. M. Lehman, J. F. Ramil, P. D. Wernick, P. D.E., and W. M. Turski, "Metrics and Laws of Software Evolution - The Nineties View," presented at Metrics '97, the Fourth International Software Metrics Symposium, Albuquerque NM, 1997.

[6] V. Basili, L. Briand, S. Condon, Y. K. Kim, and W. V. Melo, J., "Understanding and Predicting the Process of Software Maintenance Releases," presented at ICSE 18th International Conference on Software Engineering, Berlin, Germany, 1996.

[7] D. Gefen and S. L. Schneberger, "The Non-Homogeneous Maintenance Periods: A Case Study of Software Modifications," presented at ICSM IEEE Conference on Software Maintenance, Monterey CA, 1996.

[8] C. R. Cook and A. Roesch, "Real-Time Software Metrics," *Journal of Systems and Software*, vol. 24, pp. 223-237, 1994.

[9] C. K. S. Chong Hok Yuen, "An Empirical Approach to the Study of Errors in Large Software Under Maintenance," presented at 2nd ICSM, Washington, D.C., 1985.

[10] C. K. S. Chong Hok Yuen, "A Statistical Rationale for Evolution Dynamics Concepts," presented at ICSM IEEE Conference on Software Maintenance, Austin, TX, 1987.

[11] C. F. Kemerer and S. A. Slaughter, "Determinants of Software Maintenance Profiles: An Empirical Investigation," *Journal of Software Maintenance*, vol. 9, pp. 235-251, 1997.

[12] C. F. Kemerer and S. A. Slaughter, "A Longitudinal Analysis of Software Maintenance Patterns," presented at ICIS International Conference on Information Systems, Atlanta, GA, 1997.

[13] C. K. S. Chong Hok Yuen, "On Analyzing Maintenance Process Data in the Clobal and Detailed Levels," presented at ICSM 4th IEEE Conference on Software Maintenance, Phoenix, AZ, 1985.

[14] R. Kalakota and A. B. Whinston, *Electronic Commerce: A Manager's Guide*. Reading, MA: Addison-Wesley, 1996.

[15] C. F. Kemerer and S. A. Slaughter, "An Empirical Approach to Studying Software Evolution," *IEEE Transactions on Software Engineering*, vol. 25, pp. 493-509, 1999.

[16] E. Barry, C. F. Kemerer, and S. A. Slaughter, "A Mullti-Dimensional Measurement of Software Volatility," in Working Paper Series Katz Graduate School of Business University of Pittsburgh. #2003-01.

[17] E. J. Barry and S. A. Slaughter, "Measuring Software Volatility: A Multi-Dimensional Approach"," presented at ICIS International Conference on Information Systems, Brisbane, Australia, 2000.

[18] M. E. Holmes and M. S. Poole, "Longitudinal Analysis," in *Studying Interpersonal Interaction*, B. M. Montgomery and S. Duck, Eds. New York: The Guilford Press, 1991, pp. 286-302.

[19] N. F. Sabherwal and D. Robey, "An Empirical Taxonomy of Implementation Processes Based on Sequences of Events in Information System Development," *Organization Science*, vol. 4, pp. 548-576, 1993.

[20] S. Siegel and N. J. Castellan, Jr., *Nonparametric Statistics for the Behavioral Sciences*, second ed. New York: McGraw-Hill, 1988.

[21] D. C. Pelz, "Innovation Complexity and the Sequence of Innovating Stages," *Knowledge, Creation, Diffusion Utilization*, vol. 6, pp. 261-291, 1985.

*** Funded in part by National Science Foundation grants CCR-9988227 and CCR-9988315, a Research Proposal Award from the Center for Computational Analysis of Social and Organizational Systems, Carnegie Mellon University, [NSF-IGERT], and the Institute for Industrial Competitiveness, University of Pittsburgh, Katz Graduate School of Business.

Design Recovery of Interactive Graphical Applications

Keith Chan, Zhi Cong Leo Liang, Amir Michail
School of Computer Science and Engineering
University of New South Wales
Sydney, Australia, 2052
{kchan,leozc,amichail}@cse.unsw.edu.au

Abstract

Nowadays, the majority of productivity applications are interactive *and* graphical *in nature. In this paper, we explore the possibility of taking advantage of these two characteristics in a design recovery tool. Specifically, the fact that an application is interactive means that we can identify distinct execution bursts corresponding closely to "actions" performed by the user. The fact that the application is graphical means that we can describe those actions visually from a fragment of the application display itself. Combining these two ideas, we obtain an explicit mapping from high-level actions performed by a user (similar to use case scenarios/specification fragments) to their low-level implementation. This mapping can be used for design recovery of interactive graphical applications. We demonstrate our approach using LyX, a scientific word processor.*

1 Introduction

Almost all productivity applications in use today are *interactive* and *graphical* in nature. By interactive, we mean that the application takes user input (key presses, mouse clicks, etc.) and gives back an immediate response, then awaits for further input, and so on. This contrasts with older batch applications that simply take an input and terminate with the output.

By graphical, we mean that the application shows its results in a graphical manner as with a word processor or web browser say. Graphical applications typically have a graphical user interface (GUI) incorporating menus and dialog boxes to facilitate interaction. However, it is possible to have graphical applications in the sense just described that do not have such a GUI. For example, actions may be performed through keyboard commands rather than through menus say.

In this paper, we shall explore the possibility of taking advantage of these two characteristics – namely, the interactive and graphical natures of applications – in a design recovery tool. These two characteristics allow us to identify the key actions that are performed by the user in a demonstration of the application, much like use case scenarios, as well as the implementations of those actions. One can then search/browse a database of such actions and their implementations to understand the design of an application.

Intuitively speaking, an application that is interactive allows us to more easily identify actions performed by a user. Specifically, we can look for an "execution burst" that occurs when the user invokes an action. Moreover, the fact that the application is graphical gives us a way to describe the actions identified in this manner. Namely, we can describe an action by using a screenshot of the application display before and after the action is performed.

To demonstrate our approach, we have built a tool, named DRT (for Design Recovery Tool), that works with most C/C++ X Window System applications irrespective of the GUI framework used.[1] Throughout the paper, we shall demonstrate DRT using the scientific word processor LyX 1.2.1. LyX is a rather substantial X Window System application consisting of about 154,000 lines of C++ code.

Our approach is applicable to interactive graphical applications written in an event-driven programming style with alternation between user-initiated events and application responses. Most productivity software including word processors and spreadsheets is of this form. However, certain applications such as flight simulators and games are not, since the application proceeds even while the user is idle. See the discussion on future work in Section 7 for more on this latter group of applications.

We would like to emphasize how our vision for design recovery using DRT differs from other researchers doing related work. (See Section 6 for more on related work.) First, we would like to make it *very* easy to populate a database with hundreds or thousands of application actions. Thus, providing a transparent process whereby the user need only

[1] DRT can be downloaded from http://www.cse.unsw.edu.au/~drt.

0-7695-1877-X/03 $17.00 © 2003 IEEE

play with an application as actions are collected automatically in the background is a key feature of our approach. Existing work typically requires manually setting up test cases [17, 18] or specifying the criteria for the beginning and end of an action in some way [13]. Second, we would like to provide a mechanism to search and browse this large collection of actions for design recovery purposes. For example, DRT provides a *dynamic query* mechanism whereby the user can perform an action on a running application (e.g., enter math mode in LyX) to find related actions in the database (e.g., the various actions performed in math mode). It is also possible to browse actions by clicking on an action in the database (e.g., move cursor right) to find other related actions (e.g., various other cursor movements). However, the question arises: after a search or browsing query returns a set of actions, how do we know what these actions are? This is particularly an issue if the actions were performed by someone else. Of course, one could look at the functions executed by these actions to understand what happened, but this can be difficult if one is not familiar with the application code yet. Consequently, the before/after screenshot visual descriptions of actions mentioned earlier are essential in making sense of search/browsing results in our tool. As far as we know, related work (e.g., [6]) has not addressed this particular issue, where the actions are not annotated in any way by the user.

Why would one want to build large databases of application actions in the first place? Ultimately, we would like to develop a central web resource where users can easily upload their DRT action collections for various applications, possibly resulting in multiple demonstrations for the same application. Users could then search and browse this entire action collection without having to perform any demonstrations themselves. In this way, we can leverage the dynamic analysis done by a few software engineers to benefit many others. One can imagine the benefits of this approach in a large software company or in the open source community where many developers might be involved in the maintenance of an application and there is much to be gained by reusing the dynamic analysis done by others.

Action collection can be done through a demonstration of the application by either the original developers of an application (already familiar with its design) or those trying to understand its code to perform some maintenance task. The original developers of an application might use DRT to provide another form of design document that would potentially be useful to others trying to maintain the application in the future. Since it is difficult to predict which aspects of the application would need to be understood in the future, developers of an application would typically try to exercise all aspects of the application to create an comprehensive database of actions. However, in the case where a software engineer needs to understand a particular aspect of the application – and no action database already exists – he/she would only need to exercise those aspects of the application that are relevant to the maintenance task. In this paper, we shall often use the word "user" to mean either an original developer of an application already familiar with its design or a software engineer that needs to perform a software maintenance task that needs to understand the application design.

Design recovery in our approach can be done in real-time or after the fact. Indeed, DRT immediately shows captured actions in real-time as soon as they occur in the application along with functions that are particularly relevant to the action (as they are not typically called in many actions thus far). Real-time usage has two key advantages: (1) the user still remembers the action performed; and (2) the user may decide to perform other related actions to clarify the relationship with the action just performed and zero in on particular functions of interest. However, without a preexisting database of actions, more experimentation needs to be performed with the application until actions of interest are found (e.g., for various application features) and also until sufficient data is accumulated to see which functions are particularly relevant to certain actions (i.e., not called in many different contexts). After the fact usage allows one to leverage past experimentation with the application — by oneself or others — and it is in this mode of usage that before/after pictures are critical to infer the action scenario as the user likely no longer remembers the action performed, particularly if the actions are performed by others. Of course, the two modes — real-time and after the fact usage — can be combined.

The rest of the paper is organized as follows. Section 2 describes our technique for automatically detecting action boundaries. Section 3 shows how we identify functions executed by an action that are particularly relevant to that action. Section 4 presents a technique for visually describing actions using before/after screenshots. Section 5 demonstrates how one can search and browse an action collection. Section 6 discusses related work. Section 7 summarizes the paper and suggests future work.

2 Detecting Action Boundaries

To detect actions performed by a user, we need some way of knowing when an action starts and when it ends. Ideally, the action should correspond closely to the user's notion of an action. In this section, we shall describe our method for detecting action boundaries. Experimentation with interactive graphical applications of various types has shown the method to be reasonably robust.

Roughly speaking, we shall use GUI input events to determine the start of actions (e.g., mouse button down) and a combination of GUI input events and idle detection to deter-

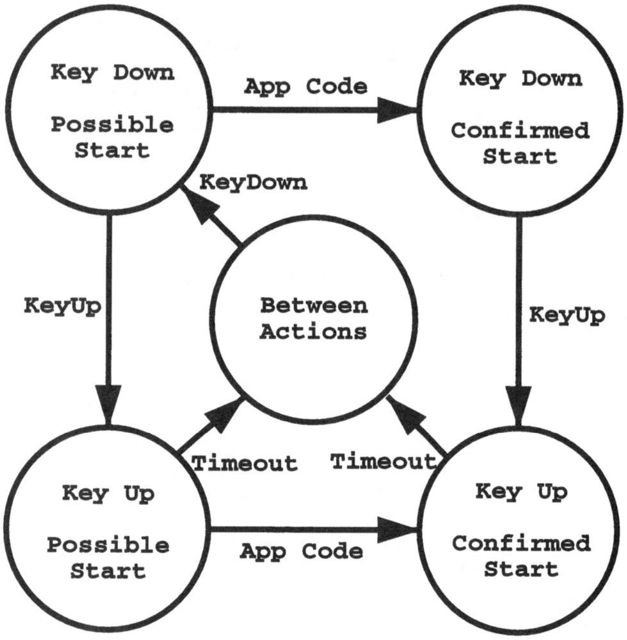

Figure 1. Action boundary detection.

mine the end of action (e.g., some time after a mouse button release when the application has gone idle).

To simplify our discussion, we shall talk only about a KeyDown event followed some time later by a KeyUp event, both of which shall refer to the same key — be it the left mouse button or the keyboard key "a" for example. All other "down" and "up" events corresponding to other keys are ignored in this time period between KeyDown and KeyUp.

Figure 1 shows the state diagram for action detection. Initially, we start out in the center state, which denotes the time spent between actions. When we receive a KeyDown event, we will be in one of the two top states. When we receive the corresponding KeyUp event, we will be in one of the two bottom states. If after receiving the KeyDown event, no application functions have been invoked (yet), we will be in one of the two left states. At this point, we have not confirmed that an action has indeed started because no application code has executed yet. If after receiving the KeyDown event, one or more application functions is invoked, we will be in one of the two right states. At this point, we have indeed started an action as application code has executed.

A transition back to the center state occurs from one of the two bottom states after a KeyUp event. In both cases, the transition occurs after a timeout during which no application functions have been invoked. (The timeout value is typically less than a second; we use a value of 0.7 seconds.) A timeout from the bottom left state indicates that we really did not have an action after all since no application code

Figure 2. Action function sequence from LyX.

was executed. A timeout from the bottom right state indicates that we have indeed found an action that just ended.

There are several subtleties to note. Observe that mouse movements without KeyDown and KeyUp events do not constitute actions even if application functions are invoked on each mouse move. However, mouse drags are considered actions because they do involve a KeyDown at the start of the drag and a KeyUp at the end. Also observe that application functions need to be called for an action to be confirmed. So for example, if the user looks through some menus but does not select any menu items, then it is likely that no action will occur as the menu code executed is typically in the GUI framework used by the application. The rationale for requiring application functions to be called for an action to occur is that actions should represent concepts inherent to the application itself. Another subtlety involves knowing when the action has completed. Observe that the action does not necessarily end when the KeyUp event is received. The reason is that the KeyDown/KeyUp pair typically initiates some application processing that occurs after the KeyUp, so it is necessary to extend the action until the application has gone idle after this processing.

While an action takes place, we keep track of all application functions that are invoked after the KeyDown event until the timeout that returns to the center state. Observe that this includes functions executed after the KeyUp event but before the timeout occurs. We shall denote an action by $A = (f_1, \ldots, f_n)$ indicating the sequence of functions f_i called, omitting subsequent repetitions of calls. For example, if an action A results in application functions f_1, f_2, f_1, f_3, f_2 being called in that order, then we denote the call sequence by $A = (f_1, f_2, f_3)$ omitting the subsequent repetitions of f_1 and f_2 but preserving the order otherwise. Omitting repetitions of calls not only speeds up DRT but also makes the output less cluttered for the user.

Finally, we observe that the user has some control over the granularity of actions through the use of timeout values and the speed with which the user interacts with the application during the demonstration. For example, if the user types a sentence quickly in a word processor, it is likely that the entire sentence would be considered a single action. (We view this as a desirable feature though others may wish to have the same results irrespective of typing speed.)

Figure 2 shows the start of a call sequence from an action performed with LyX. Each horizontal bar indicates a function call in the sequence $A = (f_1, \ldots, f_n)$, with the first few having labels indicating the actual function called. It is not clear from the start of the call sequence shown what action was performed. The functions called at the very start of the action, such as WorkArea::event_cb and WorkArea::work_area_handler are quite generic event handling functions that are executed in many contexts. The function BufferView::Pimpl::workAreaKeyPress likely indicates that the application is handling a key press action. Moreover, if we look further down, we see such functions as MathCursor::getLastCode, InsetFormulaBase::getCursorPos, and MathCursor::getPos, which hint that perhaps the user has performed some action in LyX's formula editor.

So we see that it is often difficult to understand the exact action that has taken place by simply looking at the first few functions in the call sequence. Moreover, examining all functions in the call sequence is problematic as some actions result in the execution of hundreds or thousands of functions. So we need a way to identify functions in the call sequence that are particularly relevant to the action just performed. We shall address this issue in the following section.

3 Computing Function Prevalence

Given the notion of an action $A = (f_1, \ldots, f_n)$ presented in Section 2, we now turn our attention to identifying functions f_i that are particularly relevant to A. Generally speaking, an action may result in the execution of hundreds or thousands of functions and it is crucial that we identify important functions with respect to the action to better understand the action performed and begin exploration of its implementation at key places in the source code.

While it is true that functions near the beginning of A typically start off the action, they do not necessarily do the real work. Indeed, the first function may be a callback that merely calls other functions to the real processing. Also, an action may have more than one result depending on some condition, so the outcome of the action will likely be indicated by calling one of various possible functions near the end of the call sequence.

One way to identify important functions in a call sequence is to compute a notion of "function prevalence". Those functions that are quite prevalent occur in many contexts and are not really specific to any actions. Those functions that are not prevalent occur in fewer actions and are more likely to be relevant to those actions.

A simple way to compute function prevalence is to keep a count of the number of actions in which each of the functions has been executed. The higher the count, the more prevalent the function. However, such a simple scheme has a significant problem: repeated actions will skew the count in undesirable ways.

For example, consider actions $A_1 = (f, g)$, $A_2 = (f, h_1)$, $A_3 = (g, h_2)$, and $A_4 = (g, h_1, h_2)$. Suppose the user performs actions A_1, A_3, A_4 once and action A_2 99 times. In such a case, f would have a count of 100, while g would have a count of 3. Consequently, it appears that f is in fact the least relevant function to A_1 as it occurs in so many (possibly repeated) actions. Yet, intuitively, f is in fact the most relevant function to A_1 as it only appears in two distinct actions while g occurs in three distinct actions. However, it is insufficient to simply omit repetitions of actions while computing function prevalence because some of the actions performed may indeed be very similar but not identical. Again, this would skew the action count.

We have developed a measure that captures an intuitive notion of function prevalence in the presence of identical or similar actions. Consider actions $A_1, \ldots, A_m$. First, we shall define a measure, *action distinctness*, that captures how different these actions are as a collection. Roughly speaking, if the actions $A_1, \ldots, A_m$ are very similar, then the action distinctness will be close to one, but if the actions $A_1, \ldots, A_m$ are very different, then the action distinctness will be close to m.

Second, to compute the prevalence of a function f, we simply find all the actions performed so far that resulted in the execution of f, say $A_{i_1}, \ldots, A_{i_m}$. The prevalence of f is the action distinctness of $A_{i_1}, \ldots, A_{i_m}$. In this way, the prevalence of f is low if it is executed in actions that are not that different from each other. Conversely, the prevalence of f is high if it is executed by widely different sorts of actions — which is as we would like, since a function executed in widely different contexts is not particularly specific to any of those contexts.

In Section 3.1, we define the action distinctness of a set of actions $A_1, \ldots, A_m$. In Section 3.2, we use action distinctness to compute the more robust form of function prevalence.

3.1 Action Distinctness Measure

We shall use concepts from linear algebra to define action distinctness. In particular, let vectors $V_1, \ldots, V_m$ denote the functions executed by actions $A_1, \ldots, A_m$. Supposing there are n distinct functions called by these actions collectively, each vector V_i would have dimension n, with a dimension allocated for each of the n distinct functions. Let $V_i[d]$ denote the dth entry in V_i. An entry of 1 in $V_i[d]$ indicates that the function corresponding to dimension d is executed; an entry of 0 in $V_i[d]$ indicates that it is not.

Going back to our example $A_1 = (f, g)$, $A_2 = (f, h_1)$, $A_3 = (g, h_2)$, and $A_4 = (g, h_1, h_2)$ – where we have four functions f, g, h_1, h_2 – we set up the corresponding vectors as $V_1 = (1,1,0,0)$, $V_2 = (1,0,1,0)$, $V_3 = (0,1,0,1)$, and $V_4 = (0,1,1,1)$. (The ordering of functions in the vectors is not important as long as it is the same in all vectors.)

Consider the normalized vectors $V_1/|V_1|, \ldots, V_m/|V_m|$, where $|V_i| = \sqrt{\sum_{d=1}^{n} V_i[d]^2}$. The points $P_1, \ldots, P_m$ whose coordinates correspond to these normalized vectors lie on the surface of an n-hypersphere of radius one centered about the origin. Now, consider the smallest $n-$orthotope (which is the generalization of a rectangle in n-dimensions) that just contains all the points $P_1, \ldots, P_m$ and the origin. The action distinctness measure is defined to be the sum of the square of the dimensions of this $n-$orthotope. In other words, the sum is $\sum_{d=1}^{n} \left(\max_{1 \le i \le m} \frac{V_i[d]}{|V_i|}\right)^2$.

Intuitively speaking, if the actions are quite similar, then they will have corresponding points that are close by on the hypersphere thus allowing the orthotope containing them to have small dimensions. However, if the actions are quite different, then they will have corresponding points that are spread apart on the hypersphere thus forcing the orthotope dimensions to be large. Consequently, the distinctness measure represents a collective similarity of the actions $A_1, \ldots, A_m$, with larger values indicating widely differing actions in the collection.

Returning to our example, we have normalized vectors $V_1/|V_1| = (1/\sqrt{2}, 1/\sqrt{2}, 0, 0)$, $V_2/|V_2| = (1/\sqrt{2}, 0, 1/\sqrt{2}, 0)$, $V_3/|V_3| = (0, 1/\sqrt{2}, 0, 1/\sqrt{2})$, and $V_4/|V_4| = (0, 1/\sqrt{3}, 1/\sqrt{3}, 1/\sqrt{3})$. If we view these vectors as points in 4-space, we observe that they lie on the unit 4-hypersphere. The smallest 4-orthotope that just contains these points as well as the origin $(0,0,0,0)$ has dimensions $\max(1/\sqrt{2}, 1/\sqrt{2}, 0, 0)$, $\max(1/\sqrt{2}, 0, 1/\sqrt{2}, 1/\sqrt{3})$, $\max(0, 1/\sqrt{2}, 0, 1/\sqrt{3})$, and $\max(0, 0, 1/\sqrt{2}, 1/\sqrt{3})$. Thus, the distinctness measure is $(1/\sqrt{2})^2 \times 4 = 2$. Note that A_4 does not contribute anything to the action distinctness of A_1, A_2, A_3.

The action distinctness measure satisfies the following desirable properties (proofs omitted for lack of space): (1) the order in which the actions are performed has no effect on its value (and so the order in which the user demonstrates various features of an application does not matter); (2) the repetition of actions (e.g., say $A_3 = A_4$) has no effect on its value (and so the user need not worry about avoiding repeated actions during the demonstration); (3) it is monotonically increasing as one adds more actions to the collection (which is as one would expect since adding another action to the collection should not reduce the collective distinctness of the action collection); (4) it is ≥ 1 and is actually equal to 1 with one action (and so action distinctness and action count coincide with 1 action); and (5) it is $\leq \min(m,n)$ and can actually equal $\min(m,n)$, where m is the number of actions and n is the number of functions (and so action distinctness and action count coincide when the actions are very different provided $m \leq n$).

3.2 Function Prevalence Measure

To compute the prevalence of a function f, we simply find all the actions performed so far that resulted in the execution of f, say $A_{i_1}, \ldots, A_{i_m}$. The prevalence of f is the action distinctness of $A_{i_1}, \ldots, A_{i_m}$, which is computed as described in Section 3.1.

Going back to our example, we find that: f has function prevalence $(1/\sqrt{2})^2 \times 3 = 1\frac{1}{2}$; g has function prevalence $(1/\sqrt{2})^2 \times 3 + (1/\sqrt{3})^2 = 1\frac{5}{6}$; h_1 has function prevalence $(1/\sqrt{2})^2 \times 2 + (1/\sqrt{3})^2 \times 2 = 1\frac{2}{3}$; and h_2 has function prevalence $(1/\sqrt{2})^2 \times 2 + (1/\sqrt{3})^2 = 1\frac{1}{3}$. As expected, f has a lower function prevalence than g. Also note that h_2 has a lower prevalence than h_1 even though they are both executed by two actions; the reason is that the two actions executing h_2 are more similar to each other than the two executing h_1.

Figure 3 shows the use of function prevalence in shedding light on the action shown in Figure 2. As before, horizontal bars indicate function calls, but this time we have horizontal bars for all functions in the call sequence (not just the first few). Moreover, horizontal bars now have different shading: the darker the horizontal bar (and associated label if any), the lower the function prevalence. Finally, the functions labeled are those having the lowest prevalence values. From Figure 3, we confirm our suspicion that the action involved handling a key event; indeed, we know more now as the MathCursor::up is shown in a dark shade and likely indicates that the user pressed the cursor up key in the LyX formula editor. In fact, the first dark burst of function calls has to do with moving the cursor up in the formula editor. Yet, there is another dark burst lower down in the function sequence involving functions such as BufferView::unlockInset, Paragraph::getInset,

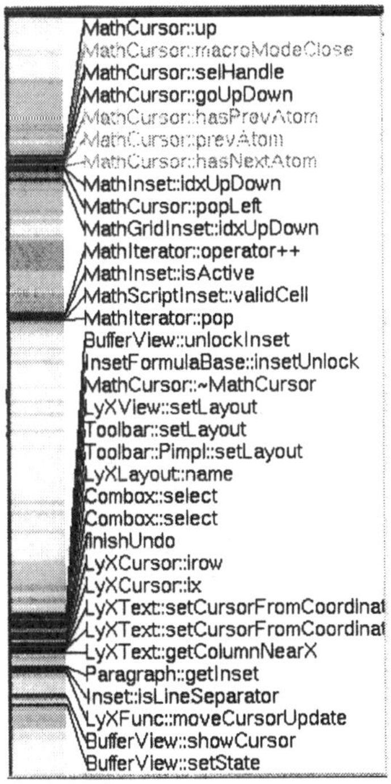

Figure 3. Adding function prevalence to the action from Figure 2.

and BufferView::showCursor. At this point, it is not clear what this second burst of functions does, but the following section on visual descriptions of actions shall shed more light on the matter.

Finally, we note that DRT incrementally updates prevalence values in real-time as new actions are performed. If we return to the action shown in Figure 3 after performing some more actions in LyX, we may find that some of the bar shading and labels shown have changed somewhat to reflect the latest function prevalence values. This is a desirable feature as the user need not repeat an action to see its bar shading/labels updated. Observe that this incremental update of function prevalence can be done quite efficiently as the only functions whose prevalence values can change are those executed by the action just performed.

4 Describing Actions Visually

In the previous section, we have shown how to describe an action by identifying functions in its call sequence that are particularly relevant to that action. However, such information is low-level and may be difficult to understand particularly if one is not familiar with the source code; the functions called are after all part of the implementation of the action. In this section, we show how to describe actions *visually* at a much higher level of abstraction that is closer to action specification.

The key idea is to take a *before screenshot* of the application display just before the action starts and an *after screenshot* of the application display just after the action ends. The timing of these screenshots is important. In particular, the before screenshot is taken just after DRT intercepts the application's KeyDown event (see Section 2) but before that KeyDown event is relayed to the application for processing. This ensures that the before screenshot captures the application display before the action has actually started. (If subsequently no application functions are executed, then no action has taken place — again, see Section 2 — and we simply disregard the before screenshot.) The after screenshot is taken after the timeout from the bottom right state in Figure 1, where we have confirmed that an action has actually taken place.

While it is possible to now describe actions using these before/after screenshots of the entire application display, it may be difficult to spot the difference between the screenshots. Consequently, DRT automatically zooms in on the region of interest and annotates the screenshots to make it more obvious what the user did at that point in the application demonstration.

To see how this works, suppose the KeyDown/KeyUp pair corresponds to a mouse button. In that case, we obtain the (x_1, y_1) coordinates of the mouse when KeyDown occurred as well as (x_2, y_2) when KeyUp occurred and we zoom in on the rectangular region (x_1, y_1, x_2, y_2) in both screenshots. In addition, we mark KeyDown with a small circle at location (x_1, y_1) in the before screenshot to indicate the mouse button press visually and we mark KeyUp with another small circle at location (x_2, y_2) in the after screenshot to indicate the mouse button release visually. Finally, we also draw a line from (x_1, y_1) to (x_2, y_2) to visually show the mouse drag in both screenshots. (If the mouse was not dragged a significant distance, we omit the drag line in both screenshots and the release circle in the after screenshot.)

If the KeyDown/KeyUp pair corresponds to a keyboard button, we try to track the cursor in the application display instead of the mouse pointer. Currently, this is done by having the application display its cursor in a unique color so that we can find it later in the before/after screenshots by scanning the bitmaps. As with mouse tracking, we again zoom in on the region in which the cursor moved and explicitly mark the cursor trail. If we do not find a cursor (some applications such as web browsers may not have them at times), we simply display the before/after screenshots in their entirety without zooming or annotation. We should note that blinking cursors may be missed in the screenshots, so we may need to modify the application code to get rid of cursor blinking (as was the case with LyX). Of course, there

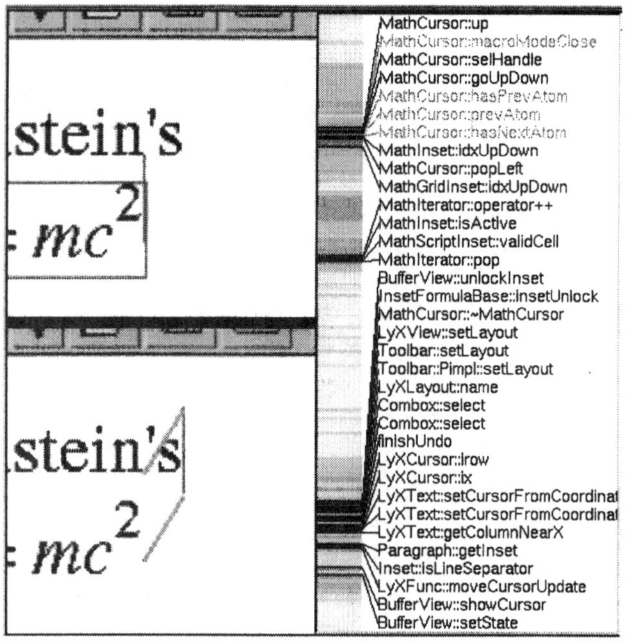

Figure 4. Adding before/after screenshots to the action in Figure 3.

are other ways to track the position of the cursor (e.g., perhaps by asking the application to send cursor coordinates more directly), but our point here is that cursor tracking is a desirable feature for focusing in on the action performed.

Figure 4 shows the addition of before/after screenshots, with zooming and a cursor trail, to the action in Figure 3. It is not surprising that the screenshots show the user moving the cursor up in the formula editor as we had inferred earlier from the function labels. What is surprising is that this upward movement has in fact caused the cursor to leave the math formula editor inset all together as made evident by the disappearance of the math formula editor frame and the movement of the cursor to standard text (just after "Einstein's"). With the addition of the before/after pictures, we now finally understand the action performed. Indeed, the call sequence makes more sense now. The first dark burst of function calls has to do with the upward movement of the cursor in the math formula editor. The second dark burst of function calls has to do with exiting the formula editor and showing a (non-formula) cursor after "Einstein's". In particular, BufferView::unlockInset refers to leaving the formula inset, Paragraph::getInset is used to move to the standard paragraph text, BufferView::showCursor is used to display the non-formula cursor in the normal paragraph mode. It is only in retrospect, after having understood the action from before/after pictures, that these function calls finally make sense. This is not surprising, as the before/after pictures are a high-level abstraction of the action closer to specification than implementation and understanding a specification is typically easier than understanding its implementation — particularly if the specification language is really simple as is the case with our before/after screenshots. Moreover, after having understood the specification, it is then easier to understand the implementation.

5 Searching and Browsing Actions

Once one obtains a collection of actions — performed by others perhaps — it is then possible to search and browse those actions to better understand the design of an application. Such an understanding can then be used to perform some maintenance task. As an example, suppose a software engineer needs to make changes to the LyX cursor code, say to fix incorrect cursor behavior while editing formulas.

Since cursor movement occurs after almost every operation in math mode (e.g., typing a character, moving the cursor explicitly with the cursor keys, etc.), we may wish to get some idea of how various aspects of the formula editor work. To get this understanding, we can search the action collection using a *dynamic query*, which involves actually performing an action on a running application. In particular, we would run LyX under DRT and perform an action (e.g., entering math mode) to see other similar actions (e.g., various formula editor actions) already in the action collection. Figure 5, (a) shows such a dynamic query where the user has entered math mode to use the formula editor. The query action is shown at the top followed by similar actions below ranked by similarity to the query action. Observe that the actions shown are all related to the formula editor although the action collection also includes non-formula editor actions. By looking at the results of this dynamic query, we immediately see typical interactions with the formula editor described visually — entering math mode, typing a summation, moving the math cursor — along with key functions responsible for implementing those interactions. These key functions include cursor related functions most relevant to the particular actions performed (such as MathCursor::up, MathCursor::goUpDown, MathCursor::script, etc.).

DRT also has a *static query* facility that allows one to search for functions whose names contain certain keywords. The set of matching functions is then used to identify actions that execute at least one of these functions. Figure 5, (b) shows the results for the static query "cursor down". Unlike dynamic queries, static queries require the user to know what words to search for (e.g., "cursor" instead of "marker" and "math cursor" instead of "formula cursor"), so some knowledge of the code is helpful to avoid vocabulary mismatch. Observe that this static query uses the implementation to find actions, whereas the dynamic query uses actions to find the implementation. Thus, the

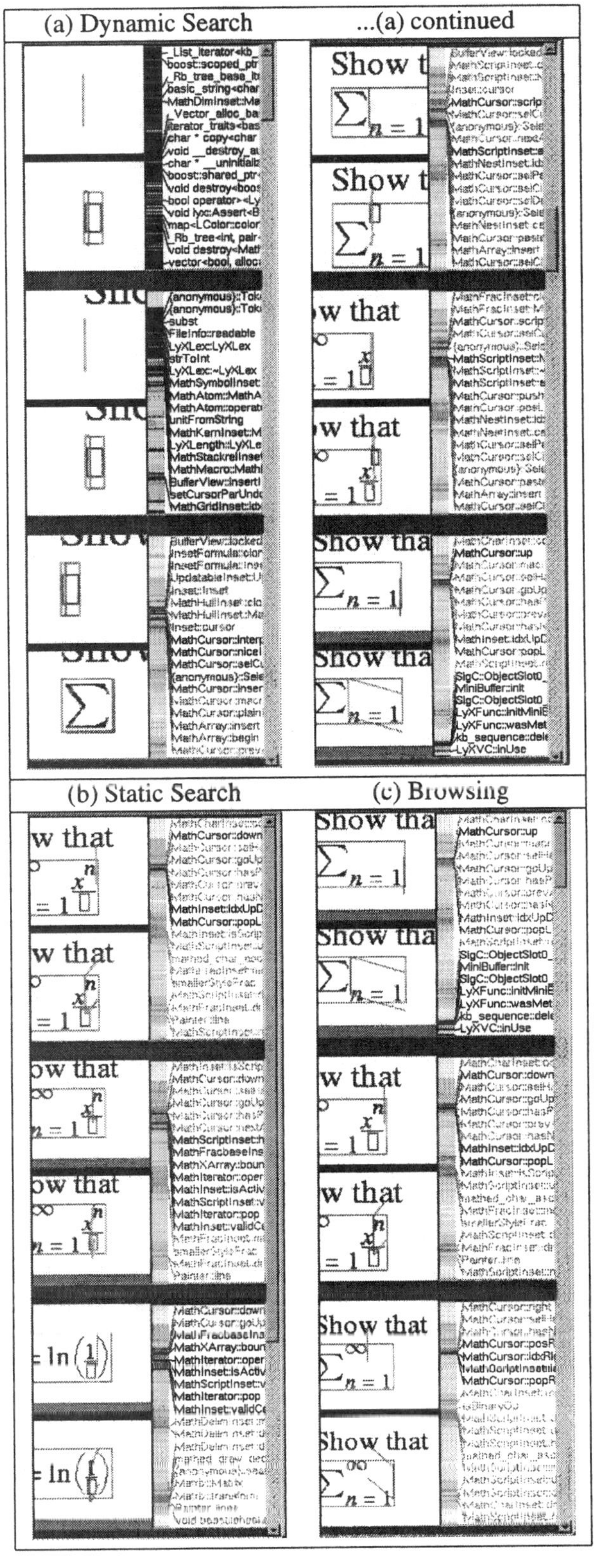

Figure 5. Searching and browsing a LyX action collection.

action/implementation mapping is used in both directions in DRT.

It is also possible to browse actions by simply clicking on an action in the ranking to see similar actions to that action. For example, suppose that after looking at the results of the dynamic query in Figure 5, (a), we decide to further explore actions (and their key functions) related to explicit cursor movement using the cursor keys in the formula editor. In a math editor, such cursor movement code is complicated by the fact that there are many different contexts in which it may occur, and we may wish to explore these various contexts (e.g., movement to the numerator in a fraction, to an exponent, etc.). To do this, we may click on the last action shown in Figure 5, (a) to obtain a list of similar actions shown in Figure 5, (c). Observe that this new list has the action that we clicked at the top followed by similar actions ranked in order of similarity to the top action. In this case, the actions shown have to do with moving the cursor in various ways and in several contexts just as one would expect. Again, to understand the implementation for these movements, one could look at the source code for the key functions shown.

For both searching and browsing, there is a *query function set* Q: (1) for a dynamic query, Q consists of all functions executed by the dynamic query action; (2) for a static query, Q consists of all functions containing all the query keywords in their names; and (3) for a browsing query, Q consists of all the functions executed by the action clicked by the user. DRT ranks actions related to this query function set using the standard cosine similarity measure used in information retrieval [19, p. 185]. In particular, let A_i' denote the set of functions from the action sequence $A_i = (f_1, \ldots, f_n)$, namely $\{f_1, \ldots, f_n\}$. Then the cosine similarity between Q and an action A_i is $\frac{\sum_{f \in Q \cap A_i'} w(f)^2}{\sqrt{\sum_{f \in Q} w(f)^2}\sqrt{\sum_{f \in A_i'} w(f)^2}}$, where $w(f)$ indicates the importance of f, which is taken to be the reciprocal of the function prevalence of f (so the lower the prevalence of f, the more important f becomes).

6 Related Work

6.1 GUISearch

DRT is inspired by our previous research on GUISearch [12]. With GUISearch, we explored the possibility of using the GUI of an application to guide search and browsing of its source code. Intuitively speaking, we can view the various menu items in the GUI as denoting informal specification fragments that tell us the purpose of the code that would be executed as a result of selecting those menu items. Consequently, one can for example search for keywords (e.g., "mail") at a higher level of abstraction (e.g., perhaps matching the menu item "Forward Mail") and discover fundamental entry points into the code (e.g., the corresponding callback doForwardMail).

DRT continues where GUISearch left off. Unlike the static GUISearch approach, DRT works dynamically so that it can (1) make use of the entire application display to provide more complete visual descriptions of the application functionality including non-GUI elements (such as text manipulation in LyX); (2) automatically detect actions performed by a user (described by these visual descriptions); (3) accurately determine the functions called in those actions; and (4) identify which of those functions are particularly relevant to the action (and not just callbacks as in GUISearch).

6.2 Software Visualization

Since DRT uses before/after pictures to describe actions, one can view the tool as a software visualization system. Other work on software visualization typically involves the development of new visualization techniques — independent of the application display — whether they be visualizations of the source code itself [1] or perhaps visualizations of more abstract entities such as algorithms and data structures [3, 8].

DRT also uses visualization to show the sequence of functions executed in an action. Each function call is represented by a horizontal bar, whose color indicates the relevance of that function to the action. This dynamic visualization is similar to the static visualizing of source code where each line of code is shown as a line of pixels color coded to highlight some aspect of the code [1].

6.3 Macro Recorders and Programming by Demonstration

Macro recorders allow users to record their actions and replay them later [5]. For example, a spreadsheet user can automate the selection of certain cells and subsequent copying to another location. DRT also allows users to record actions in an application, but for the purposes of design recovery; they are not replayed later.

Macro recorders record the user's actions verbatim. In contrast, a programming by demonstration system creates generalized programs — possibly with conditionals and loops — from the recorded actions [5]. For example, such a tool may generalize from the actions of a spreadsheet user that it should select all of the rows before row "Total". As another example, the SMARTedit system [10, 11] can generalize editing tasks such as deleting HTML comments from examples. Such generalizations can become more accurate when multiple demonstrations are given by the user for a particular task so that incorrect inferences are filtered out. We did not describe any such generalization mechanism here, but we are experimenting with identifying abstract user actions such as "move cursor" when cursor movement in several directions is demonstrated.

The work on editable graphical histories [9] introduces the notion of before/after pictures to identify past actions in a macro recorder or programming by demonstration system. As an example of this approach, the authors developed a tool that captures the user's actions in a drawing program using before/after pictures so the user could easily go back to some previous point in the session, edit the drawing at that point, and then replay subsequent drawing operations performed in the past. DRT also uses before/after pictures to visualize the application state at a very high level of abstraction.

6.4 Software Clustering

Much of the design recovery literature involves software clustering. Software clustering attempts to automatically decompose software systems into meaningful subsystems to facilitate understanding of those systems (e.g., for maintenance tasks) or to reuse subsystems in other applications [2, 4, 14, 16].

Our approach does not result in a hierarchical decomposition of subsystems. Rather, we obtain a collection of execution traces through the application — namely, the actions — that crosscut multiple subsystems. By exploring multiple execution traces through the code of some concept (e.g., different cursor movements in the formula editor), one can obtain a more general understanding of how that concept works generally.

Software clustering techniques can be divided into two categories: *knowledge-based* and *structure-based* approaches [16]. Knowledge-based approaches attempt to understand what different pieces of source code do by using reverse engineering techniques and pre-existing domain knowledge [2, 14]. For example, such a technique may recognize clusters at a conceptual level, such as a cluster of functions responsible for "reserving an airline seat".

Structure-based approaches look at simpler syntactic interactions between objects [4, 16]. For example, the objects may be functions while the syntactic interactions may be function calls. Structure-based algorithms typically identify clusters based on maximization of cohesion and/or minimization of coupling. Most software clustering researchers have concentrated on structure-based techniques as they do not require building of a knowledge base or problem domain semantics [16].

Our approach does not require any knowledge of the application domain in particular (e.g., word processing); rather, it requires knowledge of graphical interactive applications in general (e.g., the concept of a mouse drag). Such knowledge can be acquired once — and is even independent of the particular GUI frameworks used — and will be applicable to all interactive graphical applications.

6.5 Dynamic Analysis

There has been related research done on selective tracing of atomic units of activity. For example, the drive-by analysis approach employed in the Jinsight tool [13] allows users to define their own notions of execution "burst" by specifying triggers, filters, requested threads, and burst ending criteria. Jinsight returns dynamic information from the burst only, thus allowing users to prune potentially very large amounts of trace data to only those items of interest. We also have a notion of an execution burst in the DRT tool, but we predefine it as explained in Section 2 to automatically capture bursts that correspond closely to the user's notion of an action in an interactive graphical application. While Jinsight does share the generic idea of an execution burst with DRT, it does not take advantage of either the interactive or graphical aspects of applications to automatically find or describe such bursts.

However, there is an interaction-driven tool, LeNDI, for reverse engineering legacy interfaces [7, 15] that identifies the text screens encountered while an application is used and ways (e..g, keyboard input) for getting from one text screen to another. Such information can be helpful in migrating text-based legacy interfaces to newer platforms (e.g., GUIs or the web) or perhaps wrapping them for interaction with other systems. While it may seem that LeNDI is similar to DRT in the way it automatically extracts screens and transitions between them, LeNDI actually makes no connections to the corresponding burst code. The authors acknowledge that LeNDI does not shed much light on the application code behind those text-based interfaces [15]: "Clearly, if the end goal is to extend or modify the system functionality by modifying its current code, then such interaction-based understanding is insufficient because it provides only a model of the user tasks that the system supports and it completely ignores low-level design decisions such as data structures and algorithms."

Our function prevalence computation for identifying functions that are particularly relevant to an action is novel as far as we know. In what follows, we contrast our approach with previous work on mapping application features to components (e.g., functions) that implement those features.

The "software reconnaissance" technique involves running test cases with and without the desired feature and looking for code executed in the test case(s) with the feature that is not executed in the test case(s) without it [17, 18]. Whereas this approach identifies components required for a single feature, work on concept analysis goes further by deriving commonalities and variabilities between components and related features [6]. For example, using concept analysis one can find out which components are jointly needed to implement only a subset of all features.

Some recent work on mapping features to components considers metrics for quantifying the "closeness" between application components and features [20]. In other words, unlike the the feature/component mapping research just described, one now considers the *degree* to which code is related to a particular feature. As far as we know, the only work along this direction [20] develops metrics that consider the number of shared basic blocks between components and features normalized in various ways. For example, the "concentration" (resp. "dedication") between component and a feature is computed by dividing the number of shared basic blocks by the number of basic blocks in the feature (resp. the component). Our function prevalence computation also quantifies the closeness between application components (namely functions) and features (namely actions) — but in a different way. Recall that we consider a function f to be more relevant to an action A than another function g if and only if f is executed in actions that are more similar to each other than g — and in that sense, f is executed in fewer distinct contexts than g and so is more likely to be relevant to action A.

Observe that our method improves upon the shared basic block approach [20] in the following senses: (1) a helper function executed in several quite distinct actions may indeed have most of its shared blocks executed in all these actions (e.g., a helper function to get input from the user say), in which case it would have high "dedication" to these actions yet it would not be considered — as one would expect — particularly relevant to any action in our approach; and moreover, (2) it is unlikely that an action would share many of its shared basic blocks with a single function, and so the "concentration" metric would not likely alleviate the problem mentioned in (1), particularly for fine-grained components (e.g., functions).

7 Conclusions and Future Work

In this paper, we have explored a new approach to design recovery that takes advantage of the interactive and graphical nature of the vast majority of today's applications. We have described the various components of our approach — detecting action boundaries, computing function prevalence, visually describing actions using before/after screen shots, and searching/browsing action collections. We have also demonstrated each of these components using a substantial application, LyX, to show how a software engineer can use our approach to gain insight into the design of an application.

One problem we have encountered with DRT is that some applications perform frequent polling. If the polling interval is smaller than the action boundary detection timeout, then the polling will extend the action indefinitely. To resolve this issue, one can decrease the action boundary detection timeout, change the application code to perform polling less frequently, or perhaps — as future work — develop some heuristics that filter out polling code.

As discussed earlier, our approach is applicable to interactive graphical applications written in an event-driven programming style with alternation between user-initiated events and application responses. Most productivity software is of this form. However, applications such as flight simulators and games are not, since the application proceeds even while the user is idle. For future work, we wish to support this latter group of applications as well. This could be done by discovering "interesting events" (not necessarily actions initiated by the user) by mining the stream of functions executed by the application and then cross-linking these events with key frames in a video taken of the application execution.

References

[1] T. Ball and S. G. Eick. Software visualization in the large. *IEEE Computer*, 29(4):33–43, 1996.

[2] T. J. Biggerstaff, B. G. Mitbander, and D. E. Webster. Program understanding and the concept assignment problem. *Communications of the ACM*, 37(5):72–83, 1994.

[3] M. Brown. Zeus: A system for algorithm animation and multi-view editing. *Computer Graphics*, 18(3):177–186, 1992.

[4] A. Cimitile and G. Visaggio. Software salvaging and the call dominance tree. *Journal of Systems Software*, 28:117–127, 1995.

[5] A. Cypher, editor. *Watch What I do: Programming by Demonstration*. MIT Press, 1993.

[6] T. Eisenbarth, R. Koschke, and D. Simon. Feature-driven program understanding using concept analysis of execution traces. In *9th International Workshop on Program Comprehension*, pages 300–309, 2001.

[7] M. El-Ramly, P. Iglinski, E. Stroulia, P. Sorenson, and B. Matichuk. Modeling the system-user dialog using interaction traces. In *8th Working Conference on Reverse Engineering*, pages 208–217, 2001.

[8] R. R. Henry, K. M. Whaley, and B. Forstall. The University of Washington illustrating compiler. In *PLDI*, pages 223–233, 1990.

[9] D. Kurlander and S. Feiner. Editable graphical histories. In *IEEE Workshop on Visual Languages*, pages 127–134, 1988.

[10] T. Lau, P. Domingos, and D. S. Weld. Version space algebra and its application to programming by demonstration. In *17th International Conference on Machine Learning*, pages 527–534, 2000.

[11] T. Lau and D. S. Weld. Programming by demonstration: An inductive learning formulation. In *International Conference on Intelligent User Interfaces*, pages 145–152, 1999.

[12] A. Michail. Browsing and searching source code of applications written using a GUI framework. In *Proceedings of the 24nd International Conference on Software Engineering*, pages 327–337, 2002.

[13] W. D. Pauw, N. Mitchell, M. Robillard, G. Sevitsky, and H. Srinivan. Drive-by analysis of running programs. In *Proceedings for of ICSE 2001 Workshop on Software Visualization*, pages 17–22, 2001.

[14] R. C. Rich and L. M. Wills. Recognizing a program's design: A graph-parsing approach. *IEEE Software*, 7(1):82–89, 1990.

[15] E. Stroulia, M. El-Ramly, L. Kong, P. Sorenson, and B. Matichuk. Reverse engineering legacy interfaces: An interaction-driven approach. In *6th Working Conference on Reverse Engineering*, pages 292–301, 1999.

[16] V. Tzerpos and R. C. Holt. ACDC: An algorithm for comprehension-driven clustering. In *Proceedings of the Seventh Working Conference on Reverse Engineering*, pages 258–267, 2000.

[17] N. Wilde and C. Casey. Early field experience with the software reconnaissance technique for program comprehension. In *International Conference on Software Maintenance*, pages 312–318, 1996.

[18] N. Wilde and M. S. Scully. Software reconnaissance: Mapping program features to code. *Software Maintenance: Research and Practice*, 7(1):49–62, 1995.

[19] I. H. Witten, A. Moffat, and T. C. Bell. *Managing Gigabytes: Compressing and Indexing Documents and Images*. Morgan Kaufmann, 1999.

[20] W. E. Wong, S. S. Gokhale, and J. R. Horgan. Quantifying the closeness between program components and features. *Journal of Systems and Software*, 54(2):87–98, 2000.

Recovering Documentation-to-Source-Code Traceability Links using Latent Semantic Indexing

Andrian Marcus, Jonathan I. Maletic
Department of Computer Science
Kent State University
Kent Ohio 44242
330 672 9039
amarcus@cs.kent.edu, jmaletic@cs.kent.edu

Abstract

An information retrieval technique, latent semantic indexing, is used to automatically identify traceability links from system documentation to program source code. The results of two experiments to identify links in existing software systems (i.e., the LEDA library, and Albergate) are presented. These results are compared with other similar type experimental results of traceability link identification using different types of information retrieval techniques. The method presented proves to give good results by comparison and additionally it is a low cost, highly flexible method to apply with regards to preprocessing and/or parsing of the source code and documentation.

1. Introduction

Extensive effort in the software engineering community (both research and commercial) has been brought forth to improve the explicit connection of documentation and source code. A number of integrated development environments and CASE tools are particularly focused on this issue. These tools and techniques have made great strides in documentation to source code traceability for the development of new software systems. Unfortunately, many of these methods are inherently unsuited to being applied to existing and/or legacy systems.

The need for tools and techniques to recover documentation to source code traceability links in legacy systems is particularly important for a variety of software engineering tasks. These include general maintenance tasks, impact analysis, program comprehension, and more encompassing tasks such as reverse engineering for redevelopment and systematic reuse.

The major obstacle facing construction of useful tools for this type of link recovery is that the links are rarely explicit and (not without exception) based on the semantic meaning of the prose in the documentation. Relating some sort of natural language analysis of the documentation with that of the source code is an obviously difficult problem.

Our solution to this problem is to utilize an advanced information retrieval technique (i.e., latent semantic analysis) to extract the meaning (semantics) of the documentation and source code [19, 21]. Then use this information to identify traceability links based on similarity measures.

The method utilizes all the comments and identifier names within the source code to produce semantic meaning with respect to the entire input document space. This is supported well by the work of Anquetil [1] and others in determining the importance of this information in existing software. This implies the assumption that the comments and identifiers are reasonably named however, the alternative bares little hope of deriving a meaning automatically (or even manually).

A distinct advantage of using our method is that it does not rely on a predefined vocabulary or grammar for the documentation or source code. This allows the method to be applied without large amounts of preprocessing or manipulation of the input, which drastically reduces the costs of link recovery.

The following section describes the use of information retrieval (IR) methods to software systems and how latent semantic analysis works. We try to highlight the other researchers who have worked in this area in the next section and again in the following related work section. Section 4 details the traceability link recovery process and the following section describes our experiments on existing software systems. These results are then compared with the results of other researchers to highlight the validity and usability of our method.

2. IR and Program Analysis

There is a wide variety of information retrieval methods. Traditional approaches [11, 22] include such methods as signature files, inversion, classifiers, and clustering. Other methods that attempt to capture more information about the documents, to achieve better performance, include those using parsing, syntactic information, natural language processing techniques, methods using neural networks, and advanced statistical methods. Much of this work deals with natural language text and a large number of techniques exist for indexing, classifying, summarizing, and retrieving text documents. These methods produce a profile for each document where the profile is an abbreviated description of the

0-7695-1877-X/03 $17.00 © 2003 IEEE

original document that is easier to manipulate. This profile is typically represented as vector, often real valued. The method we use also has an underlying vector space model. We now present a discussion of this type of representation.

2.1 Vector Space Model

The vector space model (VSM) [23] is a widely used classic method for constructing vector representations for documents. It encodes a document collection by a term-by-document matrix whose $[i, j]^{th}$ element indicates the association between the ith term and j^{th} document. In typical applications of VSM, a term is a word, and a document is an article. However, it is possible to use different types of text units. For instance, phrases or word/character n-grams can be used as terms, and documents can be paragraphs, sequences of n consecutive characters, or sentences. The essence of VSM is that it represents one type of text unit (documents) by its association with the other type of text unit (terms) where the association is measured by explicit evidence based on term occurrences in the documents. A geometric view of a term-by-document matrix is as a set of document vectors occupying a vector space spanned by terms; we call this vector space *VSM space*. The similarity between documents is typically measured by the cosine or inner product between the corresponding vectors, which increases as more terms are shared. In general, two documents are considered similar if their corresponding vectors in the VSM space point in the same (general) direction.

2.2. Latent Semantic Indexing

Latent Semantic Indexing (LSI) [7, 8] is a VSM based method for inducing and representing aspects of the meanings of words and passages reflective in their usage.

Work applying LSI to natural language text by [5, 14] has shown that that LSI not only captures significant portions of the meaning of individual words but also of whole passages such as sentences, paragraphs, and short essays. The central concept of LSI is that the information about word contexts in which a particular word appears, or does not appear, provides a set of mutual constraints that determines the similarity of meaning of sets of words to each other.

2.3. Singular Value Decomposition and LSI

In its typical use for text analysis, LSI uses a user-constructed corpus to create a term-by-document matrix. Then it applies Singular Value Decomposition (SVD) [23] to the term-by-document matrix to construct a subspace, called an LSI subspace. New document vectors (and query vectors) are obtained by orthogonally projecting the corresponding vectors in a VSM space (spanned by terms) onto the LSI subspace.

According to the mathematical formulation of LSI, the term combinations which are less frequently occurring in the given document collection tend to be precluded from the LSI subspace. This fact, together with our examples above, suggests that one could argue that LSI does "noise reduction" if it was true that less frequently co-occurring terms are less mutually-related, and therefore less sensible.

The formalism behind SVD is rather complex and lengthy to be presented here. The interested reader is referred to [23] for details. Intuitively, in SVD a rectangular matrix $\mathbf{X}$ is decomposed into the product of three other matrices. One component matrix ($\mathbf{U}$) describes the original row entities as vectors of derived orthogonal factor values, another ($\mathbf{V}$) describes the original column entities in the same way, and the third is a diagonal matrix ($\mathbf{\Sigma}$) containing scaling values such that when the three components are matrix-multiplied, the original matrix is reconstructed (i.e., $\mathbf{X} = \mathbf{U\Sigma V^T}$). The columns of $\mathbf{U}$ and $\mathbf{V}$ are the left and right singular vectors, respectively, corresponding to the monotonically decreasing (in value) diagonal elements of $\mathbf{\Sigma}$ which are called the singular values of the matrix $\mathbf{X}$. When fewer than the necessary number of factors are used, the reconstructed matrix is a least-squares best fit. One can reduce the dimensionality of the solution simply by deleting coefficients in the diagonal matrix, ordinarily starting with the smallest. The first $\mathbf{k}$ columns of the $\mathbf{U}$ and $\mathbf{V}$ matrices and the first (largest) $\mathbf{k}$ singular values of $\mathbf{X}$ are used to construct a rank-$\mathbf{k}$ approximation to $\mathbf{X}$ through $\mathbf{X_k} = \mathbf{U_k \Sigma_k V_k^T}$. The columns of $\mathbf{U}$ and $\mathbf{V}$ are orthogonal, such that $\mathbf{U^T U} = \mathbf{V^T V} = \mathbf{I_r}$, where $\mathbf{r}$ is the rank of the matrix $\mathbf{X}$. $\mathbf{X_k}$ constructed from the $\mathbf{k}$-largest singular triplets of $\mathbf{X}$ (a singular value and its corresponding left and right singular vectors are referred to as a *singular triplet*), is the closest rank-$\mathbf{k}$ approximation (in the least squares sense) to $\mathbf{X}$.

With regard to LSI, $\mathbf{X_k}$ is the closest $\mathbf{k}$-dimensional approximation to the original term-document space represented by the incidence matrix $\mathbf{X}$. As stated previously, by reducing the dimensionality of $\mathbf{X}$, much of the "noise" that causes poor retrieval performance is thought to be eliminated. Thus, although a high-dimensional representation appears to be required for good retrieval performance, care must be taken to not reconstruct $\mathbf{X}$. If $\mathbf{X}$ is nearly reconstructed, the noise caused by variability of word choice and terms that span or nearly span the document collection won't be eliminated, resulting in poor retrieval performance.

The implementation of LSI has been empirically studied. The work in [8] investigates the effects of several term weighting schemes to instantiate the input term-by-document matrix. Evaluation was based on the precision/recall curves on the retrieval tasks with the dimensionality of the LSI subspace being fixed. Several term-weighting schemes, which combine global weights (i.e., statistics in the collection) and local weights (i.e., statistics within each document), were investigated. LogEntropy, which is a combination of a local log weight and a global entropy weight, showed superiority over the combinations of the local term frequency and global weighting schemes or no global weighting. Two well-known global weightings (i.e., Gfldf and Normal) produced performance worse than no global weighting.

Importantly, several studies have shown that the performance of LSI significantly varies over the dimensionalities of the LSI subspace [7-9]. In practice, the dimensionality is determined experimentally, or "blindly" picked by following the previous work.

Once the documents are represented in the LSI subspace, the user can compute similarities measures between documents by the cosine between their corresponding vectors or by their length. These measures can be used for clustering similar documents together, to identify "concepts" and "topics" in the corpus. This type of usage is typical for text analysis tasks. The LSI representation can also be used to map new documents (or queries) into the LSI subspace and find which of the existing documents are similar (relevant) to the query. This usage is typical for information retrieval tasks.

2.4. Why Use LSI?

A common criticism of VSM is that it does not take account of relations between terms. For instance, having "automobile" in one document and "car" in another document does not contribute to the similarity measure between these two documents.

The fact that VSM produces zero similarity between text units that share no terms is an issue, especially in the information retrieval task of measuring the relevance between documents and a query submitted by a user. Typically, a user query is short and does not cover all the vocabulary for the target concept. Using VSM, "car" in a query and "automobile" in a document do not contribute to retrieving this document (i.e., the synonym problem). LSI attempts to overcome this shortcoming by choosing linear combinations of terms as dimensions of the representation space. The examples in [7, 15] show that LSI may solve this synonym problem by producing positive similarity between related documents sharing no terms.

As the LSI subspace captures the most significant factors (i.e., those associated with the largest singular values) of a term-by-document matrix, it is expected to capture the relations of the most frequently co-occurring terms. This fact is understood when we realize that the SVD factors a term-by-document matrix into the largest one-dimensional projections of the document vectors, and that each of the document vectors can be regarded as a linear combination of terms. In this sense, LSI can be regarded as a corpus-based statistical method. However, the relations among terms are not modeled explicitly in the computation of LSI subspace, which makes it hard to understand LSI in general. Although the fact that an LSI subspace provides the best low rank approximation of the term-by-document matrix is often referred to, it does not imply that the LSI subspace approximates the "true" semantics of documents.

Another of the criticisms of this type method, when applied to natural language texts is that it does not make use of word order, syntactic relations, or morphology. However, very good representations and results are derived without this information [6]. This characteristic is very well suited to the domain of source code and internal documentation. Because much of the informal abstraction of the problem concept may be embodied in names of key operators and operands of the implementation, word ordering has little meaning. Source code is hardly English prose but with selective naming, much of the high level meaning of the problem-at-hand is conveyed to the reader (i.e., the programmer). Internal source code documentation is also commonly written in a subset of English [10] that also lends itself to the IR methods utilized. This makes automation drastically easier and directly supports programmer defined variable names that have implied meanings (e.g., avg) yet are not in the English language vocabulary. The meanings are derived from usage rather than a predefined dictionary. This is a stated advantage over using a traditional natural language type approach.

Like a number of other IR methods, LSI does not utilize a grammar or a predefined vocabulary. However, it uses a list of "stop words" that can be extended by the user. These words are excluded from the analysis. Regardless of the IR method used in text analysis, in order to identify two documents as similar they must have in common concepts represented by the association of terms and their context of usage. In other words, two documents written in different languages will not appear similar. In the case of source code, our main assumption is that developers use the same natural language (e.g., English, Romanian, etc.) in writing internal documentation and external documentation. In addition, the developer should have some consistency in defining and using identifiers.

3. Related Work

The work presented in this paper addresses two specific problems: using IR methods to support software engineering tasks and recovering source code to documentation links. The research that has been conducted on the specific use of applying information retrieval methods to source code and associated documentation typically relates to indexing reusable components [12, 13, 16, 17]. Notable is the work of Maarek [16, 17] on the use of an IR approach for automatically constructing software libraries. The success of this work along with the inefficiencies and high costs of constructing the knowledge base associated with natural language parsing approaches to this problem [10] are the main motivations behind our research. In short, it is very expensive (and often impractical) to construct the knowledge base(s) necessary for parsing approaches to extract even reasonable semantic information from source code and associated documentation. Using IR methods (based on statistical and heuristic methods) may not produce as accurate results, but they are quite inexpensive to apply. If this is then coupled with the structural information (about the program) it should produce good quality and low cost results.

More recently, Maletic and Marcus [19-21] used LSI to derive similarity measures between source code elements. These measures were used then to cluster the source code to help for the identification of abstract data types in procedural code and the identification of concept clones. In addition, these measures were used to define a cohesion metric for components. The work presented here extends these results in a new direction. At the same time, Antoniol et al. [2-4] investigated the use of IR methods to support the traceability recovery process. In particular, they used both a probabilistic method [3, 4] and a vector space model [2] to recover links between source code and documentation, and between source code and requirements. Their results were promising in each case. Additionally this work also supports the choice of vector space models over probabilistic IR. Using LSI makes the work presented here quite different in many aspects and yet provides complementary results.

4. The Traceability Recovery Process

Our traceability recovery process centers on LSI and is partially automated. However, user input is necessary and the degree of user involvement depends on the type of source code and the user's task. As mentioned, recovering the links between source code and documentation may support various software engineering tasks. Different tasks (and users) typically require different types of information. For example, there are times completeness is important. That is, the user needs to recover ALL the correct links even if that means recovering many incorrect ones at the same time. Other times, precision is preferred and the user restricts the search space so all the recovered links will be correct ones, even if this means not finding them all. Our system tries to accommodate both needs (separately of course). One way to accommodate the user needs is by offering multiple ways to recovering the traceability links. We will discuss these approaches in the section 4.3.

Figure 1 depicts the major elements in the traceability recovery process. The entire process is organized in a pipeline architecture; the output from one phase constitutes the input for the next phase. The user's involvement in the process occurs in the beginning for selecting the source code and documentation files. Then the user selects the dimensionality of the LSI subspace. After the LSI subspace is generated, the user determines

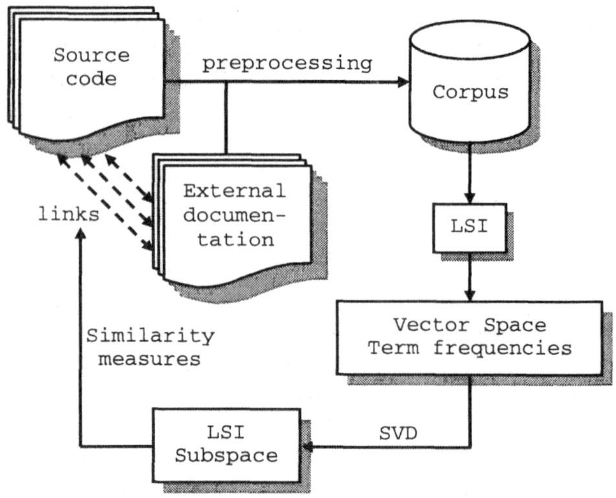

Figure1: The traceability recovery process

what type of threshold will be used in determining the traceability links.

4.1. Building the Corpus

The input data consists of the source code and external documentation. In order to construct a corpus that suits LSI, a simple preprocessing of the input texts is required. Both the source and the documentation need to be broken up into the proper granularity to define the documents, which will then be represented as vectors.

In general, when applying LSI to natural text, a paragraph or section is used as the granularity of a document. Sentences tend to be to small and chapters too large. In source code, the analogous concepts are function, structure, module, file, class, etc. Obviously, statement granularity is too small. More than that, the choice of the granularity level is influenced by the particular software engineering task. In previous experiments involving LSI and source code, we used functions as documents in procedural source code [19, 21] and class declarations in OO source code [20]. The goal there was to cluster elements of the source code based on semantic similarity, rather than mapping them to documentation.

In this application, a part of the documentation may refer to different structures in the source code (i.e., a class, a hierarchy of classes, a set of functions or methods, a data structure, etc.). Therefore, in order to allow for flexibility and simplicity, which in turn better support automation, we define each file as a document. Obviously, some files will be too large. In those situations, the files are broken up into parts roughly the size of the average document in the corpus. This ensures that most of the documents have a close number of words and thus may map to vectors of similar lengths. Of course, in some cases this break up of the files could be rather unfortunate, causing some documents from the source code to appear related to the wrong manual sections. It is a trade-off we are willing to take in favor of simplicity and low-cost of the preprocessing. If this situation is unacceptable for the user, they have the option of (re)combining a number of documents into a new one and identify which existing documents are most similar.

As far as documentation is concerned, the chosen granularity is determined by the division in sections of the documents, defined by the original authors (usually summarized in the table of content).

Some text transformations are required to prepare the source code and documentation to form the corpus for LSI. First, most non-textual tokens from the text are eliminated (e.g., operators, special symbols, some numbers, keywords of the programming language, etc.). Then the identifier names in the source code are split into parts based simply on well-known coding standards. For examples all the following identifiers are broken into the words "hot" and "chocolate": "hot_chocolate", "Hot_chocolate", "hot_Chocolate", "Hot_Chocolate", "HotChocolate", "HOTchocolate". The original form of the identifier is also preserved in the documents. Since we do not consider n-grams, the order of the words is not of importance. Finally, the white spaces in the text are normalized, blank lines separate documents, and the source code and documentation are merged.

Important to note is that in this process, no grammar based parsing of the source code is necessary. LSI does not use a predefined vocabulary, or a predefined grammar, therefore no morphological analysis or transformations are required.

One can argue that the mnemonics and words used in constructing the identifier may not occur in the documentation. That is certainly true. It is in fact the reason why we chose to also use the internal documentation (i.e., comments) in constructing the corpus. It has been shown [10] that internal source code documentation is commonly written in a subset of the language of the developer, similar to that of external documentation. In these situations, the performance of LSI is of great benefit since it is able to associate the terms in the text that are in correct natural language (and also found in the external documentation) with the mnemonics from the identifiers. These mnemonics in turn, will contribute to the similarity between to elements of source code that use the same identifiers. Of course, our assumption is that developers define and use the identifiers with some rationale in mind and not completely randomly.

As mentioned previously, we chose not to do parsing and defined files (or parts of) as documents. Several reasons motivated this choice. First, building a high quality parser for programming languages such as C++ is a non-trivial task due to the nature of the language. Second, often time's large software systems, which we target in our analysis tasks, are written using multiple programming languages. In these situations, a number of parsers are needed and this can turn the traceability problem into something simply impractical. Third, sometimes the user has access to only a part of a very large system, which may not be compile-able, thus causing a hard time for a parser. Parsing is used to extract structural information from the source code, rather than semantic (i.e., domain semantics). This type of information does help in the analysis, but we believe that the semantic analysis and the structural analysis should be performed separately and then the results combined. The traceability recovery process will link a piece of documentation to one or more pieces of code, and then structural information can be used to determine what elements of the systems (e.g., classes) are implemented in that piece of code.

4.2. Defining the Semantic Similarity Measure

Before we give a detailed explanation of this process, some mathematical background and definitions are necessary.

Notation. A bold lowercase letter (e.g., $\mathbf{y}$) denotes a *vector*. A vector is equivalent to a matrix having a single column. The ith entry of vector $\mathbf{y}$ is denoted by $\mathbf{y}_{[i]}$.

Notation. A bold uppercase letter (e.g., $\mathbf{X}$) denotes a *matrix*; the corresponding bold lowercase letter with subscript i (e.g., $\mathbf{x}_i$) denotes the matrix's i[th] column vector. The [i,j][th] entry of matrix $\mathbf{X}$ is denoted by $\mathbf{X}_{[i,j]}$. We write $\mathbf{X} \in \boldsymbol{R}^{m\times n}$ when matrix $\mathbf{X}$ has m rows and n columns whose entries are real numbers.

Definition. A *diagonal matrix* $\mathbf{X} \in \boldsymbol{R}^{n\times n}$ has zeroes in its non-diagonal entries, and is denoted by $\mathbf{X} = \mathrm{diag}(\mathbf{X}_{[1,1]}, \mathbf{X}_{[2,2]}, \ldots, \mathbf{X}_{[n,n]})$.

Definition. An *identity matrix* is a diagonal matrix whose diagonal entries are all one. We denote the identity matrix in $\boldsymbol{R}^{m\times m}$ by $\boldsymbol{I}_m$. For any $\mathbf{X} \in \boldsymbol{R}^{m\times n}$, $\mathbf{X}\mathbf{I}_n = \mathbf{I}_m\mathbf{X} = \mathbf{X}$. We omit the subscript when the dimensionality is clear from the context.

Definition. The *transpose* of matrix $\mathbf{X}$ is a matrix whose rows are the columns of $\mathbf{X}$, and is denoted by $\mathbf{X}^T$, i.e., $\mathbf{X}_{[i,j]} = (\mathbf{X}^T)_{[j,i]}$. The columns of $\mathbf{X}$ are *orthonormal* if $\mathbf{X}^T\mathbf{X} = \mathbf{I}$. A matrix $\mathbf{X}$ is *orthogonal* if $\mathbf{X}^T\mathbf{X} = \mathbf{X}\mathbf{X}^T = \mathbf{I}$.

Definition. The *vector 2-norm* of $\mathbf{x} \in \boldsymbol{R}^m$ is defined by $|\mathbf{x}|_2 = \sqrt{\mathrm{x}^T\mathrm{x}} = \sqrt{\sum_{i=1}^{m} (\mathrm{x}_{[i]})^2}$ we call it the *length* of $\mathbf{x}$.

Definition. The inner product of **x** and **y** is $\mathbf{x}^T\mathbf{y}$. The *cosine* of **x** and **y** is the length-normalized inner product, defined by

$$\cos(\mathbf{x},\mathbf{y}) = \frac{\mathbf{x}^T\mathbf{y}}{|\mathbf{x}|_2 \times |\mathbf{y}|_2} \quad (1)$$

For **x**, **y** ≠ 0; note that cos(**x**, **y**) ∈ [-1, 1]. A larger cosine value indicates that geometrically **x** and **y** point in similar directions. In particular, if **x** = **y** then cos(**x**, **y**) = 1, and **x** and **y** are orthogonal if and only if cos(**x**, **y**) = 0.

Definition. In this process a *source code document* (or simply document) *d* is any contiguous set of lines of source code and/or text. Typically a document is a file of source code or a program entity such as a class, function, interface, etc.

Definition. An *external document* (*e*) is any contiguous set of lines of text from external documentation (i.e., manual, design documentation, requirement documents, test suites, etc.). Typically an external document is a section, a chapter, or maybe an entire file of text.

Definition. The external documentation is also a set of documents $M = \{e_1, e_2, \ldots, e_m\}$. The total number of documents in the documentation is $m = |M|$.

Definition. A *software system* is a set of documents (source code and external) $S = D \cup M = \{d_1, d_2, \ldots, d_n\} \cup \{e_1, e_2, \ldots, e_m\}$. The total number of documents in the system is $n + m = |S|$.

Definition. A *file* f_i, is then composed of a number of documents and the union of all files is *S*. Size of a file, f_i, is the number of documents in the file, noted $|f_i|$.

LSI uses the set $S = \{d_1, d_2, \ldots, d_n, e_1, e_2, \ldots, e_m\}$ as input and determines the *vocabulary* *V* of the corpus. The number of words (or terms) in the vocabulary is $v = |V|$. Based on the frequency of the occurrence of the terms in the documents and in the entire collection, each term is weighted with a combination of a local log weight and a global entropy weight. A term-document matrix $\mathbf{X} \in \mathbf{R}^{v \times n}$ is constructed. Based on the user-selected dimensionality (*k*), SVD creates the LSI subspace. The term-document matrix is then projected onto the *k*-dimensional LSI subspace. Each document $d_i \in D \cup M$, will correspond to a vector $\mathbf{x_i} \in \mathbf{X}$ projected onto the LSI subspace.

Definition. For two documents d_i and d_j, the *semantic similarity* between them is measured by the cosine between their corresponding vectors $sim(d_i, d_j) = \cos(\mathbf{x_i}, \mathbf{y_i})$ The value of the measure will be between [-1, 1] with value (almost) 1 representing that the two are (almost) identical.

One important aspect to consider is the granularity of the documents. The external documentation is usually composed of paragraphs, sections, or chapters. These are then natural choices in determining the definition of an external document in particular cases. The organization of the source code differs from one programming language to another. The simplest way to determine the documents granularity is using the file decomposition. Obviously this will not suffice for all tasks. Therefore choosing classes, functions, or interfaces as source code documents is often time more desirable. Since one of the goals in for the framework to be as flexible as possible, using a full parser for each possible language is impractical. We developed a couple of simple lexical parser that can be used to split up C, C++, and Java source code into documents of different granularity levels (i.e., functions, methods, interfaces, and classes).

4.3. Recovering Traceability Links

At this point in the process the similarity between each pair of documents from *M*x*D* are computed. The user has two options, depending on the desired results. One is to determine a threshold ε for the similarity measure, which identifies which documents are considered "linked". In other words among all the pairs from *M*x*D*, only those will be retrieved which have a similarity measure greater than ε. As mentioned, a good, and widely used, heuristic is ε = 0.7. This measure corresponds to a 45° angle between the corresponding vectors. This threshold has yielded good results [18, 21] when assessing the similarity between pieces of source code. The higher the threshold used the closer the weights on the terms occurring in the documents are. One important thing to consider here is that the documents from the *M* are different in nature than the ones from *D*. Therefore, a lower threshold may yield good results. The issue of the "best" threshold for this type of corpus (i.e., combining source code and documentation) is still open and further research is needed.

Before we explain the other alternative, a way to determine the "goodness" of the results is needed. Two of the most common measures for the quality of the results in experiments with IR methods are *recall* and *precision*. In general, for a given document d_i, the similarity measure and the defined threshold will be used to retrieve a number N_i of documents, based on the LSI subspace that are deemed similar to d_i. Among these N_i documents, $C_i \le N_i$ of them are actually similar to d_i. Assume that there are a total of $R_i \ge C_i$ documents that are in fact similar to d_i. With these numbers we define the recall and precision for d_i as follows:

$$\text{Recall} = \frac{C_i}{R_i} = \frac{\#correct \wedge retrieved}{\#correct}\%$$

$$\text{Precision} = \frac{C_i}{N_i} = \frac{\#correct \wedge retrieved}{\#retrieved}\%$$

Both measures will have values between [0, 1]. If recall = 1, it means that all the correct links are recovered, though there could be recovered links that are not correct. If the precision = 1, it means that all the recovered links are correct, though there could be correct links that were not recovered. For the entire system the recall and precision are computed as follows:

$$\text{Recall} = \frac{\sum_{i=n+1}^{m} C_i}{\sum_{i=n+1}^{m} R_i} \%\,; \qquad \text{Precision} = \frac{\sum_{i=n+1}^{m} C_i}{\sum_{i=n+1}^{m} N_i} \%$$

With this in mind, choosing a higher threshold for the link recovery will result in higher precision, while lowering the threshold will increase the recall. In general, the consequence of higher precision is a lower recall (and vice versa).

A second option for the user is to impose a threshold on the number of recovered links, regardless of the actual value of the similarity measure. Thus, the user may chose to select the top θ ranked links for each document, where $\theta \in \{1, 2, 3,\ldots, n\}$. This is the approached preferred by Antoniol et al [2-4] and is a common way to deal with a list of ordered solutions. Finally, the user can opt to combine the two types of thresholds, for example to retrieved the top θ ranked links among those that have a similarity measure greater than ε.

The different choices accommodate different user needs. Using the threshold method, with a high enough threshold value, will yield high precision. Choosing the right threshold is in fact tricky. The only heuristic the user has is past experience. As mentioned, in text retrieval a 0.7 value for the threshold provided good results in a number of earlier experiments. The same threshold may or may not be best suited fro different software systems. Determining a more generally usable heuristic for selection of the appropriate threshold is an issue under investigation and future research will report on it.

Using the ranking method, the user will achieve 100% recall in a in a few number of steps. Precision however will be significantly reduced from one step to the next.

5. Experiments and Results

In the experiments presented here, we have attempted to approximate the ones done by Antoniol et al [2-4] to give us a means of relevant comparison to their work. The goal is to assess how well LSI performs in this type of software engineering task, with respect to other IR methods used by Antoniol et al. There are a number of small differences between the experiments that will be explained.

5.1. Experiment and Results for LEDA

The software system used for analysis is release 3.4 of LEDA (Library of Efficient Data types and Algorithms), a well known library developed and distributed by Max Planck Institut für Informatik, Saarbrücken, Germany (and lately by Algorithmic Solutions Software GmbH) together with its manual pages. This is the same release used by Antoniol et al.

We included in the analysis the entire library, the demo programs, and the entire manual. Table 1 contains the size of the system and manual, as well as the dimensionality used for the LSI subspace and the determined vocabulary.

Table 1. Elements of the LEDA source code, documentation, and LSI settings used in the analysis

LEDA 3.4	Count	Documents
Source code files	491	684
Manual sections	115	119
Total # of documents		803
Classes	219	In 218 files
Vocabulary	3814	-
LSI dimensions used	200 - 400	Increments of 50

We decided to use the entire manual and available source code to ensure the generation of a rich enough semantic space and vocabulary. In the end, we recovered the links for only the 88 manual sections 2.1 through 11.5 that were used in the experiments of Antoniol et al. Although we realized that using extra source code files might corrupt the results in lowering the precision, we decided on this approach since it mimics the situation when the system to be analyzed is new to the engineer and they do not know what is the core part of the system.

In addition, since the number of manual documents is much smaller than the number of source code files, we decided to trace the links from the manual to the source code, rather than vice versa (as done by Antoniol et al). The assumption is that the user can easily read the manual, and the source code is the unknown factor. A typical query would be to find out which parts of the source code are described by a given manual section. Of course, in a bottom-up type of analysis the user might ask which manual section describes a given piece of source

Table 2. Recovered links, recall, and precision using cosine value threshold. For LEDA.

Cosine threshold	Correct links retrieved	Incorrect links retrieved	Missed links	Total links recovered	Precision	Recall
0.60	81	109	33	190	42.98 %	71.01 %
0.65	68	58	46	126	53.97 %	59.65 %
0.70	49	20	65	69	71.05 %	42.63 %

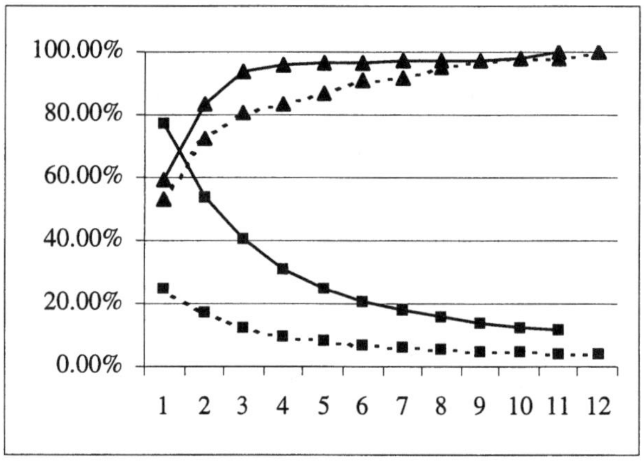

Figure 2. Recall and precision values for experiment by Antoniol and experiments with LSI using LEDA. x-axis represents the cut point and y-axis represents recall/precision values.

code. That can be established with one user query. To retrieve all the links, we believe starting from the smaller set yields better results. One more consideration determined our choice. Since our method does not require parsing of the code, its is not practical to set as starting point the implementation of a class (which can only be determined by some syntactic parsing) to recover the traceability links. Among the 219 classes, 116 are implemented in one file, 95 classes are implemented in two files, seven classes in three files, and one class in 12 files.

We found that the 88 manual sections relate to 80 classes (we did not consider the children in the inheritance hierarchies) implemented in 104 files. 34 of the manual documents relate to two source code files, 46 to one file only, and 8 to relate no class file. 10 of the files contain implementation of multiple classes, described by more than one manual section. Essentially, we found 114 correct links against which we computed recall and precision of LSI. The numbers differ from those in the Antoniol et al experiments mainly because they used classes as units of text, while we used source code files.

Before discussing our results, we should reiterate that the LEDA manual is generated, in large part, directly from the source and include sections of the code and comments. One can argue that in this case the recovery should be trivial. Although it is easier than on a different kind of system with poorer documentation (as it is often the case), it is still far from trivial. By using LEDA for these experiments, we can compare the results with previous research and better assess the quality of our experiments.

As mentioned previously, there are at least two possibilities in determining the traceability links between documentation and source code, using a semantic similarity measure. One is to use a threshold based on the value of the similarity measure and consider that a pair of documents determine a correct traceability link if their semantic similarity is larger than the established threshold. Second (as used by Antoniol et al) is to establish a cut point and consider as correct links all the top ranked pairs down to the cut point. The ranking being determined based on the semantic similarity measure between each pair of documents.

Our assumption was that using the first method with a threshold around 0.7 will yield better precision and lower recall that the second option. Table 2 summarizes the results we obtained on recovering the traceability links between manual pages and source code for LEDA. The first column (Cosine) represents the threshold value; column 2 (Correct links retrieved) represents the number of correct links recovered; column 3 (Incorrect links retrieved) represents the number of incorrect links recovered; column 4 (Missed links) represents the number of correct links that were not recovered; column 5 (Total links retrieved) represents the total number of

Table 3. Retrieved links, recall, and precision using top ranking (for LEDA).

Cut point	Correct links retrieved	Incorrect links retrieved	Missed links	Total links retrieved	Precision	Recall
1	68	20	27	88	77.27 %	59.65 %
2	95	81	19	176	53.98 %	83.33 %
3	107	157	7	264	40.53 %	93.86 %
4	109	243	5	352	30.97 %	95.61 %
5	110	330	4	440	25.00 %	96.49 %
6	110	418	4	528	20.83 %	96.49 %
7	111	505	3	616	18.02 %	97.37 %
8	111	592	3	703	15.79 %	97.37 %
9	111	680	3	791	14.03 %	97.37 %
10	112	767	2	879	12.74 %	98.25 %
11	114	853	0	967	11.79 %	100.0 %

recovered links (correct + incorrect); and the last two columns the precision and recall for each threshold.

We used 0.7 as initial threshold, and although the precision value was indeed good, the recall was rather low. Therefore, we decided to relax the selection criteria and lowered incrementally the threshold. As expected, the recall improved, but the precision deteriorated. Our goal was to determine an approximate correlation between the increase and decrease of the two measures.

To validate our hypothesis we repeated the experiment using a cut point for the best-ranked pairs of documents, as done by Antoniol et al [2-4]. Table 3 summarizes the results obtained in this case. The table is defined just as table 2, except that the first column represents the cut point rather than similarity measure threshold. As we can see, recall and precision seem to be a bit better than in the previous case, contradicting our initial assumptions. In order to compare the results with the Antoniol et al's experiments [2-4], which used both a probabilistic and a VSM IR methods, with parsing the code and morphologically analyzed the texts, we used as many number of cut points as necessary to obtain 100% recall. Figure 2 compares the precision and recall between the two sets of experiments. The values used for Antoniol's experiments are the better they had among the probabilistic and VSM. Dashed lines marked with squares and triangles show the precision and recall, respectively, obtained by Antoniol, while the solid lines indicate the same measures obtained using LSI.

The recall values we obtained are slightly better than the ones of Antoniol, LSI helps reach 100% recall value one step before their methods. The precision however, is much better for LSI in this case, with respect to the probabilistic and the VSM methods used by Antoniol. This came as no surprise considering the very reasons that motivated our preference for LSI to be used in this type of analysis and our choice of starting point (documents rather than source code).

The recall values prompted a closer inspection of the results. We expected better results by comparison (similar to the precision). As seen in table 3, all but 7 of the correct links are recovered after selecting the top 3 ranked pairs of documents. More than that, all but 3 of the correct links are recovered after selecting the top 7 ranked pairs of documents. We looked closer to the remaining 3 pairs. These were the manual sections describing the classes: *integer*, *integer matrix*, and *set*, respectively (i.e., sections 3.1, 3.6, and 4.9, respectively). As most of the other section in the manual, these describe the structure of the classes to help in and reflect the usage of them, rather than describing implementation details. Therefore, files that intensively use any of these classes will have a larger similarity measure that the files which implement the class. Even more, these particular classes are basic types, ubiquitously used throughout the LEDA package.

This fact also explains the precision values. Remember that more than half of the source code does not contribute to the implementation of the classes directly referred to by the manual sections. Again, using LSI will identify pairs of similar documents where the similarity indicates that the source code file uses the methods described in the documentation. In reality, this is a valid similarity and one can claim that in fact the manual page also relates to those source code files. We subscribe to this point of view. However, in order to perform a thorough comparison of the results, we had to define very conservatively the "correct links". The point here is that the method lends itself naturally to recover other types of links between documentation and source code.

5.2. Experiments and Results for Albergate

For a second set of experiments, we used the Albergate system, kindly provided by Giuliano Antoniol and Massimiliano Di Penta. Albergate is implemented in Java by Italian students and has 95 classes. Antoniol et al [2] analyzed 60 classes together with 16 requirements documents. We had only 58 of the classes and 13 of the requirement documents. This fact did not influence the results significantly. In this case, only three files contained the implementation for more than one class. We broke those files so that each file contained only one class. The numbers in table 4 reflect these changes. In other words, the setup for this experiment is almost identical with the one described in [2], since a document in our space corresponds to a class (in most cases). However, this is not true for all documents and a small number represent more than one class. Some of the files were large and were broken into multiple documents. Note that all the documentation is written in Italian. However, our process was essentially unchanged due to the fact our method is not dependent on a language or grammar.

Table 4. Elements of the Albergate source code, documentation, and LSI settings used in the analysis

Albergate	Count	Documents
Source code files	58	76
Requirements files	13	13
Total # of documents		89
Classes	58	76
Vocabulary	1198	
LSI dimensions used	300	

Albergate is a very different system than LEDA. First, it is implemented in Java and has documentation in Italian. Second the external documentation is in the form of requirement documents which describe elements of the problem domain, while in the case of LEDA often the manual pages referred to elements of the solution domain

Table 5. Retrieved links, recall, and precision using top rankings (for Albergate).

Cut point	Correct links retrieved	Incorrect links retrieved	Missed links	Total links retrieved	Precision	Recall
1	26	32	31	58	44.83 %	45.61 %
2	33	83	24	116	28.45 %	57.89 %
3	43	131	14	174	24.71 %	75.44 %
4	49	183	8	232	21.12 %	85.96 %
5	52	238	5	290	17.93 %	91.23 %
6	57	291	0	348	16.38 %	100.00 %

(much better represented in the source code). In addition, the requirement documents are supposed to have been written before implementation and do not include any parts of the internal documentation or the source code. Finally, the requirement documents are very short and have a fixed format with common headings. These headings have nothing in common with the problem domain and are the same in each document. The size of the system was also a concern for us. IR methods in general and LSI in particular, are designed to work on very large corpora. That is, the larger and richer (in semantics) the corpus, the better results. The entire philosophy of LSI is on the reduction of this large corpus to a manageable size without loss of information. When the corpus is small with terms and concepts distributed scarcely throughout the space, reduction of the dimensionality could result in significant loss of information. In consequence, and considering previous results, we expected lower recall and precision values than in the case of LEDA.

Table 5 summarizes the results of the traceability recovery process for Albergate. The structure of the table is the same as table 4, described above.

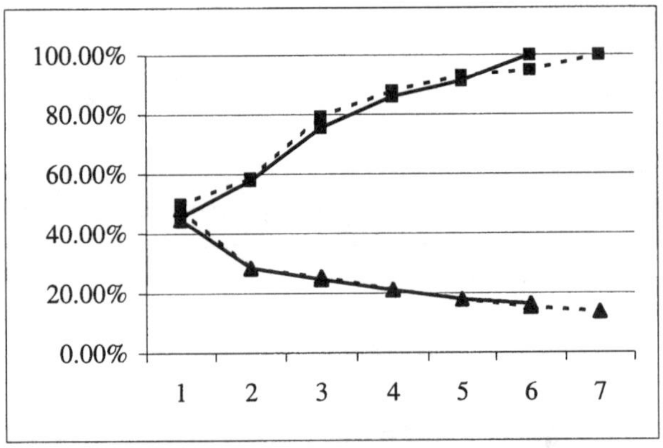

Figure 3. Recall and precision values for experiment by Antoniol and experiments with LSI using Albergate. x-axis represents the cut point and y-axis represents recall/precision values.

Confirming our hypothesis, the precision was lower, however the 100% recall target was reached faster than in the case of LEDA, with better precision. The explanation is that, unlike in the LEDA case, the uses of classes by each other are less intensive in Albergate.

Figure 3 shows graphically how our results compare with those obtained by Antoniol et al [2, 3]. Remember that this time the setup of the experiments and the benchmark mapping are almost identical. The results are very close the only significant difference is that using LSI the 100% recall is reached one step sooner (selecting the top 6 ranked pairs, rather than 7). One more thing to note is that the Albergate source code contains less than 300 lines of internal documentation (i.e., comments).

7. Conclusions and Future Work

The paper presents a method to recover traceability links between documentation and source code, using an information retrieval method, namely Latent Semantic Indexing (LSI). A set of experiments was presented and the results analyzed by comparing them with previous related research by Antoniol et al [2-4].

The method using LSI performs at least as well as Antoniol's methods using probabilistic and VSM IR methods combined with full parsing of the source code and morphological analysis of the documentation.

Our method requires less processing of the source code and documentation, implicitly, less computation. It is language, programming language, and paradigm independent, thus more flexible, and better suited for automation. These characteristics allow us to use the internal documentation in the analysis (not used by Antoniol), which we believe allows LSI to produce better results. The Albergate case is an example of this hypothesis. With almost no comments in the source code, LSI does perform at least as well as the other methods.

The results are promising enough to warrant future research. We shall repeat these experiments on other types of software systems (i.e., written in different programming languages and with different type of documentation). In addition, we will work on improving the results by combining structural and semantic information extracted from the source code and its associated documentation.

Although promising, we believe the results could be further improved. The semantic similarity measure defined using LSI (or any other IR method) could be augmented by considering structural information of the program. For example, in the case of LEDA selecting the top ranked pair of documents (cut point 1 row in table 4) the precision is very high. The recall value is of relatively low. The reason is simple. 95 of the classes are implemented in more than one file so recovering only one of them we miss a large percentage of the links. In this situation, one could use extra structural information to extend this step. For example, file include information (for C/C++), and inheritance information can be utilized to improve results. We are currently experimenting with these enhancements to the method and future work will report on the results.

Finally, we are trying to determine some good heuristics that the user and the system can use to determine the appropriate threshold value for similarity measures. This is dependent on the maintenance task that is addressed, the programming language, the quantity and quality of the documentation.

9. Acknowledgements

This work was supported in part by a grant from the National Science Foundation (CCR-02-04175).

10. References

[1] Anquetil, N. and Lethbridge, T., "Assessing the Relevance of Identifier Names in a Legacy Software System", in Proceedings CASCON 1998, December 1998, pp. 213-222.

[2] Antoniol, G., Canfora, G., Casazza, G., and De Lucia, A., "Information Retrieval Models for Recovering Traceability Links between Code and Documentation", in Proceedings IEEE International Conference on Software Maintenance (ICSM'00), San Jose, CA, October 11-14 2000, pp. 40-51.

[3] Antoniol, G., Canfora, G., Casazza, G., De Lucia, A., and Merlo, E., "Tracing Object-Oriented Code into Functional Requirements", in Proceedings 8th International Workshop on Program Comprehension (IWPC'00), Limerick, Ireland, June 10-11 2000, pp. 79 - 87.

[4] Antoniol, G., Canfora, G., De Lucia, A., and Merlo, E., "Recovering Code to Documentation Links in OO Systems", in Proceedings 6th IEEE Working Conference on Reverse Engineering (WCRE'99), October 6-8 1999, pp. 136-144.

[5] Berry, M. W., "Large Scale Singular Value Computations", Int. Journal of Supercomputer Applications, 6, 1992, pp. 13-49.

[6] Berry, M. W., Dumais, S. T., and O'Brien, G. W., "Using Linear Algebra for Intelligent Information Retrieval", SIAM: Review, 37, 4, 1995, pp. 573-595.

[7] Deerwester, S., Dumais, S. T., Furnas, G. W., Landauer, T. K., and Harshman, R., "Indexing by Latent Semantic Analysis", Journal of the American Society for Information Science, 41, 1990, pp. 391-407.

[8] Dumais, S. T., "Improving the retrieval of information from external sources", Behavior Research Methods, Instruments, and Computers, 23, 2, 1991, pp. 229 - 236.

[9] Dumais, S. T., "Latent Semantic Indexing (LSI): TREC-3 report", in The Third Text REtrieval Conference (TREC3), 1995, pp. 135-144.

[10] Etzkorn, L. H. and Davis, C. G., "Automatically Identifying Reusable OO Legacy Code", IEEE Computer, 30, 10, October 1997, pp. 66-72.

[11] Faloutsos, C. and Oard, D. W., "A Survey of Information Retrieval and Filtering Methods", University of Maryland, Technical Report CS-TR-3514, August 1995.

[12] Fischer, B., "Specification-Based Browsing of Software Component Libraries", in Proceedings of ASE, 1998, pp. 74-83.

[13] Frakes, W., "Software Reuse Through Information Retrieval", in Proceedings 20th Annual HICSS, Kona, HI, Jan. 1987, pp. 530-535.

[14] Landauer, T. K. and Dumais, S. T., "A Solution to Plato's Problem: The Latent Semantic Analysis Theory of the Acquisition, Induction, and Representation of Knowledge", Psychological Review, 104, 2, 1997, pp. 211-240.

[15] Landauer, T. K., Foltz, P. W., and Laham, D., "An Introduction to Latent Semantic Analysis", Discourse Processes, 25, 2&3, 1998, pp. 259-284.

[16] Maarek, Y. S., Berry, D. M., and Kaiser, G. E., "An Information Retrieval Approach for Automatically Constructing Software Libraries", IEEE Transactions on Software Engineering, 17, 8, 1991, pp. 800-813.

[17] Maarek, Y. S. and Smadja, F. A., "Full Text Indexing Based on Lexical Relations, an Application: Software Libraries", in Proceedings SIGIR89, Cambridge, MA, June 1989, pp. 198-206.

[18] Maletic, J. I. and Marcus, A., "Using Latent Semantic Analysis to Identify Similarities in Source Code to Support Program Understanding", in Proceedings 12th IEEE International Conference on Tools with Artificial Intelligence (ICTAI), Vancouver, British Columbia, November 13-15 2000, pp. 46-53.

[19] Maletic, J. I. and Marcus, A., "Supporting Program Comprehension Using Semantic and Structural Information", in Proceedings 23rd International Conference on Software Engineering (ICSE 2001), Toronto, Ontario, Canada, May 12-19 2001, pp. 103-112.

[20] Maletic, J. I. and Valluri, N., "Automatic Software Clustering via Latent Semantic Analysis", in Proceedings 14th IEEE International Conference on Automated Software Engineering (ASE'99), Cocoa Beach Florida, October 1999, pp. 251-254.

[21] Marcus, A. and Maletic, J. I., "Identification of High-Level Concept Clones in Source Code", in Proceedings Automated Software Engineering (ASE'01), San Diego, CA, November 26 29 2001, pp. 107-114.

[22] Salton, G., Automatic Text Processing: The Transformation, Analysis and Retrieval of Information by Computer, Addison-Wesley, 1989.

[23] Salton, G. and McGill, M., Introduction to Modern Information Retrival, McGraw-Hill, 1983.

Technical Papers

Formal Methods I

Computer-Assisted Assume/Guarantee Reasoning with VeriSoft

Juergen Dingel

School of Computing
Applied Formal Methods Group
Queen's University
Kingston, Ontario, Canada
dingel@cs.queensu.ca

Abstract

We show how the state space exploration tool VeriSoft can be used to analyze parallel C/C++ programs compositionally. VeriSoft is used to check assume/guarantee specifications of parallel processes automatically. The analysis is meant to complement standard assume/guarantee reasoning which is usually carried out solely with "pencil and paper". While a successful analysis does not always imply the general correctness of the specification, it increases the confidence in the verification effort. An unsuccessful analysis always produces a counterexample which can be used to correct the specification or the program. VeriSoft's optimization and visualization techniques make the analysis relatively efficient and effective.

1 Introduction

There has recently been a lot of interest in making formal analysis techniques more light-weight [12]. Compared to traditional formal methods, light-weight formal methods

- give more immediate feedback which allows for a more gradual learning curve and more immediate results,
- are complemented by fully automatic tools which hide the complexities of the method from the novice user, and
- offer decidability and efficiency at the expense of completeness or expressiveness.

The overall goal is to allow even novice users more effective and efficient use of formal techniques and thus pave the way for a more general adoption. The design of a number of recently developed formal analysis tools has been influenced by this goal. The software model checking tool kit Bandera [4], for instance, reduces the burden on the user by offering a much higher degree of automation than traditional model checking tools. More precisely, Bandera applies abstractions to programs and translates the result into finite state machines with little user interaction. The state space exploration tool VeriSoft [8] does away with the translation all together by analyzing source code directly. It guarantees termination by sacrificing completeness and by exploring the state space of a program only up to a certain, user-specified depth.

Assume/guarantee reasoning (sometimes also called *rely/guarantee reasoning* or *assumption/commitment reasoning*) allows compositional analysis in the presence of concurrency [14, 19, 1]. Parallel processes can be reasoned about by first reasoning about the processes in isolation and then combining the properties of each process to a property of the entire system. This kind of analysis typically is more efficient than a monolithic analysis, because the number of possible behaviours of a parallel system grows exponentially with the number of parallel processes. Moreover, a monolithic analysis does not expose the interface between components, that is, it does not shed any light on which assumptions a component makes about its environment and which guarantees it is able to give. Assume/guarantee reasoning on the other hand is based on identifying these assumptions and guarantees. This kind of information might allow the user, for instance, to replace one component safely by another or to determine which kinds of changes in the environment the component can tolerate. The maintenance of parallel or embedded systems thus often requires some kind of assume/guarantee analysis.

While the theory of assume/guarantee reasoning has been explored very thoroughly, it does seem that "it has been more widely studied than used" [21]. We attribute this phenomenon partially to the fact that assume/guarantee reasoning is not a light-weight technique. Recently, the work in [17] discussed the automatic generation of environment

0-7695-1877-X/03 $17.00 © 2003 IEEE

drivers for software components from assume/guarantee specifications for use in model checking. This work, however, focused on assume/guarantee reasoning based on temporal logic [10, 23]. In this paper we show how VeriSoft can be used without much effort to check invariant-based assume/guarantee specifications. The goal of our work is to demonstrate how an existing tool can be used to develop, debug, and check this kind of specification and thus make assume/guarantee reasoning more light-weight.

We proceed by briefly reviewing invariant-based assume/guarantee reasoning in the next section. Section 3 describes the VeriSoft tool, and Section 4 shows how it can be used to check specifications. Section 5 presents a few examples that illustrate the use of our method. Section 6 concludes and outlines further work.

2 Assume/guarantee reasoning

To explain assume/guarantee reasoning we need a semantic model of parallel computation that takes environment interference into account. Numerous such models exist. We choose transition traces due to their many pleasant theoretical properties [2], but other models could also be used.

2.1 The underlying computational model

A *transition trace* (sometimes also called *potential* or *partial computations* or *extended sequences*) is a finite or infinite sequence of the form

$$(s_0, s_0')(s_1, s_1') \dots (s_i, s_i')(s_{i+1}, s_{i+1}') \dots$$

where each s_i and s_i' is a state, that is, a mapping from program variables to values. A trace represents a possible "interactive" computation of a program in which state changes made by the program (from s_i to s_i') are interleaved with state changes made by its environment (from s_i' to s_{i+1}). We call a state change from s_i to s_i' a *program transition* and a change from s_i' to s_{i+1} an *environment transition*. The meaning $\mathcal{T}[\![C]\!]$ of a program C is then given by its set of transition traces closed under two closure conditions that correspond to the reflexive and transitive closure of a standard operational semantics. The semantics models, for instance, sequential composition through trace concatenation, iteration through repeated concatenation, and parallel composition through the fair merge of traces. A hiding operation ensures that the values of local variables are invisible outside their syntactic scope. Consider, for instance, the program

$$C_1 \equiv \begin{array}{l} \textbf{new } i = 1 \textbf{ in} \\ \quad \textbf{while } i < 3 \textbf{ do} \\ \quad\quad x := x + 1; \\ \quad\quad i := i + 1 \\ \quad \textbf{od} \\ \textbf{end} \end{array}$$

The transition trace set $\mathcal{T}[\![C_1]\!]$ of C_1 includes

$$(s_0, [s_0|x = s_0(x) + 1])(s_1, [s_1|x = s_1(x) + 1])$$

and

$$(s_0, [s_0|x = s_0(x) + 2])$$

for all states s_0 and s_1 of C_1 where $[s|x = v]$ denotes the state that is like s except that x has value v. So,

$$(x = 0 \wedge i = 0, x = 1 \wedge i = 0)(x = 5 \wedge i = 3, x = 6 \wedge i = 3)$$
$$(x = 0 \wedge i = 0, x = 2 \wedge i = 0)$$

are two traces of C_1 where $x = v_1 \wedge i = v_2$ stands for the state s in which x has value v_1 and i has value v_2, that is, $s(x) = v_1$ and $s(i) = v_2$. The first trace represents a computation in which the value of x is incremented by the program first from 0 to 1 and then from 5 to 6. Between these two increments the environment interferes and changes the values of x and i from 1 and 0 to 5 and 3, respectively. Note that the environment interference on the global occurrence of variable i does not affect the number of increments on x. This is because the global occurrence of i is shadowed in C_1 by a local occurrence. In the second trace, the program executes without interference.

However, the following three traces

$$(x = 0 \wedge i = 1, x = 3 \wedge i = 1)$$
$$(x = 0 \wedge i = 1, x = 0 \wedge i = 1)$$
$$(x = 0 \wedge i = 0, x = 2 \wedge i = 2)$$

are not traces of C_1. The first two traces describe two computations that start with $x = 0$ and end with $x = 3$ and $x = 0$, respectively. Both traces are impossible for C_1, because every uninterrupted execution of C_1 from a state in which $x = 0$ must set x to 2. In the third trace, C_1 changes the value of i. This trace also is impossible, because i is local in C_1 and thus changes to it are invisible outside its scope. In other words, the value of i cannot change across a program transition.

Note that the semantics does not require assignments to be executed atomically. More precisely, the semantics can be adapted, for instance, to account for non-atomic expression evaluation. More details about transitions traces can be found in [2].

2.2 Specifications

Various formulations of assume/guarantee reasoning exist. We will use a slight variation of the one introduced by Stirling in [22]. In this paper, a assume/guarantee specification has the form

$$[P,\Gamma]\ C\ [Q,\Delta]$$

where P and Q are state predicates and Γ and Δ are sets of state predicates. The specification holds if and only if for all transition traces t of C such that the first state of t satisfies P and every environment transition in t preserves all predicates in Γ, then every program transition in t preserves all predicates in Δ and if t is finite, the last state satisfies Q.

Definition 2.1 *We say that C satisfies the specification*

$$[P,\Gamma]\ C\ [Q,\Delta]$$

if and only if for every trace

$$t \equiv (s_0, s'_0)(s_1, s'_1)(s_2, s'_2)\ldots \in \mathcal{T}[\![C]\!]$$

such that

- $s_0 \models P$*, and*
- $s_{i+1} \models R$ *whenever* $s'_i \models R$*, for all* $0 \leq i < length(t)$ *and* $R \in \Gamma$*,*

we have

- $s_n \models Q$ *whenever t is finite with last state* s_n*, and*
- $s'_i \models R$ *whenever* $s_i \models R$*, for all* $0 \leq i < length(t)$ *and* $R \in \Delta$*.*

For instance, the assignments $x := y+1$ and $y := x+1$ satisfy following specifications

$$[odd(y),\Gamma]\ x := y+1\ [even(x),\Gamma]$$

$$[even(x),\Gamma]\ y := x+1\ [odd(y),\Gamma]$$

where Γ denotes $\{even(x), odd(y)\}$.

2.3 Proof rules

Specifications can be deduced using syntax-directed proof rules, that is, for every construct in the language we have a proof rule that describes how a specification of a composed program can be obtained from specifications of its immediate constituents. For atomic statements, and sequential and parallel compositions, for instance, the following proof rules can be used.

ATOM

$$\frac{C \text{ is an atomic statement} \qquad P \Rightarrow wp(C,Q)}{[P,\{P,Q\}]\ C\ [Q,\{R \mid R \Rightarrow wp(C,R)\}]}$$

where $wp(C,Q)$ denotes the weakest precondition of statement C with respect to predicate Q. Note that the model allows the environment to interfere before and after the execution of C. Therefore, the pre- and postconditions need to be protected from interference.

SEQ

$$\frac{[P,\Gamma_1]\ C_1\ [Q,\Delta_1] \qquad [Q,\Gamma_2]\ C_2\ [R,\Delta_2]}{[P,\Gamma_1 \cup \Gamma_2]\ C_1 \,;\, C_2\ [R,\Delta_1 \cap \Delta_2]}$$

This rule extends the corresponding rule in Hoare logic. We have $\Gamma_1 \cup \Gamma_2$ in the assumptions of the conclusion, because a predicate needs to be preserved by the environment of $C_1\,;$ C_2 if either C_1 or C_2 requires it. Similarly, we have $\Delta_1 \cap \Delta_2$ in the guarantees of the conclusion, because a predicate is guaranteed to be preserved by C_1 ; C_2 only if both C_1 and C_2 preserve it.

PAR

$$\frac{[P_1,\Gamma_1]\ C_1\ [Q_1,\Delta_1] \qquad [P_2,\Gamma_2]\ C_2\ [Q_2,\Delta_2]}{[P_1 \wedge P_2,\Gamma_1 \cup \Gamma_2]\ C_1 \parallel C_2\ [Q_1 \wedge Q_2,\Delta_1 \cap \Delta_2]}$$

where $\Gamma_1 \subseteq \Delta_2$ and $\Gamma_2 \subseteq \Delta_1$. In rule PAR, keeping track of the assumptions Γ and the commitments Δ pays off and allows the formulation of a compositional rule for parallelism. Guarantees and assumptions have to imply each other mutually. The requirements Γ_1 of C_1 have to be contained in the guarantees of C_2 and vice versa. Using PAR we can, for instance, derive

$$[P,\Gamma]\ x := y+1 \parallel y := x+1\ [P,\Gamma]$$

where P and Γ denote $even(x) \wedge odd(y)$ and $\{even(x), odd(y)\}$, respectively. It is easy to see how PAR generalizes to n-fold parallel compositions. The remaining rules and soundness proofs for a simple imperative, concurrent language can be found in [22].

3 VeriSoft

VeriSoft is a systematic testing tool developed at Bell Labs [8, 9]. It takes as input C and C++ programs in which concurrent processes communicate through either semaphores, channels, or shared memory. A process makes an update to such a communication object visible to the other processes by executing one of VeriSoft's so-called *visible actions*. VeriSoft systematically enumerates all possible sequences of visible actions a program can perform. The maximal length of the paths is limited by a user-defined parameter called *depth*. During the exploration, VeriSoft checks for livelocks (a process has no enabled transition during a sequence of more than a user-specified number of successive states), divergences (a process does not attempt to execute a visible action for more than a user-specified amount of time), deadlocks, and assertion violations. By annotating the code with *VS_assert(b)* statements, the user can check whether the boolean expression b is true at a certain program location along every execution.

VeriSoft works directly on programs written in C or C++. However, only if the program meets a few requirements will VeriSoft be able to guarantee the complete coverage of the state space (up to the specified depth). First, the program must not exhibit nested parallelism, that is, all processes must be created before the initial state is reached. For processes that are created later, VeriSoft's state space exploration may not be exhaustive leading to possibly spurious analysis results. Second, processes need to communicate via the VeriSoft communication objects (e.g., semaphores, channels, or shared variables). If an update to such a communication object is supposed to be visible to the parallel environment, the corresponding visible action needs to be used. Consider, for instance, the following program using the shared variable x.

$x := 0;$
while *true* **do**
  $x := x + 1;$
  $x := x + 1$
od

In VeriSoft, an update to shared variable x is exported, that is, made visible to the environment, by prefixing it with *VS_synchro_write_file("x")*. So, if *VS_synchro_write_file("x")* is inserted before the first increment only, the environment of the program will never be able to access x when its value is odd. If, however, *VS_synchro_write_file("x")* is inserted before the first assignment and before the second assignment, the environment will be able to access x when its value is even or odd. The placement of the visible actions thus determines the granularity of the parallel execution.

Suppose program C meets the two requirements above and C is analyzed with depth d. Then, a successful VeriSoft analysis of C guarantees that the prefix of length d of every execution of C is free of livelocks, divergences, deadlocks, and assertion violations.

VeriSoft keeps the state explosion problem in check by safely pruning the state space. More precisely, it looks for actions that are independent. Consider, for instance, two processes that update a disjoint set of shared variables.

$$x := 0 \parallel y := 1$$

Although the program has two different executions, only one of them needs to be considered, because the two assignments are independent. The order in which they are being performed does not change the behaviour of the rest of the program. This optimization is typically called *partial order reduction* and is described in, for instance, [7].

VeriSoft facilitates the implementation of test harnesses by supporting non-determinism. The statement *VS_toss(n)* non-deterministically returns an integer between 0 and n inclusive.

A graphical user interface allows paths to be displayed and states to be examined. The tree of all possible paths of the program is shown and the selection of a node in the tree runs the program up to that point and the current values of the variables can be examined. In case of an assertion violation, the path leading to the violating state is displayed. Moreover, the user can steer the program execution by stepping through each of the processes, controlling the interleaved execution and choosing the result of *VS_toss* operations.

Finally, VeriSoft allows an entire subtree of the state space to be pruned using *VS_abort(b)* where b is a boolean expression. The execution of *VS_abort(b)* causes b to be evaluated. If b is false, none of the successors of the current state is explored. The use of this statement is similar to the use of an assertion, except that no error is reported. It can be used to prune parts of the state space that the user considers uninteresting.

4 Using VeriSoft for assume/guarantee analysis

We want to use VeriSoft to determine whether or not some program C satisfies a given assume/guarantee specification φ

$$\varphi \equiv [P,\Gamma]\ C\ [Q,\Delta]$$

We assume that C does not contain any nested parallelism, since VeriSoft's analysis may be incomplete in that case. In our analysis, we will use *VS_assert* statements to indicate a violation of the specification. Therefore, we also have to assume that C does not contain any *VS_assert* statements. Finally, we assume that all shared variables in C range over natural numbers. This restriction allows the direct use of *VS_toss(n)* when generating initial states or environment transitions and thus simplifies the coding and presentation. It is, however, not strictly necessary.

To analyze C with respect to specification φ we embed C in a larger C program $S(V, \varphi, n)$ which we then analyze with VeriSoft. The parameter V is the set of variables shared between C and its environment. The natural number n denotes the *scope* of the analysis. The scope represents an upper bound on the values that the environment will generate for the shared variables and is thus reminiscent of a similar notion used in the Alloy Constraint analyzer — a tool for the automatic analysis of object models [11]. The scope of an analysis is not to be confused with the syntactic scope of a variable.

The pseudo code for $S(V, \varphi, n)$ is given in Figure 1. After declaring all shared variables, $S(V, \varphi, n)$ forks two processes: The first one blocks until the environment has completed the initialization of the shared variables, and then executes C. After termination of C, the validity of the postcondition Q is checked using *VS_assert(Q)*. The second process serves as the environment. The environment picks a candidate initial state by assigning values within the scope, that is, between 0 and n, non-deterministically to the shared variables using *VS_toss(n)*. If the candidate state satisfies the precondition P, the initialization is complete and process C is woken up. Otherwise, the state is discarded using *VS_abort(0)* and another one is picked. The environment then repeatedly monitors all program transitions and causes environment transitions. If a program transition is found to not preserve at least one predicate in Δ, the assume/guarantee specification is violated and *VS_assert(0)* is used to terminate the analysis and report the violation to the user. To cause an environment transition, a new candidate state is picked by assigning values within the scope to local copies of the shared variables non-deterministically using *VS_toss(n)*. If the transition does not preserve all predicates in Γ, the candidate state is discarded using *VS_abort(0)*. Otherwise, the current state is changed to the candidate state and the state change is made visible to C using VeriSoft's visible actions.

When run on $S(V, \varphi, n)$ and depth d, VeriSoft considers every possible initial state and every possible environment transition within scope n. Moreover, every possible interaction between the program C and the environment E is examined up to depth d. Let $SC(V, m)$ stand for the scope constraint

$$SC(V,m) \quad \equiv \quad \bigwedge_{x \in V} 0 \leq x \leq m$$

where V is a set of shared variables and m is a natural number. $SC(V, m)$ forces the values of all variables in V to lie between 0 and m. The analysis of $S(V, \varphi, n)$ with depth d produces one of three outcomes:

1. VeriSoft reports an assertion violation. In this case, C does not satisfy φ and the error trace produced by VeriSoft constitutes a counter example.

2. VeriSoft completes the exploration of all paths of $S(V, \varphi, n)$ up to depth d without reporting an assertion violation and C has terminated in the last state of every path.

   (a) If the initial state satisfies the scope constraint $SC(V, m)$, the environment preserves it, and m is less than or equal to the scope of the analysis, that is, if $P \equiv P' \wedge SC(V, m)$ and $SC(V, m) \in \Gamma$ and $m \leq n$, then C satisfies φ.

   (b) Otherwise, C may or may not satisfy φ and a violation may be found in a larger scope.

3. VeriSoft completes the exploration of all paths of $S(V, \varphi, n)$ up to depth d without reporting an assertion violation and C has not terminated in the last state of at least one path.

   (a) If the initial state satisfies the scope constraint $SC(V, m)$, the environment preserves it, and m is less than or equal to the scope of the analysis, that is, if $P \equiv P' \wedge SC(V, m)$ and $SC(V, m) \in \Gamma$ and $m \leq n$, then C may or may not satisfy φ and a violation may be found at a greater depth.

   (b) Otherwise, C may or may not satisfy φ and a violation may be found in a larger scope or at a greater depth.

Cases 1 and 2(a) provide definite answers and the most information. Case 3(b) provides the least information. In Cases 2(a) and 3(a), the parameter m of the scope constraint is within the scope n used for the analysis. This ensures the exhaustive enumeration of candidate states and transitions using *VS_toss(n)*. Case 2(b) indicates that a violation, if it exists, will only be found if the scope of the analysis is increased. Case 3(a) indicates that a violation, if it exists, will only be found if the depth is increased. The analysis is exponential in the scope and the depth. Therefore, a repeated analysis with increased parameters is not always feasible. Moreover, if C has non-terminating executions, no value of d will be large enough. In these cases, the user can at least inspect the state space generated by VeriSoft and thus attempt to get a sense whether or not the specification holds. Note that the problem of determining whether or not an assume/guarantee specification holds is undecidable. The incompleteness in Cases 2(b) and 3 thus points to the inherent difficulty of the problem, rather than to a limitation of our analysis or the VeriSoft tool.

5 Examples

We sketch a few of the analyses we have performed using VeriSoft.

```
S(V, φ, n)  ≡  declare all variables in V;
               declare and initialize fresh semaphore sem;
               [ wait(sem);   // wait till woken up by E(V, φ, n)          ||  E(V, φ, n) ]
               [ C;                                                        ||             ]
               [ VS_assert(Q);   // does final state satisfy Q?            ||             ]
               [ exit(0);                                                  ||             ]
where
E(V, φ, n)  ≡  declare local copies of variables in V;
               pick candidate state s by assigning values to the variables in V
                  using VS_toss(n);
               if s does not satisfy P then
                 VS_abort(0);   // invalid initial state
               else
                 change current state to s;
                 signal(sem);   // wake up process
                 while true do
                   copy current state into s;
                   pick new candidate state s' by assigning values to local copies of variables in V
                      using VS_toss(n);
                   if transition (s, s') does not preserve all predicates in Γ then
                     VS_abort(0);   // environment not allowed to change s to s'
                   else   // environment allowed to change s to s'
                     change current state to s';
                     "export" current state and allow process to interfere by using visible actions;
                     copy new current state into s;
                     if s' = s then   // did process change state?
                       VS_abort(0);   // transition trivially preserves all predicates in Δ
                     elsif transition (s', s) does not preserve all predicates in Γ then
                       VS_assert(0);   // violation: process not allowed to change s' to s
                 od
```

Figure 1. Pseudo code for checking $\varphi \equiv [P, \Gamma]\ \ C\ \ [Q, \Delta]$ with shared variables V in scope n using VeriSoft

5.1 Shared variables

Consider the specification φ_1

$$[odd(y), \{odd(y)\}]$$
$$x := y + 1$$
$$[even(x), \{even(x)\}]$$

When running VeriSoft on $S(\{x, y\}, \varphi_1, 3)$ it outputs the counterexample

$$(x = 0 \wedge y = 1, x = 2 \wedge y = 1)(x = 1 \wedge y = 1, x = 1 \wedge y = 1)$$

The counterexample reveals the fact that the postcondition *even(x)* was not protected from environment interference. The specification

$$[odd(y), \{even(x), odd(y)\}]$$
$$x := y + 1$$
$$[even(x) \wedge odd(y), \{even(x)\}]$$

on the other hand was found to be correct with respect to a certain scope. In scope 3, both analyses terminated at depth 14 and required about 8 seconds on a Sparc Ultra-250.

5.2 Maximum search

Let $A[1..n]$ and $M[1..n]$ be two arrays of natural numbers. We want to use n^2 parallel processes to compute $max(A)$, the maximum of A. More precisely, we want the parallel program to establish the postcondition

$$R \equiv \forall 1 \leq i \leq n. M[i] > 0 \Leftrightarrow max(A) = A[i],$$

that is, $M[i]$ is greater 0 if and only if $A[i]$ holds the maximum of A. Consider process $C_{i,j}$ consisting of just the following **if**-statement

$$C_{i,j} \equiv \textbf{if } A[j] > A[i] \textbf{ then } M[i] := 0$$

where $1 \leq i, j \leq n$. We used VeriSoft to develop and check the specification $\varphi_2(i, j, n, m)$

$$\begin{array}{l} [P_i, \{P_i, Q_{i,j}, SC_2^{n,m}\}] \\ \quad C_{i,j} \\ {[P_i \wedge Q_{i,j}, \{SC_2^{n,m}\} \cup \bigcup_{i,j=1,1}^{n,n} \{P_i, Q_{i,j}\}]} \end{array}$$

for specific values of i, j, n and m with $1 \leq i, j \leq n$ where

$$\begin{aligned} P_i &\equiv (max(A) = A[i]) \Rightarrow (M[i] > 0) \\ Q_{i,j} &\equiv (A[j] > A[i]) \Rightarrow (M[i] = 0) \\ SC_2^{n,m} &\equiv SC(V_2^n, m) \\ V_2^n &\equiv \bigcup_{k=1}^{n} \{A[k], M[k]\} \end{aligned}$$

Predicate P_i ensures that $M[i]$ is greater 0 whenever $A[i]$ holds the maximum of A. Predicate $Q_{i,j}$ on the other hand, guarantees that $M[i]$ is 0 whenever $A[i]$ cannot hold the maximum, because $A[j]$ is greater than $A[i]$. Finally, the scope constraint $SC_2^{n,m}$ keeps the entries in both arrays between 0 and m.

The performance of the analysis of

$$S(V_2^n, \varphi_2(i, j, n, m), m)$$

for $i, j \leq n$ and different lengths n of A and scopes m is given in the following table:

array length n	scope m	time for analysis
2	1	32 seconds
3	1	12 minutes
2	2	23 minutes
3	2	> 15 hours

Again, all times were obtained on a Sparc Ultra-250.

Using the generalized rule for parallel composition we conclude

$$\begin{array}{l} [\bigwedge_{i=1}^{n} P_i, \Gamma] \\ \quad C_{1,1} \parallel C_{1,2} \parallel \ldots \parallel C_{n,n} \\ {[\bigwedge_{i,j=1,1}^{n,n} P_i \wedge Q_{i,j}, \Gamma]} \end{array}$$

where

$$\Gamma \equiv \{SC_2^{n,m}\} \cup \bigcup_{i,j=1,1}^{n,n} \{P_i, Q_{i,j}\}$$

Note that the postcondition $\bigwedge_{i,j=1,1}^{n,n} P_i \wedge Q_{i,j}$ implies the desired overall postcondition R. Moreover, note that the precondition $\bigwedge_{i=1}^{n} P_i$ is true when all entries in M are greater than 0. Consequently, we can conclude that the program

$$\begin{array}{rcl} C_{max} & \equiv & \textbf{for } i = 1 \textbf{ to } n \textbf{ do } M[i] := 1 \textbf{ od;} \\ & & [C_{1,1} \parallel C_{1,2} \parallel \ldots \parallel C_{n,n}] \end{array}$$

computes the desired result when run in an environment that preserves $SC_2^{n,m}$ and P_i, $Q_{i,j}$ for all $1 \leq i, j \leq n$.

Our analysis not just revealed the interfaces of the processes, but also the interface of the entire program C_{max}. This interface is surprisingly lenient. For instance, C_{max} still works correctly if its environment subtracts a positive value from all entries that do not hold the maximum. Alternatively, if the index of the maximum in A is unique, the environment may add a positive value to it without destroying the correctness of the algorithm.

5.3 N-process tie-breaker algorithm

For a larger case study, we implemented the n-process tie-breaker algorithm [18] in C using shared variables. The code is given in Figure 2. The entry protocol in each process consists of a loop that iterates through $n - 1$ levels. A process will only be allowed to enter the critical region, if it has completed all $n - 1$ levels. The last process to enter a level l will be forced to remain on that level until another process joins that level and thus becomes last. Thus, informally, one process will always remain on each level. Since there are $n - 1$ levels and n processes, at most two processes can be on the highest level at the same time. Another, final synchronization then ensures that only one of them can complete the highest level. It is this process which will be allowed to progress into its critical region. We say that process C_i *is on level* l if and only if $in[i] = l$. We say that process C_i *is last for* l if and only if $in[i] = l$ and $last[l] = i$. If C_i is on level $1 \leq l \leq n - 2$, it is allowed to advance to level $l + 1$, if

- either it is the highest of all processes, that is, $in[j] < in[i]$ for all $1 \leq j \leq n$ with $j \neq i$,
- or, it is not last for level l.

The synchronization conditions in the entry protocol are strong enough to guarantee mutual exclusion and weak enough to ensure deadlock freedom. Eventual entry is guaranteed because the condition that a process C_i is waiting on will always eventually become true and then remain true until C_i "moves on" to the next level.

5.3.1 Monolithic reasoning

We want to show that *TIE*(n) realizes mutual exclusion for a specific n. One option is to analyze *TIE*(n) as a whole using

$$TIE(n) \equiv \textbf{new } in[1..n] = 0, last[1..n-1] = 0 \textbf{ in } C_1 \parallel C_2 \parallel \ldots \parallel C_n$$

where

```
C_i ≡ while true do
        for l := 1 to n − 1 do                          ⎫
          in[i], last[l] := l, i;                        ⎪
          for j := 1 to n such that j ≠ i do             ⎬ entry
            while in[j] ≥ l ∧ last[l] = i do skip od     ⎪ protocol
          od                                             ⎪
        od;                                              ⎭
      cr_i ; // critical region; must terminate and not change in or last
      in[i] := 0 ; // exit protocol
      nc_i // non-critical region; must not change in or last
    od
```

Figure 2. Pseudo code for the n-process tie-breaker algorithm

VeriSoft by adding a fresh, shared variable *cnt* and updating it such that the value of *cnt* always indicates the number of processes currently executing their critical region. Then, $TIE(n)$ is mutually exclusive if and only if *cnt* is always equal to one during the critical region of every process. This kind of monolithic analysis is relatively inefficient. Ascertaining that the state space of $TIE(3)$ up to depth 15 is free of violations of this assertion took over 10 hours. Analysis attempts with a greater number of processes or greater depths always had to be terminated before completion. Moreover, the monolithic analysis does not shed any light on the interface between the processes. More precisely, it does not allow us to identify which assumptions C_i makes about its environment and which guarantees it is able to make in return.

5.3.2 Compositional reasoning

We will use assume/guarantee reasoning to analyze $TIE(n)$ compositionally. VeriSoft will complement this analysis. Consider the following predicate I

$$I = \forall 1 \leq i \leq n. highest(i) \vee tower(i)$$

where

$$highest(i) \equiv \forall 1 \leq j \leq n. j \neq i \Rightarrow in[j] < in[i]$$
$$tower(i) = \forall 1 \leq l \leq in[i].in[last[l]] = l$$

Predicate I asserts that a process on level l is either the highest or that it has at least $l-1$ processes "underneath it" and that one of the processes on each level is last for that level. Figure 3 illustrates the situation in which we have 10 processes and processes 4 and 5 have risen to the top level.

Also, consider the formulas

$$top(i) \equiv in[i] = n - 1$$
$$last(i) \equiv last[in[i]] = i$$
$$B(i) \equiv highest(i) \vee \neg last(i)$$

$top(i)$ expresses that process C_i is on the highest level and $B(i)$ says that C_i is either the highest or not last for the level it is on.

We used VeriSoft to develop and check the following specification $\varphi_3(i, n, m)$

$$[I, \{I, top(i), B(i), SC_3^{n,m}\}]$$
$$C_i$$
$$[true, \{I, SC_3^{n,m}\} \cup \textstyle\bigcup_{j=1, j\neq i}^{n} \{top(j), B(j)\}]$$

where

$$SC_3^{n,m} \equiv SC(V_3^n, m)$$
$$V_3^n \equiv \{in[1], \ldots, in[n]\} \cup \{last[1], \ldots, last[n-1]\}$$

That is, if I holds initially and every environment transition preserves I, $top(i)$, $B(i)$ and the scope constraint $SC_3^{n,m}$, then every state change of C_i will preserve I and $SC_3^{n,m}$ and $top(j)$ and $B(j)$ for every process C_j in the environment of C_i. Note that the code of C_i and the specification imply that $top(i) \wedge B(i)$ always holds while C_i is in its critical region. Using PAR we get

$$[I, \{I, SC_3^{n,m}\} \cup \textstyle\bigcup_{i=1}^{n} \{top(i), B(i)\}]$$
$$C_1 \parallel C_2 \parallel \ldots \parallel C_n$$
$$[true, \{I, SC_3^{n,m}\}]$$

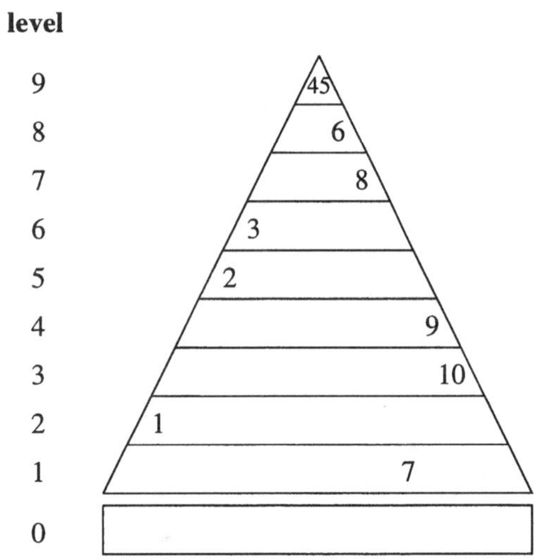

Figure 3. Illustration of a state during the execution of the tie-breaker algorithm for n=10

Since the initialization of in and $last$ in *TIE*(n) establishes I, we can thus conclude that I holds throughout every execution of *TIE*(n).

We now have all the pieces to argue that *TIE*(n) ensures mutual exclusion. For a contradiction, suppose *TIE*(n) has an execution containing a state s in which at least two processes C_i and C_j are in their critical regions. We have *top*$(i) \wedge B(i)$ and *top*$(j) \wedge B(j)$ in s. Consequently, neither C_i nor C_j is highest. Together with I, this implies *tower*$(i) \wedge$ *tower*(j) and $\neg$*last*$(i) \wedge \neg$*last*(j). Due to *tower*$(i) \wedge$ *tower*(j) and *top*$(i) \wedge$ *top*(j) both C_i and C_j have at least $n-2$ processes below them. Since there are only n processes, we can conclude that C_i and C_j are the only processes on the top level $n-1$. Due to *tower*(i) (or *tower*(j)), one of C_i and C_j must be last for level $n-1$, that is, we must have *last*$(i) \vee$ *last*(j). This, however, contradicts $\neg$*last*$(i) \wedge \neg$*last*(j). Consider Figure 3 for an illustration of the state referred to in the proof for $i = 4$, $j = 5$, and $n = 10$.

We have shown the correctness of specification $\varphi_3(i, n, m)$ by analyzing program

$$S(V_3^n, \varphi_3(i, n, m), m)$$

for various numbers of parallel processes n and scopes m. Note that in this example, the number of parallel processes n determines not only the length of the arrays in and $last$, but also the values that their entries range over, that is, the scope of the analysis. For $n = 3$, the exploration of all paths up to depth 20 took 35 minutes. For $n = 5$, it took 180 minutes. Note that the compositional analysis performs better than the monolithic analysis.

5.3.3 Changing the algorithm

Suppose that *TIE*$'(n)$ is like *TIE*(n) except that every occurrence of

$$in[i], last[l] := l, i;$$

in C_i is replaced by

$$last[l] := i \,;\, in[i] := l;$$

Intuitively, in *TIE*$'(n)$ process i becomes last for l *before* it actually has advanced to l. Predicate I is not always true along every execution of *TIE*$'(n)$. More importantly, *TIE*$'(n)$ violates mutual exclusion. For $n = 3$ our analysis required 22 seconds to find a scenario in which C_0 violated its assume/guarantee specification. For $n = 5$, the analysis required about 2 minutes. The monolithic analysis on other hand proved vastly more inefficient. The monolithic analysis of *TIE*$'(3)$, for instance, was interrupted at depth 15 after over 4 hours without having found the violation.

A fundamental limit of invariant-based reasoning is encountered when the multiple assignment is broken up differently. Suppose that *TIE*$''(n)$ is like *TIE*(n) except that

$$in[i], last[l] := l, i;$$

in C_i is replaced by

$$in[i] := l \,;\, last[l] := i;$$

TIE$''(n)$ also has executions that violate I. This is because the new, intermediate state that exists right after process i has advanced to l, but before i becomes last for l may violate the predicates *tower*(j) and $B(j)$ for some process j. We used our compositional analysis to uncover this fact. However, in contrast to *TIE*$'(n)$, *TIE*$''(n)$ does ensure mutual exclusion. The problem is that I is too strong for *TIE*$''$ and needs to be weakened by, for instance, the addition of auxiliary variables or program locations [16, 15]. We conclude this example by observing that while the kind of compositional analysis advocated in this paper has clear benefits, it also relies on the discovery of invariant properties that are strong enough to imply correctness. Finding these properties may require considerable effort. This effort is not required when using monolithic analysis.

6 Conclusion, related work and future work

We have shown how the VeriSoft tool can be used to analyze C and C++ programs compositionally using assume/guarantee specifications. The analysis is carried out with respect to a certain scope and depth. The analysis is sound in the sense that if VeriSoft says that C violates

$$[P, \Gamma] \; C \; [Q, \Delta]$$

then C has an interactive execution t from an initial state satisfying P and in an environment preserving Γ, such that either the final state of t does not satisfy Q or t has a program transition that does not preserve at least one predicate in Δ. Due to the undecidability of assume/guarantee specifications, our analysis is incomplete in the sense that it does not always produce a definite answer. In that case, a repeated analysis with a larger depth or scope may provide an answer. The complexity of the analysis grows exponentially with the depth and the scope. However, due to VeriSoft's partial order reduction, the complexity may be substantially better in many cases. The analysis always produces the (prefix of the) state space which can be animated and explored using VeriSoft.

In our examples, processes communicate through shared memory. Since VeriSoft also supports semaphores and channels, our technique can also be applied to programs that use these means of communication.

6.1 Related work

The work on using the assume/guarantee paradigm for software model checking has already been mentioned [17]. A maximally general environment is generated automatically from environment assumptions expressed in LTL or ∀CTL. The system consisting of the component and its environment are then translated into a finite state machine which is then model checked. This work differs from ours in that we consider pre- and postconditions and invariant properties only. However, the use of VeriSoft obviates the need to translate the code into a finite state machine.

VeriSoft has already been used for compositional analysis. In [3], an approach is presented that automatically closes an open system. Static analysis is used to determine which parts of the system depend on environment interaction and code that simulates all possible environment inputs is inserted. The resulting program is then analyzed with VeriSoft. Our approach also closes an open system by using VeriSoft's non-deterministic choice construct *VS_toss*, but we do so with respect to environment assumptions. In [3], the behaviour of the environment is not subjected to environment assumptions. Moreover, the approach does not show which guarantees the component can make in return.

Another related approach is presented in [24]. It suggests an assume/guarantee supervisor that monitors the execution of a parallel system and derives assumptions and guarantees of each of the components by comparing the execution with the specification of the components. The inability to discharge one of the generated assumptions of a component in its environment constitutes a specification violation by the system and is reported. This approach differs from ours in several ways. First, our analysis is more akin to systematic testing than to run-time monitoring where the input to the analysis is given by observed executions rather than the program itself. Second, in our approach the assumptions and guarantees are not generated during the analysis but have to be provided by the user.

Our analysis can be viewed as a form of systematic testing from formal specifications. A lot of work in this area already exists. The work in [5, 20, 13], for instance, describes how test input data can be generated from environment descriptions. The system output is then compared to descriptions of test oracles. These descriptions are expressed either as Lustre programs, a language for synchronous systems, or as safety properties in the form of finite state machines. The approaches are compositional in the sense that they consider the assumptions and the guarantees of the unit under test. However, the approaches differ from ours in that they are not complemented by a proof system. More precisely, there is no mechanism to combine (checked) specifications into a new specification of a larger system.

6.2 Future work

The automatic generation of the test harness $S(V, \varphi, n)$ from the program C and the specification φ is an obvious topic for future work.

Currently, our analysis seems most suited for small, yet intricate and crucial pieces of code like parallel processes in communication protocols. To make the approach more generally viable, more research is needed.

While in general no upper bound on the scope necessary to find an error can be given, it may, under certain conditions, be reasonable to assume an analog of Alloy's *small scope hypothesis*, that is, that most violations of the predicates in Δ typically are found within a small scope [11]. In light of the worst-case exponential behaviour of our analysis, it would be worthwhile to investigate this issue further.

The challenge behind finding appropriate invariants has already been mentioned at the end of Section 5.3. Approaches to automatic invariant detection may help mitigating this problem [6].

Acknowlegements

The author wishes to thank Patrice Godefroid for his assistance with VeriSoft, and the anonymous referees for their helpful comments. This work was partially supported by NSERC grants 228103-00 and 229739-00.

References

[1] M. Abadi and L. Lamport. Conjoining specifications. *ACM Transactions on Programming Languages and Systems*, 17(3):507–534, May 1995.

[2] S.D. Brookes. Full abstraction for a shared-variable parallel language. *Information and Computation*, 127(2):145–163, June 1996.

[3] C. Colby, P. Godefroid, and L.J. Jagadeesan. Automatically closing open reactive programs. In *Proceedings of the ACM SIGPLAN Conference on Programming Language Design and Implementation (PLDI'98)*, Montreal, Canada, June 1998.

[4] J. Corbett, M. Dwyer, J. Hatcliff, C. Pasareanu, Robby, S. Laubach, and H. Zheng. Bandera : Extracting finite-state models from Java source code. In *Proceedings of the 22nd International Conference on Software Engineering (ICSE '00)*, June 2000.

[5] L. du Bousquet, F. Ouabdesselam, I. Parissis, J-L. Richier, and N. Zuanon. Specification-based testing of synchronous software. In *International Workshop on Formal Methods for Industrial Critical Systems*, Berlin, Germany, April 2000.

[6] M.D. Ernst, A. Czeisler, W.G. Griswold, and D. Notkin. Quickly detecting relevant program invariants. In *Proceedings of the 22nd International Conference on Software Engineering (ICSE'00)*, pages 449–458, Limerick, Ireland, June 2000.

[7] P. Godefroid. *Partial-Order Methods for the Verification of Concurrent Systems — An Approach to the State-Explosion Problem.* Springer-Verlag, January 1996.

[8] P. Godefroid. Model checking for programming languages using VeriSoft. In *Proceedings of the 24th ACM Symposium on Principles of Programming Languages*, pages 174–186, Paris, January 1997.

[9] P. Godefroid. Software model checking in practice: An industrial case study. In *Proceedings of International Conference on Software Engineering (ICSE'02)*, Orlando, May 2002.

[10] O. Grumberg and D. Long. Model checking and modular verification. *ACM Transactions on Programming Languages and Systems*, 16(3):843–871, October 1994.

[11] D. Jackson. Automating first-order relational logic. In *Proceedings of ACM SIGSOFT Conference on Foundations of Software Engineering (FSE '00)*, San Diego, November 2000.

[12] D. Jackson and J. Wing. Lightweight formal methods. *IEEE Computer*, April 1996.

[13] L.J. Jagadeesan, A. Porter, J.C. Ramming, and L. Votta. Specification-based testing of reactive software: Tools and experiments. In *Proceedings of the 19th International Conference on Software Engineering (ICSE '97)*, 1997.

[14] C.B. Jones. Tentative steps towards a development method for interfering programs. *ACM Transactions on Programming Languages and Systems*, 5(4):576–619, 1983.

[15] Z. Manna and A. Pnueli. *Temporal Verification of Reactive Systems: Safety*. Springer Verlag, 1995.

[16] S.S. Owicki and D. Gries. An axiomatic proof technique for parallel programs. *Acta Informatica*, 6:319–340, 1976.

[17] C.S. Pasareanu, M.B. Dwyer, and M. Huth. Assume-guarantee model checking of software : A comparative case study. In *Theoretical and Practical Aspects of SPIN Model Checking*. Springer-Verlag, September 1999. LNCS 1680.

[18] G.L. Peterson. Myths about the mutual exclusion problem. *Information Processing Letters*, 12:115–116, June 1981.

[19] A. Pnueli. In transition from global to modular temporal reasoning about programs. In K.R. Apt, editor, *Logics and Models of Concurrent Systems*, NATO ASI F13, pages 123–144. Springer Verlag, 1985.

[20] P. Raymond, D. Weber, X. Nicollin, and N. Halbwachs. Automatic testing of reactive systems. In *19th IEEE Real-Time Systems Symposium (RTSS '98)*, 1998.

[21] N. Shankar. Lazy compositional verification. In *Compositionality: The Significant Difference, International Symposium (COMPOS'97)*, Bad Malente, Germany, 1998. Springer-Verlag. LNCS 1536.

[22] C. Stirling. A generalization of Owicki-Gries' Hoare logic for a concurrent while language. *Theoretical Computer Science*, 89:347–359, 1988.

[23] M. Vardi. On the complexity of modular model checking. In *Proceedings 10th Annual IEEE Symposium on Logic in Computer Science*, pages 101–111. IEEE Computer Society Press, June 1995.

[24] M. Zulkernine and R. Seviora. Assume-guarantee supervisor for concurrent systems. In *International Parallel and Distributed Processing Symposium (IPDPS'01)*, pages 1552–1560. IEEE Computer Science Press, April 2001.

Architecture, Design, Implementation

Amnon H. Eden
Center for Inquiry, Amherst, NY, and
Department of Computer Science,
University of Essex, United Kingdom
eden@acm.org

Rick Kazman
Software Engineering Institute, Pittsburgh, PA and
University of Hawaii, Honolulu, HI
kazman@sei.cmu.edu

Abstract

The terms architecture, design, *and* implementation *are typically used informally in partitioning software specifications into three coarse strata of abstraction. Yet these strata are not well-defined in either research or practice, causing miscommunication and needless debate.*

To remedy this problem we formalize the Intension and the Locality criteria, which imply that the distinction between architecture, design, and implementation is qualitative and not merely quantitative. We demonstrate that architectural styles are intensional *and* non-local*; that design patterns are* intensional *and* local*; and that implementations are* extensional *and* local.

Keywords: Software design theory, software architecture.

If people do not believe that mathematics is simple, it is only because they do not realize how complicated life is.
— J. H. von Neumann

1. Introduction

In their seminal article, Perry and Wolf [24] developed "an intuition about software architecture through analogies to existing disciplines." Building on this, Shaw and Garlan [31] suggest that "software architecture involves the description of elements from which systems are built." A considerable body of work, stemming back to DeRemer and Kron's *module interconnection languages* (MIL) [7], focuses on the specification, construction, and analysis of large software systems defined by these terms (e.g., [26], [21], [15]). For example, *architecture description languages* (ADL) combine a formal specification language with tools supporting the construction and analysis of software systems from such specifications.

Seeking to separate *architectural design* from other design activities, definitions of *software architecture* stress the following:

- "*Architecture* is concerned with the selection of architectural elements, their interaction, and the constraints on those elements and their interactions... *Design* is concerned with the modularization and detailed interfaces of the design elements, their algorithms and procedures, and the data types needed to support the architecture and to satisfy the requirements." [24]
- Software Architecture is "concerned with issues ... beyond the algorithms and data structures of the computation." [16]
- "Architecture ... is specifically not about ... details of implementations (e.g., algorithms and data structures.) ... Architectural design involves a richer collection of abstractions than is typically provided by OOD." [23]
- "Architecture ≠ Design? ... Design is an activity. Architecture, or architectural design, is design at a higher level of abstraction." [18]
- Architecture focuses on the externally visible properties of software "components." [2]

In suggesting typical "architectures" and "architectural styles", existing definitions consist of examples and offer anecdotes rather then provide unambiguous, clear notions.

In practice, the terms "architecture", "design" and "implementation" appear to connote varying degrees of abstraction in the continuum between complete details ("implementation"), few details ("design"), and the highest form of abstraction ("architecture"). But the amount of detail alone is insufficient to characterize the differences, because architecture and design documents often contain information that is not explicit in the implementation (e.g., design constraints, standards, performance goals) and therefore they cannot result from mere omission of detail. Thus, we would expect a distinction to be qualitative and not merely quantitative. A clear distinction has remained elusive and this lack of distinction is the cause of much muddy thinking, imprecise communication, and wasted, overlapping effort.

As a result, *architecture* is often used as a mere synonym for *design*. For example, the "Siemens" catalogue [4]

0-7695-1877-X/03 $17.00 © 2003 IEEE

defines "architectural patterns" that are in par with what the "Gang of Four" [14] call "design patterns".

Confusion also stems from the use of the same specification language for both architectural and design specifications. For example, the *Software Engineering Institute* (SEI) classifies UML [3] as an architectural description language [30], and it has become the industry de facto standard ADL, although UML was specifically designed to manifest detailed design decisions (and this is its most common use).

Confusion also exists with respect to the artifacts of design and implementation. UML *class diagrams* [3], for instance, are a prototypical artifact of the design phase. Nonetheless, class diagrams may accumulate enough detail to allow code generation of very detailed programs, an approach that is promoted by CASE tools such as *Rational Rose®* [28] and *System Architect®* [25]. Using the same specification language further blurs the distinction between artifacts of the design (class diagrams) from the implementation (source code.)

Intended contribution. Why are we interested in such distinctions? Naturally, a well-defined language improves our understanding of the subject matter. With time, terms that are used interchangeably lose their meaning and end up as mere platitudes, resulting inevitably in ambiguous descriptions given by developers, and significant effort is wasted in discussions of the form "by design I mean... and by architecture I mean..." The formal ontology we provide can serve as the ultimate reference point for these discussions.

The contribution of this paper is to provide insight on the largely informal dialectic by appealing to both intuition and to formal ontology. By putting these terms on a solid footing not only do we disambiguate the progressively murky discourse in "architectural specifications" but provide a foundation for formal reasoning and analysis, as well as a firm foundation for informal "chalk-talk" discussions. Finally, tools supporting design and architectural specifications, where intuitive perceptions are insufficient, will benefit by accurately defining this distinction.

Many of the required definitions were rendered informal and the proofs were omitted in this version of our work. The interested reader can find the complete definitions in [12], and additional details on the *design models* formalism can be found in [9]. Instead, we argue our points with informal illustrations and discussions.

1.1 The Intension/Locality Thesis

To elucidate the relationship between *architecture*, *design*, and *implementation*, we distinguish at least two separate interpretations for *abstraction* in our context:

- *Intensional* (vs. *extensional*) specifications are "abstract" in the sense that they can be formally characterized by the use of logic variables that range over an unbounded domain;
- *Non-local* (vs. *local*) specifications are "abstract" in the sense that they pervade *all* parts of the system (as opposed to being limited to some part thereof).

Both of these interpretations contribute to the distinction among *architecture*, *design*, and *implementation*, summarized as the **Intension/Locality thesis**:

(i) Architectural specifications are *intensional* and *non-local*;

(ii) Design specifications are *intensional* but *local*; and

(iii) Implementation specifications are both *extensional* and *local*.

Table 1. The Intension/Locality Thesis

Architecture	*Intensional*	*Non-local*
Design	*Intensional*	*Local*
Implementation	*Extensional*	*Local*

1.2 Structure of This Paper

The intension/locality thesis can be understood correctly only in the context of the ontology provided below. In Section 2 we define *design models*, which are crucial to the remainder of our discussion. Design models are abstractions which allow a formal "meaning" assigned to programs, also called "denotation". This formalism allows us to determine whether a specification is "satisfied" by a program. In Section 3, we formally define the Intension criterion and the Locality criterion. We distinguish our interpretation for "intensionality" from the accepted usage, as we define it in terms of *design models*.

Sections 4, 5, and 6, provide case studies in applying the Intension and Locality criteria using our formal ontology. In Section 4 we demonstrate that implementations in any programming language, including generics and C++ templates are *extensional* and *local*. In Section 5 we show that design patterns, such as the Factory Method, and design specifications, such as the *Enterprise JavaBeans™* and Java™ *Swing*'s MVC, are *intensional* and *local*. In Section 6 we demonstrate that architectural styles such as Pipes and Filters and Layered Architecture are *intensional* and *non-local*, and so is the Law of Demeter.

In Section 7, we discuss some of the ramifications of our criteria. The discussion of UML class diagrams in Section 7.2 reveals that class diagrams have a separate place in the hierarchy of abstractions we describe. Section 8 summarizes the contributions of this paper.

2. Setting the scene

In this section, we illustrate the formal ontology that underlies our discussion. This ontology is based on giving an abstract "meaning" to programs using *design models*.

2.1 Design models

Turing and *random-access machines* provide robust computational models that are primarily suitable for reasoning about algorithms. Other computational models and formalisms (e.g., Petri nets, statecharts, and temporal logic) facilitate reasoning about certain behavioral properties.

The discussion in architectural and design specifications, however, involves reasoning on constructs such as *classes, methods*, and *function calls*. Most other formalisms incorporate too much implementation detail and do not allow a discussion in the appropriate level of abstraction. As we seek to establish the relation between architectural or design specifications and implementations, we base our discussion on a different formalism, one which abstracts programs to a more convenient representation.

Eden and Hirshfeld [11] demonstrate how to model source code as *design models*, which are first order, finite *structures* in mathematical logic [1]. We designate a **design model** m (defined formally in [11] and [12]) to consist of a set of *atoms* and a set of *relations* among those atoms.

Table 2. A Java™ program and its denotation (adapted from [9].)

```
abstract class Decorator {
   public void Draw();
}
class BorderDecorator extends Decorator {
   public void Draw() {
      Decorator.Draw();
   }
   private int BorderWidth;
}
```

The design model of this program consists of the following:

Atoms:

"class" atoms: {Decorator, BorderDecorator, int, void}, "Method" atoms: {BorderDecorator.Draw, Decorator.Draw}

Relations:

Abstract(Decorator)

Member(Decorator.Draw, Decorator)

Member(BorderDecorator.Draw, BorderDecorator)

Inherit(BorderDecorator, Decorator)

Reference(BorderDecorator, int)

Invoke(BorderDecorator.Draw, Decorator.Draw)

ReturnType(Decorator.Draw, void)

ReturnType(BorderDecorator.Draw, void)

Table 2 depicts a detailed example of a trivial Java™ program and a design model that represents it. As this example demonstrates, an object-oriented program is abstracted to a collection of *classes* and *methods* (also *routines* or *function members*) and their relations. *Atoms* represent *classes* and *methods* that were defined in the program, such as the class `Decorator` and the method `Decorator.Draw`. *Relations* represent their correlations, such as

$$Inherit(\texttt{BorderDecorator,Decorator}) \quad (1)$$

Note that *design models* are abstractions which were made to reflect certain structural aspects of computer programs that are relevant to the discussion in software design theory. Obviously, this representation limits the type of reasoning we may perform to properties that are relevant to the discussion in classes, methods, and their interdependencies, as opposed to the discussion in dynamic properties such as *fairness* and complexity.

2.2 Specifications and instances

In this subsection, we discuss specifications and programs, and how the two correlate. We make some reasonable assumptions on the languages used to write specifications.

Let us designate $\mathcal{SPEC}$ as the set of formal languages of any order [1]. Let $\mathcal{SPEC}$* designate the set of all expressions made in some language in $\mathcal{SPEC}$. A **specification** is an element of $\mathcal{SPEC}$*.

$\mathcal{SPEC}$ includes familiar specification languages such as $\mathbb{Z}$ [32], as demonstrated in formulas (5.1) and (5.2), and LEPUS [8], as demonstrated in formula (4). $\mathcal{SPEC}$ also includes programming languages such as Eiffel, ANSI C, C++, and Java™. Naturally $\mathcal{SPEC}$ is not restricted to known programming or specification languages.

A specification is only useful if we can determine whether it is "satisfied" or not. Having chosen *design models* as our semantics we wish to ask: Does this program satisfy our specification? To answer this question, consider for example the following trivial design specification:

$$Inherit(x,y) \quad (2)$$

Expression (2) contains two free variables x, y. We say that it can be *satisfied* by any pair of atoms that belong to the relation *Inherit*. For example, from expression (1) we conclude that the pair $\langle$BorderDecorator,Decorator$\rangle$ satisfies expression (2).

Thus, we say that the pair of atoms $\langle$BorderDecorator,Decorator$\rangle$ is an **instance** of (2), and that the design model depicted in Table 2 **satisfies** expression (2). A more formal definition of *instance* appears in [12] and in [9].

From this example, it should be clear that an *instance* is not the same as a "program". Depending on the specification, a program may contain zero, one, or any number of instances. The following subsection formalizes the notion of a program.

2.3 Programs and their denotation

We expect a "program" to be a specification that is associated with only one *design model*. The association between "real" programs and design models is provided by the *denotation function*. Loosely speaking, a **denotation function** $\mathcal{D}$ has these properties:

- Its domain, denoted $\mathcal{P}_{\mathcal{D}}$, is a subset of $\mathcal{SPEC}^*$;
- $\mathcal{D}$ associates each element φ with *exactly one* design model (its *denotation*) which *satisfies* φ.

Typically, the domain of $\mathcal{D}$ contains expressions in programming languages, such as C++ and Eiffel. More formally, a **program** is an element in $\mathcal{P}_{\mathcal{D}}$. Every design model typically denotes infinitely many programs. Figure 1 illustrates a typical denotation associating programs with design models. Table 2 illustrates the denotation of a simple Java™ program and Table 3 the denotation of a C++ program.

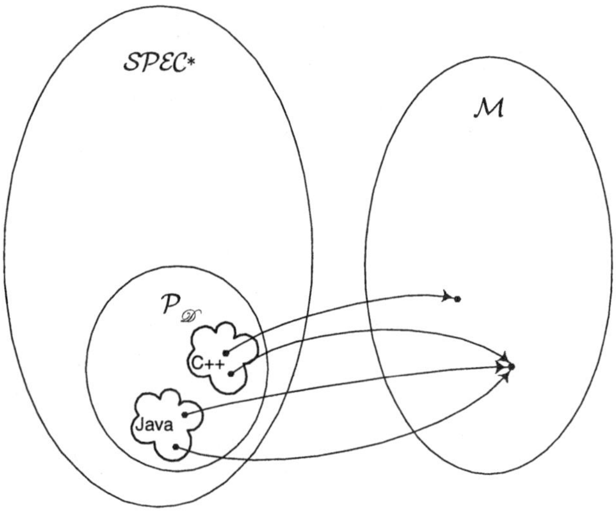

Figure 1. A typical denotation function

Observe that the set of all programs, $\mathcal{P}_{\mathcal{D}}$, is only a *small subset* of the expressions in $\mathcal{SPEC}^*$ and that there are many expressions in $\mathcal{SPEC}^*$ that are satisfied by more than one design model

We now have a well-defined notion of programs and specifications. In combination with the definition of an "instance" of a specification, we can conclusively determine whether a program satisfies a given specification:

Definition I. *We say that a program π* ***satisfies*** *specification φ iff the design model of π satisfies φ.*

This means that, for example, the Java™ program depicted in Table 2 *satisfies* expression (2).

In the following sections we will set apart architecture, design, and implementation specifications based on observing properties of the groups of programs that satisfy each specification.

3. The Intension/Locality criteria

We will now define the concepts of *intension* and *locality*, which will be applied, both formally and informally, to selected specifications in the following sections.

3.1 The Intension criterion

Perry and Wolf [24] have established that architectural specifications must be made in intensional terms. Speaking of the desired properties of an ideal specification language for software architecture they write: "We want a means of supporting a 'principle of least constraint' to be able to express only those constraints in the architecture that are necessary at the architectural level of the system description". It constrains only what it needs to, in terms of properties imposed over free variables.

Traditionally, *intensional specifications* define a concept via a list of constraints. For example, mathematical concepts are usually defined intensionally. For instance, "A *prime number* is a number that divides only by itself and by the number 1". In contrast, the North Atlantic Treaty defines the set of NATO members extensionally, namely, by itemizing its members: United States, United Kingdom, Norway, and so forth.

The notion of intensionality defined below diverges slightly from the philosophical concept. We say that a specification is intensional if and only if it has an unbounded number of instances:

Definition II. *We say that a specification is* ***intensional*** *iff there are infinitely-many possible instances thereof. Conversely, all other expressions are* ***extensional****.*

It immediately follows (as shown in [12]) that intensional specifications are also satisfied by infinitely many design models and by infinitely many programs.

3.2 The Locality criterion

Monroe et. al [23] argue that "Architectural designs are typically concerned with the entire system." Similarly, we observe that an architectural style, which pervades a system [16], manifests a property that is shared across modules of the system. This intuition motivates the Locality criterion: What distinguishes architectural from design specifications is that *architectural specifications must be met by every extension of the program.*

As a simple example, consider the rule of a "universal base class". Although the language does not require it, several C++ class libraries (e.g., NIHCL and Microsoft's MFC) are designed by this rule. Formally, this property can be expressed as follows:

$$\forall c \in \mathbb{C} \bullet (c \neq \texttt{Object}) \Rightarrow Inherit^*(c, \texttt{Object}) \quad (3)$$

(Where $Inherit^*$ is the transitive closure of the binary relation *Inherit.*) The Intension/Locality thesis argues that Universal Base Class is architectural because (a) it is intensional and (b) it pervades *all parts* of the system, i.e., *every* class must be bound to `Object`.

Subsumption. The formalization of the locality criterion requires the notion of *subsumption*. Informally, we say that design model $\mathfrak{n}$ *subsumes* $\mathfrak{m}$ if $\mathfrak{m}$ is a "sub-model" of $\mathfrak{n}$. We can also view $\mathfrak{n}$ as an "extension" to $\mathfrak{m}$, not unlike "strict inheritance" [33].

Definition III. *We say that a specification φ is* ***local*** *iff the following condition holds:*

If φ is satisfied in some design model $\mathfrak{m}$ then it is satisfied by every design model that subsumes $\mathfrak{m}$.

Essentially, Definition III states that an expression is *local* if it can be satisfied in "some corner" of our program without this being affected in how the rest of the program is like.

In the following sections, we apply the Intension and Locality criteria to selected specifications to illustrate the difference between programs, design specifications, and architectural specifications.

4. Implementations

It immediately follows from the Intension criterion (as shown in [12]) that intensional specifications are also satisfied by infinitely many design models and by infinitely many programs. This leads us to prove part (iii) of the Intension/Locality thesis:

The lemma of "extensions"*: Programs are extensional specifications.*

Following the 'principle of least constraint', we expect architectural specifications to have an unbounded number of instances, namely, to be "intensional". The same applies to design patterns. But what about other forms of specifications? Can programs be intensional?

Prima facie, it appears that some programming specifications (such as C++ templates and Eiffel generics) might also be intensional. This is not true in the context of *design models*: As demonstrated in Corollary 1, specifications in any programming language, including generics and interpreted code are, under the assumptions provided above, purely extensional:

Corollary 1. *C++ templates are extensional.*

To illustrate this, consider the design model of a C++ program with templates, such as shown in Table 3.

Table 3. A C++ program and its denotation

```
template <class C> class Stack
    {/* ... /*}
int main() {
    Stack<int> si;
    return 0;
}
```

This program is interpreted by only one design model, which consists of the following:

Atoms:

"Class" atoms: {`Stack`, `si`} "Method" atoms: {`main`}

Relations:

Generic(`Stack`)

Instantiate(`Stack`, `si`, `int`)

Return(`main`, `int`)

Corollary 1 demonstrates that although generics may be viewed as intensional with respect to other semantic frameworks, e.g., because they can be used to define other concrete constructs, the ontology we have provided assigns then with only one "interpretation". The reason is that the formal semantics we chose for the representation of programs are *design models*, which are more abstract than the machine code generated from compilation and from other formal frameworks.

To recap, the formal framework provided in Section 2 guarantees that expressions in all conventional programming languages are extensional.

5. Design specifications

By part (ii) of the Intension/Locality thesis, design specifications should be local and intensional. Since design specifications are, in practice, defined informally, we begin section with exploring the intuition behind our thesis. For the purpose of the formal analysis which follows, however, we make use of formal specifications and apply them to widely recognized designs.

5.1 Design patterns

In this subsection, we focus on an example drawn from the published patterns literature. This allows us to test our ideas on some of the most widely used design specifications.

Coplien and Schmidt [5] argue that "design patterns capture the static and dynamic structures of solutions that occur repeatedly when producing applications in a particular context". Stripped from the context of a particular application, design patterns represent *categories* of solutions, each pattern has an unbounded number of implementations (as implied by the very choice of the name "pattern"). Thus they are expected to be *intensional.*

Design patterns are commonly perceived as "less abstract" than architectural specifications. For example, they are commonly referred to as "microarchitectures" [29], that is, as if they were like architectures that only apply to a limited module. Using our terminology, we thus expect them to be *local.*

Consider, for example, the Factory Method design pattern [14]. Essentially, the pattern's solution offers three sets of participants:

1. A set of *product* classes
2. A set of *factory* classes
3. A set of *factory* methods

The collaborations between these participants are constrained as follows:

4. All *factory methods* share the same signature (thereby allowing for dynamic binding), and each is defined in a different *factory* class.
5. Each *factory method* produces instances of exactly one *products* class.

Figure 2 illustrates the general notion of the pattern. Observe that the set of $\langle$*factory-i, factory-method-i, product-i*$\rangle$ triplets is unbounded, because the number of possible *factory* and *product* classes is not bounded.

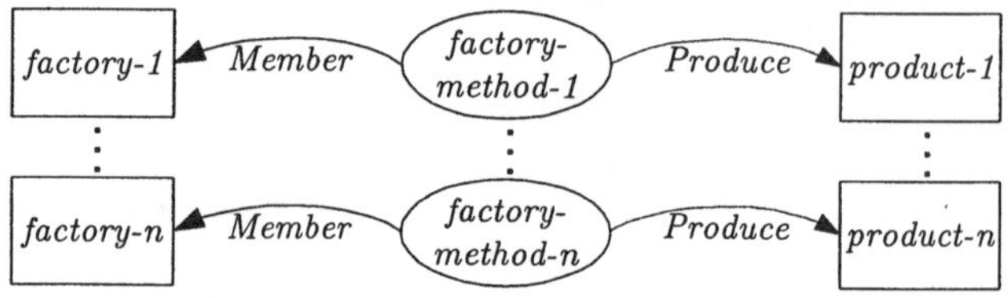

Figure 2. The general structure of the "Factory Method" pattern

For the discussion in design patterns we use LEPUS, a formal specification language for object-oriented design which is defined in detail in [8]. The five statements in the above definition of the Factory Method are formalized by expressions (4.1) to (4.5), respectively:

$$Products : \mathbf{P}(\mathbb{C}) \tag{4.1}$$

$$Factories : \mathbf{P}(\mathbb{C}) \tag{4.2}$$

$$FactoryMethods : \mathbf{P}(\mathbb{F}) \tag{4.3}$$

$$Clan(FactoryMethods, Factories) \tag{4.4}$$

$$Produce^{\leftrightarrow}(FactoryMethods, Products) \tag{4.5}$$

Expressions (4.1) through (4.3) declare two sets of *classes* and one set of *methods*. Expression (4.4) indicates that the pair $\langle FactoryMethods, Factories\rangle$ satisfies the predicate *Clan*, meaning that –

- All "factory methods" share the same signature (i.e., they share the same dispatch table);
- The relation *MemberOf* is a bijection (i.e., *one-to-one* and *onto* function) between the sets *FactoryMethods* and *Factories.*

Finally, expression (4.5) indicates that the ground relation *Produce* is a bijective function between the set *FactoryMethods* and the set *Products.*

Corollary 2. *"Factory method" is intensional and local.*

The composite expression (4.1) to (4.5) is evidently *intensional*, since each one of the free variables *Products* and *Factories* (*FactoryMethods*) can be instantiated by any number of classes (methods). To show that it is local, observe that if a design model $\mathfrak{m}$ satisfies expression (4) then it incorporates an *instance* of the pattern. It is then easy to show that any proper "extension" to $\mathfrak{m}$ (i.e., any design model that *subsumes* it) also contains the same instance of the Factory Method, namely, the same set of atoms and relations that satisfied the pattern in $\mathfrak{m}$.

The same line of reasoning can be applied to the specifications of most of the design patterns from the Gamma et. al [14] catalogue, such as the specifications in [8].

5.2 Other design specifications

The place of other design specifications within the intension/locality classification may be less obvious then that of design patterns. Thus, we have carried out our analysis on the formal rendering of two additional design specifications: MVC (Model-View-Controller) "usage pattern" in Java™ *Swing* class library, and of Enterprise JavaBeans™.

In lack of space, we cannot quote here the formal specifications but only the results of our analysis. The interested reader may find both specifications in [10], and the complete proof for this conclusion in [12]. We can report that our analysis confirms that, as predicted by the intension/locality thesis, both specifications fall under the "design" category, namely, they are intensional and local.

6. Architectural specifications

In this section, we demonstrate that, as predicted by the intension/locality thesis, two classic architectural styles are both intensional and non-local. We also demonstrate that the Law of Demeter is architectural.

6.1 Layered architecture

Garlan and Shaw [16] describe the Layered Architecture such that "An element of layer k may depend only on elements of layers $1,\ldots k$." We may formalize this description in $\mathbb{Z}$ as follows:

$$\forall e\ \exists!\, k\in\{\mathbb{N}\} \bullet Layer(e)=k \tag{5.1}$$

(i.e., each element is defined in exactly one layer), and

$$\forall x,y \bullet \quad Depends(x,y) \Rightarrow Layer(x) \geq Layer(y) \tag{5.2}$$

(i.e., the definition of each element may "depend" only on the definition of elements of same layer or of lower layers.)

***Corollary** 3. Layered Architecture is intensional and non-local.*

It is obvious that an unbounded number of programs can satisfy expression (5) (i.e., the conjunction of formulas (5.1) and (5.2)), hence it is intensional. To prove that it is non-local we show that, given any design model that satisfies (5), the same design model can be extended with a new element in the lower "layer" such that this element depends on a higher layer, thereby violating the specification.

We conclude that we may selectively apply a non-local specification only to certain parts of a program. But what does it mean? Does it compromise our results?

Discussion. Is it possible for a non-local specification, such as layered architecture, to be applied only by one part of a program? Obviously. That simply means that parts of this program satisfy the non-local rule, while other parts violate it. In fact, this property is exactly what the Locality criterion is about: We say that the Layered Architecture specification is non-local *because* it may be violated anywhere in the program.

Does it mean that non-locality is inconsequential? Quite the contrary. Non-locality is a "strong" property that qualifies *specifications*, i.e., of an expression; and by our thesis, architectural specifications are always non-local. However, they may be selectively violated in any part of the program as a conscious choice of the architect. In such case we say that this architectural style no longer characterizes this program (as a whole.) Formally:

***Corollary** 4. If a specification φ is (deliberately) violated in module m of program π, then either one of the following is true:*

- φ is not satisfied by π, or
- m is not considered part of π (i.e., it belongs to a separate program.)

In the example of Layered Architecture, a module that does "layer bridging" in a Layered Architecture program (i.e., violates the layering principle) should not be considered as part of the layered program; instead, we perceive it a separate program.

While this conclusion may seem counter-intuitive at first, it is actually a powerful view on exceptions to architectural constraints. A module that does layer bridging requires different reasoning and different management than the rest of the layered system. It not only should, but *must*, be treated as an exception, or else the power of the layering will be compromised. Exceptions to an architectural style should have attention called to them and be made the focus of intense analysis. Our reasoning provides a sound, formal basis for saying when a portion of a program is an exception to an architectural style.

6.2 Pipes and filters

According to Garlan and Shaw [16], "In a pipes and fil ter style each component has a set of inputs and a set of outputs. A component reads streams of data on its inputs and produces streams of data on its outputs."

Dean and Cordy [6] present a visual formalism defined as a context-free grammar, and formulate the pipes and filter style as depicted in Figure 3. More generally, a "program" in STSA (*) is represented as a typed, directed multigraph. An *architectural style* is defined as a context-free language. Thus, an expression in STSA defines a collection of graphs in a visual notation, such as Figure 3. Hence, according to Dean and Cordy, a "program" satisfies the pipes and filters architecture if it "parses" Figure 3. Figure 4 illustrates the kind of programs that parse the grammar defined in Figure 3.

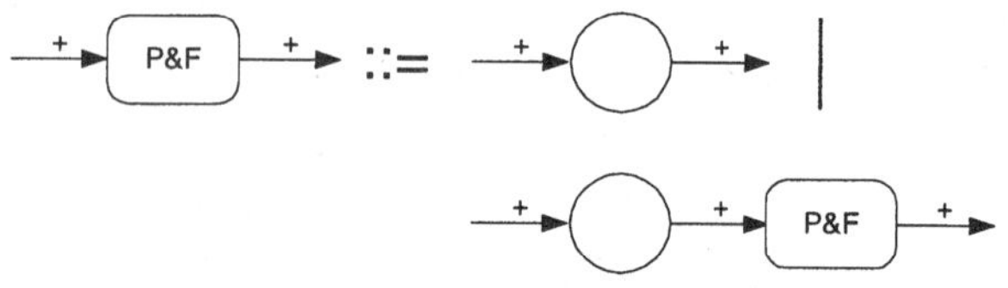

Figure 3. Pipes and Filters (adapted from [6]). Circles represent tasks, arrows represent streams. The plus sign is the BNF symbol for "one or more."

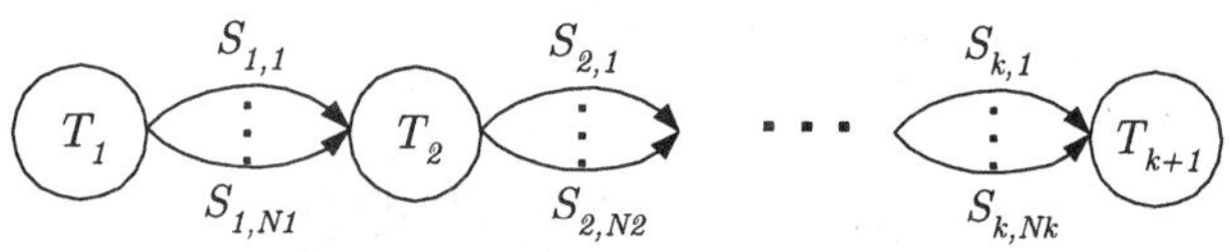

Figure 4. The general structure of programs that parse Figure 3.

Before we can reason about Figure 3, we must establish which design models satisfy an STSA diagram. For the purpose of our discussion, it suffices to restrict ourselves to diagrams of "tasks" and "streams". Let G designate a multigraph whose nodes represent "tasks" and whose arcs represent "streams". In terms of design models, tasks and streams are represented as atoms, while the relations consist of –

- the unary relations $Task(x)$ and $Stream(x)$, and
- the binary relation $Connect(x,y)$

which indicate that the directed arc representing stream x terminates at the node representing task y (or that the directed arc representing stream y begins at the node representing task x.)

It is easy to see that the general form of programs that parses Figure 3 is that of a directed multi-path, as depicted in Figure 4, and that the design models of these programs have the general form illustrated in formula (6).

* In absence of an explicit name, we use the initials of the title of [6] with reference to the formalism.

$$\begin{aligned}&Connect(T_1,S_{1,1}),\ldots Connect(T_1,S_{1,N1}),\ \ldots\\&\quad Connect(S_{1,1},T_2),\ldots Connect(S_{1,N1},T_2),\\&\ldots\\&Connect(T_k,S_{k,1}),\ \ldots Connect(T_k,S_{k,Nk}),\ \ldots\\&\quad Connect(S_{k,1},T_{k+1}),\ldots Connect(S_{k,Nk},T_{k+1})\end{aligned} \quad (6)$$

***Corollary** 5. "Pipes and Filters" is intensional and non-local.*

It is obvious that an unbounded number of programs satisfy formula (6); therefore, it is intensional. To show that (6) is non-local, observe that, for any design model that satisfies (6) we can add a new task T_{k+2} that is not connected to any other task by a pipe. Such addition violates the style's specification (in particular, there would be no *Connect* relation involving T_{k+2}). Since violates (6) *wherever* it occurs, the Pipes and Filters style must be non-local.

6.3 Law of Demeter

We have shown that two classic architectural styles meet our criteria for being "architectural" as expected. But our criteria also turn up some less expected results: The *Law of Demeter* [20] was created as a *design* heuristic. It was introduced to simplify modifications to a program and to reduce its complexity. The informal description of the law for functions is given in Table 4.

Table 4. Law of Demeter for functions

For all classes C, and for all methods M attached to C, all objects to which M sends a message must be instances of classes associated with the following classes: The argument classes of M (including C). The instance variable classes of C. (Objects created by M, or by functions or methods which M calls, and objects in global variables, are considered arguments of M.)

We may formulate the language of Table 4 as follows:

$$\begin{aligned}&\forall\ f_1,f_2,c_1,c_2\ \bullet\\&\quad Member(f_1,c_1)\ \wedge\\&\quad Member(f_2,c_2)\wedge\\&\quad Invoke(f_1,f_2)\ \Rightarrow\\&\qquad Member(c_2,c_1)\ \vee ArgOf(f_1,c_2)\ \vee\ c_1{=}c_2\end{aligned} \quad (7)$$

Evidently, formula (7) has infinitely many instances, hence it is intensional. It is also non-local. To prove this, observe that any program that satisfies (7) can be expanded with source code that violates the Law, such as demonstrated by the C++ source code in Table 5.

Table 5. An add-on to a C++ program which violates the Law of Demeter

```
struct NewName1 {
    void foo();
};
struct NewName2 {
    NewName1 y;
};
class NewName3 {
    NewName2 x;
    void bar() {
        x.y.foo();
    }
};
```

In conclusion, the Law of Demeter, which was created as a design rule, is better characterized as an *architectural* rule. The Law is not be limited to one part of the system but must be satisfied throughout. In practice, this means that any system using the Law of Demeter must create appropriate architectural practices to enforce it via coding standards, design walkthroughs, tool support, etc.

This example demonstrates the benefit of making our distinctions explicit and the power of rendering them precise, without which we would be unable to classify the Law of Demeter conclusively.

7. Analysis

Clearly, results obtained from the case studies in Sections 5 and 6 are not coincidental. The same line of reasoning used for the Factory Method can be used for many other (if not all) of the design patterns in [14], as well as for the architectural styles by Garlan and Shaw [16]. Examples drawn from other formal languages proposed for the specification of design patterns, such as *Constraint Diagrams* [19], *DisCo* [22], and *Contracts* [17], bring forth sample specifications, are clearly *intensional* as well. This motivates the following hypothesis:

The ***hypothesis of intensional specifications****. All "design patterns" and "architectural styles" are intensional.*

A direct proof would require a formalization of "all" design patterns and architectural styles. The first problem with this is that no given catalogue purports to contain "all" patterns and styles, nor do we expect such a catalogue to be possible (except perhaps in the analytic sense.) Another problem arises from the mostly informal definitions given to patterns and styles. Limited attempts have been made to prove this hypothesis (e.g.,[13],[9]), but naturally the proofs provided cannot cover all known patterns and styles. Fr this reason, our hypothesis remains as such.

7.1 Specific "design" and "architectures"

With the increase in popularity of the terms and their proliferation in the literature, the terms *design* and *architecture* often appear in a concrete context, as in "the design of this program." This usage implies that these terms can also be used with reference to extensional specifications, but only with reference to a concrete program. We suggest that "the design of program x" refers to the *instance* implemented in a program of a general design rule (e.g., design pattern.) Since instances are extensions, this resolves the apparent difficulty in the intension/locality thesis.

7.2 UML class diagrams

Since UML is used widely as a design and architectural notation, it is of particular interest to understand the place of UML diagrams in the classification we introduced: Are they local? Intensional?

Despite the wide-spread attempts towards rendering the notation with well-defined semantics (e.g., the research group known as *pUML* [27]), most types of UML diagrams have no well-defined semantics. Thus, our discussion here is largely informal, assuming that any formal interpretation for class diagrams will be consistent with the informal semantics.

In terms of design models, we can assume that any such interpretation will associate class icons with atoms of type *class*, operations with atoms of type *method*, as well as provide us with a specification of a set of associated relations. It is easy to see why the specification given by a class diagram is local; but is it intensional?

To answer this question, note that a UML class diagram is commonly viewed as an under-specification, namely, an incomplete specification; the actual implementation of the diagram may have any number of additional elements that are not mentioned in the diagram at all. Under this assumption, UML class diagrams are intensional, since there exists an unbounded number of elements that can be added to any implementation.

Unlike the formulas used in our examples, however, the abstraction that class diagrams provide is of the most rudimentary type, that is, by omitting information but without using free variables. A UML diagram provides no information on the elements that are not explicitly described. Thus, class diagrams are intensional only in a trivial sense, in the same way that the code excerpts in Table 2 and Table 3, if taken not as complete programs but just as excerpts thereof, are intensional. Clearly, this sense is quite unlike the way architectural and design specifications are intensional. The following definition facilitates this distinction:

Definition IV. *An intensional specification* φ *is* ***quasi-extensional*** *iff the set of design models that satisfy* φ*, has a single lower bound with respect to the partial-ordering relation "subsumption".*

It is easy to show that subsumption induces partial ordering on a set of design models. Definition IV, however, assigns specific importance to sets of design models that contain design model such that all other members subsume it.

Corollary 6. *UML class diagrams are quasi-extensional.*

Figure 5 illustrates the proof to this corollary. It is trivial to show also that none of the intensional specifications we quoted above is quasi-extensional.

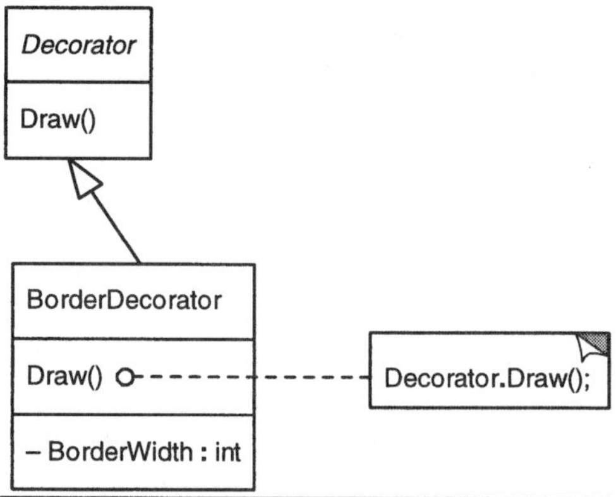

The minimal design model that satisfies this diagram appears in Table 2. Since every program that implements this diagram satisfies it, there are infinitely-many other design models that satisfy it.

Figure 5. A UML class diagram and its interpretations

8. Conclusions

We have provided a sound formal basis for the distinction between the terms *architecture*, *design*, and *implementation*, called the Intension/Locality thesis, and established it upon best practices.

What are the consequences of precisely knowing the differences between the terms architecture, design and implementation? Among others, these distinctions facilitate –

- determining what constitutes a uniform program, e.g., a collection of modules that satisfy the same architectural specifications;
- determining what information goes into *architecture* documents and what goes into *design* documents;
- determining what to examine and what to not examine in an architectural evaluation or a design walkthrough;
- understanding the distinction between local and non-local rules, i.e., between the design rules that need be enforced throughout a project versus those that are of a more limited domain.

For example, in the industrial practice of software architecture, many statements that are said to be "architectural" are in fact local, e.g., *both tasks A and B execute on the same node*, or *task A controls B*. Instead, a truly architectural statement would be, for instance, *for each tasks A,B which satisfy some property* φ*, A and B will execute on the same node and* $Control(A,B)$. More generally, for each specification we know we should determine whether it is a *design* statement, describing a purely local phenomenon (and hence of secondary interest in documentation, discussion, or analysis), or whether it is this an instance of an underlying, more general rule. (*)

Acknowledgements

We than Lutz Prechelt of the ICSE program committee for his very detailed comments. Many thanks to Jens Jahnke and Alejandro Allievi for their contributions. We thank Mary J. Anna for her inspiration. This research was supported in part by the Natural Sciences and Engineering Research Council, Canada and by the U.S. Department of Defense.

References

[1] J. Barwise, ed., (1977). *Handbook of Mathematical Logic.* Amsterdam: North-Holland Publishing Co.

[2] L. Bass, P. Clements, R. Kazman (1998). *Software Architecture in Practice.* Reading, MA: Addison Wesley Longman, Inc.

[3] G. Booch, I. Jacobson, J. Rumbaugh (1999). *The Unified Modeling Language Reference Manual.* Reading, MA: Addison-Wesley.

[4] F. Buschmann, R. Meunier, H. Rohnert, P. Sommerlad, M. Stal (1996). *Pattern-Oriented Software Architecture – A System of Patterns.* New York, NY: Wiley and Sons.

[5] J. Coplien, D. Schmidt, eds. (1995). *Pattern Languages of Program Design.* Reading, MA: Addison-Wesley.

[6] T. R. Dean, J. R. Cordy. "A Syntactic Theory of Software Architecture." *IEEE Trans. on Software Engineering* 21 (4), Apr. 1995, pp. 302—313.

[7] F. DeRemer, H. H. Kron. "Programming-in-the-large versus programming-in-the-small." *IEEE Trans. in Software Engineering* 2 (2), June 1976, pp. 80—86.

[8] A. H. Eden. "Formal Specification of Object-Oriented Design." *International Conference on Multidisciplinary Design in Engineering CSME-MDE 2001*, Nov. 21—22, 2001, Montreal, Canada.

[9] A. H. Eden. "A Theory of Object-Oriented Design." *Information Systems Frontiers* 4 (4), Nov.—Dec. 2002. Kluwer Academic Publishers.

* This final example was suggested by an anonymous ICSE reviewer.

[10] A. H. Eden. "LePUS: A Visual Formalism for Object-Oriented Architectures." *The 6th World Conference on Integrated Design and Process Technology*, Pasadena, CA, June 26—30, 2002.

[11] A. H. Eden, Y. Hirshfeld. "Principles in Formal Specification of Object Oriented Architectures." *CASCON 2001*, Nov. 5—8, 2001, Toronto, Canada.

[12] A. H. Eden, R. Kazman (2003). "On the Definitions of Architecture, Design, and Implementation". Technical report CSM-377, January 2003, Department of Computer Science, University of Essex, United Kingdom.

[13] P. van Emde Boas (1997). "Resistance Is Futile; Formal Linguistic Observations on Design Patterns." Research Report no. CT-19997-03, The Institute for Logic, Language, and Computation, Universiteit van Amsterdam.

[14] E. Gamma, R. Helm, R. Johnson, J. Vlissides (1994). *Design Patterns: Elements of Reusable Object Oriented Software*. Addison-Wesley.

[15] D. Garlan, R. Monroe, D. Wile (1997). "ACME: An Architectural Description Interchange Language." *Proceedings of CASCON'97*. Toronto, Ontario.

[16] D. Garlan, M. Shaw (1993). "An Introduction to Software Architecture." In V. Ambriola, G. Tortora, eds., *Advances in Software Engineering and Knowledge Engineering*, Vol. 2, pp. 1—39. New Jersey: World Scientific Publishing Company.

[17] R. Helm, I. M. Holland, D. Gangopadhyay. "Contracts: Specifying Behavioral Compositions in Object-Oriented Systems." *Proceedings OPPSLA/ECOOP*, Oct. 21—25, 1990, Ottawa, Canada.

[18] R. Kazman. "A New Approach to Designing and Analyzing Object-Oriented Software Architecture." Guest talk, *Conference On Object-Oriented Programming Systems, Languages and Applications – OOPSLA*, Nov. 1—5, 1999, Denver, CO.

[19] A. Lauder, S. Kent. "Precise Visual Specification of Design Patterns." *Proceedings of the 12th ECOOP, Brussels, Belgium*, July 1998. LNCS 1445. Berlin: Springer-Verlag.

[20] K. Lieberherr, I. Holland, A. Riel (1988). "Object-oriented programming: an objective sense of style." *Conference proceedings OOPLA'88*, San Diego, CA, pp. 323—334.

[21] D. C. Luckham et. al. "Specification and Analysis of System Architecture Using Rapide." *IEEE Trans. on Software Engineering* 21 (4), Apr. 1995, pp. 336—355.

[22] T. Mikkonen (1998). "Formalizing Design Patterns." *Proceedings of the International Conference on Software Engineering*, April 19—25, 1998, pp. 115—124. Kyoto, Japan.

[23] R. T. Monroe, A. Kompanek, R. Melton, D. Garlan. "Architectural Styles, Design Patterns, and Objects." *IEEE Software* 14(1), Jan. 1997, pp. 43—52.

[24] D. E. Perry, A. L. Wolf (1992). "Foundation for the Study of Software Architecture." ACM SIGSOFT *Software Engineering Notes* 17 (4), pp. 40—52.

[25] Popkin Software (2000). *System Architect 2001*. New York, NY: McGraw-Hill.

[26] R. Prieto-Diaz, J. Neighbors. "Module Interconnection Languages." *J. of Systems and Software* 6 (4), 1986, pp. 307—334.

[27] *The Unambiguous UML Consortium* page: `www.cs.york.ac.uk/puml/`

[28] T. Quatrani (1999). *Visual Modelling with Rational Rose 2000 and UML, Revised*. Reading, MA: Addison Wesley Longman, Inc.

[29] D. C. Schmidt, M. Stal, H. Rohnert, F. Buschmann (2000). *Pattern-Oriented Software Architecture*, Vol. 2: Patterns for Concurrent and Networked Objects. New York, NY: John Wiley & Sons, Ltd.

[30] SEI (2002). Carnegie Mellon's *Software Engineering Institute*. `http://www.sei.cmu.edu`.

[31] M. Shaw, D. Garlan (1996). *Software Architecture: Perspectives on an Emerging Discipline*. Upper Saddle River, NJ: Prentice Hall.

[32] J. M. Spivey (1989). *The Z Notation: A Reference Manual*. New Jersey: Prentice Hall.

[33] A. Taivalsaari (1996). "On the Notion of Inheritance." *ACM Computing Surveys* 28 (3), pp. 438—479.

Cadena: An Integrated Development, Analysis, and Verification Environment for Component-based Systems*

John Hatcliff, Xinghua Deng, Matthew B. Dwyer, Georg Jung, and Venkatesh Prasad Ranganath
Kansas State University, Department of Computing and Information Sciences
Manhattan, KS 66506, USA
{hatcliff,deng,dwyer,jung,rvprasad}@cis.ksu.edu

Abstract

The use of component models such as Enterprise Java Beans and the CORBA Component Model (CCM) in application development is expanding rapidly. Even in real-time safety/mission-critical domains, component-based development is beginning to take hold as a mechanism for incorporating non-functional aspects such as real-time, quality-of-service, and distribution. To form an effective basis for development of such systems, we believe that support for reasoning about correctness properties of component-based designs is essential.

In this paper, we present Cadena – an integrated environment for building and modeling CCM systems. Cadena provides facilities for defining component types using CCM IDL, specifying dependency information and transition system semantics for these types, assembling systems from CCM components, visualizing various dependence relationships between components, specifying and verifying correctness properties of models of CCM systems derived from CCM IDL, component assembly information, and Cadena specifications, and producing CORBA stubs and skeletons implemented in Java. We are applying Cadena to avionics applications built using Boeing's Bold Stroke framework.

1 Introduction

As software systems become more distributed, developers are increasingly turning to component-based development frameworks such Java Enterprise Beans (EJB) and the CORBA Component Model (CCM) to manage the complexities associated with building distributed systems. These frameworks aid application developers by providing services for common aspects such as distributed deployment, event notification, transactions, persistence, and security. Moreover, they use accepted design patterns (e.g., the event-oriented observer pattern) which enables a significant amount of code to be auto-generated. Component-based frameworks are also attractive because the relatively loose coupling between components facilitates reuse and allows systems to evolve gracefully as old components are switched out for new ones.

Even in the domain of distributed real-time embedded (DRE) systems where hard/soft deadlines and minimal footprint requirements traditionally have led developers to eschew sophisticated middleware solutions, component-based infrastructures are growing more popular because hardware advances allow real-time and embedded requirements to be more easily achieved. In addition, component-based infrastructures provide a framework for systematically introducing important domain aspects such time-triggered notification, real-time scheduling, and fault tolerance.

There is a wide body of literature dealing with the theory of modeling distributed systems and automated analysis of high-level state-based models using state-space exploration techniques such as model-checking. However, despite the popularity of component-based frameworks and their potential to be utilized in mission- and safety-critical applications, relatively little has been done to scale up these analysis techniques for the purpose of providing automated analysis tools for component frameworks. This is particularly the case with CCM – partly due to the fact that the CCM specification as part of CORBA 3.0 has only recently been finalized. Popular tools such as Rational Rose do not even provide design support for CCM yet.

To investigate the effectiveness of a variety of behavioral analysis techniques for component-based systems, we have built *Cadena* [1] – an integrated development environment for high-assurance CCM-based systems. The primary technical contributions of this paper are

- a framework for light-weight dependency analysis (with varying levels of precision) of component-based specifications, and
- a framework for extracting checkable transition system models from component-based specifications of sys-

*This work was supported in part by DARPA/IXO's PCES program through AFRL Contract F33615-00-C-3044, by the U.S. Army Research Laboratory and the U.S. Army Research Office under agreement DAAD190110564, by Intel Corporation under grant 11462, and was performed for the Formal Verification of Integrated Modular Avionics Software Cooperative Agreement, NCC-1-399, sponsored by Honeywell Technology Center and NASA Langley Research Center.

[1] "Cadena" is a Spanish word meaning "network". Cadena is also an acronym for Component Architecture Development ENvironment for Avionics systems.

0-7695-1877-X/03 $17.00 © 2003 IEEE

tems that use middleware services (such as event services) where extracted models incorporate the threading semantics of the relevant middleware services.

These particular capabilities were developed in response to requests from Boeing engineers working on Boeing's Bold Stroke avionics middleware infrastructure.

Boeing's Bold Stroke program is an example where CORBA middleware has been embraced in a DRE domain for the reasons outlined above [20, 21, 9]. Bold Stroke is a product-line based program providing object-oriented mission critical avionics software to a variety of military aircraft produced by the Boeing company. Avionics software acts as the center of mission control for an aircraft pilot. It manages the cockpit displays, navigation and tactical sensors as well as weapon deployments. These complex systems have hard and soft real-time deadlines involving large amounts of periodic and aperiodic processing, and support thousands of operating modes. In addition, the software developed for military aircraft is maintained and updated over the course of many years. Although the development process is repeated for each update, each update aims to preserve as much legacy software as possible to reduce cost and risk. Bold Stroke represents a significant technological advance over Boeing's previous mission computing development practices which were largely assembly code based.

During the past year, we have been interacting extensively with Bold Stroke engineers who have proposed a variety of interesting challenge problems related to component-based design and analysis. Work on Cadena is driven in large part by a desire to provide solutions to challenge problems related to behavioral analysis. Bold Stroke was initiated before the OMG CCM specification process was underway. Thus, the Bold Stroke component design, is slightly different from CCM, and therefore does not apply the CCM Interface Definition Language (IDL) (now part of OMG CORBA IDL 3.0) to auto-generate component code. In current practice, component developers receive a natural language description of functional and real-time requirements along with UML collaboration diagrams built with Rose showing component interactions, and development begins directly with C++ coding. This means that high-level designs are not tool-leveraged in any way (either for code generation or for automated analysis). Bold Stroke engineers have suggested a number interesting ways that high-level designs could be analyzed for event/data dependency and mode state information for the purpose of inferring distribution, scheduling, and real-time aspects, as well as checking for common design flaws and satisfaction of application specific requirements.

Beyond the particular domain of DRE mission/safety-critical systems, we believe that CCM and other component oriented frameworks are excellent vehicles for injecting light-weight formal methods and sophisticated automated analysis techniques across the entire software development process. In the past, it has often been difficult to get developers to write formal specifications – instead they prefer to move quickly to writing code. We believe that this is because there is little tool support for leveraging such high-level descriptions. In contrast, CCM's IDL (which defines the structure of components) and CCM's component assembly descriptions (which describe how components are connected together) are central to the use of CCM since a large percentage of a system's code is generated directly from these. These high-level descriptions can be leveraged in a number of ways: component connections can be visualized (essentially, UML collaboration diagrams can be autogenerated), useful dependency analysis can be performed at this level, light-weight behavior specifications can be incorporated, and code generation can be tailored to produce code that is more amenable to verification and certification. When applying model-checking techniques, one often struggles to find appropriate system abstraction that make state exploration tractable. CCM descriptions naturally form system abstractions, and by varying annotations on the high-level descriptions (e.g., to expose the state of mode variables, etc.) the system model processed by model-checking techniques can be easily abstracted (to hide state) or refined (to expose more state and more interesting behaviors).

Cadena provides the following capabilities for development of CCM systems.

- A collection of light-weight specification forms that can be attached to IDL to specify mode variable domains, intra-component dependencies, and component state-transition semantics. These forms have a natural refinement order so that useful feedback can be obtained with little annotation effort, and increasing the precision of annotation yields more precise analysis. In addition, Cadena specifications allow developers to specify the same information in different ways, achieving a form of *checkable redundancy* that is useful for exposing design flaws.
- Dependency analysis capabilities allow tracing inter/intra-component event and data dependencies, as well as algorithms for synthesizing dependency-based real-time and distribution aspect information.
- A novel model-checking infrastructure dedicated to event-based inter-component communication via real-time middleware enables system design models (derived from CCM IDL, component-assembly descriptions and annotations) to be model-checked for global system properties.
- Java component stub and skeleton code generated using the OpenCCM [12] CCM IDL to Java compiler.
- A component assembly framework supporting a variety of visualization and programming tools for developing component connections.
- A CCM deployment facility dedicated to the Boeing Bold Stroke architecture (static component connections with a real-time event-channel) that allows deployment code to be automatically generated.
- The Cadena tools are implemented as plug-ins to IBM's Eclipse IDE. This provides an end-to-end integrated development environment for CCM-based Java systems.

Several of these facilities are targeted directly to the avionics domain, but Cadena is useful in many respects for CCM development in general. Although Cadena currently emphasizes Java in its back-end facilities, since CCM is language-neutral, Cadena's front-end design capabilities are not Java dependent. Moreover, back-end capabilities can be easily extended in the future to other languages, for example, C++ using OpenCCM's [12] planned support for C++. Other development systems such as MetaH [24] support several important aspects for DRE systems that Cadena does not, such as timing and schedulability analysis, reliability and fault analysis, as well as sophisticated deployment strategies. The primary motivation for our work is to build a system that is robust enough for development of real systems with the goal of assessing the effectiveness of applying static analysis, model-checking, and other light-weight formal methods to CCM-based systems.

The rest of this paper is organized as follows. Section 2 gives a brief overview of CCM and the Bold Stroke architecture, and presents an example that will drive the discussion in the rest of the paper. Section 3 outlines the Cadena architecture and illustrates the various Cadena specification forms. Section 4 presents Cadena's dependency analysis facilities. Section 5 describes Cadena's model-checking facilities. Section 6 discusses related work. Section 7 assesses the current state of the tools and presents directions for future work.

2 CCM Overview and Example

To describe the features of Cadena, we will use as a running example a simple avionics system that shows steering cues on a pilot's navigational display. The pilot can choose between two different display modes — each mode yields a different set of steering cues. A *tactical* display mode displays cues related to a tactical (*i.e.*, mission) objective. A *navigation* display *mode* displays cues related to a navigational objective. Cues for the navigation display are derived in part from navigation steering points data that can be entered by the navigator.

Figure 1 presents the CCM architecture for the example system. The system is realized as a collection of components coupled together via interface and event connections. The system include three *modal components* (AirFrame, NavSteering, and TacticalSteering) whose behavior changes depending on the *mode* of the component (the mode of each component will be represented by an attribute with an appropriate enumeration type). Moreover, the system is designed to run on a single processor. For this reason, we refer to the example as *ModalSP*. Input position data is gathered periodically at a rate of 20 Hz in the GPS component and then passed to an intermediate AirFrame component (which in a more realistic system would take position data from a variety of other sensors). Both the NavSteering and TacticalSteering component produce cue data for Display based on air frame position data. The Navigator component polls for inputs from the plane navigator at a rate of 5 Hz and uses those to form NavSteeringPoints

```
#pragma prefix "cadena"
module modalsp {
 interface ReadData {
  readonly attribute any data;
 };

 eventtype TimeOut {};
 eventtype DataAvailable {};

 enum LazyActiveMode {stale, fresh};
 component LazyActive {
  provides   ReadData dataOut;
  uses       ReadData dataIn;
  publishes  DataAvailable outDataAvailable;
  consumes   DataAvailable inDataAvailable;
  attribute  LazyActiveMode dataStatus;
 };

 enum OnOffMode {enabled, disabled};
 interface ChangeMode {
  attribute OnOffMode modeVar;
 };

 component Modal1 {
  provides   ChangeMode modeChange;
  provides   ReadData dataOut;
  uses       ReadData dataIn;
  publishes  DataAvailable outDataAvailable;
  consumes   DataAvailable inDataAvailable;
 };
};
```

Figure 2. CCM/Cadena artifacts for ModalSP (excerpts)

data. This data is then used to form navigational steering cues in NavSteering. PilotControl polls for a pilot steering mode at a rate of 1 Hz and enables or disables NavSteering and TacticalSteering accordingly.

Figure 2 gives the CCM IDL that defines the component types `LazyActive` and `Modal1` for the AirFrame and TacticalSteering component instances in Figure 1. CCM components *provide* interfaces to clients on ports referred to as *facets*, and *use* interfaces provided by other clients on ports referred to as *receptacles*. Components *publish* events on ports referred to as *event sources*, and *consume* events on ports referred to as *event sinks*. In the `LazyActive` component type of Figure 2, `dataOut` is the name of a facet with interface type `ReadData`, and `dataIn` is the name of a receptacle with interface type `ReadData`. Similarly, `inDataAvailable` is the name of an event sink of type `DataAvailable`, and `outDataAvailable` is the name of an event source of type `DataAvailable`. Components can also have *attributes* such as `modeVar` that are used either in component configuration or to represent some other aspect of component state. For an attribute with name *attrname*, the IDL compiler will automatically generate an accessor method `get_`*attrname* and a mutator method `set_`*attrname*. If the attribute is declared `readonly` as in the `ReadData` interface of Figure 2, then only an accessor method is generated[2].

While CCM allows components to be dynamically created and (dis)connected, Bold Stroke applications follow typical practice in safety/mission-critical systems and em-

[2]The name of the accessor/mutator methods are dependent on the IDL to language mapping.

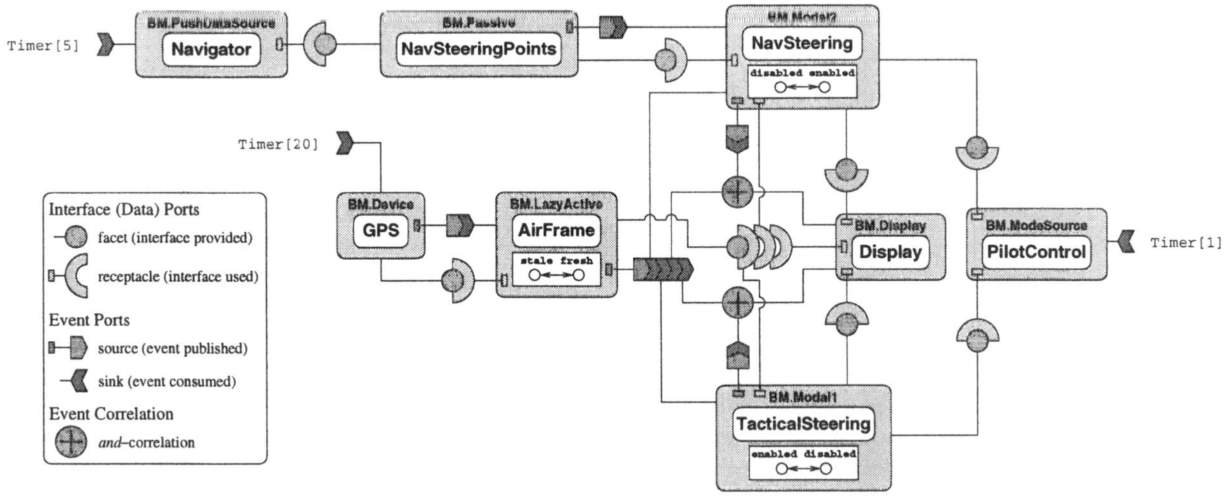

Figure 1. ModalSP – a simple avionics system

```
system ModalSPScenario {
 import cadena.common, cadena.modalsp;

 Rates 1, 5, 20;          // Hz rate groups
 Locations l1, l2, l3;    // abstract deployment locs
 ...
 Instance AirFrame implements LazyActive on #LAloc {
  connect this.inDataAvailable
       to GPS.outDataAvailable runRate #LArate;
  connect this.dataIn to GPS.dataOut;
 }
 Instance TacticalSteering implements Modal1 on l2 {
  connect this.inDataAvailable
       to AirFrame.outDataAvailable runRate 5;
  connect this.dataIn to AirFrame.dataOut;
 }
 ...
}
```

Figure 3. Cadena Assembly Description for ModalSP (excerpts)

ploy a static component allocation and configuration policy by creating and connecting components only in a system initialization phase. Dynamic reconfiguration is achieved by including components whose behavior can be deactivated based on the system mode settings.

The CORBA 3.0 specification does not provide a dedicated language for static system configuration. Cadena provides three languages for describing configurations. Graphical, textual, and forms-based descriptions are synchronized through a single internal form. Figure 3 displays a fragment of the textual Cadena Assembly Description (CAD) for the example system. In CAD, a developer declares the component instances that form a system, along with rate and distribution annotations. For receptacle and event sink ports, a `connect` clause declares a connection between a port of the current instance and a port of the component that provides the interface/event. This follows a convention that connections are declared on the client-side of an interface/event connection. Each event sink port connection uses the `runRate` clause to indicate which rate group thread should run the event handler upon event dispatch. For each instance, a developer names a location upon which the instance is to be allocated. Location names are not bound to physical locations at this point in the process, but will subsequently be mapped to CORBA specific notions such as containers and nodes at deployment time.

Incomplete specifications and incremental construction are supported by allowing rate and location variables such as `#LAloc` and `#LArate`. These act as place holders, and values for these can be inferred using the non-functional aspect synthesis algorithms presented later. Equality constraints between such variables can also be specified, and the synthesis procedures generate output that conforms to these constraints. A type-checking procedure ensures well-typed connections.

Bold Stroke applications follow a *control-push data-pull* architecture in which data is transferred between data producer and data consumer components in a two step process. First, a data producer (e.g., TacticalSteering) publishes a `DataAvailable` event indicating that it has updated some data that is ready to be consumed. Then, when a subscribing data consumer (e.g., Display) receives the event, it calls a *get data* accessor method in a facet provided by the supplier to retrieve the data. Thus, threads never block waiting for data to become available, and this simplifies the design of real-time aspects. Under this strategy, component connections come in pairs consisting of an event connection for notification that data is ready, and an interface connection for fetching the data.

The `LazyActive` component type of Figure 2 implements a variant of this strategy to handle situations where a component C (e.g., AirFrame) depends on data that is updated much more frequently than C's clients require C's data. For example, the AirFrame component does not fetch data immediately from GPS when notified, but instead simply sets its `dataStatus` attribute to indicate that its data is stale and notifies its clients (e.g., TacticalSteering) that its data is available. When a *get data* call for AirFrame data comes from one of its clients, it checks the `dataStatus` attribute to see if its data is fresh, and if it is, it returns it immediately to the calling client. If it is not fresh, it calls the GPS *get data* method, updates its own data with the return

GPS data, sets its dataStatus to fresh, and returns the new AirFrame data to the calling client.

Both NavSteering and TacticalSteering are *modal components* that have two modes (enabled,disabled). These modes are set by PilotControl via ChangeMode facets provided by the modal components. When a modal component is disabled, any events received are simply discarded by the component. When enabled, the component responds according to the control-push data-pull strategy (e.g., TacticalSteering responds to a DataAvailable from AirFrame by calling AirFrame's get data method.

In Bold Stroke applications, even though at a conceptual level component event source ports are connected to event sink ports, in the implementation, event communication is factored through a real-time CORBA event channel. Use of such infrastructure is central to Bold Stroke computation because it provides not only a mechanism for communicating events, but also a pool-based threading model, time-triggered periodic events, and event correlation. In order to shield application components from the physical aspects of the system, for product-line flexibility, and for run-time efficiency, all components are *passive* – component methods are run by event-channel threads that dispatch events by calling the event handlers ("push methods" in CORBA terminology) associated with event sink ports. The roots of computation are time-triggered events (e.g., events associated with event sinks of Navigator, GPS, and PilotControl) supplied at a specified rates by the event-channel. Dispatching of these events causes the dispatch threads to run the associated handlers which contain methods calls and publishing of subsequent events. In the current Bold Stroke implementation, the event channel thread pool has exactly one thread associated with each rate. As noted earlier in the discussion of Figure 3, each non-time-triggered event port also has a rate specified at configuration time which indicates its *rate group*, i.e., the pool thread that should run the event handler when the event is dispatched.

The event channel also provides event correlation and event filtering mechanisms. In the example system, *and*-correlation is used, for instance, to combine event flows from NavSteering and AirFrame into NavDisplay. The semantics of *and*-correlation on two events e_1 and e_2 is that the event channel waits for an instance of both e_1 and e_2 to be published before creating a notification event that is dispatched to the consumer of the correlation. The semantics of a correlator is defined by an automaton over event traces derived from the correlation expression [22].

Note that CCM IDL captures the interface properties of components – Cadena's notation for expressing component behavior is presented in the next section.

3 Cadena Architecture

Figure 4 displays the internal structure of the Cadena toolset. Cadena projects contain four high-level specification forms: a CORBA 3 IDL file that defines the structure of component types (see Figure 2), a Cadena Property Specification (CPS) file that specifies various aspects of component behavior (see Figure 5), a Cadena Assembly Description (CAD) that specifies the components instances that form the system, the connections between them, along with other real-time and distribution property information (see Figure 3), and a specification file that stores information about the desired correctness properties of the system. These input artifacts are created using customized editors built using Eclipse plug-in facilities. In particular, the CAD format has a textual editor, a graphical editor (to view systems as graphs similar to style of Figure 1)[3], and a form-based editor that allows one to easily define different projections of the component assembly (e.g., connections only, distribution and rate assignments only, etc.). The graph structure described by the CAD is the basic data structure that is used by the dependency analyzer (discussed in Section 4), the graphical view displayer, and the deployment code generator (which generates Java code to allocate and connect components).

Dependence Specifications: Figure 5 displays excerpts of the CPS file for our example system. In a CPS description, developers may declare intracomponent dependencies between ports and simple behavioral descriptions of a component's event handlers and other methods. The dependence declarations take the form *trigger-port-action* -> *response-port-action*. For example, Figure 5 declares that consumption of an event on the inDataAvailable port of a LazyActive component may trigger a publish on the outDataAvailable port in both stale and fresh modes. The absence of a dependence for the dataOut port in the fresh mode indicates that any call on dataOut should not result in an action on any other port.

A dependencydefault may have one of two settings: a none setting allows developers to start with an empty dependence relation and add new dependencies (i.e., dependences do not exist except when declared), an all setting allows developers to start with a universal dependence relation and then prune dependences (i.e., by default all possible dependencies between ports exist). In the all setting, once a port is mentioned on the left-hand-side, then only declared dependences apply for that port. For example, for Modal1 which has the all setting, the absence of declarations for the dataOut port specifies that the ports (outDataAvailable and dataIn) *do depend* on dataOut (note that is an overapproximation of the actual behavior). Dependencies are pruned in Modal1 by giving refining declarations such as those for the modeChange and inDataAvailable ports that list no dependents to the right of the ->.

Behavioral Specifications: Since transition systems for model-checking are generated from behavioral descriptions, their primary purpose is to capture (a) the actions that one wishes to reason about in temporal specifications and (b) simple control-flow relationships between these actions. Cadena supports observable actions such as event publish and consume, method call and return, data flows

[3]We do not use an actual screen shot for Figure 1 because the current version of Eclipse does not include zoom in/out capabilities, and the current layout is too large to fit on a screen.

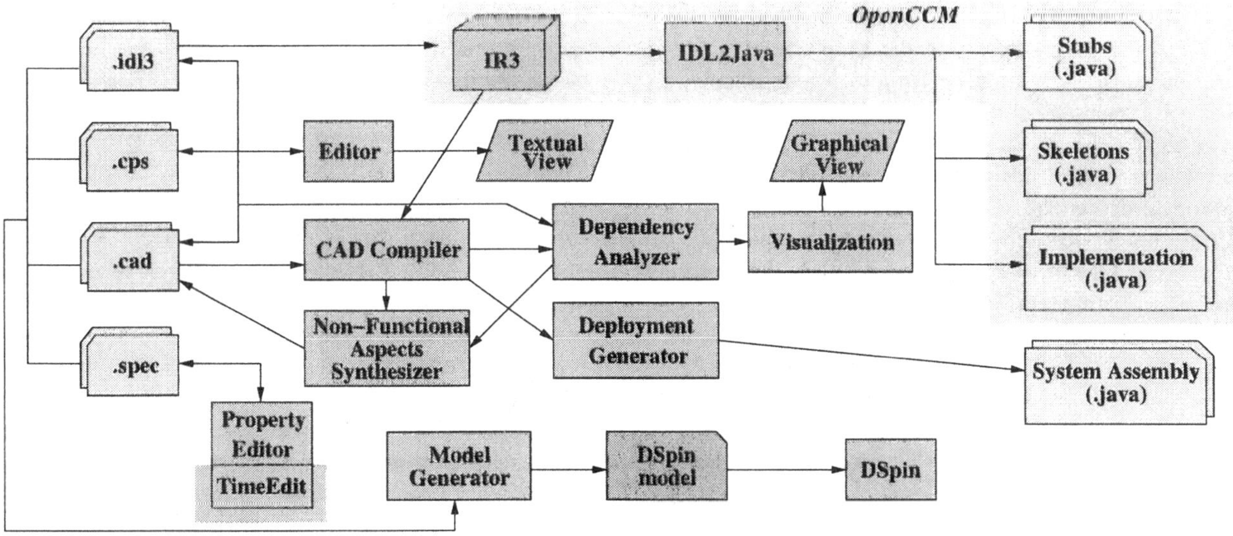

Figure 4. Cadena architecture

```
component LazyActive {
 mode dataStatus;
 dependencydefault == none;

 dependencies {
  case dataStatus of {
   stale: inDataAvailable -> outDataAvailable;
          dataOut.get_data(); -> dataIn.get_data();
   fresh: inDataAvailable -> outDataAvailable;
  }
 }

 behavior {
  any internalData;

  dataAvailable.push(_) {
   if (dataStatus == fresh)
    dataStatus = stale;
    outDataAvailable.push(_);
  }

  any dataOut.getData() {
   if (dataStatus == stale) {
    internalData <- dataIn.get_data();
    dataStatus = fresh;
   }
   return internalData;
  }
 }
}

component Device {
 behavior { ...  }
}

component Modal1 {
 mode modeChange.modeVar;
 dependencydefault == all;

 dependencies {
  modeChange ->;
  case modeChange.modeVar of {
   enabled:  inDataAvailable
             -> dataIn.get_data(),
                outDataAvailable;
   disabled: inDataAvailable ->;
  }
 }

 behavior { ...  }
}
```

Figure 5. Cadena Property Specification (CPS) (excerpts)

between system variables, assignments to mode variables. Each behavioral description in the CPS format gives both a data and control abstraction of a component's actual implementation of an event handler or method. Data abstraction is achieved by only exposing concrete values of mode variables (or other application variables with bounded domains). This was motivated by the fact that Bold Stroke engineers are primarily concerned with reasoning about modal behavior at design time since analysis of system modes and mode transitions can be leveraged in several ways. Even though concrete values of other application variables are usually not modeled, data flows between such variables can be captured. For example, `internalData <- dataIn.get_data();` in the `LazyActive` behavior models a flow from the result of the `get_data();` method into the `internalData` variable. This may abstract many actual computation steps in the actual implementation. The behavioral language contains simple control structures such as sequencing and conditionals and abstracts control by simply omitting commands from the implementation that one does not wish to observe. Note that dependence information can also be derived from behavioral specifications, and this provides a form of checkable redundancy. The intent is that developers begin with the more light-weight dependence specifications, leverage those, then only incorporate behavioral specifications when model-checking analysis is to be applied.

Code Generation: Cadena uses the OpenCCM tools [12] to generate system implementations. The OMG CORBA 3.0 specification standardizes a strategy for compiling IDL (of which the CCM IDL is part) down to CORBA IDL 2, which can then be translated to an underlying implementation language such as Java or C++. This translation process automatically generates a substantial amount of infrastructure code for tasks such as component creation and connecting and disconnecting ports. The output code contains the usual CORBA *stubs* and *skeletons*, along with skeleton *implementations* of component methods and event handlers. With this code generation, the developer only needs to implement event handlers and methods on provided interfaces. In future work we are exploring the extension of CCM-based code generation strategies to integrate code generation for component handler state-machines and global synchronization policies [8].

Methodology: When building systems with Cadena, we intend for developers to take the following steps: (1) load a library of domain-specific components and associated CPS specifications, (2) define new project-specific components and associated behavioral CPS specifications, (3) use CAD editors to configure connections between components, (4) use dependency viewer to examine dependencies, (5) use non-functional aspect synthesis tools to attach distribution and rate information (see Section 4.3), (6) specify desired global correctness properties (see Section 5.5), (7) generate a transition system model and model-check correctness properties (see Section 5), and (8) revise system based on feedback from analysis tools.

4 Dependency Analysis

Even with small systems of around 20-30 components, relationships between components and component dependences are often hard to determine from visual inspections of textual or graphical component assembly views. Bold Stroke systems can have 1000s of components, and Bold Stroke engineers have identified development of automated support for component dependency analysis and visualization as a high priority. As discussed in the previous section, Cadena provides several different layers of dependency specification and analysis with the goal of enabling incremental construction of dependency specifications – little or no specification effort should still allow useful tool feedback since a fair amount of dependency information (*inter*-component dependences) can be derived from the CAD information. Increasing the details of specifications should yield more precise visualizations and analysis. Here are the steps that we expect developers to take when creating and refining dependence information: (1) give component assembly without CPS dependence information using the global dependence default that all actions on input ports of a component C give rise to actions on all output ports of C, (2) refine by giving dependences without taking into account modal behavior, (3) refine by considering modes in CPS dependence declarations, and (4) refine by giving behavioral descriptions (which capture dependence information via control-flow properties). Bold Stroke developers currently use dependency information manually to determine non-functional aspects such as distribution, connection implementation (synchronous vs. non-synchronous calls), rate group assignment, etc. Cadena leverages partial dependence information to provide automated support for developers.

4.1 Basic notions of dependency

Given a component library and component assembly description (along with optional Cadena property specification file), Cadena's port-level dependency module builds a *port dependence graph* PDG = (N,E) where each node $n \in N$ is a component/port pair $i.p$. Edges (i.e., dependences) between PDG nodes arise from two sources: *inter-component dependences* corresponding to port connections specified in component assembly descriptions and *intra-component dependences* captured by CPS declarations in component property specifications. Whether or not intra-component dependences are generated for a particular instance C depends on the *default dependence setting* for C as discussed previously. The default setting is given by the global default dependence declaration unless a component-local default declaration exists.

For inter-component dependences, when there is a connection between $i_1.p_1$ and $i_2.p_2$ in the component assembly description, we say that $i_1.p_1$ is *event dependent* on $i_2.p_2$ (written $i_2.p_2 \overset{e}{\to} i_1.p_1$ – the arrow pointing in the direction of the event flow) if p_2 (resp. p_1) is an event source (resp. sink). Similarly, with the above connection, $i_1.p_1$ is *interface dependent* on $i_2.p_2$ (written $i_2.p_2 \overset{n}{\to} i_1.p_1$) when p_2 (resp. p_1) is a facet (resp. receptacle). For example, from the CAD information in Figures 1 and 3, we have, e.g., GPS.outDataAvailable $\overset{e}{\to}$ AirFrame.inDataAvailable and GPS.dataOut $\overset{n}{\to}$ AirFrame.dataIn.

For intra-component dependences, for an instance i of component type c, $i.p_1$ is *trigger dependent* on $i.p_2$ (written $i.p_2 \overset{t}{\to} i.p_1$) when either (1) p_2 is declared to trigger p_1 in the CPS for c, or (2) the default dependency status for c is *all* and there exists no trigger declaration for p_2 in the Cadena specification for c.

As with conventional work on dependences, a system slice for a particular point(s) of interest (referred to as the *slicing criterion*) is computed by taking the transitive closure of the PDG from the PDG node(s) corresponding to the slicing criterion. Basic slicing actions provided by Cadena include forward slice, backward slice, and slice intersections.

4.2 Mode-aware dependences

To reason about mode-aware dependences, the mode state of the system is captured formally via a mode-state vector m which holds values for one or more mode variables from the system being analyzed. In the ModalSP scenario, it is useful to consider a two-variable mode-state vector that holds the mode state of NavSteering and the mode state of TacticalSteering. Given a PDG $P = (N, E)$ for a system, a modal PDG $P_m = (N_m, E_m)$ for mode-state vector m is formed by setting $N_m = N$ and having E_m include all inter-component edges, but only intra-component edges that are enabled according to m.

Cadena provides mechanisms for collecting a set of mode-state vectors and using these to drive visualization of dependences (i.e., Cadena users can choose to visualize dependences for a particular vector). Mode-state vector sets can be entered explicitly in a form-based view or generated automatically from the state-exploration techniques discussed in the following section. For instance, for the mode-vector mentioned above, it is instructive to have a mode-based dependency view for the three mode-state vectors (disabled, disabled), (enabled, disabled), and (disabled,enabled).

4.3 Dependency-driven analyses

In the Bold Stroke development process, several non-functional system aspects that are currently designed manually can be aided or even synthesized automatically using the dependence analysis capabilities described above. These include (following the order in which they are carried out) assigning priorities/execution-rates to event consumer ports, appropriately distributing component instances to network nodes, and identifying opportunities for switching asynchronous remote event delivery (the default mechanism) to synchronous local method calls.

Rate Assignment: Automated rate assignment begins by assigning rates to each event consumer port that subscribes to a time-triggered event – the port simply is assigned the rate of the event. Using the results of the dependency analysis above, the process continues by propagating rate information along the PDG in a forwards direction and assigning the propagated rate value to each input and output port encountered. In cases where a port has more than one rate propagated to it (e.g., when event correlation is used, or when two different input ports influence an output port), the highest of the rates is propagated. The process continues until a fixpoint is reached and the resulting rates on event consumer ports bind CAD rate variables.

In the example in Figure 1, automated rate assignment would result in assigning 1Hz to the event consumer of PilotControl, and to the receptacles of PilotControl and the facets of TacticalSteering and NavSteering connected to PilotControl. Similarly, (a) all ports in Navigator, NavSteeringPoints are assigned 5Hz, and the two ports of NavSteering connected to NavSteering are assigned 5Hz, and (b) all ports in GPS and AirFrame are assigned 20Hz. There is now a conflict for the rates on the output ports of NavSteering due to the fact both 5Hz and 20Hz rates are flowing in, so the higher rate of 20Hz is used. The process continues until the remainder of the unassigned ports have a value of 20Hz.

Distribution Determination: The distribution algorithm then uses the rate information gathered above (a) to determine the traffic on the connections between components, and (b) to identify components to be deployed on a common location. In the example, the algorithm would group components closer to their trigger source with the traffic and rate information used as the arbitrating criteria.

In the example, Navigator and PilotControl would be assigned distinct locations, `l1` and `l2`. The rest of the components would be assigned location `l3` as the traffic between them is higher assuming all data and event types are of unit size. However, if the traffic on the data connection between Navigator and NavSteeringPoints was higher than the cumulative traffic on other connections on NavSteeringPoints then NavSteeringPoints would be assigned location `l1`. Although this simplistic example is not realistic, the ability to automatically leverage connection and rate information to provide developers with guidance about component distribution can be a significant advantage for large systems.

Synchronous Dispatch Optimization: For the reduction of asynchronous remote event deliveries, an event delivery between two component instance ports $i_1.p_1$ and $i_2.p_2$ that does not involve correlation can be reduced to a local method call when i_1 and i_2 are co-located and when the rates attached to p_1 and p_2 through the propagation above are the same. In the example, this optimization can be applied to all non-correlated event connections. However, if NavSteeringPoints and NavSteering were assigned different locations in the distribution step above, the optimization would not apply to that connection.

Finally, although we do not implement schedulability analysis in Cadena, we note that Cadena's dependency specifications (in particular, mode-aware dependence information) can be used to improve static scheduling. Currently, static schedulability analysis in Bold Stroke is based on summing execution costs along call-tree paths deduced from component connections only (i.e., our `all` dependence mode with no declared dependences). Cadena specifications prune away many infeasible dependences, and therefore prune away infeasible paths that may cause worst-case execution time estimates to be more conservative than necessary. This can sometimes save a surprising amount of development time since systems are often restructured in significant ways to obtain schedulable computations.

5 Model-checking Designs

As illustrated in the previous section, light-weight dependence analyses can provide a wealth of information about relationships among design components. In addition to this, Cadena supports deeper semantic analysis of design behavior using model checking. Specifically, we support reasoning about logical properties of component-based designs expressed as assertions, invariants and sequencing properties over system states and actions, such as method calls and returns and event publications and consumptions.

In order to maximize the flexibility of Cadena in targeting different classes of component-based systems, we have designed a layered translation from our extended CCM-based specification languages to the input language of the DSpin [7] model checker. The translation includes modeling of: (*i*) component interfaces and behavior, (*ii*) the semantics of middleware components through which component execution is orchestrated, and (*iii*) event and data sources and sinks in the system environment. These translation aspects have well defined interfaces that make it easy to vary, for example, the semantics of middleware functions to suit a particular application domain. In the remainder of this section, we discuss each of these aspects in turn as well as our approach to specifying the properties to be checked. Unlike much of the existing work in model checking system designs, we found it necessary to exploit knowledge of the middleware and environment to achieve models that were compact enough to check in a reasonable amount of time. We describe how we abstracted domain knowledge for the Bold Stroke architecture to encode it into our models. We conclude with a discussion of our experiences model checking properties of several variations of models generated for the design from Figure 1.

5.1 Why DSpin?

Cadena uses DSpin as its model checking engine. In principle we could use any one of a number of available model checking tools, such as Spin [14] or NuSMV [2], however, component-based designs have a number of features that are difficult to express in the low-level input languages of such tools. For example, one needs to be able to define an object, i.e., a collection of data attributes, manipulate references to an object, and invoke the methods associated with an object. It is clearly possible to map such high-level constructs onto a model checker input language as JPF [13] and Bandera [4] do, but it is much easier when the model checker supports those constructs directly. DSpin is an extension to Spin that adds support for objects, functions, and references, among other features. DSpin is implemented in such a way that it runs as least as fast as Spin for the functionality they have in common [7] and our experience is that the performance penalty for using the extensions is minimal when compared to hand-optimized models.

5.2 Component Modeling

Translating Cadena components is straightforward. A component is implemented as a group of state variables, for attributes and modes, and DSpin function references, for the receptacle methods consumed from other components. Associated with each component are a group of functions that implement the event consumer methods (i.e., handlers) and methods provided by the component.

There are two advantages to this translation: it has a natural mapping back to the Cadena model which facilitates expressing diagnostic information about detected errors and it decouples the component from other components so that models can be easily reconfigured. For example, the `NavSteering` component, shown in Figure 6, does not encode the identity of `source1` from which it reads `dataIn1`. Rather, the component has a function reference that is assigned to the appropriate method reference based on configuration information. We have generated models with static configurations to date, but it is trivial to support dynamic reconfiguration.

5.3 Modeling Middleware Services

CCM systems assume the presence of middleware services such as an event-channel with a pool for dispatching threads to execute component code.

Modeling Event Services: In our DSpin models an event publication is achieved by sending the function reference

```
any NavSteering_internalData;
mode NavSteering_componentState;
ftype Ref_NavSteering_dataIn1_getData,
      Ref_NavSteering_dataIn2_getData;
ftype Ref_NavSteering_update;

function Fun_NavSteering_source1 (mtype t) {
 printf("NavSteering: source1 handler invoked.\n");
 if
  :: NavSteering_componentState == enabled ->
   NavSteering_internalData =
       Ref_NavSteering_dataIn1_getData ();
   printf("NavSteering: publishing update.\n");
   Ref_NavSteering_update (NavSteering_DataAvailable)
  :: else
 fi
}

function Fun_NavSteering_switch_getData () : int {
 atomic {
  P <= 1 ->
   printf("NavSteering: switch getData invoked.\n");
   P = MaxPriority
 }
 return NavSteering_componentState;
}
```

Figure 6. DSpin model for NavSteering Modal Component (excerpts)

```
proctype RateGroup_1Hz () {
 ftype f;
 mtype m;
 ...
 do
  :: skip ->
   S_timeout?b;
   ...
   do
    :: Rate1_queue?[f, m] -> Rate1_queue?f(m); f(m)
    :: else -> break
   od
 od
}
```

Figure 7. DSpin model of Event Channel Rate-specific Thread

for the component's event handler and the identity of the event as a message to the process modeling the event-channel thread. That thread then invokes the event handler code for the component instance as illustrated in Figure 7, where `ftype` is a DSpin function reference and `mtype` is an enumeration encoding the events in the system.

It is easy to identify pairs of component instances where one publishes an event that is consumed by the second. Under certain constraints the behavior of those components may be sequenced, for example when they have the same rate assignments in a Bold Stroke application. Under these conditions, the generic function-event pair queuing mechanism described above may be replaced by direct calls from the component instance publishing the event to the handlers for component instances subscribed to that event. For example, all publications of *dataAvailable* events from the `NavSteering` component are made by calling the `Ref_NavSteering_update` function reference which is bound to the function in Figure 8. Sequencing execution

```
function Proxy_NavSteering_update (mtype t) {
 int i = 0;
 printf("NavSteering-Proxy: Calling subscriber methods.\n");
 do
  :: i < NavSteering_update_NumberSubscribers ->
   NavSteering_update_SubscriberList[i].Entry(t);
   i = i + 1
  :: else -> break
 od
}
```

Figure 8. DSpin Model of intra-Rate-Group Push Proxy

of event publications and consumer code yields a smaller state space [4] by reducing the data states associated with the thread queues, e.g., `Rate1_queue`.

Each event correlation in the system has its own DSpin function. This function is generated based on the automaton that defines the meaning of the correlation expression [22]. The correlation function acts as a handler for its input events, updates the state of the automaton, and when an accepting state is reached it publishes the correlated event to subscribers using the same mechanisms as described above. Since the correlation functionality is internal to the middleware service its internal steps are unobservable to the application, thus we model them as atomic transitions.

Modeling Thread Services: Middleware provides the threads on which application components execute, and it may also define a scheduling policy for those threads. When such a policy is available it can be exploited to reduce the state space of the generated model by eliminating interleavings of thread executions that violate the scheduling policy. Eliminating such interleavings also has the beneficial effect of improving the precision of analysis performed on the model.

Bold Stroke applications use rate monotonic scheduling [16] for event-channel threads. Rate monotonic scheduling is a pre-emptive priority based scheduling policy where higher rates are assigned higher priorities. Like most model checkers, DSpin does not support the definition of a specific scheduling policy, so we encode the policy directly in the DSpin model. This is achieved by guarding all component actions with a test that blocks the action if the component's priority is less than the current runnable priority, which is stored in a global variable P. The print statement of function `Fun_NavSteering_switch_getData` in Figure 6 illustrates such a guard. Guarded component actions are only enabled when the current runnable priority has been decremented to the component's priority. A decrement is performed only when there are no enabled steps in the model which can be detected by the `timeout` predicate of Spin. Since this priority decrementing process must operate independent of component or event-channel thread execution it is modeled as the separate process shown in Figure 9.

The resulting model has several interesting properties.

[4] A similar event-channel performance optimization is applied quite frequently in Bold Stroke applications.

```
active proctype PriorityHandler () {
 do
  :: timeout ->
   d_step {
    if
     :: P > 0 -> P = P - 1;
     :: else
    fi
   }
 od
}
```

Figure 9. Rate Selection Process

It assures that the highest-priority runnable action will be performed; this yields a dramatic reduction in the system state space as discussed below. Note that components running at the highest system wide priority need not have their actions guarded. This, combined with the direct call modeling of event publication and handling, means that high-priority behavior effectively executes as a single atomic step in the model. The introduction of an explicit global priority does add a state variable to the system, but note that it only changes value when no other transitions in the model are enabled. Consequently, there are no possible interleavings of the different priority values with component/thread execution and the effect on the state space is trivial.

5.4 Environment Modeling

Cadena models capture the combined behavior of a collection of component instances working in concert to respond to external inputs and to produce appropriate outputs. We use the term *environment* to describe the entities that interact with the explicitly modeled system. Since Cadena models do not attempt to accurately model data values flowing between the environment and the system the only relevant inputs are environment initiated events. The semantics of those events and the pattern of event arrival at the system will vary with each application.

Our experience suggests that accurate modeling of environment initiated events is necessary both for precision in reasoning and for state space reduction. The Cadena tools have builtin support for generating environment models for Bold Stroke system designs. These systems are driven by periodic events generated by the middleware. The rates of these events are typically harmonic to enable reasoning about schedulability via rate monotonic analysis.

Our generated transition system models do not represent time explicitly, rather they constrain the number of timeout event publishes for a given rate relative to timeout publishes for its adjacent rates. For example, in the interval defined by a pair of 5 Hz timeout events there must be four 20 Hz timeouts. Constraining the timeout events appropriately is achieved by including a separate `Timer` process in the transition system that keeps track of an abstraction of time and triggers timeout events appropriately.

For a system with harmonic rates, one could simply keep a counter, `t`, that is incremented from 0 up to the maximum rate, m, by one to maintain an abstract time. For a k Hz rate

```
proctype Timer () {
 int t = 0;
 do
  :: (t >= 6) -> t = 0
  :: (t < 6) ->
   if
    :: (t % 2) == 0 -> S_timeout15!1
    :: else
   fi;
   if
    :: (t % 3) == 0 -> S_timeout10!1
    :: else
   fi;
   if
    :: (t % 6) == 0 -> S_timeout5!1
    :: else
   fi;
   t = t + 1
 od;
}
```

Figure 10. Timeout Generation Process for 5, 10 and 15 Hz Rate Groups

group, initiation of the timeout event would then be guarded by testing that:

t % m/k == 0

m/k is guaranteed to be a whole number since the rates are harmonic. If the rates are not harmonic, then instead of the maximum rate, the counter is incremented up to the least common multiple (LCM) of the rate groups in the system and the rate specific guards use LCM rather than m in their modulo tests.

Depending on the exact rates used in a system we can reduce the granularity of abstract time and achieve a state space reduction by reducing the number of values that t will take on. To do this we scale the LCM and each of the rates down by their greatest common factor (GCF) and adjust the modulo tests appropriately. For example, if the rates in a system are 5, 10 and 15, then the LCM is 30, the GCF is 5, and we increment t from 1 up to 6. The generated timer process for such a system is shown in Figure 10.

Rather than use the event publication mechanisms described in the previous section, for timeout events we use rendezvous channels to couple the timer and the processes that model rate-specific event channel threads (see Figure 7). The rate-specific processes force all processing of published events handled by components in that rate group to complete before executing the rendezvous with the timer. Figure 11 illustrates the possible behaviors that can arise in the generated transition system as a result of Timer's behavior and the enforcement of rate monotonic scheduling. Processing in each rate group is forced to complete before the next timeout for that rate group. Processing in lower-priority rate groups can occur only after higher-priority processing has completed. No attempt is made in the transition system, however, to ensure that the amount of lower-priority processing that occurs is appropriate, either by restricting the amount that can occur (e.g., region A in Figure 11 performs an infeasibly large amount of work) or by forcing it to occur (e.g., the region between regions B and C in Figure 11 performs an infeasibly small amount of work).

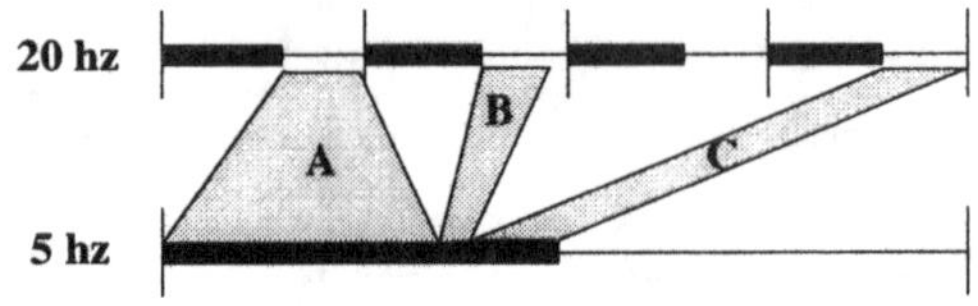

Figure 11. Interleaving of Rate Group Thread Execution

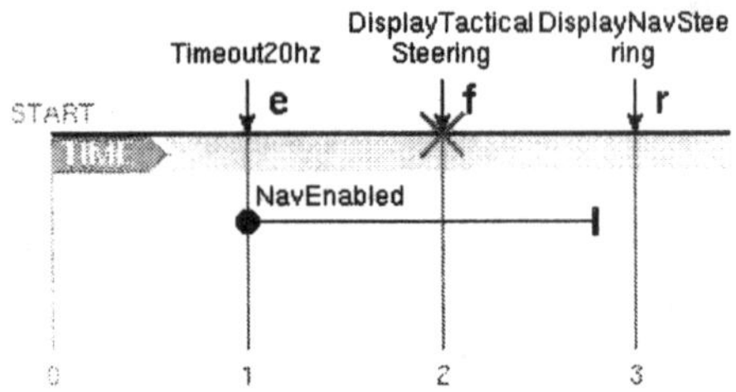

Figure 12. Timeline property

5.5 Property Specification

We divide the problem of stating correctness properties of Cadena designs into two parts: defining observations of the behavior of the system that one wishes to make and defining patterns of observations that constitute correct system behavior. Our approach is similar to the one taken in the Bandera Specification Language [5].

In Cadena designs user's may wish to reason about the call or return from a component method, the publication or consumption of an event, or the values of component modes. These basic observations can be qualified by component instance identity (e.g., a method call to a specific instance), parameter values (e.g., the return of a specific value from a method), component ports (e.g., the handling of an event on a specific component port), or rate groups (e.g., publishing an event from a specific rate group). The syntax for defining these *observables* mirrors the syntax of CCM and the Cadena extensions defined in this paper.

User's can instantiate an existing set of property specification patterns [10] with Cadena observables to form specifications of desired system behavior. In addition, Cadena generates observable definitions in a format that is compatible with the Timeedit tool [23]. Timeedit supports graphical specification of properties that are made up of complex chains of observations. Figure 12 illustrates a Timeedit specification for the constrained response property: "*when a 20 Hz timeout occurs and navigation steering mode is enabled, the display will be updated by the navigation component and not the tactical component*".

5.6 Experience

We have model checked properties of several Cadena designs. The most interesting of these is the modal scenario of Figure 1.

As a point of comparison, we generated a DSpin model for this scenario that did not enforce the rate-monotonic scheduling policy and performed an exhaustive state-space exploration for the number of timeouts issued in a single second of system execution. We ran DSpin using the maximal state compression settings available (which are the same as Spin's compression settings) and the check aborted after generating 26 million states using 1 Gigabyte of RAM. Clearly, some form of state space reduction was necessary. A state-space exploration on a model of the same design that encoded rate-monotonic scheduling for an arbitrary number of timeouts, ran in less than a minute and generated 1.4 million states using 130 Megabytes of RAM. Similar state space sizes were found for all of our checks on the modal scenario.

We attempted to check several assertions, invariants and the display mode related response property shown in the previous section. The property from Figure 12 failed on the model with non-deterministic scheduling due to the fact that execution of a 20 Hz component was preempted by a 1 Hz component. Thus, the steering component mode settings could change after the 20 Hz timeout and before the display update occurred. This is clearly infeasible in the actual system and performing the check on the rate-monotonic model described above bore that out by verifying the property.

The modal scenario is unrealistic in the number of components, but it is quite realistic in the number of rate groups. Recall that high priority component execution is effectively atomic in models that encode rate-monotonic scheduling. This suggests that the rate of growth of the state space with increasing numbers of high-priority components will be linear whereas increasing numbers of lower-priority will yield faster rates of growth. We are conducting experiments with a variety of Cadena designs of Bold Stroke applications and plan to report on the scalability of our approach.

6 Related Work

There has been a large body of work on on timing and schedulability analysis for component-based systems. As these techniques have matured, they have been integrated into environments that support the development of real-time systems. For example, MetaH [24] and Geodesic [6] are frameworks that support the reuse of components written in Ada and Java, respectively, in real-time systems. These frameworks include a range of timing analyses and automatically generate infrastructure code that coordinates the execution of component code in a way that achieves the system's timing requirements. Cadena is complementary to this work in that it targets logical properties of a system using both light-weight and heavy-weight analysis techniques.

Ptolemy [18] is a framework that allows a wide variety of formal descriptions of components and their behavior to be integrated into a single system. User's provide sufficient detail in these descriptions to allow implementations to be automatically generated. Ptolemy provides a run-time infrastructure to mediate between components that have different execution models. In contrast, Cadena models intentionally leave out detail in order to provide more abstract system descriptions that are amenable to analysis for large systems. While Cadena provides some code generation capabilities, we do attempt to generate component method implementations.

Dependence analysis has a long history of uses in program understanding, transformation, maintenance and testing (e.g., [15]). Our use of dependence analyses is essentially an adaptation of existing techniques to the level of abstraction present in CCM designs. Unlike most program dependence analyses which work from a fixed language definition, we have engineered the annotation languages in Cadena to provide a layering of detail that will allow for more precise dependences to be calculated and exploited for improved user feedback.

Model checking [3] has become extremely popular as a technology for analyzing behavioral models of software artifacts. Researchers have extracted such models from source code (e.g., [13, 4]), UML design artifacts (e.g., [19, 17]) and architectural descriptions (e.g., [1]). The difficulty with all applications of model checking is scaling it to apply to realistically large and complex systems. Recent years have seen an enormous amount of research on the systematic abstraction of models to enable more tractable reasoning. We take a different approach in Cadena by exploiting the *natural* abstractions that arise when developing high-level design models of systems.

Our model extraction techniques are based on our experiences with Bandera [4]. We have adapted those techniques to exploit knowledge of the execution environment of Bold Stroke applications. This can provide significant state space reduction, but, in support of broad applicability of Cadena to CCM-based systems it was important to engineer the model extraction framework to accommodate the semantics of different middleware infrastructures in the spirit of Garlan [11].

7 Conclusion

Component frameworks have proven to be effective in dealing with the challenges associated with building complex distributed systems. We believe that the high-level architectural descriptions used by CCM and other component oriented frameworks are an excellent vehicle for injecting light-weight formal methods and sophisticated automated analysis techniques across the entire software development process. In particular, we have built Cadena to explore how static analysis and model-checking can be integrated into CCM development by capitalizing on the use of CCM IDL to define what are, in effect, system abstractions that make such checking feasible for realistic systems.

We have applied Cadena to small and simple avionics systems based on the Boeing Bold Stroke architecture, and the initial results are encouraging. We believe that the strategies that we have developed for modeling middleware event services can scale reasonably well to larger systems. However, for systems with 1000s of components as one would find in product-line applications, we plan to investigate the use of compositional checking. In addition, there are many other forms of analysis needed for developing product-line avionics applications; Cadena current focuses on dependence analysis and behavioral analysis using model-checking techniques.

Concerning the tool itself, we believe building Cadena as a plug-in to IBM's Eclipse using the OpenCCM tools can provide a tool environment robust enough to experiment with designs of real systems. More information about the tool (with example artifacts and screen shots) can be found at `www.cis.ksu.edu/santos/cadena`.

References

[1] R. Allen and D. Garlan. A formal basis for architectural connection. *ACM Transactions on Software Engineering and Methodology*, July 1997.

[2] A. Cimatti, E. Clarke, F. Giunchiglia, and M. Roveri. NuSMV : a new symbolic model checker. *International Journal on Software Tools for Technology Transfer*, 2(4):410–425, 2000.

[3] E. Clarke, O. Grumberg, and D. Peled. *Model Checking*. MIT Press, 2000.

[4] J. C. Corbett, M. B. Dwyer, J. Hatcliff, S. Laubach, C. S. Păsăreanu, Robby, and H. Zheng. Bandera : Extracting finite-state models from Java source code. In *Proceedings of the 22nd International Conference on Software Engineering*, June 2000.

[5] J. C. Corbett, M. B. Dwyer, J. Hatcliff, and Robby. A language framework for expressing checkable properties of dynamic software. In *Proceedings of the SPIN Software Model Checking Workshop*, volume 1885 of *Lecture Notes in Computer Science*, Aug. 2000.

[6] D. de Niz and R. Rajkumar. Geodesic - a reusable component framework for embedded real-time systems. Technical report, Carnegie Mellon University, 2002.

[7] C. Demartini, R. Iosif, and R. Sisto. dspin : A dynamic extension of SPIN. In *Theoretical and Applied Aspects of SPIN Model Checking (LNCS 1680)*, Sept. 1999.

[8] X. Deng, M. B. Dwyer, J. Hatcliff, and M. Mizuno. Invariant-based specification, synthesis and verification of synchronization in concurrent programs. In *Proceedings of the 24th International Conference on Software Engineering*, May 2002.

[9] B. Doerr and D. Sharp. Freeing product line architectures from execution dependencies. In *Proceedings of the Software Technology Conference*, May 1999.

[10] M. Dwyer, G. Avrunin, and J. Corbett. Patterns in property specifications for finite-state verification. In *Proceedings of the 21st International Conference on Software Engineering*, May 1999.

[11] D. Garlan and S. Khersonsky. Model checking implicit-invocation systems. In *Proceedings of the 10th International Workshop on Software Specification and Design*, Nov. 2000.

[12] GOAL. The OpenCCM platform. `http://corbaweb.lifl.fr/OpenCCM/`, 2002.

[13] K. Havelund and T. Pressburger. Model checking Java programs using Java PathFinder. *International Journal on Software Tools for Technology Transfer*, 1999.

[14] G. J. Holzmann. The model checker SPIN. *IEEE Transactions on Software Engineering*, 23(5):279–294, May 1997.

[15] S. Horwitz and T. Reps. The use of program dependence graphs in software engineering. In *Proceedings of the 14th international conference on Software engineering*, pages 392–411. ACM Press, 1992.

[16] M. H. Klein, T. Ralya, B. Pollak, and R. Obenza. *A Practitioner's Handbook for Real-Time Analysis: Guide to Rate Monotonic Analysis for Real-Time Systems*. Kluwer Academic Publishers, 1993.

[17] D. Latella, I. Majzik, and M. Massink. Automatic verification of a behavioural subset of UML statechart diagrams using the SPIN model-checker. *Formal Aspects of Computing*, 11(6):637–664, 1999.

[18] E. A. Lee. Overview of the ptolemy project. Technical Report UCB/ERL M01/11, University of California, Berkeley, Mar. 2001.

[19] J. Lilius and I. P. Paltor. vUML: A tool for verifying UML models. In *Proceedings of the 14th IEEE International Conference on Automated Software Engineering*, 1999.

[20] D. Sharp. Reducing avionics software cost through component based product line development. In *Proceedings of the Software Technology Conference*, Apr. 1998.

[21] D. Sharp. Object oriented avionics software flow policies. In *Proceedings of the 18th AIAA/IEEE Digital Avionics Systems Conference*, Oct. 1999.

[22] H. Sipma. Event correlation: A formal approach. Technical Report Draft, Stanford University, July 2002.

[23] M. H. Smith, G. J. Holzmann, and K. Etessami. Events and constraints: a graphical editor for capturing logic properties of programs. In *Proceedings of the 5th International Symposium on Requirements Engineering*, Aug. 2001.

[24] S. Vestal. Metah user's manual. `http://www.htc.honeywell.com/metah`, 1998.

Technical Papers

Software Design

DADO: Enhancing Middleware to Support Crosscutting Features in Distributed, Heterogeneous Systems

Eric Wohlstadter, Stoney Jackson and Premkumar Devanbu
Center for Software Systems Research,
Department of Computer Science,
University of California, Davis, CA 95616
{wohlstad,jacksoni,devanbu}@cs.ucdavis.edu

Abstract

Some "non-" or "extra-functional" features, such as reliability, security, and tracing, defy modularization mechanisms in programming languages. This makes such features hard to design, implement, and maintain. Implementing such features within a single platform, using a single language, is hard enough. With distributed, heterogeneous ($\mathcal{DH}$) systems, these features induce complex implementations which cross-cut different languages, OSs, and hardware platforms, while still needing to share data and events. Worse still, the precise requirements for such features are often locality-dependent and discovered late (e.g., security policies). The DADO[1] approach helps program cross-cutting features by improving $\mathcal{DH}$ middleware. A DADO service *comprises pairs of* adaplets *which are explicitly modeled in IDL. Adaplets may be implemented in any language compatible with the target application, and attached to stubs and skeletons of application objects in a variety of ways. DADO supports flexible and type-checked interactions (using generated stubs and skeletons) between adaplets and between objects and adaplets. Adaplets can be attached at run-time to an application object. We describe the approach and illustrate its use for several cross-cutting features, including performance monitoring, caching, and security. We also discuss software engineering process, as well as run-time performance implications.*

1. Introduction

This paper is concerned with an approach to supporting the development of late-bound, crosscutting features in distributed heterogeneous systems.

Crosscutting features are those whose implementations stubbornly resist confinement within the bounds of modules. Features such as logging, transactions, security and fault-tolerance typically have implementations that straddle module boundaries even within the most sensible decompositions of systems. This issue has been discussed widely in the literature (See for example, [36, 17, 23, 9] among others; we present a sample security policy in the next section which provides an illustration). The scattered implementation of such features makes them difficult to develop, understand and maintain. To worsen matters, the requirements of such features are often *late bound*: locality dependent, discovered late, and change often—security policies again being a prime example. Programmers are thus confronted with the difficult challenge of making a scattered set of changes to a broad set of modules, often late in the game.

Distributed Heterogeneous systems (abbreviated $\mathcal{DH}$) are becoming part of the IT infra-structure in many organizations: many needed software functions are provided by systems assembled from pieces running on different platforms and programmed in different languages. Distribution arises from pressures such as globalization and mobility. Heterogeneity arises from considerations such as performance, legacy systems, weight, size, vendor specialization, and energy consumption. Crosscutting features in $\mathcal{DH}$ systems present special challenges. Feature implementations are scattered across different languages, operating systems and hardware platforms. Feature implementation elements in one platform need to correctly exchange information with existing application code, and with such elements on other platforms. Any cross-platform (remote) interactions between feature implementation elements may negatively impact application performance. In a WAN context, the presence of different, incompatible features (*e.g.* different security policies) may even cause the application to fail. In addition, the operator of a service may wish to change security policies at run-time. Some platforms may be too resource-limited or performance-constrained to support some types of software evolution techniques (*e.g.,* reflection). In some cases, source code may not be available for modification, so binary editing techniques (or middleware-based wrapping) might have to be used. However, since feature implementations may crosscut platforms, all these different techniques of software evolution should be allowed to co-exist, and inter-operate. Finally, since crosscutting feature implementations might be widely applicable, we would like to reuse them (in either source or binary form, as applicable) by changing the way they are "bound" to applica-

[1] DADO: Distributed Adaplets for Distributed Objects. We also note that a "dado" is a carpenter's tool for making cuts across the grain.

0-7695-1877-X/03 $17.00 © 2003 IEEE

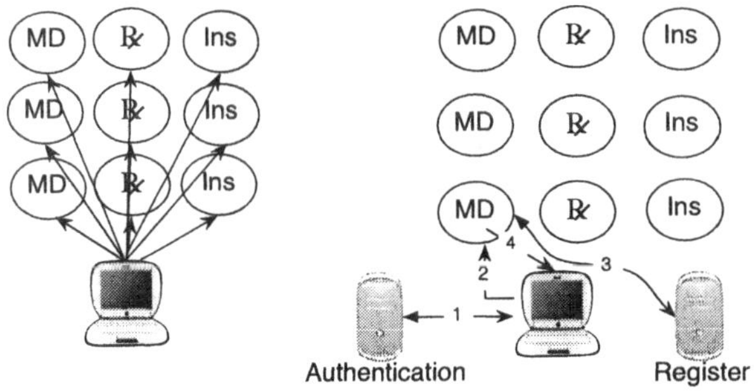

Figure 1. A distributed health-care system, with many service providers, without (*left*) and with (*right*) security. The right one enforces this security policy: the client must first get get an authentication token (1) from an authentication server, and then present this token and his request (2) to a service-provider, who then checks with the registration server (3) (to prevent multiple fraudulent requests) before servicing the request (4). Such a policy requires implementations that crosscut system and language boundaries.

tion implementations.

In this paper, we describe DADO, an approach to developing features in distributed systems that require code changes, in a heterogeneous setting, to both client- and server-side of a remote interaction. The paper begins with a motivating example in Section 2. We then survey the surrounding area in Section 3. Section 4 presents our research goals in more detail. Section 5 describes the current status of our experimental implementation of DADO (including the run-time, code-generation and deployment tools), which is based on the OMG CORBA standard. Section 6 presents some sample applications of DADO. Section 7 presents some micro-benchmarks evaluating the performance impact of DADO. In section 8 we describe closely related projects. Finally we conclude with an overall view of the work, the current limitations, and our future plans.

2. An Example

For expository reasons, we review the example used in an earlier position paper [44]. Consider a $\mathcal{DH}$ medical application (Fig. 1), with a set of clients making use of three groups of servers (shown as groups of circles with indicative labels): clinics, pharmacies, and insurers. The servers in a group could be running on different platforms (each doctor's office might use a different type of computer), but each provides the same service (e.g., through the same CORBA IDL interface). The components in this architecture communicate using $\mathcal{DH}$ middleware. In Fig. 1 (left), the original services are shown. The multiple arrows suggest drug fraud, with an unauthorized impostor client contacting multiple doctors and getting many prescriptions for the same drug, possibly getting each prescription dispensed many times, by different pharmacies, and then issuing multiple fraudulent insurance claims.

Consider injecting a *security* policy into this system, consisting of two critical elements. First, each client must be authenticated by an authentication server (*e.g.,* by a password scheme). Next each client must deal *with only one* server from each category. Thus, each client must use just one doctor (*except* for second opinions!!), one pharmacy, and one insurer within a given time interval. Fig 1 (right side) schematically indicates the new high-level architecture. A authentication server has been added to validate users, and a registration server to register client-service provider relationships.

This policy requires changes to *every component* and to *every interaction* between components. The client now has to authenticate itself to the authentication server, which provides an identity token. This token must now be added to all client-service requests. All members of each group of services must now coordinate among themselves to make sure that a client with a particular identity does not interact with more than one specific member of a group. Since malicious clients may try to induce race conditions among members of a group, they must synchronize to "commit" to serving a client.

The changes are clearly "crosscutting". Programs running on different platforms, and in different languages might need changing. Since some platforms may have performance or battery limitations, (e.g., PDAs or laptops), or be remotely located, different evolution strategies should be allowed, and allowed to inter-operate. Changes to different elements must be made consistently, to ensure correct interaction. Changes must be properly deployed in the different elements, otherwise versioning errors may result. Since the function on the server side for doctors, pharmacists and insurers is similar, it would be desirable to reuse the same policy implementation, *even if their IDL interfaces are different*, should the platforms be compatible.

Next, we survey current approaches to $\mathcal{DH}$ evolution, considering how they address programming challenges such as this one.

3. Current Approaches

There are a variety of approaches to dealing with crosscutting features. Our survey here is limited by space to be representative rather than exhaustive; no judgment of omitted or included work is implied. A more complete survey can be found in [43].

Several *language-based techniques* have been proposed. Classical syntactic program transforms [2] were perhaps among the earliest to provide the capability of broad changes to programs. Reflection [28] provided means of introducing crosscutting changes at run-time in languages such as Smalltalk. Compile-time [6, 37] reflection in C++ and Java has been developed and extended to load-time in Java using byte code editing [7]. Mixin-layers [33] also provide a way of adding features to methods in several different classes simultaneously. Implicit Context [41] is a method for separating extraneous embedded knowledge (EEK) (or crosscutting knowledge) from the design of a program, and re-weaving it back in later. Monads and monad transformers [19] have been used in lazy, pure functional languages to capture crosscutting features such as states and side-effects. They work by encapsulating the basic notion of a *computation*, and then allowing fundamental evaluation mechanisms such as value propagation to be overridden. Recently, approaches such as HyperJ [36], Aspectj [17], and Aspectual Components [20] provide differing approaches to implementing crosscutting features in Java. A detailed comparison (but see [15] for a comparison of compositional *vs.* aspectual views of program evolution mechanisms) of these differing approaches is beyond the scope of this paper; suffice to say we are interested in a $\mathcal{DH}$ setting, thus transcending language boundaries. While details vary, most of these languages provide two features: a *hook* or pattern, for describing where to insert crosscutting changes, and then a way to program the changes themselves. Since our approach uses the "hook" mechanism from AspectJ, we discuss it in more detail here.

AspectJ provides a pattern mechanism, called *pointcuts* for capturing groups of events, called *joinpoints* that may occur during a program's operation (such as method calls/receptions, constructor calls, field accesses, and exception events). The pattern-matching mechanism includes regular expression matching, with wild-carding over fragments of method names, function signatures, and types etc. Extra code, called *advice* can be associated with pointcuts, and is inserted by the AspectJ compiler into the join-points. Advice can inspect and modify data that are available at join-point events (*e.g.* method-call arguments and return values), and can create new data dynamically that is only shared with other advice. Our work uses these ideas for *modeling* crosscutting changes to distributed systems at the IDL level. However, the distribution, heterogeneity, and versioning problems that arise in our context, require new and different *implementations*.

Middleware-based approaches are certainly relevant. Some works exploit language-based reflection in the middleware [26] and other approaches use specially constructed reflective ORBs [18, 8, 16]. Communication reflection reifies the channels between client and server to address adaptation on a per-message level [5]. SOM [10] was an early approach to support reflection directly in the middleware. Interceptors [42, 24] and filters [32] provide a way of inserting extra functionality into *every* method that originates or arrives at a request broker; middleware-specific APIs provide means for interceptor code to reflect upon the details of the intercepted invocations. While these reflective methods are suitable for implementing crosscutting services [4], (and for some very idiosyncratic, and highly dynamic services may be the only way to do it) the use of the low-level reflection APIs, along with the need for frequent use of type-casting makes programming difficult and error-prone; thus it would be preferable to use more statically checkable methods when possible. Proxies and wrappers [14, 34] are another approach. However, they are typically tailored for a specific application object interface; so thus, it would not be possible to reuse a wrapper to implement the same security policy on such entirely different components as doctors and insurers.

Container models [29, 38] address this problem through code generation. They provide a fixed set of services (depending on the container vendor) to application components. Via configuration files and code-generation, services selected from a given set can be added to any component. However, some services cannot be completely located within the container. Consider that a client may not be willing to reveal his password to just any old application container, and so the initial step of authentication (password based or public-key signature based) might need to occur at a separate location that the client trusts. So the authentication exchange must be custom-programmed using an approach similar to interceptors. Programming here can be thus sometimes as hard as programming interceptor-based services.

Recently, Duclos, Estublier, and Marat [13] have proposed the model of a *Component Virtual Machine*, which captures important events in a component's lifecycle. These events can be viewed as *joinpoints*. An enhanced container implementation allows extra advice to bind to specific pointcut patterns over these joinpoints. This approach allows much easier implementation of custom services on the container side. We discuss this work in more detail later in § 8; we merely note here that our work focuses more on heterogeneous systems rather than container-based systems. Section 8 also surveys several other closely related works, that are easier to relate to ours after DADO details have been presented.

4. DADO Overview

As illustrated in Section 2, late-bound, crosscutting functions such as security require extra functional elements (which in DADO we call *adaplets*) to be located together with (potentially distributed) application software components. A client-server pair of adaplets would constitute a distributed DADO service. We begin with a discussion of the main goals of our project. Then we describe the features of DADO that address these challenges.

4.1 Desiderata

Heterogeneity and Communication Adaplets may need to exchange information and co-ordinate with each other, and/or with the application components. While this is strongly analogous to AspectJ, adaplets must communicate and co-ordinate in a *distributed heterogeneous* context. The adaptation mechanisms (source/binary transformation, runtime wrapping) may depend on the platform; even so, heterogeneous adaplets should co-exist and inter-operate correctly.

Binding and Deployment It would be desirable to support *late binding* and *flexible deployment* of DADO services. Consider that container standards such as J2EE allow independent container developers to develop services that are customized for specific applications at deployment time. Likewise, we would like to allow vendors to build services consisting of DADO services, independently of application builders, and then allow deployment experts to combine services and applications to suit their needs.

Dynamic Service Recognition Several adaplets, supporting different features, may be associated with an application component; clients and servers must deploy matching sets of adaplets. In a dynamic, widely distributed context, clients may become aware only at run-time of the adaplets associated with a server object. Thus adaplets may be need to be acquired and deployed at runtime.

Flexible Communication and Co-ordination The interaction between a matched pair of client and server adaplets may not be simple and monolithic. Under different circumstances, the client adaplet may require and request different functions (with different parameters) that are supported by a server adaplet (just as a distributed object can support several distinct methods). Likewise, the server adaplet may request different post-processing functions on the client side. A client adaplet can refer to it's server "mate" via the reserved name "`that`" (and vice versa). However, for efficiency, it would be better to have only a single invocation event through the middleware (e.g., a single CORBA synchronous call).

4.2 DADO Features

Modeling, Type-Checking, and Marshalling DADO employs an enhanced IDL and code-generation to support the following:

- Explicit IDL-level modeling of adaplets and their interaction with application components.
- Ability to implement adaplets in different languages, while supporting:
- safer interaction (via static type-checking) between adaplets, with automated generation of marshaling code.

Pointcut based Binding DADO separates services (which describe the interfaces supported by adaplets) from a deployment description, which specifies the precise deployment context of a service (using a pointcut language similar to AspectJ). This allows a deployment expert to tune the connection between DADO services and different application components. The binding language is agnostic with respect to the implementation; DADO adaplets could be incorporated into the existing application using static transformations (binary or source) or dynamic wrapping, depending on available tools, performance issues, etc.

Multiple Contextual Invocations DADO allows adaplets on the client and server side to communicate via messages. However, rather than inducing additional middleware invocations, multiple messages are piggy-backed within the single pre-existing application invocation.

Transparent Late binding DADO clients transparently (without additional programming) discover the services associated with a server, and deploy[2] additional adaplets as needed.

4.3 Process implications of DADO

Currently, the process of building $\mathcal{DH}$ systems using middleware such as CORBA includes modeling the high-level design using IDL. IDL specs are then implemented by developers, be they COTS vendors, or application builders, on different platforms and perhaps in different languages. When implementation is complete, the users of the distributed system can run ORBs on a network as suited to the application and organizational needs, and deploy the constituent application objects, along with any COTS software and ORB-provided services (naming, lifecycle, events etc.).

DADO brings three new roles into this process (see Figure 2): a *service architect*, *service programmer*, and a *service deployment specialist*. This service architect can design a $\mathcal{DH}$ service that implements a crosscutting feature, such as the ones illustrated in Section 6. This process begins with a description of a crosscutting DADO *service* as in an enhanced IDL (known as DAIDL, for DADO IDL). A service is a collection of DADO *adaplet interface* descriptions, which consist of several methods, just like a CORBA IDL interface. These interfaces are then compiled using DAIDL compilers for different target implementation languages (currently we support C++ and Java), producing marshaling routines and typing environments. The implementation then proceeds by service programmers just as with conventional middleware.

The deployment specialist binds an implemented service to a given application by specifying bindings using an AspectJ like pointcut language. The deployment specialist will need to understand both the application and the service, and select the bindings based on the specific installation. Currently, these bindings must be specified ahead of time and pre-compiled; one can then choose from different pre-compiled bindings (each of which bind a service to a set of application objects in a particular way) dynamically[3]. Duclos, Estublier and Marat's DS-CVM [13] also includes similar roles, but their implementation strategy is different, utilizing a sophisticated container architecture (we come back to this later, in § 8).

5. DADO implementation

We now present more details on the DADO features outlined in the above section. The current DADO experimental implementation is based on the OMG CORBA standard. It includes IDL language extensions for services, DADO IDL (DAIDL) compilers for C++ and Java, run-time software extensions for two different ORBs (JacORB and the TAO ORB), and tool support for the deployment of services (*i.e.,* for dynamically inserting DADO services into existing CORBA applications).

5.1 IDLs, Type-checking, and Marshalling

DADO adopts the philosophy (as does DS-CVM [13]) that IDL-level models provide an excellent software engineering methodology for distributed systems; in addition to promoting better conceptualization of the design, one can construct tools to generate useful "plumbing" code and typing environments for static type-checking. DADO IDL introduces the notion of a *service* that refers to a crosscutting feature. A service comprises client and/or server *adaplets*. Each *adaplet* supports sev-

[2]In Java, with a suitable `classloader`, adaplets could be even dynamically downloaded over the internet.

[3]This suggests another role, perhaps an *operator*, who selects services based on operating conditions.

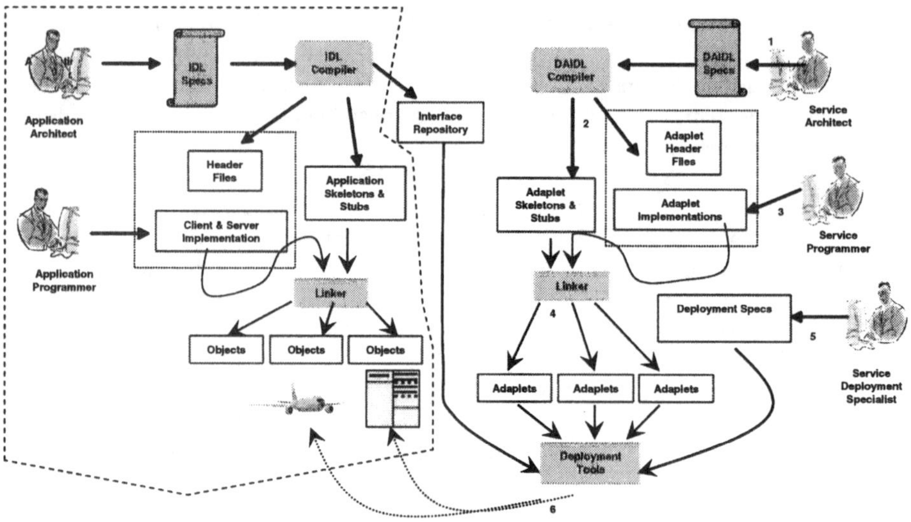

Figure 2. *DADO Development Process.* The left hand side (within the dotted lines) indicates the conventional CORBA process. On the right, the DADO service development begins (1) with modeling the interfaces to DADO adaplets using DAIDL; from this the DAIDL compiler generates (2) plumbing code, and typing contexts for adaplet implementations. The programmer writes (3) the adaplet implementations and links to get (4) the adaplets. Now, the deployment specialist produces (5) deployment specs, and these are used by deployment tools to install (6) the adaplets at the proper application object locations. Deployment can occur at compile time, link time, or run-time, depending on the instrumentation technology used (only run-time insertion is illustrated in the figure).

eral methods, which may be of 2 different kinds. *Advice* methods, identified in DAIDL by the **advice** keyword, may be bound, via pointcut patterns (like AspectJ advice, as explained later, in Section 5.3) to application objects. Advice methods basically provide additional functionality that is run *every time* certain methods defined in an IDL interface are invoked. Advice can be on the client or the server-side.

In addition to advice methods, DAIDL services can also include *request* methods (identified in DAIDL by the **request** keyword). These are a form of queued asynchronous methods (see section 5.4 on RMCI) that may be invoked by any adaplet methods. Advice and request are explained in more detail in Section 5.2.

DAIDL compilers can currently generate heterogeneous typing environments (*i.e.*, C++ header files, or Java imports), as well as stub and skeleton routines; adaplets can currently be implemented in either C++ or Java (but must be written in the same language as the application object[4]). We also note that advice adaplet methods have direct typed access to any argument in the application invocation; the actual bindings are specified in the pointcut. Programming within the context of typed stubs and skeletons, and leveraging generated marshaling and other "plumbing" code offers a distinct software engineering advantage over the current practice of "type-less" programming of late-bound services that use untyped string data in an invocation context object for data exchange.

5.2 Advice and Request

The separation of advice and request operations in the adaplet interfaces represents two levels of adaptation required to implement crosscutting distributed heterogeneous services. In this section we detail the relationship of advice and requests to the development and runtime execution of standard CORBA components and to each other.

We recall (from Section 4.3) that DADO introduces several new service-related roles into the software process: a *service architect*, *service programmer*, and a *service deployer*. When a service architect decides that some additional behavior on the client or server of a distributed application is desirable, she can add an advice operation to the interface of an adaplet. Advice operations can be specified to be client-side or server-side advice. The service deployer can then add the behavior specified by the advice interface to a specific application object by writing an appropriate pointcut. The service programmer has the obligation to implement each advice.

Some services can be implemented simply by executing advice on the client- or server-side, along with application method invocations. However, in some cases, additional information may be need to be sent along from the client to the server side adaplet (or vice versa). For example, in section 6.1 we present a service where a client side adaplet can request that a match-

[4]This is primarily for performance reasons; if adaplets are in a different language, it would be necessary to go through middleware to get from an application object to an adaplet. With a "polyglot" middleware like .NET's common language runtime, this problem can be finessed to some extent.

ing server adaplet calculate server processing time for specific invocations, and then communicate this information back to the client adaplet. This additional information conveyed between client and server adaplets is contextual. It must be associated with some original CORBA invocation. Likewise, the timing behavior by the server adaplet must occur before and after the processing of the invocation for which the client adaplet requested statistics. This type of adaptation is handled by the RMCI mechanism described below, in Section 5.4.

The service architect can include operations tagged with the `request` modifier keyword to provide an extra communication path between client and server adaplets that is associated with the current CORBA invocation. The body of client and server advice can be programmed to add request messages by using the "`that`" reference which exposes the interface of request operations available to a client adaplet by the server adaplet and vice versa. In object-oriented languages the service programmer will derive adaplet implementations from a generated abstract base class which includes an appropriately typed member variable named "`that`". "`that`" is automatically bound to a generated stub that implements RMCI semantics for each request operation.

Advice and request play different roles in adapting the dynamic execution of a distributed application. Advice operations are used to add behavior at points in the program determined by pointcut based deployment. Although the addition and removal of advice can occur dynamically at runtime it is still based on referring to static elements in the IDL interface. Pointcuts create a connection between client programs and client adaplets or server objects and server adaplets only. The connection between client adaplets and server adaplets is made through request messages and is completely dynamic. The request messages serve both to convey additional information and invoke behavior to process the information.

The exact mechanism by which the original client and server programs are modified can be platform-dependent; heterogeneity is allowed. Several options are possible, including source-code weaving, generating customized stub components, or modifying the middleware. The transmission format of request messages, however, is standardized because it must be understood by the DADO runtime on heterogeneous hosts. Our experimental implementation relies on packing request messages into the `ServiceContext` of a CORBA invocation. The `ServiceContext` is part of the CORBA protocol format for communicating invocation specific information between ORBs. Naturally, the generated request and advice typing environments are standardized, using the usual OMG IDL language mappings.

5.3 Binding and Deployment

Once built, a service can be integrated with applications by specifying a *binding*, which is done using a pointcut language. This process involves one platform-*independent* tool, which matches the pointcuts against a known set of component interfaces, and produces a digested match-table in XML format; and a separate platform-*dependent* means for actually ensuring that the adaplets get triggered when the pointcuts get activated.

The pointcut language extends the AspectJ pointcut language to specify client or server side pointcuts, extending the AspectJ regular expression syntax for the declaration of generic or cross-cutting behavior. Matching of pointcuts with invocations could be done off-line or on-line. The current DADO tool (the pointcuts pre-processor) matches pointcuts (against the IDLs of the application objects) at compile-time. This tool identifies all the IDL level events requiring adaplet intervention, and also the information in the events that should be made available to each adaplet. The output of the preprocessor is a representation of all the event/action matches as an AST (represented as XML). We call this Intermediate Joinpoint Representation (IJR). (*Note* Although this matching happens at compile-time, services with pointcuts that are already compiled into IJR can be added or removed at runtime). Of course, future tool (and associated runtime) support could allow new point cuts to be created and inserted at run-time.

In order to trigger adaplet behavior at runtime, application code must somehow be modified, or execution intercepted to capture the right events. A wide range of binary and source-code, static and dynamic instrumentation mechanisms have been reported [6, 37, 17, 30]. Middleware, also, can support highly dynamic reflective mechanisms [3]; Duclos, Estublier and Morat [13] have build a "component virtual machine" that allows great flexibility in instrumentation.

In keeping with the $\mathcal{DH}$ philosophy, *we allow heterogeneity in the implementation of the triggering mechanism.* Thus while the pointcut specifies the "high-level design" of the binding, different implementation strategies are possible. Currently, several instrumentation mechanisms are supported for translating DADO pointcuts (in IJR form) into actual trigger mechanisms. For Java, we use AspectJ [17] to insert the necessary trigger code into generated stubs and skeletons (thus avoiding the need for application implementation source code. For C++, we make use of a range of mechanisms, including TAO's smart proxies [42], and the Portable Interceptor standard in CORBA; this approach is also compatible with binary-only application components, and can work in any language, even one that does not support source-code or binary instrumentation mechanisms. However, both approaches require that adaplets be written in the same language as the application objects. Removing this restriction is certainly possible, but would require adaplets to engage a large segment of the middleware stack for cross-language interoperability with application components. Naturally, client- and server-side adaplets, *even if using different languages, different instrumentation mechanisms*, are *fully inter-operable, and portable*. The adaplet programmer remains agnostic with respect to the actual instrumentation mechanism that is used to trigger the adaplet. An adaplet can communicate with other adaplets (the matched one, or any others that it has a handle to) using the DAIDL interface description. In our implementation, this is accomplished through appropriate code generation; the generated code pumps data around by packaging it into the untyped *service context* object (See [25], Chapter 21) API in CORBA.

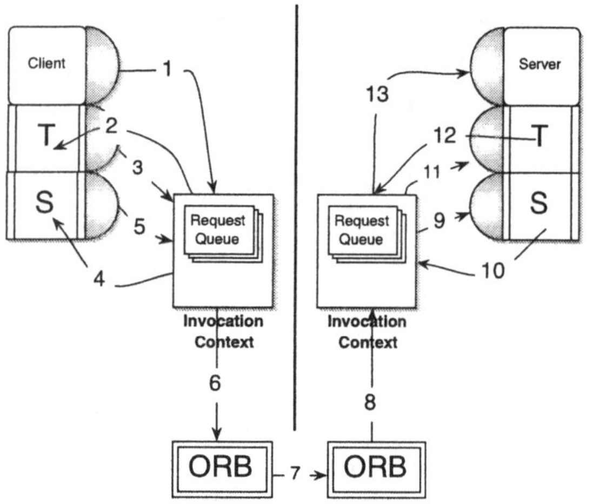

Figure 3. *Remote Multiple Contextual Invocation* Client-server application object interactions are mediated by "T" (transaction) and "S" security adaplets. Gray semi-circles denote generated marshaling code. Initial client invocation (1) is diverted by the interceptor in turn to each adaplet (2,4) until finally arriving (6) at the ORB. Adaplets use marshaling code for their invocations (3,5). Each adaplet may enqueue several one-way messages (for the server-side adaplets) which are piggy-backed as a request queue through the normal middleware invocation (7) over the WAN to the server side. The process occurs in reverse on the server side, with the requests in the queue being delivered to the corresponding adaplets. Likewise, server-side adaplets may enqueue messages to the client side adaplets which are piggy-backed on the invocation response.

5.4 Remote Multiple Contextual Invocation

Remote multiple contextual invocation (RMCI) in DADO gives service developers more ways of programming interactions between client-side and server-side adaplets. Consider that a client adaplet may require different types of actions to be taken at the server side. As a very simple example, a per-use payment service adaplet attached to a server object might accept e-cash payments, or a credit card. Another example is authentication. It could be based on kerberos-style tokens, or on a simple password. We could include both options as possible parameters, in a single method signature, along with an extra flag to indicate the active choice; this leads to poorly modularized methods with many arguments. Rather, we take the "distributed object" philosophy of supporting different requests at a single server object; we allow adaplets on either side to support several different requests. As another illustration of the use of requests, consider a generic caching service, (implemented using DADO adaplets) which can for example be attached to a stock quotation server (this example is discussed in more detail in Section 6). Client-side advice can cache values and return them instead of going to the server for each request. However, the server may want to communicate a "time-out" interval back to the client, so that it can adjust the time-out period for cached quotes based on market volatility. So it would be useful to have a special client-side request method that the server can invoke when it needs to adjust the time-out value.

DADO adaplets support a special type of one-way, asynchronous "piggy-backed" message that are sent along with an invocation (from client to server) or a response (vice versa). Since multiple services can be present simultaneously, the requests are queued on each client and packaged with the original invocation for dispatch at a server side adaplet. This also works in reverse for requests going from the server-side adaplet to the client-side adaplet. The keyword "`request`" in the DAIDL adaplet interface can be used to designate operations as having RMCI semantics.

In figure 3 we show application objects using both a security and a transaction service. Note the presence of corresponding adaplets for each service on both the client and server side. Adaplets might include both advice and request methods; the figure illustrates how the client side advice gets executed in turn. Each client adaplet may enqueue multiple requests to be executed by the server side adaplets. The requests are collected into a queue that gets piggy-backed onto the regular middleware invocation and passed through to the server side. The RMCI designation thus arises from **M**ultiple **R**emote requests contained within the *single* **I***nvocation* **C***ontext*. The implementations of these requests (regardless of adaplet's location) have full reflective access to the current active invocation, via provided APIs. Of course, if the information needed by the adaplet is known statically, there is no need to use reflection.

On the server side, the designated advice adaplet methods for each adaplet get executed, as are the enqueued requests. The server side adaplets may also enqueue requests to be executed by the client side. This feature can be used to pass information back to client-side adaplets; we illustrate with a performance monitoring example where server-side time-stamps are passed back to the client via a request adaplet method.

In essence, RMCI provides a form of dynamic per-invocation adaptation as in Lasange[39] while supporting type-checked interactions and modular design through IDL declaration.

5.5 Transparent Late Service Binding

In a WAN environment such as the internet, where servers are discovered at run-time, clients cannot predict the set of services provided by (or required by) a particular server until it is located. Static approaches that install new services based only on type information cannot easily provide this kind of late binding.

When server objects are associated with a DADO service (this can happen dynamically, from the command-line or at deployment time via configuration files) they are assigned an external object reference that is used by the client side run-time to detect the applicable services. Essentially, the references encode information about the adaplets associated with this object[5]. This information is used by the Dado interception logic on the client-side to transparently engage the corresponding client-side adaplets. Our implementations use different triggering mechanisms,

[5]Using CORBA this is possible with Tagged IOR Components.

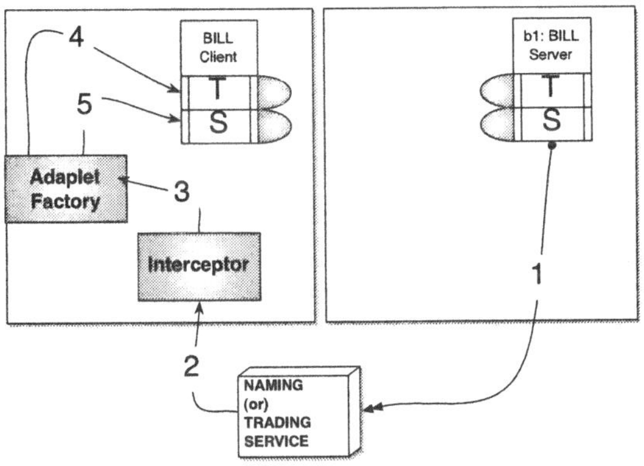

Figure 4. *Late-binding service adaptations* (1) Server object, with Security and Transaction adaplets, named "b1" of type "Bill" is registered with a Naming service. The identifiers "Transaction" and "Security" are tagged to the external object reference. When client looks up object named "b1", the returned object reference (2) is intercepted by Dado component. Dado attempts (3) to find client-side adaplets for "Transaction" and "Authentication" from client-side factory. Factory creates and binds transactions (T) and security (S) adaplets to client application object.

depending on the platform, to achieve this.This process is illustrated in figure 4. When an application object registers itself with a naming service, the reference encodes all active services (Arrow 1). Subsequently, a retrieved reference (2) is intercepted by the DADO runtime, which decodes the applicable service identifiers from the reference. It then instructs the local factory to create instances of the corresponding client-side adaplets, and injects them into the execution path of invocations originating from the client. Our current implementation assumes that the possible set of pointcuts used by servers are known statically. Different sets can be uniquely identified in the server reference. In the future we plan to address dynamic client-side detection of pointcut configurations.

If the service deployment at a server object changes dynamically, it re-registers with the naming service to alert future clients. If service deployment changes at a server while current clients are still active, the server can throw a DADO-specific exception upon their next invocation. This exception encapsulates information about the new server configuration. The client-side DADO runtime then responds by transparently reconstructing the set of client-side adaplets so that interactions may continue.

5.6 Adaplet Instance Considerations

A service developer may need to control the granularity of how server objects and clients are affected by adaplets. This may be necessary to conserve resources, by not creating too many adaplet instances, or for associating state in adaplets with particular application object instances. Currently, we provide a mechanism for associating adaplets on a one-per-ORB basis (*i.e.*, a singleton) or on a one-per-POA[6] basis. We plan to add support for per-object adaplets in the future; currently, per-object adaplet instantiation is only possible by placing objects in separate POA's.

6. Examples

We now present some sample applications of DADO. All of these examples have been implemented with a Java client on JacORB and a server on TAO. For space reasons only the DAIDL interface descriptions are presented.

6.1 Round-Trip Performance

Consider a simple performance monitor in a particular client software. One can easily write code (*e.g.*, using interceptors, see [24], or [25], Chap. 21) to attach to the client that will record the time each invocation leaves and response arrives. But the client may also want the invocation arrival-time at the server and the reply sending-time in order to compute the actual processing time. This scenario demands more cohesion between interacting client and server interceptors. This service requires three critical elements: clients must be able to ask the server for timing statistics for *some*, not all, invocations. Servers must return data through a type-checked interface. Clients need some way to modify existing software to add logic for requesting timing statistics; different means should be allowable. Finally, client- and server- adaptations should be coordinated; clients will not request timing statistics from servers unable to provide them.

```
adaplet Timing {
  client {
    advice void timedOperation();
    request timeResult(in long long received,
                       in long long sent);
  };

  server {
    request timeRequest();
};
```

```
crosscut TimeAll : Timing {
  client {
    before call(*) :
           void timedOperation();
  };
};
```

DADO service developers first write the DAIDL interfaces (above the line) of the client and server adaplets, and implement them for target languages (utilizing DAIDL tools and run-time libraries). The client adaplet has two methods. One, `timedOperation` is an advice method that can be bound to an application method. The other, `timeResult` is a request method that is used by the server-side adaplet to report back the timing results.

[6]The Portable Object Adapter is a container abstraction available in CORBA for associating policies (such as thread policies) with a number of server objects.

This `timeResult` request message can be included with the original response by the server and will be dispatched to the client side adaplet before the client application receives the response. The implementation of `timedOperation` on the client side can dynamically decide whether to invoke `that.timeRequest` or not; we note again that the special variable `that`, denoting the (other) matched adaplet is implicitly made available to both client/server adaplets.

When `that.timeRequest` is invoked by the client side advice a request message is added to the original invocation and dispatched to the server side adaplet before the server object receives the original invocation. The server adaplet can respond to a `timeRequest` by taking two timing measurements to determine the actual execution time for that application method invocation; it can then report the result back to the client, using the `that.timeResult` client-side request. We note that *the implementation of the advice is responsible for invoking the request*; there is thus no explicit modeling of this detail at the IDL level. For instance, consider a client that would like to time one out of every ten invocations. This logic could be programmed into the `timedOperation` advice by an adaplet programmer. It would be inappropriate to introduce this type of implementation detail at the IDL level. Thus the service programmer decides when request messages are triggered; however, the IDL model does allow request messages to be marshaled and triggered in a heterogeneous, yet type-checked manner.

To deploy `Timing` adaplets for a given application object, the server-side would make the service available by registering a server `Timing` adaplet component with the servers' object adapter. When clients become aware of those server objects, the DADO run-time will automatically deploy client adaplets based on the clients deployment preferences (see the `crosscut` declaration above). In this deployment the client would like all invocations to be intercepted by `timedOperation` as indicated by the wildcard. The server side doesn't need to specify any additional pointcut instructions, as the operation `timeRequest` is invoked by the client-side adaplet.

6.2 Client-Side Cache

Systems are often built without performance optimizations such as caching in mind. However, it would be nice to leverage some off-the-shelf caching behavior, without requiring extensive modifications to client and server code. We consider a feature whereby clients can cache data associated with a particular server. Consider a stock-quote server, which provides accessor and mutator methods. The accessor methods are called by clients, and mutators would be called by a data provider to "pump" data into the quote server. We would like to cache the returned quote value at the client side. When the server returns data it associates a time-to-live (TTL) value with the data, for use by the client. An invocation will be serviced using cached data from the client (without contacting the server) as long as the TTL has not expired. The server will adjust its TTL value heuristically depending on the frequency of calls (from its data provider) to its mutator method.

```
adaplet Cache {
   server {
      request requestTTL();
      advice void trackWrite(in string key);
   };
   client {
      advice any_type readcache(in string key);
      request putTTL(in long ttl);
   };};
```

The DAIDL interface for the Cache adaplet specifies two operations, `trackWrite` and `requestTTL`. The client-side cache adaplet issues `requestTTL` along with accessor operations for which it has no cached data. The server adaplet sends back the TTL value associated with the invocation, back along with the data response; it does this by issuing a `putTTL` request to the client. The server adaplet estimates the TTL values heuristically by timing the mutator operations that it receives from its stock quote providers. The `trackWrite` is the advice that is triggered to calculate TTL based on mutate operation frequency. The client-side advice `readcache` performs the caching operation. The keyword `any_type` gives `readcache` access to the return value, as a generic CORBA `any`, of the operations on which it is deployed. This design requires that the operation to be cached, the accessor operation, uses a string "unique key" argument to determine the returned data. This fits our scenario where clients access stock quote prices based on stock market symbols but may require a different interface for other applications. Consider a simple `StockQuotes` server with operations `setQ` and `getQ`. We could apply the adaplet advice hooks to introduce caching using the following deployment file ,

```
crosscut StockCache : Cache {

  client {
    around call(float StockQuotes::getQ(key)) :
          any_type readcache(in string key);
  };
  server {
    before call(void StockQuotes::setQ(key,in float)) :
          void trackWrites(in string key);
  };

};
```

The *key* arguments serve to match parameters in the application operations with parameters for use by the advice.

6.3 Security Policy

Now consider our security policy example (Section 2). Here, servers must restrict access to some operations, based both on clients' identity, and their previous history of use. Clients must be registered with a particular server for some duration. After this time has expired, clients can register with another server. This prevents clients from contacting and obtaining the same services fraudulently from multiple servers. Clients authenticate themselves using a cryptographic token. It is the clients responsibility to obtain an `Authentic::Token` which is a cryptographic object representing the verification of the clients identity. The implementation of the `contactAuthentic` advice in the client adaplet is responsible for this; this advice can be bound to application methods that must be mediated by this security policy.

Since the authentication token is specific to this service, we must include server-side request operations in the adaplet to transmit this information to the server side. The server adaplet has two request operations available for receiving the authentication information. The first time a client contacts a server, she must register (commit) to that server for a specified time interval. The request operation `register` is for use by first time clients and includes a parameter for the duration of registration. The implementation of this registration will validate the authentication token and check with a centralized registration server (not shown here) to make sure that the client isn't fraudulently registered with a different service provider.

For subsequent application object invocations within the registered duration, the client uses the second request operation `authenticInfo`, to transmit the authentication token. Now, every server operation that needs to be mediated by this security policy must trigger the policy enforcement mechanism, to check that the client is authentic, registered and still within the registration interval. The server operations that need to be restricted should be mapped to the `Wall` server adaplet operation `check` with a deployment description(not shown). An implementation of this advice can implement the policy.

```
adaplet Wall {
  server {
    request authenticInfo(in Authentic::Token tok);
    request register(in Authentic::Token tok,
                     in long duration);
    advice void check()
                     raises(NotRegistered,NoAccess);
  };
  client {
    advice contactAuthentic();
  };
};
```

The `check` implementation (in some host programming language) will contact a registration server (IDL not shown) to ensure that a client can be served. If not, (if authentication token, or registration is invalid) the operation should raise the `NoAccess` exception[7]. However, if this client is not registered with any of the servers in the group, or if the required registration interval with the current server has passed, `check` can throw a `Not Registered` exception. This gives the implementation of `contactAuthentic` a chance to catch this exception and retry the operation by sending along a request for a new registration interval (which will succeed as long as the client hasn't fraudulently registered elsewhere). Catching exceptions and retrying operations is made possible by structuring advice *around* original invocations in a fashion similar to the Decorator pattern.

The server side advice, `check` , and the client-side advice , `contactAuthentic`, can be bound to any operation that must be policy-mediated. Implementations can choose to cache security information as appropriate. However, we note that once the server has implemented and deployed the `check` advice correctly it does not have to trust the client-side advice at all; also, if the authentication service uses public-key authentication, the client-side advice does not have to leak any authentication secrets (e.g., private key) outside the client's machine.

All examples above have been implemented with the client in Java, and the server in C++. Further details of our current implementation are described in the following section. Full source code is available on `http://rickshaw.cs.ucdavis.edu`.

[7]These are implemented as a run-time `CORBA::SystemExceptions` because they occur inside of the original target operation.

7. Performance Study

The data presented is in the style of micro-benchmarks: we measure the incremental effect of the actual additional marshaling work induced by the new "plumbing" code (generated by DADO compilers), as well as other DADO runtime machinery for dispatching adaplet advice and request. For this reason, we use dummy advice and request methods that don't do any computation, so that we can focus primarily on the actual overhead of the DADO runtime machinery.

The measurements were taken for a single client server pair. The client machine was a 1.80 GHz Intel Pentium with 1GB main memory running Linux 7.1. The client middleware was JacORB 1.4 on JDK 1.4. The server machine was an 800 Mhz Intel Pentium Laptop with 512MB main memory running Microsoft Windows 2000. Server software used TAO 1.2 compiled in C++ Visual Studio. Client-side advice is invoked using modified stubs; a portable interceptor dispatches requests on the server side. The DAIDL interface to the adaplet used for performance measurement is shown below. The actual IDL interface that is bound to is not important, since we are actually just measuring the additional overhead of the adaplet run-time infrastructure; in this case, we use a simple interface with a single, synchronous method that takes a string and doesn't return anything (not shown here).

```
adaplet Test{
  client {
    advice void grabArg(in string arg);
  };

  server {
    request putArg(in string arg);
};
```

```
crosscut TestStringArg : Test {
  client {
    before call(* *(arg)) :
           void grabArg(in string arg);
  };
};
```

As can be seen above, there is one client-side advice and one server side request. The client-side advice is bound to every method call (with a single argument of type `string`) on every object by the pointcut. In our implementation, the client-side advice simply captures the string argument from the invocation and calls the server side request, passing along the string argument. The server side advice receives the string argument, and simply just passes control to the server application object. So the overhead we are measuring (beyond the normal CORBA invocation overhead) includes the additional cost of 1) intercepting the invocation on the client-side, 2) dispatching the client-side advice, 3) executing the client-side request stub, 4) marshaling the additional data transmitted by the request into the `Service-Context`, 5) transmitting the additional data over the wire 6) unmarshaling the data on the server side 7) dispatching and executing the request implementation on the server side. All measurements given above are for round-trip delays for a simple invocation that sends a "hello world" string. The data is averaged over 1000 invocations, and is given in milliseconds.

Experiment	100 Base-T	Wireless
1. Vanilla CORBA	0.65	3.49
2. with 1 advice, 1 request	1	4.17
3. with 10 advice, No request	0.68	3.65
4. with 10 advice, 10 request	1.52	7.45
5. Vanilla CORBA with equivalent raw data Payload for 10 requests	1.38	7.27

The first row is the plain unloaded CORBA call, as a baseline for comparison. The second row is a CORBA call with one adaplet advice, and one additional request. In the third row, we show the effect of "artificially" forcing a dummy advice (that doesn't transmit any requests) to dispatch 10 times. The fourth row shows the effect of executing the advice shown on the second row 10 times, thus forcing 10 request messages. The critical *fifth* row shows an interesting comparison: it measures the plain CORBA call, with additional data loaded into the service context, *exactly equivalent to 10 request messages*, without any adaplet code whatsoever. This row corresponds to the precise straw-man comparison for sending data *sans* DADO, and corresponds to the way interceptor-based services (such as Transactions and Real-Time, as per [25], page 30 of Chap. 13) are currently programmed.

As can be seen, the advice itself, which does not send any data, does not induce very large overheads (comparing rows 1 and 3, it's about 5% in both cases for 10 advice invocations) The overhead for sending requests is largely due to the base cost of transmitting data over the service context. By comparing the 100-Base-T and Wireless measurements one can see the diminishing cost of marshaling as the benefits of reduced latency from piggybacked requests increases. The motivation of RMCI is to provide type-checkable interactions and modularization of service features, we feel these measurements show the feasibility of this approach.

8. Closely Related Work

In this section, we discuss closely related work and compare them in greater detail with DADO.

Dassault Systèmes CVM The Dassault Systèmes Component Virtual Machine (DS CVM) [13] is targeted at container-based systems, and allows the implementation of custom container services. The DSCVM comprises an efficient, flexible CVM that essentially supports a meta-object protocol which can be used for instrumentation of middleware-mediated events. This allows the CVM to support the triggering of advice when the CVM executes specific events such component method invocations. Pointcut "trigger" specifications are implemented using the DSCVM events. Advice can be bound to patterns of these events, and thus be used to implement services.

DADO is complementary to DS CVM in that DADO allows elements of crosscutting services to be placed on the client site in a coordinated manner, for reasons argued earlier. DADO also operates outside of a component/container model in "bare-bones" CORBA; thus it must (and does) allow heterogeneity in the implementation of triggering mechanisms such as source transformations, binary editing etc. (See Section 5.3). The heterogeneity assumption also influences our design of type-checked information exchange between client and server adaplets, using generated stubs and skeletons (Section 5.1).

QuO The Quality of Objects (QuO) [21, 40] project aims to provide consistent availability and performance guarantees for distributed objects in the face of limited or unreliable computation and network resources. QuO introduces the notion of a "system condition", which is a user-definable measure of the system, such as load, network delay etc. System conditions can transition between "operating region"s which are monitored by the run-time environments. The novelty in QuO is that adaptations can be conditionally run to respond not only to normal middleware events, but also to region transitions.

QuO's version of adaplets are confined to a single system. Unlike DADO, Quo provides no special support for communicating information from a client-side adaplet to a server-side adaplet.

Lasagne Lasagne[39] is a framework for dynamic and selective combination of extensions in component based applications. Each component can be wrapped with a set of decorators to refine the interaction behavior with other components. Every decorator layer is tagged with an extension identifier. Clients can dynamically request servers to use different sets of decorators at run-time. An innovative aspect of Lasagne is the usage of extension identifiers to consistently turn on and off adaptive behavior. However, the use of the decorator-style constrains all extensions to have the same interface. Any additional extension-specific information must be communicated using a "context" object, without the benefits of typechecking or automated marshaling.

Software Architecture In software architecture, connectors [22, 27, 1] have proven to be a powerful and useful modeling device. Connectors reify the concern of interaction between components, and are a natural foci for some crosscutting concerns. Implementations of architectural connectors have also been proposed [12, 31, 11, 35]. Some of these provide specific services [31, 11, 35] over $\mathcal{DH}$ middleware, such as security. Our work can be viewed as providing a convenient implementation vehicle for different connector-like services in a heterogeneous environment. The DAIDL language and compiler allow service builders to write client and server adaplets that provide many kinds of "connector-style" functionality, while the DAIDL "plumbing" handles the communication details. Furthermore, the pointcut language allows a flexible way of binding this functionality to components, using pattern matching to bind events to adaplets. The question as to whether connector specifications (*e.g.*, in an ADL) can be translated to DAIDL specifications and pointcuts is interesting, and we hope to address it in future research.

9. Conclusion

We conclude here with several observations about DADO, it's limitations, and our plans for future work.

"Client-Server". First, we note that when we repeatedly discuss *"client"* and *"server"* adaplets, we are speaking of *client-server roles in a synchronous RPC-style connector!* Thus DADO is not specific to a client-server architectural style. In fact DADO adaplets may be bound to CORBA `oneway` calls, which are essentially asynchronous messages.

Design Choices. The design space of a convenient framework to implement $\mathcal{DH}$ crosscutting services is quite large, comprising many dimensions such as synchronization mechanisms, scope of data, and the handling of exceptions. The current implementation of DAIDL has made some reasonable choices, but other choices will need to be explored as other application demands are confronted. Some examples: "service-scoped" state, i.e., state that is implicitly shared between adaplets; services whose scope transcends a matched stub-skeleton adaplets; other (*e.g.*, synchronous) interactions between adaplets. We would like to implement an adaplet-per-object instance policy as well. Currently , only run-time exceptions are supported for adaplets—in the Java mapping, better static checking would be desirable.

Implementation Limitations. Currently our implementation has some limits. As outlined earlier, the marshaling needs further optimization. The Portable Interceptor approach to trigger advice prevents the modification of invocation arguments or return values; thus non-orthogonal [17] services that do affect these values must be programmed with source or binary transforms. We need to broaden our base to more languages. .NET is currently not supported, but it could be interesting. CLR [38] would allow us to write adaplets for CLR applications in any CLR compliant language.

Service interactions. Feature interactions are a difficult open research issue that DADO services must deal with eventually. We note here that it is currently possible to program interactions between two DADO services: one can write a third service that pointcuts adaplets in each, and responds to the triggering of both by preventing one from running, changing argument values, return values etc. However, we do still not have enough experience with this approach, and it remains future work.

In conclusion, DADO is an approach to programming crosscutting concerns in distributed heterogeneous systems based on placing "adaplets" at the points where the application interacts with the middleware. It supports heterogeneous implementation and triggering of adaplets, allows client- and server- adaplets to communicate in a type-checked environment using automated marshaling, provides flexibility in communication between adaplets, allows flexible binding, and late deployment of adaplets on to application objects. While much work remains to be done, we believe that the current version of DADO provides many features of interest to the software engineering community. Source code for Java using JacORB and C++ using TAO with MSVC++ is available on-line at http://rickshaw.cs.ucdavis.edu.

10. Acknowledgments

Eric Wohlstadter's and Stoney Jackson's work was supported in part by a United States Department of Education Government Assistance in Areas of National Need (DOE-GAANN) grant #P200A980307 and also from the NSF 0204348. Premkumar Devanbu gratefully acknowledge support from the NSF ITR Program, Grant No. 0085961. This material is also based in part upon work sponsored by SPAWAR and the Defense Advanced Research Projects Agency under Contract Number N66001-00-8945. The content of the information does not necessarily reflect the position or the policy of the Government and no official endorsement should be inferred. We would also like to thanks the anonymous reviewers for their detailed comments on our draft.

References

[1] R. Allen and D. Garlan. A formal basis for architectural connection. *ACM Transactions on Software Engineering and Methodology*, 6(3), 1997.

[2] B. Balzer. Transformational implementation: An example. *IEEE Transactions on Software Engineering*, 7(1), 1981.

[3] G. Blair and R. Campbell, editors. *Reflective Middleware*, 2000.

[4] L. Capra, W. Emmerich, and C. Mascolo. Reflective middleware solutions for context-aware applications. In *International Conference on Metalevel Architectures and Separation of Crosscutting Concerns (Reflection)*, 2001.

[5] W. Cazzola and M. Ancona. mChaRM: a reflective middleware for communication-based reflection. technical report disi-tr-00-09, disi, universit degli studi di genova, 2000.

[6] S. Chiba. A metaobject protocol for C++. In *Object Oriented Programming, Systems, Languages, and Applications (OOPSLA)*, 1995.

[7] S. Chiba. Load-time structural reflection in Java. In *European Conference on Object Oriented Programming*, 2000.

[8] M. Clarke, G. Blair, G. Coulson, and N. Parlavantzas. An efficient component model for the construction of adaptive middleware. In *Proceedings of the IFIP/ACM International Conference on Distributed Systems Platforms and Open Distributed Processing (Middleware)*, 2001.

[9] Y. Coady, A. Brodsky, D. Brodsky, J. Pomkoski, S. Gudmundson, J. S. Ong, and G. Kiczales. Can AOP support extensibility in client-server architectures? In *Proceedings, ECOOP Aspect-Oriented Programming Workshop*, 2001.

[10] N. Coskun and R. Sessions. Class objects in SOM. *IBM Personal Systems Developer*, Summer 1992.

[11] E. M. Dashofy, N. Medvidovic, and R. N. Taylor. Using off-the-shelf middleware to implement connectors in distributed architectures. In *International Conference on Software Engineering*, 1999.

[12] S. Ducasse and T. Richner. Executable connectors: towards reusable design elements. In *Foundation of Software Engineering*, 1997.

[13] F. Duclos, J. Estublier, and P. Morat. Describing and using non functional aspects in component based applications. In *International Conference on Aspect-Oriented Software Development*, 2002.

[14] T. Fraser, L. Badger, and M. Feldman. Hardening COTS software with generic software wrappers. In *IEEE Symposium on Security and Privacy*, 1999.

[15] W. Harrison, H. Ossher, and P. Tarr. Symmetrically and assymmetrically organized paradigms of program transformation. Unpublished manuscript, 2002.

[16] F. Hauck, U. Becker, M. Geier, E. Meier, U. Rastofer, and M. Steckermeier. Aspectix: a quality-aware, object-based middleware architecture. In *Proc. of the 3rd IFIP Int. Conf. on Distrib. Appl. and Interoperable Sys.*, 2001.

[17] G. Kiczales, E. Hilsdale, J. Hugunin, M. Kersten, J. Palm, and W. G. Griswold. An overview of AspectJ. In *European Conference on Object Oriented Programming*, 2001.

[18] F. Kon, M. Román, P. Liu, J. Mao, T. Yamane, L. C. Magalhães, and R. H. Campbell. Monitoring, Security, and Dynamic Configuration with the dynamicTAO Reflective ORB. In *IFIP/ACM International Conference on Distributed Systems Platforms and Open Distributed Processing (Middleware)*, 2000.

[19] S. Liang, P. Hudak, and M. Jones. Monad transformers and modular interpreters. In *Symposium on Principles of Programming Languages*, 1995.

[20] K. Lieberherr, D. Lorenz, and M. Mezini. Programming with aspectual components. Technical Report NU-CCS-99-01, College of Computer Science, Northeastern University, Boston, MA, March 1999.

[21] J. Loyall, D. Bakken, R. Schantz, J. Zinky, D. Karr, R. Vanegas, and K. Anderson. QuO Aspect languages and their runtime integration. In *Proceedings of the Fourth Workshop on Languages, Compilers and Runtime Systems for Scalable Components*, 1998.

[22] N. R. Mehta, N. Medvidovic, and S. Phadke. Towards a taxonomy of software connectors. In *International Conference on Software engineering*, 2000.

[23] G. C. Murphy, A. Lai, R. J. Walker, and M. P. Robillard. Separating features in source code: An exploratory study. In *International Conference on Software Engineering*, 2001.

[24] P. Narasimhan, L. Moser, and P. Mellior-Smith. Using interceptors to enhance CORBA. *IEEE Computer*, July 1999.

[25] Object Management Group. *CORBA 3.0 Specification*, 3.0 edition.

[26] R. Pawlak, L. Seinturier, L. Duchien, and G. Florin. Jac: A flexible framework for aop in java. In *International Conference on Metalevel Architectures and Separation of Crosscutting Concerns (Reflection)*, 2001.

[27] D. E. Perry and A. L. Wolf. Foundations for the study of software architecture. *ACM SIGSOFT Software Engineering Notes*, 17(4), 1992.

[28] F. Rivard. Smalltalk: a reflective language. In *Proceedings, Reflection*, 96.

[29] E. Roman, S. Ambler, and T. Jewell. *Mastering Enterprise JavaBeans*. Wiley, 2001.

[30] T. Romer, G. V. D. Lee, A. Wolman, W. Wong, H. Levy, B. N. Bershad, and J. B. Chen. Instrumentation and optimization of Win32/Intel executables using etch. In *Usenix Windows NT Workshop*, 1997.

[31] M. Shaw, R. DeLine, D. V. Klein, T. L. Ross, D. M. Young, and G. Zelesnik. Abstractions for software architecture and tools to support them. *Software Engineering*, 21(4), 1995.

[32] J. Siegel. *CORBA 3 Fundamentals and Programming*. Wiley Press, 2000.

[33] Y. Smaragdakis and D. Batory. Implementing layered designs with mixin layers. In *European Conference on Object Oriented Programming*, 1998.

[34] T. S. Souder and S. Mancoridis. A tool for securely integrating legacy systems into a distributed environment. In *Working Conference on Reverse Engineering*, 1999.

[35] B. Spitznagel and D. Garlan. A compositional approach to constructing connectors. In *Working IEEE/IFIP Conference on Software Architecture (WISCA)*, 2001.

[36] P. L. Tarr, H. Ossher, W. H. Harrison, and S. M. S. Jr. N degrees of separation: Multi-dimensional separation of concerns. In *International Conference on Software Engineering*, 1999.

[37] M. Tatsubori, S. Chiba, K. Itano, and M.-O. Killijian. Openjava: A class-based macro system for java. In *OOPSLA Workshop on Reflection and Software Engineering*, 1999.

[38] A. Troelsen. *C# and the .NET Platform*. Apress, 2001.

[39] E. Truyen, B. Vanhaute, W. Joosen, P. Verbaeten, and B. N. Jorgensen. Dynamic and selective combination of extensions in component-based applications. In *International Conference on Software Engineering*, 2001.

[40] R. Vanegas, J. Zinky, J. Loyall, D. Karr, R. Schantz, and D. Bakken. Quo's runtime support for quality of service in distributed objects. In *International Conference on Distributed Systems Platforms and Open Distributed Processing (Middleware)*, 1998.

[41] R. J. Walker and G. C. Murphy. Implicit context: easing software evolution and reuse. In *Foundations of Software Engineering*, 2000.

[42] N. Wang, K. Parameswaran, and D. Schmidt. The design and performance of meta-programming mechanisms for object request broker middleware. In *Conference on Object-Oriented Technologies and Systems (COOTS)*, 2000.

[43] E. Wohlstadter. Crosscutting adaptation in distributed heterogenous systems. Ph.D. thesis proposal, 2002.

[44] E. Wohlstadter, B. Toone, and P. Devanbu. A framework for flexible evolution in distributed heterogeneous systems. In *International Workshop on Principles of Software Evolution (4 pages)*, 2002.

Scaling Step-Wise Refinement

Don Batory, Jacob Neal Sarvela
Department of Computer Sciences
University of Texas at Austin
Austin, Texas, 78712 U.S.A.
{batory, sarvela}@cs.utexas.edu

Axel Rauschmayer
Ludwig-Maximilians-Universität München
Institut für Informatik
D-80538 Munich, Germany
axel@rauschma.de

Abstract[1]

Step-wise refinement is a powerful paradigm for developing a complex program from a simple program by adding features incrementally. We present the *AHEAD (Algebraic Hierarchical Equations for Application Design)* model that shows how step-wise refinement scales to synthesize *multiple programs* and *multiple non-code representations*. AHEAD shows that software can have an elegant, hierarchical mathematical structure that is expressible as nested sets of equations. We review a tool set that supports AHEAD. As a demonstration of its viability, we have bootstrapped AHEAD tools solely from equational specifications, generating Java and non-Java artifacts automatically, a task that was accomplished only by ad hoc means previously.

1 Introduction

Step-wise refinement is a powerful paradigm for developing a complex program from a simple program by incrementally adding details [9]. The program increments that we consider in this paper are *feature refinements* — modules that encapsulate individual features where a feature is a product characteristic that is used in distinguishing programs within a family of related programs (e.g., a product-line) [13].

There are many implementations of feature refinements, each with different names, capabilities, and limitations: layers [2], feature modules [17], meta-classes [10], collaborations [23][24], subjects [14], aspects [18], and concerns [27]. More general than traditional modules that encapsulate sets of complete classes, a feature refinement usually encapsulates *fragments* of multiple classes. Figure 1 depicts three classes, `c1`—`c3`. Refinement `r1` *cross-cuts* these classes, i.e., it encapsulates fragments of `c1`—`c3`. The same holds for refinements `r2` and `r3`. Composing refinements `r1`—`r3` yields a set of fully-formed classes `c1`—`c3`. Because refinements reify levels of abstraction, feature refinements are often called *layers* — a name that is visually reinforced by their vertical stratification of `c1`—`c3` in Figure 1. As the concepts of refinements, layers, and features are so closely related, we use their terms interchangeably. In general, feature refinements are modular, albeit unconventional, building blocks of programs.

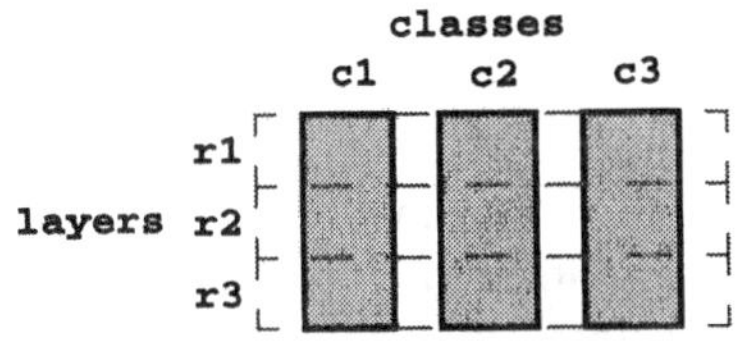

Figure 1. Classes and Refinements (Layers)

Tools that synthesize applications by composing feature refinements are *generators* whose focus has been on the production of source code for individual programs. This is too limited. Today's systems are not individual programs, but rather groups of different programs collaborating in sophisticated ways. Client-server architectures are examples, and so are tool suites, such as MS-Office. Further, systems are not solely described by source code. Architects routinely use different knowledge representations (e.g., process models, UML models, makefiles, design documents) to capture an application's design [16]. Each representation encodes different design information and is expressed in its own language or *domain-specific language (DSL)*, such as UML, OCL, XML, etc.

The contribution of this paper shows how step-wise refinement scales to the simultaneous synthesis of multiple programs and multiple non-code representations written in different DSLs. The challenge is not one of possibility, as ad hoc ways are used now. Rather, the challenge is to create a mathematical model of application synthesis that treats all representations — code and non-code, individual programs and multiple programs — in a uniform way. By expressing the refinement of representations as equations, we not only simplify tool development (as equations are ideal for program manipulation) but also lay the groundwork for specifying, generating, and optimizing application designs of considerable complexity using algebraic techniques.

1. This work was supported in part by the U.S. *Army Simulation and Training Command (STRICOM)* contract N61339-99-D-10 and *Deutsche Forschungsgemeinschaft (DFG)* project WI 841/6-1 "InOpSys".

We begin with a review of the GenVoca model, which shows how the *code* representation of an *individual* program is expressed by an equation. We then present the *Algebraic Hierarchical Equations for Application Design (AHEAD)* model that generalizes equational specifications to multiple programs and multiple representations. AHEAD is related to other methodologies, such as Aspect-Oriented Programming [18] and Multi-Dimensional Separation of Concerns [22], and thus our results are not GenVoca-specific. We review a tool set that supports AHEAD. As a demonstration of AHEAD's viability, we have bootstrapped AHEAD tools, generating over 100K LOC of Java (and other non-code artifacts) solely from equational specifications automatically, a task that was accomplished only by ad hoc means previously. We believe that this is the most sophisticated system built by automated step-wise refinement.

2 GenVoca

GenVoca is a design methodology for creating application families and architecturally-extensible software, i.e., software that is customizable via module additions and removals [2]. It follows traditional step-wise refinement [9] with one major difference: instead of composing thousands of microscopic program refinements (e.g., `x+1⇒inc(x)`) to yield admittedly small programs, GenVoca scales refinements so that each adds a feature to a program, and composing few refinements yields an entire program.

2.1 Model Concepts

Programs are *constants* and refinements are *functions* that add features to programs. Consider the following constants that represent programs with different features:

```
f        // program with feature f
g        // program with feature g
```

A *refinement* is a function that takes a program as input and produces a refined or feature-augmented program as output:

```
i(x)     // adds feature i to program x
j(x)     // adds feature j to program x
```

A GenVoca *model* of a domain a set of constants and functions. A multi-featured application is an *equation* that is a named expression. Different equations define a family of applications, such as:

```
app1 = i(f)       // app1 has features i and f
app2 = j(g)       // app2 has features j and g
app3 = i(j(f))    // app3 has features i, j, f
```

Thus, the features of an application can be determined by casually inspecting its equation.

Note that a function represents both a feature *and* its implementation — there can be different functions with different implementations of the *same* feature:

```
k1(x)     // adds k with implementation1 to x
k2(x)     // adds k with implementation2 to x
```

When an application requires the use of feature `k`, it is a problem of *expression optimization* to determine which implementation of `k` is best (e.g., provides the best performance)[2]. It is possible to automatically design software (i.e., produce an expression that optimizes some criteria) given a set of declarative constraints for a target application. An example of this kind of automated reasoning — historically called *automatic programming* [1] — is [5].

Although GenVoca constants and functions seem untyped, typing constraints do exist. *Design rules* capture syntactic and semantic constraints that govern legal compositions. It is common that the selection of a feature will disable or enable the selection of other features. The details of design rules are not germane to our paper and can be found in [3].

2.2 Model Implementation

A GenVoca constant is a set of classes. Figure 2 depicts a constant `i` that encapsulates four classes (a_i—d_i). A GenVoca function is a set of classes and class refinements. A *class refinement* adds new data members, methods, and extends or overrides existing methods of a target class. It could be implemented as a subclass of the target class, *with the provision that the subclass assumes the name of the target class.* In this sense, class refinement is different from typical subclassing in that true subclasses have names that are distinct from their parent class.

Figure 2 shows the result of applying function `j` to `i`: three classes are refined and another class is added, where the vertical lines in Figure 2 denote class refinement. That is, `j` encapsulates a cross-cut that refines classes a_j, c_j, and d_j, and adds class e_j. Figure 2 also shows the application of function `k` to `j(i)`, resulting in the refinement of two classes. In general, a forest of inheritance hierarchies is created as features are composed, and this forest grows progressively broader and deeper as the number of features increase [6].

Linear inheritance chains, called *refinement chains*, are common in this method of implementation. The rule is that

2. Different expressions represent different programs and expression optimization is over the space of semantically equivalent programs. This is identical to relational query optimization: a query is represented by a relational algebra expression, and this expression is optimized. Each expression represents a different, but semantically equivalent, query-evaluation program.

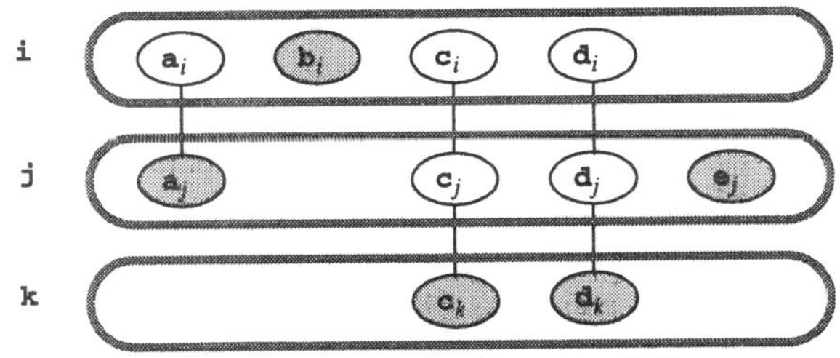

Figure 2. Simultaneous Refinement of Classes

(a) **makefile**

(b) **a foo and bar refined makefile**

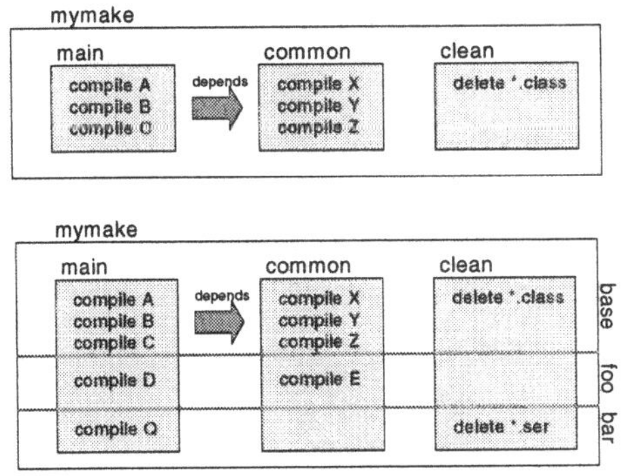

Figure 3. Makefiles and their Refinements

only the bottom-most class of a chain is instantiated, because this class implements all capabilities that were assigned to it. These classes are shaded in Figure 2. For example, the bottom-most class of the `c` refinement chain implements the capabilities defined in c_i, c_j, and c_k from features `i`, `j`, and `k` respectively. Stated another way, c_i is a class (constant) and c_j and c_k are class refinements (functions). The class `c` that is produced in Figure 2 can be expressed equationally as $c = c_k(c_j(c_i))$.

The simplest implementations of feature refinements are templates [24][29]. More sophisticated ways include generators [5][20], program transformations [8], and objects [26].

3 Scaling Refinements

Four ideas have led us to a major generalization of the GenVoca model. First, a program has many different representations besides source code. A program can be defined by UML documents, process diagrams, makefiles, performance models, design rule files, etc. in addition to code, each written in its own DSL.

Second, conventional notions of modularity must be broadened: *a module is a containment hierarchy of artifacts*. For example, an object-oriented class is a module; it encapsulates a set of data members and methods. A package is another kind of module; it encapsulates a set of `Java` and `.class` files. A J2EE EAR file is also a module; it encapsulates Java JAR files, deployment descriptors, and web archive files (e.g., HTML files). A program is yet another kind of module; its representation is expressible as a containment hierarchy of artifacts — code, makefiles, etc.

Third, the impact of refinements need not be limited to source code. When a program is refined, any or all of its representations may be changed. This is required so that all of its artifacts (code files, design rules, etc.) remain consistent. Thus if a program is represented by a containment hierarchy, a program refinement is a function that transforms containment hierarchies. That is, a refinement may alter a containment hierarchy by adding new nodes (e.g., a refined program may have new `Java` or HTML files) and refining existing nodes (e.g., existing `Java` and HTML files are updated).

Fourth, refining non-code artifacts is intuitively evident: you start with an original document and you produce an updated document. But how is this to be achieved? What general principle guides refinement? An example reveals a basic strategy that we have found to be practical. A makefile is a typical non-code artifact. Figure 3a shows a makefile with three targets: `main`, `common`, and `clean`. `common` must be built before `main`; `clean` has no dependencies. Suppose these targets are part of a `base` feature. Figure 3b shows the refinement of `base` by `foo`, which encapsulates a cross-cut of targets that adds a file `D` to compile in `main` and file `E` to compile in `common`. Figure 3b shows a further refinement of `foo(base)` by `bar`, which adds another file `Q` to compile to `main` and a new instruction (`delete *.ser`) to `clean`.

Figure 3 imposes a class-like structure on a makefile. That is, a makefile is analogous to a class and targets are analogous to methods. Refinement of makefiles refines targets and may add new targets, etc. This example illustrates the *Principle of Uniformity*: treat all non-code artifacts as classes, and refine them analogously.

Interestingly, most artifact types in use today (XML, HTML, PPT, etc.) have or can have a class-like structure and thus are *object-based*. However, these types are rarely *object-oriented* — few allow inheritance or more general refinement relationships to be defined among its files. There is, for example, no support for inheritance relationships to relate different XML schemas. For representations like XML, adding inheritance or refinement relationships seems reasonable as a plethora of tools for manipulating XML documents are available and can be used to define such relationships. However, other representations — MS Word for example — are so complex that defining inheritance relationships among Word documents seems daunting. Never the less, the idea is clear: the task to be done when introducing a new artifact type is to define what refinement means.[3] Given the ability to refine non-code artifacts, we are in the position to scale refinements in a significant way.

4 AHEAD

GenVoca expressed the *code* representation of an *individual* program as an equation. The model that we present here, called *Algebraic Hierarchical Equations for Application Design (AHEAD)*, expresses an arbitrary number of programs and representations as nested sets of equations, a form that is ideal for generators to manipulate. In this section, we show how AHEAD constants, functions, and their compositions are represented, and illustrate the power of the model. In Section 5, we review a tool set for AHEAD.

4.1 Constants and Functions

Base artifacts are *constants* and artifact refinements are *functions*. An artifact that results from a refinement chain is modeled equationally as a series of functions (refinements) applied to a constant (base artifact).

Figure 4a depicts our graphical notation for a GenVoca constant **f** that encapsulates base artifacts (henceforth called *units*) a_f—c_f. Instead of pictures, we express constant **f** mathematically as a set of constants: $f = \{ a_f, b_f, c_f \}$. Similarly, Figure 4b depicts our graphical notation for a GenVoca function **h** that encapsulates functions a_h and b_h and constant d_h. Function **h** can be expressed mathematically as a set of functions and constants: $h = \{ a_h, b_h, d_h \}$.

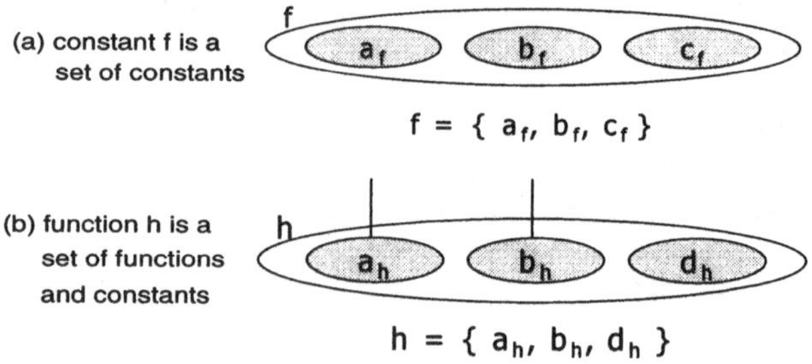

Figure 4. Constants and Functions as Sets (Collectives)

We use the term *collective* as an alternative to "set of units". The root collective (that comprises all other collectives) is also called a *model*.

4.2 Composition

Instead of writing **h(f)** to denote the composition of **h** with **f**, we henceforth write $h \bullet f$. The composition of collectives is governed by the rules of inheritance. Namely, all units of the parent (inner or right-hand-side) collective are inherited by the child (outer or left-hand-side) collective. Further, units with the same name (ignoring subscripts) are composed pairwise with the parent unit as the innermost term:

$$h \bullet f = \{ a_h, b_h, c_h \} \bullet \{ a_f, b_f, d_f \}$$
$$= \{ a_h \bullet a_f, b_h \bullet b_f, c_h, d_f \}$$

Equivalently, $h \bullet f$ is a set of equations where equation names are unit names without subscripts:

$$h \bullet f = \{ a, b, c, d \}$$
$$\text{where } a = a_h \bullet a_f$$
$$b = b_h \bullet b_f$$
$$c = c_h$$
$$d = d_f$$

Each expression in a collective defines the refinement chain of an artifact that is to be produced. Figure 5 shows this correspondence between our graphical notation and its AHEAD expression: $a_h \bullet a_f$ is the refinement chain for artifact **a** and $b_h \bullet b_f$ is the chain for **b**. Artifacts **c** and **d** are unrefined from their original definitions.

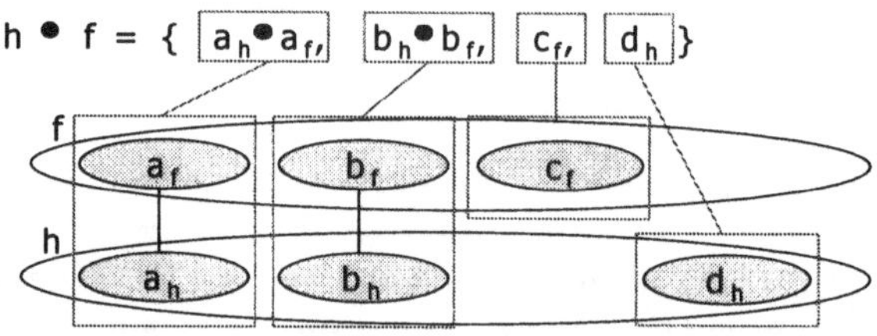

Figure 5. Expression and Refinement Chain Correspondence

Containment Hierarchies. Compound artifacts are expressed by recursion: units may themselves be collectives. Composition of compound artifacts is achieved by recursively composing collectives. Suppose a_h and a_f in Figure 5 are the collectives $a_h = \{ x_h, z_h \}$ and $a_f = \{ x_f, y_f \}$. The expression $a_h \bullet a_f$ expands to the collective $\{ x_h \bullet x_f, y_f, z_h \}$. The depth to which collectives are nested is the *rank* of the collective. **{}** is an empty collective of rank 0; **{{}}** is a collective of rank 1, and so on.

A compound artifact is a containment hierarchy. A Java program **p**, for example, is a compound artifact and thus is a non-leaf node; its leaves might be the set of Java files **{x.java, y.java, ...}** that implement it, the set of HTML files **{x.html, y.html, ...}** that **JavaDoc** produces from these Java files, the set of **.class** files **{x.class, y.class, ...}** produced by **javac**, and so on.

A feature — whether it represents an AHEAD constant or a function — is defined by a tree of artifacts. When features are composed, all of their corresponding artifacts are com-

3. Because it is possible to derive artifacts (e.g., **.class** files are derived from **Java** files via **javac**), composition operators are needed only for the most basic artifact types. Maintaining the consistency among "basic" types (e.g., English explanations of source code) is something that is accomplished manually.

posed. Thus, feature composition has a simple interpretation.

Polymorphism. The composition operator • is polymorphic. Artifacts are composed by operators that are specific to that artifact type. Java files, design rule files, XML files, etc. will each have their own unique implementation of the • operator. Thus, if there are *n* different artifact types, there will be *n* different type-specific composition operators. (As we will see in Section 5, there may be several composition operators for a given artifact type).

Further, the operator for composing collectives of rank *n* is no different than the operator for composing collectives of rank $n+1$, for $n \geq 0$. We call this the *Principle of Abstraction Uniformity*, which is a special case of the Principle of Uniformity. Imposing uniformity on all levels of abstraction produces a very compact and powerful algebra for defining and composing systems.

Scalability. OO programming languages that support parameterized inheritance can define and refine code artifacts, but are unsuitable for non-code representations. In contrast, equations elegantly express refinement relationships for *all* representations. Furthermore, *equations enable step-wise refinement and its generators to scale*. Instead of building one huge generator that deals with all possible program representations (which itself is impractical), it is *much* easier to build an elementary tool — here called a **`composer`** — that expands a high-level equation into its constituent artifact equations. The **`composer`** can then submit its generated equations to type-specific composition tools to generate the artifacts of the target system. Thus, a simple **`composer`** tool does the work of orchestrating other relatively simple tools to produce the complex set of artifacts that comprise a synthesized system.

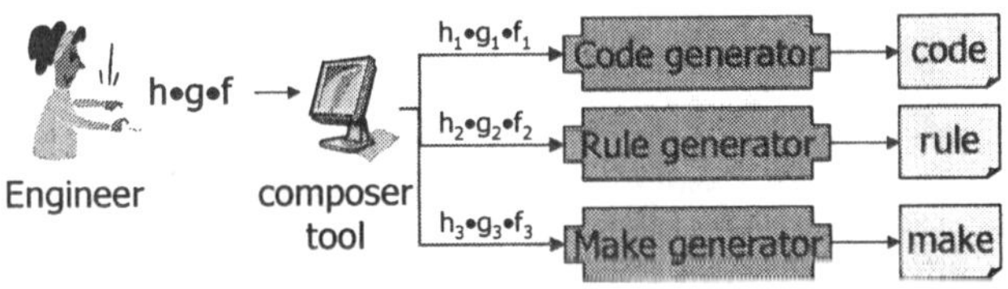

Figure 6. Organization of AHEAD Generators

4.3 Metamodels

One way in which to gauge the power of a model is its ability to express itself. A *metamodel* is a model whose instances are models. The UML metamodel is a classical example: it is a UML model whose instances are other UML models. AHEAD metamodels are collectives of models. Consider model **`M`** that contains three units **`a`**—**`c`**:

```
M = { a, b, c }
```

Metamodel **`MM`** contains three units **`AAA`**—**`CCC`**, each of which is a collective with a single unit:

```
MM = { AAA, BBB, CCC }
   = { {a}, {b}, {c} }
```

Model **`M`** is defined by an equation using metamodel **`MM`**:

```
M = AAA • BBB • CCC
```

where composition creates **`M`** by disjoint union, since none of the units share names. The following are interesting uses of metamodels.

Service Packs. A *service pack* is an update of model. A *service pack metamodel* **`SP`** contains an initial model M_0 and a series of service pack updates S_1, S_2, S_3, each of which incrementally updates a model:

$$SP = \{ M_0, S_1, S_2, S_3, \ldots \}$$

A special composition operator ♦, called *replace*, is used to apply the changes of a service pack to an existing model. If U_k and U_j are primitive (i.e., non-compound) units, the law of the replace operator is:

$$U_k \blacklozenge U_j = U_k \qquad // \; U_k \text{ replaces } U_j$$

Otherwise ♦ is identical to the composition • operator for collectives. (♦ is actually a special case of •). Thus, a model **`M`** that is up-to-date w.r.t. service pack S_3 is defined by the equation:

$$M = S_3 \blacklozenge S_2 \blacklozenge S_1 \blacklozenge M_0$$

That is, the effects of S_1 are applied to M_0 by replacing old base artifacts with new ones, and adding new artifacts. The same for S_2 and S_3. Special primitive units might be used to indicate the physical deletion (rather than replacement) of designated files.

Origami. A much more sophisticated use for AHEAD metamodels is generating equations for AHEAD tools from a single AHEAD metamodel equation. See [7].

5 AHEAD Tool Support

A simple way to implement a collective is as a file system directory. A directory's contents are either files (primitive units) or subdirectories (collectives). Figure 7a shows a collective that defines layer **`A`**; it consists of a unit, **`R.drc`** (a design rule file), and two collectives, **`Code = {X.jak, Y.jak}`** (Jak files are extended-Java files) and **`Htm = {W.htm}`**. Figure 7b depicts its representation as a directory.

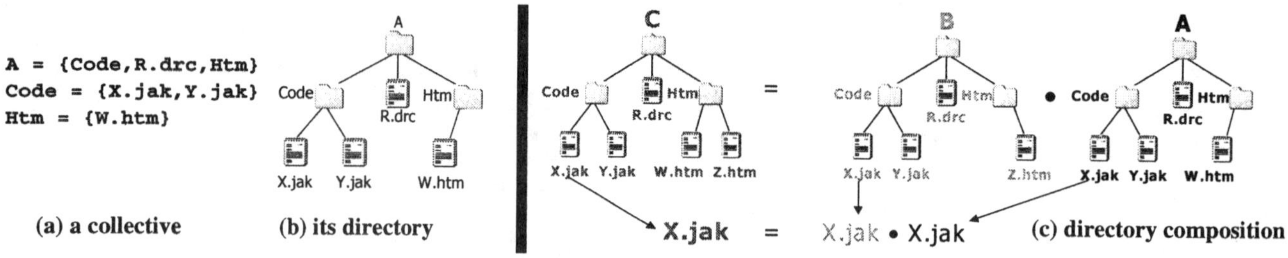

Figure 7. Collectives as Directories

Feature composition is directory composition. A composite directory is produced whose organization is isomorphic to the directories from which it was composed. Figure 7c shows a composition of features `A` and `B`, the result is feature `C`. Corresponding units in each directory are composed to produce a compound unit. For example, `X.jak` of `C` equals `X.jak` of `B` composed with `X.jak` of `A`.

Given this organization, we have built many tools to support AHEAD using the *Jakarta Tool Suite (JTS)* [4]. JTS is a set of compiler-compiler tools that use GenVoca models to build *product-lines* (i.e., families) of preprocessors for extended Java languages. Almost all AHEAD tools were built using JTS, and were written in a JTS-produced dialect of Java that includes refinement declarations, meta-programming constructs (e.g., Lisp "quote" and "unquote"), and hygienic macros. In Section 6 we describe how we recently bootstrapped our implementation where JTS is no longer used and AHEAD tools are now creating AHEAD tools. AHEAD tools are, themselves, Java language extensible — they can be created for different dialects of Java through language feature compositions.

The main tool of AHEAD is the `composer`, which takes an equation as a command-line input, and recursively expands the equation into its nested collective equivalent. It then creates a composite feature directory (whose name is that of the input equation), and invokes artifact-specific composition tools to synthesize artifact files from generated nested equations. `composer` itself is fairly simple, written in 4K lines of Java.

Other tools implement the composition operator • for specific artifact types. The first tools that we built composed code artifacts, as verifying the code synthesis capabilities of AHEAD was our first priority. Subsequently, composition tools for HTML files, makefiles, equation files (files whose contents define a single AHEAD equation), design rule files, and BNF-grammar files (for synthesizing extensible preprocessors) were constructed. We anticipate the number of artifact-composition tools to increase over time.

Because of space limitations, we review how AHEAD tools compose code and equation representations. Other tools and representations — such as makefiles and design rules — are described in [28].

5.1 Code Artifacts and Tools

Code files that are composed by AHEAD tools are not pure Java, but rather a superset of Java called Jak (pronounced "jack", short for Jakarta): this is Java extended with embedded DSLs for refinements, state machines, and meta-programming. (Remember: AHEAD tools are Java language extensible, so AHEAD can support many Java dialects).

Jak-specific tools are invoked to compose Jak files. One of two different implementations of the • operator can be used: `jampack` or `mixin`. Both take an equation as input, which defines the refinement chain of a Jak artifact, and produce a single, composite Jak file as output. A third tool, `jak2java`, translates a Jak file to its Java counterpart. Thus our two-step paradigm uses `jampack` or `mixin` to compose Jak files, and `jak2java` to derive the corresponding Java file from its composite Jak file (Figure 8).

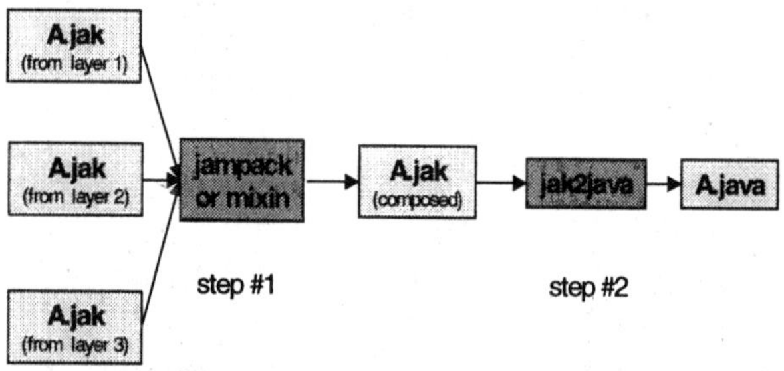

Figure 8. Composing and Translating Jak files

Source Code. A Jak file defines a code constant or function. A code constant is a single interface, class, or state machine. A Jak interface and class declaration are indistinguishable from their Java counterparts, except for a layer declaration which specifies the name of the layer to which the file belongs (see Figure 9a). More interesting is a state machine declaration, which consists of state and edge (transition) declarations. The state machine `fsm` of Figure 9b declares three states (`s1`—`s3`) and two edges (`e1`—`e2`). See [6] for more details.

```
layer A;

import java.util.*;

class k {
   int counter;

   int getCounter()
   {...}
}
```

(a) class constant

```
layer A;

import java.util;

State_machine fsm {
   States s1, s2, s3;

   Edge e1: s1 -> s2 ...;
   Edge e2: s2 -> s3 ...;
}
```

(b) state machine constant

```
layer B;

import foo.bar;

refines class k {
   int counter2;

   void method2()
   {...}
}
```

(c) class function

```
layer B;

import foo.bar;

refines State_machine fsm {
   States s4;

   Edge e3: s3 -> s4 ...;
}
```

(d) state machine function

Figure 9. AHEAD Code Constants and Functions

A code function refines an interface, class, or state machine. The **refines** modifier distinguishes constant declarations from functions. A refinement of class **k** in Figure 9a is shown in Figure 9c. It adds a new data member (**counter2**) and a new method (**method2**). Methods can be refined/extended in the usual way by overriding their superclass method and invoking that method in the extension body. A refinement of the **fsm** state machine is shown in Figure 9d. It adds another state **s4** and edge **e3** declaration.

Composition. **jampack** and **mixin** are sophisticated tools, both over 30K Java LOC in size. Their basic functionality, however, is fairly simple. **jampack** compresses refinement chains into a single interface, class, or state machine specification. The **jampack** result of composing the **k** function with the **k** constant of Figure 9 is shown in Figure 10a; the resulting class exposes the union of package imports, data members, and methods that are visible to the bottom-most class of its refinement chain. The **jampack** result of composing the **fsm** function with the **fsm** constant of Figure 9 is shown in Figure 10b. The resulting state machine exposes the union of package imports, states and edges, that are visible to the bottom-most state machine of its refinement chain.

jampack was our first tool to compose code. We soon discovered that **jampack** might not be the preferred tool. To see

```
layer C;

import java.util.*;
import foo.bar

class k {
   int counter;
   int counter2;

   int getCounter()
   {...}
   int method2()
   {...}
}
```

(a)

```
layer C;

import java.util.*;
import foo.bar;

State_machine fsm {
   States s1, s2, s3;
   States s4;

   Edge e1: s1 -> s2 ...;
   Edge e2: s2 -> s3 ...;
   Edge e3: s3 -> s4 ...;
}
```

(b)

Figure 10. jampack Compositions of Jak Files

why, a typical debugging cycle is to (a) compose Jak files, (b) translate the composite Jak file to its Java counterpart, (c) compile and debug the Java file, and (d) update the composite Jak file with bug fixes. This translate-compile-update cycle continues until no further changes are needed. Here lies the problem: **jampack** does not preserve layer boundaries, thus changes made to the composite Jak file must be manually propagated back to the original Jak layer files. This can be tedious and error prone.

mixin was created as an alternative implementation of the Jak composition operator. It preserves layer boundaries by creating within a single Jak file an inheritance hierarchy — refinement chain — of class/interface/state machine declarations, where the bottom-most declaration is concrete and all others are **abstract**. Every declaration is prefaced by a **SoUrCe** statement that identifies both the layer name and path to the file from which that instantiated declaration originated. (The case alteration in "**SoUrCe**" minimizes the likelihood of conflicting with typical program identifiers). Figure 11a-b shows the **mixin** output for the corresponding **jampack** compositions of Figure 10a-b. With the availability of **SoUrCe** statements, we have created a fourth tool, called **unmixin**, which takes a **mixin**-produced Jak file as input, and automatically propagates updates (comments as well as source statements) to the original layer files. Early experiences with **unmixin** suggest it can save a considerable amount of time during a development cycle.

There is yet another strategy: it is possible to edit the original layer files and recompose. Our experience suggests that debugging layers is similar to debugging templates: one instantiates a template to debug and develop it, and changes are eventually back-propagated to the original definition. We do not yet know which tools and processes engineers will prefer when developing software with AHEAD; this is a subject of future work.

5.2 Equation Artifacts

An *equation file* encodes an AHEAD equation. The file for `x = F•E•D` is depicted in Figure 12a; the name of the file is `x.equation` and the file itself is a text file that lists one layer per line, inner-most layer first. A refinement of an equation follows the principle of uniformity: we treat an equation as an artifact and a refinement is an equation that may reference a special layer called `super`, which refers to the parent equation. A refinement of an equation is depicted in Figure 12b, and the result of composing the equation files of Figure 12a-b is Figure 12c. If a refinement does not reference `super`, it is a constant and overrides the parent definition. Depending on the replacement of `super` in an equation file, a refinement might add new layers before, after, or around the original equation file (like before, after, and around methods).

(a) constant	(b) function	(c) composition

`D`
`E`
`F`
	`C`
	`super`
	`G`
		`C`
		`D`
		`E`
		`F`
		`G`

Figure 12. Equation Files

Equation files are useful as command-line input to `composer` and for implementing metamodels [7].

6 Applications

AHEAD is being used to build next-generation distributed *fire support simulators (FSATS)* for the U.S. Army *Simulation, Training, and Instrumentation Command (STRICOM)*. Several years ago, we built a layered prototype of FSATS [6]. As the first non-trivial test of AHEAD, we converted the prototype's source code, which included classes, interfaces, and state machines, into AHEAD layers. We also added design rule files and makefiles, so when AHEAD layers are composed, three very different representations of FSATS (code, design rules, makefiles) were synthesized. The prototype was defined by a single AHEAD equation composing 21 layers, yielding 90 files and 4500 Java LOC.

The next significant test was bootstrapping AHEAD itself. As mentioned earlier, AHEAD tools were initially built using JTS. To bootstrap AHEAD, we converted JTS source into AHEAD layers. In addition to code representations, AHEAD directories included grammar (BNF) files, which defined the syntax of optional extensions to the Java language. We used Origami, an AHEAD metamodel, to generate equations for AHEAD tools, including `jampack`, `mixin`, `unmixin`, and `jak2java`, and then used AHEAD tools to synthesize their executables [7].

To convey the complexity of this bootstrapping step, there are 69 distinct AHEAD layers constituting a code base of 33K Jak LOC. An Origami-generated equation references approximately 23 layers, where about 10 layers are shared among AHEAD tools. Each tool is generated by composing the Jak and grammar representations of each layer, and translating their representations to Java. Each AHEAD tool is sizable, having over 30K Java LOC. Thus using only equational specifications, we are generating the AHEAD tool suite whose complexity exceeds 100K Java LOC [7] *automatically*, a task that was accomplished only by ad hoc means previously. We believe this is the most sophisticated system ever produced by automated step-wise refinement.

7 Future Work

AHEAD raises many interesting questions including:

- The ability to analyze designs using tools such as model checkers will be critical to future design technologies. How do such tools fit with refinements and AHEAD designs? Preliminary results are encouraging [19].
- There are *many* operators on collectives and units, besides the • and ♦ operators. `javac`, for example, is an operator that compiles the Java files in a collective. `javadoc` is an operator that generates HTML documentation for the Java files in a collective. By equating standard tools with operators on collectives, we have an algebra for software development. Once software is specified algebraically, it is amenable to automated optimization and reasoning.
- How do the operators of refactorings and program optimizations fit into an AHEAD algebra?
- Many refinements that impact — cross-cut — different parts of programs require more sophisticated implementations of refinements than used in AHEAD. For exam-

(a)

```
layer C;

import java.util.*;
import foo.bar;

SoUrCe A "A/k.jak";
abstract class k001 {
   int counter;
   int getCounter()
   {...}
}

SoUrCe B "B/k.jak";
public class k
   extends k001 {
   int counter2;
   void method2()
   {...}
}
```

(b)

```
layer C;

import java.util.*;
import foo.bar;

SoUrCe A "A/fsm.jak";
abstract State_machine
   fsm001 {
   States s1, s2, s3;
   Edge e1: s1 -> s2 ...;
   Edge e2: s2 -> s3 ...;
}

SoUrCe B "B/fsm.jak";
public State_machine fsm
   extends fsm001 {
   States s4;
   Edge e3: s3 -> s4 ...;
}
```

Figure 11. `Mixin` Compositions of Jak Files

ple, information from multiple artifacts may be used to decide how to refine other artifacts en mass. How can such functions be modeled and implemented?

- AHEAD constants and functions are typed. The layer directories that we have composed with AHEAD have the same structure (or type), but our tools are not yet sophisticated enough to validate this assumption. A theory is needed to type refinements and artifact hierarchies.
- AHEAD has been developed with functions that have at most one parameter. There are GenVoca models with multi-parameter functions [2]. How can such functions be implemented in AHEAD? Why are functions with one parameter so common? We suspect that the answer is not how domains are represented, but rather our (implicit) use of currying which expresses a function of multiple parameters as a composition of functions with single parameters.
- Most, but not all, GenVoca models have focussed on the synthesis of programs using statically composable refinements. However, neither GenVoca or AHEAD preclude dynamic composability. How does AHEAD generalize?

8 Related Work

Among the most advanced work on generators is that of *Model Integrated Computing (MIC)* at Vanderbilt [25]. MIC embraces the concept that architects use multiple representations to specify application designs, and MIC generators have been developed to synthesize *graphical domain-specific languages (GDSLs)* that architects can use to specify their designs. Information that is collected from GDSL specifications are integrated and stored in a database. Specific artifacts of a design, ranging from source code to representations for analysis tools (e.g., model checkers), can be extracted and deduced from this database.

MIC has had great success in synthesizing software and hardware in engineering and manufacturing domains where the building blocks of systems and their composition-by-construction paradigms are well-understood. Where MIC has had less success is in areas of classical software applications where the building blocks and construction-by-composition paradigms are not well understood. We believe this is where AHEAD contributes: AHEAD shows how domains can be modularized as features and how applications of the domain are composed from them.

Domain-specific languages are recognized as a more efficient way in which to (a) specify applications and (b) integrate domain-specific analyses to validate DSL programs [30]. DSL usage is increasing and has been particularly successful in the specification of product-lines [31]. AHEAD not only embraces the use of DSLs as the primary means for specifying artifacts, but also advocates that DSL programs can be refined. (Our refinement of state machines and equation files in AHEAD are prime examples; state machines are expressed in a DSL embedded in Java; equation files are written in a stand-alone DSL). It is this scaling of refinements to code and non-code artifacts that is a distinguishing feature of AHEAD.

Aspect Oriented Programming (AOP) is a program refinement technology [18]. AHEAD essentially uses templates to express refinements. A more sophisticated way is to use special compilers to implement AHEAD functions that perform computations on a collective to determine how that collective is to be modified (or "advised"). Aspects are specifications of refinements, and aspect weavers execute these specifications on input programs. Thus, aspects provide another important kind of AHEAD function that is currently lacking in the AHEAD tool set.

Gray has shown how aspects apply to non-code artifacts [12]. AHEAD shows how both code and non-code artifacts can be refined simultaneously in collection hierarchies.

Multi-Dimensional Separation of Concerns (MDSC) is another program refinement technology [22]. We have built GenVoca generators using `Hyper/J`. Layers correspond to hyperslices, and GenVoca equations correspond to compositions of hyperslices. Further, MDSC advocates that the techniques for assembling customized code from hyperslice compositions should also work for non-code artifacts as well. This conjecture inspired work on AHEAD. The contribution of AHEAD is a simple algebraic model that supports the MDSC thesis.

9 Conclusions

The future of software engineering lies in automation. Integral to this vision is the transformation of application design from an art into a science — a systematized body of knowledge that is organized around principles, ideally expressible as mathematics. As long as application design remains an art, our abilities to automate key tasks of application design will be limited.

Generators are critical to this vision. As application complexity increases, the burdens placed on generators and their ability to synthesize multiple programs and multiple representations increases. The challenge in scaling refinement-based generators is not one of *possibility*, as there are any number of ad hoc ways in which this can be done. Rather, the challenge is to show how scaling can be accomplished in a *principled* manner, so that generators are not just ad hoc collections of tools and an incomprehensible patchwork of techniques. The significance of this point is clear: generators are a technological statement that the development of software in a domain is understood well enough to be automated. However, we must make the same claim for generators themselves: the complexity of generators must also be controlled and must remain low as application complexity scales, otherwise generator technology will unlikely have wide-spread adoption.

We have presented the AHEAD model, which offers a practical solution to the above problem. The key ideas are (1) to represent the plethora of representations that define a program — both code and non-code — as a containment hierarchy, and to treat containment hierarchies as constants. And (2) express feature refinements as functions that transform containment hierarchies; such refinements encapsulate all the changes that are to be made to the representations of a program when a feature is added.

Doing this, we discovered that application designs have an elegant hierarchical structure that is expressed by nested sets of equations. By imposing uniformity, we (1) eliminate ad hoc complexity as containment hierarchies scale; (2) enable a small number of operators to be used to manipulate AHEAD concepts; and (3) most importantly keep generators based on step-wise refinement simple as the systems they synthesize scale in complexity.

We reviewed an implementation of AHEAD and described our first non-trivial systems constructed by its principles (FSATS and AHEAD tools). We believe AHEAD takes us an important step closer to realizing a broader vision of automation in software development.

Acknowledgements. We thank Jean-Phillipe Martin, Melanie Kail, Mark Esslinger for their contributions to the design of AHEAD tools and model, and Jim Browne, Stan Jarzabek, Dewayne Perry, and Roberto Lopez-Herrejon for their helpful comments.

10 References

[1] R. Balzer, "A Fifteen-Year Perspective on Automatic Programming", in *Software Reusability II*, T.J. Biggerstaff and A.J. Perlis, Eds., Addison-Wesley, 1989.

[2] D. Batory and S. O'Malley, "The Design and Implementation of Hierarchical Software Systems with Reusable Components", *ACM TOSEM*, October 1992.

[3] D. Batory and B.J. Geraci, "Composition Validation and Subjectivity in GenVoca Generators", *IEEE Transactions on Software Engineering*, Feb. 1997, 67-82.

[4] D. Batory, B. Lofaso, and Y. Smaragdakis, "JTS: Tools for Implementing Domain-Specific Languages", *5th Int. Conf. on Software Reuse*, Victoria, Canada, June 1998.

[5] D. Batory, et al., "Design Wizards and Visual Programming Environments for GenVoca Generators", *IEEE Trans. Software Engineering*, May 2000, 441-452.

[6] D. Batory, et al., "Achieving Extensibility Through Product-Lines and Domain-Specific Languages: A Case Study", *ACM TOSEM*, April 2002.

[7] D. Batory, R.E. Lopez-Herrejon, J-P. Martin, "Generating Product-Lines of Product-Families", *Automated Software Engineering, September 2002.*

[8] I. Baxter, "Design Maintenance Systems", *CACM*, April 1992.

[9] E.W. Dijkstra, *A Discipline of Programming*. Prentice-Hall, 1976.

[10] I. Forman and S. Danforth, *Putting Metaclasses to Work*, Addison-Wesley, 1999.

[11] M. Flatt, S. Krishnamurthi, and M. Felleisen, "Classes and Mixins". *ACM Principles of Programming Languages*, San Diego, California, 1998, 171-183.

[12] J. Gray, et al. "Handling Crosscutting Constraints in Domain-Specific Modeling", *CACM* October 2001.

[13] M. Griss, "Implementing Product-Line Features by Composing Component Aspects", *First International Software Product-Line Conference*, Denver, August 2000.

[14] W. Harrison and H. Ossher, "Subject-Oriented Programming (A Critique of Pure Objects)", *OOPSLA 1993*, 411-427.

[15] W. Harrison, C. Barton, M. Raghavachari, "Mapping UML Designs to Java", OOPSLA 2000.

[16] A. Hein, M. Schlick, R. Vinga-Martins, "Applying Feature Models in Industrial Settings", *Software Product Line Conference (SPLC1)*, August 2000.

[17] K.C. Kang, et al., Feature-Oriented Domain Analysis Feasibility Study, SEI 1990.

[18] G. Kiczales, J. Lamping, A. Mendhekar, C. Maeda, C. Lopes, J. Loingtier, and J. Irwin, "Aspect-Oriented Programming", *ECOOP 97*, 220-242.

[19] H. Li, S. Krishnamurthi, and K. Fisler, "Interfaces for Modular Feature Verification", *Conf. Automated Software Engineering*, 2002.

[20] M. Mezini and K. Lieberherr, "Adaptive Plug-and-Play Components for Evolutionary Software Development", *OOPSLA 1998*, 97-116.

[21] S. McDirmid, M. Flatt, and W.C. Hsieh, "Jiazzi: new-Age Components for Old-Fashioned Java", *OOPSLA 2001.*

[22] H. Ossher and P. Tarr. "Using Multi-Dimensional Separation of Concerns to (Re)Shape Evolving Software." CACM 44(10): 43-50, *October 2001.*

[23] T. Reenskaug, et al., "OORASS: Seamless Support for the Creation and Maintenance of Object-Oriented Systems", *Jour. OO Programming*, 5(6): October 1992, 27-41.

[24] Y. Smaragdakis and D. Batory, "Mixin Layers: An Object-Oriented Implementation Technique for Refinements and Collaboration-Based Designs", to appear *ACM TOSEM.*

[25] J. Sztipanovits and G. Karsai, "Generative Programming for Embedded Systems", *Generative Programming and Component-Based Engineering (GPCE)*, Pittsburgh, October 2002.

[26] K.J. Sullivan, and D. Notkin, "Reconciling Environment Integration and Software Evolution", *ACM TOSEM*. 1, 3, July, 1992, 229-268.

[27] P. Tarr, H. Ossher, W. Harrison, and S.M. Sutton, Jr., "N Degrees of Separation: Multi-Dimensional Separation of Concerns", *ICSE 1999*.

[28] University of Texas Center for Agile Technology, "AHEAD Tool Documentation", 2002.

[29] M. Van Hilst and D. Notkin, "Using Role Components to Implement Collaboration-Based Designs", *OOPSLA 1996*, 359-369.

[30] A.van Deursen and P. Klint, "Little Languages: Little Maintenance?", *SIGPLAN Workshop on Domain-Spec. Lang.*, 1997.

[31] D. Weiss and C.T.R. Lai, *Software Product-Line Engineering*. Addison-Wesley, 1999.

Sound Methods and Effective Tools for Engineering Modeling and Analysis

David Coppit
Department of Computer Science
McGlothlin-Street Hall
The College of William and Mary
Williamsburg, VA 23185 USA
+1 757 221 3476
david@coppit.org

Kevin J. Sullivan
Department of Computer Science
151 Engineer's Way, P.O. Box 400470
University of Virginia
Charlottesville, VA 22904-4740 USA
+1 434 982 2206
sullivan@cs.virginia.edu

Abstract

Modeling and analysis is indispensable in engineering. To be safe and effective, a modeling method requires a language with a validated semantics; feature-rich, easy-to-use, dependable tools; and low engineering costs. Today we lack adequate means to develop such methods. We present a partial solution combining two techniques: formal methods for language design, and package-oriented programming for function and usability at low cost. We have evaluated the approach in an end-to-end experiment. We deployed an existing reliability method to NASA in a package-oriented tool and surveyed engineers to assess its usability. We formally specified, improved, and validated the language. To assess cost, we built a package-based tool for the new language. Our data show that the approach can enable cost-effective deployment of sound methods by effective tools.

1. Introduction

Modeling and analysis methods are at the heart of engineering. Such a method is based on a modeling language for describing systems, with a semantics in a mapping of expressions (models) to estimates of system properties (results). Functions for manipulating and analyzing models are then generally supported by software tools.

For a method to be safe and effective, its semantics must be well defined and it must be supported by high-quality tools. Semantic soundness demands an abstract, precise, compete, and validated specification of the mapping of models to results. High quality tools, on the other hand, are easy to use, rich in function, and reliable. Such a tool must provide a broad set of easy-to-learn-and-use functions matched to the needs of *engineering practice*. These functions go well beyond prototype-style barebones editing and analysis, to include printing of large models on engineering-sized paper, cut-and-paste into presentation tools, sophisticated graphical editing, etc. Engineers expect usability and functionality on par with mass-market packages, and demand it even in specialized tools. Reliability, by contrast, demands a sound semantic specification and a tool that implements it faithfully.

This paper emerges from a long-term, end-to-end experimental research program addressing the problem that, hampered by shortcomings in software engineering and languages, we are unable to deliver semantically sound methods supported by high quality tools at low cost. By experimental, we mean that we build and evaluate real tools using new techniques. By end-to-end, we mean that our work spans the life cycle and involves real customers, against whose needs results are evaluated.

Here, we address two sub-problems. First, we lack *demonstrably cost-effective* ways to ensure semantic soundness of methods too complex for informal specification. Second, we lack *low-cost* approaches to producing easy-to-use, functionally rich tools. Reliability will be addressed in forthcoming work. The contribution of this work is to show that we can, at low cost, combine well known formal methods [9] with package-oriented programming [30] to create semantically sound languages supported by richly functional, industrially usable tools. We report on the evaluation of a package-based tool, Galileo, by NASA engineers, and on the development of a similar tool, Nova, based on a formal semantics.

The rest of this paper is organized as follows. Section 2 discusses the role that formal specification should play in the development of a modeling method. Section 3 describes our approach and basic results. Section 4 introduces our experimental application domain. Section 5 describes the development of Nova using the combined approach. Section 6 presents results from the end-user evaluation of Galileo. Section 7 evaluates our work. Section 8 addresses related work. Section 9 concludes.

0-7695-1877-X/03 $17.00 © 2003 IEEE

2. Formal Semantics and Dependability

A modeling method rests on a mapping of models to analysis results. Such a mapping should be defined in both specification and implementation forms. Of the two, the specification is the more fundamental. Lacking a specification, validation of the method is difficult, there is no basis for a definitive user reference, and programmers are left to make uninformed semantic decisions and unable to test thoroughly for correct functioning.

Under such conditions, engineers cannot have justifiable confidence in the validity of a method. Yet, as Knight has observed [19], tools are increasingly used in the design of safety critical systems. Such tools should be treated as critical engineering components. He has cited numerous, serious lapses in engineering processes with respect to tools and methods. Nevertheless, the use of poorly grounded methods and tools appears widespread, putting enterprises and the public at risk.

For example, in 1996 the United States Nuclear Regulatory Commission issued an alert [23] to all operators and builders of nuclear power plants, warning of significant errors in several tools used in nuclear reactor design and analysis. Hatton and Roberts' study of seismic analysis tools showed that they produced different results even though ostensibly computing the same function [15]. A study of reliability tools by Amari et al. revealed common errors in their analysis algorithms [3].

As domain experts increasingly develop modeling and analysis methods and deploy them in tools, it is incumbent on the software engineering research community to highlight risks and impediments, and to provide approaches to mitigate and overcome them. First and foremost are the risks presented by inadequate semantic specification of methods used in critical design situations. Until these risks are addressed, our inability to develop easy-to-use tools at low cost can be viewed as a positive safety mechanism—but far from ideal. In this paper, we show it is possible to mitigate the risks substantially and cost-effectively, and, having done that, to deploy methods into industrial use through usable tools. We now sketch the approach and present our evaluation.

3. Approach and basic results

Several authors have noted that significant progress in software engineering will occur as the profession becomes increasingly specialized [17,25]. By identifying and developing practices that exploit characteristics of particular application domains, software researchers can provide developers with the means to create better software than that produced with general-purpose development methods.

A key element of our approach to tool development is based on an observation by Shaw [25]: Most applications devote less than 10% of their code to the overt function of the system—in this case analyzing models. 90% is devoted to support functionality such as text and graphical editing, data validation, etc. This means that the bulk of the development effort for a sophisticated tool is spent on a large *superstructure,* in support of a small *core.*

Our approach synergistically combines two ideas [6]. First, we address the soundness of the method and trustworthiness of the core through selective, narrowly targeted use of formal methods. Second, we provide full-featured, easy-to-learn and use superstructure at low cost by using suites of mass-market packages as components, in a style we have called package-oriented programming.

3.1. Formal methods for modeling and analysis

The first aspect of our approach is the targeted use of formal methods to define and validate of the syntax and semantics of the modeling language [9]. The savings garnered by package-oriented design can be enough to free significant resources for such applications of formal methods. We limit the scope to the *core.* It is small in relation to the tool, which limits costs, and its soundness is so essential that we expect formalizing and validating it to have disproportionate benefits.

3.1.1 Formalizing modeling languages. At the heart of our evaluation of the technical and cost effectiveness of formal methods in this domain is a specification, in Z [27], of the abstract syntax and semantics of a language for dynamic fault tree (DFT) analysis of fault-tolerant systems [5,11]. Dynamic fault trees extend static fault trees [31], originally developed for reliability analysis of the Minuteman missile system [32].

A *fault tree* is a rooted, directed graph with *basic events* as leaves and *gates* internally. Basic events model component failure events; gates, subsystem failure events; and the root, a system failure event. Given failure statistics for basic events, a probability of system failure is computable. Static fault trees have combinatorial gates (e.g., *and, or*), to model how event *combinations* lead to failures. In fault tolerant systems, *order* can matter. Dynamic fault trees thus include order-sensitive gates. Interactions amongst these gates and other modeling features complicates the semantics of DFT's to the point that the use of formal methods appears to be indicated.

An early non-formalized DFT language was implemented in Dugan's prototype DIFtree tool [14]. A revised version, also not formalized, is at the core of our deployed, package-based DFT tool, Galileo [7,29,30]. Our formal specification is the basis for a new tool, Nova.

The specification is 55 double-spaced pages of Z: about 100 schemas and axioms, structured in a denotational style, separately specifying abstract DFT syntax and the mapping of DFT's, through an intermediate semantic domain (*failure automata*), to Markov chains (MC's). Given a DFT, its MC encodes sequences of failure events. States in which the root event has occurred denote system failures. The analysis result is the likelihood of being in such a state. The mapping from MC's to probabilities is understood. The issue was the translation of DFT's to MC's. That is what the specification defines.

We developed an initial version of the specification, which we informally validated by technical reviews conducted with domain experts. We also subjected the specification to a limited formal validation. These activities provided significant benefits, creating opportunities to improve the language and existing tools. For example, no one had ever stated clearly whether failures could occur simultaneously; the language was non-orthogonal; and existing implementations had significant faults [9].

These results are not surprising. Formal methods have been used to discover and clarify complex systems many times. The question we investigated was rather that of the *cost-effectiveness* of developing and validating such specifications in collaboration with domain experts in a low-budget setting. We found that the initial development of the specification and its informal validation was cost effective and technically productive. Initial development of the specification took the authors about four months of part-time effort. Informal validation involved a sequence of about ten weekly two-hour meetings with domain experts, in which we explained, discussed, and, as needed, revised each line of specification.

3.1.2 Formal validation. We also evaluated tool-assisted formal validation, applying several tools to our specification: fuzz [26], ztc [18], and Z/Eves [24]. The first two check syntax; the third is an engineer-assisted theorem prover. On the *benefits* side, Fuzz and ztc were inexpensive to use and useful, finding both syntactic and conceptual errors. However, syntax checks are clearly not adequate to provide strong validation.

Theorem proving provides iron-clad validation of claims that the constructs denoted by a specification have stated properties. We proved two types of theorems: domain checks to show that no function is applied outside its domain, and domain-specific theorems formulated during development of the specification.

Our theorem proving revealed three specification errors. Two involved our idiosyncratic approach to specifying real-number computations in Z. Z does not represent real numbers; but we wanted to capture core mathematical formulations, which get translated directly into code. We did this by specifying real numbers as a given type and specifying standard operations on this type, abstracting away all meaningful axioms about the *real* real numbers. The errors here were not consequential.

The third error we found was non-trivial. It involved a feature of the DFT language called *coverage modeling*. Coverage modeling allows the engineer to represent three possible outcomes of a component failure: it might not propagate at all (masked transient); it might propagate normally; or it might produce an immediate system-level failure (due to a catastrophic component failure, such as an explosion). During validation, we found a fault in a failure rate computation for coverage parameters. In addition, this led us to an error in Galileo's implementation, where probability of masked failure was not correctly computed as $1-P_{\text{single point failure}}-P_{\text{covered failure}}$. The bottom line: We did find an error and are now more confident in the specification with respect to the theorems we proved, and, to some extent, beyond.

The problem we encountered with formal validation was its *cost*. We encountered three difficulties. First, the Z/Eves tool itself suffered from some of the problems we are addressing in this paper. It lacked features and had usability problems that made it costly to use. The interface was idiosyncratic and did not follow standard conventions. For example, the *File* menu disappears when the user edits a proof, and the *.zev* file extension is not automatically appended to file names when necessary. More seriously, the user has to run prior proofs before starting new ones, and each proof must be manually invoked in turn. Our validation has slightly over 100 proofs. While such problems are not inherent, they were a practical and significant productivity obstacle.

Second, the tool was computationally expensive to use. Syntax checking all paragraphs and proving all theorems required about two hours compute time on a 1.2 GHz PC. When working on proofs near the end of the specification, we dreaded having to change an early part, requiring manual re-checks of intervening paragraphs that might have depended on the changed paragraph.

Third, and perhaps most seriously, using the tool required significant expertise to formulate proof scripts. We found the prover to be robust and powerful, but we were often forced to seek guidance from its author for all but the simplest proofs. In more than one case we could not have continued without his expert guidance.

In the end, the cost of theorem proving was high enough to be nearly prohibitive *for our purposes*: given a small budget, competing demands, and hard-to-reach benefits. This is not to say the cost is too high for other purposes. However, cost did curtail our attempts to prove anything beyond elementary theorems about the formal system we constructed.

3.2. Package-oriented programming

For several years we have been evaluating the use of architecturally coherent mass-market packages as components for low cost tool superstructures. The approach, *package-oriented programming* (POP) [8,30], exploits technologies developed by industry to support tasks such as document embedding and package scripting. POP leverages the vast investments made in these tools and the economies of volume pricing. Users benefit from careful usability engineering, rich functionality, familiarity, and rich interoperability—all at very low cost.

Our evaluation is based on the use of POP to develop Galileo [7,12,29]. The ongoing development of this tool is based on feedback from industry, and especially on NASA requirements. By evaluating the results for *industrial viability* we aim to avoid false positives generated against synthetic or less demanding requirements.

It was clear that such packages could be integrated and programmed to some degree. What was not clear was whether they could be used to build real, commercially competitive tools at low cost. In earlier work, we reported that the approach is promising but risky [8]. For example, more than once we had to bend requirements to make designs work. What we now report is that the approach has enabled us to deliver the intended tool with real industrial acceptance. Section 6 presents the results of two surveys of end users who have used Galileo, and discusses adoption of the tool.

3.3. The combined approach

The approach we present combines the formal and package-based aspects in a technically and economically synergistic manner. The component-based aspect provides usability and superstructure functions, greatly reducing the cost to develop, learn, and use the software. On the other hand, the criticality and complexity of the modeling method impels us to consider using formal methods. We leverage the savings produced by the package-based approach to focus more resources on the formalization and validation of the relatively small but crucial modeling method and language. We recognize the risk that mass-market packages might somehow corrupt data passing through them and thereby output incorrect results, but we do not believe this risk to be dominant.

4. Case study: reliability engineering

As we have said, the application domain for our work is that of reliability modeling and analysis of fault-tolerant computer-based systems. In this domain, models represent failure phenomena in fault-tolerant systems with complex redundancy management. Models are analyzed to provide estimations of key properties, mainly unreliability. Analysis results are typically used in design to help engineers meet reliability requirements effectively and economically. Our case study in tool development centers on dynamic fault tree analysis. Central to this method are languages for expressing dynamic fault trees.

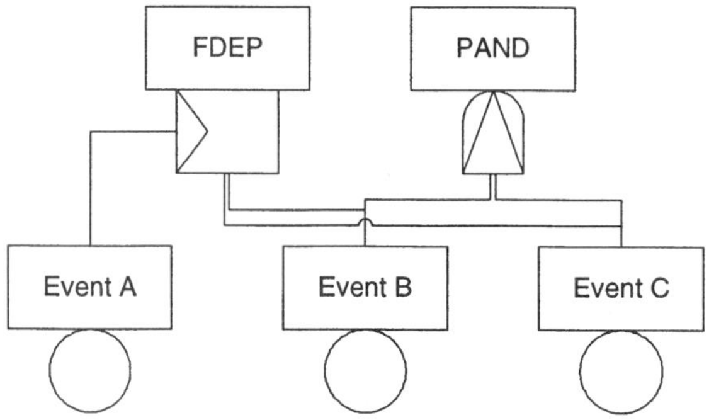

Figure 1: A small dynamic fault tree

4.1. The complex and subtle DFT language

Dynamic fault trees are more expressive than static trees, as many fault-tolerance mechanisms are sensitive to order. For example, the use of a cold spare component depends on the prior failure of the primary. Unfortunately, the addition of order-dependent semantics complicates the straightforward semantics of static fault trees.

Prior to our work, the semantics of the DFT language had been expressed only in an ad hoc way: with informal prose, isolated examples, and prototype programs [4,5,11,14]. Unfortunately, these methods are inadequate for specifying the semantics of complex languages. Informal prose descriptions are incomplete and ambiguous. Definitions for individual cases do not capture the general case. Source code implementations are precise but resistant to human understanding and validation. Moreover, in the absence of a high-level specification there is no basis for rigorous verification [9].

Consider an example DFT. See Figure 1. *PAND* is a priority-AND gate. The failure event corresponding to this gate occurs if the input events, *Event B* and *Event C,* occur in that order. *FDEP* is a functional dependence, stating that if the trigger event, *Event A,* occurs, the dependent events, *Event B* and *Event C,* occur.

This example highlighted a semantic ambiguity in the original language. Does *Event A* cause the *simultaneous* occurrence of the dependent events, or not? The original, informal semantics of the priority-AND gate did not address the issue of simultaneous failure of the inputs. If the ordering is strict, then the PAND event should not occur if the inputs occur simultaneously. If the ordering is not strict, the PAND event should occur in this case.

This kind of ambiguity is not just an academic curiosity. An engineer at Lockheed-Martin built this tree while modeling a system in an attempt to understand the semantics of the language as implemented in DIFtree. Casual explanations of the modeling approach did not address this case. Moreover, the implementation at the time was later found to answer the question inconsistently at different points in the program [9].

4.2. Inadequate tool support

Prior to our work, DFT modeling tools lacked key functionality and usability properties. Both HARP [13] and DIFTree [14] provided rudimentary graphical interfaces, and lacked many features now important in practice. DIFTree, for instance, was a successful research prototype, and served its purpose well in that capacity: to prove the worth, in principle, of a novel modeling method. However, its lack of modern features, its questionable dependability, and its being tied to Unix at a time during which reliability engineers were migrating to Windows, stood as solid impediments to the delivery of the DFT modeling method, itself, from the laboratory to practice.

5. Nova

In this section we present our efforts to build Nova, a demonstration of the feasibility of combining the two elements of our overall approach. Like Galileo, Nova is a tool for the construction and analysis of dynamic fault tree models. Compared to Galileo, Nova is an advanced prototype tool with several unique properties. First, the DFT language that it supports is a revised version based on our formal specification. Second, the implementation of the editing interface is based on more aggressive specialization of the POP components. Fault tree editing operations are implemented using components' scripting languages, rather than in separately coded procedures. Third, the analysis engine is a new implementation based on the formal semantics we have defined.

We are addressing the question of the dependability of the Nova and Galileo core implementations in work that is beyond the scope of this paper. Here, we focus on the POP-based user interface.

Figure 2 presents the Nova interface. It consists of a Word-based textual editor, a Visio-based graphical editor, and an Excel-based basic event editor. These products are parts of the Microsoft Office suite: Word is a text editor; Visio, a drawing editor; Excel, a spreadsheet. For the development of the interface, we took the opportunity to explore aggressive specialization of the POP components. For example, the figure illustrates the automatic syntax highlighting of keywords in the textual editor. For the sake of brevity, we describe only the more advanced Visio-based graphical interface.

Visio provides general graphical editing functionality such as zooming, scrolling, formatting, saving, printing. In addition, we utilized its *UpdateUI* interface to specialize our interface in several dimensions to support the editing of DFT's in their concrete graphical form.

First, we created a "stencil" of shapes for graphical depictions of the DFT modeling constructs. These shapes have dynamic behavior. For example, connectors automatically "hop" over each other, shapes move automatically to prevent overlap, and text boxes expand to accommodate long label names. Some of these features were supported natively by Visio, and others were implemented using the package's shape design capabilities.

Second, a menu and toolbar of functions has been added to perform DFT-specific operations such as changing the type of a gate or selecting a subtree. In order to implement these domain-specific operations, we took advantage of Visio's built-in macro creation capabilities. For example, consider the "change shape type" functionality. The code first checks that a shape is selected. It then displays a dialog box with the names of the various shape types. After the user makes a selection, any connections to the shape are saved and the original shape is deleted. Then the new shape is created and moved to the same location. Finally, the prior connections to the original shape are established for the new shape. By automating this fault-tree-specific editing operation, we relieve the user of having to perform each of these operations manually.

Our third type of customization was to remove or replace inappropriate Visio-native functionality. For example, Visio supports the notion of shape-to-shape connections in which the closest connection point is automatically selected. Since the DFT language makes a distinction between input and output connection points, the editor enforces a connection-point-to-connection-point policy. To do this, it detects when new connections are made by trapping the connection event raised by Visio. The editor then analyzes the type of connection, and either automatically determines the proper connection points in unambiguous cases, or queries the user otherwise.

Lastly, we enhanced the behavior of Visio to ease the task of building fault trees. For example, we found during the Galileo workshops that users often had trouble determining if both ends of a connector were properly attached. To help with this problem, we decided to implement a feature in Nova so that the connector is dashed when one end is not connected, and solid if both ends are properly connected. Implementing this feature was easy—it took only about an hour due to the programmability of the Visio package.

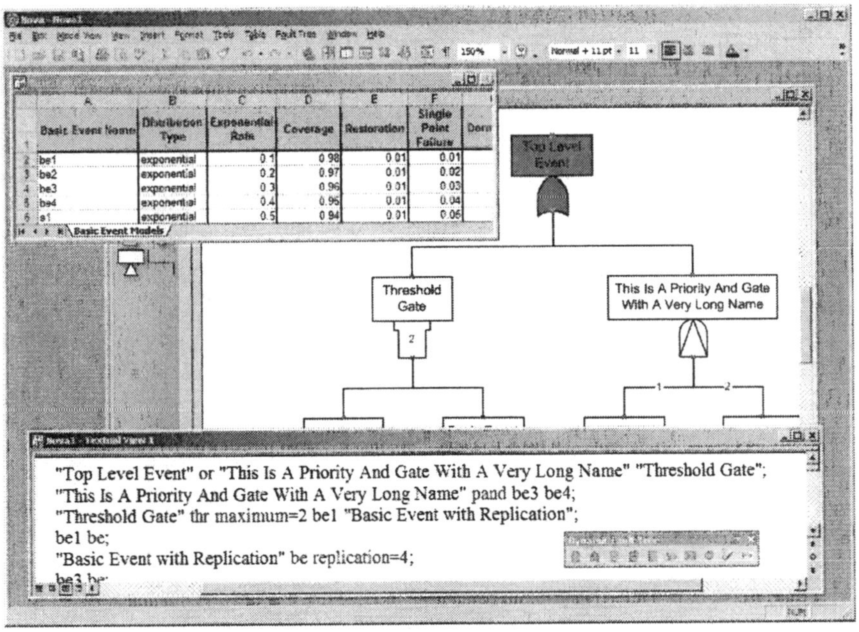

Figure 2: A screenshot of Nova

The Nova tool demonstrates the feasibility of our combined approach. It is a POP-based tool for engineering modeling and analysis implementing a modeling language having a formal, reasonably validated semantics.

6. End-user evaluation of Galileo

On the basis of the potential demonstrated by early prototype versions of Galileo, NASA Langley Research Center funded the development of a version called Galileo/ASSAP. The new tool version was required to support several new modeling and analysis constructs and to be usable in practice. It has been featured in three NASA workshops on dynamic fault-tree modeling. Engineers and managers from several NASA divisions were present at the first workshop. The second and third involved engineers from the space station and space shuttle projects.

6.1. Survey objectives and design

The workshops provided a unique opportunity to assess end user perceptions of Galileo/ASSAP. To that end, we developed two surveys and asked participants to take them. Participation was optional. To increase participation, we created a short survey with 34 key questions, and a longer survey with 77 more in-depth questions. Most of the questions were multiple-choice, with a few short-answer and ranking questions. Participants were given the opportunity to comment on every question in order to clarify their answers or give additional information. Questions were designed according to the guidelines suggested by Dillman [10]. Every effort was made to limit the range of interpretation of the questions and to reduce bias.

The overall goal of the surveys was to evaluate user perceptions of the tool in terms of usability and features. To that end, the surveys contained questions about the difficulty of performing common tasks with the tool. There were also several questions related to the user's impressions of a tool built using mass-market applications as components. Because we expected a small number of respondents and moderate variation in experience and skills, the surveys also included a number of questions designed to help us interpret the answers relative to the skills and experience of the respondents.

In order to help assess the ability of the POP approach to deliver an industrially viable tool, we also asked several questions which compares Galileo to well-established commercial tools. Questions were included to assess the users' impressions of tools that they frequently use, and to compare Galileo's features and usability.

6.2. Results

Sixteen engineers from twelve NASA groups, including NASA contractors, answered both surveys. The majority of the engineers considered themselves to be familiar with reliability modeling and analysis techniques, with five engineers using modeling and analysis tools every day. Almost half of the respondents analyze systems whose failure could lead to over US $1B lost and/or loss of life.

The two key requirements which we identified were confirmed by the surveys—the users cited "an easy-to-use user interface" and "accurate and precise analysis results" as being the two most important characteristics of a tool—above other options such as support for a range of modeling capabilities and speed. Users also confirmed our claim that dependability is crucial—a formal specification of the modeling language was second only to a comprehensive test suite as a means for increasing trust.

In terms of usability, most respondents indicated that the Word- and Visio-based views were easy to use. Compared to other tools, one said the usability was much worse, while all others said it was the same or better.

To understand user perception of Galileo features, we asked about two types of editing functionality: the functionality provided natively by the packages, and the domain-specific editing capability that we implemented by specializing the packages. The majority of users said they were satisfied with the general editing functionality, and nearly all said that the domain-specific operations met their needs well. All said the editing capabilities of Galileo were the same or better than other tools.

We also asked the users about specific features which were designed to accommodate package constraints, and which implemented modified versions of requirements. For example, views are updated using a batch approach instead of our original goal of incremental update, driven in part by the limitations of the Visio component [30]. We found that all users were satisfied with the capabilities which we were able to implement.

While learning to use Galileo, the users were told that the tool was built using Word and Visio. We asked the users several questions about these packages. All users were familiar with Word, but almost half were using Visio for the first time. When asked if their familiarity with the packages helped them use Galileo, nearly all said it helped at least a little, and several said it helped a lot. The majority of users were also satisfied with the performance of the tool, even though it uses large packages as components and is not optimized for speed.

These survey results are encouraging. End user evaluation is a key arbiter of success in the use of POP for the construction of tools. Despite the "beta" status of Galileo, the surveys indicate that the Galileo tool meets or exceeds the expectations of engineers. In most respects the tool was judged comparable with commercial tools.

When asked what surprised them the most about the tool, several users cited the usability, saying "the ease of use was better than expected", "[the] program is very user friendly", and "very friendly user interface". Several users liked the use of standard packages as components, saying they were surprised that it has "transparent linkage between Word and Visio". One user went so far as to say "the reuse of Word/Visio [is] a rather brilliant idea".

6.3. Adoption of Galileo by industry

Following their experiences using Galileo during the workshops, certain NASA engineers involved with the International Space Station (ISS) project adopted the tool. Today, the Galileo/ASSAP version of Galileo is used by the space station's fault diagnosis and repair group to model the causes of observed failures, but not for estimating failure probabilities. According to feedback from the engineers, the tool's editing interface provides capabilities that exceed those of the tools that they had been using.

In fact, the engineers have reported that Galileo's ease-of-use has led to a significant change in their practice. Previous tools required domain experts to work with reliability engineers to develop models. With Galileo, domain experts are able to model the system themselves, without having to depend on other engineers.

NASA's satisfaction with the Galileo/ASSAP tool has also led to a request for a follow-on version. This version is planned to include new features at the request of both NASA Langley Research Center (primary sponsor) and the ISS group at NASA Johnson Space Center.

The adoption of Galileo by NASA and the desire to extend the product are good indicators that the POP approach has succeeded in delivering the tool capabilities that real users value. Galileo was developed by a small team in an academic setting, and yet has features and usability that rival commercial tools and that appear able to satisfy the needs of major industrial organizations.

7. Evaluation

In earlier work, we presented less mature and separate evaluations of the constituent efforts. Previous work showed that the POP approach was promising but subject to risks, known and unknown. The survey data and industrial acceptance we present in this paper provide end user confirmation that the POP approach is capable of delivering tools with industrially viable feature sets and usability.

In terms of formal methods, we have shown that, with modest effort and basic mathematical and domain knowledge, it is possible to identify and eliminate serious semantic and implementation errors [9]. However, our experience was that the cost of formal validation was high enough to be inconsistent with a small budget.

Nova demonstrates the technical feasibility and cost-effectiveness of the combined approach. In less than two person-years, with the effort of a graduate student, advisor, and domain expert, we built a tool with usability better than Galileo's and having a formal foundation for trust.

In terms of lines of code, Nova is implemented in just under 30,000 lines of commented code. This count includes 3,100 lines of code specializing Word, 8,800 lines in specializing Visio, 9,000 lines for the analysis engine, and 5,700 lines for overall application control.

Nova has not yet been evaluated by end users, but we are confident that its interface will be as well-received as Galileo's. Nova employs more aggressive use of the POP components, resulting in better responsiveness and more sophisticated behaviors and editing operations.

8. Related work

In this section we describe three areas of related work: package-oriented programming, applied formal methods, and tool development methods.

8.1. Package-oriented programming

Lédeczi et al. [21] describe a COTS-based design environment generator exploiting packages as components. Given a meta-model of a language, their tool generates an environment. Our work focuses on the integration of applications as components. Theirs deals more with environment generation issues.

Succi et al. [28] are investigating the integration of POP components. However, they target cross-platform integration using a Java-based architecture as the integration mechanism. In contrast to our work, they do not attempt to achieve tight functional integration, and do not address user interface integration.

8.2. Applied formal methods

Efforts are underway to formalize modeling languages for software engineering, including architecture [1] and connectors [2]. The goal is to put such languages on mathematically sound foundations, enabling semantically well defined analysis methods. For example, architectural checks can assess compatibility of connectors and components using methods similar to type checking. This work supports our hypotheses about the technical value of formal methods. However, our work is more than technical. We seek to understand the benefits of formality relative to the costs. The question is, what techniques create value net of their costs, considering competing demands, and under demanding constraints?

Our experience using Z/Eves is similar to that of Knight et al. [20], who used the PVS theorem prover on a modest-sized nuclear power plant specification. They too found it hard to formulate theorems and proof strategies, and were hindered by poor tool usability.

8.3. Tool development methods

Related to our work are techniques for building general modeling and analysis environments. Examples include the Generic Modeling Environment [21], MetaEdit+ [22], and DOME [16]. The idea is to develop reusable frameworks that can be used to instantiate new tools by specifying the aspects specific to the application domain. Our work is distinct in several dimensions. First, our strategy is to address the components used to construct tools, as opposed to an overall reusable framework. In this respect our work is not incompatible with the framework approach—it is possible to use POP components within a generic framework. Second, developers of reusable frameworks are faced with the challenge of not only providing a wealth of functionality and high usability, but also making this functionality easily reusable. Lastly, many modeling languages (including DFT's) appear too complex to capture easily using the hierarchical and constraint-based semantics used by generic frameworks such as GME.

9. Conclusion

In this paper we presented and evaluated—largely in economic terms—an approach to developing sound modeling methods supported by functionally rich and easy to use software tools. Using packages as components enabled the development of an industrially effective tool at low cost, with enthusiastic acceptance by NASA engineers as evidence of acceptability. Using formal methods fundamentally improved the soundness of a complex method. The Nova tool combines these components, hosting a formally specified and validated language in an improved package-based tool. Nova demonstrates, apparently for the first time, that it is possible to develop sound methods and make them readily available for industrial use at a cost that is modest by any reasonable measure. It took less than two person years to develop the specification, implement it, and deliver it in a package-based tool.

The cost-effective verification of implementations of analysis methods is a remaining key issue, but one beyond the scope of this paper. A solution would largely complete a three-part approach to the construction of sound methods and effective tools for engineering. We have identified, are now evaluating, and will describe in a forthcoming paper, a powerful testing technique leveraging our investment in formal specification.

This work has the potential to have a significant impact on engineering practice in at least two dimensions. First, by dramatically reducing the cost barriers to developing genuinely usable modeling methods, it promises to catalyze the development of such methods and their transitioning from laboratories into practice.

Second, we see that using complex modeling methods in critical industrial, governmental, or military engineering activities without software dependability assurances based on formal foundations is fraught with risk. This paper shows that well known formal methods and a willingness to work with domain experts, although not a *silver bullet*, are enough to significantly and cost-effectively contribute to the validation, implementation and documentation of modeling methods. It is thus reasonable to start to recognize and seriously question the use of computerized modeling methods lacking documented formal semantic foundations for dependability.

Acknowledgements

This work was supported in large part by the National Science Foundation under grant ITR-0086003. We thank colleagues at NASA Langley Research Center, Johnson Space Center, and across the organization for agreeing to participate in our survey. We also warmly thank our collaborators in reliability and software engineering research, including Joanne Bechta Dugan and John Knight, for their support. Finally, we thank all of the anonymous reviewers for their constructive critiques.

References

[1] Gregory D. Abowd, Robert Allen, and David Garlan. Formalizing style to understand descriptions of software architecture. *ACM Transactions on Software Engineering and Methodology*, 4(4):319–64, October 1995.

[2] Robert Allen and David Garlan. A formal basis for architectural connection. *ACM Transactions on Software Engineering and Methodology*, 6(3):213–49, July 1997.

[3] Suprasad Amari, Joanne Bechta Dugan, and Ravindra Misra. A separable method for incorporating imperfect coverage into combinatorial models. *IEEE Transactions on Reliability*, 48(3):267-74, September 1999.

[4] Anju Anand and Arun K. Somani. Hierarchical analysis of fault trees with dependencies, using decomposition. In *Proceedings of the Annual Reliability and Maintainability Symposium*, pages 64-70, Anaheim, CA, 19-22 January 1998.

[5] Mark A. Boyd. Dynamic Fault Tree Models: Techniques for Analysis of Advanced Fault Tolerant Computer Systems. PhD thesis, Duke University, Department of Computer Science, April 1991.

[6] David Coppit. *Engineering Modeling and Analysis: Sound Methods and Effective Tools*. PhD thesis, The University of Virginia, Charlottesville, Virginia, January 2003.

[7] David Coppit and Kevin J. Sullivan. Galileo: A tool built from mass-market applications. In *Proceedings of the 22nd International Conference on Software Engineering*, pages 750-3, Limerick, Ireland, 4-11 June 2000. IEEE.

[8] David Coppit and Kevin J. Sullivan. Multiple mass-market applications as components. In *Proceedings of the 22nd International Conference on Software Engineering*, pages 273-82, Limerick, Ireland, 4-11 June 2000. IEEE.

[9] David Coppit, Kevin J. Sullivan, and Joanne Bechta Dugan. Formal semantics of models for computational engineering: A case study on dynamic fault trees. In *Proceedings of the International Symposium on Software Reliability Engineering*, pages 270-282, San Jose, California, 8-11 October 2000. IEEE.

[10] Don A. Dillman. *Mail and Internet Surveys: The Tailored Design Method*. John Wiley & Sons, 2nd edition, 1999.

[11] Joanne Bechta Dugan, Salvatore Bavuso, and Mark Boyd. Dynamic fault-tree models for fault-tolerant computer systems. *IEEE Transactions on Reliability*, 41(3):363-77, September 1992.

[12] Joanne Bechta Dugan, Kevin J. Sullivan, and David Coppit. Developing a low-cost, high-quality software tool for dynamic fault tree analysis. *Transactions on Reliability*, 49(1):49-59, March 2000.

[13] Joanne Bechta Dugan, Kishor S. Trivedi, Mark K. Smotherman, and Robert M. Geist. The hybrid automated reliability predictor. *Journal of Guidance, Control, and Dynamics*, 9(3):319-31, June 1986.

[14] Joanne Bechta Dugan, Bharath Venkataraman, and Rohit Gulati. DIFTree: A software package for the analysis of dynamic fault tree models. In *Proceedings of the Annual Reliability and Maintainability Symposium*, pages 64-70, Philadelphia, PA, 13-16 January 1997.

[15] Les Hatton and Andy Roberts. How accurate is scientific software? *IEEE Transactions on Software Engineering*, 2(10):785-797, 1994.

[16] Honeywell. DOME users' guide. URL: http://www.htc.-honeywell.com/dome/support.htm.

[17] Michael Jackson. Problems, methods and specialisation. *Software Engineering Journal*, 9(6):249-55, November 1994.

[18] Xiaoping Jia. *ZTC: A type checker for Z. Notation user's guide*. URL: http://se.cs.depaul.edu/fm/ztc.html.

[19] J. C. Knight. Safety critical systems: Challenges and directions. In *Proceedings of the 24th International Conference on Software Engineering*, pages 547-9, Orlando, Florida, 19-25 May 2002. IEEE.

[20] J. C. Knight, Colleen L. DeJong, Matthew S. Gibble, and Luís G. Nakano. Why are formal methods not used more widely? Fourth NASA Formal Methods Workshop, Hampton, Virginia, September 1997.

[21] Akos Ledeczi, Miklos Maroti, Arpad Bakay, Gabor Karsai, Jason Garrett, Charles Thomason, Greg Nordstrom, Jonathan Sprinkle, and Peter Volgyesi. The generic modeling environment. In *Workshop on Intelligent Signal Processing*, Budapest, Hungary, 17 May 2001.

[22] MetaCase Consulting. Domain-specific modeling: 10 times faster than UML. URL: http://www.metacase.com/papers/-index.html.

[23] Office of Nuclear Reactor Regulation. Requirements in 10 CFR part 21 for reporting and evaluating software errors. Technical Report NRC Information Notice 96-29, United States Nuclear Regulatory Commission, 20 May 1996.

[24] Mark Saaltink. The Z/EVES system. In *ZUM '97: Z Formal Specification Notation. 11th International Conference of Z Users. Proceedings*, pages 72–85, Berlin, Germany, 3–4 April 1997. Springer-Verlag.

[25] Mary Shaw. Prospects for an engineering discipline of software. *IEEE Software*, 7(6):15-24, November 1990.

[26] J. M. Spivey. *The fuzz manual*. URL: http://spivey.oriel.-ox.ac.uk/~mike/fuzz/

[27] J. M. Spivey. *The Z Notation: A Reference Manual*. Prentice Hall International Series in Computer Science, 2nd edition, 1992.

[28] Giancarlo Succi, Witold Pedrcyz, Eric Liu, and Jason Yip. Package-oriented software engineering: a generic architecture. IT Professional, 3(2):29-36, March-April 2001.

[29] Kevin J. Sullivan, Joanne Bechta Dugan, and David Coppit. The Galileo fault tree analysis tool. In *Proceedings of the 29th Annual International Symposium on Fault-Tolerant Computing*, pages 232-5, Madison, Wisconsin, 15-18 June 1999. IEEE.

[30] K. J. Sullivan and J.C. Knight, "Experience Assessing an Architectural Approach to Large-Scale, Systematic Reuse," Proceedings of the 18th International Conference on Software Engineering, Berlin, March 1996, pages 220-229.

[31] W. E. Veseley, F. F. Goldberg, N. H. Roberts, and D. F. Haasl. *Fault Tree Handbook*. U. S. Nuclear Regulatory Commission, NUREG-0492, Washington DC, 1981.

[32] H. A. Watson and Bell Telephone Laboratories. Launch control safety study. Technical report, Bell Telephone Laboratories, Murray Hill, NJ, 1961.

Technical Papers

Testing II

Fragment Class Analysis for Testing of Polymorphism in Java Software

Atanas Rountev
Department of Computer and Information Science
The Ohio State University
rountev@cis.ohio-state.edu

Ana Milanova
Department of Computer Science
Rutgers University
milanova@cs.rutgers.edu

Barbara G. Ryder
Department of Computer Science
Rutgers University
ryder@cs.rutgers.edu

Abstract

Adequate testing of polymorphism in object-oriented software requires coverage of all possible bindings of receiver classes and target methods at call sites. Tools that measure this coverage need to use class analysis *to compute the coverage requirements. However, traditional whole-program class analysis cannot be used when testing partial programs. To solve this problem, we present a general approach for adapting whole-program class analyses to operate on program fragments. Furthermore, since analysis precision is critical for coverage tools, we provide precision measurements for several analyses by determining which of the computed coverage requirements are actually feasible. Our work enables the use of whole-program class analyses for testing of polymorphism in partial programs, and identifies analyses that compute precise coverage requirements and therefore are good candidates for use in coverage tools.*

1 Introduction

Testing of object-oriented software presents new challenges due to features such as inheritance, polymorphism, dynamic binding, and object state [6]. Programs contain complex interactions among sets of collaborating objects from different classes. These interactions are greatly complicated by object-oriented features such as *polymorphism*, which allows the binding of an object reference to objects of different classes. While this is a powerful mechanism for producing compact and extensible code, it creates numerous fault opportunities [6].

Polymorphism is common in object-oriented software—for example, polymorphic bindings are often used instead of `case` statements [15, 7]. However, code that uses polymorphism can be hard to understand and therefore fault-prone—for example, understanding all possible interactions between a message sender and a message receiver under all possible bindings can be challenging for programmers. The sender of a message may fail to meet all preconditions for all possible bindings of the receiver [7]. A subclass in an inheritance hierarchy may violate the contract of its superclasses; clients that send polymorphic messages to this hierarchy may experience inconsistent behavior. For example, an inherited method may be incorrect in the context of the subclass [27], or an overriding method may have preconditions and postconditions different from the ones for the overridden method [6]. In deep inheritance hierarchies, it is easy to forget to override methods for lower-level subclasses [11]; clients of such hierarchies may experience incorrect behavior for some receiver classes. Changes in server classes may cause tested and unchanged client code to fail [7].

1.1 Coverage Criteria for Polymorphism

Various techniques for testing of polymorphic interactions have been proposed in previous work [37, 22, 21, 25, 10, 7, 3]. These approaches require testing that exercises *all possible polymorphic bindings* for certain elements of the tested software. Such requirements can be encoded as coverage criteria for testing of polymorphism. In this paper we focus on two such criteria. The *receiver-classes* criterion (denoted by *RC*) requires exercising of all possible classes of the receiver object at a call site [22, 21, 25, 10]. The *target-methods* criterion (denoted by *TM*) requires exercising of all possible bindings between a call site and the methods that may be invoked by that site [37, 7]. (Both criteria are discussed in more detail in Section 2.)

The testing requirements encoded by the *RC* and *TM* cri-

0-7695-1877-X/03 $17.00 © 2003 IEEE

teria have been advocated by several authors [37, 22, 21, 25, 10, 7].[1] For example, Binder points out that "just as we would not have high confidence in code for which only a small fraction of the statements or branches have been exercised, high confidence is not warranted for a client of a polymorphic server unless all the message bindings generated by the client are exercised" [7]. There is existing evidence that such criteria are better suited for detecting object-oriented faults than the traditional statement and branch coverage criteria [10].

1.2 Class Analysis for Coverage Tools

The use of coverage criteria is impossible without tools that automatically measure the coverage achieved during testing. To compute the *RC* and *TM* coverage requirements, a tool needs to determine the possible classes of the receiver object and the possible target methods for each call site. In the simplest case, this can be done by examining the class hierarchy—i.e., by considering all classes in the subtree rooted at the declared type of the receiver. While not explicitly stated, it appears that all previous work [37, 22, 21, 25, 10, 7] uses this approach to determine the coverage requirements.

Existing work on static analysis for object-oriented languages shows that using the class hierarchy to determine possible receiver classes may be overly conservative—i.e., not all subclasses may be actually possible. Such imprecision has serious consequences for coverage tools. Because of infeasible coverage requirements, high coverage can never be achieved regardless of the testing effort. In this case the coverage metrics become hard to interpret: is the low coverage due to inadequate testing, or is it due to infeasible coverage requirements? This problem seriously compromises the usefulness of the coverage metrics. In addition, the person who creates new test cases may spend significant time and effort trying to determine the appropriate test cases, before realizing that it is impossible to achieve the required coverage. This situation is unacceptable because human time and attention are much more expensive than computing time.

To address these problems, we propose to use *class analysis* to compute the coverage requirements. Class analysis is a static analysis that determines the classes of all objects to which a given reference variable may point. While initially developed in the context of optimizing compilers for object-oriented languages, class analysis also has a variety of applications in software engineering tools. In a coverage tool for testing of polymorphism, class analysis can be used to determine what are the classes of the objects that variable `x` may refer to at call site `x.m();` from this it is trivial to compute the *RC* and *TM* criteria for the call site. There is a large body of work on various class analyses with different tradeoffs between cost and precision [26, 1, 2, 28, 14, 5, 17, 13, 9, 29, 32, 34, 38, 35, 19, 31, 16, 23]. However, there has been no previous work on using these analyses for the purposes of testing of polymorphism.

[1]Other coverage criteria for polymorphism are also possible. For example, in addition to *RC*, [22] proposes coverage of all possible classes for the senders and the parameters of a message. Our work can be trivially extended to handle such criteria.

1.3 Fragment Class Analysis

The existing body of work on class analysis cannot be used directly to compute the *RC* and *TM* coverage requirements in a coverage tool. The key problem is that the vast majority of existing class analyses are designed as *whole-program analyses*—i.e., analyses that process complete programs. However, testing is rarely done only on complete programs, and many testing activities are performed on partial programs. Any realistic coverage tool should be able to work on partial programs, and therefore cannot incorporate a whole-program class analysis.

To solve this problem, we need to design class analysis that can operate on fragments of programs rather than on complete programs. We refer to such analysis as *fragment class analysis*. The first contribution of this paper is *a general method for constructing fragment class analyses for the purposes of testing of polymorphism in Java*. Using this method, fragment class analyses can be derived from a wide variety of existing (and future) whole-program class analyses [2, 5, 17, 13, 29, 34, 35, 38, 19, 31, 16, 23]. The significance of this technique is that it allows tool designers to adapt available technology for whole-program class analysis to be used in coverage tools for testing of polymorphism in partial programs.

1.4 Absolute Analysis Precision

Analysis precision is a critical issue for the use of class analysis in coverage tools. Less precise analyses compute less precise coverage criteria—i.e., some of the coverage requirements may be impossible to achieve. As discussed earlier, infeasible coverage requirements present a serious problem for coverage tools: the coverage metrics become hard to interpret, and tools users may waste time and effort trying to achieve higher coverage.

To justify the use of a particular class analysis, we need to ensure that few (if any) spurious classes are reported by that analysis. The key problem is that previous work on class analysis only addresses the issue of *relative* analysis precision: how does the solution computed by analysis Y compare to the solution computed by analysis X? However, we need information about *absolute* analysis precision: what part of the analysis solution is infeasible? The second contribution of this paper is *an empirical evaluation of the absolute precision of four fragment class analyses.* These analyses are based on four well-known whole-program class analyses: Class Hierarchy Analysis (CHA) [12], Rapid Type Analysis (RTA) [5], 0-CFA [33, 16], and Andersen-style points-to analysis [4, 34, 19, 31]. In our experiments we determined manually what parts of the analysis solution were actually infeasible. This information is essential for deciding which analysis to use in a coverage tool; however, to the best of our knowledge, such metrics of absolute precision are not available in any previous work on class analysis.

Our results show that simpler analyses such as CHA and RTA do not provide sufficient precision for the purposes of testing of polymorphism, while more advanced analyses such as 0-CFA and Andersen-style points-to analysis achieve very good precision. These findings lead to two important conclusions. First, our evaluation of CHA and RTA shows that analysis imprecision *can be a serious problem*, and it should be a primary concern when designing coverage tools. Second, our results indicate that more advanced analyses such as 0-CFA and Andersen's analysis *can achieve high absolute precision*, which makes them good candidates for inclusion in coverage tools.

1.5 Contributions

- We present a general approach for constructing fragment class analyses from a wide variety of existing whole-program class analyses. This method enables the designers of coverage tools to use whole-program class analyses for the purposes of testing of polymorphism in partial programs.
- We present an empirical evaluation of the absolute precision of four fragment class analyses. These are the first available results that measure absolute analysis precision, and they provide essential insights for constructing high-quality coverage tools for testing of polymorphism.

Outline. Section 2 describes our coverage tool for testing of polymorphism in Java. Section 3 presents the method for constructing fragment class analyses. The experimental results are described in Section 4. Section 5 discusses related work, and Section 6 presents conclusions and future work.

2 A Coverage Tool for Java

We have built a test coverage tool for Java that supports the *RC* and *TM* coverage criteria. In the context of this tool we have implemented and evaluated several fragment class analyses. In the future we plan to use the tool as the basis for investigations of other problems related to the testing of polymorphism, and more generally, problems related to the testing of object-oriented software.

```
class A { public void m() {..} }
class B extends A { public void m() {..} }
class C extends A {..}
A a;
.....
ci: a.m(); // a may refer to instances of A, B, or C
           // RC(ci) = {A,B,C}  TM(ci) = {A.m,B.m}
```

Figure 1. ***RC*** **and** ***TM*** **coverage criteria.**

To illustrate the two criteria, consider the Java classes in Figure 1. For the purpose of this example, suppose that reference variable `a` may refer to instances of classes `A`, `B`, or `C`. The *RC* criterion requires testing of call site `a.m()` with each of the three possible classes of the receiver object. Similarly, the *TM* criterion requires testing that invokes each of the two possible target methods (i.e., both `A.m` and the overriding `B.m`). Clearly, *RC* subsumes *TM*.

The input of the tool contains a set *Cls* of classes that will be tested, as well as a set *Int* of methods and fields from classes in *Cls*. These methods and fields are listed by the tool user and they define the interface to the particular functionality that is currently being tested. In general, *Int* could contain a small subset of all fields and methods from *Cls*; this corresponds to the case when the user is interested in testing only a specific subset of the functionality provided by the classes from *Cls*.

A *test suite for Int* is any arbitrary Java class that tests *Int* (i.e., calls methods from *Int* and reads/writes fields from *Int*) and does not access any methods/fields from *Cls* that are not in *Int*. We denote by $AllSuites(Int)$ the set of all possible test suites for *Int*; clearly, this set is infinite. We assume that *Cls* is closed with respect to *Int*: for any arbitrary suite $S \in AllSuites(Int)$, any class that could be referenced during the execution of S is included in *Cls*. In other words, we consider test suites that only test interactions among classes from the given set *Cls*. In general, classes from *Cls* could potentially interact with unknown classes from outside of *Cls* (e.g., with unknown future subclasses of $C \in Cls$). However, at the time the testing is performed, these unknown classes are not available and interactions with them cannot be exercised; therefore, we do not consider test suites whose execution involves such unknown classes.[2]

In addition to *Cls* and *Int*, the tool takes as input one particular test suite $T \in AllSuites(Int)$. As output, the tool reports the coverage achieved by T with respect to the *RC* and *TM* criteria.

[2]If the tester has created stub classes to simulate unknown external classes during testing, the stubs should be included in *Cls*.

```
package station;
public abstract class Link{
   public abstract void
       transmit(String message); }
class NormalLink extends Link { ...  }
class PriorityLink extends Link { ...  }
class SecureLink extends Link { ...  }
class LoggingLink extends Link { ...  }

public class Station {
   private Link link = new NormalLink();
   private int msg_id = 0;
   public void sendMessage(String m) {
  c1: link.transmit(msg_id++ + " " + m);
      if (msg_id==10)
         link = new PriorityLink(); }
   public void report(Link l)
      { c2: l.transmit("id = " + msg_id);} }

public class Factory {
   private boolean secure = false;
   public Link getLink() {
      if (secure) return new SecureLink();
      else        return new NormalLink(); }
   public void makeSecure()
         { secure = true; } }
```

Figure 2. Package `station` with two polymorphic call sites c_1 and c_2.

There are four tool components. The *analysis component* processes the classes in *Cls* and computes the requirements according the *RC* and *TM* criteria—i.e., for each call site c, it produces sets $RC(c)$ and $TM(c)$. More precisely, the analysis answers the following question: for each call site, what may be the receiver classes and target methods with respect to all possible $S \in AllSuites(Int)$? In other words, if it is possible to write some test suite that tests *Int* and exercises a call site c with some receiver class X or some target method m, the analysis should include X in $RC(c)$ and m in $TM(c)$. These computed coverage requirements are supplied to the *instrumentation component*, which inserts instrumentation at call sites to record the classes of the receiver objects at runtime (using the reflection mechanism in Java). Instrumentation is only inserted at polymorphic call sites—i.e., sites c for which $RC(c)$ is not a singleton set. The instrumented code is supplied to the *test harness* which automatically runs the given test suite T. The results of the execution are processed by the *reporting component*, which determines the actual coverage achieved at call sites.

Example. Consider package `station` in Figure 2. Class `Station` models a station that connects to the rest of the system using a variety of links. Initially, messages are transmitted using a normal-priority link. After certain number of messages have been processed, the station starts using a high-priority link. In addition, the station may be required to report its current state on some link provided from the outside. External code may use class `Factory` to gain access to normal or secure links.

```
package harness;
public abstract class Suite
   { public abstract void run(); }

package stationtest;
import station.*;
public class StationTests
 extends harness.Suite {
  public void run() {
    Station s = new Station();
    Factory f = new Factory();
    Link l;
    for (int i = 0; i < 10; i++) {
       s.sendMessage("message " + i);
       l = f.getLink();
       s.report(l); } } }
```

Figure 3. Simplified test suite.

Suppose that we are interested in testing the functionality that package `station` provides to non-package client code. In this case *Int* contains methods `Station.sendMessage`, `Station.report`, `Factory.getLink`, `Factory.makeSecure`, and `Link.transmit`, plus the constructors of classes `Station` and `Factory`. Given the package and *Int*, the tool computes sets $RC(c_i)$ and $TM(c_i)$ for the call sites in `Station`. For example, using one of the class analyses presented later, the analysis component may produce sets $RC(c_1) = \{$`NormalLink`, `PriorityLink`$\}$ and $RC(c_2) = \{$`NormalLink`, `SecureLink`$\}$ with the corresponding sets $TM(c_i)$. Given this information, the instrumentation component inserts instrumentation at the two call sites. At run time this instrumentation records the classes of the receiver objects using method `Object.getClass`.

Suppose that the tool is used to evaluate the test suite from package `stationtest` shown in Figure 3. The test harness automatically loads and executes the test suite, and then the reporting component provides the coverage results to the tool user. In this particular case, the test suite achieves 50% *RC* coverage for call site c_1 because the site is never executed with receiver class `PriorityLink`. Similarly, the *RC* coverage for c_2 is 50% because receiver class `SecureLink` is not exercised. Note that the suite achieves 100% statement and branch coverage for class `Station`, but this is not enough to achieve the necessary coverage of the polymorphic calls inside the class. To achieve 100% coverage for c_1 and c_2, we need to add at least one more iteration to the loop in `StationTests`, and we also need to introduce a call `f.makeSecure()`.

3 Fragment Class Analysis

As discussed in Section 1.3, whole-program class analyses cannot be used directly in our coverage tool because they cannot be applied to partial programs. In this context, we need fragment class analysis—that is, analysis that can be used to analyze fragments of programs rather than complete programs.

In this section we describe a general method for constructing fragment class analyses for the purposes of testing of polymorphism in Java. The method allows these fragment analyses to be derived from whole-program class analyses. Our approach can be applied to a large number of existing whole-program class analyses [2, 5, 17, 13, 29, 34, 35, 38, 19, 31, 16, 23]. The fragment analyses constructed with this method can be used in coverage tools to compute the requirements of the *RC* and *TM* coverage criteria.

Our approach is designed to be used with existing (and future) whole-program flow-insensitive class analyses. *Flow-insensitive* class analyses do not take into account the flow of control within a method, which makes them less costly than flow-sensitive analyses. The approach is applicable both to context-insensitive and to context-sensitive analyses. *Context-insensitive analyses* do not attempt to distinguish among the different invocation contexts of a method. This category includes Rapid Type Analysis (RTA) by Bacon and Sweeney [5], the XTA/MTA/FTA/CTA family of analyses by Tip and Palsberg [38], Declared Type Analysis and Variable Type Analysis by Sundaresan et al. [35], the p-bounded and p-bounded-linear-edge families of class analyses due to DeFouw et al. [13, 16], 0-CFA [33, 16], 0-1-CFA [17], Steensgaard-style points-to analyses [29, 19], and Andersen-style points-to analyses [34, 19, 31]. Our approach can be applied to all of these context-insensitive whole-program class analyses.

Context-sensitive analyses attempt to distinguish among different invocation contexts of a method. As a result, such analyses are potentially more precise and more expensive than context-insensitive analyses. In *parameter-based* context-sensitive class analyses, calling context is modeled by using some abstraction of the values of the actual parameters at a call site. *Call-chain-based* context-sensitive class analyses represent calling context using a vector of k enclosing call sites. Our approach can be applied both to parameter-based analyses (e.g., the Cartesian Product algorithm due to Agesen [2], the Simple Class Set algorithm by Grove et al. [17], and the parameterized object-sensitive analyses by Milanova et al. [23]) and to call-chain-based analyses (e.g., the standard k-CFA analyses [33, 16], as well as the k-1-CFA analyses by Grove et al. [17, 16]).

3.1 Structure of Fragment Class Analysis

Recall that the input to the tool contains a set of classes *Cls*, as well as a set *Int* of methods and fields from *Cls* that define the interface to the particular functionality that is currently being tested. A test suite for *Int* is an arbitrary Java class that calls methods from *Int*, reads/writes fields from *Int*, and does not access any methods/fields from *Cls* that are not in *Int*. $AllSuites(Int)$ is the infinite set of all possible test suites for *Int*.

The tool needs to compute the coverage requirements according to the *RC* and *TM* criteria—that is, for each method call site, to determine what may be the receiver classes and target methods with respect to all $S \in AllSuites(Int)$. More precisely, if it is possible to write some test suite for *Int* that exercises a call site c with some receiver class X or some target method m, X should be included in $RC(c)$ and m should be included in $TM(c)$.

To compute $RC(c)$ and $TM(c)$, the tool needs to use fragment class analysis. We define an entire family of such analyses in the following manner: first, we create *placeholders* that serve as representatives for the unknown code from all possible test suites $S \in AllSuites(Int)$. During the analysis, the placeholders simulate the potential effects of this unknown code. After creating the appropriate placeholders, the fragment analysis adds them to the tested classes, treats the results as a complete program, and analyzes it using some whole-program class analysis. It is important to note that the created placeholders are *not* designed to be executed as an actual test suite; they are only used for the purposes of the fragment class analysis.

3.2 Placeholders

In our approach we create a placeholder `main` method that contains a variety of placeholder statements, as shown in Figure 4. For each class $X \in Cls$, there is a placeholder variable *ph_X* that serves as a representative for all unknown external reference variables of type X (i.e., all such variables that may occur in some test suite). Different placeholder statements represent different kinds of statements that could occur in the unknown code from some test suite. For example, `ph_X = new X()` represents the fact that the unknown code may create instances of `X` and assign them to reference variables of type `X`. There are also placeholder statements that represent the effect of accessing fields and methods from *Int*. Finally, the last two categories of placeholder statements represent the possible effects of assigning variables of one type to variables of another type (including the effects of possible casting). Note that since we are targeting flow-insensitive analyses, the ordering of placeholder statements is irrelevant. For brevity, Figure 4 does not show the placeholder statements for non-default

```
main() {
  // placeholder variable ph_X for every class X ∈ Cls
  X ph_X;
  // for every class X whose constructor is in Int
  ph_X = new X();
  // for every field f ∈ Int declared in class X with type Y
  ph_Y = ph_X.f; ph_X.f = ph_Y;
  // for every method m ∈ Int declared in class X
  // with signature W m(Y,..,Z)
  ph_W = ph_X.m(ph_Y,..,ph_Z);
  // for every subclass Y of class X
  ph_X = ph_Y; ph_Y = (Y)ph_X;
}
```

Figure 4. Placeholder main method and placeholder statements.

constructors, static methods and fields, etc. The actual implementation of fragment class analyses used in our experiments handles the entire Java language.

Example. Consider again package `station` in Figure 2. Suppose that we are interested in testing the functionality that `station` provides to non-package client code. In this case the interface *Int* contains methods `Station.sendMessage`, `Station.report`, `Factory.getLink`, `Factory.makeSecure`, and `Link.transmit` (plus the constructors of `Station` and `Factory`). Given the package and *Int*, the fragment analysis creates the placeholders shown in Figure 5. Placeholder `main` is then added to `station`, and the result can be analyzed using some whole-program class analysis. In Section 3.4 we present examples of the solutions computed by two such whole-program analyses.

3.3 Analysis Correctness

A fragment class analysis is *correct* if and only if the following property holds: if there exists a test suite $S \in AllSuites(Int)$ whose execution exercises a call site c with some receiver class X, the analysis should report that X is a possible receiver class for c. This implies correctness both with respect to the *RC* criterion and the weaker *TM* criterion. We have proven that this property holds for any fragment analysis that is derived from one of the whole-program flow-insensitive analyses listed in the beginning of Section 3 [2, 5, 17, 13, 29, 34, 35, 38, 19, 31, 16, 23]. This result enables the use of a large body of existing work on whole-program class analysis for the purposes of testing of polymorphism.

The proof of this claim is based on a general framework for whole-program class analysis defined by Grove et al. [17, 16]. We have proven the correctness property for two particular precise context-sensitive instantiations of this framework (one parameter-based and one call-chain-based).

```
import station;
main() {
      Station ph_Station;
      Factory ph_Factory;
      Link ph_Link;
      String ph_String;
      ph_Station = new Station();
      ph_Factory = new Factory();
      ph_String = new String();
      ph_Station.sendMessage(ph_String);
      ph_Station.report(ph_Link);
      ph_Link = ph_Factory.getLink();
      ph_Factory.makeSecure();
      ph_Link.transmit(ph_String);
}
```

Figure 5. Placeholders for package `station`.

This result implies correctness for *any framework instance* that is less precise than one of these two specific precise instances. In particular, this guarantees the correctness of any fragment analysis that is based on one of the existing whole-program analyses listed above. Furthermore, correctness is also guaranteed with respect to a large class of future whole-program analyses that may be developed by instantiating the framework. For brevity, we omit further discussion of these claims; more details are available in [30].

3.4 Analysis Precision

The approach presented above allows us to construct fragment class analyses from a large number of existing (and future) whole-program class analyses. The quality of the information produced by the fragment analyses depends on the underlying whole-program analysis.

Consider package `station` in Figure 2. If we simply examine the class hierarchy to determine the possible receiver objects at call sites, we would have to conclude that $RC(c_i)$ contains all four subclasses of `Link`, which is too conservative and will result in infeasible testing requirements. In fact, the tool will never report that more than 50% coverage has been achieved for each of the two call sites in `Station`, even if in reality the achieved coverage is 100%.

Now suppose that we add the placeholders from Figure 5 and we run Rapid Type Analysis (RTA) [5]. RTA is a popular whole-program class analysis that performs class analysis and call graph construction in parallel. It maintains a worklist of methods reachable from `main`, and a set of classes instantiated in reachable methods. In the final solution, the set of classes for a variable `v` is the set of all instantiated subclasses of the declared type of `v`. In this example, RTA determines that class `Factory` is instantiated in `main`. This implies that call site `ph_Factory.getLink()` may be executed with an in-

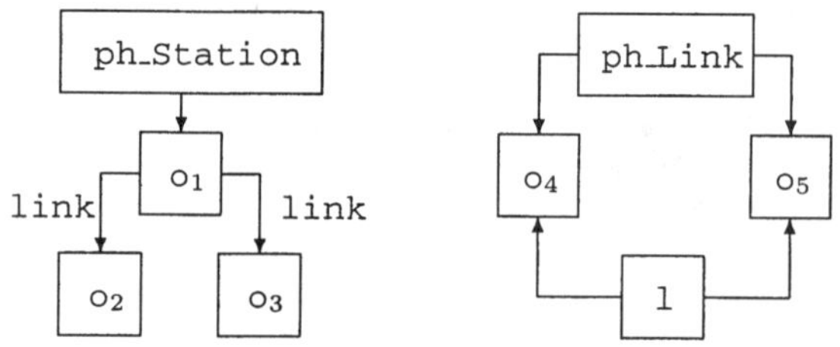

o_1: `new Station()` in `main`

o_2: `new NormalLink()` in `Station`

o_3: `new PriorityLink()` in `Station`

o_4: `new SecureLink()` in `Factory`

o_5: `new NormalLink()` in `Factory`

Figure 6. Some points-to edges computed by Andersen's analysis.

stance of `Factory`, which means that method `getLink` is reachable from `main`. While processing the body of `getLink`, the analysis determines that `NormalLink` and `SecureLink` are instantiated. Similarly, because `Station` is instantiated in `main`, `sendMessage` is determined to be reachable, which implies that `PriorityLink` may also be instantiated. At the end, RTA determines that the only instantiated subclasses of `Link` are `NormalLink`, `PriorityLink`, and `SecureLink`, and therefore $RC(c_i)$ contains only these three classes. Unlike analysis of the class hierarchy, RTA is capable of filtering out the infeasible receiver class `LoggingLink`. Still, some imprecision remains because infeasible class `SecureLink` is reported for c_1 and infeasible class `PriorityLink` is reported for c_2.

As another example, suppose that the fragment analysis uses Andersen's whole-program points-to analysis for Java [34, 19, 31]. This analysis constructs a *points-to graph* in which the nodes represent reference variables and objects, and the edges represent points-to relationships between the nodes. Figure 6 shows some of the edges in the points-to graph computed for our example. Each name o_i represent the run-time objects allocated by a particular `new` expression. (Full description of the analysis and the computed points-to solution is beyond the scope of this paper.) The points-to graph shows that field `link` may only refer to instances of `NormalLink` and `PriorityLink`, and therefore these two classes are included in $RC(c_1)$. Similarly, the points-to graph shows that $RC(c_2)$ contains `NormalLink` and `SecureLink`. Table 1 summarizes the solutions computed by the different analyses. The last row shows which receiver classes are actually feasible—i.e., which classes can be exercised by some test suite $S \in AllSuites(Int)$.

Any class analysis could potentially compute infeasible classes. In this particular case, every receiver class reported by Andersen's analysis is feasible, but in general this need

	Normal		Priority		Secure		Logging	
	c_1	c_2	c_1	c_2	c_1	c_2	c_1	c_2
Hierarchy	•	•	•	•	•	•	•	•
RTA	•	•	•	•	•	•		
Andersen	•	•	•			•		
Feasible	•	•	•			•		

Table 1. Sets $RC(c_1)$ and $RC(c_2)$ computed by the fragment class analyses.

not be true. As discussed in Section 1.4, only analyses that report few (if any) infeasible classes should be used in coverage tools. Otherwise, the coverage metrics become hard to interpret, and tool users may waste time and effort trying to satisfy infeasible testing requirements. Thus, in order to construct high-quality coverage tools for testing of polymorphism, it is necessary to have information about the imprecision of different analyses (i.e., how many infeasible classes they report). However, such measurements of imprecision are not available in previous work on class analysis. One of the major goals of our work was to obtain these measurements for several different class analyses. These results are presented in the next section.

4 Empirical Results

For our experimental evaluation we used a set of Java packages including the standard packages `java.text` and `java.util.zip`, as well as package `gnu.math` (from `www.gnu.org/software/kawa`) and package `com.lowagie.text` from the `iText` library for creating PDF files (`www.lowagie.com`). We then defined and performed several *testing tasks*. The goal of each task was to write a test suite that exercised some particular functionality provided by these packages. For example, one task exercised the functionality related to identifying boundaries in text (i.e., word boundaries, line boundaries, etc.), as provided by a set of classes from `java.text`. As another example, a task was designed to exercise the functionality from `java.util.zip` related to ZIP files. The first three columns in Table 2 briefly describe the testing tasks and the functionality they exercise.

For each task, we determined the set *Int* of interface methods and fields for the tested functionality, as well as the set of classes containing the code which implements the functionality. (This was straightforward to do by examining the documentation and the source code). In these classes, we considered all call sites that had more than one possible receiver class according to the class hierarchy. Let *PolySites* denote the set of all such call sites. Table 2 shows the number of implementing classes for each task and the number of call sites in *PolySites*.

Task	Package	Functionality	#Classes	#PolySites
task1	`java.text`	boundaries in text	12	12
task2	`java.text`	formatting of numbers/dates	13	79
task3	`java.text`	text collation	12	2
task4	`java.util.zip`	ZIP files	8	5
task5	`java.util.zip`	ZIP output streams	8	18
task6	`gnu.math`	complex numbers	8	194
task7	`com.lowagie.text`	paragraphs in PDF docs	24	199
task8	`com.lowagie.text`	lists in PDF docs	24	169

Table 2. Description of testing tasks.

For each task we wrote a test suite that exercised the tested functionality and covered all possible receiver classes for each call site from *PolySites*. Substantial effort was made to ensure that the test suites did in fact achieve *the highest possible coverage*. For each task, two of the authors (working independently of each other) thoroughly examined the code and wrote tests that exercised each possible receiver class. For each call site, the sets of exercised receiver classes obtained by the two people were carefully compared to ensure that there were no differences. As a result of this effort, for each task we had a test suite that exercised all possible receiver classes and target methods for each call site in *PolySites*.

Once we had test suites that achieved the highest possible coverage, we measured the coverage statistics reported by the tool for these suites. These statistics were based on the output of the fragment class analysis used by the tool: the analysis computed a set of possible classes/methods for each $c \in PolySites$, and the tool reported what percentage of these classes/methods was actually exercised by the test suite. In general, this reported coverage may be less than 100% because the analysis produces *RC* and *TM* requirements that are overestimates of the coverage that is actually possible—that is, the analysis may report infeasible receiver classes and infeasible target methods. Clearly, the goal of tool designers should be to use a class analysis that produces few infeasible classes/methods. As a precision metric we used the coverage that was reported by the tool for our test suites; of course, these suites in reality exercised all possible classes and methods. The better the precision of the analysis, the higher the coverage that would be reported by the tool for these suites. Ideally, the analysis would compute only feasible classes and methods, and the tool would report 100% coverage.

4.1 Fragment Class Analyses

For our experiments we evaluated three fragment class analyses. All three analyses were designed using the general approach presented in Section 3: we first created the placeholders from Figure 4, and then we ran the solution engine of a whole-program class analysis.

The first fragment class analysis (denoted by RTA_f) was derived from Rapid Type Analysis (RTA) [5]. As discussed in Section 3.4, RTA is a whole-program class analysis that computes an overestimate of the set of classes that are instantiated in methods that are reachable from `main`. This analysis belongs at the lower end of the cost/precision spectrum of class analysis.

The second fragment class analysis (denoted by AND_f) was derived from a whole-program points-to analysis for Java [31] which is based on Andersen's points-to analysis for C [4]. This whole-program analysis represents a point at the high end of the cost/precision spectrum for flow- and context-insensitive class analysis. (An example illustrating this analysis is presented in Section 3.4.)

The third fragment class analysis (denoted by 0-CFA_f) is derived from a variation of the whole-program points-to analysis from [31]. In this variation, the analysis creates a single object name for all object allocation sites for a given class—i.e., instead of having a separate object name o_i for each `new` expression as in [31], there is a single object name o_C for all expressions "`new C`". This analysis is essentially equivalent to the 0-CFA class analysis [33, 13, 16].[3]

4.2 Analysis Precision

Inside our coverage tool we used the above fragment class analyses to compute the *RC* and *TM* coverage requirements. We then ran our test suites (which in reality exercise all possible classes and methods at polymorphic call sites), and we computed the achieved coverage with respect to *RC-RTA*$_f$, *TM-RTA*$_f$, etc. More precisely, for each analysis, we computed the sum S_1 of the number of possible receiver classes over all sites in *PolySites* as determined by the analysis, as well as the sum S_2 of the number of actually observed receiver classes at these sites. The tool reported the ratio $C_{RC} = S_2/S_1$ as a coverage metric for the *RC* criterion. A similar ratio C_{TM} was computed for the

[3] The only difference is that our analysis distinguishes among occurrences of the same instance field in different subclasses that inherit that field, while 0-CFA does not make this distinction.

Task	Hierarchy		RTA_f		0-CFA_f		AND_f	
	C_{RC}	C_{TM}	C_{RC}	C_{TM}	C_{RC}	C_{TM}	C_{RC}	C_{TM}
task1	100%	100%	100%	100%	100%	100%	100%	100%
task2	67%	63%	67%	63%	76%	72%	76%	72%
task3	50%	100%	50%	100%	100%	100%	100%	100%
task4	31%	63%	45%	71%	100%	100%	100%	100%
task5	18%	21%	88%	92%	100%	100%	100%	100%
task6	76%	85%	76%	85%	97%	98%	98%	98%
task7	10%	15%	32%	48%	82%	93%	87%	93%
task8	5%	9%	18%	29%	62%	62%	62%	62%

Table 3. Reported coverage. More precise analyses result in higher reported coverage.

TM criterion. The results from these experiments are shown in Table 3. The column labeled "Hierarchy" represents the coverage with respect to the *RC* and *TM* criteria that were computed by just examining the class hierarchy. Class analyses that are more precise result in higher reported coverage percentages. In the best case, the analyses introduce no imprecision (i.e., they do not report infeasible receiver classes), and the reported coverage is 100%.

There are two important conclusions from these results. First, when using the class hierarchy or RTA_f to compute the coverage requirements, there is often a significant number of infeasible receiver classes and target methods. Thus, even for test suites that in reality achieve high coverage, the tool may report low coverage statistics. This situation is clearly unacceptable, and there is a need to use more precise analyses. Second, 0-CFA_f and AND_f perform very well, and in fact in half of the cases they achieve prefect precision. This indicates that these analyses are good candidates for inclusion in realistic coverage tools for testing of polymorphism. To the best of our knowledge, these are the first available empirical results that evaluate the absolute precision of class analysis (i.e., what portion of the analysis solution is infeasible). We believe that such measurements provide essential insights for the designers of coverage tools for testing of polymorphism.

4.3 Analysis Cost

As part of our experiments, we also measured the cost of computing the coverage requirements. All measurements were performed on a 360MHz Sun Ultra-60 machine with 512MB memory. The reported times are the median values out of three runs. Using the class hierarchy or RTA_f had negligible cost (less than 5 seconds for each task). The cost of performing 0-CFA_f and AND_f is shown in Table 4. This cost includes the time to analyze all methods that are directly or transitively reachable from the interface methods, both in classes that implement the tested functionality and in their server classes. The number of these analyzed methods is shown in the last column of Table 4. (The numbers are for AND_f; for 0-CFA_f, they are essentially the same). Clearly, the two analyses have practical cost, which makes them realistic candidates for use in coverage tools. These results are consistent with similar experiments from [31].

Task	0-CFA_f (sec)	AND_f (sec)	#Methods
task1	4.7	8.6	325
task2	12.8	25.1	752
task3	2.9	5.3	282
task4	5.3	6.4	401
task5	3.6	4.3	280
task6	12.2	35.8	386
task7	13.8	18.1	833
task8	15.4	20.4	810

Table 4. Analysis running times.

5 Related Work

Various authors have recognized the need to test polymorphic relationships by exercising all possible polymorphic bindings [37, 22, 21, 25, 10, 7, 3]. An implicit assumption in this previous work is that the bindings will be determined by examining the class hierarchy—for example, that *RC* coverage of `x.m()` will require covering all subclasses of the declared type of `x`. One key point of our work is that this approach could be overly conservative, and as a result coverage tools may introduce infeasible coverage requirements. As our results indicate, it is essential to use more precise methods for computing the possible bindings. Fortunately, there exists a large body of work on class analysis that can be used to produce more precise coverage requirements. Our work is the first investigation of the use of class analysis for the purposes of testing of polymorphism.

One key problem is that class analyses are typically designed as whole-program analyses, and therefore cannot be used directly for testing of partial programs. Some whole-program class analyses have been adapted to analyze program fragments rather than whole programs. Chatterjee and Ryder [8] present a flow- and context-sensitive points-to analysis for library modules in object-oriented software. The analysis is an adaptation of an earlier whole-program analysis [9]. Sweeney and Tip [36] describe analyses and optimizations for the removal of unused functionality in Java modules. Their work presents a method for performing RTA on program fragments. The approaches from [8] and [36] can be used to compute coverage requirements in tools for testing of polymorphism in partial programs. However, our technique for constructing fragment class analyses (presented in Section 3) is more general and can be applied to a large number of existing whole-program analyses [2, 5, 17, 13, 29, 34, 35, 38, 19, 31, 16, 23]. Furthermore, we present empirical results that evaluate the absolute precision of our fragment analyses and confirm their effectiveness.

Harrold and Rothermel [18] present a method for performing def-use analysis of a given class for the purposes of dataflow-based unit testing in object-oriented languages. Their approach constructs a placeholder driver that represents all possible sequences of method invocations initiated by client code; however, the driver does not take into account the effects of aliasing, polymorphism, and dynamic binding. The placeholder `main` method presented in Section 3 is essentially a placeholder driver that models these features. Thus, in addition to testing of polymorphism, our approach can also be used in tools for dataflow-based testing of individual classes and collections of classes.

We believe that analysis precision is a critical issue for the use of class analysis (or any static analysis) in coverage tools. In previous work, analysis precision is typically evaluated in three ways. One approach is to compare the solutions computed by two or more analyses, in order to determine the relative precision of these analyses—i.e., how analysis X compares with analysis Y. Another approach is to compare the analysis results with the behavior of the program during one particular profile run (e.g., [24, 20]). A third approach is to evaluate the effect of the analysis on a particular client application—for example, the impact on performance due to compiler optimizations. However, in the context of software engineering tools, the key issue is *absolute precision*: how close is the analysis solution to the set of all run-time relationships that are actually possible? Imprecision may lead to significant waste of human time and effort, which ultimately may result in tool rejection. This observation applies not only to coverage tools, but also to other software engineering tools (e.g., for program understanding and verification). Previous work does not contain information about the absolute precision of class analysis, which in our view is a major problem. The precision measurements in Section 4 provide valuable insights for the designers of tools for testing of polymorphism, as well as for other tools that use class analysis.

6 Conclusions and Future Work

In order to construct high-quality coverage tools for testing of polymorphism, it is necessary to use class analysis to compute the coverage requirements. We have developed a general approach that allows tool designers to adapt a wide variety of existing and future whole-program class analyses to be used for testing of partial programs. We also present the first empirical evaluation of the absolute precision of several analyses. Our results lead to two conclusions. First, analysis imprecision can be a serious problem for simpler analyses, and it should be a primary concern for tool designers. Second, more advanced analyses (such as 0-CFA and Andersen's analysis) are capable of achieving high absolute precision, which makes them good candidates for inclusion in coverage tools for testing of polymorphism.

In our future work we would like to evaluate the absolute precision of analyses that are even more precise than 0-CFA and Andersen's analysis. To choose the appropriate analyses, we plan to examine the sources of analysis imprecision. This investigation may suggest the use of existing analyses, or may guide the design of new analysis techniques that target these sources of imprecision. We also plan to obtain additional datapoints for our current analyses, and to evaluate more precise analyses using this extended dataset.

It would be interesting to generalize our approach to flow-sensitive class analyses. We do not anticipate any conceptual difficulties in addressing this problem. Intuitively, it will be necessary to change the structure of our placeholder `main` method to encode all possible sequences of placeholder statements by placing the statements in a switch statement surrounded by a loop.

We also plan to investigate other applications for which fragment class analysis is needed: for example, program understanding and dataflow-based testing of partial Java programs. Such applications require high analysis precision, and it will be necessary to obtain measurements of absolute precision similar to the ones presented in this paper.

Acknowledgments. We would like to thank the ICSE reviewers for their valuable comments, and Matthew Arnold for helping improve an earlier version of the paper. This research was supported by NSF grant CCR-9900988.

References

[1] O. Agesen. Constraint-based type inference and parametric polymorphism. In *Static Analysis Symposium*, LNCS 864, pages 78–100, 1994.

[2] O. Agesen. The cartesian product algorithm. In *European Conference on Object-oriented Programming*, LNCS 952, pages 2–26, 1995.

[3] R. Alexander and J. Offutt. Criteria for testing polymorphic relationships. In *International Symposium on Software Reliability Engineering*, pages 15–23, 2000.

[4] L. Andersen. *Program Analysis and Specialization for the C Programming Language*. PhD thesis, DIKU, University of Copenhagen, 1994.

[5] D. Bacon and P. Sweeney. Fast static analysis of C++ virtual function calls. In *Conference on Object-Oriented Programming Systems, Languages, and Applications*, pages 324–341, 1996.

[6] R. Binder. Testing object-oriented software: a survey. *Journal of Software Testing, Verification and Reliability*, 6:125–252, Dec. 1996.

[7] R. Binder. *Testing Object-Oriented Systems: Models, Patterns, and Tools*. Addison-Wesley, 1999.

[8] R. Chatterjee and B. G. Ryder. Data-flow-based testing of object-oriented libraries. Technical Report DCS-TR-433, Rutgers University, Apr. 2001.

[9] R. Chatterjee, B. G. Ryder, and W. Landi. Relevant context inference. In *Symposium on Principles of Programming Languages*, pages 133–146, 1999.

[10] M. H. Chen and M. H. Kao. Testing object-oriented programs—an integrated approach. In *International Symposium on Software Reliability Engineering*, pages 73–83, 1999.

[11] B. Cox. The need for specification and testing languages. *Journal of Object-Oriented Programming*, 1(2):44–47, June 1988.

[12] J. Dean, D. Grove, and C. Chambers. Optimizations of object-oriented programs using static class hierarchy analysis. In *European Conference on Object-oriented Programming*, pages 77–101, 1995.

[13] G. DeFouw, D. Grove, and C. Chambers. Fast interprocedural class analysis. In *Symposium on Principles of Programming Languages*, pages 222–236, 1998.

[14] A. Diwan, J. B. Moss, and K. McKinley. Simple and effective analysis of statically-typed object-oriented programs. In *Conference on Object-Oriented Programming Systems, Languages, and Applications*, pages 292–305, 1996.

[15] M. Fowler. *Refactoring: Improving the Design of Existing Code*. Addison-Wesley, 1999.

[16] D. Grove and C. Chambers. A framework for call graph construction algorithms. *ACM Transactions on Programming Languages and Systems*, 23(6):685–746, Nov. 2001.

[17] D. Grove, G. DeFouw, J. Dean, and C. Chambers. Call graph construction in object-oriented languages. In *Conference on Object-Oriented Programming Systems, Languages, and Applications*, pages 108–124, 1997.

[18] M. J. Harrold and G. Rothermel. Performing data flow testing on classes. *Symposium on the Foundations of Software Engineering*, pages 154–163, 1994.

[19] D. Liang, M. Pennings, and M. J. Harrold. Extending and evaluating flow-insensitive and context-insensitive points-to analyses for Java. In *Workshop on Program Analysis for Software Tools and Engineering*, pages 73–79, 2001.

[20] D. Liang, M. Pennings, and M. J. Harrold. Evaluating the precision of static reference analysis using profiling. In *International Symposium on Software Testing and Analysis*, pages 22–32, 2002.

[21] T. McCabe, L. Dreyer, A. Dunn, and A. Watson. Testing an object-oriented application. *Journal of the Quality Assurance Institute*, 8(4):21–27, Oct. 1994.

[22] R. McDaniel and J. McGregor. Testing the polymorphic interactions between classes. Technical Report 94-103, Clemson University, Mar. 1994.

[23] A. Milanova, A. Rountev, and B. G. Ryder. Parameterized object sensitivity for points-to and side-effect analyses for Java. In *International Symposium on Software Testing and Analysis*, pages 1–11, 2002.

[24] M. Mock, M. Das, C. Chambers, and S. Eggers. Dynamic points-to sets. In *Workshop on Program Analysis for Software Tools and Engineering*, pages 66–72, 2001.

[25] J. Overbeck. *Integration Testing for Object-Oriented Software*. PhD thesis, Vienna University of Technology, 1994.

[26] J. Palsberg and M. Schwartzbach. Object-oriented type inference. In *Conference on Object-Oriented Programming Systems, Languages, and Applications*, pages 146–161, 1991.

[27] D. Perry and G. Kaiser. Adequate testing and object-oriented programming. *Journal of Object-Oriented Programming*, 2(5):13–19, Jan. 1990.

[28] J. Plevyak and A. Chien. Precise concrete type inference for object-oriented languages. In *Conference on Object-Oriented Programming Systems, Languages, and Applications*, pages 324–340, 1994.

[29] C. Razafimahefa. A study of side-effect analyses for Java. Master's thesis, McGill University, Dec. 1999.

[30] A. Rountev. *Dataflow Analysis of Software Fragments*. PhD thesis, Rutgers University, Aug. 2002.

[31] A. Rountev, A. Milanova, and B. G. Ryder. Points-to analysis for Java using annotated constraints. In *Conference on Object-Oriented Programming Systems, Languages, and Applications*, pages 43–55, Oct. 2001.

[32] E. Ruf. Effective synchronization removal for Java. In *Conference on Programming Language Design and Implementation*, pages 208–218, 2000.

[33] O. Shivers. *Control-Flow Analysis of Higher-Order Languages*. PhD thesis, Carnegie Mellon University, 1991.

[34] M. Streckenbach and G. Snelting. Points-to for Java: A general framework and an empirical comparison. Technical report, U. Passau, Sept. 2000.

[35] V. Sundaresan, L. Hendren, C. Razafimahefa, R. Vallee-Rai, P. Lam, E. Gagnon, and C. Godin. Practical virtual method call resolution for Java. In *Conference on Object-Oriented Programming Systems, Languages, and Applications*, pages 264–280, 2000.

[36] P. Sweeney and F. Tip. Extracting library-based object-oriented applications. In *Symposium on the Foundations of Software Engineering*, pages 98–107, 2000.

[37] N. N. Thuy. Testability and unit tests in large object-oriented software. In *Proc. 5th International Software Quality Week*. Software Research Institute, 1992.

[38] F. Tip and J. Palsberg. Scalable propagation-based call graph construction algorithms. In *Conference on Object-Oriented Programming Systems, Languages, and Applications*, pages 281–293, 2000.

A Framework for Component Deployment Testing

Antonia Bertolino, Andrea Polini
Istituto di Scienza e Tecnologie dell'Informazione - "Alessandro Faedo"
Area della Ricerca del CNR di Pisa, Italy
{bertolino, a.polini}@iei.pi.cnr.it

Abstract

Component-based development is the emerging paradigm in software production, though several challenges still slow down its full taking up. In particular, the "component trust problem" refers to how adequate guarantees and documentation about a component's behaviour can be transferred from the component developer to its potential users. The capability to test a component when deployed within the target application environment can help establish the compliance of a candidate component to the customer's expectations and certainly contributes to "increase trust". To this purpose, we propose the CDT framework for Component Deployment Testing. CDT provides the customer with both a technique to early specify a deployment test suite and an environment for running and reusing the specified tests on any component implementation. The framework can also be used to deliver the component developer's test suite and to later re-execute it. The central feature of CDT is the complete decoupling between the specification of the tests and the component implementation.

1. Introduction

Component Based (CB) development is the emerging paradigm in Software Engineering. It is receiving lot of interest from both academy and industry, as testified by the spreading of devoted events (e.g., [27], [28]) and journal articles (e.g., [29], [30]), and by the launch on the market of component-oriented technological products and platforms (e.g., CCM [31], EJB [32], COM+/.Net [33]).

The captivating feature of CB development is the promise of drastically reducing the high costs of software production. A CB system is built by the assembly of already existing components, thus making true the long lasting myth of developing once for repeated deployment. Despite this very idea is older than thirty years [14], its high potential just starts being exploited.

In our opinion the major obstacles to the taking up of the CB paradigm are not technological, but relate to the process [2]. In traditional development, the process is under the control of one organization (at least in principle) and extends over a definite life cycle period. On the contrary, the process for CB software production is non-deterministically distributed across several organizations that do not necessarily coordinate or communicate with each other and the life cycle is correspondingly scattered over separate time periods. In such a distributed process we identify (among several others not of interest here) the figures of the *component developer* (in a wide sense the organization that develops and releases a component), and the *component customer* (the organization that acquires the component to assemble it within a larger system).

A new challenge that arises from the inherently distributed nature of CB production is the so-called "component trust problem", which refers to the difficulty to understand what a component really does. The trust problem is strongly related to the customer capability to validate the adequacy of a candidate component to his/her specific purposes. Obviously this question is especially hard for components built by third parties and for COTS (Component-Off-The-Shelf), which are generally delivered without the source code. However, also in the case of components reused internally to an organization, the difficulties of communication between teams and the lack of a clear documentation can produce to some extent similar effects.

Several approaches have been proposed to address the trust problem. Some [22][23] advocate a component certification strategy, with the establishment of independent certification laboratories that perform extensive testing of the components, and then publish the results. The approach relies on the conjecture that the customer puts more trust on the results provided by an independent agency than on those provided by the developer himself/herself. Moreover, in order to increase the customer confidence, the developer should adopt certified production standards.

Others authors have argued the paucity of valid accompanying information, often reduced to just the component

0-7695-1877-X/03 $17.00 © 2003 IEEE

interfaces, which anyhow provide syntactic information, insufficient for many analysis purposes. Therefore, they [18] [20] suggest approaches to augment the components with additional information (or metadata) aimed at increasing the customer understanding and analysis capability of the component behaviour. A related approach is to automatically extract models of the interfaces of a class, e.g., as Finite State Machines [26]; this information also goes in the direction of increasing the customer understanding of a component usage and scope. In the same approach, the usage of a component is assessed to identify, for instance, wrong call sequences of the component methods.

To deal with the trust problem, a focussed, coordinated initiative [16], has been launched, acknowledging that the solution cannot be univocal, instead a mix of formal and informal approaches should be applied, including formal validation, Design-by-Contract, testing techniques and others.

In this paper we focus on CB testing. As for the other development phases, the testing stage as well needs a rethinking to address the peculiar characteristics of CB development [2]. An important requirement, in our opinion, is that the customer, on the basis of what he/she expects from a searched component, and with reference to the system specification/architecture, develops a test suite and can then routinely (re)execute these tests -without too much effort- to evaluate the potential candidate components.

In [19], Rosenblum outlines a new conceptual basis for CB software testing, introducing the complementary notions of *C-adequate-for-P* and of *C-adequate-on-M* for adequate unit testing of a component and adequate integration testing of a CB system, respectively (where *C* is a criterion, *P* is a program and *M* is a component). A direct application of this model is in the formalization of the problem of adequate testing (with reference to a particular criterion) of a component released by a developer and deployed by one or more customers.

As also recognized by Weyuker [25], the tests established and run by the developer lose much of their power in the realm of the assembled system. In fact, the developer cannot account for all the possible deployment environments. On the other hand, it is illusory to hope that reuse diminishes the need for testing [25][5].

As a consequence of these considerations, a good practice could be to provide the component customer with the test cases that the component already underwent. This additional information can increase *per se* the customer's trust on the component. Moreover, the documented test cases can also be used by the customer in several manners, for instance, to better understand how to use a component, or, by means of adequate mechanisms, to re-execute them in the target environment. This practice can be particularly effective, since the retesting stage performed by the customers can take benefit by the usage of the actual implementations of the required interfaces, in place of the stubs possibly used by the developer.

In view of all the needs depicted above, we have developed the Component Deployment Testing (CDT) framework. CDT supports the functional testing of a to-be-assembled component with respect to the customer's specifications, which we refer to as *deployment testing*. CDT is both a reference framework for test development and codification and an environment for executing the tests over a selected candidate component. In addition, CDT can also provide a simple means to enclose with a component the developer's test suite, which can then be easily re-executed by the customer. The key idea at the basis of the framework is the *complete decoupling* between what concerns deriving and documenting the test specifications and what concerns the execution of the tests over the implementation of the component.

Technically, to achieve such a separation, the framework requires the capability of retrieving at run-time information on the component, mainly relative to the methods signature. In other words, the component to be tested must enable reflection mechanisms [12], allowing for the component runtime introspection. As known, this is provided by the reflection API of Java [11].

Before going ahead with the description, it is necessary to clarify what we intend by a "component". In fact, the term has not a univocal interpretation in the literature. A clarifying and often reported definition is due to Szyperski [21]: *A software component is a unit of composition with contractually specified interfaces and explicit context dependencies only. A software component can be deployed independently and is subject to composition by third parties.* For the sake of generality, we adopt a more simplified view, identifying a component as in [18] with a system or subsystem developed by one organization, deployed by one or more different organizations, and possibly provided without the source code. According to this definition, we will consider also a class or a set of class as a particular example of a component.

In the next section we expand our speculations on the needs for a revised process for CB development. In Section 3 we present in detail the CDT framework. In Section 4 we discuss the usage of the framework, its benefits and how it could be improved. We further discuss related work in Section 5, and briefly draw the conclusions in Section 6.

2. New process for CB software testing

In this section we briefly review how the software testing process is modified in the context of CB production; we discuss in particular what we mean by "Component Deployment Testing".

Traditionally, the development of complex systems involves three main testing phases. The basic phase is unit testing and concerns a relatively small executable program; for instance, in Object-Oriented systems a unit can consist of a class or a group of logically related classes. A second phase is generally referred to as integration testing. In this phase a system or subsystem obtained from the integration of several (already tested) units is tested with the purpose to evaluate their mutual interfaces and cooperation. Finally, the phase of system testing focuses on the various "ilities", or quality attributes, and on the functionalities that characterise the entire system [5]. These three phases are performed along a defined process, keeping the pace with the proceeding of system construction.

In CB development, the three traditional testing phases have to be reconsidered and extended (see Fig.1). The smallest test unit becomes here the component. **Component testing** is performed by the component developer and is aimed at establishing the proper functioning of the component and at early detecting possible failures. The tests established by the developer can rely not only on a complete documentation and knowledge of the component, but also on the availability of the source code, and thus in general pursue some kind of coverage. However, such testing cannot address the functional correspondence of the component behaviour to the specifications of the system in which it will be later assembled.

The phase of integration testing corresponds to the stage we denote by **deployment testing**, however conceptually the two tasks are very different. Even though devising a new development process for building a system by the assembly of software components is outside the scope of this paper, we can certainly assume as a minimum within such a process the following three phases:

1. a specification phase, in which the features of the required components are identified;
2. a searching phase, in which some candidate components are identified, within or outside the organization;
3. a validation phase, in which the identified components are validated, in particular by deployment testing.

With regard to point 3, we need to figure out a testing methodology that can allow for the effective testing of a component by someone who has not developed it, and within an application context that was completely unknown when the component was developed.

Performed by the component customer, the purpose of deployment testing is thus the validation of the implementation of the components that will constitute the final system. The real components identified at this stage are placed in the specific application environment and integrated with the already present components to form the logic structure of the system. It is worth noting that potential mismatches discovered by the customer during deployment testing are not in general "bugs" in the implementation. Rather they evidence the non conformance between the expected component and the tested one (and hence the need to look for other components).

Also for deployment testing (as usual for integration testing) we can consider to adopt an incremental strategy, allowing for the progressive integration of components into larger subsystems. In the presentation of CDT we will always speak in terms of a single component, however the framework could be identically applied to the deployment testing of a subsystem (we return on this in Section 4.1).

A particular case of deployment testing is when a real component comes equipped with the developer's test suite, and the customer re-executes those tests in his/her environment. These tests guarantee that the "intentions" of the developer are respected in the final environment and their execution generally lead to a more comprehensive evaluation. They can possibly include test cases not relevant for the customer's specific purposes, but that can be however useful to evaluate the behaviour of the component under customer's unexpected entries.

Finally, **system test** does not show major conceptual differences with respect to the traditional process (at this level of the analysis) and is performed by the customer when all the various components are integrated and the entire system is ready to run.

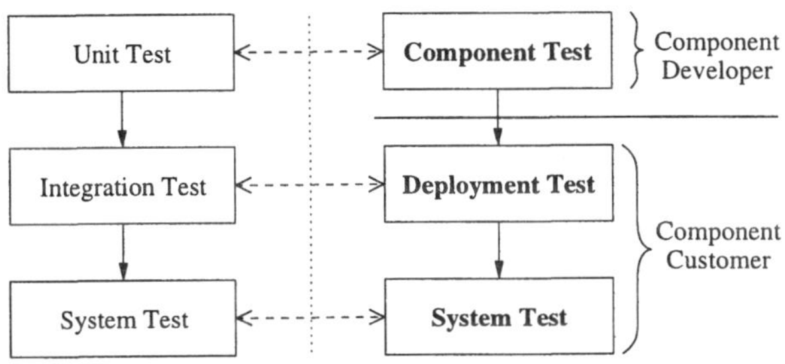

Figure 1. Adapting the test process

3. The CDT framework

In this section we introduce the CDT framework, describing its elements and how it can be used for deployment testing. To help comprehension we provide examples from the simple scenario of a component for managing bank accounts.

In our investigation we suppose that the modelling of a CB system is done by UML and specified following the guidelines expressed in [7] for CB specification (or a similar iterative process) according to which the relevant components are described in term of their provided and required interfaces. In this process we can identify two different levels of components: the *virtual components* that are the di-

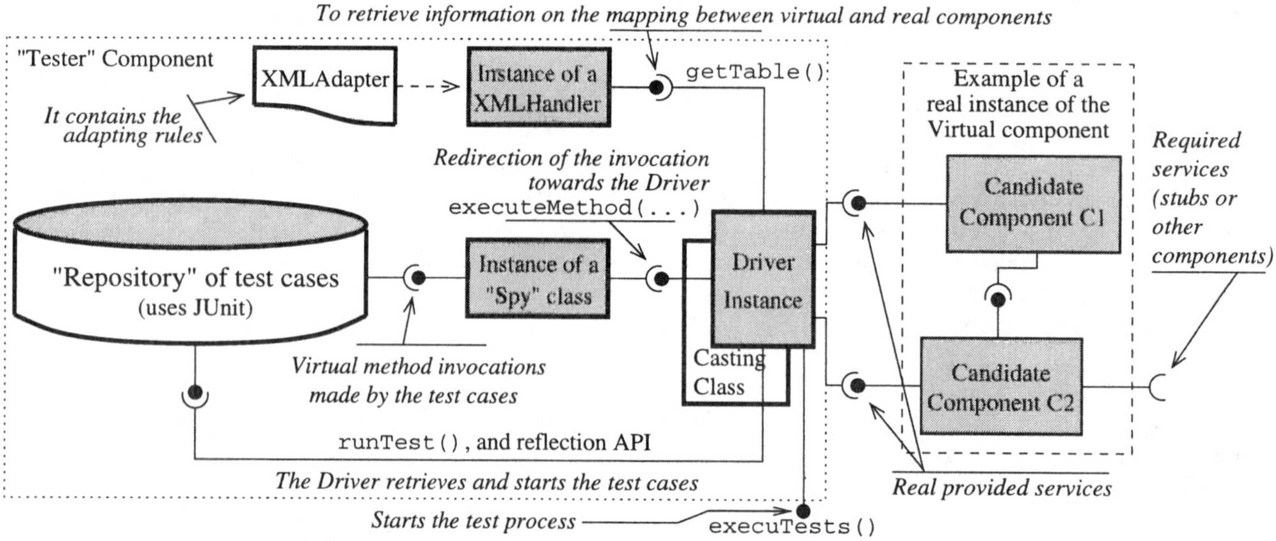

Figure 2. Schema of the framework showing the most important interactions

rect result of the analysis phase, and the *real components*, that will realize the virtual components once assmbled the final system.

3.1. Framework goals

The CDT framework has been designed to suit the needs for component deployment testing, as discussed in Section 2. CDT serves various goals:

- it allows the component customer **to early specify and document the test cases** for a searched component (independently from any possible component implementation);
- it supplies an **environment for the execution** of the specified test cases, once a candidate component is identified;
- it facilitates the **reuse of the specified test cases** for choosing among several candidate components or for substituting an existing one, making possible also the selective reuse of test cases for regression testing purposes;
- as a by-product, it can be used by the component developers **to deliver, together with a component, the test suite** used to test it, thus making easy the re-execution of those tests in the customer's application environment;
- it is a standardised, systematic means to provide a component with **additional behavioural documentation**.

A complete separation of the test derivation and documentation from the implementation of the components was instrumental to achieve these goals. The decoupling is expressly imposed by the same framework architecture, as described below.

3.2. Structure and elements of the framework

The architecture shown in Figure 2 provides an overview of the elements in the CDT framework. For explanation purposes, we can split its elements into three groups:

A. The classes "Spy" and "`TestCase_i`";

B. the XML file "XMLAdapter", and the class "`CastingClass`";

C. the package "`it.cnr.testing`" and the class "`Driver`".

The first group allows for the early codification of the test cases to be later executed on a candidate component. The tests are referred to a virtual component model specified within the "Spy" class. The elements in the second group are used to put in relation the actual component with the customer specifications. The package in the last group drives the testing by opportunely applying the various test cases to the actual component.

Although the three groups are strongly related, different teams are responsible for building and managing them, as we explain in Section 4. Besides, they are built at different stages of development.

3.2.1. The classes "Spy" and "`TestCase_i`". As already highlighted, the main feature of CDT is the decoupling between test cases specification and the actual implementation of a component candidate for assembly. A key role is played here by the classes "Spy". In short, they realize an abstraction of the components, or, in other words, they specify the functionalities expected for the components syntactically expressed by the methods of these classes.

For instance, if we consider a component for the management of bank accounts, without referring to any specific implementation, we can expect for it as a minimum the functionalities expressed by the three methods of the `Spy` class in Figure 3: `deposit`, `withdraw`, and `balance`. In reality, when we look in a repository or on the market for a bank account manager, we will find components much more complex than this, and including multiple classes. Indeed, the correspondence between the "Spy" abstract models and the actual components might result quite complicated; in general, the basic functionalities specified in the "Spy" class might be provided across several objects. We will discuss how we handle this by means of the "XMLAdapter" in the next section.

The implementation of the `Spy` methods does not have to be very elaborate (in Figure 3 only the implementation of the method `deposit` is shown). The methods act as a form of delegation towards the class `Driver` (presented in Section 3.2.3.). In fact, each "Spy" class only constitutes a syntactic reference; at run-time, the `Driver` redirects the virtual method invocations towards the corresponding ones in the real component. The name "Spy" of this kind of class was inspired by this behaviour, in that the role of "Spy" is to provide the `Driver` with the needed information about what a test case does.

After the "Spy" class has been coded, we can develop the deployment test cases taking as a reference the virtual component. Each test case is codified in a class `TestCase_i` that contains the implementation of the method `runTest`. The invocations included in the method `runTest` refer to the methods defined in the corresponding "Spy" class precisely as if it were the component under test. In Figure 4 a simple test case is shown, that invokes the methods of the class `Spy` shown in Figure 3.

We observe that the only external dependence of `Spy` and of `TestCase1` is the package `it.cnr.testing`. The latter is analysed in detail in Section 3.2.3., for the moment it is important to notice that this package is a fixed element of the approach, independent from any specific application context or system. It provides a support tool for test execution, which is developed once and for all. Therefore the classes "Spy" and `TestCase_i` can be built independently from how any candidate real component is implemented.

Finally, as shown in Fig. 2, we also use the well-known framework JUnit [9]. This is a framework developed inside the eXtreme Programming (XP) comunity. Scope of the framework is to give a means to the developer for the easy codification and execution of the test cases concurrently with the development, following the motto "*code a little, test a little, code a little, test a little...*" The framework permits also the simple storing of test cases that can be successively reused. Since we also need to store test cases, we have integrated a part of JUnit in CDT; hence we follow the same rules of JUnit to codify the test cases (see the example in Fig. 4). In this manner we have provided the developed framework with the capability of splitting the test cases in "*target equivalence classes*". This feature is particularly important when we need to modify a virtual component substituting some internal pieces, to avoide to have to re-execute too many tests.

```
package it.cnr.isti.test.bank;
import it.cnr.isti.testing.*;
public class Spy extends InformationSwap {
  /* performs a deposit and returns the
     resulting balance */
  public int deposit(String accNum, int amount) {
    Object[] parameters = new Object[]
                {accNum, new Integer(amount) };
    Object ris = driver.executeMethod(
                "deposit", parameters);
    return ((Integer)ris).intValue();
  }
  /* performs a withdraw and returns the
     resulting balance */
  public int withdraw(String accNum, int amount)
  {...}
  /* returns the account balance */
  public int balance(String accountNumber)
  {...}
}
```

Figure 3. A "Spy" class for a bank account manager

```
package it.cnr.isti.test.bank;
import it.cnr.isti.testing.*;

 /* Test codified following the JUnit schema */
import junit.framework.*;
public class BankTest extends TestCase {
  public BankTest() {}
  public void testCase_A() {
    int init=((Spy)spy).balance("123");
    int afterDeposit=((Spy)spy).deposit("123",500);

     /* Control element as specified by JUnit */
    assertEquals((init+500),afterDeposit);
    int afterWithdraw=((Spy)spy).withdraw("123",
                          init+500);
    assertEquals(0,afterWithdraw);
  }
}
```

Figure 4. A possible test-case

3.2.2. "XMLAdapter" and the classes "`CastingClass`".

As said, a class "Spy" does not represent a real component and its purpose is only to codify the desired functionality for a component, so to permit the early establishment of test cases. In this sense, we can say that the role of the "Spy" class is not

```
<MataHari>
      <testPackage name="it.cnr.isti.test.bank"/>
      <testClass name="BankTest"/>
      <realPackage name="real"/>
      <createObject class="REAL_PACKAGE.RealComp" objectName="bank"/>
      <VirtualMethod name="deposit" parameters="accNum␣amount">
            <execMethod class="TEST_PACKAGE.CastingClass" name="par2Couple" putResultIn="c">
              <parameter value="accNum"/>
              <parameter value="amount"/>
            </execMethod>
            <execMethod object="bank" name="put">
                  <parameter value="c"/>
            </execMethod>
            <execMethod object="bank" name="howMuch" putResultIn="aCouple">
                  <parameter value="accNum"/>
            </execMethod>
            <execMethod class="TEST_PACKAGE.CastingClass" name="Couple2Int" putResultIn="output">
              <parameter value="aCouple"/>
            </execMethod>
      </VirtualMethod>
      <VirtualMethod name="withdraw" parameters="accNum␣amount">
                  . . .
      <VirtualMethod name="balance" parameters="accNum">
                  . . .
      </VirtualMethod>
</MataHari>
```

Figure 5. An excerpt of the "XMLAdapter" file

different from that of an interface. At a certain stage of development, the component modelled by the "Spy" class must be instantiated: at this point it will be necessary to evaluate potential candidate components, using the developed test cases. Although the searching of the candidate components is driven by the same system specification used to build the classes "Spy", we think it reasonable to only focus on the behavioural aspects of the specification. In other words, we search for components that provide the desired functionality, but in this search we neglect possible syntactic differences.

As a result, several differences at various levels can exist between the virtual component (codified in a "Spy" class) and a real instance of it. The purpose of the "XMLAdapter" and of the `CastingClass` is to overcome these differences and to permit anyway the execution of the specified test cases. Clearly this can be done only after a real implementation for the virtual component has been identified. To establish the correspondence between the virtual component and the real instance, a customer can rely on his/her intuition of what the methods of the candidate components likely do. This intuition can be based on the signatures of the methods, and on any additional documentation that accompanies the components. Obviously this process (which is always the most delicate part of a CB development) is subject to misinterpretation (especially if the components are not adequately documented). However, deployment test execution should highlight possible misunderstandings. For instance, in our case study we have analysed the following levels of possible differences:

1. differences in the methods names and signatures:
   a. the methods have different names;
   b. the methods have the same number and types of parameters, but they are declared in different order;
   c. the parameters have different types, but we can make them compatible, through suitable transformations. It can be also necessary to set some default parameters;
2. one method in the "Spy" class corresponds to the execution of more than one method in the real implementation of the component.

Obviously the instances listed above are not mutually exclusive, and for instance it is possible to have different name methods with different signatures. It may be worth notice that the symmetric case to 2 (more methods in the "Spy" class correspond to one method in the real implementation) is not generally relevant. In fact, the "Spy" class is kept simple and typically contains a minimal number of necessary methods. If, say, two methods in the "Spy" class correspond to one method in the real implementation, then either the real implementation is not compatible, or we do not need to invoke the two methods alone, but always together and in the same sequence. If so, then it would be more intuitive to indicate only one method in the specification of the class "Spy".

Item 2 also includes the case in the list enclose also the case in which the real implementation of a virtual component is achieved combining together more candidate real

```
package real;
public class RealComp {
  private int sum;
  public RealComp() { this.sum = 0; }
  public RealComp(int sum) { this.sum = sum; }
  public void put(Couple c) {
    sum = sum + c.getSum();
  }
  public int get(Couple c) {
    int imp = c.getSum();
    if ( (sum-imp) > 0) {
      sum = sum - imp;
    } else {
      System.out.println("Not enough deposit");
    }
    return sum;
  }
  public Couple howMuch(String accNumber) {
    return new Couple(accNumber,sum);
  }
}

package real;
public class Couple {
  int sum; String name;
  public Couple(String name,int sum) {
    this.sum = sum;
    this.name = name;
  }
  public int getSum() { return sum; }
  public String getName() { return name; }
}
```

Figure 6. A real component

```
package it.cnr.isti.test.bank;
import real.*;
public class CastingClass {
  public static int Couple2Int(Couple c) {
     return c.getSum();
  }
  public static Couple par2Couple(String name,
                          Integer amount) {
     return (new Couple(name,amount.intValue()));
  }
}
```

Figure 7. The `CastingClass`

components. In this case the methods executed in a test case could belong to different real components. However we think that a good design made in a well established CB environment generally should lead to a one-to-one correspondence between virtual and real components.

In Figure 5 we have reported an excerpt of the "XMLAdapter" for the candidate component in Figure 6 and the "Spy" class in Figure 3. The file is structured in several sections delimited by specific tags. The first half of the files reports information regarding the elements to be tested and that can mostly be derived automatically. In detail, first we put the specification of the packages containing the test case classes. It can be in fact useful to group the various test cases in more packages, according to suitable criteria, so to permit a separate reuse of groups of tests. Afterwards we specified the names of the packages containing the real components (those to be tested), and then we have specified the specific classes to instantiate within those packages.

The second half of the file is more complex and reports the information on the correspondences among the various methods in the considered "Spy" class and those in the real candidate components. As an example, we have reported the specified correspondence for the method `deposit` (see Fig. 3) with regard to the real component in Figure 6. If we observe the methods in Figure 6, we note how there is no method in this class directly corresponding to the method `deposit` as specified in the relative class "Spy". However (e.g., by further analysing the class interface in the real component or from the accompanying documentation), we suspect that a compatible behaviour can be obtained by the consecutive execution of the methods `put` and `howmuch`. This case illustrates one of the trickiest case of correspondence, where nothing seems to fit at first sight. Moreover the returned type of the method `howMuch` is not the same of that expected in `deposit`, and then, for compatibility purposes, we need to perform a type conversion.

In general, type conversions can be also required for the input parameters. It is possible in principle to perform these conversions in declarative way via XML. However in some cases the conversion can be very sophisticated, disabling this possibility in practice. For this reason we have introduced in CDT the other element of this group, called the `CastingClass`, in which the "casting" between objects is specified via class methods. In Figure 7 the `CastingClass` for the example discussed is shown. It contains two methods that permit the conversion of the basic parameters in the `Spy` class to the type `Couple` in the candidate component and vice versa.

As a final consideration, the drawing up of the "XMLAdapter" is certainly not an easy task. Nevertheless this task can be partially automated and alleviated with the implementation of suitable tools and graphic interfaces.

3.2.3. The package "`it.cnr.testing`" and the class "`Driver`".

The classes contained in this package form the core of the approach. Differently from the elements described so far, that have to be implemented and customized for each new CB system, the elements contained in this package are completely independent from the application context.

There are two main elements in this package, the class `Driver` and the XML parser (named `XMLHandler`). The only duty of the latter is to retrieve the data from the XML file and organize them into suitable data structures. The information so organized can be used by the `Driver` to redirect, at run-time, the invocations made by the test cases to the associated class "Spy", towards the real methods of the selected candidate components. More precisely, in the implementation of the class `Driver` we have used the introspection mechanisms provided by the component model (in our case the reflection API of Java), to identify and invoke at run-time the methods of the candidate implementation as specified in the "XMLAdapter".

The class `Driver` is quite large and for space reasons we cannot report it entirely here, but present its most important features. There are only two public methods in the class `Driver`:

1. `executeTests()`: the invocation of this method starts the deployment test. Hence as first thing the `Driver` retrieves the information reported in the "XMLAdapter" via an instance of the XML parser (the class `XMLHandler` in Fig. 2). Obtained this information the `Driver` sets up an instance of the class "Spy" that specifies the Virtual component under test, and then instantiates the elements of the real implementation. At this point we need to identify the test cases to execute. Hence, the `Driver`, using the provided reflection mechanisms, retrieves, from the packages containing the test cases, the tests to execute, as specified in the "XMLAdapter", and provides them with the reference to the pertinent "Spy" class. This last step is mainly performed reusing the mechanisms defined in the JUnit framework. Now the `Driver` can start the testing invoking on each suite retrieved the appropriate method that as a result provides a "report" concerning the test execution.
2. `executeMethod (String name Object[] par)`: this method is invoked by the instance of the "Spy" class "to inform" the associated `Driver` object of the method executed by the test case. On the basis of this information and of the data retrieved from the "XMLAdapter", `executeMethod` invokes the corresponding method/methods in the real implementation of the component.

3.3. CDT described in terms of design patterns

Now that all the main elements of the framework have been illustrated, to help comprehension it may be useful to briefly look at it in terms of design patterns [8] (with the warning that an accurate study of a framework, even a relatively small one, in terms of design patterns would be too long to fit into one paper, see, e.g., [9]).

Among the patterns presented in [8], the CDT framework shares the intent of the *Adapter* pattern described as: *Convert the interface of a class into another interface clients expect. Adapter lets classes work together that couldn't otherwise because of incompatible interfaces.*

In fact, the CDT structure is slightly different from the one in [8], as a consequence of the high dynamic nature required to set a clear distinction between tests and component implementations, enabled by the use of introspection mechanisms, and to easily permit the integration in the framework of additional functionality. Therefore more precisely we can say that CDT realizes a *dynamic run-time adapter* that is reconfigured each time a new component is deployed (by using the "XMLAdapter" as an input). Figure 8 shows how the adapter structure can be recognized in the framework. The test case classes represent the clients of the target object constituted by an instance of a "Spy" class. The invocations made by the methods of this instance are directed to an object within `Driver` that, on the basis of the information contained in the XML file, "adapts" them to an invocation, or a sequence of invocations, of the methods of the candidate implementation. This structure is not static, but is visible only at run-time, after the instance of the class `Driver` has acquired a reference to the candidate components as consequence of the information contained in the XML file.

Moreover, it should be now clear that the duties of each instance of the class `Driver` are not limited to the adaptation of the invocations in a class "Spy", but also include the control of the test process, in particular retrieving and instancing the test cases classes and invoking on these instances the opportune method.

The choice of this kind of adaptation, i.e., the use of the XML file instead of a more static one realized implementing a class adapter, was mainly driven by the necessity of obtaining an easily extensible architecture. In particular, we want to avoid the need of building, each time, complex adapters that have to contain additional logic to perform duties as contract verification or traceability. In our solution, all this logic in fact is implemented once and for all in the `Driver` class, while in the "XMLAdapter" we only have to explain the methods correspondences.

4. Considerations on the Framework

This section explains how the CDT framework can be useful, in different regards, both to the component customer and to the component developer. We illustrate which are the main benefits gained by using the framework, and in which directions our research will continue from here.

4.1. The good news for the component customer

With reference to the phases of specification, searching and testing of a component (see Section 2), CDT can be fruitfully used to support and distribute the relative tasks among different teams. The "Spy" classes can be developed as a result of the specification phase: as said, the func-

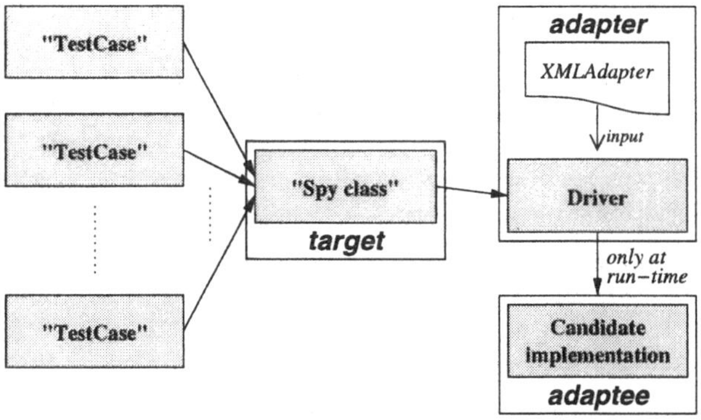

Figure 8. The CDT framework as a run-time adapter

tionalities required for a virtual component are specified as methods of the class. After that, two different kinds of team are involved: the *searching teams* and the *testing teams*. The former, on the basis of the specifications for the virtual component, looks for suitable implementation. If one seemingly good candidate implementation is found, they develop an appropriate "XMLAdapter" (the implementation, as already highlighted in paragraph 3.2.2., can consist of more real components). In parallel, the testing teams can start developing functional deployment tests with reference to the virtual component represented by the "Spy" class. When a candidate implementation is identified, and at least a test suite is ready, the deployment test phase can start.

So far, in the presentation of the CDT framework we have mainly analyzed the validation of a single virtual component, however the CDT framework can be used for incremental deployment testing without any modification. In fact, using an appropriate instance of a class "Spy" and a suitable "XMLAdapter", a set of interconnected components can be viewed as a single component that exports the necessary interfaces. More in general, we can figure out a deployment test phase that is organized in incremental steps (precisely as in traditional integration testing). In such a scenario, a component may be tested first alone, and then as part of a larger subsystem. In the latter case, the functional tests are not related to the behaviour of the component alone, but of the subsystem in which the component is integrated.

In order to simplify the integration of more virtual components, as well as the integration of more real components to form a virtual one, we have presented in [3] a particular wrapper named *WCT* (Wrapper for Component Testing) that permits the easy configuration of a system according to the specified system architecture. WCT has a similar structure of the "Tester" component in Figure 2, and its main duty is to adapt the services required by the contained component to those provided by other virtual components. A WCT foresees also mechanisms for execution tracing and contract verification. This last feature results particularly beneficial since it permits the early identification of a problem during test execution through the detection of a contract violation in the interaction between the implementations of the virtual components (this technique was presented in [6] for the testing of OO systems).

4.2. The good news for the component developer

We have discussed in the introduction the benefits that the component customer could gain from getting, together with a component, the related functional test cases. As a consequence, the opportunity to obtain the developer's test cases, established in a white-box context (i.e., with a full knowledge and access to the source code), and packaged in a way that makes them easily re-executable, can make a big difference in the component customer's choices within a competitive market. This fact could convince the developers of the advantages to identify effective methods for transferring their test suite to the customer.

In this respect, the CDT framework can also be usefully applied by the component developer to transfer executable test to the customers. The developer might define the test cases on the basis of his/her own developed "Spy" class, that in this case will obviously not show substantial differences from the actual component, and should also codify the "XMLAdapter", which will be trivial. The customer, obtained these artefacts, will be immediately able to test the component in the target environment, using the same mechanisms employed to execute the internally developed test cases. If the major advantages in the described scenario will be for the component customers, also the developer can gain benefits in codifing the test cases following the rules established in the CDT framework, in order to test successive versions of a component in which the interfaces definition could be modified.

4.3. Major benefits and further developments

In developing the framework, the main purpose was to provide the component customer with a means for the early codification of test cases in a manner completely independent from a specific real component and for easily executing them to evaluate any candidate component. We can ascribe several good qualities to the resulting framework:

1. the complete decoupling of tests and components, thus facilitating the separate reuse of these two kinds of artifacts (inside the same organization);
2. the test suite flexibility, e.g., it results extremely simple to add new test cases;
3. the grouping the test cases in different packages on the basis of relevant criteria; this feature can simplify subsequent regression test phases;

4. no specific interface implementation is requested on the candidate components.

With regard to item 4, for this same reason the framework does not permit the codification of tests that access the private elements of the components, capability that other methodologies, like Built-In Testing [24], foresee. However, by adding a simple requirement to the implementation interfaces we could obtain, using the framework, the same power of the built-in tests. Precisely, to obtain this, we have to impose that each component implements a public method that using the introspection mechanisms of the component model, redirects the invocation on the private elements, similarly to what is also presented in [10].

For instance, in Java we could impose the implementation of the method:

```
handlePrivateElement(
    String Kind,String Name,
    Object[] parameters,String op);
```

in which `Kind` ∈ {CONSTRUCTOR,METHOD,FIELD}, `Name` is the name of the private element, the vector `parameters` contains the parameters, and `op` ∈ {SET,GET} and specifies the type of the operation that must be performed when accessing a field element.

We have already noted that the framework is easily extensible with new control functionalities. An extension currently under development is the integration in the framework of mechanisms for contract verification. Design by Contract (DbC) [15] seems one of the most promising means in order to alleviate the "component trust problem". It can be exploited all along CB systems construction to evaluate the conformance of the real component to the searched one. In the area of testing, DbC can be used as a further means to validate the execution of a test case. The integration in CDT results quite simple and we think that, thanks to the fine grained control of the `Driver` on the methods invocation, the result can be effective. So far we have already integrated in the framework the possibility of instrumenting the virtual components with pre- and post-conditions that are checked at run-time. A further development on which we are working is the adding of traceability features to the framework in order to simplify the result analysis. Besides, another important piece of work that we plan is the realization of a graphical tool to support the compilation of the "XMLAdapter". Such a tool would obviously reduce the effort spent in test development and moreover it would drastically reduce the probability of errors.

5. Related work

The CDT framework is proposed as a practical contribution to alleviate the component trust problem. In the Introduction we have already extensively discussed it and have overviewed several approaches related to ours.

The special needs posed by CB development are widely discussed in [13], and a prototype environment called WREN is proposed. A strict relation clearly exists between this and our approach, in that both studies call for a process revision and start from similar requirements. However, while WREN applies in general to component composition issues, we specifically focus on the testing task. A combination of the two frameworks is not only feasible, but also desirable.

With regard to our technical solution, we are not aware of other projects specifically aimed at supporting the component customer in developing test cases for the deployment testing phase, without assuming any specific real implementation. In this respect we believe that our work is original and hopefully pioneer of an important research direction. Instead, some interesting approaches have been proposed, that the developer can use to transfer the test cases to the customer. In this direction, the authors of [17] present a tool to allow the component developer to design and run test cases. The test specification and the test results are stored into a XML document to be successively packaged with the component, thus providing to the component user a means to verify the component compliance to the specifications in the target environment.

Another well-known approach consists in enclosing the test cases as public methods of the component (the already cited Built-In Test approach [24]). The disadvantage of this methodology is the growth of component complexity, which soon makes the component hard to manage.

An interesting approach presented by Gao et al. [10] introduces the concept of a "testable bean" as a component with well defined built-in test interfaces. Goal of these interfaces is to enhance the component testability and facilitate component testing. With a mechanism that uses the introspection mechanisms of the component model, similar to what we have described above, they obtain the capability of built-in testing, but without enclosing a lot of code in the component itself.

As CB testing is a very though and expensive task, we believe that all the above approaches constitute important contributions, but that the field is far from being settled, and much more research is still needed.

6. Conclusions and future work

We introduced the CDT framework, to facilitate the testing within a customer's target environment of a component independently developed.

The central feature of the framework is the complete decoupling between the tests and the component implementation, allowing for the early codification of deployment tests, and for their reuse over different components.

This research goes in the direction of providing means to increase the trust in a component. We believe that the success of CB development passes through the adoption of a rigorous, systematic test validation process.

We have implemented a trial version of the CDT framework in Java and played it on a simple case study of a bank account manager. The empirical work demonstrated the feasibility of the idea and at the same time indicated several interesting additions to the framework structure that we plan to implement in the next future.

We plan also to investigate, in the next future, how to derive useful test cases from specifications codified in UML diagrams. In particular in a recent paper [4] we sketch some ideas on adapting Cow_Suite [1], a tool to derive test cases for OO systems, to CB development, and on how this could be integrated with the CDT framework.

7. Acknowledgements

Andrea Polini's PhD grant is supported by Ericsson Lab Italy in the framework of the Pisatel initiative. http://www.iei.pi.cnr.it/ERI

References

[1] F. Basanieri, A. Bertolino, E. Marchetti, "The Cow_Suite Approach to Planning and Deriving Test Suites in UML Projects", in *Proc. ≪UML≫ 2002*, Dresden, Germany, Sept. 30-Oct. 4, 2002, LNCS 2460.

[2] A. Bertolino, and A. Polini, "Re-thinking the Development Process of Component-Based Software" in [28].

[3] A. Bertolino, and A. Polini, "WCT: a Wrapper for Component Testing", in *Proceedings of Fidji'2002*, Luxembourg, November 28-29, 2002, to appear in LNCS.

[4] A. Bertolino, E. Marchetti, and A. Polini, "Integration of "Components" to Test Software Components", to appear in *Proceedings of TACoS 2003* workshop at ETAPS 2003, Warsaw, Poland, April 13th, 2003.

[5] R.V. Binder, *Testing Object-Oriented Systems: Models, Patterns, and Tools*, Addison-Wesley, 2000.

[6] L.C. Briand, Y. Labiche, and H. Sun, "Investigating the Use of Analysis Contracts to Support Fault Isolation in Object Oriented Code", *Proc. ACM ISSTA 2002*, Roma, Italy, July 22-24, 2002, pp. 70-80.

[7] J. Cheesman and J. Daniels, *UML Components - a Simple Process for Specifying Component-Based Software*, Addison-Wesley, 2000.

[8] E. Gamma, R. Helm, R. Johnson, and J. Vlissides, *Design Patterns. Elements of Rusable Object-Oriented Software* Addison-Wesley, 1995.

[9] E. Gamma, and K. Beck, "JUnit a Cook's Tour" available at: http://www.junit.org

[10] J. Gao, K. Gupta, S. Gupta, and S. Shim "On Building Testable Software Components", in J. Dean and A. Gravel (Eds) *Proc. ICCBSS 2002*, LNCS 2255, pp.108-121.

[11] Java Reflection Documentation, available at: http://java.sun.com/products/jdk/1.1/docs/guide/reflection/

[12] G. Kiczales, J. des Rivières, and D.G. Bobrow, *The Art of the Metaobject Protocol*, MIT Press, 1991.

[13] C. Lüer, and D.S. Rosenblum, "WREN - An Environment for Component-Based Development", in *Proc. of ACM ESEC/FSE 2001*, Vienna, Austria, September 10-14, 2001.

[14] D. McIllroy, "Mass Produced Software Components", in P. Naur and B. Randall Eds, Software Engineering: Report on a Conference by the NATO Science Committee, Brussels, 1968, pp. 138-155.

[15] B. Meyer, "Applying Design by Contract", *IEEE Computer*, vol. 25, no. 10, October 1992, pages 40-51.

[16] B. Meyer, C. Mingins, and Heinz Schmidt, "Trusted Components for the Software Industry" available at: http://trusted-components.org/documents/tc_original_paper.html

[17] J. Morris, G. Lee, K. Parker, G.A. Bundell, and C.P. Lam, "Software Component Certification", in *IEEE Computer*, September 2001, pp. 30-36.

[18] A. Orso, M.J. Harrold, and D. Rosenblum "Component Metadata for Software Engineering Tasks", in W. Emmerich and S. Tai (Eds) EDO2000, LNCS 1999, pp. 129-144.

[19] D. Rosenblum, "Adequate Testing of Component-Based Software", Univ. California, Irvine, T.R. UCI-ICS-97-34, (1997)

[20] J.A. Stafford and A.L. Wolf, "Annotating Components to Support Component-Based Static Analyses of Software Systems", *Proc. the Grace Hopper Celeb. of Women in Computing* 2001.

[21] C. Szyperski, *Component Software, Beyond Object-Oriented Programming*, Addison-Wesley, 1998.

[22] J. Voas, "Developing a Usage-Based Software Certification Process", *IEEE Computer*, August 2000, pp. 32-37.

[23] J. Voas, "Certifying Off-the-Shelf Software Components", *IEEE Computer*, June 1998, pp. 53-59.

[24] Y. Wang, G. King, and H. Wickburg, "A Method for Built-in Tests in Component-based Software Maintenance", *Proc. of the 3rd ECSMR*, 1999.

[25] E. Weyuker, "Testing Component-Based Software: A Cautionary Tale", *IEEE Software*, Sept./Oct. 1998, pp. 54-59.

[26] J. Whaley, M.C. Martin, and M.S. Lam, "Automatic Extraction of Object-Oriented Component Interfaces", *Proc. ACM ISSTA 2002*, Roma, Italy, July 22-24, 2002, pp.221-231.

[27] 5th ICSE Workshop on CBSE, Benchmarks for Predictable Assembly, Orlando, Florida, USA, May 19-20, 2002.

[28] ECBS 2002 Workshop on CBSE, Composing System From Components, April 10-11, 2002, Lund, Sweden.

[29] *IEEE Computer*, July 1999, 32 (7).

[30] *The Journal of Systems and Software*, Special Issue on CBSE, 2003, to appear.

[31] CORBA Component Model specifications: http://www.omg.org/technology/documents/formal/components.htm

[32] Enterprise Java Bean Technology: http://java.sun.com/products/ejb/

[33] .Net resources available at: http://www.microsoft.com/net/

Data Flow Testing as Model Checking*

Hyoung Seok Hong, Sung Deok Cha
Department of Electrical Engineering and Computer Science and AITrc
Korea Advanced Institute of Science and Technology
{hshong,cha}@salmosa.kaist.ac.kr

Insup Lee, Oleg Sokolsky
Department of Computer and Information Science
University of Pennsylvania
{lee,sokolsky}@saul.cis.upenn.edu

Hasan Ural
School of Information Technology and Engineering
University of Ottawa
ural@site.uottawa.ca

Abstract

This paper presents a model checking-based approach to data flow testing. We characterize data flow oriented coverage criteria in temporal logic such that the problem of test generation is reduced to the problem of finding witnesses for a set of temporal logic formulas. The capability of model checkers to construct witnesses and counterexamples allows test generation to be fully automatic. We discuss complexity issues in minimal cost test generation and describe heurstic test generation algorithms. We illustrate our approach using CTL as temporal logic and SMV as model checker.

1 Introduction

During the last two decades, there have been a number of data flow testing methods. Included are those proposed by Rapps and Weyuker[26], Ntafos[24], Ural[30], and Laski and Korel[22], which are originally developed for modules in procedural languages. These methods have been extended for interprocedural programs in procedural languages[13], object-oriented programmming languages[14], and requirements specification languages such as SDL[29, 31] and statecharts[17]. In data flow testing, we usually model a software as a flow graph which identifies the information of control flow and data flow in the software. We then establish certain associations between definitions and uses of variables required to be covered in a given coverage criterion by applying conventional data flow analysis upon the flow graph. Finally we select a finite number of paths which cover the associations as a test suite.

Model checking is a formal verification technique for determining whether a system model satisfies a property written in temporal logic and model checkers such as SMV[23] and SPIN[16] are already used on a regular basis for the verification of real-world applications. In addition to being automatic, an important feature of model checking is the ability to explain the success or failure of a temporal logic formula[5, 6, 15]. If a system model satisfies a formula, model checkers are capable of supplying an execution of the model as a witness demonstrating the success of the formula. Conversely, a counterexample is supplied when the model fails to satisfy the formula.

This paper presents a model checking-based approach to data flow testing. In our approach, the problems of data flow analysis and path selection in data flow testing are formulated in terms of model checking. We investigate four groups of coverage criteria in [26, 24, 30, 22] and characterize each coverage criterion by specifying the requirements of the coverage criterion using a set of temporal logic formulas such that the problem of test generation is reduced to the problem of finding witnesses for the set of formulas. The capability of model checkers to construct witnesses

*This research was supported in part by Advanced Information Technology Research Center at KAIST, NSF CCR-9988409, NSF CCR-0086147, NSF CCR-0209024, ARO DAAD19-01-1-0473, DARPA ITO MOBIES F33615-00-C-1707, and the Natural Sciences and Engineering Research Council of Canada under grant OGP00000976.

0-7695-1877-X/03 $17.00 © 2003 IEEE

and counterexamples allows test generation to be fully automatic. As a by-product, the characterization enables us to discuss complexity issues in minimal cost test generation. This paper illustrates our approach using CTL[4] as temporal logic and SMV[23] as model checker. The main advantages of our approach may be summarized as follows: First, the approach enables test generation from large flow graphs whose size is limited by the capabilities of current model checkers. Second, the approach allows focusing on only high-level specifications of coverage criteria written in temporal logic. All the details about test generation algoritms and their implementations are hidden in model checkers. Third, the approach is language independent in that the temporal logic formulas employed in the approach are applicable with minor modifications to flow graphs constructed from various kinds of programming languages and requirements specification languages.

Connections between data flow analysis and model checking were made in [27, 28] which show that model checking can be used to solve various data flow analysis problems including the standard bit-vector problems. Our approach extends the work of [27, 28] in that data flow testing combines data flow analysis with the path selection problem. Recently, connections between test generation and model checking have been considered especially in specification-based testing. In [20], local and on-the-fly model checking algoritms are applied to test generation. In [32], SPIN is used for on-the-fly test generation. Test generation using the capability of model checker to construct counterexamples has been applied in several contexts. In [1], the application of model checking to mutation analysis is described. In [3, 9], tests are generated by constructing counterexamples for user-supplied temporal logic formulas. In [12], the capability of SMV and SPIN to construct counterexamples is applied to test generation for control flow oriented coverage criteria. No consideration is given to data flow testing in the above work.

In [18, 19], the authors discuss the application of model checking to test generation from requirements specifications for both control flow and data flow oriented coverage criteria. The approach in [18, 19] is based on the fact that the state space of a specification is often finite and hence one can use reachability graphs instead of flow graphs for test generation. On one hand, this paper extends [18, 19] by considering more comprehensive groups of data flow oriented coverage criteria. On the other hand, the flow-graph approach we advocate here can be seen as complementary to the reachability-graph approach in [18, 19]. In the flow-graph approach one can generate tests from programs or specifications with infinite state space because the values of variables are not expanded in flow graphs. It, however, requires posterior analysis such as symbolic execution or constraint solving to determine the executability of tests and for the selection of variable values which make tests executable. The reachability-graph approach can handle only finite state space but has the advantage that only executable tests are generated which obviates the necessity of posterior analysis.

Section 2 briefly reviews the basics of flow graph and CTL which are the model and logic employed in our approach, respectively. Section 3 characterizes the coverage criteria in [26, 24, 30, 22] by associating a CTL formula, parameterized with the propositions of a given flow graph, with each entity required to be covered in a given criterion. Each formula is defined in such a way that a flow graph satisfies the formula if and only if the flow graph has an execution covering the entity described by the formula. By finding witnesses for every formula in a given criterion, we generate a test suite satisfying the criterion. Section 4 discusses complexity issues in minimal cost test generation. Typically a CTL formula can have several executions as its witness. By selecting the right witness for each formula, one can minimize the size of the test suite. We show that two optimization problems of minimal cost test generation are NP-hard and describe heuristic test generation algorithms employing the capability of model checkers to construct counterexamples. We report the experimental results obtained by applying the heuristics to a moderate flow graph. In our experience with SMV, we were able to generate test suites from flow graphs containing dozens of variable definitions and uses in seconds. Finally, Section 5 concludes the paper with a discussion of future work.

2 Flow Graph and CTL

A *flow graph* $G = (V, v_s, v_f, A)$ is a directed graph where V is a finite set of vertices; $v_s \in V$ is the start vertex; $v_f \in V$ is the final vertex; and A is a finite set of arcs. A vertex represents a statement and an arc represents possible flow of control between statements. We adopt the following convention to decorate each vertex with data flow information. Let x be a variable and v be a vertex. We say that x is *defined* at v, denoted by d_v^x, if v represents a statement assigning a value to x. We say that x is *used* at v, denoted by u_v^x, if v represents a statement referencing x. We use *DEF*(v) and *USE*(v) to denote the sets of definitions and uses at v, respectively. A sequence $v_1...v_n$ of vertices is a *path* if $(v_i, v_{i+1}) \in A$ for $1 \leq i \leq n-1$. A path is *complete* if it starts from the start vertex v_s and ends at the final vertex v_f. A *test sequence* is a complete path and a *test suite* is a finite set of test sequences. Figure 1 shows a program and its flow graph.

We view a flow graph as a Kripke structure $M = (Q, q_{init}, L, R)$ where Q is a finite set of states; $q_{init} \in Q$ is the initial state; L: $Q \rightarrow 2^{AP}$ is the function labelling each state with a subset of the set AP of atomic proposi-

```
v1: input(x, y, z);
v2: if (x > y)
v3:     then max := x;
v4:     else max := y;
v5: endif
v6: max := z * max;
v7: output(max);
```

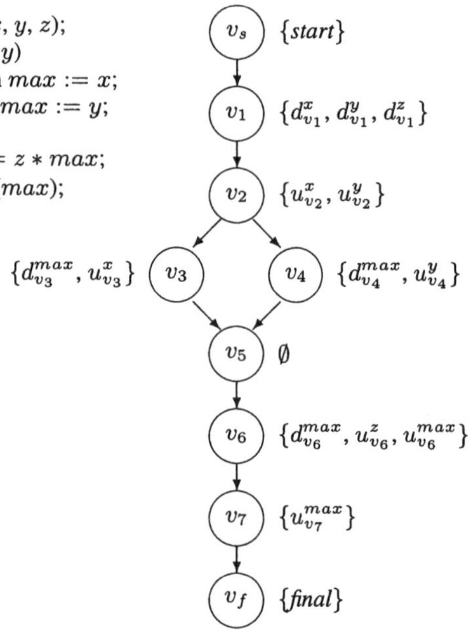

Figure 1. An example of flow graphs

tions; $R \subseteq Q \times Q$ is the transition relation which is total, i.e., for every state q, there is a state q' such that $(q,q') \in R$. The Kripke structure $M(G)$ corresponding to a flow graph G is $(V,\ v_s,\ L,\ A \cup \{(v_f, v_f)\})$ where $L(v_s) = \{start\}$, $L(v_f) = \{final\}$, and $L(v) = DEF(v) \cup USE(v)$ for every $v \in V - \{v_s, v_f\}$. The tuple (v_f,v_f) is necessary to guarantee that the transition relation be total.

Now we give a brief and informal introduction to CTL. We refer to [4] for the formal syntax and semantics for CTL. Formulas in CTL are built from path quantifiers, modal operators, and standard logical operators. The path quantifiers are **A** (for all paths) and **E** (for some path). The modal opeators are **X** (next time), **F** (eventually), **G** (always), and **U** (until). For a CTL formula f and a state q of Kripke structure M, we write $M, q \models f$ ($q \models f$ when M is understood) if q satisfies f and write $M \models f$ if $M, q_{init} \models f$. The meaning of CTL formulas can be understood as follows: "$q \models \mathbf{EX}p$" states that there is a path from q such that p holds at the next state; "$q \models \mathbf{EF}p$" states that there is a path from q such that p holds sometime in the future; "$q \models \mathbf{EG}p$" states that there is a path from q such that p holds globally in the future; "$q \models \mathbf{E}[p_1 \mathbf{U} p_2]$" states that there is a path from q such that p_1 holds until p_2 holds and p_2 eventually holds in the future. ECTL is the exitential fragment of CTL where only the path quantifier **E** is allowed and negation is restricted to atomic propositions. ACTL is the dual universal fragment of CTL.

Symbolic model checkers for CTL such as SMV represent the state space and transition relation of Kripke structures in terms of binary decision diagrams (BDDs) and use a fixpoint characterization of CTL formulas to compute the set of states satisfying a formula. For example, the set of states satisfying $\mathbf{EF}p$ is a least fixpoint of the predicate transformer τ: $2^Q \rightarrow 2^Q$ defined by $\tau(Z) = p \vee \mathbf{EX}Z$. The fixpoint computation requires standard logical operations, quantification over variables, and substitution of variables which can all be performed efficiently on BDDs.

An important feature of model checking is the ability to construct witnesses and counterexamples. Algorithms for constructing linear witnesses and counterexamples, i.e., finite or infinite paths, were developed in [5, 15] and are widely used in current model checkers. Recently, Clarke *et al.*[6] made a formal definition of witnesses and counterexamples using simulation relation. Let M be a Kripke structure, f be a ECTL formula, and g be a ACTL formula. If $M \models f$, a witness for f is a Kripke structure M' such that $M' \models f$ and M simulates M'. Dually, if $M \not\models g$, a counterexample for g is a Kripke structure M'' such that $M'' \not\models g$ and M simulates M''. They also proposed to use tree-like structures as witnesses and counterexamples for a large class of branching-time temporal logics which do not have linear witnesses.

For the purpose of data flow testing, we are only interested in linear and finite witnesses and restrict ourselves to a subclass of ECTL, which we call WCTL, defined by: A ECTL formula f is a *WCTL formula* if (i) f contains only **EX**, **EF**, and **EU** and (ii) for every subformula of f of the form $f_1 \wedge ... \wedge f_n$, every conjunct f_i except at most one is an atomic proposition. For example, $\mathbf{EF}(p_1 \wedge \mathbf{EF}p_2)$ is in WCTL while $\mathbf{EF}p_1 \wedge \mathbf{EF}p_2$ is not. For a Kripke structure M and a WCTL formula f such that $M \models f$, we define the set of *witnesses* for f with respect to M, denoted by $\mathbf{W}(M,f)$, as follows.

- $W(M,true) = Q$,
- $W(M,false) = \emptyset$,
- $W(M,p \wedge f) = \{q \mid q \models p\} * W(M,f)$,
- $W(M,f \vee g) = W(M,f) \cup W(M,g)$,
- $W(M,\mathbf{EX}f) = \{q_0q_1 \mid q_1 \models f, (q_0, q_1) \in R\} * W(M,f)$,
- $W(M,\mathbf{EF}f) = \{q_0...q_n \mid q_n \models f, (q_i, q_{i+1}) \in R$ for all $0 \leq i \leq n-1\} * W(M,f)$,
- $W(M,\mathbf{E}[f\mathbf{U}g]) = \{q_0...q_n \mid q_i \models f$ for all $0 \leq i \leq n-1$, $q_n \models g$, $(q_j, q_{j+1}) \in R$ for all $0 \leq j \leq n-1\}$ $* W(M,g)$,
- $\mathbf{W}(M,f) = \{\pi \in W(M,f) \mid \pi(0) = q_{init}\}$,

where $\Pi_1 * \Pi_2 = \{\pi \mid \exists i : \pi_i \in \Pi_1, \pi^i \in \Pi_2\}$, π_i denotes the prefix of π ending at i, and π^i denotes the suffix of π starting from i. Let $q_0...q_n$ be a witness in $\mathcal{W}(M,f)$ and M' be its corresponding Kripke structure defined as $(Q, q_{init}, L, R - \{(q,q') \mid q = q_i \text{ for some } 1 \leq i \leq n-1\})$. It is not hard to see that $M' \models f$ and M simulates M'.

Finally we extend the notion of witnesses to a set of WCTL formulas. Let M be a Kripke structure and F be a set of WCTL formulas. A *witness-set* Π for F with respect to M is a set of finite paths such that, for every formula f in F with $M \models f$, there is a finite path π in Π that is a witness for f. It is easy to see that Π is a witness-set for F if and only if it is a witness-set for $\{f \in F \mid M \models f\}$. For example, in Figure 2 we observe that $\{q_0q_1q_3q_4q_0q_2q_3\}$, $\{q_0q_2q_3q_4q_0q_1q_3\}$, and $\{q_0q_1q_3, q_0q_2q_3\}$ are witness-sets for $\{$**EF**$(a \wedge$ **EF**$c)$, **EF**$(b \wedge$ **EF**$c)\}$.

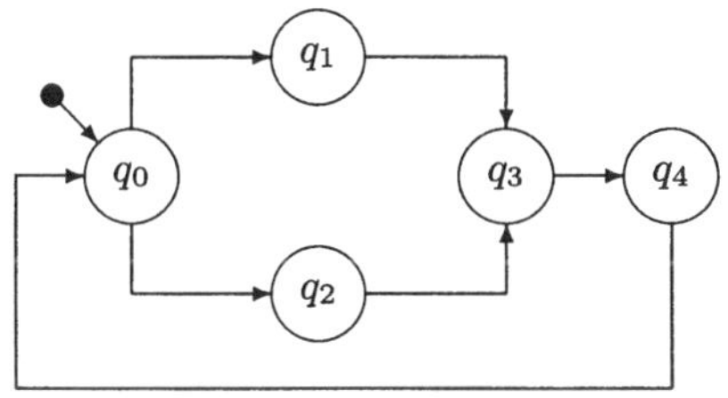

$L(q_0)=\emptyset$, $L(q_1)=\{a\}$, $L(q_2)=\{b\}$, $L(q_3)=\{c\}$, $L(q_4)=\emptyset$

Figure 2. An example of Kripke structures

3 Characterizing Data Flow Oriented Coverage Criteria

This section characterizes four groups of coverage criteria[26, 24, 30, 22] in terms of witness-sets for WCTL formulas.

3.1 Rapps and Weyuker's Criteria

Rapps and Weyuker's criteria require certain associations between definitions and uses of the same variable be covered[26]. The criteria are extended with the notion of executability by Frankl and Weyuker[11]. We first adopt the following terminology. A path $(v, v_1, ..., v_n, v')$ is a *definition-clear path from v to v′ with respect to variable* x if $n = 0$ or x is not defined at v_i for every $1 \leq i \leq n$. A pair $(d_v^x, u_{v'}^x)$ is a *definition-use pair* (in short, du-pair) if there is a definition-clear path from v to v' with respect to x. For example, consider $d_{v_1}^x$ and $u_{v_3}^x$ in Figure 1. We observe that $(d_{v_1}^x, u_{v_3}^x)$ is a du-pair through a definition-clear path $v_1v_2v_3$.

3.1.1 Characterization

We first describe how to generate a test sequence covering a pair $(d_v^x, u_{v'}^x)$. The first step is to determine whether $(d_v^x, u_{v'}^x)$ is a du-pair or not. For this, we associate the following WCTL formula with $(d_v^x, u_{v'}^x)$.

$$\textbf{wctl}(d_v^x, u_{v'}^x) = \textbf{EF}(d_v^x \wedge \textbf{EXE}[\neg \mathit{def}(x)\ \textbf{U}\ (u_{v'}^x \wedge \textbf{EF}\mathit{final})])$$

where *def*(v) is the disjunction of all definitions of x. For example, in Figure 1 we have that *def*$(x) ::= d_{v_1}^x$, *def*$(y) ::= d_{v_1}^y$, *def*$(z) ::= d_{v_1}^z$, and *def*$(max) ::= d_{v_3}^{max} \vee d_{v_4}^{max} \vee d_{v_6}^{max}$. It is not hard to see that $(d_v^x, u_{v'}^x)$ is a du-pair if and only if the Kripke structure $M(G)$ of a flow graph G satisfies **wctl**$(d_v^x, u_{v'}^x)$. Hence the problem of determining whether $(d_v^x, u_{v'}^x)$ is a du-pair is reduced to a model checking problem. After determining whether $(d_v^x, u_{v'}^x)$ is a du-pair, we generate a test sequence covering it. It is also not hard to see that a test sequence covers a du-pair $(d_v^x, u_{v'}^x)$ if and only if it is a witness for **wctl**$(d_v^x, u_{v'}^x)$. Hence the problem of generating a test sequence covering $(d_v^x, u_{v'}^x)$ is reduced to the problem of finding a witness for **wctl**$(d_v^x, u_{v'}^x)$. For example, a test sequence covering the du-pair $(d_{v_1}^x, u_{v_3}^x)$ is shown in Figure 3, which is also a witness for **EF**$(d_{v_1}^x \wedge$ **EXE**$[\neg$*def*(x) **U** $(u_{v_3}^x \wedge$ **EF***final*$)])$.

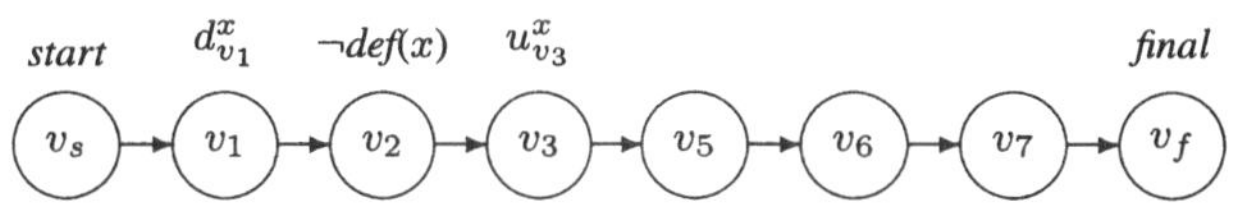

Figure 3. A test sequence covering du-pair $(d_{v_1}^x, u_{v_3}^x)$

Now we describe how to generate a set of test sequences for a set of pairs $(d_v^x, u_{v'}^x)$ according to the criteria by Rapps and Weyuker. Basically we associate a formula **wctl**$(d_v^x, u_{v'}^x)$ with every pair $(d_v^x, u_{v'}^x)$ and characterize each coverage criterion in terms of witness-sets for the formulas **wctl**$(d_v^x, u_{v'}^x)$. This reduces the problem of generating a test suite to the problem of finding a witness-set for a set of WCTL formulas.

A test suite Π satisfies *all-defs coverage criterion* if, for every definition d_v^x and some use $u_{v'}^x$, some definition-clear path with respect to x from v to v' is covered by a test sequence in Π. Let *DEF*(G) and *USE*(G) be the sets of definitions and uses in G, respectively. A test suite Π satisfies all-defs coverage criterion if and only if it is a witness-set for

$$\{ \bigvee_{u_{v'}^x \in USE(G)} \textbf{wctl}(d_v^x, u_{v'}^x) \mid d_v^x \in DEF(G)\}.$$

A test suite Π satisfies *all-uses coverage criterion* if, for every definition d_v^x and every use $u_{v'}^x$, some definition-clear path with respect to x from v to v' is covered by a test sequence in Π. A test suite Π satisfies all-uses coverage criterion if and only if it is a witness-set for

$$\{\mathbf{wctl}(d^x_v, u^x_{v'}) \mid d^x_v \in DEF(G), u^x_{v'} \in USE(G)\}.$$

In the worst case, the number of formulas can be quadractic in the size of a flow graph since the number of pairs $(d^x_v, u^x_{v'})$ can be $O(n^2)$ in a flow graph of size n. For example, for all-uses coverage criterion in Figure 1 we associate 11 formulas with the pairs $(d^x_{v_1}, u^x_{v_2})$, $(d^x_{v_1}, u^x_{v_3})$, $(d^y_{v_1}, u^y_{v_2})$, $(d^y_{v_1}, u^y_{v_4})$, $(d^z_{v_1}, u^z_{v_6})$, $(d^{max}_{v_3}, u^{max}_{v_6})$, $(d^{max}_{v_3}, u^{max}_{v_7})$, $(d^{max}_{v_4}, u^{max}_{v_6})$, $(d^{max}_{v_4}, u^{max}_{v_7})$, $(d^{max}_{v_6}, u^{max}_{v_6})$, and $(d^{max}_{v_6}, u^{max}_{v_7})$. Among them, the formulas for $(d^{max}_{v_3}, u^{max}_{v_7})$, $(d^{max}_{v_4}, u^{max}_{v_7})$, and $(d^{max}_{v_6}, u^{max}_{v_6})$ are not satisfied in Figure 1, which means that the pairs are not du-pairs.

A test suite Π satisfies *all-du-paths coverage criterion* if, for every definition d^x_v and every use $u^x_{v'}$, every cycle-free definition-clear path with respect to x from v to v' is covered by a test sequence in Π. Unlike other coverage criteria, all-du-paths coverage criterion cannot be characterized in terms of witness-sets. To generate test suites satisfying this criterion properly in our approach, we should be able to construct all cycle-free witnesses instead of only one for a given formula, which is beyond the capability of existing model checkers. In general, extending model checkers to construct all witnesses for a given formula or a subset of witnesses satisfying certain constraints is an open problem.

3.2 Ntafos' Criteria

Ntafos' criteria emphasize interactions between different variables[24]. Such interactions are captured in terms of sequences of alternating definitions and uses, called k-dr interactions. A sequence $[d^{x_1}_{v_1}\ u^{x_1}_{v_2}\ d^{x_2}_{v_2}\ u^{x_2}_{v_3}\ \ldots\ d^{x_n}_{v_n}\ u^{x_n}_{n+1}]$ is a *data flow chain* (df-chain) if, for every $1 \le i \le n$, $(d^{x_i}_{v_i}, u^{x_i}_{v_{i+1}})$ is a du-pair[30]. Note that the use $u^{x_i}_{v_{i+1}}$ and definition $d^{x_{i+1}}_{v_{i+1}}$ occur at the same vertex for every $1 \le i \le n$. A path $v_1\pi_1 v_2\pi_2 \ldots v_{n+1}$ is an *interaction subpath* of a df-chain if, for every $1 \le i \le n$, $v_i\pi_i v_{i+1}$ is a definition-clear path from v_i to v_{i+1} with respect to x_i. A df-chain consisting of $k-1$ du-pairs, $k \ge 2$, is a k-definition/reference interaction (k-dr interaction) in the terminology of [24][1]. For example, in Figure 1 we observe that $[d^x_{v_1}\ u^x_{v_3}\ d^{max}_{v_3}\ u^{max}_{v_6}]$ is a 3-dr interaction which has $v_1v_2v_3v_5v_6$ as its interaction subpath.

3.2.1 Characterization

For a sequence $\kappa = [d^{x_1}_{v_1}\ u^{x_1}_{v_2}\ d^{x_2}_{v_2}\ u^{x_2}_{v_3}\ \ldots\ d^{x_{k-1}}_{v_{k-1}}\ u^{x_{k-1}}_{k}]$, $k \ge 2$, define $\mathbf{wctl}(\kappa)$ as follows.

[1]We do not require the variables $x_1, \ldots, x_n$ and the vertices $v_1, \ldots, v_{n+1}$ be distinct. This definition is consistent with that of Clarke et al.[7] and Ntafos[25] and is different from the original one[24] which requires the vertices to be distinct.

- if κ is empty, then $wctl(\kappa) = \mathbf{EF}\mathit{final}$,
- if κ is $[d^{x_i}_{v_i}\ u^{x_i}_{v_{i+1}}] \cdot \kappa'$, then

$$wctl(\kappa) = d^{x_i}_{v_i} \wedge \mathbf{EXE}[\neg \mathit{def}(x_i)\ \mathbf{U}\ (u^{x_i}_{v_{i+1}} \wedge wctl(\kappa'))],$$

- $\mathbf{wctl}(\kappa) = \mathbf{EF}wctl(\kappa)$.

By induction on the number of pairs $(d^{x_i}_{v_i}, u^{x_i}_{v_{i+1}})$ in κ, it can be shown that κ is a k-dr interaction if and only if the Kripke structure $M(G)$ of a flow graph G satisfies $\mathbf{wctl}(\kappa)$. Moreover, a test sequence covers κ if and only if it is a witness for $\mathbf{wctl}(\kappa)$. For example, a test sequence covering the 3-dr interaction $[d^x_{v_1}\ u^x_{v_3}\ d^{max}_{v_3}\ u^{max}_{v_6}]$ is shown in Figure 4, which is also a witness for $\mathbf{EF}(d^x_{v_1} \wedge \mathbf{EXE}[\neg \mathit{def}(x)\ \mathbf{U}\ (u^x_{v_3} \wedge d^{max}_{v_3} \wedge \mathbf{EXE}[\neg \mathit{def}(max)\ \mathbf{U}\ (u^{max}_{v_6} \wedge \mathbf{EF}\mathit{final})])])$.

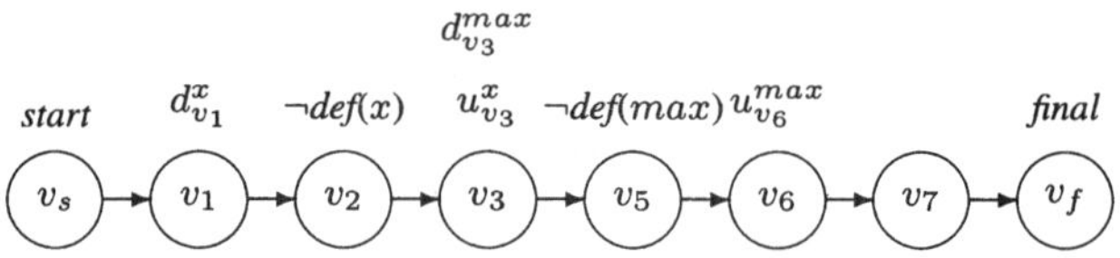

Figure 4. A test sequence covering 3-dr interaction $[d^x_{v_1}\ u^x_{v_3}\ d^{max}_{v_3}\ u^{max}_{v_6}]$

A test suite Π satisfies *required k-tuples coverage criterion* if, for every k-dr interaction κ, some interaction subpath of κ is covered by a test sequence in Π. A test suite Π satisfies required k-tuples coverage criterion if and only if it is a witness-set for

$$\{\mathbf{wctl}([d^{x_1}_{v_1} u^{x_1}_{v_2} d^{x_2}_{v_2} u^{x_2}_{v_3} \ldots d^{x_{k-1}}_{v_{k-1}} u^{x_{k-1}}_{k}])$$

$$\mid d^{x_i}_{v_i} \in DEF(G), u^{x_i}_{v_{i+1}} \in USE(G), 1 \le i \le k-1\}.$$

3.3 Ural' Criteria

Ural's criteria also emphasize interactions between different variables[30]. While Ntafos' criteria consider df-chains consisting of fixed number of du-pairs, Ural's criteria consider df-chains consisting of an arbitrary (but finite) number of du-pairs which start with inputs and end with outputs. The rationale here is to identify the functionality of a module in terms of the interactions with its environment by identifying the effects of inputs accepted from the environment on outputs offered to the environment. We say that a definition d^x_v *affects* a use $u^{x'}_{v'}$ if

- either $x = x'$ and $(d^x_v, u^{x'}_{v'})$ is a du-pair or
- there is a use $u^x_{v''}$ such that $(d^x_v, u^x_{v''})$ is a du-pair and there is a definition $d^{x''}_{v''}$, given in terms of $u^x_{v''}$, that affects $u^{x'}_{v'}$.

A pair (d^x_v, $u^{x'}_{v'}$) is an *affect-pair* if d^x_v affects $u^{x'}_{v'}$. Among the particular affect-pairs of interest to Ural's criteria are those starting with inputs and ending with outputs, which we call *io-pairs*. We define an *input* as a definition at an **input** statement and an *output* as a use at an **output** statement. For example, $d^x_{v_1}$, $d^y_{v_1}$, $d^z_{v_1}$ are inputs and $u^{max}_{v_7}$ is an output in Figure 1. We observe that the input $d^x_{v_1}$ affects the output $u^{max}_{v_7}$ through the df-chain [$d^x_{v_1}$ $u^x_{v_3}$ $d^{max}_{v_3}$ $u^{max}_{v_6}$ $d^{max}_{v_6}$ $u^{max}_{v_7}$].

3.3.1 Simple Characterization

For an affect-pair (d^x_v, $u^{x'}_{v'}$), define *CHAIN*(d^x_v, $u^{x'}_{v'}$) as the set of sequences κ = [$d^{x_1}_{v_1}$ $u^{x_1}_{v_2}$ $d^{x_2}_{v_2}$ $u^{x_2}_{v_3}$ ... $d^{x_n}_{v_n}$ $u^{x_n}_{n+1}$] such that $d^{x_1}_{v_1} = d^x_v$ and $u^{x_n}_{v_{n+1}} = u^{x'}_{v'}$. In general, there may be multiple occurrences of the same pair ($d^{x_i}_{v_i}$, $u^{x_i}_{v_{i+1}}$) in κ thereby causing the possibility of an infinite number of elements in *CHAIN*(d^x_v, $u^{x'}_{v'}$). To ensure that *CHAIN*(d^x_v, $u^{x'}_{v'}$) be finite, we consider its subset *SCHAIN*(d^x_v, $u^{x'}_{v'}$) consisting of *simple* sequences in which at most one occurrence of each pair ($d^{x_i}_{v_i}$, $u^{x_i}_{v_{i+1}}$) is allowed.

A test suite Π satisfies *all-inputs coverage criterion* if, for every input i and some output o, an iteraction subpath of some simple df-chain in *SCHAIN*(d^x_v, $u^{x'}_{v'}$) is covered by a test sequence in Π. Let *IN*(*G*) and *OUT*(*G*) be the sets of inputs and outputs in *G*, respectively. A test suite Π satisfies all-inputs coverage criterion if and only if it is a witness-set for

$$\{ \bigvee_{o \in OUT(G)} \bigvee_{\kappa \in SCHAIN(i,o)} \mathbf{wctl}(\kappa) \mid i \in IN(G)\}.$$

A test suite Π satisfies *all-outputs coverage criterion* if, for every input i and every output o, an iteraction subpath of some simple df-chain in *SCHAIN*(d^x_v, $u^{x'}_{v'}$) is covered by a test sequence in Π. A test suite Π satisfies all-outputs coverage criterion if and only if it is a witness-set for

$$\{ \bigvee_{\kappa \in SCHAIN(i,o)} \mathbf{wctl}(\kappa) \mid i \in IN(G), o \in OUT(G)\}.$$

A test suite Π satisfies *all IO df-chains coverage criterion* if, for every input i and every output o, an iteraction subpath of every simple df-chain in *SCHAIN*(d^x_v, $u^{x'}_{v'}$) is covered by a test sequence in Π. A test suite Π satisfies all-IO-df-chains coverage criterion if and only if it is a witness-set for

$$\{\mathbf{wctl}(\kappa) \mid i \subset IN(G), o \in OUT(G), \kappa \in SCHAIN(i,o)\}$$

3.3.2 Fixpoint Characterization

The above characterization of all-inputs and all-outputs coverage criteria is naive in that we need to identify all simple sequences in *SCHAIN*(i, o) for a given io-pair in order to generate a test sequence covering just one simple df-chain for the io-pair. A more faithful characterization should allow the generation of a test sequence without identifying all simple sequences in *SCHAIN*(i, o) prior to test generation. Put another way, we like to model-check a new formula $\mathbf{Q}(d^x_v, u^{x'}_{v'})$ whose semantics is defined below without model-checking all formulas $\mathbf{wctl}(\kappa)$.

> $q \models \mathbf{Q}(d^x_v, u^{x'}_{v'})$ if and only if $q \models \mathbf{wctl}(\kappa)$ for some κ in *CHAIN*(d^x_v, $u^{x'}_{v'}$).

We note that $\mathbf{Q}(d^x_v, u^{x'}_{v'})$ is not directly expressible in CTL because there is in general an infinite number of κ in *CHAIN*(d^x_v, $u^{x'}_{v'}$) and thus an infinite number of $\mathbf{wctl}(\kappa)$.

The formula $\mathbf{Q}(d^x_v, u^{x'}_{v'})$ leads to a natural characterization of all-inputs and all-outputs coverage criteria as follows: A test suite Π satisfies *all-inputs*$^+$ *coverage criterion* (resp. *all-outputs*$^+$ *coverage criterion*) if, for every input i and some output o (resp. every output o), an interaction subpath of some df-chain[2] in *CHAIN*(d^x_v, $u^{x'}_{v'}$) is covered by a test sequence in Π. A test suite Π satisfies all-inputs$^+$ coverage criterion if and only if it is a witness-set for

$$\{ \bigvee_{o \in OUT(G)} \mathbf{Q}(i,o) \mid i \in IN(G)\}.$$

A test suite Π satisfies all-outputs$^+$ coverage criterion if and only if it is a witness-set for

$$\{\mathbf{Q}(i,o) \mid i \in IN(G), o \in OUT(G)\}.$$

Finally we make a sketch of how to model-check $\mathbf{Q}(d^x_v, u^{x'}_{v'})$. Although the formula is not in CTL, it has a symbolic model checking algorithm similar to that of CTL because it can be characterized as a fixpoint of a predicate transformer. In fact, the formula is directly expressible in alternation-free mu-calculus which has a linear-time model-checking algorithm[8]. By the definition of affect-pairs, we have the following equivalence.

$$\mathbf{Q}(d^x_v,u^{x'}_{v'}) = \mathbf{EF}Q(d^x_v,u^{x'}_{v'})$$

$$Q(d^x_v,u^{x'}_{v'}) = (d^x_v \wedge \mathbf{EXE}[\neg def(v)\mathbf{U}(u^{x'}_{v'} \wedge \mathbf{EF}final)]) \vee$$

$$(d^x_v \wedge \mathbf{EXE}[\neg def(v)\mathbf{U} \bigvee_{u^x_{v''} \in USE(G)} (u^x_{v''} \wedge Q(d^{x''}_{v''}, u^{x'}_{v'}))])$$

where $d^{x''}_{v''}$ is the definition of x'' occurring at v'' for some x''. Let τ: $2^Q \rightarrow 2^Q$ be a predicate transformer defined by

$$\tau(Z) = (d^x_v \wedge \mathbf{EXE}[\neg def(v)\mathbf{U}(u^{x'}_{v'} \wedge \mathbf{EF}final)]) \vee$$

$$(d^x_v \wedge \mathbf{EXE}[\neg def(v)\mathbf{U} \bigvee_{u^x_{v''} \in USE(G)} (u^x_{v''} \wedge Z[x''/x, v''/v]))$$

where $Z[x''/x,\ v''/v]$ is the formula obtained by replacing each occurrence of x and v in Z by x'' and v'', respectively.

[2] We do not require a df-chain be simple here.

Theorem 1 *$Q(d^x_v, u^{x'}_{v'})$ is a least fixpoint of τ.*

PROOF Assume that $Z_1 \subseteq Z_2$. Then $\tau(Z_1) \subseteq \tau(Z_2)$ because $Z_1[x''/x, v''/v] \subseteq Z_2[x''/x, v''/v]$ and the modal operator **U** is monotonic. Hence τ is monotonic.

Let Z_f be $Q(d^x_v, u^{x'}_{v'})$. It is easy to see that $Z_f = \tau(Z_f)$ and hence Z_f is a fixpoint of τ.

To prove that Z_f is a least fixpoint of τ, it is sufficient to show that $Z_f = \cup_i \tau^i$ where $\tau^0(Z) = Z$ and $\tau^{i+1}(Z) = \tau(\tau^i(Z))$. We first prove that τ^i(*false*) $\subseteq Z_f$ for every i. Clearly, τ^0(*false*) $\subseteq Z_f$. Assume that τ^i(*false*) $\subseteq Z_f$. Because τ is monotonic, τ^{i+1}(*false*) $\subseteq \tau(Z_f)$. Because Z_f is a fixpoint of τ, τ^{i+1}(*false*) $\subseteq Z_f$. Hence we have the first direction $\cup_i \tau^i$(*false*) $\subseteq Z_f$. The other direction, $Z_f \subseteq \cup_i \tau^i$(*false*), is proved by induction on the number of du-pairs. Suppose that $q_0 \models Z_f$, then there is a path $q_0 q_1 ...$ covering a df-chain for $(d^x_v, u^{x'}_{v'})$. Let $j \geq 1$ be the number of du-pairs of the df-chain. We show that $q_0 \in \tau^j$(*false*) for every j. For the base case $j = 1$, we have that $x = x'$ and $q_0 \models d^x_v \wedge$ **EXE**[$\neg$*def*(v) **U** ($u^x_{v'} \wedge$ **EF***final*)]. Hence $q_0 \in \tau^1$(*false*). For the inductive step, suppose $q_0 \in \tau^j$(*false*) for $j = n$. Let $j = n + 1$ and q_k be the state in $q_0 q_1 ...$ at which the first du-pair in the df-chain ends. Then there are n du-pairs from q_k and $q_k \in \tau^n$(*false*) by the induction hypothesis. Hence $q_0 \models (d^x_v \wedge$ **EXE**[$\neg$*def*(v) **U** $\bigvee_{u^x_{v''} \in USE(G)}$ $(u^x_{v''} \wedge \tau^n$(*false*)$[x''/x, v''/v]$)]) and $q_0 \in \tau^{n+1}$(*false*). □

3.4 Laski and Korel's Criteria

Laski and Korel's criteria emphasize that a vertex may contain uses of several different variables in which each use may be reached by several different definitions[22]. Such definitions constitute the definition context of the vertex. Let v be a vertex and $\{u^{x_1}_v, ..., u^{x_n}_v\}$ be a subset of *USE*(v). An *ordered definition context* of v with respect to $\{u^{x_1}_v, ..., u^{x_n}_v\}$ is a sequence $[d^{x_1}_{v_1} ... d^{x_n}_{v_n}]$ of definitions such that there is a subpath $v_1\pi_1 v_2 \pi_2 ... \pi_n v$, called *orderded context subpath*, satisfying the following property: for every $1 \leq i \leq n$, $v_i \pi_i v_{i+1} ... \pi_n v$ is a definition-clear path from v_i to v with respect to x_i. A *definition context* of v is a set of definitions, some permutation of which is an ordered definition context of v. For example, consider the vertex v_6 in Figure 1. $[d^z_{v_1} d^{max}_{v_6}]$ is an ordered definition context of v_6 with respect to $\{u^z_{v_6} u^{max}_{v_6}\}$ whose ordered context subpath is $v_1 v_2 v_3 v_5 v_6$.

3.4.1 Characterization

Let v be a vertex and $\{u^{x_1}_v, ..., u^{x_n}_v\}$ be a subset of *USE*(v). For a sequence $\lambda = [d^{x_1}_{v_1} ... d^{x_n}_{v_n}]$ of definitions, define **wctl**(λ) as follows.

- if λ is empty, then

  wctl(λ,*nodef*) = $u^{x_1}_v \wedge ... \wedge u^{x_n}_v \wedge$ **EF***final*,

- if λ is $[d^{x_i}_{v_i}] \cdot \lambda'$, then

  wctl(λ,*nodef*) = *nodef* $\wedge\ d^{x_i}_{v_i} \wedge$ **EXE**[*nodef'* **U** *wctl*(λ',*nodef'*)]),

  where *nodef'* = *nodef* $\wedge\ \neg$*def*(v_i),

- **wctl**(λ) = **EF***wctl*(λ,*true*).

By induction on the number of definitions in λ, it can be shown that λ is an ordered definition context of v with respect to $\{u^{x_1}_v, ..., u^{x_n}_v\}$ if and only if the Kripke structure $M(G)$ of a flow graph G satisfies **wctl**(λ). Moreover, a test sequence covers λ if and only if it is a witness for **wctl**(λ). For example, a test sequence covering the ordered definition context $[d^z_{v_1} d^{max}_{v_3}]$ with respect to $\{u^z_{v_6}, u^{max}_{v_6}\}$ is shown in Figure 5, which is also a witness for **EF**($d^z_{v_1} \wedge$ **EXE**[$\neg$*def*(z) **U** ($\neg$*def*(z) $\wedge d^{max}_{v_3} \wedge$ **EXE**[($\neg$*def*(z) $\wedge\ \neg$*def*(max)) **U** ($u^z_{v_6} \wedge u^{max}_{v_6} \wedge$ **EF***final*)])])).

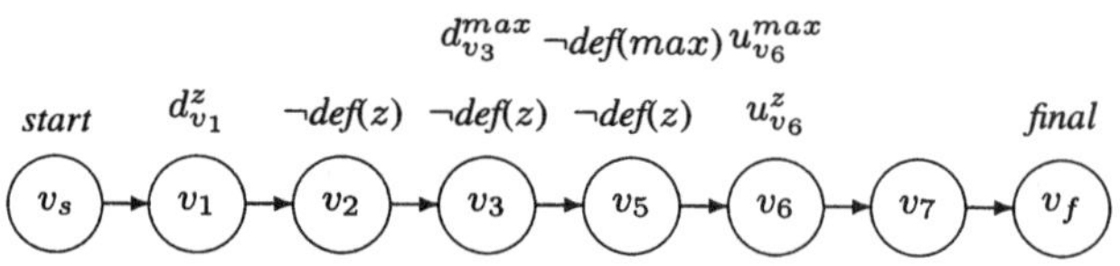

Figure 5. A test sequence covering ordered context $[d^z_{v_1} d^{max}_{v_3}]$ with respect to $\{u^z_{v_6}, u^{max}_{v_6}\}$

A test suite Π satisfies *context coverage criterion* if, for every vertex v and every definition context *dc* of v, an ordered context subpath of *dc* is covered by a test sequence in Π. A test suite Π satisfies context coverage criterion if and only if it is a witness-set for

$$\{\mathbf{wctl}(\{d^{x_1}_{v_1}, ..., d^{x_n}_{v_n}\})$$

$$\mid v \in V, u^{x_i}_v \in USE(v), d^{x_i}_{v_i} \in DEF(G), 1 \leq i \leq n\}$$

where **wctl**($\{d^{x_1}_{v_1}, ..., d^{x_n}_{v_n}\}$) is defined as **wctl**(λ_1) $\vee ... \vee$ **wctl**(λ_n), where $\lambda_1, ..., \lambda_n$ are the permutations of $\{d^{x_1}_{v_1}, ..., d^{x_n}_{v_n}\}$.

A test suite Π satisfies *ordered context coverage criterion* if, for every vertex v and every ordered definition context *odc* of v, an ordered context subpath of *odc* is covered by a test sequence in Π. A test suite Π satisfies ordered context coverage criterion if and only if it is a witness-set for

$$\{\mathbf{wctl}([d^{x_1}_{v_1}, ..., d^{x_n}_{v_n}])$$

$$\mid v \in V, u^{x_i}_v \in USE(v), d^{x_i}_{v_i} \in DEF(G), 1 \leq i \leq n\}.$$

4 Generating Minimal Cost Test Suites

This section discusses complexity issues in minimal cost test generation and describes heuristic algorithms and our experience with SMV for automatic test generation.

We wish to generate a minimal cost test suite Π with respect to one of the two costs: (i) the number of test sequences in Π or (ii) the total length of test sequences in Π. After finishing the execution of a test sequence, an implementation under test should be reset into its initial state from which another test sequence can be applied. It is appropriate to use the first cost if the reset operation is expensive, and the second one otherwise. For example, in Figure 2 we have that $\{q_0q_1q_3q_4q_0q_2q_3\}$ and $\{q_0q_2q_3q_4q_0q_1q_3\}$ are minimal in the number of test sequences, while $\{q_0q_1q_3, q_0q_2q_3\}$ is minimal in the total length of test sequences.

We first consider the Minimal Number Test Generation (MNTG) problem which is an optimization problem defined by: given a Kripke structure M and a set F of WCTL formulas, generate a minimal witness-set Π in the number of witnesses in Π. We show this problem to be NP-hard by considering its decision problem MNTG$'$: given M, F, and a positive integer k, is there a witness-set Π with $|\Pi| \leq k$?

Theorem 2 *MNTG$'$ is NP-complete.*

PROOF On input $\langle\langle M, F, k\rangle, \Pi\rangle$ where Π is a set of finite paths, we determine whether Π is a witness-set with $|\Pi| \leq k$ for F with respect to M by verifying (i) $|\Pi| \leq k$, (ii) for every $\pi \in \Pi$, π is a path of M, and (iii) for every $f \in F$, there is a witness $\pi \in \Pi$ for f. This is a polynomial time verifier and hence MNTG$'$ is in NP.

We next show that a NP-complete problem, called the Hitting Set problem, is polynomially reducible to MNTG$'$. The Hitting Set problem is defined by: given a collection of subsets C_i, $1 \leq i \leq n$, of a finite set S and a positive integer k, is there a subset $S \subseteq S'$, called hitting set, such that $|S'| \leq k$ and containing at least one element from each C_i? Given an instance of the Hitting Set problem, we construct $M = (Q, q_{init}, L, R)$ and F as follows:

- $Q = \{q_0\} \cup \{q_c \mid c \in \bigcup C_i\}$,
- $q_{init} = q_0$,
- $L(q_0) = \emptyset$ and, for every q_c, $i \in L(q_c)$ if and only if $q_c \in C_i$,
- $R = \{(q_0, q_c) \mid c \in \bigcup C_i\}$, and
- $F = \{\mathbf{EF}i \mid 1 \leq i \leq n\}$.

This reduction is in polynomial time. Clearly, $c \in C_i$ if and only if q_0q_c is a witness for $\mathbf{EF}i$. Therefore, a subset S' of S is a hitting set with $|S'| \leq k$ for the collection of C_i if and only if $\Pi = \{q_0q_s \mid s \in S'\}$ is a witness-set with $|\Pi| \leq k$. □

Second we consider the Minimal Length Test Generation (MNTG) problem defined by: given M and F, generate a minimal witness-set Π in the total length of witnesses in Π. Its decision problem MNTG$'$ is defined by: given M, F, and k, is there a witness-set Π with $\sum_{\pi \in \Pi} |\Pi| \leq k$?

Theorem 3 *MLTG$'$ is NP-complete.*

PROOF We use the same reduction as in Theorem 2. Since all paths in the Kripke structure M are of length one, the minimum total length of Π is achieved when Π contains the minimum number of witnesses. Therefore, a solution for the MLTG$'$ problem in this case will yield the same witness-set which is also a solution to the MNTG$'$ problem. □

Because of NP-hardness, we do not expect an optimal solution to the minimal cost test generation problems. Instead we describe a heuristic algorithm which can be applied to both MNTG$'$ and MLTG$'$ problems. Figure 6 describes the algorithm in a generic fashion without being specific about any coverage criteria. We directly employ the capability of model checkers to construct counterexamples by exploiting the fact that a witness for a WCTL formula is also a counterexample for its negation.

```
INPUT: a Kripke structure M and a coverage criterion C
OUTPUT: a test suite Π satisfying C

Π := ∅;
mark every entity required to be covered in C as uncovered;
repeat
    choose an entity marked as uncovered;
    let f be the WCTL formula for the entity;
    model-check f against M;
    if M ⊭ f
        mark the entity as untestable;
    else
        let π be a witness for f
        (or equivalently a counterexample for ¬f);
        let En(π) be the set of entities covered by π;
        mark every entity in En(π) as covered;
        for every π' ∈ Π such that En(π') ⊆ En(π)
            Π := Π − {π'};
        Π := Π ∪ {π};
until every entity is marked as covered or untestable
return Π;
```

Figure 6. A heuristic algorithm for test generation

Basically, we construct a witness for every formula by finding a counterexample for its negation. The algorithm is locally optimal in the sense that model checkers such as SMV find a shortest counterexample for a given formula through breadth-first search of the state space. However, it

Table 1. Results of test generation without heuristics

	all-defs	all-uses	required 3-tuples	all-inputs	all-outputs	all-IO-df-chains	context	orderded context
Number of formulas employed	24	105	139	6	22	62	105	229
Number of formulas satisfied	24	53	60	5	6	6	58	63
Number of test sequences	24	53	60	5	6	6	58	63
Total length of test sequences	487	1210	2007	92	116	116	1305	1456
Execution time (sec)	0.44	0.88	1.56	0.34	0.31	0.23	1.48	1.2
Number of BDD nodes	3130	3268	3200	1997	2043	2000	3418	3342

Table 2. Results of test generation with heuristics

	all-defs	all-uses	required 3-tuples	all-inputs	all-outputs	all-IO-df-chains	context	orderded context
Number of formulas employed	24	105	139	6	22	62	105	229
Number of formulas satisfied	24	53	60	5	6	6	58	63
Number of test sequences	4	14	23	2	3	3	14	14
Total length of test sequences	106	385	878	39	63	63	385	385
Execution time (sec)	0.86	5.13	14.39	0.37	0.40	0.35	8.08	8.23
Number of BDD nodes	5823	21498	55543	1564	2185	2183	22276	22091

would generate a number of redundant witnesses because a witness may cover more than one entity at the same time. The algorithm removes such redundant witnesses by considering only uncovered states (Line 4) and by removing an existing witness if all the entities covered by it are also covered by a new witness (Line 13 and 14). Finally we note that the computation of $En(\pi)$ in Line 11 can be done by viewing a witness $q_0 ... q_n$ as the single-path Kripke structure $(\{q_0, ..., q_n\}, q_0, L, \{(q_0, q_1), ..., (q_{n-1}, q_n), (q_n, q_n)\})$ and model-checking the WCTL formula against the Kripke structure for every entity in the coverage criterion.

We describe the experimental results obtained by applying our approach to a moderate flow graph. In the experiment, we used SMV on a standard PC and adopted the flow graph made by Ural et al. (see Figure 1 in [31]). The flow graph consists of 39 vertices, 46 arcs, 11 variables, 24 definitions, and 36 uses. We first applied our approach to the flow graph without heuristics. Table 1 summarizes the experimental results. The second row gives the number of WCTL formulas associated with each coverage criterion and the third row gives the number of WCTL formulas satisfied in the flow graph. The number of test sequences given in the fourth column is equivalent to that of formulas satisfied, because we did not remove redundant test sequences. A test sequence has a single test purpose, that is, it is intended to cover only one entity. The fifth row gives the total length of test sequences. Finally, the sixth and seventh rows give the execution time in seconds and the number of BDD nodes, respectively. Table 2 summarizes the results of test generation with heuristics in Figure 6. We removed redundant test sequences according to the heuristics and were able to significantly reduce the number and total length of test sequences with the cost of increased execution time and BDDs. For example, only 14 test sequences are necessary for all-uses coverage criterion. The test sequences cover all entities desribed by 53 formulas. The execution time was calculated by adding up the execution time of Line 6 and Line 11 in Figure 6. The number of BDD nodes was figured out in a similar manner.

5 Summary and Discussion

We have showed that test generation from flow graphs for data flow oriented coverage criteria can be automated by model checking. We investigated four groups of coverage criteria in [26, 24, 30, 22]. For a given coverage criterion, a CTL formula is associated with every entity required to be covered in the coverage criterion. A witness for the CTL formula corresponds to a test sequence covering the entity described by the formula and a witness-set for the formula set corresponds to a test suite satisfying the criterion. We also discussed complexity issues in minimal cost test generation and described heuristics for automatic test generation.

As mentioned before, one of the advantages of our approach is language independence. We are currently working on both program-based and specification-based test generation for real-world applications. In our preliminary experiments for specification-based testing, we constructed flow graphs from statecharts or a set of communicating state machines by following the methods in [17, 31] and were able to generate test suites from flow graphs with 2^{20} vertices and one hundred formulas in one minute and flow graphs with 2^{70} vertices and one hundred formulas in one hour. Of course, further experiments are compulsory to demonstrate the feasibility of our approach when applied to data flow testing with huge state space.

We are planning to extend our approach for interprocedural programs and object-oriented programs. Data flow testing of such programs is more complicated due to procedure call/return, recursion, and reference parameters as well as global variables. Data flow testing methods for such programs were proposed in [13, 14] which employ interprocedural data flow analysis. Recently, the problem of interprocedural data flow analysis has been formulated as a model checking problem[2, 10]. Combining both work together may be a starting point for developing a model checking-based approach to data flow testing of interprocedural programs and object-oriented programs.

We showed that a subclass of CTL, which we call WCTL, is expressive enough to characterize a number of data flow oriented coverage criteria except those by Ural[30]. For Ural's criteria, we extended WCTL with least fixpoints so that model checking of the resulting logic can be readily implemented in existing model checkers for CTL such as SMV. To characterize the criteria considered in this paper in a more uniform way, it is necessary to employ a logic more powerful than CTL. We are currently working with a subclass of mu-calculus[21], more specifically alternation-free mu-calculus[8], which supports the explicit use of fixpoint operators.

We cannot directly use linear time temporal logic for the characterization of data flow oriented coverage criteria, because it requires existential quantification over paths. It is, however, possible to construct a witness for a WCTL formula using linear time model checkers by exploiting the fact that a path is a witness for a WCTL formula if and only if the path is a counterexample for its negation. For example, we can construct a witness for a WCTL formula $\mathbf{EFEF}p$ by finding a counterexample for $\neg\mathbf{EFEF}p = \mathbf{AGAG}\neg p$, which is in turn equivalent to the LTL formula $\mathbf{AGG}\neg p$. This opens the possibility of applying linear time model checkers such as SPIN to data flow testing.

References

[1] P. Ammann, P. Black, and W. Majurski, "Using Model Checking to Generate Tests from Specifications," in *Proceedings of the 2nd IEEE International Conference on Formal Engineering Methods*, pp. 46-54, 1998.

[2] T. Ball and S.K. Rajamani, "Bebop: a Symolic Model Checker for Boolean Programs," *SPIN Workshop '00*, Vol. 1885 of LNCS, pp. 113-130, Springer-Verlag, 2000.

[3] J. Callahan, F. Schneider, and S. Easterbrook, "Specification-based Testing Using Model Checking," in *Proceedings of 1996 SPIN Workshop*, also Technical Report NASA-IVV-96-022, West Virginia Univeristy, 1996.

[4] E.M. Clarke, E.A. Emerson, and A.P. Sistla, "Automatic Verification of Finite-State Concurrent Systems Using Temporal Logic Specifications," *ACM Transactions on Programming Languages and Systems*, 8(2):244-263, Apr. 1986.

[5] E.M. Clarke, O. Grumberg, K. McMillan, and X. Zhao, "Efficient Generation of Counterexamples and Witnesses in Symbolic Model Checking," in *Proceedings of the 32nd Design Automation Conference*, pp. 427-432, 1995.

[6] E.M. Clarke, S. Jha, Y. Lu, and H. Veith, "Tree-Like Counterexamples in Model Checking," in *Proceedings of the 17th Annual IEEE Symposium on Logic in Computer Science*, pp. 19-29, 2002.

[7] L.A. Clarke, A. Podgurski, D.J. Richardson, and S.J. Zeil, "A Formal Evaluation of Data Flow Path Selection Criteria," *IEEE Transactions on Software Engineering*, 15(11):1318-1332, Nov. 1989.

[8] R. Cleaveland and B. Steffen, "A Linear-Time Model-Checking Algorithm for the Alternation-Free Modal Mu-Calculus," *Formal Methods in System Design*, Vol. 2, pp. 121-147, 1993.

[9] A. Engels, L. Feijs, and S. Mauw, "Test Generation for Intelligent Networks Using Model Checking," *TACAS '97*, Vol. 1217 of LNCS, pp. 384-398, Springer-Verlag, 1997.

[10] J. Esparza and J. Knoop, "An Automata-Theoretical Approach to Interprocedural Data-Flow Analysis," *FOSSACS '99*, Vol. 1578 of LNCS, pp. 14-30, Springer-Verlag, 1999.

[11] P.G. Frankl and E.J. Weyuker, "An Applicable Family of Data Flow Testing Criteria," *IEEE Transactions on Software Engineering*, 14(10):1483-1498, Oct. 1988.

[12] A. Gargantini and C. Heitmeyer, "Using Model Checking to Generate Tests from Requirements Specifications," in *Proceedings of ESEC/FSE '99* pp. 146-162, 1999.

[13] M.J. Harrold and M.L. Soffa, "Interprocedural Data Flow Testing," in *Proceedings of the 3rd Symposium on Software Testing, Analysis, and Verification*, pp. 158-167, 1989.

[14] M.J. Harrold and G. Rothermel, "Performing Data Flow Testing on Classes," in *Proceedings of the 2nd ACM SIGSOFT Symposium on the Foundations of Software Engineering*, pp. 154-163, 1994.

[15] R. Hojati, R.K. Brayon, and R.P. Kurshan, "BDD-based Debugging of Designs Using Language Containment and Fair CTL," *CAV '99*, Vol. 697 of LNCS, pp. 41-58, Springer-Verlag, 1993.

[16] G.J. Holzmann, "The Model Checker SPIN," *IEEE Transactions on Software Engineering*, Vol. 23, No. 5, pp. 279-295, May 1997.

[17] H.S. Hong, Y.G. Kim, S.D. Cha, D.H. Bae, and H. Ural, "A Test Sequence Selection Method for Statecharts," *Journal of Software Testing, Verification, and Reliability*, 10(4):203-227, Dec. 2000.

[18] H.S. Hong, I. Lee, O. Sokolsky, and S.D. Cha, "Automatic Test Generation from Statecharts Using Model Checking," in *Proceedings of the First Workshop on Formal Approaches to Testing of Software*, pp. 15-30, 2001.

[19] H.S. Hong, I. Lee, O. Sokolsky, and H. Ural, "A Temporal Logic Based Theory of Test Coverage and Generation," *TACAS '02*, Vol. 2280 of LNCS, pp. 327-341, Springer-Verlag, 2002.

[20] T. Jeron and P. Morel, "Test Generation Derived From Model Checking," *CAV '99*, Vol. 1633 of LNCS, pp. 108-121, Springer-Verlag, 1999.

[21] D. Kozen, "Results on the Propositional Mu-Calculus," *Theoretical Computer Science*, 27:333-354, 1983.

[22] J.W. Laski and B. Korel, "A Data Flow Oriented Program Testing Strategy," *IEEE Transactions on Software Engineering*, 9(5):347-354, May 1983.

[23] K.L. McMillan, *Symbolic Model Checking – an Approach to the State Explosion Problem*, Kluwer Academic Publishers, 1993.

[24] S.C. Ntafos, "On Required Element Testing," *IEEE Transactions on Software Engineering*, 10(11):795-803, Nov. 1984.

[25] S.C. Ntafos, "A Comparison of Some Structural Testing Strategies," *IEEE Transactions on Software Engineering*, 14(6):868-874, June 1988.

[26] S. Rapps and E.J. Weyuker, "Selecting Software Test Data Using Data Flow Information," *IEEE Transactions on Software Engineering*, 11(4):367-375, Apr. 1985.

[27] D.A. Schmidt and B. Steffen, "Data-flow Analysis as Model Checking of Abstract Interpretations," *SAS '98*, Vol. 1503 of LNCS, pp. 351-380, Springr-Verlag, 1998.

[28] B. Steffen, "Generating Data-Flow Analysis Algorithms for Modal Specifications," *Science of Computer Programming*, 21:115-139, 1993.

[29] H. Ural and B. Yang, "A Test Sequence Generation Method for Protocol Testing," *IEEE Transactions on Communications*, 39(4):514-523, Apr. 1991.

[30] H. Ural, "IO-df-chains criterion," ISO Working Group on Formal Methods on Conformance Testing, Draft International Standard, Sept. 1993.

[31] H. Ural, K. Saleh, and A. Williams, "Test Generation Based on Control and Data Dependencies within System Specifications in SDL," *Computer Communications*, 23(7):609-627, Mar. 2000.

[32] R. de Vries and J. Tretmans, "On-the-Fly Conformance Testing Using SPIN," *International Journal on Software Tools for Technology Transfer*, 2(4):382-393, 2000.

Technical Papers

Software Process

New Directions on Agile Methods: A Comparative Analysis

Pekka Abrahamsson[a], Juhani Warsta[b], Mikko T. Siponen[b] and Jussi Ronkainen[a]
[a]*Technical Research Centre of Finland, VTT Electronics*
P.O.Box 1100, FIN-90571 Oulu, Finland
[b]*Department of Information Processing Science*
P.O.Box 3000, FIN-90014 University of Oulu, Finland
{Pekka.Abrahamsson, Jussi.Ronkainen}@vtt.fi, {Juhani.Warsta, Mikko.T.Siponen}@oulu.fi

Abstract

Agile software development methods have caught the attention of software engineers and researchers worldwide. Scientific research is yet scarce. This paper reports results from a study, which aims to organize, analyze and make sense out of the dispersed field of agile software development methods. The comparative analysis is performed using the method's life-cycle coverage, project management support, type of practical guidance, fitness-for-use and empirical evidence as the analytical lenses. The results show that agile software development methods, without rationalization, cover certain/different phases of the software development life-cycle and most of them do not offer adequate support for project management. Yet, many methods still attempt to strive for universal solutions (as opposed to situation appropriate) and the empirical evidence is still very limited. Based on the results, new directions are suggested. In principal, it is suggested to place emphasis on methodological quality – not method quantity.

1. Introduction

Agile – denoting "the quality of being agile; readiness for motion; nimbleness, activity, dexterity in motion" (http://dictionary.oed.com) – software development methods attempt to offer once again an answer to the eager business community asking for lighter weight along with faster and nimbler software development processes. This is especially the case with the rapidly growing and volatile Internet software industry as well as with the emerging mobile application environment. The new agile methods have evoked a substantial amount of literature and debates [e.g., 1, 2, 3].

Agile proponents claim that the focal aspects of light and agile methods are simplicity and speed [4-6]. In development work, accordingly, development groups concentrate only on the functions needed immediately, delivering them fast, collecting feedback and reacting rapidly to business and technology changes [7-9].

The emerging of numerous different agile methods has exploded during the last years and is not showing any signs of ceasing. This has resulted in a situation where researchers and practitioners are not aware of the existing approaches or their suitability for varying real-life software development situations. As for researchers and method developers, the lack of unifying research hinders the ability to establish a reliable and cumulative research tradition.

The aim of this paper is to organize, analyze and make sense out of the dispersed field of agile software development methods. Based on the result of the analysis, practitioners are in a better position to understand the various properties of each method and make their judgment in a more informed way. For these purposes, an analytic framework is constructed, which guides the analysis of the different existing methods. To scrutinize the agile methods the following five perspectives are chosen: software development life-cycle including the process aspect, project management, abstract principles vs. concrete guidance, universally predefined vs. situation appropriate (i.e., fit-for-use), and empirical evidence.

The rest of the paper is composed as follows. The second section presents a short overview of the existing agile methods. The third section presents the lenses for the subsequent analysis. The fourth section presents a comparative analysis of the referred methods and the fifth section discusses the significance and the limitations of the findings. The sixth section concludes this study, recapitulating the key findings.

0-7695-1877-X/03 $17.00 © 2003 IEEE

2. An overview of agile methods

In this section the existing agile methods are identified and their objectives briefly introduced. Figure 1 shows the manifold agile software development methods and their interrelationships together with their evolutionary paths. Figure 1, purposefully, extends the considerations beyond the scope of this paper. This means that some, more philosophical meta-level expositions, which have in their turn impinged upon the preceding agile methods either directly or indirectly are included in the diagram. Figure 1 also depicts (i.e., using a dashed line) which methods (or method developers) contributed to the publication of the agile manifesto. (http://www.agilemanifesto.org).

For the purposes of this paper, agile software development in general is characterized by the following attributes: incremental, cooperative, straightforward, and adaptive [10]. Incremental refers to small software releases, with rapid development cycles. Cooperative refers to a close customer and developer interaction. Straightforward implies that the method itself is easy to learn and to modify and that it is sufficiently documented. Finally, adaptive refers to the ability to make and react to last moment changes. Due to limited space, readers are referred to [10] for further discussion on other possible characterizations. In the following, each method's objectives are briefly introduced.

Adaptive software development. Adaptive software development (ASD) [11] attempts to bring about a new way of seeing the software development in an organization, promoting an adaptive paradigm. It offers solutions for the development of large and complex systems. The method encourages incremental and iterative development, with constant prototyping. One ancestor of ASD is "RADical Software Development" [12]. ASD claims to provide a framework with enough guidance to prevent projects from falling into chaos, but not too much, which could suppress emergence and creativity.

Agile modeling. Agile modeling (AM) [13] is a new approach for performing modeling activities. It attempts to adapt modeling practices using an agile philosophy as its backbone. The key focus in AM, therefore, is on modeling practices and cultural principles. The underlying idea is to encourage developers to produce sufficiently advanced models to support acute design needs and documentation purposes. The aim is to keep the amount of models and documentation as low as possible. Cultural issues are addressed by depicting ways to encourage communication, and to organize team structures and ways of working.

Crystal family. The Crystal family of methodologies [14-16] includes a number of different methods from which to select the most suitable one for each individual project. Besides the methods, the Crystal approach also includes principles for tailoring these methods to fit the varying circumstances of different projects. Each member of the Crystal family is marked with a color indicating the 'heaviness' of the method. Crystal suggests choosing the appropriate-colored method for a project based on its size and criticality. Larger projects are likely to ask for more coordination and heavier methods than smaller ones. Crystal methods are open for any development practices, tools or work products, thus allowing the integration of, for example, XP and Scrum practices.

Dynamic systems development method. Dynamic systems development method (DSDM) [17, 18] is a method developed by a dedicated consortium in the UK. The first release of the method was in 1994. The fundamental idea behind DSDM is that instead of fixing the amount of functionality in a product, and then adjusting time and resources to reach that functionality, it is preferred to fix time and resources, and then adjust the amount of functionality accordingly. The origins of DSDM are in rapid application development. DSDM can be seen as the first truly agile software development method.

Extreme programming. Extreme programming (XP) [5, 19, 20] is a collection of well-known software engineering practices. XP aims at enabling successful software development despite vague or constantly changing software requirements. The novelty of XP is based on the way the individual practices are collected and lined up to function with each other. Some of the main characteristics of XP are short iterations with small releases and rapid feedback, close customer participation, constant communication and coordination, continuous refactoring, continuous integration and testing, collective code ownership, and pair programming.

Feature-driven development. Feature-driven development (FDD) [21, 22] is a process-oriented software development method for developing business critical systems. The FDD approach focuses on the design and building phases. The FDD approach embodies iterative development with the practices believed to be effective in industry. The specific blend of these ingredients makes the FDD processes unique for each case. It emphasizes quality aspects throughout the process and includes frequent and tangible deliveries, along with accurate monitoring of the progress of the project.

Internet-speed development. Internet-speed development (ISD) [23-25] is arguably the least known approach to agile software development. ISD refers to a situation where software needs to be released fast, thereby requiring short development cycles. ISD puts forth a descriptive, management-oriented framework for addressing the problem of handling fast releases. This framework consists of time drivers, quality dependencies and process adjustments.

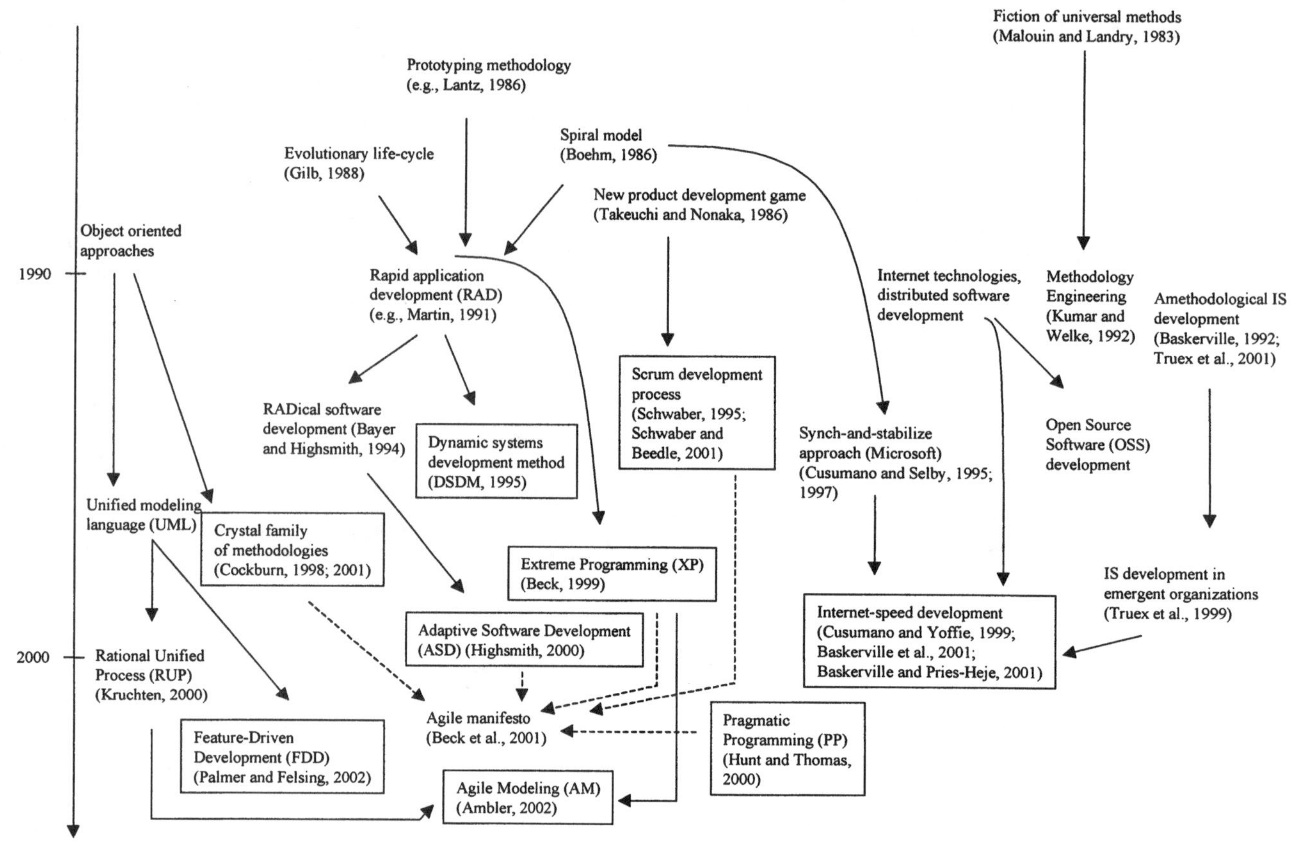

Figure 1. Evolutionary map of agile methods.

These are rules under which companies have survived in ISD. In this context the 'process adjustment' means focusing on good people instead of process, i.e., "if people are mature and talented, there is less need for process" [23, p. 56]. The framework for ISD is considered as more management and business-oriented than other related approaches. ISD draws from the "*Synch-and-stabilize*" approach by Microsoft, aimed at coping with a fast-moving, or even chaotic, software development business [26], and from emergent organizations, which are organizations having a fast pace of organizational change – an opposite to stable organizations [27]. ISD's theoretical background stems from Amethodological IS development [28, 29], which argues that software development is a collection of random, opportunistic processes driven by accident. These processes are simultaneous, overlapping and there are gaps and the development itself occurs in completely unique and idiographic forms. Finally, the development is negotiated, compromised and capricious as opposed to predefined, planned and mutually agreed.

Pragmatic programming. Pragmatic programming (PP) [30] introduces a set of programming "best practices". It puts forward techniques that concretely augment the practices discussed in the other agile methods. PP covers most programming practicalities. The "method" itself is a collection of short tips that focus on day-to-day problems; there are a total of 70 of them. These practices take a pragmatic perspective and place focus on incremental, iterative development, rigorous testing, and user-centered design.

Scrum. The Scrum [31, 32] approach has been developed for managing the software development process in a volatile environment. It is an empirical approach based on flexibility, adaptability and productivity. Scrum leaves open for the developers to choose the specific software development techniques, methods, and practices for the implementation process. It involves frequent management activities aiming at consistently identifying any deficiencies or impediments in the development process as well as the in the practices that are used.

3. Lenses for the analysis

In order to make sense and scrutinize the existing agile methods, proper analytic tools are need. Many such analytical tools have been proposed and used [e.g., 33,

34]. The following five analytical lenses were seen as relevant and complementary for addressing the research purposes of the paper (Table 1).

Table 1. Lenses for the analysis.

Perspective	Description	Key references
Software development life-cycle	Which stages of the software development life-cycle does the method cover	[35, 36]
Project management	Does the method support project management activities	[37, 38]
Abstract principles vs. concrete guidance	Does the method mainly rely on abstract principles or does it provide concrete guidance	[39]
Universally predefined vs. situation appropriate	Is the method argued to fit *per se* in all agile development situations	[37]
Empirical evidence	Does the method have empirical support for its claims	[37, 40-42]

A *software development life-cycle* is a sequence of processes that an organization employs to conceive, design, and commercialize a software product [35, 36]. A software development life-cycle perspective is needed to observe which phases of the software development process the agile methods cover. A software development life-cycle can be seen as consisting of nine phases [e.g., 43]: project inception, requirements specification, design, coding, unit test, integration test, system test, acceptance test, system in use (i.e., maintenance). Life-cycle coverage also includes that the process through which the software production proceeds needs to be identified.

Methods should be efficient (as opposed to time and resource consuming) [37]. Efficiency requires the existence of *project management* activities to enable the proper execution of software development tasks. Project management is thus a support function that provides the backbone for efficient software development [38]. Therefore, a project management perspective can be seen as a relevant dimension in the evaluation of agile software development methods.

Software development methods are often used for other purposes than originally intended by their authors [39]. For example, Wastel [44] observed that methodologies act as a social defense operating as a set of organizational rituals. Thus, in order to evaluate whether the methods can be used for other purposes than the necessary fiction of control [39], a perspective of *abstract principles versus concrete guidance* is needed. It will be evaluated whether the agile software methods provide any concrete guidance or do they rely on abstract rules of thumb. "Respect people" without instructing how to actually perform it is an example of an abstract principle. Concrete guidance, on the other hand, refers to practices, activities and work products at the different phases of the software development life-cycle.

The *Universally predefined versus situation appropriate* viewpoint stems from the works of Kumar and Welke [37], Malouin and Landry [45], and Truex *et al.*[29]. Universally predefined means a view according to which there is one method or methodology that fits as such to all (agile) development situations. In other words, a universally predefined viewpoint proposes one ready-made solution to all (agile) SW development endeavors. The view of situation appropriate, as opposed to universally predefined, holds that there can be no predetermined set of methods that would fit *per se* to all (agile) software development situations. In other words, situation appropriate refers to the extent to which a method is adjustable depending on the situation.

Empirical support is needed to see what kind of empirical evidence the agile methods are grounded upon. Clearly, one of the most important aspects of research is the use of proper research methods [46]. Since software development has a strong practical orientation, there is need for studying the different agile methods in real life situations [cf., 40, 41, 42], i.e., using empirical studies. This viewpoint explores what, if any, empirical support the different methods have.

4. Comparative analysis of the existing agile methods

In this section, the existing agile methods are compared using the analytical lenses defined in section three. Thus, for each method the software life-cycle coverage, project management support, type of guidance, situation appropriateness and the level of empirical support is evaluated. Each perspective will be analyzed separately.

Figure 2 serves for the purposes of the first three lenses. Each method is divided into three bars. The uppermost bar indicates whether a method provides support for project management (analyzed in section 4.1). The middle bar indicates whether a process through which the software production proceeds is described (pertaining to software development life-cycle analysis). The length of the bar shows which phases of software development are supported by different agile methods (analyzed in section 4.2). Finally, the lowest bar shows whether a method relies mainly on abstract principles (white color) or does it provide concrete guidance (gray color). This will be analyzed in section 4.3.

In general, a gray color in a block indicates that the method covers the perspective analyzed while a white color indicates lack of such support.

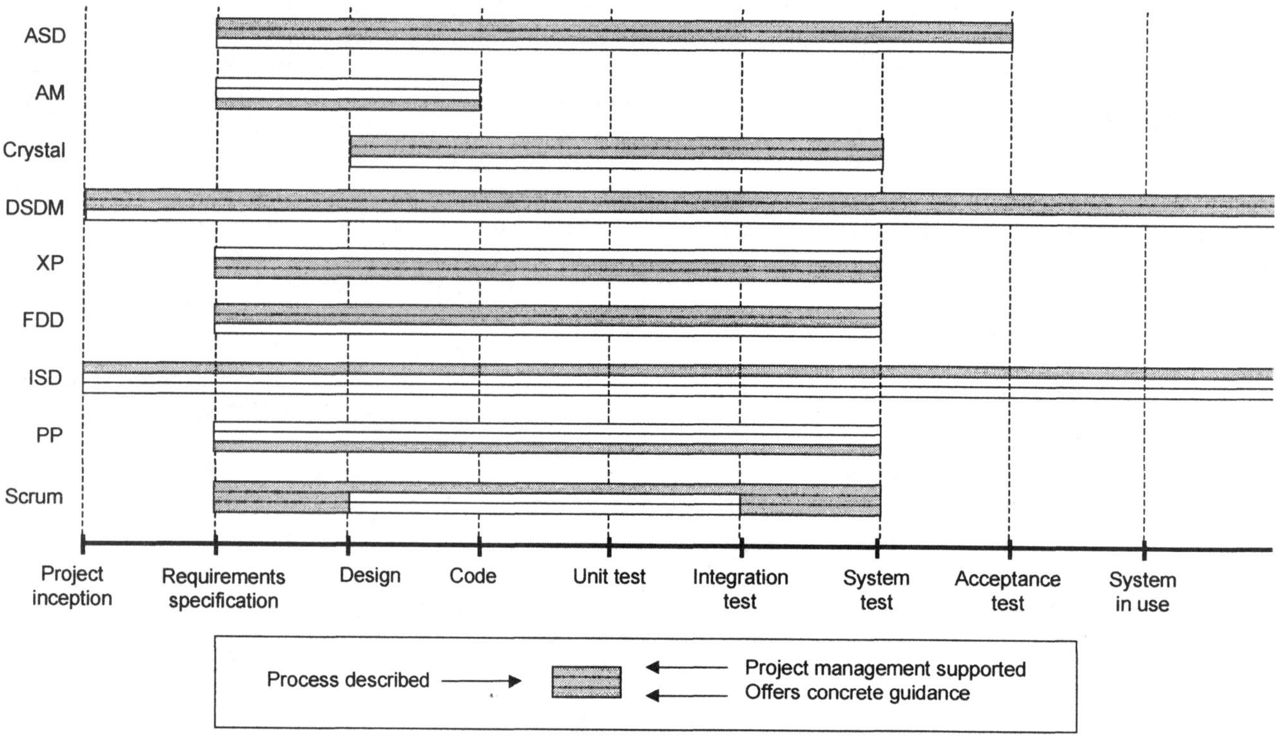

Figure 2. Comparing life-cycle, project management and concrete guidance support.

4.1. Project management

Agile software development methods differ to a large degree in the way they cover project management (uppermost bar in Figure 2). Currently, AM and PP do not address the managerial perspective. XP has recently been supplemented with some guidelines on project management [47], but it still does not offer a comprehensive project management view. Scrum, on the other hand, is explicitly intended for the purpose of managing agile software development projects. Thus, Schwaber and Beedle [32] suggest the use of other methods to complement a Scrum based software development approach, naming XP as one alternative.

The approach promoted by ASD is the *adaptive (leadership-collaboration) management model* [11]. The point of view in ASD is on changing the software development culture, essentially stating that management will also have to bend in response to changes in projects. FDD offers means for planning projects by product features, and tracking the projects' progress. FDD also believes in empowering project managers; within an FDD project, the project manager has the ultimate say on project scope, schedule, and staffing [21].

DSDM suggests a framework of controls to supplement the rapid application development approach. All of these controls are designated to increase organizational ability to react to business changes [18], which has become commonplace nowadays in all agile software development approaches. Therefore, the DSDM approach towards project management is largely about facilitating the work of the development teams, with daily tracking of the project's progress. Crystal's solution to project management focuses on increasing the ability to choose the correct method for the purpose [16].

4.2. Software development life-cycle

Figure 2 shows that different agile methods are focused on different aspects of the software development life-cycle. DSDM is an independent method in the sense that it attempts to provide complete support over all life-cycle phases. The Internet-speed development approach also addresses all the phases of the software development life-cycle but only at a managerial level. Others are more focused. ASD covers all other phases expect for project inception, acceptance test and system in use. AM aims at providing modeling support for requirements specification and design phases.

The Crystal family covers the phases from design to integration test. XP, PP, FDD and Scrum are focused on requirements speci^fication, design, implementation (except for Scrum) and testing up until the system test.

From the process perspective, AM, ISD, Scrum (for the implementation part) and PP approaches do not emphasize (or have not described) the process through which the software development proceeds. AM and PP are supplements to other methods. Thus, in the case of AM and PP the lack of a process perspective seems reasonable. However, ISD lacks clarity in this regard. In the other agile software development methods (i.e., ASD, Crystal, DSDM, XP, FDD and Scrum), the development process has been described.

4.3. Abstract principles vs. concrete guidance

The lowest bar in Figure 2 indicates whether the method relies on concrete guidance (gray color) or on abstract principles (white color).

A method that is useful and efficient should not refer to abstract principles only in forming the core of the method [39]. It is claimed that abstract principles are useless if not supported with concrete guidance [48]. Concrete guidance, in this context, refers to practices, activities and work products that characterize and provide guidance on how a specific task can be executed. For example, FDD lays down eight practices that "must" be used if compliance with the FDD development rules is to be valued [21]. They continue that the "team is allowed to adapt them according to their experience level". Especially, in the case of these "must" practices, concrete guidance should be provided how, in practice, this adaptation can be executed. If such guidance is missing (as it is, in this case), we interpret it as a reliance to abstract principles.

Based on this distinction, it was found that five out of nine agile software development methods included in the analysis place emphasis on abstract principles over concrete guidance. ASD is more about concepts and culture than software practice. Crystal, depending on the system criticality and project size, mandates certain practices but does not provide any guidance on how to execute them. DSDM states that due to the fact that each organization is different no practices are detailed [18]. Instead, organizations should develop the practices themselves. Concrete guidance on how this should be done, is not provided. Internet-speed development establishes certain practices or principles that should be in place. However, it does not offer any concrete guidance on how one should actually carry out the ideas of e.g. "always analysis" or "dynamic requirements negotiation".

AM, XP and PP have been directly derived from practical settings. Their purpose and goal is to feed collected "best practices" back into the actual practice of software development. Hence, these three methods are strong in their focus on concrete guidance. Whether the guidance they offer, however, is of value and correct falls beyond the scope of this paper (whether the guidance is supported by empirical evidence is, however, analyzed in section 4.5). Scrum defines the practices and offers guidance for the requirements specification phase as well as the integration testing phase. Implementation phases, as stated earlier, are not a part of the method.

4.4. Universally predefined vs. situation appropriate

The goal of agile software development is to increase the ability to react and respond to changing business, customer and technological needs at all organizational levels. Agile software development methods are used in a hope of nearing toward this goal. While agility refers to nimbleness, a method aiding this process needs to be nimble as well. In other words, in order to increase the level of agility, the tools (i.e., agile software development methods) used in the development process need to be agile also, i.e. situation appropriate. Situation appropriate therefore means that a method can be adjusted to different situations. A method should be flexible enough to enable adjustments to be made on-the-fly, i.e. whenever the situation calls for an adjustment. A universally predefined viewpoint proposes one ready-made solution to all agile software development endeavors.

Table 2 presents the results of the analysis regarding situation appropriateness and empirical evidence. The results are shown here using the following scale:

+ Situation appropriate, adjustable
– Universally predefined solutions, not adjustable

Empirical evidence will be discussed in the next subsection. Here, the following scale is used:

+ Some empirical evidence exists
– No empirical evidence exists

Table 2. Situation appropriateness and empirical evidence

Perspective:	Situation appropriateness	Empirical evidence
ASD	+	-
AM	+	-
Crystal	-	-
DSDM	+	-
XP	+	+
FDD	-	-
Internet speed	+	+
PP	+	-
SCRUM	+	+

Cockburn's [16] Crystal family of methodologies explicitly provides criteria on how to select the methodology for a project. The selection is made based on project size, criticality and priority [49]. Based on these factors a decision is made about which methodology should be used. However, when the project is underway the situation appropriateness is diminished. This interpretation is based on the fact that Crystal methods offer prescriptive guidance. This means that Crystal e.g. enforces certain rules such as "the projects always use incremental development cycles with a maximum increment length of four months" Thus, the adjustment is made by choosing one of the several "universal solutions" such as Crystal Clear or other.

The analysis shows further that FDD also has goals that are grounded on imperatives or prescriptive guidance similar to Crystal. Palmer and Felsing [21, p. 35] explain that FDD is "built around a core set of 'best practices'." All of these practices must be used in order to "get the full benefit that occurs by using the whole FDD process". FDD is claimed to suit for "any software development organization that needs to deliver quality, business-critical software systems on time." [21, p. xxiii]. Thus, FDD, Crystal and DSDM all represent universal prescriptions that claim to have the suitability for all agile software development situations, scopes and projects.

The DSDM Consortium [17] has published a method suitability filter in which three areas are covered: business, systems and technical [18]. The filter involves a series of questions such as "Are the requirements flexible and only specified at a high level?" or "Is functionality going to be reasonably visible at the user interface?" and some rationalization about which type of an answer would yield greater benefits if DSDM were to be applied. While the method filter is predominantly about deciding whether the method itself is applicable or not, a recent study [50] showed how the DSDM was tailored in a CMM context to a project's purposes, implying the necessary situation appropriate characteristics.

Further, the ASD, AM, XP, ISD, PP and Scrum approaches allow situation appropriate modifications. For example, regarding XP Beck [5, p.77] suggests: "If you want to try XP, ... don't try to swallow it all at once. Pick the worst problem in your current process and try solving it the XP way." Beck maintains is that there is no process that fits every project as such, but rather the practices should be tailored to suit the needs of individual projects. We interpret this in such a way that the number of adjustments is not limited. One of XP's practices, namely "just rules", implies that while the rules are followed, they can be changed if a mutual understanding among the development team is achieved. This implies that XP supports situation appropriateness.

AM and PP offer supplemental practices and concrete guidance on how and when to apply them in actual software development work. Their authors describe the situations and rationale for applying the practices suggested but refrain from offering prescriptive guidance.

4.5. Empirical evidence

This viewpoint explores what, if any, empirical support the different agile software development methods have. Table 2 presents the results of the analysis regarding the empirical evidence (right column).

While ASD, Crystal, FDD and Scrum are derived from subjective practical experience, the way they were developed is not based on reliable and systematic research. Thus their solutions lack real empirical support. AM and PP do not offer empirical support for their suggestions, either. Regarding Scrum, Schwaber and Beedle [32, p.31] claim e.g., that "*[Scrum] practices have been established through thousands of Scrum projects*". None of these projects are cited however, which invites skepticism regarding the validity of the empirical evidence. More recently, however, a study [51] can be found where Scrum was tested in real-life projects, thus showing that the body of needed industrial evidence is gradually growing, and that Scrum has some empirical support.

Internet-speed development has a degree of empirical support. It is based on qualitative case studies in nine companies [23]. We see that these cases are aimed at increasing our understanding of how Interned-speed companies survived, not proposing "laws" for making successful agile SW development.

XP is not based on systematic research but rather on the expertise and experiences of a few individual software engineers. However, parts of XP have been studied empirically. For example, empirical studies exist on pair programming [52, 53]. Maurer and Martel [54] include some concrete numbers regarding the productivity gains using XP in a web development project. Furthermore, there are some experience reports available of applying XP in industrial [e.g., 55-57] and university [e.g., 9, 58] settings. These studies provide the necessary insight on the possibilities and restrictions of XP.

DSDM has been developed by a dedicated consortium. Stapleton (1997) claims that empirical evidence exists in the form of experience reports (i.e., white papers) that are shared with the members of the consortium. However, since they are not made publicly available we interpret that the claims of DSDM are not empirically supported.

5. Discussion

In this section, the results of the comparative analysis are discussed. The purpose is to identify the principal implications for research and practice in the field of software engineering. Table 3 summarizes these implications.

Table 3. Results and implications of the study

Perspective	Description of the results	Implications
Software development life-cycle	Methods, without rationalization, cover different phases of the life-cycle.	Life-cycle coverage needs to be explained and interfaces with phases not covered need to be clarified.
Project management	While most methods appear to cover project management, true support is missing.	Conceptual harmonization is needed. Project management can not be neglected.
Abstract principles vs. concrete guidance	Abstract principles dominate the method literature and developers' minds.	Emphasis should be placed on enabling practitioners to utilize the suggestions made.
Universally predefined vs. situation appropriate	Universal solutions dominate the literature.	More work on how to adopt agile methods in different development situations is needed.
Empirical support	Empirical evidence is limited; most of the research is at conceptual level	More empirical, situation-specific, experimental work is needed; results need to be publicly available.

Software development life-cycle: Different agile methods cover different phases of the software development life-cycle. The rationalization of phases covered was, however, missing. The question that must, therefore, be raised is whether it is more profitable to cover more and to be more extensive, or cover less and to be more precise. Completeness, a notion introduced by Kumar and Welke [37], requires that a method is complete as opposed to partial. In the analysis it was realized that "completeness" is an element that must be associated both with vertical (i.e., level of detail) and horizontal (i.e., life-cycle coverage) dimensions. None of the methods evaluated were either extensive or precise. The practitioners, currently, have partial solutions to problems that cover a wider area than the methods do. It is suggested that method developers concentrate more on specialization than generalization in the areas of their expertise. On one hand, methods that cover too much ground, i.e. all organizations, phases and situations, are too general or shallow to be used. On the other hand, methods that cover too little (e.g., one phase) may be too restricted or lack a connection to other methods.

Project management: Software engineering is a practically oriented field. Yet, while most (i.e., five out of nine) agile methods do incorporate support for project management, true support is scarce. Considering this perspective from a method feasibility point of view, efficient project management is of utmost importance when agile principles such as daily builds, short release-cycles, etc. are followed. Moreover, and more importantly, the concepts of, e.g., release and daily builds differ from one method to another. This invites more confusion than clarity. It appears that the method developers are aiming for their niche by using purposefully differing terminology. Practitioners, especially project managers, are in a difficult position when a decision of the most suitable approach should be made. The operational success of any method lies on its ability to be incorporated in the software project's daily rhythm. We, thus, maintain that project management considerations need to be addressed explicitly to ensure the alignment between a developer and the project management.

Abstract principles vs. concrete guidance: Only three out of nine agile methods offer concrete guidance. Abstract principles appear to dominate the agile method literature and developers' minds. The agile community is more concerned about getting acceptance to proposed values than in offering guidance on how to use the operative versions of these values. Currently, concrete guidance exists mostly in methods that are very limited in their scope (i.e., AM) or depth (i.e., PP). More work is needed in determining how the claimed practices, activities and work products are made to operate in different organizations and situations so that practitioners have a solid base on which to constitute their decisions.

Universally predefined vs. situation appropriate: Some of the well-known agile methods (e.g., FDD) were found to be universally predefined. Nevertheless, the few methods (e.g., Crystal) that recognize the fact that "one size does not fit to all situations", still do not expound any guidance on how this fitting process may be done. This being the case, forthcoming methods and studies should pay particular attention to situation appropriateness, and offer guidance on how the methods should be used in different agile software development situations. This also requires the ability to identify the particular situations in which these fitting or adjustment activities need to be done.

Empirical support: Empirical evidence, based on rigorous research, is scarce. Only three out of nine methods have some empirical support for their claims. Yet, it should be noted that some of the methods (e.g., XP) are increasingly producing more and more empirical studies, which is bound to mature the methodological base. Lack of empirical evidence results in practitioners not having reliable evidence on the real usability and the effectiveness of particular methods. They do not know whether the existing methods really make sense – do the methods describe proven wisdom or folktales. As for researchers and method developers, the lack of empirical evidence does not help in establishing a reliable and cumulative research tradition. Currently, researchers do not have access to reliable evidence on existing works. Such information is, however, necessary in pondering which parts of the previous works have a truth in them, and to decide to which extent future research can be based on existing wisdom. Thus, more empirical work is needed to study the implications of the different agile methods in different organizations and situations. Also, it should be noted that empirical evidence – that is, if it exists – should be publicly accessible. Currently, empirical studies on DSDM are made available only to members of the consortium.

Empirical works that study the effects of particular methods, their ease of use, costs, and possible negative implications for different sizes and lines of business, are needed in particular. The empirical work should use both qualitative and quantitative research methods to study these issues.

6. Conclusions

Agile software development methods have evoked a substantial amount of literature and debates. However, academic research on the subject is still scarce, as most existing publications are written by practitioners or consultants. Yet, many organizations are considering to use or have already applied practices that are claimed to make their way of performing and delivering software more agile.

The aim of this paper is to attempt to make sense out of the jungle of emerged agile software development methods. Based on the result of the analysis, practitioners are in a better position to understand the various properties of each method and make their judgment in a more informed way. The approach chosen for the purpose was that of comparative analysis. The analytical lenses included five perspectives: software development life-cycle including the process aspect, project management, abstract principles vs. concrete guidance, universally predefined vs. situation appropriate, and empirical evidence.

We observed that methods, without rationalization, cover certain/different phases of the life-cycle. A majority of them did not provide true support for project management, and abstract principles appeared to dominate the current method literature and developers' minds. While universal solutions have a strong support in the respective literature, empirical evidence is currently very limited.

Based on the above, new directions were offered. Namely, it was suggested that emerging new agile methods need to clarify their range of applicability and explain the interfaces to those parts of the software development life-cycle which are not a part of the chosen focus. In addition it was suggested that emphasis should rather be placed on method specialization than generalization. However, this specialization should enhance the conceptual harmonization rather than to work against it. Furthermore, the project management perspective cannot be neglected, if a method is to encroach on day-to-day software development practices. Emphasis should also be placed on enabling practitioners to utilize the suggestions made. This requires placing the focus in method development on empirically validated situation-specific solutions.

The current trend on agile methods has focused on fabricating a pile of conceptual methods. Instead of hurrying to introduce yet more agile methods, the method developers should pay particular attention to address the problems described. The field is crying for sound methods, i.e. methodological quality - not method quantity.

7. References

[1] J. Highsmith, "The great methodologies debate: Part 2," *Cutter IT Journal*, vol. 15, 2002.

[2] J. Highsmith, "The great methodologies debate: Part 1," *Cutter IT Journal*, vol. 14, 2001.

[3] E. Yourdon, "Light methodologies," *Cutter IT Journal*, vol. 13, 2000.

[4] R. McCauley, "Agile Development Methods Poised to Upset Status Quo," *SIGCSE Bulletin*, vol. 33, pp. 14 - 15, 2001.

[5] K. Beck, "Embracing Change With Extreme Programming," *IEEE Computer*, vol. 32, pp. 70-77, 1999.

[6] J. Highsmith and A. Cockburn, "Agile Software Development: The Business of Innovation," *Computer*, vol. 34, pp. 120-122, 2001.

[7] B. Boehm, "Get Ready For The Agile Methods, With Care," *Computer*, vol. 35, pp. 64-69, 2002.

[8] M. Fowler and J. Highsmith, "Agile methodologists agree on something," *Software Development*, vol. 9, pp. 28-32, 2001.

[9] M. M. Müller and W. F. Tichy, "Case Study: Extreme Programming in a University Environment," presented at 23rd International Conference on Software Engineering, Toronto, 2001.

[10] P. Abrahamsson, O. Salo, J. Ronkainen, and J. Warsta, *Agile software development methods: Review and Analysis*. Espoo, Finland: Technical

Research Centre of Finland, VTT Publications 478, Available online: http://www.inf.vtt.fi/pdf/publications/2002/P478.pdf, 2002.

[11] J. A. Highsmith, *Adaptive Software Development: A Collaborative Approach to Managing Complex Systems*. New York, NY: Dorset House Publishing, 2000.

[12] S. Bayer and J. Highsmith, "RADical software development," *American Programmer*, vol. 7, pp. 35-42, 1994.

[13] S. Ambler, *Agile Modeling: Effective Practices for Extreme Programming and the Unified Process*. New York: John Wiley & Sons, Inc. New York, 2002.

[14] A. Cockburn, *Surviving Object-Oriented Projects: A Manager's Guide*, vol. 5: Addison Wesley Longman, 1998.

[15] A. Cockburn, *Writing Effective Use Cases, The Crystal Collection for Software Professionals*: Addison-Wesley Professional, 2000.

[16] A. Cockburn, *Agile Software Development*. Boston: Addison-Wesley, 2002.

[17] DSDMConsortium, *Dynamic Systems Development Method, version 3*. Ashford, Eng.: DSDM Consortium, 1997.

[18] J. Stapleton, *Dynamic systems development method - The method in practice*: Addison Wesley, 1997.

[19] K. Beck, *Extreme programming explained*. Reading, Mass.: Addison-Wesley, 1999.

[20] K. Beck, *Extreme Programming Explained: Embrace Change*, 2000.

[21] S. R. Palmer and J. M. Felsing, *A Practical Guide to Feature-Driven Development*, 2002.

[22] P. Coad, E. LeFebvre, and J. De Luca, *Java Modeling In Color With UML: Enterprise Components and Process*: Prentice Hall, 2000.

[23] R. Baskerville, L. Levine, J. Pries-Heje, B. Ramesh, and S. Slaughter, "How Internet companies negotiate quality," *IEEE Computer*, vol. 34, pp. 51-57, 2001.

[24] R. Baskerville and J. Pries-Heje, "Racing the E-bomb: How the Internet is redefining information systems development methodology," in *Realigning research and practice in IS development*, B. Fitzgerald, N. Russo, and J. DeGross, Eds. New York: Kluwer, 2001, pp. 49-68.

[25] M. A. Cusumano and D. B. Yoffie, "Software development on Internet time," *IEEE Computer*, vol. 32, pp. 60-69, 1999.

[26] M. A. Cusumano and R. W. Selby, "How Microsoft builds software," *Communications of the ACM*, vol. 40, pp. 53-61, 1997.

[27] D. P. Truex, R. Baskerville, and H. Klein, "Growing systems in emergent organizations," *Communications of the ACM*, vol. 42, pp. 117-123, 1999.

[28] R. Baskerville, J. Travis, and D. P. Truex, "Systems without method: The impact of new technologies on information systems development projects," in *Transactions on the impact of computer supported technologies in information systems development*, K. E. Kendall, K. Lyytinen, and J. I. DeGross, Eds. Amsterdam: Elsevier Science Publications, 1992, pp. 241-260.

[29] D. P. Truex, R. Baskerville, and J. Travis, "Amethodological systems development: The deferred meaning of systems development methods," *Accounting, Management and Information Technology*, vol. 10, pp. 53-79, 2001.

[30] A. Hunt, Thomas, D., *The Pragmatic Programmer*: Addison Wesley, 2000.

[31] K. Schwaber, "Scrum Development Process," presented at OOPSLA'95 Workshop on Business Object Design and Implementation, 1995.

[32] K. Schwaber and M. Beedle, *Agile Software Development With Scrum*. Upper Saddle River, NJ: Prentice-Hall, 2002.

[33] J. Iivari and R. Hirscheim, "Analyzing information systems development: A comparison and analysis of eight IS development approaches," *Information Systems*, vol. 21, pp. 551-575, 1996.

[34] T. W. Olle, H. G. Sol, and A. Verrijn-Stuart, *Information systems design methodologies: A comparative review*. Amsterdam: North-Holland, 1982.

[35] B. W. Boehm, "A spiral model of sofware development and enhancement," *IEEE Computer*, vol. 21, pp. 61-72, 1988.

[36] G. Cugola and C. Ghezzi, "Software Processes: a Retrospective and a Path to the Future," *Software Process Improvement and Practice*, vol. 4, pp. 101-123, 1998.

[37] K. Kumar and R. J. Welke, "Methodology engineering: A proposal for situation-specific methodology construction," in *Challenges and strategies for research in systems development*, W. W. Cotterman and J. A. Senn, Eds. New York: John Wiley & Sons, 1992, pp. 257-269.

[38] T. Gilb, *Principles of Software Engineering Management*. Wokingham, UK: Addison-Wesley, 1988.

[39] J. Nandhakumar and J. Avison, "The fiction of methodological development: a field study of information systems development," *Information Technology & People*, vol. 12, pp. 176-191, 1999.

[40] V. R. Basili and F. Lanubile, "Building knowledge through families of experiments," *IEEE Transactions on Software Engineering*, vol. 25, pp. 456-473, 1999.

[41] V. R. Basili, "The role of experimentation in software engineering: Past, present and future," presented at Keynote address in 18th International Conference on Software Engineering (ICSE18), Berlin, Germany, 1996.

[42] N. Fenton, "Viewpoint Article: Conducting and presenting empirical software engineering," *Empirical Software Engineering*, vol. 6, pp. 195-200, 2001.

[43] I. Sommerville, *Software engineering*, Fifth ed. New York: Addison-Wesley, 1996.

[44] D. G. Wastell, "The fetish of technique: methodology as a social defence," *Information Systems Journal*, vol. 6, pp. 25-49, 1996.

[45] J. L. Malouin and M. Landry, "The miracle of universal methods in systems design," *Journal of Applied Systems Analysis*, vol. 10, pp. 47-62, 1983.

[46] A. F. Chalmers, *What is this thing called Science?*, Third ed. Buckingham: Open University Press, 1999.

[47] R. Jeffries, A. Anderson, and C. Hendrickson, *Extreme Programming Installed.* Upper Saddle River, NJ: Addison-Wesley, 2001.

[48] D. Fiery, *Secrets of a super hacker.* Port Townsend, Washington, USA: Loompanics Unlimited, 1994.

[49] A. Cockburn, "Selecting a project's methodology," *IEEE Software*, vol. 17, pp. 64-71, 2000.

[50] M. N. Aydin and F. Harmsen, "Making a method work for a project situation in the context of CMM," presented at Product Focused Software Process Improvement (Profes 2002), Rovaniemi, Finland, 2002.

[51] L. Rising and N. S. Janoff, "The Scrum software development process for small teams," *IEEE Software*, vol. 17, pp. 26-32, 2000.

[52] L. Williams, R. R. Kessler, W. Cunningham, and R. Jeffries, "Strengthening the Case for Pair Programming," *IEEE Software*, vol. 17, pp. 19-25, 2000.

[53] J. Haungs, "Pair programming on the C3 project," *Computer*, vol. 34, pp. 118-119, 2001.

[54] F. Maurer and S. Martel, "On the Productivity of Agile Software Practices: An Industrial Case Study," 2002.

[55] J. Grenning, "Extreme Programming and Embedded Software Development," presented at Embedded Systems Conference 2002, Chicago, 2002.

[56] P. Schuh, "Recovery, Redemption, and Extreme Programming," *IEEE Software*, vol. 18, pp. 34-41, 2001.

[57] A. Anderson, R. Beattie, K. Beck, D. Bryant, M. DeArment, *et al.*, "Chrysler Goes to "Extremes". Case Study.," *Distributed Computing*, pp. 24-28, 1998.

[58] J. R. Nawrocki, B. Walter, and A. Wojciechowski, "Comparison of CMM level 2 and eXtreme programming," presented at 7th European Conference on Software Quality, Helsinki, Finland, 2002.

Efficient Authoring of Software Documentation Using RaPiD7

Roope Kylmäkoski
Nokia
Hatanpäänvaltatie 30A, FIN-33100 Tampere
roope.kylmakoski@nokia.com

Abstract

This paper presents a method, developed in Nokia, for efficient document authoring in software development projects. The method is called RaPiD7 (Rapid Production of Documentation, 7 steps). The method improves the traditional approach for document authoring in which the work is typically started by informal initiative, and the actual writing of a document is a task performed by a single individual. Traditional document authoring usually relies on inspections to verify the quality of the documentation. RaPiD7 addresses the document authoring problem by getting people involved in the documentation work earlier as a team in order to guarantee quality, calendar time efficiency, commitment and improved communication. This paper also compares RaPiD7 with some other similar approaches and presents results from a large-scale experiment with RaPiD7.

1. Introduction

In manufacturing processes, immature in their nature, it is often required to perform activities that simply verify and test artifacts produced earlier in order to meet the desired requirements, as well as the overall quality level of a product. This is because the practices and methods used are not themselves mature enough to guarantee the desired outcome. Software systems are very much developed this way today. The whole process relies on having a separate testing phase or phases in order to verify the software quality. Furthermore, not only the main phases of the software process rely on this sort of quality assurance, but the different methods used in the main phases are based on the same concept as well.

One example of such an activity is the traditional process of authoring the different documents within the projects. In this paper, traditional document authoring means the approach in which the authoring is typically started by informal initiative, and the actual writing of a document is a task performed by a single individual. Authoring documents traditionally usually rely on inspections [3] to verify the quality of the documentation. Inspections have proven to be, if used correctly, an efficient practice for discovering problems early in projects life cycle, and therefore reducing the amount of specification faults found in the testing phase. However, in the life cycle of a certain specification document, an inspection is simply a kind of testing phase. Even though we can identify and solve problems this way, in the long term the same problems will arise perpetually, unless we collect measurement data from our inspections, analyze the root causes, and act to find solutions to the root causes. By following this procedure systematically, we will eventually realize in our inspections that we have remedied all defects in the document authoring process, and thus have made the inspections obsolete as such.

According to the aforementioned reasoning, it can be stated that the inspections are only a step towards a more mature process of authoring documents. When many of the root causes of the defects found in inspections are specific to a certain environment, process or document type, many are typical to the current document authoring process itself. However, it is clear that inspections will have their role in the authoring process in areas where the root causes have not been abolished. In addition, the environments and products change over time, and therefore evidently the processes change as well. This means that after a while, we will need another process of authoring documents or new document types, and thus end up having new root causes for the defects to be found in inspections. Nevertheless, there are some root causes simply originating from the current authoring process.

Before looking at the root causes for the defects in the current authoring process, we should understand the goal of document authoring in general. At least the following issues are the key drivers for authoring documentation within software projects:

1. Gaining understanding
2. Sharing information
3. Keeping track of information shared

Gaining understanding in a successful manner is something that can be achieved only if the information is shared, and the sharing is done in a correct and

0-7695-1877-X/03 $17.00 © 2003 IEEE

unambiguous way. In the traditional authoring approach, this generally requires a lot from the writer of a document, as it does not matter what has been written, but how it is interpreted. More often than not, there are better ways to gain understanding than reading a document. Consider, for example, if you had been involved in creating this paper rather than just reading it, gaining understanding on the issues would be relatively easier. However, usually documents are among the most efficient solutions of keeping *track of information history*, in other words studying later how did people end up having a certain solution in their project.

Successful *Information sharing* expects that people read the authored documents or are able to access the necessary information otherwise. It also requires that people know what documents they should read, and how to find the right documents. It is not, however, necessary to produce a document to share information. This can be achieved also by giving training and by other means of similar kind.

How does the traditional authoring of documentation tend to fail in the aforementioned goals? Gaining understanding in the traditional way of authoring documentation is difficult. Often a single person tries to solve mostly alone all the problems. Typically, there are no proper discussions taking place with the project stakeholders resulting in problems found in the inspections after several weeks of heavy documentation work. A common observation in an inspection is that a great number of crucial decisions are still open or the decisions already made do not satisfy the different project stakeholders. Furthermore, coming up with a common agreement in such a situation is not that easy, as typically at least the author is biased in favor of the document being inspected. Even if the decisions can be made, true commitment is not guaranteed. In addition, a typical solution is to make a sort of compromise in order to keep up with the project's schedule. In the end, this may turn out to be the worst possible decision and delay the project even more.

In the traditional approach, sharing information can usually be achieved only if people read the material given for the inspections beforehand, because it appears to be difficult for people to find the time for reading the documentation later. Often people have not prepared themselves enough for the inspections to be able to contribute to the inspection resulting in poor sharing of the information and inadequate understanding of the matter in hand. Even if the material has been read, it is not necessarily understood correctly. There is a possibility that everyone will form his or her own different view on the contents. In any case, the inspection process does not force us to decide the key issues early in the projects lifecycle, and therefore we may share possibly incorrect information. This incorrect information may form basis of understanding for many people.

The following lists the most typical problems found using the traditional authoring approach:

- Using a lot of calendar time for authoring the documentation.
- The contents of the document are mostly based on the opinion of the writer
- Common theme on the contents of a document in hand cannot be defined.
- Common agreement cannot be reached due to finding the defects too late.
- There is no proper commitment.
- The approach does not enable efficient information sharing, and therefore results in inadequate level of understanding.

The following chapter provides insights to a method developed in Nokia in order to address the aforementioned problems in authoring documentation.

2. The method: RaPiD7

An acceptable level of quality in the documentation can be reached in a rather short time frame using a method called RaPiD7 (Rapid Production of Documents, 7 steps). This method enables better information sharing and gets people better committed to the decisions made. RaPiD7 forces the outcome to be produced in a relatively short time frame, forces decisions to be made before anything is written, and gets all parties involved early in the life-cycle of a document.

Simply put, RaPiD7 is a method in which the document in hand is authored in a team in consecutive workshops. The workshops are well prepared, and innovative brainstorming and problem solving methods are used. The documents are mostly written in the workshops immediately after each issue has been cleared up and decided. Typically, the document needs some polishing work after the workshop. This means in practice that a person uses approximately a day to finalize the work. The steps of RaPiD7 method are presented in figure 1.

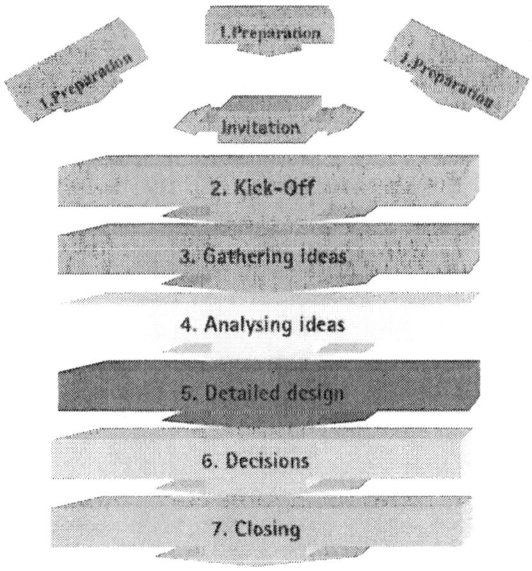

Figure 1, Steps of RaPiD7

1) Preparation step is performed for each of the workshops, and the idea is to find out the necessary information to be used as input in the workshops. This usually requires approximately two to three days of work for the first workshop, and a few hours for the following workshops. The 2) kick-off step is always performed in the beginning of the first workshop, and, if needed, in the beginning of the following workshops in order to define a common theme for the participants and to explain the goal of the workshop. In each of the workshops the steps from 3-6 are performed in a repeatable manner, according to a predefined agenda. In each of the "loops" a certain concrete issue is handled from 3) gathering the ideas related to the issue, to 4) analyzing the collected ideas, and finally 5) to make a detailed design on the selected ideas, and to actually write the document. After all aforementioned has been performed, 6) decisions on the results are made. The last step 7) is performed once in each of the workshops to see if the outcome desired has been reached or outcome desired has not been reached and a) a following workshop has been scheduled or b) a following workshop needs to be scheduled.

The process for authoring a document in consecutive workshops is presented in figure 2. Typically, authoring a document takes less than a week in calendar time. The people who would traditionally participate the inspections are the people who will participate the RaPiD7 workshops, too. In practice, this means the people that have input to give for the document in hand. The selection of the participants is crucial in the success of a workshop. Therefore, one should pay attention to making sure the right people will participate the workshops. This means both identifying the right participants but also assuring their participation. The usual number of workshops needed to author a document is between one and four, although no given figure for the number of workshops exists. The more difficult or the more unclear issues are handled, the more workshops are naturally needed. However, the workshops are usually only three to five hours long, and typically should not be longer to remain efficient. It is also important to make sure that people participate the workshops only as long as their input is needed, in order to minimize the idle time of participants. After all, if projects are planned according to RaPiD7 methodology there will be a number of workshops to participate in.

Three different levels of achievement can be perceived in implementing RaPiD7. The first and simplest level is trying RaPiD7 out according to the general idea of RaPiD7. This typically results, depending on the matter, in satisfactory results or almost satisfactory results in a single workshop. However, this approach does not usually benefit a full-scale software project significantly. The second level is to realize how workshops can be run efficiently to be able to author documentation within the timeframe of one week. To enable this some training is typically needed. The last and final level is to utilize RaPiD7 in a full-scale software project, and plan the documentation authoring in projects by scheduling consecutive workshops.

By using RaPiD7 method, the following benefits are expected to realize:

- Artifacts and specifications will be produced in a relatively short time (from couple of days to one week)
- Inspecting the documents will not be typically needed after the document has been authored in a workshop
- Communication in projects will be easier and more effective
- People can work more flexibly in teams as they all share the same information
- The overall quality of artifacts and specifications will be improved
- No re-work is needed and hence time is saved
- Schedules for workshops in projects are known early enough to plan traveling efficiently, and thus costs can be reduced

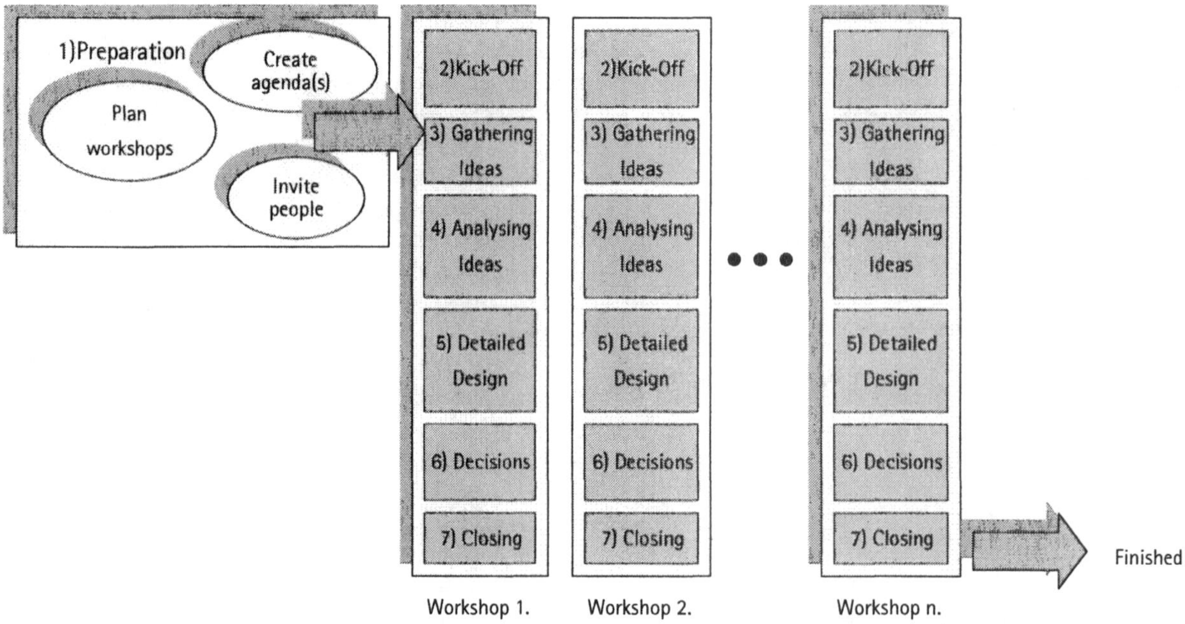

Figure 2, Creating a document using RaPiD7

RaPiD7 method can be applied for authoring nearly all types of documents. However, it suits best for documents that are not product-like in nature. Typically, these documents do not have a wide audience, and hence the focus in authoring is not on the appearance of the documents, but rather in the contents. However, RaPiD7 can always be applied when teamwork is required in the authoring process in one form or another. The way RaPiD7 is applied varies significantly depending on the case. The cases differ by the time required, the people participating the workshops and the techniques used in the workshops.

3. Related work

Other approaches similar to RaPiD7 exist, too. Although the methods resemble each other in many ways, the differences are evident. Differences are related to the goals of the methods and the scope of using the methods in software development projects. Furthermore, RaPiD7 is characterized by the starting point of its development; problems realizing in inspections. In the following, two approaches, namely JAD and Agile modeling, are discussed shortly in terms of main similarities and differences with RaPiD7.

Joint application development (JAD) is a requirements-definition and user-interface design methodology according to Steve McConnell [4]. The obvious similarity with RaPiD7 is the idea of having well structured meetings (in RaPiD7 called workshops) in order to work out system details. However, RaPiD7 is not focusing on certain artifacts or phases of software development, and actually does not state which kind of documents or artifacts could be produced using the method, but leaves this to the practitioner of the method. In JAD, the general idea is to have a workshop (or a set of workshops) rather than having unlimited number of workshops throughout the project. The goal in RaPiD7 is to benefit the whole project by creating as many of the documents as possible using RaPiD7. Furthermore, JAD sessions are always somewhat formal, whereas RaPiD7 sessions vary in formality depending on the case. This is probably why more efforts are put into the preparation work when using JAD, and why with JAD the typical "from preparation to a finished document -time" is longer than with RaPiD7. On the other hand, formal RaPiD7 workshops and JAD sessions can be quite alike. Different JAD sessions are not said to be alike [6], and while this is true for RaPiD7 too, the way RaPiD7 workshops and JAD sessions are planned is different. JAD provides many guidelines for the pre-session work and for the actual session itself, but the planning is not step based, as is the case with RaPiD7. The following lists the key differences identified between RaPiD7 and JAD:

- RaPiD7 was originally developed to improve the whole documentation authoring process in software processes instead of limited phases as was the case with JAD
- In RaPiD7 approach the document is typically finalized in shorter calendar time than with JAD

- RaPiD7 provides step approach for planning workshops
- JAD sessions are often more formal than RaPiD7 sessions

Agile modeling [1] is more like an ideology than a method. It provides set of values, principles and practices for a lightweight processes such as XP [2] describing how to perform effective modeling and documentation of software-based systems. However, agile modeling does not provide a cookbook type of approach for authoring documents, as RaPiD7 does. On the other hand, agile modeling provides a number of pragmatic ideas how to perform agile modeling sessions to produce certain kind of models. When the values, principles and practices of agile modeling are something that can be mostly adopted when using RaPiD7, the biggest differences are related to the applicability of the methods. Ambler [1] mentions in his book Agile Modeling that Agile modeling will not work best in large companies such as telecommunications firms, or not in environments where, what he calls, descriptive processes, such as RUP [5], are used. RaPiD7 has been developed and used in Nokia, which can be referred to as being a large telecommunications company. On the other hand, there is a clear and valid reason for the aforementioned hesitancy for the applicability of agile modeling. Ambler claims that in agile modeling individuals and interactions are more important than processes and tools. However, when you consider large companies it is inevitable that you will end up having more variation in the skills of your people, and therefore process discipline is more important in such environments. Even if you could hire only "good developers", as Ambler suggests for effective formation of an agile modeling team, in a large company these good developers will still have different backgrounds and knowledge base. In addition, agile modeling does not provide ways to plan the modeling sessions in your software projects whereas in JAD and RaPiD7 the planning is seen crucial for success.

It is no surprise that these different methods provide and promote similar kind of techniques for effective documentation work. This is simply because these techniques are proven to be effective. On the other hand, it is no surprise that there are differences, too. The differences are most likely consequences of different organization cultures, different origins for the methods and slightly different goals. What works in one environment might not work in the other. Hence, the variety in the methods is welcome.

4. RaPiD7 Case Study – Specification Authoring In Nokia

RaPiD7 method was developed in Nokia during years 1999-2000 based on the feedback on software inspections. The first teams took the method into use in autumn 2000. The results from the initial workshops were encouraging and the method was taken into use in several other teams, too. In addition, more work was put into developing the method and training RaPiD7 coaches that could independently take the method into use in their projects. Now hundreds of cases exist in Nokia where different artifacts and documents have been authored using RaPiD7 method.

4.1. Simple assessment

In a software development unit, size of approximately 1000 people, the results according to a software development process assessment held in 2001 are presented in Table 1. The assessment was a self-assessment in which randomly selected (anonymous) people were asked to give their opinion on predefined statements. Altogether 151 people answered the statements by expressing how the statements were reflecting the reality in their opinion (fully satisfied 100%, largely satisfied 66,7%, partially satisfied 33% and not satisfied 0%). The results in Table 1 are calculated by taking an average figure of the answers given. The way the assessment was organized reflects the way the results should be analyzed. First, these results are not exact facts, in other words, the results are not metrics from a project. Thus, the results can be biased in either favor of RaPiD7 or against the method. On the other hand, they reflect rather well the feelings of the people, and therefore are not only management wishes.

4.2. Discussion on the benefits

The results from the real life cases support mostly the expected benefits of the method presented in the previous chapter. The results show the method is being used quite widely, and that it improves the efficiency in authoring the documents in terms of calendar time (reports indicate reduction of 15-96% compared to traditional document authoring). It also shows that people feel that communication is improved, and that the method reduces the amount of defects. The results are competent keeping in mind that in a large organization there is always change resistance, and there are a number of different software development cultures, too. In general, smaller teams report even better results, as the overall results would indicate (see Table 1). These results indicate that higher use rate will give better results in terms of improved communication, authoring efficiency and defect rate reduction. Therefore, the key issue seems to be getting the

Table 1, Results of the assessment

Statement	Results 151 respondents in a unit of 1000 people	Best individual team (same team in each statement)
RaPiD7 is used for authoring documentation	50%	92%
Documents are produced within one week time	44%	92%
RaPiD7 improves communication	90%	100%
RaPiD7 reduces defects in software development	83%	100%
RaPiD7 sessions are planned adequately	45%	83%

teams to try out RaPiD7 long enough to see the benefits realizing. The first workshops, when trying to find out the right approach for a specific document type, are the most difficult ones. Actually, a typical comment found in the assessment was that using RaPiD7 becomes more efficient and better results are gained after people have become familiar using the method. On the other hand, it is apparent that to fully benefit from RaPiD7 training is required, too. Although it might be difficult to get people to change their ways of doing everyday work, typically the teams trying out RaPiD7 for some time would not give up using it.

People with different roles give different kind of feedback depending on their point of view on software development. Project managers are more satisfied as they are better aware of the status of the specification work. Something concrete is done early and the risks are realized earlier. Project managers often use the method themselves with their project team and project stakeholders in order to ensure commitment and unambiguous communication. They also use it to verify possible conflicts in schedules. Individual team leaders report that documents are produced typically in a week, newcomers are easier introduced to their work and team spirit is substantially better. In addition, team leaders feel that their team members are now taking wider responsibility as before, and this way making the teams more flexible and less vulnerable. Software designers are also more satisfied as they get an easier way to influence others work, and get comments for their work in a systematic way. Moreover, the software designers get the comments earlier than before and thus see RaPiD7 as a way to avoid frustrating rework.

4.2. Risks and threats

On the other hand, the method is not seen as a way to reduce work as such. Efforts are needed to plan the workshops, and as can be seen in table 1, effective planning is the most problematic issue in the use of the method. This indicates that people generally do not prepare themselves enough, but rather believe that miracles will happen. This is probably one of the risks of the method, because the aforementioned behavior is natural to human nature. Furthermore, there is a risk that in some cases decisions are forced in order to get a document ready fast although the facts needed are not yet known. In addition, efforts can go vain if the workshops are not run by skilled facilitators, and having skilled facilitators either requires the right kind of people or extensive training for the facilitators.

5. Conclusions

The real life cases have proven that in favorable environment, with trained people and systematic use, RaPiD7 improves the authoring process significantly in terms of calendar time efficiency, commitment and information sharing. Negative experiences in using RaPiD7 exist, too. Typically, the teams being unsuccessful in applying RaPiD7 have not received any training on RaPiD7, and therefore the method has not been applied systematically enough. On the other hand, the method is often seen as an easy solution for projects behind their plans. In these cases, the expectations tend to get too high resulting in poorly planned workshops, and in the end resulting in poor results, too. Typically, these teams start to have workshops, but do not try to finalize anything in the workshops, and therefore the document is still authored the traditional way. The idea behind the method is relatively simple, but the effective use of it is not. For the teams applying RaPiD7 systematically the reward is, however, significant. This can be perceived from results already.

6. Acknowledgements

Hundreds of people have been involved in making RaPiD7 as a working practice in Nokia. Firstly I would like to thank all the users of the method. Without the users the method would merely be a theory. Specifically, I would like to name some key people making RaPiD7 use reality. The key contributors in developing the method itself have been Riku Kylmäkoski, Oula Heikkinen, Katherine Rose and Hanna Turunen. I thank them greatly for their extensive efforts. Furthermore, I would like to thank the pilot users and teams in Nokia, especially I would like to thank Stephan Irrgang, Roland Meyer, Thomas Wirtz, Juha Yli-Olli and Miia Forssell. Without the efforts of these users we would not have such good results nor would we have RaPiD7 as an institutionalized way of working.

The deployment of the method would not have taken place without contribution from Nokia management. I would like to thank Sari Baldauf and Harri Salomaa for providing the needed management support.

Finally, I would like to thank Tuomas Lamminpää, Kai Koskimies and Ilkka Haikala for giving solid contribution by reviewing this paper several times.

7. References

[1] Ambler, Scott W, 2002. Agile modeling. John Wiley & Sons, Inc., New York.

[2] Beck, K. 2000. Extreme programming explained: Embrace change. Addison-Wesley publishing company.

[3] Gilb, Tom & Graham, Dorothy, 1993. Software inspection. Addison-Wesley publishing company.

[4] McConnell, Steve 1996. Rapid development. Microsoft Press.

[5] Rational Corporation 2002, Rational unified process home page, www.rational.com/products/rup/index.jsp

[6] Woods, Jane, Silver, Denise, 1995. Joint Application Development. John Wiley & Sons, Inc., New York.

Using Process Technology to Control and Coordinate Software Adaptation

Giuseppe Valetto
Telecom Italia Lab and Columbia University
Giuseppe.Valetto@tilab.com

Gail Kaiser
Columbia University
kaiser@cs.columbia.edu

Abstract

We have developed an infrastructure for end-to-end run-time monitoring, behavior/performance analysis, and dynamic adaptation of distributed software. This infrastructure is primarily targeted to pre-existing systems and thus operates outside the target application, without making assumptions about the target's implementation, internal communication/computation mechanisms, source code availability, etc. This paper assumes the existence of the monitoring and analysis components, presented elsewhere, and focuses on the mechanisms used to control and coordinate possibly complex repairs/reconfigurations to the target system. These mechanisms require lower-level effectors somehow attached to the target system, so we briefly sketch one such facility (elaborated elsewhere). Our main contribution is the model, architecture, and implementation of Workflakes, *the decentralized process engine we use to tailor, control, coordinate, etc. a cohort of such effectors. We have validated the* Workflakes *approach with case studies in several application domains. Due to space restrictions we concentrate primarily on one case study, briefly discuss a second, and only sketch others.*

1. Introduction

Distributed computing is becoming (or has become) a commodity. Users rely upon distributed systems for value-added services that pervade their everyday lives, such as Web-based collaboration, electronic B2B and B2C, on-demand multimedia content, ubiquitous personal messaging, and many others. These services are often built on top of a networking infrastructure as distributed systems, often constructed by composition (that is, the servers themselves are distributed amongst components, not just the client viz-a-viz server). The complexity of the behavior and interrelationships of these "systems of systems" becomes increasingly harder to analyze in advance, and keep under control in the field. That aggravates the critical problems of managing the provisioning of the service and maintaining the intended application-level, "soft" quality of service (QoS). In order to resolve poor performance or failures, often a service is interrupted, the underlying application is taken down (at least in part), and the spiral of software lifecycle iterates back to the installation or deployment phase, and sometimes even to earlier development phases.

While such a drastic response may be obligatory at times, it is desirable when possible to resolve problems with lesser impacts and costs – while the system is running and without taking it offline. This motivates the notion of *dynamic adaptation* of complex, distributed software systems and services. By that term we mean any automated and concerted set of actions aimed at modifying, at runtime, the structure, behavior and/or performance of a target software system, typically in response to the occurrence and recognition of some (adverse) conditions. Examples range from tuning functioning parameters within a component in order to optimize its performance, to component(s) migration, to architecture-wide interventions, such as on-the-fly deployment or evolution of the service as a whole.

The dynamic adaptation theme is gaining attention as an approach to addressing the ever-increasing complexity of IT infrastructures and applications. For example, the autonomic computing initiative announced by IBM [1] and the Recovery Oriented Computing work at Berkeley and Stanford [2] strongly push in that direction. But dynamic adaptation brings about several major challenges, since it can be seen as a form of automated maintenance of "live" systems – likely to be even more complex than conventional off-line maintenance.

The hardwiring of self-adaptation provisions within the application itself is still the most common approach to dynamic adaptation, but that is feasible principally only for "new" systems, or systems whose components are under the complete control of the developers. Moreover, those hardwired provisions tend to increase the overall complexity of the system, in fact intensifying maintenance difficulties, and are often developed custom, with little reuse possible across applications or domains.

For these reasons, our research has focused on solutions orthogonal to the target system's main computation, control and communication, constituting an *externalized* dynamic adaptation infrastructure. Our

0-7695-1877-X/03 $17.00 © 2003 IEEE

approach enables retrofitting legacy systems with the desired reconfiguration, self-healing, self-management, etc. capabilities, as well as similarly aiding systems built by third-party composition.

Our model for externalized dynamic adaptation is that of a layered architecture, comprised of layers for data collection, information analysis, decision/control and actuation (we use the terms *effectors* and *actuators* interchangeably for the units that perform this duty). This model is sketched briefly in section 2; more in-depth discussion of the externalized infrastructure as a whole, and in particular how its collection and analysis components have been fulfilled by our *Kinesthetics eXtreme (KX)* implementation, can be found in [18] [23].

This paper elaborates instead primarily on the decision and control role; in Section 3, we present how we have addressed it with process technology: We employ a process engine, called *Workflakes*, to coordinate the actuation layer. As with collection and analysis, many actuation approaches are possible; Workflakes integrates the *Worklets* mobile agents platform, which was originally developed for unrelated purposes and is described in [19]. A preliminary paper [5] sketched the basic ideas of the Workflakes project. This paper provides the first complete presentation and evaluation of the Workflakes model and architecture, according to our recently completed operational implementation.

KX, with and without Workflakes, has been employed in a number of case studies. We are concerned in this paper only with describing and evaluating the decision/control and actuation-coordination aspects of those target applications, through Workflakes, not the monitoring facilities or actuator details, addressed elsewhere. We present one such case study in full in Section 4 - on an industrial Internet service - with its most recent results, which subsume and update a previous report [26]. We also sum up some other case studies in their most interesting traits. Section 5 discusses related work specifically with respect to Workflakes, since as noted the other components of KX are presented elsewhere. Section 6 concludes the paper.

2. Externalized dynamic adaptation

An externalized dynamic adaptation platform can be seen at the highest level of abstraction as a feedback loop that is superimposed onto an existing distributed system for the purposes of continually monitoring and modifying its configuration, activity and performance. Since the feedback loop is handled outside of the target application, it is possible to maintain a clear separation between the reusable, common adaptation mechanisms and the target system specifics.

Furthermore, in order to be generally applicable in diverse usage and technological contexts, the infrastructure must be constructed with great attention to its interoperability with a variety of adaptation targets. Such generality in turn can be achieved via standardization of the interactions between the infrastructure components,. That enables to choose among the numerous technological options that can be used to implement the roles of probes, gauges, controllers and effectors, and to accommodate more easily within the model those that best suit the target system.

As a consequence, within the DARPA DASADA program [3] under which we conducted this research, a standard model - the proposed Common DASADA Infrastructure [25] - has emerged, which organizes the design of the feedback loop according to multiple, well-separated layers, as shown in Figure 1. The Collection layer first gathers information from the running target system, by instrumenting it with minimally invasive *probes* that report via a Probe Bus to the Interpretation layer. There, information is mapped and evaluated by *gauges*, and findings are reported to the Gauge Bus. Then the Decision and Control layer analyzes the implications of the gauge findings on the target system functioning and performance, and makes decisions on whether to carry out some dynamic adaptation(s). Adaptation actions would be performed by effectors at the Actuation layer, under the coordination of one or more *controllers*. Implementation-level *effectors* would thus adapt (i.e., reconfigure or tune) individual components, as well as connectors and other substructures of the target system.

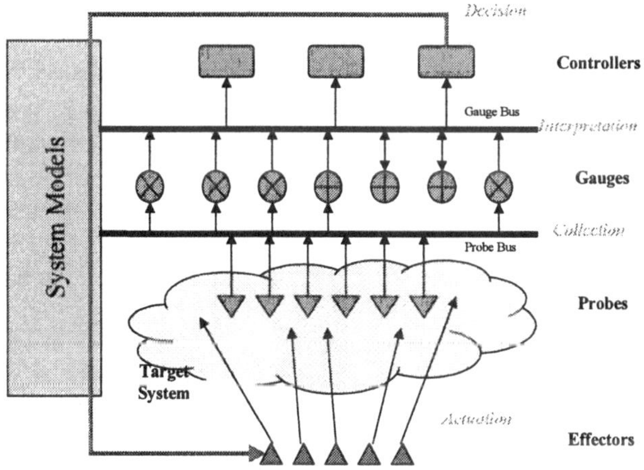

Figure 1: Dynamic adaptation infrastructure

A paramount role in this architecture is played by formal (i.e., machine-readable) models of the target system. Formal knowledge is pervasively used to drive the target instrumentation with probes, the interpretation of collected information by gauges, the decisions taken by controllers, and their coordination of the effectors' actions. That knowledge can be captured and made available to the dynamic adaptation architecture via suitable notations and models. Those models must encompass numerous aspects of the target system, like functional and non-functional properties, protocols, architecture, distribution, etc. However, dynamic adaptation does not require complete *a priori* target analysis and modeling: Models can instead be developed piecemeal and selectively, with respect to those target substructures and facets of relevance to each dynamic adaptation application.

At this level of abstraction, we are not concerned so much with indicating what form of modeling is the most suitable for any or all of those purposes: it is indeed possible that various concerns are better captured not by a single, but by multiple complementary representations. Furthermore, even proprietary or internalized models can serve well the dynamic adaptation facilities: developing exchangeable models in some "standard" formalism – as well as leveraging any pre-existing codified knowledge - is not necessary, although certainly desirable. Whereas further discussion of the modeling issues connected to dynamic adaptation is outside the scope of this paper, some indications originating from our experience are reported in the remainder, in particular related to the use of Architecture Description Language (ADL) tools.

Notice that while the architecture proposed above is largely decoupled from the running target system, this is not to say that the specific probes, gauges, controllers, effectors and the models that govern them are themselves independent of the target system. In fact, probes and effectors must often be specialized to the implementation technology; gauges and decision mechanisms must be specialized to the problem logic and the environment.

Notice also how the layered design facilitates the clear separation of the various kinds of functionality taking part in the overall infrastructure (a similar separation of concerns is advocated in other dynamic adaptation initiatives, such as [30]). In the DARPA DASADA program, much work by ourselves and others has been devoted to the development of proposals for standard probing [4] and gauging [20] APIs. The decision and control roles in a dynamic adaptation platform are however less well understood, thus further from standardization.

Finally, to effectively close the loop represented in Figure 1, the infrastructure must automate decisions on the adaptation to be carried out, orchestrate each adaptation as it occurs, and provide adequate effectors to actuate that adaptation via appropriate side effects on the target system. Workflakes explores part of that problem space, in particular how to express control, and how to organize and exert it on multiple coordinated effectors.

3. The Workflakes approach

The output of gauges represents the input to a decision process that determines whether/how the target system must be adapted. In the simplest case, some gauge may assert a fact that already carries with it unequivocally defined consequences. Other times, a variety of tools could be exploited for decision support: for example, formal architectural knowledge models of the target system, coupled with constraint analysis and architecture transformation tools, such as [16] [22], in our experience can be very effective in driving the decision and actuation phases of dynamic adaptation.

When a decision to apply some adaptation is made, a single action will sometimes suffice to fulfill it (this is the assumption of systems such as [35]). In most cases, however, the adaptation will have to be mapped onto several finer-grained and concerted activities, impacting several implementation-level elements. Then a sophisticated coordination mechanism is needed: some of those activities may be conditional, or dependent on others, or may fail, calling for contingency planning, etc.

To address that complexity, Workflakes relies on process-based coordination, and treats gauge outputs as input triggers for the enactment of a tailored adaptation process. Our choice of process technology as the coordination paradigm for dynamic adaptation is motivated by its ability of expressing even very complex patterns of coordination and dynamic dependencies in an explicit and abstract way that is also executable and reusable. Furthermore, process enactment engines are increasingly mature, even when applied, as in agent-based systems [24] and EAI [37], to completely automated rather than human coordination subjects.

A Workflakes process unfolds according to a task decomposition strategy, which in the end generates, configures, activates groups of effectors, and coordinates them towards actuating the desired side effects onto the running target system. Effectors are considered a first-class resource: they must be explicitly described in the process enacted by the Workflakes engine.

Notice that the impact of effectors can range from the adjustment of a single operation parameter, to a method call, to complex reconfigurations of the target architecture - involving many components and connectors at once. Similarly, the technologies that can be used to implement effectors may greatly vary, depending on their reach as well as the nature of their target: they are often the most target-dependent elements in our approach, and are likely to be handcrafted. However, a significant amount of standardization of the interface between the process engine and the effectors it coordinates can be achieved, and can help decoupling the control and the actuation layers across technology and application contexts.

Such an interface is relatively simple at the conceptual level, and requires means for the process engine to *look up*, *instantiate* or *recruit*, *configure* and *activate* the effectors, and for the effectors to *report back* the outcome of their work in a meaningful form for the process engine. The implementation of this conceptual interface of course varies depending on the technological underpinnings of the effectors employed.

We have to date adopted mobile agents as our effectors, which seem particularly apt for an externalized infrastructure, since by their very nature they operate on the target system from the outside. That guarantees that new forms of adaptation computations can be easily deployed at any time onto the target with minimal disruption to service operation. In particular, the current Workflakes implementation is integrated with the Worklets mobile agent platform [19]: Worklets are code-carrying agents that Workflakes selects as effectors, configures and dispatches onto the target system, as a side effect of process steps. Each Worklet carries Java mobile code snippets, and deposits them onto one or more target components, according to a programmable trajectory. Once deposited, the execution of Worklet code is governed by constructs that specify conditional execution, repetition, timing, priority, etc. The agent transport facilities and the code execution environment are provided by Worklet Virtual Machines (WVMs) residing at all "stops" in a Worklet trajectory.

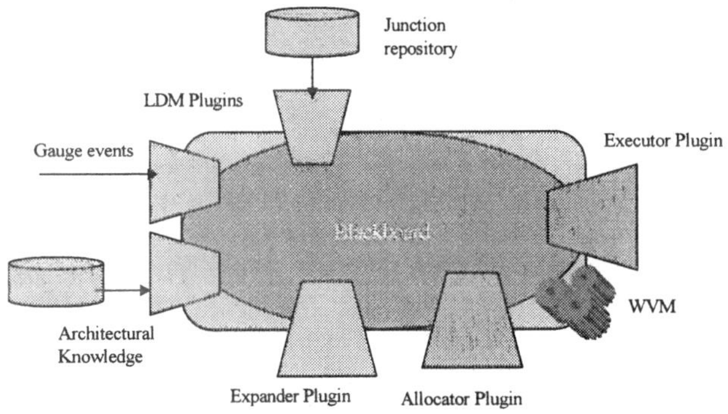

Figure 2: Representation of a typical Workflakes task processor

The current implementation of the Workflakes runtime engine relies on a specialization of the Cougaar open–source distributed platform [24]. Cougaar's decentralized task processors provide us with a number of largely autonomous controllers (as per Figure 1) for the enactment of distributed dynamic adaptation processes. Each task processor is further specified as a set of Cougaar plugins. Plugins allow to customize the functionality of task processors by inserting components that implement a particular logic or specific capability. As shown in Figure 2, a typical Workflakes task processor includes several of what Cougaar calls Logic Data Model (LDM) plugins, which are used to import and convert KX gauge events in terms of process facts, maintain internal knowledge about the target system and its state, and access a repository of effectors; an Expander plugin to load process definitions and spell them out as hierarchical decompositions of tasks; an Allocator plugin to map tasks to effectors and target components as needed; and an Executor plugin that handles the instantiation and shipment of effectors.

In Workflakes, task processors interact with Worklets in two fundamental ways. Firstly, some Worklets originate from WVMs incorporated within the task processors, and deposit their mobile code onto the target components to be adapted. Those *effectors* represent the side effects of the dynamic adaptation process onto the target system and its implementation. One of the major responsibilities of the process is therefore to decide what Worklet mobile code needs to be dispatched for a given dynamic adaptation task. That is why the repository of effectors descriptions is an essential component, and the corresponding effectors are treated as first-class process resources.

Workflakes uses Worklets also to load process definitions on the fly onto task processors, either with a pull or a push modality. The rationale for such a facility is that the dynamic adaptation of target applications is likely to call for dynamically adaptable controllers and coordinators. In Workflakes, the plugins of any task processor are initially idle and devoid of any hardcoded logic related to any particular process; for that reason, we call them *shell plugins*. The set of shell plugins launched within a task processor at start time is therefore merely indicative of the kinds of service and functionality that the cluster is meant to offer within the overall distributed Workflakes engine. Shell plugins can be activated at any time via the injection of specific *process definition Worklets*. Those Worklets dynamically deploy process fragments to the most convenient task processor for execution. Only after such deployment, shell plugins acquire a definite behavior, and start taking part in the enactment of the process. Such process delivery mechanism is effective for a centralized as well as a more scalable, decentralized process enactment architecture. It may for example be used in the pull modality for example to incrementally retrieve process fragments from a process repository when requested to handle certain specific adaptations, or in the push modality for on-the-fly process evolution across a distributed Workflakes installation.

4. Evaluation

We have carried out several experiments to validate the externalized infrastructure approach to dynamic adaptation, as embodied by KX and Workflakes specifically. Case studies to date include such varied application domains as active networking, B2C marketplaces, Internet-wide information systems and multi-channel instant messaging.

4.1. Case study: a mass-market Internet service

Figure 3 represents the architecture of a J2EE-based multi-channel instant messaging (IM) service for personal communication, which is currently offered on a 24/7/365 basis to tens of thousands of customers through a variety of channels, such as the Web, PC-based Internet chat, Short Message Service (SMS), WAP, etc.

The service runtime environment consists of a typical three-tiered server farm: a load balancer (IBM commercial software) provides a common front end to all end-users and redirects all client traffic to several replicas of the IM components, which are installed and operate on a set of middle tier hosts. The various replicas of the IM server all share a relational database and a common runtime state repository, which make up the backend tier, and allow replicas to operate in an undifferentiated way as a collective service. Some of the IM servers are wrapped within Web applications running on commercial J2EE application servers (BEA Weblogic), others may provide additional facilities, which handle access to the service through specific channels, such as SMS or WAP, and interoperate with third-party components and resources, e.g., gateways to the cell phone communication network.

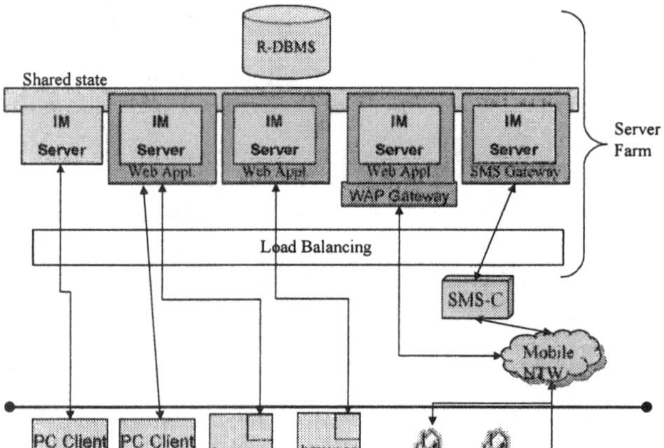

Figure 3: The IM service architecture

The case study addressed two main goals: *enhancing the QoS* perceived by end users, and *facilitating service management* by the staff in charge of supporting such a complex distributed application.

With respect to QoS, requirements focused on resolving existing load and availability problems by automating service scalability, as well as reconfiguring promptly and opportunely service parameters related to serving client requests efficiently. As for service management, requirements focused on the automation of the deployment, bootstrapping and configuration of the various service components, the continuous monitoring of those components and their interactions, and the support for "hot" service staging via automated rollout of new versions and patches.

All of those requirements are captured and addressed within a dynamic adaptation process automated by Workflakes. This process requires – among the logic and data loaded at startup onto the Workflakes engine – explicit knowledge about the service architecture and the server farm runtime environment. That knowledge is currently codified in a proprietary way.

At startup, Workflakes is given a configuration of service components that must be instantiated. Workflakes selects some hosts in the server farm for this initial deployment and sends them Worklets to execute bootstrapping code for the IM components and configure the servers with all the necessary parameters (such as the JDBC connection handle to the DBMS, the port numbers for connections by clients and other IM servers, etc.). Notice that not only the configuration information, but also the executable code of the IM server is deployed and loaded on demand, taking advantage of a code-pulling feature of the Worklets agent platform. (This approach is also followed in Software Dock [7]).

Depending on the type of the components, the deployment sub-process may change. For example, a normal IM server can be instantiated and configured by a single Worklet in one step. Web-based IM servers are notably more complex to startup and configure, since that requires first of all the spawning of a new instance of the application server, then the instantiation and parameterization of the residing Web application with respect to the hosting application server, and finally its configuration and activation as an IM component.

When a Worklet starts up an IM server, probes are simultaneously activated to track the server's instantiation and initialization. When the instantiation is successful, the process must dispatch other Worklets onto the load balancer of the server farm, which accepts traffic for the IM service, to instruct it to route it to the right host address and port for the new server. In the event of an unsuccessful initialization, instead, the likely cause is inferred by the gauge layer of the dynamic adaptation platform and reported back to the process (and also to a dashboard GUI in our implementation). Depending on the cause of that contingency, Workflakes may react in different ways: it may decide to try to bootstrap an IM server on the same host again, or on another available host, or it could skip that portion of the configuration or even abort the whole process.

Contingencies like these can be discriminated as internal or external to the process. Internal contingencies are well-known conditions that can occur in the target system and which should be provided for by specific branches of the adaptation process. External contingencies correspond either to unexpected or "new" target system conditions, or to faults within the dynamic adaptation loop itself (e.g., a communication failure between effectors and the target system components to be adapted). For those contingencies, the adaptation process should provide generic remedy strategies that are used as exceptional courses of actions, when "all else fails" or when the process needs to go back to a "safe state".

Following the initial bootstrapping phase, and after the intended service configuration is in place, Workflakes takes a reactive role, while the probing and gauging layers of the platform start monitoring and analyzing the dynamics of service usage. Certain probes and gauges are activated, to notice logging in and out of the servers, exceptions raised, service latency, number of service requests queued by the Web applications, etc.

In this case study, we are particularly concerned with load and responsiveness. Each IM server has an associated load threshold, which is best expressed in terms of the number of concurrently active clients in relationship with the memory resources of the host. When that threshold is passed, Workflakes reacts by trying to scale up the service: it selects from its system model some unused machine available in the server farm, and repeats the server bootstrapping process fragment on that machine, providing a new server replica for handling the extra load, thus achieving enhanced reliability and performance of the overall service.

For Web IM components, we are also able to reach a finer level of adaptation, exploiting the management capabilities built into the BEA Weblogic application server via Java Management eXtensions (JMX - see http://java.sun.com/products/JavaManagement), which we have integrated within the probing and effectors layers of our platform. Therefore, Workflakes can decide to intervene also in response to variations in the size of the queue of pending requests, and manipulate the details of the threading model of the Web IM application. That optimizes the degree of parallelism in processing client requests, and improves responsiveness.

We have also experimented with staging and service evolution scenarios, aiming at complete automation and minimal service disruption. It turned out that a service evolution campaign can be supported by Workflakes with relatively minor changes to the service bootstrapping process described above. The process must include tasks that gradually withdraw from the load balancer outdated server instances (thus disallowing new traffic to be assigned to them), and shut them down when traffic is absent or minimal, while another process fragment simultaneously and coordinately starts up, registers on the load balancer, and makes available to users other server instances with the new code release.

4.2 Results and lessons learned

We have been able to derive some quantitative results referring to the levels of automated support provided to the maintenance and management activities carried out onto the IM service on the field. Employing KX and Workflakes in this main case study has shown higher levels of automation, flexibility and reliability to the management of the target service and its QoS, with respect to previous labor-intensive practices. We also give some observations about the development work necessary to implement the case study.

The most significant quantitative results are:

- Reduced effort for the deployment and configuration of an IM service in the field. Current manual procedures (using Unix shell scripts and assuming DBMS and application servers pre-installed in the server farm) can take ½ to 1 person-day, with locally present experts. With KX and Workflakes, that is reduced to 1-2 minutes from a remote location.
- Reduced monitoring and maintenance effort necessary to ensure the health of the running service. A sysadmin was previously needed on-site 24/7/365, with a secondary support team of experts available on call. KX with Workflakes completely automates the monitoring of a set of major service parameters, as well as the counter-measures, for a set of well-known critical conditions.
- Reduced reaction times and improved reliability: for example, KX/Workflakes recognizes the passing of the IM load threshold in 1-2 seconds and takes approximately 40 seconds to put in place an additional server replica. Previously there was no direct overload detection: the sysadmin in charge was supposed to check the number of concurrent users from the logs and to manually start up an additional server when necessary. That was error-prone and could endanger service availability, in which case resource shortage would crash overloaded servers.
- Manageable coding complexity: KX probes, gauges and effectors are derived from generic code instrumentation templates that are then customized with situational logic. This results in rather compact code: 15 Java code lines for probes on average, usually less than 100 for effectors. In toto, the code written for the case study on top of the KX/Workflakes infrastructure was slightly above 2000 lines of Java and XML code.

Finally, other lessons we have learnt include the following qualitative considerations:

- Impact on service development: We carried out the case study positioning ourselves past the end of the development phase of the project life cycle and just prior to the deployment phase. We hence treated the target service as a complete legacy, although a legacy for which all the specifications, software artifacts and accumulated project knowledge happened to be available to the first author. Notice that also a different kind of legacy applies in the case study: the application server and the load balancer are commercial software products, which however provide sufficient APIs for carrying out our probing and actuation. Within those limitations, we were able to satisfy all the requirements of the case study.
- Relationship with architectural model: the amount of effort to analyze the target system and its behavior for dynamic adaptation purposes constituted the largest portion of the overall effort. Furthermore, a substantial portion of the software we wrote is intended to capture architectural information, relationships and inferences and represent them to KX and Workflakes. That is evidence of the strong dependency of dynamic adaptation on the ability to capture, describe and expose in an abstract and machine-readable way knowledge about the target architecture, which has motivated us to further explore integration with formal ADLs in follow-up research.
- Integrated automated management: here is where the benefit of a full-fledged process engine becomes most evident. Traditional application management is concerned with reporting warnings, alarms and other information to some knowledgeable human operator who can recognize situations as they occur, and take actions as needed. The amount of guidance and automation on the part of the management platform then may be very limited. Our approach offers instead a high level of guidance, coordination and automation to enforce what is a complex but many times largely repeatable and codifiable process.

4.3. Other case studies

Internet-scale Information Systems: the subject was ISI's Geoworlds [28], a strongly decentralized and componentized integrated Geophysical Information and Digital Library system, in experimental use for intelligence analysis at US Pacific Command (PACOM). Forms of dynamic adaptation applied to Geoworlds have varied from service parameter modification, to component repair, to global reconfigurations such as service migration.

One particularly interesting trait in this case study was that – in part building upon the lessons learned from the IM case study – we experimentally integrated architectural models and tools exploiting formal ADLs within the dynamic adaptation loop. Some of the gauges would report architecturally significant events to the CMU ABLE tool set [16], which allowed us to take dynamic adaptation decisions starting from formal architectural knowledge of the target system. That knowledge is explicit in a set of descriptions in the Acme ADL, so ABLE can decide upon and express adaptations as sets of transformations of the architectural model.

To be effected at the implementation level, transformation directives would hence be passed to Workflakes, to trigger reconfiguration processes on the deployed Geoworlds system, in accord with the architectural transformation requested. ABLE and Workflakes therefore nicely complement each other.

This juxtaposition of the architecture and implementation levels showed potential to clearly and rigorously express, reason about, validate and audit the characteristics and the effects of the modifications caused by dynamic adaptation. A difficulty we encountered and that was only partially resolved in the case study was a disconnection between the architectural model of the target system and its implementation environment; as a consequence, we have observed the need for bindings (such as those of [21]) between components and connectors in the architectural model and the runtime entities that reify the architecture in the field. Such bindings can greatly simplify the integration of ADL-based tools at all layers of our dynamic adaptation infrastructure.

The following two case studies did not directly involve the authors, but instead others applying the Workflakes system presented here:

Web Services marketplace: the subject was a prototype of an adaptive electronic marketplace. Said marketplace interfaces with a number of service components implemented as Web Services by multiple providers, and offers complex, composite service chains [27]. The dynamic adaptation platform keeps under control the basic functioning parameters of participating Web Services (such as availability, responsiveness, transaction completion ratio, etc.), analyzes their accumulated performance, and uses this information to adapt the behavior of the mediator component of the marketplace, in particular the mechanisms used in selecting service providers for composing service offers to the customers' satisfaction.

Active networking: the subject was the dynamic adaptation of active network elements, in particular active firewalls, which can be reconfigured on the fly in response to network conditions, the kind of traffic they receive, users' profiles, etc. [29]. The case study used Workflakes process-based adaptation coordination in conjunction with different implementations of the probing, gauging and effectors layers, based on TTCN-3 [36]. In response to an analysis of the network packets arriving at the firewalls and of their filtering performance and criteria, Workflakes would replace the code installed within active firewall nodes, effectively modifying their behavior. The dynamic adaptation process also includes provisions for the validation of newly installed firewall configurations through their on-line testing.

5. Related work

Given the focus of the paper and space limitations, we only compare here Workflakes in relation to other work that apparently exploits process technology to control the behavior and performance of a running application. We do not expand to comparing KX as a whole, or any of its other various constituents, or even the underlying externalized infrastructure model, to the many other approaches addressing the problem space of dynamic adaptation in whole or in part.

However, we notice that it is the externalized stance that most strongly characterizes Workflakes. Often, in fact, automated solutions to software coordination and control present structural dependencies with respect to the subjects of their coordination.

Some of those solutions can be seen as an evolution of built-in fault tolerance code. For example, [15] proposes a rule-based inference engine for decision support in application-level QoS assurance, including a coordination entity guiding a set of computational actuators. However, the coordinator and actuators must both be embedded with each target component. That makes it more difficult to define system-wide adaptations and limits the adaptations that can be carried out without rebuilding the target.

Another classic approach is that of an environment or middleware with native dynamic adaptation capabilities. Generic (i.e., not necessarily process-based) examples of dynamic adaptation middleware include Conic [14], Polylith [12], 2K / dynamicTao [13] and many others; they all offer a set of dynamic adaptation primitives as a premium for applications built with and operating on top of themselves.

Also many works that employ process technology for software control and coordination adopt in fact a middleware-like approach, by exerting the coordination "from the inside", that is, on the target's own computations. For example, [10] introduces Containment Units, as modular process-based lexical constructs for defining how distributed applications may handle self-repair and self-reconfiguration. Containment Units define a hierarchy of processes that predicate on constraints and faults, and take action to handle faults within the defined constraints. The enactment of Containment Units is under the responsibility of a process engine that is <u>integral</u> to the system being adapted, and proceeds by directing changes on the target components, which by definition is process-aware.

PIE [8] is another example of a process-based middleware, which supports federations of components. PIE adds a control layer on top of a range of inter-component communication facilities. The control layer implements process guidance via handlers that react to and manipulate the communications exchanged by the components in a federation. Dynamic adaptation is thus limited to the reconfiguration of the service architectural connectors and is carried out by plugging in appropriate handlers, as directed by the process, which intrude in the normal course of computation of the target.

TCCS [9] has considerable similarities with Workflakes, since it employs its process engine to direct the work of analogous effector agents, to carry out the dynamic adaptation tasks. However, TCCS is the epitome of the middleware approach, since it is in charge of all interactions between the system components, even normal operations; that is, the target application simply does not exist independently from its process and agent-based framework.

With each of these dynamic adaptation middlewares, all service components need to be assembled from the start according to the middleware and its primitives. This not only poses a considerable barrier with respect to legacy software, but also introduces a very strong dependency between actors and subjects of dynamic adaptation. Furthermore, the spectrum and granularity of possible adaptations is effectively restricted by the set of primitives made available by the chosen middleware. A similar observation applies also to those works that exploit the characteristics of established computing frameworks to facilitate certain aspects of dynamic adaptation, such as BARK [11], which is limited to the EJB component model.

In contrast to all of the above, Workflakes remains independent from any underlying computing framework and quite general with respect to the reach, granularity and kinds of dynamic adaptation that it can exert, since the target is fully disjoint from the dynamic adaptation engine.

The most similar approach (that we know of) may be Willow [17]. Willow proposes an architecture for the survivability of distributed applications, analogous to our vision of a superimposed feedback loop. In particular, Willow can implement reactive as well as proactive dynamic adaptation policies, which are driven by codified architectural knowledge, and enacted via a process-based mechanism built upon the previous Software Dock (re)deployment engine [7]. It appears, however, that Willow restricts itself to coarse-grained reconfigurations, such as replacing, adding and removing entire components, perhaps even composite substructures, from the target application, while presuming conventional embedded approaches for more local and refined adaptations.

6. Contributions and forecast

Workflakes is among the results of a multi-institution consortium effort concerned with instrumenting, measuring and controlling pre-existing distributed software systems. We describe/reference elsewhere our own/others' approaches to instrumenting and measuring, and note that the consortium has researched "standard" interfaces for these components to communicate with each other as well as with the control component. Workflakes is the first control component that has been developed within the consortium.

Workflakes has adequately demonstrated the process-based software adaptation controller concept in the case studies covered here. In particular, while the instrumentation and measurement facilities by themselves may reduce a feedback loop that was previously entirely manual from days or weeks to hours, Workflakes has shown that an automated controller can further reduce the consequently determined software adaptations from hours to minutes and seconds. Of course, not all adaptations can be fully automated, so our continuing research will try to better characterize those that can vs. cannot.

To investigate further the boundaries of our approach and its usability, and assess its merits as well as its drawbacks, we are also working on applying Workflakes to particularly demanding domains. One such domain is that of systems with (soft) real-time adaptation requirements, e.g., AI2TV – Adaptive Internet Interactive Team Video – where we employ KX and Workflakes to keep "in sync" multiple viewers of the same distance learning lecture video at varying compression levels, see `http://www.psl.cs.columbia.edu/ai2tv`). We compare and contrast the performance of an externalized adaptation loop – with its induced reaction latency – against middleware-oriented approaches to similar problems, such as [32] [34]. We are similarly interested to weigh the performance of Workflakes in those cases against other externalized infrastructures that employ for the coordination of actuation means different from process technology, such as [33].

Another investigation issue is how the reliability of externalized dynamic adaptation facilities may influence that of the target system, and how to minimize any adverse impacts deriving from problems and failures that may occur at the various stage of the adaptation loop.

We also plan to precisely define and develop standard interfaces for Workflakes in its role as the control component of KX, similarly to what has been done for the other infrastructure layers. That includes adopting a common, high-level process formalism suitable for describing and enacting dynamic adaptation processes (we are currently evaluating the UMass Little-JIL process language [6]), expanding the repertoire of effectors beyond mobile agents (we are currently integrating SOAP-based effectors), and being able to handle all effectors in a uniform way, independently from their technology.

Finally, another research thread is to more tightly integrate Workflakes with architecture-based modeling and analysis tools, leading to selection/construction of architecture-based repair strategies (e.g., [31] [16]), which are then spelled out and implemented as processes.

7. Acknowledgements

We would like to thank Gaurav Kc for his ongoing development of Worklets, Lee Osterweil and Nathan Combs for the frequent discussions and suggestions about Workflakes, George Heineman for help with techniques for KX and Worklets, Bob Balzer, David Garlan, Bradley Schmerl, David Wells and David Wile for their insights on the general infrastructure model and APIs' standardization, Pier Giorgio Bosco, Mario Costamagna, Matteo Demichelis, Elio Paschetta and Roberto Squarotti at TILAB for their contribution on applicability and to the IM service case study, the partner organizations and all the colleagues who worked in the OLIVES project, and the other members of the Programming Systems Lab. PSL is funded in part by Defense Advanced Research Project Agency under DARPA Order K503 monitored by Air Force Research Laboratory F30602-00-2-0611, by National Science Foundation CCR-9970790, EIA-0071954 and CCR-0203876, by Microsoft Research and by IBM. The work at TILAB is funded in part by EURESCOM project P-1108 (OLIVES).

8. References

[1] IBM Research, "Autonomic Computing Manifesto", http://researchweb.watson.ibm.com/autonomic/manifesto/autonomic_computing.pdf.

[2] A. Patterson, A. Brown, P. Broadwell, G. Candea, M. Chen, J. Cutler, P. Enriquez, A. Fox, E. Kiciman, M. Merzbacher, D. Oppenheimer, N. Sastry, W. Tetzlaff, J. Traupman, and N. Treuhaft. "Recovery-Oriented Computing (ROC): Motivation, Definition, Techniques, and Case Studies".

UC Berkeley Computer Science Technical Report UCB//CSD-02-1175, March 15, 2002.

[3] J. Salasin, "Dynamic Assembly for System Adaptability, Dependability, and Assurance (DASADA)", http://www.darpa.mil/ito/research/dasada/.

[4] B. Balzer, "Probe Run-Time Infrastructure", http://www.schafercorp-ballston.com/dasada/2001WinterPI/ProbeRun-TimeInfrastructureDesign.ppt

[5] G. Valetto, G. Kaiser, and G.S. Kc, "A Mobile Agent Approach to Process-based Dynamic Adaptation of Complex Software Systems", in *8th European Workshop on Software Process Technology*, June 2001. http://www.psl.cs.columbia.edu/ftp/psl/CUCS-001-01.pdf.

[6] A.G. Cass, B. Staudt Lerner, E.K. McCall, L. J. Osterweil, S.M. Sutton, Jr., and A. Wise, "Little-JIL/Juliette: A Process Definition Language and Interpreter", in *22nd International Conference on Software Engineering*, June 2000.

[7] R.S. Hall, D. Heimbigner, and A.L. Wolf, "A Cooperative Approach to Support Software Deployment Using the Software Dock", in *21st International Conference on Software Engineering,* May 1999.

[8] G. Cugola., P.Y. Cunin, S. Dami, J. Estublier, A. Fuggetta, F. Pacull, M. Riviere, and H. Verjus, "Support for Software Federations: The Pie Platform," in *7th European Workshop on Software Process Technology*, February 2000.

[9] S.K Shirvastava, L. Bellissard, D. Feliot, M. Herrmann, N. De Palma, and S.M. Wheater, "A Workflow and Agent based Platform for Service Provisioning", in *4th IEEE/OMG International Enterprise Distributed Object Computing Conference*, September 2000

[10] J.M. Cobleigh, L.J. Osterweil, A. Wise, and B. Staudt Lerner, "Containment Units: A Hierarchically Composable Architecture for Adaptive Systems", in *10th International Symposium on the Foundations of Software Engineering (FSE 10)*, Charleston, SC, November 2002.

[11] M.J. Rutherford, K. Anderson, A. Carzaniga, D. Heimbigner, and A.L. Wolf, "Reconfiguration in the Enterprise JavaBean Component Model", in *IFIP/ACM Working Conference on Component Deployment*, June 2002.

[12] C.R. Hofmeister, and J.M. Purtilo, "Dynamic Reconfiguration in Distributed Systems: Adapting Software Modules for Replacement", in *13th International Conference on Distributed Computing Systems*, May 1993.

[13] F. Kon, R. Campbell, M.D. Mickunas, K. Nahrstedt, and F.J. Ballesteros. "2K, A Distributed Operating System for Dynamic Heterogeneous Environments", in *9th IEEE International Symposium on High Performance Distributed Computing*, August 2000.

[14] J. Magee, J. Kramer, and M. Sloman. "Constructing Distributed Systems in Conic", *IEEE Transactions on Software Engineering*, 15(6):663--675, June 1989.

[15] H. Lutfiyya, G. Molenkamp, M. Katchabaw, and M. Bauer, "Issues in Managing Soft QoS Requirements in Distributed Systems Using a Policy-Based Framework", in *3rd IEEE International Workshop on Policies for Distributed Systems and Networks*, January 2001.

[16] B. Schmerl, and D. Garlan, "Exploiting Architectural Design Knowledge to Support Self-repairing Systems", in *14th International Conference on Software Engineering and Knowledge Engineering*, July 2002.

[17] J.Knight, D. Heimbigner, A. Wolf, A. Carzaniga, J. Hill, and P. Devanbum, "The Willow Survivability Architecture", in *4th Information Survivability Workshop (ISW-2001)*, Vancouver, B.C.,18-20 March 2002.

[18] P.N. Gross, S. Gupta, G. E. Kaiser, G.S. Kc, and J.J. Parekh, "An Active Events Model for Systems Monitoring", in *Working Conference on Complex and Dynamic Systems Architecture*, December 2001. http://www.psl.cs.columbia.edu/ftp/psl/CUCS-011-01.pdf.

[19] G. Kaiser, A. Stone, and S. Dossick, "A Mobile Agent Approach to Lightweight Process Workflow," in *International Process Technology Workshop*, September 1999. http://www.psl.cs.columbia.edu/ftp/psl/CUCS-021-99.pdf.

[20] D. Garlan, B. Schmerl, and J. Chang, "Using Gauges for Architecture-Based Monitoring and Adaptation", in *Working Conference on Complex and Dynamic Systems Architecture*, December 2001.

[21] E.M. Dashofy, A. van der Hoek, and R.N. Taylor, "An Infrastructure for the Rapid Development of XML-based Architecture Description Languages", in the *24th International Conference on Software Engineering*, May 2002.

[22] P. Oreizy, M.M. Gorlick, R.N. Taylor, D. Heimbinger, G. Johnson, N. Medvidovic, A. Quilici, D.S. Rosenblum, and A.L. Wolf, "An Architecture-Based Approach to Self-Adaptive Software", *IEEE Intelligent Systems* 14(3): 54-62, May/June 1999.

[23] G. Kaiser, P. Gross, G. Kc, J. Parekh, and G. Valetto, "An Approach to Autonomizing Legacy Systems", in *Workshop on Self-Healing, Adaptive and Self-MANaged Systems (SHAMAN 2002),* June 2002.

[24] Cougaar Home Page, "Welcome to the Cognitive Agent Architecture (Cougaar) Open Source Website". http://www.cougaar.org.

[25] Gail Kaiser, "Autonomizing Legacy Systems", invited talk at the Almaden Institute Symposium on Autonomic

Computing, April 10-12 2002 http://www.almaden.ibm.com/institute/pdf/KaiserGail.pdf

[26] Giuseppe Valetto, and Gail Kaiser, "A Case Study in Software Adaptation", in *Workshop on Self-Healing Systems (WOSS '02)*, 18-19 November 2002.

[27] A. Rocha, G. Valetto, E. Paschetta, and S. Heikkinen, "Continuous On-Line Validation of Web Services", in *International Conference on Electronic Publishing (ELPUB 2002)*, November 6-8, 2002.

[28] M. Coutinho, R. Neches, A. Bugacov, V. Kumar, K. Yao, I. Ko, R. Eleish, and S. Abhinka, "GeoWorlds: A Geographically Based Information System for Situation Understanding and Management", in *1st International Workshop on TeleGeoProcessing (TeleGeo 99)*, Lyon, France, May 6-7, 1999.

[29] P. Deussen, G. Valetto, G. Din, T. Kivimaki, S. Heikkinen, and A. Rocha, "Continuous On-Line Validation for Optimized Service Management" in *EURESCOM Summit 2002*, Hiedelberg, Germnany, October 21-24, 2002.

[30] E. Kasten, P. K. McKinley, S. Sadjadi, and R. Stirewalt, "Separating introspection and intercession in metamorphic distributed systems", in *IEEE Workshop on Aspect-Oriented Programming for Distributed Computing*, July 2002.

[31] Carnegie Mellon University, "Acme Web, The Acme Architectural Description Language", http://www-2.cs.cmu.edu/~acme/.

[32] C. Poellabauer, H. Abbasi, and K. Schwan, "Cooperative Run-time Management of Adaptive Applications and Distributed Resources", in *ACM Multimedia*, Juan-les-Pins, France, December 1-6, 2002.

[33] D. Rosu, K. Schwan, S. Yalamanchili, and R. Jha. "On Adaptive Resource Allocation for Complex Real-Time Applications", in *18th IEEE Real-Time Systems Symposium*, December 1997.

[34] R. Vanegas, J.A. Zinky, J.P. Loyall, D.A. Karr, R.E. Schantz, D.E. Bakken, "QuO's Runtime Support for Quality of Service in Distributed Objects", in *IFIP International Conference on Distributed Systems Platforms and Open Distributed Processing (Middleware'98)*, 15-18 September 1998, The Lake District, England.

[35] W. Gu, G. Eisenhauer, and K. Schwan, "Falcon: On-line Monitoring and Steering of Parallel Programs", in *Concurrency: Practice and Experience*, 10(9): 699-736, August 1988.

[36] "Tree and Tabular Combined Notation, version 3," ITU-T Recommendation Z.140, 2001 http://www.itu.int/ITU-T/studygroups/com10/languages/Z.140_0701_pre.pdf

[37] F. Cubrera, Y. Goland, J. Klein, F. Leymann, D. Roter, S. Tatte, and S. Weerawarana, "Business Process Execution Language for Web Services, Version 1.0", July 2002, http://www.ibm.com/developerworks/library/ws-bpel/

Technical Papers

Empirical Studies II

Understanding and Predicting Effort in Software Projects

Audris Mockus and David M. Weiss
Avaya Labs Research
Department of Software Technology Research
233 Mt Airy Rd., Basking Ridge, NJ 07920

Ping Zhang
Avaya Labs Research
Department of Data Analysis Research
233 Mt Airy Rd., Basking Ridge, NJ 07920

Abstract

We set out to answer a question we were asked by software project management: how much effort remains to be spent on a specific software project and how will that effort be distributed over time? To answer this question we propose a model based on the concept that each modification to software may cause repairs at some later time and investigate its theoretical properties and application to several projects in Avaya to predict and plan development resource allocation. Our model presents a novel unified framework to investigate and predict effort, schedule, and defects of a software project. The results of applying the model confirm a fundamental relationship between the new feature and defect repair changes and demonstrate its predictive properties.

Key Words and Phrases: software changes, effort estimation, project schedule, defect prediction

1. Introduction

Despite considerable research and practical experience it is still a formidable challenge to understand and predict what happens in a large software project. Even in cases where some parties have a good understanding of the consequences, the business pressures and lack of quantitative evidence often results in misguided effort and time estimation and faulty plans.

We focus on a problem of planning and managing development resource allocation in large software projects. We set out to answer very specific questions that were urgent in several high-profile projects in Avaya:

1. How much effort remains to be spent on a specific software project based on what we know now?
2. How will that effort be distributed over time?

To answer these questions we built a simple model of a software project that describes the current state and possible outcomes of a project based on various sources of information ubiquitous in software projects, thereby decreasing the need for the subjective judgment. This model proved to be flexible enough to answer a wide range of important project planning questions.

Previous work [1, 11, 13] has identified version control and problem tracking databases as a promising repository of information about a software project. We have created methods and tools to retrieve, process, and model such data at the fine level of Modification Requests (individual changes to software) in order to understand the relationships among process/product factors and key outcomes, such as, quality, effort, and interval.

This work proposes ways to use the change data to understand and predict the state of a software project. We propose a model based on the concept that each modification to software may cause repairs at some later time and investigate the model's theoretical properties and report its application to several projects in Avaya. The model assumes the basic premise of change analysis, i.e., that the people involved in a project leave traces of their work in the form of modifications to the artifacts on which they work.

We start from our motivating questions in Section 2. Section 3 describes ways to obtain data on software changes and describes a method to estimate effort for a software change. The model used to compose a project from software changes is introduced in Section 4; Section 5 describes the result of fitting such models to actual projects; Section 6 considers ways to validate these empirical results, and Section 7 outlines steps needed to model other software projects. We conclude with literature review in Section 8 and discussion.

2. Motivation

We set out with the desire to answer the two basic questions stated in 1. These questions arose in two ongoing projects and in two different contexts. In the first project the key question was whether or not the release date would be met. Would there be sufficient time and effort to complete

0-7695-1877-X/03 $17.00 © 2003 IEEE

the features scheduled for the release, including repairing any problems that arose during the development. In the second project, a new release was about to go into the field. The question was how much effort would be needed to support it once it was released. Since resources devoted to repairing problems, whether found in the field or earlier, are resources that cannot be applied to completing features or to work on other projects, the questions were critical for both projects and for other projects that were awaiting resources.

Surprisingly, the planning in both projects did not take into account that a project of larger magnitude might cause more field problems and drain more resources than a smaller project. Because of space constraints we report results only for the first project.

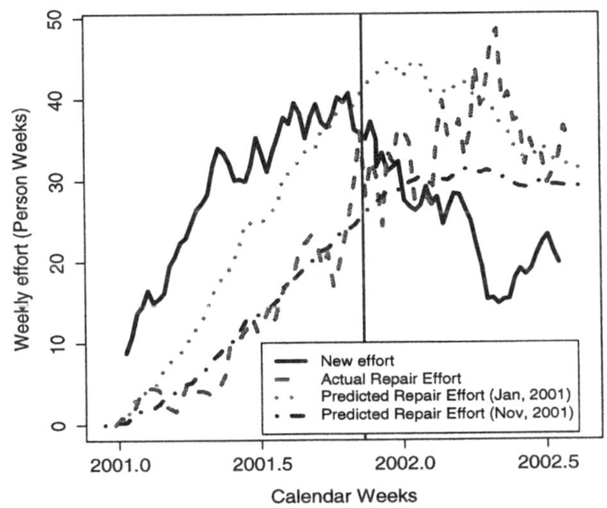

Figure 1. Actual and predicted repair effort.

The first project had an ambitious schedule. However, after a few slips the question of when and what will be complete arose. The project history is illustrated in Figure 1. The figure shows the actual effort for implementing new features (solid line), the effort of repairing defects (dashed line), and two curves of predicted effort with predictions done before the project started (dotted line) and on November 2001 (dash-dot line). The end of November is indicated by a vertical line). The details of the method used to produce the prediction are described below. There was a major release in May and new feature activities in the second quarter of 2002 will be released later via software patches or minor releases.

The predicted repair effort is fairly close to reality. However, the initial prediction at the start of the project, which is based on data from previous projects, is slightly biased because as it turns out, the new project has longer intervals until defect repairs. The revised prediction done in November 2001 uses data from the current project. Our recommendation made to the project in November 2001 was that the May 2002 target for release could not be met unless the development team refocused it's resources to repair of existing defects and away from the development of additional features. The actual effort curves after November 2001 show that the project apparently did exactly that, i.e., reducing the scope of new functionality and focusing on repair.

The next section describes background information on using change management and version control repositories to obtain information on software changes that is used to obtain and predict the the effort distribution in a software project.

3. Background

The basic premise of analyzing software changes is that software is created incrementally through a series of work items, each potentially resulting in a change. Each incremental change is recorded by a version control and, possibly, problem tracking system. The data typically contains a set of attributes such as the following:

- The identity of the person making the change.
- A short comment written by the author of the change.
- The file(s) changed and the lines changed or the file(s) contents before and after the change.

3.1. Work items in software projects

The purpose of the typical work item in a software organization is to make a change to a software entity. Work items range in size from very large work items, such as releases, to very small changes, such as a single delta (modification) to a file. A hierarchy of changes with associated attributes is shown in Figure 2.

The source code of large software products is typically organized into subsystems according to major functionality (e.g., database, user interface, etc.). Each subsystem contains a number of source code files and documentation.

The versions of the source code and documentation are maintained using a version control system (VCS) such as Concurrent Versioning System [4] commonly used for open source software projects, or a popular commercial system, such as ClearCase. We frequently deal with Source Code Control System (SCCS) [15] and its descendants. Version control systems operate over a set of source code files. An *atomic* change, or *delta*, to the program text consists of the lines that were deleted and those that were added in order to make the change. Deltas are usually computed by a file differencing algorithm (such as Unix diff), invoked by the VCS, which compares an older version of a file with the current version. Included with every delta is information

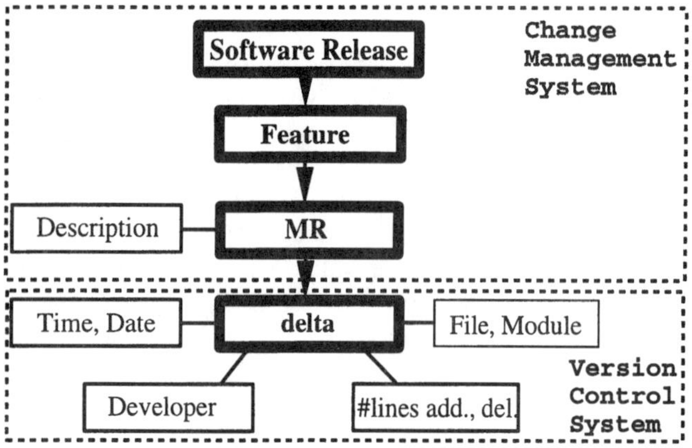

Figure 2. Hierarchy of changes and associated data sources. Boxes with dashed lines define data sources (VCS and CMS), boxes with thick lines define changes, and boxes with thin lines define properties of changes. The arrows define an "is a part of" relationship among changes, e.g., each MR is a part of a feature.

such as the time the change was made, the person making the change, and a short comment describing the change.

In addition to VCS, most projects employ a change request management system (CMS) that keeps track of individual requests for changes, which we call Modification Requests (MRs). Whereas a delta is intended to keep track of lines of code that are changed, an MR is intended to be a change made for a single purpose. Each MR may have many deltas associated with it. Some commonly used problem tracking systems include ClearDDTS from Rational, and the Extended Change Management System (ECMS) [10]. Usually such systems associate a list of deltas with each MR.

Modifications are typically made for one of the following reasons.

- Repairing previous changes that caused a failure during testing or in the field.
- Introducing new features to the existing system.
- Restructuring the code to make it easier to understand and maintain. (An activity more common in heavily modified code, such as in legacy systems.)

To understand the activities occurring in a software development project, it is critical to know which MRs belong to each of these categories. Fortunately, this information is often recorded in CMS systems as a field identifying whether the MR represents a new feature or repairs a problem. Unfortunately, the quality of this classification varies by project. In cases when it is unacceptably low for the purpose of a particular analysis we use an automatic classification technique that uses words in the MR abstract to determine the purpose of the MR [11].

Based on informal interviews in a number of software development organizations within Lucent and Avaya we obtained the following guidelines that are used to divide work into MRs:

1. Work assignments that affect several subsystems (the largest building blocks of functionality) are split into distinct MRs so that each MR affects one subsystem;
2. A work assignment in a subsystem that is too much for one person is further organized into several MRs so that each one could be completed by a single person.

For practical reasons these guidelines are not strictly enforced, so that some MRs cross subsystem boundaries and some have several people working on them.

A group of MRs associated with new software functionality is called a feature. A set of features and repairs constitute a customer delivery, also known as a release. Put another way, each release can be characterized as a base system modified and extended by a set of MRs.

3.2. The value of analyzing changes

The analysis of software changes has a number of distinct benefits that may not be immediately obvious.

- The data collection is nonintrusive, using only existing data and making analysis possible in commercial projects that are usually under intense schedule pressure and do not have time or resources to collect additional data.
- Long history on past projects is available, enabling comparison to what happened in the past and customization and calibration of the methods to the existing environment. Nonetheless, one must be mindful of changes to the environment and application that make comparisons problematic.
- The information is fine grained, at the MR/delta level. Such fine level data collection on a large scale would not be possible otherwise.
- The information is complete, all parts of software, documentation, test cases that are under version control are recorded.
- The way the version control system is used rarely changes, making data uniform over time.
- Even small projects generate large volumes of changes making it possible to detect even small effects statistically.

- The version control system is used as a standard part of the project, so the development project is unaffected by experimenter intrusion.

We believe that MRs are a very rich source of information about software development and that their analysis can evoke rewarding insights. Unfortunately drawing conclusions about characteristics such as effort, quality and interval is fraught with challenges. We describe some of these challenges in the following sections. Basic to all of them is that special care must always be taken to obtain information on how version control and change management are used in the project so as not to misinterpret the MR classifications or misunderstand the process used to create, make progress on, and record information about MRs.

3.3. Estimating change cost

While many attributes of changes are recorded by a version control system, the cost it takes to perform a change is impractical to collect. We consider cost to be paid developer time. Often we use the term effort instead, but not to refer to the actual effort or time it might take a programmer to complete a change, because the actual effort might depend on the programmer working unpaid or unrecorded overtime, on doing tasks that are not directly related to completing changes to software, such as attending meetings, learning, or, on occasions, simply being more or less productive than usual for other reasons.

While some change management systems, e.g., Sablime, include effort related fields such as estimated and actual effort, we found them to be rarely used and even when used to be extremely inaccurate. Interviews with developers in the latter cases indicates that they often put a constant number in such fields that does not depend on actual or estimated effort.

By making a few simple assumptions we can overcome this difficulty and determine, for example, what makes some changes cost more than others, as shown in [1], where the key idea is to tease out the extent of the contribution of various factors to the time a developer spends on a particular change. Our assumptions are as follows.

1. The attributes of software changes such as the identity of the individual making the change, size of the change, and types of tools used, determine the cost it takes to complete a change (more examples are in, e.g., [12]).
2. For each MR we have available the identity of the developer and the time when the MR was submitted, i.e., the time after which no work was done on that MR.
3. The work on the MR was done by the developer who submitted the MR and that work was started a short time before the submission of the MR: we used the limit of two to ten weeks before its completion for the start of an MR.
4. The developers on average spend approximately equal amounts of paid time every calendar time period (in a month, or in a week). The overtime was either not recorded or not paid in the organizations we studied so this assumption accurately reflects the cost of developer time to the organization.
5. It is possible to determine whether or not an MR is a repair or new feature. Both attributes are typically kept by a change management system, with the latter often being somewhat inaccurate. We use methods described in [11] to determine whether or not an MR is a repair.

Based on developer interviews in the commercial projects we studied these assumptions held except for infrequent instances when several developers contributed to the same MR.

3.3.1 Change effort estimation algorithm

Using the preceding assumptions we have previously developed an algorithm for estimating effort for changes [1, 7]. The algorithm consists of an initialization stage where a rough estimate of MR effort is obtained, followed by iterations. A regression model is used in each iteration of the algorithm to guide the refinement of the estimate. The code to perform the analysis is published in [7].

In the initialization step of the algorithm a table for each developer is completed (see Table 1). Table columns represent weeks, table rows represent MRs, and table cells represent the cost (developer paid time). The table is initialized as follows.

1. Put zeros in cells where no work on the MR was done (in weeks after the MR was completed and in weeks before the work has started on the MR). The MR start date is a parameter to the algorithm.
2. Put ones in column sums: we assume the monthly cost for each developer to be constant for that developer (see Table 1). The differences between developers are obtained in the model fitting stage.
3. Fill the remaining cells in each column by equally dividing the column sum among nonzero cells in that column.
4. Calculate the row sums by adding cell values in each row.

Each iteration consists of the following steps.

Table 1. An example table of effort-per-MR-per-week breakdown for one developer. The ?'s represent blank cells, whose values are initially unknown.

	W1	W2	W3	W4	W5	...	Total
MR_1	0	?	?	?	0	...	?
MR_2	?	?	?	0	0	...	?
MR_3	0	0	?	?	?	...	?
⋮	⋮	⋮	⋮	⋮	⋮		⋮
Total	1	1	1	1	1	...	12

1. A regression is fitted using a number of attributes of each MR as predictors and the fitted coefficients are used to predict MR efforts.
2. The cell values in each row are rescaled to sum up to the MR efforts predicted by the regression model.
3. The cell values in each column are rescaled to sum up to the column sums (ones).
4. A new set of row sums is calculated from the cell values.

The iteration is repeated until convergence (we stopped when the sum of the absolute values of the changes of all the fitted regression coefficients becomes less than 0.01).

The next section describes the project model we used, or the way MRs relate to each other in a software project.

4. Project Model

The main goal of our project model is to predict the amount and the distribution over time of the maintenance effort. This may be done either at an advanced stage of the development, for example, at code complete date, or it could be done at an earlier stage based on the work breakdown structure.

To perform accurate prediction we need two basic properties from the model: the model has to relate the existing effort to future effort and it has to learn (incorporate information) from completed projects. We express these two properties as the following postulates:

1. Every unit of new feature effort generates μ units of repair effort with each unit of repair effort having independent delay (the interval between the submission of the new change and the submission of the repair) with mean value of $1/\lambda$.

   The underlying thesis is that addition of a new feature may make the software violate its specifications because the new feature is not implemented correctly or because the existing functionality is exercised in a novel way. Not all defects are likely to be detected immediately because they may manifest themselves at compilation, unit testing, integration, system testing, or in the field.

2. The organization has completed some projects that are similar to the project to be predicted, e.g., similar development team, process, and software functionality. This is to ensure that the parameters μ and λ, estimated from previous projects, provide useful information to the current project.

To use the model, the new feature effort is obtained by the effort estimation techniques described above when a significant amount of new features have been implemented, or from a work breakdown structure if the prediction is done earlier in the project.

As illustrated in Figure 3, the repair starts in parallel with new feature development. The figure shows new effort (solid line), repair effort (dashed line), and predicted repair effort (dotted line) for 11 releases. Notice that in some earlier releases a significant portion of new functionality is implemented before the repair effort peaks and the later releases had more iterative development model where new feature effort is distributed more evenly throughout the project.

In the following subsections, we will briefly describe a probability model to fit the observed data. The likelihood function is a statistical concept. It is defined as the theoretical probability of observing the data at hand, given the underlying model. Empirically, it is a function of the observed data and unknown model parameters (μ and λ). Maximizing the likelihood with respect to these unknown parameters will yield the so called Maximum Likelihood Estimate (MLE) of these parameters (denoted as $\hat{\mu}$ and $\hat{\lambda}$). This is a powerful statistical technique that allows us to generalize linear regression procedures to arbitrary statistical models.

4.1. Project likelihood

Assume that the project starts at time 0 and we observe defect and new feature effort up to time t. In most cases, the link between a repair change and its root cause cannot be observed. In other words, one does not know which of the previously implemented features caused the bug, only that one of them did. Borrowing terminology from standard probability theory, our postulate 1 in the simplest case implies that the repair effort generated by one unit of feature effort follows a nonhomogeneous Poisson process with intensity function $\mu\lambda e^{-\lambda t}$, $t > 0$. Let $B_{[a,b]}$ denote the repair effort during the time interval $[a, b]$. The model implies that $B_{[a,b]}$ follows a Poisson distribution with mean

$\mu_{[a,b]} = \mu(e^{-\lambda a} - e^{-\lambda b})$. Future effort can be calculated by setting $b = \infty$, provided that one can estimate μ and λ.

Consider first the case when one feature is implemented at time 0. The data we observe can be described as n units of repair effort occurring at times $s_j, j = 1, \ldots, n$. Let $S^{(j)}$ be the order statistics of the repair times. Then the likelihood function, i.e., the joint probability distribution, of observing such data is

$$P(B_{[0,t]} = n, S^{(j)} = s_j,\ s_j \leq s_{j+1}, j = 1, \ldots, n) = e^{-\mu_{[0,t]}} \mu^n \prod_{j=1}^{n} \lambda e^{-\lambda s_j}. \quad (1)$$

The parameters μ and λ can be estimated numerically by maximizing the likelihood function.

Next, let us consider the more realistic case of observing N_{t_i} units of new feature effort at time t_i, and B_{s_j} units of repair effort at times s_j. Some slightly more tedious algebra shows that the negative log-likelihood is:

$$\sum_{t_i} \mu N_{t_i} \left(1 - e^{-\lambda(t-t_i)}\right) - B_{[0,t]} \log(\mu\lambda) - \sum_{s_j} B_{s_j} \log \left(\sum_{i:t_i < s_j} e^{-\lambda(s_j - t_i)} \right). \quad (2)$$

4.2. Limitation of the model

A problem occurs when applying the model to unfinished projects. Let us consider the simplest case of observing one unit of new feature effort at time 0 and one unit of repair effort at time s and the observation interval is $[0, t]$. When s is close to $t/2$, one can show that the MLEs are $\hat{\mu} \to +\infty$ and $\hat{\lambda} \to +0$! A similar argument can be made in more general settings. What this shows is that under fairly general assumptions it is impossible to predict what will happen in an isolated project until it reaches its late stages unless some additional information is available. We consider several ways to address this shortcoming of MLE:

1. Perform prediction in a project using estimates for one or more parameters obtained on completed projects.
2. Impose an informative prior distribution.
3. Use data from other completed projects.
4. Observe relationships between repairs and new features causing them.

The first approach is the simplest and works best when the completed projects are similar to the project under consideration. The second approach is to use a Bayesian estimation technique instead of an MLE. An informative prior would eliminate the impossible infinite values of the estimates. However, this would require an elicitation step so that an appropriate prior could be obtained from people intimately familiar with the project. While this may be the only option for a new project, it is possible to use data from completed projects in a more mature organization using, for example, a hierarchical model. Finally, modifying the problem tracking process to record the change causing the repair would provide the data needed to produce a usable estimate. Here we report the results based on the first approach.

5. Empirical Results

We fitted the model on a family of software projects each representing a release of a large real time high-availability software system. We considered 11 releases developed over more than 9 years with contributions of 494 developers via more than 27,000 MRs.

The older releases were used to fit the parameters of the project model and the estimated parameters were then used on a current release to obtain predictions of the future development effort.

The project used the Sablime system for MR tracking and a proprietary SCCS based system for version control. Certain parts of the project also use ClearCase for version control.

We consider a slightly simplified version of the development process, as follows. The developers are assigned a new feature or a defect to work on. In case of defects, they investigate the problem, make necessary changes and submit an MR for integration. In case of new features, additional tasks such as low level design and design review are performed prior to coding. After coding is complete the MR is submitted for integration by the developer. The code inspection is done afterward and any issues are resolved with additional MRs. If an MR is opened by a tester, it may take some time until someone is assigned to work on it and eventually starts working on it. In this case the MR open time may significantly precede the time when the work started. Often developers will find an issue to work on in the regular course of their activities. They may investigate the issue, complete the necessary changes in their private workspaces, and then open and immediately submit an MR for integration. In this case opening an MR does not precede the start of work. Consequently we could not use the MR open time as an accurate indicator of when the work was started.

The MR submit time, on the other hand, fairly precisely determines the completion of the work on an MR, because developers have no reason to keep an MR open after it is complete. Once an MR is submitted, it goes next to system integration build and then to system test. Such builds occur once a week or once every two weeks for the projects under investigation.

5.1. Estimation of change effort

As a baseline we assumed MRs to take at most two to ten weeks of calendar time counting backward from the date of submission. For each developer we created a table as in Table 1 with columns representing weeks and rows representing MRs. Initially the table is filled with zeros except for the four weeks up to the week when an MR was submitted. The nonzero cells are filled column by column, dividing unit weekly effort equally among the nonzero cells in the column. This corresponds to the initialization step of the algorithm described in [7, 1].

To refine these estimates we used several factors that we could measure of which we selected the ones that were shown to affect MR effort in previous studies, e.g., [1, 7], or we thought might influence MR effort:

- Developer. Login of the individual who worked on and submitted the MR.
- MR type. We classified MRs into new development (referred to as new features and enhancements in the considered projects), repair, and field problems. The last class corresponded to repairs done in response to a customer problem reported on released software.
- MR status. We discriminated among MRs that had status "nochange" indicating that no change to the code was done as a result of the MR, versus the rest.
- MR size. Logarithm of the number of lines added by the MR.
- MR size/complexity. Logarithm of the number of deltas constituting the MR.

The estimated regression coefficients and their 95% confidence intervals are presented in Table 2. The regression equation by which the coefficients affect effort is as follows:

$$E(\text{Effort}) = (\text{delta}+1)^{\alpha_1} \times (\text{lines}+1)^{\alpha_2} \times e^{\alpha_{nochange} I(nochange) + \alpha_{new} I(new) + \alpha_{field} I(field)} \times \prod_{i:\{\text{developers}\}} \beta_i I(developer_i). \quad (3)$$

where I is an indicator function. The non-field repair MR resulting in a code change is the baseline for the coefficients $\alpha_{nochange}$, α_{new}, and α_{field}. For example, a new feature MRs take $e^{0.39} \approx 1.5$ times the effort of comparable repair MRs.

Table 2 shows that the effects are in the expected direction, with field problems and large MRs requiring more effort. New feature MRs are more difficult in the considered projects than repair MRs. This is in contrast to the finding in [1], where defect repairs required more effort. The

Table 2. Results from fitting effort model.

Coefficient	Estimate	p-val	95% CI
$\alpha_{nochange}$	-0.11	0.244	$[-0.30, 0.08]$
α_{new}	0.39	0.000	$[0.23, 0.55]$
α_{field}	0.69	0.000	$[0.56, 0.82]$
delta: α_1	-0.11	0.069	$[-0.22, 0.01]$
lines: α_2	0.15	0.000	$[0.10, 0.20]$

rest of the predictors are not significant in predicting effort. The difference can be explained by the fact that [1] considers a different, even larger, software product. Furthermore, in [1] the algorithm used MR open time as an indication of when the work on an MR was started. Because new feature MRs are more likely to be opened after most of the work on the feature has been completed, e.g., low level design and prototyping, and repair MRs are more likely to be opened before the work has even started, this may have biased the estimates in [1] to make repair MRs appear more difficult than new feature MRs.

5.2. Fitting software project model

We can now use the calculated MR effort to model the project. We chose to discretize project time into work weeks because the effort estimation used weeks and because it simplified calculations. The total project effort spent during the week t_i was divided into three types: new effort N_{t_i} that was spent on MRs submitted that week that were classified as "new", repair effort B_{t_i} corresponding to repair MRs, and field effort F_{t_i} corresponding to field repair MRs.

Figure 3 illustrates the new and repair effort time series for the considered projects. The figure also shows a third curve that represents prediction of the repair effort as described in Section 5.3.

The maximum likelihood estimator for the completed projects in Table 3 gives 19 weeks delay for repair and 41 weeks of delay for field repairs. The ratio of total repair before field release to new feature effort in a project is 1.4 and for the total field problem repair effort to new feature effort is 1.7. Please note, that these are not efforts for individual MRs, but rather total efforts spent in the project on new functionality, repair, and repair of field problems.

Table 3. MLE estimates for the delay and repair to new feature effort ratio.

Type	Delay	Delay CI	Ratio	Ratio CI
Regular Repair	19	$[18, 21]$	1.36	$[1.2, 1.5]$
Field problem	41	$[33, 48]$	1.7	$[1.4, 2]$

Here we observe fairly small 95% confidence intervals

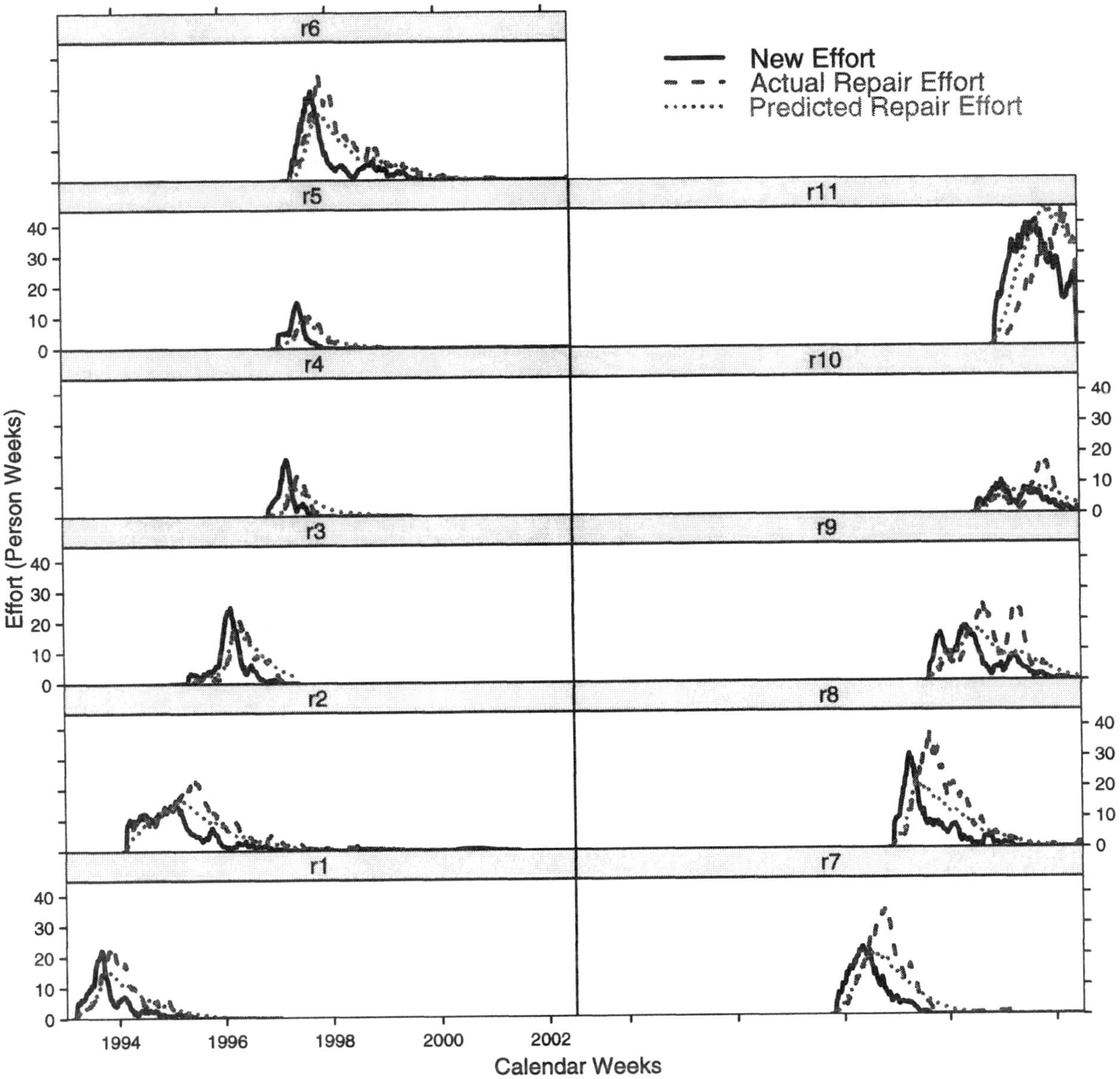

Figure 3. Effort trend broken by the type of change for several releases.

in terms of delay and in terms of the effort ratio. This gives us confidence that these estimates would accurately predict the repair effort and timing of the future projects.

Note, that total effort to implement new features represents only one quarter of the total effort in the considered software projects with repair of problems found in the field constituting almost half of the total effort. This is partially caused by the fact that the field repair MR is about twice as difficult ($e^{0.69}$) than a comparable non-field repair MR. The results for these projects confirm and make more precise the oft-heard statement that the later one finds a problem the more difficult it is to fix.

5.3. Prediction of repair effort in a project

Armed with the delay and ratio estimates from historic projects we can proceed to prediction of the repair effort. Our key assumption is that we approximately know the new feature implementation schedule and resources devoted to accomplish it. Such a plan is typically available at the end of the project planning stage before the development starts. Of course, the actual schedule might differ from the planned schedule because of a number factors, including the unplanned drain of resources to repair already released projects.

We applied our method halfway through the ongoing project in November 2001, for the project that was started in the beginning of the year and had a major release in May of the subsequent year. Consequently, we had information (new and repair MRs) of the already completed part of the project. In Figure 3 we illustrate the predicted repair effort using project model coefficients estimated in the previous section: repair delay of $1/\hat{\lambda} = 19$ weeks and repair to new ratio of $\hat{\mu} = 1.36$. According to the project model, the predicted intensity of repair effort at time t is simply an integral $\int_0^t N(s)\hat{\mu}\hat{\lambda}e^{-\hat{\lambda}s}ds$. Given our discretization of time into weeks the predicted repair effort for week t_k becomes the sum $\sum_{t_j<t_k} N_{t_j}\hat{\mu}(e^{-\hat{\lambda}t_j} - e^{-\hat{\lambda}(t_j+1)})$.

Such prediction does not take into account the fact that each project has a slightly different relationship between repairs and the new features. Consequently, if the prediction is done at the advanced stages of the project, as was the case in our study, valuable information about the project is not used. To address the problem we need to estimate project specific parameters μ and λ. However, because of reasons described in Section 4.2, it is impossible to estimate both parameters using MLE. We tried the options described in 4.2 and got similar results, but because of space considerations we report results from the simplest first option where we find a new estimate just for λ, keeping $\hat{\mu}$ estimated from previous projects. The estimate for $1/\lambda$ done in November 2001 was 48 weeks, much larger than for other projects. Figure 1 illustrates the performance of the repair schedule prediction for release r11. The first predictor uses $\hat{\mu}, \hat{\lambda}$ obtained from other projects and the second uses project specific estimate for the delay of 48 weeks.

Clearly, both predictors follow the shape of the repair activity, with the first predictor having an overly optimistic view about when the repairs will be completed and the second predictor possibly having an overly pessimistic view (the predicted repair curve continues well beyond July, 2002, the time of this writing). Only time will tell if the second predictor is in fact, overly pessimistic.

The overly optimistic performance of the first predictor that relies on the historic projects is not difficult to explain. The project under study was extremely ambitious, larger than any project undertaken before, involving new types of functionality. At the same time, the project schedule was highly optimistic for the amount of work that needs to be done, leading to various process experiments where work on numerous new features simultaneously was initiated and the job of system integration and testing was left for later stages, partly because there were not sufficient resources to do new development and sufficient testing at the same time. As is clear from the illustration, the strategy had a mixed success, with repair effort being delayed as compared to other releases.

6. Validation

Because the defects are discovered at the compilation, unit test, integration, system test, and field phases, it may make sense to consider time until repair to be a mixture distribution, each representing the phase at which the defect is discovered.

We chose to separate defects into field and non-field repair because it was possible to perform that separation and because we expected the time until discovery of field defect to be much longer than the time until discovery of other defects. The results in Section 5 indicate that, indeed, the field problems take twice as long to manifest themselves as regular defects.

At first glance it may seem that the assumption that only new feature changes generate repair changes is too restrictive. After all, fixes sometimes cause problems too. From the modeling perspective there are two ways to deal with this issue. The defects that cause other defects were caused by the new feature (it may even be the original code), so such a non-first generation repair could be attributed to the new feature change. This, of course, would increase the overall delay parameter and may require using a distribution for the delay that has a heavier tail than the Exponential distribution that we used here. We have tried using Weibull, Pareto, and Gamma distributions in the project model, but the results do not bring any surprises or significant lessons to be worth reporting. In the second approach, a complete likelihood may be written for the model where both new features and repair generate repair. We have done so, but it is computationally more complex and we have yet to apply it to real data.

We tried to incorporate all the uncertainties that we are aware of into our project model so the variability of the estimates would reflect the known uncertainties. More specifically, while estimating MR effort we considered several possible values for how long before MR submit time the work on MR may start. We considered 2, 4, 6, and 10 weeks and obtained effort estimates for each case. The results in Tables 2 involve bootstrap (a statistical term referring to calculating estimates based on multiple subsamples of the data) by sampling this parameter and by selecting 20 non-overlapping subsets of developers.

Table 3 incorporates the MR open time uncertainty by showing the mean and the confidence interval of the estimates taken over the four possible MR open times and over all 10 releases previous to R11.

Of course, from the project planning perspective the ultimate validity is the accuracy with which the repair effort and schedule could be predicted as illustrated in Figure 1.

7. Project Model Scenario

The utility of the presented model in other projects can be shown if the model is used in project planning or project understanding. In this section we outline the steps needed to apply the model in a software project. There are four basic stages: change data extraction, change data validation, and change and project modeling. In the data extraction stage access to the project systems is obtained and raw change data is extracted. In case of home-grown tools, it may be necessary to interview a person responsible for tool support to understand the structure and functionality of such systems.

The most important is data validation stage which starts from cleaning the raw change data to eliminate administrative, automatic, post-preprocessor, and other computer-generated changes. This leads to data described in Figure 2. The quality of attributes is then assessed and un- or auto-populated attributes and remaining system generated artifacts are eliminated. When engaging a new project it is important to interview a sample of developers and testers. The interview involves review of recent changes done by the interviewee to to illustrate the actual development process and to understand/validate the meaning various attribute values.

The change data is then augmented by modeling change effort [1] as described above, and, if needed, change purpose [11] or risk [12]. This stage also requires validation described in the references. It is worth pointing out, that at this point a number of important things have been learned about the software organization, including relative efforts for repair and new feature changes, effort per average change, change and effort trends over time and for different projects.

Once the relevant information on software changes is obtained, a project model is fitted for historic releases as described in Section 5.2. While we divided repair changes into post-release and pre-release repair, other classification might be desirable in other organizations. For example, classifying changes due to unit, feature, integration, and system test. For each type of repair and each project, the fitted values represent relative amount of repair effort and an average time until repair. Investigating these estimates for different projects it is important to note the variability and any patterns where the size or other characteristics of the release appear to affect the amount or delay of the repair effort.

Finally, the model may be used to predict repairs and answer other project planning questions for the upcoming project as described in Section 5.3.

8. Related Work

Our work closely relates mainly to two areas in software engineering: cost and schedule estimation and risk assessment. The software cost estimation may be roughly organized into expert and algorithmic techniques to estimate software cost and schedule.

The expert based techniques are typically best suited for projects that are not too different from projects completed in the past and where the estimator has extensive experience of estimation with these past projects (a good review of expert estimation techniques may be found in [9]). The main drawback is the subjective and non-transparent nature of the estimation process that makes it harder to justify the estimates. Often, it is also difficult to find estimators with the appropriate experience in the application and the environment in which it is developed. Our method is largely complementary to expert estimation, for example, expert estimates on the new feature effort and schedule can be fed into our model to predict the repair (and total) effort and schedule before the development has started. To help experts come up with more precise estimates they can inspect actual new feature and repair effort schedules for the past projects as shown in Figure 3.

Algorithmic techniques such as COCOMO [2, 3] may be used if the key predictors, such as size of the project, can be reliably estimated in advance and calibrated with past projects. The main drawback is that the size of the project (an input to the algorithm) may be more difficult to estimate than the cost (the output of the algorithm). While COCOMO is typically used to estimate the entire cost of the project, it may be possible to calibrate the regression used in COCOMO to estimate new feature and repair effort separately. As with expert-based techniques the estimates for new feature effort could be fed into our model and the historic MR effort data could be used to calibrate the COCOMO.

The risk assessment literature covers a number of issues, but the part most related to our work predicts the number of defects remaining in software during testing [14, 5, 6, 16]. There are two key differences with our work: we do not predict defects based on observed defect counts, but rather predict defect effort schedule based on observed new feature changes. The second difference is that testing models assume that the software does not change during testing, which is clearly not true as indicated by Figure 3. Rather, our model assumes that new features are continuously added to the software (albeit at a time varying rate) and generate defects and need for defect repair effort later on.

9. Discussion

We find it somewhat surprising that the relationship between new features and repair in a software project could be reasonably described using just two parameters: the proportion of repair effort and delay until repair. Encouragingly, these parameters vary little across projects in a single organization making them suitable for the planning of upcoming projects.

While our focus was fairly narrow: to predict repair effort and its distribution over time given the new feature effort, the project model can be applied in more general settings. For example, it could predict the number of defects based on the number and properties of new features as in [12], or predict the defects in a software module as in [8]. Furthermore a classical testing problem [5] of when to stop testing by predicting the number of defects remaining in the code base could be solved using the same model.

Since the model uses data that is available in virtually any large software project it is an appealing model for commercial software settings where all process overhead, including time-consuming data collection, are treated with skepticism.

In addition to providing a framework for answering a number of important project planning questions, the project model may help gain better insights into completed projects and may help a software organization better understand its strengths and shortcomings. One significant benefit that we expected and observed, was better understanding of a software projects constraints by people who are not directly involved in development, yet have to take important planning and resource allocation decisions.

As an example, the model applied to the projects we studied confirmed and quantified the customary wisdom that the later a defect is found the harder it is to correct (and the longer it takes to correct it). Such quantification makes it easier to justify expending resources earlier in the project to detect and correct defects before they reach the field. We leave it to future research to quantify the efficiency of various detection techniques, such as code inspections, so that one could estimate just how much effort should be expended on such a technique to make it worthwhile.

Finally, much of our ability to model projects was a result of making relatively few and minimal assumptions about how the work in a software development project proceeds based on our observations of the development process. Our observations and subsequent analysis focused on what changes were made and how they were made, i.e., how people worked to change the code, rather than focusing on properties of the code. Although we believe that analyzing code properties has its place, we also believe that analyzing changes is a rich source of insight that is usually not given proper attention.

Acknowledgments

We would like to thank all the people in Avaya, Lucent, and AT&T who provided information directly (via interviews) or indirectly (by working on the products under study.) In particular we thank S. Brown, M. Flores, D. Frost, R. Hackbarth, N. Harrison, M. Hazerodt, J. Maranzano, O. Mascarenhas, E. Moritz, S. Muchow, J. Palframan, J. Payseur, D. Sokoler, D. Turgeon and others for providing insight on development process, development tasks, project management and other aspects of the studied software projects.

References

[1] D. Atkins, T. Ball, T. Graves, and A. Mockus. Using version control data to evaluate the impact of software tools: A case study of the version editor. *IEEE Transactions on Software Engineering*, 28(7):625–637, July 2002.

[2] B. Boehm. *Software Engineering Economics*. Prentice-Hall, 1981.

[3] B. W. Boehm, B. Clark, E. Horowitz, and et al. Cost models for future software life cycle processes: Cocomo 2.0. *Annals of Software Engineering*, 1(1):1–24, November 1995.

[4] P. Cedeqvist and et al. *CVS Manual*. May be fond on: `http://www.cvshome.org/CVS/`.

[5] S. R. Dalal and C. L. Mallows. When should one stop testing software? *Journal of American Statist. Assoc*, 83:872–879, 1988.

[6] A. L. Goel. Software reliability models: Assumptions, limitations and applicability. *IEEE Trans. Software Engineering*, SE-11(12), 1985.

[7] T. Graves and A. Mockus. Identifying productivity drivers by modeling work units using partial data. *Technometrics*, 43(2):168–179, May 2001.

[8] T. L. Graves, A. F. Karr, J. S. Marron, and H. Siy. Predicting fault incidence using software change history. *IEEE Transactions on Software Engineering*, 26(2), 2000.

[9] M. Jørgensen. A review of studies on expert estimation of software development effort. *Journal of Systems and Software*, 2002. submitted.

[10] A. K. Midha. Software configuration management for the 21st century. *Bell Labs Technical Journal*, 2(1), Winter 1997.

[11] A. Mockus and L. G. Votta. Identifying reasons for software change using historic databases. In *International Conference on Software Maintenance*, pages 120–130, San Jose, California, October 11-14 2000.

[12] A. Mockus and D. M. Weiss. Predicting risk of software changes. *Bell Labs Technical Journal*, 5(2):169–180, April–June 2000.

[13] A. Mockus and D. M. Weiss. Globalization by chunking: a quantitative approach. *IEEE Software*, 18(2):30–37, March 2001.

[14] J. Musa, A. Iannino, and K. Okumoto. *Software Reliability: Measurement, Prediction, Application*. McGrawHill, New York, 1987.

[15] M. Rochkind. The source code control system. *IEEE Trans. on Software Engineering*, 1(4):364–370, 1975.

[16] N. D. Singpurwalla and S. P. Wilson. *Statistical Methods in software Engineering: Reliability and Risk*. Springer Series in Statistics. Springer-Verlag, New York, 1999.

Cost Estimation for Web Applications

Melanie Ruhe [1]
Siemens AG, Corporate Technology, Software Engineering 3
80730 Munich, Germany
melanie.ruhe@siemens.com

Ross Jeffery
University of New South Wales School of Computer Science and Engineering and CAESER
Sydney, 2052, Australia
rossj@cse.unsw.edu.au

Isabella Wieczorek [1]
Federal Ministry of Education and Research
53170 Bonn, Germany
Isabella.Wieczorek@web.de

Abstract

In this paper, we investigate the application of the COBRA™ method (Cost Estimation, Benchmarking, and Risk Assessment) in a new application domain, the area of web development. COBRA combines expert knowledge with data on a small number of projects to develop cost estimation models, which can also be used for risk analysis and benchmarking purposes. We modified and applied the method to the web applications of a small Australian company, specializing in web development. In this paper we present the modifications made to the COBRA method and results of applying the method. In our study, using data on twelve web applications, the estimates derived from our Web-COBRA model showed a Mean Magnitude of Relative Error (MMRE) of 0.17. This result significantly outperformed expert estimates from Allette Systems (MMRE 0.37). A result comparable to Web-COBRA was obtained when applying ordinary least squares regression with size in terms of Web Objects as an independent variable (MMRE 0.23).

1. Introduction

With the growing importance of web applications in general business matters, many practitioners see the measurement of web applications as a particularly valuable area of ongoing commercially relevant research. The success of web applications used to be determined by being first-to-market. Nowadays, the quality of software has become an important driver for competitiveness. Quality software applications require appropriate software development and project management processes. For project managers, cost estimation is one of the crucial steps at the beginning of any new software project. Accurate cost estimates are an essential element for being able to provide competitive bids and remaining successful in the market. Over- and underestimates of the expected costs have a significant influence on a company's reputation and competitiveness. Industry still reports difficulties with determining accurate cost estimates, even though the research on software cost estimation methods started already in the early 1960's.

Within the last decades a wealth of research focused on developing accurate cost estimation models. However, surveys indicate that only very few organizations actually use them [20] There are a number of practically relevant reasons for not using cost estimation models: Many cost estimation models are not very accurate [6]. Experience shows that model-based estimates do not perform considerably better than estimates solely based on expert judgement.

Another reason for the rare use of cost estimation models in practice is the lack of sufficient, explicit past project data to systematically build a cost estimation model. Many organizations do not have enough resources for the required measurement methods and tools. Data collection is a time-consuming process that needs to be carefully planned, because consistency and completeness are two key drivers for the usefulness of the data for effort estimation. Only data on recent projects allows for cost estimation research that is meaningful for current projects.

Another reason for the modest use of cost estimation models is the appropriate assessment of the size of a software product. The size of a software product is accepted as a key cost driver for development effort, but it requires precise measurement methods and adequate measures, which are often missing in industry.

Finally, many cost estimation models are based on standard and/or black box methods to derive a cost estimate. The lack of transparency in many cost estimation methods does not allow sufficient calibration to an organization's specific needs.

The COBRA™ (Cost Estimation Benchmarking and Risk Analysis[2]) method provides a means for developing a transparent cost estimation model when using project data internal to an organization. COBRA is a composite estimation method that utilizes expert knowledge and a limited amount of past project data to predict a project's development effort, as well as to assess the quantitative risks associated with the project. The first application of the method in the MIS context showed a very promising result achieving a Mean Magnitude of Relative Error (MMRE) of 0.09 [1].

The overall purpose of this study is to assess whether the COBRA method is appropriate for accurately estimating development effort of web applications in the context of a small company.

We investigated the appropriateness of the COBRA method in terms of two aspects: (1) To our knowledge, the COBRA method has not yet been applied to small-sized software development companies. However, it is extremely important to derive accurate cost estimates for these types of companies. Furthermore, small organizations are different from large organizations. Thus, refinements of the COBRA method to address specific needs of small companies might be required. (2) We applied the COBRA method in a new application domain, the area of web development. We know practical details about the biggest web development companies such as Microsoft and Netscape, but small niche companies develop the vast majority of

[1] This study was performed while Melanie Ruhe was a student at the University of Kaiserslautern and Isabella Wieczorek with the Fraunhofer Institute for Experimental Software Engineering (IESE).

[2] COBRA is a registered trademark of the Fraunhofer Institute for Experimental Software Engineering (IESE), Germany.

0-7695-1877-X/03 $17.00 © 2003 IEEE

Internet software [5]. Many start-up companies developing web applications suffer from underestimating the cost of a new project. Ad-hoc approaches that could be applied in the beginning of web development do not work for larger web applications.

In this study we investigated whether we could repeat the encouraging results from the first publication of the method [1]. Firstly, we adapted and applied COBRA to data collected from twelve web applications that were recently developed at a small Australian company, called Allette Systems. We then compared the derived model to the results initially published in the study by Briand et al. [1]. Furthermore, we investigated our results in comparison to the results obtained from applying ordinary least squares (OLS) regression as well as expert-based estimates to the projects developed at Allette. Consistent to the work of Briand et al., the developed model is validated using n-fold cross-validation [8].

The paper starts with a discussion of related work in Section 2, then presents our research method in Section 3, including the description of the data set, the modeling techniques and the validation criteria. The results of the case study are presented and discussed in Section 4. Section 5 finishes the paper with a summary of the results and stresses some further important conclusions from our results.

2. Related Work

We reviewed the literature with regards to three different aspects: (1) What has been achieved by empirical research studies on cost estimation within the last fifteen years? (2) What distinguishes COBRA from traditional cost estimation methods? (3) What research has been performed in the area of cost estimation for web development projects?

2.1. Empirical Research

The results of the most relevant empirical studies in the field of software cost estimation are described in the Encyclopedia of Software Engineering [6]. Existing cost estimation methods could be categorized according to Figure 1. Their strengths and weaknesses are summarized in [6].

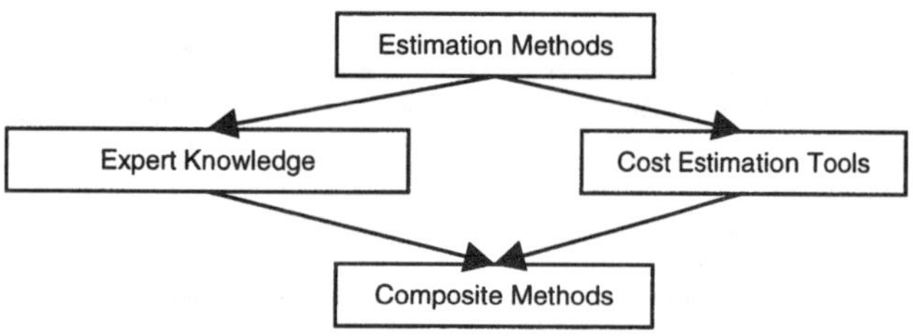

Figure 1. Effort Estimation Method Classification

Non-model based estimation methods (expert knowledge) consist of one or more estimation techniques together with a specification of how to apply them in a certain context. These methods are not involving any model building but just direct estimation. They require heavy involvement of experts to generate an estimate for every new project.

Model-based estimation methods (cost estimation tools) involve at least one modeling method, one model, and one model application method. An effort estimation model usually takes a number of inputs (e.g. a size estimate, cost factors) and produces an effort point estimate or distribution. In contrast to non-model-based estimation methods, model-based methods are not dependent on individual's capabilities but require past project data for the model building. Examples are OLS regression, the Constructive Cost Model (COCOMO), and Classification and Regression Trees (CART).

The so-called composite methods combine both of the above approaches by incorporating expert knowledge in the model building process. Composite methods usually do not require as much data as common model-based methods. Examples are Analogy [11] and COBRA [1].

The prediction accuracy of many empirical studies performed within the last fifteen years was reviewed [6, 22]. A high-level summary of the results is presented in Table 1, but only the six mostly applied estimation methods are considered. The averaged MRE values have to be interpreted with care however, because some results are obtained by tailoring the method to a specific context whereas in other studies no tailoring was performed. The numbers are used to give an overview of the results of empirical research in the area of software cost estimation.

Table 1. Descriptive Statistics of Estimation Methods Accuracy

	Number of Studies	Minimum MMRE	Maximum MMRE	Average MMRE	Std. Dev.
EXPERT	4	0.31	1.68	0.68	0.67
COCOMO	10	0.19	7.58	3.08	3.12
OLS	18	0.10	1.27	0.69	0.33
CART	5	0.47	3.64	1.19	1.37
ANOVA	3	0.42	0.57	0.48	0.08
ANALOGY	9	0.28	1.45	0.61	0.38

In general, we can conclude that stepwise analysis of variance (ANOVA) performed best considering the average MMRE. OLS regression performed considerably well compared to many other methods. Studies evaluating CART consider this type of models as a good alternative, because of their simplicity, but they seem to provide mixed results.

Analogy performed best, in 60% of the cases reported in published studies. In 30% of the cases it showed the worst predictive accuracy, hence suggesting some instability. Analogy obtained best results when using adaptation rules and heuristics to identify significant variables to measure similarity. A fully automated version of Analogy is more likely to yield good results when used on small data sets with a small number of variables. In this case, a comprehensive search for optimal similarity functions can be performed [23].

Expert judgement (EXPERT) may achieve highly accurate estimates, when being supported by a tool or combined with other cost estimation methods (e.g., analogy, regression). Using solely non-model based methods may lead to very inaccurate predictions. People also tend to underestimate the time required to do a task when they themselves are to do the work [28]. This is confirmed on small tasks by other researchers, while for larger tasks an overestimation has been observed. However, it has also been reported that bottom-up estimation helped predict projects within 6% of their scheduled dates and costs [29].

Boehm validated his COCOMO model in the 1970's on his TRW data set using the prediction level as an evaluation measure. He obtained very good results for intermediate and detailed

COCOMO, and quite poor ones for the basic COCOMO. Independent evaluations performed on other data sets have not always produced such good results. In general, the accuracy in terms of MMRE ranges form very high (i.e., 0.19) to very poor (i.e., 7.58). It was found that intermediate and detailed COCOMO do not necessarily improve the estimates and that the model systematically over-estimates effort [24]. Other studies found a bias towards underestimating effort when using COCOMO. Intermediate and detailed COCOMO may suffer from over-fitting problems. No publicly available results exist so far about the performance of COCOMO II compared to other estimation methods. Affiliate organizations are currently using COCOMO II. The COCOMO versions generated in '97 and '98 were compared with each other. It turned out that the calibration of COCOMO II by incorporating expert knowledge using Bayesian Statistics reached promising results outperforming the COCOMO II version 97 [21].

Despite the fact, that some methods obtained better results than others, very rarely studies obtained good results according to Conte's evaluation criteria [2]. Composite estimation methods, especially Analogy, grew of interest in the last couple of years because of perceived higher prediction accuracy and acceptance in industry [11]. The initially published application of COBRA was very successful in the context of a large German software development company. As reported, COBRA performed much better than commonly reported results [1]. The MMRE obtained through a cross validation was 0.09, which is very encouraging, though just an initial result. The method was, neither replicated so far, nor was it compared to standard methods, such as OLS regression or any other method.

2.2. The COBRA method

The COBRA method represents a framework of activities for developing a tailored COBRA model. Each COBRA model consists of two main components. The first component is the causal model that produces a cost overhead estimate. The causal model consists of factors affecting the cost of projects within a local environment (cost-drivers). They are characteristics of the project that are expected to significantly influence effort. The causal model is obtained through expert knowledge acquisition.

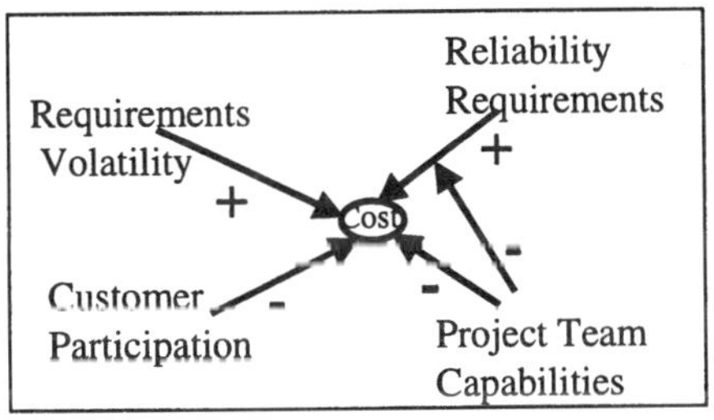

Figure 2. Causal Model Example

An example is shown in Figure 2. The arrows indicate direct relationships. A "+" and a "-" indicate positive and negative relationships, respectively. Where one arrow points to another this indicates an interaction.

This qualitative information is quantified using expert opinion. The quantification is the percentage of cost overhead above that of a nominal project. Experts have to compare in mind a nominal / optimal (i.e. a project running under optimal conditions) with a worst case project and estimate the additional cost in per cent, the cost overhead. Its uncertainty is captured for all relationships in the causal model using variables that underlie triangular distributions.

The second component of COBRA uses data from past projects that are similar according to specified project characteristics. The past project data is used to determine the relationship between cost overhead and cost. Note that this is a simple bivariate relationship that does not require a large amount of data, which explains why COBRA does not have demanding data requirements as opposed to data-driven methods.

Running Monte Carlo Simulation, the determined relationship between cost overhead and cost together with the causal model are utilized to build the COBRA model and to derive a probability distribution of effort for new projects. The probability distribution of effort can be used for various project management activities, such as cost estimation, risk assessment, and benchmarking [1].

In order to evaluate the probability that a project will be over budget, one can generate the descending cumulative cost overhead distribution for the actual project (Figure 3).

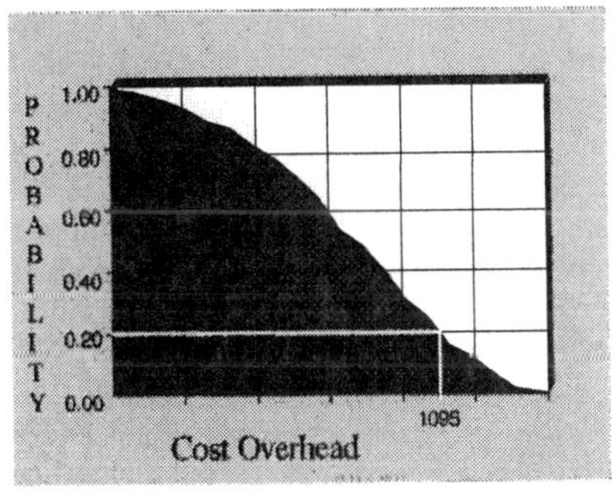

Figure 3. Cumulative Distribution Example

Let us assume that the available budget for a project is 1100 Units and that this project's cost overhead is characterized by the distribution in Figure 3. There is roughly a 80% probability that the project will stay within budget (i.e. a 20% probability to overrun 1095 units). If this probability represents an acceptable risk in a particular context, the project budget may be approved.

The advantages of COBRA over many other cost estimation methods is its applicability in environments with only little project data available. Moreover, COBRA is not restricted to a specific size measure. COBRA is more likely to be accepted in practice as the models provided are rooted to the experts' own experience that is accessible, reusable and transparent to other people. The method provides a mechanism for developing a tailored cost estimation model, thus increasing prediction accuracy. A detailed description of the COBRA method is given in [1, 26].

2.3. Web Estimation

While reviewing the literature for relevant methods in the area of web estimation, we distinguished between web hypermedia systems and web applications [10]. Web applications are technically distinct from web hypermedia systems since the user has the ability to affect the state of the system on the web server, where the business logic is implemented [12]. Hypermedia systems are much easier to predict than web applications, because web hypermedia systems are usually much smaller in terms of the expended development effort. Consequently, web applications are much more complex to develop and manage than web hypermedia systems. Thus, the focus of interest for this study is the estimation of web applications.

The literature and practical experience on web development has reported differences between traditional software applications and web applications. Web applications usually change more often in terms of their requirements, contents, and functionality than traditional software systems. In order to successfully develop and maintain quality web applications, a disciplined approach needs to be followed and better development tools need to be established. Standard software engineering approaches seem limited and cannot appropriately address all the challenges related to web development. Therefore, recent publications stress the need for web engineering and web estimation [3, 9, 15]. Web engineering is similar to software engineering, but identifies more tailored methods and techniques for web development. This is due to the fast evolution of technologies in this area combined with the little documented experience.

To our knowledge, there is only one example in the literature that investigated effort prediction models for web applications: Reifer introduced a cost estimation model called Web model (WebMo) [3, 4]. It adapts the COCOMO II model [21] to the context of web development mainly revising the COCOMO II cost factors. WebMo is based on past project data from 64 web applications, nine cost factors, and the software size measured in Web Objects. Regression analysis was applied to determine the cost estimates. The model has been calibrated and predicted "within 20% of the actual experience at least 68% of the time". However, the results of the remaining 32% estimates are not reported at all.

More research has been done on estimating effort for web hypermedia systems [9, 10], but as mentioned before, this type of web system is very different from typical web applications in terms of cost estimation issues.

3. Research Method

This research is designed as a case study. The estimation of web applications is a very new research area with only a few experiences. Thus, we firstly need to gain comprehensive knowledge about the development techniques in small web development start-ups. Case studies are seen as an ideal method for achieving inside information about a new area of interest.

3.1. Data Set

Allette Systems is a small Australian software development company, with about twenty employees. The company's main business is to develop web-based systems. Due to the projects' diversity, we categorized them in order to find a suitable, homogenous subset of projects for the COBRA application.

Project managers of Allette Systems were asked to characterize their software applications in terms of functionality, and a given categorization schema. Based on the analysis of the survey responses, we used the projects categorized as web applications for our study. The project managers of this type of projects were briefly interviewed to ensure that the identified projects were similar according to predefined subjective and objective characteristics, such as functionality, target platform, or complexity. Finally, twelve typical web applications were assessed as appropriate projects according to the requirements of the COBRA method.

The considered web applications were developed between 1998 and 2002. The web applications were very typical: financial/trading, business-to-business, and intranet applications. Nine, one, and two projects were new developments, enhancements, and re-development projects, respectively.

Table 2 presents the descriptive statistics of the general project information of the twelve Web-COBRA projects.

Table 2. Descriptive Statistics

Measure	Min	Max	Mean	Std. Dev.
Effort - Development effort in person hours (ph)	267	2504	883	710
Size - System size in Web Objects	67	792	284	227
Peak Staff - Maximum size of the project team at any time	2	6	3	1.5

The development effort spent on web applications at Allette Systems seems to be significantly higher than published effort results on web hypermedia systems (between 58 and 154 ph) [10]. Furthermore, the data collected at Allette Systems shows much higher data dispersion (710 ph) compared to the data on web hypermedia systems (26 ph). The comparison of development effort required confirms the difference in complexity between web applications and web hypermedia systems.

We measured system size using Web Objects introduced by Reifer. [3]. Web Objects are an extension of the traditional Function Points [16], addressing the needs of web development. So far, to our knowledge, no other alternative size measure for web applications has been published or initially validated.

The peak staff numbers at Allette Systems are in line with the published numbers for team size in the area of web development, which are usually small [4].

3.2. Adaptation of COBRA

The COBRA method has been modified due to the needs of a typical web development company. In the following, we outline the steps to develop our Web-COBRA model and point out the differences to the original COBRA™ method [1].

3.2.1. Refinements of the COBRA Method

Firstly, COBRA requires the identification of most important cost factors in a certain environment. In contrast to the first application of COBRA, web development as a new area of research has only few reported experiences. Hence, the literature does not provide experience on potential cost factors for this application domain. Instead of using the list of traditional cost factors and adjusting the definitions based on the expert's comments, we decided to perform personal interviews with the experts of Allette Systems using open questions [19]. We identified five experts for the interviews and provided each of them with high-level definitions of groups of cost factors related to the software product, the personnel, the software project, and the process. During the interviews the expert explained his/her specific experience with cost factors corresponding to each of the groups. This process ensured that only cost factors relevant to the area of web development were explored.

Secondly, a qualitative causal model needed to be developed. In contrast to the previous work, only direct relationships of cost factors with cost were modeled. Beside the increased complexity of the model, another drawback of modeling interactions is the necessity to ensure a common understanding among the experts of each interaction, which is not always the case. The literature does not provide adequate interview techniques for these purposes. Moreover, so far it has not been validated, whether the required additional effort to model interactions pays off and drastically improves prediction accuracy. In our study, we avoided interactions by deriving a minimal set of independent cost factors. From the authors point of view, this decision also contributes to a higher transparency of the cost estimation model. Therefore, dependent cost factors were either excluded from the causal model or their definition was adapted to ensure the orthogonality with other cost factors.

Finally, we refined the quantification of the relationships within the causal model. The previous study used a questionnaire to collect the cost overhead multipliers. In this study we performed personal interviews with Allette Systems experts to obtain the multipliers. In the previous study, an outlier analysis was performed to detect and exclude outlying multipliers. In our study, the group of experts discussed their understanding of the cost factors and the multipliers together to improve and validate the quantitative causal model. This additional step in the COBRA development process ensured that the initial multipliers were revised in terms of outliers. Therefore, no outlier analysis was performed.

In order to aggregate the multiple answers for cost overhead estimates, in the previous study alternative ways of aggregation were proposed selecting always the answer of a single expert (e.g., in each simulation run, the expert answers for each cost factor were randomly selected). In our study, we used a measure of central tendency. There are two common ways of determining the central tendency for the distribution of the data: The mean, defined as the average value, and the median, defined as the middle-most value in a set of data [19]. The median is generally more robust towards outliers. We decided to use the mean as a representative value, because outliers in the cost overhead data were excluded in the group discussion. Furthermore, weights can be used in order to take into account the different degrees of experience of the experts. No weights were used, because the experts from Allette Systems had a very similar experience. Consequently, in each simulation step each expert opinion was equally taken into account.

3.2.2. Sizing of Web Applications

An early effort estimate can only be derived from COBRA if size can be measured early on in the software development process. Therefore the literature was reviewed for a problem-oriented size measure for web-based software applications. Web Objects were chosen as the most appropriate size measure in the context of Allette Systems. In contrast to other proposed size measures for web applications, Web Objects are measurable just using the systems requirements [3]. The counting of COSMIC Full Function Points, for instance, requires at least the systems architecture [17]. Furthermore, COSMIC Full Function points are not specifically designed for web applications, whereas Web Objects are specifically tailored for web applications. Describing the full details of the work performed pertaining the sizing of web applications is beyond the scope of this paper. The interested reader is referred to a forthcoming paper on that topic.

3.3. Validation Method

3.3.1. Compared Techniques

The following three techniques are used to validate the cost estimation model.

Web-COBRA

We applied the COBRA method as described in the previous section. The system size within Web-COBRA was modelled as an uncertain variable, which underlies a triangular distribution. This decision was made to also reveal the uncertainty in the size estimation. The Web Object counting is a subjective way of measuring size, for which not much experience exists so far. In the Web-COBRA model, an uncertainty of 5% was used.

Ordinary Least Squares Regression

OLS regression is the most common modelling technique applied to software cost estimation [6]. Regression modelling is one of the most widely used statistical modelling technique for fitting a response (dependent) variable as a function of predictor (independent) variable(s). We used development effort as a dependent variable and size measured in Web Objects as an independent variable. As the data was normally distributed we used a linear model specification [8].

Allette Systems Informal Method

Allette Systems previously applied an informal method to predict development effort for web applications. The method involves the structural decomposition of a system into basic components, which are familiar in terms of estimating effort. The project managers of Allette Systems then compare the basic components with similar work that has been done and estimate the component using personal memory. The final estimate is derived by aggregating the components.

The effort estimate of Allette Systems is documented in their timesheet system. It does not necessarily represent the initial estimate, because additional tasks might be added later on in the project and effort is adjusted accordingly. The system does not mark additional tasks. Thus, the "real" initial estimates are not known for all projects.

3.3.2. Cross Validation

If one constructs a cost estimation model using a particular data set, and then computes the accuracy of the model using the same data set, the accuracy evaluation will be optimistic [11]. To avoid this, we applied a procedure known as cross-validation approach. Cross validation is a common way of validating a cost estimation model. The basic idea is to use different subsets for model building (training sets) and model evaluation (test sets).

In our case there are twelve projects in the database and each cross validation step uses eleven projects as a training set to build a new model and apply it to the remaining project (test set). Thus, a separate model is built for each of the twelve training-test-set combinations.

3.3.3. Evaluation Criteria

The estimates are compared with the actual effort by calculating the magnitude of relative error (MRE). This is a commonly used measure for the evaluation of estimation models

[2]. The magnitude of relative error as a percentage of the actual effort for a project, is defined as:

$$\text{MRE} = \left| \frac{Effort_{ACTUAL} - Effort_{ESTIMATED}}{Effort_{ACTUAL}} \right|$$

The MRE is calculated for each project in the data sets. Either the mean MRE (MMRE) or median MRE aggregates the multiple observations.

In addition, we used the prediction level Pred. This measure is often used in the literature and is a proportion of observations for a given level of accuracy:

$$\text{Pred}\,(l) = \frac{k}{N}$$

Where, N is the total number of observations, and k the number of observations with an MRE less than or equal to l. A common value for l is 0.25, which is used for this study as well. The Pred(0.25) gives the percentage of projects that were predicted with an MRE equal or less than 0.25.

Conte et al. [2] suggest an acceptable threshold value for the mean MRE to be less than 0.25 and for Pred (0.25) greater or equal than 0.75. In general, the accuracy of an estimation technique is proportional to the Pred (0.25) and inversely proportional to the MRE and the mean MRE.

We also used box-plots of residuals to graphically illustrate under- or overestimation for each estimation method.

The estimates obtained from the different methods were compared and it was tested whether the prediction accuracy of one method was significantly different from another method using a t-test [8].

4. Results and Discussion

The expert interviews revealed thirty-five potential cost factors in the area of web development, some of them are very similar to traditional cost factors, other cost factors are new. The ranking of the factors supplied the most important cost factors in the context of Allette Systems. A finally approved list of nine most important cost factors was approved at Allette Systems.

Table 3 lists the cost factors in the left column. A very high range was obtained between the minimum and the maximum cost overhead for the factors "Requirements Volatility" and "Importance of Project Management". This indicated the highest uncertainty for these two factors.

The results of the interviews for the quantification of the causal model were analyzed regarding the given cost overhead estimates (in per cent). Table 3 presents the standard deviations of the cost overhead estimates given by the five experts of Allette Systems.

Table 3. Std. Deviation after Personal Interviews

Cost Factor	Minimum	Most Likely	Maximum
Novelty of Requirements	0.10	0.15	0.11
Importance of SW Maintenance	0.19	0.24	0.53
Novelty of Technology	0.11	0.36	1.35
Developer's Technical Capabilities	0.18	0.27	0.68
Team Communication Skills	0.10	0.16	0.27
Quality of Project Management	0.14	0.29	0.61
Requirements Volatility	0.15	0.24	0.59
Quality of Specification Methods	0.14	0.19	0.30
Customer Participation	0.12	0.14	0.35

Table 3 indicates high variance in the estimates for some of the cost factors: "Importance of Software Maintenance", "Novelty of Technology", "Developer's Technical Capabilities", "Quality of Project Management", and "Requirements Volatility". Especially the maximum cost overhead shows a wide response range between the five experts.

While exploring reasons for this behavior, two options appeared: there is high variance in the expert's experience or there is a high variance in the understanding and interpretation of the cost factor definitions. In order to further investigate the situation, a group discussion with all five experts was performed. The goal of the meeting was to achieve a common understanding of the cost factors and estimate the cost overhead of each cost factor based on this. The discussion was guided in a way that avoided convergence. Each expert had to explain his/her understanding of the cost factor and estimate cost overhead.

From the experience of this group discussion we can give evidence that even though we carefully defined and tailored the cost factors to Allette Systems needs, experts still interpreted the definitions very differently in the personal interviews. Consequently, the cost overhead estimates showed a high variance. In the group discussion we came to an agreed understanding of the meaning of each cost factor and adjusted the definitions accordingly (see Table 4). After the group discussion we collected and analyzed the data again.

Table 4. Std. Deviation after the Group Discussion

Cost Factor	Minimum	Most Likely	Maximum
Novelty of Requirements	0.00	0.04	0.11
Importance of SW Maintenance	0.00	0.00	0.00
Novelty of Technology	0.05	0.12	0.31
Developer's Technical Capabilities	0.00	0.00	0.11
Team Communication Skills	0.03	0.04	0.18
Quality of Project Management	0.00	0.05	0.22
Requirements Volatility	0.04	0.22	0.00
Quality of Specification Methods	0.05	0.11	0.22
Customer Input and Motivation	0.08	0.04	0.11

Comparing the results in Table 3 with Table 4, we observe a reduction in the response variance for all the cost factors. For some cost factors there is almost no variance at all, which means the experts had the same opinion and/or experience about the cost factors influence on effort. The "Novelty of Technology" is the only cost factor with a standard deviation larger than 0.22. This may be due to different experiences regarding a novel web development technology. The "Importance of Software Maintenance" was a cost factor that showed a variance after the personal interviews but no variance at all after the group discussion. This is one example, where a high variance in the understanding of the cost factor definition was perceived in the group discussion. Therefore, we conclude that both the relevance and the tailoring of the cost factor definitions have a high influence on validity of a cost estimation model and thus the prediction accuracy.

Box plots were used to graphically illustrate the residuals between effort estimate and actual effort spent. If a residual for a certain project is negative the effort was underestimated and vice versa. Figure 4 depicts the box plots of the residuals of the three estimation methods. The estimates done by Allette Systems generally tend to underestimate development effort. OLS regression and the Web-COBRA model do not show general trends like this.

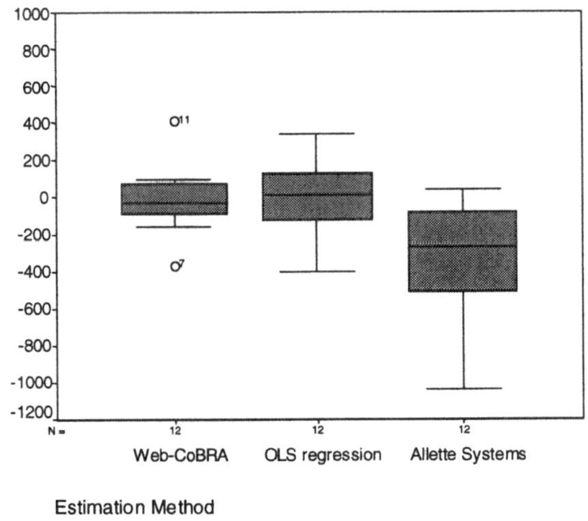

Figure 4. Box plots of the residuals

The length of the box is the interquartile range, containing 50% of all the observations. This range represents the variability of the residual values. It is the smallest for Web-COBRA. Furthermore, the upper and lower tails represent the non-outlier range. This range is very close to the box for Web-COBRA, indicating a very flat distribution. The residuals are within a range of about 100 person hours, only. Exceptions are Project 7 and Project 11, visible as the two outliers in the Web-COBRA box-plot. Usually, outlier values are outside the 1.5 box length. These two projects are very large projects in terms of development effort.

We excluded the two outliers in the cross validation when building the estimation model. The exclusion of a large project has strong effects on the regression coefficient. Thus, the estimates for large projects may be not as accurate as others. The residual represents the absolute prediction error. However, the MRE as a relative indication of the prediction accuracy is within the suggested MRE threshold of 0.25 for these two projects.

The upper and lower tail of OLS regression and Allette Systems are longer, indicating a more peaked distribution of the residuals. The box is almost twice as high for OLS regression and three times as high for Allette Systems than it is for Web-COBRA. In contrast to Web-COBRA, OLS regression more accurately (lower MRE) predicts the two large projects 7 and 11. However, for two other large projects the opposite is perceived. Thus, it seems there is no difference in prediction accuracy for larger projects between the Web-COBRA model and bivariate OLS regression

When looking at the prediction results in terms of MRE values, we observed that the enhancement project within the twelve projects was the project with the highest MRE values when applying Web-COBRA and/or OLS regression. Enhancement projects are generally more difficult to predict than other projects [18]. However, the experts at Allette Systems performed more accurately when estimating this one enhancement project.

Table 5 presents a summary of the MRE results. The different estimation methods are compared in terms of the Min, Max, Mean, and Median MRE. The Pred (0.25) indicates the prediction level.

Table 5. Results summary

Estimation Method	Min MRE	Max MRE	Mean MRE	Median MRE	Pred (0.25)
Informal estimation method (Allette)	0.12	0.68	0.37	0.36	0.25
OLS regression	0.00	0.60	0.24	0.23	0.67
Web-COBRA model	0.02	0.35	0.17	0.15	0.75

Web-COBRA performs best with a mean MRE of only 0.17 and a high Pred (0.25) value of 75% and is within the thresholds suggested by Conte et al. [2]. OLS regression conforms to only the threshold of the mean MRE (smaller than 0.25). Allette Systems prediction accuracy is low when compared to the results of OLS regression and Web-COBRA. The prediction level is low, indicated by a low value of Pred (0.25). The mean MRE is 0.37. OLS regression shows higher prediction accuracy in terms of a higher value of Pred (0.25) and a lower mean MRE value. Web-COBRA performs best with a mean MRE of only 0.17 and a high Pred (0.25) value of 75%. The estimates derived from OLS regression or Allette Systems informal method show a wider range (min MRE, max MRE) than the estimates derived from the Web-COBRA model. Hence, the median MRE is higher for the first two methods than for Web-COBRA.

Table 6 shows the results from testing whether the differences in the MRE values among the different methods are significant using the matched paired t-test.

Table 6. t-test results

Compared Methods	Mean MRE_1		Mean MRE_2	p-value
(1) Allette Systems - (2) OLS regression	0.37	vs	0.24	0.164
(1) OLS regression - (2) Web-COBRA	0.24	vs	0.17	0.242
(1) Web-COBRA - (2) Allette Systems	0.17	vs	0.37	0.005

The significance test shows that the estimates derived from the Web-COBRA model are significantly better than the Allette Systems estimates on a confidence interval of 0.99. OLS regression did not derive significantly better results than Allette Systems. Also, no significant difference in prediction accuracy could be observed between OLS regression and Web-COBRA.

Besides this objective validation of the COBRA method, we also applied a subjective method, called the technology acceptance method (TAM) [27]. This method was used to determine the appropriateness of COBRA from a practical point of view. The results from analyzing the questionnaires showed a high perceived usefulness (81%). The ease of use was evaluated 86% on average. The self-predicted usage was predicted by 91%. These results show a high appropriateness of COBRA in the context of Allette Systems.

The initial application of the COBRA method achieved a prediction accuracy of 0.09 (MMRE). The developed COBRA model included only six past projects. Furthermore, the developed causal model of cost factors involved the modeling of interactions between cost factors, which may have a positive influence on the prediction accuracy.

From a practical perspective, a strong weakness of the initial application of COBRA was its use of lines of code as size measure. This solution-oriented size measure is not available early on in the software development cycle, when the cost estimate is required. It is often more important to have an early, relatively accurate effort estimate, rather than a very accurate effort estimate later in the development process.

The WebMo is to the authors' knowledge the only published model to estimate cost for web application [3, 4]. It uses past project data on nine cost factors and system size measured in Web Objects. Reifer reports prediction accuracy in terms of relative error of less than 0.20 for 68% of 64 projects. We do not know whether this number is an aggregated number (mean/median MRE) or whether cross validation was applied, because no further details are yet published about the WebMo evaluation. Assuming that Reifer means the Pred (0.20) we can conclude that the Web-COBRA achieved about the same prediction accuracy. The disadvantage of WebMo, however, is that it is a data-driven cost estimation model, which requires more past projects than Web-COBRA.

The Web-COBRA model outperforms the cost estimation methods presented in Table 1. In the summary of previous studies (Section 2), only one single study obtained accurate predictions (MMRE less than 0.25) for two estimation methods (COCOMO and OLS) [7]. Within this study a comparison between COCOMO and OLS regression models was performed. They used two different types of factor analysis to reduce the dimensionality, i.e. number of influential factors on cost. Their approach focused on reducing the dimensionality of the cost estimation model by only including context specific cost factors. Based on the results, they conclude that model simplicity and specificity is a possible improvement to state-of-the-art estimation models.

The study on dimensionality reduction and the COBRA method have in common that only the most relevant cost factors for a specific context are used for the cost estimation model building. Therefore, we conclude that tailoring a cost model using only most important factors has a positive influence on the prediction accuracy of cost estimation models.

A distinction between the two COBRA studies and previous empirical studies may be in the homogeneity of collected past project data. A lack of precise definitions of the cost factors causes a large variation in the method's performance [6].

While developing a COBRA model, a size measurement method has to be investigated, which ensures consistent measurement. The data on the COBRA cost factors is collected with a questionnaire using a Likert-type scale as response category. The project manager has to evaluate the cost factors based on the definition of the cost factor and a worst-case statement. The questionnaire is designed in a way that ensures the easy use of the data collection instrument. Thus, COBRA also provides a means for collecting past project data rather easily and consistently. In the context of Allette Systems, the project managers filled out the questionnaire together with a researcher to assure completeness and consistency of the data. The Web Objects were counted by a researcher using the developed counting manual. Afterwards, the numbers were cross-checked with the project manager of the web application to ensure consistency.

Another important driver of the accuracy of a cost estimation model is the size measure. In the context of Allette Systems we used a size measure that is tailored to the specific needs of web applications, the Web Objects. Reifer's approach was modified in a way that is most suitable to Allette Systems. A counting manual was developed including detailed instructions and counting examples. After measuring the twelve web applications at Allette Systems and analyzing the data a significant correlation between development effort and size in Web Objects was determined. Within the Web-COBRA evaluation, bivariate OLS regression was performed, where effort is the dependent and size measured in Web Objects the independent variable. A mean MRE of 0.24 was obtained from cross validation. The results implicitly show that size is a good predictor of effort. However, from a practical point of view we know, that it is generally rather difficult to accurately assess system size at an early project stage. Thus, the authors assume that early effort estimates are likely to be more accurate when derived from a cost estimation model that also uses other characteristics than only system size.

5. Conclusions

The work presented in this paper was based on the original COBRA model provided in [1]. We modified that work by (1) instantiating a new sizing metric for web applications based on the work of Reifer [4], (2) modified the data collection and validation process for the derivation, definition and collection of cost factor s and values, and (3) changed the nature of the cost factor model to one of orthogonal drivers thereby excluding interactions between cost drivers. This modified model (Web-COBRA) was then applied in a small web application development organization and results of this compared with both bivariate OLS regression model and the subjective estimates originally used by the organization during the project development.

The results show that bivariate OLS regression predicts effort less accurately than the Web-COBRA model, even though significantly. However, from a practical point of view the subjective results of the TAM indicate a high acceptance of the COBRA method and a relatively low complexity. In contrast to this, OLS regression lacks of transparency and ease of use.

Web-COBRA produced significantly better estimates than the subjective estimates developed in the organization. We believe that it is necessary to use an orthogonal cost factor definition structure in this type of work, based on the interviews carried out in the organization. We found that common agreement on the exact interpretation of an explicitly defined cost factor cannot be assumed, and that if a white box model is to be achieved in practice, then simplicity will be an important model characteristic. This further suggests that cost factor information and values cannot be reliably captured by questionnaire in the type of organization that was involved in this study. It is necessary to validate all definitions and subjective data values through interview and cross validation between experts within the organization.

We note that it is also generally rather difficult to accurately assess system size at an early project stage. Thus, we propose that early effort estimates are likely to be more accurate when derived from a cost estimation model that also uses characteristics other than system size alone. This deeper consideration of project characteristics should lead to a better understanding of the project at hand. Whether system size alone is a good effort predictor for web applications still needs to be investigated. For web hypermedia systems it was shown that effort can be accurately predicted using only size measures [9]. We doubt that this also applies for web applications based on the experiences gained in this case study.

Several issues need to be investigated to improve the reliability and generalizability of the results. A follow-up study at Allette Systems is proposed to investigate questions regarding the acceptance of the model in the company as well as the prediction accuracy when estimating projects in the future. Further replications of this case study need to be performed in similar environments to allow more general conclusions. Instantiating Web-COBRA models in several similar environments will enable comparisons between the models.

Consistent and comprehensive comparisons between different COBRA models will require consistent size measurement. The Web Object counting approach is considered to be a future size measure for web applications, but this also needs to be validated by further case studies. Therefore, future research should focus on establishing Web Objects as a suitable future size measure for web applications.

Further case studies in small companies need to be performed to improve the understanding of their work practices. Once we achieve this, we can tailor research activities more towards the needs of small companies. Thereby, we will be able to better contribute to improved software project management in small companies.

6. ACKNOWLEDGMENTS

We would like to thank Allette Systems for supporting the research project with their project data and personal support. We are thankful to all involved employees of Allette Systems who have made this work possible. We highly appreciate the methodological details on the COBRA method that were provided by the Fraunhofer Institute for Experimental Software Engineering (IESE).

7. REFERENCES

[1] L.C. Briand, K. El Emam, F. Bomarius, COBRA: A Hybrid Method for Software Cost Estimation, Benchmarking, and Risk Assessment. *Proceedings of 20th International Conference on Software Engineering*, April 1998, pp. 390-399.

[2] S.D. Conte, H.E. Dunsmore, V. Y. Shen. *Software engineering metrics and models*. The Benjamin/Cummings Publishing Company, Inc., 1986.

[3] D. Reifer. Web-Development: Estimating Quick Time-to-Market Software. *IEEE software*, vol. 17, no. 8, November/December 2000, pp. 57-64.

[4] D. Reifer. Ten deadly Risks in Internet and Intranet Software Development. *IEEE software*, vol. 18, no. 2, March/April 2002, pp. 12-14.

[5] M.A. Cusumano, D.B. Yoffie. *Competing on Internet Time: Lessons from Netscape and Its Battle with Microsoft*. Simon & Schuster Free Press, New York, 1998.

[6] L.C. Briand, I. Wieczorek. Software Resource Estimation. *Encyclopedia of Software Engineering*. Volume 2, P-Z (2nd ed., 2002), Marciniak, John J. (ed.) New York: John Wiley & Sons, pp. 1160-1196.

[7] G.H. Subramanian, S. Breslawski. Dimensionality Reduction in Software Development Effort Estimation. *Journal of Systems and Software*, 1993, vol. 21, no. 2, pp. 187-196.

[8] W. Hayes. *Statistics*. Fifth Edition. Hartcourt Brace College Publishers. 1994

[9] E. Mendes, N. Mosley, S. Counsell. A Comparison of Length, Complexity & Functionality as Size Measures for Predicting Web Design & Authoring Effort. *Proceedings of the 2001 EASE Conference*, Keele, UK, pp. 1-14.

[10] E. Mendes, I. Watson, C. Triggs, N. Mosley, S. Counsell. A Comparison of Development Effort Estimation Techniques for Web Hypermedia Applications. *Proceedings of the IEEE Metrics Symposium*, 2002.

[11] F. Walkerden, R. Jeffery. An Empirical Study of Analogy-based Software Effort Estimation. *Empirical Software Engineering*, 42, June 1999, pp. 135-158

[12] J. Conallen. *Building Web Applications with UML*. Addison-Wesley, 2000.

[13] B.W. Boehm. *Software Engineering Economics*. Prentice Hall, NJ, 1981.

[14] L.H. Putnam. A general Empirical Solution to the Macro Software Sizing and Estimating Problem. *IEEE Transactions on Software Engineering*, 1978, vol. 4, no. 4, pp. 345-361.

[15] Y. Deshpande. Consolidating Web Engineering as a discipline. *Software Engineering Australia*, April 2002, pp. 31-34.

[16] J. Albrecht, J. R. Gaffney. Software function, source lines of code, and development effort prediction: a software science validation. *IEEE Transactions on Software Engineering*, vol. 9,1983 no. 6, pp. 639-648.

[17] T. Rollo. Sizing E-Commerce. *Proceedings of the ACOSM 2000 - Australian Conference on Software Measurement*, Sydney, 2000.

[18] T. C. Jones. *Estimating Software Costs*. McGraw-Hill, New York, 1998.

[19] Judd, Smith, Kidder. *Research Methods in Social Relations*. Sixth edition. Harcourt Brace Jovanovich College Publishers, Fort Worth, USA, 1991.

[20] F.J. Heemstra. Software cost estimation. *Information Software Technology*, 1992, vol. 34, no. 10, pp. 627-639.

[21] B.W. Boehm, C. Abts, A.W. Brown, S. Chulani, B.K. Clark, W. Horowitz, R. Madachy, D. Reifer, B. Steece. *Software Cost Estimation with COCOMO II*. Prenctice Hall, NJ, 2000.

[22] I. Wieczorek. Improved Software Cost Estimation. *A Robust and Interpretable Modeling Method and a Comprehensive Empirical Investigation*. Fraunhofer IRB Verlag, vol. 7, 2001

[23] M. Shepperd, C. Schofield, B. Kitchenham. Effort Estimation Using Analogy. *Proceedings of the 18th International Conference of Software Engineering*, 1996, pp. 170-175.

[24] C.F. Kemerer. An Empirical Validation of Software Cost Estimation Models. *Communications of the ACM*, vol. 30, no. 5, 1987, pp. 417-429

[25] S. Chulani, B. Boehm, B. Steece. Bayesian Analysis for the Empirical Software Engineering Cost Models. *IEEE Transactions on Software Engineering*, vol. 25, no. 4, 1999

[26] M. Ruhe. *The early and accurate effort estimation of web applications*. University of Kaiserslautern, diploma thesis; available via email from the author.

[27] F.D. Davis. Perceived Usefulness, Ease of Use, and Usage of Information Technology. *MIS Quarterly*, September 1989, pp. 319-340.

[28] T. DeMarco. *Controlling Software Projects*. Yourdan Press, 1982

[29] R.C. Tausworthe. The work breakdown structure in sofware project management. *Journal of Systems and Software* 1. 1980, pp. 181-189

Evaluating the Quality of Information Models: Empirical Testing of a Conceptual Model Quality Framework

Daniel L. Moody[1,2]
Guttorm Sindre[3,4]
Terje Brasethvik[3]
Arne Sølvberg[3]

[1]*Department of Software Engineering, Charles University, Prague, Czech Republic*
[2]*School of Business Systems, Monash University, Melbourne, Australia*
[3]*Department of Computer and Information Science, Norwegian University of Science and Technology, Trondheim, Norway*
[4]*Department of Management Science and Information Systems, University of Auckland, New Zealand*
email: dmoody@infotech.monash.edu.au; {guttors, brase, asolvberg}@idi.ntnu.no

Abstract

This paper conducts an empirical analysis of a semiotics-based quality framework for quality assuring information models. 192 participants were trained in the concepts of the quality framework, and used it to evaluate models represented in an extended Entity Relationship (ER) language. A randomised, double-blind design was used, in which each participant independently reviewed multiple models and each model was evaluated by multiple reviewers. A combination of quantitative and qualitative analysis techniques were used to evaluate the results, including reliability analysis, validity analysis, interaction analysis, influence analysis, defect pattern analysis and task accuracy analysis.. An analysis was also conducted of the framework's likelihood of adoption in practice. The study provides strong support for the validity of the framework and suggests that it is likely to be adopted in practice, but raises questions about its reliability and the ability of participants to use it to accurately identify defects. The research findings provide clear directions for improvement of the framework. The research methodology used provides a general approach to empirical validation of quality frameworks.

1. INTRODUCTION

1.1 The Importance of Conceptual Model Quality

The traditional thrust of software quality assurance has been to use "brute force" testing at the end of the development process [56]. However empirical studies show that more than half the errors which occur during systems development are the result of inaccurate or incomplete requirements [30, 34]. Requirements errors are also the most common cause of failure in systems development projects [54, 55].

This suggests that substantially more effort should be spent to quality assure conceptual models, in order to catch requirements defects as soon as they occur, or to prevent them from occurring altogether [64]. Empirical studies have shown that moving quality assurance effort up to the early phases of development can be 33 times more cost effective than testing done at the end of development [58]. However, it is during requirements analysis that the notion of software development as a craft rather than an engineering discipline is strongest, and quality is therefore most difficult to assess. There are few guidelines for evaluating the quality of conceptual models, and little agreement even among experts as to what makes a "good" model. As a result, the quality of conceptual models in practice is almost entirely dependent on the competence of the analyst [28, 35].

0-7695-1877-X/03 $17.00 © 2003 IEEE

1.2 Previous Research on Conceptual Model Quality

There have been a number of frameworks proposed in the literature for evaluating the quality of conceptual models [e.g. 3, 27, 28, 32, 33, 37, 57, 62]. The most serious deficiency in the existing literature is the lack of empirical justification: most frameworks are either justified based on theory or the author(s)' experience. Theoretical justification is limited because methods have no "truth" value—the validity of a method is an empirical rather than a theoretical question [24, 48]. Also, software engineering is replete with examples of methods which are theoretically sound but do not work in practice, and vice versa. Experiential justification is limited because personal experience is subject to bias. Also, a method which works well when used by one person may not work for another [63].

1.3 Objectives of this Paper

This paper conducts an empirical analysis of the quality framework proposed by Lindland et al [33] for evaluating information models. The broad research questions addressed are:

- Does the framework provide a reliable and valid basis for evaluating the quality of information models? Reliability and validity are important characteristics of any quality evaluation method [16, 17].
- Is the framework likely to be adopted in practice? This is an issue that is rarely addressed in IS design research, despite the fact that this is critical for research to have an impact on practice.

This is the first quantitative study of the use of a quality framework to quality assure information models.

2. CONCEPTUAL MODEL QUALITY FRAMEWORK

In this section, we define the conceptual model quality framework developed by Lindland et al [33]. This represents the *a priori* theory being tested by this research.

2.1 Overview of the Framework

The conceptual model quality framework tested in this research study is based on semiotic theory (the theory of signs), and has been developed for evaluating conceptual models of any type (e.g. data models, process models, interaction models). The quality of a conceptual model is defined with respect to four components or *sets*:

- The model (M) is the set of statements that has been represented.
- The language (L) is the set of all statements that are possible to make according to the grammar of the language.
- The domain (D) is the set of statements that would be correct and relevant to make about the problem domain, often called the Universe of Discourse (UoD), the part of the world to be modelled.
- The interpretation (I) is what the audience of relevant stakeholders think is expressed in the model.

2.2 Quality Categories

The framework defines three *quality categories* and separates between *quality goals* and *means* to reach the goals. The quality categories are based on the three levels of semiotic theory [41], and are defined by equations on the sets described above:

- Syntactic quality is a relationship between the model and the language. The goal is *syntactic correctness*, which can be described as $M \setminus L = \emptyset$, i.e., there are no statements included in the model that are not part of the language.
- Semantic quality is a relationship between the model and the domain. Here two goals can be identified:
  - *Validity*: $M \setminus D = \emptyset$, i.e., there are no statements in the model that are not correct and relevant about the domain
  - *Completeness*: $D \setminus M = \emptyset$, i.e., there are no statements that are correct and relevant about the domain, but are not included in the model
- Pragmatic quality is the relationship between the model and the audience's interpretation. For each stakeholder, the goal is *comprehension*, which can be defined as $M \setminus I_i = \emptyset$ & $I_i \setminus M = \emptyset$, i.e., there are no statements in the model which are not in the stakeholder's interpretation of the model, and vice versa.

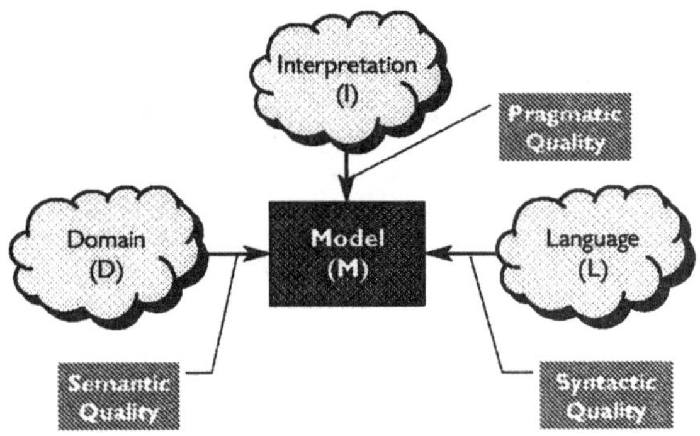

Figure 1. Conceptual Model Quality Framework

3. RESEARCH METHODOLOGY

3.1 Validation of IS Design Methods

The question of how to validate IS design methods has been a longstanding issue in the IS field [e.g. 18, 24, 44, 45, 46, 60, 63]. There are inherent problems evaluating any design method since there is typically no theory, no hypotheses, no experimental design and no data analysis to which traditional evaluation criteria can be applied [60]. As a result, IS design research tends to emphasise the development of new design methods while addressing the evaluation of methods in only a limited fashion [8, 13, 18, 36, 61, 63]. The Method Evaluation Model [39] is a theoretical model for evaluating IS design methods, which incorporates two aspects of method "success": actual efficacy and adoption in practice. It combines Methodological Pragmatism, a theory for validating methodological knowledge [48], and the Technology Acceptance Model (TAM), a theoretical model for explaining and predicting user acceptance of information technology [15]. The constructs of the model and the relationships between them are summarised in Figure 2. This model has been validated using both laboratory and field experiments [39].

The definitions of the constructs are:

- Actual Efficiency: the extent to which the method reduces the effort required to perform the task;
- Actual Effectiveness: the extent to which the method improves the quality of the result;
- Perceived Ease of Use: the extent to which a person believes that using the method would be free of effort;
- Perceived Usefulness: the extent to which a person believes that the method would be useful;
- Intention to Use: the extent to which a person intends to use the method;
- Actual Usage: the extent to which the method is actually used.

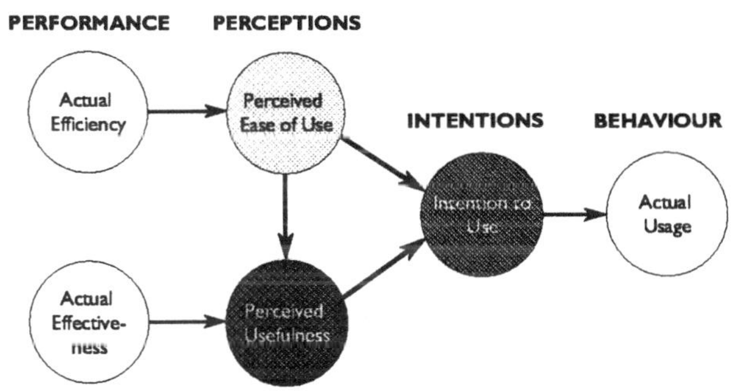

Figure 2. Method Evaluation Model

Actual Efficiency and Actual Effectiveness measure whether the method actually improves task performance, while Perceived Ease of Use and Perceived Usefulness represent perceptions of the method's efficiency and effectiveness.

3.2 Research Design

The research design is summarized in Figure 3. This shows the experimental treatment, experimental tasks, materials and dependent variables. A randomised, double-blind design was used, in which each participant reviewed multiple models and each model was evaluated by multiple reviewers.

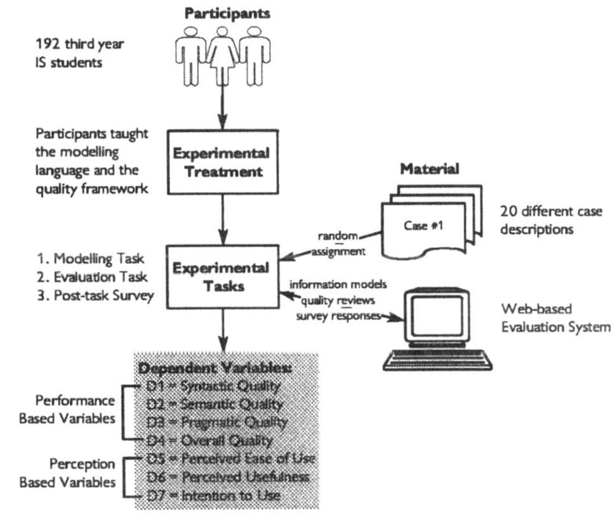

Figure 3. Research Design

3.3 Participants

There were 192 participants in this study, all 3rd year Information Systems students at the Norwegian University of Science and Technology. Computer Science or Information Systems students have been used in most previous experimental studies of conceptual modelling [e.g. 4, 5, 6, 21, 31, 42, 51, 52, 59].

3.4 Experimental Treatment

To prepare the participants for the evaluation task, they were given the original paper defining the framework [33], two 45 minute lectures explaining the framework and a 45 minute lecture explaining the evaluation exercise itself.

3.5 Experimental Tasks

Modelling Task. A total of twenty different case descriptions were prepared for use in the experiment. This was done to minimise the chance of collaboration between participants. Each participant had two weeks to develop an information model to meet the requirements of the case they were assigned, and submit it using a web-based system. The modelling language used was an extended Entity Relationship (ER) notation, called the Referent Modelling Language [7, 20, 53].

Evaluation Task. Following completion of the information modelling task, three reviewers were assigned to evaluate each model. Models were randomly assigned to reviewers, and reviews were double blind (reviewers did not know whose models they were evaluating, and modellers did not know who their reviewers were). Each participant was assigned cases which were different to each other and to the one they had modelled themselves. Participants had one week to complete the evaluation task, and record the results of their reviews using the web-based evaluation system.

Post Task Survey. Finally, participants were required to answer a post task survey, which measured their perceptions of the framework, also using the web-based system. The survey consisted of 16 closed questions and 3 open questions. The closed questions consisted of 6 items used to measure Perceived Ease of Use, 8 items to measure Perceived Usefulness and 3 items to measure Intention to Use. Each item was measured on a 5-point Likert scale, using the opposing-statements format. The order of the items was randomised to avoid monotonous responses [23].

3.6 Dependent Variables

We distinguish between two types of dependent variables:

- Performance based measures: How well did subjects perform the evaluation task?
- Perception based measures: How effective did subjects perceive the framework to be?

These types of measures represent the difference between actual efficacy and perceived efficacy as defined in the Method Evaluation Model.

Performance Based Variables. Four dependent variables were used to evaluate performance on the evaluation task: Syntactic Quality, Semantic Quality, Pragmatic Quality, and Overall Quality. A total of 550 ratings of each type (syntactic, semantic, pragmatic, overall) were collected as part of the study (an average of three per model). These were used to assess the reliability and validity of the evaluation framework (actual efficacy). All four quality ratings were given on a 7 point Likert scale, from 1 (poor) to 7 (excellent). As well as rating the models, reviewers were required to identify all defects in the models, classified by quality category.

Perception Based Variables. We define three perception-based dependent variables for evaluating the framework. These are all constructs defined in the Method Evaluation Model.

- Perceived Ease of Use: this was measured using five items on the post-task survey (Questions 1, 10, 11, 14 and 16).
- Perceived Usefulness: this was measured using eight items on the post-task survey (Questions 2, 5, 6, 7, 9, 12, 13 and 15).
- Intention to Use: this was measured using three items on the post-task survey (Questions 3, 4 and 8).

Items used to measure these constructs were based on the items defined for the corresponding constructs in the Technology Acceptance Model, which have been shown to have high levels of reliability and validity [9, 14, 23].

3.7 Theoretical Model

The relationship between all dependent variables and their empirical indicators are shown in Figure 4. In the diagram, circles indicate latent variables, rectangles indicate observed variables (empirical indicators), dotted lines indicate measurement relationships, while solid lines indicate causal relationships. The empirical indicators associated with the performance based variables represent the different reviewer ratings, while those for the perception based variables are the items on the post task survey.

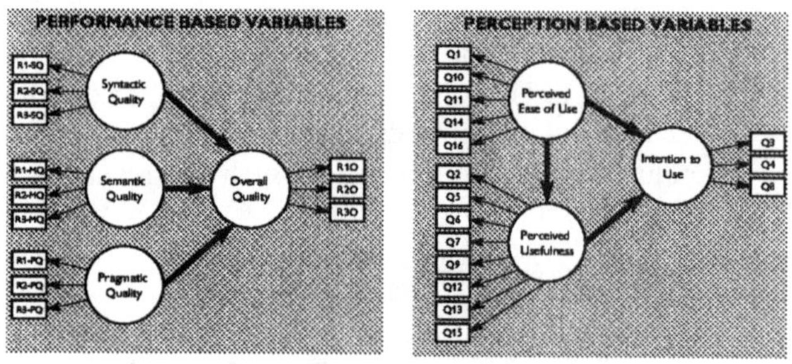

Figure 4. Theoretical Model

4. RESULTS AND DISCUSSION

4.1 Summary of Analyses

The results were evaluated by a combination of quantitative and qualitative analysis techniques. Each of these analyses addresses a sub-question of one of the research questions defined at the beginning of this paper:

1. Reliability analysis: How consistently were reviewers able to apply the framework?
2. Validity analysis: Are the quality categories necessary, sufficient and independent determinants of information model quality?
3. Influence analysis (weight estimation): What was the relative influence of each quality category on decisions about the overall quality of a model?
4. Interaction analysis: What are the relationships between the quality categories?
5. Defect pattern analysis: What was the frequency of errors in each quality category?
6. Task accuracy: How accurately were participants able to identify quality defects using the quality framework?
7. Perceived ease of use: How easy did participants find the framework to use?
8. Perceived usefulness: How useful did participants find the framework?
9. Intention to use: Were the participants likely to use the framework in the future?

Analyses 1-6 evaluate the framework's *actual efficacy* in performing the task. Analyses 7-9 evaluate the framework's *perceived efficacy*. Analyses 1-4 are quantitative analyses, analyses 5-6 are qualitative analyses, while analyses 7-9 involve a combination of the two (both closed and open questions were included in the post-task survey). Mixing qualitative and quantitative research methods can lead to a more comprehensive understanding of a phenomenon [25].

4.2 Reliability Analysis

Reliability was evaluated by measuring the inter-rater reliability between different reviewers of the same model. The results are summarised in Table 1. While there is no definitive standard for reliability, alphas of 0.7 or above are generally considered to be acceptable in the literature [43].

Table 1. Reliability Levels for Each Quality Category

CONSTRUCT	CRONBACH'S α
Syntactic Quality	.6508
Semantic Quality	.6617
Pragmatic Quality	.7043
Overall Quality	.7293

The observed levels of reliability for two of the quality categories (syntactic and semantic) are clearly lower than acceptable, which suggests that the definition of these categories needs to be refined. This was confirmed by the qualitative analysis, which showed that participants confused the two categories. The most encouraging result of this analysis is that overall quality assessments were at an acceptable level of reliability. The likely explanation for this is that consideration of quality within each category led to an overall increase in reliability, even if there was some ambiguity in the classification of defects.

4.3 Validity Analysis

To assess the validity of the quality framework, we need to address the following questions [1, 40]:

- *Completeness (sufficient)*: Do the set of quality categories include all aspects of quality of information models? Are there any aspects that have been left out?
- *Parsimony (necessary)*: Are all the quality categories necessary for evaluating information models? Are they all relevant determinants of information model quality?
- *Independence (orthogonal)*: Are the quality categories independent of each other? Do they overlap?

A regression analysis was carried out using the quality categories (syntactic, semantic, pragmatic) as independent variables and Overall Quality as the dependent variable (Figure 5). The results of the regression analysis were:

- Adjusted $r^2 = 0.877$
- Significance (p) = 0.000
- Pearson correlation coefficient (r) = .937

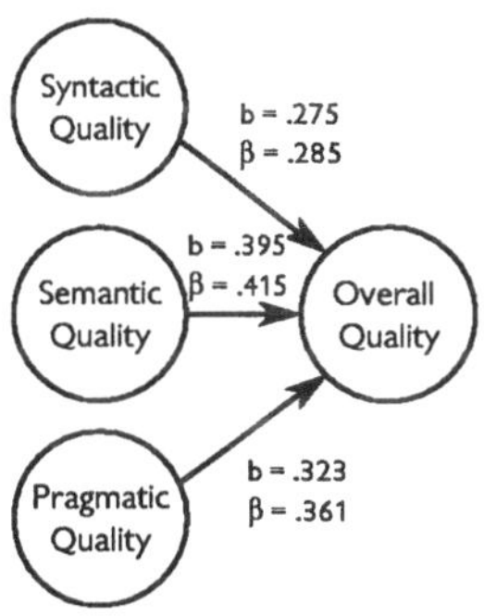

Figure 5. Regression Model for Validity Analysis

Completeness of Quality Categories. The r^2 statistic measures the proportion of the variance of the dependent variable explained by the independent variables. In this case, the quality categories account for almost 90% of the variance in Overall Quality. Ratings of overall quality are almost entirely explained by variations in ratings for the individual quality categories. This provides strong evidence that the model is fully specified (i.e. that there are no missing independent variables) and therefore that the set of quality categories is complete.

Parsimony of Quality Categories. Table 2 shows the the size and significance of the separate effects of each independent variable on the dependent variable. All independent variables (quality categories) were found to have highly significant effects ($\alpha < .01$) on the dependent variable (Overall Quality). *Effect size* (ES) has been suggested by a number of researchers as an index of practical meaningfulness [10, 22, 49, 50]. In multiple regression, the standardised regression coefficient (β) is most commonly used as a measure of effect size [47]. As shown in Table 2, Syntactic Quality has a "small" effect ($\beta > .1$) while Semantic and Pragmatic Quality have "medium" effects ($\beta > .3$), following Cohen's guidelines for effect size [10]. This means that all relationships are practically meaningful as well as statistically significant, which provides strong evidence that all quality categories are relevant determinants of the quality of an information model.

Table 2. Multiple Regression Results

QUALITY CATEGORY	STATISTICAL SIGNIFICANCE (p)	EFFECT SIZE (b)	TOLERANCE
Syntactic	.000	.285	.478
Semantic	.000	.415	.455
Pragmatic	.000	.361	.475

Independence of Quality Categories. Collinearity analysis was also conducted to evaluate the independence of the quality categories. As shown in Table 2, Tolerance values are well above .2 for all quality categories, which means there is no evidence of multicollinearity between the quality categories. This suggests that they are all independent determinants of Overall Quality.

4.4 Influence Analysis

Regression analysis was used to evaluate the separate effects of each quality category on judgements of overall quality. The regression equation which resulted was:

Equation 1. *Overall Quality = .275 Syntactic Quality + .395 Semantic Quality + .323 Pragmatic Quality + .021*

The coefficients for each variable in the regression equation measure the effect of each quality category on judgements about the Overall Quality of a model. For example, an increase of one unit in Syntactic Quality is associated with an increase of .275 in Overall Quality. However the relative size of the standardised regression coefficients (β) for the variables indicates their relative influence in determining overall quality. This shows that Syntactic Quality contributes 27% to the total variance explained, Semantic Quality 39% and Pragmatic Quality 34%. As expected, Semantic Quality had the greatest effect on decisions about overall quality of a model—these represent mismatches between the model and user requirements, so are the most costly and visible type of errors.

4.5 Interaction Analysis

Bi-variate correlation analysis was conducted to test for interactions between the different quality categories. Strong positive correlations were found between all quality categories:

- Syntactic and Semantic Quality ($r = .669$, $p = .000$)
- Syntactic and Pragmatic Quality ($r = .652$, $p = .000$)
- Semantic and Pragmatic Quality ($r = .672$, $p = .000$)

Correlations are non-directional, but our theoretical explanation for the observed correlations is that they represent causal relationships (shown in Figure 6). Improving syntactic quality is expected to improve semantic quality, as a model that is not syntactically correct will have ambiguous semantics. Improving syntactic quality is expected to improve pragmatic quality because a model that is not syntactically correct will be difficult to interpret. Improving pragmatic quality is expected to improve semantic quality, as a model that is difficult to interpret will be difficult to match against the real world.

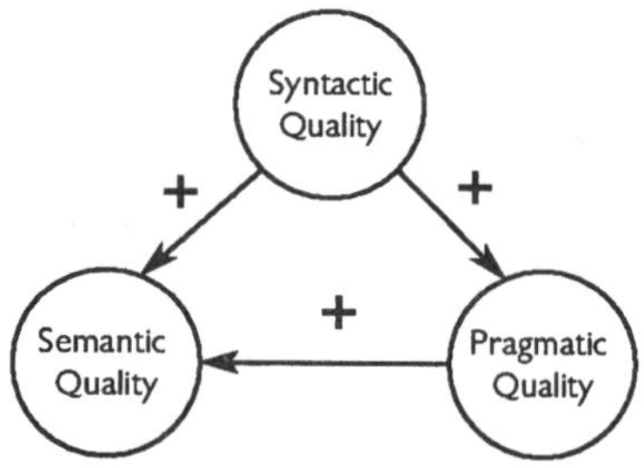

Figure 6. Interactions Between Quality Categories

Three alternative multiple regression models were developed to test this explanation (these represent all possible causal combinations of the variables):

- Model 1: Syntactic Quality + Semantic Quality → Pragmatic Quality
- Model 2: Syntactic Quality + Pragmatic Quality → Semantic Quality
- Model 3: Semantic Quality + Pragmatic Quality → Syntactic Quality

The results of the analysis are summarised in Table 3. While all regression models were statistically significant, Model 2 (our *a priori* theory) provides the best fit (as evidenced by the higher variance explained).

Table 3. Alternative Regression Models

MODEL	ADJUSTED r^2	SIGNIFICANCE
1	.524	.000
2	.543	.000
3	.521	.000

4.6 Defect Pattern Analysis

Rather than evaluate all 192 models and 550 reviews, a random sample of 32 models and 96 reviews were selected. The most frequent defects were (defined in terms of average number of defects per model):

- Cardinality errors on relationships (4.5).
- Missing attributes (3.6).
- Missing names for relationships(2.6).
- Missing entity types (1.3).
- Erroneous use of aggregation, membership and generalisation connectors (1.0).
- Missing relationships (0.5).
- System components as entity types (0.4), e.g., "System" or "Database".
- Activities modelled as entity types (0.4).

Entities without attributes and relationship types without names fall into the category of syntactic errors (given that the notation requires that all entities should have attributes, and all relationships should be named). Otherwise, most of the others fall into the semantic category, and are mostly incompleteness defects (something mentioned in the case description but not covered by the model).

The high level of errors in cardinality of relationships indicates a systematic problem in the information modelling notation and/or the teaching of it. Relationship cardinalities are a basic element of information modelling syntax and one would not expect such high error rates for such a basic syntactic error. Further analysis showed that participants found the conventions used for cardinalities confusing, as they were the reverse of notations they had learnt in previous courses. This explains the high level of errors and also the high level of underreporting of errors. This illustrates how the quality framework can provide useful diagnostic information about the effectiveness of modelling notations and teaching methods used.

4.7 Task Accuracy

Task accuracy was measured by inspecting the sample reviews and comparing them to expert reviews:

- Ratio of Type 1 errors (false negatives): where defects exist in the model but are not identified by reviewers. On average, 75% of the defects went unreported.
- Ratio of Type II errors (false positives): when defects are identified which are not defects at all. Of the defects identified by the participants, 92% were genuine defects, so 8% were Type II errors.
- Ratio of Type III errors (classification errors): where defects are correctly identified but classified in the wrong category. About 20% of the errors were wrongly categorised. Most of these were confusion between syntactic and semantic quality, which explains the lower reliability for these quality categories.

This analysis shows that participants were not able to apply the framework accurately to identify defects, with very high levels of underreporting. While this could be partly attributed to their lack of experience in information modelling, it also suggests a possible deficiency in the framework. A clear weakness of the framework is that quality categories are defined at such an abstract level. Decomposing the framework to a lower level of detail would help to improve identification of defects and would also improve the reliability of evaluations.

4.8 Likelihood of Adoption in Practice

Measurement Validity. To evaluate the results for Perceived Ease of Use, Perceived Usefulness and Intention to Use, it is necessary first to evaluate the validity and reliability of the survey items used to measure them.

Factor analysis was conducted on the items used in the post-task survey using the principal components extraction method and varimax rotation. The initial factor analysis resulted in four factors being extracted using the Kaiser criterion. Q5 (Perceived Ease of Use) and Q14 (Perceived Usefulness) formed a fourth factor, and were therefore eliminated from the analysis. Factor weights derived from the analysis were then used to estimate the value of the underlying theoretical constructs.

Reliability analysis was conducted on the items used to measure Perceived Ease of Use, Perceived Usefulness and Intention to Use (excluding Q5 and Q14). As shown in Table 4, high levels of reliability were found for all constructs, with Cronbach's alpha > .7 in all cases, which is considered acceptable [43].

Table 4. Item Reliabilities for each Construct

CONSTRUCT	CRONBACH'S α
Perceived Ease of Use	.7055
Perceived Usefulness	.8661
Intention to Use	.9036

Significance Testing. One-sample t-tests were conducted for each construct to see if they were significantly different to 3 (the "zero point" of the Likert scale use). Table 5 summarises the results of the significance testing. Overall, participants found the framework easy to use, useful, and intended to use it in the future ($\alpha < .01$).

Table 5. Significance of Responses

CONSTRUCT	MEAN	STDEV	SIGNIFICANCE	Y/N
Perceived Ease of Use	3.77	.570	.000	YES
Perceived Usefulness	3.72	.665	.000	YES
Intention to Use	4.04	.665	.000	YES

4.9 Analysis of Causal Relationships

In the Method Evaluation Model (Figure 2), a number of causal relationships are hypothesised:

- Perceived Ease of Use → Perceived Usefulness
- Perceived Ease of Use + Perceived Usefulness → Intention to Use

These relationships were evaluated using regression analysis.

Perceived Ease of Use fl Perceived Usefulness. The results for this regression analysis were:

- $r^2 = .647$
- $\alpha = 000$
- $r = .804$

The Pearson correlation coefficient (r) is greater than .5, which corresponds to a "large" effect (r is used as a measure of effect size in simple regression) [11]. This means that the relationship between Perceived Ease of Use and Perceived Usefulness is both statistically significant ($\alpha < .01$) and practically meaningful. The resulting regression equation was:

Equation 2. *Perceived Usefulness =.937 Perceived Ease of Use + ?182*

Perceived Ease of Use + Perceived Usefulness fl Intention to Use. The results for this regression analysis were:

- Adjusted $r^2 = .322$
- $\alpha = 003$
- $r = .610$

The Pearson correlation coefficient is greater than .5, which corresponds to a "large" effect [11]. This means that the relationship between the variables is both statistically significant ($\alpha < .01$) and practically meaningful. The resulting regression equation was:

Equation 3. *Intention to Use =.035 ?Perceived Ease of Use + .682 Perceived Usefulness +1.333*

The significance levels and effect sizes for each independent variable in Equation 3 are shown in Table 6 below.

Table 6. Multiple Regression Results

VARIABLE	SIGNIFICANCE (p)	EFFECT SIZE (b)
Perceived Ease of Use	(.897)	.035
Perceived Usefulness	.035	.582

The relationship between Perceived Usefulness and Intention to Use was found to be significant ($\alpha < .05$) with a large effect size ($\beta > .5$), while the relationship between Perceived Ease of Use and Intention to Use was neither statistically significant ($\alpha < .05$) nor practically meaningful ($\beta < .1$). This is consistent with many of the studies of the Technology Acceptance Model (on which the Method Evaluation Model is based), which have found that the relationship between Perceived Ease of Use and Intention to Use is not significant after controlling for the effects of Perceived Usefulness [9, 15].

5. CONCLUSION

5.1 Summary of Findings

This paper has conducted an empirical analysis of the conceptual model quality framework proposed by Lindland et al [33]. The validation approach combines both quantitative and qualitative research approaches, providing triangulation of method. While the quantitative analyses suggested that participants were able to successfully apply the framework (based on reliability and validity analysis), the detailed qualitative analysis showed that their evaluations included high levels of underreporting and misclassification of defects. This suggests that use of quantitative analysis techniques on their own can lead to deceptive results.

Overall, the quality framework was found to be valid, with the quality categories found to be necessary, sufficient and independent. It was perceived to be both easy to use and useful in evaluating information models and participants intended to use it in the future. The research findings provide clear direction for future research, which will focus on refining the framework to address the limitations identified, particularly in terms of accurate identification of defects, as highlighted in the qualitative analysis. Finally, the paper conducts a further empirical test of the Method Evaluation Model, which showed the measurement instrument had a high level of reliability and validity and validated two of the three causal relationships in the model.

The results for each of the research questions defined at the beginning of the paper are summarised in Table 7:

Table 7. Summary of Findings

RESEARCH QUESTION	RESULT
1. Task Performance (Actual Efficacy)	
1.1 Is the framework reliable?	Partially - two quality categories had reliability levels lower than acceptable but overall quality was acceptable
1.2 Is the framework valid?	Yes – the quality categories were found to be necessary, sufficient and independent
1.3 What is the relative influence of each quality category on decisions about overall quality?	Syntactic Quality 27% Semantic Quality 39% Pragmatic Quality 34%
1.4 What are the interactions between the quality categories?	Syntactic → Semantic Syntactic → Pragmatic Pragmatic → Semantic
1.6 How accurately were participants able to identify defects?	75% Type I errors 8% Type II errors 20% Type III errors
2. Adoption In Practice (Perceived Efficacy)	
2.1 Did participants find the framework easy to use?	Yes
2.2 Did participants find the framework useful?	Yes
2.3 Are participants likely to use the framework in practice?	Yes

5.2 Theoretical Contributions

The major theoretical contribution of this paper is that it conducts the first quantitative analysis of a conceptual model quality framework. The lack of empirical validation is a major weakness in the conceptual model quality literature, and this paper demonstrates a systematic approach to testing and improving such frameworks. It could also be used to compare the effectiveness of different frameworks, using a multiple group design. The validation approach addresses issues of reliability and validity, which are important requirements of any quality evaluation process, as well as the issue of adoption in practice, which has been largely ignored in IS design research. The results of the analyses provide clear direction for future research, as well as identifying problems in the information modelling technique and teaching methods used. More generally, the validation approach described in this paper could be applied to validate and improve any quality framework. There is nothing about the approach that is specific to conceptual modelling. It could just as easily be used to evaluate a framework for software quality, a framework for user interface design quality or a framework for website design quality.

5.3 Limitations and Further Research

The major limitation of this study, and it is a significant one, is the nature of sample population used. In general, the population from which one selects subjects for a research study should be representative of the population to which the researcher wishes to generalise results [12]. Computer Science or Information Systems students have been used in most previous experimental studies of conceptual modelling [e.g. 4, 5, 6, 21, 31, 42, 51, 52, 59]. However external validity is a significant problem in most laboratory experiments involving undergraduate students, and has been identified as a major issue in IS research in terms of its relevance to practice [19, 26, 38]. It is also one of the major limitations of experimental research in the social sciences generally [2].

The question therefore remains: would similar results have been found if practitioners (which is the population to which we wish to generalise) had been used instead? The argument could be made that undergraduate students have little or no practical experience in information modelling, and therefore do not have the knowledge or expertise to properly evaluate the quality of information models. Lacking such experience, students may have been tempted to score overall quality simply as an average of their scores for syntactic, semantic, and pragmatic quality. Such averaging would inflate the validity of the quality framework. Similarly, both validity and reliability might be inflated by defensive reviewing (i.e. assigning scores of 3-5 rather than 1-2 or 6-7). These are valid criticisms and difficult to argue against convincing.

For this reason, we do not see this study as the end of the validation process but only the *beginning*. This study has provided useful empirical data about the framework and pilot-tested the validation approach, but the results must be interpreted with caution. The generalisability of the results to practice is questionable because of the nature of the participants used. For this reason, a similar study is planned using experienced practitioners, possibly with a refined version of the quality framework. Some refinement of the framework has already taken place [29], but the results of this study suggest the need for other refinements.

REFERENCES

[1] Alexander, C. (1968): *Notes On The Synthesis Of Form*, Boston: Harvard University Press.

[2] Babbie, E.R. (1998): *The Practice of Social Research*, Belmont, California: Wadsworth Publishing.

[3] Batini, C., S. Ceri, and S.B. Navathe (1992): *Conceptual Database Design: An Entity Relationship Approach*, Redwood City, California: Benjamin Cummings.

[4] Batra, D., J.A. Hoffer, and R.P. Bostrom (1990): Comparing Representations with Relational and EER Models, *Communications of the ACM*, **33** (2), February: p. 126-139.

[5] Bock, D.B. and T. Ryan (1993): Accuracy in Modelling with Extended Entity Relationship and Object Oriented Data Model, *Journal Of Database Management*, **4** (4): p. 30-39.

[6] Bodart, F., A. Patel, M. Sim, and R. Weber (2001): Should the Optional Property Construct be used in Conceptual Modelling: A Theory and Three Empirical Tests, *Information Systems Research*, **12** (4).

[7] Brasethvik, T. and J.A. Gulla (2002): A Conceptual Modeling Approach to Semantic Document Retrieval, In A. Banks Pidduck (Ed.) *14th International Conference on Advanced Information Systems Engineering (CAiSE'02)*, Toronto: Springer Verlag, May 27-31.

[8] Bubenko, J.A. (1986): Information Systems Methodologies - A Research View, In *Information Systems Design Methodologies: Improving The Practice*, T.W. Olle, H.G. Sol, and A.A. Verrijn-Stuart (Eds.), North-Holland.

[9] Chau, P.Y.K. (1996): An Empirical Assessment of a Modified Technology Acceptance Model, *Journal of Management Information Systems*, **13** (2).

[10] Cohen, J. (1988): *Statistical Power Analysis for the Behavioural Sciences (2nd ed.)*, 2nd ed, Hillsdale, NJ: Lawrence Earlbaum and Associates.

[11] Cohen, P.A. (1981): Student Ratings of Instruction and Student Achievement: A Meta-Analysis of Multi-Section Validity Studies, *Review of Educational Research*, **51**: p. 281-309.

[12] Cooper, D.R. and P.S. Schindler (1998): *Business Research Methods (6th edition)*, 6th ed, Singapore: McGraw-Hill International.

[13] Curtis, B. (1986): By The Way, Did Anyone Study Any Real Programmers?, In *Empirical Studies of Programmers*, E. Soloway and S. Iyengar (Eds.), Ablex: Norward, N.J.

[14] Davis, F.D. (1989): Perceived Usefulness, Perceived Ease of Use and User Acceptance of Information Technology, *MIS Quarterly*, **13** (3).

[15] Davis, F.D., R.P. Bagozzi, and P.R. Warshaw (1989): User Acceptance of Computer Technology: A Comparison of Two Theoretical Models, *Management Science*, **35** (8): p. 982-1003.

[16] Deming, W.E. (1986): *Out of the Crisis*, Cambridge, MA: MIT Center for Advanced Engineering.

[17] Evans, J.R. and W.M. Lindsay (2002): *The Management and Control of Quality (5th Ed.)*, Cincinnati, Ohio: South-Western (Thomson Learning).

[18] Fitzgerald, G. (1991): Validating New Information Systems Techniques: A Retrospective Analysis, In H.E. Nissen, H.K. Klein, and R. Hirschheim (Eds.), *Information Systems Research: Contemporary Approaches And Emergent Traditions*: North-Holland,

[19] Galliers, R.D. (1994): Relevance and Rigour in Information Systems Research: Some Personal Reflections on Issues Facing the Information Systems Research Community, In *Proceedings of the IFIP TC8 Conference on Business Process Reengineering: Information Systems and Challenges*, Gold Coast, Australia,

[20] Gulla, J.A. and T. Brasethvik (2000): On the Challenges of Business Modelling in Large-scale Reengineering Projects, In *4th International Conference on Requirements Engineering (ICRE 2000)*, Schaumburg, IL: IEEE Computer Society Press, 19-23 June 2000.

[21] Hardgrave, B.C. and N.P. Dalal (1995): Comparing Object Oriented and Extended Entity Relationship Models, *Journal Of Database Management*, **6** (3).

[22] Harris, M.J. and R. Rosenthal (1985): Mediation of Interpersonal Expectancy Effects: 31 Meta-Analyses, *Psychological Bulletin*, **97**.

[23] Hu, P.J. and P.Y.K. Chau (1999): Examining the Technology Acceptance Model Using Physician Acceptance of Telemedicine Technology, *Journal of Management Information Systems*, **16** (2), Fall: p. 91-113.

[24] Ivari, J. (1986): Dimensions Of Information Systems Design: A Framework For A Long Range Research Program, *Information Systems Journal*, (June).

[25] Kaplan, B. and D. Duchon (1988): Combining Qualitative and Quantitative Methods in Information Systems Research: A Case Study, *MIS Quarterly*, December.

[26] Keen, P.G.W. (1991): Relevance and Rigour in Information Systems Research: Improving Quality, Confidence, Cohesion and Impact, In *Information Systems Research: Contemporary Approaches and Emergent Traditions*, H.-E. Nissen, H.K. Klein, and R. Hirschheim (Eds.), Elsevier Science Publishers (North Holland).

[27] Kesh, S. (1995): Evaluating The Quality Of Entity Relationship Models, *Information And Software Technology*, **37** (12).

[28] Krogstie, J., O.I. Lindland, and G. Sindre (1995): Towards a Deeper Understanding of Quality in Requirements Engineering, In *Proceedings of the 7th International Conference on Advanced Information Systems Engineering (CAISE)*, Jyvaskyla, Finland, June.

[29] Krogstie, J. (1998): Integrating the Understanding of Quality in Requirements Specification and Conceptual Modelling, *Software Engineering Notes*, **28** (1).

[30] Lauesen, S. and O. Vinter (2000): Preventing Requirement Defects, In *Proceedings of the Sixth International Workshop on Requirements Engineering: Foundation for Software Quality (REFSQ'2000)*, Stockholm, Sweden, June 5-6 2000.

[31] Lee, H. and B.G. Choi (1998): A Comparative Study of Conceptual Data Modelling Techniques, *Journal Of Database Management*, **9** (2), Spring: p. 26-35.

[32] Levitin, A. and T. Redman (1994): Quality Dimensions of a Conceptual View, *Information Processing and Management*, **31** (1).

[33] Lindland, O.I., G. Sindre, and A. Sølvberg (1994): Understanding Quality In Conceptual Modelling, *IEEE Software*, **11** (2), March: p. 42-49.

[34] Martin, J. (1989): *Information Engineering*, Englewood Cliffs, N.J.: Prentice Hall, 3 v.

[35] Moody, D.L. and G.G. Shanks (1994): What Makes A Good Data Model? Evaluating the Quality of Entity Relationship Models, In P. Loucopolous (Ed.) *Proceedings of the Thirteenth International Conference on the Entity Relationship Approach*, Manchester, England, December 14-17.

[36] Moody, D.L. and G.G. Shanks (1998): Evaluating and Improving the Quality of Entity Relationship Models: An Action Research Programme, *Australian Computer Journal*, November.

[37] Moody, D.L. and G.G. Shanks (1998): What Makes A Good Data Model? A Framework For Evaluating And Improving The Quality Of Entity Relationship Models, *Australian Computer Journal*, August.

[38] Moody, D.L. (2000): Building Links Between IS Research and Professional Practice: Improving the Relevance and Impact of IS Research, In R.A. Weber and B. Glasson (Eds.), *International Conference on Information Systems (ICIS'00)*, Brisbane, Australia, December 11-13.

[39] Moody, D.L. (2001): *Dealing with Complexity: A Practical Method for Representing Large Entity Relationship Models (PhD Thesis)*, Melbourne, Australia: Department Of Information Systems, University of Melbourne.

[40] Moody, D.L. and G.G. Shanks (2003): Improving the Quality of Data Models: Empirical Validation of a Quality Management Framework, *International Journal of Information Systems*, **forthcoming**.

[41] Morris, C.W. (1970): *Foundations of the Theory of Signs*, Chicago: Chicago University Press.

[42] Nordbotten, J.C. and M.E. Crosby (1999): The Effect of Graphic Style on Data Model Interpretation, *Information Systems Journal*, **9**.

[43] Nunally, J. (1978): *Psychometric Theory (2nd edition)*, New York: McGraw Hill.

[44] Olle, T.W., H.G. Sol, and A.A. Verrijn-Stuart, eds. *Information Systems Design Methodologies: A Comparative Review*. 1982, North Holland: Amsterdam.

[45] Olle, T.W., H.G. Sol, and C.J. Tully, eds. *Information Systems Design Methodologies: A Feature Analysis*. 1983, North-Holland: Amsterdam.

[46] Olle, T.W., H.G. Sol, and A.A. Verrijn-Stuart, eds. *Information Systems Design Methodologies: Improving the Practice*. 1986, North-Holland: Amsterdam.

[47] Pedhazur, E.J. and L.P. Schmelkin (1991): *Measurement, Design and Analysis: An Integrated Approach*, Hillsdale, NJ: Lawrence Erlbaum Associates Inc.

[48] Rescher, N. (1977): *Methodological Pragmatism: Systems-Theoretic Approach to the Theory of Knowledge*, Oxford: Basil Blackwell.

[49] Rosenthal, R. and D.B. Rubin (1979): A Note on Percent Variance Explained as a Measure of Importance of Effects, *Journal of Educational Psychology*, **74**.

[50] Rosenthal, R. (1983): Assessing the Statistical and Social Importance of the Effects of Psychotherapy, *Journal of Consulting and Clinical Psychology*, **51**.

[51] Shoval, P. and M. Even-Chaime (1987): Database Schema Design: An Experimental Comparison Between Normalisation and Information Analysis, *Database*, **18** (3), Spring: p. 30-39.

[52] Shoval, P. and S. Shiran (1997): Entity-Relationship and Object-Oriented Data Modeling: An Experimental Comparison of Design Quality, *Data & Knowledge Engineering*, **21**: p. 297-315.

[53] Sølvberg, A. (1999): Data and what they refer to, In *Conceptual Modeling, Current Issues and Future Directions (Selected Papers from the Symposium on Conceptual Modeling, Los Angeles, CA, held before ER'97)*. P.P. Chen, et al. (Eds.), Springer Verlag: Berlin, p. 211-226.

[54] Standish Group (1995): *The CHAOS Report into Project Failure*, The Standish Group International Inc. Available on-line at http://www.standishgroup.com/visitor/chaos.htm.

[55] Standish Group (1996): *Unfinished Voyages*, The Standish Group International Inc. available on-line at http://www.standishgroup.com/visitor/voyages.htm.

[56] van Vliet, H. (2000): *Software Engineering: Principles and Practice (2nd edition)*: John Wiley & Sons.

[57] von Halle, B. (1991): Data: Asset or Liability?, *Database Programming and Design*, **4** (7), July.

[58] Walrad, C. and E. Moss (1993): Measurement: The Key to Application Development Quality, *IBM Systems Journal*, **32** (3): p. 445-460.

[59] Weber, R.A. (1996): Are Attributes Entities? A Study Of Database Designers' Memory Structures, *Information Systems Research*, June.

[60] Weber, R.A. (1997): *Ontological Foundations Of Information Systems*, Melbourne, Australia: Coopers And Lybrand Accounting Research Methodology Monograph No. 4, Coopers And Lybrand.

[61] Westrup, C. (1993): Information Systems Methodologies in Use, *Journal of Information Technology*, **8**.

[62] Witt, G.C. and G.C. Simsion (2000): *Data Modeling Essentials: Analysis, Design, and Innovation*, The Coriolis Group.

[63] Wynekoop, J.L. and N.L. Russo (1997): Studying Systems Development Methodologies: An Examination Of Research Methods, *Information Systems Journal*, **7** (1), January.

[64] Zultner, R.E. (1992): The Deming Way: Total Quality Management for Software, In *Proceedings of Total Quality Management for Software Conference*, Washington, DC, April.

Technical Papers

Program Analysis

Whole Program Path-Based Dynamic Impact Analysis

James Law
Computer Science Dept.
Oregon State University
Corvallis, OR
law@cs.orst.edu

Gregg Rothermel
Computer Science Dept.
Oregon State University
Corvallis, OR
grother@cs.orst.edu

Abstract

Impact analysis, determining when a change in one part of a program affects other parts of the program, is time-consuming and problematic. Impact analysis is rarely used to predict the effects of a change, leaving maintainers to deal with consequences rather than working to a plan. Previous approaches to impact analysis involving analysis of call graphs, and static and dynamic slicing, exhibit several tradeoffs involving computational expense, precision, and safety, require access to source code, and require a relatively large amount of effort to re-apply as software evolves. This paper presents a new technique for impact analysis based on whole path profiling, that provides a different set of cost-benefits tradeoffs – a set which can potentially be beneficial for an important class of predictive impact analysis tasks. The paper presents the results of experiments that show that the technique can predict impact sets that are more accurate than those computed by call graph analysis, and more precise (relative to the behavior expressed in a program's profile) than those computed by static slicing.

1. Introduction

A frequent problem with software is that changes to a system, however small, may have unintended, expensive, or even disastrous effects [13]. Software change impact analysis, often called simply *impact analysis*, is a family of approaches for addressing this problem [2, 3, 14, 16, 22].

Impact analysis is often used to assess the effects of a change on a system after that change has been made, but a more proactive approach uses impact analysis to *predict* the effects of change before it is instantiated [3]. For instance, software maintainers may wish to consider several methods for implementing a change and choose one that has the lowest estimated impact on cost or schedule. Predictive impact analysis can allow maintainers to work to a plan, rather than simply deal with consequences.

Impact analysis techniques can been partitioned into two classes: traceability analysis and dependency analysis [3]. We focus on the latter. Impact analysis techniques based on dependency analysis [1, 5, 6, 7, 9, 10, 11, 19, 23] attempt to assess the affects of change on semantic dependencies between program entities, typically by identifying the syntactic dependencies that may signal the presence of such semantic dependencies [17].

We focus on three traditional dependency-based impact analysis techniques: call graph based analysis, and static and dynamic program slicing [3].[1] Each of these approaches has advantages and disadvantages:

- Transitive closure on call graphs, cited as a fundamental technique for predicting change impact [3]; is relatively inexpensive; however, it can be highly inaccurate, identifying impact where none exists and failing to identify impact where it does exist.
- Static slicing (see [21] for a summary), can predict change impact conservatively (safely); however, by focusing on all possible program behaviors, it may return impact sets that are too large, or too imprecise relative to the expected operational profile of a system, to be useful for maintainers.
- Dynamic slicing can predict impact relative to specific program executions or operational profiles, which may be useful for many maintenance tasks, but it sacrifices safety in the resulting impact assessment.
- Static and dynamic slicing techniques are relatively computationally expensive, requiring data dependence, control dependence, and alias analysis, whereas call graph based analysis is comparatively inexpensive.
- All three approaches rely on access to source code to determine the static calling structure or dependencies in that code, and require a relatively large amount of effort to recompute the information needed to assess impact on subsequent releases of a software system.

[1] Other common techniques include expert judgment and code inspection; however, these are not easily automated. Moreover, expert predictions of the extent of change impact have been shown to be frequently incorrect [12], and performing impact analysis by inspecting source code can be prohibitively expensive [16].

0-7695-1877-X/03 $17.00 © 2003 IEEE

In this paper, we present a new technique for performing impact analysis based on *whole path profiling* [8]. Our technique, `PathImpact`, uses relatively low-cost instrumentation to obtain dynamic information about system execution, and from this information builds a representation of the system's behavior which it uses to estimate impact.

`PathImpact` provides a different set of cost-benefits tradeoffs than the three techniques outlined above – a set which can potentially be beneficial for an important class of predictive impact analysis tasks. The technique is dynamic, requiring no static analysis of the system. The resulting impact estimate is thus not safe, but because it is drawn only on operational behavior, it can be used in cases where safety is not required to provide more precise information relative to a specific operational profile or set of executions than static analysis. The technique is call-based, and thus identifies impact at a coarser level than that provided by fine-grained analyses, but it is much more precise than call graph based analysis, and requires no dependence analysis. The instrumentation on which the technique is based has a relatively low overhead and can be performed on binaries, so the technique does not require access to source code. The technique also accommodates system evolution at relatively low cost.

We present results of a controlled experiment comparing `PathImpact` to transitive closure on call graphs and static slicing, in relation to a real software system, a large set of changes, and a wide range of inputs and test suites. The results of the experiment show that the technique can predict impact sets that are far more accurate than those computed by call graph analysis, and more precise (relative to the behavior expressed in a program's profile) than those computed by static slicing.

2. Costs-Benefits Tradeoffs for Dependency-Based Impact Analysis Techniques

Call graphs are commonly used by programmers to estimate the potential impact of software change [3]. The underlying assumption is that a change in some procedure p in program P has a potential change impact on any node reachable from p in P's call graph G. The transitive closure of G calculates all potential impact relationships between procedures in P under this assumption.

Call graphs are well understood and relatively easily constructed, and transitive closure on call graphs is simple to perform. However, calling behavior is much more complex than call graphs indicate. Calling behavior may include entering and exiting a procedure without calling any other procedures; entering a procedure, calling one other procedure and exiting; or entering a procedure and making any number of calls to many other procedures in any order. A call graph captures the local structure of potential calls by a single procedure, but ignores these other aspects of calls. As a result, call graph based analysis can lead to imprecise

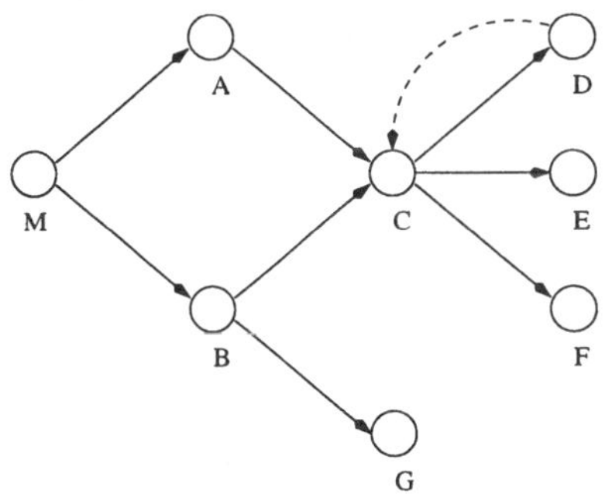

Figure 1. Example call graph. An arc from node *M* to node *A* denotes that procedure *M* may call procedure *A*; the dashed arc denotes a back-edge in the call graph and signals the presence of recursion.

impact sets. For example, in the call graph in Figure 1, *M* transitively calls all other procedures in the program. We cannot determine from the call graph what conditions cause propagation of change impact from *M* to other procedures.

Another limitation of the call graph is that it does not capture impact propagation due to procedure returns. Suppose we propose to change *E*. The effects of the change could propagate through returns to *C*, *B*, *A*, and *M*. A typical call graph has no information on returns, and inferring such information may cause errors. We can infer that *E* returns to *C*; however, we cannot infer whether, following the return to *C*, impact propagates into *A*, *B*, both, or neither.

In contrast to call-graph based techniques, techniques based on static slicing rely on calculation of fine-grained dependency relationships. Static slicing is conservative (safe); it accounts for all possible program inputs and behaviors. When safety is required, this conservatism is important; however, impact analyses that rely on the results may return large impact sets of little use to maintainers. More important, these sets may claim the existence of impacts that do not occur relative to the expected operational profile of the system; for non-safety-critical systems, it may be more cost-effective to consider impact relative to expected usage.

Dynamic slicing overcomes these drawbacks of static slicing by focusing on static dependencies that have been involved in program executions, at the potential cost of safety. Both dynamic slicing and static slicing, however, require fine-grained dependence analysis entailing additional expense in computational support and instrumentation.

Further, fine-grained analysis of dependencies may be inappropriate in many predictive impact analysis situations. Predictive impact analysis requires maintainers to specify the approximate location of changes, but knowing the precise statements that will require modification, and the precise variables that will be involved in those modifications, may not be practical. Further, when modifications involve deleting code, it may not be obvious what slicing criteria to invoke, at the fine-grained level, to predict potential impact.

Working at the coarser-grained level of functions or methods simplifies the impact analysis task, because it requires maintainers to determine only a set of functions or methods that will be changed, and not the precise syntax of the required changes. This suggests that analysis at the level of calls may be more appropriate in practice.

Finally, call-graph based and slicing-based approaches all rely on access to source code to determine the static calling structure of or dependencies in that code. In practice, systems often contain or consist primarily of components for which source code is not available. Approaches for analyzing binaries may lessen this problem, but another alternative is not to analyze them at all, but simply to instrument them, and it is this alternative that we consider.

3. Dynamic, Whole Program Path-Based Impact Analysis

The use of dynamic path information collected at the level of procedure calls helps address the foregoing problems. Our approach can be summarized as follows: if we propose to change procedure p, we concern ourselves only with impact that may propagate down any (and only) dynamic paths that have been observed to pass through p. Therefore, any procedure that is called after p, and any procedure which is on the call stack after p returns, is included in the set of potentially impacted procedures.

By examining program paths, yet limiting impact to observed call orders and call-return sequences, we can improve considerably on the precision of the more simple call graph based techniques, while also approaching the accuracy of more detailed techniques based on static slicing. Also, since program binaries can be instrumented [4, 20], we can avoid requiring program source code. While this approach remains subject to the limitations of dynamic information, it can yield impact sets that are more accurate relative to a specific operational profile.

As an example, suppose we have a single execution trace, shown by the string of letters along the top of Figure 2, for the program whose call graph appears in Figure 1. Function returns are represented in this string by r, and program exit by x. Informally, if we propose to change procedure E, we can estimate the dynamic impact of the change relative to this execution by searching *forward* in the trace to find procedures that are called directly or indirectly by E and procedures that are called after E returns. By searching *backward* in the trace we can discover the procedures E returns into. In the case of this trace, E makes no calls, but E returns into C, A, and M. E cannot return into D since D is immediately followed by a return, and likewise for B. Therefore, we can conclude that the set of potentially impacted procedures due to a change in E is { M, A, C, E }.

A small amount of bookkeeping is necessary to reconstruct the behavior of the program from a trace such as that

```
M B r A C D r E r r r r x
```

Figure 2. Single execution trace.

```
M B r A C D r E r r r r x M B G r r r x M B C F r r r r x
```

Figure 3. Multiple execution traces.

given in Figure 2. Unmatched function returns encountered in the trace determine which procedures are returned into. For example, counting forward from E we encounter three more returns (r) than procedure names (including E). This indicates that three functions were returned into. Searching backwards we pair the three unmatched returns with any procedure names that do not have associated returns. For instance, searching backward from E we look for three procedure names, but skip D and B because we encounter a return immediately before each of them indicating that they returned before E was called. (An alternative approach uses instrumentation that explicitly identifies the procedure responsible for each return. In this case impact can be estimated solely by searching forward in the trace. However, this has disadvantages which we discuss in Section 4.1.)

Multiple execution traces can be processed by concatenating traces, and proceeding in the same manner as for a single trace, but not crossing the termination symbol while searching either forwards or backwards. For example, Figure 3 shows a series of execution traces. If we propose to change G, the potentially impacted procedures are G,B, and M. If we propose to change C the potentially impacted set is { M, A, B, C, E } from the first trace and { M, B, C, F } from the third trace, giving a union of { M, A, B, C, E, F }.

An obvious difficulty with this approach involves tracking executed paths, since traces of this sort may be long. Therefore, practical techniques must restrict the length of traces to be viable. In the next section we show how methods for compressing traces [15] can be used to greatly reduce the size of the trace, constructing a directed acyclic graph representation called a whole path DAG [8]. Then we present algorithms that calculate impact directly from this DAG. We further show how this DAG can be incrementally updated, facilitating its continued use for impact analysis as a program and its operational profile evolve.

4. Algorithms

Our technique requires programs to be instrumented at procedure (or method) entry and exit. This produces a trace containing procedure names, function returns, and program exits in the order in which they occur across multiple executions. The `SEQUITUR` data compression algorithm [15] is used to reduce the size of the trace that is collected, generating a grammar. The whole path DAG representation developed by Larus [8] is used to represent the grammar. We next review the SEQUITUR data compression algorithm focusing on its application in our context, and its representation as a whole path DAG; then, in Section 4.2 we present our dynamic impact algorithms and algorithms for incrementally updating the DAG.

4.1. The SEQUITUR data compression algorithm and whole path DAG

The SEQUITUR algorithm examines a trace generated by a program and removes redundancies in the observed sequence of events by creating a grammar that can *exactly* regenerate the original trace. The trace may contain loops and backedges. SEQUITUR is an online algorithm – this means it can process traces as they are generated, rather than requiring the entire trace to be available. To facilitate re-use of the collected trace, only the resulting SEQUITUR grammar need be stored.

Figure 4 displays the SEQUITUR algorithm.[2] The algorithm constructs a grammar by appending each token seen to the end of rule $\mathcal{T}$ and searching the resulting rule and all other production rules for redundancy. If the tail of the new end of the compressed trace matches any of the production rules the appropriate substitution is made. Then, if any redundancy is found a new production rule is added and substituted in the compressed trace. The algorithm also checks each time a replacement is made to ensure that each production rule is used more than once. If any rule is used just once its production is substituted where it is used and the rule is removed from the grammar. This prevents the retention of rules that do not contribute to compression.

In our case, we apply this algorithm to a set of one or more concatenated traces, each consisting of tokens indicating calls and returns, as shown in Figure 3. Each individual trace is terminated by a special symbol x, generated by the instrumented program on exit. For an example of the SEQUITUR algorithm's operation, consider the trace shown in Figure 3. The rule $\mathcal{T}$ is initially empty:

$\mathcal{T} \rightarrow$

Using the program trace shown in Figure 3 the algorithm begins appending symbols, starting with M and continuing until it finds a duplicate digram:

$\mathcal{T} \rightarrow MBrACDrErrrr$

At each step the algorithm checks to see if the last two tokens (a digram) in the string are duplicated (without overlap). In this case rr appears twice, so the algorithm constructs a grammar rule and applies it to $\mathcal{T}$ (we use numbers as tokens to denote production rules, to distinguish them from the tokens in the execution traces):

$\mathcal{T} \rightarrow MBrACDrE11$
$1 \rightarrow rr$

[2] We present the algorithm given in [15]; in [8] Larus introduces a modification to the SEQUITUR algorithm which we have not used.

```
algorithm SEQUITUR( S )
input     Execution Trace S
output    Grammar G

    Grammar G
    Rule T
    for each token in S
      append token to end of production for T
      if duplicate digram appears
        if other occurrence is a rule g in G
          replace new digram with non-terminal of g.
        else
          form a new rule and replace duplicate
          digrams with the new non-terminal.
      if any rule in G is used only once
        remove the rule by substituting the production.
    return G
```

Figure 4. SEQUITUR algorithm.

After applying the new rule the algorithm continues appending tokens and seeking redundancies. In this case another redundancy, MB, is found, and a second rule is created:

$\mathcal{T} \rightarrow 2rACDrE11x2$
$1 \rightarrow rr$
$2 \rightarrow MB$

The grammar is complete when there are no more tokens to process; in this case the result is:

$\mathcal{T} \rightarrow 2rACDrE113G43CF4rx$
$1 \rightarrow rr$
$2 \rightarrow MB$
$3 \rightarrow x2$
$4 \rightarrow 1r$

Following processing, the resulting grammar for these traces contains terminals (function names, r, and x) and rules, that can contain both terminals and other rules.

The SEQUITUR algorithm runs in time $O(N)$, where N is the trace length. The size of the compressed trace is $O(N)$ worst case (no compression possible) and $O(\log N)$ best case [15]. Programs containing loops may generate extremely long traces; however, loops will introduce redundancies that SEQUITUR takes advantage of.

The SEQUITUR grammar can be stored as it is constructed in the form of a *whole path DAG* [8]. Each node in the whole path DAG is a rule in the SEQUITUR grammar. A directed acyclic graph is constructed by connecting the members of each production rule to their rule or non-terminal node. The whole path DAG for the above SEQUITUR grammar is shown in Figure 5. Note that the outgoing edges from any node are ordered by the members of the production rule. The size of the whole path DAG is equal to the size of the SEQUITUR grammar plus the sum of the lengths of the production rules, since each DAG node represents a grammar rule and the sum of the lengths of the production rules equals the number of DAG edges.

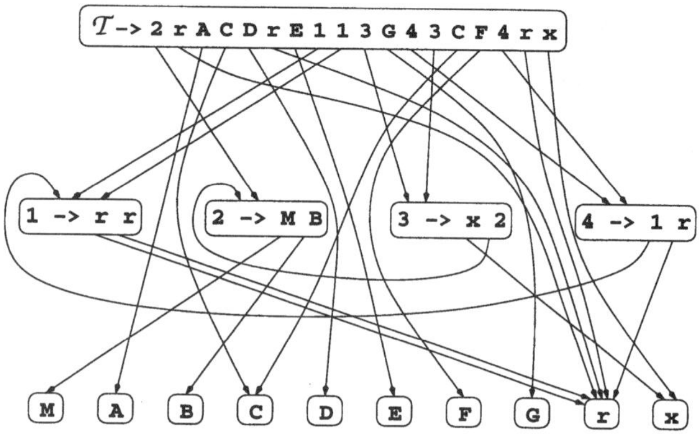

Figure 5. Whole path DAG.

4.2. Path impact algorithm

The PathImpact algorithm for estimating impact is shown in Figure 6. One way to visualize its operation is to consider beginning at a procedure node in the DAG, and ascending through the DAG performing recursive forward and backward in-order traversals at each node, stopping when any trace termination symbol is found. Traversing the DAG in this manner yields an impact set equivalent to that which would result by traversing the uncompressed traces.

Any changed procedure is a terminal, so PathImpact begins at that terminal, ascending upwards in the DAG searching forward for procedures that were called after the changed procedure, and searching backward for procedures that are returned into. This is implemented in the function up shown in Figure 7. The integer *act.stat* is used to signal the end of an execution trace and set the Boolean values of *fwd* and *bwd* accordingly. Up uses two functions, forward and backward, to search for terminals in the grammar that should be added to the impact set *I*; these functions are shown in Figures 8 and 9, respectively.

The integers *act.retn* and *act.skip* perform the necessary bookkeeping functions while searching forward, governing which functions are returned into while searching backward. Forward matches function names and returns, and passes the number of unmatched returns to backward in the structure named *act* and variable named *retn*.

Backward uses *act.retn* to determine how many procedures to include in the impact set. When Backward has added a number of procedures equal to *act.retn*, the search backwards in this trace can stop. Backward must also match function returns and names while searching backwards, since functions that return before the changed function is executed cannot be returned into. The variable *skip* controls this by incrementing when a return is encountered and decrementing when a procedure name is found. Procedures are added to *I* when *skip* is zero.

Since the SEQUITUR grammar forms a DAG, and a DAG has no cycles, the traversal performed by PathImpact must terminate. It is relatively easy to verify that PathImpact is correct for an uncompressed trace such as the one given in Figure 3. Since the SEQUITUR grammar exactly reproduces the uncompressed trace, the introduction of intermediate nodes in the DAG due to the formation of grammar rules does not affect the ability to retrieve the trace via the graph traversal. Since each trace records a sequence of actual calls and returns the calling context is always preserved. As long as the trace termination symbols are always appended to the end of each execution, and as long as they are honored while searching, PathImpact computes the predictive impact set outlined in Section 3.

```
algorithm PathImpact( G, c )
input     Whole Path DAG G
input     Changed Procedure c
output    Impact Set, I
    struct Action contains:
        integer skip = initially 0
        integer retn = initially 0
        integer stat = initially 0
    Set I = set of potentially impacted procedures, initially empty.
    boolean fwd = initially true.
    boolean bwd = initially true.
    Action act.
    if node c exists in G
      add c to I
      for each node p whose production contains c
        up( p, c, fwd, bwd, act )
```

Figure 6. PathImpact **algorithm.**

```
algorithm up(p, c, fwd, bwd, act )
input     Node p
input     Node c
input     boolean fwd
input     boolean bwd
input     Action act
output    Action
    Node t
    if( fwd == true )
      t = c
      while t has a successor in prod rule of p
        t = successor of t
        act = forward( t, act )
        if( act.stat == -1 )
          fwd = false
          break
    if( bwd == true )
      t = c
      while t has a predecessor in prod rule of p
        t = predecessor of t
        act = backward( t, act )
        if( act.stat == -1 )
          bwd = false
          break
    if( fwd == false AND bwd == false )
      act.stat = -1
      return act
    for each node q whose production contains p
      up( q, p, fwd, bwd, act )
```

Figure 7. Up **function in** PathImpact.

```
algorithm forward( g, act )
input    Node g
input    Action act
output   Action
    Node t
    if( g is a procedure )
        if( g is a program exit )
            act.stat = -1
            return act
        if( g is a function return )
            act.retn++
            return act
        add g to I
        act.retn–
        return act
    t = first element of production rule of g
    act = forward( t, act )
    if( act.stat == DONE )
        return act
    while t has a successor in prod rule of g
        t = successor of t
        act = forward( t, act )
        if( act.stat == DONE )
            return act
    return act
```

Figure 8. `Forward` **function in** `PathImpact`.

Applying `PathImpact(E)` to the whole path DAG in Figure 5 for a proposed change in procedure E, the algorithm first adds E to the impact set, I. Next, since the only rule whose production contains E is the rule $\mathcal{T}$, `PathImpact` calls `up(`$\mathcal{T}$`,E,true,true,act)`. Procedure `up` searches forward to find procedures directly and transitively called by E. The immediate successor of E in rule $\mathcal{T}$ is *1*, therefore up calls `forward(1,act)`. `Forward` searches recursively for the end-of-trace symbol, x, and counts returns. The production rule for *1* results in two calls of `forward(r,act)`. The value of *act.retn* after these two calls is 2. Then control returns to up in rule $\mathcal{T}$, where the next successor of E is considered. Since the next successor is another *1*, another call of `forward(1,act)` and two more calls of `forward(r,act)` result, and the value of *act.retn* is 4. The next successor in the production rule for $\mathcal{T}$ is *3*. `Forward(3,act)` causes a call to `forward(x,act)`. Since x is the end-of-trace symbol, `forward` sets *act.stat* to -1 and returns. The value of *act.stat* causes up to break out of the forward searching loop, set the value of *fwd* to false, and begin searching backwards for procedures that E returns into.

`Backward` uses the value of *act.retn* and its own count of return symbols encountered, *act.skip*, to determine which procedures in the trace are actually returned into. The search starts by calling `backward(r,act)` since r is the immediate predecessor of E in the production for rule $\mathcal{T}$. Since r is a procedure return `Backward` increments the value of *act.skip*. The subsequent call, `backward(D,act)`, decrements *act.skip* rather than adding D to the impact set I. The next predecessor in the production for rule $\mathcal{T}$ is the procedure C. Execution of the call `backward(C,act)` adds procedure C to the impact set and decrements *act.retn*. Subsequent calls to `backward(2,act)` result in the addition of A and M to the impact set I and the decrementing of *act.retn* to 1. An execution that terminated abnormally would count fewer returns in *act.retn* and, consequently, cause `backward` to terminate sooner. In this example, since there is no next predecessor, the algorithm ends. The resulting impact set for `PathImpact(E)` is { M, A, C, E }.

```
algorithm backward( g, act )
input    Node g
input    Action act
output   Action
    Node t
    if( g is a procedure )
        if( g is a program exit )
            act.stat = -1
            return act
        if( g is a procedure return )
            act.skip++
            return act
        if( act.skip > 0 )
            act.skip–
            return act
        if( act.retn > 0 )
            add g to I
            act.retn–
            return act
    t = last element of production rule of g
    act = backward( t, act )
    if( act.stat == DONE )
        return act
    while t has a predecessor in prod rule of g
        t = predecessor of t
        act = backward( t, act )
        if( act.stat == DONE )
            return act
    return act
```

Figure 9. `Backward` **function in** `PathImpact`.

Similarly, `PathImpact(G)` results in the impact set { M, B, G } and `PathImpact(F)` results in the set { M, B, C, F }. The worst-case running time of `PathImpact` is $O(N)$, where N is the uncompressed length of the concatenated traces. `PathImpact` does not require additional space above that required by the whole path DAG.

We are also interested in the ability to incrementally update a whole path DAG as a program and its operational profile evolve. Adding a trace to the whole path DAG can be easily accomplished due to the on-line nature of the `SEQUITUR` algorithm. Removing a trace simply involves deleting a section of the compressed trace and associated edges and adjusting the grammar. Adjusting traces in response to a deleted procedure requires removing traces containing that procedure from the whole path DAG, via simple modification of `PathImpact`. Beginning at the procedure that has been removed from the system, we search upwards, forwards, and backwards locating the traces where the procedure occurs and then remove each trace from the DAG. Addition of a procedure requires identification of traces containing procedures changed to call that procedure; these can then be deleted per the foregoing approach and collected again, and new versions inserted as above.

Finally, we return to a point raised in Section 3, where we mentioned the possibility of altering the instrumentation to explicitly identify returning procedures rather than returning a common symbol. Doing so can reduce the cost of searching the DAG, since we then need to search only in a forward direction. However, doing so would also approximately double the size of the traces considered, since each return would require a procedure name plus a special character to indicate a return. Also, pairs of returns would no longer match other pairs of returns unless they were associated with the same two procedures, in the same order, reducing possibilities for compression.

Therefore, a tradeoff exists between the cost of searching and the amount of compression obtainable. The SEQUITUR grammars generated in our experiments (see Section 5) were reduced to approximately one fifth of the average trace size of 1 MB. Larus reports reducing a 2GB trace to approximately 100 MB [8]. We would intuitively expect SEQUITUR to achieve better compression on larger traces. Due to the large number of SEQUITUR grammars generated in our experiments we have chosen to emphasize possible compression over a reduction in searching.

5. Empirical Validation

The research questions we wish to investigate are whether PathImpact computes an appropriate impact set relative to a specific operational profile or set of dynamic executions, and how that impact set compares to those computed by dependency-based impact analysis algorithms. To investigate these questions we performed an experiment comparing the impact sets calculated by PathImpact to those calculated by approaches based on transitive closure on the call graph and function-level static slicing.

5.1. Experiment materials

As an subject for our experiment we used a program developed for the European Space Agency; we refer to this program as space. Space is an interpreter for an antenna array definition language (ADL). Space has approximately 6200 non-blank, non-comment lines of C code and 136 functions. The developers of Space found 33 faults during the program's development. We found five additional faults [18]. We created 38 single fault versions, each containing one of the known faults. We excluded two versions that could not be analyzed by our tools.[3] The remaining 36 versions served as our experiment subjects, allowing us to model a process of performing predictive impact analysis on a function in which a fault is about to be corrected.

To provide input sets for use in determining dynamic behavior, we used test cases created for space for earlier experiments [18]. These test cases consisted of 10,000 randomly generated test cases and 3,585 test cases generated by hand to ensure coverage of every branch in the program by at least 30 test cases. This pool of test cases was used to generate 1000 branch coverage adequate test suites containing on average approximately 150 test cases each. We randomly selected 50 of these test suites. The selected test suites in aggregate contained 7773 test cases including 2886 duplicates. To examine impact on single executions, we eliminated the duplicate test cases to obtain another set of 4887 individual test cases. We collected execution trace information for the individual test cases and for the test suites.

5.2. Experiment methodology

5.2.1 Measures

As discussed in Sections 1 and 3, the transitive closure and static dependency-based slicing techniques for impact analysis may over- or underestimate change impact, relative to a specific set of program behaviors as captured in a profile, a specific execution, or a test suite. Overestimates force maintainers to spend additional, unneeded time investigating potential impacts; underestimates may cause maintainers to omit, in their investigations, important potential impacts.

Thus, in this study, we examine these over- and underestimates. To do this, we compare the relative size and contents of the impact sets computed by transitive closure, PathImpact for single program executions, PathImpact for test suites, and function-level static slicing, for each of the faulty versions of space.

5.2.2 Impact analysis techniques

To calculate static function-level slices for each version we used the Codesurfer tool by *GrammaTech*.[4] In Codesurfer a function-level static forward slice uses all the dependencies identified by data and control dependence analysis in the changed procedure or procedures to identify dependent functions. We implemented the algorithm for impact analysis based on transitive closure, and we implemented the PathImpact algorithm.

5.2.3 Design

In this experiment, the three impact analysis techniques are our independent variables. Our dependent variables are the sets of functions identified as impacted by each technique.

We applied each impact analysis techniques to each version of space, calculating the number of functions that would be returned as potentially impacted by correction of

[3] On one version, the fault caused it to crash on nearly all executions, so no usable traces were produced. On a second version, the Codesurfer tool was unable to calculate accurate dependencies for a large array.

[4] Available from: GrammaTech, Inc. 317 North Aurora Street Ithaca, NY 14850, or http://www.grammatech.com.

the faulty function. For the transitive closure and function-level slice techniques this calculation was performed only once per version, since they are static and not dependent on test executions. For the PathImpact algorithm, we applied the algorithm once for each of the 4887 tests for each version. From the impact set resulting from each test, we calculated the differences between impact sets. The results for suites is based on the DAG created by concatenating all the executions from tests in a suite, including duplicates.

5.2.4 Threats to validity

We have studied only one program and set of changes, and we cannot claim that these are representative of programs and changes generally. Also, our tests do not represent operational profiles, and the test suites we use represent only one type of suite that could be found in practice. Additional studies of other programs, change distributions, and types of inputs are needed to address such threats to external validity. However, space is a "real world" program and its faults are actual faults, its test suites constitute one type of suite that could be used in practice.

A second concern involves our measures of impact. We would like to know how the impact sets returned by our algorithm correlate with true dynamic impact over the test suites. Such a measure would be difficult to obtain, however, given the general undecidability of precisely determining impact, and would most likely have to be accomplished at least partially through expensive and error-prone human calculations. However, our comparisons of the sets returned by various impact analysis techniques provide important perspective on their relative power.

Finally, we have considered only one static slicing implementation; other implementations may obtain different results. Also we have not yet compared our technique to dynamic slicing techniques, since no implementations were readily available and an appropriate implementation will require considerable effort to create. However, we intend to accomplish such a comparison in the future.

5.3. Analysis and results

We now present our results, beginning by presenting and discussing data. Section 5.4 discusses implications.

5.3.1 Data

Figure 10 provides a view of the data we collected. Column one lists the version of space. Column 2 (**TC**) shows the size of the impact set resulting from transitive closure. The columns under the heading "**Individual Traces**" list measures of the impact set calculated by the PathImpact algorithm relative to the size and contents of the transitive closure set and static slicing set using individual program executions. The columns under the heading "**Test Suites**" show the same for executions of entire test suites. The column heading **PI/TC** is the average ratio of the size of the PathImpact set to the size of the transitive closure set. **PI-TC** is the average number of functions that are members of the PathImpact set, but not members of the transitive closure impact set. Likewise, **TC-PI** is the average number of functions that are members of the transitive closure impact set, but not members of the PathImpact set. **PI/FS** is the average ratio of the size of the PathImpact set to the size of the static slicing impact set. **PI-FS** is the average number of functions that are members of the PathImpact set, but are not members of the static slicing impact set. Similarly, **FS-PI** is the average number of functions that are members of the static slicing impact set, but not members of the PathImpact set. All of the average measures are obtained across either the sets of individual test executions, or the sets of test suites. We have calculated ratios so that the results can be compared across versions and test suites.

5.3.2 Analysis of impact sets

As Figure 10 shows, the transitive closure sets included far fewer procedures than those of the other two impact approaches. On examination of the changes it can be seen that this is due to the locations of the changed procedures in the call graph, most of which were relatively "deep" in the call graph (with the exception of version 30). The impact set calculated using PathImpact generally included (on average) many more procedures, and the set calculated using function-level static slicing contained the most.

Figure 11 contains a scatter-plot comparing sizes of the PathImpact sets to the sizes of the corresponding function-level static slice sets, for both test suite and individual test executions. Most of the data points lie on or below the $x = y$ line, with the exception of some of the cases involving versions 19, 20, and 21, which we discuss below. This graphically shows that PathImpact using single program executions calculates generally smaller sets than function-level static slicing with an increasing difference in the set sizes as the set size gets larger. PathImpact sets using test suite execution displayed a somewhat wider range of differences, with maximums approximately equal to the size of the static slicing impact sets.

We calculated paired t-test statistics between each of the four impact sets. In each of the comparisons the t-statistic was outside of the 95% confidence interval, the p-value was zero, and the null hypothesis (that the sets had the same mean) was rejected.

To directly compare the size of the **PI** sets with the size of the **TC** and **FS** sets across program versions we expressed the size of **PI** as a percent of **TC** or **FS** for each of the single execution impact sets and for the 50 test suites. Columns 3, 7, 10, and 14 in Figure 10 show the average relative size of **PI** for each version.

The **PI** sets were considerably larger than the **TC** sets, four and a half times larger in the case of single traces and nine and a half times larger for the test suites, and displayed

Vers	TC	Individual Traces							Test Suites							
		PI/TC	PI-TC	TC-PI	PI	PI/FS	PI-FS	FS-PI	PI/TC	PI-TC	TC-PI	PI	PI/FS	PI-FS	FS-PI	FS
1	3	14.8	41.6	0.0	44.6	0.45	1.0	55.4	33.0	96.0	0.0	99.0	1.00	1.0	1.0	99
2	3	16.6	46.8	0.0	49.8	0.44	1.0	64.2	36.5	106.4	0.0	109.4	0.97	1.0	4.6	113
3	2	22.4	42.8	0.0	44.8	0.37	1.0	76.2	56.5	111.0	0.0	113.0	0.94	1.0	8.0	120
4	3	6.0	14.9	0.0	13.0	0.18	1.0	82.1	6.3	16.0	6.3	19.0	0.19	1.0	81.0	99
5	3	4.6	10.9	0.0	13.9	0.18	1.0	100.1	7.0	18.0	0.0	21.0	0.18	1.0	93.0	113
6	2	8.0	14.0	0.0	16.0	0.13	1.0	105.0	15.5	28.6	0.0	30.6	0.26	1.0	90.4	120
7	4	1.8	5.4	2.2	7.3	0.40	0.5	11.2	4.1	13.3	1.0	16.3	0.90	1.0	2.7	18
8	3	1.7	3.2	1.2	5.0	0.72	0.5	2.5	2.7	5.0	0.0	8.0	1.14	1.0	0.0	7
9	6	2.9	14.0	2.6	17.4	0.51	0.7	17.3	5.4	27.7	1.0	32.7	0.96	1.0	2.3	34
10	4	4.1	14.4	2.1	16.4	0.48	0.6	18.2	7.0	25.0	1.0	28.0	0.82	1.0	7.0	34
11	5	3.2	13.0	2.0	16.0	0.47	0.4	18.4	6.4	28.1	1.0	32.1	0.94	1.0	2.9	34
12	4	3.4	12.6	3.0	13.6	0.52	0.5	12.9	3.6	13.6	3.0	14.6	0.56	0.7	12.1	26
13	14	1.6	13.4	5.0	22.4	0.55	0.7	19.3	2.9	29.0	2.0	41.0	1.00	2.0	2.0	41
14	6	4.5	21.3	0.2	27.1	0.40	1.0	41.9	10.9	59.7	0.0	65.7	0.96	1.0	3.3	68
15	6	3.2	14.0	0.6	19.4	0.31	1.0	44.6	7.7	40.4	0.0	46.4	0.74	1.0	17.6	63
16	7	0.9	3.7	4.4	6.3	0.57	0.5	5.3	1.6	5.0	1.0	11.0	1.00	1.0	1.0	11
17	6	3.7	17.2	1.0	22.2	0.52	0.6	21.4	6.9	36.2	1.0	41.2	0.96	1.0	2.8	43
18	4	3.8	12.6	1.0	15.6	0.56	0.5	12.9	4.2	13.6	1.0	16.6	0.59	0.7	12.1	28
19	1	4.0	3.0	0.0	4.0	1.33	1.0	0.0	1.3	3.0	0.0	4.0	1.33	1.0	0.0	3
20	1	7.0	6.0	0.0	7.0	1.17	1.0	0.0	6.9	5.9	0.0	6.9	1.14	1.0	0.1	6
21	1	7.0	6.0	0.0	7.0	1.17	1.0	0.0	6.9	5.9	0.0	6.9	1.14	1.0	0.1	6
22	5	1.7	4.8	1.4	8.4	0.93	1.8	2.4	1.9	5.5	1.0	9.5	1.05	2.0	1.5	9
23	1	10.7	9.7	0.0	10.8	0.60	1.0	8.2	16.4	15.4	0.0	16.4	0.91	1.0	2.6	18
24	14	1.6	13.2	5.0	22.3	0.52	0.6	21.3	3.0	29.0	1.0	42.0	0.98	1.0	2.0	43
25	6	1.1	5.0	4.3	6.8	0.21	0.2	25.5	4.8	25.8	3.0	28.8	0.90	1.0	4.2	32
26	18	2.0	26.3	8.4	35.9	0.40	0.9	55.0	5.0	72.9	1.0	89.9	1.00	1.0	1.1	90
27	7	0.9	3.7	4.4	6.3	0.57	0.6	5.3	1.6	5.0	1.0	11.0	1.00	1.0	1.0	11
28	17	1.9	20.5	4.7	32.8	0.42	1.0	47.2	3.9	50.0	0.0	67.0	0.85	1.0	13.0	79
30	16	0.4	0.0	10.2	5.8	0.07	0.0	73.2	0.8	0.0	3.5	12.5	0.16	0.0	66.5	79
31	12	2.1	17.0	4.1	24.9	0.23	1.0	85.1	7.7	81.7	1.0	92.7	0.85	1.0	17.3	109
32	3	2.6	5.9	1.2	7.7	0.48	0.8	9.1	5.3	13.8	1.0	15.8	0.99	1.0	1.2	16
33	3	3.0	7.0	1.0	9.0	1.00	1.0	1.0	3.0	7.0	1.0	9.0	1.00	1.0	1.0	9
35	5	1.3	4.5	3.2	6.4	0.35	0.5	12.1	3.3	12.5	1.0	16.5	0.91	1.0	2.5	18
36	1	7.0	6.0	0.0	7.0	0.12	1.0	50.0	49.0	48.0	0.0	49.0	0.88	3.0	10.0	56
37	13	1.3	10.8	6.4	17.4	0.51	0.6	17.2	2.6	22.0	1.0	34.0	1.00	1.0	1.0	34
38	13	1.4	11.2	6.3	17.9	0.52	0.6	16.8	2.6	22.0	1.0	34.0	1.00	1.0	1.0	34
Avg		4.56				0.51			9.51				0.87			
Std Dev		4.78				0.29			13.12				0.27			

Figure 10. Impact sets and their relationships calculated in the experiment.

a large standard deviation. Averaged across all the versions the **PI** impact sets were about one half (51%) of the size of the **FS** impact sets using single executions and 87% of their size using test suites. In the case of versions 19, 20, and 21, **PI** was larger than **FS** by one function. On inspection we found that in every case the additional function was the same. This extra function executes near the end of nearly every test and has no static dependencies (its purpose is simply to pause program execution after displaying output to the screen). Since the function nearly always executes it is nearly always included in **PI**, but since it has no static dependencies it is never included in **FS**. In practice, maintainers familiar with the system could cause it to be excluded from future impact consideration.

5.4. Discussion

Our goal was to compare the impact sets calculated by our four target approaches when performing predictive impact analysis relative to a specific set of program behaviors captured by a specific input set. We now comment on some of the implications of our results.

The sets shown in Figure 10 show that `PathImpact` caught a large number of procedures which would be missed by transitive closure, but did not include as many

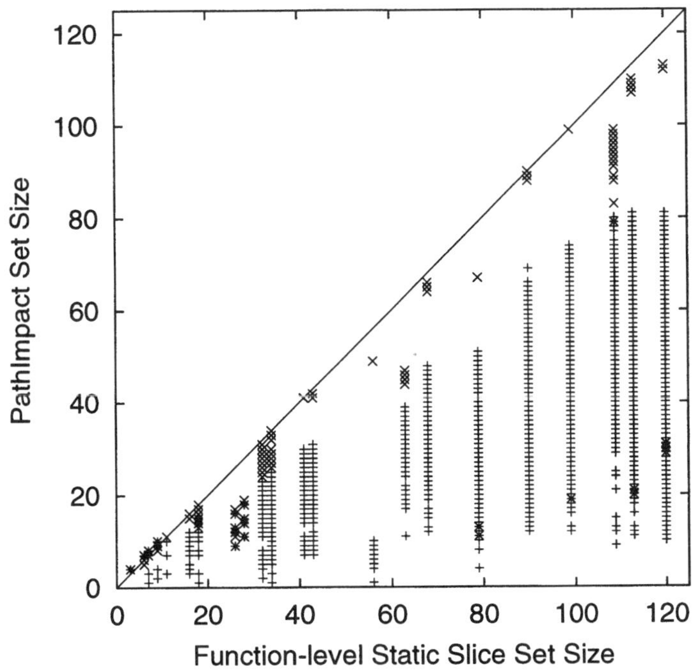

Figure 11. **Impact set size comparison. Single traces are shown as "+", suites are shown as "×".**

procedures as function-level static slicing. This is good on both counts since it is moderated by the fact that the included procedures *actually* executed, and thus could have propagated actual impact.

The impact sets observed for transitive closure were unreliable, having more to to with the location of the change in the call graph than the behavior of the program. This reinforces the notion that impact propagation is more dependent on the behavior of the program than the program's structure. `PathImpact` moderates the results of transitive closure and static slicing in cases where we have an interest in specific program behavior embodied in an operational profile or a specific set of tests.

Function-level static slicing is also, in some sense, a reflection of the program's structure. Static slices represent every possible behavior rather than actual behavior. In our experiments, this sometimes led to overestimation of change impact using static slicing. However, the test suites used, while showing considerable variation, often came remarkably close to agreement with the static slicing impact sets. Further, cases in which profile-based impact analysis overestimates impact are fewer, and the amount of overestimation is less, than with static slicing.

Of course, the extent to which the estimate from `PathImpact` matches actual impact is entirely dependent on the appropriateness of the operational profile or set of tests used. But it is these situations, where that appropriateness holds, that are our focus.

We have not presented execution time or slow-down statistics since our initial implementation processes stored traces with Java programs, rather than using a fully online implementation. A fully online implementation would build the DAG as the instrumentation executes and not save the uncompressed traces, and would be considerably more efficient than our prototype. Nonetheless, the simulation times we observed were relatively small. The time required to generate the DAG was less than one minute per test suite, and the time required to calculate an impact set was at most several seconds.

6 Conclusions and Future Work

The call graph of a program has severe limitations for predicting the impact of program changes. Static slicing is much more precise than transitive closure on call graphs, but may be expensive. It also may return unnecessarily large impact sets if the goal is to predict impact relative to a set of dynamic behaviors as present in a user profile or test suite.

We have thus introduced a new approach to function-level impact analysis, based on dynamic information obtained through simple program instrumentation. Our approach does not rely on availability of program source code and does not require static dependency calculations. In our approach dynamic traces are compressed using the `SEQUITUR` data compression algorithm [15], and a directed acyclic graph (DAG) is constructed following Larus [8]. We then use the `PathImpact` algorithm presented in this paper to predict dynamic change impact. The results of our experiment show that `PathImpact` can provide potentially more useful predictions of change impact than function-level static slicing in situations where specific program behavior is the focus.

Future work includes experimentation with a wider range of programs, an examination of the sensitivity of our techniques to test input data, and consideration of object-oriented and distributed programs. Future implementations will address performance issues such as program slowdown and impact calculation times. We also intend to investigate statistical measures of impact such as density functions for the predicted impact sets. While this research has investigated the application of an approach at the level of a procedure, we intend to apply this model to other levels, such as components. We intend to investigate scalability to large systems by adapting the local level of modeling according to various criteria, such as local usage or complexity measures. We also plan additional empirical comparisons with conventional dynamic slicing techniques. While typical dynamic slicing techniques operate at a different level (statement-level versus procedure-level) than our techniques, the behavior of impact analyses based on dynamic slicing may be more directly comparable to our techniques than those based on static slicing.

Eventually, a thorough understanding of our technique will require an examination of the return on investment (ROI) in practice. By this examination, we hope to determine the extent to which the technique can save software maintainer's time and improve the quality of systems undergoing maintenance.

Acknowledgements

This work was supported in part by the NSF Information Technology Research program under Award CCR-0080900 to Oregon State University. Phyllis Frankl, Alberto Pasquini, and Filip Vokolos provided the `space` program and randomly generated tests. A special thanks to Chengyun Chu for creating the additional tests for `space`.

References

[1] H. Agrawal and J. Horgan. Dynamic program slicing. In *Proceedings: SIGPLAN '90 Conference on Programming Language Design and Implementation. SIGPLAN Notices.*, pages 246–56, White Plains, June 1990. ACM.

[2] R. S. Arnold and S. A. Bohner. Impact analysis - towards a framework for comparison. In *Proceedings of the International Conference on Software Maintenance*, pages 292–301, Montreal, Que, Can, Sept. 1993. IEEE.

[3] S. Bohner and R. Arnold. *Software Change Impact Analysis.* IEEE Computer Society Press, Los Alamitos, CA, USA, 1996.

[4] C. Cifuentes and M. V. Emmerik. UQBT: Adaptable Binary Translation at Low Cost. *Computer*, 33(3):60–66, Mar. 2000.

[5] S. Horwitz, T. Reps, and D. Binkley. Interprocedural Slicing Using Dependence Graphs. *ACM Trans. Prog. Lang. Syst.*, 12(1):27–60, Jan. 1990.

[6] M. Kamkar. An Overview and Comparative Classification of Program Slicing Techniques. *Journal of Systems Software*, 31(3):197–214, 1995.

[7] B. Korel and J. Laski. Dynamic slicing in computer programs. *Journal of Systems Software*, 13(3):187–95, 1990.

[8] J. Larus. Whole Program Paths. In *Proc. SIGPLAN PLDI 99*, pages 1–11, Atlanta, GA, May 1999. ACM.

[9] M. Lee. *Change Impact Analysis of Object-Oriented Software.* Ph.D. dissertation, George Mason University, Feb. 1999.

[10] M. Lee, A. J. Offutt, and R. T. Alexander. Algorithmic Analysis of the Impacts of Changes to Object-oriented Software. In *TOOLS-34 '00*, 2000.

[11] L. Li and A. J. Offutt. Algorithmic analysis of the impact of changes to object-oriented software. In *Proceedings of the International Conference on Software Maintenance*, pages 171–184, Monterey, CA, USA, Nov. 1996. IEEE.

[12] M. Lindvall and K. Sandahl. How well do experienced software developers predict software change? *Journal of Systems and Software*, 43(1):19–27, Oct. 1998.

[13] J. L. Lions. ARIANE 5, Flight 501 Failure, Report by the Inquiry Board. *European Space Agency*, July 1996.

[14] J. P. Loyall, S. A. Mathisen, and C. P. Satterthwaite. Impact analysis and change management for avionics software. In *Proceedings of IEEE National Aerospace and Electronics Conference, Part 2*, pages 740–747, Dayton, OH, July 1997.

[15] C. Nevill-Manning and I. Witten. Linear-time, incremental hierarchy inference for compression. In *Proc Data Compression Conference (DDC 97)*, pages 3–11. IEEE, 1997.

[16] S. L. Pfleeger. *Software Engineering: Theory and Practice.* Prentice Hall, Englewood Cliffs, NJ, 1998.

[17] A. Podgurski and L. Clarke. A formal model of program dependences and its implications for software testing, debugging, and maintenance. *IEEE Trans. Softw. Eng.*, 16(9):965–79, Sept. 1990.

[18] G. Rothermel, R. H. Untch, C. Chu, and M. J. Harrold. Test Case Prioritization: An Empirical Study. In *Proceedings of the International Conference on Software Maintenance*, pages 179–188, Oxford, UK, Sept. 1999.

[19] B. G. Ryder and F. Tip. Change impact analysis for object-oriented programs. In *ACM SIGPLAN – SIGSOFT workshop on on Program analysis for software tools and engineering*, pages 46–53. ACM Press, 2001.

[20] A. Srivastava, A. Edwards, and H. Vo. Vulcan: Binary Transformation in a Distributed Environment. Technical Report MSR-TR-2001-50, Microsoft Research, 2001.

[21] F. Tip. A survey of program slicing techniques. *Journal of Programming Languages*, 3:121–189, 1995.

[22] R. J. Turver and M. Munro. Early impact analysis technique for software maintenance. *Journal of Software Maintenance: Research and Practice*, 6(1):35–52, Jan. 1994.

[23] M. Weiser. Program slicing. In *5th International Conference on Software Engineering*, pages 439–49, San Diego, CA, Mar. 1981. IEEE.

Precise Dynamic Slicing Algorithms*

Xiangyu Zhang Rajiv Gupta
The University of Arizona
Dept. of Computer Science
Tucson, Arizona 85721

Youtao Zhang
The Univ. of Texas at Dallas
Dept. of Computer Science
Richardson, TX 75083

Abstract

Dynamic slicing algorithms can greatly reduce the debugging effort by focusing the attention of the user on a relevant subset of program statements. In this paper we present the design and evaluation of three precise *dynamic slicing algorithms called the full preprocessing (FP), no preprocessing (NP) and limited preprocessing (LP) algorithms. The algorithms differ in the relative timing of constructing the dynamic data dependence graph and its traversal for computing requested dynamic slices. Our experiments show that the LP algorithm is a fast and practical precise slicing algorithm. In fact we show that while precise slices can be orders of magnitude smaller than imprecise dynamic slices, for small number of slicing requests, the LP algorithm is faster than an imprecise dynamic slicing algorithm proposed by Agrawal and Horgan.*

1. Introduction

The concept of program slicing was first introduced by Mark Weiser [10]. He introduced program slicing as a debugging aid and gave the first *static slicing* algorithm. Since then a great deal of research has been conducted on static slicing and an excellent survey of many of the proposed techniques and tools can be found in [8] and [5]. Other works on slicing have explored the applications of slicing in greater depth. Some examples of such works include the use of slicing in debugging sequential and distributed programs as well as testing sequential programs [2, 6].

It is widely recognized that for programs that make extensive use of pointers, the highly conservative nature of data dependency analysis leads to highly imprecise and considerably larger slices. For program debugging, where the objective of slicing is to reduce the debugging effort by focusing the attention of the user on the relevant subset of program statements, conservatively computed large slices are clearly undesirable. Recognizing the need for accurate slicing, Korel and Laski proposed the idea of *dynamic slicing* [7]. The data dependences that are exercised during a program execution are captured precisely and saved. Dynamic slices are constructed upon users requests by traversing the captured dynamic dependence information. An exception to this approach is various works on forward computation of dynamic slices [11, 12] which precompute all dynamic slices prior to users requests. While no experimental data is reported in [11, 12], the execution times of this approach can be expected to be high. Therefore in this paper we take the standard approach of computing only the dynamic slices requested by the user.

It has been shown that precise dynamic slices can be considerably smaller than static slices [9, 5]. The data in Table 1 shows the effectiveness of dynamic slicing. For each of the benchmark programs, we computed 25 distinct dynamic slices half way through the program's execution (`@Midpoint`) and another 25 at the end of program's execution (`@End`). The average (AVG), minimum (MIN) and maximum (MAX) precise dynamic slice sizes that were observed are given in the precise dynamic slices *PDS* column. In addition, the number of distinct statements in the program (*Static*) and the number of distinct statements that are executed (*Executed*) are also given. For example, program `126.gcc` contains 585491 static instructions and, during the collection of the execution trace, 170135 of these instructions were executed at least once. When 25 precise dynamic slices were computed, they had average, minimum and maximum sizes of 6614, 2, and 11860 instructions respectively. As we can see, the *PDS* values are much smaller that the *Static* and *Executed* values. Thus, dynamic slices greatly help in focusing the attention of the user to a small subset of statements during debugging.

While precise dynamic slices can be very useful, it is also well known that computing them is expensive. Therefore researchers have proposed *imprecise* dynamic slicing algorithms that trade-off precision of dynamic slicing with the costs of computing dynamic slicing. However, while such algorithms have the potential of reducing the cost of slicing,

*Supported by a grant from IBM and National Science Foundation grants CCR-0220334, CCR-0208756, CCR-0105355, and EIA-0080123 to the University of Arizona.

0-7695-1877-X/03 $17.00 © 2003 IEEE

Table 1. Effectiveness of Dynamic Slicing.

Program	Static	Instructions Executed	PDS			IDS-II/PDS			IDS-I/PDS		
			AVG	MIN	MAX	AVG	MIN	MAX	AVG	MIN	MAX
`126.gcc` @ End	585491	170135	6614	2	11860	2.01	1	5188.25	3.82	1.75	13759.5
`126.gcc` @ Midpoint	585491	144504	2325.8	2	7405	2.69	1	1953.25	6.60	1	4804.75
`099.go` @ End	95459	61350	5382	4	8449	1.20	1	946.30	2.27	1	3328.04
`099.go` @ Midpoint	95459	55538	3560	2	6900	1.43	1	1321.83	2.55	1	5353.50
`134.perl` @ End	116182	21451	765	2	2208	3.43	1	96.15	4.26	1	973.75
`134.perl` @ Midpoint	116182	20934	601	2	2208	3.04	1	813.5	4.80	1	953.25
`130.li` @ End	31829	10958	834	2	834	5.96	1	41.9	12.87	1	667.5
`130.li` @ Midpoint	31829	10429	48	2	584	17.33	1	1036.00	53.40	4.35	1339.5
`008.espresso` @ End	74039	27333	350	2	1304	3.90	1	48.57	5.54	1	1273.8
`008.espresso` @ Midpoint	74039	21027	295	2	1114	3.65	1	300.25	9.78	1	1133.75
Average						4.46	1	1174.6	10.59	1.41	3358.7

they have also been found to greatly increase reported slice sizes thus diminishing their effectiveness. In [3], Atkinson *et al.* use *dynamic points-to* data to improve the accuracy of slicing. Unfortunately, their studies indicate that "improved precision of points-to data generally did not translate into significantly reduced slices". In [4], Gupta and Soffa proposed *hybrid slicing* technique which uses limited amounts of control flow information. However, it does not address the imprecision in data dependency computation in presence of pointers. We implemented two imprecise algorithms, *Algorithm I* and *Algorithm II*, proposed by Agrawal and Horgan [1] and compared the sizes of the imprecise dynamic slices (*IDS-I* and *IDS-II*) with corresponding precise dynamic slices (*PDS*). The ratios *IDS-I/PDS* and *IDS-II/PDS* are given in Table 1. As we can see, imprecise slices can be many times larger than precise dynamic slices. In the worst case, for program `gcc`, the imprecise dynamic slice *IDS-II* was over 5188 times larger than the precise dynamic slice. The *IDS-I* sizes are even larger. Therefore, so far, all attempts to address the cost issue of dynamic slicing have yielded unsatisfactory results. Given the inaccuracy of imprecise slicing algorithms, we conclude that it is worthwhile to spend effort into designing efficient precise dynamic slicing algorithms.

We observe that once a program is executed and its execution trace collected, precise dynamic slicing typically involves two tasks: *[preprocessing]* which builds a dependence graph by recovering dynamic dependences from the program's execution trace; and *[slicing]* which computes slices for given slicing requests by traversing the dynamic dependence graph. We present three precise dynamic slicing algorithms that differ in the degree of preprocessing they carry out prior to computing any dynamic slices. The *full preprocessing* (*FP*) algorithm builds the entire dependence graph before slicing. The *no preprocessing* (*NP*) does not perform any preprocessing but rather during slicing it uses *demand driven analysis* for recovering dynamic dependencies and caches the recovered dependencies for potential future reuse. Finally the *limited preprocessing* (*LP*) algorithm performs some preprocessing to first augment the execution trace with summary information that allows faster traversal of the trace and then during slicing it uses demand driven analysis to recover the dynamic dependences from the compacted execution trace. Our experience with these algorithms shows:

- The FP algorithm is impractical for real programs because it runs out of memory during the preprocessing phase as the dynamic dependence graphs are extremely large. The NP algorithm does not run out of memory but is slow. The LP algorithm is practical because it never runs out of memory and is also fast.

- The execution time of the practical LP algorithm compares well with that of the imprecise *Algorithm II* proposed by Agrawal and Horgan. The LP algorithm is even faster than *Algorithm II* if a small number of slices are computed. Also, the latency of computing the first slice using LP is 2.31 to 16.16 times less than the latency for obtaining the first slice by *Algorithm II*.

Thus, this paper shows that while imprecise dynamic slicing algorithms are too imprecise and therefore not attractive, a carefully designed precise dynamic slicing algorithm such as the LP algorithm is practical as it provides precise dynamic slices at reasonable space and time costs.

The remainder of the paper is organized as follows. In section 2 we present the precise slicing algorithms. In section 3 we present our experimental studies. Related work is discussed in section 4. Conclusions are given in section 5.

2 Precise Dynamic Slicing

The basic approach to dynamic slicing is to execute the program once and produce an execution trace which is processed to construct dynamic data dependence graph that in turn is traversed to compute dynamic slices.

The *execution trace* captures the complete runtime information of the program's execution that can be used by a dynamic slicing algorithm – in other words, there is sufficient information in the trace to compute precise dynamic slices. The information that the trace holds is the full *control flow trace* and *memory reference trace*. Therefore we know the complete path followed during execution and each point where data is referenced through pointers we know the address from which data is accessed.

A *slicing request* can be specified both in terms of a program variable and in terms of a memory address. The latter is useful if the slice is to be computed with respect to a field of a specific instance of a dynamically allocated object. Data slices are computed by taking closure over data dependences while full slices are computed by taking closure over both data and control dependences.

For a dynamic slice to be computed, dynamic dependences that are exercised during the program execution must be identified by processing the trace. The precise algorithms that we present differ in the degree to which dependences are extracted from the trace prior to dynamic slicing. The *full preprocessing* (*FP*) algorithm follows an approach that is typical of precise algorithms proposed in the literature [7, 1]. The execution trace is fully preprocessed to extract all dependences and the full dynamic dependence graph is constructed. Given this graph, any dynamic slicing request can be handled by appropriate traversal of the graph. The *no preprocessing* (*NP*) algorithm does not precompute the full dynamic data dependence graph. Instead, dynamic data dependences are extracted in a *demand-driven* fashion from the trace during the handling of dynamic slicing requests. Therefore each time the execution trace is examined, only dependences relevant to the slice being computed are extracted from the trace. Finally the *limited preprocessing* (*LP*) algorithm differs from the *NP* algorithm in that it augments the execution trace with trace-block summaries to enable faster traversal of the execution trace during the demand-driven extraction of dynamic dependences. Next we describe the above algorithms in detail. Our discussion primarily focuses on data dependences because the presence of pointers primarily effects the computation of data dependences.

2.1 Full Preprocessing

In developing our slicing algorithms one goal that we set out to achieve was to develop a dynamic data dependence graph representation that would not only allow for computation of precise dynamic slices, but, in addition, support computation of a dynamic slice for any variable or memory address at *any execution point*. This property is not supported by the precise dynamic slicing algorithm of Agrawal and Horgan [1]. We take the statement level control flow graph representation of the program and add to it edges corresponding to the data dependences extracted from the execution trace. The *execution instances* of the statements involved in a dynamic data dependence are explicitly indicated on the dynamic data dependence edges thus allowing the above goal to be met.

Consider a situation of memory dependences between stores and loads. A statically distinct load/store instruction may be executed several times during program execution. When this happens different instances of a load instruction may be dependent upon different store instructions or different instances of the same store instruction. For precise recording of data dependences we associate the instances of load and store instructions among which dependences exist. A slicing request not only identifies the use of a variable by a statement for which the slice is needed, but also the specific instance of the statement for which the slice is needed.

Consider the example shown below in which we assume that the load instruction is executed twice. The first instance of the load reads the value stored by the store on the left and the second instance of the load reads the value stored by the store on the right. In order to remember this information we label the edge from the load to the store on the left/right with (1,1)/(2,1) indicating that the first/second instance of the load's execution gets its value from first instance of execution of the store on the left/right respectively. Therefore when we include the load in the dynamic slice, we do not necessarily include both the stores in the dynamic slice. If the dynamic slice for the first instance of the load is being computed, then the store on the left is added to the slice while if the dynamic slice of the second instance of the load is being computed then the store on the right is added to the slice.

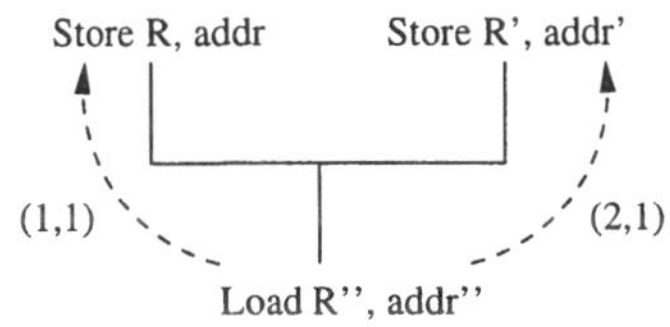

Thus, in summary this precise dynamic slicing algorithm first preprocesses the execution trace and introduces labeled dependence edges in the dependence graph. During slicing the instance labels are used to traverse only relevant edges. We refer to this algorithm as the *full preprocessing* (FP) algorithm as it fully preprocesses the execution trace prior to carrying out slice computations.

The example in Figure 1 illustrates this algorithm. The dynamic data dependence edges, from a use to its corresponding definition, for a given run are shown. For readability we have omitted the dynamic data dependence edges for uses in branch predicates as computation of data slices do not require these edges; only the edges for all non-predicate uses are shown. Edges are labeled with the execution instances of statements involved in the data dependences. The precise dynamic slice for the value of z used in the only execution of statement 16 is given. The data dependence edges traversed during this slice computation include: $(16_1, 14_3)$, $(14_3, 13_2)$, $(13_2, 12_2)$, $(13_2, 15_3)$, $(15_3, 3_1)$, $(15_3, 15_2)$, $(15_2, 3_1)$, $(15_2, 15_1)$, $(15_1, 3_1)$, and $(15_1, 4_1)$.

Note that it is equally easy to compute a dynamic slice at any earlier execution point. For example, let us compute the slice corresponding to the value of x that is used during the first execution of statement 15. In this case we will follow the data dependence edge from statement 15 to statement 4 that is labeled $(1,1)$; thus giving us the slice that contains statements 4 and 15.

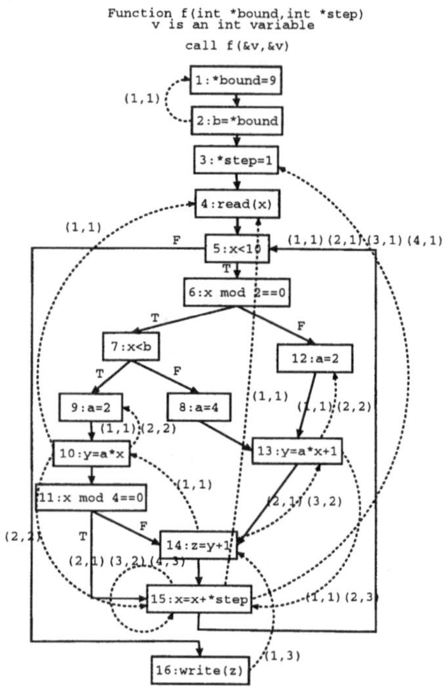

Figure 1. The path taken by the program on input $x = 6$ is $\{1_1 2_1 3_1 4_1 5_1 6_1 7_1 9_1 10_1 11_1 14_1 15_1 5_2 6_2 12_1 13_1 14_2 15_2 5_3 6_3 7_2 9_2$ $10_2 11_2\ 15_3 5_4 6_4 12_2 13_2 14_3 15_4 5_5 16_1\}$. The precise dynamic slice for use of z by the only execution of statement 16 is {16,14,13,12,4,15,3}.

2.2 No Preprocessing

The *FP* algorithm first carries out all the preprocessing and then begins slicing. For large programs with long execution runs it is possible that the dynamic dependence graph requires too much space to store and too much time to build. In fact our experiments show that too often we run out of memory since the graphs are too large. For this reason we propose another precise algorithm that does not perform any preprocessing. We refer to this algorithm as the *no preprocessing* (NP) algorithm.

In order to avoid a priori preprocessing we employ *demand driven analysis* of the trace to recover dynamic dependences. When a slice computation begins we traverse the trace backwards to recover the dynamic dependences required for the slice computation. For example, if we need the dynamic slice for the value of some variable v at the end of the program, we traverse the trace backwards till the definition of v is found and include the defining statement in the dynamic slice. If v is defined in terms of value of another variable w, we resume the traversal of the trace starting from the point where traversal had stopped upon finding the definition of v and so on. Note that since definitions we are interested will always appear earlier than the uses, we never need to traverse the same part of the trace twice during a single slice computation.

In essence this algorithm performs partial preprocessing for extracting dynamic dependences relevant to a slicing request as part of the slice computation. It is possible that two different slicing requests involve common dynamic dependences. In such a situation, the demand driven algorithm will recover the common dependences from the trace during both slice computations. To avoid this repetitive work we can *cache* the recovered dependences. Therefore at any given point in time, all dependences that have been computed so far can be found in the cache. Therefore when a dependence is required during a slice computation, the cache is first checked to see if the dependence is already known. If the dependence is cached we can directly access it; otherwise we must recover it from the trace. Thus, at the cost of maintaining a cache, we can avoid repeated recovery of same dependences from the execution trace.

We will refer to the two versions of this demand driven algorithm, that is, without caching and with caching, as *no preprocessing without caching* (NPwoC) and *no preprocessing with caching* (NPwC) algorithms.

As an illustration of this algorithm let us reconsider the example of Figure 1. When the *NP* algorithm is used, initially the flow graph does not contain any dynamic data dependence edges. Now let us say the slice for z at the only execution of statement 16 is computed. This will cause a single backward traversal of the trace through which the data dependence edges $(16_1, 14_3)$, $(14_3, 13_2)$, $(13_2, 12_2)$, $(13_2, 15_3)$, $(15_3, 3_1)$, $(15_3, 15_2)$, $(15_2, 3_1)$, $(15_2, 15_1)$, $(15_1, 3_1)$, and $(15_1, 4_1)$ are extracted. When caching is used, in addition to obtaining the slice, these edges are added to the program flow graph. Now if the slice for the use of x in the 3rd instance of statement 14 is computed, all dependences required are already present in the graph and thus the trace in not reexamined. On the other hand, if the slice for the use of x by the 2nd instance of statement 10 is requested, the trace is traversed again to extract additional dynamic data dependences.

2.3 Limited Preprocessing

While the *NP* algorithm described above addresses the space problem of the *FP* algorithm, this comes at the cost of increased time for slice computations. The time required to traverse a long execution trace is a significant part of the cost of slicing. While the *FP* algorithm traverses the trace only once for all slicing requests, the *NP* algorithm often traverses the same part of the trace multiple times, each

Table 2. Benchmark Characteristics

Program	Lines of C Code	Num. of Funcs	Code Size (Bytes)	Instructions Executed			Trace Size (Bytes)		
				(1)	(2)	(3)	(1)	(2)	(3)
`126.gcc`	207483	2001	283070464	103156356	112037569	104650291	500000391	500000757	500000215
`099.go`	29629	372	27512832	117503888	120467852	62271885	500000788	500000747	250000022
`134.perl`	27044	277	87438967	32729474	55416461	111023934	132807387	250000192	500000438
`130.li`	7741	357	7964444	122017736	21590453	109323294	581574086	99999705	500000365
`008.espresso`	14850	361	22432108	1142979	37512537	20203629	4665571	124988145	79512147

time recovering different relevant dependences for a different slicing request.

In light of the above discussion we can say that *NP* algorithm does too little preprocessing leading to high slicing costs while *FP* algorithm does too much preprocessing leading to space problems. For example, during our experiments we found that a run of *FP* over a trace of around one hundred million instructions for `126.gcc` is expected to generate a graph of size five gigabytes. Therefore next we propose an algorithm that strikes a balance between *preprocessing* and *slicing* costs. In this precise algorithm we first carry out *limited preprocessing* of the execution trace aimed at augmenting the trace with summary information that allows faster traversal of the augmented trace. Then we use demand driven analysis to compute the slice using this augmented trace. We refer to this algorithm as the *limited preprocessing* (LP) algorithm.

This algorithm speeds up trace traversal as follows: the trace is divided into *trace blocks* such that each trace block is of a fixed *size*. At the end of each trace block we store a *summary of all downward exposed definitions* of variable names and memory addresses. During the backward traversal for slicing, when looking for a definition of a variable or a memory address, we first look for its presence in the summary of downward exposed definitions. If a definition is found, we traverse the trace block to locate the definition; otherwise using the *size* information we skip right away to the start of the trace block.

Since the summary information contains only downward exposed definitions, the number of checks performed to locate the definition being sought is smaller when the summary information is used in contrast with using the trace itself. Thus, if the block is skipped, the net effect is fewer comparisons between the address of the variable whose definition is being sought and addresses defined within the trace block. On the other hand, if the block is not skipped, more comparisons are needed because both the summary information and the trace block are examined till the definition is located. Note that the cost of comparisons, and the size of the summary information, can also be reduced by representing the summary information using bit vectors. Moreover, since the dynamic slices are quite small in comparison to the trace size, it is expected that many of the traversed trace blocks will not contribute to the dynamic slice and would therefore be skipped after examination of the summary information. Thus, fewer address comparisons will be performed in practice, and even more importantly, the I/O cost during trace traversal will be greatly reduced.

3 Experimental Evaluation

3.1 Implementation

For our experimentation we used the *Trimaran* system that takes a `C` program as its input and produces a lower level intermediate representation (IR) which is actually the machine code for an EPIC style architecture. This intermediate representation is used as the basis for slicing by our implementations of the algorithms. In other words, when slicing is performed, we compute the slices in terms of a set of statements from this IR. Our implementation supports computation of both data slices as well as full slices that are based both upon data and control dependences. However, when computing slices for C programs, the key source of imprecision is the presence of pointers. Therefore in our experiments we focus primarily upon computation of dynamic data slices.

In the low level IR the usage of registers and presence of memory references has been made explicit by the introduction of load and store instructions. An interpreter for the IR is available which is used to execute instrumented versions of the IR for obtaining execution traces consisting of both the control flow trace and memory trace. In our implementation we read the execution trace in blocks and buffer it to reduce the I/O cost. Some of the programs we use make use of *longjmps* which makes it difficult to keep track of the calling environment when simulating the call stack. We handle this problem by instrumenting the program to explicitly indicate changes in calling environment as part of the trace. This additional information in the trace is used during traversal of the trace.

To achieve a fair comparison among the various dynamic slicing algorithms, we have taken great care in implementing them. The dynamic slicing algorithms that are implemented share code whenever possible and use the same basic libraries.

Table 3. Precise Dynamic Slice Sizes for Additional Inputs.

Program	Static	Instructions Executed(2)	PDS(2)			Instructions Executed(3)	PDS(3)		
			AVG	MIN	MAX		AVG	MIN	MAX
`126.gcc` @ End	585491	136269	1268	2	10702	194162	7359	2	15388
`099.go` @ End	95459	56051	4982	2	6934	46497	1268	2	5178
`134.perl` @ End	116182	15327	98	2	611	22897	151	2	599
`130.li` @ End	31829	8462	21	2	232	8854	19	2	323
`008.espresso` @ End	74039	22897	448	4	1443	19356	227	2	1229

3.2 Benchmark Characteristics

The programs used in our experiments include `008.espresso` from the `Specint92` suite, and `130.li`, `134.perl`, `099.go` and `126.gcc` from the `Specint95` suite. The attributes of the programs, including the number of lines of `C` code, number of functions, and the generated code size are given in Table 2. Each of the programs were executed on three different inputs and execution traces for the three inputs were collected. The number of instructions executed and the sizes of execution traces for these program runs are also given in Table 2. We can see that both the programs and the execution traces collected are quite large.

The system used in our experiments is a 2.2 GHz Pentium 4 linux workstation with 1.0 GB RAM and 1.0 GB of swap space.

3.3 Precise Slicing Algorithms

In order to study the behaviors of the proposed precise dynamic slicing algorithms we computed the following slices. We collected execution traces on 3 different input sets for each benchmark. For each execution trace, we computed 25 different slices. These slices were performed for latest executions of 25 distinct values loaded using load instructions by the program. That is, these slices were computed with respect to the end of program's execution (`@ End`). For the first program input, in addition, we computed 25 slices at an additional point in program's execution: `@ midpoint` - after half of the execution.

Slice sizes. Let us first examine the sizes of slices to establish the relevance of dynamic slicing for program debugging. In Table 1, in the introduction, the precise dynamic slice sizes of the programs on the first input for both `@ End` and `@ midpoint` were given and it was observed that the number of statements in the dynamic slice is a small fraction of the distinct statements that are actually executed. Thus, they are quite useful during debugging. In Table 3, the precise dynamic slice sizes for the other two program inputs for `@ End` are given. As we can see, similar observations hold for different inputs for each of the benchmarks. Thus, dynamic slicing is effective across different inputs for these pointer intensive benchmarks.

Slice computation times. Next we consider the execution times of *FP*, *NPwoC*, *NPwC*, and *LP* algorithms. Our implementation of the *LP* algorithm does not use caching. Figure 2 shows the cumulative execution time in seconds as slices are computed one by one. The three columns in Figure 2 correspond to the three different inputs. These graphs include both the preprocessing times and slice computation times. Therefore for algorithms which perform preprocessing the time at which the first slice is available is relatively high as before the slice is computed preprocessing must be performed.

First we note that in very few cases the *FP* runs to completion, more often it runs *out-of-memory* (OoM) even with 1 GB of swap space available to the program and therefore no slices are computed. Clearly this latter situation is unacceptable. This is not surprising when one considers the estimated graph sizes for these program runs given in Table 4 (the estimates are based upon the number of dynamic dependences).

Table 4. Estimated Full Graph Sizes.

Program	Size (MB)		
	(1)	(2)	(3)
`126.gcc` @ End	4931.4	5064.7	5055.9
`099.go` @ End	2366.6	2276.5	1076.2
`134.perl` @ End	1975.8	5629.2	8977.5
`130.li` @ End	1808.6	316.2	1614.3
`008.espresso` @ End	26.4	755.5	409.3

When we consider the other precise algorithms, that is, *NPwoC*, *NPwC* and *LP* algorithms, we find that they all successfully compute all of the slices. Therefore clearly these new algorithms make computation of precise dynamic slices feasible.

Now let us consider the *no preprocessing* algorithms in greater detail. We note that for the *NPwoC* algorithm there is a linear increase in the cumulative execution time with the number of slices. This is to be expected as each slicing operation requires some traversal of the execution trace. Moreover we notice that for *NPwC* that uses caching, the cumulative execution time increases less rapidly than *NPwoC*, which does not use caching, for some programs but not for others. This is because in some cases dependences are found in the cache while in other cases they are not present in the cache. In fact when there are no cache hits, due to the time spent on maintaining the cache, *NPwC* runs slower

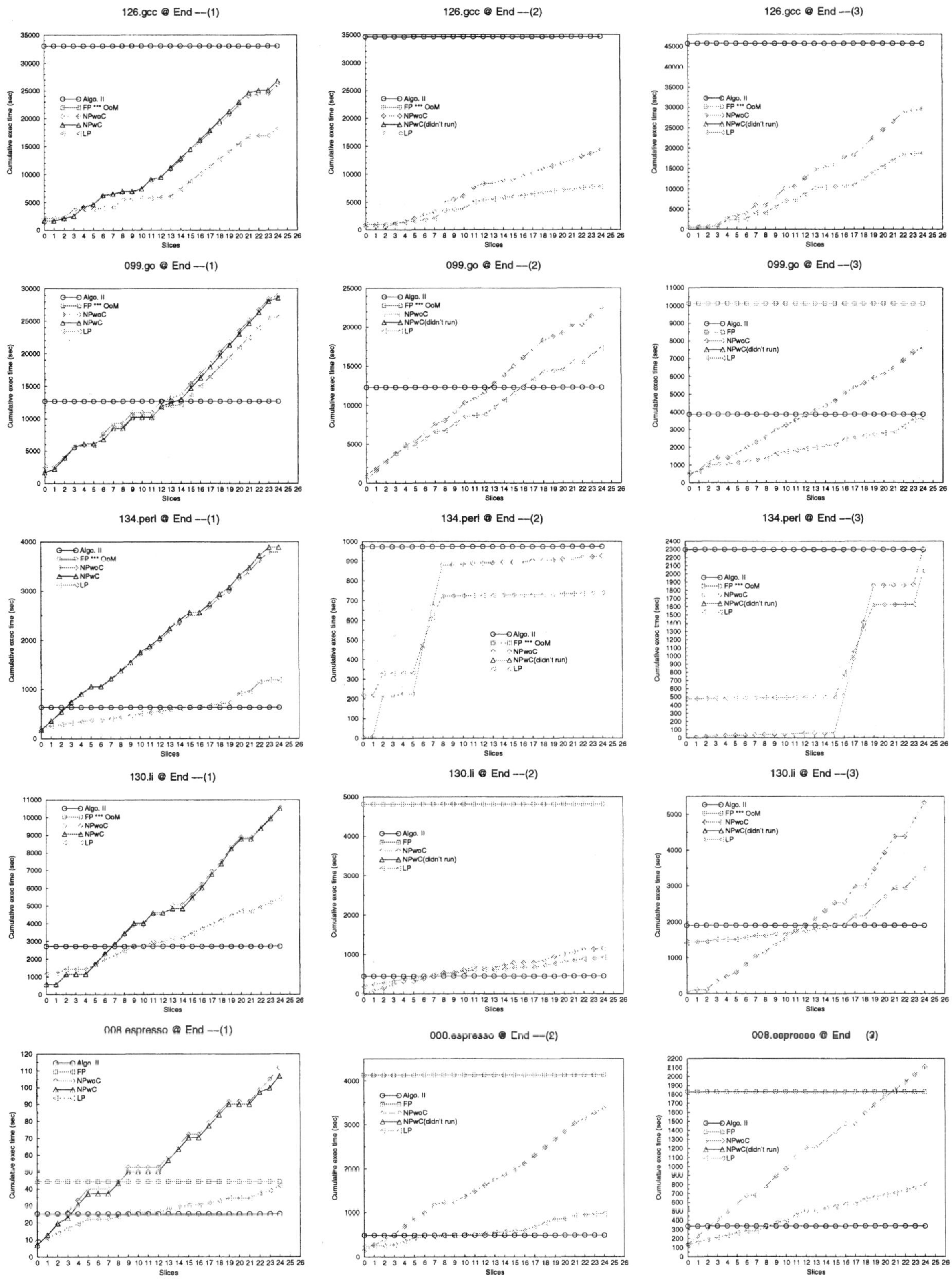

Figure 2. Execution Times.

than *NPwoC*. Since the impact of caching was minimal for the first input, we did not run the *NPwC* version on the other two inputs.

When we look at the results of using *LP* algorithm we find that the limited preprocessing indeed pays off. The *LP* cumulative execution time rises much more slowly than the *NPwoC* and *NPwC* curves. Since limited preprocessing requires only a single forward traversal of the trace, its preprocessing cost is small in comparison to the savings it provides during slice computations. The execution times of the *LP* algorithm are 1.13 to 3.43 times less than the *NP* algorithm for the first input set (see Table 5). This is not surprising when one considers the percentage of trace blocks that are skipped by the *LP* algorithm (see Table 6). Each trace block consisted of the trace of 200 basic blocks. Varying the trace block size makes little difference as the percentage of trace blocks skipped is quite large.

Table 5. Cumulative times: *NP* vs *LP*.

Program	*NP/LP*		
	(1)	(2)	(3)
`126.gcc` @ End	1.43	1.833	1.58
`099.go` @ End	1.13	1.31	2.09
`134.perl` @ End	3.19	1.25	1.14
`130.li` @ End	1.95	1.25	1.53
`008.espresso` @ End	2.67	3.43	2.65
Average	2.07	1.81	1.80

Table 6. Trace Blocks Skipped by *LP*.

Program	% Blocks Skipped		
	(1)	(2)	(3)
`126.gcc` @ End	90.43	97.63	89.39
`099.go` @ End	57.52	65.38	91.7
`134.perl` @ End	92.42	98.99	98.26
`130.li` @ End	99.02	99.51	99.70
`008.espresso` @ End	96.6	97.15	98.68
Average	87.20	91.73	95.65

3.4 LP vs. Imprecise Algorithm II

In this section we compare the performance of our best precise dynamic slicing algorithm, the *LP* algorithm, with Agrawal and Horgan's *Algorithm II*. We do not include data for *Algorithm I* because as shown by the data presented in Table 1, *Algorithm I* is extremely imprecise even in comparison to *Algorithm II*.

Before describing the results it is important to understand the differences between the *LP* algorithm and *Algorithm II*. Both algorithms do not run out of memory and hence solve the problem of large graph sizes. The *LP* algorithm solves this problem by demand-driven construction of relevant part of the precise dynamic dependence graph. *Algorithm II* solves the same problem by constructing an imprecise dynamic dependence graph where the instances of statements among which dependences exist are not remembered. This approximation greatly reduces the size of the graph which is constructed in a single pass over the trace. Thus all the preprocessing is carried out once in the beginning and then slices can be computed very quickly by traversing this graph.

A question that may arise is whether the performance of *Algorithm II* can be further improved by applying the demand-driven approach and limited preprocessing used by the *LP* algorithm. Since the approximate dynamic dependence graph constructed by *Algorithm II* is already small, there is no point in building it in a demand-driven fashion. Moreover, given the approach taken by *Algorithm II*, the demand-driven construction of the approximate dynamic dependence graph will only further slow down *Algorithm II*. This is because *Algorithm II* constructs the complete approximate dynamic dependence graph in a single pass over the trace. If demand-driven approach is used, to extract subset of dependences from the trace, the entire trace may have to be traversed for extracting these dependences. Thus, repeated passes over the trace would have to be carried out to extract different subsets of dependences which will further slow down *Algorithm II*. On the other hand, the *LP* algorithm has to build the precise dependence graph in a demand-driven fashion because the complete graph is too large. Furthermore, since *Algorithm II* traverses the trace only once, there is no point in augmenting the trace with summary information because such augmentation would also require a complete traversal of the trace.

Slice sizes. The data presented in the introduction already showed that precise dynamic slices are much smaller than the imprecise dynamic slices computed using *Algorithm II*. In Table 7 similar data for the two additional inputs is given. As we can see, the same observation holds across these additional inputs.

We have already compared the slice sizes of *LP* and *Algorithm II*. However, since the results of such comparisons are dependent upon the variables for which slicing is performed, we also developed a novel *slice independent* approach for comparing the algorithms by simply comparing the dynamic dependence graphs constructed by them and measuring the imprecision in these dependence graphs that is introduced by *Algorithm II*. This method is motivated by the fact that the imprecision in dynamic dependence graph constructed by *Algorithm II* is the root cause of resulting imprecision in the dynamic slices computed by this algorithm.

The number of dynamic dependences recovered by the precise algorithm is exact. However, when the imprecise algorithm is used, the imprecision is introduced in the dynamic dependence graph in form of false dependences. Therefore if we compute the equivalent number of dynamic dependences for the imprecise algorithm they will be higher than those for the precise algorithm. The greater the number

Table 7. IDS-II vs. LP: Inputs (2) and (3).

Program	IDS-II/PDS(2)			IDS-II/PDS(3)		
	AVG	MIN	MAX	AVG	MIN	MAX
126.gcc @ End	6.80	1	4167	2.03	1	6533.5
099.go @ End	1.39	1	4124	1.95	1	162.5
134.perl @ End	8.65	1	737	8.92	1	703
130.li @ End	9.09	1	178.5	3.08	1	21.50
008.espresso @ End	2.09	1	60.95	8.26	1	1561.5
Average	5.6	1	1853.49	4.85	1	1796.46

Table 8. Slice Independent Comparison of Algorithms.

Program	Number of Dynamic Memory Dependences					
	Input (1)		Input (2)		Input (3)	
	Algorithm-II	Precise	Algorithm-II	Precise	Algorithm-II	Precise
126.gcc	35378836	8632906	74601341	8546040	38311969	8686760
099.go	148995060	10079908	114054794	8768685	42549505	3852822
134.perl	22114062	2923947	6853213	4668814	13566847	9307883
130.li	310899820	10150987	6175836	1828449	37056110	9284206
008.espresso	374329	77217	14414220	1232534	6686934	918732

of false dependences, the greater is the degree of imprecision.

Let us say statement S is executed many times and some of its instances are dependent upon values computed by statement T and others on values computed by statement U and in addition S refers to some addresses that are also written by statement V although there is no true dependence between S and V. *LP* algorithm makes each instance of S dependent upon a single instance of either T or U. *Algorithm II* introduces twice the number of dependences as the *LP* algorithm because it makes each instance of S dependent upon both T and U.

We computed the equivalent number of dynamic memory dependences (i.e., dependences between a store and a load operation) present in the dynamic dependence graphs constructed for *Algorithm II* and *LP* algorithm. The results of this computation are given in Table 8. As we can see, the number of dynamic memory dependences for *Algorithm II* are several times that of the number of dynamic memory dependences for the *LP* algorithm. For example, for the first input set, 126.gcc's execution produces a dynamic data dependence graph containing 35378836 memory dependences for *Algorithm II* and 8632906 memory dependences for the precise algorithm. Thus, imprecision of *Algorithm II* leads to a 4.1 fold increase in the number of dynamic memory dependences.

We also compared the performance of the two algorithms for two types of slices, *data slices* (based upon transitive closure over data dependences) and *full slices* (based upon transitive closure over both control and data dependences). We observed that while the overall sizes of full slices were several times (3 to 9 times) greater than data slices, the relative performance of the two algorithms was similar. For the first input, while precise data slices computed by the *LP* algorithm were 1.2 to 17.33 times smaller than imprecise data slices computed by *Algorithm II*, precise full slices were 1.09 to 1.81 times smaller than imprecise full slices. More detailed data is omitted due to space limitations.

Execution times. The execution times for *Algorithm II* for slices computed at the end of execution are shown in Figure 2. Table 9 shows the preprocessing and slice computation times of these two algorithms. When we compare the execution times of the two algorithms we observe the following:

- @ End of execution the total time (i.e., sum of preprocessing and slicing times) taken by *LP* is 0.55 to 2.02 times the total time taken by *Algorithm II*.
- @ Midpoint of execution the total time taken by *LP* is 0.51 to 1.86 times that of *Algorithm II*.
- The latency of producing the results of the first slice using *LP* is 2.31 to 16.16 times smaller than that of producing the first slice using *Algorithm II*.

On examining the graphs in Figure 2 we notice that if we compute only a small number of slices, then the precise *LP* algorithm in fact outperforms *Algorithm II* even in terms of the runtime performance. This is because *Algorithm II* requires that all preprocessing be performed before slicing can begin while *LP* performs much less preprocessing. For each program there is a number L such that if at most L slices are computed, *LP* algorithm outperforms *Algorithm II*. The value of L is higher for execution runs with longer traces as the length of the trace determines the preprocessing time for *Algorithm II*. For the slicing of gcc @ End we can compute all 25 slices precisely using *LP* algorithm in time which is less than the time it takes for *Algorithm II* to

Table 9. Preprocessing + Slicing Times: Algo. II vs. LP for Input (1).

Program	Algorithm II	LP
`126.gcc` @ End	33014.1 + 11.46	727.82+17556.48
`126.gcc` @ Midpoint	9271.64+ 5.24	347.61+4371.21
`099.go` @ End	12671.8 + 5.37	893.92+24766.14
`099.go` @ Midpoint	6039.56 +3.21	455.17+8582.18
`134.perl` @ End	631.32 + 0.76	190.18+996.82
`134.perl` @ Midpoint	407.83+0.32	94.16+543.20
`130.li` @ End	2725.32 + 3.43	858.08+4493.45
`130.li` @ Midpoint	1747.38+1.89	464.71+2736.54
`008.espresso` @ End	25.15 + 0.11	7.83+33.98
`008.espresso` @ Midpoint	15.39+0.03	3.74+25.01

carry out preprocessing. On the other hand, for `espresso @ End` we can compute around 10 slices using *LP* algorithm in the same amount of time as it takes *Algorithm II* to carry out preprocessing. We also compared the performance of *LP* and *Algorithm II* for the first input trace at execution midpoint (i.e., `@ Midpoint`). The results are presented in Figure 3. As we can see, at this earlier point in program executions similar observations hold.

4 Related Work

Agrawal and Horgan proposed two imprecise and two precise dynamic slicing algorithms in [1]. We have already compared the performance of our algorithms with the imprecise algorithms in detail. The first precise algorithm they propose, *Algorithm III*, is quite similar to our *FP* algorithm. The difference is in the dynamic dependence graph representation. While *FP* labels dependence edges with instances, Agrawal and Horgan construct multiple instances of nodes and edges. In practice, we found our representation to be more compact.

To reduce the size of the dependence graph, Agrawal and Horgan also proposed another precise algorithm which is *Algorithm IV* in their paper. *Algorithm IV* is based upon the idea of *forward computation* of dynamic slices where slices for all variables can be maintained at all times, and when a statement is executed, the new slice of the variable just defined can be computed from the slices of the variables whose values are used in the definition. *Algorithm IV* maintains the current dynamic slices in terms of the dynamic dependence graph. A new node is added to the dynamic dependence graph only if following the execution of a statement the dynamic slice of the defined variable changes. Thus, the size of the graph is bounded by the number of different dynamic slices. As shown in [8], a program of size n can have $O(2^n)$ different dynamic slices.

Essentially *Algorithm IV* precomputes all of the dynamic slices. While this idea results in space savings, the precomputation time of *Algorithm IV* can be reasonably assumed to be much higher than the preprocessing time in *FP*, in

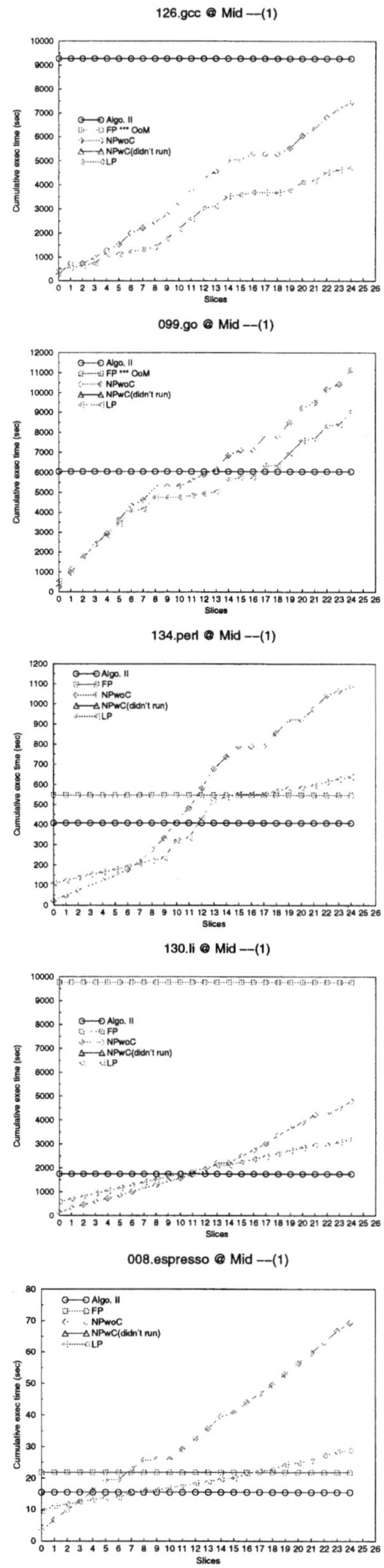

Figure 3. Execution Times `@Midpoint`.

which the direct dependences are merely added as edge labels but no slices are computed. Given the fact that *LP* is faster than *FP*, it is going to perform even better in comparison to *Algorithm IV*. Furthermore, the dynamic dependence graph produced by *Algorithm IV* can be used only to compute dynamic slices for the last definitions of variables. All the algorithms we have developed can be used to compute dynamic slices corresponding to any executed definition of any variable at any program point. In other words, in order to produce a compacted graph, *Algorithm IV* sacrifices some of the functionality of *Algorithm III*.

In [11] another algorithm for forward computation of dynamic slices was introduced which precomputes and stores all dynamic slices on disk and later accesses to them in response to users requests. This algorithm saves sufficient information so that dynamic slices at any execution point can be obtained. Like *Algorithm IV*, it will also take a long time to respond to user's first request due to the long preprocessing time. Some applications of dynamic slicing, such as debugging, may involve only a small number of slicing requests. Thus, the large amount of preprocessing performed is not desirable. Our *demand driven* approach represents a much better choice for such situations.

Korel and Yalamanchili [12] introduced another forward method which computes executable dynamic slices. Their method is based on the notion of *removable blocks*. A dynamic slice is constructed from the original program by deleting *removable blocks*. During program execution on each exit from a block, the algorithm determines whether the executed block should be included in a dynamic slice or not. It is reported in [8] that executable dynamic slices produced may be inaccurate in the presence of loops.

Finally no experimental data is presented to evaluate the forward computation of dynamic slices in any of the above works [1, 11, 12]. In this paper we have shown that it is important to consider practical design tradeoffs when developing a precise backward slicing algorithm. Any similar issues that may exist in the design of algorithms that perform forward computation of dynamic slices have yet to be studied by anyone.

5 Conclusions

In this paper we have shown that a careful design of a dynamic slicing can greatly improve its practicality. We designed and studied three different precise dynamic slicing algorithms: *FP*, *NP*, and *LP*. We made the use of *demand driven analysis* (with and without caching) and *trace augmentation* (with trace block summaries) to achieve practical implementations of precise dynamic slicing. We demonstrated that the precise *LP* algorithm which first performs limited preprocessing to augment the trace and then uses demand driven analysis performs the best. In comparison to the imprecise *Algorithm II* it runs faster when a small number of slices are computed. Also, the latency of computing the first slice using *LP* is 2.31 to 16.16 times less than the latency for obtaining the first slice by *Algorithm II*.

In conclusion this paper shows that while imprecise dynamic slicing algorithms are too imprecise and therefore not an attractive option, a carefully designed precise dynamic slicing algorithm such as the *LP* algorithm is practical as it provides precise dynamic slices at reasonable space and time costs.

References

[1] H. Agrawal and J. Horgan, "Dynamic Program Slicing," *ACM SIGPLAN Conference on Programming Language Design and Implementation* (PLDI), pages 246-256, 1990.

[2] H. Agrawal, R. DeMillo, and E. Spafford, "Debugging with Dynamic Slicing and Backtracking," *Software Practice and Experience* (SP&E), Vol. 23, No. 6, pages 589-616, 1993.

[3] D.C. Atkinson, M. Mock, C. Chambers, and S.J. Eggers, "Program Slicing Using Dynamic Points-to Data," *ACM SIGSOFT 10th Symposium on the Foundations of Software Engineering* (FSE), November 2002.

[4] R. Gupta and M.L. Soffa, "Hybrid Slicing: An Approach for Refining Static Slices using Dynamic Information," *ACM SIGSOFT 3rd Symposium on the Foundations of Software Engineering* (FSE), pages 29-40, October 1995.

[5] T. Hoffner, "Evaluation and Comparison of Program Slicing Tools." *Technical Report*, Dept. of Computer and Information Science, Linkoping University, Sweden, 1995.

[6] M. Kamkar, "Interprocedural Dynamic Slicing with Applications to Debugging and Testing," *PhD Thesis*, Linkoping University, 1993.

[7] B. Korel and J. Laski, "Dynamic Program Slicing," *Information Processing Letters* (IPL), Vol. 29, No. 3, pages 155-163, 1988.

[8] F. Tip, "A Survey of Program Slicing Techniques," *Journal of Programming Languages* (JPL), Vol. 3, No. 3, pages 121-189, September 1995.

[9] G. Venkatesh, "Experimental Results from Dynamic Slicing of C Programs," *ACM Transactions on Programming Languages and Systems* (TOPLAS), Vol. 17, No. 2, pages 197-216, 1995.

[10] M. Weiser, "Program Slicing," *IEEE Transactions on Software Engineering* (TSE), Vol. SE-10, No. 4, pages 352-357, 1982.

[11] A. Beszedes, T. Gergely, Z.M. Szabo, J. Csirik, and T. Gyimothy, "Dynamic Slicing Method for Maintenance of Large C Programs," *5th European Conference on Software Maintenance and Reengineering* (CSMR), March 2001.

[12] B. Korel and S. Yalamanchili. "Forward computation of dynamic program slices," *International Symposium on Software Testing and Analysis* (ISSTA), August 1994

An Empirical Study of Predicate Dependence Levels and Trends

David Binkley
Loyola College
Baltimore MD
21210-2699, USA
binkley@cs.loyola.edu

Mark Harman
Brunel University
Uxbridge, Middlesex
UB8 3PH, UK
Mark.Harman@brunel.ac.uk

Keywords: Dependence Analysis, Program Slicing

Abstract

Many source code analyses are closely related to and strongly influenced by interdependence among program components. This paper reports results from an empirical study of the interdependences involving program predicates *and the formal parameters and global variables which potentially affect them.*

The findings show that it is possible to eliminate from consideration approximately 30% of the formal parameters, 50% of the 'touched' global variables, and 97% of the 'visible' global variables.

Another important and encouraging finding is a strong inverse correlation between the number of formal parameters and dependence level. The fact that no such correlation was found for global variables provides evidence to support the conjecture that global variables are harmful.

1. Introduction

Of the many software engineering applications supported by source code analysis, a large number are highly sensitive to dependences between program components. However, despite its importance, there is little published work on empirical assessment of the *level* of program dependence expected, nor how it varies within and between programs.

Results concerning dependence levels and trends are important for dependence-sensitive applications. Such applications can require considerable analysis effort (by both humans and machines). For example, human program comprehension is an inherently expensive task. Program slicing [1, 5, 8, 13, 16] has been used to reduce this expense, by focusing attention on a particular 'slice' of the source code [2, 3, 4, 7, 10]. Slices are constructed using dependence analysis. The lower the dependence level, the smaller the slice, and consequently, the greater the saving in human analysis effort.

Automated analysis can be expensive too. For example, consider the automated search for branch-coverage adequate test data [9, 11, 14, 15]. Here, the potential savings from dependence analysis are dramatic; *linear* dependence level reductions cause *exponential* search space reductions.

This paper introduces empirical program dependence level and trend analysis. The results of which have significant impact upon dependence-sensitive applications. Specifically, the contributions of the empirical study are as follows:

- Results for dependence levels reveal that, for a typical predicate, it is possible to ignore
  - 30% of formal parameters in the scope,
  - 50% of the global variables potentially used or defined by a call to the predicate's procedure, and
  - 97% of the global variables in scope.
- The study provides evidence of a strong correlation between an increase in the number of formal parameters visible to a predicate and the proportion actually used. There is no such correlation for either kind of globals.
- Visualizations are introduced for human analysis and interpretation of dependence level and trend results for individual programs.

The rest of the paper is organized as follows: Section 2 outlines the experimental setup, while Sections 3 and 4 report the results of the study. Section 5 shows that dependence analysis is practical with regard to both its theoretical complexity and actual computation time. Section 6 summarizes the paper.

0-7695-1877-X/03 $17.00 © 2003 IEEE

Name	Size KLOC	Predicates	Predicates per KLOC	Description
replace	0.6	84	140	Regular expression string replacement
copia	1.2	45	38	European Space Agency (ESA) signal processing code
compress	1.9	88	46	Data compression utility
which	5.4	136	25	Unix utility
barcode	5.9	365	62	Barcode generator
space	11.5	593	52	European Space Agency (ESA) ADL interpreter
ed	13.6	2627	193	Unix editor
prepro	14.8	619	42	European Space Agency (ESA) array pre-processing code
bc	16.8	432	26	Calculator
findutils	18.6	1819	98	File finding utilities
diffutils	19.8	2212	112	File comparing routines
flex2-4-7	21.2	911	43	BSD scanner (version 2.4.7)
flex2-5-4	21.5	1306	61	BSD scanner (version 2.5.7)
espresso	22.1	2497	113	logic simplification for CAD (from SPECmark)
ijpeg	28.2	2038	72	JPEG compressor (from SPECmark)
ntpd	45.6	3061	67	daemon for the network time protocol
a2ps	62.9	5984	95	postscript formatter
gnugo	81.7	5244	64	Gnu game player
sendmail	85.7	4991	23	Linux mail daemon
spice	167.0	15527	93	Digital circuit simulator
average	28.3	2529	73	

Figure 1. Subject programs

2. Experimental setup

This section describes the subject programs, the statistical tests used, and the data collection process.

2.1. The subjects

The study concerns 20 C language subject programs that range in size from 600 LOC to 167K LOC. Three programs were obtained from the European Space Agency (ESA), while the remaining 17 consist of publicly available utilities and application programs. Figure 1 presents summary information concerning the subjects. Interestingly, predicate density (predicates per KLOC) appears independent of program size, with an average of 73 predicates per KLOC.

2.2. Statistical tests

Pearson's linear correlation is used to construct quantitative models of the data. Such correlations measure linear associations between variables. The output is a *correlation coefficient*, reported as the value R, and the coefficients of a linear *model*. The statistical significance of R can be summarized as 0.8 - 1.0 strong association, 0.5 - 0.8 moderate association, and 0.0 - 0.5 weak or no association. A negative value indicates an inverse correlation. For the effect of X, Y, and Z on A, the resulting model coefficients, m_i, belong to the linear equation

$$A = m_1X + m_2Y + m_3Z + b.$$

2.3. Dependence data collection

The dependence data was collected by a modification of the standard System Dependence Graph (SDG) based backward interprocedural slicing algorithm [6]. An SDG represents a program as a collection of Procedure Dependence Graphs (PDGs), the nodes of which represent statements and predicates and the edges of which represent control and data-dependences between nodes. Interprocedural dependence edges connect PDGs to form the SDG. The final step in the construction of the SDG is the addition of '*summary*' edges at call-sites. These transitive dependences edges represent certain paths of dependence edges through called procedures from vertices representing initial parameter values to vertices representing final parameter values.

The formal parameters and global variables that potentially affect a branch node b of procedure P can be computed by slicing with respect to the vertex for b and reporting the formal parameters of P and global variables whose vertices occur in the slice. It turns out that this approach is inefficient because it needlessly discovers components of other procedures that are in the slice. Therefore, the slicing algorithm was modified to compute 'local' slices. Based on the two-pass algorithm of Horwitz et. al.[6], only intraprocedural edges are considered when computing a local slice. Collecting parameters in a local slice is equivalent to collecting parameters in the full slice.

3. Dependence level

For a predicate p, *dependence level* refers to the proportion of *parameters* that p depends upon. In this definition, the term *parameter* refers to formal parameters and global variables. Globals variables are further broken down into *visible globals*, those in scope at p, and *du-globals*, the subset of the visible globals potentially defined or used by a call to the function that contains p. This distinction is interesting because du-globals represent a first approximation to those globals upon which p depends. As will be seen, this first approximation is rather crude.

In order to visualize dependence levels three variables must be depicted:

Predicate Count. The number of predicates summarized by a data point. Data points summarizing a larger number predicates carry more weight.

Max-Parameters. The maximum number of parameters in scope (visible) at a predicate. Large maxima are more interesting because of the greater potential for savings.

Parameters-Used. The number of parameters that affect a predicate according to the dependence analysis described in Section 2.3. The smaller this number the better for dependence-sensitive applications.

In these definitions "parameters" referees to formals and globals taken together. When only formals are being considered the terms *Max-Formals* and *Formals-Used* are used. Similar specialization is done when only globals are considered

It is important to understand the difference between max-parameters and parameters-used. In the absence of any dependence analysis, *every* formal parameter and *every* global variable must be considered to potentially affect a predicate. Dependence analysis can reduce this number, but by its very nature, must be conservative: determining whether a formal definitely affects a predicate is undecidable. Therefore, a safe (conservative) approximation is computed; parameters-used excludes only those parameters that can be *guaranteed* not to affect a predicate.

Program	Max Formals	Average Formals Used	Predicate Count
`replace`	1	1.0	8
	2	1.5	11
(*)	3	2.2	8
	4	3.6	47
	6	5.0	10
`prepro`	0	0.0	11
	1	1.0	137
	2	1.2	62
	3	1.1	176
	4	1.3	98
	5	1.1	53
	6	1.0	10
	7	1.6	18
	8	1.4	24
	9	1.0	4
	10	0.7	15
	11	1.0	5
	12	1.0	6

Figure 2. Example formals data

3.1. Dependence level visualizations

To visualize the dependence level data, two graphical devices are introduced: the *Dependence Skyline* and the *Dependence Bubble Chart.* This section introduces these visualizations and illustrates their interpretation for two of the smaller programs.

Figure 2 shows formal parameter dependence data for the programs `replace` and `prepro`. The column labeled 'Predicate Count' indicates the number of predicates summarized in each row of the table. The difference between the columns labeled 'Max Formals' and 'Average Formals Used' indicates the reduction (and hence savings in analysis time) which can be achieved by separating formals that may actually affect a predicate from those merely in scope.

For example, consider the third row (marked '(*)' in Figure 2). This row summarizes predicates in procedures with three formal parameters. Such predicates, by definition, are influenced by at most three formal parameters. As shown in the 'Predicate Count' column, there are 8 such predicates. For these predicates, the average number of formals depended upon (shown in the column labeled 'Average Formals Used') is 2.2.

Compare this row with the row immediately below it in the table. For predicates with 4 formal parameters in scope, an average of 3.6 actually affect the predicates. At first

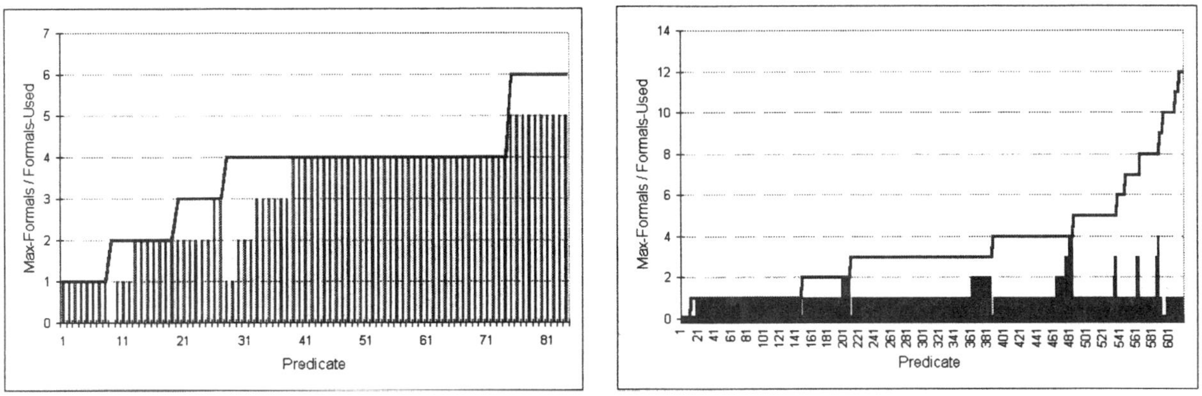

`replace` Dependence Skyline   `prepro` Dependence Skyline

Figure 3. Dependence skylines. Bars indicate actual predicate dependence. The horizon line running across the top of the dependence skyline is the 'theoretical maximum' – the number of formals in scope. Predicates are ordered left-right by Max-Formals. The space between these two indicates ignore-able formal parameters. The larger this space the greater the potential saving.

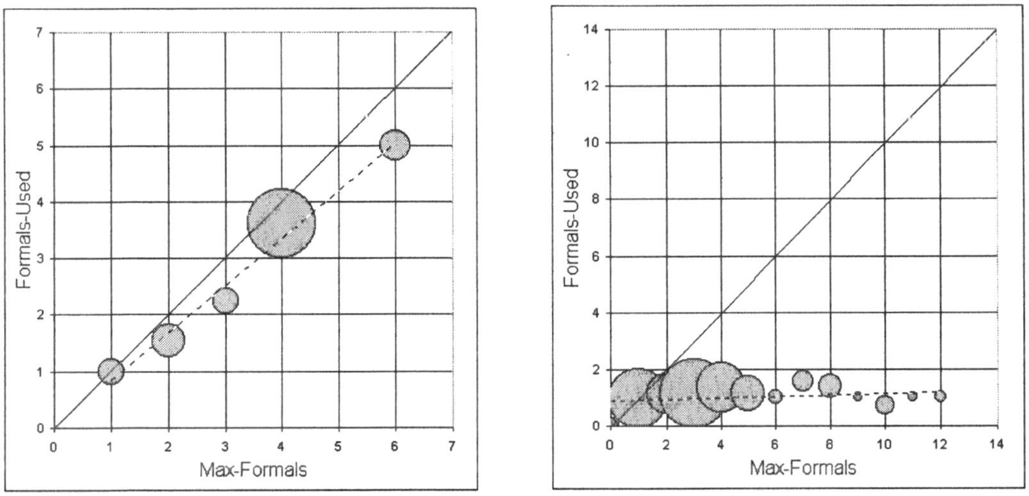

`replace` Dependence Bubble Chart   `prepro` Dependence Bubble Chart

Figure 4. Dependence bubble charts. In these dependence bubble charts, bubble size indicates predicate-count. The solid line at 45° indicates the maximum possible dependence. The further the bubbles are from this line, the greater saving. The dotted line indicates the linear trend.

glance, this row seems to be telling a similar story: most of the formal parameters affect each predicate. However, Row 4 is more interesting than Row 3 because it summarizes almost six times as many predicates. This highlights the importance of the predicate count attribute.

The raw data summarized in Figure 2 is shown in graphical form using dependence skylines in Figure 3. A dependence skyline shows each predicate on the X axis (sorted by max-parameters and, within that, sorted by parameters-used). The Y axis denotes usage of parameters (both the theoretical maximum and the actual count revealed by dependence analysis). The 'horizon line' which monotonically increases as it travels left to right across the top of the dependence skyline indicates the value of max-parameters, while the usage bars indicate the value of parameters-used.

For example, the data for predicates in procedures with 3 formal parameters (marked with '(*)' in Figure 2) appears in the dependence skyline at points with X values 20 through 27 in the left of Figure 3. Over this range, the horizon line (showing max-formals) is horizontal and represents all predicates with three visible formal parameters. The first six bars in this range have height 2, while the last two have height 3. (This gives the average height of 2.2 as shown in Figure 2.)

In general, the gap between the horizon line and the usage bars is a measure of the reduction achieved. A larger gap represents a greater reduction. In the `replace` dependence skyline, there is very little space between the horizon line and the usage bars. However, the `prepro` dependence skyline (displayed on the right of Figure 3) tells a different story: here dependence analysis leads to big savings in subsequent analyses. There is significant space, especially on the right-hand side of the graph, where the greatest savings are to be found.

For a small example like `replace`, the dependence skyline replicates the tabular data in full detail. However, for a larger example, like `prepro`, the dependence skyline provides only a general *feel* for the raw data; it is unrealistic to separate out individual bars due to the large number of data points.

For larger data sets, dependence bubble charts can often better display the three dependent attributes. In such charts, the X axis denotes max-parameters, while the Y axis denotes parameters-used. Thus, the line $y = x$ represents the worst case (*i.e.*, a predicate can reference no more that the visible parameters). For reference, this line is drawn as the solid line in all dependence bubble charts. Also drawn is a dashed line that represents the linear trend (computed using a linear least squares fit). Finally, bubble size represents predicate-count.

For example, consider `replace`'s dependence bubble chart for formal parameters shown on the left of Figure 4. The largest bubble summarizes the data from Row 4 of the table in Figure 2. Here, the average number of formals used by all predicates from `replace` with 4 formals in scope is just under 4. Recall from Figure 2, the actual value is 3.6. Also, as can be quickly seen, this bubble is considerably larger than the others. In fact, it summarizes over half of the predicates in the program. The second largest bubble represents predicates in procedures with two formals (visually, these can be seen to depend upon an average of approximately 1.5 of the 2 available formal parameters).

The `prepro` dependence bubble chart appears on the right of Figure 4. Three important facts can be readily seen. First, divergence from the solid $y = x$ line very clearly highlights the *tremendous savings* which occur from dependence analysis of `prepro`. Second, the relative size of the bubbles indicates that most of this saving is to be expected in procedures with fewer than 5 formal parameters. Third, the dashed trend line indicates that formals-used is effectively constant (independent of the number of formals available). This trend line may have important implications for subsequent maintenance and evolution of `prepro`.

3.2. Using the visualizations

Twelve representative formal parameter dependence bubble charts appear in Figure 5. The corresponding charts for du-globals appear in Figure 6 (the data for visible globals appears in Figure 8, in a single dependence bubble chart). In Figures 5 and 6, programs are presented in corresponding locations and are ordered (roughly) by increasing complexity. Note that the axes scales are not the same in each chart. While some normalization has been done, complete normalization causes charts for smaller values to be unreadable.

The dependence bubble charts provide useful information about the dependence trends in the software. They highlight trends and anomalies which can be used to inform maintenance and evolution decisions. For example, since lower levels of dependence are desirable for many applications, programs that display a greater divergence of trend line from the max line are preferred. Also of interest are the changes in dependence bubble charts over different releases of the software, which provide feedback on software evolution. Finally, individual bubbles can provide valuable insights. The rest of this section illustrates the ways in which dependence bubble charts can be used to visualize aspects of program dependence.

Consider the overall picture for formal parameter dependence across the 12 programs shown in Figure 5. There are some clear general coding styles present: a linear increase in predicate dependence is exhibited by `replace`, `find-utils`, `espresso`, `flex`, and `sendmail`. In contrast, for `copia`, `compress`, `barcode`, and `spice` the level of dependence is almost constant. That is, the dependence level is independent of max-formals. Comprehension for this second set of 'constant dependence' programs is likely to be easier; there will be fewer values to consider for typical predicates (*e.g.*, slices constructed from the program's predicates will tend to be smaller).

Turning to individual programs, consider the formal and global dependence bubble charts for the programs `copia` and `prepro`. Both these programs show an almost constant trend in dependence for formals and du-globals. This suggests that these programs will be more tractable in comprehension tasks and might be thought of, *inter alia*, as providing evidence of improved prospects for testability and maintainability. Of course, as `prepro` is a far larger program, the results are more significant for `prepro` than for `copia`.

Next, consider the du-global dependence for the two releases of the program `flex`. The later release, `flex2-5-4`, shows a marked increase in the slope of the trend line, indicating that the level of dependence on globals is on the increase. This suggests poorly planned maintenance, which increased either the number of globals variables or the pred-

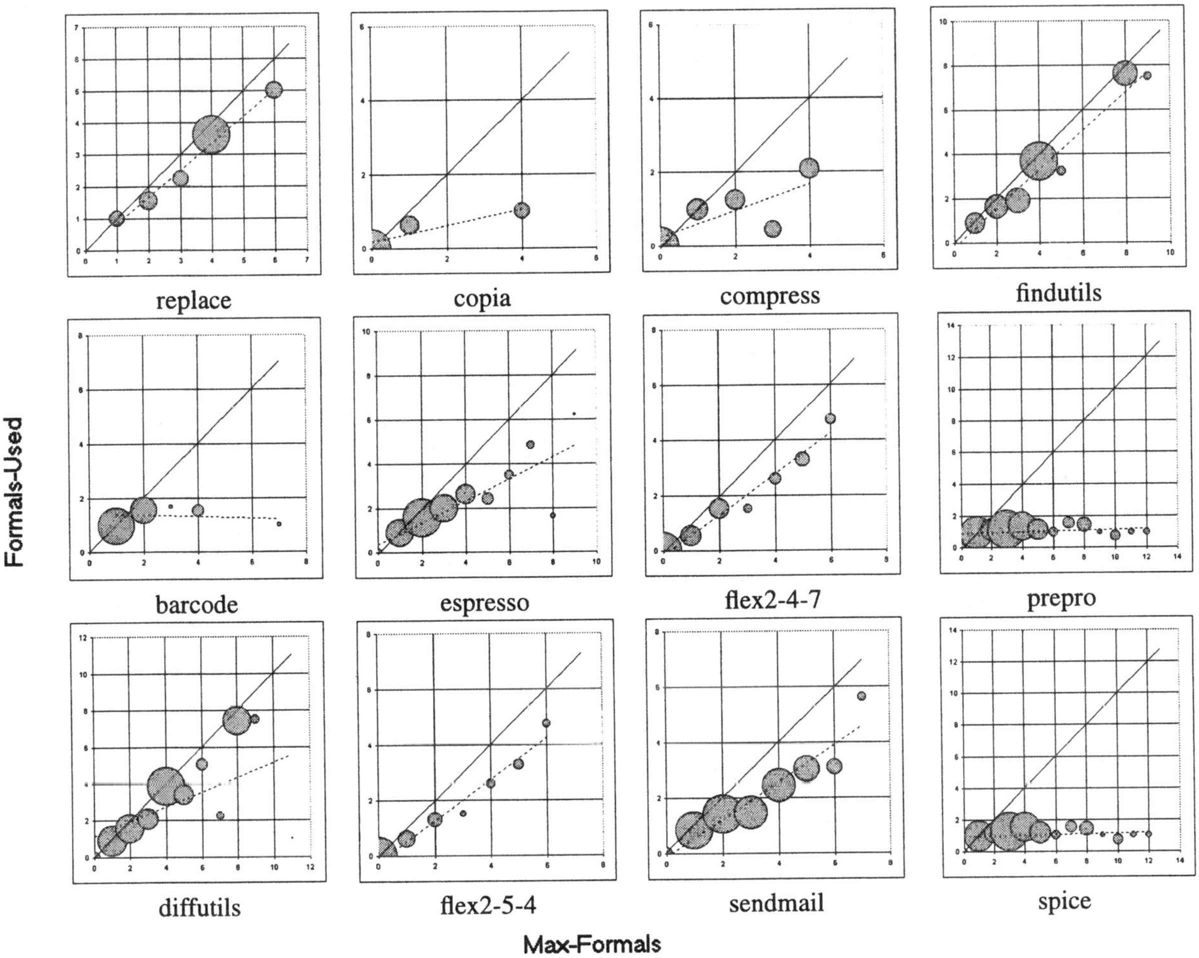

Figure 5. Dependence level for predicates upon formal parameters

icate dependence on globals. Either of which increases the comprehension effort required to understand the control behavior of the program. This can be expected to produce problems during future maintenance and evolution activities.

Looking at a trend line provides a summary of a program. However, the individual bubbles can provide further detail. For example, are they close to the trend line or do they vary wildly? This impacts predictability. Furthermore, programs with large bubbles towards the upper right are potentially problematic. An excellent example of this is `sendmail`, which, as seen in Figure 6, has several large bubbles on the upper right of the chart; thus, it may be hard to analyze. In contrast, the large bubbles for `diffutils` are toward the lower left of the dependence bubble chart. `Diffutils` will be comparatively easy to analyze.

4. Results over all predicates

One of the major goals of this study is to determine trends in predicate dependence levels. This section reports key findings over all 50579 predicates considered. Three related questions are asked that relate dependence level and first formals and then the two kinds of globals. The first question to be addressed is

> *'How does the dependence level change as the number of available formal parameters increases?'*

As seen in Section 4.2, the answer, put simply, is that

> *'As the number of formals available increases, the dependence level drops.'*

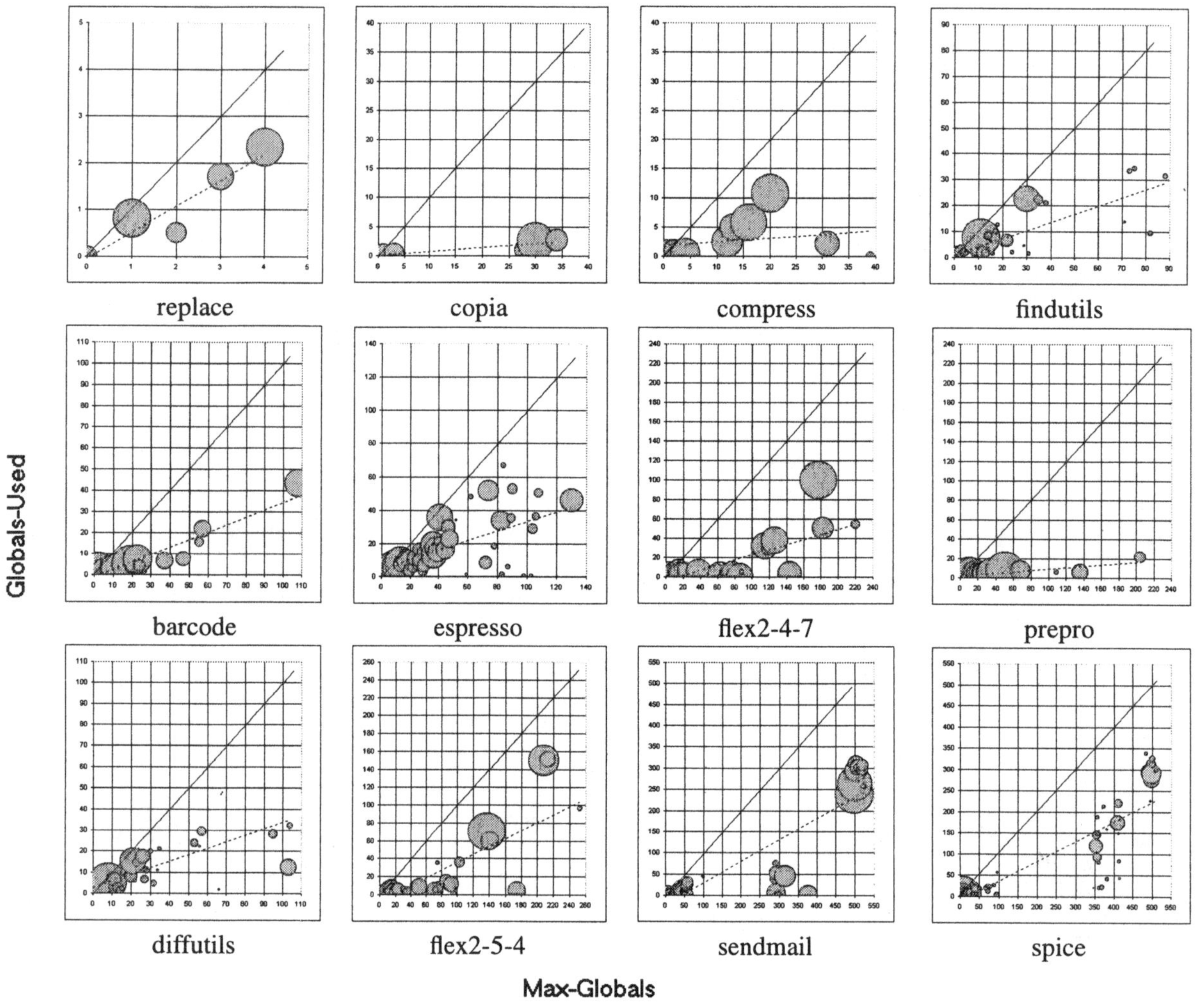

Figure 6. Dependence level for predicates upon du-global variables

This is an important and optimism-inducing finding. For example, impossibly large search spaces for test data generators may present more tractable problems than previously thought.

A similar question can be asked for globals. Sadly (but importantly), a similar result *does not* hold (for visible globals or for du-globals). This provides evidence for the assertion:

'Global variables are harmful.'

That is, programs with a large number of global variables may present intractable problems for dependence-sensitive applications. The "silver lining" here comes from the relatively low percentage of visible globals used by a typical predicate.

4.1. All predicate visualizations

Analysis of the data for formals shows that it is *piecewise linear.* This analysis introduces a third variable that has the value 0 up to a pivot point where it takes on the value *max-formals − pivot-point.* Using a piecewise linear model, the pivot-point occurs at max-formals of 8 or 10 ($R = 0.96$ and $R = 0.95$, respectively). There is little to choose between these two. Visually the split starts at max-formals of 10, where the figures clearly show different dependence profiles. For this reason, the visualizations are split into two diagrams; one for values of max-formals less than 10 and one for max-formals at least 10. This piecewise linearity is starkly evident in the trend lines of the two dependence bubble charts. The following two equations separate out the two pieces. For max-formals less than 10 the model is

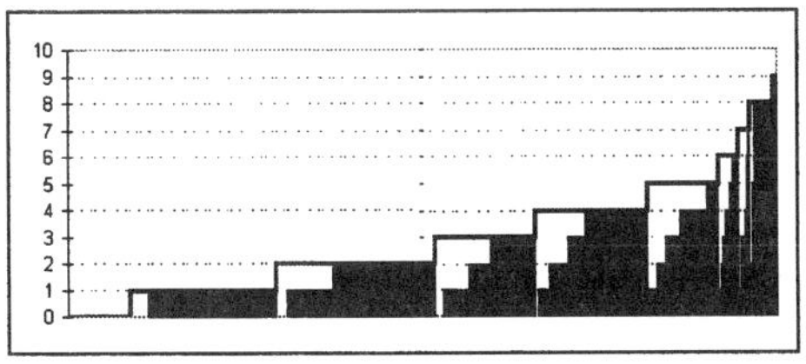

Max-Formals < 10

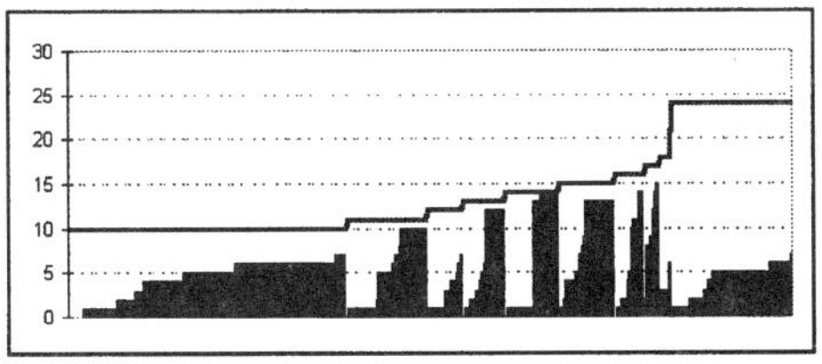

Max-Formals ≥ 10

Figure 7. Dependence skylines for all 50579 predicates

$$\textit{formals-used} = 0.14 + 0.68 \times \textit{max-formals}.$$

For max-formals at least 10 the model is

$$\textit{formals-used} = 8.54 - 0.16 \times \textit{max-formals}.$$

In essence, the number of formals-used increases linearly at roughly $0.68 \times$ *max-formals* until max-formals is 10, where formals-used begins a slight decline, but is rather independent of max-formals.

The decreasing dependence on formal parameters, can be readily appreciated visually in both dependence skylines and dependence bubble charts. The dependence skyline for all 50579 predicates is shown in Figure 7. The corresponding dependence bubble charts are shown at the top of Figure 8.

The bottom two dependence bubble charts in Figure 8 summarize the data for global variables. When considering du-globals, the trend line for globals is just below the '$y = x/2$' line and reflects the 48% average usage. The resulting model is

$$\textit{globals-used} = 0.47 \times \textit{max-du-globals} - 13$$

with an R value of 0.83 (a strong linear association).

For visible globals the R value of 0.40 indicates there is no linear correlation. Thus, there are two possibilities. The more likely case is that max-visible-globals is simply not a good predictor of globals-used; however, it is it is possible that some non-linear relationship exists. These models are important, because they show that predicate dependence levels do not fall as the number of available globals increases.

4.2. All predicate dependence level

In this final analysis section, the perspective changes from the relationship between max and used, to the relationship between max and *dependence level* (*i.e.*, percentage used). Scatter plots showing this relationship for formals, du-globals, and visible-globals appear in Figure 9.

Over all 20 programs, there is strong evidence for an inverse linear correlation between max-formals and dependence level. The resulting trend line is captured by the model

$$\textit{dependence-level} = 86\% - 2.8\% \times \textit{max-formals}$$

with an R value of -0.833. While the linear model fit better explains the data, the average dependence level for formals is 72%.

No linear correlations exist for globals. When considering du-globals (center chart in Figure 9) R has the values 0.080. For all visible globals (lower chart in Figure 9) it has the value -0.27. Both indicate no linear correlation.

5. Theoretical and actual time complexity

The previous two sections show the significant benefits possible using dependence analysis. However, these benefits can only be realized if it is possible to compute the dependence information in reasonable time. Fortunately, this is possible. This section describes the predicted and actual computational effort required to compute the dependence information presented in Sections 3 and 4.

The algorithmic complexity of the analysis can be given in terms of the size of a procedure, S, and the number of predicates, P. The complexity of a brute force algorithm is $O(P \times S)$. This algorithm takes P slices, each having linear ($O(S)$) complexity. It is possible to reduce this to $O(S)$ assuming $O(1)$ bit vector operations, by propagating bit vectors over a topologically sorted DAG produced by finding strongly connected components (SCCs) in the subgraph reachable from predicate vertices [12]

The actual data was collected on a PII 450 with 386Mb memory using an implementation of the brute force algorithm. The average time per predicate was 7.6ms. Statistical modeling of the computation time shows a tight fit with that predicted by its complexity. Using the sum of the number of edges and nodes in a PDG as the size measure, S, yields the following model

$$Analysis\ time = 0.000017 \times P \times S$$

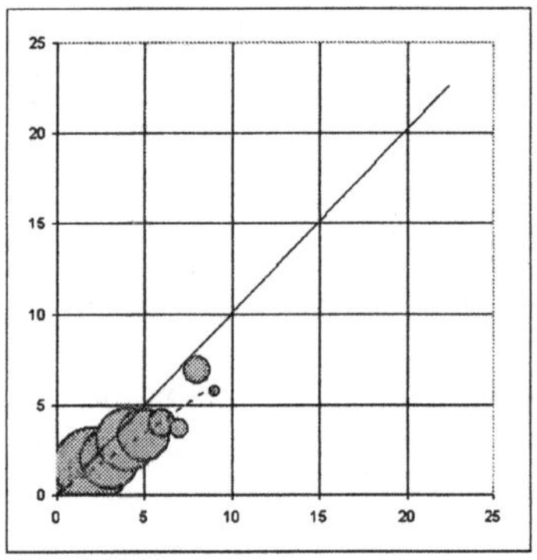

Max-Formals < 10

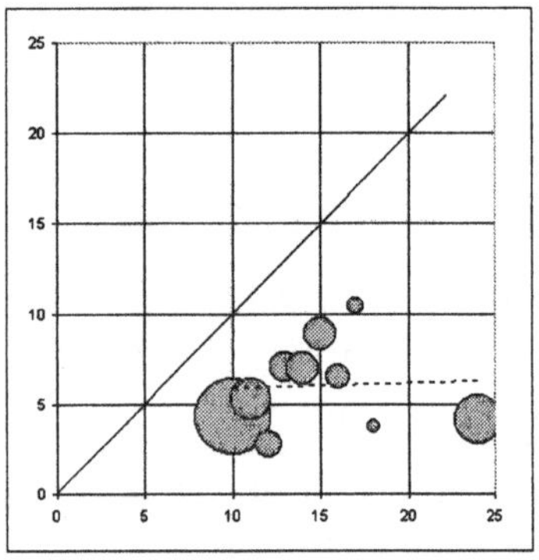

Max-Formals ≥ 10

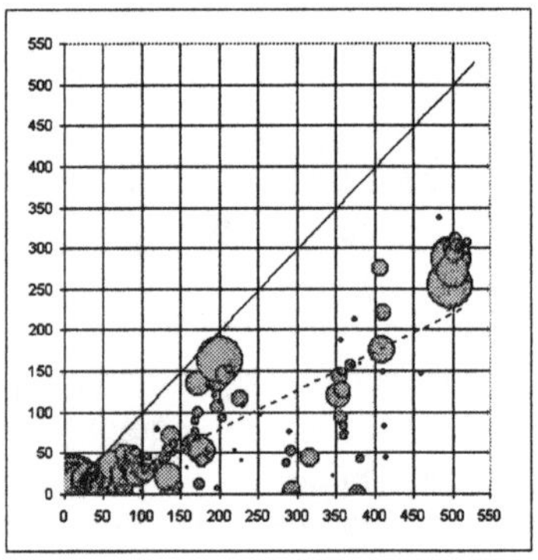

All du-Globals

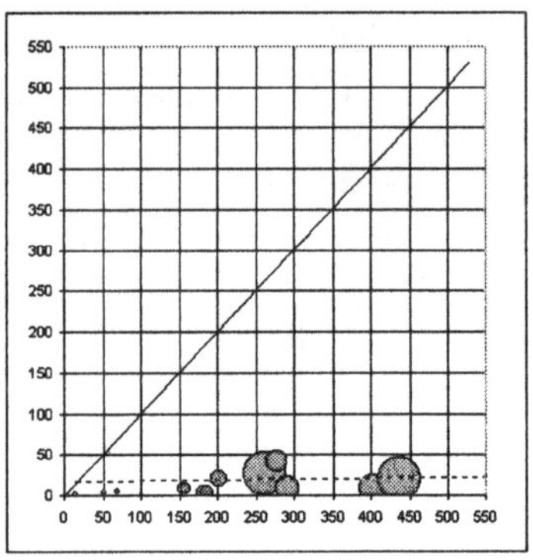

All visible Globals

Figure 8. Bubble charts for all 50579 predicates

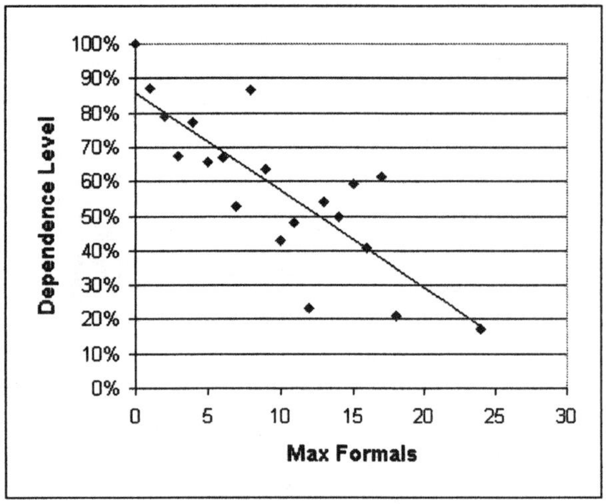

Declining Dependence Level on Formals

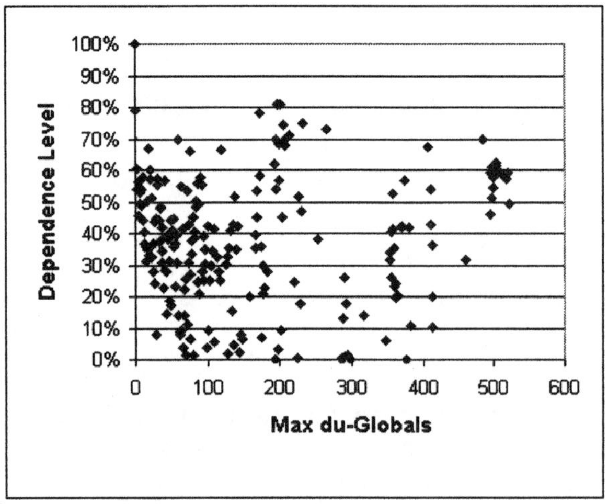

Non-Declining Dependence Level on du Globals

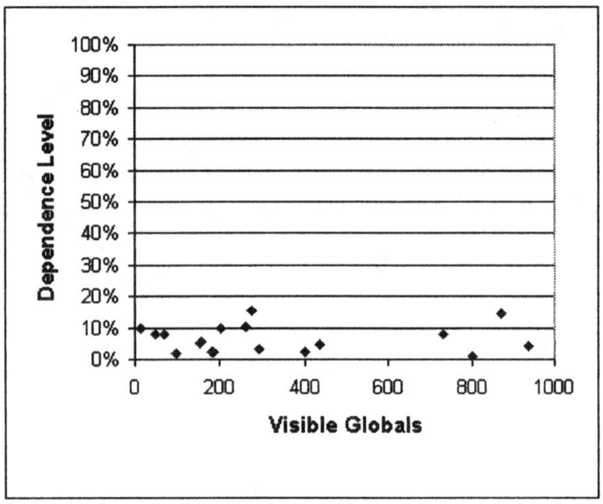

Non-Declining Dependence Level on visible Globals

Figure 9. Predicate dependence trends

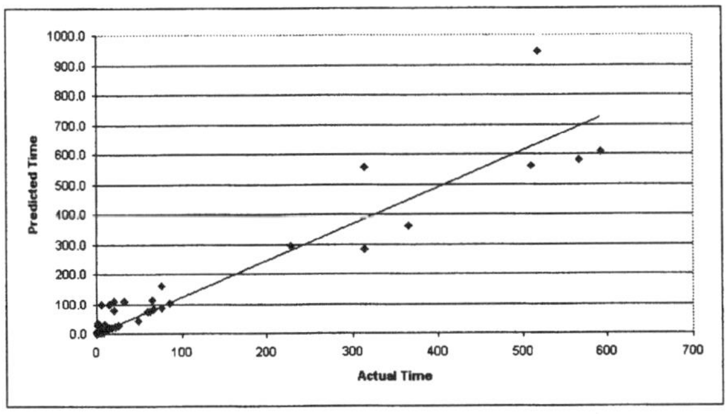

Figure 10. Actual computation time vs. predicted. Times are per predicate in milliseconds.

with $R = 0.99995$. Furthermore, the *t*-score for the coefficient of $P \times S$ is 7881, which, being much greater that 1.94, is statistically significant. This indicates an excellent fit as seen the scatter plot of actual and predicted time shown in Figure 10. Note that most of the points in the plot occur right on the line with values less then 20.

6. Summary

Program predicates form the backbone of the logic of a program and the basis for much analysis (both automatic and manual). Clearly, not *all* predicates in *all* programs depend upon *all* the formal parameters and globals variables.

This paper presented results from a study of predicate dependence level (both upon formal parameters and global variables). The results are very encouraging, showing that initial dependence analysis is cost-effective, worthwhile and can lead to significant reductions in subsequent (human and mechanical) analysis effort.

The results also show important differences between formal parameter dependence and global variable dependence. While there is an inverse correlation between the number of formal parameters and dependence level, no such finding was observed for global variables.

7. Acknowledgements

The authors wish to thank GrammaTech Inc. (`http://www.grammatech.com`) for providing CodeSurfer, Gregg Rothermel for providing the `space` program, Chris Morel for his statistical guidance, and Erin Dyet who assisted with the visualizations. Mark Harman is supported, in part, by EPSRC Grants GR/R98938, GR/M58719, GR/M78083 and GR/R43150 and by two development grants from DaimlerChrysler. Dave Binkley is supported by National Science Foundation grant CCR-9803665.

References

[1] D. W. Binkley and K. B. Gallagher. Program slicing. In M. Zelkowitz, editor, *Advances of Computing, Volume 43*, pages 1–50. Academic Press, 1996.

[2] D. W. Binkley, M. Harman, L. R. Raszewski, and C. Smith. An empirical study of amorphous slicing as a program comprehension support tool. In 8th *IEEE International Workshop on Program Comprehension (IWPC 2000)*, pages 161–170, Limerick, Ireland, June 2000. IEEE Computer Society Press, Los Alamitos, California, USA.

[3] A. De Lucia, A. R. Fasolino, and M. Munro. Understanding function behaviours through program slicing. In 4th *IEEE Workshop on Program Comprehension*, pages 9–18, Berlin, Germany, Mar. 1996. IEEE Computer Society Press, Los Alamitos, California, USA.

[4] K. B. Gallagher. Evaluating the surgeon's assistant: Results of a pilot study. In *Proceedings of the International Conference on Software Maintenance*, pages 236–244. IEEE Computer Society Press, Los Alamitos, California, USA, Nov. 1992.

[5] M. Harman and R. M. Hierons. An overview of program slicing. *Software Focus*, 2(3):85–92, 2001.

[6] S. Horwitz, T. Reps, and D. W. Binkley. Interprocedural slicing using dependence graphs. *ACM Transactions on Programming Languages and Systems*, 12(1):26–61, 1990.

[7] B. Korel and J. Rilling. Program slicing in understanding of large programs. In 6th *IEEE International Workshop on Program Comprenhesion (IWPC'98)*, pages 145–152, Ischia, Italy, 1998. IEEE Computer Society Press, Los Alamitos, California, USA.

[8] L. D. Larsen and M. J. Harrold. Slicing object-oriented software. In *Proceedings of the 18th International Conference on Software Engineering*, pages 495–505, Berlin, 1996.

[9] C. Michael, G. McGraw, and M. Schatz. Generating software test data by evolution. *IEEE Transactions on Software Engineering*, (12):1085–1110, Dec. 2001.

[10] J. Ning, A. Engberts, and V. Kozaczynski. Automated support for legacy code understanding. *Communications of the ACM*, 37(5):50–57, 1994.

[11] R. P. Pargas, M. J. Harrold, and R. R. Peck. Test-data generation using genetic algorithms. *The Journal of Software Testing, Verification and Reliability*, 9:263–282, 1999.

[12] R. E. Tarjan. Testing flow graph reducibility. *Journal of Computer and System Sciences*, 9(3):355–365, Dec. 1974.

[13] F. Tip. A survey of program slicing techniques. Technical Report CS-R9438, Centrum voor Wiskunde en Informatica, Amsterdam, 1994.

[14] N. Tracey, J. Clark, and K. Mander. Automated program flaw finding using simulated annealing. In *International Symposium on Software Testing and Analysis*, pages 73–81. ACM/SIGSOFT, March 1998.

[15] J. Wegener, A. Baresel, and H. Sthamer. Evolutionary test environment for automatic structural testing. *Information and Software Technology Special Issue on Software Engineering using Metaheuristic Innovative Algorithms*, 43(14):841–854, 2001.

[16] M. Weiser. Program slicing. *IEEE Transactions on Software Engineering*, 10(4):352–357, 1984.

Technical Papers

Software Architecture I

Comparison of Two Component Frameworks: The FIPA-Compliant Multi-Agent System and The Web-Centric J2EE Platform

Michelle Casagni Margaret Lyell
The MITRE Corporation
{ mcasagni, mlyell } @mitre.org

Abstract

This work compares and contrasts two component frameworks: (1) the web-centric Java 2 Enterprise Edition (J2EE) framework and (2) the FIPA-compliant multi-agent system (MAS). FIPA, the Foundation for Intelligent Physical Agents, provides specifications for agents and agent platforms. Both frameworks are component frameworks; servlets and Enterprise Java Beans (EJBs) in the case of J2EE and software agents in the case of MAS. Both frameworks are specification based. Both frameworks mandate platform responsibilities towards their respective component(s).

We develop a framework with which to structure the comparison of the component frameworks. We apply this comparison structure in the context of a 'Data Access' scenario to application development in the respective component frameworks. Furthermore, we have prototyped this scenario in each of the two component frameworks. We conclude with a discussion of the benefits, drawbacks, and issues of developing new applications in each of the component frameworks.

1. Introduction

Recent work by Griss and Pour [10] advanced the thesis that agent components are a potential foundation for "flexible, intelligent, Web-based enterprise application systems". In contrast, a leading contemporary component-based Web-centric architecture is that of the Java 2 Enterprise Edition (J2EE) platform. The question of how applications developed for the Web-centric, client-server, n-server tier, component-based architecture that is prevalent today will interoperate with applications developed in a software agent framework is the larger question that motivates our efforts. In this work, we develop a framework for comparing and contrasting the features of two classes of component frameworks: (1) the client-server, Web-based component architecture and (2) the software agent framework. In our work, we take the J2EE platform as the exemplar of the former. We consider only software agent components and multi-agent system (MAS) frameworks that are compliant with specifications set forth by the Foundation for Intelligent Physical Agents (FIPA). There are similarities between these two specification-grounded component frameworks. Obviously, both frameworks include components; servlets and Enterprise Java Beans in the case of J2EE and software agents in the case of FIPA-MAS. Both frameworks mandate platform responsibilities towards their respective component(s). There are also obvious differences in the nature of the components. For example, the paradigm that is software agents resides at a higher semantic level than that of the EJB or servlet component. Software agents have additional properties such as task-orientation, autonomy, and social-ability (communicative ability and co-cooperativeness) [23].

Efforts reported in the literature have involved disparate assessments of each of the individual component frameworks. EJBs have been evaluated against the quality attributes of (1) modifiability, (2) performance, and (3) availability in the work of [15]. With regard to software agent frameworks, previous assessments of MAS have not focused on FIPA-compliant systems nor have they utilized FIPA specifications. Rather, an architectural evaluation of MAS, organized by design patterns, has been given by [22]. This work considered the effect of MAS behavior on attributes of: (1) performance predictability, (2) security, (3) resiliency to modifiability of the environment, and (4) availability.

We develop a framework with which to structure the comparison between the J2EE framework and the FIPA-compliant agent framework. Our 'comparison structure' is informed by previous efforts that dealt with single framework assessment. We include consideration of design patterns and (an expanded set of) quality attributes as features in our comparison. Additional features in our comparison structure are a set of Design Properties for components and component-based applications. We discuss how these propagate into the quality attributes. (The propagation concept was put forth in another context by Bansiya [2].) Our comparison structure also considers the framework features that support component hosting,

0-7695-1877-X/03 $17.00 © 2003 IEEE

as well as design ramifications for the components due to framework considerations.

We apply the comparison structure in the context of a 'Data Access' scenario in order to highlight the similarities and differences that arise in the same application developed for the two different component frameworks. Additionally, we prototyped the 'Data Access' scenario in each of the component frameworks. The prototyping effort permits application of the 'resource consideration' and 'performance' elements of the comparison structure to each of the component-based solutions. Furthermore, the prototyping effort can potentially reveal absent features of the comparison structure.

2. Comparison structure

2.1. Comparison elements

The comparison structure consists of three sets: (1) Design Property Features, (2) Framework Impact Features, and (3) Quality Attributes. Design properties subdivide into those that pertain to a single component and to those that pertain to the overall application (composed of multiple components). We assume that the components in each of the frameworks have been developed in accordance with established Object Oriented (OO) design principles, and do not address this level. Use of a J2EE platform implies that component development will utilize Java. This situation does not strictly hold in the realm of FIPA-compliant software agent platforms. However, the vast majority of FIPA-compliant software agent platforms are developed in Java; individual agent development largely employs Java.

Comparison of the two frameworks draws on the J2EE specifications [14] and the FIPA specifications [8]. Elements of the comparison structure also require information pertaining to a platform implementation of the two respective frameworks. We use WebLogic (v6.1) and FIPA-OS (v2.0) as the exemplar implementations in Java. Other Java implementations of the FIPA specifications exists; for example, JADE [12]. However, this work is one thread of a larger effort that is utilizing FIPA-OS. (WebLogic is an established commercial platform [3]. FIPA-OS [9] is an open source reference implementation of the FIPA specifications developed by an industry team. The industry team and a developer community continue to add enhancements.)

The first set of elements in the comparison structure concerns Design Properties. Elements of this set, with their definitions are:

- Design Properties, Application Level
  - *Design Size*: Number of components in the application.
  - *Functional Cohesiveness*: A measure of how the aggregate components provide a unified 'application' to the user.
  - *Coupling*: Interactions among components that form an application.
- Design Properties, Component Level
  - *Inheritance / Templating*: Presence of base level requirements that must be satisfied in order to be a component, along with rules on component instantiation.
  - *Encapsulation*: A measure of how well the component is concerned with one 'topic'.
  - *Complexity*: A measure of the depth and breadth of a component's functionality.

The second set of elements in the comparison structure concerns Framework Impact issues. Elements of this set are:

- Framework Features supporting Component Hosting
  - *Platform Configuration Support*
  - *Descriptive Files*
  - *Packaging*
  - *Deployment*
  - *Services Offered by Platform to Component*
- Design Ramifications for Components due to Framework Considerations
  - *Component Access*
  - *Resource Restrictions Placed on Components by Platform*
  - *Design Pattern Usage*

The third set of elements in the comparison structure involves the Quality Attributes. Elements of this set, with their definitions are:

- *Availability*: Properties that promote or detract from the component or system's ability to perform its function.
- *Usability*: Assessment is from three viewpoints:
  - *Developer POV*: Properties that promote or detract from component development.
  - *Deployer POV*: Properties that promote or detract from component deployment.
  - *User POV*: Properties that promote or detract from application usage.
- *Modifiability*
  - *Maintainability*
    - *Extendibility*: Properties that support or hinder component or system modifications in order to incorporate new requirements.
    - *Reusability*: Properties that support or hinder a component's use in a new case without excessive effort.
  - *Flexibility:* Properties that promote or hinder the system's ability to respond to environmental changes (resources no longer available) without affecting the application's defined functionality.

- *Resource consideration*: Infrastructure-supplied resources expected to be utilized by the application.
- *Performance: (Restricted definition)* Timing measurements.

2.2. Application of comparison structure to component frameworks

Space limitations preclude an exposition of the full comparison structure applied to the two component frameworks. We present only selected elements in the comparison of the FIPA-compliant agent framework and the J2EE web-centric framework. For additional details, see [4].

A metric for *design size* is given by counting both the number of EJBs and servlets in the application hosted by the J2EE Platform, and the number of software agents in the multi-agent system that participate in the application. *Coupling*, another application level design property is highlighted in Table 1. The metric in table 1 yields the worst case for coupling between the components.

With regard to *inheritance/templating,* a component level comparison element, there are EJB specifications [7] regarding which interfaces must be implemented in order to develop {Entity, Session, or Message-Driven} EJBs. These interfaces extend specific 'javax.ejb' classes. Consider, for example, a Session EJB 'YYY'. In order to construct a Session Bean, a Remote interface and a Home interface must be defined. Remote interface 'YYY' must extend javax.ejb.EJBObject. Home interface 'YYYHome' must extend javax.ejb.EJBHome. The implementation 'YYYEJB' must implement javax.ejb.SessionBean.

In contrast, the FIPA specifications do *not* address this issue. Rather, the issue of agent templates or inheritance is the purview of the specific FIPA-compliant agent platform. For the case of the FIPA-OS platform, an application agent can extend a FIPA-OS agent. Specific tasks that an agent performs can extend the FIPA-OS Task class. Agents can also be part of an inheritance chain; the leaf agent is non-abstract.

Design patterns are used for application development in both of the component frameworks. In software agent systems, design patterns offer an approach to organizing roles and relationships in the multi-agent society. Common design patterns include the Mediator or Broker patterns, the Wrapper pattern, and the Peer-to-Peer pattern [11]. Within the J2EE framework, design patterns are employed to facilitate the connection of one component to another, potentially across tiers. Several design patterns have been mentioned in Table 1. Additional common patterns [20, 21] are the Service Locator pattern, used in a Session EJB, to hide the complexity of JNDI lookup calls, and the Model, View, Controller (MVC) pattern used in

Table 1. Design property: coupling

	EJBs and J2EE Framework	**Software Agents and FIPA-compliant MAS**
Definition Refinement	Interactions among EJBs or among servlets and EJBs.	Interactions among software agents in a MAS.
Comments	Interactions are via method invocation on business methods. (Business methods are defined in the Remote Interface.) HttpServlets are invoked by Get or Post methods from the client.	Interactions between two agents are via messaging. Messages are exchanged according to Interaction protocols. (FIPA defines standard semantically meaningful performatives and Interaction protocols.)
Issues	DESIGN ISSUE: Business Delegate and Façade Design patterns seek to minimize direct exposure of an EJB's business methods (to general clients). This controls granularity of access to EJBs. Entity EJBs may interact with each other. This is not desirable; it is mitigated via use of the Aggregate Entity Design pattern.	DESIGN ISSUE: Several agents in the MAS may form a sub-group. Communication to the sub-group may be restricted to only one agent in the sub-group.
Metric	Sum of [the number of Business Methods of each EJB multiplied by the number of remaining EJBs.] (Upper bound)	Sum of [number of Interaction protocols that an agent understands multiplied by the number of potential communicating agents in the MAS.]

servlets to separate the control logic from the presentation logic.

In the area of framework-driven design ramifications, specifically that of *component access* and *resource restrictions placed on components by platform*, it is noted that framework constraints are more severe on EJBs than on FIPA-compliant software agents. The J2EE application container mediates access to EJBs. An EJB should not act as a network server, nor listen, accept or multicast on a socket [1]. Furthermore, the application container manages resources, such as file I/O and threading, for the components. Resource restrictions placed on the EJB component affects design decisions, as will be evidenced in Section 3. In contrast, an agent in a FIPA-compliant MAS is free to use whatever resources it needs.

Another discriminator between the two component frameworks is the degree to which they support component hosting. In the area of *packaging*, the J2EE framework provides for servlets and other web components to be packaged in a '.war' file. EJB '.jar' files and relevant '.war' files can be packaged together in an '.ear' file. FIPA specifications do not address 'packaging' of software agent components that together form an application or offer functionality.

Table 2 looks at the *services that are offered by platforms* in each of the frameworks. The FIPA-compliant agent platform excels at offering a software agent component support for advertising its services and support for dynamically finding other agents and the services they offer. The J2EE platform excels in offering managed resources, such as database connections and Java Message Service destination channels. The J2EE platform, through the application container, also offers the Entity EJB components managed mapping of its data to database tables.

The quality attribute of *usability* is considered from multiple vantage points. With regard to the end-user, applications hosted in the J2EE platform generally offer the user a web-browser interface. Software agent systems do not offer a standard human-user interface to the system. Rather, the FIPA specifications focus on software agent to software agent interactions. Good functional cohesiveness of EJB components, together with appropriate design pattern usage, allows presentation of a unified application to a user. Reduced coupling among EJBs improves performance for the end-user.

From a deployer point-of-view, the J2EE platform offers standard directories for deploying '.war' files into the web container, and for deploying '.jar' and '.ear' files into the application container. Such files contain the Java classes that comprise the components. It is the FIPA-OS platform, rather than the FIPA specifications, which addresses software agent deployment. An agent loader allows automatic deployment of agents. A control GUI is also available for manual sequencing of agent start-up. Executable scripts can be used to control startup of individual agents, and allow for command line parameter passing. In the FIPA-OS agent system, attention is given to the mechanics of deployment, but not the organization of the deployment.

Table 2. Framework support for component hosting: services offered by the platform to the component

J2EE Platform	EJB lifecycle management, network access, security, transaction management, resource management, container managed persistence (Entity EJB). Platform offers servlet threading. Lookup provided by JNDI API.
FIPA-Compliant MAS Platform	Agent Management System (AMS) provides lifecycle management, white pages services. Directory Facilitator (DF) provides yellow pages services. Message transport services, for messages between agents on single FIPA-compliant platform and to other FIPA-compliant platforms. FIPA specifications provide a Service Description (SD) for any agent wishing to advertise its services with the DF. [The SD consists of descriptive {name,value} property pairs as well as sets of Interaction protocols understood by the agent/agent-service, set of ontologies used, and sets of agent content languages understood.] **NB: Specific to FIPA-OS** Conversation Managers and Task Managers are provided.

The deployer does not receive any assistance in the identification of resources from the FIPA-compliant software agent framework. The resources that a software agent must utilize, such as a JMS topic channel or a database connection, are not linked to the software agent in any standard manner. This is in contrast to what is offered by the J2EE specifications; resources required by components must be specified in standardized xml deployment descriptor files.

In MAS, a distinction is drawn between open and closed multi-agent systems. In an open MAS, a new software agent component joins the system; dynamic discovery by other agents permits the new agent to offer its services and be useful. However, the FIPA specifications do not require that an agent provide the necessary information for effective usage as part of its Service Description advertisement. For example, the agent is not required to list the Interaction protocols that it speaks. In a closed MAS, all of the software agent components and their Interaction protocol usage are considered known at design time.

These issues have implications for both *availability* and *reusability* in a FIPA-compliant MAS. Consider a scenario in which the "usual" agent offering a service becomes unavailable. A search for an alternative agent that offers the service is made using only key words for the service as search parameters. (The search can span multiple agent platforms.) Initial search results identify two other agents, SA1 and SA2, that offer the service. Neither SA1 nor SA2 advertise the Interaction protocols that they speak. Agent SA1 speaks a different Interaction protocol from the one that the requesting agent knows, but the requesting agent finds this out only when it communicates with SA1 and its request is not understood. At this point, the service is still unavailable to the requesting agent. The requestor then turns to agent SA2; it does speak the same Interaction protocol and handles the request. If FIPA specifications required agents to list the Interaction protocols they understand as part of their Service Description, requesting agents would be more likely to include Interaction protocol information in their search parameters. This could lessen the period of service unavailability.

With regard to *reusability*, in order to determine if an existing software agent component could be utilized in a new application, the developer has to inspect the code. The developer gains information as to what Interaction protocols, agent content languages and ontologies the software agent understands only by inspecting the code.

In contrast, the J2EE framework enhances component *reusability* and *availability*. The Remote Interface of an EJB lists the business methods that may be invoked on that component. This facilitates the use of that component in a new application. Failover strategies are not mandated by the J2EE specifications. However, commercial vendors do address this topic; enhancing the availability of an EJB component.

This section concludes with presentation of additional factors that affect *maintainability* in Table 3. In Section 4, two elements of the comparison structure, *resource consideration* and *performance*, are applied to each of the component frameworks in the context of a 'Data Access' scenario. This scenario has been prototyped and is described in the next section.

Table 3. Maintainability

	Component Level	**J2EE Platform Level**
Servlet	Excessive coupling (to EJBs) detracts from reuse; mitigated by use of MVC pattern. Good encapsulation facilitates maintainability.	Use of logical name and JNDI promotes reuse. Web container offers support to servlets, JSP's and HTML pages; promotes extendibility.
Enterprise JavaBean (EJB)	EJBs are portable among different vendor implementations of J2EE; promotes reusability. Good encapsulation facilitates maintainability. Encapsulation of JNDI information in Session EJB, and use of Service Locator Design pattern promotes maintainability.	Use of logical name and JNDI promotes reuse. Application container offers middleware support to EJBs; promotes reuse.
	Component Level	**FIPA-Compliant Agent System Level**
Software Agent	Good encapsulation, with clearly defined agent role, promotes agent reuse. An agent role with multiple responsibilities and complex task structure is not easily extended. User-defined Interaction protocols detract from agent reuse.	No requirement to provide elements of Service Description hinders reuse. Registration and searching functionality are supported by the system, supports adding new agents to meet new requirements (extendibility).

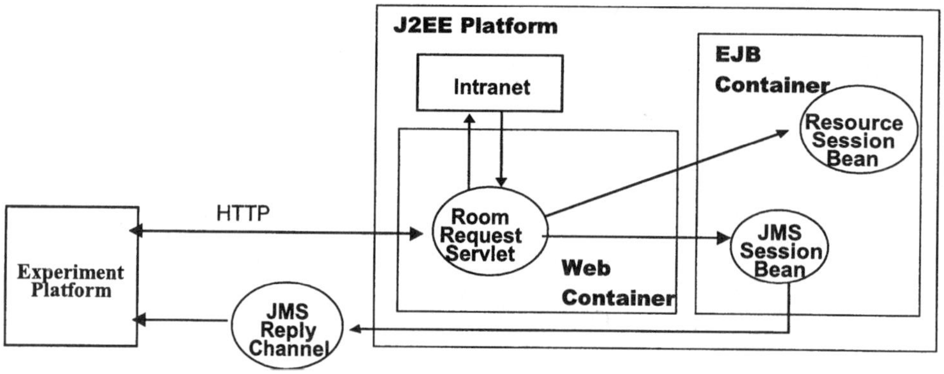

Figure 1. J2EE Hosted System Architecture

3. Data access scenario

A 'Data Access' scenario is used to provide a set of requirements for designing and implementing an application in both the J2EE platform and a FIPA-compliant Multi-Agent System. The experimental prototype further elucidates differences between the framework architectures and allows us to obtain basic performance results.

Users of the Experiment Platform, a pure Java application that is not based on agent frameworks or J2EE technology, are collaborating via a chat application and need to access information not available to them locally. To provide a reasonable example of data access from another platform, the experiment consists of answering a request based on both time sensitive information (changes frequently) and static information. Our scenario is to find a room available at a specific time that contains certain equipment and holds a specific number of people. The availability of a room is determined by searching an Intranet and the resources for each room are retrieved from a local data store.

In part I of the 'Data Access' experiments, a "Find Room Request" is generated by the Experiment Platform application. This request is processed by an application that is hosted by the J2EE framework. In part II of these experiments, the "Find Room Request" is processed by an application developed in a FIPA-MAS framework.

3.1. J2EE hosted application analysis and design

The analysis and design of the J2EE-based system began with a determination of which modes of communication to use between the Experiment Platform and the J2EE framework components. Using typical design choices for component development as a guideline, we iterated the identification of components in the framework to host the object functionality as we considered various communication options. Object-oriented analysis and design techniques as discussed in [19] were then used to design the objects, object attributes, relationship among objects and behavior of objects.

Resource restrictions placed on the components by the platform affected the design. For example, guidelines for developing Enterprise Java Beans [1] preclude them from accepting socket connections or listening on a port. Therefore, these components cannot listen directly for messages from the Experiment Platform. A Message-Driven Bean [7] could be hosted by the J2EE platform to receive requests from the experiment platform using the Java Message Service (JMS) [1]. To satisfy the scenario requirements, this approach requires an EJB to use the java.net.URLConnection class in order to check the schedule on the Intranet. The development guidelines do not restrict a URLConnection resource in an EJB, but this is not a typical usage.

Servlets, on the J2EE platform, are typically involved in a synchronous, request-response communication using the HTTP protocol. We wanted to design an asynchronous request-response to allow for the possibility of the "Find Room Request" not being fulfilled immediately. To provide an asynchronous solution, both HTTP and JMS were selected for communication between the Experiment Platform and the application hosted by the J2EE framework. HTTP was selected as the protocol for contacting the servlet, rather than JMS. This was for two reasons. First, servlets are typically HTTP servlets. Secondly, the effective use of JMS in a servlet requires session pooling, development of a new servlet engine and potentially modifications to the web container. We did not undertake this level of re-engineering. More recently, a Jakarta Commons Sandbox component, Messenger [18], is addressing this issue. (Note that the Sandbox area of the Commons project contains experimental (Not-Yet-Proposed) components [13].)

The design process involved mapping the entities from the Analysis phase into the proper components in the J2EE framework. UML sequence and class diagrams

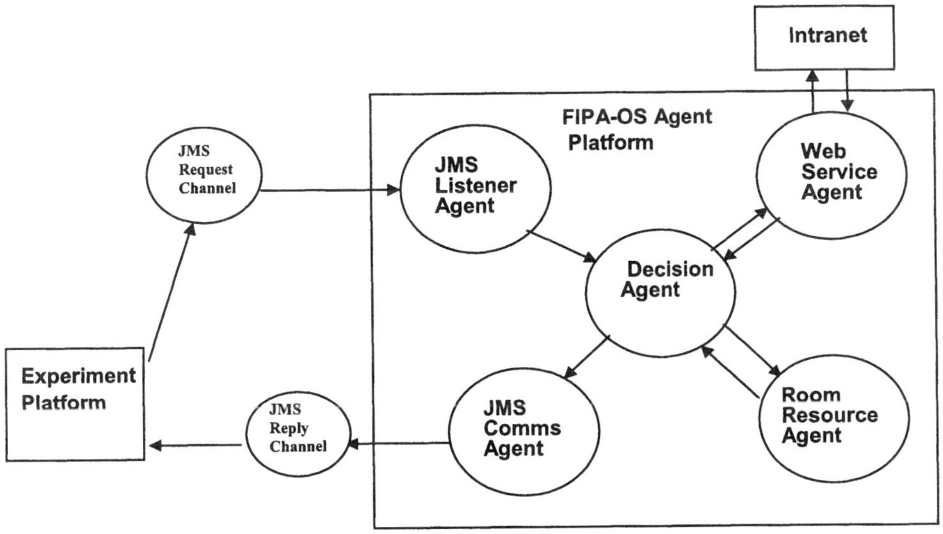

Figure 2. Multi-Agent System Architecture

were created to assist in this process. The final components of the J2EE application (Figure 1) consist of a Servlet and two Enterprise Java Beans. The servlet receives the "Find Room Request". It contains the logic to satisfy the request, but must invoke methods on the EJBs in order to process it. One EJB acts as a local datastore by holding static room data. It compares the static room resources against the requested resources. The other EJB generates and publishes the response as a JMS message. These operations do not require state, therefore, these components have been implemented as stateless session EJBs.

3.2. Multi-agent system application analysis and design

A similar analysis of communication modes was performed for the multi-agent system. Options presented by sockets, HTTP or JMS solutions presented no issues regarding resource usage restrictions according to the FIPA specifications. However, agents in a multi-agent system inherently communicate asynchronously. We wanted to develop the multi-agent system application according to common usage patterns. Thus, JMS is the optimal choice to use for the asynchronous communications. Previous demonstrations have shown that an agent in the FIPA-OS system can send JMS messages [16]. The JMS Comms Agent developed for that demonstration is reused in this multi agent system.

We employed a combination of the Multi-agent Systems Engineering (MaSE) methodology [5] and the Gaia methodology [24] for the analysis and design processes of the software agents in the multi-agent system. Note that for this prototype, we are developing a "closed" agent system. That is, all of the agents, with their responsibilities, resource needs, activities, and Interaction protocols, are known at the design phase. We began by capturing the system requirements as goals in a goals-hierarchy tree using the MaSE approach. These goals provided a task-oriented view of the system that laid out a foundation for describing the roles and responsibilities.

Table 4. Roles and Responsibilities Model

Roles	Responsibilities
Message Sender (=> JMS Comms Agent)	• Send "find room" results
Message Receiver (=> JMS Listener Agent)	• Receive "find room" requests and forward to Decision Maker for processing
Decision Maker (=> Decision Agent)	• Parse the "find room" request and obtain information to process it • Analyze the information to determine which rooms meet the request criteria • Generate the "find room" reply
Room Resource Holder (=> Room Resource Agent)	• Contain the list of resources for each room • Provide a list of rooms that meet the resource requirements
Web Service Provider (=> Web Service Agent)	• Search the Intranet for the room schedule • Provide a list of rooms available at the specified time

We followed an approach described by the Gaia methodology to generate the analysis phase products: a Roles model (Table 4) and an Interaction model. Each role in the Roles model has associated responsibilities. These roles evolved into five software agents in the final design (Figure 2): JMS Comms Agent, JMS Listener Agent, Decision Agent, Room Resource Agent, and Web Service Agent. The responsibilities are modeled as tasks. The interactions between the agents are in accordance with the FIPA Request Interaction Protocol.

The Interactions model revealed several design patterns. Roles within the system only interact with the Decision Maker role. This behavior is similar to that of the Mediator pattern as described by Hayden [11]. From the roles Message Receiver and Message Sender, we identify an agent design pattern that allows for an interface to a different framework. These roles, implemented as the JMS Listener Agent and the JMS Comms Agent, act as gateways into and out of the multi-agent system. The Gateway pattern is described in [4].

4. Application of comparison structure to prototype

4.1. Design properties

Design property metrics were applied to each application design solution of the 'Data Access' scenario. The *design size* of each application in the two component frameworks is roughly the same. The J2EE framework solution design size is three, with one servlet and two EJBs. The FIPA-compliant multi-agent solution design size is five, with five individual agents.

The *design patterns* employed in each approach highlight the *coupling* within that framework. In the J2EE framework, the servlet controls processing of the request. It invokes the stateless session EJBs to retrieve information for finding a room. In doing so, the servlet implements a Controller pattern [20]. Similarly, the Mediator pattern and the Gateway pattern organize agent interactions within the multi-agent system. The Decision Agent is responsible for interacting with other agents in the system to fulfill the "Find Room Request". Communication into and out of the multi-agent system is through the gateway agents.

All of the components in each framework use *inheritance/templating*. The servlet in the J2EE framework inherits from javax.http.servlet.HTTPServlet. The EJBs extend the javax.ejb.EJBHome and javax.ejb.EJBObject classes for their home and remote interfaces and implement the javax.ejb.SessionBean class. In the multi-agent system, each agent extends the FIPA-OS Agent class and specific tasks extend the FIPA-OS Task class.

The servlet in the J2EE framework *encapsulates* the logic of processing a "Find Room Request" by controlling the entire process of fulfilling the request. The EJBs *encapsulate* a single business process; one EJB searches the room resources and the other generates and publishes the JMS reply. Within the multi-agent system, each agent *encapsulates* its roles and responsibilities through the use of tasks.

Both the applications developed for the 'Data Access' scenario demonstrate *functional cohesiveness*. The servlet in the J2EE framework provides a single point of entry into the application. The EJBs provide the servlet with the additional functionality required to process the request in its entirety. Likewise, in the FIPA-compliant multi-agent system, the JMS Listener Agent provides a single point of entry into the system. The Decision Agent relies on the other agents within the system in order to complete the "Find Room Request".

4.2. Performance

Basic performance tests were done on the prototype applications. The end-to-end times for the "Find Room Request" from the Experiment Platform to the J2EE framework, and from the Experiment Platform to the FIPA-compliant MAS were measured. The networking for the prototype extends over a subnet. JMS and the J2EE framework are hosted on one machine. A second machine hosts the Experiment Platform and the MAS.

Overall, the application in the J2EE framework processes the request faster than the application in the multi-agent system. Most of the delay experienced using the multi-agent system is due to a 'Wait Task'. An agent discharges its responsibilities through execution of asynchronous tasks. Wait tasks are typically designed for use in situations such as polling, searching or acquiring a resource from another agent.

We used a 'Wait Task' to poll the incoming message queue. We experimented with 'Wait Task' times ranging from 100 ms to 10,000 ms; although it is unlikely that 100 ms would be used in practice. More typical 'Wait Task' times are between 5,000 and 10,000 ms. The 'Wait Task' time must be adequate for the agent system application. Wait tasks designed for polling could result in thrashing with too small a wait time. Conversation timeouts could result from too long a wait time when agents are waiting for search results or resources.

Table 5 contains some of the timing results obtained for the 'Data Access' prototypes. Each set of measurements is the average of ten experimental runs, with standard deviation indicated. The full set of performance results is given in [4].

Table 5. Performance Results

	Experiment Platform to J2EE Hosted Application	Experiment Platform to FIPA-MAS (Wait Task 5,000 ms)
Set 1	177 ms +/- 48 ms	3,021 ms +/- 1,586 ms
Set 2	134 ms +/- 37 ms	3,133 ms +/- 1,714 ms
Set 3	213 ms +/- 30 ms	3,202 ms +/- 1,021 ms
Set 4	306 ms +/- 184 ms	3,017 ms +/- 937 ms
Set 5	229 ms +/- 66 ms	2,932 ms +/- 1,557 ms
Set 6	137 ms +/- 21 ms	2,106 ms +/- 1,543 ms

4.3. Resource usage

Infrastructure resources utilized by the respective applications to process the "Find Room Request" in both the J2EE framework and the FIPA-compliant Multi-Agent System are listed in Table 6.

Table 6. Resource Usage

Resources Used	WebLogic 6.1 J2EE Platform	FIPA-OS Agent System
Comm (transport) protocols from/to user	JMS, HTTP	JMS
Components	Control/Decision Logic Servlet Resource EJB (stateless session bean) JMS-EJB (stateless session bean)	JMS Listener Agent JMS Comms Agent Decision Agent Resource Agent Intranet Agent
Deployment Components	Ejb-xml files (deployment descriptors, dd) Web-xml files (dd) War and EJB jar files (executables)	Bat Files Agent Loader Descriptor File
Framework Infrastructure Elements	Web Container Application (EJB) Container JMS Service	FIPA-OS platform with 2 agents: Agent Management System (AMS) and Directory Facilitator (DF) JMS Service

4.4. Developer experience

One of the authors (M. Casagni) served as the developer of the J2EE components and the software agent components. Her key development experiences are discussed in this section.

She was an experienced Java/J2EE developer, but did not have prior exposure to software agents and FIPA specifications. The detailed design provided a solid baseline, and she found implementation of the J2EE system straightforward. However, developing the prototype revealed some issues that were not apparent at design time. For example, use of a property file for global information such as URLs appeared to be a good design idea. Since guidelines indicate that EJBs should not access files, this required many parameters to be passed to them.

The property file was not an issue in the MAS as FIPA specifications indicate agents can access any resources they need. The Room Resource and Intranet Search components for both systems had similar designs, so she was able to reuse the business logic code in the respective agents. The parallel processing capabilities of a MAS allowed for the subtasks of scheduling a room and comparing the room resources to occur in parallel. In the J2EE system these tasks were performed sequentially.

The developer found the asynchronous, concurrent task structure inherent in agent design to be challenging. In particular, coding of the Decision Agent required more time and effort as she had to determine how to track the completion of multiple subtasks before initiating later tasks. Another implementation challenge was in properly incorporating the JMS resource into the agent task structure. The successful method involved having the Agent implement the MessageListener and execute a WaitTask. Whenever a JMS message was received, it was placed on a local list that was processed each time the WaitTask completed.

5. Related work

We are not aware of other work that performs a side-by-side comparison of a web centric architecture, the J2EE framework, to that of a FIPA-compliant software agent system. However, assessments have been done on the individual frameworks. Two such efforts were referenced in the Introduction section.

A recent effort due to Eiter and Mascardi [6] serves to compare software agent development environments (ADE). In general, the ADEs selected for this study were not FIPA-compliant. The authors determine a set of criteria for evaluating agent development environments and apply these criteria to several development tools and multi-agent system application scenarios. The end result is a set of guidelines for selection of a multi-agent system development kit.

6. Conclusions and future directions

We have developed a 'comparison structure' in order to elucidate the differences and similarities between the two component frameworks in a principled manner. We have applied this 'comparison structure' to a 'Data Access' scenario. In this section we highlight some of the results of our structured comparison between the two frameworks.

Certain similarities relate to application design. For example, an application should involve communication among its components, but excessive coupling is inconsistent with good design in both frameworks. Details in the realization of good design of components within the two frameworks do differ. For example, EJBs are single threaded, with their lifecycle managed by the container. Software agents are generally multi-threaded to reflect their task structure.

A difference in typical component usage occurs across the two frameworks. In the case of the J2EE framework, the servlet controls the communication to the EJB components, invoking (methods in) them in a sequential pattern. In the MAS, the interaction among components is asynchronous and can be done in parallel. For example, in the 'Data Access' prototype, the communication between the Decision Agent and the Resource Agent, and the Decision Agent and the Intranet Agent are done in parallel. The MAS framework is more suited to parallel processing than is the J2EE framework. (Of course, the application intrinsically must contain elements that can be parallelized.)

The MAS framework is more supportive of an 'open system' configuration, involving new software agents that join an established group at run-time. The FIPA-MAS infrastructure mandates a Directory Facilitator that supports lookup for services based on an ontologically-grounded Service Description. However, the FIPA-MAS framework does not mandate all infrastructure elements that would be useful in an 'open system'. For example, an ontology server is not required.

A 'closed system' MAS is closer to the J2EE framework than the 'open system' MAS. In this case, the software agent components are known at application design time, as are the EJB and servlet components. However, the J2EE framework specifications offer more support to the application developer, especially one attempting to reuse components. The Remote Interface must be specified for an EJB, thus exhibiting the business methods of that EJB. The FIPA specifications do not mandate that a software agent exposes the Interaction protocols that it understands. A developer must resort to the code base in order to determine them.

The J2EE specifications offer more support to the system deployer. These specifications offer a standard structure for component deployment and for component-resource association. Resource usage, such as database connections or JMS topic channels, is managed by the J2EE platform. Neither component deployment nor component-resource association is addressed by FIPA specifications. However, the FIPA-OS agent platform does provide an agent loader for deployment.

There are a number of commercial implementations of the J2EE specifications. As a result, the reliability of the J2EE platform is greater than that of the FIPA-MAS implementations. Performance benchmarks are available for different vendor implementations of the J2EE platform, thus enhancing predictability of performance. In implementations of the FIPA specifications, reliability is the responsibility of the application developer. Performance studies of such implementation platforms are sparse. A recent study investigated the FIPA-OS platform [17]. Performance tuning can involve fine-grained tuning of an individual software agent component's task parameters.

If an application is inherently parallel, or if the majority of communications within the system will be asynchronous, or if the application is conceived to be an open system which will grow dynamically, then the designer is advised to consider the FIPA-MAS framework. In doing this, the system designer will have to provide for reliability. Selecting a FIPA-MAS approach will also require more performance testing. System deployment procedures will also have to be developed.

We plan to apply the 'comparison structure' to other scenarios. Also, efforts are planned in the area of MAS infrastructure and reliability.

7. References

[1] Allamaraju, S., K. Avedal, R. Browett, J. Diamond, J. Griffin, M. Holden, A. Hoskinson, R. Johnson, T. Karsjens, L. Kim, A. Longshaw, T. Myers, A. Nakhimovsky, D. O'Connor, S. Tyagi, G. Van Damme, G. van Huizen, M. Wilcox, S. Zeiger, *Professional Java Server Programming, J2EE Edition*, Wrox Press Ltd., Birmingham, UK, 2000.

[2] J. Bansiya and C.G. Davis, "A Hierarchical Model for Object-Oriented Design Quality Assessment," *IEEE Transactions on Software Engineering*, Vol. 28, No. 1, January 2002, pp. 4-17.

[3] BEA WebLogic web site, http://www.bea.com/

[4] M. Casagni, M. Lyell., L. Rosen, G. Vecellio, J. Warren, and H. Xiao "Architecture Comparison of J2EE Framework and FIPA-Compliant Software Agent Framework Using a Data Access Scenario," MTR 02W0000026, The MITRE Corporation, May 2002.

[5] S. DeLoach, M. Wood, and C. Sparkman, "Multi-agent Systems Engineering," *International Journal on Software Engineering and Knowledge Engineering*, Vol 11, No. 3, June 2001, pp. 231-258.

[6] T. Eiter and V. Mascardi, "Comparing Environments for Developing Software Agents," INFSYS Research Report 1843-01-02, Institut Für Informationssysteme, Technical University, Vienna, March 2001.

[7] Enterprise Java Beans Specification 2.0 web site http://java.sun.com/products/ejb/docs.html

[8] FIPA specifications, See web site, http://www.fipa.org/

[9] FIPA-OS project hosted at the web site, http://sourceforge.net/projects/fipa-os/

[10] M. Griss and G. Pour, "Accelerating Development with Components", *Computer*, Vol. 34, No. 5, May 2001, pp. 37-43.

[11] S. Hayden,, C. Carrick, and Q. Yang. "Architectural Design Patterns for Multiagent Coordination." *In Proc. of the International Conference on Agent Systems* (Agents'99), Seattle, WA, May 1999.

[12] JADE project web site http://sharon.cselt.it/projects/jade/

[13] Jakarta Commons website http://jakarta.apache.org/commons/components.html

[14] "Java 2 Platform Enterprise Edition Specification v1.3", Sun Microsystems, July 2001.

[15] A. Liu, L. Bass, and M. Klein, "Analyzing Enterprise Java Beans Systems using Quality Attribute Design Primitives," Technical Note, CMU/ SEI-2001-TN-025,Carnegie Mellon University, 2001.

[16] M. Lyell, L. Rosen, G. Vecellio, H. Xiao , "Interoperability through Messaging: An Investigation of Software Agent Frameworks as Compared with the J2EE Framework,", WN 01W0000022, The MITRE Corporation, May, 2001.

[17] M. Lyell , H. Xiao , L. Rosen, M. Casagni, G. Vecellio, J. Warren , "Performance Study of Software Agent Systems Using the FIPA OS V2.0 Agent Platform," MTR 02W0000032, The MITRE Corporation, May, 2002.

[18] Messenger, Jakarta Commons component, website http://jakarta.apache.org/commons/sandbox/messenger/

[19] Rumbaugh, J., M. Blaha, W. Premerlani, F. Eddy, W. Lorensen, *Object-Oriented Modeling and Design*, Prentice Hall, Englewood Cliffs, NJ, 1991.

[20] Stelting, S. and Maassen, O, *Applied Java Patterns*, Prentice Hall, Palo Alto, CA, 2002.

[21] Sun Java Center J2EE Patterns web site, http://developer.java.sun.com/developer/restricted/patterns/J2EEPatternsAtAGlance.html

[22] S. Woods and M. Barbacci,, "Architectural Evaluation of Collaborative Agent-Based Systems," Technical Note, CMU/ SEI-99-TN- 025, ESC-TR-99-025, Carnegie Mellon University, 1999.

[23] M. Wooldridge and N.R. Jennings, "Intelligent Agents: Theory and Practice," *Knowledge Engineering Review*, Vol. 10, No.2, 1995, pp. 115-152.

[24] M. Wooldridge, N.R. Jennings, and D. Kinny: "The Gaia Methodology for Agent-Oriented Analysis and Design," *Autonomous Agents and Multi-Agent Systems*, Vol. 3, No. 3, 2000, pp. 285-312.

Design Pattern Rationale Graphs: Linking Design to Source

Elisa L.A. Baniassad & Gail C. Murphy
University of British Columbia
2366 Main Mall Vancouver Canada V6T 1Z4
{bani,murphy}@cs.ubc.ca

Christa Schwanninger
Siemens AG, CTSE 2
Otto-Hahn-Ring 6, 81739, Munich Germany
christa.schwanninger@siemens.com

Abstract

A developer attempting to evolve a system in which design patterns have been applied can benefit from knowing which code implements which design pattern. For instance, the developer may be able to understand the purpose, or to assess the flexibility of the code, more quickly. The degree to which the developer benefits depends upon their understanding of the pattern. Achieving an in-depth understanding of even a simple pattern can be difficult as pattern descriptions span several pages of text, and discuss interrelated design concepts and choices. To enable a developer to effectively trace the design goals associated with a pattern to and from source, we have developed the Design Pattern Rationale Graph (DPRG) approach and associated tool. A DPRG makes explicit the relationships between design concepts in a design pattern, provides a graphical representation of the design pattern text, and supports the linking of those concepts to implementing code. In this paper, we introduce the DPRG approach and tool, and present case studies to show that a DPRG can, at low-cost, help a developer identify design goals in a pattern, and can improve a developer's confidence about how those goals are realized in a code base.

1 Introduction

> A design pattern names, abstracts, and identifies the key aspects of a common design structure that make it useful for creating a reusable object-oriented design. ...[A design pattern] describes when it applies, whether it can be applied in view of other design constraints, and the consequences and trade-offs of its use. [6, p. 3-4]

A developer who has chosen to implement a particular design pattern as part of building a software system must make choices amongst the implementation alternatives presented in the pattern. For instance, in the OBSERVER design pattern [6], which provides a solution for notifying registered dependents (observers) when a particular object (a subject) changes state, the developer must decide how to transmit information related to the change. One option is the push model in which the subject sends all observers detailed information whether or not each observer needs it: This approach can limit the reusability of observers. Another option is the pull model in which the subject may send little information, requiring interested observers to request needed details: This approach can be inefficient because an interested observer has to try to determine what changed.

A developer who is later asked to perform an evolution task involving this code, such as adding a new feature or fixing a defect, can benefit from knowing that it represents the OBSERVER pattern. For instance, the developer may be able to understand the purpose of the code more quickly, to posit how the code works, or to understand the flexibility of the code. The developer may be able to recognize the pattern by comments in the code, by the names chosen for the classes or methods in the code, through the use of a pattern finding tool (e.g., [18]), or through the use of a pattern generation or encoding technique (e.g., [22, 8])

The degree to which a developer benefits from knowing that a piece of code implements a particular pattern depends upon the developer's understanding of the design pattern. If the developer knows many of the possible implementation variants and understands their relationship to design goals, the developer can work with the code effectively. Achieving an in-depth knowledge of even a single pattern can be difficult as the pattern description may span several pages of text and may include several diagrams. The OBSERVER pattern, for instance, is eleven pages long and discusses more than seven significant implementation choices, including how to store the subject-to-observer mapping, and how unexpected updates can be handled. Trying to understand which variant was implemented, why that variant was chosen, and the effect of that variant on design goals requires careful reading and analysis of the pattern. In the open source and industrial code that we have examined, the original developers have seldom provided this kind of *ra-*

0-7695-1877-X/03 $17.00 © 2003 IEEE

tionale in any comments or documentation associated with the code. A developer encountering the code must thus recall or find the rationale in the text of the design pattern itself. In a small exploratory study we conducted involving the Visitor [6] and Reactor [19] design patterns, we found that pattern-experienced developers had difficulty answering detailed questions about how the pattern worked based on a reading of the pattern alone [1].

To enable a developer to trace the design goals associated with an implementation of a pattern to and from source code implementing the pattern, we have developed the Design Pattern Rationale Graph (DPRG) approach and associated tool. A DPRG makes explicit the relationships between design concepts in a design pattern, provides a graphical representation of the design pattern text, and supports the linking of the design concepts to the implementing source code. With a DPRG, a developer can navigate from a design concept in the pattern to other relevant parts of the pattern, and to the implementation of the concept in source code. A developer can also navigate from a class or method in the source to relevant parts of the pattern. This support helps a developer reason about their code in the context of the relevant design concepts. Our tool is lightweight: A DPRG can be built and linked to source at reasonable cost.

In this paper, we present the DPRG approach and tool in the context of a simple scenario (Section 2). We also present a number of case studies we have conducted with pattern-experienced developers to validate the utility of the approach (Section 3). In the latter part of the paper, we discuss outstanding issues with our approach (Section 4), compare to related efforts (Section 5), and summarize (Section 6).

2 Design Pattern Rationale Graphs

To introduce the concept of a DPRG, and to explain how a DPRG can be used by a developer, we consider a simple scenario. In this scenario, a developer has been asked to improve the efficiency of a drawing editor built on the JHotDraw object-oriented framework [9]. The design of JHotDraw relies on several design patterns, including OBSERVER. In our scenario, the developer has decided to investigate the efficiency of a part of the code implementing the OBSERVER pattern. We describe the format of the DPRG, how one is created, and how one is used.

2.1. Overview

A DPRG consists of three levels (Figure 1): pattern, source, and link. Our current DPRG tool requires one DPRG per instance of a design pattern in the source.

The pattern level consists primarily of sentence chains—graphical representations of the sentences comprising the

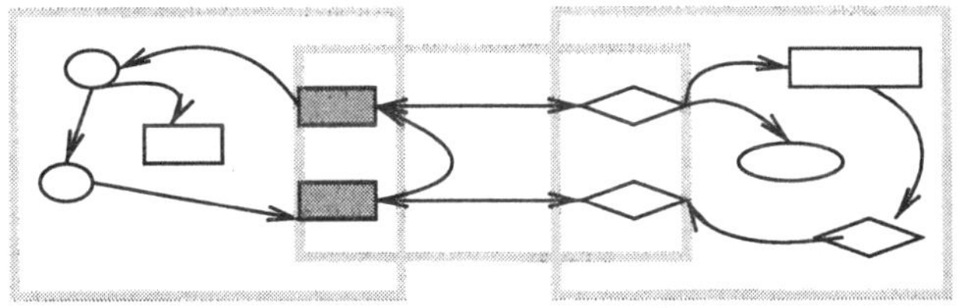

Figure 1. Three Levels of a DPRG.

text of the design pattern of interest. These chains are a direct translation, formed semi-automatically, from the design pattern text. The left area of Figure 2 shows two sentence chains from an OBSERVER DPRG including one corresponding to the part of the following sentence from the pattern "pull model may be inefficient because Observer classes must ascertain what changed without help from the Subject" [6, p.298]. Noun phrases in a sentence chain are are shown as rectangular nodes; verb phrases are shown as oval nodes.[1] Edges associating noun and verb phrases are annotated with the parts of the sentence that serve to connect the phrases in the pattern text. A developer reads this sentence from the DPRG by locating the root of a verb phrase chain, such as `may be`. The subject of this verb can be found by following edges into the verb, in this case, `pull model`. The object of the verb can be found by following edges out of the verb, such as `inefficient`. Diamond-shaped nodes are sequence nodes; when order matters, they indicate the order in which sentence chains should be read.

Noun phrases that represent a pattern design element are represented by a single (gray rectangular) node in the DPRG pattern level, enabling the DPRG to bring together all parts of the pattern text related to that element.[2] For example, the `observer` node in the DPRG in Figure 2 is a design element node, and thus brings together, in this fragment, two sentences related to the concept from the pattern text. Dashed edges associate these nodes with phrases that modify them. In this figure, there are two such associations: *update efficiency*, and *observer classes*. When reading sentences, such node-pairs should be read together.

The source level contains information about structural relationships derived from the code base. Nodes in this level are entities from the code, such as classes and methods. Edges are relationships between entities, representing structural associations such as calls between methods, or inheritance relationships between classes. In the area marked *Source Level* of Figure 2, seven source level nodes representing JHotDraw elements are shown. A developer can determine from this representation that the `PolyLineFig-`

[1] A noun or verb phrase may consist of a single noun or a single verb.

[2] Our tool colour codes the nodes according to their role in a sentence to make it easier to read a DPRG.

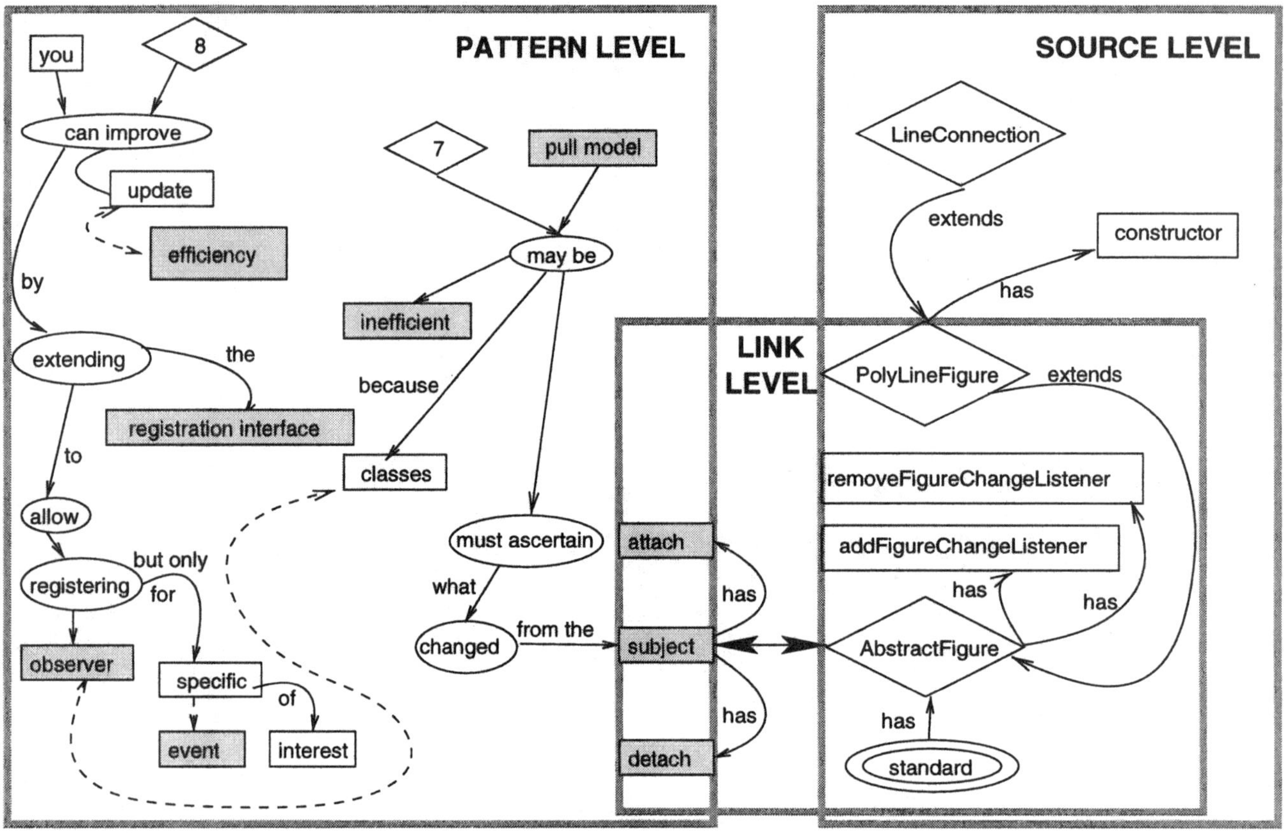

Figure 2. Three queries on a DPRG of OBSERVER**/JHotDraw: a regular expression query for** **efficien**, **a link level expansion of** *subject*, **and a source level expansion of** `PolyLineFigure`

`ure` class extends the `AbstractFigure` class, that `AbstractFigure` is contained in the `standard` package and has two methods, `removeFigureChangeListener` and `addFigureChangeListener`, and that the `LineConnection` class extends the `PolyLineFigure` class, which has a constructor.

The link level represents the association between elements from the design pattern and entities in the source. The link level contains nodes from the pattern level, nodes from the source level, and edges associating the two. The left most portion of the graph in Figure 2 shows a portion of the link level where the pattern-level `subject` node has been associated with the JHotDraw `AbstractFigure` class.

2.2. Creating a DPRG

A developer must create each level of the DPRG. Effort invested in creating the pattern level can likely be amortized over the linking of that pattern level to different implementations of the pattern. Effort invested in creating the source level can be amortized over the investigations of different patterns for that source base.

Pattern Level Creation Creating the pattern level requires three inputs: the text comprising the pattern, a dictionary of design elements—participants, and concepts—specific to the pattern, and an encoding of the structure section of the pattern.

Providing the text is straightforward: it can be extracted from a digital representation of the pattern. The only sections that are not used from the pattern text are those that relate to sample code, and to known uses of the pattern. The developer must annotate the text to include sequential information by adding the word, "first", to the beginning of the first sentence in a set of steps, and the word, "then", to the beginning of each subsequent sentence. We have not found this step onerous; it took one of the authors less than 10 minutes to annotate the text of the OBSERVER pattern.

To help the developer provide the dictionary of keywords, our DPRG tool extracts a list of noun phrases found in the pattern text. The developer then peruses this list, and identifies those noun phrases that are design elements. For the OBSERVER DPRG, the design elements identified included `change request`, `notify` and `observer`. Nouns not chosen as design elements included `need`, `state`, `class`, and `call`. It took developers in one of our studies (see Section 3), approximately 10 minutes to identify 28 (of 400) noun phrases from the OBSERVER pattern text as design elements. A developer using a DPRG can easily refine the keywords chosen as design elements, and regenerate the DPRG pattern level, if needed.

Providing the encoding of the structure section consists of extracting the participants and their relationships from the structural diagram within the pattern, and recording the information in a simple textual format. The relationships of interest are the same as those described below for the source level. These associations are shown in Figure 2 as link level edges between the pattern level nodes: The `subject` has `attach` and `detach` methods. This information could be automatically analyzed and extracted from a digital representation of the pattern; our DPRG tool does not yet have this capability.

Given these inputs, the DPRG tool automatically creates the pattern level. Using a parts-of-speech tagger called LTCHUNK [15], the DPRG tool identifies the noun and verb phrases in each sentence of the pattern text. Each sentence is then processed individually. Except for noun phrases included in the dictionary, each occurrence of a noun or verb phrase introduces a new node into the pattern level. The first node identified in a sentence, whether a noun or a verb phrase, is considered a source node. Each subsequent node encountered in the same sentence is considered a destination node, and causes the introduction of an edge between the source and destination nodes. When a node based on a verb phrase is encountered, the source node is reset to the verb phrase node. Edges are labeled by any phrase linking the noun and verb phrases.

Source Level Creation To create the source level, the developer runs a third-party program database tool that can extract entities and relationships—source models—from the code base. For the JHotDraw example, we used the Chava tool [13], which operates on Java class files, and post-processed its output with a simple script to massage the data into the format expected by our DPRG tool.

The source models we used for the examples and studies presented in this paper included: the *extends* relation between classes, the *calls* relation between methods, the *has* relation between any source entity, such as a class has methods, the *accesses/writes* relations describing when a method reads/writes the value of a field, the *implements* relation between classes and interfaces, and the *takes* relation where a method takes a type as a parameter.

Link Level Creation Links between the pattern and source levels in a DPRG are specified by the developer through the use of the DPRG tool's *links view*. To initialize this view, the developer provides one or more seeds: A seed describes an entity in the source level that the developer believes corresponds to an entity from the structure section of the pattern. For instance, for the OBSERVER example, the developer may seed an entry associating the `FigureChangeListener` interface from JHotDraw with the `observer` pattern entity. Positing this relationship requires minimal perusal of the code, and some understanding of standard Java coding conventions.

Given this seed, the tool can infer additional links. For instance, after two iterations, our tool presented a number of possibilities in the *links view*,[3] including the following:

```
U, update
U, subject state
N, subject, AbstractFigure
A, attach, addFigureChangeListener
A, detach, removeFigureChangeListener
A, notify, figureInvalidated
```

Each entry in the links view depicts its status: a `U` indicates an unlinked pattern-level node entry, such as `subject state`; an `N` indicates a link inferred by the tool, such as `subject-AbstractFigure`; and an `A` indicates a link a developer has accepted as accurate, such as `attach-addFigureChangeListener`. From the *links view*, a developer can inspect a link, exclude unwanted links, or infer additional links.

Inspecting a link results in a display of a portion of the DPRG that shows the pair of nodes comprising the link, and all nodes which have an edge to or from one of the nodes in the pair. Edges between these surrounding nodes are also included. Inspecting the inferred `subject-AbstractFigure` link results in display of the link level shown in Figure 2. The context shown in this view supports the inferred link since the methods of `AbstractFigure` could play the roles of the `attach` and `detach` methods from the pattern.

Excluding a link flags the link in the view as excluded. An excluded link is not considered in further inference. At any time, a developer can reaccept a previously excluded link.

When a developer chooses to infer additional links, the tool iterates across all seeded and accepted links. For each such link, the tool compares the relationships emanating from the source entity node with those emanating from the pattern level node. Where the relationships agree, the end points of the matching relationships are suggested as new links.

A developer continues seeding, inferring, and excluding links until satisfied that the pattern is linked to the code base. In one of our studies (Section 3), developers were able to link JHotDraw to OBSERVER, and to investigate the con-

[3]The *links view* is a simple textual window. We have chosen not to reproduce the window for space considerations, showing only the content.

nection in the context of an assigned task, in approximately one hour despite being unfamiliar with the code base.

2.3. Investigating a DPRG

To select relevant portions of the DPRG to view to aid with the task at hand, a developer can use two kinds of query operations: regular expression searching, and node expansion.

A regular expression query applies to the pattern level, and results in the inclusion of all sentence chains containing nodes that satisfy the expression, and all sequence nodes that point into those sentence chains. This kind of query is used to focus on a particular concept within a pattern. The developer can begin investigating efficiency in an implementation of the OBSERVER pattern using this kind of query by searching for the regular expression **efficien** to capture nouns involved with both efficiency and inefficiency, such as *efficient*, *efficiency*, *inefficient*, and *inefficiency*. The result of this query is shown in the pattern level of Figure 2. Viewing these results, the developer sees that the "pull model may be inefficient".

Node expansion queries support navigation between different levels of a DPRG. For example, expanding the *subject* node in the link level of Figure 2 reveals a node representing the `AbstractFigure` class in JHotDraw, which corresponds to the `subject`, and also reveals the other link level nodes neighboring the *subject* and the `AbstractFigure` nodes. To better understand the context of `AbstractFigure`, the developer can expand the class `polyLineFigure` at the source level, resulting in the source level portion of Figure 2, in which all source level nodes neighboring the expanded node are displayed.

To further investigate *efficiency*, the developer decides to expand the `pull model` pattern level node for more information about the concept (results not shown). Expanding a node at the pattern level results in a view of all sentence chains and all sequences that contain the expanded node. This query results in a DPRG that includes the following fragments of sentence chains: "the pull model sends minimal notification", and the pull model "emphasizes the ignorance of the subject". One sentence chain mentions another option, the *push model*, as an alternative strategy.

Based on an investigation of the results of these queries, the developer determines that efficiency might be improved by investigating the push model. Changing to the push model would likely require modifications to the notification mechanism. Thus, the developer decides to perform a regular expression query for **notif**. The sentence chains displayed include a node called `notify method`. To see how this node relates to the code base of interest, the developer expands the `notify method` node at the link level, and finds the `FigureInvalidated` method. The developer now has a concrete location in the code from which to consider the change task.

3 Case Studies

We make three claims about the DPRG approach:

1. Confidence — Access to a DPRG will improve a developer's confidence about which design goals are relevant to a (part of a) code base.
2. Completeness — Given a DPRG, a developer can effectively navigate to all design goals related to (a part of a) code base.
3. Lightweightness — Developers can create DPRG at reasonable cost.

We use the term design goal to refer to a property desired in the system, such as avoiding race conditions, or easing the introduction of a new algorithm.

We chose to evaluate each of these claims in a separate case study.

3.1. Confidence Study

The purpose of this study was to investigate whether access to a DPRG can improve a developer's confidence that design goals, such as efficiency and synchronization, are achieved in a code base. The study consisted of two cases. In each case, the subject, a developer from Siemens AG, was asked to use a DPRG to revisit an investigation task they had recently finished. The investigator provided the pattern level of a DPRG for a pattern chosen as relevant by the subject, and a source model of the subject's code base. The subjects were given a 35 minute tutorial on how to use a DPRG. The subjects were alloted one hour to apply the DPRG tool to their system. During a session, the subjects worked only with the DPRG.

Validity We informed each subject that the intent of the study was to observe their use of the DPRG tool when investigating design goals. When we analyzed their use of the tool and their responses to an interview, we focused on what information a subject learned about their system. If the developer learned something about the goals associated with their code, we consider their confidence was increased. We did not ask subjects directly about their confidence to avoid hypothesis guessing and evaluation apprehension. The subjects did ask questions about the DPRG approach during a session; the investigator was careful to limit responses to the use of the DPRG and did not provide direct assistance with the task. Our choice of using tasks completed previously by the subjects may have affected the results because the subjects may have been unwittingly wary of admitting they missed information when they performed the task.

Case #1 As part of an earlier task on a system that supported the visualization of object connections in a distributed system, the subject had implemented a locking mechanism to allow only one method of an object to execute at one time. The subject later learned about the MONITOR OBJECT pattern [3], which synchronizes concurrent method execution within an object to ensure only one method runs at any given time within the object. The subject believed that this design pattern closely represented her implementation. The subject had attempted to match her implementation to the pattern previously with limited success.

Actions The subject started by seeding three links, including an association between a class, `Monitor Condition`, in the pattern and a method, `TransmitCallID`, in the code base. The subject then used the DPRG tool to infer additional links, resulting in a suggestion by the tool that the `TransmitCallID` method be associated with the `synchronized method` pattern element. After inspecting the suggested link, the subject wanted to know more about synchronization in the pattern and thus chose to search for "block" at the pattern level. This query resulted in 18 sentences, one of which included the phrase: "if a synchronized method must block or cannot make immediate progress, it can wait on one of its monitor conditions". The subject then revisited the inspection view of the `synchronized method–TransmitCallID` link, and expanded the `synchronized method` node at the pattern level. From the resulting graph, the subject learned about the relationships between the `synchronized method` and the `monitor object`.[4] Specifically, the following sentence was displayed: "A monitor object therefore contains a monitor lock that serializes the execution of its synchronized methods, as well as one or more monitor conditions used to schedule the execution of synchronized methods within a monitor object". At this point, the subject reported that their initial seeding of the `TransmitCallID` method with the `monitor condition` class was incorrect, and that the proposed link from the `synchronized method` to the `TransmitCallID` method was correct. The subject then expanded the `monitor object` at the pattern level, revealing the caller of the `synchronized method` to be the `client`. After some investigation, the subject noted that the methods exported by the `monitor object` are often synchronized.

At the end of the session, the subject stated that they believed the code matched the MONITOR OBJECT pattern.

Results Before using the DPRG, the subject was unsure whether her code implemented the design pattern despite having spent time attempting to make the correspondence. The subject also did not have a good understanding of the pattern as can be seen from her initial seeding attempt. Before accepting the tool's suggestion on a different link, the subject investigated the context for various portions of the pattern. After the study, the subject stated that she believed her implementation was structurally similar to the solution described in the pattern. Furthermore, the subject was able to articulate that her solution shared the pattern design goals of method synchronization, and of allowing only one synchronized method in an object to run at a time to prevent race conditions. The subject was also able to articulate that the code and the pattern shared the drawback that it may be difficult to change the synchronization policy. We infer that this subject's confidence about their understanding of the relationship between design goals and the code base increased after using the DPRG.

[4]The `monitor object` is used by the `monitor condition` class.

When asked whether the DPRG tool had been helpful, the subject said:

> I didn't even really understand which part of my code is really a condition and which is the synchronize method. I didn't know this before. [The DPRG] helps because you really have a crosscutting view, you can read it in the sentence, and you can match this to the method you see in the code. But [the pattern] is quite difficult to understand so it helps to have this [pattern level] view and this matching into the source code.

Case #2 The second subject was instrumenting methods in a system pertaining to certain design patterns to enable the generation of sequence diagrams from system execution traces. This study involved the FORWARDER-RECEIVER pattern, which consists of a forwarder, who upon receipt of a message, sends the message on to a receiver. The subject reported only a cursory understanding of the FORWARDER-RECEIVER pattern at the start of the study, and reported being familiar with the code base.

Actions The subject began by positing one seed that related a class in the code to the forwarder, and then used the tool to infer more links. The tool suggested that two methods in the pattern, the `marshal` method, which prepares a method for forwarding, and the `sendMsg` method, which performs the action, as possible links for the `sendCmdAsynch` and `sendCmdSynch` methods in the code. The subject did not recognize the role of the `marshal` method. To investigate, she inspected the suggested link, and expanded the `marshal` method at the pattern level. Upon reading the displayed description, the subject noted that it was likely that this functionality had been absorbed into the `sendCmdAsynch` method and `sendCmdSynch` methods.

The subject then chose to investigate the `sendCmdSynch` and `sendCmdAsynch` methods. She was reminded that the code base to which she was adding tracing had taken two approaches to implementing the pattern. Given the linking of each of these methods to `marshall`, she was unsure of the pattern's intent with relation to asynchronous versus synchronous approaches. To investigate further, she performed a search for "asynch", which resulted in several sentences, including one stating that the developer "must decide whether the receiver should block until the message arrives". The subject said that she was unware that the pattern had not required both the asynchronous and synchronous options, but she now understood that the original developers had implemented both options.

The subject then performed a pattern-level search for the regular expression "blocking", which resulted in several sentences, including the following: "if the underlying IPC mechanism does not support non-blocking, the developer could use a separate thread to handle communication". The results of the query also included the information that certain timeout values were involved in the non-blocking implementation. The subject indicated that this was likely the approach taken in the asynchronous version of the implemented code.

Results Using the DPRG tool, the subject learned about differences between the concrete design provided in the pattern and the implementation of the pattern in the system being studied. The subject used information from the pattern level to investigate the differences until she was satisfied the differences were consistent with intent of the pattern. The subject also learned about options in the pattern of which she was unaware. With the help of the DPRG tool, she was able to focus on the pertinent parts of the pattern, and was able to then explain the code. We infer from her explanations that her confidence about which design goals were met in the system increased after the use of the DPRG tool.

3.2. Completeness Study

To verify that relevant design goals that are described in a design pattern can be identified from portions of code, we conducted a case study that involved two industrial software developers with expertise in both patterns and a particular code base, and one DPRG tool user (an author on this paper) who was unfamiliar with both the patterns and the code base. The experts worked together to report design goals relevant to certain portions of the Zen CORBA ORB [23]. The implementation of this system was based on a number of design patterns. Based on information provided by the experts, the investigator created several DPRG's. The tool user was then asked to report the design goals related to the code linked in the provided DPRGs. The user used expansion queries from the link level up to the pattern level to prepare the results reported. Three design patterns were used in the study: CACHING [11], THREAD SPECIFIC STORAGE [3] and STRATEGY [6].

Validity To ensure the DPRG tool user did not fish for high-level goals, the user was not informed of any target design goals, and was restricted in the kinds of searches allowed.

Results The tool user identified six of the seven goals identified by the experts, and noted eleven additional goals. The one goal missed was the *avoidance of blocking overhead* in the THREAD SPECIFIC STORAGE pattern. This goal is not described explicitly in the design pattern text; it thus falls outside the scope of the DPRG..

When the expert participants were asked to examine the list of eleven additional goals, they reported that all were considered applicable, though of secondary importance. From these results we conclude that the DPRG representation and tool do enable a developer to effectively navigate to the relevant high-level design goals.

3.3. Lightweightness Study

To be useful, it must be possible for a developer to create and use a DPRG at reasonable cost. To investigate whether our approach meets this goal, we conducted a study in which two industrial developers from Siemens AG were given the task of finding portions of JHotDraw code related to efficiency in the OBSERVER pattern using a DPRG that they had to create. We provided the subjects with the source level for JHotDraw, and the massaged text and encoded structure section of the OBSERVER pattern. We provided these inputs as the need to provide this information is dependent upon the current state of the tool, and is not central to the approach. To create the DPRG, the subjects had to create the dictionary to be used in pattern level creation, and had to create the link level.

Validity The developers had access only to the DPRG tool. The task we chose stressed information across the levels of the DPRG. The session time allotted was sufficient for the task.

Actions Each participant was able to create the dictionary, and the initial unlinked DPRG with relative ease; the first subject completed in 10 minutes, the second in 15 minutes. The subjects then began the task of finding the code related to efficiency. Completing this task required linking the pattern to the source level. The first subject completed the task in 70 of the 120 allotted minutes, reporting that the code implementing the subject's registration interface effects efficiency. The second subject, after the full 120 minutes, had correctly identified several links including an `observer` and a `subject`, but was unable to locate the attach method.

Results The first subject demonstrated that it was possible to create a DPRG for an unfamiliar code base and complete the task in a short amount of time. The second subject was able to address efficiency at the pattern level, but had taken a source-centric approach to linking, and was hindered by the inability of the DPRG tool to support browsing of the source model and source. This subject spent considerable time reading the source model itself in database form.

3.4. Synthesizing Results

The investigation paths followed by the subjects in the confidence and lightweightness studies support our motivations for introducing the DPRG approach.

First, the investigation paths spanned all levels of the DPRG (Figure 3). Each dot in a graph in Figure 3 corresponds to a query or operation performed by a subject. The queries and operations are connected to make the progress between levels clearer. The location of a dot in the graph is based on the type of query that was performed. If a participant performed a pattern-level query (either a regular expression search or a node expansion) on a node that was not included in the link level, the corresponding dot is shown within the pattern-level only. Expansion of pattern level nodes in the link level are shown in the upper link level area. Source level node expansions on nodes in the link level are shown in the lower link level area. Expansions of source level nodes not included in the link level are shown at the lowest level. Queries shoen in the middle of the link level area are interactions with the linking portion of the tool: either link inferences, or link inspections.

These investigation paths show that the subjects did not intuit how design goals likely played out in the source, nor how the code related to the goals. Instead, they chose to browse the levels of the DPRG to make the connections.

Second, at some point, all of the subjects performed two or more queries at the pattern level when traversing to, or from, the source level, rather than merely switching between a point in the pattern and the source level. These actions are shown in grey in Figure 3. For example, the second grey portion of (A) shows a movement from a low-level pattern element, the `synchronize method` of the MONITOR OBJECT pattern, up to its design context involving serialization and scheduling. This pattern is also visible in (B) in the first grey segment, which involved moving up from a more concrete pattern level node to its design context in the FORWARDER-RECEIVER pattern. Similarly, a down ward movement is seen in portion (C) and (D), in which developers were concretizing their information on *efficiency* in the OBSERVER pattern.

Although the generalization of our results is limited, we believe our claims about the DPRG approach likely apply to other development settings for three reasons. First, the confidence study used two realistic cases; industrial developers examining their own systems and revisiting investigation tasks that they had previously performed. Second, across the three studies, six patterns from four sources were used. Finally, the results of the less realistic completeness and lightweightness studies are corroborated by the experiences of the developers participating in the confidence study.

4 Discussion

Why not use grep? A DPRG of a pattern, even when not linked to source, can be used to understand a pattern. However, the DPRG approach, whether linked or not linked to source, is not intended to replace either the reading or textual searching of design patterns. Instead, it provides complementary support. Whereas a lexical search typically results in a user sequentially visiting each result in the text, the results of a regular expression search on a DPRG are a graph that presents the information separately from its structure in the document. An obvious limitation of this presentation is a lack of context for a sentence matching a query. On the other hand, a different presentation of the sentence may lead to a different focus on the information by a user. The ability of a DPRG to collect crosscutting information and present it in the context of a design element can also make it easier to understand some aspects of a pattern. For instance, in the CACHING pattern, it is possible, by reading on the verb nodes surrounding the `Resource User` element, to learn that the resource user acquires something, uses something, accesses something, and calls something.

Overlapping patterns With our current tool, a DPRG can represent only one pattern. Since one portion of a code base may represent more than one pattern, it may be useful to consider extending a DPRG to represent multiple patterns whose implementations may or may not overlap. There are two hurdles to providing this support.

First, the same term may mean different things in different patterns. Since a DPRG presents only local context for nodes, it may be difficult to identify which pattern-level nodes refer to which pattern and which meaning. Visual cues or filtering to differentiate the sentence chains from different patterns might be sufficient to overcome this hurdle.

Second, the developer gains from a DPRG representing multiple patterns when it is useful to display information in response to a query from multiple patterns. It is an open question whether it is helpful to show the results if they are not integrated. An integrated display, for instance, would make explicit the relationships between the patterns, as when one pattern refers to another. Any significant integration of pattern information would require a deeper automatic semantic analysis.

Improving link inference Our current approach for inferring links does not consider the names of pattern or source model entities. Several developers who have used the tool have noted that an ability to express lexical rules for inclusion, exclusion, or prioritizing of links would be helpful. For instance, when linking a pattern level method with a name like "acquire", a developer might suggest tar-

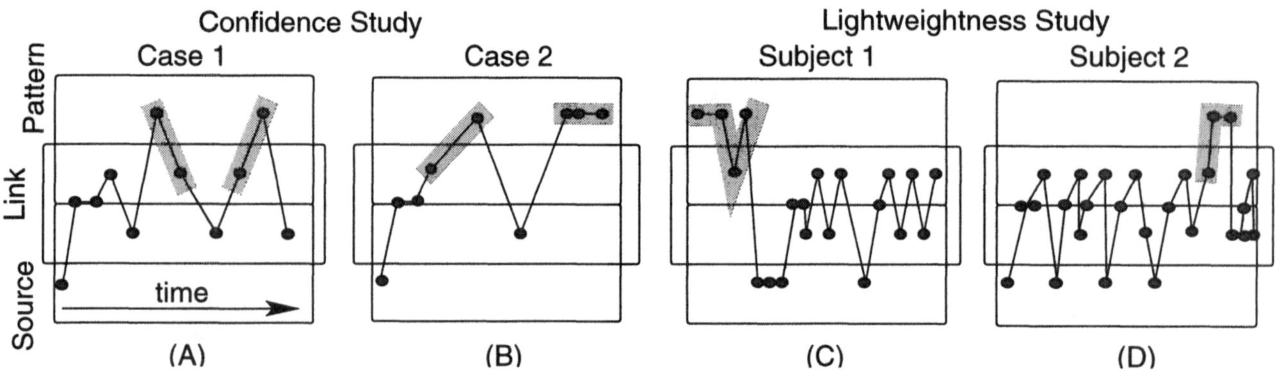

Figure 3. Subjects' Investigation Paths

get strings, such as "get" or "acquire", and might suggest exclusion strings such as "set", or "release".

Pattern level reusability We expect that the pattern level of a DPRG can be used many times for different systems. We have not yet tested this hypothesis. It may be that its reusability is limited if the dictionary choices made by a developer are task- or source-base specific.

Consideration of task applicability We believe a software developer can apply a DPRG for a software evolution task either top-down or bottom-up. For instance, in the first case in our study on developer confidence (Section 3.1), the developer was aware that that a pattern applied to part of a particular code base, and thus proceeded top-down, generating a DPRG to investigate how design goals in the pattern text related to the code. This top-down approach is also illustrated in the scenario presented in Section 2.3. The second case in the confidence study is illustrative of a bottom-up approach: the developer started at a portion of code and wanted to consider how how that code related to a particular design pattern.

5 Related Work

Expressing Design in Code With literate programming, Knuth suggested that programs should be human-readable in addition to being executable [12]. In this style of programming, documentation and code are combined in a single artifact: tools are then used to produce appropriate views for humans or computers. Griswold has advocated the embedding of knowledge about interdependencies between parts of a system into code through the use of information transparency techniques, such as such as naming conventions, formatting style, and placement within the source [7]. The degree to which a developer evolving the code benefits from these kinds of approaches depends on the quality and extent of the design expressed in the code. Although DPRGs apply in a narrower context, they can provide deep design information for pattern-related code even when such information has not been encoded beforehand.

Several researches have investigated generative and language-based approaches to ease the use, and subsequent recognition, of design patterns in code. For instance, in the Generic Pattern Implementation [22] approach based on C++ templates, a developer tags a location in the code where a particular pattern is to be used; code to configure the concrete instance of that pattern can then be generated automatically. As another example, Hannemann and Kiczales have shown how aspect-oriented programming can improve the modular expression of some kinds of patterns, improving the reusability, composability, and pluggability of patterns [8]. These approaches can help a developer use and recognize patterns, but they do not help a developer understand the subtleties of a pattern and its implementation

Inferring Design from Code Reverse engineering techniques produce abstract models of a software system, such as a subsystem diagram (e.g., Rigi [16]) or a sequence diagram (e.g., Shimba [21]), from source code or execution traces. These models can help a developer understand how a system works, but they do not describe *why* particular choices were made in the implementation. Pattern mining techniques help a developer search for and recognize design patterns in the source code of a system (e.g., [18, 10]). DPRGs are complementary to pattern mining techniques: A DPRG can be used to help a developer understand the pattern once found.

Verifying Design Design conformance tools check whether the implementation of a system conforms to an intended design. PatternLint is one example tailored to design patterns [20]. Rules about conformance and non-conformance to the structure of a pattern are specified in a logic fact base. These rules are compared against structural features, such as the calls between classes, extracted from source code. PatternLint can help a developer understand how an implementation may or may not structurally correspond to a pattern. The DPRG approach can also help in assessing conformance; it is less automatic than PatternLint but it can provide more detail about implementation variants, and can be used to match against partial implementations of a pattern.

Capturing Design Rationale A number of techniques help a developer capture design rationale and link it to code. These techniques vary in what rationale is captured, how it is captured, and how it is represented. In the LaSSIE system [4], for instance, an action-object format is used to capture and integrate architectural, conceptual, and implementation information about a system. In the DESIRE framework [2], an object-oriented domain model is used as the basis to guide the recovery of design concepts, and to link those concepts to a code base. These techniques both require a significant investment of developers time to encode the knowledge base prior to its use. The DPRG approach can be applied at much lower cost, albeit to a narrower range of code.

Other techniques focus on lower-cost capture and linking. Lougher and Rodden tool, for instance, allows developers performing maintenance tasks to annotate code with text and graphics, enabling the capture of rationale and the sharing of information over time [14]. The SLEUTH tool takes a generative approach by helping a developer to link existing design documentation to source [5]. Links are formed based on regular expressions specified by a developer. Links within the design documents are limited to pre-specified anchor points; links to source are limited to files. In contrast, the DPRG approach links design information on the basis of dictionary words that can be easily re-specified, and supports links to specific program elements. Both Lougher and Rodden's tool and SLEUTH require the maintenance of information added to development artifacts, whereas the DPRG approach can be applied on demand.

6 Summary

Parnas used the term *ignorant surgery* to refer to changes made to a software system by developers who do not understand the original design concepts behind the code [17]. When ignorant surgery occurs, the structure of a system tends to degrade, leading to increased costs for subsequent evolutionary tasks.

Design Pattern Rationale Graphs (DPRG) are intended to reduce occurrences of ignorant surgery by making the design rationale behind parts of a system associated with design patterns accessible to a developer. A DPRG makes the relationships amongst design concepts in a pattern explicit, and enables the linking of the concepts to the parts of a system implementing the pattern. The cost of creating and linking a DPRG is reasonable; a developer can create a DPRG within the context of a particular evolutionary task.

Through a series of case studies, we have shown that DPRGs show promise in improving a developer's confidence about the design goals related to a piece of code, that a developer can effectively access all relevant design goals represented in a DPRG from code, and that the approach can be applied within a short amount of time.

7 Acknowledgments

This work has been funded in part by Siemens AG and in part by a University of British Columbia fellowship. We would like to thank all of the participants in the case studies for their time and feedback. We thank M. Robillard, J. Hannemann and Y. Coady for insightful comments on an earlier draft. We also thank the anonymous reviewers for their input.

References

[1] E. Baniassad. *Linking Design to Source Using Design Pattern Rationale Graphs.* PhD thesis, Univ. of British Columbia, 2002.

[2] T. Biggerstaff, B. Mitbander, and D. Webster. Program understanding and the concept assignment problem. In *CACM*, pages 72–83, 1994.

[3] F. Buschmann, R. Meunier, H. Rohnert, P. Sommerlad, and M. Stal. *Pattern-Oriented Software Architecture: A System of Patterns*, volume 1. Wiley & Sons, 1996.

[4] P. T. Devanbu, R. Brachman, P. Selfridge, and B. Ballard. Lassie: a knowledge-based software information system. In *Proc. of Int'l Conf. on SE*, pages 249–261, 1990.

[5] J. C. French, J. C. Knight, and A. L. Powell. Applying hypertext structures to software documentation. *Info. Proc. and Mngmt*, 33(2):219–231, 1997.

[6] E. Gamma, R. Helm, R. Johnson, and J. Vlissides. *Design Patterns: Elements of Reusable Object-Oriented Software.* Addison-Wesley, 1995.

[7] W. Griswold. Coping with crosscutting software changes using information transparency. In *Proc. of Reflection 2001*, pages 250–265, 2001.

[8] J. Hannemann and G. Kiczales. Design pattern implementation in Java and Aspectj. In *Proc. of OOPSLA*, pages 161–173, 2002.

[9] jhotdraw software. `http://www.jhotdraw.org`.

[10] R. K. Keller, G. Knapen, B. Lagu, S. Robitaille, G. SaintDenis, and R. Schauer. The SPOOL design repository: Architecture, schema and mechanisms. *Adv. in Soft. Eng.: Topics in Evolution, Comprehension, and Evaluation*, pages 269–294, 2000.

[11] M. Kircher and P. Jain. Caching architectural design pattern. In *Tech. Rep. of Corporate Technology, Siemens AG*, Munich, Germany, 2002.

[12] D. Knuth. Literate programming. *Computer Journal*, 27(2):97–111, 1984.

[13] J. Korn, Y. Chen, and E. Koutsofios. Chava: Reverse engineering and tracking of java applets. In *Working Conf. on Rev. Eng.*, pages 314–325, 1999.

[14] R. Lougher and T. Rodden. Group support for the recording and sharing of maintenance rationale. *Soft. Eng. Journal*, pages 295–306, November 1993.

[15] LTCHUNK. `http://www.ltg.ed.ac.uk/index.html`.

[16] H. Müller and K. Klashinsky. A system for programming-in-the-large. In *Proc. of Int'l Conf. on SE*, pages 80–86, 1988.

[17] D. Parnas. Software aging. In *Proc. of Int'l Conf. on SE*, pages 279–287, 1994.

[18] L. Prechelt and C. Kramer. Functionality versus practicality: Employing existing tools for recovering structural design patterns. *J. of Universal Computer Science*, 4(12):866–882, Dec. 1998.

[19] D. Schmidt, M. Stal, H. Rohnert, and F. Buschmann. *Pattern-Oriented Software Architecture: Patterns for Concurren and Networked Objects*, volume 2. Wiley & Sons, 2000.

[20] M. Sefika, A. Sane, and R. Campbell. Monitoring compliance of a software system with its high level design models. In *Proc. of Int'l Conf. on SE*, pages 387–397, 1996.

[21] T. Systa, K. Koskimies, and H. Müller. Shimba – an environment for reverse engineering java softare systems. *Soft.: Pract. and Exp.*, 31(4):371–394, 2001.

[22] J. Vlissides and A. Alexandrescu. To code or not to code, part i and ii. C++ Report, March and June 2000.

[23] Zen CORBA ORB. `http://www.zen.uci.edu`.

A Component Architecture for an Extensible, Highly Integrated Context-Aware Computing Infrastructure*

William G. Griswold, Robert Boyer, Steven W. Brown, and Tan Minh Truong

Department of Computer Science and Engineering
University of California, San Diego
La Jolla, CA 92093-0114
E-mail: {wgg,rboyer,sbrown,mtruong}@cs.ucsd.edu

Abstract

Ubiquitous context-aware computing systems present several challenges in their construction. Principal among them is the tradeoff between easily providing new context-aware services to users and the tight integration of those services, as demanded by the small form factor of the devices typically found in ubiquitous computing environments. Performance issues further complicate the management of this tradeoff.

Mechanisms have been proposed and toolkits developed for aiding the construction of context-aware systems, but there has been little consideration of how to specialize, organize, and compose these mechanisms to meet the above requirements. We motivate and describe a software architecture that provides the desired integration and extensibility of services in a context-aware application infrastructure. A key result is the fissioning of intuitive class organizations, both across layers and within layers, to achieve the required integration of services and separation of concerns.

1 Introduction

The small end-user devices found in ubiquitous computing environments place tough requirements on applications. Users want to grasp information quickly, navigate representations fluidly, and respond easily. These requirements drive systems toward tight integration—where every component knows about all other components—in order to simultaneously meet performance expectations and create a composite view that succinctly expresses vital information.

These challenges are critical in a young fast-moving field like context-aware computing. A typical system might regularly undergo the addition of new kinds of context sensors, modeled entity types, services, or end-user devices. To reduce fragile coupling among components, software engineering principles argue for anticipating future changes and introducing separation of the identified concerns. The question, then, is how to achieve separation (e.g., through modularization) without sacrificing too much integration or performance. Mechanisms have been proposed and toolkits developed for easing the construction of context-aware systems [4, 10, 16], but there has been little consideration of how to specialize, organize, and compose these mechanisms to meet the above requirements.

Over the past year and a half we have been building the UCSD ActiveCampus context-aware infrastructure for ubiquitous computing, exploring the challenges of simultaneously supporting extensibility and tight integration. ActiveCampus has been online for a year and now comprises eight integrated end-user services [8]. It is available to everyone at UC San Diego, and is in active use by our extended group. We are now in the process of deploying ActiveCampus to our base of 700 HP Jornada users.

Our experiments with a traditional layered approach [5] combined with a hybrid of the mediator and observer design patterns [15] yielded significant leverage. However, maintaining a high level of integration and performance while maintaining a decoupling of services from modeled entities and from each other required additional architectural constraints and mechanisms. These include stripping the entity object down to a collection of compact context identifiers, employing a service introspection mechanism with an extended service interface, and a scoped, context-indexed data cache. These result in a significant change to the roles of the principal layers in the architecture.

In the following, we first identify the key dimensions of extensibility in a context-aware ubiquitous computing environment, based on our experience with ActiveCampus. These provide a groundwork for the key dimensions of componentization required for an extensible, integrated context-aware computing application infrastructure. Second, we consider current approaches, including the Context Toolkit [4], discussing the extent to which it meets these needs, and what challenges remain. Third, we present our architecture and its evolution to better meet the requirements. Finally, we discuss the implications of this architecture and lay out some open problems.

2 Background and Motivation

Building on previous definitions, Dey et al. define context as "any information that can be used to characterize the sit-

*This work is supported in part by an HP Mobility Grant gift, support from the California Institute for Telecommunications and Information Technology (Cal-(IT)^2), and the ActiveWeb project, funded by NSF Research Infrastructure Grant 9802219.

0-7695-1877-X/03 $17.00 © 2003 IEEE

uation of entities (i.e. whether a person, place or object) that are considered relevant to the interaction between a user and an application, including the user and application themselves," where relevance is defined with respect to the user's current task [4]. Context might include, for example, the proximity and availability of colleagues.

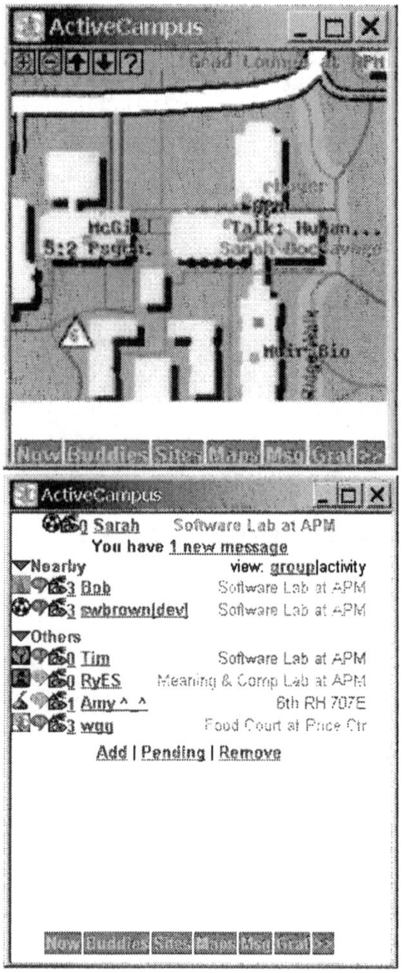

Figure 1. The Map and Buddies services of ActiveCampus. The Map service shows an outdoor or indoor map of the user's vicinity, with buddies, sites, and activities overlaid as links at their location. The Buddies service shows colleagues and their locations, organized by their proximity. Icons to the left of a buddy's name are buttons that show the buddy on the map, send a message to the buddy, and look at graffiti tagged on the buddy. Other services are reached by the button bar or clicking items embedded in the views.

Following Winograd [16], we expand on this definition slightly. Providing a context-aware application through computing devices in a ubiquitous computing setting supposes that the application *cum* device, as an artifact in the environment, is useful for completing some human-directed task. Hutchins characterizes such artifacts by their ability to efficaciously store, superimpose, and relate multiple representations of information about a task [11]. The artifact then can reduce a person's cognitive effort to recognize important relationships and recall key information, thus permitting the person to allocate unused cognitive resources to other aspects of the task. A classic example artifact is the alidade, which combines a compass, a prism, and a magnifier to adjoin a magnified scene on top of a compass reading, with a single vertical line passing through the center of each. The part of the scene that is bisected by the line is at the heading bisected by the same line. Thus, as compared to using a compass alone, it is possible to take an accurate magnetic heading in the context of visible landmarks with little cognitive effort.

Thus, for the purposes of this paper, we define an end-user context-aware application to constitute the selection, superimposition, and rendering of representations of task-relevant context, including the superimposition of application operations available for the next step of the task. Because many tasks are emergent and human behavior is often opportunistic, the available actions may include "switches" in the task.

To motivate the dimensions of extensibility and integration required for such an artifact, consider two screenshots of ActiveCampus services (application views) for a user named Sarah, shown in Figure 1. The services show mostly the same information—Sarah's physical proximity to other entities that are present at the time—but in rather different representations. The "task" is to help Sarah, a new student, engage the complex milieu of campus life in the face of obstructions and distractions.

The Map service represents Sarah centered geospatially on a map of her surroundings, with nearby buddies and static entities (e.g., departments) superimposed as well. Once Sarah orients the map to her physical space, she can use this representation to construct a plan for how to reach any of the entities on the map. Clicking on any of her buddies will list a set of services that are available on that buddy (e.g., show map centered on them, send them a message, show digital graffiti on them, show their profile).

The Buddies service also represents Sarah situated with respect to her buddies, distinguishing buddies that are near, as well as their activity level. By showing only buddies and by giving their locations by name, Sarah can conceptualize her active buddies at a relatively high level of detail. If Sarah knows the places by name, she can quickly find her way to a nearby buddy. If not, she can click on her buddy's personal icon to see her buddy centered on the map. The same services available via a click-through on the map are available directly in this service's display, to the left of each buddy name. Also, the area below the title bar is reserved for other services to notify the user of events, like the arrival of new messages.

Finally, below both services is a "button bar" of services for one's self, such as editing of privacy settings; these are a superset of the services available on a buddy.

Dimensions of Extensibility. From these two services, we can observe many possible dimensions of extensibility, largely driven by innovation. In particular, someone might want to improve the system by adding one of the following, with the resultant consequences on preexisting components:

- A new service, such as a contextual alarm service [3]. This would require adding the new service to the button bar and giving the alarm service the ability to notify users of triggered alarms through other services. If a user were allowed to add alarms for their buddies ("Hey Brad, check out the 'new books' table at the bookstore!"), then an alarm icon should appear next to each buddy on the Buddies service as well.
- A new kind of context or sensor input format, such as a latitude/longitude representation of location generated by a GPS device. Consumers of location, like the Map service, must be able to cope with locations generated via this device.
- A new kind of modeled physical entity, such as a web cam, which may also come with new kinds of context. Such entities would need to show up in the maps and entity lists of services to show where they are positioned and give access to their functionality.
- A new representation, such as 3-D image of a location. Such representations would have to be correlated to locations reported from sensor devices.
- A new end-user device, such as a pen PDA (personal digital assistant), which uses sound and LED's for output and sound and button clicks for input. Services would need to produce representations that are suitable for 'display' on such a device.

One issue we do not consider is the mobility of a user's work products as the user moves through a heterogeneous computing environment. Aura addresses this issue [13].

Tight Integration. Given the above considerations, it is natural to consider a component architecture that defines a component category for each dimension of extensibility, with standardized interface rules for each category. The interface rules would be defined so that the typical changes under each category could be made behind the component interface, thereby hiding the impacts of those changes from other components in the system.

One challenge in determining such rules is to balance the separation of the component changes against the integration of component functionality. A narrow interface might be easy for a component implementor to satisfy, but might be hard for component integrators to use as wished. Using the Map and Buddies services as examples, we see two immediate needs for tight integration: dense information display and contextual access to one service from another.

Because service representations and actions must often be rendered on devices with compact displays, the information displayed about each entity and service must be customized to fit the exact needs of the current service and limitations of the device. The Buddies service, for example, selectively uses small icons, shortened names, and their careful juxtaposition to maximize the display's utilization. This means that the service must require each of the displayed entities and services to satisfy queries for small icons or short names of themselves and entity locations. Yet, other services benefit from larger icons or full names of entities and locations.

On the Map service, a click on the map shows a set of location-based services available at that location, such as the tagging of digital graffiti. This ability to contextually access one service from another is the very definition of tight integration. Yet, for that integration to be fully realized, a newly introduced service (such as digital graffiti) must be able to insinuate itself into the list of possible actions at that location. If that insinuation is to be modular, then it must be realizable through the Map service's interface, rather than by editing the service's code.

The upshot, is that we need to design an architecture with component contracts that are easy for implementors to satisfy (i.e., supporting innovation), yet whose behaviors are rather open (i.e., enabling integration).

3 Current Approaches

The most developed prior work in this area is Dey's Context Toolkit [1, 4]. To ease the prototyping of a context aware application, it offers a small set of generic 'base' classes from which an application developer can derive application-specific classes. These classes are organized around high-level context-aware application functions: collecting sensor data, combining data from multiple sensors, and translating sensor data into alternate formats. Each of these classes contains all the infrastructure required for distributed peer-to-peer storage, communication via XML over HTTP, and software event monitoring:

- *Context Widget,* accepts and stores context coming from a sensor, abstracting away the details of the sensor. For example, a location widget might gather time-stamped locations coming from a GPS device. Context is stored in dynamically typed attribute–value pairs. It provides event notification functionality to signal the arrival of new data. Context widgets also abstract away actions on actuators (e.g., a light switch), and in this case they are called *Services*.

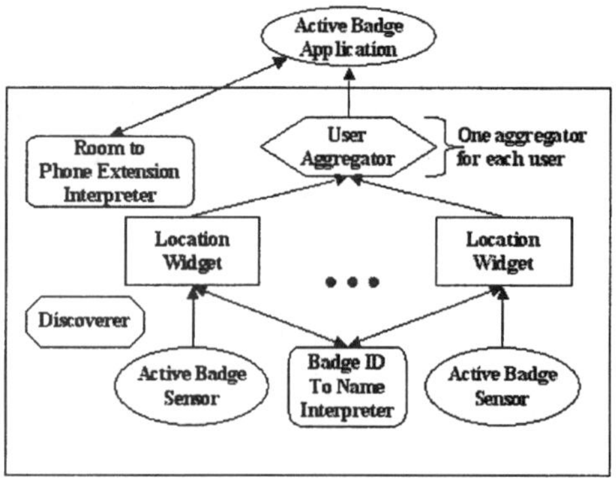

Figure 2. Architecture diagram for the ActiveBadge application using the Context Toolkit [4].

- *Context Aggregator,* subclassed from Context Widget, aggregates the context of multiple Widgets, and inherits their attribute–value pairs. By listening to events from the Widgets it aggregates, an aggregator can stay aware of changes in the context it monitors.
- *Context Interpreter,* takes one representation of context and generates an alternate representation, such as taking a GPS reading and producing a map.
- *Discoverer,* helps applications find one of the above resources by name or capability in the network.

Abstracting away each functional requirement as a class is useful in accommodating key dimensions of change. Yet, as is typical of a *toolkit*, the Context Toolkit stops short of dictating architectural standards that would enable an application based on the Toolkit to interoperate or integrate with applications of complementary functionality [10]. Indeed, such standards could hinder rapid development. Another concern is that the Toolkit's fine-grained distributed object model entails significant inter-object communication costs and precludes some efficient data organizations, among other issues [10, 16].

A key question is how a resource like the Context Toolkit could best be used to define an extensible suite of context-aware applications (what we call services) that share their context-aware underpinnings, their functionality, and even their displays to users. For example, the typical Context Toolkit application contains a number of context widgets, a couple of context aggregators that join those widgets into observable entities (e.g., *user*), a few context interpreters for the translation and interpretation of context, and an application object that hooks all these up (Figure 2). The application object then interacts with the user objects and context interpreters to produce interactive displays for end users. How then should two applications be fused together? As one possibility, should the user entities in each be merged into a large user object to eliminate redundancy, distributed processes, and event propagation from context widgets? Or should they be left separate, each with their redundant data at risk of becoming inconsistent or causing performance problems? Suppose just one of these applications is used at a time, in sequence, defined by the end user's emergent needs? Is there a way that unnecessary computation from the separately running applications, or the fused application, could be avoided?

In response to questions like these, Hong and Landay advocate a centralized service infrastructure approach [10]. The infrastructure would dictate architectural rules that would ensure that an innovator's component would interoperate with others that hew to the same rules. These rules would include how data and functional responsibilities are allocated to components, how those components relate to each other, and how their interfaces are defined [7, 12].

Along these lines, Hong is developing a Context Specification Language and infrastructure [9]. Winograd proposes a data-centric, two-level blackboard that decouples data from computations [16]. The lower *Event Heap* tuple-space abstracts away the complexities of coping with ephemeral sensor data. The upper *Context Memory* level tuple-space supports a persistent object view of the world. In separating computations from data, this proposal shares some of the same motivations and architectural ideas as those presented here, but does not directly address the issue of service integration.

4 The ActiveCampus Architecture

As advocated by Hong and Landay, we've taken a centralized client-server approach to providing a context-aware application infrastructure. The ActiveCampus server infrastructure supports all functions that it can provide internally, with only the sensing of context and its rendering to end user devices operating outside the server. This both eases administration of the system and minimizes the requirements placed on sensors and display devices, whose resources for computation and program development tend to be quite limited. Most importantly, centralization provides greater freedom to allocate behavior to components and organize those components to meet the needs of extensibility, integration, and performance. Also, newly deployed services can integrate with and leverage the existing running services.

At the highest-level there are two aspects of the system's component architecture: the interfaces to external components, and the internal system architecture. We briefly discuss the interfaces to external components before discussing the internal architecture.

Sensor-reporting is supported by providing a pair of components connected via XML/SOAP RPC (top two levels of Figure 3, on the left). One component runs on the device to capture and send data, and the other runs on the server to receive the data and marshal the raw data into the system database. Both components are typically written in C++. Display to devices (and interaction with them) is componentized similarly, with additional support for HTML transport.

Most of the responsibility for the operation of the context-aware system is managed within the centralized infrastructure, implemented as a web server running PHP and backed by an SQL database. We present our architecture of the centralized infrastructure by first discussing our initial design failures, and then follow with a complete architectural description, as diagrammed in Figure 3.

4.1 Early Design Experience

Context-aware computing, especially in a multi-application setting, is both representationally and behaviorally complex. To address these challenges, we settled on a layered design to incrementally provide behavior and assert system-wide properties [5]. The principal layers were, bottom-up: Data Storage (i.e., the database), Data Abstraction (e.g., sensor data and entity objects), Object Correlation (e.g., mapping raw sensor data to internal forms, as well as services themselves), and Environment Proxy (i.e., transport to external devices). To aid the incorporation of new services into ActiveCampus, our initial idea hinged on centralizing the data of *entities*—the people, departments, devices, and places modeled by the system—in typed entity objects so as to ease their handling by the many services we anticipated incorporating. In particular, sensor data would be accepted and processed into entity objects, and aggregate entity objects would then be the base of data for providing services.

Three problems emerged with this design as services were added to ActiveCampus:

Entity definitions experienced churn and bloat. The evolution of user identity in ActiveCampus is instructive. The identity of a person entity began as a unique internal ID and a login name. Soon a screen name and icon were added. Then the icon was split into a large icon (for clarity) and a small icon (for compactness). Each of these extensions, motivated by a service enhancement, is in fact just adding an *alternate representation* of the user's identity. Moreover, there is no apparent end in sight; we anticipate adding "earcons" [2] to enable hands-free and eye-free perception of context. From a software design perspective, it is troubling that every service enhancement has entailed enhancements to other objects in the system; the development of services was not being simplified.

Services were not decoupled from each other. Because of the small end-user displays, the fusion of service elements, not just entity data, seemed required to provide concise yet meaningful representations of context. For example, the Buddies service indicates what services are available on buddies, and will notify the user when a new message has arrived. In our initial design, these requirements led to services explicitly calling each other.

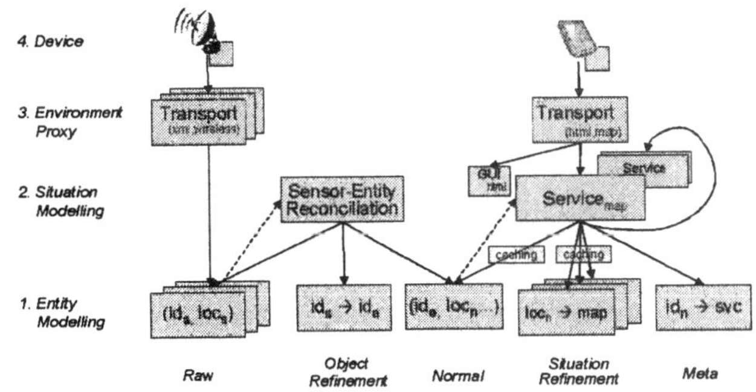

Figure 3. A graphical depiction of the essential elements of the revised ActiveCampus software architecture, focusing on the capture of user location and displaying it on a map.Boxes denote components, solid arrows denote calls, and dashed arrows represent event notifications.

Performance was becoming unacceptable. As more services were added and entity objects grew, database access to entities became a bottleneck. Even if a service was using only a small part of an entity, it had to pay for the bloat introduced by other services. This was exacerbated by services calling each other, which resulted in re-querying entity data. Naive efforts at reducing re-querying by data sharing increased the coupling of services through the sharing.

4.2 Internal Component Architecture

Our analysis of these problems resulted in the architecture shown in Figure 3. There are five layers, top to bottom, the last not shown. Boxes denote components, solid arrows denote calls, and dashed arrows represent event notifications. We briefly outline the architecture here, and then further motivate and elaborate the architecture with respect to the three observed problems:

4. *Device*: In the top Device layer, components run on devices and connect to ActiveCampus through RPC.
3. *Environment Proxy*: The Proxy layer marshals data between Devices and ActiveCampus's internals.
2. *Situation Modeling*: The Situation Modeling layer synthesizes the situation of an individual entity from multiple available data sources. For example, it translates quirky sensor representations to internal forms and associates them with entities. It also assembles and superimposes contextual representations of entities for end-user display (i.e., service execution). From the Context Toolkit's point of view, these are Context Interpreters.
1. *Entity Modeling*: The Entity Modeling layer represents entities (e.g., users and sensors) in several forms: raw external representations (e.g., a dynamically assigned network address), fast-indexing normal forms (e.g., a

permanently assigned unique integer), and forms for presentation (e.g., a screen name). It also represents the static relationships among them. From the Context Toolkit's point of view, the components are (left to right) Context Widgets, Context Interpreters, Context Aggregators, and Context Interpreters.

0. *Data* (not shown): The data layer provides for efficient storage and retrieval of data, in our case through an SQL database. The data layer may store data differently than apparently organized in the Entity Modeling layer for reasons of performance.

We point out three salient features of this architecture before going into the deeper discussion. One, a key feature of this architecture is how the representations of the Entity Modeling layer are integrated by the Situation Modeling layer, using a hybrid mediator–observer design pattern [6, 15]. Two, introspective mechanisms are used by services to refer to each other generically, thereby avoiding explicit service coupling. Three, caching mechanisms interposed between the Entity Modeling and Situation Modeling layers cope with performance problems.

4.2.1 Entity Bloat: The Entity and Situation Layers

Our first mistake was to confuse an entity's *intrinsic* data with the *presentation* of that data. Consider again entity identity. In database design or object-oriented design, an entity can be uniquely identified with an integer or object reference. The other forms of 'identity' discussed above, like screen name, are merely *alternate representations* (i.e., presentations) of that identity. Being alternate rather than intrinsic representations (and since their introduction is driven by the enhancement of services rather than entities), they can be associated to the entity through separate relations that are referenced through the unique identifier. These alternate representations are not necessarily unique (e.g., multiple persons may have the same screen name). The same observation applies for all intrinsic entity data, especially data that can be represented in multiple ways, such as locations.

Entity Normalization. Following through with this insight entails the following architectural rules for representing entities relating entities to other data:

- Only data that is intrinsic to an entity is part of its object. Alternate representations of intrinsic data should be stored separately.
- Intrinsic data should be represented in a compact normal form that is suitable for use as an index for fast retrieval of alternate representations.
- Any kind of context (e.g., location) should be standardized into an indexable "normal form" representation as well. For example, all location indices are required to be $\{x, y, z\}$ tuples with a fixed origin, orientation, and distance scale. Any representation to be retrieved using that kind of context should be indexed by its standardized index representation. For example, maps should be directly retrievable with normal-form location tuples. Thus, any location, regardless of its source, can be used to retrieve data from any location-indexed representation.
- All associations (mappings) of context (e.g., buddy membership, *(id_1, id_2)*) should be represented using their indexed forms. The association of alternate representations (e.g., *(Sarah, Brad)*) should be reserved only for final display.[1]

With these rules, adding a new service has no impact on an entity. For example, a service that requires the addition of earcons results in adding a new component that maps between entities and earcons. The independence of both the representation and its mapping from the service makes it reusable by other services without further coupling services. Moreover, it is now trivial to translate from a user to a location to a map, as each is guaranteed to be indexed against standardized indexed representations.

Entity and Situation Modeling. Raw sensor data, by its nature, is not in entity-normal form. It is a "pre-entity" abstraction of entities until translated into a normal form and re-stored as entities. For example, the network MAC address of a wireless device may be used to identify it in the system until it can be converted into an internal system ID.

The pre-normal status of sensor data is true in another way as well: although a device itself is a modeled system entity, it is also used for computing the context information for another entity, like a person, who is only loosely associated with the device. For example, a person may carry a wireless PDA, whose wireless signals can be used for geolocating the person. However, it is all too easy for the person to leave the PDA in the office when going to lunch. Yet, the cell station providing connectivity for the cell phone in the person's pocket may continue to generate legitimate data about the their location.

Such sensor data must be processed in light of other context data to derive a probably-correct entity-centric interpretation. This indeed is what our Object Correlation layer had done, although with a simple one-to-one mapping that did not allow for many-to-many mapping of context to entities.

Now that we have distinguished both the presentation forms and the pre-entity sensor forms of an entity from its normal form, it becomes apparent that the Data Abstraction layer is really an Entity Modeling layer, providing these

[1] Although an object's identity is classically represented by the object reference itself, we use a unique integer ID suitable for database queries. This could be hidden from applications through abstraction, but we have chosen not to do so.

three dimensions of entity modeling. Also, because of the complexity of mapping first from raw sensor data to normal-form entities, and then from entities to their rich presentation by services, it is appropriate to reconceptualize our Object Correlation layer. We rename it the Situation Modeling layer to signify its role of processing data from multiple entities in a context to discern or present the *situation* of an entity.

The complex relationship between these three forms of entity data deserve special architectural attention. Even though the states of entities are derived from sensor data, entities have no direct dependence on them or the processing of their data. For example, new forms of sensing or sensor processing should have no direct impact on entities. Applying design patterns to this problem suggests a hybrid mediator–observer design that manages the sensor–entity relationship through an independently operating component [6, 15]. In our case, the Sensor-Entity Reconciliation component, operating as a third party, mediates the complex sensor–entity relationship by receiving change notifications from the sensor components and propagating updates to the appropriate entities. This separation protects entities from implementation changes in the sensor domain. This pattern is also applied in relating entities to the views generated by services; here, services themselves are the mediators between entities and views.

In contrast to this separation, the Context Toolkit's structure encourages Context Aggregators (e.g., entities) to directly connect to Context Widgets (to aggregate them). The translation of Widget data for use by an Aggregator is performed by a Context Interpreter that is called by either the Widget or the Aggregator. Context Interpreters are simple passive input–output translators without the native capability to function as a mediator between Widgets and Aggregators.

4.2.2 Service Coupling: Introspective Interaction

The decoupling of entities and services does not do away with the service coupling observed earlier. Using the Buddies service as an example, the question is how the service could come to know, with low inter-service coupling, (a) what services are available on a user's buddy, (b) what services want to notify the user of something, and (c) how to render service activators and notifications on its view?

To help decouple services, we employ a registration mechanism, along with interface rules for services to follow so the mechanism can work:

Service Structure. All services are designated to run on behalf of an entity, usually a user, called the *subject*. Most services also can be run on the accessible context of an entity different than the subject, known as the *object*. For example, if the Maps service is run by Sarah on Brad, she will see the map view centered on Brad, rather than herself.[2]

To support inter-service integration, all services objects are required to support the following methods:

```
boolean compatible(id subj, &optional id obj)
     id   renderID(id subj, &optional id obj)
```

The compatibility method is a type check to determine whether the types of the subject and object can support the successful execution of the service (e.g., they are of subtype Locatable and hence provide a location).

The `renderID` method indicates how to render the target service's activation button, without specifying the representation of that button (i.e., keeping entity references in normal form). For example, the `renderID` call on the Map service returns the object's (buddy's) ID if `object` is bound. In the Buddies service, the buddy's map service is indicated by the buddy's small icon (but other services might wish to render the Map service as text). Thus, the Buddies service passes the `renderID` result to the small-icon mapping component to retrieve the icon. As a way of providing state information about the service, a call on `renderID` might even return an ID for a state (e.g., "Available") rather than the ID for the service, subject, or object.

Active services must also provide an implementation of this method:

```
id msgWaiting(id subject, &optional id object)
```

which lets a rendering service test whether the active service has a notification for the subject. If so, the method returns a non-null entity ID for the notification that can be rendered a number of ways, like the ID returned from `renderID`. This test permits general notifications when `object` is omitted, and object-specific notifications when `object` is provided (e.g., new messages from `object`).

Registration. When a top-level service comes online, it is registered as available and is assigned a unique entity identifier by the system. If the service needs to be run regularly to notify users of important information, it also registers itself as an *active* service. Additionally, the developer of the service will provide values for the representations of a service's activation button: short name, icon, and tooltip.

Introspection. To render the services for an entity, a rendering service R iterates over the registered services S. For each service S_i, R calls S_i's `compatible` method with the invoking user as the subject and the entity (e.g., buddy) as the object. For those calls returning true, R calls S_i's `renderID` method with the same arguments. R then uses the returned ID to obtain a representation of S_i's activation button.[3]

[2]The object could be a set of entities, but the need for this has not yet emerged, in part because the subject's own context includes associated entities like buddies that serve as the implied objects of the service.

[3]For developers who want absolute control over the rendering of their service's display, they might introspect on the available services merely to detect that a new one has been added and notify the developers.

Similarly, R can iterate over all active services with waiting messages, A_i, using A_i's `msgWaiting` method to get an ID for use in rendering A_i's notification.

4.2.3 Speed: Scoped, Context-Indexed Caching

Decoupling services and unbundling intrinsic entity data from renderable representations of entities potentially compromises performance. A service like Buddies queries large amounts of entity data itself, then delegates to passive services for rendering of the buddies, and finally checks with active services for notifications. Many of these checks on other services use data already retrieved by the top-level service. However, to minimize service coupling, this data is not part of the inter-service interfaces. To address this problem, the ActiveCampus infrastructure provides a simple two-level caching mechanism.

To implement this mechanism, we take advantage of the fact that ActiveCampus applications can tolerate inconsistent and stale data. As an example of tolerable inconsistency, it is not critical that a person's location and their buddy's location be reported for the exact same point in time. As an example of tolerable staleness, a person's location from 10 seconds ago is a reasonable approximation of their location now. Data that has minimal tolerance for inconsistency and staleness (e.g., passwords) is not cached.

Caching is achieved through the memoization of method calls into the Entity Modeling layer. To bound the staleness of Normal Entity data, we scope their memoization to the lifetime of a top-level call to a service. If the service itself causes changes to data (e.g., the user is manually asserting a change in their location), the service is responsible for updating the cache.

Because the renderable representations of entities are relatively stable and have weak consistency requirements (e.g., the change of a buddy's icon is not critical), they may be cached across an entire user session (e.g., login). Because this data is indexed by its normal form, efficient lookup is possible.

5 Discussion

We have designed a context-aware software architecture around the criteria of extensibility, integration, and performance. Surprisingly, moving away from the Context Toolkit's focus on rapid prototyping causes several aspects that may appear in a single Toolkit object to be dispersed across several components in ActiveCampus. The dispersion both spans layers and occurs within a layer. In the following, we discuss this outcome and its consequences.

Fissioning Objects across Layers. Employing the traditional architectural themes of layering of abstractions and mediation of representations implies a rather faceted design in contrast to the Context Toolkit. In particular, we spread its "built-in" functions of abstraction, distribution, and storage across three different layers. This allows exclusion of unneeded elements, independent control of the implementation of each aspect, and assigning the development of each to an expert (e.g., a database specialist) who can integrate their functions over many objects if needed (e.g., database table organization).

This separation also permits the placement of other components in between. Most notably, we found it beneficial to place context interpreters in layer 2 of the system, above data abstraction but below distribution. Moving this functionality above distribution would have hurt performance, and of course moving below abstraction would have exposed too many representation details. Theoretically, this decoupling should also permit us to "move the line" that separates the internal and external components of ActiveCampus, giving external agents greater control, computational responsibility, and the ability to provide services. For example, a service component could be pushed above the proxy line by providing a pair of proxy components that handles the service's calls to the internal architecture. To be successful, however, there would be performance and consistency issues to be resolved.

Intralayer Fissioning of Modeled Entities. Other than the fusion of abstraction, storage, and distribution, the Context Toolkit's class design is relatively neutral about how classes should be combined into an application. One architectural rule of the Context Toolkit is that Context Aggregators are a subclass of Context Widgets. This particular insight is represented in our architecture by placing our sensor representations and other entities in the same layer of the architecture. However, we have added several additional architectural rules to meet our goals of extensibility, integration, and performance. First, we stripped our entity objects of any presentation data, instead using normal-form indices to represent entity context that can be used to index into presentation representations. This leaves raw sensor data in a pre-entity form and presentation data in a entity-independent form.

Intralayer Fissioning of Situation Modeling. The consistency of the various forms of entity representation is maintained by the Situation Modeling layer, and driven by events outside the system. Interestingly, Dey et al. have explored the addition of a situation abstraction to the Context Toolkit [4]. What we observe here is that achieving consistency across views of an entity requires analysis of an entity's situation. Thus, sensor–entity reconciliation is both a context interpreter and a situation abstraction. This fusion of functions and roles in a single object suggests that packaging an abstraction like "situation" in an object could be problematic. "Context interpretation" is a basic system function that can be reused in a number of ways. However, this particular context interpreter fulfills the role of pre-entity situation analysis. Likewise, an ActiveCampus service also performs situation modeling for rendering efficacious views to end-users for performing their own situation analysis. In some sense our services are "aggregated interpreters", fulfilling the Context Interpreter function in the same way that Context Aggregators fulfill the Context Widget function.

What we see then is that the Situation Abstraction that Dey and Abowd write about is more of a system-wide *role* fulfilled by a layer, rather than a reusable abstraction (although we note that the facade design pattern is a layer-like object [6, p. 185]). In particular, the situation of an entity is two stages of interpretation by the Situation Modeling layer. The U.S. Department of Defense's data fusion paradigm suggests that are at least five levels (really phases) of situation modeling [14]:

0. *Sub-Object Data Association and Estimation*: signal-level data association and characterization.
1. *Object Refinement*: combines data from multiple sensors and other sources to determine position, kinematics, and other attributes.
2. *Situation Refinement*: develops interpretation of the relationships among the objects and events in the context of the operational environment.
3. *Significance Estimation*: intent prediction and consequence prediction.
4. *Process Refinement*: monitors the fusion process to refine the process itself and guide acquisition of additional data.

To a first approximation, our two situation modeling components in Figure 3 perform fusion levels (0,1) and 2, with an end-user performing the last two levels with the assistance of the displays produced by level 2.

Given ActiveCampus's Entity and Situation Modeling layers, with refinement moving to the right, enhancing ActiveCampus with significance estimation modeling would involve adding two new columns on the right side of the architecture. In particular, services would store analyzable versions of their superimposed representations to a new Entity Situation component in the Entity Modeling layer, which would be consumed by new Significance Estimation components in the Situation Modeling layer.

Situation Elaboration via Inter-service Introspection. Rich situation modeling requires services to communicate with each other. Given a mechanism that can generically enumerate the available services, one way to avoid a complete fusion of such services is a generic inter-service interface that allows one service to render small amounts of information for other services, or perhaps even surrender control. For this purpose we identified the key service meta-functions of: (a) checking compatibility with the entities on which they might be run, (b) providing hints as to how to render their activators, and (c) notifying entities of important context information. Normal-form entity identifiers play a key role in fulfilling the separation, as they enable services to communicate in terms of representation-neutral identifiers rather than a particular presentation that may be inappropriate to the rendering of the top-level service.

Future Work. This architecture has not been fully tested. It has been successful in decoupling existing services, but new ones have yet to be added. The ultimate success of the architecture will hinge on whether new entities and services manifest the characteristics of interaction we've seen in the past, or instead manifest unanticipated ones.

One dimension of change we have not addressed to date is the addition of radically new device types. ActiveCampus, for the most part, has taken a lowest-common-denominator approach to the rendering of services, assuming that all devices can render text and small images straightforwardly via web browsers. Advanced javascripting techniques had to be avoided because the PDA web browsers provided inconsistent levels of support. ActiveCampus responds to the standard device pragmas that browsers provide, but not in a sophisticated way. Someone who wished to use ActiveCampus through a device such as a pen PDA, which used sound and LED's for output and sound and button clicks for input, would be disappointed.

Supporting a radically new device—without creating a duplicate set of services for it—might be handled by designing services around a strategy pattern [6, p. 315] that is parameterized by the renderable representations. A service then could be created by a factory [6, p. 107] that instantiates the service's representation strategy according to the device's output characteristics.

6 Conclusion

The construction of a ubiquitous context-aware computing system faces the difficult tradeoff between the tight integration of application services and the ease with which they can be added to the system. Performance considerations further complicate the management of tradeoffs.

We have motivated and described a software architecture that provides the necessary separation of concerns for the above considerations in a context-aware application infrastructure, and reported on our use of this architecture in the construction of the ActiveCampus system. We found that a hybrid mediator observer design pattern structured by layering provides significant leverage. However, maintaining a high level of integration and performance while maintaining a decoupling of services from modeled entities and other services requires additional architectural constraints and mechanisms. These include stripping the entity object representation down to a collection of context index identifiers, employing a service introspection mechanism with additional rules for service interfaces, and a scoped, context-indexed data cache.

Acknowledgements

We thank Jeremy Weir, Jolene Truong, Tim Foley, Neil McCurdy, David Harbottle, R. Benjamin Shapiro, Greg Jay, Rommel Pesigan, David Hutches, Jadine Yee, Justin Lee, Steve Lau, Daniel Wittmer, Antje Petzold, Jean Aw, Linchi Tang, Joseph Chow, Adriene Jenik, Jim Hollan, and Jason Chen for their help. We thank UCSD's Facilities office, especially Roger Andersen, Robert Clossin, and Kirk Belles, for their expertise and resources. We thank Intel's Network Equipment Division for donating network processors and Symbol Technologies for their technical support.

References

[1] K. D. A. *Providing Architectural Support for Building Context-Aware Applications.* PhD thesis, Georgia Institute of Technology, College of Computing, December 2000.

[2] M. Blattner, D. Sumikawa, and R. Greenberg. Earcons and icons: Their structure and common design principles. *Human-Computer Interaction*, 4(1):11–44, 1989.

[3] A. K. Dey and G. D. Abowd. Cybreminder: A context-aware system for supporting reminders. In *Intl. Symposium on Handheld and Ubiquitous Computing (HUC'00)*, pages 172–186, 2000.

[4] A. K. Dey, D. Salber, and G. D. Abowd. A conceptual framework and a toolkit for supporting the rapid prototyping of context-aware applications. *Human-Computer Interaction*, 16(2-4):97–166, 2001.

[5] E. W. Dijkstra. The structure of the "THE"-multiprogramming system. *Communications of the ACM*, 11(5):341–346, May 1968.

[6] E. Gamma, R. Helm, J. Vlissides, and R. E. Johnson. *Design Patterns: Elements of Reusable Object-Oriented Software.* Addison-Wesley, Reading, MA, 1995.

[7] D. Garlan and M. Shaw. An introduction to software architecture. In V. Ambriola and G. Tortora, editors, *Advances in Software Engineering and Knowledge Engineering*, volume 1, pages 1–39. World Scientific Publishing Company, Singapore, 1993.

[8] W. G. Griswold, R. Boyer, S. W. Brown, T. M. Truong, E. Bhasker, G. R. Jay, and R. B. Shapiro. Activecampus - sustaining educational communities through mobile technology. Technical Report CS2002-0714, UC San Diego, Department of CSE, July 2002.

[9] J. I. Hong. Context fabric: Infrastructure support for context-aware systems. Qualifying Exam Proposal, 2001.

[10] J. I. Hong and J. A. Landay. An infrastructure approach to context-aware computing. *Human-Computer Interaction*, 16(2-4):287–303, 2001.

[11] E. Hutchins. *Cognition in the Wild.* MIT Press, Cambridge, 1995.

[12] D. E. Perry and A. L. Wolf. Foundations for the study of software architecture. *SIGSOFT Software Engineering Notes*, 17(4):40–52, October 1992.

[13] J. P. Sousa and D. Garlan. Aura: an architectural framework for user mobility in ubiquitous computing environments. In *3rd Working IEEE/IFIP Conference on Software Architecture*, 2002.

[14] A. N. Steinberg, C. L. Bowman, and F. E. White. Revisions to the JDL data fusion model. In *Proceedings of SPIE AeroSense (Sensor Fusion: Architectures, Algorithms and Applications III)*, pages 430–441, Orlando, Florida, 1999.

[15] K. J. Sullivan and D. Notkin. Reconciling environment integration and component independence. In *Proceedings of the SIGSOFT '90 Fourth Symposium on Software Development Environments*, pages 22–33, December 1990.

[16] T. Winograd. Architectures for context. *Human-Computer Interaction*, 16(2-4):401–419, 2001.

Technical Papers

Formal Methods II

A Compositional Formalization of Connector Wrappers

Bridget Spitznagel
Carnegie Mellon University
5000 Forbes Ave
Pittsburgh, PA 15213
sprite@cs.cmu.edu

David Garlan
Carnegie Mellon University
5000 Forbes Ave
Pittsburgh, PA 15213
garlan@cs.cmu.edu

Abstract

Increasingly systems are composed of parts: software components, and the interaction mechanisms (connectors) that enable them to communicate. When assembling systems from independently developed and potentially mismatched parts, wrappers *may be used to overcome mismatch as well as to remedy extra-functional deficiencies.*

Unfortunately the current practice of wrapper creation and use is ad hoc, resulting in artifacts that are often hard to reuse or compose, and whose impact is difficult to analyze. What is needed is a more principled basis for creating, understanding, and applying wrappers. Focusing on the class of connector wrappers *(wrappers that address issues related to communication and compatibility), we present a means of characterizing connector wrappers as protocol transformations, modularizing them, and reasoning about their properties. Examples are drawn from commonly practiced dependability enhancing techniques.*

1. Introduction

Increasingly systems are implemented as compositions of independently-developed components that must be integrated into working systems using various interaction mechanisms, such as remote procedure call, event buses, pipes, etc. For such systems a serious problem is dealing with component mismatches that arise when the expectations of a component do not match those of other components or of the environment into which it is placed [4].

For example, a component selected for use in some software system may not use the same units of measurement or the same data format as the rest of the system. Or, a COTS component may not gracefully tolerate out-of-range input data produced by other components.

In this setting the traditional approach of directly rewriting or modifying the software to solve the problem may not be feasible, since components are often built by third parties, or are sufficiently complex that rewriting them is not cost-effective.

One widely used technique to deal with this problem is to use wrappers. Informally a *wrapper* is new code interposed between component interfaces and communication mechanisms. The intended effect is to moderate the behavior of the component in a way that is largely transparent to the component or the interaction mechanism.

For example, a unit conversion mismatch might be resolved by a data conversion wrapper that intercepts data entering or leaving the offending component, and converts it to the units expected by the rest of the system. Or, in the case of a component that does not gracefully handle out-of-range data, a wrapper might be constructed to harden the component by rejecting illegal input, allowing only well-tolerated inputs to reach the component, and thereby increasing the reliability of the system as a whole [15].

Unfortunately the current practice of wrapper creation and use is ad hoc and something of a black art. To overcome a (perhaps unforeseen) difficulty quickly, a one-off wrapper is written specifically for that problem in that software system. Consequently as somewhat random pieces of code, wrappers are often hard to reuse elsewhere, analyze, compose with one another, modify, and maintain.

As a result, many important questions that might arise cannot be answered. For example: How does a specific wrapper, interposed between a component and a connector, affect the protocol of that connector? Are existing properties of the protocol maintained; does a desirable new property emerge? Do two potential wrapping efforts interact in bad ways? Does it matter in which order the wrappers are applied? Does a wrapper violate the interface expected by the component that is being wrapped? Does a wrapper require modifications to the source code of a component?

In principle, such questions could be answered in an ad hoc fashion themselves, for example, by writing a formal description of the affected part of the system as it would stand after the incorporation of the wrapper. However this task would have to be repeated each time another wrapper is added, and yields no general understanding. Moreover, the wrappers themselves would still not enjoy the usual desired properties of reusability, maintainability, and so on.

What is needed is a more principled basis for wrapper creation and application, ideally providing three desirable capabilities: First, we would like to be able to *specify* a wrapper itself, independent of any particular context of use. Second, we would like to use this specification to understand things such as *impact* of its use, its effects on the communication protocol between components, compositional properties, etc. Third, we would like to be able to relate the wrapper specification to an *implementation* using tools and techniques that help enforce that the implementation corresponds to the specification.

In this paper we address the first two of these issues for an important subclass of wrappers, namely *connector wrappers*.[1] As we detail later, these wrappers are used to repair or augment communication-related properties of a system, such as the two examples above. As we will show, it is possible to specify this class of wrappers as modularized protocol transformations, whose properties can be reasoned about using standard notations and tools. We give examples drawn from commonly practiced dependability-enhancing techniques, show the application of these example wrappers to two connector specifications, demonstrate the ease of composition of this kind of wrapper specification, and illustrate how analyses can be used to confirm whether the wrappers actually achieve their intended purpose.

2. Related Work

The widespread use of wrappers (which, in part, motivates this work) has given rise to efforts directed at standardized support for wrapper insertion. System-level support mechanisms, usually called *interceptors*, have become increasingly available for implementations of some commonly used connectors. Interceptors facilitate the insertion of arbitrary application-level wrapper code. Such code may be used to enhance fault tolerance [13] and security [3] of COTS components, or to add instrumentation [8]. However, by their nature these efforts are specific to a connector implementation and/or set of system libraries; and, generally speaking, do not address the questions posed in section 1, which are concerned with what is going on in the wrapper itself rather than the means of wrapper emplacement.

Our work builds on process algebras such as CSP and CCS [6, 12]. In particular, it applies to FSP [11] some of the structure of Wright [1] in order to describe protocols of software connectors, and to describe connector wrappers as transformations of these protocols. Wright's decomposition of connectors into interfaces (roles) and interactions (glue), enables explicit identification of the communicating parties and their obligations, as well as compatibility checks. The work described in this paper, however, goes beyond that of previously published work on Wright by further decomposing the connector and promoting reusability of "wrapper" interaction elements.

We also make use of the idea, drawn from software architecture, of treating a software connector as a separate first-class entity [18], on a par with software components. Building on the idea of first-class connectors, and with similar goals to our work, Lopes, Wermelinger, and Fiadeiro have investigated the notion of "higher-order" connectors as a formal framework in which to create connectors compositionally. They base their work on CommUnity, a Unity-like parallel program design language [9]. The categorical semantic underpinnings of their work gives it a somewhat different form of compositional framework, as compared to the use of process algebras (as in our work).

Mismatch resolution, a problem that gives rise to some wrappers, has also been tackled in software architecture. When two mismatched components are unable to communicate via existing connectors, one alternative to wrappers is to construct or modify a *connector* to resolve the mismatch [19]. Another technique, Flexible Packaging [2], separates the component's functionality (ware) from its assumptions about the communication infrastructure (packaging); mismatches in packaging can then be overcome by replacing the ware's packaging with one that is a better match for the rest of the system. The flexible packaging approach is elegant, but lack of adoption by component providers makes it unlikely to replace practitioners' use of wrappers in the immediate future.

Also related to this work is protocol synthesis, which deals with a protocol's composition from (or decomposition into) simpler protocols. Ensemble [21] enables the construction of an adaptive protocol composed of stacked micro-protocol modules. The x-Kernel [14] project has also used micro protocol composition to design and implement a dynamic architecture for flexible protocols that take advantage of operating system support for efficient layering. Conduits+ [7] also provides a framework for network protocol software, with a focus on reuse aided by design patterns; layered protocols are composed from conduits (software components with two distinct "sides") and information chunks (which flow through the conduits). The work described here has a somewhat different goal: to describe the impact of application-level wrapper code on a pre-existing protocol, rather than to construct a fresh protocol (and corresponding connector implementation) from scratch.

[1] We address the third issue in [20].

3. Overview of Approach

Informally a *wrapper* is new code interposed between component interfaces and infrastructure support (e.g., between application-level code and communication facilities such as RPC). The intent of the code is to alter the behavior of the component with respect to the other components in the system, without actually modifying the component or the infrastructure itself.

An important class of wrappers are those that are primarily designed to affect the communication between components. We refer to these as *connector wrappers*. Connector wrappers encompass a wide range of behaviors, including things such as changing the way data is represented during communication, the protocols of interaction, the number of parties that participate in the interaction, and the kind of communication support that is offered for things like monitoring, error handling, security, and so on.

Moreover, since connector wrappers focus on modifying the behavior of shared communication infrastructure, they are not inherently speci£c to the particular components being wrapped. As a result, they have a greater potential for reuse and generalization. For example, a connector wrapper that adapts a communication to use encrypted data could be reused between many components.

3.1. Goals

Our goal is to provide a more formal, disciplined approach to connector wrapper design (and indirectly implementation), so that we can understand their behavior and other properties. Speci£cally, there are three important classes of properties that we would like to analyze:

- Soundness: Having introduced a wrapper (or sequence of wrappers), does the resulting communication mechanism still work? Does a wrapper introduce new deadlocks, failure modes or race conditions?
- Transparency: Does a wrapper change the interface of the communicating parties? Since the goal of wrappers is to avoid directly modifying the components in a system, transparency is an important feature to verify.
- Compositionality: What are the compositional and algebraic properties of a set of wrappers? This includes issues such as commutativity (can the ordering of two wrappers be exchanged?), inverses (does one wrapper undo the effects of another?), idempotence (does it matter if we apply the same wrapper twice?), and other more speci£c properties of a composition of several wrappers.

a → P	Action Pre£x
a → P | b → Q	Choice
P || Q	Parallel Composition
label:P	Process Labelling
P/{new/old}	Relabelling
P\{hidden}	Hiding
when (n<T) a → P	Guarded Action
P+ {a,b,c}	Alphabet Extension
STOP, ERROR	prede£ned processes
set S = $\{a, b, c\}$	de£nes a set S
range R = 0..5	de£nes a range R
[v:S]	binds variable v to a value chosen from S

Table 1. FSP quick reference

3.2. Protocol Transformation

To address questions like these, our approach is to de£ne a connector wrapper formally as a *protocol transformation*. In effect, a wrapper converts the protocol de£ning one connector into a new protocol de£ning the altered connector. The basic operations that comprise a protocol transformation may include redirecting, recording and replaying, inserting, replacing, and discarding particular events.

Building on past work in this area, we adopt an approach based on process algebras [6, 12]. Process algebras provide a way to talk about patterns of events, and are supported by a number of useful analysis tools. In particular, we use FSP[2]. (Other process algebras would have worked equally well: we chose FSP because it is simple enough for non-experts to use but can still provide a useful set of analyses, such as whether a connector protocol will deadlock or whether a safety or liveness property is violated.)

To describe a connector protocol in FSP, we use an approach similar to Wright [1]. A connector is de£ned as a set of processes: there is one process for each interface or "role" of the connector, plus one process for the "glue" that describes how all the roles are bound together. These $n+1$ processes are placed in parallel with the roles relabelled. Checks are performed on the resulting composite processes using tools such as model checkers.

Formally, for a connector with roles $R_1 \ldots R_n$ and glue G, the semantics of the connector is given by Expression 1.

$$R_1 \| \ \ldots \| \ R_n \| \ G \qquad (1)$$

[2]A quick reference for some FSP operators is given in Table 1; for further information see [11]. Processes describe actions (events) that occur in sequence, and choices between event sequences. Each process has an *alphabet* of the events that it is aware of (and either engages in or refuses to engage in). When composed in parallel, processes synchronize on *shared* events: if processes P and Q are composed in parallel as $P \| \ Q$, events that are in the alphabet of only one of the two processes can occur independently of the other process, but an event that is in both processes' alphabets cannot occur until both processes are willing to engage in it.

Caller = (call → return → Caller).
De£ner = (call → return → De£ner).
Glue = (caller.call → de£ner.call → Glue
  | de£ner.return → caller.return → Glue).
||ProcCall = (caller:Caller || de£ner:De£ner || Glue).

Figure 1. Simple procedure call

To illustrate, Figure 1 shows a simple procedure-call connector. The connector has two roles, Caller and De£ner. Each engages in a call event followed by a return event. In the parallel process ProcCall, the role processes execute concurrently with the Glue process, synchronizing on shared events; here the event labels in each role process have been pre£xed with a label unique to that role (caller or de£ner), so each role shares events only with the glue, not directly with other roles. The glue describes the interaction of the roles: a call event at the Caller role is followed by a call at the De£ner role, and a return event at the De£ner role is followed by a return at the Caller role. ProcCall can then be checked for deadlock, without needing any speci£cation of the components whose communication it describes. (Later, the protocol of the component interfaces should be checked for conformance to the role speci£cations, which are effectively standing in for these future components.)

Our protocol transformation takes a connector of the form given in Equation 1 and, by adding and modifying processes in that connector, produces a new connector with the same general form. The chosen approach (outlined in the next section) makes it easy to compose, or chain together, several such transformations, to achieve a complex result from several simpler modular wrappers.

4. Connector Wrapping

The core of this wrapper-description technique is the interposition of a new process between a role process R and a glue process G. In an implementation this would correspond informally to the interposition of a new piece of code, the wrapper.

First, we decouple R and G from one another; formally this is done by renaming. Next, we add a new process W that synchronizes with both R and G. This wrapper process W re-links the two decoupled processes by intermediating between the original and the renamed events. W has the opportunity to redirect, record/replay, insert, replace, or discard the events communicated between R and G. W may be parameterized to facilitate reuse in a broader range of contexts.

Let $A_{RG} = \alpha(R) \cap \alpha(G)$ be the set of events shared by R and G. The £rst step is performed by renaming these events in *one* of the two processes, ensuring that the two processes no longer synchronize directly. For the second step, a new process W is placed in parallel with the role processes and glue process. W translates between the events in A_{RG}, in the alphabet of R, and their counterparts in the renamed alphabet of G. W in parallel with G can be thought of as a new composite glue process, G_W.

We can derive the semantics of the newly wrapped connector, given in Equation 2, by taking the original equation 1, adding W (a wrapper for one of the roles $R_1 \ldots R_n$), and replacing G with $f(G)$, where $f(G)$ is the relabelled version of G.

$$R_1 \| \ldots \| R_n \| W \| f(G) \qquad (2)$$

Some classes of wrappers may also increase the number of roles; this is done by introducing additional new processes with which W synchronizes:

$$R_1 \| \ldots \| R_n \| W \| f(G) \| R_{n+1} \ldots \| R_{n+k} \qquad (3)$$

4.1. Bene£ts

This approach isolates the wrapper from the rest of the original connector; though the core concept is not dif£cult to grasp, the technique can be powerful when used consistently and yields several bene£ts including composability, traceability, and reusability.

These wrapper speci£cations are readily composable; we can treat $W \| f(G)$ as a new *composite* glue, and apply a new wrapper W_2 to the W-wrapped connector:

$$R_1 \| \ldots \| R_n \| W_2 \| f_2(W \| f(G)) \qquad (4)$$

Traceability is facilitated by the decompositional structure of the transformed speci£cation, which separates the effects of a sequence of changes to the protocol so that a problem detected by a model checker can more easily be traced back to the change responsible for introducing the problem. Pinpointing the source of such a problem would be more dif£cult with a monolithic speci£cation of the protocol. Furthermore, the structure in the speci£cation is not arbitrary but corresponds readily to the structure of the implementation, facilitating traceability of a problem detected in one of several wrapper processes by a model checker to the one of several wrappers in the implementation that would contain a corresponding bug. This correspondence between wrapper processes and wrapper implementations can be enforced by implementation generation tools.

Parameterization techniques enable the construction of *reusable* wrapper speci£cations, applicable to a range of connector speci£cations. Generalization can be taken further[3], describing patterns or templates for types of wrappers in terms of their actions (redirect, record/replay, insert,

[3]Owing to space considerations, this technique will not be covered in this paper.

```
Caller = (call → return → Caller).
De£ner = (call → return → De£ner).
Glue = (caller.call → de£ner.call→ Glue
        | de£ner.return → caller.return → Glue).
Wrap = (caller.call → wrap.caller.call → Wrap
        | wrap.caller.return → caller.return → Wrap).
||WrapPC = (caller:Caller || de£ner:De£ner
           || Glue/{wrap.caller/caller} || Wrap).
```

Figure 2. "No Effect" wrapper

replace, or discard) on events; this enables automatic generation of instances of some kinds of wrapper speci£cations given a connector speci£cation and a set of inputs including the wrapper template and the affected elements of the connector.

We will illustrate the basic structure of wrapper application with three brief examples. These examples will then be used to show composition of wrappers (section 6). Then we will demonstrate parameterization of a wrapper and apply it to a different connector protocol (section 7).

5. Examples

We begin with a trivial wrapper to illustrate the basic structure of its application to a connector speci£cation. Then we introduce a connector with two classes of faults and describe two fault-tolerance wrappers.

5.1. First Wrapper: "No Effect"

Figure 2 shows the representation of a wrapper that does nothing. Such wrappers can be generated automatically from the FSP representation of a connector. Though trivial, this example provides a starting point for the construction of more complex wrappers.

The intermediary process, Wrap, simply relays events from the Caller role to the Glue role and vice versa. The new Wrap is added to the composite process WrapPC, and all events in the glue that begin with the label caller are relabelled to begin with wrap.caller so that the glue and the caller no longer synchronize directly.

If the wrap events in WrapPC are hidden from observers by means of the hiding operator, and the labelled transition system drawn by LTSA (Labelled Transition System Analyzer, a tool provided with FSP) is compared to the depiction of the original connector, it becomes apparent by inspection that the two are equivalent. Equivalence can be checked more formally by treating one version as a safety property of the other version.

```
Caller = (call → TryCall),
      TryCall = (return → Caller | err → Caller).
De£ner = (call → return → De£ner | crash → END) \{crash}.
Glue = (caller.call → TryCall
        | de£ner.return → caller.return → Glue),
      TryCall = (de£ner.call → Glue | caller.err → Glue).
||FaultyRPC = (caller:Caller || de£ner:De£ner || Glue).
```

Figure 3. Procedure call with timeouts

5.2. Another Connector

The remaining examples of wrappers will embody common dependability enhancements. In order to illustrate their application, we introduce a connector in which the caller occasionally receives errors (Figure 3).

The FaultyRPC connector is subject to timeout errors that can occur whenever the caller is attempting to contact the de£ner.[4] The timeouts are represented by the glue's choice of the caller.err event. These timeouts may be transient in nature, perhaps due to problems in the communications channel, or may be due to the permanent silent failure of the de£ner component.[5]

The task of a dependability-enhancing wrapper for this connector is to hide the errors from the caller: it must be possible for a err-unaware caller not merely to avoid deadlock but also to make progress.

We will apply two wrappers to this connector: one that hides transient faults, and one that hides the failure of the de£ner. Transient faults can be masked by re-sending the request that had timed out. (This technique is in common practice; examples, such as retransmission in TCP [16], abound.) To mask the component failure, one possible technique is to provide a more reliable[6] backup, to be used when a failure is diagnosed. (This technique is a stripped-down instance of a general well-known method for introducing redundancy, which includes recovery blocks and N-version programming [10].)

5.3. Second Wrapper: "Retry"

We begin with a wrapper that will retry inde£nitely, and then show how it may be revised to retry only a £nite number of times. The wrapper intercepts any timeout error sent

[4]Timeouts when the de£ner is replying to the caller can also be modelled by adding another choice branch to the glue.

[5]The possibility of subsequent recovery of the failed component can be modelled, but is not included in this example for simplicity. Also, although a non-transient failure could also be due to a failure in the communications channel (such as being severed by a backhoe), for this example we will model only the failure of the component.

[6]It may be lacking in other key qualities such as performance, for which the primary may be generally preferred, as in [17].

to the client, and send out a new call event to the glue (to be relayed to the de£ner) instead: see Figure 4.

The structure of the composite RetryRPC is essentially identical to that of the WrapPC already seen (Figure 2). The RetryAll process is very similar to the previous no-effect Wrap process, with the addition of a new choice branch triggered by the retry.caller.err sent by the glue.[7]

This wrapper illustrates interception and replacement of events without change to the interfaces of the connector[8]. Wrappers can also enable the addition of new participants (roles) to the communication, as shown in a subsequent example.

5.3.1 Checking Results

Having applied this wrapper to our faulty connector, we would like to know several things: Is the result sound, or will it deadlock? Is the wrapper transparent to the caller role, or has it changed the interface? Have errors been hidden from the caller role? Does the caller role always make progress, or (as we expect) can the system become wedged: unable to make progress? We can use the LTSA model checker to con£rm that RetryRPC is deadlock-free as well as to answer the remaining questions.

FSP allows us to de£ne "safety properties" that constrain event ordering of legal events and prohibit illegal events. The £rst part of a safety property is a *process* de£ning the legal event ordering; the second part of a safety property is a *set* of any events that should be considered illegal. FSP also allows us to de£ne "progress properties"; a progress property speci£es a *set* of desirable events, and the system is considered to be making progress when at least one of these events occurs in£nitely often. Safety and progress properties can be checked with LTSA.

To con£rm that the caller's interface need not change, we restate the original caller role as an FSP safety property. The "process" part of this safety property would be the caller role; we'll leave empty the "set" part of this safety property. LTSA will show a safety violation and event trace, if the legal event ordering is not followed.

To con£rm that errors will not reach the caller role, we write another safety property: the NoErrors property shown in Figure 5. Here, event ordering is unconstrained (the "process" part of the property is simply STOP), and there is one

```
Caller  = (call → return → Caller).
De£ner = (call → return → De£ner
          | crash → END) \{crash}.
Glue = (caller.call → TryCall
        | de£ner.return → caller.return → Glue),
    TryCall = (de£ner.call → Glue | caller.err → Glue).
RetryAll = (caller.call → retry.caller.call → RetryAll
           | retry.caller.return → caller.return → RetryAll
           | retry.caller.err → retry.caller.call → RetryAll).
||RetryRPC = (caller:Caller || de£ner:De£ner
           || Glue/{retry.caller/caller} || RetryAll).
```

Figure 4. Applying RetryAll

```
property NoErrors = STOP + {caller.err}.
progress CallerOk = {caller.return}
||RetryRPC = (caller:Caller || de£ner:De£ner
           || Glue/{retry.caller/caller} || Retry
           || NoErrors ).
```

Figure 5. Safety and progress

```
Caller = (call → return → Caller).
De£ner = (call → return → De£ner | crash → END) \{crash}.
Glue = (caller.call → TryCall
        | de£ner.return → caller.return → Glue),
    TryCall = (de£ner.call → Glue | caller.err → Glue).
const T = 3
Retry = Retry[0],
  Retry[n:0..T] = (caller.call → retry.caller.call → Retry[0]
  | retry.caller.return → caller.return → Retry[0]
  | when (n<T) retry.caller.err → retry.caller.call → Retry[n+1]
  | when (n==T) retry.caller.err → caller.err → Retry[0]).
||RetryRPC = (caller:Caller || de£ner:De£ner
           || Glue/{retry.caller/caller} || Retry).
```

Figure 6. Applying Retry

illegal event, caller.err. LTSA will show a safety violation and event trace, if an illegal event can occur.

To con£rm that the caller will *make progress* in the case of a failed de£ner, we de£ne the progress property CallerOk. Its set of desirable events contains simply caller.return. In this example, just as we expect, LTSA reports a progress violation and the trace shows the failure of the de£ner.

5.3.2 Revising the Wrapper

Figure 6 shows a revised wrapper that re-sends at most 3 times in a row, using a parameterized local process that is incremented on each retry (and is reset on each non-error branch). It can be substituted for the RetryAll wrapper previously shown.

[7] Wrapper processes such as this one may also be generated automatically using tools that we are developing; £rst by generating the no effect wrapper particular to the desired connector and then by modifying the no-effect wrapper according to a connector-independent template, e.g. adding a choice branch as seen here.

[8] In the case of in£nite Retry, one might *choose* to replace the original role R_0 with a more speci£c interface R_1 that does not engage in error events; in£nite Retry is nevertheless a transparent addition for our purposes, because the event traces accepted by R_1 are a *subset* of those that R_0 accepts, so a component that was compatible with R_0 will still be compatible with R_1.

```
Caller = (call → return → Caller).
De£ner = (call → return → De£ner | crash → END) \{crash}.
Glue = (caller.call → TryCall
        | de£ner.return → caller.return → Glue),
    TryCall = (de£ner.call → Glue | caller.err → Glue).
Backup = (call → return → Backup).
BGlue = caller.call → de£ner.call → BGlue
        | de£ner.return → caller.return → BGlue).
Failover = (caller.call → pri.caller.call → Failover
        | pri.caller.return → caller.return → Failover
        | pri.caller.err → bk.caller.call → ToBk),
  ToBk = (caller.call → bk.caller.call → ToBk
        | bk.caller.return → caller.return → ToBk).
||FailoverRPC = (caller:Caller || pri.de£ner:De£ner || pri:Glue
    || bk.de£ner:Backup || bk:BGlue || Failover).
```

Figure 7. Applying Failover

Retransmission masks one of the two kinds of errors to which the FaultyRPC connector is subject. The £nite-retry wrapper produces a wrapped connector that is subject only to errors that are (probably) symptoms of a failed de£ner. We show later how this connector can be wrapped in turn to mask de£ner failure. Such chaining is common practice in fault tolerance, to achieve a greater coverage of possible failure situations by using a combination of several techniques drawn from broad classes (such as detection, diagnosis, containment, masking, compensation, and repair [5]; classi£cations vary but in general are ordered from the less drastic, lighter weight to the last-ditch, heavier weight techniques and are used in that order). This practice further motivates our compositional approach.

5.4. Third Wrapper: "Failover"

In order to mask the potential failure of the de£ner, we introduce component redundancy, which requires adding a new participant in the communication. The wrapper in this example (Figure 7) triggers the switch from primary to backup and performs the subsequent redirection of calls from the caller component to the backup. The local process ToBk, de£ned within the Failover process, redirects calls to the backup.[9]

[9]Note that we have modeled the simple case in which the primary never recovers. Slight modi£cation of Failover would be required to handle the case in which the primary may eventually recover: just as the Failover process has a trigger to switch to ToBk, ToBk could be given a trigger to switch back to the primary, or if the primary's recovery is also silent, ToBk could employ a counter (similar to the Retry process) and periodically attempt use of the primary.

```
||ReOver = (caller:Caller || pri.de£ner:De£ner
    || pri:( Glue/{retry.caller/caller} || Retry )
    || bk.de£ner:Backup || bk:BGlue || Failover).
```

Figure 8. Composing Retry and Failover

```
property NoErrors = STOP + {caller.err}.
progress CallerOk = {caller.return}
||ReOver = (caller:Caller || pri.de£ner:De£ner
    || pri:( Glue/{retry.caller/caller} || Retry )
    || bk.de£ner:Backup || bk:BGlue
    || Failover || NoErrors ).
```

Figure 9. Safety and progress, revisited

```
||ReReOver = (caller:Caller || pri.de£ner:De£ner
    || pri:( Glue/{retry.caller/caller} || Retry )
    || bk.de£ner:Backup
    || bk:( Glue/{retry.caller/caller} || RetryAll )
    || Failover).
```

Figure 10. Retry and RetryAll and Failover

6. Composition

Now we have wrappers that embody two reliability-enhancing techniques, each suited to one of the failure modes of the original faulty connector. Naturally we wish to compose the two wrappers. Our incremental approach makes this straightforward. Had we taken another approach to specifying wrapped connectors, such as simply modifying the existing glue processes rather than placing a new intermediary process beside them, the results of applying a single wrapper might have appeared simpler, but composition of wrappers would be quite dif£cult.

To compose these two wrappers, the reference to the Glue process in FailoverRPC is replaced with the enhanced "glue" of RetryRPC, as in Figure 8 (the elements that came from RetryRPC's "glue" are shown in bold font).

These two wrappers are *not commutative* (readily evident as the replacement of the Glue in RetryRPC with the enhanced "glue" of FailoverRPC yields a non-equivalent state machine in LTSA), thus it is important to get the order of application right; fortunately it is fairly intuitive to translate the desired effect "try x; if that's not enough, try y" into the right order "wrap with x, then wrap the composite with y".

Consider again the questions posed in section 5.3.1. By reusing the NoErrors and CallerOk safety and progress properties, as shown in Figure 9, we con£rm that errors are still hidden from the caller role, and furthermore that the caller *will* now make progress.

Finally, this example assumes no transmission dropouts between the caller and the backup de£ner (BGlue will not

```
set C = {caller}
set D = {de£ner}
set COut = {call}
set CIn = {return}
set NewLabel = {wrap}
Wrap = ([r:C].[e:COut] → [NewLabel].[r].[e] → Wrap
       | [NewLabel].[r:C].[e:CIn] → [r].[e] → Wrap).
||WrapPC = (caller:Caller || de£ner:De£ner
           || Glue/{[NewLabel].[r:C]/[r]} || Wrap).
```

Figure 11. Parameterized "No Effect"

generate errors on its own). To eliminate the unrealistic BGlue, we can replace it with an unreliable glue that has been wrapped with the RetryAll wrapper (Figure 10; the elements that came from RetryAll's "glue" are shown in bold font).

7. Parameterizing for Reuse

The wrapper processes in the preceding examples are hardcoded for the speci£c connector that they wrap. It is preferable to write more generalized and reusable wrapper processes via parameterization, so that they can be applied in a different context to a different connector type. We now see how to generalize the earlier examples to accomplish this in a straightforward way, and apply the result to a different connector.

7.1. Revisiting "No Effect"

Figure 11 shows how generalization can be performed for the simple "no effect" wrapper. To apply the wrapper to a connector, we must £ll in the italicized regions, de£ning several global variables: the set C of "caller" roles, the set COut of events that callers may initiate, the events CIn that callers may receive, and a one-element set NewLabel containing the label to tag the glue and the wrapper with. In the Wrap process, values of variables are drawn from these sets and are bound within a sequence.

For example in the £rst line of Wrap, for the £rst event, any value of r drawn from C is acceptable, and any value of e drawn from COut. In this application, each set has only one element, so the only corresponding event is caller.call. The next event in the sequence will pre£x the [r].[e] event (bound to caller.call) with a label drawn from the one-element set NewLabel. The result is wrap.caller.call.

Similarly, in the composite process WrapPC, the relabelling of the Glue can be parameterized to ensure it matches the labels used in the Wrap process; the label drawn from NewLabel will be added to the beginning of each event pre£xed with any label in C. The £nal lines of the £gure

```
set C = {caller}
set COut = {call}
set CIn = {return}
set CErr = {err}
set L = {retry}
set CInit = {call}
const T = 3
Retry = hide[e:CInit] → Retry[0][e],
  Retry[n:0..T][olde:COut] =
  ([r:C].[e:COut] → [L].[r].[e] → Retry[0][e]
  | [L].[r:C].[e:CIn] → [r].[e] → Retry[0][olde]
  | when (n<T)  [L].[r:C].[e:CErr]
                 → [L].[r].[olde] → Retry[n+1][olde]
  | when (n==T) [L].[r:C].[e:CErr]
                 → [r].[e] → Retry[0][olde])\{hide}.
||RetryRPC = (caller:Caller || de£ner:De£ner
             || Glue/{[L].[r:C]/[r]} || Retry).
```

Figure 12. Parameterized Retry)

show the pattern for the composite process of a wrapped connector that uses this wrapper; the italicized roles should be £lled in with the names of the actual roles.

7.2. Revisiting "Retry"

Parameterization of the Retry wrapper, shown in Figure 12, is similar. This wrapper must remember which event the caller attempted to transmit, so that that speci£c event can be repeated. Note the set CInit, used to initialize the cached event. Due to limitations of FSP syntax, a hidden event (hide) is used to select an element of CInit to provide the initial value for the second parameter of Retry[0..T][COut] since non-numeric values cannot be expressed directly in this circumstance. This value is not used unless an error is received before the caller has sent an event (which cannot happen in the example connectors shown here).

7.3. Applying to a New Connector

Figure 13 shows a new example connector. Here operation must begin with an open event, and end with a close event. During normal operation the client makes requests, and the server responds with a range of numeric values. Only the server can choose the returned value, and only the client can choose when to close. Timeouts (shown in bold font) may occur when the client is attempting to send requests or to close the connection. This connector *will deadlock*, since the client role is not expecting an error. The deadlock is eliminated when we apply the parameterized retry wrapper of Figure 12.

```
range M = 0..5
Client = (open → Run),
  Run = (request → result[v:M] → Run | hide → Close),
  Close = (close → END) \{hide}.
Server = (open → Run),
  Run = (request → hide[e:M] → result[e] → Run
        | close → END) \{hide}.
Glue = (client.open → server.open → Glue
       | client.request → server.request → Glue
       | server.result[v:M] → client.result[v] → Glue
       | client.close → server.close → END).
       | client.request → client.err → Glue
       | client.close → client.err → Glue
||Conn = (client:Client || server:Server || Glue).
```

Figure 13. Another connector

```
set C = {client}
set COut = {open, request, close}
set CIn = {result[v:M]}
set CErr = {err}
set L = {retry}
set CInit = {open}
||RetryRPC = (client:Client || server:Server
             || Glue/{[L].[r:C]/[r]} || Retry).
```

Figure 14. Applying parameterized Retry

Figure 14 shows the elements that must be £lled in to apply the Figure 12 wrapper to the Figure 13 connector.

The Retry pattern can also be applied to connectors with more than two roles, such as a client-server connector with multiple client roles. However, if the glue process constrains the behavior of the role processes (perhaps by allowing or disallowing nesting of calls), the wrapper process must cooperate in enforcing this constraint. In the approach we have been using this is achieved by patterning the wrapper on the results of exposing only a subset of events (those engaged in by the roles that will be adjacent to the wrapper) in the glue process, similar to the "no effect" wrapper.

7.4. Detecting Errors

Mistakes in the construction and application of parameterized wrappers can still be caught by the safety and progress analyses described earlier. This becomes increasingly useful as wrappers are composed and the speci£cation size increases.

For example, Figure 15 shows a plausible mistake in the application of a parameterized Failover. The event err (shown in bold font) is listed in the set of events that are acceptable as input to the caller; this would allow some error events to be relayed to the caller, at the whim of the Failover

```
set C = {caller}
set COut = {call}
set CIn = {return, err}
set CErr = {err}
Caller = ...
De£ner = (call → return → De£ner | crash → END) \{crash}.
Glue = (caller.call → TryCall
       | de£ner.return → caller.return → Glue),
  TryCall = (de£ner.call → Glue | caller.err → Glue).
Backup = (call → return → Backup).
BGlue = (caller.call → de£ner.call → BGlue
        | de£ner.return → caller.return → BGlue).
Failover = ([r:C].[e:COut] → pri.[r].[e] → Failover
           | pri.[r:C].[e:CIn] → [r].[e] → Failover
           | pri.[r:C].[CErr] → bk.[r].call → ToBk),
  ToBk = ([r:C].[e:COut] → bk.[r].[e] → ToBk
         | bk.[r:C].[e:CIn] → [r].[e] → ToBk).
||FailoverRPC = (caller:Caller || pri.de£ner:De£ner || pri:Glue
    || bk.de£ner:Backup || bk:BGlue || Failover).
```

Figure 15. Parameterized Failover

process. This mistake is caught by the NoErrors property (used to check that the wrapper does its intended job, as seen earlier in Figure 5), no matter whether the caller process accepts err, as in Figure 3, or ignores err, as in Figure 7. Once diagnosed, the problem can be resolved by removing err from CIn.

7.5. In Review

The initial examples of wrappers were hard-wired and could only be used for one particular connector speci£cation. In implementation, this would correspond to particular pieces of code that could be applied in systems where a particular connector implementation is used (such as a Java RMI connector, an example of an RPC-style connector), but could not be applied to some other arbitrary connector implementation (such as a Unix pipe, or even a different implementation of RPC).

Here in section 7 we have shown how to write parameterized wrappers that are applicable to, and reusable across, *multiple* connector types. This generalization is straightforward to accomplish. The parameterized wrappers are not dif£cult to apply to connector speci£cations. Furthermore, even if a mistake is made, it can be readily detected (as shown in 7.4).

In implementation, this generalization into parameterized wrapper patterns, which are then applied to particular connector types, could correspond to the use of a tool or "wizard" that is prompted with a wrapper pattern plus a small amount of information about a connector, This tool would then generate an instance of a wrapper implementation suitable for that particular connector implementation (which may be a CORBA connector, a Java Message Service connector, etc.). We use this approach in [20].

8. Discussion

An important consideration when producing a formal specification, or a family of formal specifications (as we have proposed), is the resulting engineering properties of the formal artifact. Our approach has two important properties: *compositionality* and *traceability*. Here compositionality refers to the ability to combine wrappers to create a more complex composite wrapper, as in Figure 8. Traceability refers to the ability to determine where something "came from", so that if a problem is discovered, its source can be located in a particular section of the model, and the corresponding affected section of the implementation can be determined, and vice versa.

As we have demonstrated in the example of section 6, this wrapper specification technique exhibits ease of composition. The effects of event redirection, insertion, replacement, deletion, etc., are achieved by interposing a new process, rather than by actually editing an existing process. As a result composition of the wrappers is straightforward. To apply an existing wrapper it is only necessary to classify events into a small number of sets and to perform a renaming on the glue. (It is naturally also easy to remove a wrapper.) If layers of enhancement were added instead by, for example, performing directives that state how to mutate the glue process into a monolithic enhanced glue process (such as, after each event e of type T, add a new event $f(e)$), either automatically or by hand, the result would become increasingly difficult to modify further, and removal of an arbitrary enhancement would not be straightforward.

Traceability between the protocol specification and the implementation is promoted by the essential similarity of their respective structures. When wrappers are actually implemented, it is generally as a layer of enhancements interposed between the component interface and the communication infrastructure; this interposition may be supported by interceptors or system-level trickery, but in any case leaves the component and the infrastructure essentially undigested and unchanged. By using a similar wrapping technique in the protocol specification, its structure remains similar to the structure of the implementation (implementation wrappers correspond to wrapper processes in the specification), enabling the tracing of attributes from a substructure of one to the corresponding substructure of the other.

It is worth noting that, while there are many contexts in which wrappers must ideally achieve a transparent effect, in other cases it is desirable for information available to one wrapper to be exposed to a subsequent wrapper (when ordinarily this information would deliberately be concealed). Often this can be achieved, without adversely impacting any intervening wrappers, by using parameterization that is already in place. For example[10], consider a system with three high-performance Definer components and one slow but reliable Backup component. We apply the parameterized Retry and Failover wrappers to each of three FaultyRPC connectors. Now we wish to apply a new LoadBalancer wrapper which, given a caller.call event, redirects it to *one* of the three wrapped connectors and thus, ultimately, to either the corresponding Definer or the single Backup component. Clearly it would be wise to expose the failure of a component to LoadBalancer so that it has the opportunity to refrain from using it. This can be done by adding a tag to [r].[e] in the Failover process, and extending the set CIn of any wrappers between Failover and LoadBalancer to include these tagged events.

Finally, one important question is, can this formalism correspond to implementation as hinted at in section 7.5? To what extent can it be related back to the "real world"? To answer this question is beyond the scope of this paper, but in other work [20], transformation patterns are encoded as operations on stub generation tools. For example we have shown how to create and apply transformation patterns that are very similar to the kinds of wrappers described here. Using the stub generation tools, implementations of these transformations have been generated for Java RMI, a commonly used RPC-style connector implementation, and this work has been extended to Java Message Service, an event-style connector.

9. Conclusion

This work provides a formal framework for reasoning about wrappers and their effect on interaction mechanisms via protocol enhancement. We have illustrated the use of this technique for dependability-oriented wrappers and shown how compositionality is achieved, and how analyses may be used to confirm desired attributes, such as whether a wrapper preserves existing interfaces while also masking communication errors. This approach allows practitioners to break a complex modification into incremental, more easily understood parts, and reason about wrappers' effects in advance of their implementation.

More generally, this work also provides an example of a formal abstraction or model that has a good engineering basis, providing not just a means of principled reasoning, but one that also has an increased degree of compositionality, checkability, traceability, and maintainability.

An additional contribution of this work is to demonstrate usefulness of the Wright approach, which separates a connector into interfaces and their interactions.

[10] Thanks are due to an anonymous reader of an earlier draft who suggested this scenario

Several questions were posed in section 3. We have addressed a number of them, showing how to answer them for at least the speci£c examples shown.

- Soundness: Given a connector and a wrapper, we have shown how to construct a wrapped connector, on which a model checker can be used to determine whether the wrapper introduces new deadlocks.
- Transparency: The interfaces of a wrapped connector can be checked to ensure conformance.
- Compositionality: We show how to compose several types of wrappers and reason about that composition, including determination of noncommutativity. Checking other algebraic properties, such as idempotence and inverses, can be addressed in a manner similar to transparency conformance checks.

Work is ongoing to complete a set of genericized protocol transformation patterns comparable, and complementary, to the common patterns of connector implementation enhancement described in other work [20]. The examples given here illustrate the rudiments of the approach, giving semantics for a subset of the enhancement patterns, and thus supporting increased understanding of the results of their application and composition. Our other wrapper speci£cations (not included here due to space) include compression, encryption, logging, authorization, and voting wrappers, dynamic protocol selection and a limited set of protocol mismatch-repair wrappers.

10. Acknowledgments

This research has been supported by NSF under grant CCR-0113810, by DARPA under contract F30602-00-2-0616, and by NASA under the High Dependability Computing Program from NASA Ames cooperative agreement NCC-2-1298. The views and conclusions contained in this document are those of the authors and should not be interpreted as representing the of£cial policies, either expressed or implied, of NSF, DARPA, NASA, or the U.S. government. We would like to thank Philip Koopman, Mary Shaw, Jeannette Wing, and the members of the ABLE group.

References

[1] R. Allen and D. Garlan. A formal basis for architectural connection. *ACM Transactions on Software Engineering and Methodology*, July 1997.

[2] R. DeLine. *Resolving Packaging Mismatch.* PhD thesis, Carnegie Mellon, School of Computer Science, 1999. Issued as CMU Technical Report CMU-CS-99-141.

[3] T. Fraser, L. Badger, and M. Feldman. Hardening COTS software with generic software wrappers. In *IEEE Symposium on Security and Privacy*, pages 2–16, 1999.

[4] D. Garlan, R. Allen, and J. Ockerbloom. Architectural mismatch, or, why it's hard to build systems out of existing parts. In *Proceedings of the 17th International Conference on Software Engineering*, Seattle, Washington, April 1995.

[5] W. L. Heimerdinger and C. B. Weinstock. A conceptual framework for system fault tolerance. Technical Report CMU/SEI-92-TR-33, Carnegie Mellon University, 1992.

[6] C. Hoare. *Communicating Sequential Processes.* Prentice Hall, 1985.

[7] H. Hueni, R. E. Johnson, and R. Engel. A framework for network protocol software. *Proceedings of OOPSLA'95*, pages 358–369, 1995.

[8] G. Hunt and D. Brubacher. Detours: Binary interception of win32 functions. In *Proceedings of the 3rd USENIX Windows NT Symposium*, pages 135–143, Seattle, WA, July 1999.

[9] A. Lopes, M. Wermelinger, and J. L. Fiadeiro. A compositional approach to connector construction. In *Recent Trends in Algebraic Development Techniques*, volume LNCS 2267, pages 201–220. Springer-Verlag, 2001.

[10] M. R. Lyu. *Software Fault Tolerance.* John Wiley and Sons, 1995.

[11] J. Magee and J. Kramer. *Concurrency: State Models and Java Programs.* John Wiley and Sons, 1999.

[12] R. Milner. *Communication and Concurrency.* Prentice Hall, 1989.

[13] P. Narasimhan, L. E. Moser, and P. M. Melliar-Smith. Exploiting the internet inter-ORB protocol interface to provide CORBA with fault tolerance. In *Proceedings of the 3rd USENIX Conference on Object-Oriented Technologies and Systems (COOTS).* USENIX, 1997.

[14] S. W. O'Malley and L. L. Peterson. A dynamic network architecture. *ACM Transactions on Computer Systems*, 10(2):110–143, May 1992.

[15] J. Pan, P. Koopman, D. Siewiorek, Y. Huang, R. Gruber, and M. L. Jiang. Robustness testing and hardening of CORBA ORB implementations. In *Proceedings of the International Conference on Dependable Systems and Networks (ICDSN/FTCS)*, pages 141–150, July 2001.

[16] J. Postel. Transmission control protocol. Technical report, RFC-793, 1981.

[17] L. Sha, J. Goodenough, and B. Pollack. Simplex architecture: Meeting the challenges of using COTS in high-reliability systems. *Crosstalk*, April 1998.

[18] M. Shaw. Procedure calls are the assembly language of system interconnection: Connectors deserve £rst-class status. In *Proceedings of the Workshop on Studies of Software Design*, May 1993.

[19] M. Shaw. Architectural issues in software reuse: It's not just the functionality, it's the packaging. In *Proceedings of the Symposium on Software Reuse (SSR'95)*, April 1995.

[20] B. Spitznagel and D. Garlan. A compositional approach for constructing connectors. In *The Working IEEE/IFIP Conference on Software Architecture (WICSA'01)*, pages 148–157, Royal Netherlands Academy of Arts and Sciences Amsterdam, The Netherlands, August 2001.

[21] R. van Renesse, K. Birman, M. Hayden, A. Vaysburd, and D. Karr. Building adaptive systems using Ensemble. Technical report, Cornell/TR97-1638, 1997.

Modular Verification of Software Components in C*

Sagar Chaki Edmund Clarke Alex Groce
Carnegie Mellon University
{chaki|emc|agroce}@cs.cmu.edu

Somesh Jha
Univ of Wisconsin
jha@cs.wisc.edu

Helmut Veith
TU Vienna
veith@dbai.tuwien.ac.at

Abstract

We present a new methodology for automatic verification of C programs against finite state machine specifications. Our approach is compositional, naturally enabling us to decompose the verification of large software systems into subproblems of manageable complexity. The decomposition reflects the modularity in the software design. We use weak simulation as the notion of conformance between the program and its specification. Following the abstract-verify-refine paradigm, our tool MAGIC first extracts a finite model from C source code using predicate abstraction and theorem proving. Subsequently, simulation is checked via a reduction to Boolean satisfiability. MAGIC is able to interface with several publicly available theorem provers and SAT solvers. We report experimental results with procedures from the Linux kernel and the OpenSSL toolkit.

1 Introduction

State machines have been recognized repeatedly as a cardinal point in the software development process; in fact, variants of state machines have been proposed for virtually all software engineering methodologies, including, most notably, Statecharts [25] and the UML [9]. The sustained success of state machines in software engineering derives from the fact that state machines provide for both a concise mathematical theory, and an intuitive semantics of system behavior which naturally allows for visualization, hierarchy, and abstraction.

Traditionally, state machines are mainly used in the design phase of the software life-cycle; they are intended to guide and constrain the implementation and the test phase, and may later be reused for documentation purposes. In most cases, however, the assertion that a state machine safely abstracts the existing implementation is kept implicit and informal.

With the rise of Internet-based technologies, the significance of state machines has only increased. In particular, security protocols and communication protocols are naturally specified in terms of state machines. Similar applications of state machines can be found in other safety-critical domains including medicine and aerospace.

Moreover, the dramatic change of focus from relatively monolithic systems to highly distributed and heterogeneous systems whose development cycles are interdependent, calls for new specification methodologies; for example, in August 2002, IBM, Microsoft, and BEA announced the publication of three specifications (WS-Coordination, WS-Specification, BPEL4WS [3]) which "collectively describe how to reliably define, create and connect multiple business processes in a Web services environment". We foresee state machines being used for *contracts* describing software capabilities. In both cases – protocol specification and distributed computation – we observe that state machines are no longer just tools for internal use, but are increasingly introduced into the public domain.

In this paper, we describe our tool MAGIC (**M**odular **A**nalysis of pro**G**rams **I**n **C**) which is capable of verifying whether a state machine (or, more precisely, a labeled transition system) is a safe abstraction of a C procedure; the C procedure in turn may invoke other procedures *which are themselves specified in terms of state machines.*

Our approach has a number of tangible benefits:

- *Utility.* The capability of MAGIC to verify formally the correctness of state-machine specifications closes an evident gap in many software development methodologies, most notably, but not only, for security-related system features. In the future we envision that tools based on ideas from MAGIC will assist the contracting process with third party software providers.

- *Compositionality.* MAGIC verification can be used early on during the development cycle, as specifica-

*This research was supported by the NRL-ONR under Grant No. N00014-01-1-0796, by the NSF under Grant No. CCR-9803774, CCR-0121547 and CCR-0098072, by the Army-ARO under Grant No. DAAD 19-01-1-0485, the Austrian Science Fund Project NZ29-INF, the EU Research and Training Network GAMES and graduate student fellowships from Microsoft and NSF. Any opinions, findings and conclusions or recommendations expressed in this material are those of the authors and do not necessarily reflect the views of NSF or the United States Government.

0-7695-1877-X/03 $17.00 © 2003 IEEE

tions can be plugged in for missing system components. Compositionality evidently fosters concurrent development by independent groups of developers.

- *Complexity.* State-space explosion [18] remains the bottleneck of most automated verification tools. Due to compositionality, the size of the individual system parts to be verified by MAGIC remains manageable, as demonstrated by our experiments. Moreover, the verification process in MAGIC is reduced to computing a *simulation relation between finite state systems*, for which we can provide highly efficient algorithms.

- *Flexibility.* Internally, MAGIC uses several theorem provers and SAT solvers. The open design of MAGIC facilitates the easy integration of new and improved tools from this quickly developing area.

Consequently, we believe that MAGIC like tools have the potential to become indispensable in the software engineering process. In the rest of this section we describe the technical contributions of this paper.

Labeled Transition Systems as Specification Mechanism. In the literature, several variants of state machines have been investigated; purely state-based formalisms such as Kripke structures [18] are often used to model and specify systems. For the MAGIC framework, however, we employ *labeled transition systems* (LTS), which are similar to Kripke structures but for the fact that state transitions are labeled by *actions*.

From a theoretical point of view the presence of actions does not increase the expressive power of LTS. In our experience, however, it is more natural for designers and software engineers to express the desired behavior of systems using a combination of states and actions. For example, the fact that a lock has been acquired or released can be expressed naturally by *lock* and *unlock* actions. In the absence of actions, the natural alternative is to introduce a new variable indicating the status of the lock, and update it accordingly. The LTS approach certainly is more intuitive, and allows both for a simpler theory and for an easier specification process. A simple example of an LTS is shown in the left part of Figure 1. A formal definition will be given in Section 2.

In the MAGIC framework, we use actions to denote externally visible behaviors of the system being analyzed, e.g. acquiring a lock. Actions are atomic, and are distinguished simply by their names. Often, the presence of an action indicates a certain behavior which is achieved by a subprocedure in the implementation. Since we shall analyze a procedural language, namely C, we will model the termination of a procedure (i.e., a return from the procedure) by a special class of actions called *return actions*. Every return action a is associated with a unique return value $RetVal(a)$. Return values are either integers or *void.* All actions which are not return actions are called *basic* actions.

The use of LTSs is also motivated by work in concurrency. Process algebras like CCS [33], CSP [28] and the π-calculus [34] have been used widely to reason formally about message passing concurrent systems. In these formalisms, actions are crucial for modeling the sending and receiving of messages across channels. Process algebras lead very naturally to LTSs. Thus, even though we currently only analyze sequential programs, we believe that the use of LTSs will facilitate a smooth transition to concurrent message-passing programs in the future.

Procedure Abstractions. The goal of MAGIC is to verify whether the implementation of a system is safely abstracted by its specification. To this end, MAGIC verifies individual procedures against the respective LTS. In our implementation, it is possible to handle a group of procedures with a tree-like call graph as a single one by inlining; for simplicity, we speak only of single procedures in this paper. Figure 1 describes a simple case of a procedure *proc* and a corresponding LTS. We will use *proc* as a running example.

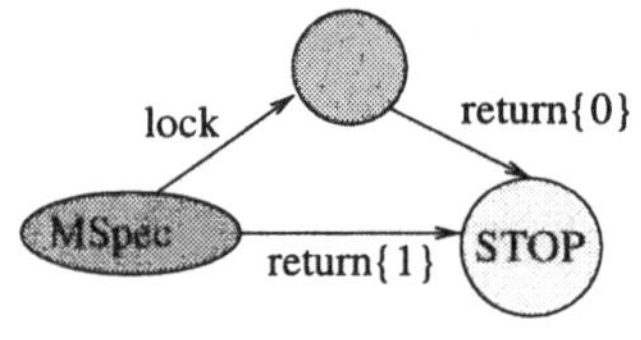

Spec State Machine

```
int proc()
{
  if(do_lock())
    return 0;
  else
    return 1;
}
```

Code to be analysed

Figure 1. The example M_{Spec} and $proc$.

In practice, it often happens that single procedures perform quite different tasks for certain settings of their parameters. In our approach, this phenomenon is accounted for by allowing multiple LTSs to represent a single procedure. The selection among these LTSs is achieved by *guards*, i.e., formulas, which describe the conditions on the procedure parameters under which a certain LTS is applicable.

This gives rise to the notion of *procedure abstraction* (PA); formally a PA for a procedure $proc$ is a tuple $\langle d, l\rangle$ where

- d is the declaration for *proc*, as it appears in a C header file.

- l is a finite list $\langle g_1, M_1\rangle, \ldots, \langle g_n, M_n\rangle$ where each g_i is a guard formula ranging over the parameters of *proc*, and each M_i is an LTS with a single initial state.

The procedure abstraction expresses that $proc$ conforms to one LTS chosen among the L_i's. More precisely, $proc$

conforms to L_i if the corresponding guard g_i evaluates to true over the *actual arguments* passed to *proc*. We require that the guard formulas g_i be mutually exclusive so that the choice of L_i is unambiguous. The goal of MAGIC then is to prove that a user-defined PA for *proc* is valid. The role of PAs in this process is twofold:

1. A *target PA* is used to describe the desired behavior of the procedure *proc*.
2. To assist the verification process, we employ valid PAs (called the *assumption* PAs) for library routines used by *proc*.

Thus, PAs can be seen both as conclusions and as assumptions of the verification process. Consequently, our methodology yields a scalable and compositional approach for verifying large software systems. Figure 2 illustrates this by depicting the call graph of an implementation and the verification steps; note that due to compositionality no particular order of these steps is required.

Without loss of generality we will assume throughout this paper that the target PA contains only one guard G_{Spec} and one LTS M_{Spec}. To achieve the result in full generality, the described algorithm can be iterated for each guard of M_{Spec}.

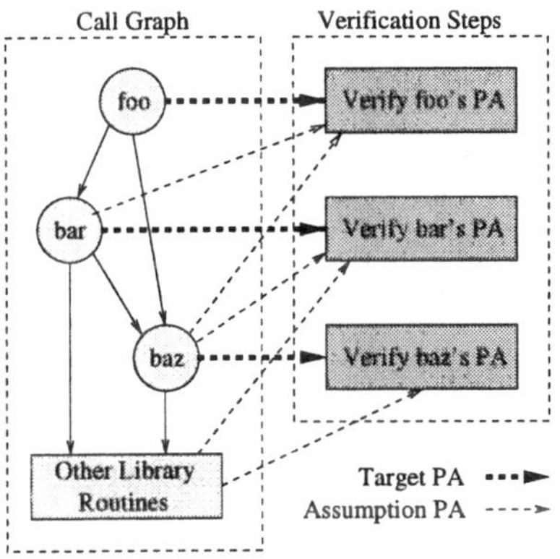

Figure 2. Compositional verification.

Algorithms and Tool Description. The MAGIC tool follows the well-known *abstract - verify - refine* paradigm [13, 16, 21, 27]:

- **Step 1 : Model Creation.** Extract an LTS M_{Imp} from *proc* using the assumed PAs and the guard G_{Spec}.

  In MAGIC, the model is computed from the control flow graph (CFG) of the program in combination with an abstraction method called *predicate abstraction* [16, 19, 37]. To decide properties such as equivalence of predicates, we use theorem provers. The details of this step are described in Section 3.

- **Step 2 : Verification.** Check whether M_{Spec} safely abstracts M_{Imp}. If this is the case, the verification successfully terminates; otherwise, extract diagnostic feedback and perform step 3.

  In MAGIC, the verification step amounts to checking whether a *simulation relation* holds between M_{Spec} and M_{Imp}, cf. Section 2. We reduce simulation to the satisfiability of a certain Boolean formula, thus deferring the solution to highly efficient SAT procedures. The details of this step are described in Section 2.

- **Step 3 : Refinement.** Use the diagnostic feedback to determine the reason behind the failure of the safe abstraction property. If the cause is a bug in *proc* we are done. Otherwise the property fails because M_{Imp} is not a sufficiently precise model for *proc*. In this case return to step 1 to compute an improved M_{Imp}.

At its current stage of development, MAGIC performs the first two of these steps automatically, while the third step is manually guided. The input to MAGIC consists of (i) a set of preprocessed ANSI-C files representing *proc* and (ii) a set of specification files containing textual descriptions of M_{Spec}, G_{Spec} and *predicates* for predicate abstraction. The textual descriptions of LTSs are given using an extended version of the FSP notation by Magee and Kramer [30]. For example, the LTS shown in Figure 1 is described textually as follows:

```
MyLock = ( lock -> return {$0 == 0} -> STOP
         | return {$0 == 1} -> STOP ).
```

The schematic in Figure 3 explains the software architecture of MAGIC. **Model Creation** is handled by Stage I and II of the program. In Stage I the input files are parsed and the control flow graph (CFG) of the C program is constructed. Simplifications are made so that the resulting CFG only has simple statements and side-effect free expressions. Then relevant predicates at each control location are computed and the CFG is annotated with them. In Stage II, M_{Imp} is extracted from the annotated CFG using the assumed PAs, G_{Spec} and the predicates. As described later, this process requires the use of theorem provers. MAGIC can interact with several public domain theorem provers viz. Simplify [36], CVC [39], ICS [23] and CPROVER [29].

Verification is performed in Stage III. As mentioned above, simulation here is reduced to Boolean satisfiability. MAGIC can interface with several publicly available SAT solvers viz. Chaff [35], FGRASP [31] and SATO [40]. We also have our own efficient SAT solver implementation which leverages the specific nature of SAT formulas that arise in this stage to deliver better performance than the public domain solvers. MAGIC does not generate diagnostic feedback yet, nor does it support automatic model

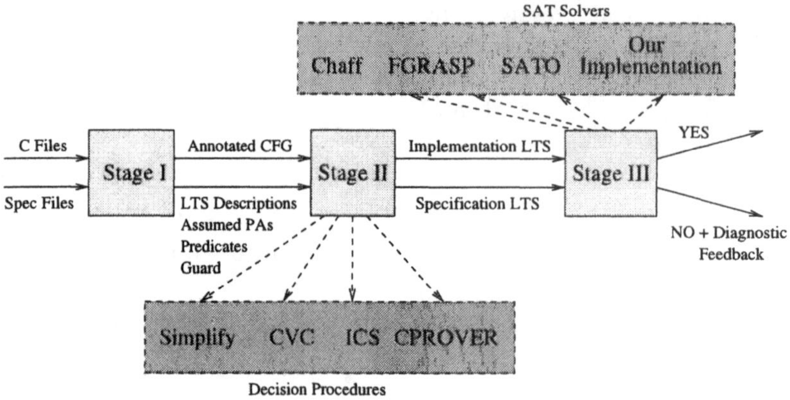

Figure 3. Overall architecture of MAGIC.

refinement. We consider this a significant area for future research.

Related Work. During the last years advances in verification methodology as well as in computing power have promoted renewed interest in software verification. The resulting systems – most notably Bandera [1] and Java PathFinder [5, 26], ESC Java [4], SLAM [7], BLAST [2] and MC [22, 24] – are increasingly able to handle industrial software. Among the six mentioned systems, the former three focus on Java, while the latter three all deal with C. Java verification is quite different from C, because object orientation, garbage collection and the logical memory model require specific analysis methods. Among the C verification tools, MC (which stands for meta-compilation) has a distinguished place because it amounts to a form of pattern matching on the source code, with surprisingly good results for scanning relatively simple errors in large amounts of code. SLAM and BLAST are closely related tools, whose technical flavor is most akin to ours. SLAM is primarily optimized to analyse device drivers, and is going to be included in the Windows development cycle. In contrast to SLAM which uses symbolic algorithms, BLAST is an on-the-fly reachability analysis tool. MAGIC is the only tool which uses LTS as specification formalism, and simulation as the notion of conformance. This choice reflects the area of security currently being our primary application domain.

Except for MC, the mentioned tools are based on variations of *model checking* [15, 18], and they all require abstraction methods to alleviate the state explosion problem, most notably data abstraction [17] and the more general predicate abstraction [37]. The abstraction method used in SLAM and BLAST is closest to ours. However, due to compositionality, we can afford to invest more computing power into computing abstractions, and are therefore able to improve on Cartesian abstraction [12]. Generally, we believe that the form of compositionality provided by MAGIC is unique among existing software verification systems.

Virtually all systems using abstraction interface with theorem provers for various purposes. The software architecture of MAGIC is designed as to facilitate the integration of various theorem provers. In addition, MAGIC is the only tool in this area which attempts to transfer the enormous success of SAT procedures in hardware verification [14] to software.

2 Transition Systems and Simulation

A labeled transition system (LTS) M is a 4-tuple (S, S_0, Act, T), where (i) S is a finite non-empty set of states, (ii) $S_0 \subseteq S$ is the set of initial states, (iii) Act is the set of actions, and (iv) $T \subseteq S \times Act \times S$ is the transition relation.

We assume that there is a distinguished state $STOP \in S$ which has no outgoing transitions, i.e., $\forall s' \in S, \forall a \in A, (STOP, a, s') \notin T$. In addition we assume the presence of a distinguished action in the set Act, which we denote by ϵ. If $(s, a, s') \in T$, then (s, s') will be referred to as a a-transition and will be denoted by $s \xrightarrow{a} s'$. If s is reachable from s' via zero or more ϵ-transitions, we will denote this by $s \xrightarrow{\epsilon^*} s'$. The relation $\Rightarrow$ is defined as follows: $s \stackrel{a}{\Rightarrow} s'$ iff there exist s_1 and s_2 such that $s \xrightarrow{\epsilon^*} s_1 \xrightarrow{a} s_2 \xrightarrow{\epsilon^*} s'$.

Conformance via Simulation. In the context of LTS, *simulation* [33] is the natural notion of conformance between a specification LTS and an implementation LTS. We will therefore use simulation as our notion of conformance between the specification LTS and the program. Compared to conformance notions based on trace containment [13], simulation has the additional advantage that it is computationally less expensive to check. Among the many technical variants of simulation [33], we choose *weak simulation* because it allows for a limited form of asynchrony between the LTSs, i.e., one step of the specification LTS may simulate multiple steps of the implementation. This feature of weak simulation is crucial to our approach, because one step in M_{Spec} typically corresponds to multiple steps in M_{Imp}.

Weak Simulation. Let $M = (S, S_0, Act, T)$ and $M' = (S', S'_0, Act, T')$ be two LTSs. A relation $E \subseteq S \times S'$ is called a *weak simulation* between M and M' iff (i) for all $s \in S_0$ there exists $s' \in S'_0$ such that $(s, s') \in E$, and (ii) $(s, s') \in E$ implies that for all actions $a \in Act \setminus \{\epsilon\}$ if $s \stackrel{a}{\Rightarrow} s_1$, then there exists $s'_1 \in S'$ such that $s' \stackrel{a}{\Rightarrow} s'_1$ and $(s_1, s'_1) \in E$. We say that LTS M' *weakly simulates* M (denoted by $M \preceq M'$) if there exists a weak simulation relation $E \subseteq S \times S'$ between M and M'. In the rest of the paper, we use the convention that the terms *simulation* and *simulates* will always mean *weak simulation* and *weakly simulates* respectively.

Algorithm for Computing Weak Simulation. The existence of a simulation relation between M and M' can be checked efficiently by reducing the problem to an instance of Boolean satisfiability [38]. Interestingly the SAT instances produced by this method always belong to a restricted class of SAT formulas known as the *weakly negated* HORN formulas. In contrast to general SAT (which has no known polynomial time algorithm), satisfiability of weakly negated HORN formulas can be solved in linear time [20]. As part of MAGIC, we have implemented an online linear time HORNSAT algorithm based on [10]. MAGIC can also interface with public domain general SAT solvers like Chaff [35], FGRASP [31] and SATO [40].

3 Model Creation

Let $M_{Spec} = (S_{Spec}, S_{0,Spec}, Act_{Spec}, T_{Spec})$ and the assumption PAs be $\{PA_1, \ldots, PA_k\}$. In this section we show how to extract M_{Imp} from *proc* using the assumption PAs, the guard G_{Spec} and the predicates. The extraction of M_{Imp} relies on several principles:

- Every state of M_{Imp} models a state during the execution of *proc*; consequently every state is composed of a control component and a data component.

- The control components intuitively represent values of the program counter, and are formally obtained from the CFG of *proc*.

- The data components are *abstract representations* of the memory state of *proc*. These abstract representations are obtained using predicate abstraction.

- The transitions between states in M_{Imp} are derived from the transitions in the control flow graph, taking into account the assumption PAs and the predicate abstraction. This process involves reasoning about C expressions, and will therefore require the use of a theorem prover.

In the rest of this section, we will describe these steps in detail.

Control Flow Graph. The CFG of *proc* is a finite graph describing the flow of control in *proc*. The nodes of the CFG are called control locations, and intuitively correspond to the values of the program counter; the edges denote transfer of control. Ordinary C code however contains nested procedure calls, expressions with side-effects and other similar constructs that make it difficult to construct precise CFGs. In order to alleviate this problem, our tool first performs a set of natural simplifications on *proc* before constructing its CFG. The simplified procedure body contain only *normal assignments* (e.g. `x = y + 5;` or `*x = *y + 10;`), *call assignments* (e.g. `x = foo(y + 5);`), *branches* (e.g. `if (x) { ... } else { ... }`), *gotos* and *returns* (e.g. `return (*y + 5);`). The left hand side of assignments must always be either a variable or a single address dereference (such as `*v = 5;`). Note that in the resulting program loop statements such as `while` and `for` are substituted by appropriate `if` and `goto` statements. Moreover, we can assume that each variable has a unique scope, and each procedure always terminates with explicit `return` statements. These preprocessing steps are not very complicated, and are omitted here. The CFG for our example *proc* is shown in Figure 4.

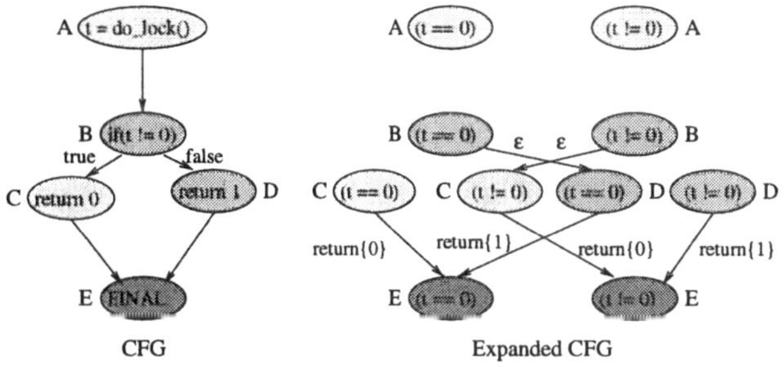

Figure 4. CFG and expanded CFG.

Control Locations. After this simplification, the definition of control locations becomes straightforward: Each normal assignment, call assignment, goto and return statement gives rise to a control location with a unique successor. In contrast, a branch yields a control location with exactly two successors. We assume that for each control location in the CFG, the associated conditions and statements are available. In addition, we introduce a unique final control location and make it the unique successor of all return control locations. Depending on the statement to which the control location is referring we speak of normal assignment locations, branch locations etc. Formally, $\mathcal{C}$ denotes the set of control locations of *proc*.

Expanding the Control Flow Graph. The CFG is the simplest reasonable finite model of *proc*. However, for verification purposes the CFG is too imprecise because it models only control flow, but ignores data (memory). On the other hand, it is computationally unfeasible to model the memory explicitly.

We will now show how to incorporate *abstract* memory state information into the CFG. To this end, we will consider a set of properties at each control location. These properties are described by C expressions similar to those used as branching conditions. Thus, if we have k data properties, each of which can be true or false, then each control location corresponds to 2^k possible states in our model, each of them corresponding to a particular valuation of the properties considered. Intuitively, the construction of the LTS M_{Imp} proceeds stepwise:

1. Construct the CFG.

2. Construct an expanded CFG $M_{Exp} = (S_{Exp}, S_{0,Exp}, Act_{Spec}, T_{Exp})$ as follows:

   - For each control location c, we include 2^k states in S_{Exp}; each state thus is a combination of a control location and a valuation of the considered properties.
   - Consider an edge (c_1, c_2) in the CFG. Then c_1 and c_2 correspond to 2^k states in S_{Exp} each. Consequently, (c_1, c_2) may be correspond to up to $2^k \times 2^k$ transitions in T_{Exp}. However, not all of them will be included because not all transitions are consistent with the abstract memory state information. We will use a theorem prover to determine which of these transitions indeed are admissible. We will only rule out transitions whose admissibility can be disproved by the theorem prover.

3. M_{Exp} is a more precise model of *proc* than the CFG. However it does not model the behavior of the library routines called by *proc*. To achieve this we incorporate the assumption PAs into M_{Exp}. This step also requires the use of a theorem prover. The LTS obtained after incorporating the assumption PAs is M_{Imp}.

In the following two sections, we will describe step 2 of this process in detail; in Section 3.4, we will explain step 3.

3.1 Predicate Abstraction

Predicate abstraction is an approach to model abstractly the state of a system by a set of logical predicates [19, 37]. We use predicate abstraction techniques only to model the memory state. As we aim to verify C programs, it is natural to express these properties by pure (side-effect free) Boolean C expressions. Since we assumed the scope of each variable to be unique, this definition is unambiguous.

Thus, we shall use C expressions very much in the same way as quantifier-free first order formulas. Because of this conceptual proximity we will use logical connectives such as $\wedge$, $\vee$ and $\neg$ instead of their C equivalents `&&`, `||` and `!`.

In order to describe abstract memory states, let us fix a certain set $\mathcal{P} = \{P_1, \ldots P_k\}$ of expressions which we call the *predicates*. Note that we do not use float and string constants in predicates at the current stage of the implementation. Given a concrete memory state m and a predicate P, we say that m satisfies P iff P evaluates to true (i.e., a non-zero numerical value) during the execution of *proc* when the memory state is m. A valuation for $\mathcal{P}$ is a vector $v_1, \ldots v_k$ of Boolean values, such that v_i expresses the Boolean value of P_i. $\mathcal{V}$ denotes the set of all valuations, i.e., the set of abstract memory states. Intuitively, a concrete memory state m is modeled by $v_1, \ldots v_k$ if for $1 \leq i \leq k$, m satisfies P_i iff v_i is true.

A valuation v typically models many concrete memory states. This set is characterized by a formula (called the *concretization* of v) which expresses truth or falsity of the involved properties in the natural way: Given a valuation $v = v_1, \ldots v_k$, the concretization $\gamma(v)$ is defined as $\bigwedge_{i=1}^{k} P_i^{v_i}$ where $P_i^{v_i}$ is equal to P_i if v_i is true, and equal to $\neg P_i$ if v_i is false. Thus, $\gamma(v)$ describes the property captured by the valuation v; all memory states which are modeled by v satisfy $\gamma(v)$.

Example 1 *In our example, $\mathcal{P}$ contains a single predicate $(t == 0)$ and therefore has two valuations - [true] and [false]. Hence $\gamma([true]) := (t == 0)$ and $\gamma([false]) := \neg(t == 0)$. Thus [true] models all concrete memory states where the variable t is equal to* 0 *and false models all concrete memory states where the variable t is not equal to* 0.

State Space of M_{Exp}. We combine the control flow graph and the predicate abstraction to obtain the state space $S_{Exp} := \mathcal{C} \times \mathcal{V}$ of M_{Exp}. Thus a state of M_{Exp} is a pair $\langle c, v \rangle$ where $c \in \mathcal{C}$ and $v \in \mathcal{V}$. It models all execution states of *proc* where the control location is c and where the memory state is modeled by v. In Section 3.3 we show how to compute the transitions between states in S_{Exp}; in Section 3.4 we show how to extend M_{Exp} to incorporate the specification PAs. Before we can do this, we need to give some details about our use of theorem provers.

3.2 Application of Theorem Provers

We will use theorem provers to reason about C expressions. Since these expressions may involve integer as well as Boolean arithmetic, and, importantly, pointer arithmetic, the logic involved is quite complicated, and certainly undecidable.[1] It is therefore important to our approach that we use the theorem prover *conservatively*, i.e., we only assume logical relationships which the theorem prover actually can prove.

In this section, we will describe the principles of our usage of theorem provers so as to give an intuition of our approach. The logical intricacies involved (including, for example, uninterpreted function symbols to model the heap) are handled by our tool, but would exceed the scope of this paper, and are therefore omitted.

For the construction of the abstract transition relation it will often be necessary to determine whether two C expressions e_1 and e_2 are mutually exclusive. To this end, we use the theorem prover to compute a meta-predicate $\mathcal{A}(e_1, e_2)$ with the following properties:

- If $\mathcal{A}(e_1, e_2)$ is false, then e_1 and e_2 are provably mutually exclusive.
- If $\mathcal{A}(e_1, e_2)$ is true, then this indicates that the theorem prover could not prove that e_1 and e_2 are mutually exclusive, either because they indeed are not mutually exclusive, or because proving mutual exclusiveness was beyond the capabilities of the theorem prover.

The meta-predicate $\mathcal{A}$ has a crucial role in the definition of the transition relation. We will see that the definition of $\mathcal{A}$ ensures that the abstraction is safe. We illustrate the use of $\mathcal{A}$ by the following important example:

Given any C expression e_1 and a normal C assignment s, we define the *weakest precondition* of e_1 with respect to s in the same way as [11] and denote it by $\mathcal{WP}(s, e_1)$. Intuitively, $\mathcal{WP}(s, e_1)$ is a C expression which denotes the weakest assumption that has to be true *before* the execution of s in order for e_1 to become true *after* the execution of s. Given s and e_1, $\mathcal{WP}(s, e_1)$ can be computed as follows:

- If s is the assignment statement $v = e_2$ then $\mathcal{WP}(s, e_1)$ is obtained from e_1 by replacing all occurrences of v in e_1 with e_2.
- If s is an assignment statement of the form $*v = e_2$, then we have to take into account aliasing possibilities as well. For example if e_1 is the expression $a == 5$ then $\mathcal{WP}(s, e_1)$ is $((v == \&a) \wedge (e_2 == 5)) \vee ((v != \&a) \wedge (a == 5))$.

[1] It follows from the famous negative solution to Hilbert's tenth problem [32] that checking the equivalence of two C expressions is undecidable even for simple integer arithmetic; even when we restrict the range of the variables to 32 bit, the question is computationally very hard.

Let $Asgn$ be the set of normal C assignments in P. The relation $Update \subseteq \mathcal{V} \times Asgn \times \mathcal{V}$ denotes how normal assignments affect the valuations, and is defined as follows.

$$Update = \{(v_1, s, v_2) \mid \quad \mathcal{A}(\gamma(v_1), \mathcal{WP}(s, \gamma(v_2))), \; v_1, v_2 \in \mathcal{V}, s \in Asgn\}$$

Intuitively $Update(v_1, s, v_2)$ means that if *proc* is in a memory state modeled by v_1, and the assignment statement s is executed, then we need to admit the possibility that a memory state abstracted by v_2 can be reached.

3.3 Transition Relation T_{Exp}

We are now ready to define the transition relation $T_{Exp} \subseteq S_{Exp} \times Act_{Spec} \times S_{Exp}$ for M_{Exp}.

Consider any two states s and s' of M_{Exp}. We have already seen that state $s = (c, v)$ models all concrete states of *proc* whose control component is c and whose data component is modeled by v. Let t and t' denote two concrete states modeled by s and s' respectively. If there is a concrete transition for any such t and t' then we must include a transition (s, s') in T_{Exp}. This approach guarantees that M_{Exp} is a sound model of *proc*.

The rest of this section describes a procedure to decide whether to include such a transition (s, s') in T_{Exp} or not. We will make a case distinction by the type of c. If c is a final location, then there are no outgoing transitions from s. Otherwise c can be of five different types and we consider each type separately.

Goto. Let c' be the unique successor control location of c. Then we include $((c, v), \epsilon, (c', v))$ in T_{Exp}. Thus we change the control state according to the program flow and keep the data state unaltered.

Normal Assignment. Let z be the assignment statement at c and c' be the unique successor control location of c. For every valuation v' such that $Update(v, z, v')$, we include $((c, v), \epsilon, (c', v'))$ in T_{Exp}. Thus we let the control state change according to the control flow of the program and allow any data state change not disproved by the theorem prover.

Branch. Recall that in the CFG, every branch has two successors. Let e be the branching condition, and let c'_T and c'_E be the *true* and *false* successors of c. If $\mathcal{A}(\gamma(v), e)$, then we include $((c, v), \epsilon, (c'_T, v))$ in T_{Exp}. If $\mathcal{A}(\gamma(v), \neg e)$, then we include $((c, v), \epsilon, (c'_E, v))$ in T_{Exp}. Thus we allow for any successor control state that is not provably impossible and we keep the data state unchanged.

Return. Let e be the return expression at the return location c in *root* and c' be the unique successor location of c. Note that c' must be the final location. For all return actions $a \in Act_{Spec}$, if $\mathcal{A}(\gamma(v), (e == RetVal(a)))$ (i.e., if the return value described by the action is possibly equal to the value actually returned) then we include $((c, v), a, (c', v))$ in T_{Exp}. If there is no return action $a \in Act_{Spec}$, then we include $((c, v), \epsilon, (c', v))$ in T_{Exp}.

Call Assignment. Since we do not incorporate the specification PAs at this stage, we do not include any transitions originating at call assignment locations. These transitions will be explained in Section 3.4.

Initial States. The initial states are those states which are consistent with the guard G_{Spec}. Thus, $S_{0,ECFG}$ is the set of states (c, v) where $\mathcal{A}(\gamma(v), G_{Spec})$ and c is the initial location of CFG.

Example 2 *The expanded CFG for our example is shown in Figure 4. Since there are two valuations, there are two states corresponding to every control location in the actual CFG. The corresponding control locations and states in the M_{Exp} have the same color and are marked with the same letter. In addition every state corresponding to valuation v is marked with $\gamma(v)$ ($\neg(t == 0)$ is written $(t! = 0)$.)*

3.4 Inlining the Specification PAs

In this section, we show how to conclude the construction of M_{Imp} by incorporating the assumption PAs into M_{Exp}. Recall that the purpose of this step is to model calls made by *proc* to library routines. Intuitively, this is achieved by inline copies of appropriate LTSs between call assignment locations and their respective successors in the CFG.

M_{Imp} is obtained from M_{Exp} by adding new states and transitions: Consider a state (c, v) where c is a call assignment, and let c' be the unique successor of c in the CFG. Let `x = lib(...);` be the call assignment statement at c. Assume that *proc* is not a function pointer; we will deal with this special case later. Let $\langle g_1, P_1\rangle, \ldots, \langle g_n, P_n\rangle$ be the guard and LTS list in the assumption PA for `lib`. For each i, we do the following:

1. Let g'_i be the guard obtained from g_i by replacing every parameter of *lib* by the corresponding argument passed to it at c. If $\mathcal{A}(g'_i, \gamma(v))$, then proceed, otherwise move on to the next guard.

2. Let $P_i = (S_i, Act_i, \{s_{0,i}\}, T_i)$. For each state $s \in S_i$ which is not *STOP*, introduce a new state $(c \cdot s, v)$ into S_{Imp}. These states represent the inlined states of P_i.

3. Add a transition $((c, v), \epsilon, (c \cdot s_{0,i}, v))$ into T_{Imp}. This transition connects the call location state to the initial inlined state.

4. For each transition $(s, a, t) \in T_i$ where t is different from STOP, add a transition $((c \cdot s, v), a, (c \cdot t, v))$ into T_{Imp}.

5. For each transition $(s, a, \text{STOP}) \in T_i$ where a is *not* a return action, and for each v' such that $\mathcal{A}(\gamma(v), \gamma(v'))$ is true, add $((c \cdot s, v), a, (c', v'))$ into T_{Imp}.

6. For each transition $(s, a, \text{STOP}) \in T_i$ where a is a return action, and for each v' such that $Update(v, x = RetVal(a), v')$ is true, add $((c \cdot s, v), \epsilon, (c', v'))$ into T_{Imp}.

If *lib* is a function pointer, then we repeat the construction described above for each possible target of *lib* listed by the user.

Example 3 *The assumption LTS for* `do_lock` *is shown at the top of Figure 5. The M_{Imp} obtained by incorporating the LTS for* `do_lock` *into M_{Exp} of Figure 4 is shown at the bottom. The corresponding states in M_{Exp} and M_{Imp} are colored identically. Similarly the states of the LTS for* `do_lock` *and the corresponding inlined states in M_{Imp} have identical colors. It is clear that M_{Imp} is simulated by the M_{Spec} in Figure 1.*

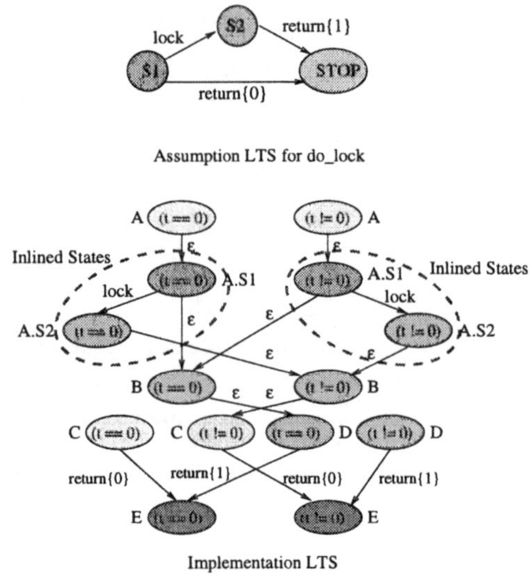

Figure 5. LTS for `do_lock` **and** M_{Imp}**.**

3.5 Enhancements and Implementation Issues

We now describe several enhancements to the above described basic framework that we have implemented in

MAGIC, but have been omitted to keep the presentation simple.

Making predicate abstraction more efficient. The set of valuations $\mathcal{V}$ is exponential in the number of predicates in $\mathcal{P}$. MAGIC also uses the theorem prover to group together predicates that are mutually exclusive. Since at most one predicate in such a group can be true at any time the number of possible valuations of that group is equal to the size of the group. This reduces the size of the state space dramatically. For example suppose we had four predicates originally and we formed two groups of two predicates each. Then the number of possible valuations reduces from sixteen to four.

Even though we have assumed a fixed set of predicates $\mathcal{P}$ in the above discussion, MAGIC allows different sets of predicates. Since not all predicates are *useful* to be abstracted at all control locations, using them indiscriminately would be inefficient. A similar method has been used by BLAST [27].

Automatic predicate discovery. The effectiveness of predicate abstraction relies critically on the set of predicates. The model extraction process described above requires that the predicates be supplied externally. However, if directed, MAGIC can also try to discover suitable sets of predicates. We do not discuss the full details of this predicate discovery process in this paper. However in almost all of our experiments MAGIC manages to automatically discover good predicate sets and correctly prove/disprove the simulation property with them.

Interfacing with theorem provers. As explained before, during the construction of M_{Imp} we use efficient theorem provers. We have integrated MAGIC with various publicly available theorem provers. In some cases, like Simplify [36], CVC [39] and ICS [23], the version of the software available to us can only be used via command line arguments. We run them as separate processes and interface with them via their standard inputs and outputs. In other cases, like CPROVER [29], the software is available as libraries with well-defined APIs and we link them directly with MAGIC. Also in all the cases we cache results to avoid redundant calls to the theorem prover.

4 Case Studies

Our experiments were guided by three general goals: First, we wanted to assure the correctness of the tool by experimenting with examples where the correct outcome was already known. Second, we wanted to evaluate the relative performances of various publicly available software (theorem provers, SAT solvers) that were integrated into our system. Third, we wished to validate the usefulness of our tool in handling large real life examples.

Regression Tests. The first two goals were achieved by a suite of 10 regression tests of small size. All these tests were derived from actual Linux kernel code. Figure 6 describes the source of each test briefly. LOC indicates the number of post-processed lines of C. The name of the procedure analysed is given in italics in the description. A modified procedure means that the source code was changed so that it would no longer be safely abstracted by the specification LTS. The library to which the procedure belongs is given in brackets after the procedure name.

Regression	LOC	Description
lock-y	27	*pthread_mutex_lock* (pthread)
unlock-y	24	*pthread_mutex_unlock* (pthread)
socket-y	60	*socket* (socket)
sock_alloc-y	24	*sock_alloc* (socket)
sys_send-y	4	*sys_send* (socket)
sock_sendmsg-y	11	*sock_sendmsg* (socket)
lock-n	27	modified *pthread_mutex_lock*
unlock-n	24	modified *pthread_mutex_unlock*
sock_alloc-n	24	modified *sock_alloc*
sock_sendmsg-n	11	modified *sock_sendmsg*

Figure 6. Descriptions of regression tests.

Verifying OpenSSL. To achieve the third goal we opted to work with OpenSSL [6], an open source implementation of the publicly available SSL [8] specification. This protocol is used by a client (typically a web browser) and a server to establish a secure socket connection over a malicious network using public and symmetric key cryptography.

A critical component of the protocol is the *handshake*. First we verified that the *openssl-0.9.6c* implementation of the server side of the handshake conforms to its specification. This implementation is encapsulated in a single procedure of about 347 lines of C. We constructed the target LTS M_{Spec} manually by reading the SSL specification [8]. The LTS had 28 states and 67 transitions. A total of 19 predicates and PAs for 14 library routines were supplied externally. We carried out two experiments. The first was done with the correct target LTS. The second was done with a modified the target LTS (of same size) so that a correct implementation would no longer be simulated by it. Next we repeated identical experiments with the client side implementation. It was encapsulated within a single procedure of 345 lines. The target LTS had 28 states and 60 transitions. A total of 18 predicates and PAs for 12 library routines were supplied externally.

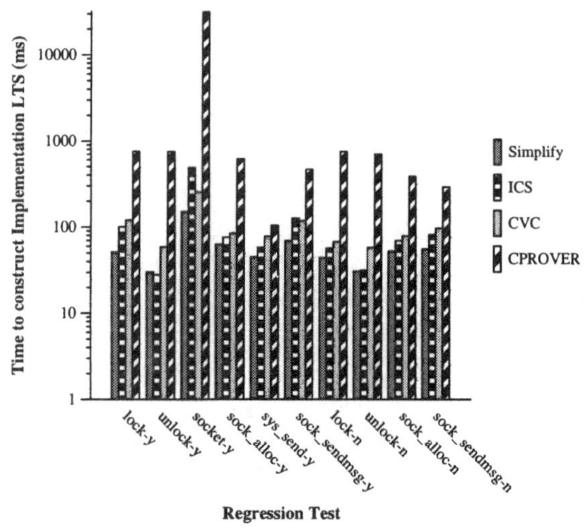

Figure 7. Time to construct M_{Imp}.

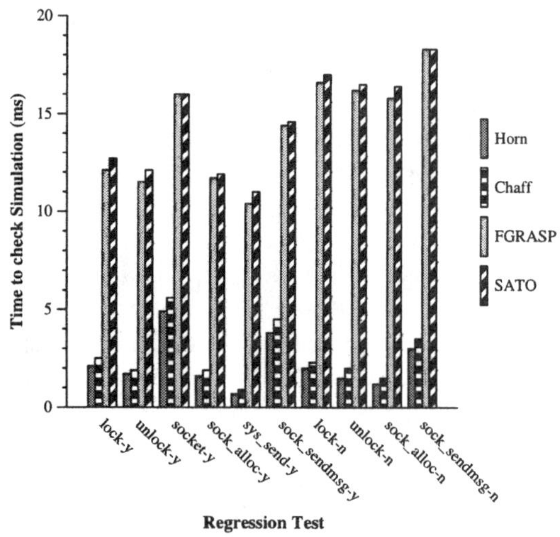

Figure 8. Time to check simulation.

Regression Test Results. All our experiments were done on a 1.4 GHz AMD Athlon machine with 1 GB of RAM running RedHat Linux 7.1. Figure 7 summarizes the performance results for various theorem provers obtained via the regression suite. The y-axis (drawn in log scale) shows the time needed to construct M_{Imp} in milliseconds which is a clear indicator of the performance of the theorem prover. Similarly, Figure 8 summarizes the performance results for various SAT solvers obtained via the regression suite. The y-axis indicates the time in milliseconds needed to check simulation since this is the step where the SAT solver is used.

OpenSSL Results. In the case of the OpenSSL server experiments, the fact that the correct specification LTS safely abstracts the OpenSSL implementation was then proved by our tool in 255 seconds using about 130 MB of memory. The tool also successfully verified that the modified specification LTS does not safely abstract the implementation in 247 seconds using 115 MB of memory. For the client experiments the corresponding figures were 226 seconds, 107MB and 227 seconds, 111MB. Owing to compositionality we did not have to verify the validity of the assumption PAs used for these experiments.

Comparison of Theorem Provers and SAT Tools. A closer look at the two bar graphs reveal several consistent trends. First, for the purposes of our tool, the theorem provers can be arranged in decreasing order of efficiency as follows: Simplify, ICS, CVC and CPROVER. The first three theorem provers have comparable efficiency and seem clearly superior to CPROVER. Second, the SAT solvers can also be arranged in decreasing order of efficiency as follows: Horn, Chaff, FGRASP and SATO. Of the external solvers we used Chaff seems to be easily the best, almost matching our own HORNSAT based implementation. FGRASP and SATO are less easily distinguishable.

The difference in performance between general SAT solvers and the HORNSAT solver we implemented becomes prominent for the larger OpenSSL example. The time required for checking simulation for the first OpenSSL server experiment and the first OpenSSL client experiment were 42 seconds and 32 seconds respectively when using our HORNSAT solver. In comparison the same figures for Chaff were 386 seconds and 265 seconds respectively.

Negative Results. The reported figures were obtained using user supplied predicates. When we repeated the experiments using automatically discovered predicates, higher execution times were observed. The reason is that our automatic predicate discovery process yields more predicates than are necessary. This leads to a larger number of states in M_{Imp} and hence to greater execution times. We believe that improving the predicate discovery technique is a good area for further research.

5 Future Work

There is enormous potential for extending the basic framework implemented by MAGIC. In conclusion we list notable areas for future research: (i) generation of diagnostic feedback and automatic model refinement, (ii) abstraction techniques for more precise modeling of the heap, (iii) extending the MAGIC infrastructure to OO languages like Java and C++, (iv) handling concurrency, and (v) automatic predicate discovery.

References

[1] Bandera. *http://www.cis.ksu.edu/santos/bandera.*

[2] BLAST. *http://www-cad.eecs.berkeley.edu/ rupak/blast.*

[3] Business Process Execution Language for Web Services. *http://www.oasis-open.org/cover/bpel4ws.html.*

[4] ESC-Java. *http://www.research.compaq.com/SRC/esc.*

[5] Java PathFinder. *http://ase.arc.nasa.gov/visser/jpf.*

[6] OpenSSL. *http://www.openssl.org.*

[7] SLAM. *http://research.microsoft.com/slam.*

[8] SSL 3.0 Specification. *http://wp.netscape.com/eng/ssl3.*

[9] Unified Modeling Language. *http://www.uml.org.*

[10] G. Ausiello and G. F. Italiano. On-line algorithms for polynomially solvable satisfiability problems. *Journal of Logic Programming*, 10(1,2,3 & 4):69–90, January 1991.

[11] T. Ball, R. Majumdar, T. D. Millstein, and S. K. Rajamani. Automatic predicate abstraction of c programs. In *SIGPLAN Conference on Programming Language Design and Implementation*, pages 203–213, 2001.

[12] T. Ball, A. Podelski, and S. K. Rajamani. Boolean and Cartesian abstraction for model checking C programs. *Lecture Notes in Computer Science*, 2031:268–??, 2001.

[13] T. Ball and S. K. Rajamani. Automatically validating temporal safety properties of interfaces. *Lecture Notes in Computer Science*, 2057, 2001.

[14] A. Biere, A. Cimatti, E. Clarke, and Y. Zhu. Symbolic model checking without BDDs. *Lecture Notes in Computer Science*, 1579:193–207, 1999.

[15] E. M. Clarke, E. A. Emerson, and A. P. Sistla. Automatic verification of finite-state concurrent systems using temporal logic specifications. *ACM Transactions on Programming Languages and System (TOPLAS)*, 8(2):244–263, April 1986.

[16] E. M. Clarke, O. Grumberg, S. Jha, Y. Lu, and H. Veith. Counterexample-guided abstraction refinement. In *Computer Aided Verification*, pages 154–169, 2000.

[17] E. M. Clarke, O. Grumberg, and D. E. Long. Model checking and abstraction. *ACM Transactions on Programming Languages and System (TOPLAS)*, 16(5):1512–1542, September 1994.

[18] E. M. Clarke, O. Grumberg, and D. Peled. *Model Checking*. MIT Press, 2000.

[19] S. Das, D. L. Dill, and S. Park. Experience with predicate abstraction. In *Computer Aided Verification*, pages 160–171, 1999.

[20] W. F. Dowling and J. H. Gallier. Linear time algorithms for testing the satisfiability of propositional horn formula. *Journal of Logic Programming*, 3:267–284, 1984.

[21] M. B. Dwyer, J. Hatcliff, R. Joehanes, S. Laubach, C. S. Pasareanu, H. Zheng, and W. Visser. Tool-supported program abstraction for finite-state verification. In *International Conference on Software engineering*, pages 177–187. IEEE Computer Society, 2001.

[22] D. Engler, B. Chelf, A. Chou, and S. Hallem. Checking system rules using system-specific, programmer-written compiler extensions. In *Symposium on Operating Systems Design and Implementation*, 2000.

[23] J.-C. Filliatre, S. Owre, H. Ruess, and N. Shankar. ICS: Integrated canonizer and solver. In *Computer-Aided Verification*, 2001.

[24] S. Hallem, B. Chelf, Y. Xie, and D. Engler. A system and language for building system-specific, static analyses. In *SIGPLAN Conference on Programming Language Design and Implementation*, 2002.

[25] D. Harel. Statecharts: A visual formalism for complex systems. *Science of Computer Programming*, 8(3):231–274, June 1987.

[26] K. Havelund and T. Pressburger. Model checking JAVA programs using JAVA pathfinder. *International Journal on Software Tools for Technology Transfer*, 2(4):366–381, 2000.

[27] T. A. Henzinger, R. Jhala, R. Majumdar, and G. Sutre. Lazy abstraction. In *Symposium on Principles of Programming Languages*, pages 58–70, 2002.

[28] C. A. R. Hoare. Communicating sequential processes. *Communications of the ACM (CACM)*, 21(8):666–677, August 1978.

[29] D. Kroening. Application specific higher order logic theorem proving. In S. Autexier and H. Mantel, editors, *Proc. of the Verification Workshop - VERIFY'02*, pages 5–15, July 2002.

[30] J. Magee and J. Kramer. *Concurrency: State Models & Java Programs*. Wiley, 2000.

[31] J. P. Marques-Silva and K. A. Sakallah. GRASP – a new search algorithm for satisfiability. In *IEEE/ACM International Conference on Computer-Aided Design*, November 1996.

[32] Y. Matiyasevich. *Hilbert's Tenth Problem*. MIT Press, 1993.

[33] R. Milner. *Communication and Concurrency*. Prentice-Hall, 1989.

[34] R. Milner. *Communicating and Mobile Systems: the π-Calculus*. Cambridge University Press, 1999.

[35] M. Moskewicz, C. Madigan, Y. Zhao, L. Zhang, and S. Malik. Chaff: Engineering an efficient sat solver. In *Design Automation Conference*, June 2001.

[36] G. Nelson. *Techniques for Program Verification*. PhD thesis, Stanford University, 1980.

[37] S. Graf and H. Saidi. Construction of abstract state graphs with PVS. In O. Grumberg, editor, *Computer Aided Verification*, volume 1254, pages 72–83. Springer Verlag, 1997.

[38] S. K. Shukla. *Uniform Approaches to the Verification of Finite State Systems*. PhD thesis, SUNY, Albany, 1997.

[39] A. Stump, C. Barrett, and D. Dill. CVC: A cooperating validity checker. In *Conference on Computer-Aided Verification*, 2002.

[40] H. Zhang. SATO: An efficient propositional prover. In *Conference on Automated Deduction*, 1997.

Architectural Interaction Diagrams: AIDs for System Modeling*

Arnab Ray   Rance Cleaveland
Department of Computer Science
SUNY at Stony Brook
Stony Brook, NY, 11794-4400 USA
{arnabray,rance}@cs.sunysb.edu

Abstract

This paper develops a modeling paradigm called Architectural Interaction Diagrams, *or AIDs, for the high-level design of systems containing concurrent, interacting components. The novelty of AIDs is that they introduce interaction mechanisms, or* buses, *as first-class entities into the modeling vocabulary. Users then have the capability, in their modeling, of using buses whose behavior captures interaction at a higher level of abstraction than that afforded by modeling notations such as Message Sequence Charts or process algebra, which typically provide only one fixed interaction mechanism. This paper defines AIDs formally by giving them an operational semantics that describes how buses combine subsystem transitions into system-level transitions. This semantics enables AIDs to be simulated; to incorporate subsystems given in different modeling notations into a single system model; and to use testing, debugging and model checking early in the system design cycle in order to catch design errors before they are implemented.*

1. Introduction

Pre-implementation modeling of software systems has been accepted as good software engineering practice for some time. The utility of such *design-time* artifacts is that they allow users to model systems at a high level, without worrying about implementation details, in order to study high-level structure and behavior and isolate design bugs early in the development cycle. While not nearly as widespread as in other areas of engineering, the use of modeling tools for software systems is growing rapidly, as notations such as Statecharts [6] and Message Sequence Charts (MSCs) [1], and commercial languages such as UML [3] and Simulink®/ Stateflow®[1] [7], gain adherents.

Despite the many benefits of modeling, however, one may identify a common shortcoming *vis à vis* modeling notations for concurrent and distributed systems: they force users to adopt low-level communication primitives too early in the design cycle. For example, in Statecharts, synchronous broadcast is the only communication mechanism, while in MSCs only asynchronous point-to-point message-passing is allowed. Given the diversity of high-level communications primitives available to implementors (multi-casting, shared memory, CANbus, HTTP, etc.), the paucity of interaction mechanisms in these modeling notations severely limits their usefulness in modeling systems containing interacting components. In particular, the problem that arises is that the interaction discipline of the underlying modeling language becomes tightly bound to the system modeling, which becomes guided more by what the modeling language permits rather than the *actual* interprocess communication mechanism the system designer might have access to during implementation.

The goal of this paper is to devise a formal framework in which high-level interaction mechanisms can be defined and used to support the mechanical analysis of system behavior. Our theory, which we call *Architectural Interaction Diagrams* (AIDs), supports a highly parameterizable notion of interprocess communication, freeing designers from artificial constraints on how his/her design components may interact with one another. The definition of the notation also allows submodels given in different notations to interoperate. In contrast to existing modeling notations, the framework is extensible in that it allows the user to implement his/her own interprocess communication; new interprocess primitives can be added and made a part of the language itself.

Our approach also supports the decoupling of a system's interactions from the internal workings of its subsystems. This decoupling of interaction from behavior has

*Research supported by Army Research Office grants DAAD190110003 and DAAD190110019, and National Science Foundation grants CCR-9988489 and CCR-0098037.

[1]Simulink and Stateflow are registered trademarks of The MathWorks, Inc.

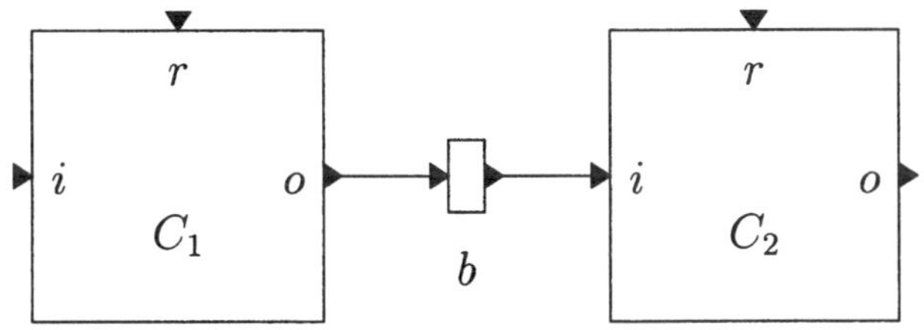

Figure 1. A sample architecture interaction diagram.

great significance in terms of platform-independent modeling of software systems. One of the important issues that arises when porting software from one platform to another is the different inter-process communication primitives provided by the new platform. In conventional modeling, the software components would have to be re-examined and re-adjusted to take into account the new system of inter process communication. In AIDs, all the designer has to do is to use system-defined buses or his/her own definitions without having to adjust the different software components themselves. Of course, it would still be incumbent on the designer to verify that changing the buses still yields correct over-all behavior.

The rest of the paper is arranged as follows. The next section gives an intuitive introduction to AIDs and discusses related work. We then give a formalization of AIDs in Section 3, including a precise definition of the structure of AIDs and how they execute. Section 4 discusses some example interaction mechanisms definable in AIDs, while the final section presents future work and our conclusions.

2. An Introduction to AIDs

The goal of AIDs is to give precise mathematical meaning to diagrams such as the one in Fig. 1. The diagram depicts a model containing two component models, C_1 and C_2. Each component is embedded inside an interface containing input (i, r) and output (o) "ports" that the components may use to interact with their environments. These ports may be left unlinked, indicating an "open connection", or they may be linked to *interaction mechanisms*, or *buses* (b). Buses contain their own ports and are responsible for combining submodel transitions involving the bus's ports into system-level transitions. A main goal of this paper is to give a highly flexible framework for defining buses that permits many different interaction disciplines to be captured uniformly.

Fig. 2 illustrates another important aspect of AIDs, namely, that models can be nested hierarchically, with component ports "exported" to enclosing interfaces. This figure also contains a bus, q, with a different graphical representation than b. The intention is that q represents a FIFO reliable channel, while b represents synchronous hand-shaking. Thus, the model in this diagram employs two different communication mechanisms.

Related Work. AIDs builds on the Graphical Calculus of Communicating Systems (GCCS) presented in [4]. Like AIDs, GCCS supports the hierarchical construction of models of communicating subsystems, and the language is also given a formal operational semantics in which subsystem transitions are combined into system transitions. However, GCCS includes only a single interaction mechanism, binary handshaking, and thus suffers from the same drawbacks for modeling interaction that the languages mentioned in the introduction do.

Our approach is also akin to that adopted in [13], where *infra-models* are proposed as a mechanism for supporting interoperability among different modeling notations. Infra-models share a syntactic similarity to Petri Nets: such models are hypergraphs consisting of nodes (= places, in Petri-Net terminology) and hyperedges (= transitions). Infra-models augment standard Petri Nets by an ability to define firing rules that are different from traditional Petri Net firing rules; these are used to capture different notions of synchrony. However, the work lacks a precise mathematical account of how infra-models interact with component models.

AIDs also share a similarity to the *architectural styles* work presented in [5, 16]. There, the authors define architectural styles to be reference models for system architectures, and they observe that architectural styles exhibit four kinds of properties.

1. They provide a vocabulary of design elements, which are classified in their terminology as component and connector types.

2. They define a set of configuration rules or topological constraints. Examples of topological constraints are if the processes engage in single or multi-party communication.

3. They define a semantic interpretation for compositions of components that give such compositions a well defined meaning.

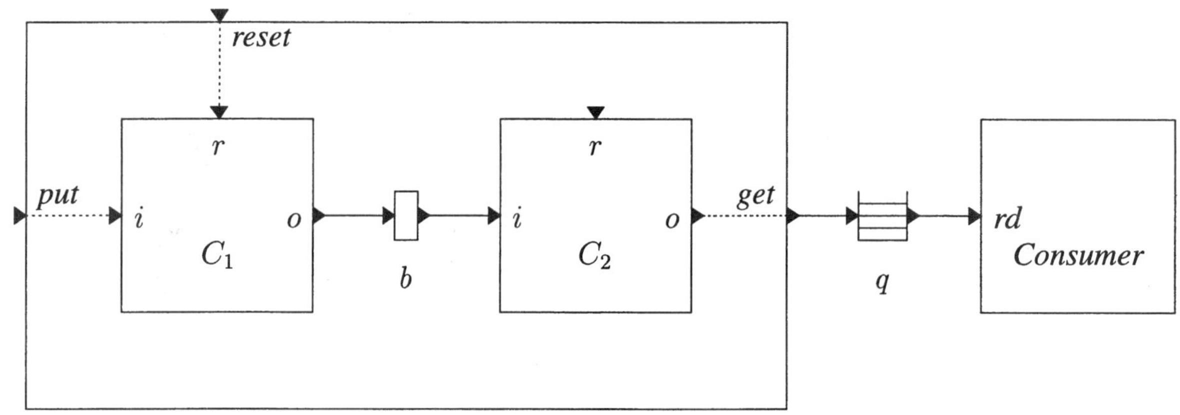

Figure 2. A nested AID.

4. They define analyses that can be performed on systems built in that style.

AIDs can be readily thought of as a tool for creating architectural styles according to the criteria above. Component types for AIDs consist of the processes that are plugged in while the connector types denote the different kind of buses that are supported by the framework. However, AIDs supports a much wider range of interaction disciplines than traditional architectural description languages.

Like AIDs, WRIGHT [15, 16] also treats interprocess communication structures (called connectors) as first class entities of the modeling vocabulary. Connectors in WRIGHT are semantically same as the components; to define a new type of connector, one "implements" it as a process, using CSP's native handshake coordination mechanism. (The reason for this is that WRIGHT is built on top of CSP.) The disadvantage of this approach in relation to ours is that these implementations can be subtle (think of implementing multi-casting using handshaking) and error-prone. In contrast, buses in AIDs are given a much more declarative and concise semantics. The other disadvantage involves state explosion. In general, WRIGHT connectors will contain significant internal computation, since they must encode the intended interaction semantics in terms of CSP's. A single interaction among components involving such a connector may therefore give rise to a number of transitions, with the possibilities of interleavings with other ongoing interactions leading to significant state-space growth. In contrast, our semantics guarantees that any interaction involving a bus generates exactly one system-level transition.

The aims of the Ptolemy project [10] are very similar to those for AIDs. In a Ptolemy model, a system model contains a topology of subsystems and interaction mechanisms, together with a definition of how the interaction mechanisms cause submodels to interact. Thus all interaction devices at the same "level" of a model have the same semantics. The advantage of AIDs is that different buses may be freely intermixed at the same level in a system model; in Ptolemy, multiple levels of submodeling would have to be introduced to achieve this effect. In addition, the AIDs semantic framework for buses gives a uniform paradigm for defining interaction behavior; the Ptolemy approach, on the other hand, is rather more *ad hoc*, making it difficult for users to add to the interaction mechanisms supported.

Coordination languages have generally been applied in the domain of programming languages in the coding phase of the software life cycle. Examples of such coordination languages in the programming language domain include Linda [12], Javaspaces [8] and TSpaces [14]. AIDs, as mentioned before, are a design notation, although they share some of the same motivations as coordination languages, specifically, the capability to integrate subsystems given in different languages into a single system.

Process-algebra-based tools like the CWB-NC [17] provide support for specifying architectural designs in a variety of input languages. Unlike traditional architecture description languages, process algebras have a precise semantics, and indeed have been used to define the semantics of several ADLs [2, 11, 16]. They also have a capacity for hierarchical modeling. However, process algebras, like GCCS, typically only include a single primitive process-interaction mechanism.

3. Formalizing AIDs

This section is given over to a mathematically rigorous definition of AIDs and how they execute. The goal of this effort is, first, to make precise what the different elements of an AID are, and second, to develop a foundation for mechanically analyzing their behavior. In the rest of this paper we fix the following.

- $\mathbb{W}$ is an infinite set of *write ports.*

- $\mathbb{R}$ is an infinite set of *read ports*, with $\mathbb{R} \cap \mathbb{W} = \emptyset$.
- $\mathbb{V}$ is a nonempty set of *values*.

Intuitively, $\mathbb{W}$ and $\mathbb{R}$ contain all the possible port names that may be used to define a given system, while $\mathbb{V}$ contains all the values that may be used. In this paper our focus is on interaction rather than data manipulation, so we do not impose any additional structure on $\mathbb{V}$. We also use the following definitions in what follows.

- $\mathbb{O} = \{w\,!\,v \mid w \in \mathbb{W}, v \in \mathbb{V}\}$ is the set of *output actions*.
- $\mathbb{I} = \{r? \mid r \in \mathbb{R}\}$ is the set of *input actions*.

The sets $\mathbb{O}$ and $\mathbb{I}$ represent interactions that a system may engage in with its environment: outputting, and inputting.

3.1. I/O Labeled Transition Systems

The basic components of the AID theory are *I/O labeled transition systems* (IOLTSs). These are defined as follows.

Definition 3.1 *An* I/O labeled transition system (IOLTS) *is a tuple $\langle Q, T, q_0\rangle$, where Q is a set of states, $q_0 \in Q$ is the start state, and $T = T_{\text{write}} \cup T_{\text{read}} \cup T_{\text{internal}}$ is the transition relation such that:*

1. $T_{\text{write}} \subseteq Q \times \mathbb{O} \times Q$,
2. $T_{\text{read}} \subseteq Q \times \mathbb{I} \times (\mathbb{V} \longrightarrow Q)$, *and*
3. $T_{\text{internal}} \subseteq Q \times Q$.

An IOLTS encodes the operational behavior of a system, with Q being the set of system states and q_0 the initial state. State transitions may take one of three forms.

- An *output transition* $\langle q, w\,!\,v, q'\rangle \in T_{\text{write}}$ indicates a state change from q to q' when value v is written out to the environment on write port w.
- In *input transition* $\langle q, r?, f\rangle \in T_{\text{read}}$, f is a function mapping values to states. This transition indicates a state change from q to $f(v)$ if the system's environment supplies value v on read port r.
- An *internal transition* $\langle q, q'\rangle \in T_{\text{internal}}$ represents an execution step that the system can engage in without any interaction with its environment.

In what follows, if $P = \langle Q, T, q_0\rangle$ is an IOLTS then we write:

- $q \xrightarrow{w\,!\,v}_P q'$ if $\langle q, w\,!\,v, q'\rangle \in T$;
- $q \xrightarrow{r?}_P f$ if $\langle q, r?, f\rangle \in T$; and
- $q \xrightarrow{\tau}_P q'$ if $\langle q, q'\rangle \in T$.

If $t \in T$ then we use $src(t), tgt(t) \in Q \cup (V \to Q)$ to refer to the source and target of t: $src(t) = q$ and $tgt(t) = q'$ if $t = \langle q, w\,!\,v, q'\rangle$ or $t = \langle q, q'\rangle$, and $src(t) = q$ and $tgt(t) = f$ if $t = \langle q, r?, f\rangle$. We also define the following.

- $Q(P)$ refers to the state set of P, while $q_0(P)$ is the initial state of P.
- $T_{\text{write}}(P), T_{\text{read}}(P)$ and $T_{\text{internal}}(P)$ refer to the write, read and internal transition sets of P (so $T = T_{\text{write}}(P) \cup T_{\text{read}}(P) \cup T_{\text{internal}}(P)$).
- The *write interface*, $WI(P) \subseteq \mathbb{W}$, of P is the set of write ports that P might use as it executes:

  $$WI(P) = \{w \in \mathbb{W} \mid \exists q, q' \in Q, v \in \mathbb{V}.\, q \xrightarrow{w\,!\,v}_P q'\}.$$

- The *read interface*, $RI(P) \subseteq \mathbb{R}$, of P is the set of read ports that P might use as it executes:

  $$RI(P) = \{r \in \mathbb{R} \mid \exists q \in Q, f \in \mathbb{V} \to Q.\, q \xrightarrow{r?}_P f\}.$$

3.2. Defining AIDs

We now define the structure of AIDs. An AID may take one of two forms.

1. It may be an IOLTS.
2. It may be a *network* containing other AIDs embedded in interfaces and connected together into a communication topology, as depicted in Figs. 1 and 2.

The theory imposes no restrictions on how an IOLTS AID is described concretely: it could be a Statechart, or a term in process algebra, or a program. The only requirement is that the model have identifiable read and write transitions.

The remainder of this section is devoted to defining the structure of networks. From the figures, one may identify the following components of a network AID.

- AIDs describing subsystems.
- Interfaces, containing read and write ports, surrounding subsystems.
- Connections between ports in a subsystem and ports in an interface (cf. the dotted lines in Fig. 2).
- Buses.
- Links from interface ports to buses.

We first give mathematical accounts of interfaces and buses and then use them to define networks formally.

Interfaces. An interface consists of a set of read ports and a set of write ports. Mathematically, an interface I is a pair $\langle W, R\rangle$, where $W \subseteq \mathbb{W}$ and $R \subseteq \mathbb{R}$ are the *write and read interfaces*, respectively, of I. We write $W(I)$ for the write interface of I and $R(I)$ for the read interface of I.

Buses. In AIDs buses handle interactions between subsystems. As such, they have two responsibilities: the transfer of data between senders and receivers, and the synchronization of sender/receiver transitions, depending on the semantics of the interaction mechanism. For example, consider a synchronous binary handshaking interaction mechanism. Not only must a bus implementing this mechanism deliver a data value from a sender to a receiver, but it must also ensure that senders and receivers block until a communication partner is ready to execute. In the case of bounded-buffer non-lossy communication, on the other hand, senders should be blocked when the buffer is full, while receivers should be blocked when the buffer is empty. In shared memory neither senders ("writers") nor receivers ("readers") ever block. Providing a common framework for explicating these subtleties is a central goal of the AIDs theory.

Our treatment of buses is inspired by the work on *action transducers* of [9]. In particular, we wish to view buses as "transducers" that combine transitions of subsystems connected to the bus into system-level transitions, according to the synchronization discipline the bus is intended to capture. These considerations underly the following definition.

Definition 3.2 *A* bus *is a tuple of form* $\langle I, B, T, b_0\rangle$, *where* I *is an interface,* B *is a set of states,* $T \subseteq B \times 2^{(W(I)\times\mathbb{V})} \times 2^{R(I)} \times 2^{W(I)} \times 2^{(R(I)\times\mathbb{V})} \times B$ *is the transition relation, and* $b_0 \in B$ *is the start state. Every transition* $\langle q, WV, R, W, RV, q'\rangle \in T$ *is also required to satisfy the following:*

$$\begin{array}{rcl} R & \supseteq & \{r \mid \exists v \in \mathbb{V}.\langle r, v\rangle \in RV\} \\ W & \subseteq & \{w \mid \exists v \in \mathbb{V}.\langle w, v\rangle \in WV\} \end{array}$$

If $M = \langle I, B, T, b_0\rangle$ is a bus and $\langle b, WV, R, RV, b'\rangle \in T$ is a transition, then we write

$$b \xrightarrow[WV\ R]{W\ RV}_M b'.$$

We also write $W(M) = W(I)$ and $R(M) = R(I)$ for the write and read interfaces, respectively, of M, and $B(M)$, $T(M)$ and $b_0(M)$ for the state set, transition relation, and initial state of M, respectively.

Intuitively, a bus contains a read/write interface, a set of states reflecting the internal status of the bus, a transition relation, and an initial state. Buses are similar to IOLTSs, but the transition relation is significantly different and requires more comment. A bus transition of form

$$b \xrightarrow[WV\ R]{W\ RV}_M b'$$

is intended to be read as: "if the bus is in state b, and subsystems connected to the bus enable write transitions as indicated in WV and read transitions as enabled in R, then the bus fires read transitions as indicated in RV and write transitions as indicated in W and goes to state b'." This firing of selected read and write transitions in systems connected to the bus is also done atomically: thus one bus transition may "consume" several transitions from the components connected to it. Also, "writing" to a bus is interpreted with respect to components connected to a bus: so write ports on a subsystem are connected to write ports on a bus, and similarly for read ports.

AIDs. We now have the machinery needed to define AIDs. The definition below develops two notions simultaneously: AID, and the principal read/write interface of an AID.

Definition 3.3 *An* architecture interaction diagram (AID) *is either:*

1. *an IOLTS* P, *with principal write interface* $PWI(P) = WI(P)$ *and principal read interface* $PRI(P) = RI(P)$*; or*
2. *a network* $N = \langle \bar{C}, \bar{M}, L\rangle$, *where:*
   (a) $\bar{C} = \langle C_1, \ldots, C_n\rangle$ *is a tuple of components, where each* $C_i = \langle S_i, I_i, G_i\rangle$ *consists of an AID* S_i, *an interface* I_i, *and a* gate definition G_i *(gate definitions are defined below);*
   (b) $\bar{M} = \langle M_1, \ldots M_k\rangle$ *is a tuple of buses; and*
   (c) $L \subseteq (\{1, \ldots, n\} \times (\mathbb{W} \cup \mathbb{R})) \times (\{1, \ldots, k\} \times (\mathbb{W} \cup \mathbb{R}))$, *the link set, satisfies: if* $\langle\langle i, p_1\rangle, \langle j, p_2\rangle\rangle \in L$ *then*
      i. $p_1 \in \mathbb{W}$ *if and only if* $p_2 \in \mathbb{W}$*;*
      ii. $p_1 \in W(I_i) \cup R(I_i)$*;*
      iii. $p_2 \in W(M_j) \cup R(M_j)$*;*
      iv. $\langle\langle \ell, p_1'\rangle, \langle j, p_2\rangle\rangle \in L$ *iff* $\ell = i$ *and* $p_1' = p_1$.
      v. $\langle\langle i, p_1\rangle, \langle \ell, p_2'\rangle\rangle \in L$ *iff* $\ell = j$ *and* $p_2' = p_2$.

   $PWI(N) = \{\langle i, w\rangle \mid w \in W(I_i) \wedge \forall j, w'.\langle\langle i, w\rangle, \langle j, w'\rangle\rangle \notin L\}$ *is the principal write interface of* N, *while* $PRI(N) = \{\langle i, r\rangle \mid r \in R(I_i) \wedge \forall j, r'.\langle\langle i, r\rangle, \langle j, r'\rangle\rangle \notin L\}$ *is the principal read interface. Also,* $|N|_C = n$ *is the number of components in* N, *while* $|N|_M$ *is the number of buses.*

Intuitively, a network contains a list of components, each containing a subsystem description, an interface, and a *gate* (see below) that defines how the ports of the subsystem are connected to the interface. It also contains a list of buses and a link set connecting component ports to bus ports so

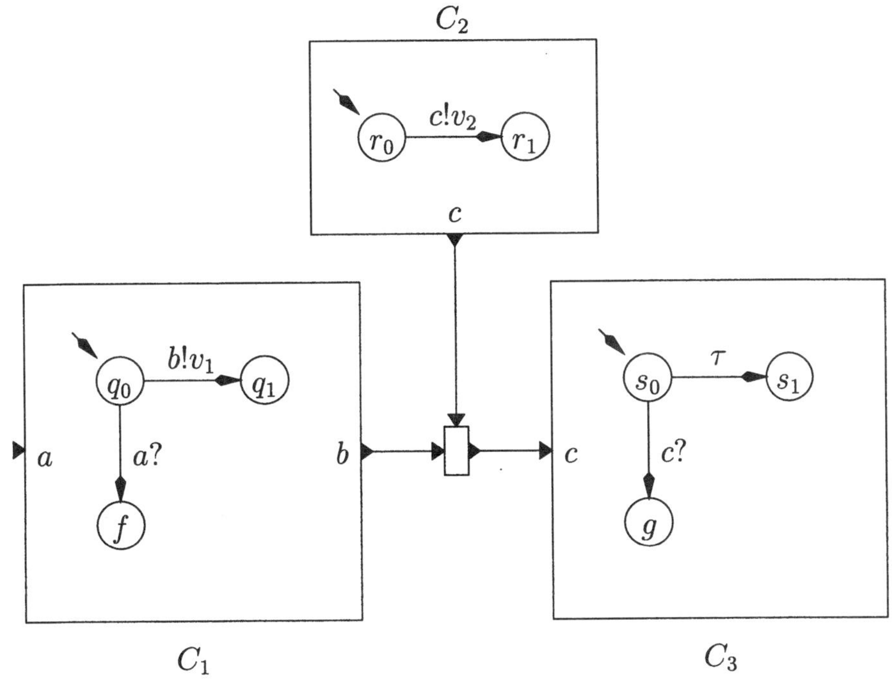

Figure 3. A network AID; subsystems are IOLTSs.

that: write ports are connected to write ports, and read ports to read ports, and each port (bus or component) has at most one link to it. The principal write and read interfaces of N contain the component number / port pairs describing ports on given interfaces that are not connected to a bus by a link.

We now define gates as follows.

Definition 3.4 *Let S be an AID and I an interface. Then a* gate $G \in (PWI(S) \cup PRI(S)) \to (W(I) \cup R(I))$ *is a one-to-one partial function satisfying:*

1. *If $p \in PWI(S)$ and $G(p)$ defined, then $G(p) \in W(I)$.*

2. *If $p \in PRI(S)$ and $G(p)$ defined, then $G(p) \in R(I)$.*

This definition defines a gate to be a connection between write ports in a system and write ports in an (enclosing) interface, and similarly for read ports. The fact that G is a one to one partial function guarantees that every port in S is connected to at most one port in I, and vice versa. Note that if S is an IOLTS, then $PWI(S)$ and $PRI(S)$ contain ports, while if S is a network then these sets contain pairs comprising an interface index and a port. Also note that since G is one-to-one, its inverse G^{-1} is a partial function.

Finally, we use the following notation in what follows. If N is a network then we write $C(N, i)$ for the ith component of N and $M(N, i)$ for the ith bus. If $C(N, i) = \langle S_i, I_i, G_i \rangle$ then we use $S(N, i)$, $I(N, i)$ and $G(N, i)$ to refer to S_i, I_i and G_i, respectively.

3.3. Semantics of AIDs

A chief aim of this paper is to equip AIDs with an operational semantics describing the execution steps that individual AIDs may engage in. As an example of what this semantics should do, consider the network AID N in Fig. 3, which consists of three components, each subsystem of which is an IOLTS. Also assume that the bus implements binary synchronous handshaking. If we represent the current state of the system as a vector of system / bus states, and the bus only contains one state, b_0, then semantics should allow us to infer execution steps like the following.

$$\langle q_0, r_0, s_0, b_0 \rangle \xrightarrow{a?}_N \lambda v. \langle f(v), r_0, s_0, b_0 \rangle \quad (1)$$
$$\langle q_0, r_0, s_0, b_0 \rangle \xrightarrow{\tau}_N \langle q_0, r_0, s_1, b_0 \rangle \quad (2)$$
$$\langle q_0, r_0, s_0, b_0 \rangle \xrightarrow{\tau}_N \langle q_1, r_0, g(v_1), b_0 \rangle \quad (3)$$
$$\langle q_0, r_0, s_0, b_0 \rangle \xrightarrow{\tau}_N \langle q_0, r_1, g(v_2), b_0 \rangle \quad (4)$$

In Step 1, component C_1 awaits an input from its (unconnected) port a while the other components idle (the λ expression is the standard *anonymous function* notation from the λ-calculus; it is explained later). Similarly, in Step 2, C_3 executes its internal computation step while the other components idle. The last two steps show synchronizations over the bus between C_1 and C_3 (Step 3), and between C_2 and C_3 (Step 4).

Mathematically, we define the semantics in the Structural Operational Semantic (SOS) style, by showing how a single AID may be viewed as an IOLTS whose transition relation reflects the execution steps of the AID. Also in line with SOS, the definition of the transition relation of an AID is given inductively using inference rules that explain how transitions of subsystems are combined to form transitions of systems. More precisely, given an AID N we wish to associate with N an IOLTS $\langle Q_N, T_N, q_N \rangle$. If $N = \langle Q, T, q_0 \rangle$ is itself an IOLTS, the association is obvious: take $Q_N = Q, T_N = T$ and $q_N = q_0$.

Now suppose that $N = \langle \bar{C}, \bar{M}, L \rangle$. What should Q_N, T_N and q_N be? In the case of Q_N, each system state should record current state information for each component and bus, and the initial state should contain the initial states of each component and bus. This leads to the following.

Definition 3.5 *Let $N = \langle \bar{C}, \bar{M}, L \rangle$ be a network AID, and let $n = |N|_C$ and $k = |N|_M$. Then:*

1. $Q_N = C_N \times M_N$, *where:*

$$\begin{aligned} C_N &= \{\langle q_1, \ldots, q_n \rangle \mid q_i \in Q(S_i)\} \\ M_N &= \{\langle b_1, \ldots, b_k \rangle \mid b_i \in B(M_i)\} \end{aligned}$$

2. $q_N = C_N^0 \times M_N^0$, *where* $C_N^0 = \langle q_0(S_1), \ldots, q_0(S_n) \rangle$ *and* $M_N^0 = \langle b_0(M_1), \ldots, b_0(M_k) \rangle$.

Thus, the states for N's IOLTS consists of a state vector for N's components and another state vector for N's buses, with the start state for N containing the start states for each component and bus. We often represent these states as pairs $\langle \bar{s}, \bar{b} \rangle$, where $\bar{s}$ and $\bar{b}$ are the subsystem- and bus-state vectors, respectively. We also use the following notation on vectors. Let $\bar{v} = \langle v_1, \ldots, v_n \rangle$ be a vector. Then:

- $\bar{v}[i] = v_i$.
- $\bar{v}[i := u]$ is the vector obtained by modifying the ith component of $\bar{v}$ to be u:

$$\bar{v}[i := u] = \langle v_1, \ldots, v_{i-1}, u, v_{i+1}, \ldots, v_n \rangle.$$

It remains now to define T_N. This is done using SOS rules, each of which has the following general form.

$$\frac{\text{Premises}}{\text{Conclusion}}$$

Intuitively, a rule states that when the premises are true, the conclusion holds. In our case, a conclusion will state the existence of an element of the transition relation, T_N, while the premises will refer to transitions of subsystems and buses as well as conditions about the structure of N.

In preparation for defining T_N, we first give rules showing how transitions of subsystems may be "lifted" to transitions of components. Recall that a component has form $C = \langle S, I, G \rangle$, where S is an AID, I is an interface, and G is a gate function. The idea behind these rules is to convert transitions of S, which involve S's ports, into "equivalent" transitions that involve ports on I. In what follows we fix $C = \langle S, I, G \rangle$.

The first two SOS rules define write transitions for C. The first rule handles the case when S is an IOLTS

$$\frac{w \in W(I), G^{-1}(w) = w', q \xrightarrow{w'\,!\,v}_S q'}{q \xrightarrow{w\,!\,v}_C q'}$$

This rule says that a component C can engage in an output transition labeled $w\,!\,v$ if: w is part of the write interface of I; and the IOLTS S can output v on a port w' that is connected to w (captured by the predicate $G^{-1}(w) = w'$).

The next rule handles the case in which the write port in question is on a subsystem that is a network rather than an IOLTS. To emphasize the fact that we are referring to a network we consider C as $C = \langle N, I, G \rangle$

$$\frac{w \in W(I), G^{-1}(w) = \langle i, w' \rangle, \bar{s}[i] \xrightarrow{w'\,!\,v}_{S(N,i)} q_i'}{\langle \bar{s}, \bar{b} \rangle \xrightarrow{w\,!\,v}_C \langle \bar{s}[i := q_i'], \bar{b} \rangle}$$

This rule is more complicated than the previous one because the port of S to which w is connected (w') exists on a specific interface within N (the ith one, in the rule), and the rule must ensure that it is the ith subsystem of N that writes on w'. Note that $s[i]$ is the state component of the ith subsystem within N.

The next two rules define the read transitions for C. The rules are similar to the ones above in that they define how S's read transitions may be "lifted" to component-level read transitions. Since the targets of read transitions must be functions, however, the rules use notation, from the λ-calculus, for defining anonymous functions: $\lambda x.e$ is a function that, when applied to a value v, returns the result of evaluating expression e with v substituted for x. The first rule handles the case in which the subsystem contributing the read transition is an IOLTS.

$$\frac{r \in R(I), G^{-1}(r) = r', q \xrightarrow{r'?}_S f}{q \xrightarrow{r?}_C f}$$

This rule says that if read port r has a gate connection to a read port in an IOLTS subsystem, and the IOLTS subsystem can perform a read transition on its read port, then the overall system can perform a read transition involving r.

The second rule handles the situation in which S is a network N.

$$\frac{r \in R(I), G^{-1}(r) = \langle i, r' \rangle, \bar{s}[i] \xrightarrow{r'?}_{S(N,i))} f_i}{\langle \bar{s}, \bar{b} \rangle \xrightarrow{r?}_C \lambda v.\langle \bar{s}[i := f_i(v)])], \bar{b} \rangle}$$

The greater complexity of this rule is driven by the same considerations involving the analogous write-transition rule defined above. Note again that any value input as a result of a read transition is "fed into" the subsystem responsible for engendering the transition.

The last rule handles internal transitions of S.

$$\frac{q \xrightarrow{\tau}_S q'}{q \xrightarrow{\tau}_C q'}$$

Internal transitions of S become internal transitions of C.

Having defined component transitions, we may now give the SOS rules for a network N. The first defines $(T_{\text{write}})_N$ in terms of component-level write transitions.

$$\frac{\langle i, w\rangle \in PWI(N), s[i] \xrightarrow{w\,!\,v}_{C(N,i)} q'_i}{\langle \bar{s}, \bar{b}\rangle \xrightarrow{w\,!\,v}_N \langle \bar{s}[i := q'_i], \bar{b}\rangle}$$

This rule states that if a component can engage in a write transition, then N can as well, with all other components remaining idle, provided that the write port involved in the ocmponent transition is not connected to a bus. This last condition is captured formally by the requirement that $\langle i, w\rangle \in PWI(N)$, i.e. that port w on interface I_i is in the principal write interface of N.

The second rule defines $(T_{\text{read}})_N$ similarly.

$$\frac{\langle i, r\rangle \in PRI(N), s[i] \xrightarrow{r?}_{C(N,i)} f'_i}{\langle \bar{s}, \bar{b}\rangle \xrightarrow{r?}_N \lambda v.\langle \bar{s}[i := f_i(v)], \bar{b}\rangle}$$

Note that the target of the transition is a function that, given a value v, "routes" v to the ith component of N.

The third rules lifts internal component transitions to network-level ones.

$$\frac{s[i] \xrightarrow{\tau}_{C(N,i)} q'_i}{\langle \bar{s}, \bar{b}\rangle \xrightarrow{\tau}_N \langle \bar{s}[i := q'_i], \bar{b}\rangle}$$

The final rule is the most important of the semantics, since it defines how buses combine subsystem transitions into system transitions. The basic idea underlying the rule is this. A bus transition may be thought of as consisting of an "enabling condition" and a "firing condition". The former requires that certain transitions be enabled on component ports that are connected to different bus ports. The latter then indicates which of the enabled transitions actually fire when the bus transition fires, thus causing state changes in the components as well as the bus.

To capture this intuition formally, we first introduce some auxiliary notions.

Definition 3.6 *Let N be a network.*

1. *An* annotated component transition *of N is a pair $\langle i, t\rangle$ such that $t \in T_{C(N,i)}$ is a transition of the ith component of N. We use AT_N to represent the set of all annotated component transitions of N.*

2. *A set A of annotated transitions of N is* enabled *in system state $\langle \bar{s}, \bar{b}\rangle$ if, for every $\langle i, t\rangle \in A$, $src(t) = \bar{s}[i]$.*

3. *A set $A \subseteq AT_N$ is* independent *if for every $\langle i_1, t_1\rangle, \langle i_2, t_2\rangle \in A$, if $i_1 = i_2$ then $t_1 = t_2$. In other words, A is independent if every component contributes at most one transition to A.*

4. *A set $A \subseteq AT_N$ is* maximally independent and enabled *for system state $\langle \bar{s}, \bar{b}\rangle$ if it is independent and enabled in $\langle \bar{s}, \bar{b}\rangle$ and no proper superset of A satisfies these properties. We write $MIE(N, \langle \bar{s}, \bar{b}\rangle, A)$ when this is the case.*

5. *Let $A \subseteq AT_N$. Then the* forward image, *$F(A, N)$ of A along the link set of N is defined as follows.*

$$\begin{aligned} F(A,N) &= F_w(A,N) \cup F_r(A,N) \text{ where} \\ F_w(A,N) &= \{\langle j, w, v\rangle \mid \exists \langle i, t\rangle \in A.\, t = \langle q, w'\,!v, q'\rangle \\ &\quad \wedge \langle \langle i, w'\rangle, \langle j, w\rangle\rangle \in L(N)\} \\ F_r(A,N) &= \{\langle j, r\rangle \mid \exists \langle i, t\rangle \in A.\, t = \langle q, r'\,?, f\rangle \\ &\quad \wedge \langle \langle i, r'\rangle, \langle j, r\rangle\rangle \in L(N)\} \end{aligned}$$

Intuitively, $F(A, N)$ records the bus ports (and values) used by a set of annotated transitions.

6. *Let $t = \langle b, WV, R, RV, W, b'\rangle \in T(M(N, j))$ be a transition of the jth bus in network N. Also let $A \subseteq AT_N$. Then A* triggers *t if the following hold.*

   (a) *$F_w(A, N) \cap \{\langle j, w, v\rangle \mid w \in W(M(N, j)), v \in \mathbb{V}\} = \{\langle j, w, v\rangle \mid \langle w, v\rangle \in WV\}$.*

   (b) *$F_r(A, N) \cap \{\langle j, r\rangle \mid r \in R(M(N, j)), v \in \mathbb{V}\} = \{\langle j, r\rangle \mid r \in R\}$.*

   Intuitively, A triggers t if the only actions involving $M(N, j)$ that A includes are exactly those encoded in WV and R.

7. *Let $t = \langle b, WV, R, RV, W, b'\rangle \in T(M(N, j))$ be a bus transition, and let $A \subseteq AT_N$ be such that A is independent and A triggers t. Also let $\langle \bar{s}, \bar{b}\rangle$ be a state of N. Then $APPLY(A, j, t, \langle \bar{s}, \bar{b}\rangle) = \langle \bar{s'}, \bar{b}[j := b']\rangle$, where $\bar{s'}$ is defined as follows for $1 \leq i \leq |N|_C$.*

$$\bar{s'}[i] = \begin{cases} s'_i & \text{if } \exists t, j, v.\langle i, t\rangle \in A, \\ & \langle j, w, v\rangle \in F_w(\{t\}, N), \\ & w \in W \text{ and } s'_i = tgt(t) \\ f_i(v) & \text{if } \exists t, j, v.\langle i, t\rangle \in A, \\ & \langle j, r\rangle \in F_r(\{t\}, N), \\ & \langle r, v\rangle \in RV \text{ and } f_i = tgt(t) \\ s_i & \text{otherwise} \end{cases}$$

Intuitively, $APPLY(A, j, t, \langle \bar{s}, \bar{b} \rangle)$ uses bus transition t in bus j, together with the transitions in A that involve ports in the "firing condition" of t, to update the system state. Write transitions in A whose ports are connected to "firing ports" in t execute, causing their components' sub-states to change. Read transitions in A whose ports are similarly connected also fire, drawing values from RV in order to update their state. Finally, the bus state changes as indicated by the bus transition.

With these definitions, we can now state the final SOS rule for networks as follows.

$$\frac{\begin{array}{l} t = \langle \bar{b}[j], WV, R, RV, W, b' \rangle \in T(B(N,j)), \\ MIE(N, \langle \bar{s}, \bar{b} \rangle, A), \\ A \text{ triggers } t \end{array}}{\langle \bar{s}, \bar{b} \rangle \xrightarrow{\tau}_N APPLY(A, j, t, \langle \bar{s}, \bar{b} \rangle)}$$

4. Examples

This section presents several concrete examples of different interaction mechanisms that may be encoded as buses in AIDs. These examples are intended to illustrate the expressiveness of the AIDs theory, on the one hand, and also the relative ease with which new forms of interprocess communication may be defined within the theory.

4.1. Synchronous message passing

The Graphical Calculus of Communicating Systems (GCCS) [4] supports synchronous message passing as its only form of communication. This form of communication is common in process algebras as well, and we show how it may be encoded as a bus.

Buses in GCCS place no limit on how many subsystems are allowed to use them. They require all senders and receivers to block until at least one sender and receiver are enabled; then an exchange of data occurs, with the selected sender and receiver free to continue executing.

A bus $M_S = \langle I, B, T, b_0 \rangle$ encapsulating synchronous binary handshaking may be defined as follows.

- $I = \langle \mathbb{W}, \mathbb{R} \rangle$. This reflects the fact that there is no limit on the number of links to M_S.
- $B = \{b\}$ consists of a single state.
- T is defined below.
- $b_0 = b$.

T contains all transitions of the form

$$b \xrightarrow[WV\ R]{W\ RV} b$$

where:

- $WV \neq \emptyset, R \neq \emptyset$
- $\exists \langle w, v \rangle \in WV, r \in R. W = \{w\}, RV = \{\langle r, v \rangle\}$.

In other words, a bus transition is enabled any time there is at least one reader and writer, and the result of firing the transition is to cause exactly one writer and one reader to execute, with the value output by the writer being shifted to the reader. Note that the bus never changes state; the only role of M_S's transitions is to synchronize the transitions of users of the bus.

One may verify that the SOS rules for AIDs ensure that, if several processes are connected to bus M_S, then all interaction consists of binary handshaking.

Note that connection limitations may be imposed on buses like M_S by altering its interface. So, for example, if one wanted to define synchronous communication buses in which each bus has exactly one writer and reader, then one could define such a bus exactly as M_S with the exception that the interface would be $\langle \{w\}, \{r\} \rangle$, where $w \in \mathbb{W}$ and $r \in \mathbb{R}$.

Finally, based on this semantics, one may infer the transition numbered 3 in Section 3.3 by noting that: $q_0 \xrightarrow{b!v_1}_{C_1} q_1$, $r_0 \xrightarrow{c!v_2}_{C_2} r_1$, and $s_0 \xrightarrow{c?}_{C_3} g$; that this set is maximally independent for the network N in Fig. 3; that there is a bus transition whose triggering condition involves all three transitions and whose firing condition selects the transitions from C_1 and C_3; and that $APPLY$ causes these transitions to fire, with the value v_1 being shifted from C_1 to C_3.

4.2. Asynchronous Communication

One may find many different forms of asynchronous communication used in modeling distributed systems: bounded / unbounded buffer, shared variables, etc. All involve a shared data structure into which writers deposit data and from which readers extract data. In this section we give a general scheme for defining non-lossy asynchronous communication primitives and show how it may be specialized to implement asynchronous mechanisms.

We begin by defining a generalized "storage structure".

Definition 4.1 *A* storage structure *is a tuple $\langle B, put, get \rangle$, where B is the set of states, $put \in \mathbb{V} \times B \rightarrow B$ is a partial function, and $get \in B \rightarrow (\mathbb{V} \times B)$ is a partial function.*

Intuitively, the states of a storage structure indicate "what's stored", while put and get insert and extract, respectively, data stored in a state. As an example, consider how a storage structure corresponding to a five-place FIFO buffer might be defined, where $\mathbb{V}^*$ is the set of sequences of values, $|\ell|$ is the length of sequence ℓ, and $\cdot$ is the sequence concatenation operator.

- $B_{FIFO} = \{\ell \in \mathbb{V}^* \mid |\ell| \leq 5\}$.

- $put_{FIFO}(v,\ell) = \ell \cdot v$ if $|\ell| < 5$, and is undefined otherwise.
- $get_{FIFO}(v \cdot \ell) = (v,\ell)$; $get_{FIFO}(\ell)$ is undefined if ℓ is empty.

A storage structure may also be given for a shared variable. In this case, the states of the variable correspond to the values that the variable can hold.

- $B_{SV} = \mathbb{V}$.
- $put_{SV}(v',v) = v'$.
- $get_{SV}(v) = (v,v)$.

Both put_{SV} and get_{SV} are total functions. Note that get_{SV} does not change the state of a variable, reflecting the fact that read operations on a shared variable do not change the state of the variable.

Given a storage structure $D = \langle B_D, put_D, get_D\rangle$ and distinguished storage state $b_D \in B_D$, we may define an asynchronous D-bus $\langle I,B,T,b_0\rangle$ as follows.

- $I = \langle \mathbb{W}, \mathbb{R}\rangle$.
- $B = B_D$.
- T is defined below.
- $b_0 = b_D$.

T contains all bus transitions of the form

$$b \xrightarrow[WV\ R]{W\ RV} b'$$

such that $WV \neq \emptyset$ or $R \neq \emptyset$, and: either $RV = \emptyset$ and

$$\exists \langle w,v\rangle \in WV.\, W = \{w\} \wedge b' = put_D(v,b),$$

or $W = \emptyset$ and

$$\exists r \in R, v \in \mathbb{V}.\, get_D(b) = \langle v,b'\rangle \wedge RV = \{\langle r,v\rangle\}.$$

In other words, M_D does not limit the connections coming into it, and its transitions are candidates for firing if at least one writer or reader wants access *and the relevant put_D or get_D operations are defined in the current storage state*. If e.g. $get_D(b)$ is undefined, then no reads can be performed because the condition "$get_D(b) = ...$" is untrue.

By varying the definition of the storage structure D, one can implement many different asynchronous communication disciplines. Even more flexibility can be afforded if *get* and *put* are allowed to be relations rather than functions; in this case, nondeterminism as to the result of those operations can be modeled, allowing e.g. nondeterministic delivery orders. Finally, lossy-channel behavior can be modeled by adding in transitions of the form:

$$b \xrightarrow[WV\ R]{\emptyset\ \emptyset} b'$$

. Such transitions are internal bus transitions and can be used to model spontaneous state changes within a bus. What is interesting about AIDs is that they provide a common framework to which many subtle differences in asynchronous communication can be easily accounted for.

4.3. Broadcast Communication

In broadcast communication there is a single writer that talks with all readers who happen to be listening. Process algebras like CCS and GCCS do not provide natural support for broadcast. On the other hand, AIDs can readily accommodate broadcast.

A bus $M_{MC} = \langle I,B,T,b_0\rangle$ encapsulating broadcast communication may be defined as follows.

- $I = \langle \mathbb{W}, \mathbb{R}\rangle$. This reflects the fact that there is no limit on the number of connections to M_{MC}.
- $B = \{b\}$ consists of a single state.
- T is defined below.
- $b_0 = b$.

T contains all transitions of the form

$$b \xrightarrow[WV\ R]{W\ RV} b$$

where:

- $WV \neq \emptyset$
- $\exists \langle w,v\rangle \in WV. W = \{w\}, RV = \{\langle r,v\rangle \mid r \in R\}$.

A bus transition is enabled any time there is at least one writer enabled, and the result of firing the transition is to cause one writer and all enabled readers to execute, with the value output by the writer being sent to the readers. Note that in contrast to the case of bi-party message passing, the value of the writer is sent to all the readers who expressed interest rather than just sending it to one reader among all of them.

5. Conclusions and Future work

In this paper we have presented the theory of architectural interaction diagrams (AIDs), which extend traditional software-architecture modeling notations in two respects. On the one hand AIDs have a flexible scheme for modeling process interaction mechanisms encapsulated as "buses". Rather than having to rely on the fixed set of low-level communication primitives most modeling notations have, AIDs permits users to use buses that encapsulate sophisticated interaction protocols. On the other hand, AIDs are also equipped with a formal operational semantics defining how each AID "executes", and in which any interaction among components is modeled as a single execution step. This semantics permits the behavior of AIDs to be mechanically analyzed, either via simulation and testing or (in certain cases) by model checking. In principle AIDs may also be used as a model-interoperation language, since the basic elements of an AID are semantic objects (labeled transition systems) that may be defined concretely in any number of other modeling notations.

We see the fundamental contributions of this work as being three-fold. On one hand it brings to the table a rich and extensible set of communication primitives. No other modeling language we are aware of provides users with such flexibility in using system communication primitives and adding his/her own. Secondly, it enforces a modeling paradigm that separates the internal working of the component from its interaction with other components. Thirdly, it provides a framework by which components specified in different modeling languages but possessing an underlying LTS semantics can be compiled together to provide a fully simulate-able heterogeneous system.

Regarding future work, we would like to build tool support for AIDs so that diagrams may be built, simulated, and model-checked. We anticipate doing this using the CWB-NC [17], which already has parameterizable analytical routines in place. We would also like to study other interaction mechanisms in order to formalize them as buses; such a library that clearly explicates the often subtle distinctions between different schemes would be useful. We plan to study the encoding of high-level middle-ware mechanisms such as CANbus as buses and to explore the development of an environment in which models given in disparate modeling notations (Statecharts, say, and MSCs) may be combined into a single, mathematically coherent system description using AIDs. Finally, we wish to investigate the extent to which the structure of AIDs may be used in service of *modular model checking*. Modular model checking consists of abstracting the environment of a process by constructing interface processes which denote the part of the environment that can affect the process in question. In AIDs, the buses provide a natural interface which encapsulates all the interaction behavior of the environment. In modular model checking, one has to transform the environment to an interface process by restricting the environment to only those transitions that can affect the component in question. AIDs provides one with a natural way of extracting this interface process without taking recourse to any transformations. since the buses to which the process is connected constitute the environment's interface with the process in question. This extraction of the interface process for a process via the buses it is connected to is a by-product of the separation of interaction and internal working that AIDs enforces. Future work consists in formalizing this intuition.

References

[1] Message sequence charts (MSC). *ITU-TS Recommendation Z.120*, 1996.

[2] M. Bernardo, P. Ciancarini, and L. Donatiello. On the formalization of architectural types with process algebras. In *8th ACM Intl. Symp. on the Foundations of Software Engineering*, pages 140–148, San Diego, CA, Nov. 2000. ACM Press.

[3] G. Booch, I. Jacobson, and J. Rumbaugh. The unified modeling language user guide.

[4] R. Cleaveland, X. Du, and S. Smolka. GCCS: A graphical coordination language for system specification. *COORDINATION 2000,Lecture Notes in Computer Science*, 1906:284–298, 2000.

[5] D.Garlan, R.Allen, and D.Ockerbloom. Exploiting style in architectural design environments. *Proceedings of SIGSOFT'94: The Second ACM SIGSOFT Symposium on the Foundations of Software Engineering*, 1994.

[6] D.Harel. Statecharts:a visual formalism for complex systems. *Science of Computer Programming,8*, pages 231–274, 1987.

[7] http://www.mathworks.com. The MathWorks.

[8] S. M. Inc. Javaspaces specifications. 1998.

[9] K.Larsen and L. Xinxin. Compositionality through an operational semantics of contexts. *Journal of Logic and Computation*, 1(6):761–795, 1991.

[10] E. Lee. Overview of Ptolemy project. *Technical Memorandum*, 6(3):213–249, 2001.

[11] J. Magee, N. Dulay, S. Eisenbach, and J. Kramer. Specifying distributed software architectures. In *Proc. of the 5th European Software Engineering Conf.*, volume 989 of *Lecture Notes in Computer Science*, pages 137–153. Springer Verlag, 1995.

[12] N.Carriero and D.Gelertner. Linda in context. *Communications of the ACM*, 32(4):445–458, 1989.

[13] M. Pezzé and M. Young. Constructing multi-formalism state-space analysis tools: using rules to specify dynamic semantics of models. pages 239–250, 1997.

[14] P.Wyckoff, S. McLaughry, T.J.Lehman, and D. Ford. Tspaces. *IBM Systems Journal*, 37(3), 1998.

[15] R.Allen and D.Garlan. Formalizing architectural connection. *16th International Conference on Software Engineering*, 1994.

[16] R.Allen and D.Garlan. A formal basis for architectural connection. *ACM Transactions on Software Engineering and Methodology*, 6(3):213–249, 1997.

[17] R.Cleaveland and S.Sims. Generic tools for verifying concurrent systems. *Science of Computer Programming*, 41(1):39–47, 2002.

Technical Papers

Software Understanding

Hipikat: Recommending Pertinent Software Development Artifacts

Davor Čubranić and Gail C. Murphy
Department of Computer Science
University of British Columbia
201-2366 Main Mall, Vancouver BC
Canada V6T 1Z4
E-mail: {cubranic, murphy}@cs.ubc.ca

Abstract

A newcomer to a software project must typically come up-to-speed on a large, varied amount of information about the project before becoming productive. Assimilating this information in the open-source context is difficult because a newcomer cannot rely on the mentoring approach that is commonly used in traditional software developments. To help a newcomer to an open-source project become productive faster, we propose Hipikat, a tool that forms an implicit group memory from the information stored in a project's archives, and that recommends artifacts from the archives that are relevant to a task that a newcomer is trying to perform. To investigate this approach, we have instantiated the Hipikat tool for the Eclipse open-source project. In this paper, we describe the Hipikat tool, we report on a qualitative study conducted with a Hipikat mock-up on a medium-sized in-house project, and we report on a case study in which Hipikat recommendations were evaluated for a task on Eclipse.

1. Introduction

A software developer who joins an existing software development team must come up-to-speed on a large, varied amount of information before becoming productive. Sim and Holt, for instance, interviewed newcomers to a project and found that they had to learn intricacies about the system, development processes being used, and the organizational structure surrounding the project, amongst others [15]. In collocated teams, this knowledge is often gained through mentoring: An existing member of the team works closely with the newcomer, looking over their shoulder, and imparting the oral tradition of the project, as the newcomer works on their first assigned tasks [15, 6].

Newcomers to open-source software projects cannot rely on this traditional approach. Communication between members of a team who are separated geographically and across time zones do not have access to such lightweight, high-bandwidth communication channels as the lunch table. Instead, these newcomers must try to find their way amongst the huge amount of archived, electronic information that is maintained as part of the project, such as the source repository, the bug database, and postings to newsgroups. Finding one's way, for instance, through the over 50,000 e-mail messages archived for the Apache open-source project (covering the period from February 1995 to May 1999 [11]) or through the one hundred or so postings *each* weekday to the Eclipse open-source project newsgroup,[1] is indeed a daunting task.

To help a newcomer in this situation become productive more quickly, we propose a tool that *recommends* existing artifacts from the development that are relevant to a task that the newcomer is trying to perform. In essence, we consider all of the artifacts that have been produced—the versions of the source, the bugs, archived electronic communication, web documents—as an implicit group memory. The tool plays two roles. First, the tool infers links between the artifacts that may have been apparent at one time to members of the development team but that were not recorded. Second, using these links, the tool, in a role similar to that of a mentor, suggests possibly relevant parts of the group memory given information about a task a newcomer is trying to perform. To investigate this hypothesis, we have built a tool called Hipikat,[2] we have instantiated Hipikat for the Eclipse open-source project, and we have conducted two exploratory studies: one using a mock-up of Hipikat on a medium-sized in-house project, and one using the Hipikat prototype on Eclipse.

In this paper, we begin with an overview of the structure of open-source projects, with a specific focus on Eclipse (Section 2). We then describe our approach to forming a

[1] `www.eclipse.org`

[2] Hipikat means "eyes wide open" in the West African language Wolof.

0-7695-1877-X/03 $17.00

group memory (Section 3), describe the Hipikat tool (Section 4), and present our exploratory studies into the effectiveness of the approach (Section 5). A discussion of the approach and tool follows (Section 6), as does a comparison to related efforts (Section 7).

2. Open-Source Projects

Outside the basic principle that the source code be freely available to anyone wishing to view or modify it [12], open-source projects vary in size, application domain, implementation language, team organization, and licensing model. Although there are differences between projects, a set of open-source best-practices is emerging, and a non-trivial project will typically produce the following four electronic artifacts.

1. *CVS source repository* Most projects use CVS [2] to provide version control support. The repository contains a complete history of the code base.

2. *Issue-tracking system* An issue-tracking system is typically used to submit and track bugs and feature requests on-line. Some systems, such as Bugzilla,[3] allow the posting of comments within tracked items, enabling the capture of discussion about the direction of bug fixes and feature implementations.

3. *Communication channels* Since project members are typically widely distributed, communication tends to be asynchronous, and to be supported electronically [5]. The culture of open-source projects is to keep all communication public; mailing lists and newsgroups are used more frequently than person-to-person mail. These archives are typically available on-line.

4. *Online documentation* Available documentation is most often code-oriented: reference manuals and programming guides are common; architectural descriptions and design-level documentation are rare. Documentation is usually distributed through a web site.

2.1. Eclipse.org

We are focusing our research efforts on one particular open-source project, the Eclipse extensible integrated development environment project. The Eclipse platform was originally developed by IBM, and was subsequently released under an open-source license. The platform can be extended through *plug-ins*. Basic Eclipse distribution includes plug-ins for Java development and for communication with CVS.

[3] `www.mozilla.org/projects/bugzilla/`

The Eclipse project mostly matches the earlier description of open-source projects: it includes a CVS repository with open read-only access, public newsgroups and mailing lists, a web site with documentation, and uses Bugzilla. At this time, there are two fairly distinct groups of developers: IBM employees who are working on the runtime of the platform, and on bundled plug-ins (the Eclipse *core*), and a much larger community of third-party plug-in developers, who range from large commercial software developers to hobbyist programmers. This division is reflected in the project's artifacts. For example, most newsgroups postings are questions about using and accessing the core API. Compared to the Mozilla project,[4] there is little discussion or give-and-take within the issue-tracking system, likely because the Eclipse project is in its early stages compared to Mozilla, which after four years as an open-source project has a sizeable portion of developers outside the Netscape Communications Corporation in which the system originated.

3. Approach

Our approach has two parts. First, we form the implicit group memory from the artifacts and communications stored in a project's history. Second, we present to the developer artifacts selected from this implicit group memory that may be relevant to the task being performed.

Figure 1 shows the schema we use to represent a project's implicit group memory. There are four types of artifacts represented in the schema: bug and feature descriptions (e.g., items in Bugzilla, source file revisions (e.g, checked in a CVS source repository), messages posted on developer forums (e.g., newsgroups and mailing lists), and other project documents (e.g., design documents posted on the project's web site). These artifacts are created by project members, represented by `Person` in the diagram.

Entries in the project's issue-tracking system are a locus within the schema because these entries typically represent a logical unit of work on the project. Source revisions are checked into the source repository to respond to one of these entries; newsgroup postings and mailing list messages often contain discussion that either results in a new entry or that is about an existing entry; other documentation may contain information about a particular entry, such as specific design trade-offs related to a feature request.

A given project may not contain all artifacts or links described in the schema. In general, missing *artifacts* result in a loss of the portion of the schema related to the artifact. In a small number of cases, such as structural design documentation, a missing artifact might be reverse engineered from other project artifacts; for example, some limited kinds of

[4] `www.mozilla.org`

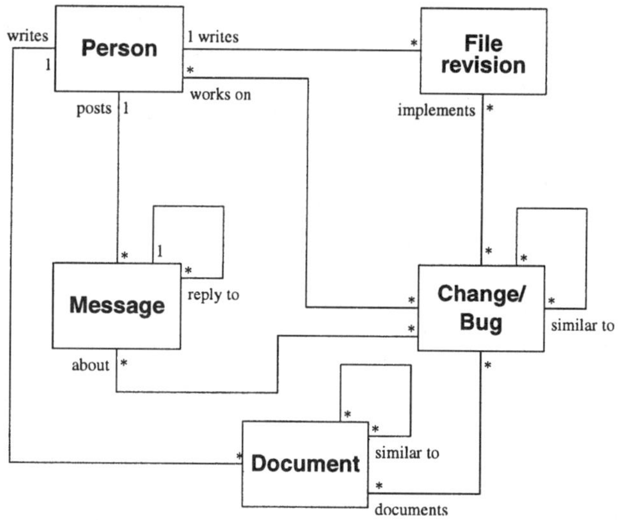

Figure 1. Artifact linkages schema

design documentation might be regenerated from source. Missing *links* are easier to infer as information contained within the project artifacts, and meta-information available about those artifacts, can be exploited. For instance, some links between feature requests and file revisions might be inferred if there is a project convention to include in a check-in comment associated with the revision a reference to the issue-tracking system entry that describes the feature request. Other links between entries in the issue-tracking system and file revisions might might be inferred based on meta-information, such as when particular project artifact's were created or touched; for example, it is likely that the author of a bug fix checked in source revision(s) close to the time that the bug was closed in the issue-tracking system.

The schema is also used to direct the selection of relevant artifacts in response to a query. For example, once a developer has started working on a task, such as a request to make a particular change to the system, the developer may be interested in other tasks that have been completed within the same subsystem, or with a similar description. Following the `similar_to` links may lead to tasks that are helpful. Once a similar task has been identified, following the `implements` links will lead to source revisions that implemented the task of interest. These revisions may help a developer identify code that may have to be modified or understood for the task at hand. The completed similar tasks may also have related discussions about which design options were examined, and which decisions were made that may impact the task at hand.

Abstractly, a tool implementing our approach has to implement three distinct functions.

1. **Identification** As artifacts are added to a project's history, the implicit group memory must be formed, including inference of missing links and artifacts.
2. **Selection** In response to queries, relevant artifacts must be identified and returned.
3. **Update** The project's archives must be monitored for additions and changes that result from the development and evolution of the system. The implicit group memory must be updated to reflect the additions and changes.

4. Hipikat Prototype

The Hipikat prototype is a client-server system. Hipikat is instantiated currently for the Eclipse project, but has been designed to be adapted easily to other open-source projects that follow the general model described in Section 2.

The client, when commanded by the user, issues a request for suggestions to the server, and displays returned results to the user. There are three parameters in any request from the client for suggestions. Two of the arguments are required: the first identifies anonymously the user,[5] and the second identifies artifact for which related items are sought. An optional third argument is intended to further describe the context of the query for additional tailoring of recommendations, although it is not used at this time. The server replies with a list of matches that the client then formats and presents in human-readable format.

4.1. Hipikat Client

Since Eclipse is self-hosted, we wrote the client as a plug-in that works within the IDE. This approach permits the Hipikat client to integrate seamlessly into a full-featured work environment, and to thus be used in combination with other software engineering tools plugged into Eclipse. For example, an Eclipse developer can use both Hipikat and the Java search feature that comes bundled with the default Eclipse distribution.

A developer who wants to make a query to Hipikat selects an artifact in their Eclipse project workspace, such as a class in a Java package browser, and chooses "Query Hipikat" from a pop-up context menu. (See Figure 2 for a full list of places in the IDE where such queries can be made.) Identifier of the selected artifact is passed as the second argument in the request to the Hipikat server, described in Section 4.2.

Additionally, the Hipikat artifact database can be searched based on search terms specified by the developer. This functionality is accessed through a pane in the regular

[5]Users are represented in the query to facilitate future extensions to selection mechanisms such as user-modelling and collaborative filtering. In the interests of privacy, user ids used in queries do not personally identify the user.

Bug report open in the Bugzilla editor
CVS-managed file open in the Java editor
File in the CVS Repository view
Revision in the CVS Resource History view
CVS-managed file in the workspace Navigator
Item recommended in the Hipikat Results view
Bugzilla search match in the Search results view
Java class or method in Outline and Hierarchy views

Figure 2. Places where Hipikat query can be done in Eclipse

Eclipse search dialog, which also supports plain-text and Java-specific searches.

The results of a query or search are displayed in a Hipikat view within Eclipse (see Figure 5). The recommendations are grouped by artifact type and by selection criteria as determined by the identification submodule that reported a link. A recommendation can be opened for viewing, either within Eclipse or through an external viewer (e.g., a Web browser) depending on the artifact. We also provide access to Eclipse's revision comparison functionality to allow a developer to view a (CVS) artifact's differences from the preceding revision; for instance, to allow a developer to focus on particular changes to the source base. A Hipikat user can reorganize the recommendation lists, delete unwanted items, or move items towards the top or bottom of the list. Currently, this feature is purely for a user's direct benefit and convenience; in the future, this feature is intended be used to rate recommended items so that collaborative filtering capabilities can be added. Lastly, any recommendation can be used in another Hipikat query to help support easy traversal of the links in the group memory.

4.2. Hipikat Server

The server implements the three functions described earlier: identification, update, and selection. As Figure 3 shows, each function is encapsulated in a module. Each module is divided into submodules based on an artifact or link type for which it is responsible.

Update The update module for Eclipse has four submodules: one each for Bugzilla, CVS, newsgroups, and the Web site. Each update submodule monitors the project artifacts as appropriate for its type: The Web site is scanned by crawling the links, the CVS repository is monitored by parsing the history of updated files as gathered via `cvs update` commands, news articles are downloaded using the NNTP protocol from the Eclipse news server, and issue items are parsed from the output of Web front-end to Bugzilla.[6] New and changed artifacts are inserted into Hipikat's artifact database, and change listeners in the identification module are notified of the updates.

The artifact database saves primarily the *metadata* from the new and changed artifacts that are needed to establish relationships between the artifacts. For instance, for a CVS revision, the author and check-in time will be retained. Text, such as the bug descriptions or check-in comments, is indexed, both for the purpose of searching and for making similarity comparisons, but otherwise artifacts contents (i.e., the actual source of a Java file under CVS) that are not used to make recommendations are not kept.

Identification The identification submodules register with the update module as listeners for changes on artifact types for which they are responsible. There are currently four such submodules: check-in comment matcher (*log-matcher*), check-in time matcher (*activity-matcher*), text similarity matcher, and newsgroup thread matcher. When informed of a new instance of an artifact, or a change to an existing artifact, the identification submodules attempt to infer links within the implicit group memory, following the schema from Figure 1.

The *log-matcher* and the *activity-matcher* infer the `implements` links between a source revision and an issue ticket based on conventions used by Eclipse project developers. The *log-matcher* responds to changes in the CVS database, scanning CVS check-in comments for text that looks like bug id's (e.g., "Fixes bug *id*" or "*id*: ..."). The *activity-matcher* listens to updates to Bugzilla, taking advantage of the fact that Bugzilla is increasingly used to keep track of *all* the work done in the project, not just bugs reported by users. Since a developers will usually post a message on Bugzilla (and change the issue ticket's status) shortly after relevant source changes have been checked in, the *activity matcher* looks for checkins that are close to (within six hours of) activity occurring in a Bugzilla item. Checkins are further grouped into likely work units by looking for all checkins by a given developer within a small time window, similar to the strategy employed by Mockus, Fielding, and Herbsleb in their study of Mozilla development process [11].

The text similarity matcher works in two phases. First the text of new artifacts is indexed and each artifact—for example, a Bugzilla description and its comments, or a document on the project Web site—is turned into a *document vector* whose dimensions correspond to words in the vocabulary. The component magnitudes are the weights of words in the document and are calculated using a product of the term's *global weight*, indicating its overall importance in the entire collection, and *local weight*, which

[6] A production system could interface directly with the Bugzilla SQL database.

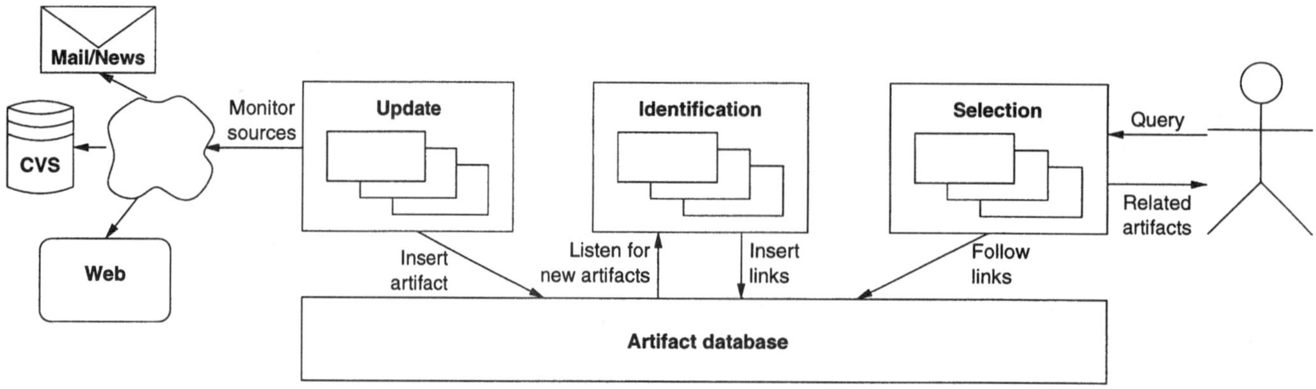

Figure 3. Hipikat server architecture

depends only on the frequency of terms within each document. We use log-entropy[7] combination for the two weights: The local weight is calculated as $L(i,j) = log(1+tf_{ij})$ and the global weight is calculated as $G(i) = 1 - \frac{1}{log(N)}\sum_{j=1}^{N} p_{ij}log(p_{ij})$, where tf_{ij} is the number of times term i occurs in document j, N is the number of documents in the collection, $p_{ij} = \frac{tf_{ij}}{d_i}$, and d_i is the number of documents containing term i.

In the second phase, the text similarity matcher uses a standard information retrieval vector-space cosine similarity measure [14] to infer `is_similar_to` links between artifacts. Specifically, the similarity between two documents is calculated as $sim(d_i, d_j) = \frac{d_i \cdot d_j}{\|d_i\|\|d_j\|}$. A selection submodule is responsible for using the computed measures to recommend a small set of nearest neighbours to an artifact.

This text similarity approach is also used in user-specified search queries: A user's query is treated just as another document vector, allowing matching artifacts to be sorted by relevance based on their degree of similarity to the search query.

Finally, the simplest identification submodule is the newsgropu thread matcher, which looks for "References" headers in newsgroup articles and reconstructs conversation threads of a newsgroup posting and subsequent replies.

Selection Lastly, selection works by following links from the artifact specified in client's request. Submodules are specialized to make recommendations for a subset of artifact types and their links—for example, one module makes recommendations on CVS and Bugzilla artifacts by following `implements` (and its reverse, `is_implemented_by`) links. Recommendations from all selection submodules to a given query are merged together before a final list is returned to the user.

Implementation The server is written as a Web application running within Tomcat.[7] The server and client communicate using SOAP [3].

To make a query, the client makes a remote procedure call, `getRecommendations`, with the three arguments described earlier: the anonymous user making the query, the id of an artifact for which recommendations are sought, and the currently unused third argument to provide additional context for making recommendations. The id for an artifact includes both a type (for quick selection of appropriate modules to handle the request), and a further unique identifier within the artifact type name space, as appropriate to the type (e.g., file path and revision number for a CVS artifact).

The server replies with an XML-formatted list of matches which is modelled on the "What's Related" service provided by Alexa.com and available in all major browsers. The recommendations are wrapped in a `RecommendationList` XML element (Figure 4). Each item recommended by the server is represented as a `Recommendation` element, with children `key`, `name`, `reason`, and `confidence`. The `key` element uniquely identifies the recommended artifact and is used if the user decides to open it or make a subsequent query on it. The `name` element is a human-readable description of the artifact and depending on its type can be a CVS file name, a one-line summary of a Bugzilla item, subject and author of a newsgroup posting, etc. The `reason` element describes why the item was recommended, and `confidence` expresses the relative strength of this relationship. The confidence value can be descriptive, as in "Same discussion thread" for a newsgroup posting, or numeric in the case of a text similarity measure.

The Eclipse project produces all of the kinds of artifacts in our schema. As of September 2002, our Hipikat server knows about 21,668 Bugzilla items (incorporating 72,536 additional comments), 125,429 CVS revisions,

[7] `jakarta.apache.org/tomcat`

```
<RecommendationList>
  <Recommendation>
    <key>cvs:dev.eclipse.org:/home/eclipse/...
        org.eclipse.team.cvs.ui/src/org/eclipse/team/...
        internal/ccvs/ui/actions/TagAction.java:1.13</key>
    <name>org.eclipse.team.cvs.ui/src/org/eclipse/team/...
        internal/ccvs/ui/actions/TagAction.java:1.13</name>
    <reason>Bug ID in revision log</reason>
    <confidence>High</confidence>
  </Recommendation>
  <Recommendation>
    <key>bugzilla:12367</key>
    <name>[CVS Repo View] ``Define Branch Tag''...
        confusing?</name>
    <reason>Text similarity</reason>
    <confidence>0.6240631</confidence>
  </Recommendation>
  ...
</RecommendationList>
```

Figure 4. A sample response from Hipikat server.

36,864 newsgroup postings, and 1,459 Web pages (including those used solely to group frames and navigation functions) associated with the Eclipse project.

5. Validation

5.1. Initial Qualitative Study

Our first investigation of the Hipikat approach focused on whether recommendations of relevant artifacts were of any help to developers working on a change task, and if so, which kinds of recommendations were used. We also wanted to determine if there were recommendations developers would have found useful but that Hipikat did not suggest. For this initial assessment, we chose to manually build the implicit group memory for a medium-sized software system that was under development in our research lab. We then trialled a mock-up of Hipikat for this implicit group memory as part of an assignment for a graduate software engineering class held in our department.

The medium-sized software system used was the AVID visualization tool, which allows a developer to analyze the execution of a software system off-line in terms of an architectural view of the system [17]. AVID is written in Java and comprises 12,853 non-comment, non-blank lines of code organized in 177 classes and 16 packages.

Since the AVID development did not use a bug-tracking system, we analyzed its CVS repository, extracted about two dozen distinct change tasks from its history, including both bug fixes and new functionality, and entered these tasks as items in a Bugzilla database. We then built up the implicit group memory for the project, which consisted of change tasks, CVS revisions, documentation, project-related emails, and links between these artifacts. Although we formed the links manually, we followed the principles described in Section 3: revisions were linked to change tasks based on similarity of the check-in comments to task descriptions, documentation was associated through text similarity, and associations between change tasks were inferred using text similarity and overlap in source files that were changed as part of a task. These links were realistic: They contained both relevant and irrelevant suggestions since they were based on the information recorded. For instance, change tasks that contained similar words in their description may have been about something totally different, and groups of CVS checkins often included some revisions that were not related to the check-in comment or the rest of the group.

The mock-up client was a stand-alone Java application that allowed the user to browse the CVS repository the on-line documentation, and change task database. When the client displayed an artifact, it would issue a background request to the Hipikat server for items related to the displayed artifact, and would display a list of related artifacts returned in a side pane. The client also included a "bookshelf" where users could create notes as they worked and keep links to artifacts they accessed often.

The assignment in the graduate software evolution class consisted of having students implement two changes to AVID that we had selected from previously completed changes on a development branch of the system. Students were grouped into pairs; each pair was asked to use the mock-up for one change and one of Rigi[8], Chava[9], or jRMTool[10] for the other. We randomized the assignment of tools to the changes, and we randomized the order in which we asked the pairs to make the changes. Following the completion of the assignment, we invited students to participate in the study by sharing their assignment reports with us. Seven pairs (out of twelve in the class) agreed and gave us a copy of their assignment reports. We analyzed the comments in the reports and interviewed six of the subjects.

Overall, the subjects reported that Hipikat helped them to start the assigned task. In particular, suggestions of relevant previous changes to AVID that were based on textual similarity to the change at hand helped to identify the classes and methods that the subject needed to understand or modify to complete the assigned task:

> The suggestions on the side pane on the left gave us the starting point of classes to look for. We then used a bottom-up approach—browsed through the source code to see whether it is relevant to the change task. (Pair 5)

One potential problem with our approach is that a new-

[8] www.rigi.csc.uvic.ca

[9] www.research.att.com/sw/tools/chava/

[10] www.cs.ubc.ca/\~murphy/jRMTool/doc/index.html

comer receiving suggestions may not have sufficient knowledge of the system to determine readily what a suggestion means and whether it is relevant. For the most part, the subjects in our study were able to distinguish which suggestions were likely relevant, and which were the result of apparent similarity However, some pairs reported difficulty in assessing relevance without "wasting a lot of effort" (Pair 5) investigating a suggestion. We also had reports of a pair missing a relevant suggestion because they lacked knowledge about the overall structure of the system, and realizing its relevance only once they have figured out the solution on their own.

> For the implementation of the change we ignored the existance [sic] of the AbstractQueryManager although the Hipikat tool more or less directly pointed us to it through the change task for [...] (Pair 7)

The usefulness of suggestions made by Hipikat depends on the context in which a suggestion is made and on the experience of the developer(s) receiving a suggestion as can be seen by the following two comments which talk about the same change task and the same set of recommendations:

> Unfortunately, none of the change tasks previously recorded in Hipikat bore much resemblance to the change we were attempting aside from identifying a file... (Pair 2)

and

> Hipikat definitely helped us during the first part of the task. ... We quickly found a related task [...] We confirmed that this task was related by examining the CVS differences in files that Hipikat indicated were involved in the change. This meant we knew which methods we needed to look at. (Pair 4)

The results of this initial study showed that it was possible to make reasonable suggestions using the inferences we had posited, and that those suggestions were (sometimes) useful to developers. We proceeded to implement the Hipikat prototype for Eclipse, incorporating two enhancements from the initial study: we added the return of a reason for a recommendation to a user, and we changed the user interface from automatically suggesting related artifacts to making suggestions based on a query from the user.

5.2. Case Study: An Eclipse Change Task

As an initial step in the evaluation of our Hipikat prototype for Eclipse, we undertook a case study in which we used Hipikat to aid the performance of a change task on Eclipse. We selected a completed enhancement for Eclipse that was logged in Bugzilla, and created an implicit group memory for Eclipse based on the project artifacts that were in existence when that Bugzilla item was entered. The subject in this study was the first author on this paper. At the time of this case, he had experience with Eclipse plug-in development, but had not contributed to the core of the Eclipse project and was in a position similar to that of a newcomer to the Eclipse.org project. We chose a completed enhancement to enable us to compare our solution with that developed by the Eclipse team.

The enhancement request we selected deals with the behaviour of Eclipse's CVS repository browser. The browser displays the files and directories residing in the repository, and shows their existing branches and tagged versions. The repository supports basic operations such as checking out files (from either a trunk or version branch, as well as a tagged version), viewing a file's revision history, and creating new branches and tagged versions. However, when a new version is created through the browser, a manual refresh (potentially requiring the overhead of communication with the server) is necessary before the new version appears in the browser. The desired enhancement is to have the browser update automatically in this situation.[11] We describe the subject's use of Hipikat for the study as if it was currently occurring to provide the context of how the tool was used.

The subject starts off by opening the Bugzilla item describing the modification request describing the task at hand in Eclipse. The subject then makes a Hipikat query from the context menu of the viewer displaying the modification request. A list of similar items appears in the search result window, Since this is an unsolved request, the list includes only other Bugzilla items selected for their textual similarity to the change task at hand (Figure 5).

Near the top of the list is bug 11419, whose one-line description of "Automatically add version to repo[sitory] view when tagging", sounds similar to the current change task. A double-click opens it, and the subject determines that it describes functionality almost equivalent to the functionality that is desired. The difference is that bug 11419 describes functionality that was activated from the context menu for files in Eclipse workspace; the equivalent of the CVS "tag" command, as opposed to "rtag" in the CVS repository browser. Since bug 11419 is marked as "fixed", the functionality must have been added into Eclipse. The subject makes another Hipikat query to get files related to the completed enhancement, hoping to learn something from the fix (Figure 6).

At the top of the results list for this query are file revisions that Hipikat retrieved following the `imple-`

[11] Bug 116, accessible at URL: `bugs.eclipse.org/bugs/show_bug.cgi?id=116`.

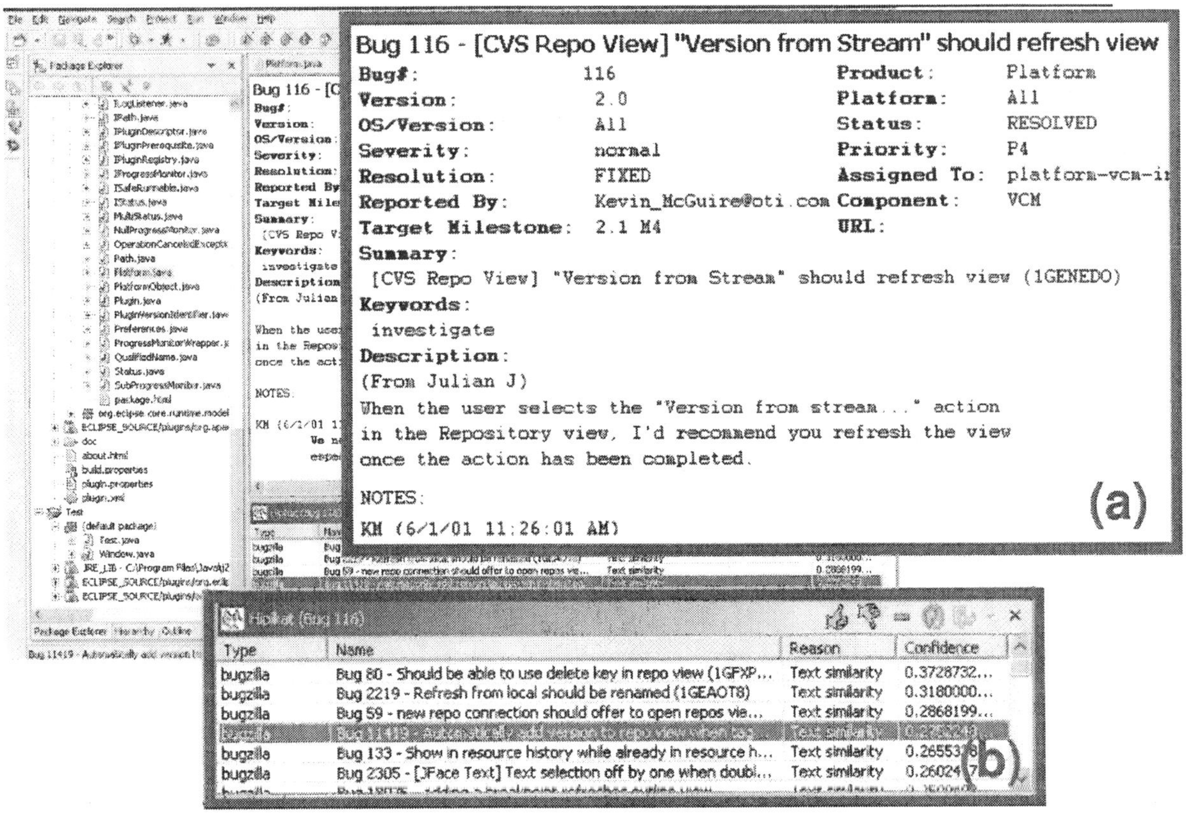

Figure 5. A screenshot of Hipikat being used within Eclipse IDE during the change task case study. Zoomed-in rectangles show the change task, bug 116 (a), and list of related artifacts (b)

mented_by links. In this case, there is a single file, *TagAction.java rev. 1.13*, which was recommended because the bug id 11419 appeared in its check-in comment, and because of the temporal proximity of its check-in to the closing of the item in the Bugzilla database. To focus on what it was that this revision changed in the code, the subject uses the context menu in the "Hipikat results" view to request a diff of the file to its preceding revision. The view comparing the revisions shows that the fix centers on a call to the CVS UI plugin's *RepositoryManager* from within TagAction class's execute method. The call is not entirely straightforward, because it also requires interaction with the model of CVS resources to find the tagged file's project in the workspace, and to map that file to the remote folder in the CVS repository.

At this point, the subject uses Eclipse built-in facilities to view the code of classes TagAction and RepositoryManager, as well as the classes in the model that are used in the TagAction's code (e.g., IResource, ICVSRemoteResource, and CVSTag). With the subject's attention focused on just this part of the code base, it does not take long to figure out how tags are created in the model and updated in the view.

What remains is figuring out why the code works when called from the *Tag as Version* in the context menu on a file in the workspace, but not in the CVS Repository browser. Debugging the current version of TagAction, which includes the changes added in version 1.13, by, for instance, inserting a breakpoint, can help the subject identify quickly that it is not the action that is invoked for the CVS Repository browser's menu.

A look at the XML file that defines a plugin's contributions to various context menus shows that TagAction is executed only when the *Tag as Version* option is chosen from the context menu on items of type IResource, which are directories and files in the Eclipse workspace. Further on in the same file, the subject sees that for the context menu on items of type ICVSRemoteResource, TagInRepositoryAction is the action executed, so the subject starts to look at the code for that class.

Upon inspection of TagInRepositoryAction, the subject sees that its execute method is almost identical to the execute method in TagAction before changes implemented in the revision fixing bug 11419. This logi-

Type	Name	Reason
cvs	...internal/ccvs/ui/actions/TagAction:1.10	Bug ID in revision log
bugzilla	Bug 12367 - [CVS Repo View] "Define Branch Tag" confusing?	Text similarity
bugzilla	Bug 8185 - Branch should automatically version	Text similarity
	...	

Figure 6. The top few artifacts related to bug 11419

cally leads the subject to apply the same approach in `TagInRepositoryAction`, which indeed solves the change task, as evidenced by the the fix implemented by Eclipse developers.

6. Discussion

Lessons from validation

For software change tasks, an inquiry episode has been defined as consisting of a developer asking a question, conjecturing an answer, and then searching through the code and documentation to verify or reject the conjecture [16]. Since the search space is so large, newcomers tend to have difficulty coming up not only with a good conjecture, but also the way of searching through the documentation and code to verify it. In our case studies, we found that Hipikat was most useful at the beginning of a major inquiry episode. A developer can query from a Bugzilla item describing the change, producing a set of similar bugs: Some of these bugs may serve as starting points for a newcomer to make more informed conjectures. Specifically, recommended fixed bugs will have associated source, which the developer can use to identify code possibly relevant to the current change.

Most of the time, the recommendations to bugs and source are still just entry points. The developer must still evaluate the code and understand how it works. For this part of the task, other source-based discovery tools, such as the Java search feature of Eclipse, can be used to help the developer focus on understanding a manageable (and relevant) portion of the system.

A more fundamental issue with Hipikat is that the quality and number of items recommended affects the newcomer's performance on the task. When the recommendation list is long, the newcomer can have trouble determining if any of the recommendations are relevant. In the study described in Section 5.1, we found that newcomers sometimes had difficulty assessing recommendations. Some newcomers who were recommended a fixed bug with many associated source files investigated all of associated files in sequence, even when there was little basis to believe a file was relevant for the current change. Reporting the amount of code involved in a revision when presenting the recommendations may alleviate this problem somewhat, although obviously no machine-based solution will work in all cases.

Eclipse We chose the Eclipse project as our testbed for two main reasons. First, Eclipse is a large system, comprising over 800,000 lines of Java code, for which a rich history of project artifacts is available. Second, we could integrate our tool into Eclipse, making it more accessible to Eclipse developers. Since Eclipse shares similar processes and structure with other open-source projects—for instance both Eclipse and Mozilla use Bugzilla to track all work done in a project—our approach may reasonably apply to other targets.

Accuracy Our link inference algorithms are approximate. Out of 9,418 bugs marked fixed as of August 24, 2002 in the Eclipse Bugzilla database, the Hipikat log- and activity-matcher identification submodules inferred revision links for 5,688 (60%) of these bugs. The two submodules linked a further 2,810 bugs to revisions even though these bugs were not marked fixed; most of these links are probably false, the result of bugs that have been reopened or that have been erroneously left open, or that refer to revisions implementing test cases for still-unsolved bugs. Over two thirds of these false links are ranked with lower confidence because they are for activity that is significantly distant from the time of the check-in: The confidence in a link inferred by the activity-matcher progressively decreases when this distance is over five minutes.

It remains to be seen how users will treat Hipikat recommendations in view of their approximativeness. Will a user give up on certain kinds of recommendations entirely once they conclude, rightly or wrongly, that they are not helpful, as happened during testing of our mock-up? Will Hipikat's "confidence" measures make sense? Since it has been shown that expressing confidence as a numeric value in recommenders makes little sense to users [8], we try to use textual descriptions wherever possible. In some places, like text similarity, there is no such obvious explanation and it remains to be seen whether users will make use of the numeric value (vector cosine), or if they will simply go through the list and view recommended artifacts, possibly filtering based on the short description of the artifact that is included in the recommendations view.

Beyond Search The Eclipse web site supports a search

function. However, this search is of limited functionality, in part, because of the high amount of noise in its matches. As an example of the noise, the search includes the text of source files so that any query involving a class name will yield matches for *all* revisions of that class and other classes that use it. More fundamentally, searching is by definition useful when the user knows on what to search. Hipikat, on the other hand, allows a user who is working on a change task and who is unsure of where to start or what to look for to simply say "tell me about what might be similar to what I'm doing".

Role of Task We use Bugzilla entries as focal points to which other artifacts are linked. This organization makes sense in view of the fact that Bugzilla is increasingly used to keep track of *all* the work done in the project. The same process happened in Mozilla—which is now much further along this path, thanks to its longer duration and more diversified developer community—and we expect that as Eclipse evolves in the same way, all revisions implementing more than trivial changes will have corresponding Bugzilla items.

Furthermore, while Bugzilla is normally used with a Web browser front end, including viewing and editing of Bugzilla reports into Eclipse gives us a simple way of tracking what the developer's current change task is. Although we are not currently using it to refine the recommendations, having access to Bugzilla within the IDE lowers the barrier to use Hipikat on change tasks and makes it more likely it will be applied in the early stage of change task planning where it is most likely to be helpful.

Collaborative filtering and user modelling Currently, the identification of links between artifacts in Hipikat is purely content-based; it depends solely on the contents of artifacts, such as when artifacts are compared based on text similarity, and on metadata, such as in the bug activity matcher identification submodule. Collaborative-based techniques could be used to enhance link identification. For example, newsgroup postings from authoritative sources, such as developers who checked in revisions on the same subject, could be given higher priority when making recommendations.

Schema-based selection could also be further refined through the use of a user model. For example, the CodeBroker [18] reuse recommender keeps track of components in a reuse repository that a developer has often accessed in the past, assumes that these components are well-known, and thus does not include the components in its recommendations. Although collaborative filtering would, by definition, have to be done in the Hipikat server, user modeling could be done partly or even entirely by the client.

7. Related Work

Many existing approaches have attempted to use the artifacts associated with a software development, other than source, to aid in software evolution tasks. These approaches vary in their degree of automation and in their specificity to a task.

Several systems mine version control information. The VE editor can display the revision in which a given line was changed together with its check-in description, and supports browsing of the code through a sequence of versions [1]. The Expertise Recommender system (ER) uses the author information recorded in a program's change history to generate recommendations of people who might have some expertise on a given problem [10]. Neither of these tools attempts to integrate version information with other artifacts. For example, we have found in practice that a problem report often contains information beyond that in a version check-in description.

Initial steps towards integrating software artifacts with developers' communication were made by Lougher and Rodden [9], whose system allowed maintenance engineers to make annotations on the code, capturing rationale and making long-term collaboration possible. Their approach requires the user to look at the exact spot in the source code to see the annotation, which may not be as useful for a relative newcomer trying to grasp tens of thousands of lines of source. Anchored Conversations [4] coupled actual conversations between collaborators, either real time chats or asynchronous messages, with the work artifact for in-context discussion, but suffers from the same drawback when dealing with a multi-megabyte artifact corpus.

Similar to Hipikat, Ye and Fischer's CodeBroker [18] uses information retrieval methods to determine software artifacts to suggest in the context of a developer's current task. However, CodeBroker is tailored to helping a developer on small-scale reuse tasks: The tool monitors a developer's use of a text editor watching for the method declarations and the descriptions of those methods in comments, the tool uses that information as a query to a library to find potential components that could be reused instead of a new component being created. In contrast, when used as a reuse tool, Hipikat works at the granularity of a task, providing such information as documents describing how a component is to be used with other components. The CodeBroker approach also relies on a developer properly formatting documentation in the component being defined, and in the presence of properly formatted documentation in the components in the reuse library. Hipikat avoids placing any additional requirements on the developers, making use of information that is potentially more informal. In this regard, Hipikat is more similar to the *Remembrance Agent* [13], which used information sources, such as user's email folders and text notes, to present documents relevant, or similar, to the one currently being edited.

Mockus, Fielding, and Herbsleb have described building logical work units from CVS revisions by looking at revisions that were checked in by a single author within a small time interval and that share the same comment [11]. We relax their technique by allowing different check-in comments. The advantage of relaxing this constraint is that we may be more inclusive of the revisions that are part of the same change. The disadvantage is the increased cognitive load place don the developer who has to decide if a recommendation based on this information is relevant. We do note in the recommendations a lower-level of confidence when this inference heuristic is used and the check-in comments do not match. We further extend Mockus et al's method by attempting to match the checkin with the activity in the issue-tracking system as an additional way to link the code revisions with the descriptions of tasks in which developers were engaged.

8. Summary

The archives of a software development project can serve as an implicit group memory about the design of the system, decisions made over the course of the development, "tricks" for solving bugs, amongst many other kinds of information. Although the archives are stored and often accessible through common search techniques, the information is not integrated into a group memory. In this paper, we have described Hipikat, a tool that forms an implicit group memory for a project by inferring links between stored artifacts, and that then recommends pertinent parts of the group memory (artifacts) to a developer working on a task. Through two qualitative studies, we have shown that this approach shows promise for helping a newcomer perform a task effectively on an unfamiliar system.

Acknowledgments

This research was funded, in part, by NSERC and IBM (Ottawa Software Lab), as part of the Consortium for Software Engineering Research. We would like to thank the students of CPSC 507 in the fall of 2001 for their participation in our initial qualitative study.

References

[1] D. L. Atkins. Version sensitive editing: Change history as a programming tool. In *System Configuration Management 98*, pages 146–157. Springer-Verlag, 1998.

[2] B. Berliner. CVS II: Parallelizing software development. In USENIX Association, editor, *Proceedings of the Winter 1990 USENIX Conference*, pages 341–352, Jan. 1990.

[3] D. Box, D. Ehnebuske, G. Kakivaya, A. Layman, N. Mendelsohn, H. F. Nielsen, S. Thatte, and D. Winer. Simple object access protocol, `http://www.w3c.org/TR/SOAP`, 8 May 2000.

[4] E. F. Churchill, J. Trevor, S. Bly, L. Nelson, and D. Čubranić. Anchored Conversations: chatting in the context of a document. In *CHI 2000*, pages 454–461, 2000. ACM Press.

[5] D. Čubranić and K. S. Booth. Coordinating open-source software development. In *WETICE 1999*, pages 61–65, 1999. IEEE Computer Society Press.

[6] M. Cusumano and R. Selby. *Microsoft Secrets: How the World's Most Powerful Software Company Creates Technology, Shapes Markets, and Manages People.* The Free Press, 1995.

[7] S. Dumais. Improving the retrieval of information from external sources. *Behaviour Research Methods, Instrument, and Computers*, 23(2):229–236, 1991.

[8] J. L. Herlocker, J. A. Konstan, and J. Riedl. Explaining collaborative filtering recommendations. In *CSCW 2000*, pages 241–250, 2000.

[9] R. Lougher and T. Rodden. Supporting long term collaboration in software maintenance. In *COOCS=93*, pages 228–238, 1993.

[10] D. W. McDonald and M. S. Ackerman. Expertise Recommender: A flexible recommendation system and architecture. In *CSCW 2000*, pages 231–240, 2000. ACM

[11] A. Mockus, R. T. Fielding, and J. Herbsleb. Two case studies of open source software development: Apache and Mozilla. *ACM Transactions on Software Engineering and Methodology*, 11(3):1–38, July 2002.

[12] B. Perens. The open source definition. In C. DiBona, S. Ockman, and M. Stone, editors, *Open sources: voices from the open source revolution.* O'Reilly, 1999.

[13] B. J. Rhodes and T. Starner. Remembrance agent. In *PAAM '96*, pages 487–495, 1996.

[14] G. Salton and M. J. McGill. *Introduction to Modern Information Retrieval.* McGraw-Hill, New York, 1983.

[15] S. E. Sim and R. C. Holt. The ramp-up problem in software projects: A case study of how software immigrants naturalize. In *ICSE 1998*, pages 361–370, 1998. IEEE Computer Society Press / ACM Press.

[16] M.-A. D. Storey, K. Wong, and H. A. Müller. How do program understanding tools affect how programmers understand programs? *Science of Computer Programming*, 36(2–3):183–207, Mar. 2000.

[17] R. J. Walker, G. C. Murphy, B. Freeman-Benson, D. Wright, D. Swanson, and J. Isaak. Visualizing dynamic software system information through high-level models. In *OOPSLA 1998*, pages 271–283, 1998. ACM Press.

[18] Y. Ye and G. Fischer. Information delivery in support of learning reusable software components on demand. In Y. Gil and D. B. Leake, editors, *IUI 2000*, pages 159–166, 2002. ACM Press.

Toward an Understanding of the Motivation of Open Source Software Developers

Yunwen Ye[1,2]
[1]*Department of Computer Science*
University of Colorado
Boulder, CO80309-0430, USA
yunwen@cs.colorado.edu

Kouichi Kishida[2]
[2]*SRA Key Technology Lab*
3-12 Yotsuya, Shinjuku
Tokyo 1600-0004, Japan
k2@sra.co.jp

Abstract

An Open Source Software (OSS) project is unlikely to be successful unless there is an accompanied community that provides the platform for developers and users to collaborate. Members of such communities are volunteers whose motivation to participate and contribute is of essential importance to the success of OSS projects. In this paper, we aim to create an understanding of what motivates people to participate in OSS communities. We theorize that learning is one of the motivational forces. Our theory is grounded in the learning theory of Legitimate Peripheral Participation, and is supported by analyzing the social structure of OSS communities and the co-evolution between OSS systems and communities. We also discuss practical implications of our theory for creating and maintaining sustainable OSS communities as well as for software engineering research and education.

1. Introduction

The wide success of Open Source Software (OSS) has recently attracted much attention. Software engineering researchers and commercial companies alike have been trying to learn lessons from the success of OSS and apply some of them to the development of proprietary and closed systems [1, 4, 12]. There are abundant lessons in OSS to be discovered and learned, but there is still very limited, if any, understanding of what motivates so many software developers to dedicate their time, skills, and knowledge to OSS systems with no monetary benefits.

Many definitions about OSS exist. In this paper, we define Open Source Software as those systems that give users free access to and the right to modify their source code. OSS grants not only developers but also all users, who are potential developers, the right to read and change its source code. Developers, users, and user-turned-developers form a *community of practice*. A community of practice is a group of people who are informally bounded by their common interest and practice in a specific domain. Community members regularly interact with each other for knowledge sharing and collaboration in pursuit of solutions to a common class of problems. An OSS project is unlikely to be successful unless there is an accompanied community that provides the platform for developers and users to collaborate with each other. Members of such communities are volunteers whose motivation to participate and contribute is of essential importance to the success of OSS projects.

This paper describes a conceptual framework to analyze the motivational issues in OSS. It argues that *learning is one of the major motivational forces* that attract software developers and users to participate in OSS development and to become members of OSS communities. The argument is grounded in the learning theory—*Legitimate Peripheral Participation (LPP)*, developed by Lave and Wenger [10]. The essential idea of LPP is that learning is situated in social situations, and learning takes place when members of a community of practice interact with each other in their daily practice.

The paper is organized as follows. To lay the foundation, Section 2 discusses the roles and structure of OSS communities in general, and Section 3 uses an example for further illustration. Section 4 introduces the theory of LPP. Section 5 elaborates our theory that learning is one of the motivational forces. Section 6 discusses the practical implications of our proposed theory, followed by a summary.

2. OSS Communities

The right to access and modify source code itself does not make OSS projects different from most "Closed Source Software" ones. All developers in a project in any software company would have the same access privilege. The fundamental difference is the *role transformation* of the people involved in a project. In Closed Source Software projects, developers and users are clearly defined and strictly separated. In OSS projects, there is no clear distinction between developers and users: all users are potential developers. Borrowing terms from programming languages, if we think of *developers* and

0-7695-1877-X/03 $17.00 © 2003 IEEE

users as types, and *persons* involved in a project as data objects, Closed Source Software projects are static-binding languages in which a *person* is bound to the type of *developer* or *user* statically, and OSS projects are dynamic-binding languages in which a *person* is bound to the type of *developer* or *user* dynamically, depending on his or her involvement with the project at a given time.

2.1. Roles in OSS Communities

The distinct feature of *role transformation* in OSS projects leads to a different social structure. People involved in a particular OSS project create a community around the project, bounded by their shared interest in using and/or developing the system. Members of an OSS community assume certain roles by themselves according to their personal interest in the project, rather than being assigned by someone else. Our previous research studying four different OSS projects has found that a member may have one of the following eight roles [13].

Project Leader. The Project Leader is often the person who has initiated the project. He or she is responsible for the vision and overall direction of the project.

Core Member. Core Members are responsible for guiding and coordinating the development of an OSS project. Core Members are those people who have been involved with the project for a relative long time and have made significant contributions to the development and evolution of the system. In those OSS projects that have evolved into their second generation, a single Project Leader no longer exists and the Core Members form a council to take the responsibility of guiding the development, such as the Apache Group and the PostgreSQL core group.

Active Developer. Active Developers regularly contribute new features and fix bugs; they are one of the major development forces of OSS systems.

Peripheral Developer. Peripheral Developers occasionally contribute new functionality or features to the existing system. Their contribution is irregular, and the period of involvement is short and sporadic.

Bug Fixer. Bug Fixers fix bugs that either they discover by themselves or are reported by other members. Bug Fixers have to read and understand a small portion of the source code of the system where the bug occurs.

Bug Reporter. Bug Reporters discover and report bugs; they do not fix the bugs themselves, and they may not read source code either. They assume the same role as testers of the traditional software development model. The existence of many Bug Reporters assures the high quality of OSS, because "given enough eyeballs, all bugs are shallow. [16]"

Reader. Readers are active users of the system; they not only use the system, but also try to understand how the system works by reading the source code. Given the high quality of OSS systems, some Readers read the systems to learn programming. Another group of Readers exists who read an OSS system not for the purpose of improving the system per se but for understanding its underlying model and then using the model as a reference model to implement similar systems [1].

Passive User. Passive Users just use the system in the same way as most of us use commercially available Closed Source Software. They are attracted to OSS mainly due to its high quality and the potential to be changed when needed.

Not all of the eight types of roles exist in all OSS communities, and the percentage of each type varies. Different OSS communities may use different names for the above roles. For example, some communities refer to Core Members as Maintainers. The difference between Bug Fixers and Peripheral Developers is rather small because Peripheral Developers might be mainly engaged in fixing bugs.

2.2. Community Structure

Although a strict hierarchical structure does not exist in OSS communities, the structure of OSS communities is not completely flat. The influences that members have on the system and the community are different, depending on the roles they play. Figure 1 depicts the general layered structure of OSS communities, in which the role closer to the center has a larger radius of influence. In other words, the activity of a Project Leader affects more members than that of a Core Member, who in turn has a larger influence than an Active Developer, and so on. Passive Users have the least influence, but they still play important roles in the whole community. Although they do not directly contribute to the development of the system technically, their very existence contributes socially and psychologically by attracting and motivating other, more active, members, to whom a large population of users is the utmost reward and flattery of their hard work [16]. Metaphorically speaking, those Passive Users play a role similar to that of the audience in a theatrical performance who offers values, recognition, and applause to the efforts of actors.

Each OSS community has a unique structure depending on the nature of the system and its member population. The structure of an OSS community differs in the percentage of each role in the whole community. In general, most members are Passive Users. For example, about 99% of people who use Apache are Passive Users. The percentage drops sharply from Readers to Core Members. Most systems are developed by a small number of developers [12, 14].

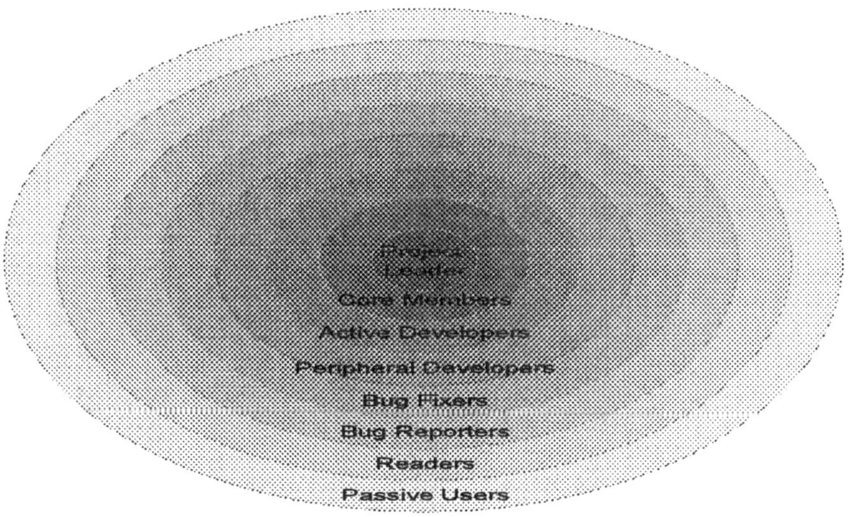

Figure 1: General structure of an OSS community

2.3. Co-evolution of OSS Systems and OSS Communities

The roles and their associated influences in OSS communities can be realized only through contributions to the community. Roles are not fixed: members can play larger roles if they aspire and make appropriate contributions. As members change the roles they play in an OSS community, they also change the social dynamics, and thus reshape the structure, of the community, resulting in the evolution of the community itself.

For an OSS project to have a sustainable development, the system and the community must co-evolve. A large base of voluntarily contributing members is one of the most important success factors of OSS. The evolution of an OSS community is effected by the contributions made by its aspiring and motivated members. Such contributions not only transform the role and influence of their contributors in the community and thus evolve the whole community, but also are the sources of the evolution of the system. The opposite is also true. Any modification, improvement, and extension made to an OSS system—whether it is a bug fix, a bug report, or a patch—not only evolves the system but also redefines the role of the contributing members and thus changes the social dynamics of the OSS community (Figure 2).

Unlike a project member in a software company whose role is determined by managers and remains unchanged for a long time until the member is promoted or leaves, the role that an OSS member plays in the community might constantly change, depending on how

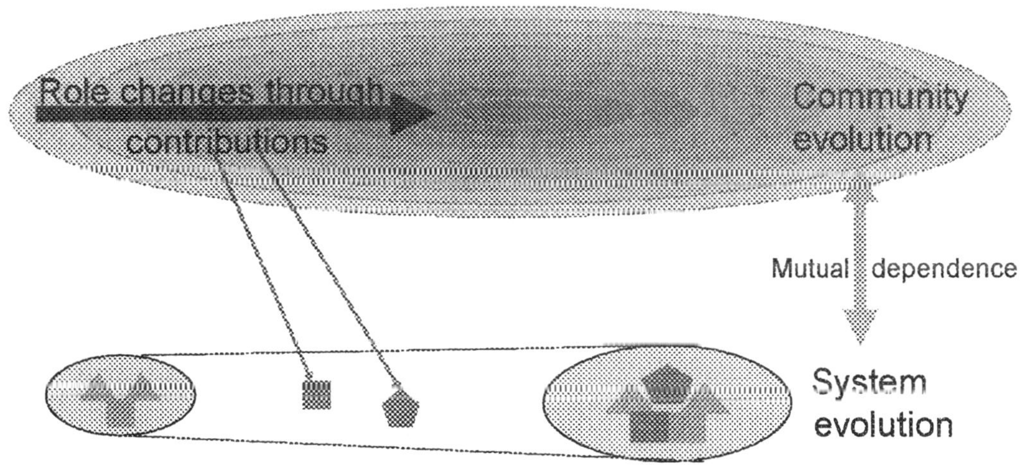

Figure 2: The co-evolution of OSS systems and OSS communities

much the member wants to get involved in the whole community. The role is not preassigned, and is assumed by the member as he or she interacts with other members. An aspiring and determined member can become a Core Member through the following path.

New members are attracted to an OSS community because the system can solve one of their own problems. The depth and richness of good OSS systems often drives motivated members to want to learn more, to read the system [18]. The new members now migrate from being Passive Users to being Readers. As they gain more understanding of the system, they are able to fix the bugs that are either encountered by themselves or reported by others. They may also want to add a new twist to the system to make the system more powerful and more suitable for their own tasks. As their developed programs are made publicly available to other community members, their roles as Bug Fixers and Peripheral Developers are recognized and established in the whole community. The more contributions they make, the higher recognition they earn, and finally, they will enter the highly selected "inner circle" of Core Members.

The above path describes an abstract and idealized model of role changes of aspiring members. Not all members want to and will become Core Members. Some are always Passive Users, and some stop somewhere in the middle. The important point is that Open Source Software makes it possible for an aspiring and technically capable software developer to play a larger role through continual contributions. On the other hand, for OSS projects to sustain, their communities have to be able to regenerate themselves through the contributions of their members and the emergence of new Core Members and Active Developers. Otherwise, the development of projects will stop when current active contributors leave. Because all OSS developers are volunteers who are not bound by any kind of formal contracts, they may leave at any moment for various reasons.

3. An Example—The GIMP Project

In this section, we use the GIMP (Gnu Image Manipulation Program, http://www.gimp.org) project as an example to illustrate the different roles in and the structure of an OSS community, as well as the co-evolution of OSS systems and OSS communities.

3.1. The GIMP System

GIMP is a system that processes images in Linux. The system was initially created by two students, Spencer Kimball and Peter Mattis, at the University of California at Berkeley. They released version 0.51 to public on Nov. 29, 1995. This version had a plug-in mechanism for other developers to add new features easily. It was not stable at that time, but because it was one of the earliest graphics manipulation programs in Linux, it attracted many users, some of whom became developers by contributing plug-ins and helping stabilize the system. A mailing list called GIMP-Developer was soon created to discuss and share those extensions. On June 9, 1997, Kimball and Mattis released version 0.99.10, which was their final release because they graduated, started full-time employment, and no longer had time to be involved in GIMP development. The absence of Project Leaders halted further development of GIMP for about 20 months. Finally, Federico Quintero, who had developed the Color Gradient Editor for GIMP since version 0.60, assumed the role of Project Leader by coordinating the efforts of other developers and making formal release, until he left for other OSS projects. At that time, the GIMP community had well developed, and a team of Core Members, who had made major contributions to the system for a long time, formed to control and coordinate the development effort.

3.2. The GIMP Community

Like most OSS communities, the GIMP community is a virtual community. It relies on the GIMP-Developer mailing list for interested users and developers to discuss the development and use of the system, to report bugs, and to submit patches for bug fixes and new features. Analyzing the emails sent to the mailing list is one way of understanding the structure of the community. 7525 emails were sent to the mailing list between August 31, 1999 and August 02, 2002, and 913 members sent at least one email. The largest number of emails a person has sent is 817, and 502 members have sent only one email. The member who sent the most emails is currently in charge of release. Table 1 shows the compositional structure of the GIMP community based on the email traffics in the GIMP-Developer mailing list.

Table 1: The frequency of emails sent by members to the mailing list

No. of emails	No. of members	Total no. of emails
> 200	5	2237
101 - 200	8	1197
51 - 100	10	695
26 - 50	29	1061
11 - 25	47	741
5 - 10	73	471
3 - 4	107	352
2	134	267
1	502	502
Total	915	7525

Table 2: Number of code contributions and the defined roles of contributing members

No. of contributions	No. of contributors	Breakdown of the contributors according to their defined roles in the GIMP community				
		Core Members	Active Developers	Peripheral Developers	Bug Fixers	Bug Reporters
>250	3	3	0	0	0	0
101-250	4	0	4	0	0	0
51-100	11	0	10	1	0	0
21-50	15	1	12	2	0	0
3-20	47	0	21	26	0	0
1-2	82	0	0	82	0	0
Not credited in change log	25	0	0	0	10	15
Total	**197**	**4**	**47**	**111**	**10**	**15**

Table 2 displays the number of code contributions made by members to the GIMP system and the defined roles of those contributing members. We counted the number of contributions made by each person by analyzing the change log of the system. 162 persons are formally credited for the development of the system core, and about half of them (82) made only one or two contributions. The bulk of the system has been developed by 18 persons, who each made more than 50 contributions and combined to contribute more than 71% of the changes of the code. However, because counting only the number of contributions does not differentiate the importance and quality of contributed code, the number itself, albeit an important indication, does not define the roles of contributors that are recognized by the community.

The GIMP community has a quite clear definition of roles. As we have mentioned before, because the two persons who initiated GIMP have left, all GIMP developers are the second generation and four Core Members are in charge of guiding the development and are responsible for public release; 47 Active Developers are granted write access to directly contribute to the source code tree; and 111 Peripheral Developers exist whose contributions must be integrated into the released systems by Core Members or Active Developers. 476 emails are directly related to bug reports and fixes and involve 106 members, among which 10 Bug Fixers and 15 Bug Reporters are not credited in the change log. It is possible that some of the Peripheral Developers are primary Bug Fixers, but we could not find data to differentiate their roles. Core Members are the most influential figures in the GIMP community because they are the final decision makers; Active Developers can directly modify the system, and the contributions made by Peripheral Developers and Bug Fixers must be approved by Active Developers or Core Members before they are integrated.

Table 3: The co-relation between community activity and code contribution in the GIMP project

ID	No. of emails	No. of contributions	Defined role	Role transformation process
g1	817	1244	Core Member	In charge of release after 2000/12
g2	601	111	Active Developer	One of the earliest contributing members
g3	345	95	Active Developer	Granted write access in 2001/1 after contributing 10 patches
g4	245	33	Peripheral Developer	Numerous patches
g5	229	32	Peripheral Developer	Patches; responsible for a separate project Gimp-Print, a print plugin for both GIMP, Ghostscript and other systems
g6	184	5	Peripheral Developer	Numerous patches
g7	179	70	Active Developer	Granted write access in 1999/9 after contributing 7 patches
g8	155	1038	Core Member	Become active developer in 1998/2 after contributing 10 patches, become core in 2001/11
g9	141	69	Active Developer	Granted write access in 1999/9 after contributing 6 patches
g10	140	60	Active Developer	Not active since 2001/6

3.3. The Co-Evolution of GIMP System and Community

Table 3 reveals the co-relation between the active participation in the GIMP-Developer mailing list and the contributions made to the GIMP system by showing the code contributions made by the 10 most active participants in the mailing list. It is easy to see that all of them are involved in the development of the system, and 7 of them are Core Members or Active Developers.

Table 3 also illustrates the role transformations of community members, as discussed in Section 2.3. For example, `g1` and `g8` were trusted to the Core Member status due to their continuous contributions to the system and the community. Most Active Developers have earned their status of directly committing source code after they had made many contributions in the form of submitting patches as Peripheral Developers (see `g3`, `g7`, `g8` and `g9`).

4. Legitimate Peripheral Participation

Before we proceed to argue that learning is one of the motivations that attracts many users to become active contributors and drive them to contribute more to OSS systems, we need to understand how learning takes place in communities of practice by introducing the theory of *Legitimate Peripheral Participation* developed by Lave and Wenger [10] based on their studies of several communities of practice.

Communities of practice embody knowledge that is often tacit in the practice of and interactions among competent practitioners. Schön describes such knowledge as *knowing-in-action*, which practitioners demonstrate spontaneously and intuitively in their action and reaction to the constantly changing context but are unable to describe [17]. Because knowing-in-action is highly situated in the context in which it is demonstrated, learning cannot be thought of as a process of gaining, through instruction, a discrete body of abstract knowledge that learners will then transport and reapply in later contexts. Instead, learning in community should be viewed as an integral constituent of participation in the community of practice, as a process of constructing knowing through social interaction with other members of the community, of changing relationships with other members of the community, and of transforming roles and establishing identities from a journeyman to a master in the community.

LPP locates learning in the transformation of roles learners assume in the participation of community practice. Learners experience learning not as a result of being taught, but through direct engagement in the social, cultural, and technical practice of the community. Learners' entering a community entails their *legitimate participation* in real practice as collaborative partners of more competent practitioners. During collaborative participation, learners are granted legitimate access to the knowing of masters that can only be observed and understood within its context. Due to the limited capability of learners, their full participation is impossible. At first, they can only *peripherally participate* in small and easy tasks. Through legitimate participation as peripheral participants, learners create their own learning curriculum by developing a global view of the community and what there is to be learned. Learning unfolds during the interaction and collaboration with not only the masters but also other learners. As learners gain more knowledge, they become competent in undertaking more important roles, resulting in changing relationships with other members and transforming their roles in the community. Gradually, they move toward the center of the community and eventually establish their identities as competent masters in the community.

LPP refers both to the role transformation and identity development of individual members from learners to masters, and to the reproduction and evolution of the community. A community is a social unity defined by the coupling relations among its members, practice, and the outside world. The ontogenetic development of the identity of new members—from entrance as learners to becoming masters with respect to new learners who also become masters over time—changes their relations with the community as well as the relations among other members, resulting in the evolution, or the phylogenic development, of the community. The identity of the community is conserved and reproduced through the ontogenetic development of its new members who learn via legitimate peripheral participation and become masters that embody the mature practice and structural characteristics of the community.

The intertwined relationship between the ontogenetic development of the identity of an individual member and the conservation of the identify of community provides an anchor to understand the altruistic behaviors that so many OSS developers have demonstrated by contributing their time and knowledge for the benefit of the whole community. By establishing their own identities or shaping the identities of others through voluntary participation in the community practice, members help reproduce and preserve the community. This process is also in their own interests because their identity, skills, and reputation as master rely on the continuous existence of the community. Therefore, from the perspective of the community to which each member belongs, an individual's altruistic behavior is "altruistically" selfish and "selfishly" altruistic [11].

5. Learning as the Motivation

Without software developers who are motivated to start and contribute to OSS projects, OSS projects cannot succeed. Factors that affect motivation are both intrinsic (cognitive) and extrinsic (social). The precondition for motivating developers to get involved in OSS projects is that they must derive an intrinsic satisfaction in their involvement in OSS projects. Relying purely on altruism makes OSS unsustainable. Intrinsic motivation is positively reinforced and amplified when social structure and conventions of the community recognize and reward the contributions of its members.

Raymond has postulated that "scratching a personal itch" is the intrinsic motivation for OSS developers [16]. Although many developers get involved in OSS development due to the need for functionality, many OSS developers are not motivated by utility only. For example, neither Kimball nor Mattis, who started the GIMP project, had any graphic arts needs. They did not start the project because they wanted to use it [7].

We argue that learning is one of the driving forces that motivate developers to get involved in OSS projects because it provides the intrinsic satisfaction for OSS developers, and the role transformation in OSS communities that go along with learning offers the extrinsic motivation.

Software systems are cognitive artifacts whose creation is a process of knowledge construction that requires both creativity and a wide variety of knowledge about problem domains, logic, computer, and others. In this sense, software systems, like books, are a form of knowledge media. Many OSS systems come into existence as results of the learning efforts of their original developers who try to understand how to model, or to change, the world with computational systems, as we will explain in Section 5.1. When the source code become accessible to users, the knowledge and creativity therein also become accessible, providing the initial learning resource that attracts users to form a community of practice around the system. By participating in the community, developers and users learn from the system, from each other, and share their learning with each other, as we will discuss in detail in Section 5.2.

5.1. Learning Experience of OSS Initiators

Initiators of new OSS projects may be motivated by *explorative learning* or *learning by doing*. These two forms of learning are not mutually exclusively; they may exist simultaneously to inspire the initiation of an OSS project.

Explorative learning. This form of learning is similar to most scientific research in which learners (e.g., scientists, practitioners) attempt to find new ways of doing things or of overcoming an existing problem. OSS systems are viewed by GNU developers as "scientific knowledge to be shared among mankind" [6]. Larry Wall started Perl because he ran into a problem he couldn't solve with existing tools, and he wanted to explore a way of doing things better [20]. Similarly, John Ousterhout initiated his Tcl/Tk project because he wanted to create a reusable tool command language for his many research systems [15]. Atsushi Aoki started Jun—a Smalltalk and Java library for manipulating 3D graphics and multimedia data, because he wanted to explore the possibility of handling both geometry and topology of 3D graphics [1].

Learning by doing. In this form of learning, the learners want to deepen their understanding of a certain domain by actually engaging in practical tasks that allow them to apply their existing knowledge and to perfect their current skills. By definition, hackers, who are behind almost every OSS systems, are people who enjoy "exploring the details of programmable systems and how to stretch their capabilities" through programming rather than theorizing [1]. Linus Torvalds started Linux partially because he wanted to learn more about the architecture of Intel 386, and the perfect way of doing so was to develop an operating system for it [3]. Peter Mattis described his "original impetus for GTK was simply (his) wanting to understand how to write a UI toolkit" [7].

5.2. Learning Experience of Later Participants

When the results of the above, more often than not, individual learning efforts are distributed in the form of open source, they provide resources and opportunities for other developers to learn. Most developers who start an OSS project are master programmers, and their systems are the products of fine craftsmanship and examples of excellent programming practice. When those systems are freely distributed, they grant developers in the world the *legitimate* access to the skill and knowledge embedded in such systems. Similar to the way that we learn to write by reading literature, reading existing source code of expert programmers is a powerful path to the mastery of programming art. We believe that many developers are attracted to OSS projects because they want to learn something. As Michael Tiemann, founder of Cygnus, put it: "It was this depth and richness that drove me to want to learn more, to read the GNU Emacs Manual and the GNU Emacs source code. [18]" We also believe that OSS participants learn a lot from their OSS experience. As Patrick Volkerding, creator of the Slackware distribution of Linux, commented: "My experience with Linux has taught me a lot of valuable skills. It looks like the project has saved me from a life of COBOL. What more could I ask for than that? [8]"

The learning experience of later participants of OSS projects does not stop at passive absorption by reading source code; it also happens when new participants engage in bug reports, maintenance, and further development of OSS projects. In most cases, new

[1] Jargon Dictionary, available at http://info.astrian.net/jargon/terms/.

participants do not become Core Members suddenly. As we have analyzed in Section 2.3 conceptually and illustrated in detail with the GIMP example in Section 3, they have to earn their status and recognition in the community gradually by making small contributions at first. In other words, they start with *peripheral participation* by, for example, reporting and fixing bugs. By doing so, they learn by doing and their skills improve. As their skills are gradually recognized in the community based on their contributions, they are trusted to bigger and more challenging tasks, and move toward the "inner circle" of the community, becoming competent full participants and exerting larger influence (Figure 2).

Active participation of new members creates opportunities for them to interact with other more knowledgeably skilled developers, and gives them *legitimate* access to the expertise therein. The existence of OSS communities enables new participants to ask questions about a variety of aspects of the OSS systems and to acquire help in using, understanding, modifying, and extending the systems. One study on the communication patterns of the FreeBSD Newconfig project has found that 18.8% of the emails in the mailing list of the project are questions, and 49.9% of the emails are responses that include answers to questions, agreement, disagreement, and additional information [21]. Questions and answers are also very common in the GIMP-Developer mailing list. Such communities create social networks of knowledge in which all participants share their knowledge and learn from each other.

Another major function of the mailing list is to provide a platform for developers to discuss the functionality, design, and implementation of the system. In other words, the mailing list displays the ongoing process of creating the product. The process is yet another learning resource for newcomers, who are given the opportunity not only to see how the system is developed as it is being developed, but to understand the culture of the community and make it theirs by observing how skilled developers talk, work, and collaborate with each other.

5.3. Social Aspects of Extrinsic Motivations

The social fabric inherent in OSS communities reinforces the intrinsic motivation for participating in OSS projects as a form of learning. Only in a society where technical supremacy is highly appreciated can developers acquire good reputations among their peers by displaying their skills through free distribution, and often wider acceptance, of their systems. The good reputation attracts attention, trust, and cooperation from others and lays the foundation for advancing the original developers' agenda and the establishment and development of OSS communities.

Members close to the center of the community (Figure 1) enjoy better visibility and reputations than do peripheral members. The road to the core has to be paved by contributing more to the project and interacting more with their members (Figure 2). As new members contribute to the system and the community, they are rewarded with higher recognition and trust in the community, and higher influence as well. In the GIMP community, most developers who have contributed a lot are given the right to directly contribute to the system. Some even become Core Members.

Rewarding contributing members with higher recognition and more important roles is also important for the sustainability of the community and the system development, because it is the way that the community reproduces itself (Section 4). In the GIMP community, 29 Active Developers have not been active for at least a year, but the community is still prospering because many new developers have become competent participants along the path of LPP. From the log of source code commitments, we have found that 25 developers started contributing code in the recent two years.

5.4. An Oriental Perspective

The viewpoint of learning as a motivation that intrinsically drives people to get involved in OSS development and that extrinsically rewards them with higher social status and larger influence in OSS communities is in parallel with a tradition of Eastern culture. Intellectual property is a very new concept in Eastern culture; instead, scholars have long pursued intellectual prevalence by commanding high recognition and respect from the people, especially the ruling class and intelligentsia, through the free distribution of their writings. Writings are treated as the heritage and public assets of the whole society and they are free to all. More importantly, all writings are open to interpretation. In fact, most scholars build their own theory and knowledge by commenting and annotating the writings of earlier scholars while they are reading. Although comments and annotations are often the products of the scholars' own efforts of understanding, assessing, and learning the writings produced by others, they become free learning resources and inspire further modifications and interpretations. The hallmark of an established scholar is the authority of interpreting the writings of a well-respected ancient scholar (e.g. Confucius), and only those who can integrate the ideas of their ancestors and contemporaries alike and convince others with their freely distributed writings can acquire such status.

6. Discussions

Realizing that learning is one of the major driving forces for OSS development has practical implications in managing OSS projects and raises several questions in software engineering education and research.

6.1. Creating Opportunities for LPP

Learning through LPP is not a result of direct and intentional teaching; instead, it is enabled by legitimate participation in practice and legitimate access to learning resources—products and process—available in the community. The openness of the produced system, the development process, and the communications among members in OSS communities enables learning by watching and invites learning by doing, and thereby is directly related to the learning experience of the people involved [9]. Although all OSS communities are open to certain forms of participation and access, the different control structure inherent in each OSS community due to considerations of system quality [13] creates different degrees of openness that allows the legitimate participation and access of community members.

Table 4 shows the possible combinations of openness in two dimensions: product (row) and process (column). In the product dimension, *open release* means that only formally released versions are accessible to all community members; and *open development* means that all interim developing versions are accessible. In the process dimension, *closed process* means that the discussion of system development is conducted mostly within the "inner circle", often through a strictly controlled mailing list which is not accessible to other members; *transparent process* means that although only the "inner circle" is involved in the development process, but their discussion is readable by other members; *open process* means that the development decision is conducted in public space, allowing the participation and access of all interested parties. To encourage learning-motivated participation requires the highest degree of openness in both dimensions because it offers more learning resources. However, it may also reduce the Project Leader's control over the system. This conflict needs to be balanced by those who want to make their systems open source.

The possibility for newcomers to participate peripherally is another key point in LPP. To attract more users to become developers, the system architecture must be designed in a modularized way to create many relatively independent tasks with progressive difficulty so that newcomers can start to participate peripherally and move on gradually to take charge of more difficult tasks. The way a system is partitioned has consequences for both the efficiency of parallel development—a prerequisite to OSS—and for the efficiency of knowledge acquisition. This adds an extra dimension of importance to the modularity of software systems because it ensures the possibility of legitimate peripheral participation of new members. The plug-in architecture of GIMP is quite effective in engaging new developers. Linux could not be such successful without its well designed modularity [19].

Table 4: Openness of OSS communities

	Open release	**Open development**
Closed process	GNU; Jun	APACHE
Transparent process	Tcl/Tk	PostgreSQL
Open process		GIMP

Another approach to afford peripheral participation is to intentionally under-design the system by leaving some non-critical parts unimplemented to facilitate easy participation. The TODO list most OSS systems have creates guidance for participation. Rather than just listing TODO items, grouping them according to their estimated difficulty might provide a better roadmap for newcomers to start participation at periphery.

6.2. Advice for OSS Practitioners

Developers at the center of OSS communities should not only focus on the development of the system itself, but also pay enough attention to the creation and maintenance of a dynamic and self-reproducing OSS community. Core Members and Active Developers should also strive to create an environment and culture that fosters the sense of belonging to the community and mechanisms that encourage and enable newcomers to move toward the center of the community through continual contributions. It is very important for the community to be responsive to the questions and contributions of newcomers to sustain their interest and encourage their further participation. Old members should remember that they are also the learning resources for newcomers. One possible mechanism is to have skilled members take turns in the mailing list to answer questions of newcomers, to help new contributors perfect their code contributions.

People who want to start an OSS project need to consider how many learning opportunities it offers, and how easy it is for others to participate legitimately and peripherally. For example, a system developed with COBOL is probably less attractive to OSS developers than a system developed with Java because the demands for COBOL developers are much lower in today's world. A system with large size and cumbersome architecture, such as the early version of Mozilla, is also difficult to attract OSS participants [2].

6.3. Impacts on Education and Research

The existence of many OSS projects provides a possibility for educators to change the way of educating and training new software professionals in schools [5]. By integrating OSS projects with university classes, students are given the chance to learn programming by reading the existing systems developed by world-class professionals. At the same time, they can work together with skilled developers and gain practical experience in developing systems of industry scale and strength. From such collaborations, students also acquire the communication skills of presenting ideas effectively and of taking feedback from other developers, which are essential in practical development settings that invariably require teamwork. Moreover, introducing students into OSS projects will foster the next generation of OSS developers and sustain the further development of the OSS movement.

Given the importance of learning in OSS communities, the importance of the skill of reading programs and tools that support program reading and understanding should be stressed more [1]. Current software engineer education and research focuses mostly on system writing. However, as we all know from our language learning experience, to become good writers, we have to learn to read first, and read a great amount of good literature.

7. Summary

In this paper, we have tried to create an understanding of what motivates people to participate in OSS development. We applied the LPP theory to understand how to form and sustain OSS communities that are essential to the success of OSS projects. We argued that learning is one of the major driving forces that motivate people to get involved in OSS communities. We discussed how our theory can inform software engineering researchers and OSS practitioners.

OSS is a very complicated phenomenon that is related to technology, human behaviors, economics, culture, and society. We do not claim that our theory clarifies all those complicated, intertwined relationships, but we do believe that it creates a better theoretical understanding of OSS from a new analytical angel, and provides practical guide to the management and development of OSS projects.

Acknowledgment.
The authors thank Kumiyo Nakakoji and Yasuhiro Yamamoto for their valuable feedback. The research was supported by the National Science Foundation, Software Engineering and Language Program, Grant CCR-0204277.

References

[1] Aoki, A., K. Hayashi, K. Kishida, K. Nakakoji, Y. Nishinaka, B. Reeves, A. Takashima, and Y. Yamamoto. "A Case Study of the Evolution of Jun: An Object-Oriented Open-Source 3D Multimedia Library," in *Proceedings of 23rd International Conference on Software Engineering (ICSE'01)* (Toronto, Canada, 2001), IEEE Press, 524-533.

[2] Baker, M., *The Mozilla Project and Mozilla.org*, at http://www.mozilla.org/editorials/mozilla-overview.html, accessed on 2/11, 2002

[3] DiBona, C., S. Ockman, and M. Stone. eds. *Open Sources: Voices from the Open Source Revolution*. 1999, O'Reilly & Associates: Sebastopol, CA.

[4] Dinkelacker, J., P.K. Garg, R. Miller, and D. Nelson. "Progressive Open Source," in *Proceedings of 24th International Conference on Software Engineering (ICSE'02)* (Orlando, FL., 2002), ACM Press, 177-186.

[5] Dvorak, G. "Collective Education," *Ubiquity*, 2001. **2**(16): http://www.acm.org/ubiquity/views/g_dvorak_1.html

[6] FSF, *GNU Philosophy*, at http://www.gnu.org/philosophy/philosophy.html, accessed on 2/11, 2002

[7] HackVan, S., *Where Did Spencer Kimball and Peter Mattis Go?*, at http://devlinux.com/, accessed on 2/11, 2002

[8] Hughes, P. "Interview with Patrick Volkerding," *Linux Journal*, 1994. **1994**(2es): 3.

[9] Hutchins, E. *Cognition in the Wild*. The MIT Press, Cambridge, MA, 1994.

[10] Lave, J., and E. Wenger. *Situated Learning: Legitimate Peripheral Participation*. Cambridge University Press, Cambridge, UK, 1991.

[11] Maturana, H.R., and F.J. Varela. *The Tree of Knowledge: The Biological Roots of Human Understanding*. Shambhala Publicaions, Boston, MA, 1998.

[12] Mockus, A., R. Fielding, and J. Herbsleb. "A Case Study of Open Source Software Development: The Apache Server," in *Proceedings of 2000 International Conference on Software Engineering (ICSE2000)* (Limerick, Ireland, 2000), 263-272.

[13] Nakakoji, K., Y. Yamamoto, Y. Nishinaka, K. Kishida, and Y. Ye. "Evolution Patterns of Open-Source Software Systems and Communities," in *Proceedings of International Workshop on Principles of Software Evolution (IWPSE 2002)* (Orlando, FL, 2002), 76-85.

[14] O'Reilly, T. "Lessons from Open-Source Software Development," *Commun. ACM*, 1999. **42**(4): 33-37.

[15] Ousterhout, J. "Scripting: Higher Level Programming for the 21st Century," *IEEE Computer*, 1998. **31**(3): 23-30.

[16] Raymond, E.S., and B. Young. *The Cathedral and the Bazaar: Musings on Linux and Open Source by an Accidental Revolutionary*. O'Reilly, Sebastopol, CA, 2001.

[17] Schön, D.A. *The Reflective Practitioner: How Professionals Think in Action*. Basic Books, New York, 1983.

[18] Tiemann, M. "Future of Cygnus Solutions," in *Open Sources: Voices from the Open Source Revolution*, DiBona, C., S. Ockman, and M. Stone. (eds.), O'Reilly, Sebastopol, 1999, 71-89.

[19] Torvalds, L. "The Linux Edge," *Commun. ACM*, 1999. **42**(4): 38-39.

[20] Wall, L. "The Origin of the Camel Lot in the Breakdown of the Bilingual Unix," *Commun. ACM*, 1999. **42**(4): 40-41.

[21] Yamaguchi, Y., M. Yokozawa, T. Shinohara, and T. Ishida. "Collaboration with Lean Media: How Open-Source Software Succeeds," in *Proceedings of 2000 International Conference on Computer Supported Cooperative Work (CSCW'00)* (Philadelphia, PA, 2000), ACM Press, 329-338.

Tools for Understanding the Behavior of Telecommunication Systems

André Marburger
Aachen University of Technology
Department of Computer Science III
Ahornstraße 55, 52074 Aachen, Germany
marand@cs.rwth-aachen.de

Bernhard Westfechtel
Aachen University of Technology
Department of Computer Science III
Ahornstraße 55, 52074 Aachen, Germany
westfechtel@cs.rwth-aachen.de

Abstract

Many methods and tools for the reengineering of software systems have been developed so far. However, the domain-specific requirements of telecommunication systems have not been addressed sufficiently. These systems are designed in a process- rather than in a data-centered way. Furthermore, analyzing and visualizing dynamic behavior is a key to system understanding. In this paper, we report on tools for the reengineering of telecommunication systems which we have developed in close cooperation with an industrial partner. These tools are based on a variety of techniques for understanding behavior such as visualization of link chains, recovery of state diagrams from the source code, and visualization of traces by different kinds of diagrams. Tool support has been developed step by step in response to the requirements and questions stated by telecommunication experts at Ericsson Eurolab Germany.

1. Introduction

Reengineering of large and complex software systems has proved a difficult task. According to the "horseshoe model of reengineering" [4, 10], reengineering is divided into three phases. *Reverse engineering* is concerned with step-wise abstraction from the source code and system comprehension. In the *restructuring* phase, changes are performed on different levels of abstraction. Finally, *forward engineering* introduces new parts of the system (from the requirements down to the source code level).

For reengineering, many methods and tools have been developed. To a large extent, however, previous work has been *data-centered* since it focuses on structuring the data maintained by an application. In particular, numerous approaches have addressed the migration of legacy business applications — written, e.g., in COBOL — to an object-based or object-oriented architecture [5, 15, 23]. This task requires the grouping of data and functions into classes with corresponding attributes and methods. Another stream of research has dealt with programming languages such as C++ and Java which already provide language support for object-oriented programming [17].

Reengineering of *process-centered* applications has been addressed less extensively so far [25]. For example, a telecommunication system is composed of a set of distributed communicating processes which are instantiated dynamically for handling calls requested by its users. Such a system is designed in terms of services provided by entities which communicate according to protocols. Understanding a telecommunication system requires the recovery of this conceptual world from the actual source code and other sources of information.

The *E-CARES*[1] research cooperation between Ericsson Eurolab Deutschland GmbH (EED) and Department of Computer Science III, Aachen University of Technology, has been established to develop methods, concepts, and tools for the reengineering of complex legacy telecommunication systems. E-CARES has been driven strongly by the requirements of software engineers who are involved in the design and implementation of GSM networks for mobile communication. The subject of study is Ericsson's Mobile-service Switching Center (MSC) for GSM networks called AXE10. The AXE10 software system comprises approximately 10 million lines of code spread over about 1,000 executable units, and has an estimated lifetime of about 40 years. Thus, there is an urgend need for tool support to improve program evolution and maintenance.

In E-CARES, a prototypical environment — called *E-CARES prototype* [14] — is being developed which addresses the reengineering of telecommunication systems. So far, tool support covers only reverse engineering, i.e., the first phase of reengineering. While *structural analysis* is covered as well, we put strong emphasis on *behavioral analysis* since the structure alone is not very expressive in the case of a telecommunication system.

[1] *E*ricsson *C*ommunication *AR*chitecture for *E*mbedded *S*ystems [13]

0-7695-1877-X/03 $17.00 © 2003 IEEE

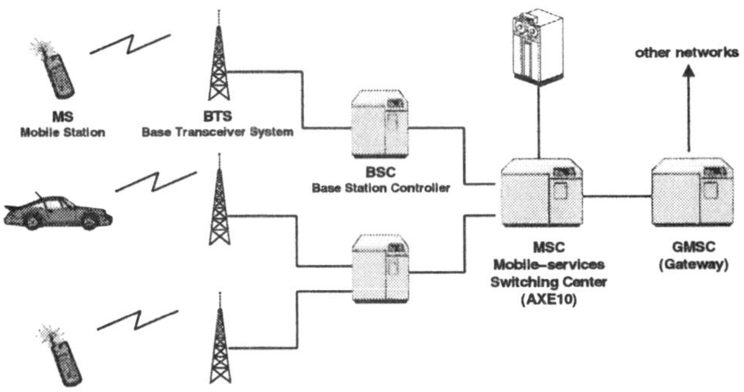

Figure 1. Simplified sketch of a GSM network

The rest of this paper is structured as follows: Section 2 motivates our research and explains its background. Section 3 gives an overview of the E-CARES prototype. Section 4 briefly describes structural analysis. Section 5, the core part of this paper, presents a variety of techniques which support the understanding of behavior. Section 6 introduces metrics — for both structure and behavior — which further improve the understanding of telecommunication systems. Section 7 discusses related work, and Section 8 concludes this paper.

2. Background

The *mobile-service switching centers* are the heart of a GSM network (Figure 1). An MSC provides the services a person can request by using a mobile phone, e.g., a simple phone call, a phone conference, or a data call, as well as additional infrastructure like authentication. Each MSC is supported by several Base Station Controllers (BSC), each of which controls a set of Base Station Transceivers (BTS). The interconnection of MSCs and the connection to other networks (e.g., public switched telecommunication networks) is provided by gateway MSCs (GMSC). In fact, the MSC is the most complex part of a GSM network. An MSC consists of a mixture of hardware (e.g., switching boards) and software units. In our research we focus on the software part of this embedded system.

Figure 2 illustrates how a *mobile originating call* is handled in the MSC. The figure displays logical rather than physical components according to the GSM standard; different logical components may be mapped onto the same physical component. The mobile originating MSC (MSC-MO) for the A side (1) passes an initial address message (IAM) to a GMSC which (2) sends a request for routing information to the home location register (HLR). The HLR looks up the mobile terminating MSC (MSC-MTE) and (3) sends a request for the roaming number. The MSC-MTE

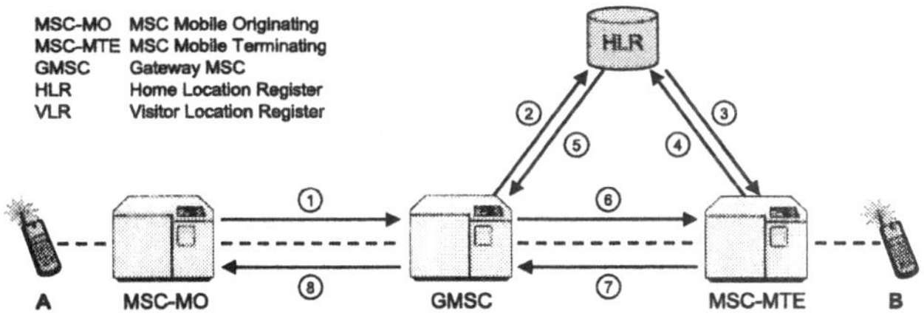

Figure 2. Mobile originating call

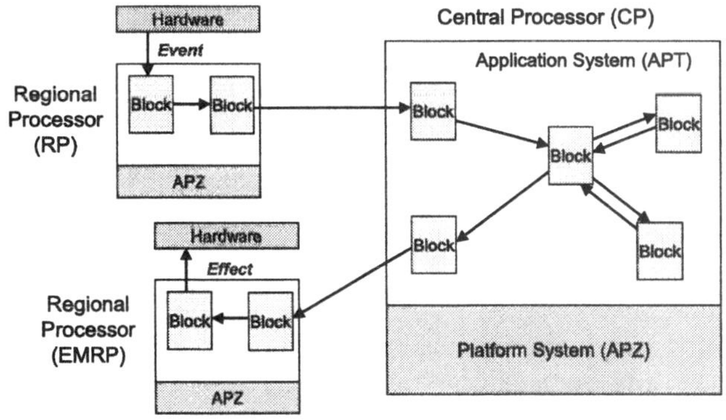

Figure 3. System architecture

assigns a roaming number to be used for addressing during the call and stores it in its visitor location register (VLR, not shown). Then, it (4) passes the roaming number back to the HLR which (5) sends the requested routing information to the GMSC. After that, the GMSC (6) sends a call request to the MSC-MTE. The MSC (7) returns an address complete message (ACM) which (8) is forwarded to the MSC-MO. Now, user data may be transferred between A and B.

Ericsson's implementation of the MSC is called *AXE10*, whose *system architecture* is shown in Figure 3. Each MSC has a central processor which is connected to a set of regional processors for controlling various hardware devices by sensors and actors. The core of the processing is performed on the central processor. The AXE10 software is composed of blocks which constitute units of functionality and communicate by exchanging signals (see below). On each processor, a runtime system (called APZ) is installed which controls the execution of all blocks executing on this processor. An event raised by some hardware device is passed from the regional processor to the block handling this event on the central processor. In response to the event, an effect may be triggered on another hardware device.

The executable units of the AXE10 software system are implemented in Ericsson's in-house programming language *PLEX* (*P*rogramming *L*anguage for *EX*changes), which was developed in about 1970 and has been extended since then. PLEX is an asynchronous concurrent real-time language designed for programming of telecommunication systems.

The programming language has a *signaling paradigm* as the top execution level. That is, only events can trigger code execution. Events are programmed as signals.

A PLEX program is composed of a set of *blocks* which are compiled independently. Each block consists of a number of sectors for data declarations, program statements, etc. (see Figure 8, which will be explained more thoroughly in Section 5). Although PLEX does not support any further structuring within these sectors, we have identified some additional structuring through coding conventions in the program sector. At the beginning of the program sector all signal reception statements (*signal entries*) of a block are coded. After these signal entry points, a number of *labeled statement sequences* follows. The bottom part of the program sector consists of *subroutines*.

The control flow inside a program sector is provided by `goto` and `call` statements. The `goto` statement is used to jump to a label of a labeled statement sequence. Subroutines are accessed by means of `call` statements. Both `goto` and `call` statements are parameter-less. That is, they affect only the control flow, but not the data flow.

Inter-block communication and data transport is provided by different kinds of *signals*. As every block has data encapsulation, signals are able to carry data. Therefore, signals may affect both the control flow and the data flow.

At runtime, every block can create several *instances* (processes). This again is not a feature of the PLEX programming language but achieved by means of implementation tricks and coding conventions. Therefore, these instances are managed by the block and not by the runtime environment.

3. E-CARES prototype

In the E-CARES project, we design and implement tools for reengineering of telecommunication systems and apply them to the AXE10 system developed at Ericsson. The basic architecture of the E-CARES prototype is outlined in Figure 4. The solid parts indicate the current state of realization, the dashed parts refer to further extensions.

Below, it is crucial to distinguish between the following kinds of analysis: *Structural analysis* refers to the static system structure, while *behavioral analysis* is concerned with its dynamic behavior. Thus, the attributes "structural" and "behavioral" denote the outputs of analysis. In contrast, *static analysis* denotes any analysis which can be performed on the source code, while *dynamic analysis* requires information from program execution. Thus, "static" and "dynamic" refer to the inputs of analysis. In particular, behavior can be analyzed both statically and dynamically.

We obtained three sources of information for the static analysis of the structure of a PLEX system. The first one is the *source code* of the system. It is considered to be the core information as well as the most reliable one. Through code analysis (parsing) a number of structure documents is generated from the source code, one for each block. These structure documents form a kind of textual graph description. The second and the third source of information are *miscellaneous documents* (e.g., product hierarchy description) and the system *documentation*. As far as the information from these sources is computer processable, we use parsers and scripts to extract additional information, which is stored in structure documents, as well.

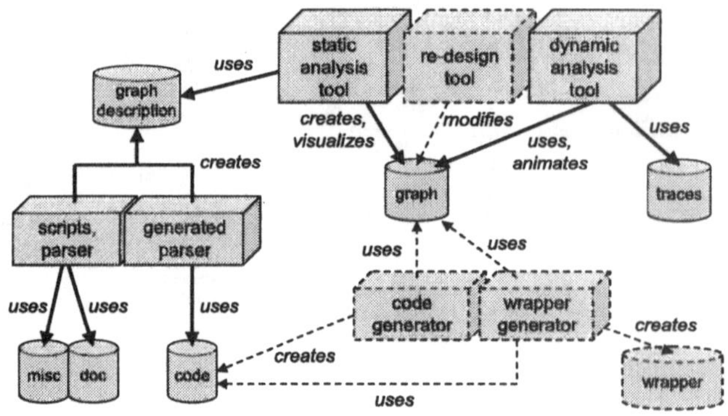

Figure 4. Prototype architecture

The *static analysis tool* processes the graph descriptions for individual blocks and creates corresponding subgraphs of the structure graph representing the overall application. The subgraphs are connected by performing global analyses in order to bind signal send statements to signal entry points. Moreover, the subgraphs for each block are reduced by performing simplifying graph transformations [13]. The static analysis tool also creates views of the system at different levels of abstraction. In addition to structure, static analysis is concerned with behavior (e.g., extraction of state machines or of potential link chains from the source code).

There are two possibilities to obtain dynamic information: using an emulator or querying a running AXE10. In both cases, the result is a list of events plus additional information in a temporal order. Such a list constitutes a *trace* which is fed into the *dynamic analysis tool*. Interleaved with trace simulation, dynamic analysis creates a graph of interconnected block instances that is connected to the static structure graph. This helps telecommunication experts to identify components of a system that take part in a certain traffic case. At the user interface, traces are visualized by collaboration and sequence diagrams.

Both the static and the dynamic analysis tool calculate *metrics* which were designed to improve the understanding of both structure and behavior. These metrics are visualized e.g. in the underlying structure graph (see Section 6).

The dashed parts of Figure 4 represent planned extensions of the current prototype. The *re-design tool* will be used to map structure graph elements to elements of a modeling language (e.g., ROOM [20] or SDL [8]). This will result in an architecture graph that can be used to perform architectural changes to the AXE10 system. The *code generator* will generate PLEX code according to changes in the structure graph and/or the architecture graph. The *wrapper generator* will enable reuse of existing parts of the AXE10 system written in PLEX in a future switching system that is written in a different programming language, e.g., C++.

To reduce the effort of implementing the E-CARES prototype, we make extensive use of generators and reusable frameworks [14]. Scanners and parsers are generated with the help of JLex and jay, respectively. Graph algorithms are written in PROGRES [19], a specification language based on programmed graph transformations. From the specification, code is generated which constitutes the application logic of the E-CARES prototype. The user interface is implemented with the help of UPGRADE [1], a framework for building interactive tools for visual languages.

4. Structural analysis

The static structure of a PLEX program is represented internally by a *structure graph*, a small (and simplified) example of which is shown in Figure 5[2]. In the example, there is a subsystem which contains two blocks A and B. The subgraphs for these blocks are created by the PLEX parser. The subgraph for a block — the block structure graph — contains nodes for signal entry points, labels, (contiguous) statement sequences, subroutines, exit statements, etc. Thus, the block structure graph shows which signals may be processed by the block, which statement sequences are executed to process these signals, which subroutines are used for processing, etc. In addition, the block structure graph initially contains nodes representing outgoing signals. Subsequently, a global analysis is carried out to bind outgoing signals to receiving blocks based on name identity. In our example, a signal H is sent in the statement sequence X of block A. This signal is bound to the entry point of block B. From the signal edges between statement sequences and signal entry points, more coarse-grained communication edges may be derived (between blocks and eventually between subsystems).

Externally (at the user interface), the structure graph is represented by multiple *views* [13]. The product hierarchy is displayed in a *tree view*. Furthermore, there is a variety of *graphical views* which display the structure graph at different levels of abstraction (internals of a block, block communication within a subsystem, communication between subsystems). For example, Figure 13 shows block communications within a subsystem of AXE10 (see Section 6 for further explanations). The user may select among a set of different, customizable layout algorithms to arrange graphical representations in a meaningful way. He may also collapse and expand sets of nodes to adjust the level of detail. Graph elements representing code fragments are connected to the respective source code regions, which may be displayed on demand in *text views*.

[2]For the time being, please ignore all graph elements for link chains (lc), which will be explained in Section 5.

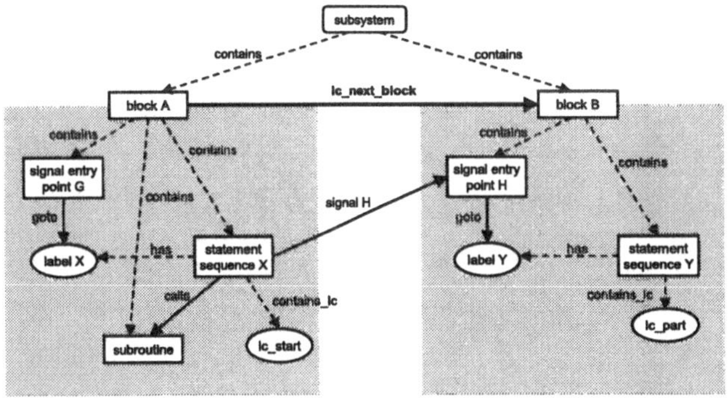

Figure 5. Cut-out of a structure graph

5. Behavioral analysis

5.1. Motivation

As stated in Section 1, we found that the static system structure is not very expressive in the case of telecommunication systems. These highly dynamic, flexible, and reactive systems handle thousands of different calls at the same time. The numerous services provided by a telecommunication system are realized by re-combining and re-connecting sets of small (stand alone) processes, block instances in our case, at runtime. Each of these *block instances* realizes a certain kind of (internal) mini-service. Some of the blocks can even create instances for different mini-services dependent on the role they have to play in a certain scenario.

Therefore, structural analysis as described in Section 4 is not sufficient to understand telecommunication systems. For example, the structure graph does not contain any information on how many instances of a single block are used to set up a simple phone call. In Figure 6, a so-called *link chain* for the GSM-layer 3 part of a simple mobile originating call is sketched. Link chains describe how block instances are combined at runtime to realize a certain service. Each node represents a block instance. An edge between two nodes indicates signal interchange between these blocks. Each link chain consists of a main part (directed edges) and side-links for supplementary services (authentication, charging, etc.). The directed edges between elements of the main link chain indicate its establishment from left to right; communication is bidirectional in all cases. In correspondence to

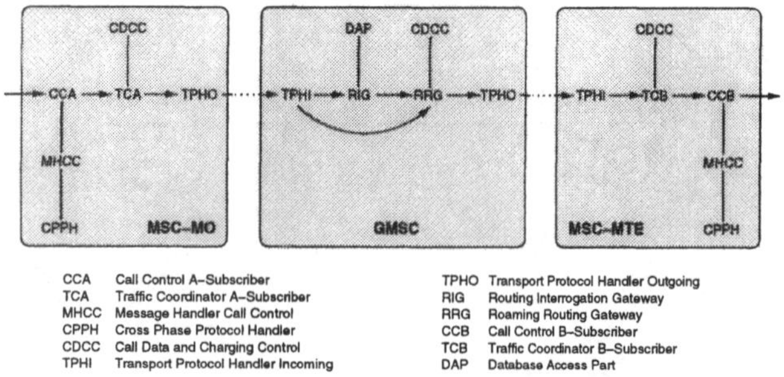

Figure 6. Simplified link chain for mobile originating call at GSM-layer 3

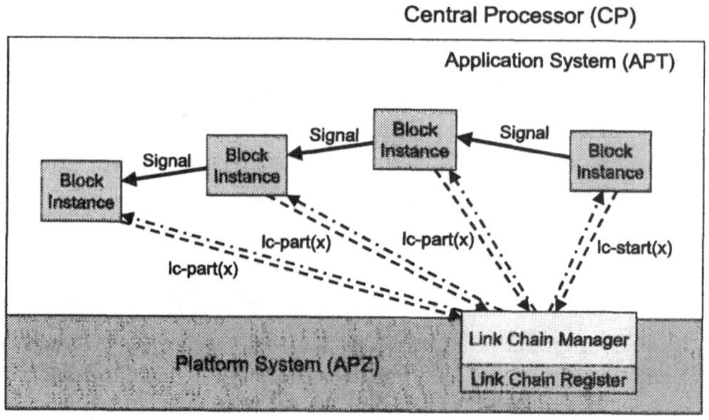

Figure 7. Link chain handling

Figure 2, the link chain in Figure 6 is divided into the three parts MSC-MO, GMSC, and MSC-MTE.

This simple example shows that there are, e.g., three instances of the charging access (CDCC), two message handler instances (MHCC), and two instances of the CPPH protocol handler block needed to setup a mobile originating call. This kind of behavioral information is very important to telecommunication engineers. Sections 5.2 and 5.4 describe how information on link chains can be derived via static and dynamic analysis, respectively.

Furthermore, each block in Figure 6 implements at least one *state machine*. State machines are a common modeling means in the design of telecommunication systems. Therefore, telecommunication experts are interested in having a good knowledge about the state machines implemented in a block and their operation at runtime. Extraction of state machines from source code is discussed in Section 5.3.

5.2. Static link chain analysis

In case of the AXE10, link chains can be obtained from static analysis by making use of an *error recovery* mechanism implemented in the system. The mechanism allows to kill processes specific to an erroneous link chain if normal error recovery fails. Each block instance that is the initiator of a new link chain first notifies the *Link Chain Manager* (LCM) of the APZ via an lc_start message (Figure 7). The LCM creates a new *Link Chain Identifier* (LID), stores it in the *Link Chain Register*, and returns it to the initiating block instance. Now the LID will be implicitly attached to every signal the initiating block instance sends to any other block instance. If another block instance is requested, it notifies its participation in a link chain by sending an lc_part message to the LCM which in turn will respond by sending an acknowledgment containing the currently valid LID from the Link Chain Register. The LID will now be implicitly attached to the second block's signals as well etc.

The lc_* messages to the platform system are represented by corresponding PLEX statements in the source code. Thus, these statements are detected and inserted into the structure graph during structural analysis (see Figure 5). The static link chain analysis searches for the occurrence of an lc_start statement in a given block's structure graph and marks the surrounding statement sequence. All signals sent after the link chain initiation notification by this statement sequence do transmit an LID[3]. Thus, these signals are traversed to the receiving blocks. Next, the block structure graph of each receiving block is traversed starting from a signal entry point which one of the signal edges is connected to. If an lc_part statement is reachable from this signal entry, an lc_next_block edge is inserted into the structure graph between sending and receiving block.

In Figure 5, block A contains an lc_start statement in statement sequence X. Furthermore, signal H triggers the execution of statement sequence Y in block B which contains an lc_part statement. As a result, a new edge of type lc_next_block is inserted into the structure graph to indicate that A and B can take part in the same link chain.

After having performed static link chain analysis on the structure graph, it is possible to visualize which blocks *potentially* take part in the same link chain and which block triggers the participation of which other blocks. Indeed, if the static link chain analysis is performed for the whole structure graph, the result is the union of *all* link chains that can occur at runtime. Nevertheless, this information is very useful as most link chains appear to be constructed from smaller, invariant link chains. Additionally, the scope of a static link chain analysis can be limited by selecting a starting block. In this case, only blocks are considered that are reachable from the starting block via a path of signals. Here, link chain analysis also accepts lc_part statements as initiators of a 'new' link chain because an intermediate block of a real link chain might have been selected as starting point. Furthermore, certain classes of telecommunication services

[3]To be precise, the lc_start statement must not be part of a conditional statement to make sure that subsequently sent signals do transmit an LID. Otherwise, only signals in the same conditional context do so.

(e.g., voice calls) always have a kind of basic common link chain. Smaller chains representing different supplementary services are just linked in on demand. In combination with system traces (see Section 5.5), it is possible to identify the basic common link chains.

5.3. State machine extraction

The information extracted from the source code and other sources of information, its representation, and its visualization have to meet the demands of both the reengineer and the system experts involved. In particular, telecommunication systems are often planned and modeled using *state machines*. That is, system experts think in terms of state machines and protocols. Thus, the design process is process- and behavior-centered rather than data-centered, and blocks are just implementations of one or more state machines. Though PLEX does not provide any language elements for state machine implementation, the knowledge of some (informal) design rules at Ericsson and additional manual analysis of a couple of PLEX blocks allowed to develop an algorithm to detect state machines in and extract them from a block's source code or structure graph, respectively.

The example code in Figure 8 represents the main patterns used to implement state machines in PLEX. Every block contains declarations of a stored (DS flag) data record (BlockTRecord), a file to store several of these records, and a pointer (BlockTPointer) to the record currently used in execution. Each of these records represents a block instance. A block implements a state machine if its stored record contains a symbol variable of a string-valued enumeration type whose name contains the substring STATE. Additionally, the set of possible values of this state variable must enclose the values IDLE and SEIZED. Furthermore, each signal entry (ENTER <signal name>) is immediately followed by a case statement whose condition queries the current value of the state variable. Each branch of this case statement triggers different executions in the block (instance). Accordingly, a state change is represented by an assignment to the state variable. A design rule determines that a block must change its state at most once per execution cycle. No state change corresponds to a feedback loop in the underlying state machine. Furthermore, after a state change and a possibly subsequent signal sending statement, a block has to terminate immediately by means of an EXIT statement.

Hence, using this information we can conclude from the example in Figure 8 that block T owns a state variable named STATE. This state variable can have – among others – the values IDLE, SEIZED, SETUP, and DISC. When receiving (consuming) SignalA in states IDLE or SEIZED, the block will change to state SETUP and send SignalB. This results in the lower three states and two transitions on the right

```
...
! Declare Sector !
DECLARE
 ...
 RECORD BlockTRecord;
  ...
  SYMBOL VARIABLE STATE = (IDLE, SEIZED, SETUP, DISC, ...) DS;
  ...
 END RECORD;
 POINTER BlockTPointer(BlockTRecord);
 ...
END DECLARE;

! Program Sector !
PROGRAM;
 ! Begin Interface !
 ENTER SignalA WITH SignalDataA;
   CASE BlockTPointer:STATE IS
     WHEN IDLE, SEIZED DO
       GOTO SequenceY;
     OTHERWISE DO
       GOTO UnexpectedState;
   ESAC;

 ENTER SignalC WITH SignalDataC;
   CASE BlockTPointer:STATE IS
     WHEN DISC DO
       GOTO SequenceZ;
     OTHERWISE DO
       GOTO UnexpectedState;
   ESAC;
 ...
 ! End Interface !

 SequenceY)
   ...
   BlockTPointer:STATE = SETUP;
   SEND SignalB WITH SomeData;
   EXIT;

 SequenceZ)
   ...
   BlockTPointer:STATE = IDLE;
   SEND SignalD WITH AgainSomeData;
   EXIT;
 ...
END PROGRAM;
...
```

Figure 8. Example code with relevant statements for state machine extraction

side of Figure 9. That is, a cut-out of the block's state machine has been extracted. The rest of the state machine can be extracted stepwise by analyzing the source code for each signal entry as originator again and again. But compared to a graph-based algorithm this procedure is inefficient for large systems like the AXE10.

The *graph-based state machine extraction algorithm* traverses a block's structure graph trying to find a path from a signal entry to a statement sequence that contains an assignment to the state variable. In each run, the starting states from the conditional clauses of the case statement and the name of the incoming signal are stored. If a state assignment is found, a state transition from the starting state to the new state is inserted into the block's state diagram. The state transition is annotated with the incoming and the outgoing signal. Additional information that is necessary

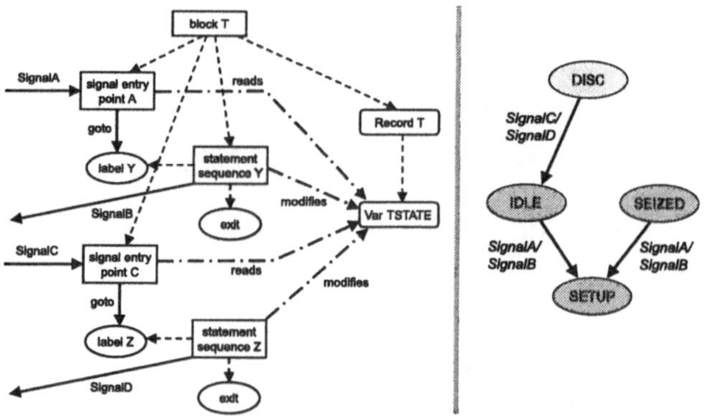

Figure 9. State machine extraction on structure graph

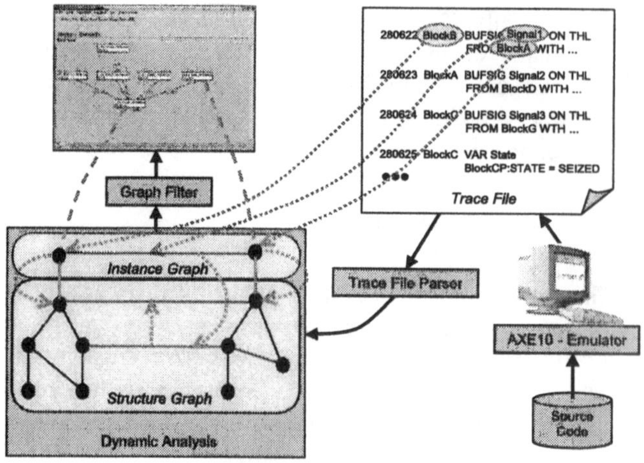

Figure 10. Obtaining dynamic information

for the state machine extraction and that is not represented by elements of the structure graph (e.g., conditional statements) is stored in attributes of nodes and edges. Therefore, all information that is needed for the extraction is obtained in a single run of the PLEX parser.

In the sample graph of Figure 9 corresponding to the source code in Figure 8, the transition from DISC to IDLE can be obtained by starting with signal entry C. The conditions for the branches of the subsequent case statement are stored in the corresponding GOTO edges. On state DISC, the execution of block T is continued at statement sequence Z which modifies the state variable STATE, sends signal SignalD, and terminates its execution.

The result of the state machine extraction is a state machine of a block that might be too large. That is, it may contain too many transitions. A reason for this anomaly is given by nested if-clauses that query the current value of different variables. At runtime only a small amount of all possible pairs of values of these variables might be valid. That is, only a subset of all possible execution paths through this part of the source code might be possible in reality. The identification of those state transitions that are valid is possible in combination with trace information (see Section 6).

Another problem arises from the fact that blocks can have several state machines inside – one for every mini-service they implement. The algorithm is designed to extract all state machines in parallel in a single pass.

5.4. Tracing

As stated in Section 3, there are two possibilities to obtain dynamic information: using an emulator or querying a running AXE10. In the latter case, the complexity of the information traced has to be reduced to avoid that the system gets into timing problems and becomes instable. Besides error handling, tracing jobs have the highest priority in a running AXE10. Therefore, intense tracing can cause abnormal behavior, e.g., through an increased number of missed time constraints and the resulting system recovery actions. Furthermore, tracing an AXE10 that is in normal operation – handling thousands of calls at the same time – results in trace files containing information on all of these calls. This huge amount of information makes it difficult to focus on a special call scenario, which is one of the goals of tracing. If real-time issues are not regarded, there is no need to query a running switching system. Consequently, we decided to use the AXE10 emulator. However, the procedure described below and the dynamic analysis tool are the same for both sources of dynamic information.

First, the tracing facility of the emulator is configured. The configuration determines which information (e.g., signal interchange, data access) is to be captured in a trace file and which parts of the system should be observed (e.g., several blocks in a certain subsystem). Currently, we are interested in the following information: signals, sending and receiving block (instance) of a signal, data transferred with a signal, signal priority, and assignments to certain (state) variables. After the configuration has finished, the running emulator starts to capture all actions whose tracing has been switched on (Figure 10). Now the testing equipment can be used to set up a call scenario of interest, e.g., a mobile originating call, and trigger the execution of telecommunication services implemented in the AXE10.

The dynamic analysis tool and the associated trace file parser read a selected trace file stepwise – action by action – on demand. Every action is analyzed to identify the participating entities (block instances, signals, etc.) of the instance graph. The instance graph is then modified accordingly – new elements are inserted and existing ones are updated. Some modifications are also propagated into the static structure graph. For example, every block instance is connected

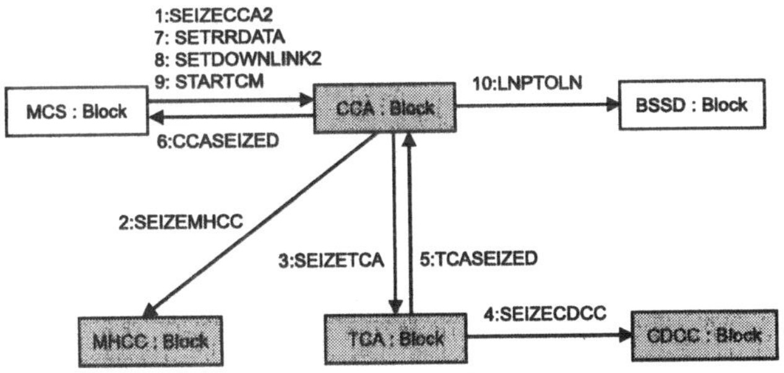

Figure 11. Example of a collaboration diagram

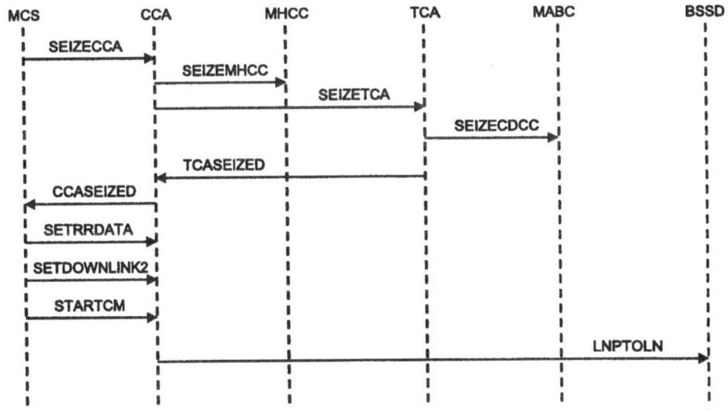

Figure 12. Example of a sequence diagram

to its corresponding block in the structure graph and the activation of a block instance results in the activation of the corresponding block.

During their daily work, telecommunication experts need different views on the traffic cases they analyze. Sometimes they just need a complete overview, sometimes they focus on the inter-work of two block instances, and sometimes the development of a call over time is their main interest. Therefore, dynamic analysis provides three different *working modes*: In *step mode*, the dynamic analysis process is interactive. That is, the reengineer triggers the analysis of each action in the selected trace file manually. In *run mode*, the analysis tool processes the whole trace in one run. This mode has been implemented to create complete diagrams for re-documentation purposes. In *animation mode*, the actions in a trace file are processed successively in adjustable time intervals. The animation mode is used to produce a slow motion replay of the actions that took place in the systems software with respect to a certain call scenario. For convenience, it is possible to switch between the three working modes at any time.

All changes to the instance graph are directly visualized in the dynamic analysis tool. Here, a reengineer is able to refine and adjust the amount of information displayed by means of a complex graph filter interactively. Furthermore, he can choose between two kinds of diagrams that are commonly used in the telecommunications domain: *collaboration diagrams* and *sequence diagrams* similar to those provided in the UML [2]. Collaboration diagrams can be used in all three working modes of the analysis tool whereas sequence diagrams are mainly used for re-documentation purposes. For example, the collaboration diagram in Figure 11 and the sequence diagram in Figure 12 show the same trace at the same stage. The different grey scales of the block instances in Figure 11 illustrate that the block instances belong to different subsystems.

The dynamic analysis tool has proved its value for system analysis and system understanding in several tests and discussions with the expert group from Ericsson supporting our research. However, in complex traces, huge amounts of information are obtained from the emulator. As a result, numerous elements are inserted into the instance graph that have to be visualized to the user at once. In step mode and even worse in animation mode, the user often gets confused by the quantity of information after some time and might even lose his track. There are two complementing possibilities to support the user in understanding complex call scenarios: limiting the observation scope of a trace and extending the visualization with aging.

The *limitation* of the *observation scope* is necessary anyhow to suppress noise in traces that results from periodic jobs like access statistics in order to focus on special aspects. Limitation means that observation is only activated for selected blocks, signals, and variables of a traced system in the emulator configuration. All other blocks etc. are ignored; e.g., tracing could be limited to a certain subsystem. But the block instances that take part in a certain call scenario are always spread over various parts of the AXE10. Hence, there are e.g. signals coming from the ignored parts to observed blocks and vice versa. This leads to missing links (signals) in the control flow of a trace, in the instance graph, and in the diagrams produced by the dynamic analysis tool. Therefore, a heuristic has been implemented in the dynamic analysis tool that inserts *synthetic signals* during trace analysis to keep traces connected. For example, the heuristic marks signals sent to unobserved block instances (*out signal action*), tracks the following signal actions for a corresponding *in signal action*, and inserts an appropriate synthetic incoming signal if it is missing[4]. For this purpose, the dump of the emulator configuration that corresponds to the current trace file is used to extract information on observed entities. This is necessary to keep the diagrams correct. Similarly, if another block is activated out of turn after a signal has been sent to the ignored part of a system, there

[4]For each signal a pair of signal actions must be captured for a trace file to be correct – an outgoing signal action at the sending block instance and an incoming signal action at the receiving block instance. But, signal actions are only captured for observed blocks.

must have been communication in the ignored part which has not been captured. This circumstance can also be represented by an appropriate synthetic signal during dynamic analysis that summarizes this unknown communication.

In addition, the user is supported during trace analysis through the *aging* of the *representation elements* in the visualization of the instance graph. Consider a collaboration diagram view, which represents the current state of a call's link chain. Some elements in this diagram remain inactive while others participate continuously in the current part of the trace. But this difference in the amount of participation is not noticed easily in complex traces. Therefore, all elements in the collaboration diagram which have not participated recently in a current trace are faded out continuously. If an element participates again, it is re-displayed immediately. This procedure guarantees that the visualization focuses on elements that determine the current behavior. Keeping in mind that a call link chain develops over time and that it creates temporary side links that are never released explicitly for efficiency reasons, visualization aging is a good means to analyze the evolution of a call over time.

5.5. Combining analyses

So far, the direct analysis of a system's runtime behavior has been addressed. But there are additional applications for a combination of analyses. In Section 5.2 we have mentioned that link chains for a certain class of calls (e.g., voice calls) have a common *basic link chain* that is extended by *side links* representing different supplementary services (e.g., charging). Traces can be used to identify basic link chains and supplementary side links. The procedure is similar to feature analysis as described in [7].

Always, several traces of the system are needed. To identify the basic link chain of a class of calls, a number of traces of different voice calls is needed. All these traces are now processed by the dynamic analysis tool to produce corresponding instance graphs. Next, the logical and operation over all instance graphs is used to create an instance graph that represents the intersection of all instance graphs that result from trace analysis. This intersection graph corresponds to the common basic link chain of all these traces.

To find out whether a side link inherently belongs to a given type of call (e.g., a mobile originating call), additional traces are needed that belong to other types of calls. Now, all elements that are part of the other calls can be subtracted from the instance graph of the first trace which results in a set of elements that inherently belong to this kind of call.

The state machines statically extracted from source code can be reused in the dynamic analysis of a systems runtime behavior. Remember that state changes were captured in trace files as well. In combination with a trace it is possible

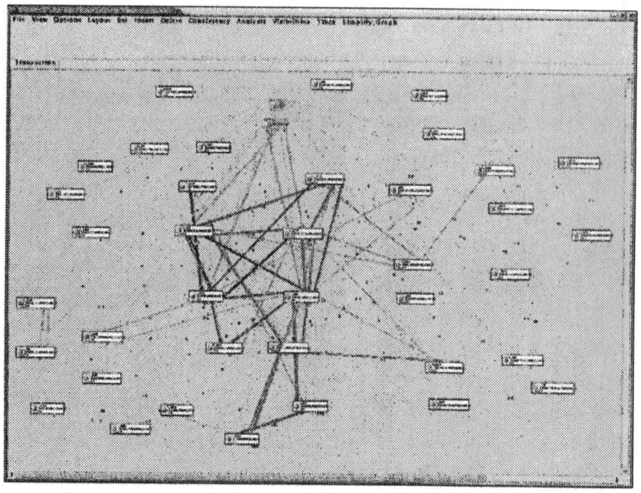

Figure 13. Static communication weights

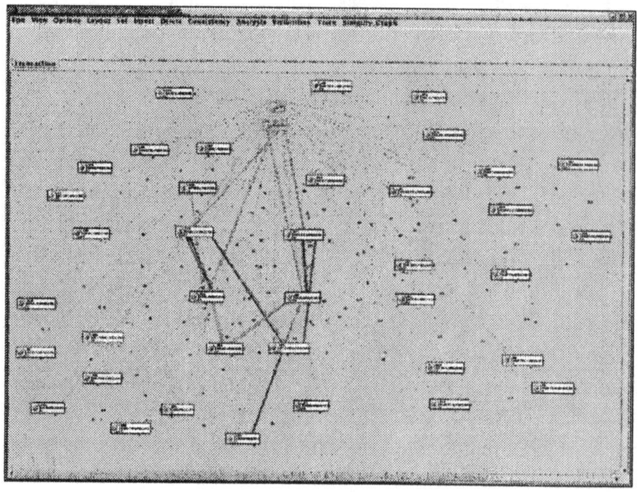

Figure 14. Dynamic communication weights

to animate the state machines of a marked set of blocks and visualize them to the telecommunication expert.

6. Metrics

As presented so far, the E-CARES prototype provides qualitative information on the structure and behavior of a telecommunication system. In addition, telecommunication experts are interested in quantitative information. The *metrics* introduced in this section further improve the understanding of a telecommunication system. Usually, metrics are used for assessment (e.g., of the complexity of a system), but so far we have not used them for this purpose.

Metrics are used to assign *weights* to graph elements. These weights are defined with the help of both static and dynamic information. They are attached to both structural and behavioral graphs. At the user interface, weights are visualized with the help of different representation attributes, e.g., colors, size of boxes, or thickness of edges.

As an example, Figure 13 shows a view on the structure graph which displays communications at the block level. *Static weights* are assigned to communication edges based on the number of types of signals sent from the source to the destination. Colors and thickness of edges are used to represent communication weights. The thick lines at the center of the diagram indicate where the main traffic occurs. Telecommunication experts at Ericsson considered this information useful to distinguish "communication highways" from "secondary roads". Similarly, weights may be attached to blocks based on the code size so that is easier to understand where the main functionality is implemented (not shown in the figure).

Static weights provide general information on potential executions. However, the telecommunication expert may be interested more specifically in what happens in a specific trace (or a set of traces). To this end, we offer *dynamic weights*. For example, each communication edge is weighted by the number of signals sent along this edge in a specific trace. Again, we may display these weights in the structure graph. By comparing Figure 14 to Figure 13, the user may recognize the specific behavior in a certain trace. It is also possible to hide all elements which do not participate at all in the trace under study. In this way, the user may compare expected and actual behavior. Alternatively, weights may be displayed in a collaboration diagram, which provides a more detailed view on the execution since it shows individual block instances.

As a final example, let us briefly discuss the assignment of weights to elements of state machines. In Subsection 5.3, we mentioned that static analysis may produce a state diagram which is too large. To detect potentially dead elements, state transitions are weighted according to the number of occurrences in some trace (or in a set of traces). State transitions with weight 0 may be obsolete.

7. Related work

The E-CARES prototype is a reengineering environment designed for telecommunication systems. In particular, it is based on domain-specific architectural concepts. A telecommunication system is modeled as a set of active components which communicate by sending and receiving signals. Thus, modeling is process-centered. Since the static system structure is not very expressive, analysis of behavior plays a crucial role in E-CARES.

In contrast, many other reengineering tools such as e.g. Rigi [16] or KOGGE [6] primarily focus on the static system structure. Moreover, they are typically data-centered; consider e.g. tools for the reengineering of COBOL programs as described in [5, 15, 23]. Here, recovery of units of data abstraction and migration to an object-oriented software architecture play a crucial role [3]. More recently, reengineering has also been studied for object-oriented programming languages such as C++ and Java. E.g., TogetherJ or Fujaba [17] generate class diagrams from source code.

Reengineering of telecommunication systems follows different goals. Telecommunication systems are designed in terms of layers, planes, services, protocols, etc. Behavior is described with the help of state machines, message sequence charts, link chains, etc. Thus, reengineering tools are required to provide views on the system which closely correspond to system descriptions given in standards, e.g., GSM. Telecommunication experts require views on the system which match their conceptual abstractions.

In this paper, we focus on tools and techniques for behavioral analysis offered by the E-CARES prototype. Below, we compare these to other approaches.

In the literature, a lot of work is described on the extraction of dynamic information from object-oriented systems. The motivation for the need of dynamic information is quite similar to ours: In object-oriented systems the runtime behavior of a system is neither predictable nor understandable by just performing different kinds of static analysis on the system's source code. Source code analysis does not provide enough information to understand a software system completely because there are components and relations that only exist during its runtime.

There are different methods described how to extract or gather dynamic information. In the majority of these methods, the code of the target system is instrumented so that a trace is produced of the components executed in each test case. The level of instrumentation ranges from very low level instrumentation where the components of a trace are branches in the target system control flow [25] to the instrumentation of class or method entry and exit points [22] or inter-process messages [12, 24], respectively. Low level instrumentation of a production system brings with it a significant performance penalty since trace information is generated each time the system passes through an conditional statement like `if`, `switch`, or any other decision points. In general, for a large real-time system like the AXE10 switching system low level instrumentation would be too difficult. In particular, if we ran a low level instrumented system, we would experience severe timing problems within the system. This would result in unusable traces.

Another approach that can be found nowadays is the utilization of debugger and profiler logs to gather dynamic information [7, 9, 21]. In the end, debugger and profiler just provide a more convenient, more efficient but also more indirect way of instrumenting source code or byte code, respectively. Considering real-time systems, if too much information is queried this could result in unusable traces as well. Fortunately, we can use an emulator to execute the AXE10 source code as is – no instrumentation is necessary. The output of tracing information is a configurable built in functionality of this emulator. Additionally, the virtual time mode of the emulator guarantees that complex test cases are possible without running into timing problems.

There are different proposals for the representation of dynamic information to a reengineer. In most cases, either collaboration diagrams or different variations of sequence diagrams are used [21]. Others [9, 18] use different kinds of non-standard graph representations. In rare cases, there are even more elaborate representations like the piano-roll representation in [12]. We have chosen to implement both a collaboration diagram view and a sequence diagram view because these kind of representations are very common to telecommunication engineers. Furthermore, we have implemented different inspection modes for traces (manual step-by-step inspection, slow-motion replay with aging, and batch processing for re-documentation purposes). This provides a reengineer with maximum flexibility in the processing and utilization of dynamic information.

When comparing the E-CARES approach of dynamic information retrieval to other approaches, we found that the majority of approaches collect this information from a running system. There are only a few approaches [11] that derive behavioral information via static analysis. In E-CARES both static and dynamic analysis are utilized to retrieve information on a systems' behavior. Furthermore, information retrieved from static and dynamic analysis can be combined to overcome each others' deficits: E.g., for state machine extraction, code coverage is guaranteed via static analysis while the precise dynamic information can be used to search for potentially invalid transitions. That is, information can be exchanged between static and dynamic views.

In the literature, the post-processing of dynamic information ranges from slicing of program structures, feature location in code [7], and state machine extraction [22] to re-documentation of the current implementation. The E-CARES prototype currently comprises state machine extraction and re-documentation; the implementation of program slicing (which is related to architecture extraction in our case) and feature location is still under construction.

8. Conclusion

We have presented tools for understanding the behavior of telecommunication systems. These tools were developed in close cooperation with telecommunication experts from Ericsson. We followed an evolutionary approach to tool development, i.e., functionality was added incrementally in response to the requirements stated by the telecommunication experts. In this way, we took a step towards an environment which is based on domain-specific concepts.

So far, approximately 500,000 lines of PLEX code plus several ten thousands of lines of additional documents have been processed, analyzed, visualized, and inspected on different levels of abstraction. Understandably, the exact and detailed results are confidential and cannot be discussed here. According to the telecommunication experts, the E-CARES prototype allows to visualize the AXE10 software systems in terms of their daily use, e.g., block dependencies, state diagrams, link chains, and sequence diagrams. For that, no tools have been available so far. In particular, the dynamic analysis tool has proved its value for system analysis and system understanding. Therefore, we are convinced that analyzing and visualizing the dynamic behavior of telecommunication systems is key to system understanding. Furthermore, we believe that only the combination of static and dynamic as well as structural and behavioral analysis – integrated in an interactive reengineering framework – allows to obtain best possible results.

The current E-CARES prototype is domain dependent to a certain extent. In particular, the structure graph is tightly bound to the PLEX programming language, i.e., nodes of the structure graph correspond to PLEX constructs such as blocks, signal declarations, signal send statements, etc. At Ericsson, other programming languages, e.g., C and C++, are used, as well. To support multi-language systems, we have started to divide the structure graph into programming language dependent and language independent aspects. The final goal is a flexible and extensible reengineering system that consists of a core system which is extended with specific functionality in form of plug-in modules. For this purpose, we are currently defining general interfaces between the different parts of the system, e.g., between parsers and static analysis tool, etc. The visualization of extracted information in form of different views, e.g., structural views, sequence diagrams, collaboration diagrams, and state machines, are independent of the current subject of study. Even the underlying analyses can be readily applied to other real-time systems, provided that the needed information is available and storable in terms of our structure graph.

Additionally, we need a neutral representation at the architecture level. Therefore, we are currently extending the E-CARES prototype such that it builds a ROOM model from analyzed programs. Others, like SDL or the component model of UML 2.0 will be explored in the future.

Finally, we will extend the E-CARES prototype to cover re-design. That is, we intend to support the restructuring and extension of existing systems in addition to reverse engineering, which has been our focus so far.

Acknowledgments The E-CARES project is funded by Ericsson Eurolab Deutschland GmbH (EED); support is gratefully acknowledged. We would like to thank the following members of EED for their constant active support, critical feedback, and patience: Martin Blumbach, Jörg Bruss, Axel Jeske, Per Ljungberg, Ari Peltonen, Andreas Thülig, Dietmar Wenninger, and Andreas Witzel.

References

[1] B. Böhlen, D. Jäger, A. Schleicher, and B. Westfechtel. UPGRADE: Building interactive tools for visual languages. In *Proceedings of the 6th World Multiconference on Systemics, Cybernetics, and Informatics (SCI 2002)*, volume I (Information Systems Development I), pages 17–22, Orlando, Florida, July 2002.

[2] G. Booch, J. Rumbaugh, and I. Jacobson. *The Unified Modeling Language User Guide*. Addison Wesley: Reading, MA, 1999.

[3] G. Canfora, A. Cimitile, A. De Lucia, and G. Di Lucca. Decomposing legacy systems into objects: An eclectic approach. *Information and Software Technology*, 43(6):401–412, 2001.

[4] E. J. Chikofsky and J. H. Cross II. Reverse engineering and design recovery: A taxonomy. *IEEE Software*, 7(1):13–17, 1990.

[5] K. Cremer, A. Marburger, and B. Westfechtel. Graph-based tools for re-engineering. *Journal of Software Maintenance and Evolution: Research and Practice*, 14(4):257–292, Aug. 2002.

[6] J. Ebert, R. Süttenbach, and I. Uhe. Meta-CASE in practice: A case for KOGGE. In *Proceedings 9th International Conference on Advanced Information Systems Engineering CAiSE 1997*, LNCS 1250, pages 203–216, Barcelona, Spain, June 1997.

[7] T. Eisenbarth, R. Koschke, and D. Simon. Aiding Program Comprehension by Static and Dynamic Feature Analysis. In *Proceedings International Conference on Software Maintenance ICSM 2001*, pages 602–611, Florence, Italy, Nov. 2001.

[8] J. Ellsberger, D. Hogrefe, and A. Sarma. *SDL - Formal Object-oriented Language for Communicating Systems*. Prentice Hall, 1997.

[9] J. Gargiulo and S. Mancoridis. Gadget: A Tool for Extracting the Dynamic Structure of Java Programs. In *Proceedings International Conference on Software Engineering and Knowledge Engineering SEKE 2001*, Buenos Aires, Argentina, June 2001.

[10] R. Kazman, S. G. Woods, and J. Carrière. Requirements for integrating software architecture and reengineering models: CORUM II. In *Working Conference on Reverse Engineering*, pages 154–163, Hawai, USA, Oct 1998.

[11] R. Kollmann and M. Gogolla. Capturing Dynamic Program Behavior with UML Collaboration Diagrams. In *Proceedings European Conference on Software Maintenance and Reengineering CSMR 2001*, pages 58–67, Lisbon, Portugal, Mar. 2001.

[12] K. Lukoit, N. Wilde, S. Stowell, and T. Hennessey. TraceGraph: Immediate Visual Location of Software Features. In *Proceedings International Conference on Software Maintenance ICSM 2000*, pages 33–39, San Jose, California, USA, Oct. 2000.

[13] A. Marburger and D. Herzberg. E-CARES research project: Understanding complex legacy telecommunication systems. In *Proceedings 5th European Conference on Software Maintenance and Reengineering CSMR 2001*, pages 139–147, Lisbon, Portugal, 2001.

[14] A. Marburger and B. Westfechtel. Graph-based reengineering of telecommunication systems. In *Proceedings of the International Conference on Graph Transformations ICGT 2002*, LNCS 2505, pages 270–285, Barcelona, Spain, Oct. 2002.

[15] L. Markosian, P. Newcomb, R. Brand, S. Burson, and T. Kitzmiller. Using an enabling technology to reengineer legacy systems. *Communications of the ACM*, 37(5):58–70, 1994.

[16] H. A. Müller, K. Wong, and S. R. Tilley. Understanding software systems using reverse engineering technology. In *The 62nd Congress of L'Association Canadienne Francaise pour l'Avancement des Sciences ACFAS 1994*, pages 41–48, Montreal, Canada, May 1994.

[17] U. Nickel, J. Niere, and A. Zündorf. Tool demonstration: The Fujaba environment. In *Proceedings of the 22nd International Conference on Software Engineering ICSE 2000*, pages 742–745, Limerick, Ireland, Nov. 2000.

[18] T. Richner and S. Ducasse. Recovering High-Level Views of Object-Oriented Applications from Static and Dynamic Information. In *Proceedings International Conference on Software Maintenance ICSM 1999*, pages 13–22, Oxford, England, Sept. 1999.

[19] A. Schürr, A. J. Winter, and A. Zündorf. Graph grammar engineering with PROGRES. In *Proceedings 5th European Software Engineering Conference ESEC 1995*, LNCS 989, pages 219–234, Barcelona, Spain, Sept. 1995.

[20] B. Selic, G. Gullekson, and P. T. Ward. *Real-Time Object-Oriented Modeling*. John Wiley & Sons: Reading, MA, 1994.

[21] T. Systä. On the Relationships between Static and Dynamic Models in Reverse Engineering Java Software. In *Proceedings 6th Working Conference on Reverse Engineering WCRE 1999*, pages 304–313, Atlanta, Georgia, USA, Oct. 1999.

[22] T. Systä and K. Koskimies. Extracting state diagrams from legacy systems. In *Object-Oriented Technology ECOOP'97*, LNCS 1357, Jyväskylä, Finland, 1997.

[23] H. J. van Zuylen, editor. *The REDO Compendium: Reverse Engineering for Software Maintenance*. John Wiley & Sons: Chichester, UK, 1993.

[24] N. Wilde, C. Casey, J. Vandeville, G. Trio, and Hotz Dirk. Reverse engineering of software threads: A design recovery technique for large multi-process systems. *Journal of Systems and Software*, 43(1):11–17, 1998.

[25] N. Wilde and M. Scully. Software reconnaissance: Mapping program features to code. *Journal of Software Maintenance: Research and Practice*, 7(1):49–62, 1995.

Technical Papers

Consistency Management and Quality Assurance

Palantír: Raising Awareness among Configuration Management Workspaces

Anita Sarma, Zahra Noroozi, and André van der Hoek
Department of Information and Computer Science
University of California, Irvine
Irvine, CA 92697-3425 USA
asarma@ics.uci.edu, znoroozi@yahoo.com, andre@ics.uci.edu

Abstract

Current configuration management systems promote workspaces that isolate developers from each other. This isolation is both good and bad. It is good, because developers make their changes without any interference from changes made concurrently by other developers. It is bad, because not knowing which artifacts are changing in parallel regularly leads to problems when changes are promoted from workspaces into a central configuration management repository. Overcoming the bad isolation, while retaining the good isolation, is a matter of raising awareness among developers, an issue traditionally ignored by the discipline of configuration management. To fill this void, we have developed Palantír, a novel workspace awareness tool that complements existing configuration management systems by providing developers with insight into other workspaces. In particular, the tool informs a developer of which other developers change which other artifacts, calculates a simple measure of severity of those changes, and graphically displays the information in a configurable and generally non-obtrusive manner. To illustrate the use of Palantír, we demonstrate how it integrates with two representative configuration management systems.

1. Introduction

One of the core functions of any configuration management system is to coordinate access to a common set of artifacts by multiple developers who are all working on the same project. While ideally project management assigns the developers tasks that are mutually exclusive, the reality is that changes made by one developer regularly affect another's work [21,22,31].

The various approaches that different configuration management systems take to address this situation can be distinguished into two classes: pessimistic and optimistic. In the pessimistic approach, a developer must lock artifacts before making any modifications. Such a lock prevents other developers from making concurrent modifications, and in essence serializes the set of changes to the artifacts. In the optimistic approach, multiple developers can change the same artifacts at the same time (perhaps on branches [37], or alternatively using independent change sets [39]). Conflicts may then arise, but semi-automated differencing and merging tools help in identifying and resolving them (albeit only a subset [26]).

Both approaches rely on workspaces to partition the work of developers. While these workspaces are essential to shield developers from the effects of other changes in other workspaces (good isolation), they have the unfortunate side effect of creating a barrier that prevents developers from knowing which other developers change which other artifacts in parallel (bad isolation). In a typical configuration management system, a developer becomes aware of other' activities only at three specific points in time: when they obtain artifacts from the repository and place them in their workspace; when they put modified artifacts back from their workspace into the repository; and when they explicitly query the repository. Even then, in the pessimistic approach they only know what artifacts other developers have locked for future changes and in the optimistic approach they only become aware of what changes already have occurred. From a coordination point of view, this is an undesirable and limited situation.

To alleviate this situation, we have built Palantír, a novel configuration management workspace awareness tool that deliberately breaks bad isolation while retaining good isolation. A crucial aspect of Palantír is that it inverts information flow from pull to push. Instead of informing developers of other efforts only when they themselves perform some configuration management operation (e.g., check in or check out), Palantír increases awareness by *continuously* sharing information regarding operations performed by all developers. Specifically, Palantír informs a developer of which other developers change which other artifacts, calculates a simple measure of severity of those changes, and graphically displays the information in a configurable and generally non-obtrusive manner.

Palantír architecturally separates specific workspace wrapper components from a generic visualization compo-

0-7695-1877-X/03 $17.00 © 2003 IEEE

nent. Each workspace wrapper supports one particular configuration management system and intentionally has no further functionality than to emit events regarding the operations performed by different developers. The generic visualization component continuously collects and interprets the events, presenting a developer with an up-to-date picture of the workspace activities of others. Connecting the components is the Siena event notification service [7], whose distributed event filtering mechanism is leveraged to only deliver the necessary subset of events to each developer's visualization.

Constructing a system as Palantír raises many questions regarding, among others, which information should be shared, how to avoid overloading developers with information, scalability, and general effectiveness of the approach in helping developers coordinate their tasks. The aim of this paper is not to provide an absolute answer to all of the questions, but rather to serve as an initial investigation into the feasibility of increasing workspace awareness in configuration management systems. As such, the basic research question we seek to answer is whether Palantír can enhance existing configuration management systems with workspace awareness.

The remainder of this paper is organized as follows. In Section 2, we discuss background information regarding awareness in configuration management systems. Next, we discuss the overall approach and high-level architecture of Palantír in Section 3. Section 4 discusses the current implementation of Palantír. We demonstrate how Palantír can be integrated with two existing configuration management systems, namely RCS [35] and CVS [4], in Section 5. While old, these two systems represent the core of virtually every configuration management system, and cover both a pessimistic (RCS) and an optimistic (CVS) approach. We discuss related work in Section 6, and conclude in Section 7 with an outlook at future work.

2. Background

Awareness is characterized as "an understanding of the activities of others, which provides a context for your own activity" [15]. The kind of information needed to create awareness depends on the particular activity in which a group of people is participating, but generally includes such information as who is part of the group, what tasks they perform, how active they are, what changes they make, and which objects they manipulate [23].

Awareness as a concept applies to many different activities, but within the discipline of computer science it is generally associated with the field of computer-supported collaborative work (CSCW). There, efforts have largely focused on the use of awareness for coordination purposes, for example in multi-user editors (e.g., MMM [5] and Suite [13]) or collaborative workspaces (e.g., BSCW [3] and TUKAN [32]). The basic underlying theory is that providing users with appropriate contextual information allows them to make much more sophisticated decisions in coordinating their individual and group activities than any automated approach ever could. A few studies on the use of awareness in particular domains confirm this hypothesis and discuss the benefits of awareness as a coordination mechanism [12,14,15,18,19,27].

At the heart of any configuration management system is the need to coordinate the changes made by different developers in different workspaces. It is therefore surprising that the use of awareness has not received much attention, especially considering the apparent success in other domains. In fact, the focus has largely been on eliminating the need for awareness altogether. The philosophy is that workspaces are sacred places in which a developer must be able to make their changes in complete isolation. Not only should the artifacts be shielded from potentially interfering changes made concurrently by other developers, developers themselves should not have to know who else makes changes, how active they are, which artifacts they modify, and so on [6,10,11].

Current configuration management systems provide extensive and automated support for maintaining this kind of total workspace isolation [10]. Unfortunately, current mechanisms are highly inadequate from a coordination point of view (see Table 1). In a pessimistic configuration management system, locking is used to coordinate activities and only one developer may change an artifact at a time. Conflicts in which two or more developers change the same artifact *(direct conflicts)* are avoided, but at the expense of project delays if one developer must access an artifact currently locked by another developer. Furthermore, conflicts in which changes by one developer to one artifact negatively affect changes by another developer to another artifact *(indirect conflicts)* cannot be avoided.

Optimistic configuration management systems support parallel work with either branches [37] or change sets [39], and in essence coordinate parallel activities via the use of merge tools that combine changes to an artifact by one developer with changes to the same artifact by another developer. Most merge tools can automatically resolve most direct conflicts, but unfortunately cannot handle overlapping changes, leading to a regular need for manual problem resolution. Indirect conflicts are not addressed.

Ideally, the above drawbacks of the pessimistic or optimistic approach never occur. Then, either approach will succeed in maintaining the image of workspace isolation by automatically coordinating the activities of individual developers. In reality, however, the ideal case cannot be enforced. More often than not the illusion of workspace isolation vanishes when complex direct or indirect conflicts arise that the automated procedures cannot handle [21,22,31].

Table 1. Different coordination mechanisms.

	Coordination mechanism	*Direct conflicts*	*Indirect conflicts*
Pessimistic	Locking before changes are made	Avoided, at the expense of project delays	Not addressed
Optimistic	Automated merging after changes are made	Resolved, except for overlapping changes	Not addressed

The root cause of why current configuration management systems perform poorly when it comes to coordination can be found in the following three observations:

- While coordination must be among workspace activities, current configuration management systems coordinate those activities based on information in the central repository only. Consequently, available information is restricted to which artifacts may potentially change (because they are locked) or which artifacts already have been changed by another developer (because they now must be merged).
- Coordination information is available to a developer only when they themselves: (1) attempt to lock an already locked artifact, (2) must merge an artifact, or (3) make an explicit request. As a consequence, information flow is irregular, limited to the particular artifact at hand, and typically out-of-date with respect to the actual state of the other workspaces.
- Coordination mechanisms focus on avoiding and resolving direct conflicts, but ignore indirect conflicts altogether. As a result, the conflicts that are perhaps the most difficult to discover and resolve remain elusive from a coordination point of view.

We are not alone in making the above observations and concluding that the use of awareness can make a difference in how configuration management systems are used in coordinating the activities of developers [21,27]. In fact, many developers already use some home-grown conventions that keep other developers up-to-date, for example via e-mails that are sent when some set of artifacts is checked out or checked in.

A few configuration management systems have started to include functionality for automatically creating awareness among developers (e.g., Coven [8], CVS [4], COOP/Orm [25]). Even some Open Source development portals, such as SourceCast [9] and SourceForge [33], provide some simple awareness mechanisms attached to their configuration management functionality. In general, however, these approaches have serious limitations in terms of what information is shared, when the information is shared, and how the information is presented to the developers (see Section 6). Perhaps most limiting is that all of the aforementioned systems inform developers only of direct conflicts concerning individual artifacts. An overall view of other developer's workspace activities is missing. Especially when compared with the successful awareness approaches developed in the field of CSCW, the potential for a principled, rich awareness mechanism that complements existing configuration management systems has not been realized as of yet.

3. Approach

To introduce awareness in current configuration management systems, we have developed Palantír, a novel configuration management workspace awareness tool that provides developers with insight into other workspaces. Palantír itself is not a configuration management system and does not provide any traditional configuration management functionality such as artifact storage, workspace management, differencing and merging, or locking. Instead, Palantír builds on top of existing configuration management facilities and concentrates on the *collection*, *distribution*, *organization*, and *presentation* of relevant workspace information.

The architecture of Palantír is shown in Figure 1. Arrows represent information flow. Grey ovals represent components traditionally found in configuration management systems; they are used unchanged. White ovals are Palantír components that incrementally implement its functionality. A WORKSPACE WRAPPER collects and subsequently emits relevant workspace events that the generic EVENT SERVICE distributes to other developers. The INTERNAL STATE receives and stores the events, which are extracted and organized by an EXTRACTOR before they are shown to a developer by a VISUALIZATION component.

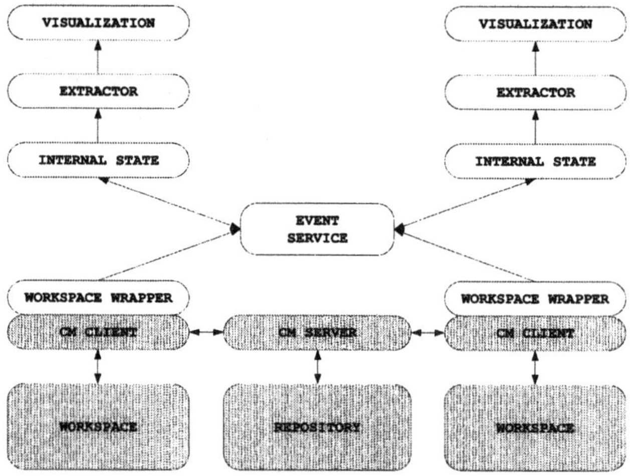

Figure 1. Palantír architecture.

The key observation underlying the Palantír architecture is that it inverts information flow from pull to push. Rather than informing developers of other efforts only when they themselves perform some configuration management operation, Palantír increases awareness by *continuously* sharing information regarding operations performed by all developers. As a result, Palantír not only frees developers from having to manually collect and interpret information from the configuration management repository, but in the process provides them with a more complete, accurate, and up-to-date picture concerning the activities in the other workspaces.

The architecture of Palantír is purposely constructed to address a number of concerns.

- **Non-obtrusiveness.** Developers should not have to change the way they interact with their particular configuration management system. Palantír, therefore, relies on simple workspace wrappers that, other than emitting events regarding the actions by the developers, have no further functionality. As discussed in Sections 4.2, these wrappers can normally be implemented with a minimal level of intrusiveness and without altering the state of a workspace.

- **Scalability.** Informing a developer of all activities in all workspaces overloads their cognitive senses and, in fact, is not necessary. Rather, Palantír uses the distributed event filtering mechanism provided by its event notification service of choice (Siena [7]) to only inform a developer of relevant activities in other workspaces. Relevant activities are defined as all activities pertaining to the artifacts in the local workspace, as performed in parallel by other developers in their remote workspaces (see Section 4.3).

- **Flexibility.** Not every configuration management system requires the same level of awareness. By separating internal data management from data extraction and information visualization, Palantír offers a flexible architecture in which different visualizations can be used. Currently, Palantír offers two such visualizations: a simple ticker tape similar to the one provided by Elvin [20] and a fully graphical visualization that presents a detailed overall view of the state of other workspaces. Other visualizations can easily be developed and added to the framework.

- **Configurability.** Not always will a developer want to be aware of all activities in all workspaces. Sometimes, it is desirable to select only a few developers or artifacts that one wants to monitor. The EXTRACTOR component of Palantír provides exactly this capability and can filter, in a number of ways, the events stored by the INTERNAL STATE component. Other selection mechanisms can easily be added.

4. Implementation

We have built a prototype implementation of Palantír on top of the generic Siena event notification service [7]. For each of the Palantír components identified in Figure 1, we highlight its design considerations and implementation details below. Given that Siena is used as an external service, we do not discuss its details. We do, however, illustrate how we leverage Siena for event filtering in order to achieve scalability within Palantír. We begin our discussion by introducing the events that Palantír uses internally.

4.1 Events

At the heart of Palantír are the events that describe the ongoing activities in each workspace. Of importance in the design of these events is the fact that Palantír must interoperate with different configuration management systems and cannot count on each of those systems to follow the same configuration management policy [36]. Rather than capturing actions (e.g., check in, check out, synchronize), events therefore represent particular *states* in which an artifact may be in a workspace. The resulting set of events is listed in Table 2, along with their interpretations and detailed data constituting each event.

Regardless of the particular configuration management system that is used, most artifacts will go through one of two cycles of events. Artifacts that change typically trigger the following sequence of events: (1) POPULATED, (2) CHANGESINPROGRESS, (3) CHANGESCOMMITTED, and (4) UNPOPULATED. Of course, the pair CHANGESINPROGRESS and CHANGESCOMMITTED may be repeated if a developer continues to make changes to the artifact before removing it from the workspace. Artifacts that must be present in a workspace for ancillary purposes trigger a simpler series of events: POPULATED followed by UNPOPULATED.

Exactly *when* these two event sequences are triggered depends on the particular configuration management system, its configuration management policy, and the specific wrapping mechanism that is used. Important, however, is that most, if not all, configuration management policies can be mapped onto the above two sequences of events in one way or another (see Section 5).

Most of the other events capture infrequent, but nonetheless critical workspace activities. The event CHANGESREVERTED captures the fact that a developer has undone some changes and reversed an artifact back to its initial, unchanged state in the workspace. The event SYNCHRONIZED is similar, but instead signifies that an artifact has been updated to reflect its latest state in the repository. Finally, the events ADDED, REMOVED, RENAMED, and MOVED capture the results of adding, removing, renaming and moving artifacts in the project hierarchy—all events that may indicate potential conflicts amongst workspaces.

Table 2. Palantír events.

Event	*Meaning*	*Data*
POPULATED	Artifact has been placed in a workspace	artifactID, parentArtifactID
UNPOPULATED	Artifact has been removed from a workspace	artifactID
SYNCHRONIZED	Artifact has been synchronized with repository	syncArtifactID, artifactID
CHANGESINPROGRESS	Artifact has changed in the workspace	wsArtifactID, artifactID, comment
CHANGESREVERTED	Artifact has been returned to its original state	artifactID, wsArtifactID
CHANGESCOMMITTED	New version of artifact has been stored in repository	newArtifactID, wsArtifactID, comment
ADDED	New artifact has been added	artifactID, parentArtifactID, comment
REMOVED	Artifact has been removed altogether	artifactID
RENAMED	Artifact has been renamed	artifactID, newName
MOVED	Artifact has been moved from one artifact to another	newArtifactID, newParentArtifactID, artifactID
SEVERITYCHANGED	Amount of change to an artifact has changed	artifactID, min, actual, max, explanation

The last event, SEVERITYCHANGED, has no direct relation to any particular configuration management operation. It is used by Palantír as a mechanism for communicating a measure of the amount of change that an artifact has undergone at a given point in time. Simply knowing which artifacts are changing in other workspaces is useful, but having an associated indication of severity conveys more information. Small changes typically will be easy to reconcile. Large changes may signify a regression towards potentially difficult conflicts in an eventual integration.

A trivial severity measure is binary and simply indicates whether or not any kind of change has occurred. A slightly more complicated measure of severity can be calculated by dividing the number of lines that has been added, removed, and changed by the total number of lines in an artifact. A domain-specific configuration management system could even institute a measure that depends on the type of artifact being managed (e.g., by tracking interface changes in a particular programming language).

Of note is that the event SEVERITYCHANGED only provides a way of communicating severity, but does not prescribe a particular severity measure. In fact, different configuration management systems may use different severity measures as implemented in their respective workspace wrapper. In general, it should be noted that one configuration management system should adopt one kind of severity measure throughout in order to provide a uniform view to all of its developers.

Palantír events must distinguish incarnations of the same artifact in different workspaces. Additionally, they must distinguish an artifact that is in a workspace in its original, repository-equivalent state from that same artifact in that same workspace after it has undergone some changes. At the same time, however, Palantír must be able to detect related artifacts in order to be able to identify potential conflicts. For these three reasons, Palantír defines artifact identifiers incrementally and uses different parts of the identifier for different purposes (e.g., organizing artifacts per workspace, sorting versions of artifacts, matching artifacts in different workspace to each other). The resulting structure of artifact identifiers is as follows:

object-id:name:version:[REP|WS]:author-id

The object identifier uniquely identifies an artifact in the configuration management repository and is typically assigned by the configuration management system. (If not, an equivalent can often be obtained by using the path to the version archive of the artifact in question.) Because the object identifier may not be human readable, and because it sometimes identifies an artifact as a whole rather than a specific version, the name and version of an artifact are an integral part of the Palantír artifact identifier. To distinguish an artifact that has changed from one that has not, the qualifiers WS and REP are used (WS indicating that the artifact's contents are unique to the workspace, REP indicating that the contents are still the same as the original version in the repository). Finally, to distinguish different workspaces, a unique author identifier is used as an integral part of the artifact identifier.

As an example, consider the following artifact identifier:

17608:write.c:1.1:WS:Ellen

It identifies version 1.1 of artifact 17608 in the configuration management repository as it has been materialized in the workspace of ELLEN under the name WRITE.C.

Currently, artifact identifiers as described above make two simplifying assumptions. First, they assume that each developer has a single workspace. Second, they assume that each artifact is placed in a workspace only once. These limitations are a result of the prototype nature of Palantír. They can be easily overcome by enhancing the artifact identifier slightly to make it unique per author's workspace and per copy of an artifact in a workspace.

4.2 Workspace wrapper

Workspaces and their access mechanisms differ per configuration management system. While most of the architecture of Palantír can be independent of that fact because it is driven by the generic events defined in the previous section, workspace wrappers must be specific to a configuration management system in order to translate its workspace conventions into Palantír events. To do so, a workspace wrapper should execute the following steps for each action performed by a developer: (1) intercept the action, (2) interpret the action, (3) determine whether the action is relevant to Palantír, (4) if relevant, gather appropriate information concerning the action, and (5) construct and emit an event.

Some of the more advanced configuration management systems, such as CM/Synergy [34] and ClearCase [1], provide integrated triggering mechanisms and associated scripting languages that ease the development of a workspace wrapper. Other systems do not have such facilities, and their command line interface must be wrapped with a separate program. Such a program should take the place of the original executable and operate by first invoking the original executable and then emitting events as necessary. In both wrapping techniques a slight delay in user response will be incurred due to the added complexity of constructing and emitting events. The interaction mechanism of the user with the configuration management system, however, remains the same and the workspace wrapper operates in a non-obtrusive way without altering the state of a workspace.

4.3 Internal state

The internal state component maintains an overview of the activities in both the local and remote workspaces that is independent of the particular visualization that a developer may use. This is necessary because a typical visualization can only show a subset of all workspace activities without cognitively overloading a developer. Nonetheless, the overall state of the workspaces must be maintained as a cache such that a developer can change the viewpoint of their visualization without having to wait for all necessary information to be obtained on demand.

In addition to maintaining the details of the various workspace activities, the internal state component serves a second critical role in Palantír. In particular, it is the component that is responsible for subscribing to relevant types of events and processing the individual events that it receives from Siena as a result of those subscriptions. Scalability is of a pertinent concern in the particular set of subscriptions that Palantír maintains. Rather than simply receiving every event concerning every artifact, Palantír leverages the structure of artifact identifiers to only subscribe to events regarding artifacts that are in the current workspace. Some indirect conflicts may be missed as a result of this policy. The benefit of achieving a first level of scalability in terms of the number of events that must be handled, combined with the benefit of not overloading a user with information regarding all artifacts in all workspaces, however, clearly outweighs this issue. Especially since studies have shown that workspaces generally overlap only partially rather than completely [31], we can expect significant savings in the number of events that must be handled by each internal state component.

An additional benefit of this approach is that Siena internally uses the subscriptions to optimize event routing among its distributed event servers [7]. While Siena's servers already can handle a significant number of events per second, this optimization improves their overall performance even further.

A timing problem arises when two developers each populate their workspace with some of the same artifacts. One developer will be first, and their internal state component will subscribe to the relevant events and receive notifications as the other developer populates their workspace. The developer that is second, however, will not be aware of the activities of the first developer since its internal state component creates its subscriptions after the relevant notifications were sent. To address this issue, Palantír has a small set of internal bootstrap events that it uses to synchronize new workspaces with the state of other, previously existing workspaces.

As a consequence of its central role in processing events and sharing bootstrap information with other workspaces, the internal state component should always be executing for every workspace. While a developer may choose not to run any visualizations, they must always start the internal state component such that at least other developers can benefit from Palantír and become aware of potential conflicts as they arise.

4.4 Extractor

While the internal state component of Palantír provides a first cut at automatically selecting the events of interest (namely those performed in other workspaces but pertaining to the artifacts in the local workspace), users often can narrow these down even further. Guided by their experience over time, they may for example decide that the only events of interest are those with a severity measure of fifty percent or higher. Alternatively, they may wish to only monitor a few select workspaces, since their knowledge of project context may help them in selecting only those developers who are working on closely related tasks that have a high chance of interfering.

Specifically for this purpose, the Palantír architecture contains an extractor component that, based upon a set of developer preferences, selects a subset of all events to be visualized. Shown in Figure 2, this component allows a developer to select which types of events they want to know about, by which authors, over which time span, and with what minimal severity. In this particular case, a developer is interested in a number of different events, by Ellen only, over the past 5 minutes, with a severity of at least fifty percent.

4.5 Visualization

The last component in the architecture of Palantír is the visualization component. It is responsible for organizing and displaying the activities as they happen in the various workspaces. Thus far, we have built two visualizations, both of which can be used in parallel. The first is a simple ticker tape similar to the ticker tape of Elvin [20]. Shown in Figure 2, it scrolls through the set of events as selected by the extractor component. While limited in displaying one event at a time, it serves an important role as a non-obtrusive alert mechanism. For example, Figure 2 shows a ninety percent severity for a CHANGESCOMMITTED event, which almost certainly necessitates further investigation.

Note that the order in which events appear in the ticker tape can be sorted according to event, author, or severity.

Shown also in Figure 2, the fully graphical visualization complements the ticker tape with a mechanism to maintain an overall view of workspace activities. Instead of focusing on one event at a time, the fully graphical visualization organizes and colors the events such that they highlight potential conflicts among workspaces. For example, the first stack highlights that, in addition to the workspace owner, two other developers are in the process of making changes to the artifact EDIT.

The visualization is hierarchical, and supports browsing of the artifacts much like a web browser. Severity measures are displayed as change bars, and can be used to help localize the source of a potential conflict. For example, if a high-level artifact shows a high severity value, a developer can double click on the artifact to see and examine severity values of its constituents; one or more of those values is likely to be high and causing the conflict.

Several other features of the fully graphical visualization are of note. First, it shows pair-wise conflicts among developers. Second, it sorts the individual artifacts per severity, such that the artifacts with the highest severity appear first in the window. Both these features make it easier to recognize and localize potential conflicts.

As a final note, we observe that the fully graphical visualization helps in detecting potential indirect conflicts. It highlights all relevant workspaces activities with associated severity values, not just those for direct conflicts.

5. Two Example Integrations

To evaluate the effort involved in enhancing an existing configuration management system with Palantír, we implemented two integrations: one with RCS and one with CVS. While old, these two systems represent the core of virtually every configuration management system. Moreover, they are examples of a pessimistic (RCS) and an optimistic (CVS) approach. We discuss each integration below, and conclude the section with some observations regarding other potential integrations.

5.1 RCS

RCS [35] is a simple configuration management system that, while supporting branching, is often used with locking only. Our particular integration is geared towards that (pessimistic) mode of operation.

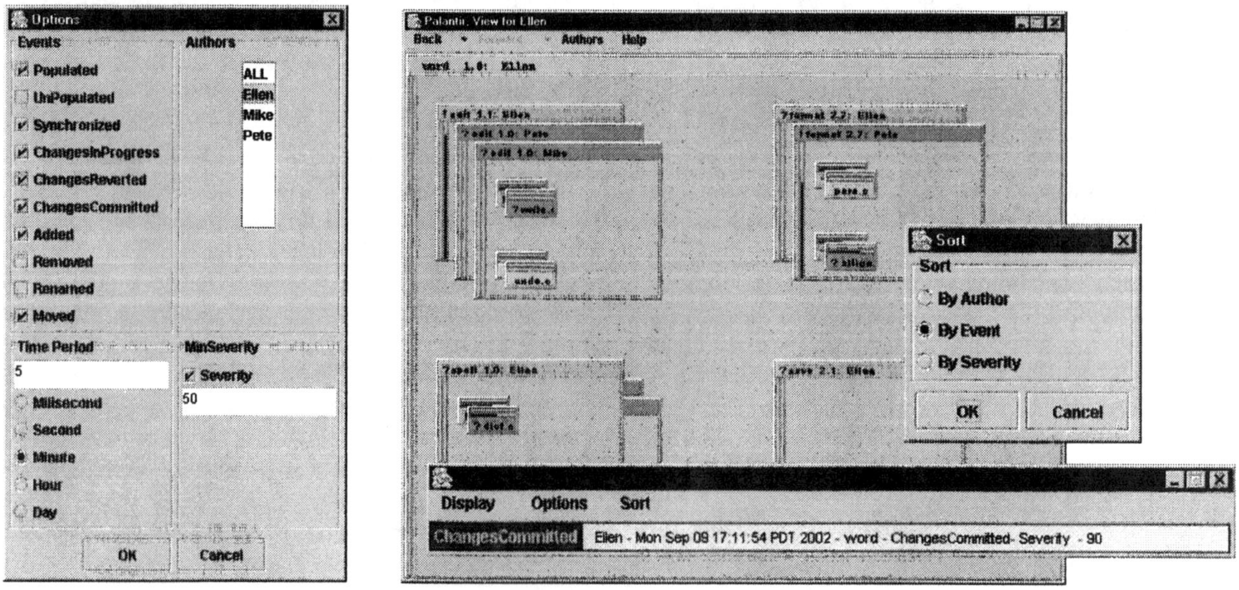

Figure 2. Extractor ("Options" window), ticker tape, and fully graphical visualization.

We were able to develop a workspace wrapper for RCS within the span of a single day. The wrapper constitutes about 500 lines of Java code, and largely concerns wrapping the RCS executable with our own executable that invokes RCS, calculates a severity measure, and emits corresponding events. Individual RCS commands are mapped, per artifact, onto Palantír events as follows.

check out: POPULATED
check-out + lock: [POPULATED +] CHANGESINPROGRESS
uncheck-out: CHANGESREVERTED
check-in: SEVERITYCHANGED + CHANGESCOMMITTED

The end result of this mapping is that developers become aware of which other developers are modifying which artifacts, but until the artifacts are checked in, they do not know the actual severity of the changes. This drawback could easily be overcome by building a simple workspace daemon that periodically calculates and emits the severity of each artifact currently locked.

The severity measure used in our RCS integration is the same as we use for the CVS integration. Using the output of the DIFF program, we calculate the percentage of lines that has been added, removed, and modified.

Compared to just RCS, its integration with Palantír has the advantage that developers are aware of which other artifacts are being modified in parallel, know at all times which new versions of artifacts are available, and have at least the opportunity to detect potential indirect conflicts.

5.2 CVS

CVS [4] is an optimistic configuration management system that allows parallel work. The integration of Palantír with CVS was also performed in a single day, and again constitutes about 500 lines of Java code. The particular mapping of commands to events, however, is slightly different (once again, per artifact).

check out: POPULATED
edit: CHANGESINPROGRESS
update: SYNCHRONIZED
commit: [CHANGESINPROGRESS +] SEVERITYCHANGED + CHANGESCOMMITTED

In addition to these commands, we also wrapped the addition and removal of artifacts. This represents a particularly interesting event since additions and removals are local to a workspace until the parent artifact is checked in. This represents a clear case in which Palantír shares workspace information that otherwise would not be known to others.

A single CVS command recursively operates on all artifacts in a workspace, and thus, can emit multiple events. Of particular interest is CVS EDIT, which announces to CVS that an artifact will be modified (see Section 6.1). It is not mandatory that this command is used before an artifact is changed and committed. In such cases, a commit should first result in the emission of a CHANGESINPROGRESS and awareness in effect is delayed. Again, this could be overcome by building a simple daemon.

Compared to just CVS, its integration with Palantír has the advantage that developers are more rapidly aware of potential conflicts, know of planned artifact additions and removals, and know at all times when new versions of artifacts are available and what their change severity is.

5.3 Other potential integrations

Integrating other configuration management systems may in fact be easier and more powerful than RCS or CVS. Newer configuration management systems provide trigger mechanisms and associated scripting languages in which to implement a workspace wrapper. One particularly interesting feature of some newer configuration management systems is their use of a virtual file system to implement workspaces. The virtual file system intercepts every read and write to an artifact. Palantír could leverage this mechanism to send out a SEVERITYCHANGED event every time an artifact is edited or modified. As compared to the RCS and CVS integrations, this would result in the most up-to-date workspace information possible.

6. Related work

Palantír builds upon work in the areas of configuration management and computer-support collaborative work. We discuss relevant contributions in each area below.

6.1 Configuration management

CVS [4] already provides what is perhaps the oldest awareness mechanism in the field of configuration management. Through the use of watches, developers specify which artifacts they want to monitor. Before changing an artifact, developers must announce their intent of doing so by invoking the CVS EDIT command. This triggers notifications to be send, usually via e-mail, to those developers who are watching the artifact in question. Compared to Palantír, CVS watches require explicit manual action, provide limited awareness information concerning direct conflicts only, and do not scale due to the use of e-mail as the presentation mechanism.

Coven [8] supports awareness through soft locks. Before changing any artifacts, developers place soft locks with associated messages on those artifacts. When another developer attempts to place a soft lock on an artifact that already has a soft lock, that developer is presented with the message attached to the lock. They then are given the option to abort, which has no further effect, or continue, which informs the other developers that parallel work is now ensuing. Coven suffers drawbacks similar to CVS: it requires extra manual actions and it provides, via e-mail, limited information concerning direct conflicts only.

EPOS [30] and Adele [17] do not directly address awareness, but rather provide sophisticated mechanisms to coordinate artifact sharing among workspaces. EPOS supports four different policies that can be instituted among different pairs of workspaces: (1) all artifacts are shared immediately, (2) artifacts are pushed to other workspaces, (3) artifacts are pulled from other workspaces, and (4) artifacts are implicitly propagated through the central repository [38]. Adele extends this model with programmable process support for specifying sharing policies on a per-artifact (type) basis [16]. In both cases, the primary objective is workspace integration, not awareness, and Palantír complements the functionality provided.

6.2 Computer-supported collaborative work

BSCW [3] is a web-based, shared, centralized workspace with integrated versioning facilities that allow it to be used as a configuration management system. Awareness is provided statically, via web-based icons that enrich the web page for each artifact with information concerning its state, and dynamically, via a Monitor Applet that continuously informs authors of what activities are taking place in the central workspace. Compared to Palantír, BSCW lacks pair-wise comparisons, severity information, and a mechanism to scope the events of interest.

TUKAN [32] and COOP/Orm [25] are distributed, cooperative software development environments that support fine-grained editing and versioning of artifacts. In TUKAN, authors can select different collaboration modes and, upon accessing or modifying an artifact, are informed via "weather" icons whether potential conflicts exist with other authors. In COOP/Orm, active diffs instantly communicate changes to other developers who can see those changes both in the version tree and the actual artifact. Unfortunately, both TUKAN and COOP/Orm provide awareness on a per-artifact basis and only when the artifact is actually accessed. An overall view of activities in other workspaces, such as provided by Palantír, is lacking.

State Treemap [28] is an awareness widget for multi-synchronous groupware that relies on many of the same concepts as Palantír. Its visualization component shows which artifacts are being modified (both locally and remotely) and which artifacts already have been committed to the configuration management repository. Out-of-sync artifacts and potential conflicts, thus, are quickly discovered. Because State Treemap lacks author information, it does not provide pair-wise workspace comparisons. Severity information is also missing, though an enhancement for change impact calculations is underway [29].

Other approaches, such as Elvin [20], iScent [2], and CoVer [24], are subsumed by the systems discussed.

7. Conclusions

Any configuration management system exhibits a fundamental tension between the need for individual developers to work in isolated workspaces and the need for the overall team to maintain control over the integration of the individual changes into the overall system. To address this tension, we have developed Palantír, a novel configuration management workspace awareness tool. Palantír deliberately, but non-intrusively, breaks workspace isolation by continuously informing developers of the activities of others developers. By letting developers know who modifies which artifacts by how much, Palantír complements current automated procedures with the capability of human *intervention* when potential problems are recognized.

Palantír exhibits three key properties: (1) its coordination mechanism is based on workspace rather than repository information, (2) it continuously instead of sporadically informs developers of other ongoing efforts, and (3) it provides an overall view of other workspaces that supports the detection of both direct and indirect conflicts. The resulting system increases awareness among developers, and helps them in coordinating their tasks such that future integration problems can be avoided.

The current incarnation of Palantír represents only the beginnings of our investigations into the use of awareness in configuration management systems. Now that we have demonstrated that it is indeed possible to enhance existing configuration management systems with awareness, we intend to develop additional visualizations, explore the use of virtual file systems as a way of creating a more informative workspace wrapper, and investigate the use of a measure of change impact to complement our measure of change severity. Additionally, we will integrate Palantír with an industrial-strength configuration management system to study whether it truly scales and whether we can empirically determine its impact on coordination among developers in an actual, real-life development setting.

Acknowledgments

We thank the other members of our research group for their valuable suggestions during the design, implementation, and testing of Palantír.

This research is supported by the National Science Foundation under Grant Number CCR-0093489. Effort also sponsored by the Defense Advanced Research Projects Agency, Rome Laboratory, Air Force Materiel Command, USAF under agreement numbers F30602-00-2-0599 and F30602-00-2-0607. The U.S. Government is authorized to reproduce and distribute reprints for governmental purposes notwithstanding any copyright annotation thereon. The views and conclusions contained herein are those of the authors and should not be interpreted as necessarily representing the official policies or endorsements, either expressed or implied, of the Defense Advanced Research Projects Agency, Rome Laboratory or the U.S. Government.

References

[1] L. Allen, et al. *ClearCase MultiSite: Supporting Geographically-Distributed Software Development.* Proceedings of the International Workshop on Software Configuration Management: ICSE SCM-4 and SCM-5 Workshops Selected Papers, 1995: p. 194-214.

[2] K.M. Anderson and N.O. Bouvin. *Supporting Project Awareness on the WWW with the iScent Framework.* Proceedings of the International Workshop on Awareness and the WWW, 2000.

[3] W. Appelt. *WWW Based Collaboration with the BSCW System.* Proceedings of the Conference on Current Trends in Theory and Informatics, 1999: p. 66-78.

[4] B. Berliner. *CVS II: Parallelizing Software Development.* Proceedings of the USENIX Winter 1990 Technical Conference, 1990: p. 341-352.

[5] E.A. Bier and S. Freeman. *MMM: A User Interface Architecture for Shared Editors on a Single Screen.* Proceedings of the ACM Symposium on User Interface Software and Technology, 1991: p. 79-86.

[6] C. Burrows and I. Wesley, *Ovum Evaluates Configuration Management.* Ovum Ltd., Burlington, Massachussetts, 1998.

[7] A. Carzaniga, D.S. Rosenblum, and A.L. Wolf, *Design and Evaluation of a Wide-Area Event Notification Service.* ACM Transactions on Computer Systems, 2001.

[8] M.C. Chu-Carroll and S. Sprenkle. *Coven: Brewing Better Collaboration through Software Configuration Management.* Proceedings of the Eighth International Symposium on Foundations of Software Engineering, 2000: p. 88-97.

[9] CollabNet, *SourceCast*, http://www.collabnet.org/products/sourcecast/, 2002.

[10] R. Conradi and B. Westfechtel, *Version Models for Software Configuration Management.* ACM Computing Surveys, 1998. 30(2): p. 232-282.

[11] S. Dart. *Concepts in Configuration Management Systems.* Proceedings of the Third International Workshop on Software Configuration Management, 1991: p. 1-18.

[12] C.R.B. De Souza, S.D. Basaveswara, and D.F. Redmiles. *Supporting Global Software Development with Event Notification Servers.* Proceedings of the ICSE 2002 International Workshop on Global Software Development, 2002.

[13] P. Dewan and R. Choudhary, *A High-Level and Flexible Framework for Implementing Multi-user Interfaces.* ACM Transactions on Information Systems, 1992. 10(4): p. 345-380.

[14] S.E. Dossick and G.E. Kaiser. *A Metadata-Based Distributed Software Development Environment.* Proceedings of the Seventh European Software Engineering Conference together with the Seventh ACM SIGSOFT International Symposium on the Foundations of Software Engineering, 1999: p. 464-475.

[15] P. Dourish and V. Bellotti. *Awareness and Coordination in Shared Workspaces.* Proceedings of the ACM Conference on Computer-Supported Cooperative Work, 1992: p. 107-114.

[16] J. Estublier. *Defining and Supporting Concurrent Engineering Policies in SCM.* Proceedings of the Tenth International Workshop on Software Configuration Management, 2001.

[17] J. Estublier and R. Casalles, *The Adele Configuration Manager*, in Configuration Management, W.F. Tichy, Editor. 1994: p. 99-134.

[18] G. Fitzpatrick, S. Kaplan, and T. Mansfield. *Physical Spaces, Virtual Places and Social Worlds: A Study of Work in the Virtual.* Proceedings of the Computer-Supported Collaborative Work '96, 1996: p. 334-343.

[19] G. Fitzpatrick, et al., *Supporting Public Availability and Accessibility with Elvin: Experiences and Reflections.* Computer Supported Cooperative Work, 2002 (to appear).

[20] G. Fitzpatrick, et al. *Augmenting the Workaday World with Elvin.* Proceedings of the Sixth European Conference on Computer Supported Cooperative Work, 1999: p. 431-451.

[21] R.E. Grinter. *Using a Configuration Management Tool to Coordinate Software Development.* Proceedings of the Conference on Organizational Computing Systems, 1995: p. 168-177.

[22] R.E. Grinter, *Supporting Articulation Work Using Software Configuration Management Systems.* Computer Supported Cooperative Work, 1996. 5(4): p. 447-465.

[23] C. Gutwin and S. Greenberg. *Workspace Awareness for Groupware.* Proceedings of the CHI'96 Conference Companion on Human Factors in Computing Systems, 1996: p. 208-209.

[24] A. Haake and J.M. Haake. *Take CoVer: Exploiting Version Support in Cooperative Systems.* Proceedings of the INTERCHI'93, 1993: p. 406-413.

[25] B. Magnusson and U. Asklund. *Fine Grained Version Control of Configurations in COOP/Orm.* Proceedings of the Sixth International Workshop on Software Configuration Management, 1996: p. 31-48.

[26] T. Mens, *A State-of-the-Art Survey on Software Merging.* IEEE Transactions on Software Engineering, 2002. 28(5): p. 449-462.

[27] A. Mockus and J. Herbsleb. *Expertise Browser: A Quantitative Approach to Identifying Expertise.* Proceedings of the 2002 International Conference on Software Engineering, 2002.

[28] P. Molli, H. Skaf-Molli, and C. Bouthier. *State Treemap: an Awareness Widget for Multi-Synchronous Groupware.* Proceedings of the Seventh International Workshop on Groupware, 2001.

[29] P. Molli, H. Skaf-Molli, and G. Oster. *Divergence Awareness for Virtual Team through the Web.* Proceedings of the Integrated Design and Process Technology, 2002.

[30] B.P. Munch. *Versioning in a Software Engineering Database - the Change-Oriented Way.* Ph.D. Thesis, DCST, NTH, 1993.

[31] D.E. Perry, H.P. Siy, and L.G. Votta, *Parallel Changes in Large-Scale Software Development: An Observational Case Study.* ACM Transactions on Software Engineering and Methodology, 2001. 10(3): p. 308-337.

[32] T. Schummer and J.M. Haake. *Supporting Distributed Software Development by Modes of Collaboration.* Proceedings of the Seventh European Conference on Computer Supported Cooperative Work, 2001: p. 79-98.

[33] SourceForge.net, *SourceForge*, http://sourceforge.net/, 2002.

[34] Telelogic, *CM/Synergy*, http://www.telelogic.com/products/synergy/cmsynergy/index.cfm, 2002.
[35] W.F. Tichy, *RCS, A System for Version Control.* Software - Practice and Experience, 1985. 15(7): p. 637-654.
[36] A. van der Hoek, et al., *A Testbed for Configuration Management Policy Programming.* IEEE Transactions on Software Engineering, 2002. 28(1): p. 79-99.
[37] C. Walrad and D. Strom, *The Importance of Branching Models in SCM.* IEEE Computer, 2002. 35(9): p. 31-38.
[38] A.I. Wang, et al. *Improving Cooperation Support in the EPOS CM System.* Proceedings of the European Workshop on Software Process Technology, 1998: p. 75-91.
[39] D. Wiborg Weber. *Change Sets versus Change Packages: Comparing Implementations of Change-Based SCM.* Proceedings of the Seventh International Workshop on Software Configuration Management, 1997: p. 25-35.

Consistency Management with Repair Actions

Christian Nentwich, Wolfgang Emmerich and Anthony Finkelstein
Department of Computer Science
University College London
Gower Street, London WC1E 6BT, UK
{c.nentwich,w.emmerich,a.finkelstein}@cs.ucl.ac.uk

Abstract

Comprehensive consistency management requires a strong mechanism for repair once inconsistencies have been detected. In this paper we present a repair framework for inconsistent distributed documents. The core piece of the framework is a new method for generating interactive repairs from full first order logic formulae that constrain these documents. We present a full implementation of the components in our repair framework, as well as their application to the UML and related heterogeneous documents such as EJB deployment descriptors. We describe how our approach can be used as an infrastructure for building higher-level, domain specific frameworks and provide an overview of related work in the database and software development environment community.

1 Introduction

Software engineers today make use of many informal and semi-formal notations during development, the Unified Modeling Language (UML) [18] being the most notable example. Large systems are increasingly developed in a distributed fashion, making it necessary to provide support for the distribution of development artifacts.

The goal of this work is to support software engineers in managing the consistency of their artifacts. Consistency management typically encompasses the specification of consistency constraints, consistency checking, and acting on inconsistency, or repair. In previous work on xlinkit [15], we have shown how a tool-independent service built on open, extensible and light-weight web technology can provide a strong consistency checking mechanism. The aim of this paper is to complete the circle and complement xlinkit with a strong, yet light-weight and tool-independent repair mechanism.

The main contribution of this paper is a tool-independent framework for repairing distributed documents. The core piece of this is a novel evaluation semantics that automatically derives a complete and correct set of repair actions from xlinkit's first order logic constraints. These repair actions serve to guide the user towards making effective corrections to documents: to enable them concentrate on editing operations that can provably eliminate inconsistency, and to reassure them that all possible resolution options are presented.

The semantics has been fully implemented in the form of a repair action administration and execution tool. We discuss the design, features, and implementation of these programs. We give examples of how the approach can be used to repair inconsistent UML documents and related heterogeneous documents such as Enterprise JavaBeans (EJB) [12] deployment descriptors. Finally, we explain how the infrastructure provided by our solution supports the construction of higher-level repair frameworks such as precedence or workflow-driven repair.

The paper progresses from here as follows: we provide some background on the consistency checking mechanisms of xlinkit, which forms an essential part of the remaining discussion. We then present the architecture of our repair framework and discuss the repair action generation semantics, followed by an overview our implementation and options for higher-level repairs. The paper concludes with an account of related work and an outline of future work.

2 Background

xlinkit is a framework for checking the consistency of distributed, heterogeneous documents. It comprises a language, based on first order logic, for expressing constraints between such documents, a document management mechanism and an engine that checks the documents against the constraints. A full description of xlinkit, including a formal specification of its semantics, its scalability and an evaluation can be found in [15]. The application of xlinkit to checking distributed and heterogeneous software engineering artifacts is described in [16, 17].

0-7695-1877-X/03 $17.00 © 2003 IEEE

xlinkit builds on open technologies, most notably the eXtensible Markup Language (XML) [1] and XPath [3] to provide a lightweight and tool-independent consistency checking service for distributed documents. By combining first order logic with XPath expressions, xlinkit supports the specification of constraints over XML documents. Figure 1 is an example of an xlinkit *consistency rule* that implements a constraint from the UML Core package, *"The AssociationEnds must have a unique name within the Association"*. This rule can be applied to UML models encoded in the XML Metadata Interchange (XMI) [19] format, the standard UML interchange format.

```
<forall var="a" in="//UML:Association">
  <forall var="x" in="$a/*/UML:AssociationEnd">
    <forall var="y" in="$a/*/UML:AssociationEnd">
      <implies>
        <equal op1="$x/@name" op2="$y/@name"/>
        <same op1="$x" op2="$y"/>
      </implies>
    </forall>
  </forall>
</forall>
```

Figure 1. Sample consistency rule

One of the main contributions of xlinkit is that it provides a strong diagnostic for inconsistency: Instead of returning boolean values as the result of formula evaluation, it creates n-ary hyperlinks that connect inconsistent elements. Figure 2 shows the link generated by checking the constraint in Figure 1 against an inconsistent XMI document. It relates the association with the two association ends that have the same name, providing all the diagnostic information necessary to identify the elements causing the inconsistency.

```
<xlinkit:ConsistencyLink rule="as.xml#id('r1')">
  <xlinkit:State>inconsistent</xlinkit:State>
  <xlinkit:Locator
    xlink:href="inc.xml#//UML:Association[2]"/>
  <xlinkit:Locator
    xlink:href="inc.xml#//UML:Association[2]/*
                         /UML:AssociationEnd[1]"/>
  <xlinkit:Locator
    xlink:href="inc.xml#//UML:Association[2]/*
                         /UML:AssociationEnd[2]"/>
</xlinkit:ConsistencyLink>
```

Figure 2. Sample consistency link

Raw XML hyperlinks form a solid basis for further processing or tool integration, but they are not particularly useful to the end-user in their raw form. xlinkit provides a report generation tool, *Pulitzer*, that enables rule writers to attach diagnostic messages to inconsistent links. It processes these messages and generates HTML or XML report pages. Figure 3 shows a "report fragment" for our sample UML rule. It uses the `locator` variable to refer to the endpoints of the link in Figure 2, and retrieves information, in this case the name of the association and the name of its roles, for display. We will show later in this paper the result of processing this fragment.

```
<report:linkdescription state="inconsistent">
  The association
  <font color="red">
  <i>%@=gettext($locator[1]/@name)%</i></font>
  has two ends with the same role name,
  <font color="red">
  <i>%@=gettext($locator[2]/@name)%</i></font>.
</report:linkdescription>
```

Figure 3. Report Fragment

3 Architectural Overview

A consistency management system that performs a check and explains to the user which elements are contributing to an inconsistency is only partly complete. This section serves to introduce the architecture of the repair framework we have constructed to complement the xlinkit checker.

The aim of our work is to present to the user a simple set of options, or *repair actions*, to choose between when an inconsistency occurs. Figure 4 gives an overview of our architecture as a UML collaboration diagram.

The *repair administrator* creates repair actions by static analysis of a set of constraints. It is important that the actions are of high quality and not faulty, meaning in practice that they should be complete and correct:

- *There are no actions that can be taken to remove an inconsistency other than those generated by the generator.*
- *Any of the actions generated by the generator can remove an inconsistency.*

While our semantics can guarantee completeness and correctness, the repair administrator may still want to make use of their domain knowledge to disable actions that should not be offered to the user. For example, if an association has two equal role names, we can delete the association, delete either association end or rename either role. The repair administrator will know that it does not make sense to remove association ends – unary associations do not exist in the UML – and so can disable these two actions. The final output of the repair administrator is a parameterized set of actions that needs to be instantiated with actual inconsistent data.

When a linkbase is produced by the check engine, the user can process it with the *repair manager*. This tool will instantiate the correct set of repair actions for each inconsistency and present the available choices to the user, minus

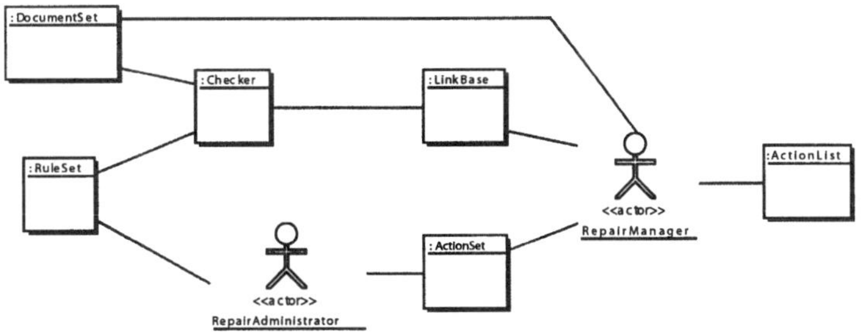

Figure 4. Repair Architecture

any actions disabled by the administrator. After selecting the actions for each violation, or choosing not to take action, the user can instruct the tool to execute the repair.

We deliberately restrict the scope of the architecture to the output of concrete actions. Document modification is an implementation-specific mechanism and we did not wish to restrict our work to any particular technology. Simple implementations that can be provided include: a document update tool that makes copies of the original documents and returns modified instances – the only option when pure http is used and there is no way to modify the documents,– a tool that modifies remote documents over the web using infrastructure such as WebDAV [10], or full integration into proprietary tools, which would require a language to map from actions to component invocations.

With this brief overview in mind, we now discuss the core piece of the architecture, which is the repair action generator built into the repair administrator.

4 Repair Action Generation

The core contribution of this paper is the denotational semantics that maps xlinkit's first order logic language to repair actions that can be used to interactively correct rule violations. In this section we provide a formal definition of this semantics, a step-by-step explanation and several examples.

$$
\begin{array}{rcl}
formula & ::= & \forall \mathbf{var} \in XPath(formula) \mid \\
& & \exists \mathbf{var} \in XPath(formula) \mid \\
& & formula \ \mathbf{and} \ formula \mid \\
& & formula \ \mathbf{or} \ formula \mid \\
& & formula \ \mathbf{implies} \ formula \mid \\
& & \mathbf{not} formula \mid \\
& & RelativePath = RelativePath \mid
\end{array}
$$

Figure 5. Rule language abstract syntax

The input to our repair action generator will be xlinkit formulae. Figure 5 shows the abstract syntax of our rule language. The meaning of the quantifiers is the same as that in standard first order logic. For a full definition see [15].

In our repair system, there are three types of modifications that can be made to a document: *Add*, *Delete* and *Change*. While change could be represented by deletion followed by addition, we retain it as an atomic action as it simplifies comprehension by the user – changing a value is an intuitive concept and the user only has to select one action.

$$
\begin{array}{rcl}
Action & ::= & Add\ Accessor \mid \\
& & Delete\ Accessor \mid \\
& & Change\ Accessor\ RelativePath \\
Accessor & ::= & Direct\ LocatorNumber \mid \\
& & Lookup\ XPath \\
XPath & ::= & AbsolutePath \mid RelativePath
\end{array}
$$

Figure 6. Repair actions

Each of the three actions are parametrized by the target of their modification. We refer to this as the action's *Accessor*. Accessors come in two forms, *Direct Accessors* and *Lookup Accessors*. Direct Accessors point to information relative to a hyperlink locator generated by xlinkit, while Lookup Accessors require the user of the repair manager to select an item interactively. The reason for this distinction will become clear from the definition of the semantics.

Figure 6 defines the abstract syntax of repair actions. We define an XPath to be either an absolute path, which starts from the root of a document, or a relative path, which starts with a variable reference. Due to space constraints, it is not possible to present a more detailed grammar of the XPath language in this paper. Change actions have an additional path parameter, which must be a path relative to the accessor: the meaning is that we wish to change a property, identified by the relative path, of some element, identified by the accessor.

We will in the following make use of the function

$getvar(RelativePath)$, which retrieves the variable name from a relative path. Because the function can be implemented using simple string manipulation and formalisation would require a complete grammar for XPath, we will not go beyond this informal definition.

Our semantics maps formulae to a set of sets of repair actions. It maps to multiple sets because formulae that include the logical connectives *and*, *or* or *implies* can fail in multiple ways. Each set of actions will be an alternative, and the correct one must be chosen after a consistency check, when the hyperlink locator information becomes available. Our semantics will make use of the cartesian operator $\wp(\wp(Action)) \times \wp(\wp(Action))$ in order to prepend a set of sets of actions to each set in a set of actions. For example, abstractly, $\{\{a, b\}\} \times \{\{c\}, \{d\}\}$ becomes $\{\{a, b, c\}, \{a, b, d\}\}$. We will also make use of the function $locator(variable)$, which returns the hyperlink locator number xlinkit has assigned to a particular variable. The function is implemented in xlinkit and is not formally defined here.

We can now discuss the denotational action generation semantics. The discussion will provide an overview of the semantics, and will be followed by several examples.

Figure 7 defines the function $\mathcal{D}_i$, the main function for mapping a formula to repair actions. It takes as a subscript parameter a set of variable bindings, $\sigma : \mathbf{var} \times XPath$, which is assumed to be empty when the function is first invoked, and a set of variables that can be referenced by locators, τ, which is also assumed to be empty in the beginning. The function subscript is short for "inconsistent", that is the function is defined to work under the assumption that the formula has been violated. Its task is to pick out and act on the violating elements.

For example, suppose a formula of the form $\forall \mathbf{var} \in XPath\ (\phi)$ has been violated. Then for some assignment of the variable, ϕ evaluates to *false*. There are two ways this inconsistency can be removed: delete the element currently assigned to the variable, or remove the inconsistency recursively by fixing ϕ. It is easy to show that there are no other ways this inconsistency can be removed: adding a new element cannot make the existing element more consistent, and neither can changing a property of the element, since the quantifier does not check for properties – although the subformula may, in which case the recursive definition will generate the appropriate repair action.

The logical connectives are defined depending on the evaluation of the subformulae necessary to make them inconsistent. If both subformulae need to evaluate to a certain result to make the result inconsistent, the sets of actions are joined using a cartesian product. Choosing any of the actions in the combined set will then be sufficient for removing the inconsistency. For example, if $a \wedge b = false$ then making either a or b true will make the overall result true.

Some connectives can fail in multiple ways. The different modes of failure are combined using the union operator and become alternatives. It is only after a check has been executed that information on how a formula has failed becomes available and the correct set of actions can be selected. For example, the definition of *and* takes three possibilities into account: the first subformula fails, the second subformula fails, or both subformulae fail and their results are joined using the cartesian product. By contrast, if *or* fails we know that both subformulae must be false and simply join their actions.

Some logical connectives invert the meaning of the repair semantics. For example, *not* requires us to look for assignments that make its subformula *consistent* for an overall inconsistent result. Similarly, in order to find a failure for *implies*, we must treat its first subformula as consistent and the second as inconsistent. The function $\mathcal{D}_c$, also defined in Figure 7, provides this inverted mapping. The goal in this function is to assume that the outcome of a formula will be *true* and to construct repair actions that prevent this.

In many cases, it is not possible to point to a definite element for modification. The simplest such case is a formula involving existential quantification, for example $\exists\ \mathbf{var} \in XPath(\phi)$. If this formula is violated, then no element exists for which the subformula ϕ evaluates to true. There are two ways of acting: add a new element that matches the XPath and for which ϕ is true, or select one of the elements on the path and make ϕ true for it. It will, however, not be possible to point to definite elements in the repair actions for ϕ anymore we cannot choose automatically for which variable assignment ϕ should be corrected. An example of this will be given in the next subsection.

As soon as an existential quantifier is encountered while in inconsistent mode, or a universal quantifier in consistent mode – in this case the subformula was consistent for all assignments and the choice which element to change can again not be made automatically –, the semantics switches to the "no information" functions in Figure 8. In these functions, no direct accessors are generated and all actions require selection.

Predicates are treated differently from logical connectives and quantifiers. We have included only equality as an example in this paper. An equality comparison in xlinkit compares elements relative to variables. In order to fix a violated equality comparison, we generate change actions. Take for example the formula $\$x/@name = \$y/@name$, which compares the name attributes of nodes x and y, which must have been bound by some outer formula. It is not possible to decide in general which side of the equality has caused the inconsistency, so we always generate two change actions. The $change$ function in Figure 7 shows how this is done: if the variable that an argument is relative to is present in τ, and can thus be accessed through a locator, we gener-

$$
\begin{aligned}
change(RelativePath, \sigma, \tau) &= Change\ (Direct\ locator(getvar(RelativePath)))\ RelativePath, \\
&\quad if\ getvar(RelativePath) \in \tau \\
&= Change\ (Lookup\ \sigma(getvar(RelativePath))),\ otherwise
\end{aligned}
$$

$$
\begin{aligned}
\mathcal{D}_i &: formula \rightarrow \wp(\wp(Action)) \\
\mathcal{D}_i\llbracket \forall \mathbf{var} \in XPath\ (formula)\rrbracket_{\sigma,\tau} &= \{\{Delete\ Direct\ locator(\mathbf{var})\}\} \times \\
&\quad \mathcal{D}_i\llbracket formula\rrbracket_{(\{(var,XPath)\}\cup\sigma),(\{var\}\cup\tau)} \\
\mathcal{D}_i\llbracket \exists \mathbf{var} \in XPath\ (formula)\rrbracket_{\sigma,\tau} &= \{\{Add\ Lookup\ XPath\}\} \times \mathcal{N}_i\llbracket formula\rrbracket_{\{(var,XPath)\}\cup\sigma,\tau} \\
\mathcal{D}_i\llbracket formula_1\ \mathbf{and}\ formula_2\rrbracket_{\sigma,\tau} &= \mathcal{D}_i\llbracket formula_1\rrbracket_{\sigma,\tau} \cup \mathcal{D}_i\llbracket formula_2\rrbracket_{\sigma,\tau} \cup (\mathcal{D}_i\llbracket formula_1\rrbracket_{\sigma,\tau} \times \mathcal{D}_i\llbracket formula_2\rrbracket_{\sigma,\tau}) \\
\mathcal{D}_i\llbracket formula_1\ \mathbf{or}\ formula_2\rrbracket_{\sigma,\tau} &= \mathcal{D}_i\llbracket formula_1\rrbracket_{\sigma,\tau} \times \mathcal{D}_i\llbracket formula_2\rrbracket_{\sigma,\tau} \\
\mathcal{D}_i\llbracket formula_1\ \mathbf{implies}\ formula_2\rrbracket_{\sigma,\tau} &= \mathcal{D}_c\llbracket formula_1\rrbracket_{\sigma,\tau} \times \mathcal{D}_i\llbracket formula_2\rrbracket_{\sigma,\tau} \\
\mathcal{D}_i\llbracket \mathbf{not}\ formula\rrbracket_{\sigma,\tau} &= \mathcal{D}_c\llbracket formula\rrbracket_{\sigma,\tau} \\
\mathcal{D}_i\llbracket RelativePath_1 = RelativePath_2\rrbracket_{\sigma,\tau} &= change(RelativePath_1, \sigma, \tau) \times change(RelativePath_2, \sigma, \tau)
\end{aligned}
$$

$$
\begin{aligned}
\mathcal{D}_c &: formula \rightarrow \wp(\wp(Action)) \\
\mathcal{D}_c\llbracket \forall \mathbf{var} \in XPath\ (formula)\rrbracket_{\sigma,\tau} &= \{\{Add\ Lookup\ XPath\}\} \times \mathcal{N}_i\llbracket formula\rrbracket_{\{(var,XPath)\}\cup\sigma,\tau} \\
\mathcal{D}_c\llbracket \exists \mathbf{var} \in XPath\ (formula)\rrbracket_{\sigma,\tau} &= \{\{Delete\ Direct\ locator(\mathbf{var})\}\} \times \\
&\quad \mathcal{D}_c\llbracket formula\rrbracket_{(\{(var,XPath)\}\cup\sigma),(var\cup\tau)} \\
\mathcal{D}_c\llbracket formula_1\ \mathbf{and}\ formula_2\rrbracket_{\sigma,\tau} &= \mathcal{D}_c\llbracket formula_1\rrbracket_{\sigma,\tau} \times \mathcal{D}_c\llbracket formula_2\rrbracket_{\sigma,\tau} \\
\mathcal{D}_c\llbracket formula_1\ \mathbf{or}\ formula_2\rrbracket_{\sigma,\tau} &= \mathcal{D}_c\llbracket formula_1\rrbracket_{\sigma,\tau} \cup \mathcal{D}_c\llbracket formula_2\rrbracket_{\sigma,\tau} \cup (\mathcal{D}_c\llbracket formula_1\rrbracket_{\sigma,\tau} \times \mathcal{D}_c\llbracket formula_2\rrbracket_{\sigma,\tau}) \\
\mathcal{D}_c\llbracket formula_1\ \mathbf{implies}\ formula_2\rrbracket_{\sigma,\tau} &= \mathcal{D}_i\llbracket formula_1\rrbracket_{\sigma,\tau} \cup \mathcal{D}_c\llbracket formula_2\rrbracket_{\sigma,\tau} \\
\mathcal{D}_c\llbracket \mathbf{not}\ formula\rrbracket_{\sigma,\tau} &= \mathcal{D}_i\llbracket formula\rrbracket_{\sigma,\tau} \\
\mathcal{D}_c\llbracket RelativePath_1 = RelativePath_2\rrbracket_{\sigma,\tau} &= change(RelativePath_1, \sigma, \tau) \times change(RelativePath_2, \sigma, \tau)
\end{aligned}
$$

Figure 7. Repair actions - Direct accessor cases

ate a direct change action. Otherwise, we generate a lookup action and the user has to select an item to change.

4.1 Examples

In order to clarify the semantics and show how it can work in practice, we now present some simple examples that cover the different action generation functions.

The formula $\forall\ x \in$ "$/a$"($\exists\ y \in$ "$/b$"($\$x/@name = \$y/@name$)) would be processed as follows: function $\mathcal{D}_i$ generates a delete action for the inconsistent x, $\{\{Delete\ 1\}\}$, where 1 is the locator number returned by xlinkit. It then calls $\mathcal{D}_i$ recursively to process the existential quantifier. We know that for some x, we cannot find any y for which the equality comparison is true, so we add the action $\{\{Add\ Lookup$ "$/b$"$\}\}$ and call $\mathcal{N}_i$ on the equals predicate. Evaluation of the *change* function returns two actions, $\{\{Change\ Direct\ 1$ "$@name$", $Change\ Lookup$ "$/b$" "$@name$"$\}\}$, which can be read as "change the name of locator 1, or change the name of some b". We can modify the name of a directly, because it is present as a locator, but have to let the user choose which b is to be modified. The actions are all combined using the times operator to form a set of four alternative actions for the user to choose.

If we modify the formula slightly to read $\forall\ x \in$ "$/a$"($not(\exists\ y \in$ "$/b$"($\$x/@name = \$y/@name$))) the evaluation proceeds differently. The same action is generated for the universal quantifier, but $\mathcal{D}_c$ is called on the existential quantifier instead of $\mathcal{D}_i$. In this case there is no uncertainty: if a violation occurs, it is because an element that should not be there, is present anyway. Thus $\mathcal{D}_c$ creates the action $\{\{Delete\ 2\}\}$ where 2 is the locator number returned by xlinkit. The change function also returns the slightly different set of actions, $\{\{Change\ Direct\ 1$ "$@name$", $Change\ Direct\ 2$ "$@name$"$\}\}$. Since we know the element that should not be there is referenced by a locator we do not have to offer a choice to the user.

4.2 Additional Considerations

The most important question to ask of our semantics is whether its results are correct and complete. The size restrictions for this paper do not permit us to answer this question, but we note that both properties can be shown to hold by structural induction over the formulae. A simple exam-

$$
\begin{array}{rcl}
\mathcal{N}_i & : & formula \rightarrow \wp(\wp(Action)) \\
\mathcal{N}_i[\![\forall \mathbf{var} \in XPath\ (formula)]\!]_{\sigma,\tau} & = & \{\{Delete\ Lookup\ XPath\}\} \times \mathcal{N}_i[\![formula]\!]_{\{(var,XPath)\}\cup\sigma,\tau} \\
\mathcal{N}_i[\![\exists \mathbf{var} \in XPath\ (formula)]\!]_{\sigma,\tau} & = & \{\{Add\ Lookup\ XPath\}\} \times \mathcal{N}_i[\![formula]\!]_{\{(var,XPath)\}\cup\sigma,\tau} \\
\mathcal{N}_i[\![formula_1\ \mathbf{and}\ formula_2]\!]_{\sigma,\tau} & = & \mathcal{N}_i[\![formula_1]\!]_{\sigma,\tau} \times \mathcal{N}_i[\![formula_2]\!]_{\sigma,\tau} \\
\mathcal{N}_i[\![formula_1\ \mathbf{or}\ formula_2]\!]_{\sigma,\tau} & = & \mathcal{N}_i[\![formula_1]\!]_{\sigma,\tau} \times \mathcal{N}_i[\![formula_2]\!]_{\sigma,\tau} \\
\mathcal{N}_i[\![formula_1\ \mathbf{implies}\ formula_2]\!]_{\sigma,\tau} & = & \mathcal{N}_c[\![formula_1]\!]_{\sigma,\tau} \times \mathcal{N}_i[\![formula_2]\!]_{\sigma,\tau} \\
\mathcal{N}_i[\![\mathbf{not}\ formula]\!]_{\sigma,\tau} & = & \mathcal{N}_c[\![formula]\!]_{\sigma,\tau} \\
\mathcal{N}_i[\![RelativePath_1 = RelativePath_2]\!]_{\sigma,\tau} & = & change(RelativePath_1,\sigma,\tau) \times change(RelativePath_2,\sigma,\tau)
\end{array}
$$

$$
\begin{array}{rcl}
\mathcal{N}_c & : & formula \rightarrow \wp(\wp(Action)) \\
\mathcal{N}_c[\![\forall \mathbf{var} \in XPath\ (formula)]\!]_{\sigma,\tau} & = & \{\{Add\ Lookup\ XPath\}\} \times \mathcal{N}_c[\![formula]\!]_{\{(var,XPath)\}\cup\sigma,\tau} \\
\mathcal{N}_c[\![\exists \mathbf{var} \in XPath\ (formula)]\!]_{\sigma,\tau} & = & \{\{Delete\ Lookup\ XPath\}\} \times \mathcal{N}_c[\![formula]\!]_{\{(var,XPath)\}\cup\sigma,\tau} \\
\mathcal{N}_c[\![formula_1\ \mathbf{and}\ formula_2]\!]_{\sigma,\tau} & = & \mathcal{N}_c[\![formula_1]\!]_{\sigma,\tau} \times \mathcal{N}_c[\![formula_2]\!]_{\sigma,\tau} \\
\mathcal{N}_c[\![formula_1\ \mathbf{or}\ formula_2]\!]_{\sigma,\tau} & = & \mathcal{N}_c[\![formula_1]\!]_{\sigma,\tau} \times \mathcal{N}_c[\![formula_2]\!]_{\sigma,\tau} \\
\mathcal{N}_c[\![formula_1\ \mathbf{implies}\ formula_2]\!]_{\sigma,\tau} & = & \mathcal{N}_i[\![formula_1]\!]_{\sigma,\tau} \times \mathcal{N}_c[\![formula_2]\!]_{\sigma,\tau} \\
\mathcal{N}_c[\![\mathbf{not}\ formula]\!]_{\sigma,\tau} & = & \mathcal{N}_i[\![formula]\!]_{\sigma,\tau} \\
\mathcal{N}_c[\![RelativePath_1 = RelativePath_2]\!]_{\sigma,\tau} & = & change(RelativePath_1,\sigma,\tau) \times change(RelativePath_2,\sigma,\tau)
\end{array}
$$

Figure 8. Repair actions - no information cases

ple was given earlier in this section in the explanation of action generation for the universal quantifier.

Clearly, additional actions could be generated for equality comparisons: we could delete the properties referenced by the predicate, e.g. delete the *name* attributes referenced in the example. We have deliberately chosen not to include these actions in the semantics because we found that in practice these properties are in almost all cases mandatory. Deleting them would thus simply lead to a violation of document structure.

It is possible to provide some support for default values for node changes in the case of equality: if $a = b$ is violated, then the only way to remove the inconsistency is to set a equal to b and vice-versa. We can thus offer a default value of b for changes to a and the other way round. This approach will not work once the equality predicate occurs in a negative formula: if $not(a = b)$ is violated then we cannot determine a default value – the only criterion is that after the change the two values must not be equal.

5 Implementation

We have implemented a framework for repair action generation and execution and tested it in several application domains. This section presents the implementation of the repair administrator and repair manager tool and its application to UML models.

The first step in the architecture we outlined in Section 3 was the generation of repair actions from constraints. Figure 9 shows a snapshot of our repair administrator tool. The administrator has selected the example rule from Figure 1, and the tool has generated the repair actions. For each action, the administrator can enter a natural language description that is comprehensible to the user, or leave the default description generated by the action generator.

The administrator has decided that deleting the ends of the association should not be an option available to the user, but they should instead rename either of the role names or delete the whole association. The delete actions for the association ends have thus been disabled and have turned red. In the *diagnostic message* section, the administrator can enter a diagnostic message that describes the inconsistency as a whole. When everything has been entered, the set of actions and messages is saved in a report fragment in XML format for use by the repair execution tool.

Figure 10 shows how default value generation is handled in the case of add-actions. The rule displayed at the top says that for every class stereotyped "EJBImplementation" in the UML model, there must be a Session Bean or Entity Bean declaration in the Enterprise JavaBeans deployment descriptor. If such an entry does not exists, one option is to add one. In this case, we have selected the "From File" option and selected an existing entry in the XML browser (not shown). All text elements of the tree fragment have been parametrized by the tool and will be offered as text fields for the user to fill in when they execute the repair manager. If no sample file is available, the administrator can automatically construct the default value to add from

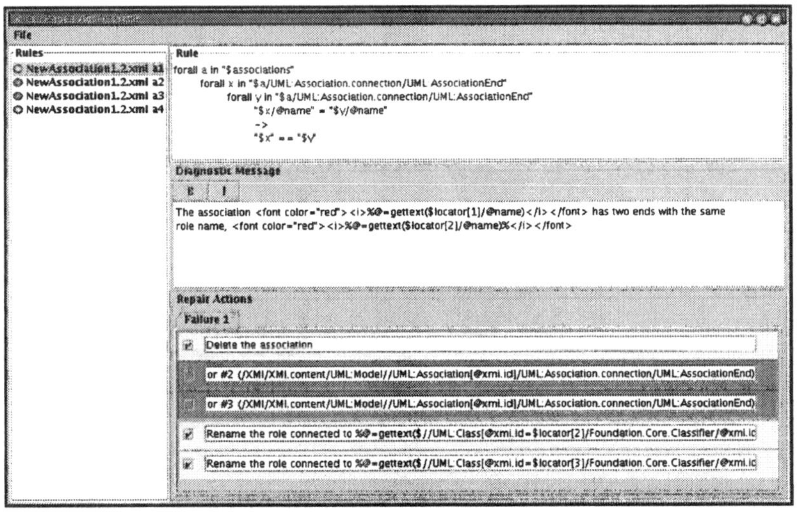

Figure 9. Repair Administrator Tool

an XML Schema [6] instead.

Figure 11 shows a snapshot of the repair manager tool. We have fed into the tool a linkbase generated by checking an inconsistent UML model. On the left-hand side, the user can see which rules have been violated. Rules are flagged red if no repair actions have yet been chosen for them and turn green as soon as one or more actions are chosen. Notice that only the two types of actions permitted by the administrator are present, and that the role and class names have been substituted from the UML model. Changing either name will fix the inconsistency, so we have entered a new value for the role connected to the "SalesAssistant" class. We can now click the "Execute Actions" button and a suitable back-end can modify the files, as explained in Section 3.

The repair execution tool can also easily check for contradictory repair actions. The way this is done depends on the action: Two change actions cannot modify the same property of the same element to hold two different values; and no action of any type must access a path that is logically beneath the path of a delete action. If either of these scenarios occurs, the user must deselect one of the actions.

6 Advanced Repair

Using our repair action generator as an infrastructure tool we can build higher level repair frameworks.

An advanced repair framework in our sense is one that restricts the set of repair actions automatically in some way, so as to minimize or even eliminate user interaction. The simplest type is a *static precedence relationship* where certain types of artifacts take precedence over others. For example, if a UML model is inconsistent with a Java class we may dictate that the model should override the class. This can be implemented by removing those repair actions that refer to elements in the UML model and only allowing those that modify Java classes.

A more sophisticated approach would be to construct *dynamic precedence relationships*. In this approach, the override relationship would change over time. For example, during design it may be appropriate for the UML model to override Java classes but during an implementation phase, when source code evolves more quickly and models become outdated, we may wish to invert this relationship. We could use an off-the-shelf workflow system or a simple event notification mechanism such as Emu [8] to implement such a system.

7 Evaluation

Since the repair action semantics can be proven to generate correct and complete repair actions, this evaluation section concentrates mainly on practical issues we encountered during testing.

We have applied our repair generator the the full set of rules in the UML Foundation/Core package. On the whole, the action generator performed very well and it is possible for somebody with knowledge of the documents to intuitively grasp the meaning and consequence of actions. We have however identified several problems that must be addressed before this framework can become a practical proposition.

The biggest problem is the interaction of repair actions with the grammar of documents and with actions generated by other constraints. These cases are currently not addressed at all and are investigated further in the section on

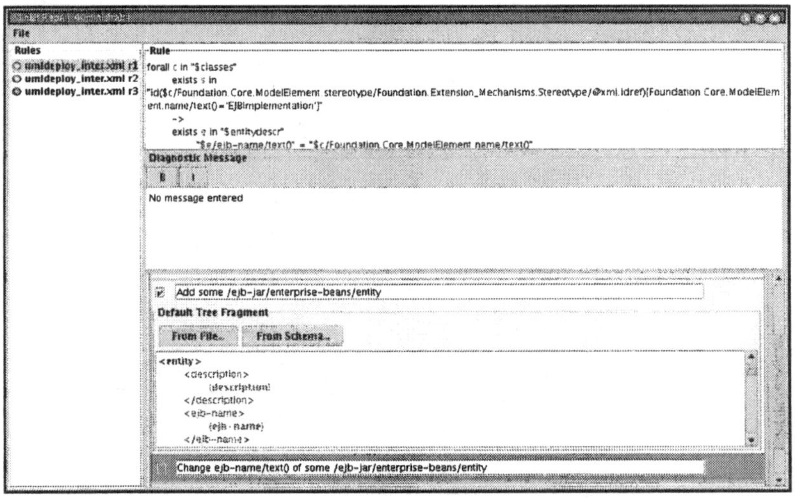

Figure 10. Default Tree Fragment Generation

future work.

It is also not clear at the moment whether the localized view of one single inconsistency at a time may cause problems with multiple interconnected inconsistencies. For example, a single class may violate several constraints, but deleting it could automatically fix all of them. One possible way of approaching this problem would be to provide a more "global" overview of problems where a single element causes multiple inconsistencies. This could help to reduce user disorientation. Another possibility is the automatic selection of actions for elements that contribute to multiple inconsistencies as soon as the user chooses to fix the element once.

Finally, another common problem we have identified is the apparent complexity of the paths the action generator prints out for the administrator, for example the paths in the second and third action in Figure 9. This complexity is mainly due to the complexity of the XMI notation. In the case of our evaluation, the repair administrator also wrote the constraints, so it was easy to identify these paths as pointing to association ends. If the administrator was a pure UML domain expert, we would have to provide additional support such as intelligent abbreviation or translation.

8 Related Work

The problem of repairing integrity violations has received attention in the areas of software development environments and databases. In this section we give a brief account of work most closely related to ours.

The software engineering community has produced a substantial body of work on Software Development Environments. The goal of systems like ESF [20], GoodStep [5] or IPSEN [14], to name but a few, is to integrate different tools and to ensure consistency across heterogeneous artifacts. These environments include change propagation mechanisms that can restore consistency in a dependency graph when changes are made. GoodStep includes a scripting language for adding domain-specific repair mechanisms, for example to add a variable declaration at the right level of scope when a variable reference is invalid. To the best of our knowledge, none of them include mechanisms for automatically transforming a declarative constraint language into repair actions without user intervention or hand-coding. In addition, these environments typically require a central repository and cannot support the loose style of fully distributed development.

Active integrity maintenance through triggering in a software development environment is discussed in [21]. The paper gives examples of an algorithm that can transform a constraint into condition-action repair actions that are executed when a constraint is violated. The approach is powerful in that it works automatically from a declarative specification. It also relies on a fast triggering mechanism rather than a complete consistency check, which is expensive, but it can only handle simple boolean constraints and no support for distribution is indicated.

The process of making changes to transactions or databases to recreate a state of integrity is referred to in the literature as *integrity constraint maintenance*. The common goal of work in this area is to prevent expensive transaction roll-back by making amendments that prevent constraint violation before committing. Approaches typically differ by the expressiveness of the constraints they permit – though none of them support unrestricted first order logic formulae, – the underlying data model they are trying to support, the level of user interaction, and the guarantees that can be

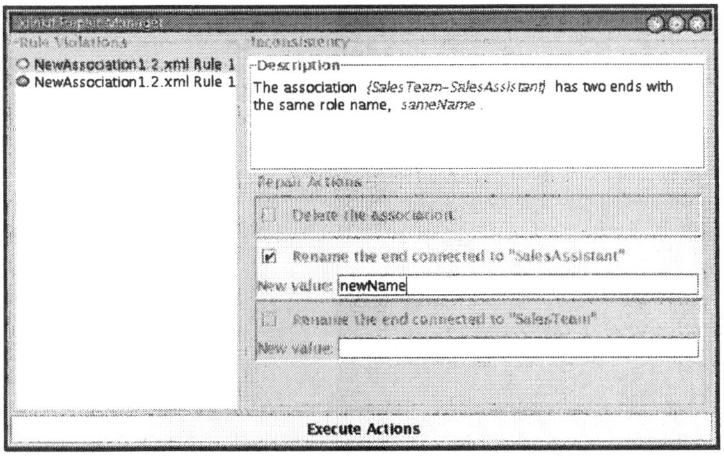

Figure 11. Repair Manager Tool

made about repairs. In the following, we present some of the most relevant work in the area.

The rule generator described in [2] takes restricted constraints over relational databases of the form ∀∃ and generates set of repair actions. The actions and constraints are ordered so as to generate a minimal set of actions that are self-contradictory and cannot be executed automatically. Because the approach builds on restricted formulae, constraint checking can be performed quickly through "violation queries". User interaction is treated using a low-level text mechanism but no tool support is discussed.

A similar class of constraints is analyzed in [9]. The paper includes an additional section on repair strategies, which discusses mechanisms for reducing the set of repair actions made available to the user. These include optimisations on the number of changes necessary to the database or to the transaction that triggered the repairs. These strategies differ from the higher-level repairs proposed here as they are analytical and do not build on domain knowledge.

Repair actions have also been a topic of interest in deductive databases. In [13], a system is described that generates actions from closed, range-restricted first order logic formulae. The repair algorithm can automatically find repairs for violated existential formulae without user intervention. For this, the algorithm relies on the rules of the database and the closed-world assumption. These mechanisms are not available in the case of distributed, semi-structured documents, hence the need for a lookup mechanism in our generator.

Compensating transactions [11] are similar in approach but make use of transaction operations as well as database data to undo dirty reads caused by lack of isolation between multiple transactions. This is not possible in our scenario as we treat the data "as-is", and have no information on modification by the user.

Finally, our previous work on consistency checking [15, 17] complements the work presented here. This includes evaluations of case studies that checked UML documents against other types of representations, for example source code, and an assessment of performance.

9 Future Work

There are many theoretical and practical questions that we cannot address in this paper.

The first concerns the interaction of repair actions with the syntax of documents. Repair actions that make a document consistent with respect to some xlinkit constraint, but at the same time violate the document's grammar should not be permitted – the grammar of a document is a lower-level mechanism and takes precedence. It is not possible to statically compare our constraints against a DTD or Schema to predict whether this behaviour must necessarily occur [7], but it should be possible to incrementally revalidate a document after executing each action and to retract the action if it violates the grammar.

A more complex problem arises when the repair action for one constraint forces the user to violate another. Since the equivalence problem for first order logic formulae is undecidable, it is not possible to predict in advance whether two formulae are contradictory. An iterative process that is capable of detecting repair cycles, similar to that in [9], could be used to address this problem.

We are also interested in comprehensive architectures for consistency management in various application domains. Tighter integration of consistency management mechanisms invariably raises domain specific problems. We have already applied xlinkit to checking the integrity of financial derivative trade data [4] and will extend our work in this area to include repair.

10 Conclusion

We have presented in this paper a novel framework for repairing inconsistent distributed documents. The framework is supported by a strong semantics that can translate first order logic constraints into repair actions that are correct and complete.

By combining the powerful diagnostic capabilities of xlinkit with this framework we have laid the foundations for a comprehensive architecture for managing the consistency of distributed and heterogeneous software engineering specifications.

We have shown the application of the framework to UML models encoded in XMI, and will continue to investigate its usefulness in other application domains.

The xlinkit check engine is available with full source code for academic research, and has already been taken up by several research groups. We welcome further request to use the check engine, and will make our repair action tools available as soon as the implementation stabilises. For more information please visit `http://www.xlinkit.com`.

Acknowledgements

We gratefully acknowledge financial support from Zuhlke Engineering for Christian Nentwich.

References

[1] T. Bray, J. Paoli, C. M. Sperberg-McQueen, and E. Maler. Extensible Markup Language. Recommendation http://www.w3.org/TR/2000/REC-xml-20001006, World Wide Web Consortium, Oct. 2000.

[2] S. Ceri, P. Fraternali, S. Paraboschi, and L. Tanca. Automatic Generation of Production Rules for Integrity Maintenance. *ACM Transactions on Database Systems*, 19(3):367–422, September 1994.

[3] J. Clark and S. DeRose. XML Path Language (XPath) Version 1.0. Recommendation http://www.w3.org/TR/1999/REC-xpath-19991116, World Wide Web Consortium, Nov. 1999.

[4] D. Dui, W. Emmerich, C. Nentwich, and B. Thal. Consistency Checking of Financial Derivatives Transactions. *Objects, Components, Architectures, Services and Applications for a Networked World, Lecture Notes in Computer Science*, 2591, 2003. To Appear.

[5] W. Emmerich. GTSL — An Object-Oriented Language for Specification of Syntax Directed Tools. In *Proc. of the 8th Int. Workshop on Software Specification and Design*, pages 26–35. IEEE Computer Society Press, 1996.

[6] D. C. Fallside. XML Schema Part 0: Primer. Recommendation http://www.w3.org/TR/2001/REC-xmlschema-0-20010502/, World Wide Web Consortium, MAY 2001.

[7] W. Fan and L. Libkin. On XML Integrity Constraints in the Presence of DTDs. *Journal of the ACM*, 49(3):368–406, 2002.

[8] S. Fickas, T. Beauchamp, and A. R. Mamy. Monitoring Requirements: A Case Study. In *Proceedings of the 17th IEEE International Conference Automated Software Engineering*, 2002. To appear.

[9] M. Gertz. An Extensible Framework for Repairing Constraint Violations. In *Workshop on Foundations of Models and Languages for Data and Objects*, pages 41–56, 1996.

[10] Y. Y. Goland, J. Whitehead, A. Faizi, S. Carter, and R. Jensen. Extensions for Distributed Authoring on the World Wide Web – WebDAV. Internet Draft (Work in Progress) http://www.ietf.org/internet-drafts/draft-ietf-webdav-protocol-10.txt, IETF, Nov. 1998.

[11] H. F. Korth, E. Levy, and A. Silberschatz. A Formal Approach to Recovery by Compensating Transactions. In D. McLeod, R. Sacks-Davis, and H. J. Schek, editors, *Proceedings of the 16th International Conference on Very Large Data Bases, Brisbane, Queensland, Australia*, pages 95–106. Morgan Kaufmann, August 1990.

[12] V. Matena and M. Hapner. Enterprise JavaBeans Specification v1.1. Technical report, Sun Microsystems, DEC 1999.

[13] G. Moerkotte and P. C. Lockemann. Reactive Consistency Control in Deductive Databases. *ACM Transactions on Database Systems*, 16(4):670–702, December 1991.

[14] M. Nagl, editor. *Building Tightly Integrated Software Development Environments: The IPSEN Approach*, volume 1170 of *Lecture Notes in Computer Science*. Springer Verlag, 1996.

[15] C. Nentwich, L. Capra, W. Emmerich, and A. Finkelstein. xlinkit: a Consistency Checking and Smart Link Generation Service. *ACM Transactions on Internet Technology*, 2(2):151–185, May 2002.

[16] C. Nentwich, W. Emmerich, and A. Finkelstein. Static Consistency Checking for Distributed Specifications. In *Proceedings of the 16th International Conference on Automated Software Engineering (ASE)*, pages 115–124, Coronado Island, CA, Nov. 2001. IEEE Computer Science Press.

[17] C. Nentwich, W. Emmerich, A. Finkelstein, and E. Ellmer. Flexible Consistency Checking. Research Note RN/01/40, University College London, Dept. of Computer Science, 2001. Submitted for Publication.

[18] Object Management Group. *Unified Modeling Language Specification*, March 2000.

[19] Object Management Group, 492 Old Connecticut Path, Framingham, MA 01701, USA. *XML Metadata Interchange (XMI) Specification 1.1*, Nov. 2000.

[20] W. Schäfer and H. Weber. European Software Factory Plan – The ESF-Profile. In P. A. Ng and R. T. Yeh, editors, *Modern Software Engineering – Foundations and current perspectives*, chapter 22, pages 613–637. Van Nostrand Reinhold, NY, USA, 1989.

[21] S. D. Urban, A. P. Karadimce, and R. B. Nannapaneni. The Implementation and Evaluation of Integrity Maintenance Rules in an Object-Oriented Database. In *Proceedings of the Eighth International Conference on Data Engineering*, pages 565–572, Los Alamitos, 1992. IEEE Computer Society Press.

Automated Support for Classifying Software Failure Reports

Andy Podgurski, David Leon, Patrick Francis,
Wes Masri, Melinda Minch
Electrical Engineering & Computer Science Dept.
Case Western Reserve University
Cleveland, OH 44106
1-216-368-6884
andy@eecs.cwru.edu, dzl@po.cwru.edu,
paf9@po.cwru.edu, qds1@hotmail.com
mlm24@po.cwru.edu

Jiayang Sun, Bin Wang
Statistics Department
Case Western Reserve University
Cleveland, OH 44106
1-216-368-0630
jiayang@sun.cwru.edu, bwang@laplace.cwru.edu

Abstract

This paper proposes automated support for classifying reported software failures in order to facilitate prioritizing them and diagnosing their causes. A classification strategy is presented that involves the use of supervised and unsupervised pattern classification and multivariate visualization. These techniques are applied to profiles of failed executions in order to group together failures with the same or similar causes. The resulting classification is then used to assess the frequency and severity of failures caused by particular defects and to help diagnose those defects. The results of applying the proposed classification strategy to failures of three large subject programs are reported. These results indicate that the strategy can be effective.

1. Introduction

Some recent software products such as Netscape *Communicator*, *Mozilla*, and Microsoft *Visual Studio.NET* have the ability to detect certain of their own runtime failures and, with the user's permission, report these to the software's developer via the Internet. A transmitted failure report includes information characterizing the state of the software at the time the failure was detected, which is intended to assist developers in diagnosing the failure's cause. Some applications, including the *Visual Studio.NET* beta version, have a feature that allows a user to transmit a failure report (bug report) to the developer whenever they believe the application has behaved incorrectly, that is, even if the application did not detect a failure itself. The report typically contains the user's characterization of the failure and may also contain information about the application state. Such automated support for reporting failures and collecting diagnostic information is a significant advance in software development technology. Traditionally, developers have relied upon users to report software failures by email or telephone and to provide detailed information about the conditions under which they occurred so their cause could be diagnosed. Often, however, users are unable to provide adequate information even when they are questioned by support personnel.

Although automated failure reporting and collection of diagnostic information facilitates debugging, it is also likely to exacerbate another problem encountered by software developers: they often receive many more failure reports than they have time to investigate thoroughly. Developers attempt to classify and prioritize the failure reports they receive, so they can address at least the most significant ones. With automated problem reporting, the number of failure reports received by developers seems likely to increase dramatically. If so, manual classification and prioritization of these reports may become infeasible.

This paper proposes automated support for classifying reported software failures so as to facilitate prioritizing them and diagnosing their causes. A classification strategy is presented that involves the use of supervised and unsupervised pattern classification[1] and multivariate visualization. These techniques are applied to execution profiles in order to group together reported failures with closely related causes. Failures are initially

[1] *Supervised* pattern classification techniques require a training set with positive and negative instances of a pattern; *unsupervised* techniques do not.

0-7695-1877-X/03 $17.00 © 2003 IEEE

classified *before* their cause is investigated manually. Limited manual investigation may then be done to confirm or, if necessary, refine the initial classification. The resulting classification is then used to assess the operational frequency and severity of failures caused by particular defects and to diagnose those defects. We report the results of applying the proposed classification strategy to failures of three large subject programs. These results indicate that the strategy can be effective.

We now outline the remainder of the paper. Section 2 explains how classification of failures facilitates maintenance. Section 3 outlines our strategy for classifying failures. Sections 4-7 describe the phases of the strategy in detail. Section 8 describes our experimental results. Section 9 surveys related work. Finally, conclusions and future work are presented in Section 10.

2. How classification helps

(*Note on terminology: We use the terms "software failure" and "failure" as synonyms for "failed program execution".*)

When software has many users it is common for different users to report failures that are due to the same defect, although this may not be obvious from the users' descriptions of the failure. Thus, if users report m failures over some period during which the software is executed n times in total, it is likely that these failures are due to a substantially smaller number k of distinct defects. Let $F = \{f_1, f_2, \ldots, f_m\}$ be the set of reported failures. For simplicity, assume that all reported failures are actual ones and that each failure is caused by just one defect. Then F can be partitioned into $k < m$ subsets $F_1, F_2, \ldots, F_k$ such that all of the failures in F_i are caused by the same defect d_i for $1 \leq i \leq k$. We call this partition the *true failure classification*. Knowledge about the true failure classification is valuable to software developers for the following reasons:

- k is the number of defects responsible for reported failures.
- $|F_i|/n$ is an estimate of the frequency with which defect d_i causes failures in the field.
- The failures in F_i are the executions that are most relevant to diagnosing the defect d_i and to determining its severity.
- To diagnose and repair d_i, it should usually suffice to investigate at most a few of the failures in F_i in detail.

Although in principle developers can determine the true failure classification exactly by manually diagnosing the cause of each failure f_i, $1 \leq i \leq m$, this may be impractical, and it largely defeats the purpose of prioritizing reported failures. Instead, we propose using automatic classification and multivariate visualization techniques to *approximate* the true failure classification with much less human effort. The approximation is unlikely to be exact, because of estimation error and because the techniques we employ are based on *correlations* that may or may not indicate *causation*. Nevertheless, we hypothesize that even a rough approximation to the true failure classification can be of great practical value to developers. Moreover, it is possible to refine the initial classification as more information is obtained.

Classifying program *crashes* and *aborts* is an important special case of the failure classification problem that is typically easier to solve than the general case, provided that information about the program state just before each crash or abort, such as a call-stack trace, is available. For example, in postings on the *Mozilla* project [22] the fact that multiple crashes occurred at the same instruction and with the same call stack is used as evidence that the crashes have the same cause.[2] Note that this paper addresses the more difficult general case of failure classification, where a user may not realize that a failure has occurred until well after the defective code that caused it has executed.

3. Classification strategy

The basic strategy we present for approximating the true failure classification has four phases:

1. The software is instrumented to collect and transmit to the developer either execution profiles or captured executions, and it is then deployed. (Captured executions can be replayed offline to obtain whatever kind of profile is desired [27].)
2. Execution profiles corresponding to reported failures are combined with a random sample of profiles of operational executions for which no failures were reported. This set of profiles is then analyzed to select a subset of all profile features[3] (a projection) to use in grouping related failures. The feature selection strategy is to:

---

[2] James Larus of Microsoft Research informed one of the authors (Podgurski) that Microsoft Corporation internally uses automated heuristics to classify crash reports produced by its products.

[3] By a *feature* of an execution profile we mean an attribute or element of it. For example, a function call profile contains an execution count for each function in a program, and each count is a feature of the profile.

a. Generate candidate feature-sets and use each one to create and train a pattern classifier to *distinguish failures from successful executions.*
b. Select the features of the classifier that performs best overall.

3. The profiles of reported failures are analyzed using cluster analysis and/or multivariate visualization techniques, in order to *group together failures whose profiles are similar with respect to the features selected in phase (2).*
4. The resulting classification of failures into groups is explored in order to *confirm it or, if necessary, refine it.*

The result of approximating the true failure classification using this strategy is a partition $C = \{G_1, G_2, ..., G_p\}$ of F. We call C the *approximate failure classification*. For it to be useful, all or most of the groups G_i should contain all or mostly failures with closely related causes.

Phases (1)–(4) of the classification strategy are described in Sections 4–7, respectively.

4. Applicable forms of profiling

The kind of information that can be used in automatically classifying arbitrary software failures is not limited to the kind of information that is typically considered in debugging, e.g., the value of the program counter, the values of key variables, and the contents of the call stack when a failure occurs. Any kind of execution profile can be used that is potentially relevant to the occurrence of failures and that can be collected from the field without inconveniencing users unduly. This includes both generic and application-specific profiles characterizing such aspects of a program's execution as its control flow, data flow, input values and other variable values, and event sequences. For example, profiles might include execution counts for basic blocks, conditional branches, functions, definition-use chains, or state transitions. Profiles can be augmented with information obtained from users when they reported failures, e.g., by having them complete a form.

Both the causes of failures and their effects are relevant to classifying them, and hence the form of profiling should be chosen to reflect both if possible. Since failures often involve small parts of a large program, profiles should generally be as detailed (fine-grained) as possible, considering profiling overhead and analysis costs. Coarse-grained profiles are unlikely to distinguish between different defects in the same fragment of code.

5. Feature Selection

The second phase in our strategy for approximating the true failure classification involves selecting a subset of all profile features to use in grouping failures. This step is necessary because execution profiles typically have thousands of features, many of which are not relevant to the occurrence of failures. For example, a profile might contain an execution count for each basic block in a large program. We hypothesize that *the profile features that are most relevant to classifying failures according to their causes are the features that are most useful for distinguishing reported failures from successful executions.*

The approach to feature selection used in the experiments reported in Section 8.1.2 is a modification of the probabilistic wrapper method of Liu and Setiono [21].[4] Random sets of features of given size are generated iteratively. Each set of features and one part of the profile data is used to train a classifier. The misclassification rate of each classifier is estimated using another part of the profile data, and the features used by the classifier with the smallest estimated misclassification rate are chosen for use in phase (3) of our classification strategy.

Many types of statistically-based classifiers have been developed by researchers [6][9]. This paper does not address the issue of which of these types of classifiers is best suited to classifying program failures. Its goal is to provide evidence that *some* classifiers are useful for this purpose. Hence, in the experiments reported in Section 8, we employ a widely-used but relatively simple type of classifier: *logistic regression* models. Binary logistic regression is a type of statistical regression in which the dependent variable Y represents one of two possible outcomes or responses, such as failure or success in the case of a program execution [9]. In logistic regression, the expected value $E(Y \mid \mathbf{x})$ of Y given the vector of predictor values $\mathbf{x} = (x_1, x_2, ..., x_p)$ is $\pi(\mathbf{x}) = P(Y = 1 \mid \mathbf{x})$. The conditional probability $\pi(\mathbf{x})$ is modeled by

$$\pi(\mathbf{x}) = \frac{e^{g(\mathbf{x})}}{1+e^{g(\mathbf{x})}}$$

where the *log odds ratio* or *logit* $g(\mathbf{x})$ defined by

$$g(\mathbf{x}) = \ln\left(\frac{\pi}{1-\pi}\right) = \beta_0 + \beta_1 x_1 + ... + \beta_p x_p$$

is a linear function of $\mathbf{x}$. Each coefficient represents the change in log odds of the response per unit change in the

[4] In the *wrapper* approach to feature selection, candidate feature sets are evaluated by using them to train classifiers, whose misclassification rates are estimated.

corresponding predictor. When logistic regression is used for classification, the coefficients of $g(\mathbf{x})$ are estimated from a sample of $\mathbf{x}$ and Y values to obtain an estimator $\hat{g}(\mathbf{x})$ for $g(\mathbf{x})$. The outcome for input $\mathbf{x}$ is classified as a 1 if an only if $\hat{g}(\mathbf{x}) > 0$, that is, if and only if the estimated odds of a 1 exceed the estimated odds of a 0.

6. Grouping related failures

We consider two alternative approaches to grouping related failures in phase (3) of our classification strategy. The first approach calls for applying automatic *cluster analysis*[5] to the sub-profiles induced by the profile features selected in phase (2). The second approach involves applying a *multivariate visualization* technique such as multidimensional scaling to the aforementioned sub-profiles to produce a two-dimensional scatter plot display representing the similarity or dissimilarity of the sub-profiles to each other. This display is then inspected and clusters are identified visually.[6]

6.1 Automatic cluster analysis

Ideally, the process of grouping failures according to their likely causes would be fully automated. This suggests applying automated *cluster analysis* [8] to the sub-profiles induced by the profile features selected in phase (2) of our classification strategy. Cluster analysis algorithms identify clusters among a set of objects according to the similarity or dissimilarity of their feature vectors, as measured by a *dissimilarity metric* such as *d*-dimensional Euclidean distance or Manhattan distance. Roughly speaking, objects that are more similar to one another than to other objects are placed in the same cluster. In order to automatically group failures according to their causes, it is necessary to *estimate* the number of clusters among them. Although many approaches to finding the "best" number of clusters in a population have been proposed (see [8] for examples), the problem is quite difficult, because there are often several "reasonable" ways to cluster the same population. Hence, we have concluded that it is unwise to depend solely on automatic cluster analysis to group reported failures according to their likely causes. We propose instead that cluster analysis be used together with other techniques, such as multivariate visualization.

One widely used measure of the goodness of a clustering into c clusters, which we employ in Section 8, is the index due to Calinski and Harabasz [3]:

$$CH(c) = \frac{B/(c-1)}{W/(n-c)}$$

where B is the total *between-cluster* sum of squared distances, W is the total *within-cluster* sum of squared distances from the cluster centroids, and n is the number of objects in the population. To use $CH(c)$, its value is plotted for c = 2, 3, ... n, and local maxima are considered as alternative estimates of the number of clusters.

6.2 Multivariate visualization

Multivariate visualization methods such as *multidimensional scaling* (*MDS*) represent a set of objects characterized by dissimilarity or similarity measurements as points in a low dimensional space such as a two-dimensional display [2]. A two-dimensional display produced with MDS is a kind of scatter plot. The points are positioned so that the distance between each pair of points approximates the dissimilarity between the corresponding objects. An arbitrary dissimilarity matrix can be input to multidimensional scaling, so it can be used with a variety of dissimilarity metrics.

We propose that multidimensional scaling be used to display the sub-profiles induced by the profile features selected in phase (2) of our classification strategy, so that groups of related failures can be identified by visual inspection of the resulting scatter plot. We hypothesize that apparent clusters of points in the display will often correspond to such groups of failures. With visualization, users can judge themselves which failures are most closely related, rather than relying on a fixed clustering criterion as in automatic cluster analysis. A drawback of visualization for this purpose is that in projecting high dimensional data onto just two dimensions, small dissimilarities may be poorly represented in the display. Approaches to addressing this issue are presented in [19]. To better distinguish individual clusters, automatic cluster analysis should be used together with visualization. Clusters found automatically can be highlighted in an MDS display, e.g., by coloring their points or drawing their convex hulls.

We have developed a visualization tool that supports MDS of large sets of execution profiles and provides features useful for classifying failures, including ones for: selecting a group of points in the display and determining the corresponding executions; magnifying regions of the

[5] Cluster analysis is an example of unsupervised learning.

[6] Note that if profiles of successful executions are unavailable clustering can be done based on *all* profile features, at the cost of some precision.

display; and highlighting specified sets of points such as clusters.

7. Confirming or refining the initial classification

Given an initial approximation to the true failure classification, a software developer might choose to use it "as is" for the purpose of prioritizing reported failures. However, it is prudent to do some additional work to confirm or, if necessary, refine the initial classification. This can be done by:

1. Selecting a few failures (two or more) from each group of failures.
2. Attempting to determine if the failures selected from a group actually have closely related causes, using conventional debugging techniques.
3. Attempting to determine if similar groups contain failures with the same cause.

Step (2) is especially important with clusters that are elongated or are "loose", because such clusters have high internal dissimilarity. If all of the failures selected from a group turn out to have closely related causes, this is further evidence that all or most of the failures in the group do. Otherwise the initial classification should be refined. Step (3) is applicable to neighboring clusters.

One criterion for deciding which failures to select from a group is that ones with *maximally dissimilar profiles* should be chosen. For example, one might select one failure from each end of an elongated cluster. Such failures can be selected automatically or by inspection of a scatter plot display. If the selected failures have the same or similar causes, one might conclude that all of the failures between them in the cluster do also. If they have dissimilar causes, one should seek a good place to split the cluster into two or more pieces.

8. Experimental validation

In order to evaluate the effectiveness of our classification strategy, we implemented its first three phases with three large subject programs. Automatic cluster analysis was used to classify failures, and the resulting clusters were then examined manually. To be thorough, we examined all or most of the failures in each cluster rather than sampling just a few failures from each cluster as described in Section 7.

8.1 Experimental methodology

8.1.1 Subject Programs, Inputs, and Profiles. The three subject programs for this study were all compilers: the *GCC* compiler for C [7] and the *Jikes* [15] and *javac* [14] Java compilers. These programs were chosen for several reasons: they are large; they can be executed repeatedly with a script; source code for a number of versions is available; and self-validating test suites are available for them. Unfortunately, we did not have access to failure reports from ordinary users. Instead, our classification strategy was applied to the failures detected by self-validating tests.

Version 2.95.2 (Debian GNU/Linux) of the *GCC* compiler for C was used. Only the C compiler proper was profiled. The compiler was executed on a subset of the regression test suite for *GCC*, consisting of tests that actually execute compiled code. These came from the test suite shipped with *GCC* 3.0.2, which included tests for defects still present in version 2.95.2. *GCC* was executed on 3333 tests and failed 136 times. Version 1.15 of *Jikes* and *javac* build 1.3.1_02-b02 were executed on the *Jacks* test suite (as of 2/15/02) [11], which tests adherence to the Java Language Specification [12]. *Jikes* was executed on 3149 tests and failed 225 times; *javac* was executed on 3140 tests and failed 233 times. Note that the *Jacks* test suite contains tests that are specific to the *Jikes* and *javac* compilers. *GCC* and *Jikes*, which are written in C and C++ respectively, were profiled using the GNU test coverage profiler *Gcov*, which is distributed with *GCC*. To profile *javac*, which is written in Java, a simple profiler was written by using the Java Virtual Machine Profiling Interface [13]. For each test t of one of the subject programs, the generated profile consisted of a vector of counts, with one count per function in the program. The count for each function f indicated how many times f was executed during test t. Note that *GCC* had 2214 functions, *Jikes* had 3644 functions, and *javac* had 1554 functions.

8.1.2 Feature Selection. Phase (2) of our classification strategy was implemented using the *S-PLUS 6* statistical computing environment [26]. Logistic regression (LR) models were used as classifiers. These were implemented using the *S-PLUS* function *glm*. An *S* language program was written to iteratively generate 400-500 candidate models per data set and to fit and evaluate them. Each model included 500 randomly selected features.[7] The *S* program output the best model

[7] The number of candidate models generated and the number of features used were selected based on preliminary experiments. They represent a tradeoff between classifier performance and total training time.

of a given type. To avoid underestimating the misclassification rate of models, the original set of profiles for each subject program was randomly partitioned into three subsets (*Train*, *TestA*, and *TestB*) comprising 50%, 25%, and 25% of the original set, respectively. The profiles in *Train* were used to train candidate models; those in *TestA* were used to pick the best model (i.e., for model validation); those in *TestB* were used to produce a final estimate of the best model's misclassification rate.

The measure used to pick the best model was the average of the percentage of misclassified failures and the percentage of misclassified successes. This measure gives more weight to the misclassification of failures than does the overall misclassification rate. For each of the data sets (*GCC*, *javac*, and *Jikes*), the final logistic regression model correctly classified at least 72% of failures and at least 91% of successes. It is notable that *S-PLUS* reported that a substantial number of selected features were not used in the fitted logistic regression models, because they were linearly dependent on other features. We did not use those features for clustering or visualization either.

8.1.3 Cluster Analysis. To group failures together automatically, we used the *S-PLUS* cluster analysis algorithm *clara*, which is based on the *k-medoids* clustering criterion [18]. To estimate the number of clusters in the data, the Calinski-Harabasz index $CH(c)$ was plotted for $2 \leq c \leq 50$ and its local maxima were examined.

8.1.4 Visualization. For each subject program, the sub-profiles induced by the features of the best classification model were displayed using the *hierarchical MDS* (*HMDS*) algorithm described in [19]. This algorithm was designed to minimize the error in representing small dissimilarities between execution profiles.

8.1.5 Manual Examination of Failures. In many cases, we were able to diagnose the specific cause of a group of failures. In other cases, this was not possible, but other evidence was found that certain failures had the same cause. The nature of such evidence varied with the subject program. The *GCC* failures were manually classified by exploiting the organization of the *GCC* test suite and information about later versions of the compiler. Each execution test in the *GCC* test suite involves compiling a simple source file and executing the resulting program. For each source file, multiple tests are run, each with a different optimization level as some defects are triggered only at certain optimization levels. Since each source file is designed to reveal a specific defect, we evaluated our automatic classification strategy with respect to whether it grouped together multiple failures corresponding to the same source file. We also checked manually whether different source files triggered the same defect.

Table 1. Comparison of automatic clustering and manual classification for *GCC* data set.

Number of clusters	% size of largest group of failures in cluster with same cause	Total failures (136)
21	100	77 (57%)
1	83	6 (4%)
3	75,75, 71	23 (17%)
1	60	5 (4%)
1	24	25 (18%)

For 12 of the 29 source files associated with *GCC* failures, we were able to identify bug fixes in later versions of the compiler that prevent the failures the files induce, and we verified that each fix worked when applied to the version under test (2.95.2). The remaining *GCC* failures were classified by determining when the corresponding test case stopped failing. For example, if test A is fixed in the CVS version as of January 2000 and test B keeps failing until July 2001, then we have reason to believe that they failed because of different defects. This required checking out, building, and testing enough versions of the compiler to separate most tests, but it was still less time-consuming than finding and porting specific bug fixes. Because of the possibility of regression defects introduced by changes to the compiler, the resulting classification is not certain, but we believe it is a good approximation. Only 3 pairs of source files were found to induce failures caused by the same defect. Thus, the *GCC* failures were apparently caused by 26 different defects.

The automatic clusterings of the *javac* 1.3.1 and *Jikes* 1.15 failures were examined manually in two stages. In the first stage, the failures in each cluster were examined to see if they actually had the same cause. In cases where the failures in a cluster had different causes, we were often able to identify sub-clusters consisting of failures with the same cause. In the second phase, the groups of related failures identified in the first phase were displayed using hierarchical MDS, and overlapping groups were examined manually to determine if the failures they contained actually had the same cause.

In order to determine if different *javac* 1.3.1 failures had the same cause, the following activities were

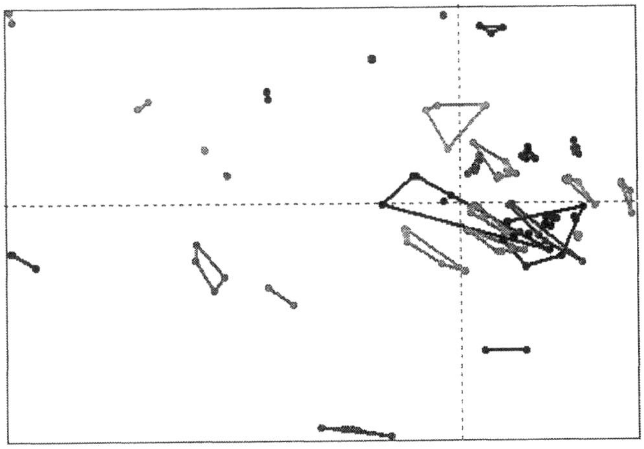

Figure 1. HMDS display of the *GCC* failure profiles after feature selection. Convex hulls indicate results of automatic clustering into 27 clusters.

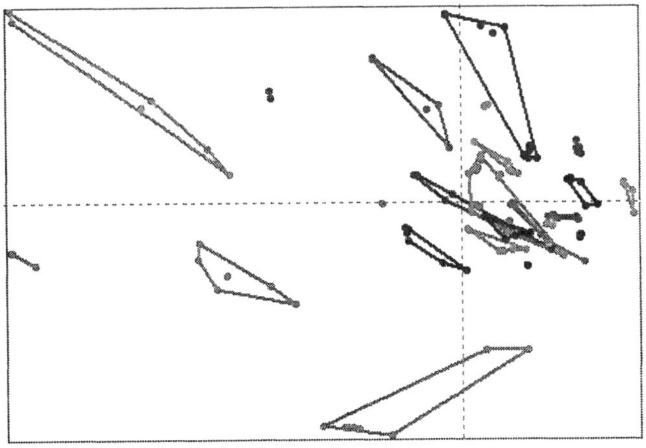

Figure 2. HMDS display of the *GCC* failure profiles after feature selection. Convex hulls indicate failures involving same defect.

attempted in the order listed until one of them succeeded, although activity (5) was always conducted:

1. *Debugging javac 1.3.1.* The causes of many of the *javac* 1.3.1 failures were diagnosed using conventional debugging techniques.
2. *Comparing the javac 1.3.1 and javac 1.4 code bases.* A few of the tests that caused *javac* 1.3.1 to fail were found to succeed with *javac* 1.4 due to identified bug fixes.
3. *Examining error codes.* It was found that the input files corresponding to many of the *javac* 1.3.1 failures formed groups: the files in each group were erroneously accepted by *javac* 1.3.1 but were rejected by *javac* 1.4 with the same error code.
4. *Inspecting failure-causing source files.* It was found that many of *javac* 1.3.1 failures were caused by language constructs present in multiple source files.

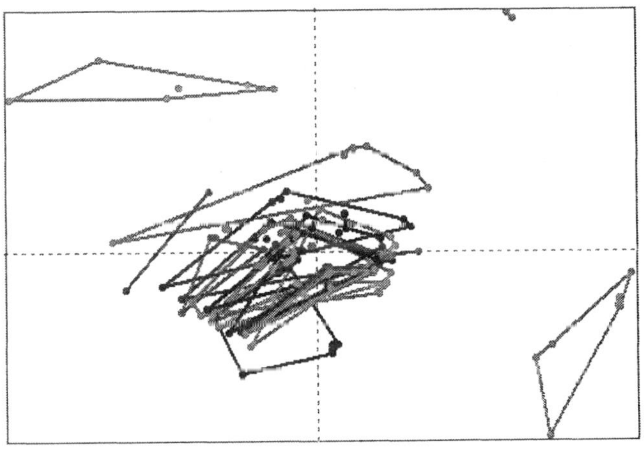

Figure 3. HMDS display of the *GCC* failure profiles before feature selection. Convex hulls indicate failures involving same defect.

5. *Checking the association between tests and Java Language Specification sections.* Some of the *javac* 1.3.1 failures were classified based on the fact that they involved tests of a language rule described in a particular *JLS* section.

To determine if different *Jikes* 1.15 failures had the same cause, the same five activities were attempted, with versions 1.15 and 1.16 of *Jikes* used in place of versions 1.3.1 and 1.4 of *javac*. Most groups of related failures were identified using activity (1) or activity (3).

8.2 Results

8.2.1 GCC. The *GCC* failures were automatically clustered into 27 clusters, as suggested by the Calinski-Harabasz index. The failures in each cluster were analyzed manually to determine the percentage size of the largest subgroup with the same apparent cause. The results are summarized in Table 1. Most of the clusters were comprised of failures caused by the same defect. Five clusters, of sizes between 5 and 8, contained failures caused by two different defects. One cluster, however, contained 25 failures caused by 7 different defects. Overall, in 26 of the 27 automatically generated clusters, the majority of failures appear to have the same cause. Figure 1 shows a hierarchical MDS display of the *GCC* failures, calculated using the profile features selected in phase (2) of our classification strategy. Convex hulls indicate the results of automatic clustering.

Figure 2 is another HMDS display of the *GCC* failures, in which convex hulls are drawn around each

Table 2. Results of manual examination of automatic clustering for *javac* data set.

Number of clusters	% size of largest group of failures in cluster with same cause	Total failures (232)
9	100	70 (30%)
5	88, 85, 85, 85, 83	64 (28%)
4	75, 67, 67, 57	49 (21%)
2	50, 50	20 (9%)
1	17	23 (10%)

Table 3. Results of manual examination of automatic clustering for *Jikes* data set.

Number of clusters	% size of largest group of failures in cluster with same cause	Total failures (225)
12	100	64 (29%)
5	85, 83, 80, 75, 75	41 (18%)
4	70, 67, 67, 56	25 (11%)
8	50, 50, 50, 43, 41, 33, 33, 25	76 (34%)

group of failures that manual analysis indicated were caused by the same defect. In this display, groups of failures corresponding to particular defects are well separated, suggesting that visual classification of failures is likely to be successful. Comparing Figure 1 to Figure 2 confirms that automatic clustering tended to group together failures with the same cause. However, these figures also indicate that automatic clustering erroneously split some groups of failures with the same cause. Of these 26 groups of failures, 5 had their failures split across two clusters, 2 had their failures split across 3 clusters, and one more was split across 4 clusters.

Figure 3 is an HMDS display of the *GCC* failures that was calculated using *all* profile features. As in Figure 2, convex hulls are drawn around each group of failures that manual analysis indicated were caused by the same defect. There is much more overlap of these convex hulls than in Figure 2. It turns out that Figure 3 overemphasizes the effect of optimization levels. For each source file, high optimization tests are placed to the left of the display, while low optimization tests are on the right. The difference between Figures 2 and 3 illustrates the importance of feature selection in our classification strategy.

8.2.2 javac. The *javac* failures were automatically clustered into 26 clusters. The failures in each cluster were examined manually to determine the percentage size of the largest subgroup with the same apparent cause. Table 2 summarizes the results for different groups of clusters comprising 21 clusters. (The remaining 5 clusters comprised 4 singletons and 1 cluster of size 2 whose elements could not be classified decisively.) Overall, in 22 of 26 automatically generated clusters (85%), a majority of failures had the same cause. Note that two large clusters formed by automatic clustering were found to be heterogeneous. Manual analysis revealed that both clusters had several sub-clusters, each consisting of failures with the same apparent cause.

Figure 4 is a hierarchical MDS display of the *javac* 1.3.1 failures. Convex hulls have been drawn around

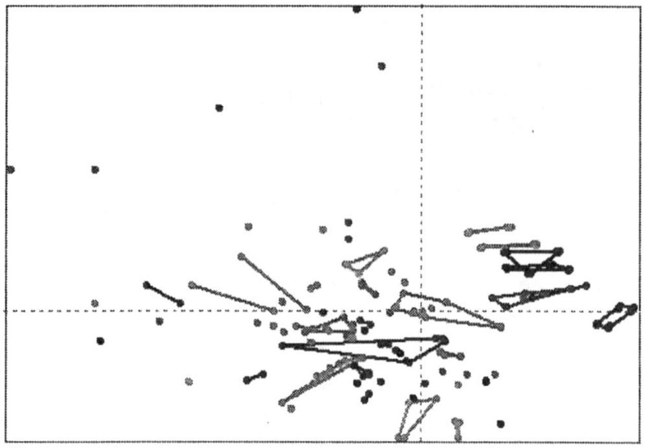

Figure 4. HMDS display of the *javac* failures. Convex hulls indicate the results of manual classification.

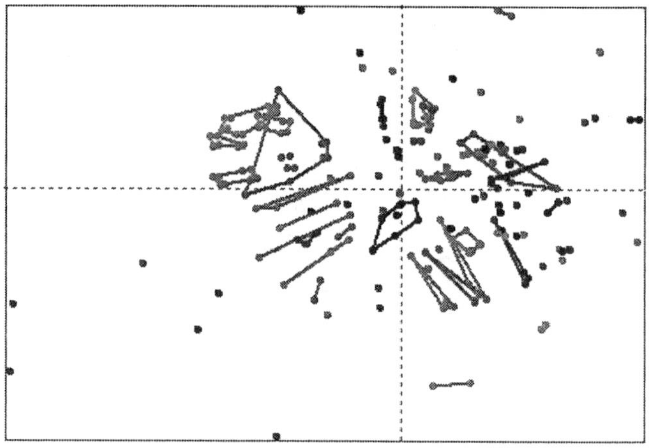

Figure 5. HMDS display of the *Jikes* failures. Convex hulls indicate the results of manual classification.

groups of failures that manual classification indicated have the same cause. Some of the convex hulls are compact and well separated from others, but some are elongated or overlap. Automatic clustering performed well in identifying the groups of failures whose convex hulls were well separated from those of other groups, even when they were elongated. It is unlikely that the elongated clusters would be identified by inspection of the HMDS display, although sub-clusters would. The groups of failures in the upper right quadrant of Figure 4 whose convex hulls overlapped noticeably were subject to further manual analysis. It was found that the failures in the overlapping groups actually had the same cause. Automatic clustering erroneously split those groups.

8.2.3 Jikes. The *Jikes* failures were automatically clustered into 42 clusters. The failures in each cluster were analyzed manually to determine the percentage size of the largest subgroup with the same apparent cause. Table 3 summarizes the results for 29 of the 42 total clusters. (The remaining 13 clusters comprised 9 singletons and 4 clusters whose elements could not be classified decisively.) Overall, in 30 of 42 automatically generated clusters (71%), the majority of failures appear to have the same cause.

Figure 5 is a hierarchical MDS display of the *Jikes* 1.15 failures. Convex hulls have been drawn around groups of failures that manual classification indicated have the same cause. As with the HMDS display of the *javac* failures, some of the convex hulls are compact and well separated from others, but some are elongated or overlap. Automatic clustering again did a good job of clustering the groups of failures whose convex hulls were well separated from those of other groups, even when the convex hulls were elongated. The groups of failures in the top left quadrant of Figure 5 whose convex hulls overlap were subjected to further manual analysis, which revealed that the failures in those groups had the same cause. This was also true of one of the pairs of overlapping groups in the top right quadrant of Figure 5.

8.3 Summary

In most of the clusters created by automatic clustering, a majority of failures appeared to have the same cause. However, automatic clustering created a few large, non-homogeneous clusters with sub-clusters consisting of failures with the same cause. The sub-clusters were evident in the corresponding HMDS displays. In other cases automatic clustering erroneously split groups of failures with the same cause, but the HMDS displays did not provide clear evidence that these groups were homogeneous. Overall, groups of failures with the same cause tended to form fairly cohesive clusters in the HMDS displays. Small, tight clusters in the displays were quite likely to contain failures with the same cause, although they were not always maximal.

8.4 Threats to Validity

All of the subject programs used were compilers. Therefore, it is possible that our results may not generalize to other types of software. Also, hand crafted test inputs were used rather than operational inputs. Test inputs like those in the *GCC* and *Jacks* test suites are generally smaller than typical compiler inputs and so the corresponding profiles may be less "noisy" than profiles of operational inputs would be.[8] Additional evaluation of the classification strategy is necessary, especially with different kinds of software and with actual failure reports from users.

9. RELATED WORK

Several previous papers have addressed issues closely related to failure classification and prioritization. Agrawal, *et al* describe the *χSlice* tool, which analyzes system tests to facilitate location of defects [1]. *χSlice* visually highlights differences between the *execution slice* of a test that induces a failure and the slice of a test that does not. Reps, *et al* investigate the use of a type of execution profile called a *path spectrum* for discovering Year 2000 problems and other kinds of defects [25]. Their approach involves varying one element of a program's input between executions and analyzing the resulting spectral differences to identify paths along which control diverges. Jones, *et al* describe a tool for defect localization called *Tarantula*, which uses color to visually map the participation of each statement in a program in the outcome of executing the program on a test suite [16].

Hildebrandt and Zeller describe a *delta debugging* algorithm that generalizes and simplifies failure-inducing input to produce a *minimal test case* that causes a failure [10]. Their algorithm, which can be viewed as a feature-selection algorithm, is applicable to failure classification in the case that failure-causing inputs reported by different users simplify to the same minimal failure-causing input. Note that Hildebrandt and Zeller's approach requires an automated means of detecting whether a simplified input causes the same kind of failure as the original input.

[8] On the other hand, operational inputs may tend to form more cohesive groups, which would aid our strategy.

Podgurski, *et al* used cluster analysis of profiles and stratified random sampling to improve the accuracy of software reliability estimates [24]. Leon, *et al* describe several applications of multivariate visualization in *observation-based* (software) *testing*, including analyzing synthetic test suites, filtering operational tests and regression tests, comparing test suites, and assessing bug reports [20]. Dickinson, *et al* present a technique called *cluster filtering* for filtering test cases [4][5]. This technique involves clustering profiles of test executions and sampling from the resulting clusters. They present experimental evidence that cluster filtering is effective for finding failures when unusual executions are favored for selection. Note that the aforementioned work on observation-based testing differs from the work reported here in three main respects:

- The goal of the previous work was to identify possible failures in set of mostly successful executions. The goal of the current work is to identify groups of failures with closely related causes among a set of reported failures.
- The previous work did not involve user feedback; the current work depends upon failure reports from users.
- The previous work applied unsupervised pattern classification techniques to complete program profiles. The current work uses supervised pattern classification techniques to select relevant profile features prior to clustering or visualization.

Finally, Julisch and Dacier demonstrated that a form of *conceptual clustering* is effective for grouping similar *alarms* from intrusion detection systems (IDS) [17]. We note that IDS alarms are typically generated by matching intrusion *signatures*, hence the attack type is at least partially known. Alarms typically have many fewer features than execution profiles do, and most features of alarms are relevant to classifying them. In many cases, relatively few features of an execution profile are relevant to classifying a particular type of failure or attack. Thus, dimensionality reduction is a much more critical issue in clustering profiles than it is in clustering alarms. On the other hand, our approach may be useful for classifying profiles of intrusions reported by *anomaly detection* systems [23].

10. CONCLUSIONS

The results of applying our classification strategy to *GCC*, *Jikes*, and *javac* suggest that the strategy is effective and scales to large programs, although this must be confirmed with other subject programs of different types. It is especially notable that the strategy performed well with a relatively simple type of classifier and with coarse-grained execution profiles; it may perform even better with more powerful classifiers and more detailed profiles. It is especially important to evaluate our strategy with deployed software and with failure reports from users. Other basic issues to be resolved in future work include the best choices of methods for profiling, classification, clustering, and visualization and the best way to integrate these methods during failure classification. Finally, we note that our approach may be useful for classifying computer intrusions reported by anomaly detection systems.

11. ACKNOWLEDGEMENTS

This work was supported by National Science Foundation award CCR-0098325 to Case Western Reserve University.

12. REFERENCES

[1] Agrawal, H., Horgan, J.J., London, S., and Wong, W.E. Fault location using execution slices and dataflow tests. 6th IEEE Intl. Symp. on Software Reliability Engineering (Toulouse, France, October 1995), 143-151.

[2] Borg, I. and Groenen, P. Modern Multidimensional Scaling: Theory and Applications. Springer-Verlag, New York, 1997.

[3] Calinski, R.B. and Harabasz, J. A dendrite method for cluster analysis. Communications in Statistics 3, 1-27.

[4] Dickinson, W., Leon, D., and Podgurski, A. Finding failures by cluster analysis of execution profiles. 23rd Intl. Conf. on Software Engineering (Toronto, May 2001), 339-348.

[5] Dickinson, W., Leon, D., and Podgurski, A. Pursuing failure: the distribution of program failures in a profile space. 10th European Software Engineering Conf. and 9th ACM SIGSOFT Symp. on the Foundations of Software Engineering (Vienna, September 2001), ACM Press, 246-255.

[6] Duda, R.O., Hart, P.E., and Stork, D.G. Pattern Classification, 2nd edition. Wiley, New York, 2001.

[7] GCC. The GCC Home Page, www.gnu.org/software/gcc/gcc.html, Free Software Foundation, 2002.

[8] Gordon, A.D. Classification. Chapman and Hall/CRC, Boca Raton, 1999.

[9] Hastie, T., Tibishirani, R., and Friedman, J. The Elements of Statistical Learning: Data Mining, Inference, and Prediction. Springer-Verlag, New York, 2001.

[10] Hildebrandt, R. and Zeller, A. Simplifying failure-inducing input. 2000 Intl. Symp. on Software Testing and Analysis (Portland, August 2000), ACM Press, 135-145.

[11] Jacks, International Business Machines Corporation, Jacks Project, www.ibm.com/developerworks/oss/cvs/jacks/, 2002.

[12] Java Language Specification, Sun Microsystems, Inc., java.sun.com/docs/books/jls/second_edition/html/j.title.doc.html, 2000.

[13] JavaTM Virtual Machine Profiler Interface (JVMPI). http://java.sun.com/j2se/1.3/docs/guide/jvmpi/jvmpi.html, 2001.

[14] Javac, Sun Microsystems Inc., Java™ 2 Platform, Standard Edition, java.sun.com/j2se/1.3/, 1995 – 2002

[15] Jikes, IBM developerWorks, www-124.ibm.com/developerworks/opensource/jikes/, 2002.

[16] Jones, J.A., Harrold, M.J., and Stasko, J. Visualization of test information to assist fault localization. 24th International Conference on Software Engineering (Orlando, May 2002).

[17] Julisch, K. and Dacier, M.. Mining intrusion detection alarms for actionable knowledge. 8th ACM SIGKDD International Conference on Knowledge Discovery and Data Mining (Edmonton, Alberta, July 2002).

[18] Kaufman, L. and P.J. Rousseeuw. Finding Groups in Data. John Wiley & Sons, New York, 1990.

[19] Leon, D., Podgurski, A., and Dickinson, W. Visualizing distances between executions. Technical Report #02-12, EECS Dept., Case Western Reserve University.

[20] Leon, D., Podgurski, A., and White, L.J. Multivariate visualization in observation-based testing. 22nd Intl. Conf. on Software Engineering (Limerick, Ireland, June 2000), ACM Press, 116-125.

[21] Liu, H. and Setiono, R. Feature selection and classification: A probabilistic wrapper approach. 9th Intl. Conf. on Industrial and Engineering Applications of AI and ES, 1996, 284-292.

[22] The Mozilla Project, www.mozilla.org.

[23] Noel, S., Wijesekera, D., and Youman, C.. Modern intrusion detection, data mining, and degrees of attack guilt. Applications of Data Mining in Computer Security, edited by D. Barbar'a and S. Jajodia, Kluwer Academic Publishers, 2002.

[24] Podgurski, A., Masri, W., McCleese, Y., Wolff, F.G., and Yang, C. Estimation of software reliability by stratified sampling. ACM Trans. on Software Engineering and Methodology 8, 9 (July 1999), 263-283.

[25] Reps, T., Ball, T., Das, M., and Larus, J. The use of program profiling for software maintenance with applications to the Year 2000 Problem. 6th European Software Engineering Conf. and 5th ACM SIGSOFT Symp. on the Foundations of Software Engineering (Zurich, September 1997), ACM Press, 432-449.

[26] S-PLUS 6 statistical software. www.insightful.com.

[27] Steven, J., Chandra, P., Fleck, B., and Podgurski, A. jRapture: a capture/replay tool for observation-based testing. 2000 Intl. Symp. on Software Testing & Analysis (Portland, Oregon, August 2000), ACM Press, 158-167.

Experience Reports

Case Studies

Fault-tolerance in a Distributed Management System: a Case Study

Robert Smeikal
Vienna University of Technology
Gusshausstrasse 27-29/384
A-1040 Vienna, Austria
smeikal@ict.tuwien.ac.at

Karl M. Goeschka
Frequentis Nachrichtentechnik GmbH
Spittelbreitengasse 34
A-1120 Vienna, Austria
goeschka@acm.org

Abstract

Our case study provides the most important conceptual lessons learned from the implementation of a Distributed Telecommunication Management System (DTMS), which controls a networked voice communication system. Major requirements for the DTMS are fault-tolerance against site or network failures, transactional safety, and reliable persistence. In order to provide distribution and persistence both transparently and fault-tolerant we introduce a two-layer architecture facilitating an asynchronous replication algorithm. Among the lessons learned are: component based software engineering poses a significant initial overhead but is worth it in the long term; a fault-tolerant naming service is a key requirement for fail-safe distribution; the reasonable granularity for persistence and concurrency control is one whole object; asynchronous replication on the database layer is superior to synchronous replication on the instance level in terms of robustness and consistency; semi-structured persistence with XML has drawbacks regarding consistency, performance and convenience; in contrast to an arbitrarily meshed object model, a accentuated hierarchical structure is more robust and feasible; a query engine has to provide a means for navigation through the object model; finally the propagation of deletion operation becomes more complex in an object-oriented model. By incorporating these lessons learned we are well underway to provide a highly available, distributed platform for persistent object systems.

1. System Context

High availability is not only demanded for safety-critical networked voice communication systems (VCS) but also for the management systems controlling them. In our case, these VCS networks are managed by a **D**istributed **T**elecommunication **M**anagement **S**ystem (DTMS) as illustrated in figure 1. Multiple DTMS servers are connected via a WAN and every DTMS server configures, controls and monitors its associated VCS systems. Every DTMS stores VCS parameter data using an object-oriented model.

Following the general design principles of Component-based Software Engineering (CBSE) [6] like strong component coherence and well-defined interaction standards, we consider the following requirements, which are relevant for availability considerations:

Fault-tolerance: The system has to be tolerant against network and site failures. This is achieved through replicating object-states to other sites.

- All objects need to be available for read access at any available site at all times even in presence of arbitrary system degradation scenarios.
- For write access it is sufficient
  - if objects are available at all sites during periods of healthy system condition.
  - if objects are available at a particular site (which we call their home site) during periods of degraded system condition.

Moreover, the framework itself has to be fully distributed. A single unique framework component must not exist in order to avoid *any* single point of failure throughout the whole system.

Transaction: The objects shall be able to participate in transactions. Typically, small write and large read transactions need to be performed frequently.

Persistence: The persistent objects' data shall be written to a stable storage.

Transparency: Clients shall not be aware of distribution, replication and persistence issues, which are therefore transparent to clients.

In our case, both, distribution *and* persistence, have to be transparent *and* fault-tolerant, where ***fault-tolerance*** is the

0-7695-1877-X/03 $17.00 © 2003 IEEE

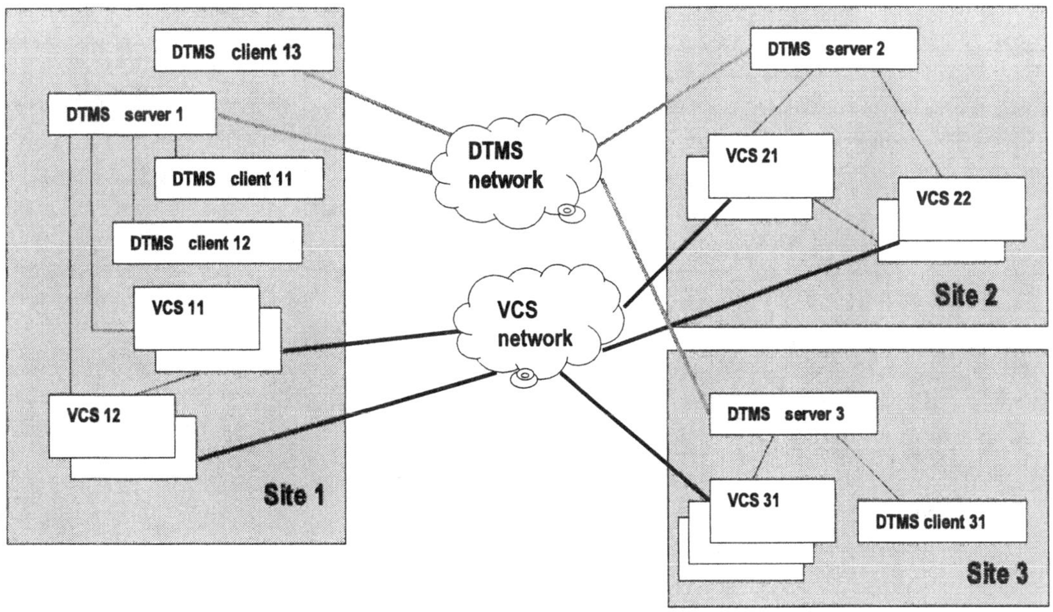

Figure 1. DMTS overview.

ability of a system to continue functioning while a failure is still unrepaired or even undetected [7]. Since fault-tolerance needs to be incorporated into the system architecture itself, we replicate the persisted object to other sites, in order to provide enough redundant information to replace any failed object dynamically. In the best case, the application is available if *any* site is available, because now objects can be restored at every site.

Replication as a means to provide fault-tolerance is well suited and a plethora of replication protocols exist. However, the deployment of replication requires the management of the replicated object data and introduces the new requirement of transparency of the replication. Moreover, if deployed in an object-oriented, persistent and distributed software system, managing multiple physical copies that constitute the state of a single logical copy poses problems on conventional concepts of such systems, which are usually designed to operate on a single copy:

- the preservation of consistency among different logical objects
- the concurrent access to logical objects
- the transactional access to logical objects
- handling of object identities, which are unique among logical objects

The contribution of this case study is to describe the major rationale for the key decisions and to derive general lessons, which we believe can be learned from our experience.

The major findings are:

- Distribution and replication need to be installed as two-layer architecture. This way, conventional distribution mechanisms can be deployed unaltered.
- Fail-safe naming services are a key requirement to fail-safe distribution.
- Performance requirements are more difficult to ensure due to the complexity of the systems.

Both authors have been heavily involved in the DTMS development project:

Karl M. Goeschka is Chief Scientist at Frequentis Nachrichtentechnik GmbH with headquarters in Austria and several subsidiaries in other countries (USA, Canada, Germany). Frequentis is world market leader for fast and highly available voice communications in air traffic ontrol. The products are also used for public safety and safe communications. Due to the innovative character of the DTMS development he is also the responsible manager of this project.

Robert Smeikal is a research assistant at the Vienna University of Technology in Austria. He is currently working on his Ph.D. and engaged in consulting the development team at Frequentis concerning practical and conceptual software engineering issues.

2. DTMS Architecture and Components

Figure 2 depicts the system architecture using a component diagram (Unified Modeling Language UML syntax).

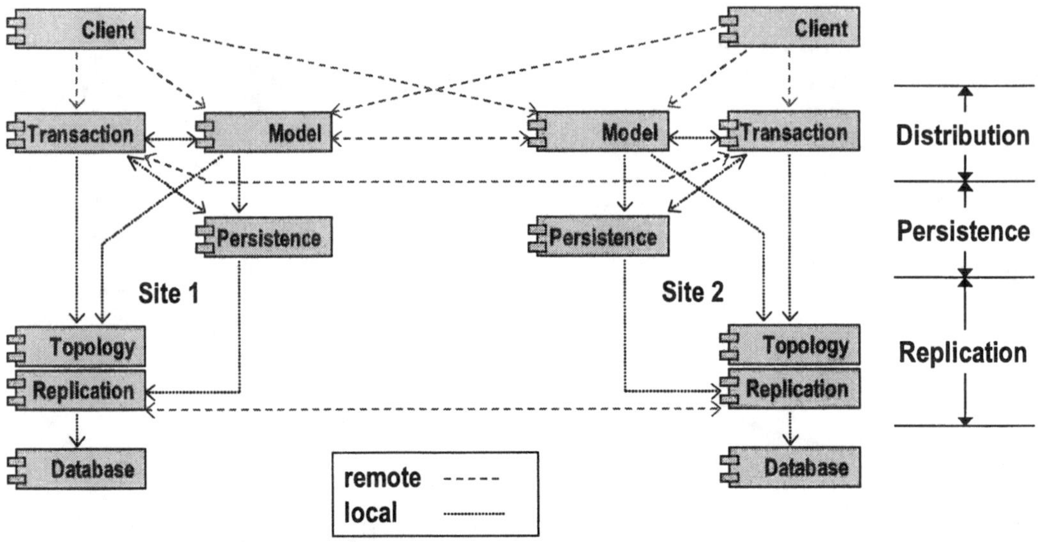

Figure 2. Proposed architecture.

The picture shows how components use each other either locally or remotely. A single site consists of the following components: **Transaction**, **Model**, **Persistence**, **Topology**, **Replication** and **Database**. **Client** components do not belong to a site. A client can be connected to an arbitrary site. Please note, that remote communication is established between components of the same type only (eg. local **Replication** and remote **Replication**). As denoted on the righthand side, the **Model** and **Transaction** components belong to the distribution aspect, the **Persistence** component to the persistence aspect and the **Topology** and **Replication** component to the replication aspect of the architecture.

Model. The **Model** component contains the model of the VCS. This model

- is complex, i.e. it consists of many classes, small object-states and few object-states per class.
- requires complex validation, i.e. many algorithmic constraints involving many object-states.
- requires complex read operations concerning many objects, e.g. assemble information for configuration of the VCS.

Each model object has a system wide unique ID. Each class has an associated factory, which can be located using the class name (kind of naming service). The factory creates and deletes objects. The factory validates object-constraints.

Objects and factories register at component **Transaction**. Objects store their serialized object-state at **Persistence**. Factories query **Topology** for the currently responsible site and initialize accordingly using either remote **Model** or local **Persistence**. Factories provide Interoperable Object References (IORs, refer to CORBA [1]) pointing at their associated local or remote objects given an ID or another query. Factories obtain IORs pointing at remote objects by communicating with remote factories. Clients can obtain IORs for every object at every associated factory.

Transactional behavior and persistence are mandatory for all model objects. Therefore, all model objects implement the the `validate()`, `commit()`, `rollback()`, and `store()` method.

Client. The **Client** component performs invocations on objects in local or remote **Model**, where the physical location of the model object is transparent to **Client**. An arbitrary number of **Client** components can operate on the model concurrently. The **Client** component starts and finishes transactions at **Transaction**.

Topology. The **Topology** component maintains a list of all sites and their availability and provides information about the currently responsible site for a particular object. It is queried by the **Model** and **Transaction** components. Therefore, **Topology** tells other components at which site they have to look for an object, also if the home site of that object cannot be contacted.

Transaction. The **Transaction** component is responsible for serializing concurrent transactions. It coordinates the invocation of `commit()`, `rollback()`, and `validate()` on the objects in the **`Model`**, it controls the transaction context at **`Persistence`** and it coordinates distributed transactions in co-operation with remote **`Transaction`** components (2-phase commit [3]).

Currently, the smallest unit of lock granularity is a whole site. Since write transactions are not expected to last long and validation involves many object-states from different classes, this is sufficient. We differentiate between write and read transactions.

Persistence. The **`Persistence`** component stores and retrieves serialized object-states using the **`Replication`** component. Additionally, it provides methods to access object-states in a transactional way, which are used by **`Transaction`**. **`Persistence`** does not distinguish between object-states that are home at the local site and object-states that are home at a remote site, but always persists to and retrieves from the local **`Replication`** component. Factories always ask their local **`Persistence`** component for retrieving persisted object-states. An object persists itself providing its ID, its type and its object-state to **`Persistence`**, which in turn provides transactional access to the stable object-store.

Database. The Database component essentially encapsulates the actual stable storage. It provides function primitives to persist and retrieve data. It may also encapsulate local database redundancy for even higher availability.

Replication. The **`Replication`** component is at the heart of the architecture, as it implements the replication algorithm. It performs a replication protocol in accordance with **`Replication`** at other sites to propagate object-states, to build constructed object-states, and to calculate their object readiness accordingly. It uses the **`Database`** component to persist data locally and it provides methods to access the stored object-states.

3. Lessons learned

We provide the most important lessons learned with a focus on conceptual aspects rather than implementation details or findings regarding particular COTS (commercial off the shelf) products and tools.

Semantics of methods versus read/write: There is a considerable amount of theory on the subject of exploiting method semantics in order to increase availability of certain methods (e.g. [8], where "intersection relations" capture the information flow among method invocations). In practice, we have not been able to deploy any further classification of methods than read-methods and write-methods, especially in regard to common use cases. Apart from a significant increase of implementation complexity (consider a replication mechanism, which knows about method semantics of every object type and calculates the objects' availability accordingly) it renders the system incomprehensible from the users' point of view.

Mapping of object identity to object reference: Obtaining an object reference (i.e. locating an object) given an object identifier (i.e. an object name) is always of concern if objects are instantiated out of process or even remotely (compare the CORBA Naming Service [1] or the Java Naming and Directory Interface [2]). Though such a naming service is already needed for basic persistence, the matter gets complicated if objects might live in different places due to a particular degradation scenario. On the one hand, the naming service maintains information about the references to objects (where a reference also determines the objects' location), on the other hand, the replication component decides where objects are instantiated if degradation occurs. Thus, the mapping of identity to reference is very dependent on the underlying mechanisms instilled to provide failure tolerance. Furthermore, the required fail-safe naming service has to be available at every site at every time, because the naming service itself has to be fault-tolerant as well.

In our case we resolve an object identifier using two steps. At first, the **`Topology`** component is queried for the presently responsible naming service (the factories in the DTMS), which can be either remote or local depending on the degradation scenario. Secondly, the object identifier is finally resolved.

Additionally, the mandatory use of object identifiers to store references (we call them "soft references") introduces the problem of either having to resolve an identity every time the respective reference is used (which usually yields bad performance) or to maintain a kind of identity/reference cache within every object.

Granularity: Defining the unit of granularity for system operations is a fundamental design decision. It can vary for different parts of the system entailing different implementation complexity and system behavior. The boundaries of granularity in an object-oriented model range from single attributes to the whole model.

We experienced that single objects as unit of granularity are a reasonable approach, mainly because objects are designed to be the units of coherence especially from the use-cases' point of view. However, we use different granularity in different components:

Persistence: Persisting object data using whole objects as unit of granularity was comparatively easy to achieve, because we generate the necessary code from the modelling information using the APIs (application programming interfaces) of our CASE (computer aided software engineering) tools (Rational in our case).

Transactions and concurrency: Currently, a site is the unit of lock granularity. Since this is clearly not sufficient, we strive to use object granularity here as well. This entails the ability of each object to associate method invocations with a particular transaction context and to calculate whether a commit is possible or not. Additionally, more complexity is introduced because of "indirect" write operations due to object relationships and because of the necessary locking of "uninvolved" objects that are used during validation of constraints. We plan to generate the necessary code, which obviously is far more complex.

Two-layer architecture: The design of our two-layer architecture focuses mainly on one requirement: Read access to every object must be possible at all times, while write access must be possible *at a particular site* (its home site) at all times. To free the object implementation from the additional burden of handling synchronous replication (propagate the data and coordinated commit using an atomicity control protocol like in group communication [4]), we decided to use asynchronous replication (commit first, propagate afterwards using queues). Asynchronous replication jeopardizes consistency, if multiple instances of a single object live in the system (e.g. an objects is accessed before changes from a remote site arrive). Therefore, during periods of a healthy system, we use a conventional setup of a distributed system: Every object is instantiated only once, objects communicate with other objects in an synchronous way and concepts of distributed computing can be smoothly applied. This makes up the upper layer, called distribution layer. Furthermore, persisted object-data is propagated asynchronously to prepare the system for a degraded scenario. This makes up the lower layer, called replication layer. All of the above considerations apply to model objects only, combined in the the "model" component. In contrast, "system" components exist at every site and manage the distributed model objects.

Derived from our experience, the lesson here is to use asynchronous replication of object data rather than synchronous replication at the instance level.

CBSE: Persistence and Transaction are usually considered as services of the component model implementation (CMI), but since orthogonality is desired (i.e. replace the replication algorithm) CMI itself should be component-based. The DTMS is not implemented using a particular component model implementation but its design is based on a basic principle of CBSE: strong coherence of concern and accompanying interface standards. From our experience, this approach increases the effort at the beginning of the project, but later on the coordination is reduced significantly, both in terms of technical and organizational issues. So far, our software is used in three projects for different customers on different platforms (Microsoft Windows and Sun Solaris) and only two components were altered to accommodate customer requirements: The rest of the framework remains unchanged and is stable.

However, also a disadvantage of CBSE was encountered. Due to the strict encapsulation of components, multiple mappings from component-internal interfaces to component-external ("provided") interfaces are necessary instead of one single invocation (object to object). That yields a loss in runtime performance, which can pile up considerably as the size of the system grows. Therefore, there is a hidden trade-off between component coherence and runtime performance.

WAN-Bandwidth: During the design phase of the project we did not distinguish between in-process, out-of-process and CORBA calls, because we expected the middleware to hide any related issues from the application programmers point of view. Though this is true, we afterwards experienced that such a unregulated use of CORBA calls congested our 2MBit WAN links dramatically. Apart from CORBA optimization, we had to reconsider carefully where CORBA calls are really necessary.

Object-states to database mapping: We designed our database scheme to accommodate object-states in a generic way using a table with three columns: object id, object type and serialized XML-formatted object-data. This setup provides the flexibility to handle changes in the model without altering either the database scheme or the persistence and replication component. However, we experienced some drawbacks:

- Since no static validation can be applied, the database allows inconsistency of object-states. Though obvious, this proved to be quite unpleasing, because now even small failures in the object model may render the database in an inconsistent state.

- Queries that operate directly on the database are very laborious to implement, since neither pure SQL nor pure XPath/XQuery can be used.

- XML is readable for a human consumer, but this comes at the price of a large amount of redundant information. The size of the XML data is increasing quickly as the size of the system grows and therefore becomes increasingly inefficient to handle. In turn the human readability of these large and complex structures vanishes. Thus, we currently develop a binary format to substitute XML at the database level.

Hierarchical structure: The hierarchy has proven to be one of the most robust, feasible and practical structures [9]. On the other hand, the structure of the model cannot be limited, because many-to-many relations are needed as well as additional arbitrary associations. Therefore, we found it useful to build a hierarchical structure by means of aggregation references. We introduced a model rule, demanding each object to be reachable by exactly one aggregation hierarchy.

Query engine: Two simple types of query are supported: Get object by ID and get all objects of a certain type. For efficient UI implementation purposes, additional queries for navigation through the object hierarchy are essential, e.g. get the ancestor or get the descendants of an object where additional conditions on attributes are fulfilled. Though a descriptive query language like OQL (object query language [1]) is desirable, the mentioned queries are sufficient.

Propagation of delete operation: When an object instance is to be deleted, there may exist other objects referencing this object. Similar to relational databases, it has to be determined whether or not the reference or the referencing object has to be deleted. This may result in cascading delete operations or in delete restrictions when constraints would be violated. Sometimes this results in quite complex delete implementations on the client side. We do not have an appropriate general solution yet, but we consider this to be an important issue for further investigation.

4. Future work

The following improvement possibilities have been identified:

- Support for a query engine, that allows descriptive queries using OQL.
- Support for finer granularity of locking to yield better concurrency of model access for clients.
- Invocation of write methods at model objects at all sites even during system degradation is a major future requirement.
- A better exploitation of transaction types (currently read/write-available) regarding the trade-off between availability of object-states and consistency requirements is desired [5, 10].

By improving these current system weaknesses we are well underway to provide a highly available, distributed platform for persistent object systems.

References

[1] *http://www.omg.org/*. The Object Management Group.

[2] *http://www.sun.com/*. Sun Microsystems.

[3] P. Bernstein, V. Hadzilacos, and N. Goodman. *Concurrency Control and Recovery in Database Systems*. Addison-Wesley, 1987.

[4] K. Birman. The process group approach to reliable distributed computing. *Communication of ACM*, 36(12):37–53, December 1993.

[5] H. Garcia-Molina and G. Wiederhold. Read-only transactions in a distributed database. *ACM Transactions on Database Systems*, 7(2):209–234, June 1982.

[6] G. Heineman and W. Councill. *Component-Based Software Engineering*. Addison-Wesley, 2001.

[7] A. Helal, A. Heddaya, and B. Bhargava. *Replication Techniques in Distributed Systems*. Kluwer Academic Publishers, 1995.

[8] M. Herlihy. A quorum consensus replication method for abstract data types. *ACM Transactions on Computer Systems*, 4(1):32–53, February 1986.

[9] P. Kahn. Information architecture: a new discipline for organizing hypertext. In *Proceedings of the twelfth ACM conference on Hypertext and Hypermedia*, pages 1–2. ACM, September 2001.

[10] D. Skeen. Achieving high availability in partitioned database systems. In *Proceedings of the International Conference on Data Engineering*, pages 159–166. IEEE, 1985.

The Deployer's Problem: Configuring Application Servers for Performance and Reliability

Mukund Raghavachari Darrell Reimer Robert D. Johnson
IBM T.J.Watson Research Center
19 Skyline Drive, Hawthorne, NY 10532
raghavac@us.ibm.com

Abstract

Frameworks such as J2EE are designed to simplify the process of developing enterprise applications by handling much of the complexity of concurrency, transaction, and persistence management. An application server that supports such a framework implements these concerns, freeing the application developer to focus on the task of implementing the business logic aspect of the application. In such frameworks, the deployer, the individual(s) who configures the application server to manage concurrency, transaction and persistence correctly and efficiently, plays a central role. A deployer has few tools to assist with performing this complicated task. Incorrect configuration can lead to application failure or severe underperformance. We outline the problems facing the deployer of applications, present a methodology that can assist the programmer with the task of configuring application servers, and present two case studies that validate the usefulness of our methodology.

1 Introduction

The development of large-scale business applications can involve many concerns — concurrency management, transaction management, persistence, security, presentation, business logic, etc. Frameworks such as J2EE [8] are designed to simplify this process by supporting the separation of concerns [7]. The application developer can, for the most part, focus on implementing the business logic aspect of an application; the *application server* on which the application is deployed handles much of the complexity of concurrency, transaction, and persistence management. In this framework, the *deployer*, the individual who configures the application server to manage concurrency, transaction and persistence correctly and efficiently, plays a central role.

Several factors combine to make the deployer's task complex. Firstly, the deployer must understand the application's semantics well. For example, the application determines which data must be persisted to a database. It is the deployer's duty to configure the application server's persistence management to match the application's desired semantics. Even armed with good documentation on the application's structure and behavior (which is rare in practice), the deployer task is not simple. Subtle interactions in the application among accesses to data that are persistent can, as we shall see in a case study in this paper, affect the configuration of an application server.

Secondly, the hardware and software systems with which the application interacts can affect its deployment significantly. The application server, the operating system on which it runs, network characteristics, the back-end database and/or legacy software with which it communicates, the number of machines and the topology of the system all affect the available concurrency and persistence capabilities of the application. For example, the configuration of an application server is different depending on whether the back-end database is dedicated or shared.

Finally, the workload of the application can affect the configuration of the application server. The workload determines which aspects of the application will be used most heavily and how much concurrency is required. The ability to predict the workload is essential not only in tuning the system, but in determining the topology of the system — how many machines to devote to running the application, how powerful a database is necessary, etc.

Currently, a deployer has few tools at her disposal. Application servers are designed to be flexible because their performance depends on many external factors — application semantics, hardware/software configuration, workload; deployers are provided with knobs to tune all components of the application server. Other tools available to a deployer are best-practice guides [6, 5] and rule-based profilers (based on the best practices) that suggest configuration settings based on usage data. The sophistication of these guides and profilers has improved steadily as more experience has been gained with complex business application

0-7695-1877-X/03 $17.00 © 2003 IEEE

deployments, but they suffer from a fundamental problem. Best practices are heuristics that cannot possibly cover the entire space of applications, hardware/software topologies, and workloads. We shall present a case-study in this paper where the best configuration of the application server conflicts with the best practice suggestion.

Without adequate tools, application servers are configured using a mixture of rules-of-thumb, intuition, and trial-and-error. An incorrect configuration can result in application failure or underperformance. Since the natural tendency on application failure is to assume a bug in the application, configuration-based problems are often difficult and expensive to trace.

In this paper, we focus on the problem of configuring an application server for an application given a hardware/software topology and a workload. We have developed a tool/methodology that address the problem of determining the correct configuration of application server parameters. The goal of this paper is threefold:

1. To present some of the issues involved in configuring an application server while deploying applications in a framework such as J2EE. The increased adoption of J2EE and frameworks such as .NET and Web Services makes the development of tools for helping the deployer in such systems essential.

2. To describe the tool/methodology we have developed for facilitating the deployment task.

3. To provide case-studies that validate the usefulness of our tool/methodology.

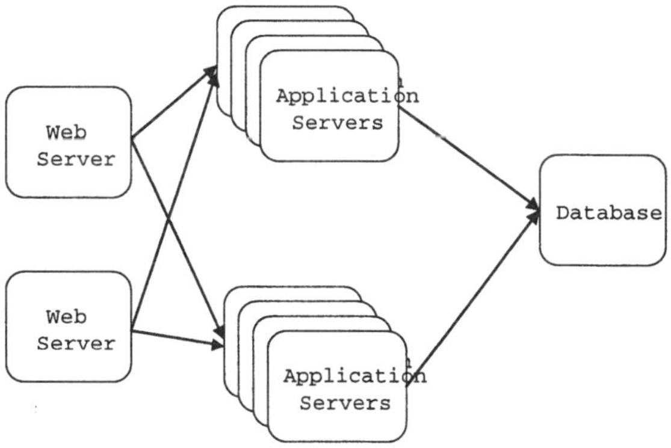

Figure 1. Structure of a conventional J2EE-based application server deployment.

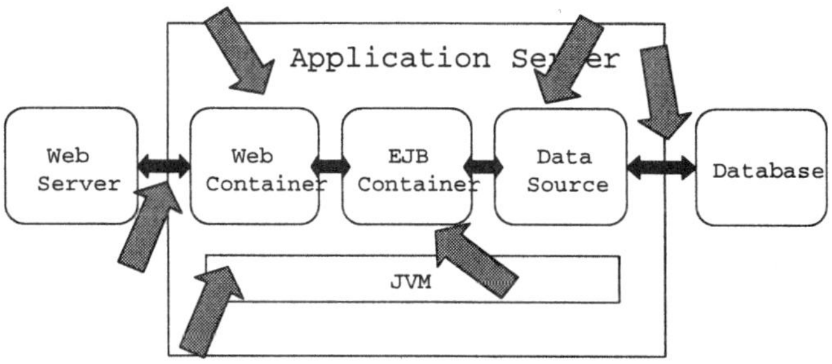

Figure 2. Structure of a J2EE-based application server. Arrows depict point where configuration parameters may affect behavior.

2 Anatomy of an e-Business Topology

A conventional topology of an application server deployment is shown in Figure 1. The Web servers (or HTTP servers) serve to direct requests from the internet to the application servers. The application servers are connected to a back-end database where enterprise data are persisted.

The structure of a J2EE-based application server is depicted in Figure 2. The application server is generally written in Java itself, and therefore, the entire system executes in one or more Java Virtual Machines (JVM). The application server is partitioned with respect to presentation, business logic, and data layers. The *web container* corresponds to the presentation layer. It manages interactions with the web server. Browser requests are routed through the web servers to the web container, where either a static HTML page is returned or the execution of a Java Server Page (JSP) or servlet is launched. The JSP or servlet may in turn interact with the business logic layer, and ultimately, synthesizes the HTML returned to the user. The web container determines the concurrency of the servlets by controlling how many threads may execute at a time.

The *EJB container* corresponds to the business logic layer. The container manages the creation and execution of the Enterprise Java Beans (EJB) deployed on the server. Furthermore, it controls the transactional behavior of the EJBs, their concurrency, and their caching. It also controls the interactions of the EJBs with the *data sources*, which correspond to the data layer. A *data source* is an abstraction of a database. It manages connections to the database in a connection pool to avoid the expensive operation of creating connections. When an EJB no longer requires a connection to a database, rather than closing the connection, it returns the connection to the pool for later reuse. Furthermore, the data source maintains a statement cache that is used to reduce the cost of processing frequently executed SQL statements.

For the purpose of this paper, we shall focus on a small subset of configuration parameters, which are listed and described in Table 1.

Table 1. Application Server configuration parameters considered in this paper

Parameter	Description
Web Container Thread Pool Minimum	Minimum number of threads in the web container. Represents the minimum amount of concurrency.
Web Container Thread Pool Maximum	Maximum number of threads in the web container. Represents the maximum amount of concurrency.
Thread is Growable	Denotes whether the web container thread pool maximum number is a hard or soft limit, that is, whether the thread pool size can be extended if necessary.
EJB Container Thread Pool size	Maximum number of threads in the EJB container.
Data Source Connection Pool Minimum	Represents the minimum number of connections in the connection pool.
Data Source Connection Pool Maximum	Represents the maximum number of connections in the connection pool.
Statement Cache	Represents the number of executed SQL statements that are cached.
JVM minimum heap size	Minimum amount of memory allocated to the JVM in which the application server (and the applications deployed on it) executes.
JVM maximum heap size	Maximum amount of memory allocated to the JVM in which the application server executes.

3 Application Server Configuration

Broadly speaking, the problem facing a deployer of an application is the following: the deployer has a finite amount of resources — CPU time, memory, I/O — that must be rationed out to the components of an application server. Ideally, a deployer could use analytic models to determine the proper allocation of resources. For the business applications that are found in practice, the derivation of analytic models is difficult for the following reasons:

- The applications are complex, distributed, and multi-threaded where the interactions between the components of the system cannot be characterized easily.
- Different hardware and operating systems have varying performance characteristics for threading, JVM performance, etc.
- The performance of the server may depend on external factors such as the load on the database, network congestion, etc.
- The components of the application server are not independent. Allocating more CPU resources to the web container will result in more servlets being executed, which in turn, will cause a greater demand on the EJB container, and through the EJBs, on the database.

Furthermore, the task of the deployer is complicated by the fact that the application must be deployed on the server before it can be stress tested. As a result, when an application fails or underperforms severely, it is difficult to determine the correct source of the problem — application error or incorrect deployment. Given these obstacles, a deployer generally relies on intuition, experience, and best practices to allocate resources to the different components of an application server. When these fail, determining and fixing the cause of the problem is time consuming and expensive.

In this section, we present a simple method for determining good configurations and case studies of the use of this method.

3.1 A Method for Finding Good Configurations

A method that we have found useful in determining good configuration values for the deployment of an application is the following:

1. For each configuration value of interest, select a reasonable range. For example, for the JVM heap max value, we could select a range from 256–512 MB.
2. For each configuration value of interest generate a random value from the range chosen for it in Step 1.
3. Deploy the application using the set of configuration values generated in Step 2.
4. Drive a workload against the application server and measure performance characteristics, e.g response time and throughput.
5. Repeat Steps 2–4 as necessary. We shall refer to an experiment consisting of executing Steps 2–4 as a *run*.

The purpose behind this method is to explore the configuration space randomly, and to learn from the results, characteristics of the application, the interactions between the configuration values, and good sets of configurations. For our method to be successful, the application must behave somewhat consistently, that is, not exhibit wide swings in performance for a given configuration. When applications satisfy this requirement, changes in performance

Table 2. Range of values for each of the configuration parameters of interest.

Parameter	Description
Web Container Thread Pool Minimum	10 ... 35
Web Container Thread Pool Maximum	35 ... 100
Thread is Growable	true, false
EJB Container Thread Pool size	5 ... 50
Data Source Connection Pool Minimum	5 ... 25
Data Source Connection Pool Maximum	15 ... 40
Statement Cache	50 ... 500
JVM minimum heap size	64 ... 256
JVM maximum heap size	256 ... 768

across runs can be attributed to the effects of changes in configuration values. Statistical techniques such as multiple regression can then be used to infer useful information from the results of the runs. We shall now use two case studies to demonstrate the utility of this method.

3.2 Case Study — Manufacturing Application

We first study an application that simulates the operation of a manufacturing company. The application and workload driver were developed independently, and it was our task to deploy the application on an application server.

In Table 2, we list the range of values that we considered for each configuration parameter of interest. These were chosen to cover the range of values that are considered reasonable for such an application. We have developed a tool for generating a random point in the configuration space, deploying an application with those configuration values, driving a workload against the application server and recording throughput and response time in an automated fashion. The generation of random configuration values performs simple consistency checks, for example, that the minimum value for the web container thread pool be less than the maximum number. The time taken for one run is approximately 15 minutes, of which 12 minutes is devoted to driving the workload.

The topology of our deployment is as shown in Figure 3. We ran the Web Server (IHS 1.3.19) and the application server (WebSphere 4.03) on the same machine and the database (DB2 7.2 fixpack 5) on a separate machine. The application server and the database machine are identical machines. We had detailed documentation describing the structure of the application to guide us.

The first step, as mentioned previously, is verifying that the application behaves deterministically with respect to a given configuration. We performed 15 experiments using the same set of configuration values and found low variance

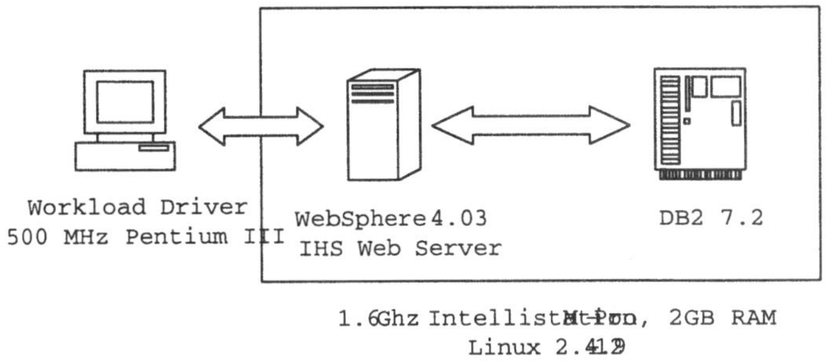

Figure 3. Hardware configuration used in experiments.

in the throughput across runs (stdev/mean = 1.1%).

Figure 4 shows the results of 25 runs with varying sets of configuration parameters. As can be seen from the figure, the configuration of an application server can have a substantial effect on performance. The maximum throughput obtained is 14 times the minimum throughput. In fact, the behavior of the application appears to be bimodal — the peaks and troughs are fairly consistent. To explain better the cause of this difference, we shall focus on the two parameters that are the cause of this behavior: EJB container thread pool size and the data source connection pool maximum.

In Figure 4b, we plot throughput as a function of the difference between maximum data source connection pool size and EJB container thread pool size. It can be seen that when the data source connection pool maximum is greater than the EJB container thread pool size (the difference is positive), the throughput of the system is good. When the opposite is true, the system performs poorly.

An examination of application logs when the system behaved poorly revealed that there were a significant number of transaction rollbacks which affected throughput. The cause of this behavior is the manner in which the application accesses the database. Under certain circumstances, a component of the application requires more than one connection to the database. Under load, the situation can arise where each thread executing in the EJB container pool has grabbed one connection and is waiting to obtain another. If there are fewer connections than threads then no progress can be made. Eventually, the threads time out waiting for connections and rollback their transactions. On receiving notification of the rollbacks, the application attempts to restart the transactions leading to the same situation again. Few transactions ever get completed.

Our diagnosis of this problem was aided by the fact that the application under consideration had been tested and validated previously. Therefore, we did not have to consider application bugs as a cause. In practice, determining the source of such performance problems is difficult since it in-

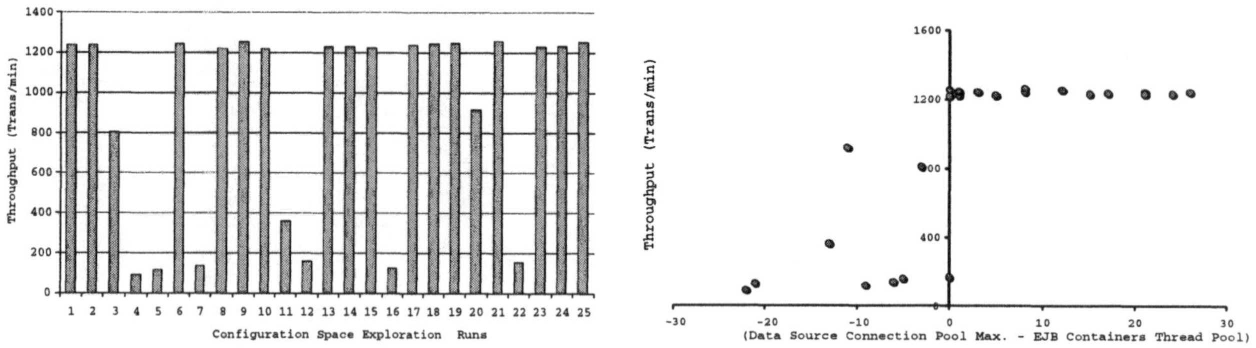

(a) (b)

Figure 4. (a) Average Response Time for each of the 25 random configuration space exploration runs. (b) Throughput as a function of maximum active data source connections and EJB containers

volves non-deterministic behavior and is sensitive to workload and the topology on which the applications run.

The remedy in our case study was to increase the data source connection pool size maximum so that it was greater than the EJB container thread pool size. Following best practices, however, would have let to the opposite conclusion. The accepted notion in tuning application servers is to constrain resources as one gets further away from the client. In other words, to have more web container threads than EJB container threads, and more EJB container threads than data source connections. The rationale behind this theory can be explained by the following quote from the WebSphere 4.0 tuning guide [5]:

> To effectively configure WebSphere in this fashion, the queues furthest upstream (closest to the client) should be slightly larger. Queues further downstream should be progressively smaller... In many cases, only a fraction of the requests passing through one queue will enter the next queue downstream ... For example, in an application that spends 90% of its time in a complex servlet and only 10% making a short JDBC query, on average 10% of the servlets are using database connections at any time, so the database connection queue can be significantly smaller than the Web container queue.

The basis for the suggestion that the allocation of resources be constrained to the components further from the client is the following. For a given application, there is an ideal number of connections to the database. Allocating an amount greater than that can lead to a decrease in throughput. Given this ideal data source connection size, there is an ideal number of EJB container threads that can execute concurrently. This number is generally larger than the number of data source connections because not all threads require database connections. The difficulty facing the deployer is in determining these ideal numbers, but as a general rule-of-thumb, this practice of scaling down resources works well.

In our particular application, this rule is inappropriate because the number of connections required by the threads can be greater than the number of threads. When such a situation arises, there can be two solutions — increase the number of data connections, or modify the application so that each thread uses at the most one connection. The benefit of our method for determining configuration values is that within 25 runs, this problem was illustrated clearly.

3.3 Case Study — Trade

The second application we consider is a simulation of a brokerage application, Trade V2.7 [3]. Again, the application was developed independently. Furthermore, as with the manufacturing application, there was low variance between runs using the same configuration parameters. In 15 runs, the standard deviation/mean was 0.6%. In other words, changes in the performance between runs with different configuration parameters can be attributed to the changes in configuration parameters.

Figure 5 provides the results of 25 runs with random configuration values. For this application, the difference between maximum and minimum average response times is less drastic — 14%. In Table 3, we provide the correlation between each configuration parameter and the response time. In other words, for each configuration parameter, we have 25 values and the average response time obtained with the parameter set at those values. We report the correlation coefficient between these values and average response time.

The two parameters that stand out from Table 3 are the web container thread pool maximum and the statement cache size. The sign of the correlation, positive or negative, implies how these knobs should be tuned. The positive correlation for web container thread pool maximum and average response time implies that increasing the number of web container threads will increase response time,

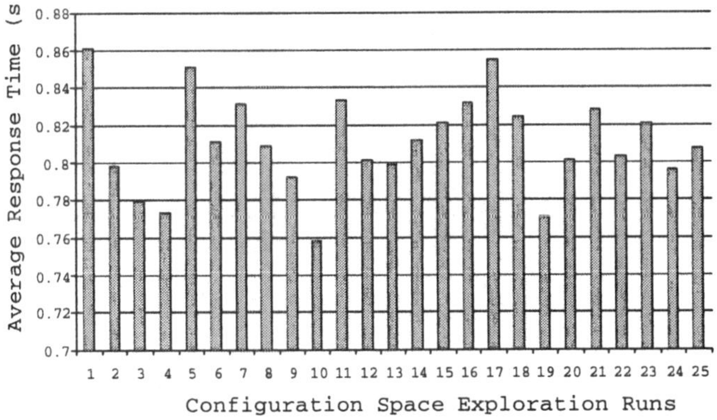

Figure 5. Average Response Time for each of the 25 configuration space exploration runs.

Table 3. Pairwise correlations between configuration parameters and average response time

Parameter	Correlation
Web Container Thread Pool Min.	-.1
Web Container Thread Pool Max.	.68
EJB Container Thread Pool Size	.13
Data Source Connection Pool Max.	.2
Data Source Connection Pool Min.	.31
Statement Cache	-.56
JVM Min. Heap Size	-.22
JVM Max. Heap Size	-.08

and therefore, this knob should be turned downwards. Conversely, the negative sign on the statement cache correlation implies that this value should be raised.

On further analysis of our application, our conclusions were justified. The application's execution is compute-bound. Having too many threads can lead to thrashing, and therefore, lowering the thread count is justified. Furthermore, the documentation suggests setting the statement cache to a setting higher than the default value.

4 Related Work

We are unaware of any work discussing the problems faced by deployers in frameworks such as J2EE. Most tools for J2EE-based applications, for example, from Sitraka [1], Precise [2], and Wily [4] focus on profiling and problem determination at the application level and do not address the configuration problem directly. Best practices guides [6] and application server documentation [5] are of great utility in understanding how to tune in the common case, but as we saw from our case study, can lead to problems when the application under consideration does not fit the class of applications covered by these guides.

5 Discussion

The configuration space exploration methodology is a simple and cost effective mechanism for understanding the performance behavior of an application. In a sense, our methodology treats the entire system as a "black box," and derives information by probing the system at appropriate points. While this information can be useful in itself as we have shown in our case studies, its value increases when used in conjunction with good application documentation. Furthermore, an initial set of runs that explores the configuration space randomly can lead to insights that can drive a more focused set of tests. For example, consider the Trade case study in the previous section. Determining that the web container thread pool maximum and statement cache are the most relevant parameters suggests that these dimensions of the configuration space should be explored in greater detail.

A useful outcome of explorations of the behavior and deployment of J2EE applications would be a classification of applications into specific categories, for which more focused best practices can be derived. For example, database-heavy applications generally have different characteristics (and different configuration parameters) than static web page based applications. The configuration exploration methodology could be used to determine which of these broad classes an application falls into and present suggestions on that basis.

References

[1] Performasure. http://www.sitraka.com.

[2] Precise/Indepth for the J2EE platform. http://www.preciseso ft.com.

[3] Trade 2 performance benchmark. http://www.ibm.com/soft ware/webservers/appserv/wpbs_download.html.

[4] Wily introscope 3.0. http://www.wilytech.com.

[5] IBM WebSphere application server advanced edition tuning guide. Technical report, IBM, 2001. http://www.ibm.com/software/webservers/appserv/doc/v40 /ae/infocenter/was/pdf/nav_Tuneguide.pdf.

[6] G. Cuomo. WebSphere application server standard and advanced editions - a methodology for production performance tuning. Technical report, IBM, 2001. http://www-1.ibm.com/support/docview.wss?uid=swg27000616&aid=1.

[7] H. Ossher, P. Tarr, W. Harrison, and S. Sutton. N-degrees of separation: Multi-dimension separation of concerns. In *Proceedings of the 1999 ICSE*, May 1999.

[8] B. Shannon. J2EE specification, v1.3. Technical report, Sun Microsystems, 2001. http://java.sun.com/j2ee/j2ee-1_3-fr-spec.pdf.

From Scenarios to Code: An Air Traffic Control Case Study

Jon Whittle Jyoti Saboo
QSS Group/NASA Ames Research Center
{jonathw,jsaboo}@email.arc.nasa.gov

Richard Kwan
Raytheon/ NASA Ames Research Center
rkwan@mail.arc.nasa.gov

Abstract

Two high profile workshops at OOPSLA and ICSE, an IEEE Computer article by David Harel and a growing number of research papers have all suggested algorithms that translate scenarios of a system's behavior into state machines. One of the uses of such algorithms is in the transition from requirements scenarios to component design. To date, however, most efforts have concentrated on the algorithmic details of the proposed translations. Less work has been done on evaluating these algorithms on a realistic case study. In this paper, we do exactly that for the algorithm presented in [10]. Our study is a component of an air traffic advisory system developed at NASA Ames Research Center.

1 Introduction

There has been a lot of interest recently in the possible role of algorithms that generate state machines automatically from scenarios of intended system behavior — witness, for example, successful workshops at the ICSE02 and OOPSLA01 conferences. A scenario is a trace of an individual execution of a (software) artifact [9]. Scenarios are widely used because they describe concrete interactions and are therefore easier for customers and domain experts to use than an abstract model. Many popular software processes advocate the development of scenarios as an initial software design activity. These scenarios are then used as a starting point to develop more detailed designs, e.g., in the form of state machines. An obvious question to ask is whether this transition can be partially automated. In fact, Harel raised this question in his original paper on statecharts [2] and researchers are now beginning to investigate it (e.g., [4, 5]). To date, however, the focus has been on developing algorithms to translate from scenarios to state machines. The transition is essentially from a *global* scenario-based view (in which interactions between all system components are considered) to *local* component-based views (in which a state machine is given for each component as a precursor to implementation). To the authors' knowledge, there have been no significant case studies in using these algorithms to translate from requirements scenarios to state machines. In this paper, we do exactly that — we apply the algorithm from [10] to the weather control logic subsystem of CTAS (Center TRACON Automation System) which is under development at NASA Ames Research Center. The objective of this study was to assess whether it is possible to use scenario-to-state machine algorithms (s2s-algorithms) to reliably develop models of a distributed system. A preliminary version of this paper appeared in [11].

2 Background

A scenario can be thought of as a particular path through the (intended or actual) behavior of a system. Scenarios can be either exemplary – in which one concrete path is described – or complete, in which a more abstract representation describing multiple concrete instances is given. Scenarios typically involve multiple components of a system. Scenario-to-state machine algorithms can be used on both complete and exemplary scenarios. Their application to exemplary scenarios is generally useful for exploring an incomplete set of requirements to validate or extend it. In contrast, complete scenarios can be used to fully specify a system and complete state machines can be derived from them. In this paper, we will consider the complete case. In addition, we will assume that scenarios are given as UML sequence diagrams and our translation algorithm [10] will output UML statecharts.

The major challenge for s2s-algorithms lies in the fact that each scenario is usually written in isolation from the others. To obtain a local model of each component, the scenarios have to be weaved together in such a way that only behavior relevant to that component is extracted and merged together. Most s2s-algorithms have as their basis a translation in which messages received by a component in a scenario are considered as trigger events in the component's statechart. Similarly, messages sent to a component are considered as actions for that component (see figure 1[1]).

[1]As usual, `a/b` denotes that `a` is a trigger event and `b` is the action carried out in response to the trigger.

0-7695-1877-X/03 $17.00 © 2003 IEEE

What distinguishes different s2s-algorithms is in the way they identify same states in different scenarios and hence weave the scenarios. [7] weaves scenarios based only on a common prefix in the messages and hence cannot merge states that are the same but do not stem from the same sequence of messages. SCED [4] applies merging based on the names of the actions but this does not allow the same action to have a different effect in different states. [5] and others use special state labels to explicitly identify points in different scenarios. [10] allows the user to give more declarative constraints (in the form of message pre/post-conditions) from which state identities can be derived. In this case study, we will use the s2s-algorithm from [10] extended with the state labels feature. State labels fit this particular problem well because the scenarios were well defined.

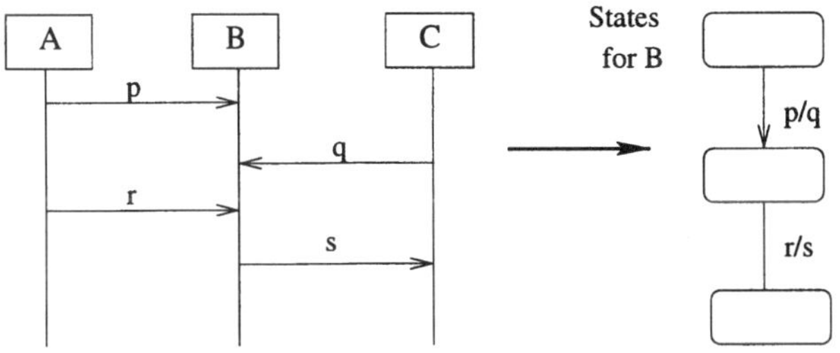

Figure 1. The basic idea underlying most s2s-algorithms

3 The Case Study

CTAS (Center TRACON Automation System) [1] is a set of tools designed to help air traffic controllers manage the increasingly complex air traffic flows at large airports. The project began in 1991 and prototypes are now deployed at Denver and Dallas/Fort Worth airports. Extensions to the core CTAS system are constantly being integrated and incorporate the latest developments from research into air traffic control systems. Figure 2 gives an overview of the software architecture for CTAS. CTAS consists of a set of advisory tools and a set of processes that support these tools. In Figure 2, CM is the Communications Manager which handles all communications between the various advisory tools and support processes. TS is the Trajectory Synthesizer which generates 4D trajectories and ETAs that all CTAS tools depend on. RA (Route Analyzer) generates all possible future routes for an aircraft. PFS (Profile Selector) assigns runways for approaching aircraft. PGUI and TGUI are graphical user interfaces. WDAD is a script that is responsible for gathering weather data files from hosts and making them available on the CTAS network file system. WDPD is responsible for converting raw weather files provided via WDAD into binary weather files usable by CTAS.

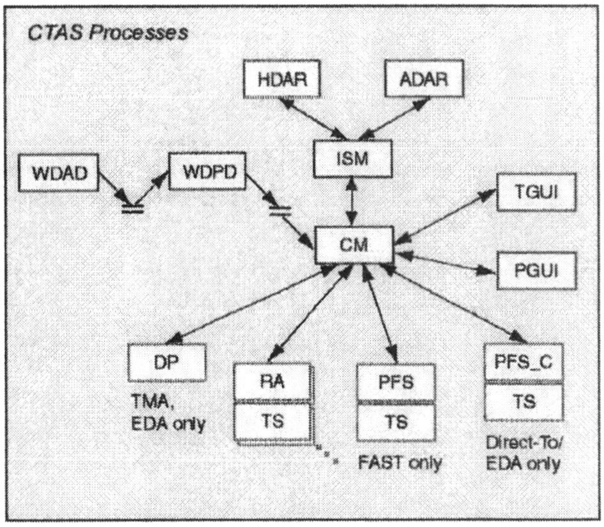

Figure 2. CTAS Architecture Description (taken from `http://www.ctas.arc.nasa.gov`)

One of the most crucial parts of an air traffic control system is the subsystem that deals with weather data. Adverse weather conditions can grind an entire traffic control system to a halt, so it is imperative that each of the components of CTAS is notified of weather forecast updates. The subject of the case study is the subsystem of CTAS that deals with weather data updates. The top-level requirement of this system is that every client that uses weather data should be notified of a weather update and all clients should begin using the updated weather data at the same time. The logic that implements this subsystem is defined by ten pages of English textual requirements. For each weather update, a Weather Cycle is invoked to update all weather aware clients. Similarly, the Weather Cycle is invoked to provide weather data to new clients. The Weather Cycle is split into two subcycles – one for the overall control of the update, and one to keep track of the relative states of the clients. Each requirement describes the behavior of the CM according to the current stage in the cycle, for example:

```
2.8.9
The CM should perform the following actions when
the Weather Cycle status is 'post-initializing'
and the newly connected weather-aware client has
responded no to the CTAS_USE_NEW_WTHR message
(i.e., wthr_status = FAILED_USE)
  (a) it should set the Weather Cycle status to
      'done';
  (b) it should enable the F2 weather control
      panel ''set'' button
  (c) it should send a CM_CLOSE_CONNECTION message
      to the newly connected client
```

4 Objectives

The complete set of requirements describes a state machine expressing the weather update logic component of CTAS, where each requirement describes a partial path through the state machine (i.e., a partial scenario). These partial scenarios also overlap — the requirements designer wrote down each requirement without regard for how it interacts with other requirements.

The code that implements the weather update logic had already been implemented manually in C. The objective of the case study was to reproduce this code directly from the requirements scenarios. The personnel on the case study consisted of a software developer from the CTAS team (not the original developer of the code), one of the researchers who developed the s2s-algorithm [10] and a student. The requirements were translated into UML sequence diagrams from which state machines were automatically generated using the tool from [10]. The commercial tool Rational Rose RealTime [3] was then used to generate C++ code from the state machines. This code was integrated into the existing system and tested against the original, manually developed weather control logic code. Twenty of these requirements were written as UML sequence diagrams. In general, the researcher and student came up with the sequence diagrams and then iterated with the CTAS engineer. The other main role of the CTAS engineer was to integrate the code generated from the statecharts into the existing CTAS system and perform testing on it. To summarize the results, this exercise showed that it is possible to generate code directly from UML sequence diagrams. This code passed all test cases. Figure 3 gives the sequence diagram for the requirement 2.8.9 above. Figure 4 shows a portion of the statechart generated for CM. It includes 2.8.9.

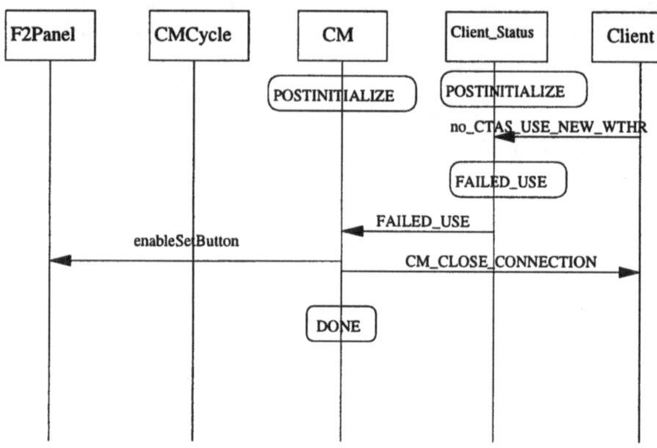

Figure 3. Scenario 2.8.9

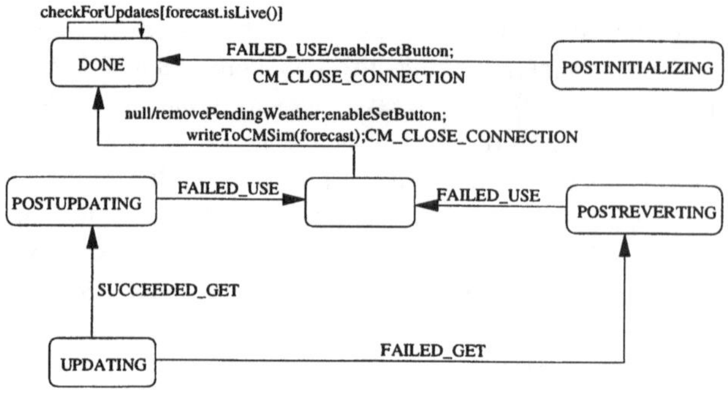

Figure 4. Part of the generated statechart

5 Observations

5.1 Requirements as sequence diagrams

All s2s-algorithms use some form of sequence chart as their input language — either UML sequence diagrams, high-level message sequence charts (hMSCs) or similar. Sequence diagrams are an attractive choice because of their simplicity. For added expressivity, however, we used an extended version of sequence diagrams with explicit state labels. For this case study, the requirements are already state-oriented — states are used both as preconditions to scenarios and within scenarios to synchronize the states of a subsystem (e.g., client or panel).

Initially, the authors began modeling the requirements directly as a set of state machines. This turned out to be a surprisingly difficult exercise, however. The CM has a number of states corresponding to the current state of the Weather Cycle: unknown, preinitializing, initializing, postinitializing, preupdating, updating, postupdating, postreverting and done. Each weather-aware client has these states in addition to states describing whether or not the client has received new weather data and whether or not it is able to use this new weather data (succeeded_get, failed_get, succeeded_use, failed_use). In order to capture the requirements correctly, the states of the CM and of the clients must be tightly coupled together. These couplings are distributed across the entire requirements document and so capturing them directly as state machines is a time consuming and error-prone task. In contrast, translating the twenty requirements into sequence diagrams took about one hour of clerical work.

There were, however, a number of issues that could not easily be expressed as sequence diagrams (or any other sequence chart notation). Many of the messages in the requirements are universal or existential messages — that is, the scenario is dependent on receipt of a message from *all* (alternatively, *any one of*) the instances of a classifier. It is unclear how to represent this on a sequence diagram.

Of course, this could be done by attaching a textual note but the difficulty is representing this information in such a way that a synthesis algorithm can generate appropriate states for it. One possibility is to use UML's constraint language, OCL ([8]). The requirement that "all connected weather-aware clients have responded yes to the CTAS_USE_NEW_WTHR" message could be written as `Client.allInstances()-> forall(i | receive(CM, yes_CTAS_USE_NEW_WTHR, i))` where $receive(i, m, j)$ denotes the receipt of message m from instance j by instance i. The problem with using OCL is that the user is given too much freedom to specify arbitrary constraints that may or may not be relevant to synthesis. The synthesis algorithm would need to look for OCL patterns to trigger the generation of the appropriate state machine transitions. This would rely on the user specifying the constraint in the form given above rather than a semantically equivalent one. An alternative is to include special textual (or graphical) syntax to denote existentiality or universality. In general, however, this may be inadequate if there turns out to be a large number of special cases like this one. In this case study, it turned out to be sufficient to encode the universality (or existentiality) directly in the messages — i.e., to send a message to all clients, a new message *send_to_all* is created. This is adequate but, in general, it seems beneficial to be able to express this kind of information explicitly.

Sequence diagrams are currently inadequate for describing generalized scenarios. A generalized scenario is one that describes a set of possible scenarios rather than a single trace. We give two examples of generalized scenarios here. Firstly, one may wish to specify that a message can be sent or received at any point during an interaction. In hMSCs, this could be expressed using coregions. Alternatively, a group of messages may be order independent — i.e., there is a scenario for each possible ordering of the messages and all are valid. Clearly, describing each of these scenarios individually is time consuming. For hMSCs, ordering of messages can be left underspecified using coregions. Many generalized scenarios (but not all) can be expressed using hMSCs. However, current s2s-algorithms cannot generate appropriate states for generalized scenarios. Hence, the use of these algorithms can lead to mismatches between the input sequences and the generated state machines. One possible approach to including generalized scenarios in s2s-algorithms is to generate hierarchical states. For example, the requirement that a component can receive messages m_1, m_2, m_3 in any order can be succinctly expressed using orthogonal states and the join operator (which impedes progress until all its input transitions have fired) — see Figure 5.

The use of state labels alone is also insufficient in general. The continuation from one sequence diagram to another can be expressed by state labels (see Figure 3) but a better solution would have been to use hMSCs. hMSCs include a notation for specifying how individual sequence charts connect using continuation, iteration and choice operators. On the other hand, hMSCs are more complex than sequence diagrams. Note, also, that state labels are still needed in hMSCs for connecting points in the middle of a sequence chart.

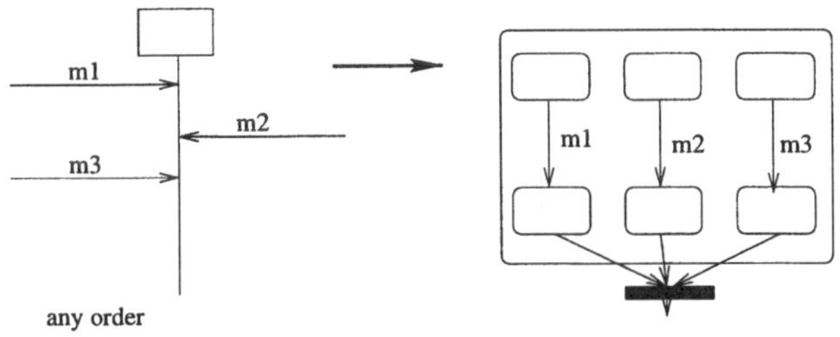

Figure 5. Translating Generalized Scenarios

In total, twenty requirements were translated into sequence diagrams. The procedure was mostly painless, the main detail being in deciding on which components to represent in the diagrams. For example, we decided to represent Client_Status explicitly as a component but could alternatively have represented it as a variable. One suggestion for s2s-algorithms is to allow the user to specify how a component should be translated — currently, all algorithms will generate a state machine for each component in the sequences. However, it may be useful to be able to give a component explicitly in the sequence diagram but then implement it in the design or code as a variable. For details on the structure of the sequence diagrams, see section 6.

5.2 Translating into statecharts

The twenty sequence diagrams were translated into statecharts using the algorithm in [10]. The requirements centred around the behavior of CM and Client_Status so statecharts were generated only for these components. There were not enough messages to make it meaningful to generate a statechart for F2Panel. For Client, no information was specified as to when it should send its messages so a highly non-deterministic state machine could have been generated and possibly used to generate test cases, but this was not done (test cases were developed manually).

The major barrier in the use of s2s-algorithms currently is in avoiding over-generalization of the input scenarios. Many forms of generalization are possible – e.g., generalizing a concrete instance to a variable, generalizing a message to be sent to *all* instances of a class – but most of these probably cause more problems than they solve because it is very difficult to identify over-generalizations in a generated state machine (it requires thoroughly understanding the state machine and failure to do so may result in bugs). There is one form of generalization that is crucial for s2s-algorithms to work well, however – that of merging same states from different scenarios. If no attempt is made to merge states, the result is a state machine with essentially one branch for each scenario that contains a lot of redundant states and duplication of transitions. A variety of approaches to this problem have been proposed. Our algorithm [10] takes a heuristic approach – states can be merged if they have an identical sequence of transitions above some given length leading into and out of them.

Figure 4 illustrates the benefit of merging. There are three transitions with the trigger FAILED_USE. In two cases, the paths following FAILED_USE in the corresponding scenarios are the same and so are merged. In the third case, merging is not appropriate because the following path is an alternative. In general, merging in this way produces a much more concise and readable state machine. Research still needs to be done, however, on the best ways to introduce merging. Using our heuristic approach, over-zealous merging can still occur — in this case study, a small number of over-generalizations had to be modified by hand.

The other major observation made during application of the s2s-algorithm was that there were some "hidden dependencies" in the sequence diagrams. Consider Figure 1. According to the semantics of the algorithm, component C is only dependent on messages q and s, and hence, only q and s will appear in C's state machine. However, it may be that message q can only be sent once p has been received by B (alternatively, sending q may be independent of p). We term such a dependency "hidden". Our s2s-algorithm has no way to detect hidden dependencies and the resulting state machines will not synchronize components correctly in such cases. Our solution was to add an explicit handshake between components B and C. This solution worked well but tool support for detecting hidden dependencies would have been useful. Early research in this area has begun [6] but we did not try out these techniques on this case study.

5.3 Generating code

Once state machines were generated for the CM and Client_Status components, the Rational Rose RealTime tool was used to generate C++ code. This code was then integrated into the existing CTAS code base. This was generally a straightforward process. Each action in the transitions corresponded to a method in the original code base. In the original design, the weather update subsystem of CM is polled from its environment every two seconds. Once polled, the module runs to completion, finishing by sending a message to one or more clients. At this point, the weather update subsystem yields the focus of control. In order to facilitate this, the state machines generated were given additional triggers. Yielding of focus of control can occur in a given number of states. When control is regained, execution should continue from the exit state. These states were given a trigger that is called from the environment. This mechanism gives the same behavior as the two second polling in the original design.

At the point of integrating the code, a small number of misunderstandings were discovered in the way the scenarios had been written. These modifications were made to the state machine and code re-generated. Unfortunately, in the time crush that was now ensuing, changes were not reflected in the scenarios. This leads us to the conclusion that a crucial part of this technology should be to automatically maintain consistency between sequence diagrams and state machines. This could be done with a "backwards direction" algorithm that keeps track of the changes to the state machine and suggests corresponding changes in the scenarios. Although there has been some research on this topic, a good solution has not yet been found.

Rose RealTime generates code that includes its own runtime services library. The CTAS team were not ready to accept a third party library such as this because of concerns about reliability. As a result, the code was generated using RealTime *passive classes* which do not require a runtime library. State machines for passive classes, however, have a synchronous model of execution — all triggers are just function calls so there are no event queues on state machines. The main problem with this is that the sequence diagrams were written assuming an asynchronous model. As a result, the state machine did not exhibit the expected behavior. This mismatch necessitated some minor changes to the state machines.

6 Results Summary

Tables 1 and 2 give some basic statistics on the problem scenarios and the generated artifacts for the portion of the weather control logic subsystem considered in this paper. If we had used hMSCs instead of sequence diagrams extended with state labels, we could have avoided inserting most of the state labels. The RoseRT comments referred to in the table are special comments introduced by the RoseRT code generator to keep track of which code is auto-generated for the purposes of round-trip engineering.

Whilst the authors believe this case study to provide evidence that transitioning mostly automatically from scenarios to code is possible, it should be noted that this case study has a number of characteristics that may or may not be shared with other examples. Firstly, the requirements were very well developed. They represent a complete and consistent view of the system and hence, there were very few and only minor iterations in developing the scenarios. In a case where the s2s-algorithm was being used to help

General data	
# of sequence diagrams	17
# of components per diagram	3-6
Messages data	
total # of messages	75
# of messages per diagram	2-12
average # of messages per diagram	4.4
# of messages that don't appear in state machines	0
State labels data	
# of state labels	45
# of state labels avoided by hMSCs	36

Table 1. Sequence diagram statistics

	CM	Client_Status
# states	12	11
# LOC generated by RoseRT	986	640
# LOC w/out RoseRT comments	672	404

Table 2. State machine statistics

develop the requirements, additional results would be observed. Secondly, the length of the sequence diagrams (in terms of number of messages) turned out to be quite small on average. This is because the requirements were already well structured. This might not be the case for examples in which the requirements were vague. Thirdly, it is interesting to note that the requirements already identify most of the states (e.g., postinitialize) that appear in the state machine. Clearly, the scenarios were written from a state-based perspective which may have made the transition to state machines easier. In summary, though, we believe that this case study represents a realistic example that provides interesting results to the researchers in this field.

7 Conclusions

This case study has shown that it is possible to generate code mostly automatically from scenarios of the intended behavior. Although there are still some hurdles to overcome, we believe it would have been possible for the CTAS engineer to carry out this process independently. Interestingly, the engineer could very easily understand the sequence diagrams but had trouble understanding the statecharts generated. The hardest part of the process was actually in integrating the generated code into the existing CTAS system. In particular, the messages had to be mapped to existing method calls and the previous implementation made use of variables to represent the weather cycle that became obsolete but were still used by other components.

In generating statecharts from scenarios, simple algorithms work the best. The more advanced features of our particular algorithm were not used and we would conjecture that other complex mechanisms designed to avoid overgeneralization would cause too much confusion. Current s2s-xalgorithms are generally good enough to do a reasonable job. The main area that is not currently well supported is in maintaining the consistency of the different viewpoints under modifications to the generated artifacts.

References

[1] D. Denery, H. Erzberger, T. Davis, S. Green, and B. McNally. Challenges of air traffic management research: Analysis, simulation and field test. In *AIAA Guidance, Navigation and Control Conference*, 1997.

[2] D. Harel. Statecharts: A visual formalism for complex systems. *Science of Computer Programming*, 8:231–274, 1987.

[3] *Rational Rose RealTime*. Rational Software Corporation, Cupertino, CA, 2002.

[4] T. Systä. Incremental construction of dynamic models for object oriented software systems. *Journal of Object Oriented Programming*, 13(5):18–27, 2000.

[5] S. Uchitel and J. Kramer. A workbench for synthesizing behavior models from scenarios. In *Proceedings of the 23rd IEEE International Conference on Software Engineering (ICSE01)*, Toronto, Canada, 2001.

[6] S. Uchitel, J. Kramer, and J. Magee. Detecting implied scenarios in message sequence chart specifications. In *Proceedings of the 9th European Software Engineering Conference (ESEC01)*, Vienna, Austria, 2001.

[7] A. van Lamsweerde. Inferring declarative requirements specifications from operational scenarios. *IEEE Transactions on Software Engineering*, 24(12):1089–1114, 1998.

[8] J. Warmer and A. Kleppe. *The Object Constraint Language: Precise Modeling with UML*. Addison-Wesley Object Technology Series. Addison-Wesley, 1999.

[9] K. Weidenhaupt, K. Pohl, M. Jarke, and P. Haumer. Scenarios in system development: Current practice. *IEEE Software*, pages 34–45, March/April 1998.

[10] J. Whittle and J. Schumann. Generating Statechart Designs From Scenarios. In *Proceedings of International Conference on Software Engineering (ICSE 2000)*, pages 314–323, Limerick, Ireland, June 2000.

[11] J. Whittle and J. Schumann. Statechart synthesis from scenarios: an air traffic control case study. In *Proceedings of Workshop on Scenarios and State Machines at ICSE2000*, 2002.

Experience Reports

Automotive Software Engineering

Software Technology in an Automotive Company - Major Challenges

Klaus Grimm
DaimlerChrysler AG, Research and Technology
Alt-Moabit 96A, 10559 Berlin, Germany
klaus.grimm@daimlerchrysler.com

Abstract

The automotive industry is one of the sectors which has been affected significantly by the industrial software revolution during the last few years. Competitive challenges, which are of major relevance for the growing number of software-based automotive innovations, are presented by a dramatic growth in system complexity, rising time and cost pressure, and high quality demands.

All these requirements lead to a number of software-related challenges which will be of significant competitive importance for the automotive industry in the future. Asides from the question of whether an automotive company decides to develop software in-house or whether this is carried out by suppliers, every automotive key player has to hold or to build up specific software competencies. The most important competence areas are the software development process, software quality management including supplier cooperation, the overall architecture of the in-vehicle software, as well as the ability to specify, to integrate and to test the system.

1. Introduction

The importance of software is increasing dramatically in nearly all sectors of industry. In the area of business administration, software has become an indispensable core technology. However, more and more products and innovations in most technical fields are also based on software. Traditional application fields are aeronautics, and space and defence systems in which software has already played an important role for a few decades. During the past few years software has also become established in many industrial sectors and products which had been determined by mechanical and electrical engineering traditionally. Within the automotive industry, for example, more and more innovations are based on electronics and software to enhance the safety of the vehicles but also to improve the comfort of the passengers and to reduce consumption and emission.

The increasing share of software in the car is accompanied by certain trends and requirements, such as rising time and cost pressure and high quality demands. These trends are presented in the next section, followed by a description of general problem areas in section 3 and technical challenges facing the automotive company in section 4. The core competencies required to meet these challenges are outlined in section 5. Section 6 provides a survey of current activities and results gained by automotive software technology research at DaimlerChrysler. The article closes with a short summary and the outlook for future work.

2. Software-related trends

The share of software within a vehicle is steadily growing. At the same time more and more competitive differentiation is realized by means of software-based functions. Current examples are intelligent powertrain control, the Electronic Stability Program ESP, and the active distance control DISTRONIC which recently entered the market as a comfort feature of the new Mercedes-Benz S-Class. DaimlerChrysler experts estimate that 80 percent of all future automotive innovations will be driven by electronics, 90 percent thereof by software. Leading automotive companies will not be able to reach their future strategic goals such as accident-free driving or significant reduction of consumption and emission without software. This will further increase the amount and importance of software in the automotive industry.

The rising share of software in the vehicle is accompanied by a growing complexity of the systems. In the past every single control device had to fulfil a single dedicated task such as electronic injection or airbag control, and the devices were simply connected by point-to-point connections if there was any direct link at all. In the early nineties, more and more functions, such as the Anti Slip Control, were developed which could only be realized by the cooperation of different sub-functions and control devices coupled by a single network like the CAN (Controller Area Network) bus. In the late nineties the engineers started to couple control units using multiple networks such as CAN bus and MOST (Media Oriented System Transport) bus. Thereby, functions were designed which e.g. required the combination of vehicle dynamics and navigation information. Nowadays, functions such as Teleaid are developed which comprise several networks and which are also coupled to the outer-car world via radio link. Teleaid provides the automatic alert of an emergency service in case of an accident detected by the airbag control. A current example for the high degree of software-related complexity of today's cars, shown in figure 1, is provided by the current S-Class of Mercedes-Benz which contains more than 50 controllers, more than 600,000 lines of code, three different bus systems and approximately 150 messages and 600 signals.

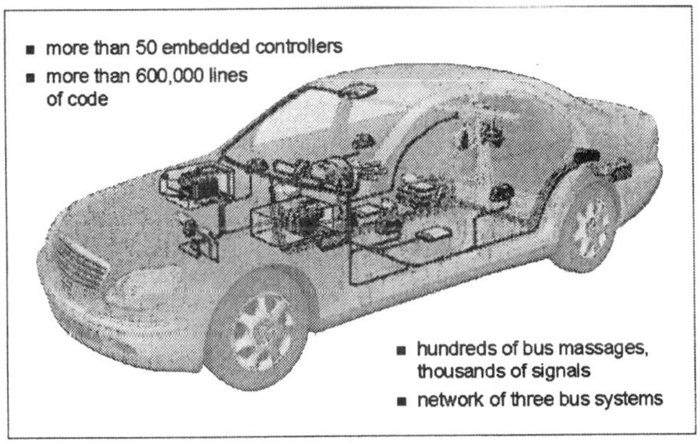

Figure 1. The complexity of the current Mercedes-Benz S-Class

The growing use of software-based automotive functions has led to software gaining a significant impact on the quality of the car. Nowadays, automobiles have to fulfil high software quality demands in order to satisfy the customer and to be in line with legal requirements. The most important quality criteria are reliability, availability, and safety. As more and more interfaces to the driver are realized by software, user friendliness and ease of use also become important quality demands. A mature software development process including cooperation with suppliers, a comprehensive quality management and powerful methods and tools is required to fulfil the high quality requirements.

The automotive industry has to face enormous time and cost pressure. Particularly premium class producing companies have to launch their innovations quickly and to achieve a short time to market in order to gain competitive advantages and to underline their premium image. To the same extent as innovations are driven by software, the share of development cost, as well as warranty and goodwill costs incurred by software, increases. Approximately 25 percent of the cost of the current Mercedes-Benz S-Class is already incurred by electronics, including software. As shown in figure 2, this proportion will rise by up to 40 percent during the next ten years due to additional safety and comfort systems as well as modern entertainment and infotainment services. On the other hand, the use of software offers a much higher flexibility than can be achieved by realizing innovations with conventional automotive technologies only. Especially appropriate software architectures allow fast innovations and a high degree of flexibility and reuse as well as leading to a significantly more efficient software development.

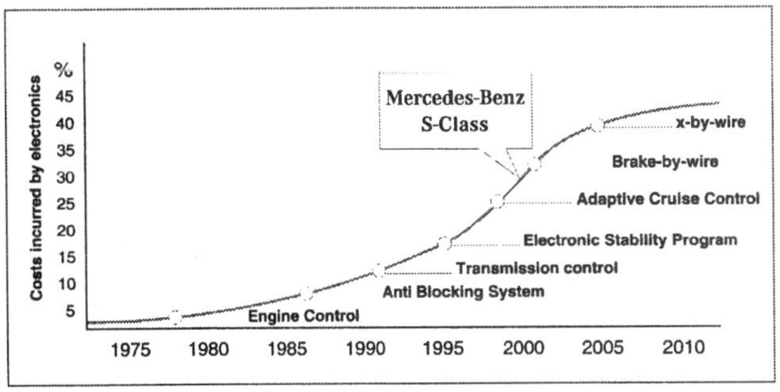

Figure 2. Proportion of cost incurred by electronics

In contrast to the traditional technologies used in the automotive industry, such as mechanical and electrical engineering, the use of software is subject to a fast succession of technologies. These fast changes hold the danger that software-based innovations become obsolete early and that technologies which were used to realize the innovations are replaced quickly by more powerful ones. Particularly in the field of telematics, innovation cycles are much shorter than the current development cycles of new vehicle models. In order to safeguard innovations and corresponding investments as long as possible, the software technologies to be used in automotive development have to be selected very carefully. Furthermore, the software-based system, its architecture and its interfaces have to be designed openly and flexibly enough to follow the short telematics innovation cycles and to facilitate the easy replacement of old-fashioned telematics equipment during the life-time of a specific vehicle model.

3. General problem areas

Regarding software-based innovations in vehicles, the depth of the added value created by software at the automotive company represents an important aspect. Currently, a lot of software development is undertaken by suppliers. But more and more automotive companies have decided to develop some of those parts of their software in-house which allow competitive differentiation. Whether an automotive company develops its software in-house or not, it has to face several software-related challenges.

The control of the increasing complexity of the systems represents a core challenge. The complexity problem affects different phases and elements of system development, especially the specification of the requirements, the design and the architecture of the systems as well as the integration and testing of the sub-functions and sub-systems. Complexity control becomes even more difficult if several suppliers are involved in the development of the system.

An indispensable prerequisite for the efficient development of dependable software-based systems is a mature requirements specification. In practice, this objective is very difficult to achieve, particularly because not all requirements are clear or stable right from the start, and a lot of changes in the requirements become necessary in the course of development due to technical or customer-related reasons. In-house experience has shown that, on average, more than 40 percent of errors which occur during the use of an automotive software-based function are attributable to requirements errors caused by immature specifications.

The development of electronic control units for automotive use becomes even more complicated if it takes place in cooperation between an automotive company and suppliers. In many projects the hardware and major parts of the software are developed by suppliers, while software functions which allow competitive differentiation are built by the automotive company. In this case, even more emphasis has to be put on the maturity of the requirements specification and the integration and testing aspects. The entire development process, as well as quality management, has to include the suppliers' part and the aspects of distributed development.

Due to the high time and cost pressure, the productivity of the software development is of great importance for an automotive company. One objective within this context is the increasing reuse of development results such as requirements, models, functions, and software components. Today, the degree of reuse is low. There is a lack of constructive prerequisites such as an open and flexible software architecture to facilitate reuse and integration of existing code into newly built systems. As a consequence, some functions are built nearly from scratch for each vehicle model.

The efficiency of the software development and the quality of the software-based systems can be improved significantly by the use of appropriate methods and tools. Nowadays, methodological and tool support exists for different single tasks and phases of development. Unfortunately, there is no chain of methods and tools which seamlessly support the whole development cycle from requirements specification to integration and testing. As a consequence, gaps between phases have to be covered manually, which is an error-prone and time-consuming exercise. Furthermore, tracing of information such as requirements or design decisions and change management are awkward, involved and costly. This missing seamlessness of processes, methods and tools is already an unavoidable problem in the field of software technology. Its dimension increases if one considers the interdependencies of software and other core disciplines of automotive development such as electrical and mechanical engineering. Currently, each discipline has its own processes, methods and tools. The lack of harmonization between these worlds causes many expensive errors or changes in the course of the development of a new vehicle model.

4. Technical challenges

The use of software in vehicles is characterized by certain technical circumstances and challenges.

Apart from telematics applications such as navigation, in-vehicle software generally forms part of an embedded system. This requires a close connection between software and hardware development or at least, if standard hardware is used, a consequent consideration of hardware aspects during all software development stages. In many cases, hardware components have to be simulated in early software development phases as they are not yet available or their availability is limited or costly.

Very often embedded systems in a car have to fulfil hard real-time requirements. For instance, an airbag controller only works correctly if it reacts within a precisely defined period of time if an accident is detected. In practice, both design and testing of real-time properties are complicated tasks and require a lot of modeling, simulation, and practical trials.

An additional challenge is provided by the growing complexity, namely the high degree of connectivity between the electronic control units. Not only the design of the overall system, including an appropriate, open and flexible software architecture, but also the integration and testing of the system are complex and elaborate tasks.

The use of embedded systems in the vehicle is accompanied by real-time requirements and also by limited capacity of storage. This limitation is often the result of space or cost restrictions. Due to the large number of cars which are to be equipped with certain components or electronic control units the cost of each single unit has a perceptible influence on the profit margin of a vehicle model.

As software is used to realize more than simple comfort functions, high reliability and safety requirements have to be met by the systems. This requires a proper and mature development process and the use of appropriate state-of-the-art methods in all development phases.

Suitable and powerful constructive and analytical measures have to be taken to ensure and to prove the required system safety and reliability, taking into account all relevant software aspects.

The increasing use of software-based driver interfaces and new MMI-concepts makes strong demands on the ergonomics of the system. The system has to be easily and intuitively usable by the driver without causing any dangerous situations, for instance by distracting him from the traffic.

5. Required technological core competencies

The discussion of the general trends and problem areas and the more detailed technical challenges show that an automotive company has to have or to develop certain software-related competencies. In most cases, the importance of these competencies is independent of whether the actual software coding takes place in-house or is carried out by suppliers.

Requirements engineering is the most important competency to avoid errors in early development stages and to reduce cost caused by requirements changes. Requirements engineering comprises appropriate techniques for elicitation, specification, modeling, and management of requirements. In particular, requirements tracing and change management are necessary to control the technical and economic impact of requirements or design changes.

As efficiency and time to market are of high competitive importance, the automotive company has to be able to define, analyze, assess and improve its development process systematically. A high degree of process maturity does not automatically guarantee high efficiency and quality, but it is an important prerequisite for both the manufacturer and the supplier.

The software architecture is a central element of the system of software-based innovations. Hence, the automotive company has to be able to design and maintain an open and extendable overall architecture and corresponding interfaces in order to facilitate the fast integration of innovations and the flexible replacement or reuse of software components and control devices.

Systematic testing is indispensable in order to detect errors as early as possible. This applies to software developed in-house as well as – to an even larger extent – to software supplied by partner companies. Special emphasis has to be placed on the aspect of integration of different components from different sources. In early development stages appropriate analysis and testing techniques, such as reviews, inspections and simulations, have to be applied to specifications and design models. Apart from functional behavior, performance aspects such as real-time system properties also have to be considered.

Software quality management has to cover the entire development process including the aspects of software acquisition and cooperation with suppliers. In order to avoid errors occurring due to method or tool inconsistencies and corresponding manual work, the automotive company has to be able to integrate appropriate methods and tools to achieve a seamless chain of computer support. Finally, usability engineering is an important competency to provide user-friendly software-based driver interfaces. The aspect of usability has to be taken into account throughout the whole development process starting with the specification of requirements in order to avoid late and, hence, expensive changes.

An additional requirement is caused by the growing complexity of the systems accompanied by the combination of functions of different areas such as vehicle dynamics, powertrain management, and telematics. As a consequence, appropriate architectures, as well as specification, modeling and testing techniques, are required which reconcile the different scientific disciplines involved, such as software engineering, control engineering and communication technology.

Model-based development is an essential technological competency if the automotive company carries out in-house software development. It facilitates early simulation and error detection as well as automatic generation of target code. Thereby, development becomes more efficient and the quality of the system can be improved significantly.

6. Selected research activities and results

In order to take the current trends and the resulting challenges and requirements into account, a Software Technology Research Lab was established at DaimlerChrysler in 1998. The work is divided into the areas of Process Organization, Software Architectures, as well as Methods and Tools and serves all business units of DC. The most important application areas are placed within the automotive sector. Both for the Passenger Cars Division as well as for Commercial Vehicles innovative solutions are being developed in the fields of vehicle dynamics, powertrain, comfort electronics, telematics, and sales. In addition, specific software technology topics are worked on for subsidiary companies, in particular for the European Aerospace and Defense Company EADS.

6.1. Processes

Based on established process standards such as the V-model propagated by the German Ministry of Defense, several similar process models have been developed at different automotive companies. Recently, a process-oriented software quality management handbook was released at DaimlerChrysler providing clear guidelines for the different software development steps. Experience has shown that specific reference models are required for the different automotive application areas such as vehicle dynamics, powertrain, body electronics, and telematics. The differing requirements are mainly related to the duration of the respective development cycles, to the degree of dependence from vehicle prototypes and trial rides, and to the involvement of the end-user. For instance, in the field of vehicle dynamics software development is closely coupled with the development of vehicle prototypes, whereas the integration of many cooperating, complex subsystems and the direct involvement of the driver is of greater importance in the area of body electronics.

In projects which involve not only the development of pure system functionality but also the design of user interfaces, e.g. for telematics and body electronics applications, the reference models are extended by the sub-process of "user-centric design and development". This sub-process aims at the seamless integration of all usability aspects into the entire software development process [1].

Major elements of DaimlerChrysler's research into requirements engineering are described in [2]. The work is focused on methodological aspects such as elicitation, specification, and refinement of requirements. It is complemented by corresponding analytical measures such as early simulation of requirements and the derivation of test cases from specifications. Requirements management represents another important area of work comprising the structure, administration, and tracing of requirements across the entire system life cycle. An essential result of this research work is a generic information model for requirements management which has been tailored to several automotive and aerospace applications. In order to provide powerful computer support the model has been mapped to different existing requirements management tools such as DOORS.

The specific problems occurring during cooperation with suppliers are tackled in a project focused on software acquisition management [3]. An appropriate process model has been developed which comprises the organization, the methodological support and the establishment of an efficient process for cooperation with suppliers. Emphasis is placed on quality and risk management on the part of the customer as well as on interaction with the corresponding procedures on the part of the supplier. Furthermore, a specific technique has been defined for the assessment of suppliers and their products.

6.2. Methods and tools

Major progress has been made in the area of methods and tools for automotive software development during the last few years. Tools for model-based development have found their way into the automotive development departments, and computer support has also been established in the areas of requirements management and testing.

At DaimlerChrysler Research significant effort has been made during the last five years to improve the methodological foundations of automotive software development, as well as the integration of tools and systematic and efficient testing. Test tools in particular contribute to a significant increase in test efficiency.

The design of test cases has a decisive impact on the quality of a test. Apart from common test criteria related to the coverage of the program code the required and specified functions of the system for the test must be considered. The Classification-Tree Method [4] and the Classification-Tree Editor CTE [5] have been developed by DaimlerChrysler Research in order to guarantee a systematic and comprehensible approach to the design of functional test cases. Both method and tool have been tried out successfully in numerous DaimlerChrysler projects, and have become established in development standards and environments of different business units and divisions. An extension of the approach is currently under development which explicitly considers the aspects of embedded systems with continuous input sequences.

The test system TESSY provides computer support for the testing of modules written in C [5,6]. It covers all testing activities from test case design to test execution, test evaluation, and test documentation. The functional test case design is supported by means of the Classification-Tree Editor CTE as an integral part of TESSY. Furthermore, host and target testing, automatic regression testing, and completely automated run-time testing are provided by the system. TESSY is being successfully used in different divisions of DaimlerChrysler, for instance for testing motor control units and powertrain management.

The tool MTest provides a powerful computer support for testing on the level of system models [7]. Thereby, errors made when modeling software-based functions can be detected early, i.e. before the actual coding process starts. Test cases defined for testing the model can easily be reused in later phases for testing software components and the completed system. MTest is based on the modeling tool Matlab/Simulink and is mainly used in the area of vehicle dynamics at present.

In the area of embedded systems, the correct behavior of the system depends on the fulfillment of functional as well as of real-time requirements. At DaimlerChrysler Research a new approach to real-time testing has been developed which is based on the use of evolutionary algorithms [8]. It has been successfully tried out in the areas of motor electronics and airbag control. The objective of the evolutionary test is to detect errors within the run-time behavior of the system. Input situations are searched for which lead to extremely short or extremely long execution times causing the system to fail the specified timing requirements. The search for these input situations is regarded as an optimization problem to be tackled by means of evolutionary algorithms. The target function of the optimization is provided by the execution times. The input domain of the system defines the search space.

6.3. Software architectures

As the architecture of the software is an essential element of the system ability of an automotive company, DaimlerChrysler Research currently works on both the design and the evaluation of in-vehicle software architectures. In the course of an evaluation an existing architecture or a draft version is analyzed with regard to different criteria in order to check whether or not given requirements are met, for instance concerning complexity or extendibility [9]. In general, the development of an architecture is based on a control circle between design and evaluation. In particular, the interplay between these tasks becomes very important if changes occur in the course of the software development. As the software architecture in a vehicle also depends on the mechanical and the electrical architecture there is also a mutual interdependency between the physical construction of the vehicle and the architecture of the software.

Currently, new architectural concepts are being tried out in DaimlerChrysler research cars. For example, an integration platform for the dynamic configuration and control of software modules has been developed for innovative driver assistance systems. This platform, called Agent Network System ANTS, is based on agent technology. The major advantage of this approach is the fact that the system can be flexibly extended by additional algorithms and control units and that existing software can be reused very easily. Furthermore, the architecture facilitates the cooperation and fusion of functional units which can be used for different applications in the form of a unit construction system.

DaimlerChrysler's research in the field of software architecture also comprises domain engineering and generative programming [10].

7. Conclusion and outlook

Due to the increasing use of software in the processes and products of automotive companies, software has a significant impact on product quality and company productivity. In order to meet the corresponding challenges and requirements, specific software competencies are required which cover both in-house software development as well as cooperation with suppliers. At DaimlerChrysler's Software Technology Research Lab innovative and powerful approaches are elaborated which comprise the areas of process organization, software architectures, and methods and tools. Numerous research results, such as systematic requirements engineering processes and testing techniques, could already be transferred successfully to projects, processes and development environments of DaimlerChrysler business units. Amongst other things, future work will focus on the model-based development of distributed systems, on the elaboration of a product line approach for future in-vehicle software architectures, and the integration of processes, methods and tools from the different areas of software, mechanical, and electrical engineering.

8. References

[1] E. Metzker, and M. Offergeld, "An Interdisciplinary Approach for Successfully Integrating Human-Centered Design Methods Into Development Processes Practiced by Industrial Software Development Organizations", *Proc. of 8th IFIP Conference on Engineering for Human Computer Interaction 2001 (EHCI '01)*, Toronto/Canada, Springer, pp. 21-36.

[2] M. Weber, and J. Weisbrod, "Requirements Engineering in Automotive Development - Experiences and Challenges", *IEEE Software*, January/February 2003, pp. 16-24.

[3] T. Gantner, and G. Getto, "Software Acquisition Processes - Research and Implementation at DaimlerChrysler", *Proc. of the Second World Congress for Software Quality*, Yokohama, Japan, September 2000.

[4] M. Grochtmann, and K. Grimm, "Classification Trees for Partition Testing", *Software Testing, Verification and Reliability*, Vol. 3, No. 2, pp. 63-82.

[5] www.razorcat.com/development

[6] www.hitex.de

[7] A. Rau, M. Conrad, H. Keller, I. Fey, and C. Dziobek, "Integrated Model-based Software Development and Testing with CSD and Mtest", *Proc. of International Automotive Conference*, Stuttgart, May 11-12, 2000.

[8] J. Wegener, *Evolutionärer Test des Zeitverhaltens von Realzeit-Systemen* (german), Aachen, Shaker Verlag, 2001.

[9] R. Trauter, "Software-Architekturbewertung", Tutorial (german), NetObjectDays, Erfurt, October 2000.

[10] K. Czarnecki, and U. Eisenecker, *Generative Programming: Methods, Tools, and Applications*, Addison-Wesley, 2000.

Experience Reports

Process Analysis and Improvement

Experiences on Defining and Evaluating an Adapted Review Process

Thomas Gantner, Tobias Barth
DaimlerChrysler AG
Ulm, Germany
{Thomas.Gantner, Oliver_Tobias.Barth}@DaimlerChrysler.com

Abstract

This paper presents our experiences with the introduction of a review process for software requirements documents in a development project of the Passenger Car Development business unit (PCD) of DaimlerChrylser AG. As software quality management and quality assurance must be carefully integrated into existing company processes or business cultures, we had to substantially adapt the review process to the specific needs of the above project and its context characteristics. The chief difference to the traditional procedure for conducting reviews as, for example, set out in [1] or [2] is that our review process has a strong workshop character with an emphasis on one of the most crucial success factors for reviews: sufficient time for the individual preparation of the reviewers. We also describe the phase of analyzing the effort and defect data captured with respect to cost benefit aspects and the quality of the reviewed documents in relation to each other.

1. Introduction

With the growing importance of software-based car innovations, more than 80% of the new innovative features are software driven, carmakers are faced with a new situation. Traditionally, electronic engineering in the automotive industry focuses strongly on building complex hardware systems controlled by a relatively small piece of embedded software. Recent and rapid changes in soft- and hardware technology enable the integration of the production of complex software (information) systems in the overall car development process. As a consequence, car manufacturers have to improve their know-how in the field of developing and acquiring large and complex software packages.

As the greatest part of the automotive software is developed by external suppliers, PCD has to write and deliver requirements documents of high quality to the supplier(s). Therefore, the introduction of an efficient and effective review process for these requirements documents is a key factor for achieving success in the development projects.

At the moment, we at DaimlerChrysler Research are supporting a project for Chassis Control Systems at PCD targeting the introduction and carrying-out of requirements document reviews. This business unit develops software systems that help to increase driving comfort and driving security (e.g. ABS or ESP). The fact that safety aspects are a major topic in the development of these systems greatly heightens the need for mature quality assurance activities.

We started our activities by performing a pilot review for a requirements document. The review process used and the problems faced with this pilot application in the specific project context are introduced in section 2. Section 3 presents the adapted or changed review process (compact reviews) we employed for the requirements documents written in our development project, including the preparation phase of the reviews and the subsequent analysis of the reviews. Section 4 summarizes the developed approach and some lessons learned. A shorter version of this paper can be found in [3].

2. Reviews and related issues in the specific context

As mentioned in the introduction, we started our project support activities with a pilot review for one requirements document from the given project context. For the pilot application, we utilized a traditional review process as illustrated in figure 1 and described in more detail in [1] or [2].

0-7695-1877-X/03 $17.00 © 2003 IEEE

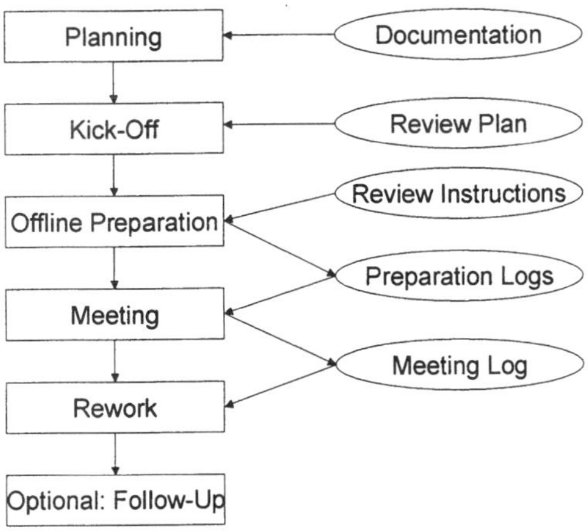

Figure 1. A traditional review process

The pilot application was intended to have 3 reviewers, each to represent a different perspective [4]: one reviewer was to represent the perspective of the reference documents which the requirements document under investigation was based on, the second reviewer assumed the perspective of deriving system test cases from the requirements document, and the third reviewer represented an author of another requirements document with a close connection to the reviewed document. Thus, thorough analysis of the document from all three reviewers was a primary goal for the pilot application.

The review meeting was scheduled for 3 weeks after the kick-off meeting and the distribution of the material which was necessary for the individual preparation of the reviewers. During these 3 weeks the reviewers were to give a short weekly report concerning their preparation status. It soon became clear that two of the reviewers had great problems in their preparation. As these two reviewers work in an open-plan office, it was at times difficult for them to find enough time and quiet for an effective preparation. In contrast, the third reviewer, who did a very thorough and deep review, had a workplace at home, allowing him to avoid many of the problems the other two had to deal with.

The pilot application therefore offered us some valuable insights for the review process within the new project:

- How to assure that enough preparation time is spent by the reviewers?
- How to manage efficient reviews for the 21 requirements documents, which in total described the whole set of requirements, that were to be addressed in the system?
- How to analyze whether the chosen approach was successful?

Another key aspect from a learning perspective was that each author of a requirements document should at least once take on the role of a reviewer for another requirements documents. Thus, in addition, the authors should learn how a reviewer feels when reading the documents written by another person.

3. Our approach: compact reviews

In this section we set out our approach of performing compact reviews on requirements documents under consideration of the general conditions in the project and the objectives described above.

3.1 Planning

General structure. Due to the objectives to be met and our experiences gained with former reviews in the given context, we decided to organize the reviews as workshops instead of offline individual preparation followed by the discussions with the authors. A chief disadvantage of the "classical" way of performing reviews is that they are spread over a longer period of time and management has less control over the progress than it does in a compact workshop. Our goal was to perform all reviews within one or two weeks, moderated and controlled by us as project-external observers.

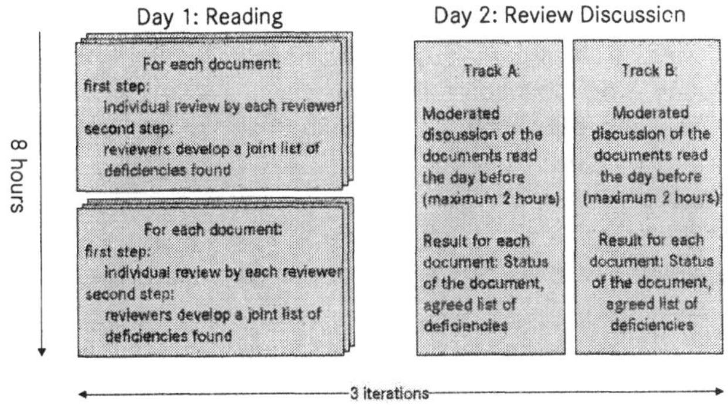

Figure 2. Structure of the review workshops

So, we defined a general structure for the review workshops with one day for reading documents (Day 1) and with the review discussions with the authors of the documents on the following day (Day 2) (see figure 2).

Each reading session for a requirements document was divided into two parts: the first part was the individual reading done by each inspector, the second a summarization of the individual inspection reports to a joint report of all inspectors for the analyzed document. This additional step helped to focus the discussion with the author on the critical insufficiencies, making the discussions on the following day more efficient. For example, in some cases we managed to cover more than 60 findings in only one or two hours. In addition to that, only one inspector actually had to participate in the discussion the next day, since all the findings were summarized in the joint review report. The inspectors were able to decide for themselves, which of them was to attend the review discussion part for the document to be reviewed. Of course, at least one of them had to be present. In the end, for 10 requirements documents only one inspector was present at the discussion session with the author. At no point did the absence of the other inspectors cause severe problems. Therefore we can claim that this reduction in effort spent did not have a negative impact on the quality of the review process.

As a guideline for the inspectors we prepared a checklist and a template for the inspection reports (these were identical for both the individual and joint reports). These templates were to be in electronic form so they could easily be summarized to a joint report. First the findings were classified by the inspectors with respect to the severity of the finding on a three point scale ("question", "optimize", "critical") and were then categorized by type: "formality", "consistency", "interface", "testability", "simplicity" and "completeness". Of course, the classification of the findings by severity was helpful for the authors when they had to correct or improve the requirements documents. The classification of the findings by type was found not really useful, as in many cases it was not clear which type a specific finding could be mapped to. Thus, we actually did not utilize this kind of information in the subsequent analysis of the review process, since the results might be misleading. As far as defect classification is concerned, the optimal solution would be a type classification which is orthogonal, lowering the danger of ambiguity. Yet, this would necessitate more effort for the preparation of the reviews.

Of course, the aim of the discussions on Day 2 was to present the insufficiencies to the author and not to correct them [5]. The author should understand the items set out in the inspection report in order to do the rework. The discussion should be moderated to keep the attendees from trying to correct the document, to prevent personal attacks, and to facilitate meeting the schedule. At the end of the discussion, each document was to be accorded a review status (e.g. "OK", "OK after rework done", "re-review needed") which then was communicated to management. Insufficiencies belonging to more than one document were listed separately and discussed with management afterwards.

As each reading day had as many as three parallel tracks and the day for the review discussions had two, we had to perform the structure shown in figure 2 three times in order to review all 21 requirements documents.

Characterization and calculation of estimated time. For a smooth flow of the workshops, an estimation on how much time the reviewers would need for reading each document was an essential success factor. Coming up with a good estimation of the time needed for reading a characterization of the requirements documents only by the number of pages is not sufficient. Therefore, we characterized each document according to the number of pages, the complexity of the text (4-point-scale from easy-to-read/understand up to difficult-to-read/ understand) and the target depth of reading (4-point-scale from quick reading up to intensive reading). Categorization of complexity was done by us on the basis of a document scan-through, to assess whether the structures contained such as text, diagrams, and tables were easy to read/understand or not. The categorization concerning target depth of reading was effected by a key player person in the project, who had a good overview on the project and the criticality of the content of the requirements documents under investigation.

The next step was to enter these data into a two-dimensional portfolio (Complexity/Target Depth). High complexity and intensive reading indicates that more time for reading is necessary, whereas low complexity and quick reading indicates less effort. We defined 6 priority-classes from 10 minutes down to 1 minute of reading time per DIN A4 page [6] in the portfolio. As the chief result of these steps, we had calculated one priority-class per document (How much time will it take to read and understand one DIN A4 page of this document on average?). Multiplied by the number of pages, we came up with an estimation of how long it would approximately take to read each document (Figure 3). Of course, we had to add some extra time for each requirements document to accommodate producing the joint review report. In the normal case, the addition of one or two hours sufficed, depending on the priority class of each requirements document.

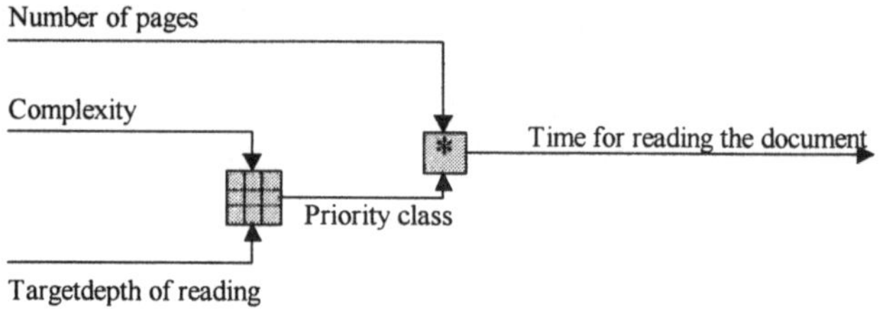

Figure 3. Time estimated for reading a document

On the basis of these calculations it was then possible to plan the agenda in more detail. Together with the project management, we defined the inspectors for the documents and fixed the agenda for the three iterations of the presented flow. As many people were involved in the reviews, this was not a trivial task. However after a number of iterations we came up with a plan that, in the end, worked quite well.

3.2 Applying the approach

All reviews were performed as scheduled with only slight deviations from the agenda. Only two documents could not be read completely within the planned time based on the presented estimation approach: one document took only a bit longer than estimated, the other document which was found to take much more time than planned had already been classified as critical before the reviews started (so this overrun was no surprise). For this document, we suggested that the inspectors split the documents into parts with each inspector reading a different part. While the document was read in total, this also meant that in this case we were not able to cover all the perspectives mentioned. The inspectors, however, decided to read the same parts, since they found the joint discussion on the commonly read parts extremely helpful.

All in all, we were very satisfied with our approach of estimating the time for reading. All the authors were pleased with the effective reading done by the inspectors. The time discipline was good and almost all the inspectors came to the reading sessions they were scheduled for.

In the review discussions we observed no personal attacks against the authors. A slight hitch was that some inspectors tried to solve the problems instead of just explaining the findings to the author. In these cases it was beneficial to have the moderators for interruption. In addition to the findings in the documents, some major points which needed a more general discussion in the project were found and recorded by the moderators. On the whole, the discussions were very efficient because of the well-prepared joint inspection reports: the planned maximum of two hours for the corresponding review discussions was never exceeded. On average the meetings for the review discussions took only an hour.

Another benefit of the review process introduced was that the quantitative data gathered by the moderators during the review process were very reliable, as the complete review process was totally under control of the moderators. By data reliability, we mean that, for example, the recorded effort data were very close to the real effort expended by the process participants. Of course, this was a key prerequisite for the quantitative analysis described in the next section.

3.3 Analysis

After performing the workshop, we compiled a statistical analysis based on the quantitative data (number of deficiencies found, time spent for the reading phases and the discussions) gathered by the moderators during the workshops. As our project principal has asked us not to divulge proprietary information, we are unfortunately not able to present absolute values for the data or provide quantitative information for the axes of the following diagrams. Nevertheless, we think the data analysis shown here is valid and meaningful, as the basic data used are real data and the knowledge of the absolute data is not necessary for the aspects analyzed and the conclusions derived.

As stated, the 21 requirements document were almost completely reviewed. On average, 1.1 insufficiency per page was found in the requirements documents. More precisely, the minimum value determined was 0.5, with the maximum value 2.3. Roughly 45% of the insufficiencies were denoted as "critical", i.e. it was deemed essential that these deficiencies be remedied before the respective requirements document was handed over to the supplier commissioned to realize the new system. Another issue analyzed was how much time on average was required to identify a (critical) deficiency in the documents. This was naturally very interesting information for the project management, aiding them in deciding if there was a positive cost-benefit relation for the reviews. As the value for the total deficiencies and the critical deficiencies was less than one hour, the project management was convinced that the project's investment in the reviews was valuable. Similar reviews in future projects are planned.

Of course, a more detailed cost-benefit analysis based on past data from projects which were not run through such a review process would be more helpful for deciding whether the chosen approach was successful or not–assuming that the historical data are meaningful and valid. However, in this case, the conclusions from the analysis of the data done in the review process were strong and detailed enough for the project management.

For us as the designer of the review process, the assumption that there is a close relationship between the time spent in reading and the number of deficiencies found was another target for analysis. A linear regression analysis with the variables *reading time* (independent variable) and *critical deficiencies* (dependent variable) showed with the resulting correlation coefficient that 66% of the variance in the dependent variable can be explained by the variance in the independent variable. The F-test with a significance level of 0.05 illustrated that this result is statistically significant–a strong hint that thorough individual preparation supported by sufficient time for reading is a key success factor for effective reviews.

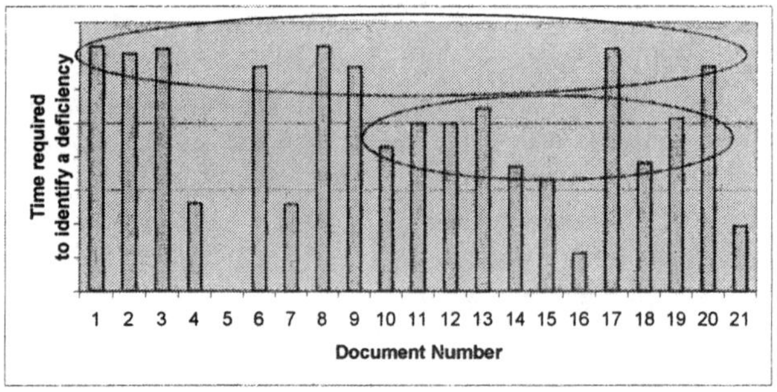

Figure 4. Time needed to identify a deficiency

A further interesting result of our analysis is portrayed in Figure 4. Examining the information on how much time was needed to identify a deficiency for each approved document, it became apparent that the documents could be separated into classes in which the documents have similar values for the analyzed metric.

This result was a trigger for a further analysis: the goal was to find out which documents did not seem to be as mature as we wanted them to be by analyzing how easy it was to identify deficiencies in these documents. These are the documents the project has to focus when starting the rework and further quality assurance activities. Documents where many critical deficiencies in a short reading time could be found are slated to be candidates for intensive rework and further quality assurance activities. Figure 5 illustrates that there were a number of documents with these characteristics.

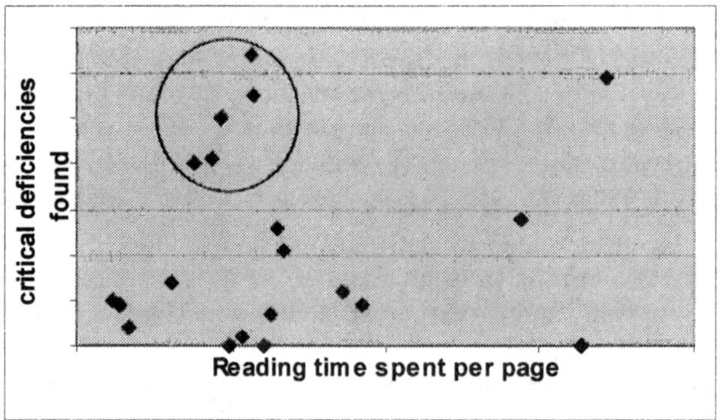

Figure 5. Short reading time–many critical deficiencies

In an initial step, we presented the results of this quantitative analysis in anonymously to the project, i.e. in figures 4 and 5, for example, we did not show the mapping of the document numbers or data points to the real requirements documents. The underlying reason, of course, was that we did not want to trigger a discussion on the quality and competence of the authors. Yet all the people involved had a great interest in clarifying which requirements documents seemed to be conspicuous according to the quantitative analysis and in determining whether this information as derived by the quantitative analysis corresponded to the subjective feeling the people had as to the quality of the requirements documents.

To investigate this issue further, we asked a key player in the project with a good overview of the requirements documents which requirements documents he would classify as critical on the basis of his subjective assessment of the document quality. In addition, this person was requested to add some arguments showing why he had classified these documents as critical.

The key player classified 6 documents as critical. From these 6 documents, 4 requirements documents were also identified as critical by the quantitative analysis, i.e. for these 4 documents either many critical deficiencies were found or critical deficiencies were found with a relatively low reading time spent per page. So, for the 4 documents at hand, the subjective classification of the key player and the quantitative analysis were strongly indicative of a need for further activities for improving the quality of the documents.

Now, the interesting question for the other 2 documents arises: why did the key player classify them as critical, but the quantitative analysis didn't? Interestingly, the argument the key player brought forth for his rating of these 2 documents not marked by quantitative analysis was that although the requirements document covered the expected aspects, these aspects were not addressed in sufficient detail.

A number of explanations for this observation occur: one is that the key player expected higher granularity in the requirements documents than the inspectors did. So the inspectors neglected to mark this as a defect. A further explanation is that the inspectors–when they did agree with the key player's point of view–marked the missing detail as a general finding. Thus this problem does not correlate with the number of defects found, which was some basic information for the quantitative analysis. A look at the detailed review reports shows that, according to a general comment made, parts of one of the two requirements documents were in fact classified as too complex.

4. Conclusions

We presented the defined approach for performing requirements documents reviews in a difficult project context which made a thorough individual preparation for the inspectors more laborius. We based our approach on the experience we gained in a pilot application in the given context. The main characteristic of our approach is that the reviews possess a workshop character with the requirement that the inspectors develop a joint list of deficiencies at the end of the preparation phase. Thus, the reviews could be performed in a compact fashion by strictly following the schedule for the workshop and by minimizing potential disturbing influences. The key goals were to provide an environment where a thorough individual preparation for identifying as many deficiencies as possible is supported and the review discussions with the authors of the documents could be performed efficiently. Both goals seem to have been met, as the inspectors very much appreciated the review approach and since the review discussions necessitated less time than expected and were performed in a pleasant atmosphere. Another chief advantage of the chosen review approach was that the overall process was under the control of the moderators. As a consequence the quantitative data (effort spent, deficiencies found) gathered during the review process seem to be a very sound basis for further analysis as shown here. Since the quantitative analysis conducted strongly hinted at a positive cost-benefit relation for the reviews and at the possibility of identifying "critical" documents as a basis for further quality assurance activities, the project management intends to incorporate our approach into document reviews in future projects. In summary, we can state that the introduced approach for performing reviews in a compact, efficient and effective way met with the intended success.

The analysis activities also showed that the quantitative analysis in general corresponded with the subjective rating of an experienced key player in the given context. Yet it also showed that a "blind" belief in quantitative data can be misleading. This is, of course, not new, but common sense has to be used when interpreting quantitative data.

As mentioned, the involved project manager intends to conduct document reviews in the described manner in future projects. To support this, we documented the procedure and the lessons learned in an experience package, together with the documents and material that were produced in planning and conducting the described review process in this pilot application. This experience package is based on a technique [7] developed by one of our colleagues.

Naturally there are some details of the described review process that can be improved in the future. For example, the time planned for the review discussions can be corrected on the basis of the experiences made. We planned a maximum of two hours for these sessions. Experience showed that this threshold can eventually be cut, which will improve the efficiency of the reviews. A further aspect targeted is enhanced support of the quasi online development of a joint list of the deficiencies found by the reviewers through a suitable infrastructure.

5. References

[1] Gilb, Tom; Graham, Dorothy: *Software Inspection.* Addison Wesley, Reading, Mass., 1993.

[2] Ebenau, Robert G.; Strauss Susan H.: *Software Inspection Process.* Mc Graw Hill, 1994.

[3] Barth, Tobias; Gantner Thomas: *An Efficient and Effective Software Review Process in a Difficult Project Context.* Proceedings CONQUEST 2002, Nuremberg, 2002.

[4] Basili, V.; Green, S.; Laitenberger, O.; Lanubile, F.; Shull, F.; Sorumgard, S.; Zelkowitz, M.: The Empirical Investigation of Perspective-based Reading. *Journal of Empirical Software Engineering*, 2(1):133-164, 1996.

[5] Wallmüller, Ernest: *Software Qualitätsmanagement in der Praxis*, 2.Auflage, München, Wien, Carl Hanser Verlag, 2001.

[6] http:\\www.ruediger-weingarten.de .

[7] Schneider, Kurt: *LIDs: A Light-Weight Approach to Experience Elicitation and Reuse*, Proceedings PROFES 2000, Oulo, Finland, 2000.

Towards Systematic Recycling of Systems Requirements

Nadine Heumesser, Frank Houdek
DaimlerChrysler AG,
Research and Technology
P.O. Box 23 60
89013 Ulm, Germany
{nadine.heumesser, frank.houdek}@daimlerchrysler.com

Abstract

Many (technical) systems are not developed from scratch but as an evolution of existing systems. Consequently, a large portion of the system requirements employed can be recycled when building the next version of the product. Usually, this recycling step is performed unsystematically, i.e. simply by copying and modifying complete requirements documents.

In this paper, we present in a case study a lightweight requirements recycling approach which evolved from observations and concrete needs of projects at DaimlerChrysler Passenger Car Development. The basic idea of the approach is separation of model-dependent from model-independent requirements on the same level of abstraction. This notion is supported by document structures, criteria for identifying reusable requirements and tool support.

The paper presents the core elements of the approach and provides observations and valuable experiences we made in the projects.

1. Introduction

Over the last few years the amount of software in cars has increased dramatically. Premium cars nowadays may contain up to 80 electronic control units (ECU), which make hundreds of software-based functions available either to the user or to other ECUs. In particular those functions and features that are innovative and provide competitive advantages are implemented using software.

Typically, development and production of ECUs is handled completely or partly by external suppliers who ask the car manufacturers for precise specifications of the related systems. And for this reason, the quality of the system requirements specification (SRS) plays a crucial role. It directly impacts the final quality of the ECUs and their interaction in the finished product – the car.

As a rule, specification and development of ECUs for a new car model does not start on 'the green field' but is instead based on existing descriptions and concepts. An SRS is built by reusing, modifying, and enhancing these specification documents. By reusing specification fragments, associated information such as test specifications and basically the underlying experience is reused. So on the up side, reused specifications are of higher quality than any built-from-scratch specification can ever be as they incorporate knowledge accumulated over time and across various product lines.

Nevertheless, the reuse processes currently employed are ad-hoc. Reworking and enhancing a document of several hundred pages so that it is complete, correct, and consistent is challenging. Hence, in 1999 we started collaborating with the instrument cluster group at DaimlerChrysler Passenger Car Development to improve their requirements reuse process.

As a main result we defined a recycling[1] approach which bases on their particular situation and addresses their reuse needs explicitly. The approach has been validated in two instrument cluster development projects where it proved to be applicable.

The approach focuses on the separation of model-independent requirements (i.e. the core functionalities) from model-dependent requirements (e.g. the communication protocols used, implementation of visual display, threshold values, or detectable defects) on the same level of abstraction. To be precise, we do not use any different kind of language or representation in either part. Although our approach may be characterized as generation based [1], we do not introduce a meta-level. Both model-independent and model-dependent requirements are written on the level of technical specifications, i.e. using natural language. Model-dependent aspects are suppressed merely by avoiding concrete interfaces, constants, etc. Instead, we use only symbolic names in the independent

[1] Internally we use the term requirements *recycling* instead of requirements *reuse,* for reuse sometimes leaves an unpleasant aftertaste, as it is associated with often unfulfilled expectations of achievable effects with code reuse. Interestingly, the term requirements recycling has already been picked up by others as the workshop *"Recycling requirements for system product families"*, Imperial College, London, 14th April 2002 demonstrates.

description that are instantiated in the model-dependent parts.

This concept is not merely new. The foundations for this concept can be found in work by Parnas et al [8]. Kuusela and Savolainen [7] show a similar approach applied at Nokia to manage requirements for product lines.

The remainder of the paper is structured as follows. Section 2 offers a brief overview of our application environment. Section 3 presents the recycling approach itself. Our observations and the lessons learned from real applications are summarized in Section 4. We end in Section 5 with conclusions and a brief discussion of further work.

2. Current Situation and Constraints

In this section, we give a brief overview of the application context in our case study, the instrument cluster group at DaimlerChrysler Passenger Car Development. Additionally, we identify the constraints and requirements that our requirements recycling approach has to fulfill if it is to be accepted in the instrument cluster group.

2.1. Instrument Cluster

An instrument cluster is a complex ECU connected to various other ECUs by a communication bus (see Fig. 1).

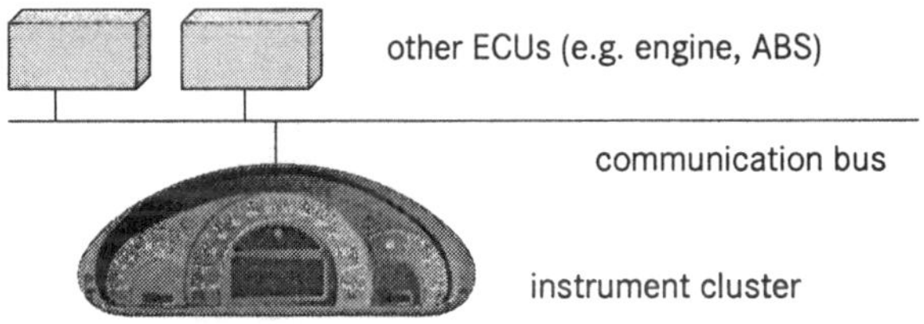

Figure 1: Example instrument cluster.

The cluster has to observe various legal constraints (e.g. for speedometer). As the component is visible to the driver, it not only has to fulfill high quality and reliability demands but also needs to meet aesthetic requirements. In addition to conventional instrument cluster functions, e.g. speedometer or tank indicator, it offers advanced functions to the user via a built-in display (e.g. a travel manager). And what is more important, it provides services to other ECUs such as information about the current state of the car or data for maintenance purposes.

Specification documents (SRSes) for instrument clusters consist of anywhere from 200 to 600 pages, describing requirements on the system level. This implies that our reuse approach has to be very careful:

(R1) not to extend the length of specification documents significantly by requesting amounts of additional information (e.g. meta-information), and

(R2) to be able to handle complex and voluminous specification documents (scalability).

2.2. Development Context

Specifying requirements for an instrument cluster for a specific car model incorporates three major tasks:

- *Clarifying and negotiating requirements* with all the stakeholders affected within DaimlerChrysler. As a car can be seen as a highly distributed system, there are numerous interfaces to other ECUs.
- *Describing the functionality* on a detailed technical level. The various ECUs are developed by separate groups (internally or by outside suppliers). Thus the requirements for a single ECU have to be very precise, especially in the area of interface specification. As a consequence, the specifications are extremely fine-grained, dealing with bits and bytes, milliseconds, etc. A large portion of the specification is dedicated to fault management, e.g. what has to happen if an expected input is missing, is out of range or is delayed.
- *Interacting with the development unit,* e.g. answering questions, tracking open points, evaluating prototypes.

The engineers responsible for instrument clusters consider themselves domain experts, not requirements engineering specialists. Thus, our reuse approach has to meet further requirements:

(R3) it must be applicable for 'ordinary' engineers and should not require special skills such as mastering formal notations. Instead, it should rely on commonly used elements such as natural language specification texts [4].

Usually, workload is high and several car models are specified and developed simultaneously. Consequently, our reuse approach

(R4) has to avoid additional overhead in all phases of its life-cycle. Especially during the ramp-up phase a great deal of additional effort shouldn't be necessary [6].

Also, our reuse approach must be able

(R5) to deal with simultaneous projects with different involved parties (e.g. different suppliers). This affects both tool support and concepts for evolution.

2.3. Current Reuse Approach

Reuse of existing documents is every-day work. As legacy documents compile experience and knowledge, it makes perfect sense to derive new documents from existing ones. The reuse approach usually used, however, is copy-rename-edit, i.e. legacy documents (or parts of them) are copied into a new context and then modified. Bearing in mind that SRSes tend to become very lengthy, it is likely that modifications, deletions or insertions may not touch on all the relevant requirements. So, we end up with inconsistencies and contradictions.

When copying existing requirements, we are sometimes unable to follow up on the rationales for a particular behavior. This means that the new specification may contain requirements that made sense in the context of the old system (where, for instance, we had to perform a signal conversion) whereas, in the new context, the requirement makes no sense at all (for instance, the conversion may already be performed by the sender of the signal). This implies that our reuse approach

(R6) should help to separate concerns, i.e. needs to group requirements that belong together and identify interfaces among various groups

(R7) should also help to capture requirements rationales, i.e. underlying assumptions and explanations.

Usually, specification documents are treated as individual text files, which are then modified using word processors. Here, of course, we find the usual drawbacks of such a practice, i.e. there is no real simultaneous working, only local copies of documents and discussions about the most recent versions. To avoid complete confusion when moving towards an integrated, reuse-based process, our approach thus has to

(R8) rely on a repository-based working environment (tool) for all requirements.

3. Recycling Approach

This section introduces our requirements recycling approach. First, we sketch the basic concept. From there, we go on to derive the ingredients which were necessary to make the concept applicable and then introduce them.

3.1. The Concept

The basic idea emerged from analysis of various existing specification documents. Large portions of different SRSes were similar or even identical (as new documents were created by copying and editing existing ones). On the detailed level, however, we found a number of deviations. Reasons for such deviations are largely implied by different environments (e.g. different communication messages, car parameters such as the engine power or maximum speed, size of indicators or display resolution).

Another essential observation was that all these documents dealt more or less with the same functionalities. Over time, the instrument cluster group built a common understanding of the relevant key concepts.

This observation stimulated the idea of separating model-dependent from independent concerns. For each functionality, we describe *all* the requirements in the model-independent part. While doing so, we use only abstract interfaces and parameters to avoid the dependent information. This kind of information is provided in the model-dependent part. Figure 2 sketches this idea graphically. Ideally, the model-dependent part can be seen as a 'wrapper' which offers instantiation information for all the interfaces and parameters identified.

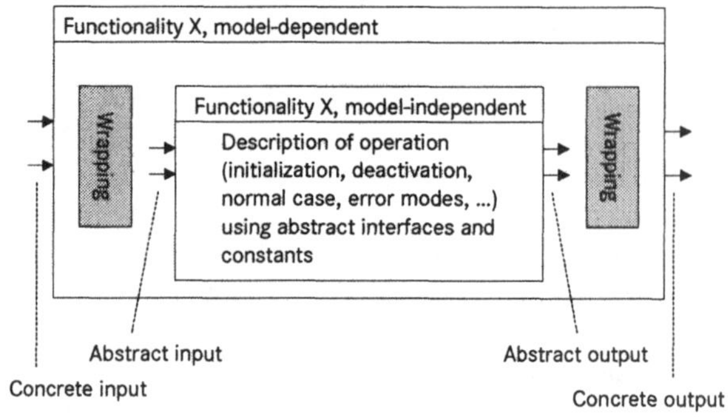

Figure 2: Separation of model-dependent from model-independent parts.

It is vital to note that this separation does not introduce several levels of abstraction in terms of overview and detail: instead it introduces abstraction in terms of concrete and abstract interfaces and parameters.

The term *parameter* may need further explanation: parameters are variable elements in the context of the model-independent description. Examples are maximum values for the speedometer or the ability to handle a recall-command (see example in Section 3.3). In a concrete implementation, parameters may be handled in different ways. Some are hard coded, others may be stored in a re-writeable memory, and others cannot be localized in the final product at all as they result in shorter or longer code.

Example: If a particular tank indicator does not support low-fuel warning (i.e. parameter low_fuel_warning = not available), then the implementation of the tank indicator will not incorporate any code for this warning.

In cases where the functionality for a particular car model cannot be covered solely by the model-independent requirements, we have to add new requirements in the dependent part. In rare situations we also encounter the case that the model-dependent requirements completely over-rule the independent ones (see Figure 3)

Situation: The particular functionality is ...	The content of model-dependent description ...
... an instantiation of the model-independent description	... is only a mapping of abstract interfaces to concrete ones and an instantiation of parameters
... an instantiation of model-independent description with modifications	... is a mapping of interfaces, an instantiation of parameters and a list of added requirements (which might invalidate series-independent ones)
... different to the model-independent ones	... provides a new functionality description without reference to the model-independent requirements

Figure 3: Various forms of interaction of model-independent and dependent specifications.

3.2. Applying the Concept

To make the basic concept work, we need several ingredients:

- *Criteria for recycling candidates,* as it is likely that not all parts of an SRS can be recycled equally effectively.
- *Documentation structure* that supports the documentation of functionalities in accordance with the basic concept without imposing too much documentation overhead.
- *Tool support/configuration* which assists in making the approach applicable and helps to take the environmental constraints identified in Section 3 into account (e.g. parallel work or access rights).

All these issues have to be handled by an integrated *requirements engineering process*. As it is likely that the common functionality descriptions will emerge over time, the requirements engineering process has to provide a *concept for evolution,* i.e. a way to evolve the model-independent description and decide about propagation of changes to all car models that are currently in the pipeline. In the context of this paper, however, we omit process and evolution concept.

3.3. Criteria for Recycling Candidates

Reviewing existing specification documents, it became obvious that not all parts were equally suited for recycling. Instead, we found three levels of reusability:

- *Domain requirements*, i.e. requirements that can be considered stable in a given environment. Typical examples are requirements set for physical or electromagnetic properties. Once identified, these requirements can be recycled as black-box components. Document analysis and a workshop with domain experts were used to identify these requirements and to prepare them as reusable assets.
- *Functionality requirements*, i.e. requirements that deal with functionalities of the system under development. These are essential recycling candidates, as they are similar from one model to the next, but not identical. They differ in the concrete interfaces at the least, but may also differ in the functionality itself. Identifying them on the coarse-grain level was fairly simple, as the instrument cluster group members had a good understanding of the key features and functionalities of their systems. Digging deep into detail, however, revealed some problems. We had to work hard on the term *functionality* – where does a functionality start and end, which requirements belong to a functionality and which do not. Here, we found the model-view-controller pattern [2] valuable as it helped to separate optical aspects (e.g. data on the display) from processing aspects.

  Example: The travel manager[2] was quickly identified as a functionality on the coarse level. But which parts of the travel manager can be recycled easily and which cannot? While the basic behavior is identical throughout the car models, there are subtle differences. Some travel managers provide automatic reset on restart only, whereas others provided re-access to previous travel data on demand. Details such as the information presented on the display may vary also, i.e. the number of significant digits or the display layout may differ. The model-view-controller pattern helped to differentiate the various aspects of the travel manager and, in the end, led to the reusable core ('model' part of pattern, see Figure 4).

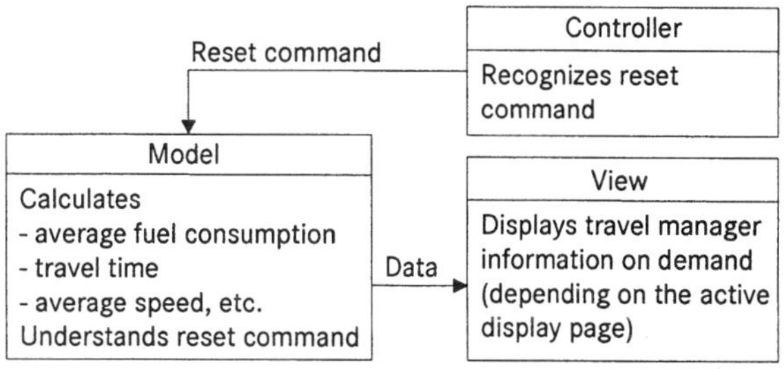

Figure 4: Model-view-controller pattern applied for a generic travel manager.

  As a consequence of this analysis, when considering what goes into the reusable core, we incorporated not only the behavior that was common to all existing implementations but also model-specific features if we envisioned that they might be relevant for some car models in the future. For instance, the generic travel manager functionality performs an automatic reset on restart (common to all models) and is able to handle the re-access command (currently available only in some models). Here we see a difference to many reuse approaches which focus only on commonalities among all ancestors. On the other hand, we didn't attempt to envision potential modifications to the functionality which might happen at some time in the future (except some very likely ones). So we did not spend much effort in forecasting and planning, as would be characteristic for product line approaches [3].

  In our experience, the functionality-driven approach helps to divide a system into manageable parts without being too coarse-grained or excessively fine-grained (R2 and R6).
- *Model-specific requirements*, i.e. requirements that are particular for a given car model. Currently we are treating all requirements that do not belong to one of the two above categories as model-specific. Prominent candidates are MMI requirements (e.g. text allocation

[2] The travel manager displays information on the current driving style, such as average fuel consumption or average speed.

in the display, fonts, size and shape of indicators, user interaction, and response behavior), hardware requirements (e.g. size, weight, connectors, casing), or communication requirements (e.g. information sent and received via CAN-bus). Keeping the model-view-controller pattern in mind, we currently treat both view and controller parts as model-specific.

This classification is somewhat coarse as it treats requirements that could be seen as recycling candidates as model-specific. Future work will target refining this model to enlarge the portion of reusable requirements.

To give an idea of the absolute and relative size of requirements, Figure 5 sketches the percentage and number of requirements in the three categories.

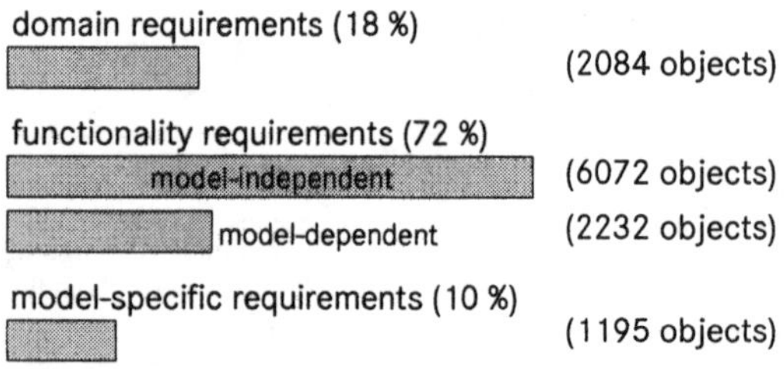

Figure 5: Absolute and relative number of requirements in the three levels of reusability for one car model (absolute figures counted as DOORS objects, see Sec. 3.5).

3.4. Documentation Structure

An uncomplicated, easy way to handle document structure was a key challenge for our approach (see R1 and R3 in Section 2). We left domain requirements and model-specific requirements completely untouched, i.e. they are written in the same style as before. Figure 6 shows an example of a simple functionality documentation.

Concerning functionality requirements, we extended the current ways of documenting requirements (i.e. natural language text with drawings, tables, etc.) by adding absolutely necessary elements implied by the basic concept, i.e. interface and parameter definitions. To make the functionality requirements more comprehensive, we also appended an overview section which consists of a short introduction describing the core behavior in a few sentences and a figure depicting all inputs, outputs, and parameters. The figure itself is generated automatically using interface and parameter information.

Another essential factor are the meta-requirements for the environment. This section is chiefly dedicated to requirements set for *view* or *control* according to the model-view-controller pattern. For instance, if a functionality can trigger a warning message, the necessity for this warning message is described in this section. Yet, details about this warning message (i.e. layout) are of no interest here.

X. Engine Stop Time

X.1 Modification history

<omitted>

X.2 Overview

X.2.1 Relationship to other functions

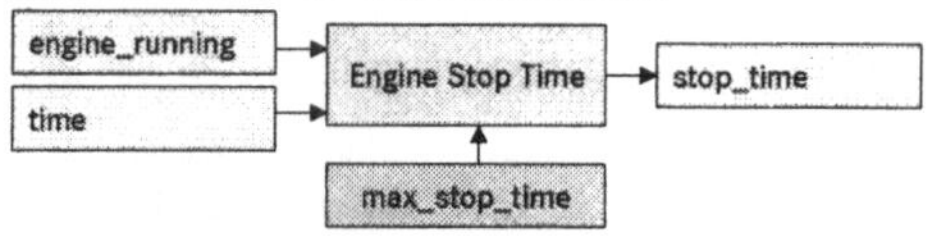

X.2.2 Core functionality

The function calculates the time since the engine has been turned off in minutes (up to a fixed value). This value is needed by the engine to optimize engine restart.

X.3 Functionality description

At first activation, stop_time is max_stop_time. When the engine has been started, stop_time is decremented by 10 every minute until it has reached 0. As long as the engine is running, stop_time keeps the value 0. When the engine stops running, stop_time is incremented every minute by 1 until it reaches max_stop_time.

If there is no valid information about the engine state available, it is assumed that the engine is not running.

Setting the system into hibernation mode and waking it afterwards should not affect stop_time in the sense that after waking the system, stop_time provides the same value as it would have done without interruption by hibernation mode. During hibernation mode, however, no information is provided.

X.4 Interfaces and parameters

X.4.1 Inputs

Name	Description	Values
engine_running	Is engine running?	true/false/error
time	System time	hh:mm:ss

X.4.2 Outputs

Name	Description	Values
stop_time	Duration engine isn't running	0..max_stop_time

X.4.3 Parameters

Name	Description	Values
max_stop_time	Max. perceived stop time	Integer (minutes)

X.5 Appendix

<omitted>

X.6 Meta-Requirements

– none –

X.7 Specific requirements for car model XYZ

X.7.1 Modification history

<omitted>

X.7.2 Overview of model-specific requirements

Compliant with model-independent description.

X.7.3 Model-specific requirements

– no modifications –

X.7.4 Instantiation of interfaces and parameters

X.7.4.1 Inputs

Name	Source
engine_running	[internal] functionality engine run detection
Time	[CAN] by clock module

X.7.4.2 Outputs

Name	Sink
stop_time	[CAN] e_stp_tm

X.7.4.3 Parameters

Name	Source	Defaultvalue
max_stop_time	[hard coded]	1200 (minutes)

X.7.5 Appendix

<omitted>

Figure 6: Example of documentation structure for one functionality (alienated from real functionality).

Example: Let us go back to the travel manager example (Section 3.3). Here, meta-requirements would be the request for a display page that presents the calculated data and the request for a recall command (if this part of the travel manager functionality is used at all).

3.5. Tool Support/Configuration

From a technical perspective, there is no need for explicit tool support. In principle, the recycling approach described can be implemented simply by using a word processor. From an administrative point of view, however, tool support is inevitable. As our approach has to support several development projects in parallel (R2, R5), we need mechanisms that support concurrent work. Additionally, we need mechanisms for access control (R5). It is essential that not everyone should be able to modify or even read particular requirements. Some support of the broad range of documentation types used (e.g. text, pictures, attached documents) should be also be implemented. Thus we decided to use the tool DOORS from Telelogic. In previous projects we gained some experience with this tool and it seemed to us that DOORS would be able to cope with the above-mentioned requirements very well.

In DOORS, requirements are arranged in various modules composed of objects. Each object has a unique identifier and a main attribute that can contain any text and/or heading as well as embedded OLE objects or pictures. Each object has additional attributes: some of them are maintained automatically (e.g. author, creation date), while others may be user defined (e.g. status or rationale). Objects may be arranged hierarchically to represent the structure of a document. Two objects can be connected by means of a bi-directional link. Baselines can be used to freeze the current state of work with a version label. On the basis of baselines and individual object histories, previous states of work can be viewed and restored.

Figure 7 sketches the organization of two development projects (model XYZ and model UVW) by means of modules in DOORS. Each module in the folder 'workbench', which contains all reusable functionality requirements, is structured according to Figure 6. All other modules that are relevant for the SRS are structured as per their particular content (e.g. introduction according to existing templates or an item list of requirements on electromagnetic compatibility).

Clustering requirements in separate folders within the workbench has the great advantage that all relevant information is grouped together, thus supporting concentrated work on a particular functionality at one time (R2).

The fine-grained separation of information into isolated modules has the advantage of simple access rights and eases parallel work (R5). The only trade-off is that more complex document definition schemes are needed to compile one SRS for a particular car model out of the available modules. As we have automated this process, it does not really have a negative impact on daily work (R4).

A number of additional attributes (status, modification rationale) helped to improve daily work as well.

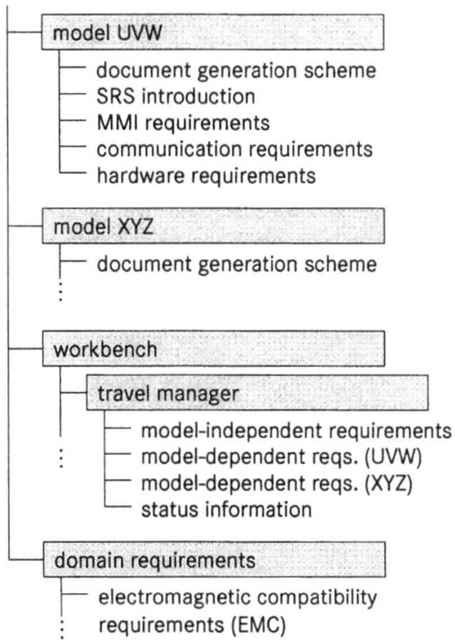

Figure 7: Organization of information (gray-shaded boxes are folders, text lines are DOORS modules).

4. Lessons Learned

In this section we present the experience gained and observations made within two instrument cluster projects at DaimlerChrysler Passenger Car Development. On the whole, the approach was accepted very well. It seems that we maintained a balance between innovation and tradition, i.e. the approach provides enough benefit to be employed without imposing too much overhead (R4).

In the following discussion we categorize the observed effects as either primary or secondary . Primary effects are effects that can be traced directly back to our requirements recycling approach. Secondary effects are side-effects which are not directly related to requirements recycling but to accompanying activities such as usage of a requirements management tool or refined processes. Additionally, we present issues observed during the implementation of our approach.

4.1. Primary Effects

By restructuring existing specifications according to our recycling structure (see Figure 6), we achieved a greater degree of uniformity and higher quality. There are two chief reasons for this:

- The documentation structure used requires information that in the past was often missed. As interfaces and parameters are mentioned explicitly, important requirements (which often affect interfaces) are less likely to be mentioned in subordinate sections, diagrams, etc.

- During restructuring, many questions about rationales for a specific behavior arose. In the past, these unclear requirements were often copied meaninglessly to new SRS *("there must be a reason for this requirement, so I'm keeping it").* The effect of digging into rationales has been fostered by the fact that a significant portion of restructuring was done by non-instrument cluster people (e.g. researchers) who were able to ask even more 'stupid questions'. Incorporating answers to these questions and rationales into requirements (R7) helped to improve quality significantly [5].

Both the notions of separating model-independent from model-dependent requirements and grouping information according to functionalities in the workbench had considerable influence on the working processes. Cooperation amongst engineers has increased as awareness of effects of individual changes has risen. Unnecessary variations between models are reduced. With model-independent/dependent requirements, we introduced something like a *provider-user concept.* The engineer responsible for a particular car model considers the model-independent requirements as master requirements that must be complied with. Foreign requirements are no longer incorporated in new contexts.

Our recycling approach also helped to cut the time needed to create a new version of an SRS with higher quality (R4). While merely copying and renaming an existing SRS is also a pretty quick job, the resulting SRS is just not tailored to the new product. By picking exactly the functionalities needed on the model-independent level according to a previously defined feature list, we create an initial SRS version that is correct. Of course, many adaptations which are necessary are missing, but we have not incorporated any unnecessary requirements.

If functionality has to be modified by additional requirements in the model-dependent part, we have to ensure the consistency of the whole picture. This job became significantly easier as dependent information is either part of the corresponding model-independent description or can be identified via the function interfaces.

4.2. Secondary Effects

Many secondary effects are due to the tool support introduced. Having a requirements management tool in place had some positive effects on daily work:

- There is one commonly used repository for all requirements (R8). Thus, there is no question about which is the most recent version of a document. And every engineer has the chance to 'just have a look' at the requirements of other models, as they are only a module away. Before, engineers had to navigate through the folders to identify the relevant document.
- Recognizing the possibility to store existing documents as OLE objects within DOORS, the engineers tended to misuse the tool as a document management system, i.e. storing all related documents in one location. The positive effect of this is that all relevant information is available in one place. The trade-off, however, it that an SRS is no longer a plain document but becomes a hypermedia object.
- User access management made it possible to locate all the information in the repository. Even confidential information, e.g. encoding algorithms, can be stored in the repository now and no longer has to be kept in private folders.
- Simultaneous work is now much easier than it used to be (when we had to deal with monolithic SRS documents). Reasons are the finegrained module structure and DOORS's ability to handle concurrent access.
- The ability to create customized views makes it easy to answer questions other than *"what's in the SRS?".* For instance, we record open points in the modules and denote them as 'open'. A customized view enables us to generate an open-point SRS, i.e. a document containing all currently open issues.

4.3. Problems Encountered

It is unlikely that a situation can be changed without introducing some (at least temporarily) negative side-effects.

Although we tried to minimize the overhead of information introduced due to reusable requirements (R1), there is no getting around this (interfaces, parameters, introduction, meta-requirements; see Section 3.4). Here, we observed two reactions:

- The need for the overhead information (approximately 20% in terms of length) is not always accepted as it makes the documents harder to read.
- The uniform structure sometimes differs from the individually chosen style of writing. Thus the feeling that a requirement 'belongs' to an engineer is reduced.

Restructuring information to align it with the new structure is linked with a significant amount of work that needs to be carried out in addition to the daily workload (in contrast to R4). This could have been a major problem introducing our approach would hit. Fortunately, we were able to mitigate this issue. Key aspects here were as follows:

- The approach can be introduced incrementally, i.e. it is not mandatory to migrate all relevant functionalities at one point in time.
- We, as researchers, were able to contribute additional manpower which was beneficial when used in the re-

structuring process. A side-effect of this was incorporation of additional explanations that arose due to answers to our 'stupid questions' (R7).

- If there is uncertainty about separation of model-dependent from model-independent information (e.g. for a new functionality) it is possible to treat this functionality as a model-specific functionality, i.e. to postpone restructuring until enough evidence about model-dependence/independence is available.

Another issue came up with selection of the requirements management tool DOORS. People no longer work solely with a word processor; they use a database. This has several drawbacks:

- The final product (the SRS document) is not directly present on the screen. If a complete SRS is needed, the user has to generate it. Depending on the size of the document, generation may consume several hours. A quick printout of a few pages, for instance, is not sensible.
- Although the tool can be used intuitively in most cases, training is required to exploit its full functionality. This takes time and requires individual commitment.

The 'new visibility', i.e. having information available for all persons involved had a psychological drawback. Many people were for some reason afraid to present incomplete work to their colleagues. They preferred to leave the information on their home directories until it could be presented in full. A main reason for this is the experience that incomplete work which was used by others (without notification of the author) tends to cause a lot of trouble and rework. A consequence for our approach is that we have to emphasize the role of the status attributes introduced. Others may not use requirements that are declared to be 'in the pipeline'.

5. Conclusions and Future Work

Recycling of requirements is a key challenge for environments used to build similar but evolving systems. In this paper, we presented in a case study an approach for requirements recycling (or reuse) which has been implemented for ongoing instrument cluster projects within DaimlerChrysler Passenger Car Development for more than two years. At the heart of this approach lies the separation of model-independent from model-dependent requirements by means of documentation structures. Although this approach can be characterized as generation-based (the model-independent information has to be instantiated for a particular car model), we do not introduce a separate level of abstraction. Moreover, the general description is augmented and tailored by model-specific information. The positive aspects of this approach are three-fold: there is no need for specific education or training (e.g. formal notations) and special-purpose tools are not called for, and the approach does not substantially change the way requirements are formulated. Thus implementation in productive environments is fairly easy.

For future activities we see a wide range of promising extensions:

- We have to work on criteria to define the parts of an SRS that should be restructured for recycling and those that need not. The currently implemented functionality-driven approach works, but it seems that there are other areas that can also be recycled effectively,.
- The overhead information introduced by our approach (a model-independent list of interfaces and parameters and its instantiation in the model-dependent part) is currently part of the generated SRS document. For the sake of readability it seems feasible to suppress this information in the generated documents.
- Downstream work-products (except test cases) are not considered so far, as external suppliers perform most development activities. Nevertheless it seems sensible to incorporate some downstream work-products in the future.

Acknowledgements

We would like to acknowledge our colleagues in Sindelfingen who helped us to keep our approach applicable. We learned a lot and had a great time. Thanks, folks.

References

[1] T. Biggerstaff, A. Perlis (Ed.). *Software Reusability. Volume 1, Concepts and Models.* ACM Press Frontier Series, 1989.

[2] F. Buschmann, R. Meunier, H. Rohnert, P. Sommerlad, and M. Stal. *A System of Patterns.* John Wiley & Sons. 1996.

[3] P. Clemens and L. Northrop. Software Product Lines: Practices and Patterns. Addison Wesley, 2001.

[4] A.M. Davis. *Predictions and Farewells.* IEEE Software. Vol. 15, No. 4, pp. 6-9, 1998.

[5] F. Kiedaisch, M. Pohl, J. Weisbrod, S. Bauer, and S. Ortmann, *Experiences on Outsourcing Requirements Specifications*, In Proc. of EuroSPI'01, pp. 10-16 to 10-31, 2001.

[6] A.v. Knethen, B. Paech, F. Kiedaisch, and F. Houdek. *Systematic Requirements Recycling through Abstraction and Traceability.* In Proc. of the IEEE Joint Int. Requirements Eng. Conf, pp. 273-281, Sept. 2002.

[7] J. Kuusela and J. Savolainen. *Requirements Engineering for Product Lines.* In Proc. of the 22nd Int. Conf. on Software Eng., ICSE'00, pp. 61-69, June 2000.

[8] D. Parnas, P. Clements, and D. Weiss. *The Modular Structure of Complex Systems.* IEEE Transaction on Software Engineering. Vol. 11, pp. 259-266, 1985.

Tricks and Traps of Initiating a Product Line Concept in Existing Products

Christof Ebert & Michel Smouts
Alcatel, Paris, France & Antwerp, Belgium
Contact: christof.ebert@alcatel.com

Abstract

Many industries are hampered with introducing the product line concept into already existing products. Though appealing, the concept is very difficult to introduce specifically into a legacy environment. All too often the impacts and risks are not considered adequately. This article describes the introduction of a product line approach in Alcatel's S12 Voice Switching System Business Unit. Practical impacts during the introduction are described as well as tricks and traps. The article not only summarizes the key software engineering principles, but also provides empirical evidence and practical techniques on which to build.

***Keywords**: product lines, portfolio management, roadmapping, prioritization, process improvement*

1. Introduction

The recent evolution in the telecommunication markets has stimulated a focus on short cycle time, while continuing to deliver competitive advantage to network operators. Equipment suppliers thus deliver individualized solutions to the operators with very short reaction time. To better address these challenges within its voice networking business, Alcatel introduced a product line concept for switching products.

Product line architecture and approaches to introduce product families recently received increased attention within software engineering literature – for the obvious business impacts as described above. The majority of results originate from telecommunication infrastructure products [1,2,3,4,5,6]. While initial focus was on effective configuration and change management [1,5], the scope grew towards validation [2], and identifying marketing and organizational constraints and effectively reducing them [3,4,6,7,9].

To achieve sustainable and thus successful product families we must carefully integrate with upfront processes, such as marketing, requirements management or portfolio management. So far the introduction of a product line concept was only addressed from a requirements engineering and architecture perspective [3,6]. This article thus builds a bridge from the concept of a product line to its introduction in an existing set of products and markets.

Alcatel is the world's leading telecommunication equipment supplier. Like architects, Alcatel designs, builds and evolves telecommunications networks, according to its customers needs. Specific and dedicated solutions for customers have been provided in this market for many years. The challenge today is to build upon technology platforms, while still offering tailored solutions.

The study describes switching products within Alcatel's voice networking business. Alcatel is registered for the ISO 9001 standard. The majority of development locations in this business unit have been assessed at CMM L3. The *Alcatel 1000 S12* is a digital switching system that is currently used in over 50 countries world wide with over 180 million installed lines. It provides a wide range of functionality (line concentrators, small local exchanges, transit exchanges, international exchanges, network service centers, and intelligent networks). It is scaleable from small remote concentrators to large local exchanges. This wide range of functionality in an existing product is the real challenge for introducing a product line concept.

The typical size is over 4.5 million source statements, which is customized for network operators. In terms of functionality, *S12* covers almost all areas of software and computer engineering. This includes operating systems, database management, and distributed real-time software.

The product line concept has been applied in other Alcatel products such as mobile terminals, or satellites for quite awhile. The challenge for the *S12* products was *moving* from a project- and market perspective towards a global product line concept, and *not starting over from scratch*.

The paper is organized as follows. Section 2 outlines how the product line concept fits into existing product development. Section 3 characterizes success factors that facilitate product lines. Finally, section 4 summarizes concrete results from this observational case study. We have tried to abstract as much as possible from any specific observation related to the products used in this study.

2. Product Lines in Existing Development

The perceived flexibility of software-driven products often results in an amount of variants and local evolutions which make it impossible to synchronize development activities, be it corrective or additive. The absence of clear linkages to business value invites over-engineering, that is, implementing functions that may only rarely be used or adding excessive functions that are not necessary to attain the desired business results.

Over-engineering not only wastes resources, but more importantly, it produces a proliferation of variants and complexity, as each further enhancement has undesired side effects with other features. We faced this evolution in a product that was customized for a multitude of markets, however not synchronized in the way it was customized. As each customization reused big portions of software in a white box approach (i.e. minor internal changes to the reused components which are embedded), any major change to the architecture would foster generic evolution of the product creating huge overheads, specifically for retesting existing functionality. No customer is willing to pay these costs.

Traditional answers are related towards improving configuration management and introducing white-box reuse. This happened years ago but without the big effects on both cycle time and productivity. The existing legacy architecture was not supporting the move towards separating domain from application development. Frequently a small feature change for one application product would create major impact because of the many ripple effects. Developing a fully new product would certainly solve the issue with complex legacy architecture but was not feasible in its entire business environment. Components could be reengineered, but not the entire product.

As an answer to these challenges we decided to introduce a rigid coherent worldwide product line concept for "switching" products. We introduced this incrementally to to better manage change and avoid major uncertainty on marketing and customer reaction This meant gradually merging related releases to few product lines, instead of a big-bang approach.

We envisioned the product line concept based on a few generic releases that are further customized according to specific market requirements around the world. Having only one product domain release and customize that for all market-specific application products would be the best - theoretic - solution. It was however not feasible, since many markets were at that point (mid 90's) not yet prepared for such change.

Such evolution from isolated products towards clustered product families that are increasingly aligned is primarily a question of effective requirements management. It starts on the marketing front-end where such product line must be specified in its basic layout. Customer profiles and their business needs must be mapped to global market evolution and our own products' evolution streams. Similarities will be detected. The key drivers for future sales will build the skeleton for an increasingly global release roadmap. A master roadmap is generated with a visible heartbeat of annual or bi-annual domain releases. From this master roadmap market-specific application releases are derived. Requirements management links these different roadmaps and ensures that features evolve synchronously.

3. Tricks and Traps

3.1 Strongly coordinate marketing and engineering

A major objective of introducing the product-line concept is to reduce design variety and focus on reuse. When introducing lawful interception functionality into our different switching systems during 1997/98 timeframe we had to fully design it into several major products, because the systems had so many differences that it was impossible to reuse even key design elements. Design effort and integration cost multiplied, as did the project risks. The change took over 2 years for all major markets. The solution looked the same, but the development effort was not sustainable in several product lines.

Why this discrepancy? Marketers are primarily interested in solutions, not immediately technical features. With respect to stakeholders the model of a product line has to address their questions. What functionality at what price can I offer the customer? What solution space can I address? What are the features I can configure in a concrete solution? What operational impacts would result for the customer or for the supplier? What supply chain impacts need to be addressed in due time to ensure volume delivery?

Marketing is the external success factor for product lines. Without sufficient forecasting and influencing markets and communicating roadmaps and portfolios back to markets, no product line concept will sell. There certainly is a heavy impact on roadmap definition, i.e. product and program management (fig.1). While individual and market-specific management of products asks "only" for sufficient engineering resources, an aligned global product line concept means that marketing and R&D are fully aligned.

This is indicated in fig.1 as an evolution from left to right. On the left side we see ad hoc releases with individual synchronization points that are not planned upfront, and often generate huge overheads for development and market introduction. The right side depicts a roadmap view with number of releases and their individual market-specific application products. Not necessarily each market has to follow the frequency of the baseline. We use a one-year period for the baseline. It's thus sufficient to have a three-year product roadmap to allow individual markets to plan when a change should be introduced.

The evolution of a baseline release from version n to version n+1 is driven by market needs. This is indicated in fig.2, which from left to right shows version n and version n+1. The middle part shows two application products for markets A and B. Both require certain changes to be successful in the respective market. Changes should be on top, not happening within the domain product's design unless a business case justifies the additional cost of making late changes to the base line.

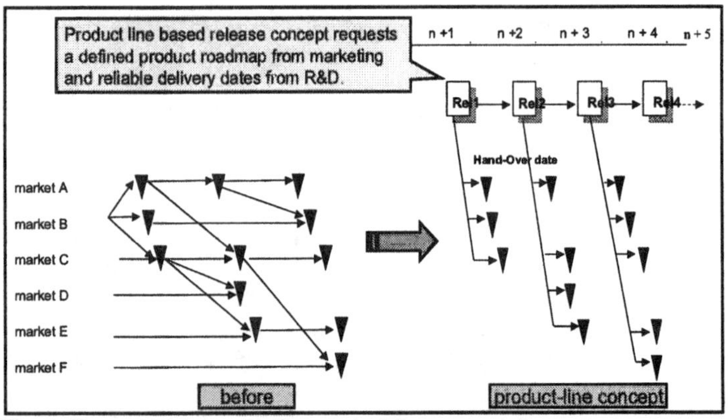

Fig. 1: To avoid interrupts, the product line approach needs to gradually evolve out of previously ad-hoc and isolated market roadmaps

Not all changes that happened for markets A and B can be taken into the next baseline release n+1. Both markets had introduced functionality and thus changes to the baseline, which they need to maintain individually also for release n+1 - or to give up. Again, it shows how close marketing and engineering must cooperate to have successful product line architecture in place.

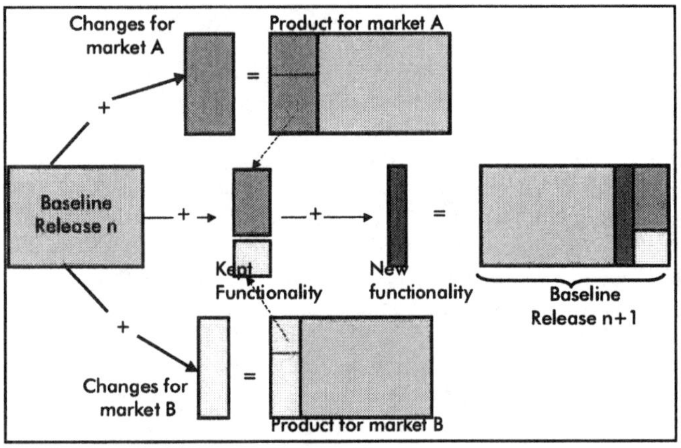

Fig. 2: The evolution of a baseline release with inputs from application releases.

What did we achieve? While the product-catalogues look more impressive due to offering more features simultaneously to markets, the amount of design effort for a specific feature has been reduced. Portfolio management is reduced to few major product lines, with variants following suit. Today the roadmap of all market-specific releases is reliable and easy to maintain. The time for changes until they ripple through into key markets has been cut by more than half. Transparency and visibility is available for product managers and sales. Cycle time is reduced for the market-solutions. Increased predictability means less heavy changes late in the life cycle.

3.2 Express requirements clearly and with business focus

Requirements are reused and also identify reuse concepts. Impact analysis is based on requirements, as well as priority setting and portfolio management. What are the requirements? How do they relate between markets and correlate with each other? What is their impact? What markets have asked for it and for what reason? Are they necessary for a solution or just inherited from an incumbent approach perhaps becoming obsolete in meantime? To address these questions requirements must be documented in a structured and disciplined way. They must be expressed allowing both technical as well as business judgment.

Before the move to product lines requirements often had an almost technical character. For instance, timer durations or database entries were specified, where the solution had only required finding appropriate solutions for proper interworking. Alignment was impossible due to unsynchronized cycles and unclear separation between needs and implementation.

Today any incoming requirement is reviewed with the product catalogue and global product evolution in mind to also evaluate marginal value versus marginal costs.

Specific costs together with the investment for the generic evolution for developing an application product must generate at the bottom line a return on domain assets. We have the classic case of R&D investment that would pay back - if well invested - down the road in the individual market products. If the percentage is insufficient the concept will fail sooner or later. If relationships between features are not obvious before the configuration, additional costs during application releases reduce the returns dramatically. The ROA value is a good business indicator for a product line concept as it shows which program to further merge or even cancel as a product.

3.3 Reinforce a reliable release roadmap

A successful product line is driven on a reliable release roadmap. Reliable means stable release timing. A baseline, on which a multitude of application projects depend, must not be late or miss key functionality. This translates into the following steps.

- Identify commonalties and dependencies between the different market-specific solutions.
- Evaluate existing functionality according to value, complexity, extendibility, and cost.
- Determine a roadmap that gradually and with defined steps brings together related functionality.

- Decide which functionality or variants would not be preserved and agree migration strategy towards standard functionality.
- Define within the functional specification determined areas for change and evolution, and agree with marketing and sales.
- Provide a functional (content) roadmap for both the product family, and the markets.
- Model the system in front of this baseline of common functionality and determined evolution.
- Reengineer the development process towards time boxing with reliable results in terms of cost and quality. This means to reduce the degree of freedom to functional content alone.
- Restructure the system (i.e. generic product) to reduce complexity (e.g. separate functional layers in different components, move specific functionality on separate servers).
- Strictly split at the beginning of each new product life cycle between what will be handled by domain engineering and what will be handled by application engineering.

During introduction of the product line generic release we focused on a few subsystems, which created most overhead while implementing specific changes. The total amount of changed source statements for the first iteration of the global product was in the range of twice what we typically did for a major release in one market. Effort however accumulated afterwards with integration and regression testing in the different markets. We did that change in iterations to better manage the risk of not passing major regression needs. Over a period of three years we had two major upgrades. Introducing the product line concept to a legacy environment thus often will not save any cost in the first one to two iterations.

3.4 Reuse contents across markets

Many product line concepts start from reusing artifacts [3]. Reusing contents makes the difference. Properly expressed requirements form a high-level abstraction of the functional and nonfunctional behavior of the product. Formalizing such a description helps in identifying reusable aspects of systems at a level independent of any particular solution or component structure. This high level is of limited value in practice.

Requirements must be explicit per release and still linked with each other across the entire family of domain and application projects. This also is the biggest preparation effort to decide on the viability of the entire concept. Instead of capturing design artifacts and cluster them to features, one aspect that needs to be redone from scratch when introducing a product line concept is structuring and organizing requirements.

A requirements database helps with this effort. Contents include requirements, implementation status of each requirement, priorities, estimated cost, value assessment, mapping to releases – especially future releases to communicate the roadmap –, relationships between requirements, and links to related implementation and test details.

Variants and versions typically differ between 5..20% of their content. To provide access to what solutions already exist for a given need, it's mandatory to keep all requirements and their variants in one database. For managing requirements, features and portfolio, we use interacting tools. A tailored commercial tool is used for the feature catalogue, traceability and release mapping. Portfolio is managed in a dedicated roadmap database. Requirements change management is embedded within the global change management, which also provides defect management.

For an existing system with existing markets and products, each product would initially be dumped into this database, and then – manually – similarities are clustered with respect to underlying design decisions.

3.5 Introduce prioritization and link with planning

Product lines are only successful if the underlying domain releases arrive in due time with necessary quality level and the major functional contents. From a software engineering perspective this is an obvious contradiction. Impacts cannot be fully assessed and micro-managed in advance, neither can risks or people skills. Thus a buffer has to be foreseen to achieve results in due time. Buffers are typically implemented by anticipating flexible content that is achieved by priority setting and incremental builds [1,8]. This might work in independent products but for a domain release unknown content is a major flaw. What would marketing and sales build if contents were only clear after two thirds of cycle time?

Prioritization as well as related planning concepts must be adjusted for the domain engineering to make product families successful. For simplicity, we distinguish just two priorities and link them directly to customer and market needs. There was not much experimentation, rather the need to get some rules introduced as easy as possible. Two priorities have the advantage to always consider a simple "Occam razor" or portfolio box of perceived marginal value for our customers: high versus low.

We try to split functionality changes into steps to avoid too many major features that would heavily impact planning. For the domain release we need some lower priority features that are not a mandatory functionality of a major application release. An additional instrument is to leave some lead-time buffer between generic release and application releases.

3.6 Foster incremental development

Successful introduction of a product line concept is highly impacted by work organization and effective work split. For global product lines, we strongly suggest building coherent and co-located teams of fully committed engineers. Coherence means that the work is split during development according to feature content, which allows assembling a team that can implement a set of related functionality. Collocation means that engineers working on such a set of coherent functionality should sit in the same building, perhaps the same room. Full allocation finally implies that engineers working on a project should be available from the start and should not be distracted by different tasks in other projects.

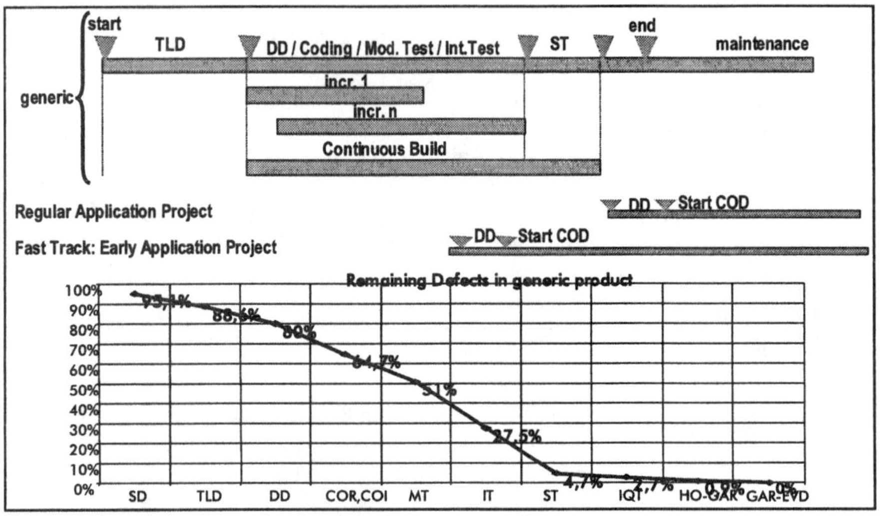

Fig. 3: Defect detection ratio after introducing the product line concept. Top shows the phases of the generic product, bottom shows defect percentage (of total).

The changes we introduced towards achieving real incremental development within the product line development can be summarized as follows:

- Analyze requirements from the beginning in the view of how they could be clustered to related functionality, which later could be delivered as an increment.
- Analyze requirements before project start with multi-functional expert teams. Analyzing by different functions that later implement, test, or market the product, ensures that assumptions and decisions are shared.
- Analyze context (data structures that are common for all subsystems) impacts of all increments upfront before start of development.
- Provide a project plan that is based on these sets of clustered customer requirements and allocates development teams to each set.
- Review the project plan with the portfolio and resource planning to ensure availability of skills from the pool of engineers.
- Ensure that each increment is developed within one dedicated team, although a team might be assigned to several increments in a row.
- Base the progress tracking of development and test on the integration and testing of a single customer's requirements.
- Increments are extensively feature tested by an independent test line.

3.7 Stimulate rigorous configuration management

Rigorous configuration management is mandatory to achieve consistency in a product line. This includes processes and underlying tools support for configuration control, change management, and requirements management. We very much aligned the guiding business processes for change management (including service request management), the specific R&D processes (including need for a globally effective build control board), and the underlying tools to implement these processes. Configuration management systems are today the same, including implemented processes and roles.

Corrections cannot easily be copied from one code branch to the other due to their impacts on ongoing development, such as new functionality with different local flavors that had been already added. Effective synchronization of the individual corrections involves thus global visibility of all defects, impacts of defects, correction availability, and evaluation of impacts of the corrections. Nobody is forced to use corrections. A trade-off between stability and reliability is made before implementing a single change.

Clearly the achieved quality level determines release cycles and overall periodicity of the product line and its customization releases. Fig. 3 indicates with concrete figures this relationship. The various lifecycle phases are abbreviated as follows: SD: system design, TLD: top level design, DD: detailed design, COR/COI code reading and code inspection, MT: module test, IT: integration test, ST: system test, IQT: internal qualification test, HO: handover, GAR: general availability release, EVD: end of volume deployment. If coding of the first application project starts with the generic product in ST, less than 5% of defects remain for potential cross-impacts on the derived product. We also anticipate a fast track for exceptional cases where a key functionality in the generic release must go into a market without delays.

4. Results

The success of introducing product lines in existing products depends on several factors, which we call the tricks of successful introduction of product lines:

- Strongly coordinate marketing and engineering
- Document requirements clearly and with business focus

- Reinforce a reliable release roadmap
- Reuse contents across markets
- Introduce prioritization and link with planning
- Foster incremental development
- Stimulate rigorous configuration management.

There are however also the traps.

- It's not obvious from a business perspective that in all legacy environments the change would be feasible. Architecture constraints can be a major hurdle.
- If a product has reached maturity and is close to its phase-out, the needs are small to make all described changes, while it could still be valuable to have for the phase-out and next product introduction an aligned content and behavior.
- If organizational patterns don't distinguish between the domain development and the variety of customizations or applications, it will always be a mixture and not a product line.
- If not appropriately marketed, product lines will fail, especially in investment products, where customers are used to dedicated solutions.
- Insufficient project and program or portfolio management make the product lines invalid. Milestones must be committed and held to. Trust between engineering and sales or product management is absolutely crucial.
- Adherence to agreed content evolution on the other hand is mandatory for sales and product managers.

Still, the bottom-line is positive if the tricks are used, while the traps are avoided:

- Shorter cycle-time for products from inception to release. Fig.4 summarizes the cycle time for releases according to size and change volume. The 4 curves from top to bottom indicate 4 different standard sizes of products in our portfolio. The top is the biggest and has over 100 KLOC changed code. The lowest is for small changes. All categories show a drastically reduced cycle time that came with the introduction of more focused product line management.
- Faster introduction of completely new functionality into all markets. With aligned baselines a major change – though still costly in its development and integration – can be easily deployed in other variants. Instead of a long sequence of release cycles, the change will be effective with next major domain release.
- Less cost for introducing major changes, as they are built in upfront and shared across markets. Small changes for a specific market could still be cumbersome, however it's known upfront, and marketing can steer via prizing mechanisms.
- Availability of a trusted and liable baseline roadmap with well specified feature content across markets. This certainly is of big help to ensure that product and program management are aligned with each other and especially with engineering.
- Full visibility of existing feature content and traceability to design work products and test cases. Having this visibility and traceability allows for fast development or adjustments for small changes. The previous overhead for stabilizing and qualification has been reduced.

Introducing a product line concept in an existing set of related products in many cases can prove the underlying business case, but it needs careful planning, evaluation, and execution. If side effects stemming from legacy environment, culture, organization and sales and engineering processes are not tackled simultaneously, the product line concept will remain a phrase without business value.

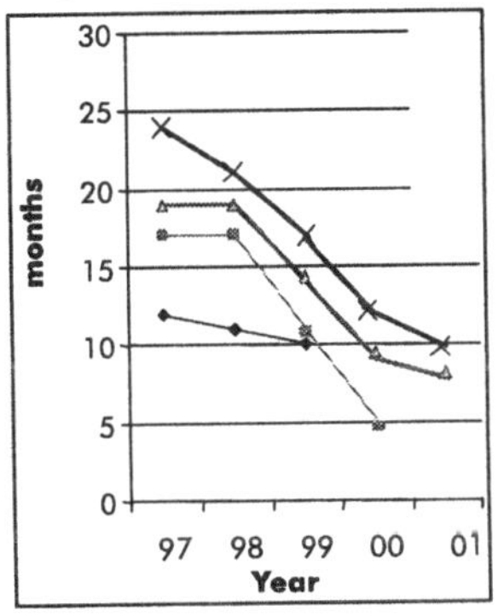

Fig. 4: Focus on product lines helped to substantially reduce cycle time.

References

[1] Karlsson, E.A. et al: Daily Build and Feature Development in Large Distributed Projects. Proc. Int. Conf. on Software Engineering 2000, pp. 649-658. IEEE Comp. Soc. Press. Los Alamitos, USA, 2000.

[2] Ebert, C.: Improving Validation Activities in a Global Software Development. Proc. Int. Conf. on Software Engineering 2001. IEEE Comp. Soc. Press, Los Alamitos, USA, 2001.

[3] Weiss, D.M. and C.T.R.Lai: Software Product line Engineering. Addison Wesley. Reading, USA, 1999.

[4] Bunnell, D.: Making the Cisco Connection. John Wiley, New York, 2000.

[5] Perry, D.E., H.P.Siy and L.G.Votta: Parallel Changes in Large Scale Software Development: An Observational Case Study. Proc. Int. Conf. on Software Engineering, IEEE Comp. Soc. Press, pp. 251-260, 1998.

[6] Kuusela, J. and J.Savolainen: Requirements Engineering for Product Families. Proc. Int. Conf. On Software Engineering 2000. IEEE Comp. Soc. Press, Los Alamitos, USA, pp. 61-69, 2000.

[7] Knauber, P. et al: Applying Product Line Concepts in Small and Medium-Sized Companies. IEEE Software. Vol. 17, No. 4, pp. 88-95, 2000.

[8] McConnell, S.: Software Project Survival Guide. Microsoft Press. Redmond, USA, 1998.

[9] Bosch, J.: Software Product Lines: Organizational Alternatives. Proc. Int. Conf. On Software Engineering 2001. IEEE Comp. Soc. Press, Los Alamitos, USA, pp. 91-100, 2001.

Experience Reports

Process and Tools

About the Development of a Point of Sale System: an Experience Report

Stefan Berner
IBM Switzerland
stefan.berner@ch.ibm.com

Abstract

This report comprises some experiences, which were made during the development of a point of sale (POS) system. Specific about the project is the fact that it started as an attempt to develop customizable standard software, and then was restructured to deliver a unique project solution. This report details the situation before and after the restructuring, and discusses the experiences made through the ongoing development. These experiences relate mostly to three areas, which are: software project management, prototyping, and testing.

Introduction

This report comprises some experiences made during the development of a distributed point of sale (POS) system. There are a couple of technical experiences, but most experiences presented here are non-technical by nature and related to people and processes. It must be noted that the project this report relates to, was not an IBM project. Nevertheless, the analysis and compilation has been done within the IBM IT Consulting & Testing Group at IBM Switzerland.

As mentioned in the abstract, this report is about a project that has been reorganized; the report does not focus on the reorganization itself, but on the way, it was managed afterwards. In order to better present the experiences they have been grouped into three groups.

- First, the experiences with the development process (after the restructuring of the project), estimations and productivity.
- Second, the experiences with the requirements analysis through explorative prototyping.
- Third, experiences related to system testing, the deployment of the system, and some pre-production related activities.

Beforehand and to facilitate the understanding, a brief description of the POS system and its embedding will be given, followed by a comprehensive outline of the different project situations and phases.

System Overview

As mentioned, the system to be developed was a point of sale system. Its intended use was to assist the sales process of life insurances. The system was developed for the life insurances division of a large bank. This bank intended to enter the life insurance market with a complete portfolio of products. Instead of building a new sales organization, the existing infrastructure (branch offices) should be used. Therefore, the POS system should enable finance people and bank clerks to offer and sell life insurances to bank customers.

The POS system was realized in common multi-tier architecture with a relational database in the background, CORBA as middleware, and Java as the main language to realize both, the business components on the middleware, and the client components in form of a thin client. Front end was an applet running in a web browser. (see Fig. 1)

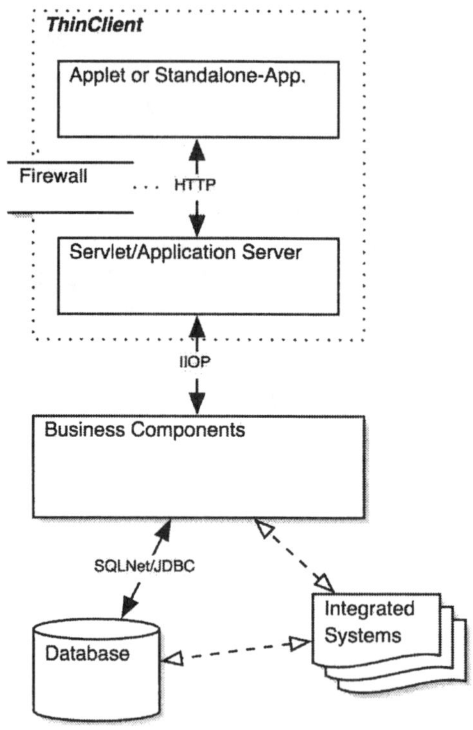

Fig. 1: Hi-level architecture of the system

0-7695-1877-X/03 $17.00 © 2003 IEEE

Project Situation

The company, which realized the POS system, had a reasonable amount of experience with management systems for life insurances and also with POS systems, for insurance brokers. Yet, a POS system for non-insurance-brokers (bank clerks) and in this technology (multi-tier, CORBA, Java, etc.) had only been realized before on a very small scale and not for a complete product portfolio.

Involved in the project were four parties: (1) the client company (a bank), (2) the company to operate the system (an IT service provider), (3) the company which should develop the insurance products (a financial services consulting company), and (4) finally the company which should provide the management system and develop the POS (a software firm for the insurance sector).

The Project before the Reorganization

The company (4) had another customer – an insurance company (ic) – who ordered a similar system, and two additional customers, who were potentially interested in a system like this. So, the idea was to develop a customizable POS system once, and adapt this system to each customers needs. Before the project started some basic decisions were made about the overall technical architecture. These decisions turned out to be robust and scalable. However, the requirements of each individual system and more important the potential differences between those systems were not completely understood.

It was clearly recognized that the development of a customizable system would take more effort than the development of a single project solution. Surprisingly, the time frame for the development was not adapted. This meant de facto that it was planned to develop/produce a completely new standard software and customize it for at least two clients in the same time frame the development of a single system would have taken. To cope with this problem the development team was enlarged to an overall size of 35 people distributed on two locations.

The attempt to develop the customizable POS standard software was more difficult than expected. There were a couple of technical problems as a direct result of weak early phases, some communication problems due to the distributed development. However, the most severe problems were related to an unworkable plan based on a timeframe and goals, which were too ambiguous and led to a 'we don't have the time to be efficient' situation. The development became increasingly difficult and progress stayed far beyond expectations. The development was stopped after 9 months, right at the time the first customer (1) – the bank mentioned at the beginning of the paper – wanted to enter the pre-production phase. At this time, an initial version of the system should have been developed and customized to the needs of the first customer in order to allow for first comprehensive tests. In reality only parts of the system had been developed. The system or better the parts of it that were ready had three major problems:

- P-1 *What had been developed was for two reasons not what the customer wanted.* (a) The system did not really fit to the sales processes of the customer and (b) it was too complicated to be usable by non-insurance people. Yet, the customer's wants and needs were not entirely clear, but it was sure that the actual system would not fit. The system was close to what the other customer – the insurance company (ic) – wanted. The system at this point was more similar to an insurance management system than to a POS system. In retrospection, this is not too surprising because: (I) there was no real requirements analysis, and (II) the customer 'insurance company (ic)' was located nearer to the developers, and (III) insurance management systems are the systems the developing company (4) has a lot of experience with.
- P-2 *The actual architecture was problematic and not really compliant with the original idea.* Due to time constraints the design phase was considerably shortened, and so it was not clear to all the developers where or on which tier to put which functionality. Hence, too much business logic was coded into the presentation and user interface layer. The middleware was used more like a connector to the database. This led to massive integration problems – especially with external sub systems – and explains at least partially why the development became increasingly difficult.
- P-3 *The overall quality of the system was unsatisfactory.* For example: the system was difficult to install, its behavior and look and feel was inconsistent between different subsystems, connections to other systems terminated unexpectedly, etc. Mainly this was because there were no explicit activities towards system integration and no dedicated and controlled environment where an integration could be placed and tested.

Despite the delay, both customers (1) and (ic) still wanted their system. In this situation it was decided to suspend the plans to develop a customizable POS standard software and split the project into (two) independent projects and independent development teams. Each project should deliver an individual project solution to its customer. It was up to each project to decide, which parts of the system developed so far could or should be reused.

In this report, we will now focus solely on the development of the system for the customer (1) – the bank.

The Project after the Reorganization

After the reorganization the team, which was assigned to develop the POS system for the bank was sized to eight people. This team started in a situation where it not only had to cope with the three major problems mentioned before (wrong system, problematic architecture, low quality) but also with three additional problems:

P-4 The team had considerable experience with the technology used, but nobody in the team had built such a system before.

P-5 The customer committed to the development, but it was not clear how long the patience of the customer would last.

P-6 No documentation existed (de facto) about the parts of the system that had been developed so far. The initial developers were (de facto) not available, because they were busy and located at another site.

The Steps after the Reorganization

In this situation but mostly because of the problems P-1 and P-5 it was decided and agreed to a development process based on explorative prototyping [4]. This approach should ensure to get the system right on the second time and to be able to present something to the customer as soon a possible. It was further agreed to involve the customer as close as possible in order to validate results continuously and make the progress transparent. In detail, the following activities were identified in order to 'survive' the situation and get the development done:

A-1 Regarding architecture and code quality, decide which parts of the existing (ill-fated) system can be reused and which parts have to be redeveloped.

Out of six components[1] two were reused (5,6), two were reused but completely reengineered (2,4) and the other two (1,3) – including the most important one – were redeveloped. Where wrong components had been built, it was necessary to redevelop them. Where the component had been built wrong, the component was reengineered.

A-2 Establish an integration, test and release environment, which is essentially similar to the productive environment and allows for continuous integration during development.

Two people (to an equivalent of 1.5 full time employees) out of a team of eight were dedicated to integration and integration test (later on also to packaging, delivery, and installation support).

[1] The six components were responsible for: (1) insurance sales (policies and calculations), (2) customer management (integrated), (3) capital market data, (4) printing (web-based), (5) access control/security, and (6) a thin client framework.

A-3 Decide if and where an incremental development of the system is possible. Start or resume the development of the components, which are not subject to incremental development.

Only one component – insurance sales – was identified to be developed in increments. Nevertheless, this was the largest and most important one. It was responsible for the control of the sales process for all insurance products. The other components were developed conventionally.

A-4 Do some research to find out the increments in which the system can be developed. Determine the vertical cuts and number of increments. Besides, prepare the framework to allow for incremental development.

Overall, there were four increments identified until completion. The increments, in which the system was developed, were the categories of the insurance products. In order to develop the increments in a structured way, the framework was extended to allow for (i) a controlled inclusion of newly developed product-plug-ins and (ii) a coexistence of prototypical parts and real parts.

A-5 Select the first increment, build an explorative prototype of the user interface, and ensure feasibility of the supporting business components.

Prototyping started with the most difficult product. The complete user interface was built using a GUI builder. The result of the prototyping was a plug-in of the increments user interface. It could be plugged in into what would be the system once for validation purposes. The prototype had a little control logic but no business logic.

A-6 Review the prototype together with the customer to get the requirements clear. Also, present the current state of the development. Get commitment from the customer to proceed this way.

Here workshops were organized every 4 weeks to validate the prototype together with the cus-

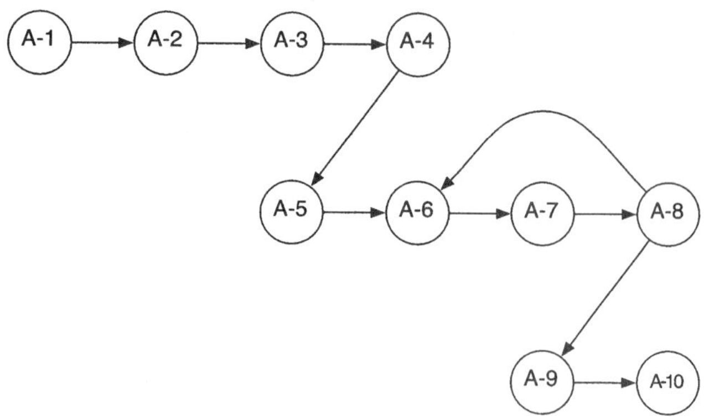

Fig. 2: Succession of activities

tomer. Demonstrated was also the progress of the development. At the end of a workshop the current state and the planned state of system for the next workshop was clearly communicated. The final requirements were documented and the customer was expected to explicitly commit to these requirements. Thereafter, the realization of the validated part was launched (or at least scheduled).

A-7 Get the system complete on all layers/tiers for the selected/next increment. This meant, design and develop the business components, integrate them with other systems, and finally, put all together with the client components and user interface.

As a prototype was built using a GUI builder the code for the prototype was generated and not thrown away. Even at the point an increment was horizontally complete, it was still possible to modify the user interface using the GUI builder.

A-8 Until vertically complete: Meanwhile prototype the user interface for the next increment. Establish a baseline of the system consisting of prototypical and real parts. Then proceed with activity A-6 for this cycle/increment (see Fig. 2).

As planned it needed four increments to get the system complete for all 10 insurance products.

A-9 Deliver a test system to allow the customer to do installation -, functional -, volume - and performance tests in his environment. The test system must be at least horizontally complete for one insurance product.

Due to technical problems, the pre-production environment of the customer was not ready. Subsequently, instead of testing the system in his environment the customer used our test and release environment to test the system. This allowed for all functional, but only for limited installation -, volume -, and performance tests.

A-10 Finally, finish the development and deliver the complete POS system.

Progression after the Reorganization

Development Time. After the reorganization the overall development of the system needed 14 month. After 9 months the system was complete and testable by the customer. After 12 months the system entered the pre-production phase, and after 14 month (and two failed attempts) it finally went productive.

System Size. Developed had been around 190000 lines of Java code (counted lines not statements) or almost exactly 2000 classes (not counted were IDL definitions, Perl scripts, and SQL statements). Reused from the first development were around 400 classes.

The supporting frameworks and class libraries (thin client framework, persistence framework, JUnit, chart libraries, CORBA, JDK, etc.) contributed almost another 6000 classes. However, not all of these classes were part of the delivered system.

Experiences and Lessons Learned

In this section the experiences with this approach will be presented. Please note, these are the experiences of one project, and therefore do not need to be universally valid.

Development Process, Estimations, Productivity

- Continuous integration was essential to ensure a consistent system over all phases. Integration had been one of the more serious problems (P-3) before. Consequently, the process after the reorganization emphasized on continuous integration and validation. We integrated frequently but in contrast to XP-like techniques [1] we did coordinate the integration process.
- Continuous integration helped also to get the development to speed. Everybody (especially the developers) could see the progress in the development of the system as a whole and their part in it. That seemed to motivate people a lot.
- Integrators have to be very communicative. By pure chance this was the case here, but in retrospection it was crucial. For example, the team committed to some necessities before a piece of software would be eligible for check-in and integration (no compiler errors, unit-tested, versioned, etc.). The integrators consequently enforced these rules. They needed – and had – the capability to reject a component without worrying the developer.
- Two persons (1.5 full time employees) out of a team of eight on integration, integration test, etc. was a good size and surely not too much. Consistent integration does not happen by chance but pays out a lot on the long run. Especially when there is a considerable amount of (changing) interfaces to other systems.
- Integrational activities are difficult to justify, because they tend to appear unproductive – at least from a certain point of view. It needs a high degree of perseverance to steadily justify the assignment of almost two developers 'just for such unproductive' things like integration, integration test, etc.
- Clear assignment of developers to parts or components of the system helped to ensure quality (this one is a classic [3] but too often ignored). Every-

body in the team knew insufficient quality would bounce back. I am not sure to which degree this would be the case with collective code ownership or comparable approaches.

- The absence of hectic activities in combination with a high productivity and delivery on time can create the impression that there are to many people in the team. It is nothing new that structured approaches tend to balance workload and avoid peaks. But exactly this can become a problem in a culture were hectic pre-deadline activities are normal and expected. Instead of looking closely at the development process or some numbers the reasoning often goes like this: "There are no hectic activities before a workshop, not even before a delivery. Hence, there must be too many people on the team. So the team size can be reduced without any further effect." These (fatal) conclusions have a lot to do with the ability of the management to see when a development is running fine and when not (see also next point).
- (Except for team internal use) It is a waste of time to communicate measurements/numbers about system size or productivity – e.g. LoC per Developer and Month – if nobody else does it in the company. Because they could not be seen in direct comparison to other projects, statements like "2000/LoC per month and developer" were often simply not understood. Does this number mean a high or low productivity?

Requirements Analysis and Explorative Prototyping

- Prototyping helps to get the requirements quickly. Especially in a situation where the customer's wants and needs are not entirely clear – or at least not clearly documented.
- Use explorative prototyping to get the most important requirements clear but do not 'over-prototype' a system. Typically, we used prototyping to ensure that the POS system supports the processes in the approved manner and the individual screens contain the right information.
- Micro-changes in the user interface – even in the late phases – can comfortably be handled using to GUI builder tools. As the user interface was almost completely built with a GUI builder and we were capable to rearrange it at any time, we did use prototyping only sparsely to decide where to put a field on a screen.
- Presenting a prototype after a short time of development restores (a lot of) trust for both customer and developers. The climate in the project changed from tensed to relaxed, and after the third workshop, the climate was very optimistic (which can be dangerous too).
- Do not expect the customer to explore the prototype on his own. This has do be done in a planned and moderated workshop. In addition to the workshops we made some attempts to get further feedback, e.g. by providing stand-alone versions of the prototype. The feedback here was very meager and you can control neither the distribution of the prototype nor the way of its presentation.
- If you make clear what (part of the system) you are presenting and what the actual state of the development is no false expectations will come up. We had no 'why isn't the system ready' effect due to our prototyping approach.
- It is a waste of time to build the screens of a GUI by hand – at least the standard ones. The tools e.g. [5] – are quite ripe here and allow for roundtrips and a modification of the layout at any time. Even if the system is near completion. We did not need to touch the generated code at any time.
- Building a prototype is no replacement for a written specification, but it eases the creation of a specification significantly. It eased the making of a specification because to a reasonable amount the specification consisted of annotated screen shots taken from the prototype. Btw, this document became important when it came to late changes. At this time, nobody was interested in the prototype anymore.
- Prototyping does not prevent from late changes, but it minimizes the risk for major errors. There were a couple of minor issues where the system had to be changed due to wrong, changed or new requirements, but the major ones were found during the workshops.

System Testing, Deployment, Pre-Production

- JUnit tests [2] helped a lot but with a large number of them, they tend to become very complex. Organizing them along a test scenarios and referencing this scenario in the header of the JUnit-test-case helped to keep them concise.
- Without proper load and performance testing it remains unknown for which quantity structure the developed system performs comfortable. Often the system performs comfortable for a quantity structure, which corresponds somehow to the size of the development team. A team of eight persons often produces a system, which performs comfortable for eight simultaneous users (but no more).

- Load and performance testing is simply not effective without tool support. At least for a quantity structure that exceeds the capabilities of the development team to manually generate user load.
- Do not allow the system to go directly into production without a complete test cycle at the pre-production stage (system and systems integration test). As already mentioned, the customer had some technical problems with its pre-production environment right at the time the test system was about to be delivered. To avoid further delay, the tests were done in the environment of the developing company (4). This was sufficient for the functional tests but clearly not sufficient for all kinds of load and performance tests.
- The absence of a usable pre-production environment at the customer site is more than a major inconvenience. Not only that the absence prevents from proper load and performance testing, it also makes it really difficult and time consuming to track down even the simplest things. A productive system without a pre-production environment is virtually a nightmare.
- Be very cautious to give your customer access to your test and change management tools – in fact do not do it. The idea behind seems attractive – to share the same tool environment in order to allow for a quick communication between customer test team and development. But, usually the customer – of course – has other requirements than the development team. Until these tools allow for such simple things like a customer side priorisation of changes and a developer side priorisation of the same changes they simply lead to many discussions when used collaboratively.
- The deployment of the system must not be underestimated. Installation and operation support is necessary and must be provided by the development team if the system is supposed to go productive without further delay – even if it is explicitly not the responsibility of the development team to provide this kind of support. It is not sufficient to provide only the software (including comprehensive documentation) and first time help. There was also avoidable trouble and delay due to unclear responsibilities on the customer and hosting side.

Summary

Concluding and given the same situation, explorative prototyping would be a thing to be done again and the same way it has been done. The same is valid for the emphasis on a steady integration and an explicit allocation of resources to this task. Problem areas were testing in the later phases of the project. Testing problems arouse during or with the early tests by the customer. Some of these problems were technical problems (pre-production system not ready), some process related (change management was established to late), and some due to missing skills (customer does not now how and what to test). This things need to be trained (and more thoroughly planned).

One of the most interesting things – at least for the author – is still what happens when the culture of the development team (mostly structured approach, absence of hectic activities, etc.) is different from the development culture of the company and how the development is then seen from the outside. In retrospection, some kind of mimicry like 'make the team to appear stressed before a release' seems to be a more successful approach than the attempt to convince certain people that certain activities are mostly counterproductive and mere a symptom of poor planning.

Many of the experiences reported here are not new, but a confirmation of the classic messages – including the fact that the classic messages are often unknown or ignored. So, I would assume that most of the experiences made here are not specific to the development of a distributed point of sale system. A qualitative comparison and evaluation with projects, which are similar in terms of size, effort and duration would be quite interesting.

References

[1] K. Beck, Extreme Programming Explained: Embrace Change, Addison-Wesley, 1999.

[2] K. Beck, Gamma, E., JUnit Test Infected: Programmers Love Writing Tests, Java Report, vol. 3, nr. 7, July 1998.

[3] B.W. Boehm, Seven Basic Principles of Software Engineering, Journal of Systems and Software 3 (1983), pp. 3-24.

[4] C. Floyd, A Systematic Look at Prototyping. In: Budde, R., et al. (eds): Approaches to Prototyping. Springer, Berlin, 1984, pp. 1-18.

[5] IBM, Visual Age for Java, Version 3, http://www3.ibm.com/software/ad/vajava/

Effective Experience Repositories for Software Engineering

Kurt Schneider *and* Jan-Peter von Hunnius
DaimlerChrysler Research Center, Ulm, Germany
{Kurt.Schneider, Jan.Hunnius}@DaimlerChrysler.com

Abstract

Software development and acquisition require knowledge and experience in many areas of software engineering. Experience helps people to make decisions under uncertainty, and to find better compromises. Experience-based process improvement considers experience as a prerequisite for competent behavior in software development. There is usually a repository to store experiences and to make it available for reuse. At DaimlerChrysler, we have been building those repositories for more than five years. We learned to concentrate on certain properties that seem to be key success factors for experience repositories. During our experience-based work in business units, five key quality aspects have been identified that determine the chances for success of an experience repository. The quality criteria can be used to analyze a given repository; or they can be applied to guide the construction of more effective experience repositories.

1. Introduction: Experience Repositories

Software process improvement often follows the CMM for software or a similar maturity approach (e.g. SPICE/ISO 15 504). During the improvement activities, experiences play an important role:

- They may determine which improvement step should be carried out first.
- Experienced people can anticipate the acceptance and impact of an improvement activity.
- Fine-grained experience with a certain process step may help to fine-tune processes, thus optimizing their efficiency.
- Experience helps to anticipate how constraints and organizational structures will react to change that comes with improvement activities.

Basili has promoted experience-based improvement for a long time. His concept of an "Experience Factory" [1] describes a learning software organization built around a so-called "Experience Base". At DaimlerChrysler, we were inspired by the Experience Factory concept. We adapted the concept and implemented a similar learning software organization [2].

Repositories for experiences play a crucial role in all variants of experience-based process improvement no matter how authors call them [3-5]. While the importance of a repository is often acknowledged, the difficulty of producing an *effective* tool is often underestimated. An experience repository is a persistent storage device for experiences. They are often called (or mistaken as) "experience databases". However, deep software engineering knowledge and experience can benefit from being structured in a very different way than a database. In this paper, we present five quality aspects for experience repositories. We used them for a fast assessment of a repository's profile. They can also guide an effort to develop an effective repository.

In section 2, experience-based process improvement is sketched. Experience repositories are often built or purchased for such a situation. Our SEC project advocated experience exploitation in our business units. We present and discuss our five key quality attributes for effective software engineering experience repositories (section 3). Section 4 provides some of our lessons learned in practice that led us to select the above set of key qualities. In section 5, we discuss how the key qualities can be used in analytical and in constructive ways. We conclude the paper by pointing out that the repository is a necessary, but not a sufficient prerequisite for an effective learning organization.

2. Experience-based process improvement

Several DaimlerChrysler business units have participated in an initiative to benefit from experiences in software engineering. Among them is a large IT department that is responsible for developing and acquiring software for administrative business processes. Our research project SEC (Software Experience Center [2]) coordinated and supported all activities. We supported experience identification and elicitation; experience engineering and experience reuse. In particular, we constructed several versions of experience repositories [6].

0-7695-1877-X/03 $17.00 © 2003 IEEE

Software process improvement usually focuses on a certain aspect of a software process, or on a specific support process, such as software risk management. In the example of risk management (and in several others alike) we started with a textbook process and continued adapting and improving it [7]. Finally, a simple but highly optimized risk management process was defined and disseminated that suits the needs of the respective business unit. Many experience-based improvement steps are subtle and their importance is not obvious to outsiders [8]. For example, it turned out to be crucial to develop our own potential risk-checklist rather than using a (more comprehensive) generic list provided by an external consultant. Many of those issues were identified during feedback or experience elicitation workshops [9]. It is not easy to elicit valuable experiences, since they are often implicit or tacit. This is a commonly held insight. However, spreading experiences in an effective way is not much easier: For example, it is not sufficient to "make experiences available on the Intranet". During our several attempts to establish experience repositories, we gained a number of insights in frequent traps or common misunderstandings that surround experience reuse [10]. This insight helped us to build more effective experience repositories.

3. Key success factors for experience repositories

3.1. Purpose of quality attributes

Experience repositories are software systems, too. Therefore, a general set of quality attributes could be applied to rate repository quality [11]. However, we needed a more efficient approach: By highlighting only a few selected aspects, we wanted to *focus* and speed up a repository evaluation. While it may be desirable for an experience repository to run fast (generic quality aspect: *speed*), other aspects are much more important – and much more specific for experience handling (e.g. *maintainability* as described below). We tried to provide a small, distinctive list of aspects that allows to diagnose and to guide therapy of experience repositories – and to do it *fast*.

There are different kinds of experience: In the area of service and maintenance support, fine-grained experience is common. Case-based reasoning approaches [12] or expert systems have proven useful to handle those. We are instead dealing with experience on sophisticated software engineering processes such as code inspections, risk management, or quality gates. In this area, we often face a smaller number of bigger junks of experience. Some of those lessons learned are subtle and some are rather drastic, as our risk management example shows [8].

3.2. Overview of important quality aspects

A repository is supposed to hold experiences in a format that facilitates their reuse by many people. Before going into any technical detail, we present the five challenges that will often limit the benefit of such a repository. A user will face the qualities in the following order:

User guidance. Most users have to do a job and are very busy. They expect a system to provide direct support in their respective work or task; many users want to be guided. They want to immediately start reusing, not analyzing experiences.

Usability. When a user has been granted access to the repository, and maybe received some instructions on its use, he or she should be able to use the system as it is intended – and to benefit. As with many software systems, poor usability can scare a user away. Experience-related systems suffer from a number of misconceptions about how they will be used [10].

Process conformance. Systems that are highly usable conform to the tasks they are supposed to support. For example, hints and experiences about risk management can be organized according to the risk management process steps. By making an improved process the center piece and backbone of an experience repository, navigation, orientation and search are highly improved. Much of the structure comes for free: it is the structure of the underlying software process.

Feedback mechanism. This is a highly specific quality aspect. Experience is a material that calls for continuous update and rework. Therefore, the repository should not only allow, but encourage feedback through several channels. Email, electronic black boards, FAQs, phone and personal contacts should be encouraged, and specific variants of those channels should be developed (e.g. risk analysis chat [13]). Any threshold for giving feedback needs to be lowered.

Maintainability. Once new input or feedback arrives, it must be analyzed and integrated into preexisting contents. There can be technical and organizational support to facilitate this operation. Polishing or gold-plating should be avoided because they only delays updates and maintenance. Frequently occurring restructuring should be made particularly easy for the same reason. For example, a simple change in the backbone process should not cause extensive manual rework of more than one file.

4. Lessons learned that support key qualities

In [6], the whole story of our attempts to develop efficient experience repositories has been told in chronological order. Below, we take a different approach: we organize selected lessons learned around the five above-mentioned quality attributes, and provide observations to substantiate why we consider those quality attributes key success factors.

All cases reported below have two sides: We learned how to improve an aspect and why to consider it a key aspect only after we had violated it and produced a less satisfactory solution. For all reported cases, we learned and improved to reach a solution that has worked better in practice. Based on this fact we claim: The success of a repository depends more on our key success factors than on other quality attributes – although the latter may also be somewhat important (e.g., speed, portability, interoperability etc.). Most cases taught us more than one lesson.

Be specific. In our earlier attempts, we provided containers for software engineers to put their experiences in. We provided sophisticated forms to enter experiences [6]. Collected information was entered into a web-based tool that resided on top of a database. Searching facilities were optimized. *Lessons learned:* The contents of the database were unordered and provided no guidance to a user. Many comments referred to (different) processes, but none of them could be used as backbone. The tool was fairly usable, and maintainability in terms of entering, deleting or modifying experience packages was good. However, the initial emptiness combined with poor structuring (no process orientation, no feedback options) drastically limited the benefit of this repository.

One process at a time. Most repositories we have seen in other companies collect all kinds of experiences in one place. *Lessons learned:* For us, it was a breakthrough to concentrate on one process at a time. For example, reviews and inspections, with all preparation, session, and rework included, make a process of appropriate size. Risk management was another successful example. The effect was that only those people used the repository who were interested in the respective process. Others did not even have to search in vain. Those who entered the repository had a much easier time navigating through less material, all of which was more or less relevant to their task (i.e.: process) at hand. We found it not too difficult to engineer several experiences about the same task into a (best) practice description around a simple process description.

Usability counts. We had a usability expert evaluate one of our repositories. After this, we simplified the structure and page layouts. *Lessons learned*: Before, novices had a hard time getting to the point where they could start working. They left the repository and never returned. In this situation, even the most valuable insights would have been wasted – users never got to see them. A business unit used the revised version and encountered no severe usability problems. Their feedback referred to the contents, not the repository. We take this a positive sign that the tool did no longer get in the way of its users.

One-way communication fades away. One of our repositories had a perfect layout and structure – but it was hard coded. In a way, we had expected the inspection process to be complete and supported with so many experiences that we expected no further improvements. *Lessons learned:* Of course, there is always room for experience-based improvement. Checklists can be revised, and business unit culture may change, causing change in processes. Users were asked to write to an email address, but not in a very encouraging way. Also, reasonable feedback could not easily be incorporated in the repository since a change affected many static HTML pages. If users see no change and no reaction to their feedback, they stop visiting the repository – and will miss updates when they finally occur.

5. Exploiting key qualities

The above case stories taught us to focus on the five quality aspects as decisive properties of an effective experience repository. There are two ways to capitalize on knowing these key success factors. Both aspects are expanded and combined below:

- Analyzing existing repositories
- Guidance when constructing a new repository

5.1 Fast repository assessment and profile

When a business unit considers working with an experience repository, there are usually suggestions to use an existing product. Some groups already have their own information exchange platforms they want to consider. In such a situation, it is useful to present a short checklist of criteria that help to make a decision.

We started such a checklist about three years ago. Since then, it has guided our work, but it has also been modified and improved. However, we did not have to retract any *key* quality. We use the criteria in the form of a simple Microsoft Excel sheet. For each of the key quality criteria, a set of about 5-7 subcriteria are listed (Table1, our newest version). Again, we do not strive for completeness or full coverage, but for a fast way to determine a rough profile of a product.

A person evaluating a tool would answer each criterion or question while working with the system. The answer is coded as a number between 0 (not fulfilled) and 1 (fully achieved). Excel calculates averages and draws a profile.

We find it detrimental to use fractional numbers. Evaluators are encouraged to enter 0 or 1, and only rarely respond with a number in between. We value clear profiles over misleading precision. As a consequence, our evaluation results provide only inputs to the decision process. Evaluation results – in particular the profile, not the overall average – can support an informed decision. However, one should not rely on a three-digit evaluation number alone when it comes to selecting a product.

Table 1. Checklist of Key Quality Aspects

User Guidance	
Is a new user properly introduced into the area of interest?	
Is the process well described?	
Are commented templates available for all required documents?	
Are frequently asked questions listed, answered, and can the answers be easily found?	
Can the community of practice discuss using the repository?	
Usability	
Is everything available (e.g. tools, documents) that is needed to use the experience repository?	
Is help (e.g. hint windows, descriptions within the text, general instructions) available where needed?	
Are messages and screens easy to understand?	
Are buttons and menus where users expect them to be?	
Does the system layout conform to familiar systems (e.g. the organization's Intranet)?	
Process Conformance	
Does the process described in the experience repository conform to the process as defined by the organization?	
Does the process described in the experience repository conform to the process the employees really follow?	
In case of an update of the process definition, is the update visible in the experience repository as well as in daily work?	
Is the defined process the "Best Known Practice"?	
Does feedback have an impact on the process?	
Feedback	
Is there a chance to identify at which point within the repository a user sent a given feedback - without referring to it manually?	
Can feedback be given without such a context?	
Can feedback be made visible to all users?	
Can questions be answered so that the answer appears in the feedback part of the repository? Are questions and answers visibly related?	
Can feedback be kept private?	
Maintainability	
Is the content maintainable through the experience repository and only with the assistance of standard tools?	
Is content kept separate from layout?	
Is the information well structured and modularized?	
Does new or modified information require only few changes to existing data or simple process changes?	
Does the maintaining expert benefit from using the experience repository?	

A profile as an evaluation result tells us how close a given tool gets to the requirements for an experience repository. An ideal profile has all bars up; a low value indicates weaknesses in the respective quality aspect.

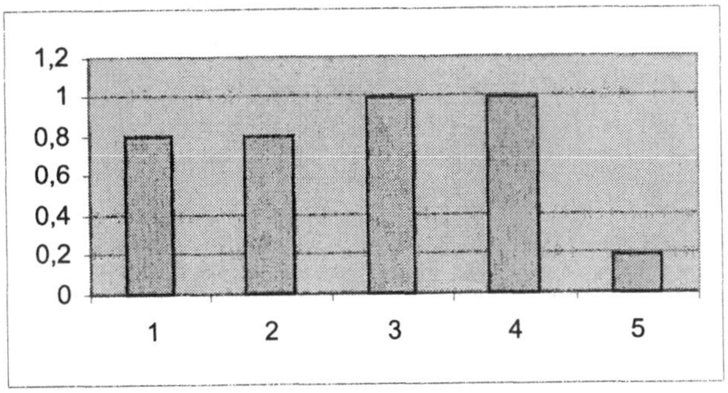

Figure 1. Example repository profile

Figure 1 shows the profile of an experience repository that has good potential. Only maintainability (5) is very low, since many frequently changing aspects are hard-coded. Of course, products or tools can be evaluated using our checklist, even if they were not intended to serve as experience repository. A generic database might score high in terms of maintainability. But it will lose points when it comes to process conformance or feedback mechanisms. Nothing general can be said about user guidance, since it is not a standard feature of a database to guide users in their daily tasks, supported by experiences. However, such guidance can be implemented on top of a database layer. We recommend to evaluate entire products, not individual layers.

5.2 Benchmarking

When we first initiated our list of criteria, we had a different application in mind: we wanted to get feedback on how well our self-constructed repository was developing. We wanted to compare our current version of the emerging experience repository both with our expectations, and with emerging repositories of others. In this scenario, an evaluation as described above allowed us to compare profiles and argue about advantages and disadvantages that surfaced in the evaluations. We evaluated different repositories, from simple newsgroups to public servers on the Internet (e.g., the family of BSCW servers that is offered by the German Fraunhofer Gesellschaft). Each family of generic tools has a typical profile. We used the analytical dimension of our key quality criteria as a tool to take a break and compare what we had achieved so far. In hindsight, we might have used the quality attributes in a more constructive way. But we first had to learn our lessons that led us to criteria below.

5.3. Developing a repository

The order of quality attributes below conforms to the order they need to be considered during development. This order differs from the one in which users encounter the quality aspects (see section 2).

User guidance. There is always a tradeoff between generality of a tool and its power to support a specific task. In order to increase user guidance, we make sure we really understand in which way users will make use of the repository. When it comes to experience reuse, those requirements are often neglected since it seems so obvious what one could do with experience. In practice, however, it makes a big difference whether people find experience reports or ready-to-use (best) practices. After our evolution of experience repositories, we assume the latter (best practices – *what to do*) guide a user better than any experience package can (*what happened before*). Best practice descriptions have very different storage and search characteristics than experience packages. This affects how the entire tool needs to be structured. More than that, it changes the "mental model" of what the repository is supposed to do for the users. Once this fundamental decision for best practice over experience packages has been made, the other questions from the list of criteria can offer more detailed advice: they tell developers what else they need to keep in mind in order to provide powerful user guidance.

Process conformance. In our experience-based process improvement work, processes have always been a core element. Those of our experience repositories were most effective that used one specific process (e.g., risk management or reviews) as backbone for contents and tool structure. In short, process seems to be a good candidate to organize a repository. Therefore, process orientation should be considered whenever a repository supports best practices. All information is attached to the respective process steps. Templates and checklists can be reached from the part of the process description in which they will be applied. A slightly hierarchical two- or three-level process facilitates searching for information and material: Browing along a graphical process sketch makes excessive search machines obsolete. Process orientation is a concrete architecture for an effective repository.

Usability. It is advisable to apply techniques for a higher usability. A specific aspect of usability is *familiarity* by using terminology and figures user know from their work – instead of experience-slang or knowledge management terms. Good familiarity is easier to achieve when the repository is focused on only one or a few topics and is not intended to cover all software engineering experiences. If such a comprehensive repository is necessary, it should contain sub-repositories that are structured around single topics each. Familiarity can be reached at least for the sub-topics. Besides familiarity, usability includes aspects like *expectation conformance, consistency of concepts*, etc. There are standards to assist usability engineering (e.g., ISO 9241). Our list of criteria can only scratch the surface of what makes a repository usable. For constructing an experience repository, it is advisable to apply usability engineering from the beginning.

Feedback. Software experts and managers make many experiences when they are not working at the computer. They should have an easy way to report those. We have experimented with capturing forms, interviews and tuned elicitation workshops [9]. However, working with a best practice or associated material can also remind them of something they did or saw before. Very often, one finds a reason why a piece of presented material is not applicable or needs adaptation in the specific situation the user is in. Therefore, the activity of (trying to) reuse others' experiences is a good catalyst for eliciting new observations and experiences. A surfaced insight must be immediately captured – or it will sink back to oblivion. Therefore, fast and easy feedback options must be offered by the tool. Contextualized email or Web-form feedback are options: At every point of the supported process, users can initiate feedback. The email or message will be automatically indexed with the process step or location it was sent from. This allows easier analysis and engineering – and even automatic placement of the feedback. Experience engineers or librarians will still be needed at some point to respond to feedback, and to weed out inconsistent or obsolete comments. Fischer calls this the indispensable "reseeding" task [14].

Maintainability. Feedback and input such as new experiences challenge an experience repository with a high rate of change. The architecture of the system must be able to handle frequent change with a minimum delay. However, the scope of change is mostly known in advance: The underlying process may change on the level of single process steps, or in the sequence of steps. For each step, comments and experiences may be added, modified or deleted. All changes will affect support material that is also assigned to parts of the process. Obviously, maintainability can be enhanced by a design that does not hard-code any of the above elements or relationships. In particular, the process itself should be a flexible parameter that can be modified with a minimum of manual work. An update in one place should automatically ripple through all its graphical representations, navigation between steps, and menus that offer access to this navigation We have created two generators that take in descriptive texts, figures, and supportive files. One is written in Delphi. It generates a set of static HTML pages and JavaScripts to navigate between them. A more advanced implementation uses dynamic JavaServlets with an XML backend. Despite their technological differences, they both score high in maintainability. We see a drastic reduction of cycle time, and even building a new experience repository for a new topic was shortened by half or more in our first attempts.

6. Conclusions

Software engineering relies on experiences, and companies need to capitalize on their experiences by capturing and reusing them. In this paper, we have concentrated on complex coarse-grained experiences that often are qualitative. They are encountered when a software process is being improved.

In all approaches of experience reuse, repositories play a central role. However, selecting or developing such a repository is a demanding task. We found many misconceptions about the mission and capabilities of an experience storage and dissemination tool. Experiences should not be stored on a dusty shelf, but engineered into best practices and processes that guide user work.

We have compiled our five-year-long experience in building, revising, and improving experience repositories for DaimlerChrysler business units into a checklist of key quality attributes. Each attribute is measured by an intentionally short list of questions. Answers are calculated into a profile of the evaluated repository. We would not defend every detail of our criteria – but the approach and the key quality criteria should be applicable in a wide range of environments.

Profiles can be used as selection criteria for purchasing a repository. They can also be used to refocus and guide in-house development of an efficient experience repository. The five key quality attributes provide general guidance for developers. In addition, some consequences described above make very concrete suggestions for designing, structuring, and developing an effective experience repository for software engineering issues.

All discussions about effective storage, however, must not distract companies and responsible people from a basic truth that is often neglected: Repositories are important, but they are not sufficient to make a software organization effectively learn from experiences [10, 15]. Without a learning attitude and some appreciation for continuous process improvement, even the best repository will not make experiences "fly".

In our SEC project and in our business units we have seen how an effective experience repository can greatly support an organization that is seriously trying to improve by learning from software engineering experience.

7. References

1. Basili, V., G. Caldiera, and D.H. Rombach, *The Experience Factory*. Encyclopedia of Software Engineering. 1994: John Wiley and Sons.
2. Houdek, F. and K. Schneider, *Software Experience Center. The Evolution of the Experience Factory Concept.*, in *International NASA-SEL Workshop*. 1999.
3. Conradi, R. and T. Dingsoyr. *Software Experience Bases: A Consolidated Evaluation and Status Report.* in *Profes*. 2000. Oulu, Finland.
4. Davenport, T.G.P., *Knowledge Management Case Book - Best Practises*. 2000, München, Germany: Publicis MCD, John Wiley & Sons. 260.
5. Henninger, S. *Using Software Process to Support Learning Software Organizations*. in *Workshop on Learning Software Organizations*. 1999. Kaiserslautern, Germany.
6. Schneider, K. and T. Schwinn, *Maturing Experience Base Concepts at DaimlerChrysler.* Software Process Improvement and Practice, 2001. **6**: p. 85-96.
7. Kontio, J., G. Getto, and D. Landes. *Experiences in improving risk management processes using the concepts of the Riskit method.* in *Sixth International Symposium on the Foundations of Software Engineering (FSE-6)*. 1998. Orlando, USA.
8. Schneider, K. *Key Success Factors and Traps for Software Risk Management.* in *Conference on Engineering in Software Technology (CONQUEST 2002)*. 2002. Nürnberg, September 19-20, 2002: Arbeitskreis Software-Qualität Franken e.V. (ASQF).
9. Schneider, K. *LIDs: A Light-Weight Approach to Experience Elicitation and Reuse.* in *Product Focused Software Process Improvement (PROFES 2000)*. Oulo, Finland: Springer.
10. Schneider, K., *What to Expect from Software Experience Exploitation.* Journal of Universal Computer Science (J.UCS). www.jucs.org,, 2002. **8**(6): p. 44-54.
11. Boehm, B., *Software Engineering Economics.* 1981: Prentice Hall, Englewood Cliffs, NJ.
12. Tautz, C., Althoff, K.-D., Nick, M. *A Case-Based Reasoning Approach for Managing Qualitative Experience.* in *17th National Conference on AI (AAAI-00). Workshop on Intelligent Lessons Learned Systems.* 2000.
13. Schneider, K. *Experience Magnets - Attracting Experiences, not Just Storing Them.* in *Conference on Product Focused Software Process Improvement PROFES 2001*. 2001. Kaiserslautern, September 2001.
14. Fischer, G., *Seeding, Evolutionary Growth and Reseeding: Constructing, Capturing and Evolving Knowledge in Domain-Oriented Design Environments.* Automated Software Engineering, 1998. **5**(4): p. 447-464.
15. Schneider, K.B., Victor R.; von Hunnius, J., *Experience in Implementing a Learning Software Organization.* IEEE Software, 2002. **19**(3).

The Software Engineering Impacts of Cultural Factors on Multi-cultural Software Development Teams.

Greg Borchers
Sharp Laboratories of America
gborchers@sharplabs.com

Abstract

This paper is based on our experiences in trying to apply software engineering practices to development projects staffed by developers from three distinct cultures; Japan, India, and the United States. The development of commercial software products has always been difficult. The standard balancing act that occurs between features, schedules, and resources is at the core of the difficulty. We found that cultural differences also had a large impact on our software engineering work.

Much has been written and said about software engineering methods that can be applied to development projects to reduce and control these core difficulties. Methods that were thought to be "best practices" turned out to be ineffective or very difficult to implement. Our understanding of the possible root causes for these difficulties greatly increased when we began to study some of the cultural dynamics within the team. This paper describes our observations in terms of how these cultural factors impacted the software engineering techniques used on the projects.

1. Introduction

This paper is based on two separate software development projects conducted over the past 4 years. Both projects involved the contributions of software developers from India, Japan and the United States. In both projects, the software development effort was shared between the three teams. Each team contributed differently over the course of the project, with primary project management coming from the team in the United States. The Japanese teams were part of the parent company, the U.S. team was part of the research lab leading the projects, and the Indian teams were part of offshore development groups at both internal subsidiary and external contract development sites.

The author of this paper served in both technical lead and project management roles at various times over the course of 4 years on these 2 projects. This paper will compare our experiences with some cultural background information based on the works of Geert Hofstede. Several instances exist where the parameters described in his work match very closely to the observations we saw in the behavior and problems on our projects. Until we studied some of the cultural factors, we had difficulty in understanding software development problems that we were having. This paper presents these insights in a way that will hopefully allow others to learn from our experiences.

This paper is structured to include short review of the parts of Hofstede's work that are relevant to our projects in the U.S., Japan and India. This is followed by a list of the cultural dimensions and the potential influence of these on our software engineering efforts. The conclusions section explains what feel are the important observations, and proposes future areas of study.

2. Cultural Studies and Measurements

Author's Note:

"A chance reading of a book by Geert Hofstede started the kernel of interest in the cultural factors that were influencing some of the problems on our software project. I read that first book on a plane flight from India back to the United States. As I read through the chapters on Power Distance, Uncertainty Avoidance, and Individualism, I began to see how some of the patterns Hofstede was describing were playing out as realities in the behaviors among the team members on our software project. When I finally got to the chapter comparing all the factors quantitatively, I saw the measurements that jumped out at me as possible explanations for the team behaviors that I was seeing."

There were three measurements in Hofstede's cultural study that were interesting from a software project perspective. In his book, each measurement was expressed in terms of an index. The results were based on survey research done at a large multinational computer company. Data was collected between 1967 and 1973. The first edition of the book summarizing the research is

0-7695-1877-X/03 $17.00 © 2003 IEEE

titled "Culture's Consequences" and was printed in 1980. [1] The cultural indexes generated as part of the study, were computed scores that range from approximately 0 to 100. (See the book for more details on scoring.) The primary measurements that were found to be interesting for looking at our software development project were:

Power Distance (PDI)

Human inequalities can be expressed in terms of prestige, wealth, and power. The most interesting aspect of this measurement from a software development perspective is in the way it applies internally to organizations. Power distance exists in all organizations. Many things about how a software team behaves are based on the cultural norms of the organization within which the team exists. The "always connected" nature of software development projects that are spread across different cultures does not necessarily change the way the power distance impacts behavior locally.

High values for Power Distance Index (PDI) correspond to higher levels of perceived inequality. In the development of software, the inequality of bosses and subordinates is the most relevant example. In high PDI cultures the boss has greater authority over subordinates, than in cultures with lower PDI.

Uncertainty Avoidance (UAI)

The tolerance for uncertainty about the future is the core element of this measurement. In proportion to this tolerance, cultures create many different coping mechanisms. Some of these coping mechanisms have large impacts on the way that software development teams can be expected to operate.

Cultures with high values for Uncertainty Avoidance Index (UAI) possess more highly evolved coping mechanisms to reduce the feelings of uncertainty. Examples of these coping mechanisms in the software development field could include rigorous adherence to waterfall development models, restrictive change control systems and elaborate process models creating procedures for dealing with every possible event during development.

Individualism (IDV)

The strength of the relationship between an individual and their societal group is the primary measurement in this dimension. The ways that people live and work together are the visible effects of this dimension. How people feel about their position in a group, and their overall attitude toward their group, are major factors that influence how software development teams function. This dimension influences the initial formation and continuance of software development teams.

High values for Individualism Index (IDV) correspond to cultures in which individuals live independently from the groups that they belong to. These cultures with high IDV have relatively weak relationships between individuals and the groups that they belong to. For software development this index impacts the ability of a software team to form strong bonds between the team members, and act cohesively. It also impacts the ability of individual team members to excel independently as "star performers" within the team.

Measurements:
Here is the data from the Hofstede study for USA, Japan, and India.

	PDI	UAI	IDV
India	77	40	48
Japan	54	92	46
United States	40	46	91

The graph below shows the relative values for these three indices for the three countries that are part of our current software development effort. In summary, the data shows the following trends:

Here is a graph depicting the relative scores.

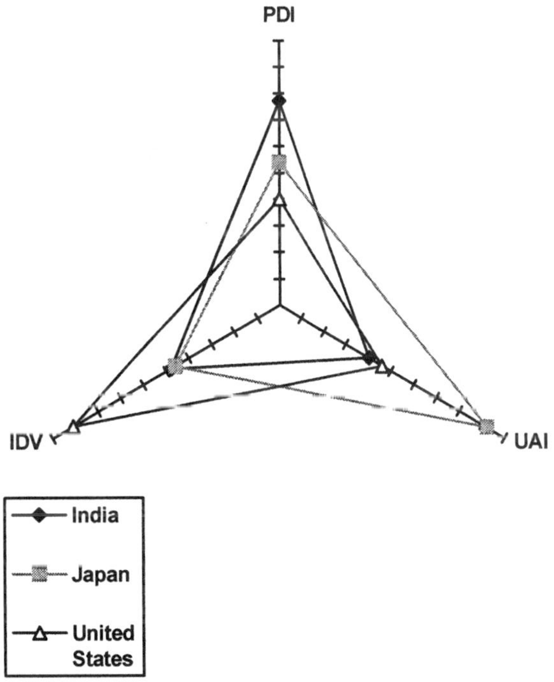

PDI:
India has the highest power distance index, then Japan. The USA has the lowest PDI.

IDV:
The USA has the highest score by for individualism by a large margin. India and Japan have a lower IDV, and are at about the same level.

UAI:
Japan has the highest score for uncertainty avoidance, by a large margin. India and Japan have a lower UAI, and are at about the same level.

3. Discussion

When we first faced software project problems on our multi-cultural development team, it was easy to ignore the impacts of culture. In the first phases of facing this problem, our software engineering training had us reaching into our "software process" bag of tricks in an attempt to solve every issue. The next phase was denial. Each team started to believe that other team was just incompetent. Finally, we became more comfortable with the fact that each team did have the strength to do their part of the task. We began to realize that each part of the team would be operating under their own norms, not all of which would make sense to everyone else.
The next sections describe the impact that the different indices described by Hofstede, seem to have had on our software projects.

Power Distance

This is the factor that is the most difficult to understand from an American perspective. Much of the modern software engineering and project management is filled with techniques that work well in an American culture. Foremost among these is the "team of respected peers" notion. Many successful software teams in the USA have taken the approach that the "project manager is just along for the ride." Many successful software project managers have used this approach with great results. This approach has been shown to have strong advantages, particularly when it can be used to build a sense of team accountability for the software product being delivered. Jim McCarthy describes this approach quite well in his book "Dynamics of Software Development." He states:

"Before the program manager can be worth anything to the team, he or she must be thoroughly disabused of the notion that he or she has any direct control. Fortunately, in the healthy team, no one needs to take any special steps to see that this happens: the program manager's teammates will quickly disabuse him or her of any delusions of control that he or she may be harboring"[2]

This statement describes a healthy team situation for a team composed of developers with a low PDI, and high IDV. However, the cultural bias for power distance index becomes a factor when the American project manager expects that the teams in India and Japan will "push back" on issues the same way that teams of American developers usually do. PDI impacts Japanese and Indian teams when they have the expectation that their relationship to an American project manager will be a purely subordinate one. The reality is that the three cultures come together with different cultural expectations for leadership. The practical solution is that the software project leadership has to be dispersed. Each team must have local leaders in place. This is a good idea for any distributed team, even within a mono-cultural project, but it becomes a critical success factor when the teams are from different cultures. At a minimum, the local leads for each team must be aware of the cultural differences. Ideally these individuals will need to be the most "culturally aware" of anyone on the project. Providing incorrect leadership based on mismatched cultural norms for PDI is a very easy mistake to make. It is also an easy mistake to recover from. Local leadership is the answer.

Individualism

Individualism is easy to understand from an American perspective. However, the impacts on a multi-cultural software project are subtle. In our experience, we could see where the Indian teams formed close interpersonal bonds within the teams. These teams seemed to be very much composed of friends. The same appeared to be happening in the Japanese part of the team, although it was harder to tell. The American teams also had what would be considered a good camaraderie. This factor was difficult to consider. Perhaps the only evidence we have seen is that during a "bug fixing" phase on a project, the Indian developers seemed to fix each others bugs even though they were not assigned to do so. The American team tended to only work on their assigned bugs without voluntarily fixing the bugs assigned to others.

Another influence that IDV had is that being singled out for public praise is not viewed positively in some cultures with low IDV. In Japanese cultures, the praise of an individual in a public way is not always interpreted the same way it would be for American or Indian team members.[3] IDV and PDI may also have an interaction effect. In cultures with low IDV and high PDI there may be no good way to single out a developer in a subordinate role who is performing well. While American developers would typically enjoy this type of praise, Japanese or

Indian teams might consider this type of praise to be disturbing.

The influence of IDV on software development probably goes deeper than we were able to observe just by our normal day-to-day software development work. Further investigation with survey-based research may be needed to better understand the impact of IDV on software teams. However, as a general rule, it is good to be aware of the potential cultural differences when considering actions that would positively (or negatively) single out an individual on a team in a culture that has a low IDV.

Uncertainty Avoidance

Uncertainty avoidance is easy to see in the different ways that each culture approaches the design and analysis phases of software development. UAI was easier to observe than the impact of IDV, or PDI. The approach to design, documentation, as well as project management and tracking, are easily observable areas where UAI has an impact. Another area of impact that is less observable is the manner in which "the consensus to move forward" is achieved.

Software design techniques can be characterized on a spectrum that ranges from "code is design" to "design as a monument built of paper." Both ends of the spectrum have value when applied in the right situations. Cultures with high UAI tend towards a more "design upfront" approach. The removal of uncertainty through iterative design, consensus reaching, and consideration for all possibilities seems to be a common approach for teams with a high UAI. Teams with a low UAI, might call this "analysis paralysis." This is a natural tension that was relieved through prototyping. The teams were able to move forward when prototyping was used. Purposeful prototype projects seemed to satisfy the need for uncertainty avoidance. The goal focused prototypes allowed early development effort to proceed smoothly. This was probably because it allowed for a "controlled uncertainty" within the constraints of each prototype's goal. This was a case where the desire to avoid uncertainty worked together with the desire to get started. The result was an iterative milestone delivery approach that worked for all teams.

UAI impacted documentation, in that while the American and Indian teams felt that documentation was a necessary exercise, the Japanese teams relied on the documentation for achieving understanding. This may have been a secondary effect of the English language constraint. (Not really a cultural issue, but it does affect teams that have a language barrier.) The Japanese team members achieved better communication through written documentation than spoken communications. However, it was face-to-face meetings that produced the best communications.

The impact of UAI on project management and tracking was fairly large. Up-front planning was definitely required for our projects and the natural tension between getting started, and reaching consensus before starting provided an interesting challenge. From a project planning perspective, the mix of UAI tendencies was probably a good thing. The urge to start was tempered by the urge to plan. In the end, we probably had the right mix of both.

The need for project tracking details was high for the Japanese teams. Whereas the Indian and American teams with a low UAI were comfortable knowing only that "bug fixing would continue until the product shipped", many times an estimate was requested by the Japanese teams for "exactly when will each of the bugs be fixed." The reality was that the best way to run the projects turned out to be somewhere in-between these two points of view. It could be said that a "temporarily high UAI" sets in during the final phases of any software project that is about to ship. At the end, everyone wants to avoid uncertainty. To meet the project tracking needs, a multicultural team at distributed sites, will need to develop a more detailed tracking & reporting system than might be required for a mono-cultural team in a single location. This extra tracking detail was required in our projects because of large differences in time zones, and the reliance on written communication.

Software Architecture Impacts

One interesting area that emerged from our projects is the idea that software architecture seems to be culturally influenced. The design approach varies, particularly in the area of how abstractions are chosen. It seems to vary from team to team on our projects. We were not able to pinpoint a pattern that we could describe here. Further study might reveal whether teams from different cultures tend to use different architectural patterns. These differences were not large in our projects. This was probably because we tried to have a common software architecture model for the entire project. However, within the modules produced by each team, it seemed like different styles prevailed.

Configuration Management Impacts

While it is possible to have decentralized development teams, we found it essential to have centralized configuration management. In particular, a daily build from a central source, with a highly visible result, was a useful practice. By making the current state of the product a daily public announcement, good integration practices are encouraged. Our experience confirmed that breaking the daily build, and having that fact publicly announced via email, is not a considered a good thing by developers from any culture.

Integration across cultural boundaries is difficult. The amount of communication required between remote developers working on an integration area will quickly exceed their ability to communicate with each other. We found that adding architectural layers for no other reason than minimizing the code that needed to be integrated was a useful idea. It seems that physical boundaries are good ways to align the team assignments. For example, separate DLLs were assigned to each team. Changing the software architecture to match the team structure proved useful, although to a greater extent, software architecture drove the team structure.

Certain activities caused havoc with configuration management. These included performance tuning and bug fixing. This was because the nature of these tasks often caused the work to cross module boundaries, and thereby cultural boundaries too. Keeping track of the changes once the changes start to cross the module boundaries, brought up the normal issues associated with integration. These integration tasks were made more difficult by the fact that the module boundaries were aligned with the cultural boundaries.

4. Conclusions

The risk of forming conclusions based on cultural observations is that whatever is said can be misconstrued as a stereotype. This is true. Conclusions made about a group based solely on their cultural background will be generalizations that don't hold true for all cases. However, a summary of the observations seen on our projects can be made. The reader can draw their own conclusions about how this applies to their own multi-cultural software development situations.

Indian teams seem to be able to "go with the flow", and have a good ability to work with moderate levels of uncertainty. Software teams with a high PDI as exists in Indian culture are at risk of being "jerked around" by changing requirements. Requirements churn can come from project leaders who unknowingly make statements such as "wouldn't it be cool if the software could do X." The Indian team's reaction might be to implement that feature before the next meeting! The cohesiveness of the teams formed seem to be high. The low IDV helps Indian teams form strong bonds between individuals on the team. In addition, the high PDI may actually strengthen the teams' cohesiveness.

Japanese teams seem to have high cohesiveness much like the Indian teams. The high UAI of Japanese culture tends to slow the decision making process, and actually may be helpful for development projects that require more deliberate software processes. It seems that the negative impact of uncertainty avoidance can be rediced if uncertainty is broken into small doses. This can be done through short duration prototyping efforts with a well-defined purpose. The relatively high PDI together with the high UAI seem to cause Japanese teams to "seek approval before acting" more often than might be the case in other teams. As long as prototyping was used, this was not a problem. If left unchecked, this tendency seems to move software project teams towards waterfall development styles.

American teams benefit from low uncertainty avoidance in that they are culturally well suited for iterative development and prototyping. However, the tendency to "wallow in uncertainty" may be a drawback of this low UAI. Some American teams seem to enjoy the chaos, often to the detriment of project progress. American software development teams are notoriously difficult to lead for project leaders more accustomed to a hierarchical style. The low PDI, and high IDV of American culture impacts the styles of leadership that can be successful for software development. For software project managers, the high IDV suggests that many of the project tracking and task assignment activities be done carefully, with forethought towards the personal impacts on the team members.

The impact of culture on Software Architecture was not easy to draw conclusions about. However, it seems like there were some patterns. Hopefully, future research will be able to comment on this. It is possible that the Open Source community might be the best "ongoing field experiment" on which to base these observations. Our two projects were too small a sample to draw any conclusions in this area.

As a United States research and development laboratory for a Japanese parent company, we receive more training in the area of cultural impacts than most software engineers do. While our awareness is somewhat elevated, the impact of cultural factors for our projects was still greater than we initially anticipated.

In summary, the impact of cultural factors on our software engineering efforts caught us off-guard. Initially, it was thought that rigorous software processes could smooth over any and all cultural differences. However, as we observed on our projects, it was not that simple. It was more successful to adapt and adjust our expectations to the realities of the cultural impacts.

References

[1] Hofstede, G. *Culture's Consequences* Sage Publications, London, 1980.

[2] McCarthy, J. *Dynamics of Software Development,* Microsoft Press, Redmond Washington, 1995, p 48.

[3] Ferraro, G. P. *The Cultural Dimensions of International Business,* Prentice Hall, New Jersey, 2002, p. 101.

This paper does not necessarily reflect the opinions of Sharp Corporation. The conclusions and observations made, are made solely by the author alone.

Experience Reports

Software Architecture II

Why Can't They Create Architecture Models Like "Developer X"? An Experience Report

George Fairbanks

School of Computer Science
Carnegie Mellon University
5000 Forbes Ave, Pittsburgh PA 15213 USA
george.fairbanks@cs.cmu.edu

Abstract

A large financial company, struggling with legacy systems that did not interoperate, performed a pilot project to teach software architecture to an enthusiastic application development team. Experienced mentors, including the author, worked with the application team for seven months to complete their engineering goal successfully. However, the mentors were unsuccessful in their attempt to train any of the six members of the application team to create architecture models on their own, though they were able to create them collaboratively with the mentors. This surprising result is due to the application team's strong preference for concrete artifacts over abstract ones. Even more surprising, an application developer from a different project, "Developer X", read the architecture modeling documentation on an internal website and, without mentoring, created architecture models within a few days. In light of this failure to teach software architecture, two short-term strategies are suggested for the use of software architecture in companies.

1. Introduction

Many companies struggle with systems that do not interoperate, so-called "stovepipe systems". The techniques of software architecture promise to help by providing high-level views of the system and by identifying components [10]. A seemingly reasonable approach is to train each software development team to use architecture models, provide the models to senior architects, and re-engineer applications to interoperate and share components. In contrast to earlier reports in academic environments [7, 1] the developers in our pilot project found it hard or impossible to create these architecture models without assistance. This result is important for two reasons: First, it is surprising to find that all six developers on the project had trouble learning to create architecture models. Second, the difficulty in training the necessary developers will cause organizational difficulties for companies seeking to use software architecture techniques.

I learned these lessons inside a large financial company during a pilot project to institute a software process that included architecture modeling techniques. For seven months, the author and other mentors experienced in teaching architecture and component-based development guided an enthusiastic team through their first use of the software process. The engineering goal was to specify an existing single-tier system for third-party re-implementation as a multi-tier J2EE [11] application. The educational goal was to provide sufficient training on the new software process so that the team could continue to create architecture models after the mentors had gone. The team was composed of both programmers and analysts. All knew the domain well and many were involved in the creation of the original application. This was their first exposure to software architecture and their first time creating specifications for a third-party contractor. Prior to the pilot project, the team members had proven themselves effective in designing and implementing large upgrades to the system.

The engineering goal of the project was achieved in that specifications, including architecture models, were delivered for implementation. The training goal was not achieved because when the application team worked alone they produced poor architecture models despite months of mentoring. It had been assumed that each application team could provide their architecture models to a central architecture group that would use them to redesign applications for integration. The results of this pilot suggest that this approach may not work as intended.

While the pilot project was in progress, a developer from another project, "Developer X", sent the architecture group an email requesting an evaluation of his architecture model.

0-7695-1877-X/03 $17.00 © 2003 IEEE

His architecture model was quite good. This was of interest to the architecture group because Developer X had never received training or mentoring and had only read the architecture group's documents on the corporate intranet a few days earlier. Developer X's success suggests that the process and documentation was adequate and the failure to teach the application team to create architecture models was related to their aptitude in working with abstractions.

The remainder of this report proceeds as follows. Section 2 describes the rationale for the pilot project and new software process. Section 3 provides details on the project schedule, mentoring, and activities. Section 4 describes the observations on the project successes and failures, including the surprising success of Developer X. Section 5 investigates several hypotheses that explain the observations. Section 6 provides conclusions including two short-term workarounds and suggests long-term strategies to make software architecture accessible to more developers.

2. The Software Process

The new software process used in this project had four sources of inspiration. The first was the Catalysis [4] approach to system description, which describes how to use UML [5] precisely and relate models at different levels of abstraction. It gives guidance on how to specify and use components.

The second source of inspiration was Cheesman and Daniels' [2] work that provides advice on which levels of abstraction to choose, pragmatic UML notations, and nomenclature for creating component systems.

Third, the Model Driven Architecture (MDA) approach from the Object Management Group [9] provides ideas on how to integrate applications based upon consistent domain models across many applications.

Fourth and finally, the standard concepts from the software architecture community provided the building blocks for the construction of the architecture [8].

The new software process allows precise modeling of the business process, software architecture, components, and connectors. The notation used in architecture modeling was proprietary, but it embodied standard architecture modeling ideas like components, connectors, roles, and ports that are found in architecture description languages such as Acme [6]. By combining selected software engineering technologies, this process is designed to address the challenges that are found when integrating legacy systems. Although currently proprietary, the process is expected to be published in the future.

Product Line Architecture (PLA) techniques were not used on this project because they cannot be used to integrate existing systems, even though they can be quite effective when designing and implementing new systems [3].

3. The Project

This section describes the context, calendar, and activities during the pilot project. Due to confidentiality concerns, some details have been omitted or generalized but sufficient detail is provided to illuminate the principles involved.

Two peer groups inside the company were involved in the project. The architecture group, of which the author was a part, consisted of mentor/educators experienced in component-based development and architecture modeling. The software application team consisted of both analysts and programmers. The application team had recently decided to try outsourcing to a third party for implementation and had requested assistance from the architecture group.

The application team had been updating and maintaining a medium-sized two-tier application used by customer service representatives. With new requests to make some application functions available over the internet, the team chose to re-engineer the application to run under J2EE on multiple tiers. The engineering goal of the team was to produce architecture and component specifications to deliver to the third party implementers.

With agreement from the application team, the architecture group assigned a mentor to co-locate with the group and guide them through a software process that included the creation of architecture models of the existing system and planned improvements. The architecture group hoped that these architecture models could be used to identify reusable components and provide insight into the structure of the application to enable interoperation with other applications. Another goal was to train the application team sufficiently so that in the future they could create architecture models without the mentors present.

The sequence of events was roughly as follows. We modeled the business context and desired quality objectives. The high level architecture of the new system was designed and component choices made. Design proceeded until it was discovered that the existing system contained functionality not present in the new system design. In a painstaking process, the application team analyzed the code and transformed it into prose readable by subject matter experts. Since a rules engine was part of the new design, they converted some procedural logic into declarative rules. They created specifications for each component at two levels: a logical level and an API-level. The third party implementers then coded the specifications in Java.

When the application team was asked to produce architecture models without assistance from the mentors, the resulting architecture models lacked abstraction and made inappropriate references to concrete artifacts.

4. Successes, Failures, and Developer X

This section discusses the project successes and areas of difficulty. Generally, when the application team and the mentors collaborated they produced quality results. Without the mentors, the application team tended to produce models lacking abstraction. However, after reading the architecture group's online documentation another developer in the company produced abstract models without mentor assistance.

4.1. Success at Collaboration

The project was successful when the mentors and application team worked together to create architecture models. Frequently the mentor would facilitate a working session. Ideas would be jointly sketched, debated, reworked, agreed to, and finally recorded. In this style of interaction, the application team would supply facts about how the system worked and the mentor would incorporate them into the architecture model on the board using correct notation. This style of interaction worked because the mentors knew the software process and modeling techniques while the application team knew the problem domain of the system.

The collaboration between the architecture group and the application team was successful at producing a model of the system that neither group could have produced individually and demonstrates that the pairing of individuals with these skill sets is viable.

4.2. Failure in Abstraction

Though effective, these joint mentor and application team working sessions were not without friction. The mentor frequently acted as the gatekeeper between the architecture model and what he perceived as unnecessary details. For example, the application team preferred to show the AS/400 computer and the Sybase database as large deployed components, while the mentors instead preferred to show a batch connection to another system.

The application team trusted the mentors to judge the appropriate detail, but a lack of understanding combined with that trust may have caused problems elsewhere. The mentors discovered late in the project that the application team had not volunteered details on some of the system functions related to data caching coherency that were relevant to the architecture. This was certainly not malicious and probably based on an incorrect guess at what details were important at the architecture level.

When specifying components without mentor assistance, the application team repeatedly produced detailed specifications of a component's internal implementation but presented these as specifications of the interface. This is a problem because another programmer using the component should only want to know how to use the component, i.e., the interface specification, not how to re-implement the component. The application team did not omit the interface specification but instead delivered a duplicate of the implementation specification. After working collaboratively with the mentor, they were able to build an appropriate interface specification and agreed that the new interface specification was better.

The application team appeared more comfortable discussing their system using concrete terms. They resisted the use of abstract model attributes. In one case, data interchange requirements necessitated a single character database field to encode a combination of three independent properties. The application team resisted the abstract representation of this as three separate properties. Similarly, another database field name was "employeeFlag", but it did not identify employees nor was its datatype Boolean. The application team resisted renaming this attribute in the abstract models. At other times, the application team would convey the domain requirements in terms of database entries, as in "Q is allowed to do R if there is a matching entry in the S table," instead of in domain language "Q can do R if Q has a registered entitlement."

4.3. Surprising Success of Developer X

At one point during the pilot, a developer who worked on a separate project, Developer X, sent an email to the architecture group. Developer X had read the architecture group's internal website and had produced architectural models of his system. He asked the architecture group to review his models and, in the architecture group's opinion, his architecture models were quite good. He obtained these results without mentoring and without months of effort.

Clearly there was an enormous difference in the success of Developer X compared to the application team. The application team was given months of daily guidance from experienced mentors and feedback on how to improve their modeling yet their architecture models continued to be of poor quality. Developer X, either from former related experience or through natural ability, possessed great skill in extracting the essence of the software and creating architecture models to represent it. This idea and others are analyzed in the next section.

5. Hypotheses

Many hypotheses for the observed failures have been suggested. Many of these are listed here along with a discussion on how well the hypothesis fits with the observed facts. When necessary, additional details that support, disprove, or otherwise affect a hypothesis are also noted. The first hypotheses to be presented are the ones that have strong evidence to suggest that they are not true.

- *The application team was resistant or otherwise not trying hard enough.* From beginning to end, the team kept trying to learn the techniques and was excited to learn. This pilot project was not a case where a software process was forced upon an unappreciative team. In fact, at the end of the pilot the application team decided to keep using the new software process.

- *The team was incompetent.* When working on the new process, the application team was unsure of themselves and progressed slowly. I observed a distinct difference in the team's apparent competence when working on their usual duties. When responding to maintenance requests they were confident and quick. This team had successfully maintained the system for years and had designed and implemented significant upgrades.

- *Architecture modeling is too hard for anyone or is too hard on real-world projects.* However, when the application team and the mentors collaborated they produced good architecture models.

- *The new software process was poor, the materials were defective, or the mentoring process was flawed.* A few of the mentors believed this hypothesis for some time despite the substantial history the mentors had in teaching this material. While improvements to the process, materials, and mentoring are always possible, the mentors stopped believing the hypothesis to be a large influence once they saw Developer X's work.

- *The architecture group engaged in a game of "bring me a rock" by changing the acceptance criteria of the application team's models.* The game is impossible to win because the answer can always come back "No, a darker one" or "No, a flatter one." This is inconsistent with what the architecture group observed. The application team consistently brought the same rock, architecture models that were always at the API or data representation level.

The following hypotheses cannot be refuted given the scope of this project, but are unlikely to be true given the experience on the project.

- *The lack of software architecture ability on the pilot project was statistically abnormal and other projects will not be so unlucky.* This is indeed possible, but a cautious reader should treat this report like a sighting of a natural disaster and be aware that they can happen. This project showed six developers, not just one, who were ineffective in creating software architectures. A larger study of the developer population could better test this hypothesis.

- *"Old habits die hard" and that the team needed longer to learn the new techniques.* Perhaps a year-long project would show different results. However, if the training process takes more than seven months of continuous mentoring then it is likely not cost-effective to perform the training at all.

Based on the cumulative evidence and especially the differing abilities of Developer X and the application team, the hypothesis most likely to be true is the following.

- *Many developers are unskilled in working with abstractions, a skill necessary to create architecture models.* While I believe this based upon this pilot project and other observations, the evidence from one pilot program cannot prove this. A more conservative hypothesis that is directly supported by this pilot program is that some developers have great difficulty creating architecture models. Both hypotheses are significant enough to interfere with company-wide use of architecture models, as is described in the next section.

6. Conclusions

Viewed very generally, the finding of this report is not surprising: The project revealed a difference in ability of developers to perform a task, namely creating architecture models. However, this finding is interesting for two reasons. First, it had been assumed by many, including the architecture group, that software architecture would be a readily teachable skill. This project uncovered six competent, experienced developers who showed little aptitude for creating architectural models.

Second, if this finding generalizes then it limits the way companies can use software architects. The traditional approach to adopting a new technique is simply to train people to use it, but this pilot shows that a software architecture training program may be ineffective.

This project gave us no direct guidance on how to predict if a developer will be good at creating architecture models. As long as this is not known, companies will spend time and money attempting to train developers with poor abstraction skills. I speculate, however, that developers with poor abstraction skills self-select certain job types that allow them to emphasize their skills at manipulation of concrete artifacts. It follows that certain jobs, perhaps maintenance programming, may be disproportionately lacking developers trainable in software architecture.

Since the architecture group still believes in the benefits that software architecture can bring to the field of software engineering, we are determined to work through or around this difficulty. Turning from the problem of how to obtain good software architects, to the problem of how to use the ones that are available, I identify two short-term strategies.

6.1. Central Architecture Group

The first strategy is send architects from a central architecture group to collaboratively create architecture models with the application teams. The architects know the domain of software architecture and the team representatives know the domain of their application. As this pilot showed, they can work together for a short time to create a reasonable architecture model. This approach may not work if the ratio of architects to teams is low because the architects would be stretched too thin. Furthermore, changes to the application may warrant another collaboration session with an architect, consuming more time and effort.

As this project demonstrated, there are times when the collaboration approach is deficient. Details concerning the caching behavior of the application were not shared with the mentor because the application team did not think they were relevant to the architecture model. Also, though this project was lucky to have mentors who were experienced at facilitating modeling sessions, all projects will not be so lucky.

6.2. An Architect for Each Application

A second strategy is to require application teams to develop their own architecture models. This requires each team to have at least one software architect. While the existence of architecture modeling skills cannot be taken for granted, companies can deliberately seed each team with trained architects. This application architect has the benefit of both knowing the domain of the application as well as having architecture modeling skills, which avoids the "unmentioned details" problem that a collaborative effort can have. Also, incremental modifications to the architecture models can be done painlessly as the application evolves since an application team member can do the incremental modifications.

This approach is not without problems. It assumes that a large pool of developers can be identified and trained in software architecture techniques. At least one architect must be present on each application team, which will invariably require inter-team transfers of personnel. As mentioned above, the application teams lacking architecture skills may not be uniformly distributed across the company, further complicating inter-team transfers. Finally, the architecture models created by part-time architects may not be quite as good as models created by full-time architects.

6.3. Future Work

In the longer term, the goal should be to expand the pool of developers who can be taught to use software architecture effectively. Similar to the way that the lesson plans for teaching of calculus and programming have evolved to make them more effective and widen their audience, the teaching materials for software architecture need to improve. As training materials become more mature, the pool of developers who are able to use software architecture should also grow.

7. Acknowledgements

Great thanks to those on the architecture group and application team who inspired this report and to Jim Herbsleb, Mary Shaw, the participants in her Wordwright course, Patrick Riley, and Marianne Berkovich who provided extensive improvements to the report argument and structure. The author wishes to acknowledge support through the High Dependability Computing Program from NASA Ames cooperative agreement NCC-2-1298.

References

[1] P. Bucci, T. J. Long, and B. W. Weide. Teaching software architecture principles in cs1/cs2. Proceedings 3rd International Software Architecture Workshop, 1998.

[2] J. Cheesman and J. Daniels. UML Components: A Simple Process for Specifying Component-Based Software. The Component Software Series. Addison-Wesley, 2000.

[3] P. Clements and L. M. Northrop. Software Product Lines: Practices and Patterns. Addison-Wesley, 2001.

[4] D. D'Souza and A. Wills. Objects, Components, and Frameworks With Uml: The Catalysis Approach. Addison-Wesley Object Technology Series. Addison-Wesley, 1998.

[5] M. Fowler and K. Scott. UML Distilled: A Brief Guide to the Standard Object Modeling Language. Addison-Westley, 1999.

[6] D. Garlan, R. Monroe, and D. Wile. Acme: An architecture description interchange language, 1997.

[7] D. Garlan, M. Shaw, C. Okasaki, C. Scott, and R. Swonger. Experience with a course on architectures for software systems. Proceedings of the Sixth SEI Conference on Software Engineering Education, 1992.

[8] N. Medvidovic and R. N. Taylor. A classification and comparison framework for software architecture description languages. IEEE Transactions on Software Engineering, 26(1), January 2000.

[9] J. Mukerji. Model driven architecture. Technical report, Object Management Group, 2001.

[10] M. Shaw and D. Garlan. Software Architecture: Perspectives on an Emerging Discipline. Prentice Hall Publishing, 1996.

[11] I. Sun Microsystems. Java 2 Platform, Enterprise Edition Specification, Version 1.3, August 2001.

The Co-Evolution of a Hype and a Software Architecture: Experience of Component-Producing Large-Scale EJB Early Adopters

Lutz Prechelt and Daniel J. Hutzel
abaXX Technology AG, Stuttgart
{lutz.prechelt|daniel.hutzel}@abaxx.com

Abstract

abaXX.components was one of the first API software products fully based on Enterprise JavaBeans™ (EJB) technology. We describe the evolution of its architecture as it moved from simply taking the initial EJB hype for the truth, through several intermediate stages, to using EJB simply as one of several encapsulated implementation techniques. So far, the public perception of how to use EJB properly evolved along a similar path, lagging 6 to 12 months behind.

1. Introduction

abaXX Technology was founded in April 1999 and was possibly the first software company that based all of its work on Enterprise JavaBeans (EJB) and other Java2 EnterpriseEdition (J2EE) Technology.

This report describes the architectural evolution of abaXX's main suite of software products, called abaXX.components, a collection of components and frameworks for building web-based e-business/eCRM applications of all kinds (primarily process-based end-customer portals). The authors are responsible for devising and evolving this architecture and for explaining it to abaXX customers.

2. The software: abaXX.components

abaXX.components is written entirely in Java and uses many technologies of the J2EE and Web world such as Servlets, Java ServerPages (JSP), Enterprise JavaBeans (EJB), JNDI, JDBC, JMS, XML, XSL-T, and others.

abaXX.components comprises frameworks and small-grained and large-grained application components in the following functional areas: web-frontend programming (including portlets), portal-process modeling and programming (workflow), integration of content providers (such as content management systems), email/fax/sms messaging, document generation, user tracking and automatic personalization, e-commerce, and advice/configuration applications.

Most of the product has the form of APIs (separated into client API and extension API), the rest is tools (e.g. the graphical workflow modeler), source code examples, and a complete Web-GUI application called AdministrationCenter for business-view administrators. An application using abaXX.components is always custom software; the implementation project involves a significant part of programming rather than just configuration.

Despite its heavy use of many J2EE technologies including EJB, the product directly supports various application servers such as IBM WebSphere 4.0, BEA Weblogic 5.1 and 6.1, and JBoss 2.6 and 3.0, which are by far less compatible to one another than one might expect.

Our goals for evolving abaXX.components can be summarized as follows:

- continously improving the power, performance, openness, extensibility, and ease-of-use of the components;
- maximizing the flexibility and extensibility of the resulting custom applications;
- exploiting improvements in the application server infrastructure;
- continously adapting newly evolving standards (such as Apache Struts for frontend programming) and new technological trends (such as web services) without breaking backwards compatibility to earlier versions.

3. Enterprise JavaBeans (EJB) quick intro

While this report assumes some technical familiarity with EJB, here is a quick quick overview for all other interested readers.

Enterprise JavaBeans [3] is the name of a technology specification featuring software components (think of each as one logical class) that reside within an EJB container. The EJB container is a major element of a J2EE application server. There are two flavors of enterprise beans: Entity beans represent business/domain objects and session beans represent business services. The EJB specification has seen versions 1.0, 1.1, and 2.0 (2.1 is

0-7695-1877-X/03 $17.00 © 2003 IEEE

under way) and starting with EJB 2.0, there is also an extension of session beans not discussed here called MessageDrivenBeans.

Clients access an enterprise bean through a remote proxy interface. The EJB container intercepts each call and transparently inserts additional functionality that provides added value to the caller. This additional functionality comprises life-cycle management, automatic transaction control, automatic persistence management (for entity beans), resource management, access control, remoting, load balancing, and fail-over management (with replication).

The central idea behind EJB and the whole point in using it is the added value from these implicit functions.

4. Enterprise JavaBeans™ (EJB) quick history

The initial hype around EJB claimed that EJB solved essentially all of the problems around all of the above aspects and did so with essentially no disadvantages. Which, of course, is just not true at all.

Rather, the main drawbacks of EJB are:

- The programmer no longer has full control over the above-mentioned characteristics, which sometimes leads to inefficiencies and/or awkward designs.
- Client calls to an EnterpriseBean are always remote calls and hence quite run-time expensive.
- The development of an EnterpriseBean is inconvenient, as it involves many files (home interface, remote interface, implementation class, standard deployment descriptor, application-server-specific deployment descriptor).
- The configuration and use of an EJB container is complex and full of pitfalls.
- Exposing EJB interfaces to application programmers through a Client API can impose dangerous impacts on system performance and robustness. This is because application programmers would then be bothered with the complexity of dealing with remote objects.

In younger times, partial countermeasures against many of these disadvantages have been introduced by the J2EE community:

- The J2EE BluePrints design patterns [4] describe how best to cope with the first, second, and last,
- The notion of local interface, introduced in EJB 2.0 solves the second for the case when the client is another EJB in the same container,
- Modern IDEs and CASE tools cope reasonably well with most of the third.

Since we were early adopters, however, we were usually too early for these developments and had to find our own solutions. The resulting archtectural evolution is described in the following sections.

5. Evolution phase 1: Naïveté

"Is it important? Then it's an EJB."

When EJB appeared, the hype and public perception essentially said "Just do it. EJB will solve your problems." When we started developing with EJB technology, we decided to follow just this approach, in order to see where it would work and where not.

Roughly speaking, in the first version of abaXX.components, each business service was a session bean and each business object – even any persistent object – was an entity bean.

The resulting software worked, but the runtime performance was rather poor, due to EJB-born brute-force remoting, transaction management, and locking overhead.

6. Evolution phase 2: Repair

"If we don't fix this, we're dead."

It turned out that in our typical web applications, say, for e-commerce, most of the operations were read-only accesses to many different entity beans during catalog browsing. But for retrieving, say, 20 entity beans with an EJB finder method, the early application servers would execute as many as 21 SQL queries in the database: one for obtaining the keys and for each bean. And instantiating and returning an entity bean is also a costly operation.

So we had to invent a remedy. It consisted of two pieces:

For every entity bean *Mybean*, we would introduce a corresponding normal (i.e. non-remote) Java class *MybeanData* with the same set of attributes. We called these objects *Lightweights*. The J2EE design patterns today call this idea *Value Objects* or *Transfer Objects*. Each EntityBean *Mybean* would have a method *getByValue()* for obtaining a *MybeanData* instance and a method *updateByValue(MybeanData)* for setting all its attributes from a single *MybeanData* with just one remote call.

For reading multiple records from the database in a single step for browsing (read-only) purposes, we created a simple and very efficient object-relational mapping framework called *Retrieve*. Based on a SQL select clause declared in each Lightweight class, Retrieve can obtain large sets of *MybeanData* objects from the database quickly. Selection and ordering criteria are encapsulated in *Filter* and *Sorter* classes, respectively, so that the business logic is kept completely free from SQL code.

Retrieve is similar to what the J2EE design patterns today call a *Fast Lane Reader*.

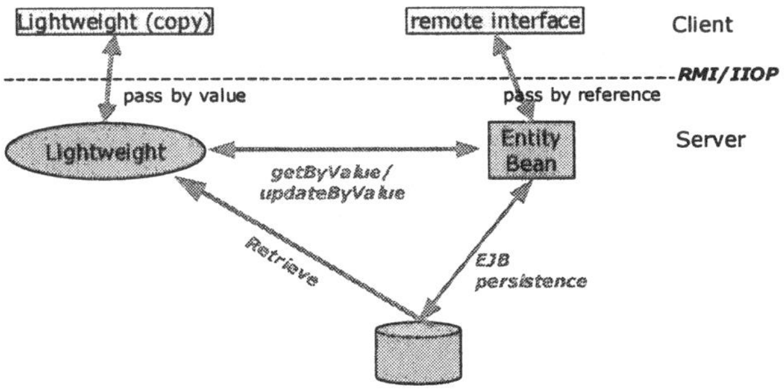

With these additions, it was possible to create reasonably efficient applications.

Meanwhile the hype around EJB split into two groups of people: Those who had not yet tried out the technology were still mesmerized. The others were somewhat sobered, invented Value Objects themselves or dropped using EntityBeans altogether.

With our two additions (and a few extensions such as a *Service Locator*, called *IContext*), we were sufficiently satisfied for a while and just took EJB for granted: There were plenty of EJBs in our software and it worked.

7. Evolution phase 3: Emancipation

"EJBs shouldn't be central at all."

However after a while it became more and more clear that the Value Objects were much more important for most of the application programmers most of the time compared to the EntityBeans themselves. So we turned the previous view of EJB use upside down and made the following changes to our architecture and APIs:

- We now considered the Lightweight to be the business object, rather than the EntityBean.
- Consequently, we now named the Lightweight *Mybean* (rather than *MybeanData*) and the EntityBean *MybeanEJB* (rather than *Mybean*) and stowed the EntityBeans away out of sight in separate subpackages.
- All business logic used Lightweight objects only, never EntityBeans.
- Access to EntityBeans was restricted to *Manager* classes. A Manager class provides explicit create-read-update-delete (CRUD) functionality for one or a few types of closely related business objects. Its implementation uses a SessionBean; for representing the business objects, its API reflects the respective Lightweight classes only; its implementation uses EntityBeans.
- The Manager class is not a SessionBean itself, it only uses a SessionBean for its core functionality.

This kind of Manager services and their implementation is a combination of both, *Session Facade* and *Business Delegate* patterns in the J2EE patterns catalog: a mechanism that decouples the EJB tier from its clients. The architecture has now effectively downgraded enterprise beans from the heart and soul of the architecture to a mere implementation mechanism.

By this time, the EJB hype had largely worn off. Some people now viewed EJB as an unnecessary and expensive luxury, others understood that it is well-suited for situations where strong scalability and availability is required and where transaction security is critical, such as in financial services. The latter group had begun to search for ways of using EJB in a selective manner.

8. Evolution phase 4: Independence

"Use EJB only if you really want to."

We searched, too, and found that given the previous changes, the rest of the way was not very long.

So far, we already had provided an EJB-free client API. Only those few programmers who needed to modify or extend one of our components would still see the EJBs (in the separate extension API).

The remaining step was to introduce what we now call EJB-on-demand[1]: Simply by setting a load-time configuration option, programmers can (at least for many of our components) decide on a service-by-service basis where EJBs are to be used and where a plain Java solution should be used instead. The latter does not have the added value gained from the management features of the EJB container, but also requires fewer resources and, if no EJB services are used at all, simplifies the infrastructure and its operation enormously.

In terms of the product implementation, this is relatively easy to achieve for the services: In EJB mode, the client API *Myservice* is implemented by a simple wrapper *RemoteMyservice* that delegates to the SessionBean *MyserviceEJB*, which in turn delegates to the core plain Java solution *LocalMyservice* (which does the actual work). In non-EJB mode, *Myservice* is directly implemented by *LocalMyservice*.

Which of these two options is active is hidden by the Service Locator *IContext*, which is called to instantiate a *Myservice* object and will return either a *LocalMyservice* or a *RemoteMyservice*. Obviously, this scheme can be

[1] This is a generalization of a notion introduced by Gartner Group as *dual topology* [1]: Application Servers should be offered in a variant for lightweight applications not using EJB as well as one for full-blown J2EE applications including EJBs. *EJB-on-demand* extends this idea to application components.

extended to cover still other possibilities than just an EJB versus a non-EJB implementation, as is exemplified by the figure shown below about our User Management Service (UMS) that implements the UserRegistry interface.

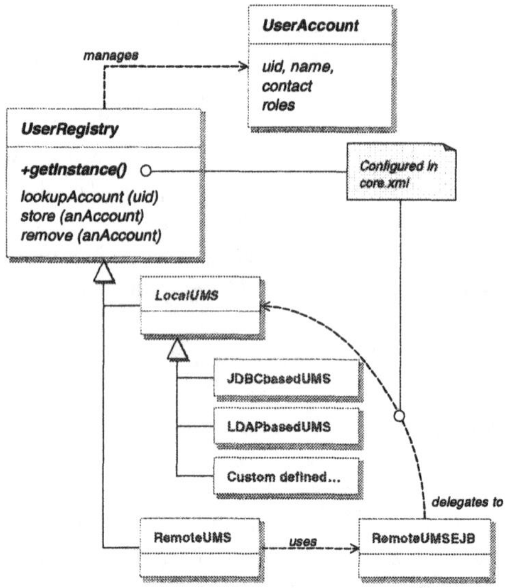

For Manager services, that is, if EntityBeans are involved, the EJB-less implementation requires a little more work: MyserviceEJB will then directly implement the service using EntityBeans, whereas LocalMyservice is a separate implementation using JDBC or whatever other persistence mechanism is to be used.

And the EJB hype? As of today, where the pros and cons of EJB are much better understood, many projects think quite hard about whether they should employ EJB or rather try to get by without it.

EJB-on-demand is a nice way out of this dilemma: One can build an application in such a way that it can start without EJB and be upgraded later, but largely without rework of any client code. And the external application components (if it's abaXX.components) can just be switched to EJB mode without any additional implementation work at all.

9. Conclusion

Here is a summary of the lessons we learned from the above during over 3 years of developing abaXX.components.

About following a hype: Following a technological hype (either with the masses or even ahead of the masses) may be viable, but not necessarily efficient. If we had taken the time to evaluate EJB more thoroughly before building the large number of components that we did, we could have gotten to where we are with less effort.

About developing an API-based software product: The most dangerous aspect of starting with a less-than-perfect architecture for a high-level API-based software product is backwards compatibility. There were 8 releases of abaXX.components so far, two of them not being backwards compatible to the one before. The first of these steps was relatively easy; we made it after just half a year, with only two customers involved. The recent second one was quite difficult, as our customers now have systems in operation that represent over 80 Million US$ of investments. We have managed to contain incompatible changes to a small number of places in the API and are providing a backwards compatibility add-on package, but we don't yet know how costly the migration of a large project solution really will be and whether our customers will do it.

About the EJB technology: After all we have done, we are still unsure whether we love or hate EJB technology. Some of the promises hold true: EJB and J2EE application servers are now a rock-solid foundation for business-critical, large-scale, transaction-intensive systems. On the other hand there are so many design flaws, omissions, oddities, and pitfalls in EJB that it is really hard to be enthusiastic about it [2]. One thing, however, we are sure about: If one is to build a suite of reusable application components based on EJB, it is a good idea to hide the EJB aspects of the implementation behind simple, non-EJB interfaces.

References

[1] Yefim Natis: *Application Server Scenarios: From Stovepipes to Services*, Gartner Research AV-14-5983, October 2001.

[2] Robin Sharp and Dinu Fancellu: *101 Damnations of EJB*, http://www.softwarereality.com/programming/ejb, February 2002.

[3] Sun Microsystems: *Enterprise JavaBeans 2.0 Final Specification*, September 2001.

[4] Sun Microsystems: *J2EE BluePrints Design Patterns*, http://java.sun.com/blueprints/patterns.

Quantifying the Value of Architecture Design Decisions: Lessons from the Field

Mike Moore
NASA Goddard Space Flight Center
mike.moore@nasa.gov

Rick Kazman,
Software Engineering Institute Carnegie Mellon University and *University of Hawaii*
kazman@sei.cmu.edu

Mark Klein
Software Engineering Institute, Carnegie Mellon University
mk@sei.cmu.edu

Jai Asundi
School of Management University of Texas, Dallas
asundi@utdallas.edu

Abstract

This paper outlines experiences with using economic criteria to make architecture design decisions. It briefly describes the CBAM (Cost Benefit Analysis Method) framework applied to estimate the value of architectural strategies in a NASA project, the ECS. This paper describes the practical difficulties and experiences in applying the method to a large real-world system. It concludes with some lessons learned from the experience.

1. Introduction

For the past three years we have been developing and road-testing a method for doing architecture-based economic analyses of software-intensive systems. We have called this method the CBAM (Cost Benefit Analysis Method). The method was first described in [6] and revisions have been described in [1], and [7]. The purpose of this paper is not to discuss the CBAM, but rather to discuss the lessons learned from applying it to a large real-world project over several years. We applied the CBAM to NASA's ECS project in two distinct phases of the project's development, and the results from these experiences have helped us improve the method. In this paper we outline our experiences in eliciting economic data from stakeholders and in analyzing and interpreting this data. We describe the changes made to the CBAM based on our successes and failures, and we describe the benefits that it brings to a large development effort.

2. The ECS Project

The ECS problem was framed as follows: we had a limited budget to maintain and enhance the current system. From a prior analysis, in this case an architecture evaluation using the ATAM (Architecture Tradeoff Analysis Method) [5], a large set of desirable changes to the system was elicited from the stakeholders of the system, resulting in a large set of ASs (Architectural Strategies). The problem facing us was to choose a (much) smaller subset of ASs for implementation. The CBAM was applied to the problem so that we could justify decisions based on the economic criterion of return on investment (ROI).

The CBAM begins with the assumption that the *business goals* of a system influence the architectural decisions made. For example, the choice of a tri-modular redundant server will be influenced by a business need for a highly reliable/available system that the system's stakeholders are presumably demanding. This AS will in turn influence various quality attributes of the system (such as performance, modifiability, availability, security etc.) These quality attributes (QAs) will in turn accrue benefit to the system as defined by the business goals. For example, the high availability server will result in $X worth of more business due to additional sales, or an unstable system will result in $Y worth of lost business per year, or $Z worth of lawsuits filed against the corporation each year.

Each architectural decision will also incur a cost. They can be considered to be software investments as described in [2] or more precisely, investments under uncertainty [3]. The aim of the CBAM was to maximize the ROI for the architecture design decisions and explore the possibility of embedded options within these decisions—options that are opened/closed due to the design choice being made. For example, the implementation of one particular architectural strategy could preclude the implementation of another.

2.1. Operationalizing the CBAM

Any simple description of the steps of a method glosses over many of the problems with actually *operationalizing* such a method. Creating a method that asked questions that stakeholders could actually answer, and imposing only small demands on the stakeholders (in terms of the amount of work that they had to do) turned out to be non-trivial.

0-7695-1877-X/03 $17.00 © 2003 IEEE

For example, within the original version of the CBAM, we assumed that the effects of the ASs on the QAs are additive. We also assumed that each QA has a weight proportional to its importance in the system and that it was possible to elicit these weights from stakeholders. To do this, we asked the stakeholders to individually rate each QA such that the sum of their scores was 100. Hence, by design, $\Sigma(QAScore_j) = 100$ and for all j, $QAScore_j >= 0$.

We then elicited from the stakeholders an estimate of the impact resulting from the application of each AS, in terms of how it affects each quality attribute of the system. This impact estimate was termed the "contribution score", $Contrib_{i,j}$ where this describes the impact of AS_i on QA_j. Based upon the *QAScore* and the *Contrib* score the total benefit of each AS was calculated as:

$$Benefit(AS_i) = \Sigma_j(Contrib_{i,j} \times QAscore_j)$$

The units of benefit are 'utils' and the return for a single AS (in units of utils/person-month) is calculated as:

$$Return(AS_i) = Benefit(AS_i)/Cost(AS_i)$$

This return score is relative to all other ASs and hence is only useful for rank ordering them. A relative scoring (such as a rank ordering) was sufficient for our investigations, since one of NASA's concerns was to decide how to spend its budget, by implementing the top *r* ASs.

3. The CBAM Experience

Using the above framework we conducted the initial CBAM exercise with three facilitators from the SEI (Software Engineering Institute) and seven stakeholders from the ECS project. For the initial exercise the facilitators spent 8 hours meeting with the stakeholders, spread over 2 days. The stakeholders also spent time on their own for rating the ASs and estimating the costs of the ASs.

Eight QAs were elicited (Maintainability, Operability, Relavailability, Scalability, Performance, User satisfaction, Flextensibility and Security). There were 58 distinct ASs put forth by the architect of the ECS. We estimated that we had the resources to implement only 6 to 10 of these ASs (depending on the specific costs of strategies chosen)!

In this exercise the stakeholders' responses were kept from each other to prevent undue influence of some stakeholders on the others. The concordance of the stakeholders on the QA ratings was 0.838 which reflects a high degree of agreement. On the other hand the AS contribution ratings varied considerably. The concordance rating here was only 0.326 which indicates a low level of agreement regarding the effects of the AS on the respective QAs. This experience taught us a number of important lessons about operationalizing the CBAM.

3.1. Dealing with large numbers of ASs

The experience taught us that we needed to explicitly compare all the stakeholders' judgments to understand, and to further probe, areas where they differed. Such differences of judgment could be interpreted in two ways:

1. They are true differences of opinion among the stakeholders, and hence represent uncertainty, or

2. They are based on differing understanding of the AS and QA, and hence the stakeholders are actually rating different things.

Differences of the second kind need to be eradicated as much as possible. But how to do this? Karlsonn and Ryan [4] describe the Analytical Hierarchy Process for rank ordering requirements. This method, though effective, is quite cumbersome for dealing with a large number of strategies each of which affect multiple quality attributes. With the 58 ASs that we had in the ECS study, this would mean making 1653 comparisons! Even if we could prune the number of ASs to 25, it would mean 300 comparisons which is still quite large and for more time consuming than the stakeholders would put up with.

3.2. Short attention spans

Stakeholders typically have very short attention spans and tolerances for new "methods". The stakeholders are typically very busy and their time working on elicitation exercise is highly valued. We needed to be able to show them the benefits of the exercise itself and justify their time spent on it. Thus, when eliciting information, we had to be realistic about the time that it will take the stakeholders to complete any exercise and must strive to keep this time to a minimum.

3.3. The "Interpretation" problem

In dealing with a multi-attribute decision problem such as ours, it is theoretically convenient to view QAs like performance, security, availability etc. as attribute dimensions that we can reason about and for which we can choose desirable or undesirable levels. However, the notion of a QA is an abstract concept. In our experience, despite providing precise definitions for the QAs, the stakeholders showed considerable subjectivity in their interpretations of the QAs. Furthermore, from one context to another (for example, from one scenario to another) the interpretation of the QA could change, thus exacerbating the "interpretation" problem.

3.4. Stakeholders "game" the system

Stakeholders, once they realize how the analysis is going to be carried out will try to "game" the system. They might do this by providing favorable values for their favorite scenario or AS. This is typically done to further some hidden agenda. This tendency can mitigated by making the elicitation procedure open to discussion and by making the recorded values arise from *consensus*, rather than a voting procedure. This further has the benefit that it reduces the time to dispel misunderstandings and the resultant variance in scores. Though consensus-based valuation runs the risk of the values being unduly influenced by a few powerful personalities, it is the duty of the project manager to ensure that the right personnel have appropriate influence in the proceedings. This, in turn, ensures that the right stakeholders have appropriate influence on the final value recorded.

3.5. Knowing the state of the system

Though it seemed obvious to us that stakeholders would be able to quantify the effect of a change to their system, we found that these judgments were highly variable. We discovered that this was due to considerable variation among the stakeholders in their understanding of the *current* state of the system. It is typical in large systems that stakeholders will be experts only in their particular subsystem and will be only partially aware of the other subsystems. As a consequence they are not fully capable of characterizing the current state of the system and hence the precise effect of a particular change. Thus, characterizing the current state of the system is an important exercise before trying to measure the effect of a change.

3.6. The dialogue is important

What are the important benefits from the CBAM exercise? We assumed, when we embarked on the exercise, that the most important benefit was having a disciplined process that would result in a well-reasoned choice of ASs for NASA to pursue. However, it turns out that just as important was the dialogue and the discussion that the method fosters amongst the stakeholders. This dialogue forces them to discuss the various alternative strategies in terms of their utilities, and this discussion results in greater understanding of the scenarios that motivate the ASs, the utility of various response levels for these scenarios, and the ASs themselves. These discussions lead to a better understanding of how particular scenarios are important or how some set of ASs affect a particular QA. In our experience this exchange of ideas leads to results that better appeal to intuition.

4. CBAM Version 2

Armed with the experience of the first attempt at quantifying the benefit information we have developed a new version of the CBAM, described in [7]. The salient features of CBAM 2 are:

• It is now an *iterative* procedure where we refine our understanding of the system's benefits via the elicitation of progressively more information (scenarios, ASs, and utility levels). This iterative process helps the stakeholders understand the method's calculations as well as giving them preliminary results so that they see the benefit of performing the exercise. The steps of the CBAM are run in iterations. Each iteration progressively adds information via additional elicitation from the stakeholders. For example after the initial iteration, follow-on iterations add estimates of risk and uncertainty and correlations among the ASs.

• We have introduced scenarios to represent each of the QAs. Instead of talking about the QA of "relavailability", for example, we introduce a specific scenario that addresses the QA, e.g. "Reduce data distribution failures that result in hung distribution requests requiring manual intervention." This helps in providing a concrete context for the stakeholders to understand the impact of an AS.

• We now elicit the current state of the system, to provide all stakeholders with a common basis of understanding to inform their decision-making.

• Perhaps most important, we now explicitly determine the sensitivity of Utility to each QA. Rather than elicit a single value for an AS's effect on a QA, we ask the stakeholders to give a utility value for several different response measures (e.g. for the data distribution scenario above, the stakeholders might give {response measure, utility value} pairs of {10% hung, 10}, {5% hung, 80}, {1% hung, 95}, and {0% hung, 100}). These sets of pairs define Utility-QA level *curves*. These curves aid the stakeholders in understanding how utility varies with changing QA responses, and hence how the value of the system changes as different response levels are achieved.

An example of such a graph is shown in Figure 1. As we see in the graph on the left, we have elicited the QA response levels for the worst-case (W), Best case (B), Current (C) and Desired (D) cases. The respective utility values for these response levels are elicited. Depending on the AS chosen, the expected case (E) is plotted on the curve.

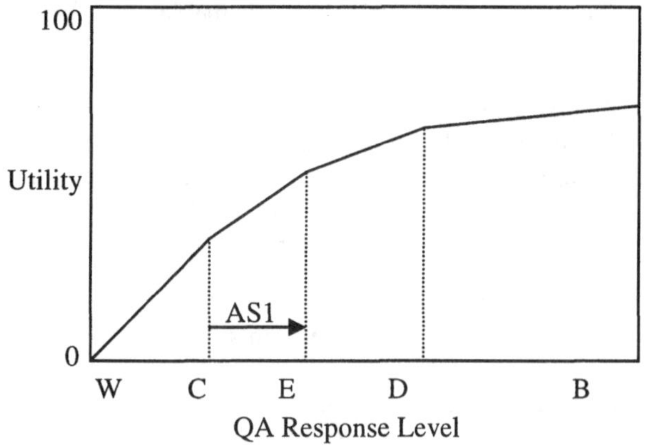

Figure 1. A QA Response/Utility Curve

5. Applying CBAM 2

We now turn to an application of the CBAM to a real-world system as an example of the method in action. The Earth Observing System is a constellation of NASA satellites that gathers data about the Earth for the U. S. Global Change Research Program and other scientific communities worldwide. The Earth Observing System Data Information System (EOSDIS) Core System (ECS) collects data from various satellite downlink stations for further processing. The mission of the ECS is to process the data into higher-form information and make it available in searchable form to scientists world-wide.

The ECS problem was framed as follows: management had a limited budget to maintain and enhance the system. From a prior ATAM analysis [5] a set of desired changes to the system was elicited from the stakeholders, resulting in a large set of ASs. The problem facing management was to choose a (much) smaller subset of ASs for implementation, as only 10-20% of what was being proposed could actually be funded. Management used the CBAM to help make a rational decision based on the economic criterion of return on investment.

5.1. Collate Scenarios

We began by eliciting a set of scenarios from the assembled stakeholders. Because the ECS stakeholders had previously been used ATAM, this step was relatively straightforward for them. A subset of the raw scenarios put forward by the stakeholders were as shown in Table 1. Note that the scenarios are not yet all well formed and some do not even have defined responses.

5.2. Refine and Prioritize Scenarios

These scenarios were then refined, paying particular attention to precisely specifying their stimulus/response measures. The worst, current case, desired, and best case response goals for each scenario were elicited. Having the team of stakeholders perform this refinement together helped drive out any differences in interpretation of the scenarios. It also helped the team members reach a common understanding of the current system state.

TABLE 1. Collected Scenarios

Scenario	Scenario Description
1	Reduce data distribution failures that result in hung distribution requests requiring manual intervention.
2	Reduce data distribution failures that result in lost distribution requests.
3	Reduce the number of orders that fail on the order submission process.
4	Reduce order failures that result in hung orders that require manual intervention.
5	Reduce order failures that result in lost orders.

Based on this representation of the scenarios, the stakeholder team proceeded to vote. This close-knit group chose to discuss each scenario and arrive at a determination of its weight via consensus. The votes allocated to the entire set of scenarios were constrained to total 100, as shown in Table 2. Although the stakeholders were not constrained to make the votes multiples of 5, they felt that this was a reasonable resolution, and that more precision in the votes was not needed and could not be justified. It also helped the team quickly reach consensus on the relative importance of the scnearios.

TABLE 2. Refined Scenarios with Votes

Sce-		Response Goals			
nario	Votes	Worst	Current	Desired	Best
1	10	10% hung	5% hung	1% hung	0% hung
2	15	> 5% lost	<1% lost	0% lost	0% lost
3	15	10% fail	5% fail	1% fail	0% fail
4	10	10% hung	5% hung	1% hung	0% hung
5	15	10% lost	<1% lost	0% lost	0% lost

5.3. Assign Utility

In this step the utility for each scenario was determined by the stakeholders, again by a consensus process. A utility score of 0 represents no utility; a score of 100 represents the most utility possible. The results of this process are given in Table 3. This step proved to be one of the most valuable because it helped the team quickly reach a consensus on how they thought the system should evolve.

TABLE 3. Adding Votes and Utility Scores

Scenario	Votes	Utility Scores			
		Worst	Current	Desired	Best
1	10	10	80	95	100
2	15	0	70	100	100
3	15	25	70	100	100
4	10	10	80	95	100
5	15	0	70	100	100

5.4. Develop ASs for Scenarios and Elicit Expected Response Levels

Based upon the requirements implied by the above scenarios, a set of 10 ASs was developed by the ECS architects. Recall that an AS may affect more than one scenario. To account for these complex relationships, we determined the expected quality attribute response level that each AS was predicted to achieve with respect to *each* relevant scenario. A subset of the ASs, along with the determination of the scenarios that they address is shown in Table 4. For each AS/scenario pair, the response levels that the AS is expected to achieve with respect to that scenario is shown (along with the current response, for comparison purposes).

TABLE 4. Architectural Strategies and Scenarios Addressed

AS	AS Name	Scenarios Affected	Current Response	Expected Response
1	Order persis tence	3	5% fail	2% Fail
		5	<1% lost	0% lost
4	Order seg-mentation	4	5% hung	2% hung
5	Order re-assignment	1	5% hung	2% hung
6	Order retry	4	5% hung	3% hung
7	Forced order completion	1	5% hung	3% hung

5.5. Determine Expected Utility and ROI

Once the expected response level of each AS with respect to a set of scenarios was characterized, we could calculate the *utility* of this expected response level. To do this we consulted the utility scores for each scenario's worst, current, desired, and best responses for all of the affected attributes. Using these scores we could interpolate the utility of the expected response levels for the AS/scenario pair. Using the votes from Table 2 as weights and the delta benefit scores, a total benefit for each AS could now be calculated.

To complete the analysis, a cost estimate for each AS was done, and based on these a return on investment was calculated for each architectural strategy. Using the ROI, we are then able to rank each of the architectural strategies. This is shown in Table 5. Note that these ranks differ from the AS numbers (which were the stakeholders' intuitive initial rankings of the ASs). For example, AS 7 has the third highest rank. If the stakeholders were using intuition alone they may well have overlooked this AS. This is evidence of the usefulness of a *method*, as opposed to ad hoc design decision making.

TABLE 5. ROI of Architectural Strategies

AS	Cost	Total AS Benefit	AS ROI	AS Rank
1	1200	950	0.79	1
4	200	100	0.5	3
5	400	120	0.3	7
6	200	50	0.25	8
7	200	70	0.35	6

5.6 Iteration II

In the second iteration, a number of important risk factors were discussed by the team that were not given significant consideration in iteration I, due to time constraints (and the triage focus of iteration I). Each risk pertained to one or more of the ASs that had been previously proposed. For each risk factor its probability of occurrence, the impact that it would have if it did occur, and any mitigation strategy were discussed and assessed.

The outcomes of the risks as well as the probabilities of their occurence were elicited in iteration II. Based on these elicited values expected cost and benefit ranges were determined. (Note that during iteration I we had *single values* for cost and benefit; now we have ranges.) The min and max values of these ranges are interpreted as end points of confidence intervals. These probability functions allowed us to produce a matrix that shows the confidence that we have in the rank orderings (from Table 5) given the additional information that we have collected regarding the uncertainties. This matrix is shown in Table 6.

TABLE 6. Probability that AS(row) > AS (column)

	AS1	AS4	AS5	AS6	AS7
AS1	0.5	0.64	0.82	0.94	0.69
AS4	0.36	0.5	0.89	0.99	0.6
AS5	0.18	0.11	0.5	0.89	0.05
AS6	0.06	0.01	0.11	0.5	0
AS7	0.31	0.4	0.95	1	0.5

Management, viewing these rankings and their associated probability values, used this information in some cases to commit to certain ASs, and in other cases to get better estimates of costs and benefits of two attractive alternatives that were too close to differentiate (i.e. when the probability that one is greater than the other is between 0.4 and 0.6).

5.7. Results

The most obvious results of the CBAM were an ordering of architectural strategies based upon their predicted ROI and a probability that shows the confidence in this position. But the benefits of the CBAM extend far beyond the qualitative outcomes. There have been palpable social and cultural benefits as well. The CBAM process provided a great deal of structure to what was largely unstructured discussions where requirements and architectural strategies and personal opinions are freely mixed together, and where stimuli and response goals are not clearly articulated. The CBAM process forced our stakeholders to make their scenarios clear in advance, to assign utility levels to specific response goals, and to prioritize scenarios based on the resulting determination of utility. The CBAM forced our stakeholders to address risks and their resulting effects explicitly, rather than simply stating an "unease" with a particular technical direction.

6. Conclusions

Elicitation of information from real world projects is difficult. As researchers we are charged with creating methods that are usable, by real-world engineers in real projects. These methods need to produce useful results quickly, and at a reasonable "price", in terms of the time of the stakeholders. As we have discovered in our experiences with the CBAM, solving a problem in theory and in practice are very different. We have already modified the CBAM considerably as a result of the two applications of this method to the ECS.

The new version of the CBAM is an iterative elicitation process combined with a decision analysis framework. It incorporates scenarios to represent the various QAs. The stakeholders explore the decision space by eliciting Utility-QA response level curves to understand how the system's utility varies with changing attributes. The consensus basis of the method allows for active discussion and clarification amongst the stakeholders. The traceability of the design decision permits updating and continuous improvement of the design process over time.

In spite of the practical difficulties in running such methods, we believe that the application of economic techniques is inherently better than the ad-hoc approaches that projects (even quite sophisticated projects) employ today. We cannot prove the optimality of our techniques Because we use expert judgments our techniques may not be optimal but they are at least satisficing. Our experience with the CBAM tells us that giving people appropriate tools with which to frame and structure their discussion and their decision making is an enormous benefit to the development of a software system.

7. References

[1] J. Asundi, R. Kazman and M. Klein, "Using Economic Considerations to Choose Amongst Architecture Design Alternatives", CMU/SEI-2001-TR-035, SEI, Carnegie Mellon University, 2001.

[2] B. Boehm, *Software Engineering Economics*, Prentice Hall, 1981.

[3] A. Dixit, R. S. Pindyck, *Investment Under Uncertainty*, Princeton University Press, New Jersey, 1994.

[4] J. Karlsson, K. Ryan, "A Cost-Value Approach for Prioritizing Requirements", *IEEE Computer*, September/ October 1997.

[5] R. Kazman, M. Barbacci, M. Klein, S. J. Carriere, S. G. Woods, "Experience with Performing Architecture Tradeoff Analysis", *Proceedings of the ICSE 21*, Los Angeles, CA, May 1999, 54-63.

[6] R. Kazman, J. Asundi, M. Klein, "Quantifying the Costs and Benefits of Architectural Decisions", *Proceedings of the ICSE 23*, Toronto, Canada, May 2001, 297-306.

[7] R. Kazman, J. Asundi, M. Klein, "Making Architecture Design Decisions: An Economic Approach", CMU/SEI-2002-TR-035, SEI, Carnegie Mellon University, 2002.

Experience Reports

Testing and Fault Correction

Assessing Test-Driven Development at IBM

E. Michael Maximilien
IBM Corp. and NCSU
5505 Six Forks Road
Raleigh, NC 27609

maxim@us.ibm.com

Laurie Williams
North Carolina State University
Department of Computer Science
Raleigh, NC 27695-8207

williams@csc.ncsu.edu

Abstract

In a software development group of IBM Retail Store Solutions, we built a non-trivial software system based on a stable standard specification using a disciplined, rigorous unit testing and build approach based on the test-driven development (TDD) practice. Using this practice, we reduced our defect rate by about 50 percent compared to a similar system that was built using an ad-hoc unit testing approach. The project completed on time with minimal development productivity impact. Additionally, the suite of automated unit test cases created via TDD is a reusable and extendable asset that will continue to improve quality over the lifetime of the software system. The test suite will be the basis for quality checks and will serve as a quality contract between all members of the team.

1 Introduction

IBM Retail Store Solutions (RSS) is located primarily in Raleigh, North Carolina. As one of the founding members of the Java for Point of Sale (JavaPOS) specification, IBM participated in the creation of the standard and specification with Sun, NCR and Epson. The JavaPOS specification defines a set of JavaBeans (software services) to allow access to point of sale (POS) devices (e.g. printers, cash drawers, magnetic stripe readers, bar code readers or scanners) in Java applications. The specification defines a set of properties, methods, and events applicable for each device class and the semantic model for the behavior of the devices. Over the past three years, the RSS division has implemented the JavaPOS specification for a wide array of devices on various operating systems (e.g. Windows, Linux, and IBM's own retail operating system 4690-OS[1]).

Though the development team has a broad experience with the JavaPOS[2] specification and the POS devices, we have noticed that for each revision of the deliverable, the defect rate after Functional Verification Test (FVT) was not being reduced as we had expected. As a result, the development and management teams were open to new approaches to development. We proposed a development practice based on the eXtreme Programming (XP) [1] test-driven development (TDD) [2] approach. With TDD, all major public classes of the system have a corresponding unit test class to test the public interface, that is, the contract of that class [8] with other classes (e.g. parameters to method, semantics of method, pre- and post-conditions to method). This practice was used by the new JavaPOS[3] development and test teams. The team was made up of nine full-time engineers. Five of the engineers were located in Raleigh (including the team lead); four were located in Guadalajara, Mexico. Additionally, part-time resources for project management and for performance were dedicated to the team.

In this paper, we examine the efficacy of the TDD approach, to alleviating the recurrent quality and testing problems, of the new JavaPOS project. The remainder of this paper is organized as follows. Section 2 provides an overview of traditional and TDD unit testing techniques. Section 3 discusses our view of expected gains and business risks upon transitioning to TDD. Section 4 discusses our experiences with TDD in our software development organization. Section 5 presents our results and lessons learned. Finally, Section 6 summarizes our findings and future work.

2 Unit Testing

[1] http://www2.clearlake.ibm.com/store/support/html/driver.htm

[2] IBM, NCR Epson and Sun http://javapos.com

[3] We use "new JavaPOS" for the JavaPOS release where we used the TDD development process. JavaPOS Legacy is the moniker we use for the previous releases.

0-7695-1877-X/03 $17.00 © 2003 IEEE

This section provides an overview of traditional unit testing and the emerging test-driven development practice.

2.1 Prior Unit Test Approaches

The prior approach to unit testing at IBM RSS was an ad-hoc approach. The developer coded a prototype of the important classes and then created a design via UML class and sequence diagrams [6]. We define *important classes* to be utility classes, classes which collaborate with other classes, and classes that are expected to be reused. This design was then followed by an implementation stage that sometimes caused design changes, and thus some iteration between the design and coding phases. Real unit testing then followed as a post-coding activity. One of the following unit test approaches was chosen:

- After enough coding was done, an interactive tool was created by the developer that permitted the execution of the important classes.
- Unit testing was executed using an interactive scripting language or tool, such as jython[4], which allows manual interactive exercising of the classes by creating objects and calling their methods.
- Unit testing was done by the creation of independent ad-hoc driver classes that test specific important classes or portions of the system which have clear external interfaces.

In all cases, the unit test process was not disciplined and was done as an afterthought. More often than not, no unit tests were created, especially when the schedule was tight, the developer got side tracked with problems from previous projects, or when new requirements that were not clearly understood surfaced. Most of the unit tests developed were also thrown away and not executed during the FVT phase or when a new release of the software was developed.

2.2 Test-Driven Development

With TDD, before writing implementation code, the developer writes automated unit test cases for the new functionality they are about to implement. After writing test cases that generally will not even compile, the developers write implementation code to pass these test cases. The developer writes a few test cases, implements the code, writes a few test cases, implements the code, and so on. The work is kept within the developer's intellectual control because he or she is continuously making small design and implementation decisions and increasing functionality at a relatively consistent rate. New functionality is not considered properly implemented unless these new unit test cases and every other unit test case written for the code base run properly.

As an example of how the unit tests are structured is to consider a typical method that takes one input parameter, returns an output value, and could throw an exception. Such a method would then have a unit test for (1) a valid parameter value which expects a valid return and (2) an invalid value causing appropriate exception; boundary values are typically selected. The unit test method could be longer than the method itself. Often the unit tests are not exhaustive but rather test the typical expected behavior with valid parameters and a few negative paths. Furthermore, additional unit test methods are sometimes added for each method when its behavior is dependent on the object being in a particular state. In these cases, the unit test starts with the correct method calls that put the object in the correct state.

Some professed benefits to TDD are discussed below:

- In any process, there exists a gap between decision (design developed) and feedback (functionality and performance obtained by implementing that design). The success of TDD can be attributed to reducing that gap, as the fine granular test-then-code cycle gives constant feedback to the developer. An often-cited tenet of software engineering, in concert with the "Cost of Change" [3], is that the longer a defect remains in a software system the more difficult and costly it is to remove. With TDD, defects are identified very quickly and the source of the defect is more easily determined.
- TDD entices programmers to write code that is automatically testable, such as having functions/methods returning a value, which can be checked against expected results. Benefits of automated testing include the following: (1) production of a reliable system, (2) improvement of the quality of the test effort, (3) reduction of the test effort and (4) minimization of the schedule [5].
- The TDD test cases create a thorough regression test bed. By continuously running these automated test cases, one can easily identify if a new change breaks anything in the existing system. This test bed should also allow smooth integration of new functionality into the code base.

With XP, developers do little or no up-front design before embarking in tight TDD cycles consisting of test case generation followed by code implementation. However, many of the benefits listed above can be realized in essentially any development process simply by shifting from *unit test <u>after</u> implementing* to *unit test <u>before</u> implementing*.

[4] http://www.jython.org

3 Assessing Expected Gains and Risks

In our past experiences, the ad-hoc approach to unit testing usually leads to last minute or even no testing at all. Therefore, when we set out to build the new implementation of the JavaPOS services, the management team was open to a new unit testing practice as long as we could articulate our expected long term advantages. Since this was the first time that IBM RSS had taken such an approach to software development, there were many unknowns and questions that the management and development teams wanted answered:

- *Defect Rate.* How will this rigorous approach affect the defect rate in the short term (current release) and the longer term (future releases)?
- *Productivity.* What is the impact to developer productivity (lines of code (LOC) per person-month)?
- *Test Frequency.* What will be the ratio of interactive vs. automated tests? How often will each of these types of test be run?
- *Design.* Does the use of the TDD practice yield systems that have a more robust design? We assess the robustness of design by examining the ease of handling late requirements and supporting new devices and services.
- *Integration.* Does TDD and its resulting automated regression test assets allow for smoother code integration?

Many in the development and management team were concerned that this rigorous approach would impact productivity so much that we would not be able to keep our schedule dates. Further, there was some resistance from the developers at first, since many were not only new to TDD but also some were somewhat unfamiliar with Java. All but two of the nine full-time developers were novices to the JavaPOS specification and the targeted POS devices. The domain knowledge of the developers had to be built during the design and development phases.

To alleviate the productivity concerns, we decided to be very careful in the scheduling phase. Since we had an existing similar system, we decided to measure the LOC of the existing system and to extrapolate and predict the LOC of the new system. We used an average productivity rate of 400 LOC per person-month as per the finding of an internal audit of our process by an IBM consultant. This productivity rate was determined to be justified for our development team by studying past historical data. This rate included time for design, unit testing, and code implementation. This rate is also appropriate for the type of software that we develop in which essential money [4] is at risk.

4 IBM RSS Experiences

In the past, unit test was usually an afterthought after code had been developed and was *working*. With TDD, test cases are developed up front as a means to reduce ambiguity and to validate the requirements, which for the JavaPOS comes in the form of a full detail standard specification. We found that such up-front testing drives a good understanding of the requirements and an up-front design. In XP projects, such up-front testing proceeds without any "big design up front," commonly referred to as BDUF [1]. However in our system, the requirements were stable, and we chose to do up-front design via UML class and sequence diagrams. This design activity was interspersed with the up-front unit test creation.

After creating a "spike" [1] of the system by implementing an end-to-end service for one device, each logical portion of the system was layered and completely designed using UML class and sequence diagrams. For each important class, we enforced complete unit testing. We define *complete testing* as ensuring that the public interface and semantics (the behavior of the method as defined in the JavaPOS specification) of each method were tested utilizing the JUnit[5] unit testing framework. For each public class, we had an associated public test class; for each public method in the class we had an associated public test method in the corresponding unit test class. Our goal was to achieve 80 percent of the important classes covered by <u>automated</u> unit testing. By automated we mean requiring no human interaction and thus unit test that can be batched and executed automatically. Each design document included a unit test section that listed all important classes and the public methods that would be tested. Some unit tests would also contain methods that tested particular variations on behavior, e.g. the printer has an asynchronous printing capability and the regular print methods behave differently in synchronous vs. asynchronous mode.

To guarantee that all unit tests would be run by all members of the team, we decided to set up automated build and test systems both locally (in Raleigh) and remotely (in Guadalajara). Daily, these systems would extract all the code from the library build and run all the unit tests. The Apache ANT[6] build tool was used. After each automated build/test run, an email was sent to all members of the teams listing all the tests that successfully ran and any errors found. This automated build and test served us as a daily integration and validation for the team. At first this build test was run multiple times a day locally and remotely. Eventually, we decided to alternate the build between locations and to only run the build tests once a

[5] http://junit.org

[6] Apache Software Foundation http://www.apache.org/jakarta/ant

day. Figure 1 summarizes the development and test process used by the team.

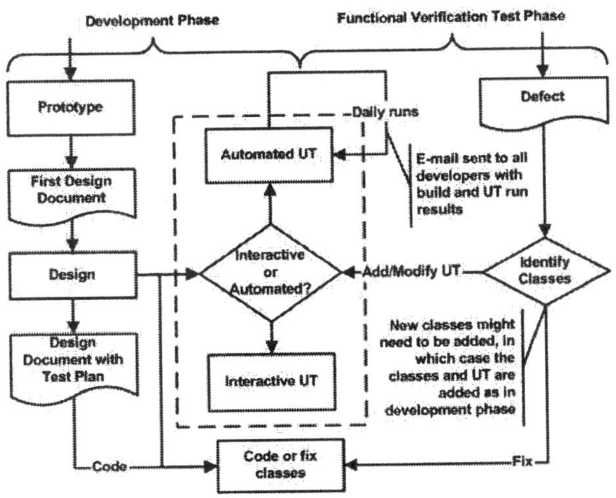

Figure 1: Summary of development and test process (UT = Unit Test)

For every project at IBM RSS, various metrics are collected during the FVT phase to keep track of the test progress and to predict the start of regression and the end of the test. We define the start of regression as the date when 100% of the FVT tests have been attempted. (This does not imply that the defects from these attempted tests are all resolved.) We predict the number of new and changed lines of code in the project and the number of total defects that will be found during the FVT based on historical data. From these predictions, a defect and test progression curve is calculated with weekly points that forecast the number of executed tests cases and the expected number of defects for each week of the project. For the new JavaPOS project, we entered test with 71.4 KLOC of new code and 34 KLOC of JUnit code; the total predicted defects for our process was 286 defects or 4 errors/KLOC. Generally, new development projects within RSS are estimated at 8 errors/KLOC; the test team demonstrated their confidence in the TDD approach by utilizing a 50% reduction in their estimate.

Another set of data that we collected during the development phase is the number of KLOC from all different modules (source and test code) and the number of JUnit tests for each module. For approximately 71 KLOC, we wrote approximately 2390 automated unit test cases. Additionally, over 100 automated JUnit performance test cases were written.

The new JavaPOS team experienced approximately a 50% reduction in defect density in FVT. Figure 2 displays the defect density for a comparable JavaPOS legacy implementation that was recently updated; TDD was not used. On this project, the realized defect density was consistently higher than the projected density and averaged 7.0 errors/KLOC. The development and test teams for this legacy project were fully experienced with the specification, code and devices (this is the third release of that project). Comparatively, Figure 3 displays the defect density for the relatively inexperienced new JavaPOS team that employed the TDD practice. Our actual defect density averaged 3.7 errors/KLOC. We attribute this quality increase to the use of the TDD practice.

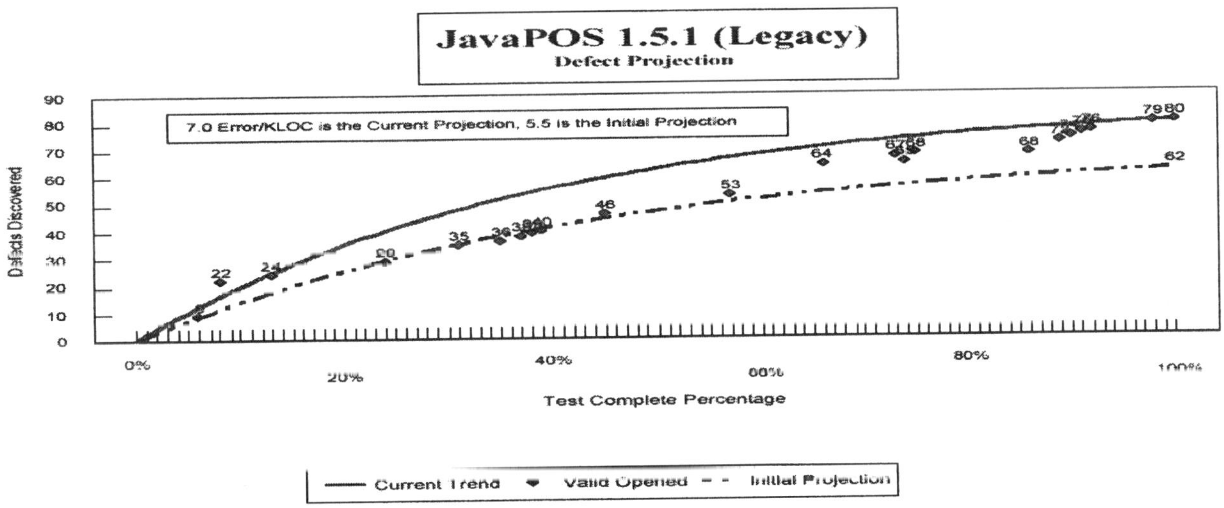

Figure 2: FVT Defect Projection - Ad-Hoc Testing Project

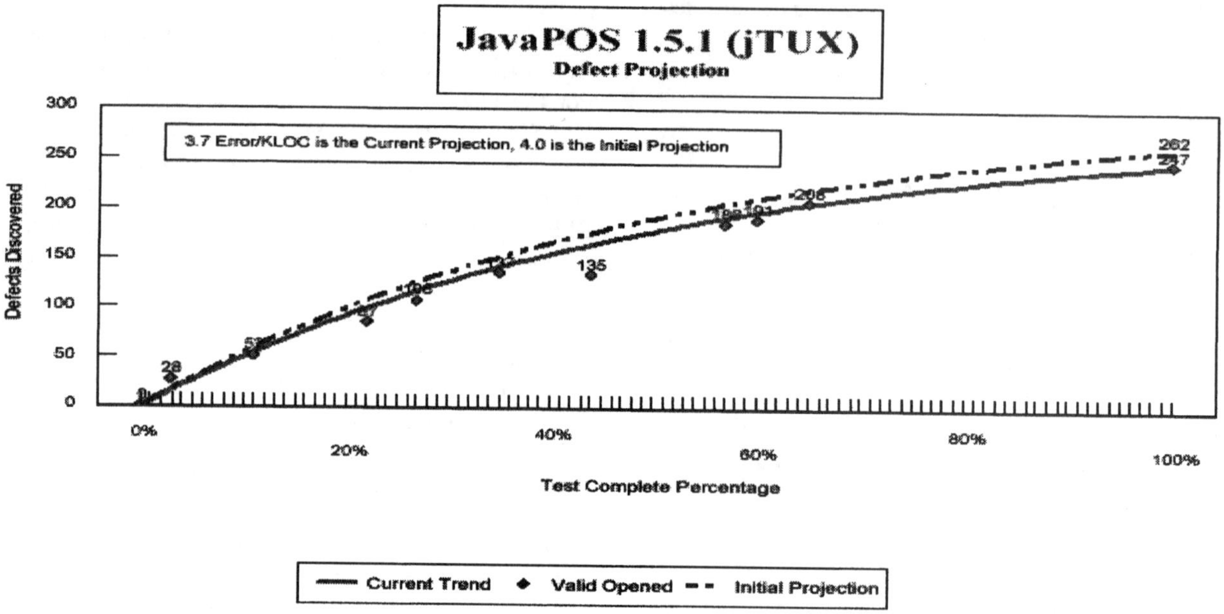

Figure 3: FVT Defect Projection - TDD Project

5 Results and Lessons Learned

In this section, we first share the business results from our adoption of TDD. Next, we share our lessons and suggestions for team transitioning to TDD. Our business results are now discussed:

- *Defect Rate.* With TDD, unit testing actually happens. In our prior approaches, testing was an afterthought. With TDD, unit testing is an integral part of code development. As a result, we achieved a dramatic 50% improvement in the FVT defect rate of our system.
- *Productivity.* Because the project is still in the final phases of regression test, we cannot compute exact productivity numbers. However, we know the project is on schedule. We expect our productivity numbers to be at or slightly below the 400 LOC/person-month estimate. Other studies have also found a slight decrease in developer productivity when employing the TDD practice [7, 9]. We also must attribute some credit toward our productivity to the new use of Microsoft Project Central[7], which many believe has improved our project management practices and kept the developers consistent about making visible progress on their tasks.
- *Test Frequency.* We wrote approximately 2500 automated tests and 400 interactive tests. Eighty-six percent of the tests were automated, exceeding our 80% target. The interactive tests were rarely run; the automated tests were run daily.
- *Design.* We believe that the TDD practice aided us in producing a product that would more easily incorporate late changes. A couple of devices (albeit, not overly complex devices) were added to the product about two-thirds of the way through the schedule.
- *Integration.* In the past, we only integrated code into the product once we were close to FVT. The daily integration certainly saved us from late integration problems. The success (or failure) of the daily integration served as the heart beat of the project and minimized risk because problems surfaced much earlier.
- *Morale.* The developers are very positive about the TDD practice and have continued its use.

Additionally we have gained experiences with transitioning to TDD we wish to share with other teams. We list these in order of importance.

- Start the TDD from the beginning of project. Set the expectation that team members that fervently apply the unit test paradigm may initially appear less productive or frustrated at the time it takes to create the unit tests. Assure them that the practice will have ultimately minimal impact to their productivity.
- For a team new to TDD, introduce automated build test integration towards the second third of the

[7] http://www.microsoft.com/office/project/default.asp

development phase—not too early but not too late. If this is a brand new project, adding the automated build test towards the second third of the development schedule allows the team adjusts to and become familiar with TDD. Prior to the automated build test integration, each developer should run all the test cases on their own machine.

- Convince the development team to add new tests every time a problem is found, no matter when the problem is found. Thus, at least one new test should confirm the presence of and removal of each valid, opened defect. By doing so, the unit test suites improve during the development and test phases. This part of the process needs to be communicated early and enforced by reminders and monitoring of unit test count.
- Get the test team involved and knowledgeable about the TDD approach. The test team should not accept new development release if the unit tests are failing.
- Hold a thorough review of an initial unit test plan, setting an ambitious goal of having the greatest number of automated tests, since automated tests can be easily integrated and run automatically without necessitating human intervention. We used 80% automated tests as a minimum goal. We cannot overemphasize the importance of constantly running in a daily automatic build; tests run should become the heartbeat of the system as well as a means to track progress of the development. This also gives a level of confidence to the team when new features are added. If new classes and tests are added and the next build test is successful, the team can have a higher confidence in the change.
- Encourage fast unit test execution and efficient unit test design. Test execution speed is very important since when all tests are integrated the complete execution can become quite long for a decent project and constant test execution. Results are important early and often, to provide feedback on the current state of the system. Further, the faster the execution of the tests the more likely developers themselves will run the tests without waiting for the automated build tests results.
- Take all opportunities to encourage development team to add unit tests to their code. This can be done by monitoring which subsystems have more unit tests relative to how big that subsystem is and acknowledging the developer of the subsystem.

6 Summary and Future Work

The new JavaPOS development team in the IBM Retail Store Solutions organization transitioned from an ad-hoc to a TDD unit testing practice. Through the introduction of this practice the relatively inexperienced team realized about 50% reduction in FVT defect density when compared with an experienced team who used an ad-hoc testing approach for a similar product. They achieved these results with minimal impact to developer productivity. Additionally, the suite of automated unit test cases created via TDD is a reusable and extendable asset that will continue to improve quality over the lifetime of the software system. The test suite will also be the basis for quality checks and will serve as a quality contract between all members of the team.

7 Acknowledgements

We would like to thank the Raleigh and Guadalajara teams for an outstanding job executing this new process and for their trust that this new process of up-front unit testing would pay off. The results and actual execution of the ideas came from their hard work. We especially acknowledge Mike Hyde and Dale Heeks from the FVT team for creating Figures 2 and 3. We also want to thank the IBM RSS management teams for their willingness to try a new approach to development without prior data on whether this would be effective or not. We also thank the NCSU Software Engineering reading group for their comments and review of initial drafts of this paper. Finally, we want to acknowledge Kent Beck for devising and documenting the TDD approach and for co-authoring the JUnit testing framework.

8 References

[1] Beck, K., *Extreme Programming Explained: Embrace Change*. Reading, Massachusetts: Addison-Wesley, 2000.

[2] Beck, K., *Test Driven Development -- by Example*. Boston: Addison Wesley, 2003.

[3] Boehm, B. W., *Software Engineering Economics*. Englewood Cliffs, NJ: Prentice-Hall, Inc., 1981.

[4] Cockburn, A., *Agile Software Development*. Reading, Massachusetts: Addison Wesley Longman, 2001.

[5] Dustin, E., Rashka, J., and Paul, J., *Automated Software Testing*. Reading, Massachusetts: Addison Wesley, 1999.

[6] Fowler, M., *UML Distilled*. Reading, Massachusetts: Addison Wesley, 2000.

[7] George, B. and Williams, L., "An Initial Investigation of Test-Driven Development in Industry," ACM SAC, Mel, FL, 2003.

[8] Meyer, B., "Applying Design by Contract," *IEEE Computer*, vol. 25, pp. 40-51, October 1992.

[9] Muller, M. M. and Hagner, O., "Experiment about Test-first Programming," presented at Conference on Empirical Assessment in Software Engineering (EASE), 2002.

An Analysis of the Fault Correction Process in a Large-Scale SDL Production Model

Dolores Zage Wayne Zage
Software Engineering Research Center
Ball State University
Muncie, IN 47306 USA
+1 765 285 8642
{dmzage, wmzage }@bsu.edu

Abstract

Improvements in the software development process depend on our ability to collect and analyze data drawn from various phases of the development life cycle. Our design metrics research team was presented with a large-scale SDL production model plus the accompanying problem reports that began in the requirements phase of development. The goal of this research was to identify and measure the occurrences of faults and the efficiency of their removal by development phase in order to target software development process improvement strategies. The number and severity of problem reports were tracked by development phase and fault class. The efficiency of the fault removal process using a variety of detection methods was measured. Through our analysis of the system data, the study confirms that catching faults in the phase of origin is an important goal. The faults that migrated to future phases are on average eight times more costly to repair. The study also confirms that upstream faults are the most critical faults and more importantly it identifies detailed design as the major contributor of faults, including critical faults.

1. Introduction

The authors have been studying design metrics as indicators of fault-prone software components in research supported by the Software Engineering Research Center. Over a fifteen-year validation period, on projects over a wide variety of application areas, these design metrics have been shown to target fault-prone design components [14,15,16,17]. The research reported in this paper is an extension of that previous metrics work with the goal of exploring the distribution of faults, their types and techniques of fault removal in the interest of providing improvements in the software development process.

The study data is a large-scale industrial software system written in the Specification and Description Language (SDL). SDL is a standard language for the specification and description of systems. Its more recent versions contain object orientation, remote procedure calls and non-determinism [7]. SDL is used in telecommunications, as well as in other real-time, distributed and communicating systems to increase productivity, reduce faults and improve maintainability.

This analysis has study data collected as early as the requirements phase. Such thorough fault reporting is relatively uncommon and is most helpful in determining the origin and resolution of faults in the development process. The authors were granted access to problem reports from an organization with a level 5 CMM rating. Once the requirements had reached a satisfactory level of stability, problem reports were submitted and catalogued. This study data is also valuable because the software was developed utilizing an SDL development process. Figure 1 displays a comparison of a conventional development process and one that employs SDL. The use of SDL can accelerate and simplify the engineering process. To capture the customer requirements as scenarios, message sequence charts (MSCs) are used to model use cases for the SDL development. MSCs describe the communication behavior of the system components and their environment by means of message interchange. The set of MSCs is automatically transformed into an executable SDL model. The SDL Design Tool, SDT, provides the capability to do simulations, system verification and validation automatically. In conventional development, simulations can be executed, but must be developed as a by-product to the system code. As reported by the International Telecommunication Union, SDL and MSC tools have captured 32% of the real-time software development tool market and their share is growing [8].

The data in this study consists of an SDL production model containing 1600 SDL components (processes, states, state transitions and procedures), accompanied by 603 problem reports. Our research team had the task of tracking each fault identified in the problem reports back to its SDL component. The researchers spent two days with the lead developers to gain insight into the actual system and the contents of the problem reports. Each problem report consisted of 35 fields that included the development cycle phase of origin and phase found, severity class, a

0-7695-1877-X/03 $17.00 © 2003 IEEE

fault class, detection method and the effort required to resolve the fault. In addition, a separate analysis section was appended to each report detailing the description of the problem, the problem history, the suggested cause and solution and subsequent changes to the model.

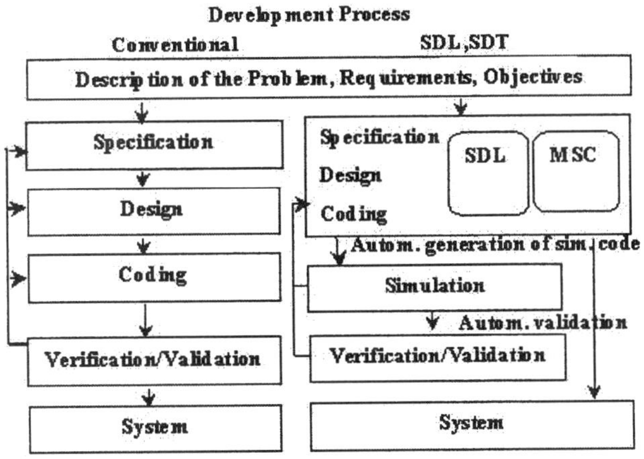

Figure 1. Comparison of a conventional and an SDL development process [10]

2. Analysis of problem reports

The analysis began by focusing on the categorization of problem reports by severity class and development phase. As seen from Table 1, the greatest number of reports stemmed from faults attributed to detailed design. This phase also accounts for the maximum number of faults designated as critical. Of these 11 faults, 5 of them were removed in detailed design, leaving 6 to be found later in the development life cycle. Some reports have indicated that coding errors are more severe than design errors [12]. Our results indicate that detailed design in particular is the phase that contains the most critical faults in this SDL model.

Table 1. Number and severity of problem reports by development phase

	critical	major	minor	cosmetic	enhancement	unknown	total
Requirements	4	28	51	2	3		88
Preliminary Design		13	92	6	2		113
Detailed Design	11	70	135	37	1		254
Coding	2	5	3	2			12
Testing	1	4	9	3	2		19
unknown	1	14	15	2	1	84	117
total	19	134	305	52	9	84	603

For these study data, 75% (455/603) of the reports originated in the upstream phases of software development. This is a marked difference over the projects studied in the Marick Report [11]. The average percentage of the upstream faults in that survey was 39%. The variation in these studies may be attributed to the differences between the conventional and the SDL development processes. It has been shown that faults identified earlier in the development process are cheaper to fix than faults identified late in the process [6]. Very few (2.5%) of the total faults reported originated in the coding phase. This outcome can be attributed to the development environment, since SDL by its nature stresses design over coding. Thus design is maximized (along with the potential to originate faults) and coding is minimized. However, pushing faults into the upstream phases may reduce the total cost of the entire system. The emphasis on design in turn leads to a situation where the bulk of the faults originate in the design phases of development.

A literature search for comparable studies revealed that most of the previous change data study systems were written in procedural languages. For example, the empirical investigations from projects in the NASA/GSFC Software Engineering Laboratory were primarily coded in Fortran [1]. Moreover, the SEL change data were collected during the software phases of coding, testing, acceptance and maintenance, whereas the change data from this study began with the requirements phase. One analysis that perhaps can be comparable with projects based on data derived from a different project and environment studies is the distribution of errors by fault type. In a study by Basili and Perricone, the error distribution by type recorded errors stemming from requirements and functional specification problems at 63% [1]. In this same study, it was noted that this high percentage was consistent with another project's evaluation, even though they were not similar projects. However, typical error distributions from the other ground-support software systems had low percentages of requirements and functional specifications errors, with approximately 8% in these categories. The reason for the difference was postulated as the high application experience level of the developers. In our study, 15% of the problem reports originated in the requirements phase. Our developers are experienced telecommunication practitioners and SDL allows a developer to explore the requirements space through an executable model. Commencing the recorded change procedure with the requirements phase and allowing for executable specifications may have influenced the slightly larger increase of problem reports (15% vs. 8%) stemming from the requirements phase.

The sorting of the reports into the fifteen different fault classes is presented in Table 2. Note that the largest category, containing almost 20% of the reports, was named "unknown". This category contains the reports that did not list a fault type. The two fault classes of "data" and "interface" combined contain 33% (200/603) of the reports. An interface fault interacts with other components or drivers through calls, macros, control blocks or a parameter list. Ninety of the 118 interface faults and 73 of 82 data faults entered the system during the design phase of software development.

Table 2: Number and severity of problem reports by fault class

	critical	major	minor	cosmetic	enhancement	unknown	total
Constr/lim			2				2
data	2	13	39	27	1		82
err-handling		1	7				8
initialize	2	4	6	1			13
interface	2	32	74	7	3		118
logic	4	22	50	3			79
non-test			2	1			3
nonstd	2	2	1				5
other	2	15	32	2	2		53
perf/effi			1				1
rel/repeat		1					1
reqment	4	27	68	4	1		104
test - def			6	2			8
test - str		1		3			4
user - int		1	1				2
unknown	1	15	16	2	2	84	120
total	19	134	305	52	9	84	603

The separation of each fault class into problems that were detected within the development phase (in-phase) and those that were detected in a later software development phase (post-phase) was completed to determine the latency for various fault types (Table 3). Observing the six classes of faults that contain over 10 reports and not including the category "unknown" (Table 2), three fault classes, namely "data", "initialize" and "reqment" roughly possess an even distribution between in-phase and post-phase discovery (Table3). Only logic faults are discovered earlier: 2/3 are in-phase, 1/3 are post-phase. The two classes that exhibited the opposite pattern of discovery were the classes of "other" and "interface". Only 1/5 of the "other" reports were identified in-phase while 4/5 slipped into later phases. Interface faults also were discovered later, with 2/5 being discovered within the phase and 3/5 sliding into later phases.

When observing the remaining nine fault classes, which make up approximately just 6% of all the reports (34/602), six of the nine are identified mostly in-phase and the remaining three are identified post-phase. Of these three post-phase fault classes, two, "rel/repeat" and "user-int" had higher than the 5.1 hour average effort per problem report (Table 7). In fact, the single problem report denoting the fault class of "rel/repeat" expended 24 hours to remove the fault.

Table 3. Fault class separated by in- and post-phase discovery

	in-phase	post-phase
constr/lim	100%	0%
data	47.0%	53%
err-handling	91%	9%
initialize	51%	49%
interface	41%	59%
logic	66%	34%
non-test	74%	26%
nonstd	74%	26%
other	29%	71%
perf/effi	0%	100%
rel/repeat	0%	100%
reqment	50%	50%
test - def	100%	0%
test - str	100%	0%
user - int	0%	100%

In a fault classification for a Hewlett Packard division system provided in Table 4, logic faults are the major source of problems, followed by documentation and computation [4]. Logic and computation are most likely to occur during coding. Our system has very few coding errors, and with its emphasis on the design phase, logic faults are minimized (Table 2) and removed with efficiency (Table 3). Interesting in itself is that a category employing the concept of "other" appears in both classifications and has a significant percentage of the total faults. In this study, the faults classified as "other" have a poor in-phase discovery rate. It is well known that finding faults later magnifies the effort to correct, which is also verified by this study. The fault classification "other" has the second highest effort/report. Implications are that one-of-a-kind types of classifications that are placed into this catch-all category should be carefully scrutinized. Unique fault types require more effort. This statement was also observed in this study's fault class distribution where the classes that have a small number of reports such as "rel/repeat" and "user-int" are responsible for a higher than average effort/report.

Table 4. Fault classification from a Hewlett Packard division system

Hardware	4%	Other Code	11%
Process/InterProcess	5%	Computation	18%
Requirements	5%	Documentation	19%
Data Handling	6%	Logic	32%

This historical fault classification can be useful as long as the same process and activities are executed and as long as the recording of the type of fault provides true insight into the nature of the fault. A concern is that 29% of the reports either did not record a fault class or selected the category "other".

3. Observations on the fault removal process

A second focus in this study was to measure the effectiveness and efficiency of the fault removal process. Table 5 (first percentage in each rectangle) identifies the source of the fault and phase in which that fault was identified. As observed from Table 5, 31% of the requirements faults were eliminated in the requirements phase, 30% of requirements faults were eliminated in preliminary design, 15% during detailed design and the remaining were removed during testing. When observing the large percent of coding faults removed during the testing phase, recall that there were a total of only 12 coding faults in all. However, 51% of the detailed design faults slipped into the testing phase. One could say that detailed design faults had only one chance (phase) in which to be discovered, but intra-phase fault detection was 15% higher during preliminary design. It seems reasonable to conclude that practitioners could have benefited from further review during detailed design.

Unfortunately, a number of faults pass from one phase to the next as seen in Figure 2. The information in Table 5 displays the efficiency of fault removal by phase, but it does not present the cumulative effect of this slippage for the entire process. In Figure 2, the vertical arrow going into each box represents faults injected at that step. The horizontal arrow going out of each box represents the faults removed at that step. The curved arrow represents the faults passed to the next step. As also observed from Table 5, the requirements phase has a 31% (28/88) removal efficiency. In preliminarily design, the removal efficiency increases to 57% (99/(113+60)) thus raising the cumulative efficiency to 63%. This increasing trend does not continue through detailed design. The removal efficiency decreases to 49% and the cumulative efficiency remains stable. Since there are so few coding faults, it is not reasonable to comment on that phase. Once again, as seen from the previous analysis in this paper, detailed design is the least efficient fault removal phase.

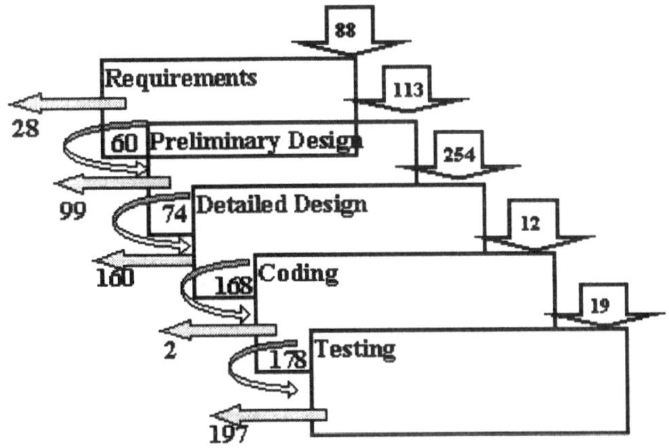

Figure 2. Profile of injected, removed and remaining faults by phase

The other important aspect to efficiency is the effort required to remove the faults. If only a marginal difference exists between correcting the fault earlier than later, then many techniques can be applied at anytime for improving the fault removal process. This investigation confirms that it is costly to wait. The total effort expended to remove 236 intra-phase faults was 250.5 hours while it took 1964.8 hours to remove the 248 inter-phase faults. Faults undetected within the originating phase took approximately eight times more effort to correct. In fact, the problem doesn't get better as time passes. Faults found in the field are at least an order of magnitude more expensive to fix than those found while testing [3]. This also confirms Boehm's classic result [2] that propagating faults to later phases of development produces a nearly exponential increase in the effort, and thus in the cost, of fixing those faults.

Table 5 (second percentages) quantifies the effort expended to remove faults during each phase of software development for this SDL project. From this table, one can determine that upstream faults that passed into the testing phase will require significantly more effort to remove than those removed earlier. The first column contains the requirement faults data. Removing 31% of the requirement faults in the requirements phase took 8% of the total effort.

The remaining 69% of the requirement faults required 92% of the total effort to remove those faults in subsequent phases. Preliminary design, column two, had a similar relationship of faults captured within the phase of origin. However, the disparity of the effort applied to the intra and inter-preliminary design faults was not as dramatic as that of requirement analysis, but it is still significant. The third column of Table 5 shows that the 49% of the detailed design faults that were caught in the detailed design phase consumed only 10% of the total effort. The remaining detailed design faults consumed 90% of the total effort.

Table 5. Percentage of faults detected in each phase by phase of origin/ Percentage of effort to correct faults by phase

Phase of Origin \ Phase Found	Requirements	Preliminary Design	Detailed Design	Coding	Testing
Requirements	**31% / 8%**	**30% / 5%**	**15% / 2%**	**0% / 0%**	**24% / 85%**
Preliminary Design		**64% / 21%**	**21% / 12%**	**0% / 0%**	**15% / 67%**
Detailed Design			**49% / 10%**	**0% / 0%**	**51% / 90%**
Coding				**16% / 4%**	**84% / 96%**
Testing					**100% / 100%**

The SDL language is based on the concept of extended finite state machines and also includes constructs for behavior and data description, complex system structuring, a visual action language and an execution model [9]. There is a rich set of SDL tools that provide SDL designers the capability for model testing and autocoding [13]. Autocoding provides the benefit that specified behavior is exactly implemented and no conformance testing is needed. In Table 6, data columns 1 and 2 describe a typical development fault stream for a large non-SDL telecommunication system [5]. Data in columns 3 and 4 are from this SDL study. As observed in both studies, faults are often detected at the end of the development process despite being present in the earlier phases. However, the SDL system data reveals that the SDL development process was much better in detecting faults earlier. And even if the design and implementation faults introduced figures are totaled (80% and 78% respectively), because technically, SDL has no implementation phase, the faults detected are 22% and 53%, or a 2.4 times improvement for the system designed with SDL. This improvement is perhaps due to the fact that SDL facilitates a continuous design flow through the whole system in contrast to a conventional software development process. As established in this paper and confirmed in earlier studies, the earlier defects are identified, the less costly they are to remove.

The detection methods employed to uncover errors also were reviewed. The problem reports were categorized by the detection method identified in the report. There were eleven methods recorded in the problem reports as seen in Table 7. Only 3% of the reports did not record the detection method. The most expensive error detection method was integration test. On the average this detection method consumed 17.2 hours per recorded report. Note however, that approximately half of the integration test reports did not report effort. Of these reports with no effort recorded, nine were terminated and thirteen were labeled new. Additional information on the thirteen new reports could affect the average for the integration test method. However, the integration test detection method contained the highest three total efforts of the 483 reports that had recorded effort information. Thus it is possible that this average will increase.

Table 6: Comparing non-SDL and SDL fault streams

	non -SDL		**SDL**	
Phase	Faults introduced	Faults detected	Faults introduced	Faults detected
Requirements	20%	1%	18%	6%
Design	38%	2%	76%	53%
Implementation	42%	20%	2%	0%
Testing	0%	77%	4%	41%

Another observation that can be seen from Table 7 is that the detection methods of author code and group code review constitute a very minor portion of the total detection methods. Author code review appears only twice, and group code appears five times. Two conclusions come to mind: either this method was not used extensively to uncover faults or it has a very poor record in uncovering faults. However, another review category, namely manual review, uncovered 92 faults. The average effort per report using a manual review was in the top half based on effort expended of the eleven methods recorded.

Table 7: Number and effort by detection method

Detection Method	Total Number of Reports	Reports Without Effort Value	Reports With Effort Value	Total Effort	Avg of Detection Method Effort – Reports With Effort Value	% of Detection Method
INTEGRATION TEST	74	36	38	652.95	17.2	12.3%
SYSTEM TEST	71	35	36	522.85	14.5	11.8%
AUTHOR CODE REVIEW	2	0	2	23	11.5	0.3%
RANDOM UNPLANNED TEST	23	5	18	202.25	11.2	3.8%
MANUAL REVIEW	92	10	82	383.25	4.7	15.3%
IN-HOUSE NORMAL USE	68	4	64	290.5	4.5	11.3%
REGRESSION TEST	22	0	22	98.75	4.5	3.6%
FUNCTIONAL TEST	56	9	47	149.75	3.2	9.3%
GROUP CODE REVIEW	5	2	3	2.25	0.8	0.8%
INTERACTIVE TEST	173	2	171	118.75	0.7	28.7%
NOT GIVEN	16	16	0	0	0.0	2.7%
CUSTOMER USE	1	1	0	0	0.0	0.2%
TOTALS	603	120	483	2444.3	5.1	100.0%

The detection method of interactive test uncovered 29% of the total faults. These faults consumed 118.75 removal hours. Thus the faults that were uncovered by interactive tests were the least costly. Analyzing the 173 problem reports listing interactive test as the detection method, 141 of the faults were discovered within the development phase, while the 32 remaining faults were from previous phases. The source for 89 of these interactive reports was test problems. Perhaps the reason that interactive tests uncovered problems with less effort is that this method uncovered only the least severe problems. When the reported severity classes for the reports listing the interactive test as the detection method were compiled, it was found that 52% of all the cosmetic and 39% of all the minor class severity reports were identified by interactive tests. Interactive test has a greater share of minor and cosmetic faults than the other 11 detection method categories, and thus it should have the greatest efficiency per test. However, this method was also responsible for uncovering four critical problems while only consuming less than 4 hours effort. Only in-house normal use and system test uncovered as many critical faults, but each method required additional effort at 11 hours for in-house and over 65 hours each for system test.

It is also interesting that reports listing critical faults do not consume the most effort, but the reports cataloging enhancements and major faults consume the most per enhancement or fault. The majority of the reports designate the severity level as minor. These data can be seen in Table 8.

Table 8: Severity class cardinality and effort

Severity Class	Number	Effort	Average Effort per Report
Critical	19	117	6.2
Major	134	1103.7	8.2
Minor	305	1005.1	3.3
Cosmetic	52	66	1.3
Enhancement	9	152.5	16.9
Unknown	84		0
Total	**603**	**2444.3**	**4.1**

Sixty-two percent of the reports recorded less than one hour of effort to correct the problem. These 62% accounted for only 7% of the total effort. There are only 29 reports with effort recorded at 20 hours or more, and yet they consume 1380 hours or 56% of the total effort for all of the reports listed. In other words, 5% of the reports took 56% of the effort. Seven of the 29 reports listed requirements as the phase of origin. Two reports in this set listed preliminary design as the phase of origin. Eighteen reports listed detailed design. The phases of coding and integration testing each listed one. As previously noted, the phase of detailed design has the most reports identifying the severity level as critical. It is also the phase of origin of the most time consuming reports to fix.

All of the 29 reports with effort recorded at 20 hours or more were uncovered during later stages of development. The majority of them were uncovered during integration (8) and system testing (12) phase. The fault class of these 29 reports was also explored. Fourteen of the reports listed interface as the fault class. From Table 2 the percentage of interface faults for the entire set of reports is approximately 20%. When considering only the 29 reports with effort greater than 20 hours, interface fault now constitutes 48%. As expected, the other fault classes of data, logic, and other roughly approximate the same proportion as in the total report population. Requirement faults have less than the expected distribution at 2 reports. This perhaps can be explained by the fact that all of these reports stem from the later stages of development and the majority, if not all of requirement fixes have had time to resolve themselves. Surprisingly the fault classes with very few reports in the total report set such as err-handling, initialize, rel/repeat are represented within these 29 reports. This suggests that uniqueness has its price in terms of effort.

The problem reports also contain documentation on the history of the report. For example, the submission date, the submitter, and the resolve date are included in the information. Also included is whether a problem was cloned from another problem set, for example the associated hardware problem reporting. Of the 29 reports, 16 (55%) were cloned. In the entire database of 603 reports, there were 62 reports that were cloned. Of these 62 reports only 24 had recorded an effort detection method of which 16 took over 20 hours to correct.

The detection methods by each development phase were analyzed to determine which methods are most likely to uncover certain fault categories. This analysis did not uncover any surprising results. The detection methods divided themselves more by their availability to perform the test. For example, in-house normal use was the best at identifying problems with requirements. Interactive test was the best method in finding preliminary design and detailed design problems. Random unplanned test and system test also discovered requirement problems, but these required more than thirty hours each on average.

The detection methods categorized by fault class were compiled. There were 11 detections methods. The top three fault classes, data, requirement and interface faults, which made up over 50% of the reports, were isolated. The distribution of the type of methods used to uncover all of the various fault classes exhibited the same pattern of discovery methods for the individual fault classes of data, requirement, and interface. This implies that even if a tester has the knowledge of the fault class, the detection methods applied would be similar to when this information is not available.

4. Analysis of model changes

When the changes for each problem report were traced back to their originating module, only 37% of the approximately 1600 modules in the SDL production system had changes. Recall that these problem reports began with the requirements phase and ended with maintenance, thus these changes are the aggregate changes for the entire development process over the entire model. As expected from the modules that had changes, most of them only had one change (Table 9). The greatest number of changes for a module was 16. This particular module was a setup module and even with its sixteen changes, the effort associated with these sixteen changes was over 26 hours.

Table 9: Percentage of modules with 1 to 16 changes

# of changes	%	# of changes	%
1	42.5%	9	0.5%
2	22.5%	10	0.5%
3	14.5%	11	0.2%
4	8.4%	12	0.3%
5	4.9%	13	0.3%
6	1.7%	14	0.0%
7	2.0%	15	0.0%
8	1.4%	16	0.2%

The modules that required 2 changes were isolated to determine if fault classes occur in pairs. Since there were 15 fault classes, pairs of faults can occur in a total of 105 fault class combinations (15*14/2). When analyzing the 150 modules that required 2 changes, only 19 combinations were found, and three of the pairs occurred 12%, 13% and 14% of the total 105 two-change modules.

5.Conclusions and future research directions

These study data were generated from a system developed using a formal specification and description language, SDL, and a system engineering approach that facilitates a continuous design process. These factors may influence resulting fault patterns. Perhaps equally interesting are the outcomes that were consistent with those in studies involving a conventional development process, namely, the cost of removing faults, parallelism in fault classes and the finding that unique faults require more effort to repair.

The results also indicate that detailed design is the phase that introduces the most critical faults in a developing system. Detailed design is also the least efficient fault-removal phase. Moreover, this investigation confirms that it is very costly to remove faults if they are not detected in their phase of origin. The types of fault-detection methods used to uncover the various fault classes exhibit the same pattern of discovery, suggesting that even if a tester has the knowledge of the fault class, the detection methods applied would be similar to when this information is not available. The results of this study suggest that a further analysis of a system during detailed design is needed to capture a relatively high number of faults that often slip through to downstream life cycle phases.

In the future, a detailed analysis of the module changes will be performed in order to offer further guidance during testing. In addition, we will explore whether the functionality of the module can be used to identify appropriate fault-detection techniques.

6. Acknowledgements

The research presented in this paper was funded by Motorola Corporation through the Software Engineering Research Center (SERC), a National Science Foundation Industry/University Cooperative Research Center (NSF Grant No. EEC-0120799).

7. References

1. Basili, Victor, Barry T. Pericone, "Software Errors and Complexity: An Empirical Investigation", *Communications of the ACM*, January 1984, Volume 27, Number 1

2. Boehm, B. W. "Software Engineering", *IEEE Transactions on Computers,* December 1976, pp. 1226-1241.

3. Dalal, S.R., J.R. Horgan, and J.R. Kettenring, "Reliable Software and Communication: Software Quality, Reliability, and Safety", *Proceedings of the 15th International Conference on Software Engineering,* 1993, pp. 425-435.

4. Daran, M., and P. Thévenod-Fosse, "Software Error Analysis: A Real Case Study Involving Real Faults and Mutations", *ISSTA '96*, pp. 158-171.

5. Ebert, Christof, Evalutation and Application of Complexity-Based Criticality Models, Proceedings of METRICS '96, 1996, IEEE.

6. Eick, S. G., et al, "Estimating Software Fault Content Before Coding", *Proceedings of the 14th International Conference on Software Engineering*, 1992, pp. 59-65.

7. Ellsberger, J., D. Hogrefe, and A Sarma, *SDL, Formal Object-oriented Language for Communication Systems*, Prentice Hall, Europe, 1997.

8. International Telecommunication Union, "ITU Adopts New Releases of SDL and MSC Specification and Description Languages", http://www.itu.int/newsarchive/press_releases/1999/np-7.html, Geneva, 1999.

9. International Telecommunication Union, Recommendation Z.100, "Specification and Description Language" (SDL), http://www.itu.ch , Electronic Bookshop, Geneva, 1996

10. Kellerer, W., Spezifikation, Simulation und Implementierung eines Sicherungsprotokolls mit SDL, Master's thesis, Lehrstuhl fur Kommunikationsnetze, TU Munich, 1995.

11. Marick, B., "A Survey of Software Fault Surveys", Report No. UIUCDCS-R-90-1651, Dept. of Computer Science. U. Illinois at Urbana-Champaign, December 1990.

12. Rubey, R.J., Quantitative Aspects of Software Validation, *Proceedings of the 1975 International Conference on Reliable Software - SIGPLAN Notices,* Vol. 10, June 1975, pp. 246-251.

13. SDT, *SDT Reference Manual.* Telelogic, Malmo, 1996.

14. Wong, W.E., J.R. Horgan, W. Zage, D. Zage and M. Syring, "Applying Design Metrics to Predict Fault Proneness: A Case Study on a Large Scale Software System," *Software-Practice and Experience*, Vol. 30, No. 14, November 25, 2000, pp. 1587-1608.

15. Zage, W., D. Zage, J. M. McGrew, and N. Sood, "Using Design Metrics to Identify Error-Prone Components in SDL Designs", *Proceedings of the 9th International SDL Forum*, Montreal, Canada, June 1999.

16. Zage, W., D. Zage, E. Wong, J. R. Horgan, and M. Syring, "Applying Design Metrics to a Large-Scale Software System", *Proceedings of the Ninth International Symposium on Software Reliability Engineering (ISSRE '98)*, Paderborn, Germany, November 1998.

17. Zage, W. and D. Zage, "Evaluating Design Metrics on Large-Scale Software", *IEEE Software Journal,* July 1993, pp. 75-81.

Requirements Discovery during the Testing of Safety-Critical Software

Robyn R. Lutz
Jet Propulsion Laboratory
and Iowa State University
rlutz@cs.iastate.edu

Inés Carmen Mikulski
Jet Propulsion Laboratory
Pasadena, CA 91109-8099
ines.c.mikulski@jpl.nasa.gov

Abstract

This paper describes the role of requirements discovery during the testing of a safety-critical software system. Analysis of problem reports generated by the integration and system testing of an embedded, safety-critical software system identified four common mechanisms for requirements discovery and resolution during testing: (1) Incomplete requirements, resolved by changes to the software, (2) Unexpected requirements interactions, resolved by changes to the operational procedures, (3) Requirements confusion by the testers, resolved by changes to the documentation, and (4) Requirements confusion by the testers, resolved by a determination that no change was needed. The experience reported here confirms that requirements discovery during testing is frequently due to communication difficulties and subtle interface issues. The results also suggest that "false positive" problem reports from testing (in which the software behaves correctly but unexpectedly) provide a rich source of requirements information that can be used to reduce operational anomalies in critical systems.

1. Introduction

This paper describes the role of requirements discovery during the testing of a safety-critical software system. Difficulties with requirements have been repeatedly implicated as a source of both testing defects [2, 7] and accidents in deployed systems [3, 10]. In an effort to improve our understanding of how requirements discovery occurs during testing, and how such discoveries are resolved (or are not resolved) prior to deployment, we investigated the requirements-related problems reported during testing of a safety-critical system currently under development. Analysis of the problem reports generated during integration and system testing of the software distinguished four common mechanisms for requirements discovery and resolution:

(1) *Incomplete requirements, resolved by changes to the software.* As often occurs, testing caused several previously unidentified requirements to surface. These new requirements usually involved complicated interface issues between software components or between hardware and software. Several of the incomplete requirements involved fault protection, of special concern in safety-critical systems.

(2) *Unexpected requirements interactions, resolved by changes to the operational procedures.* A closely related mechanism for requirements discovery was the identification during testing of unexpected interactions among the existing requirements. Typically, these interactions resulted in new required sequencing of activities when the interleaved processes unexpectedly caused incorrect behavior or did not achieve the required precondition for correct execution of the software.

(3) *Requirements confusion by the testers, resolved by changes to the documentation.* Testing revealed some significant misunderstandings on the part of the testers regarding what the requirements actually were. In these cases the software worked as required and the requirements were correct, but the software's behavior was unexpected. The corrective action was not to fix the software, but to enhance the documentation in order to better communicate the required software behavior or requirements rationale.

(4) *Requirements confusion by the testers, resolved by a determination that no change was needed.* In this mechanism testing also revealed a gap in requirements understanding. However, the problem report was judged to be a "false positive," i.e., indicating failure where the software in fact behaved correctly. We found that in some cases where the software behaved correctly but unexpectedly, an opportunity was missed to prevent similar, subsequent, requirements confusion by the operators of the deployed system. We propose some guidelines for distinguishing and responding to such situations.

The research described in this paper was carried out at the Jet Propulsion Laboratory, California Institute of Technology, under a contract with the National Aeronautics and Space Administration. It was funded by NASA's Office of Safety and Mission Assurance, Center Initiative UPN 323-08. The first author's research is supported in part by National Science Foundation Grants CCR-0204139 and CCR-0205588.

0-7695-1877-X/03 $17.00 © 2003 IEEE

The experience reported here suggests that problem reports generated during testing are an underused source of information about potential requirement-related anomalies that may occur after the software is deployed. Test defect reports provide a unique source of insights into future users' gaps in domain knowledge, misidentification of requirement rationales, and erroneous assumptions regarding required sequences of activities. In this limited sense, testing problem reports may provide a preview of some possible operational problems. The main contributions of the paper are (1) to identify the common mechanisms by which requirements discovery and resolution occurred during testing, and (2) to report the lessons learned regarding how such discoveries can be better used to reduce future requirements anomalies in the deployed system.

The rest of the paper is divided into sections as follows. Section 2 describes the approach used to investigate requirements discovery during testing. Section 3 discusses and evaluates the results in the context of some illustrative examples. Section 4 briefly compares the experience described here to others' findings. Section 5 summarizes the lessons learned.

2. Approach

The data for this analysis consisted of the 171 completed problem reports (PRs) written by project test teams during integration and system testing of the Mars Exploration Rovers (MER). MER, to be launched in 2003, will explore Mars with two robotic rovers equipped to search for evidence of previous water. The size of MER's flight software is roughly 300K Lines of Code, implementing approximately 400 software requirements of varying degrees of granularity. Although the software was delivered in a series of builds, we do not distinguish here among the builds due to the relatively small number of PRs.

The on-line problem reports (PRs) filled out by the project consist of three parts. The first part describes the problem and is filled out by the tester when the problem occurs. The second part is filled out by the analyst assigned to investigate the problem. The third part is filled in later with a description of the corrective action that was taken to close out the problem.

The approach we selected for the analysis of the PRs was an adaptation of Orthogonal Defect Classification (ODC) [1]. ODC provides a way to "extract signatures from defects" and to correlate the defects to attributes of the development process (Fig. 1). Our ODC-based approach uses four attributes to characterize each PR: Activity, Trigger, Target, and Type. The Activity describes where the defect surfaced, e.g., Integration Test or System Test. The Trigger describes the environment or condition that had to exist for the defect to appear. In the testing environment, the trigger was usually the testing of

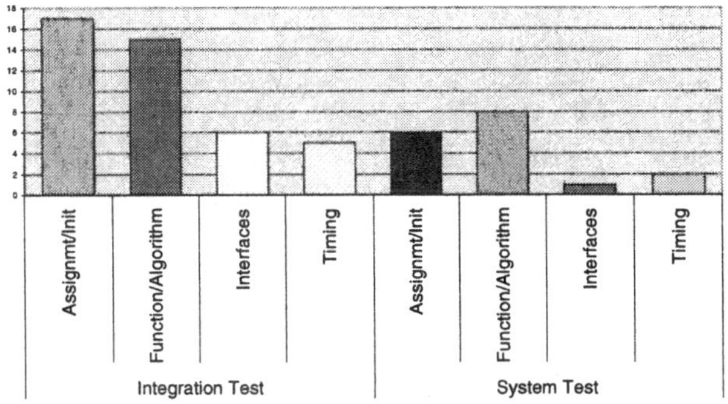

Figure 1. Types of Corrections for Testing Reports

a single command or of a capability sequence (i.e., a software requirement scenario). The Target describes the high-level entity that was fixed in response to the problem report, e.g., Flight software, Ground software, etc. The Type describes the actual correction that was made, i.e., "the meaning of the fix" [1].

The two authors classified the PRs using the adapted ODC. Both of us have experience on flight projects at JPL but neither are directly involved with the testing of the MER software. MER engineers generously assisted us with answers to our process and domain questions.

Following the ODC approach, we defined each classification attribute and the possible values it could take in a document that was reviewed by MER project personnel. Adaptation of the standard ODC categories to the spacecraft domain was driven by the need to capture core properties of the anomalies seen during testing. In order to improve repeatability and reduce bias, the process of classification involved three steps in which (1) each analyst separately classified the set of anomalies, (2) inconsistent classifications were highlighted and each analyst had an opportunity to correct any clear errors in her own classifications (e.g., missing fields), and (3) they analysts jointly reviewed the remaining inconsistencies and resolved them through discussion. A detailed description of the classification process and of efforts to remove bias is provided in [9].

The work reported here is part of a multi-year pilot study to reduce the number of safety-critical software anomalies that occur post-launch. This paper reports the first experience using the adapted ODC technique on a spacecraft currently under development. The motivation was to mine the testing problem reports for insights into how requirements discovery during testing can be used to forestall or mitigate some critical software anomalies during operations.

3. Results and analysis

We here describe each of the four mechanisms for

requirements discovery and resolution identified during analysis of the problem reports (PRs) generated in integration and system testing of the spacecraft software. A subsection describes each mechanism in terms of the ODC classification values that characterize it, provides a more in-depth causal analysis of some typical examples, and evaluates the adequacy of the corrective action taken to resolve the requirements discovery.

3.1 Incomplete requirements, resolved by changes to the software

Sixty-five of the completed 171 integration and system tes' ,g PRs were resolved by a change to the flight software (Fig. 2). In ODC terms, the Target for these sixty-five PRs was "Flight Software." Twenty-three of the Flight Software PRs had an ODC Type of "Assignment/Initialization." These PRs were resolved by changes to parameters in the light of new system knowledge. They entailed discovery of new requirements knowledge, but not of new functional requirements. Two typical examples of these PRs are, in one case, a change to the value of the variable "max" to avoid unintended triggering of fault protection and, in another case, a change to require that a component come up disabled rather than enabled after a reboot.

Another twenty-three of the sixty-five Flight Software testing PRs had an ODC Type of "Function/Algorithm." Some of these changes involved design or implementation issues such as testing of functions not yet delivered in the current build. However, the PRs of interest to us from a requirements perspective are the ten that entailed more substantial changes to the flight software as the result of knowledge gained during testing.

Each of these ten PRs was resolved by requiring a new software function. Many of the corrective actions taken to close these PRs involved additional reasonableness checks on preconditions and post-conditions. Several involved startup/restart scenarios, or the correct triggering of recovery software. New requirements included an additional health check, a parameter validation check, an inhibit to checks of disabled software, distinguishing unavailability from non-response of a unit, turning off encoding in some cases, ignoring false out-of-order messages, providing a new capability to copy a rate to a register, an additional check so a warning does not occur in a shutdown mode, and a new capability to command a hardware unit.

An additional seven of the Flight Software PRs had an ODC Type of "Timing," and seven more had an ODC Type of "Interfaces." In these types, as well, the role of testing in the discovery of new requirements was evident. Due to space constraints, we only mention briefly that several resulted in new requirements to insert delays in the software to compensate for interface delays. It is

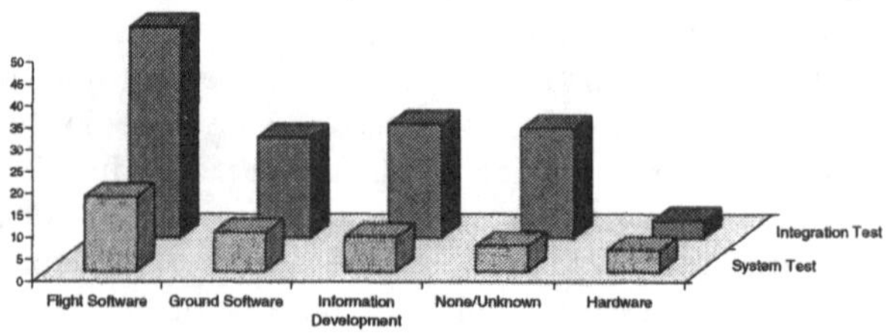

Figure 2 . Fixing Testing Problem Reports

worth noting that no PRs documented extra requirements (where the flight software did more than it should).

3.2 Unexpected requirements interactions, resolved by changes to the operational procedures

The previous subsection described new requirements that were discovered during testing and resolved by changes to the flight software. In this subsection we describe unexpected requirement interactions that were discovered during testing and fixed, not by changes to the software, but instead by changes to the procedures that will constrain operational activities.

This mechanism for requirements discovery tended to involve emerging requirements, not discovered until testing, on the sequencing or timing of activities in interfacing software components or software/hardware interfaces. The ODC Target for these thirteen PRs was "Information Development" and the ODC Type for these PRs was "Missing or Incomplete Procedures." This second mechanism is a special case of the incomplete requirements described above, involving new knowledge and requirements that must be enforced on interactions. However, this mechanism differs from the first mechanism described above in that achievement of the new requirement is here allocated to procedures rather than to software.

Most of these PRs dealt only with testing procedures and were not relevant to operations or maintenance. However, three of them involved discovery during testing of unexpected requirements interactions. In each of these three cases, responsibility for the requirement was allocated to operations. For example, in one PR testing revealed that unless a spacecraft component was re-calibrated before use, it triggered fault-protection software. The discovery of this requirement for sequential activities (first calibrate, then use) was allocated to an operational procedure.

In another, a tester observed that, contrary to expectations, an off command was issued redundantly by a software fault monitor. Analysis showed that this behavior was correct, but idiosyncratic. The corrective action was to avoid these redundant commands during operations by carefully selecting the high and low limits to preclude the state observed in testing. It is easy to see how, even with a documented procedure in place, this situation might recur in operations.

This third mechanism for requirements discovery is of interest in preventing operational anomalies because corrections made to procedures still depend on the correct implementation of the procedure by the operator of the deployed system each time the relevant scenario arises. We were thus interested in whether some of the new requirements for constraining interactions, levied on the operational procedures, might be better handled in software. Given the small number of s in the study, no conclusion was appropriate. However, the examples suggest that in long-lived systems, the tradeoff between easy but operator-dependent procedural fixes and more costly but operator-independent software fixes should be considered.

3.3 Requirements confusion by the testers, resolved by changes to the documentation

The previous two subsections both described requirements discovery mechanisms in which the testers' expectations were consistent with the required software behavior. Testing revealed missing requirements that had to be added in order to achieve the correct, and expected, behavior. The requirements discovery mechanism described in this section is different in that the testers' expectations regarding the required software behavior were incorrect. The resolution was to try to remove the source of the testers' confusion by improving the documentation of the existing requirements and their rationale.

Fourteen of the 171 testing PRs were resolved by changes to the documentation. The ODC Target for these PRs was "Information Development" and the ODC Type was "Documentation." (Only PRs that changed just documentation but not software or procedures are labeled this way).

Four of the PRs of type "Documentation" revealed erroneous requirements assumptions by the testers. For example, in one case, the tester incorrectly assumed that certain heaters remain on during the transition from one mode to another, as the spacecraft transitions from the pre-separation mode of the Mars lander to the entry/descent mode (as the lander enters the Martian atmosphere). The tester's assumption was reasonable but incorrect. In fact, there is a software requirement on another component to turn the heaters off when this transition occurs. Documentation of this fact was added to the Functional Design Document and the procedure writers were notified of the update in order to correct the misunderstanding prior to launch.

In these PRs it was requirements confusion, rather than new requirements that were discovered during testing. The perceived inconsistency between the test results and the required behavior was inaccurate. The corrective action was not to fix the software but the source of confusion. This resulted in improved communication of the rationale for the existing behavior in the existing project documentation

3.4 Requirements confusion by the testers, resolved by a determination that no change was needed.

The final mechanism for requirements discovery is similar to the previous one except that no fix is made, even to documentation. Thirty of the 171 testing PRs have an ODC Target of "None/Unknown" and an ODC Type of "Nothing Fixed." The reason that nothing was fixed is that these PRs were "false positives," raising an alarm when nothing was broken. Our interest in investigating this mechanism was to see if any of these PRs described requirements confusion or requirements interactions that could potentially recur in flight operations. If so, it might be that some change to documentation or procedure was indicated.

As expected, for most of the PRs there was, in fact, nothing to fix. For example, thirteen of the thirty PRs referred to problems that were no longer relevant (e.g., the current build removed the issue); two were clearly one-time operator errors (e.g., misreading the test results); and three were relevant only to the test environment but not to flight. However, eight of the thirty raised possible flight concerns, although in each case the software worked as required. We describe several of these more fully here, since they support our claim that false positives encountered during testing often provide a useful window into latent requirements misunderstandings during operations.

For example, in one case the PR stated as an error that commands issued when a remote unit was off were not rejected as expected, but instead were completed when the unit rebooted. Although the software operated correctly, the PR revealed a gap in understanding of the rationale for the software's required behavior (a gap, by the way, that was shared by the analysts). Since this requirements confusion could apparently reappear in a post-launch operational scenario, it may merit additional documentation to preclude a similar mistake by an operator.

Another PR of Type "Nothing Fixed" describes a situation in which one component, attempting to communicate with another component, received warning messages indicating that an invalid response had occurred. In fact, the communication attempt happened to occur during a few-millisecond timeout that takes place in some particular scenarios. This behavior is, in fact, correct and required, and subsequent communication attempts will be normal. However, the effect of the timeout is rather subtle.

In a third example, the tester incorrectly assumed that a telemetry (data download) channel output the value of a counter when the channel instead provided the value of the counter's high-water mark (the highest value yet recorded for the counter). Thus, even when the counter was reset, the telemetry value remained constant. The requirements rationale is sound -- that the fault-protection software needs information regarding the worst case over a time interval, not just the current snapshot of a frequently reset counter. However, the requirements misunderstanding by the tester is reasonable and suggests that a similar erroneous assumption might be possible later.

Testing PRs often provide detailed descriptions of sequences of input, states, error messages, and even partial dumps in order that the test scenario can later be duplicated. This level of detail is extraordinarily useful in allowing an analyst to pinpoint not only whether an error has occurred but also the source of any confusion regarding the required behavior. Incorrect assumptions (e.g., about the effect of specific commands on the state of the system) and gaps in domain knowledge (e.g., of hardware idiosyncrasies or transients) can often be identified from the details in the problem reports.

3.5 Implications for testing

Given limited project resources (in terms of schedule and budget), should these "false-positive" testing reports be documented further? Based on the problem reports seen here and on past experience with operational anomalies [8, 9], we suggest the following guideline: *if the situation described in the problem report could recur in operations, and if the requirements confusion or misunderstanding of required interactions could also recur in operations, then the problem report may merit additional attention.* Using this guideline, each of the three examples above would have involved additional corrective actions.

For example, one such false-positive PR recorded a perceived discrepancy between two time tags that should be identical. In fact, the software worked as required. The two time tags were two different representations of the same time (cumulative number of seconds since a standard base time and the translation of that value to the current UTC, the Universal Time). This misunderstanding by the tester is one that could be repeated by an operator or maintenance programmer with conceivably hazardous effect, so may merit additional documentation.

Experience with the MER testing PRs also suggests that PRs related to certain critical activities always merit additional attention even if the PR merely records requirements confusion. Thus, if the testing PR involves fault protection software, critical control software, critical maneuvers or activities (e.g., engine burns), or critical mission phases (e.g., insertion of the spacecraft into a planetary orbit), then the problem report should take into account measures to prevent the required behavior that surprised the testers from later surprising the operators.

3.6 Implications for operations

False-positive problem reports from testing (when the software behavior was correct but unexpected, so nothing was fixed) have significant value in a development organization if the requirements confusion or emerging domain knowledge that led to them can be identified and remedied. Especially in a long-lived spacecraft system where turnover of operational personnel is to be expected, loss of knowledge regarding requirement rationale can be substantial. It appears that testers' requirements confusion may provide some small degree of "crystal ball" insight into possible future post-release misunderstandings and, thus, the opportunity to mitigate those gaps, whether by documentation, training, or changes to software or procedures. Techniques to trace the requirements misunderstandings encountered during testing into operations are at this time an open problem.

Some results from a recent study by the authors confirm that the requirements discovery mechanisms found in testing can affect safety-critical operations. This ODC-based study profiled 199 safety-critical software anomalies recorded post-launch on seven spacecraft [9]. One of the surprises to emerge from that study was that some procedures needed for post-launch operations were not in place, and that these omissions contributed to 21% of the safety-critical anomalies. Another finding related to requirements discovery was that in most of the anomalies of Type "Nothing Fixed" (14% of the total), what was originally reported as a safety-critical anomaly was in fact the required behavior of the spacecraft, i.e., requirements confusion. Better understanding of the various requirements-discovery mechanisms in testing has as its primary goal to prevent slippage of requirements-related testing problems into operations.

4. Related Work

Most work on the analysis of testing defects has focused on measuring the quality or readiness of the software for release (see, e.g., [2]). In our study, the focus was instead on how to use the requirements discoveries made during testing (either of incomplete software or of incorrect human assumptions) to reduce critical defects during operations.

The results reported here tend to confirm the central role that Hanks, Knight, and Strunk have found for problems communicating domain knowledge [3]. Weiss, Leveson, Lundqvist, Farid, and Stringfellow specifically implicate requirements misunderstanding in several recent disasters, stating, "software-related accidents almost always are due to misunderstanding about what the software should do" [10]. In this regard, the instances of requirements confusion found here are somewhat similar to the examples of mode confusion by pilots and other operators that Leveson and others have described.

Previous work by one of the authors found that safety-related testing defects on two earlier spacecraft arose most commonly from (1) misunderstanding of the software's interfaces with the rest of the system and (2) discrepancies between the documented requirements and the requirements needed for correct functioning of the system [7]. A recent study by Lauesen and Vinter found similar results for non-critical systems, with slightly more than half the defect reports being requirements defects and the major source being missing requirements [5]. Several defect classification methods (see, e.g., [6, 1]) include communication failures as root causes or as defect triggers. However, these approaches tend not to distinguish requirements confusion in which the reported software behavior is actually correct from other kinds of communication failures, as we found helpful here. These studies also focus on ways to prevent requirements defects from reaching testing, whereas we were more interested in how to use testing problem reports to prevent defects from reaching operations.

Harold recently suggested the use of "test artifacts" for software engineering tasks in describing future directions for work, but added that "this research is in its infancy" [4]. The experience described here suggests that testing problem reports may be useful test artifacts that can be more effectively mined for requirements insights to reduce post-deployment anomalies.

5. Conclusion

The results reported here distinguish four common mechanisms for requirements discovery and resolution during the integration and system testing of a safety-critical software system. One of the lessons learned was that requirements discovery during testing is frequently due to communication difficulties and subtle interface issues. Requirements discovery in testing thus drove changes not only to the software but also to the operational procedures and to the documentation of requirements rationale. Another lesson learned was that false-positive problem reports from testing (where the software behaves correctly but unexpectedly) provide a rich source of insights into potential requirements-related anomalies during operations. This information may be able to be used to reduce operational anomalies in critical systems.

Acknowledgments. The authors thank Daniel Erickson and the Mars Exploration Rover engineers and test teams for their assistance and feedback.

References

[1] R. Chillarege, I. S. Bhandari, J. K. Chaar, M. J. Halliday, D. S. Moebus, B. K. Ray, and M.-Y. Wong, "Orthogonal Defect Classification—A Concept for In-Process Measurements, *IEEE Trans on SW Eng*, Nov. 1992, pp. 943-956.

[2] S. Gardiner, ed. *Testing Safety-Critical Software*, Springer-Verlag, London, 1999.

[3] K. S. Hanks, J. C. Knight, and E. A. Strunk, "Erroneous Requirements: A Linguistic Basis for Their Occurrence and an Approach to Their Reduction," *Proc. 26th NASA Goddard SW Eng Workshop*, IEEE, Greenbelt, MD, Nov., 2001.

[4] M. J. Harold, "Testing: A Roadmap" in *The Future of Software Engineering*, A. Finkelstein, ed., ACM Press, New York, 2000.

[5] S. Lauesen and O. Vinter, "Preventing Requirements Defects: An Experiment in Process Improvement," *Requirements Engineering Journal*, 2001, pp. 37-50.

[6] M. Leszak, D. E. Perry, and D. Stoll, "A Case Study in Root Cause Defect Analysis," *Proc 22nd Intl Conf SW Eng (ICSE'00)*, IEEE CS Press, Los Alamitos, CA, 2002, pp. 428-437.

[7] R. Lutz, "Analyzing Software Requirements Errors in Safety-Critical, Embedded Systems," *Proc IEEE Intl Symp Req Eng*, IEEE CS Press, 1993, pp. 126-133.

[8] R. Lutz and I. C. Mikulski, "Operational Anomalies as a Cause of Safety-Critical Requirements Evolution," *The Journal of Systems and Software*, to appear.

[9] R. Lutz and I. C. Mikulski, "Empirical Analysis of Safety-Critical Anomalies During Operations," submitted to *IEEE Trans on SW Eng*.

[10] K. A. Weiss, N. Leveson, K. Lundqvist, N. Farid, and M. Stringfellow, "An Analysis of Causation in Aerospace Accidents," *Space, 2001*, Aug., 2001.

Software Engineering Education and Training

Extreme Programming

Introducing Software Engineering by means of Extreme Programming

Görel Hedin, Lars Bendix, Boris Magnusson
Department of Computer Science
Lund Institute of Technology
Sweden
{gorel|bendix|boris}@cs.lth.se

Abstract

This paper reports on experience from teaching basic software engineering concepts by using Extreme Programming in a second year undergraduate course taken by 107 students. We describe how this course fits into a wider programme on software engineering and technology and report our experience from running and improving the course. Particularly important aspects of our set-up includes team coaching (by older students) and "team-in-one-room". Our experience so far is very positive and we see that students get a good basic understanding of the important concepts in software engineering, rooted in their own practical experience.

1. Introduction

Teaching software engineering is difficult since many of the practices are motivated by large projects and large organisations of which the students have little or no experience. As many other universities we have previously been running an introductory software engineering course based on a small project. The project has been run in a scaled down waterfall style in order to illustrate basic concepts such as requirements analysis, specification, design, implementation, testing, documentation, and delivery. This traditional set up, with little or no support from faculty during the project, has always been problematic. In particular, it has been difficult to motivate and enforce all the practices for such a small project. With only one iteration, the waterfall model has no place for students to improve. The result has too often been that a few students on each team have been doing most of the work, drowning in details and deadlines rather than grasping concepts, and the rest of the team has learned even less.

In spring 2002 we changed the course completely, renaming the course to Programming in Teams (PT) and adopting Extreme Programming (XP) as the basis for the course. Although our gut feeling is that all of the XP practices are very valuable, our main goal was not to teach XP per se, but to use XP as a vehicle for teaching the basic concepts in software engineering. In running a practical project there is the need for following a method, and in using XP as the basis we have found it easy to give the students a solid basic understanding of not only the important concepts mentioned above, but also of, e.g., iterative development, configuration management, and team communication. In particular, the highly iterative nature of XP, where the participants get rapid feedback at all levels, makes it ideal in a teaching situation.

As a side effect, the PT-course also gives the students practical skills in testing, configuration management, and refactoring, they can immediately use in their projects in later courses. We find such skills to be much easier to teach in the new XP-based set up of the course.

The PT course is designed to fit into the larger picture of the curriculum where many different aspects of software engineering and technology are treated. We view the curriculum as being composed of three layers. At the bottom layer there are first and second year courses teaching basic programming and object-oriented design. In these courses the students work individually or in pairs. At the middle layer we find the PT course, which is focused on programming in small teams. At the top layer we find courses that address software development issues in larger organisations and/or more advanced topics.

The content of the classical introductory software engineering course is placed in the top layer, while the students only have experience from individual work thus creating a mismatch that is hard to bridge. By having the practical experience from the XP-based PT course, we think that the students later on can easier appreciate, understand, and critically discuss the concepts taught at the third level. At the top layer we also find a Coaching course – the second course in our scheme. Here the students learn about team coaching and software architecture. Each student in the coaching course acts as a coach for one of the teams in the PT course. The top layer also includes advanced software engineering courses on, e.g., requirements elicitation, configuration management, etc. In all of these courses the students can benefit from their

0-7695-1877-X/03 $17.00 © 2003 IEEE

practical experiences from a small, yet complete, project in the PT course.

The rest of this paper is structured as follows: In section 2 we give a short background on the XP methodology and explain how we have adapted it for the PT course. In sections 3 and 4 we give more in-depth treatment of our experiences from applying the different practices in the course. Section 5 elaborates on the lessons learned and compares with related work. Section 6 concludes the paper and gives directions for future work.

2. The Team Programming Course

Course format

The course is organised in a theory part followed by a project part. This fit nicely into two consecutive study periods of seven weeks each (corresponding to the spring term).

The first part is a theory part with 6 lectures of 2 hours each covering: introduction; overview of XP practices; testing and pair programming; configuration management; simple design, refactoring, and architecture; and planning and estimation. At the seventh lecture the students were given a one-hour quiz that they must pass in order to be allowed into the project part of the course. Also, the project and product to develop were introduced at this lecture.

During the theory part there are also 3 lab sessions of 2 hours each in order to introduce the main practices and the tools. These labs covered: planning (which was conducted as a so called Extreme Hour [1]); test first and pair programming (using JUnit); and configuration management (using CVS). During these labs the students work in groups of 15-20 students, presence is compulsory and a short quiz is done at the beginning of each lab in order to ensure that the students are sufficiently prepared to get full benefit from the lab. The Extreme Hour was done in a classroom, whereas the other two labs were done in the computer lab working in pairs.

The second part of the course is a project part where the students are grouped into teams of 8-10 students that do an XP-style project in 6 iterations during 6 weeks of study. Presence is compulsory for all group activities during the project. Each team was coached by a pair of older students, who were, at the same time, taking the Coaching course. In the last (7th) week of the study period, the resulting products are demonstrated and evaluated. This is done by peer evaluation, letting each team try out another team's product and review their documentation. These reviews were presented orally in groups of three teams at a time.

An iteration starts on Wednesdays with a two-hour planning meeting where the coach and the team follow up on the previous iteration and plan for the next one. The following Monday, the whole team and the coach meet in the lab for 8 hours, a "long lab session", of program development. In the meantime, each student is expected to spend around 6 hours of "spike time" on experimenting and studying particular issues. Spikes could be done individually, in pairs, or in larger groups. However, actual program development (which is checked into the common team repository) takes place *only* during the long lab sessions. Thus, each student spends a total of (2+6+8)*6=96 hours on the project, or 2.4 man weeks spread out over the 7 week study period, not counting the final evaluation.

As main literature we chose the book "XP Installed" [2], and supplemented this with some articles [3, 4, 5, 6]. We find the book a good practical introduction to XP, but it is very different from the normal text books that students usually have. It is aimed at practitioners and explains a particular method (XP) without any broader outlook or objectivity. We solved this by presenting the book as a "handbook" for the particular method used, rather than the objective final truth.

In the first course instance there were 12 teams of a total of 107 students. Students were assigned to labs and teams in a random fashion, with the goal of making everyone's schedule work out. All teams developed essentially the same product (a system for tracking races in the motorcycle sport Enduro) and were given the same set of requirements (user stories in XP). All teams also had the same person as customer (one of the authors).

In most other course projects we give fixed requirements that the system should fulfil. This course is very different. Here we give the students a fixed time box (planning time, spike time, and long lab time), and expect them to do the best of this time, producing as much as they can of the requirements (user stories), while learning as much as they can in the process.

How can we grade a course that is time boxed and builds so much on team work? We grade it only pass / no pass, and for passing it is required to be actively participating in all the scheduled activities. Students could apply for an exemption from the scheduled activities due to illness or exceptional circumstances. In order to make up for their absence, these students got additional spike time tasks that were valuable for their team and which was presented to both us and the team.

XP as used in the real world

XP is a so-called agile methodology [11] promoting a highly iterative work model with the aim of producing high-quality software and allowing quick adaptation to changing requirements. It is centred around the 12 practices of: Planning Game, On-site Customer, Pair Programming, Collective Code Ownership, Continuous Integration, Small Releases, Metaphor, Simple Design, Coding Standard, Testing, Refactoring, and Forty-hour Week [7].

In a typical XP project the team may consist of around 6-8 developers, a coach, and a customer that is "on-site" and therefore available for informal discussions. The development work will typically be organised in short iterations of around 2-3 weeks between which planning meetings are held. The intervals between releases is also short, for some projects on a daily basis and for others after a few iterations, the goal being to let the customer give feedback as often as possible and to be able to steer the project direction.

XP in an educational setting

The PT course is set up to fit into the normal study periods at our university. The study year is divided into 4 periods of 7 weeks each, and each student normally follows around three courses at the same time. The students are studying for a Master of Science in Computer Engineering, and they are used to quite dense and intensive courses.

In our educational setting there are a couple of major differences from a real XP project. First of all, we have accelerated the iterations substantially. Instead of letting the students do normal 2-3 week iterations, they do six 1-day iterations of development (during a 6 week period), and 3 releases (one release at the end of every second iteration). This way, they get several rounds of feedback through the repeated iterations and releases, while not having to spend an unreasonable amount of time on development.

Secondly, the students are in a learning situation. Not only do most of them have no experience from being part of a software development team, but they also have quite limited programming experience in general. Therefore, they need help both with what to do regarding the project, but also with programming as such.

There are several other differences as well such as the developers being graded (pass / no pass) rather than paid, the customer being a professor rather than a real customer.

Additional practices

Our goal has been to apply the 12 XP core practices more or less according to the book. In addition, we have applied a number of practices, most of which are also described by XP practitioners, but usually not mentioned among the core practices. These are: First Iteration, On-Site Coach, Team-in-one-room, Spike Time, Reflection, and Documentation. Because we run a number of iterations we had the opportunity to tune and refine the practices somewhat during the project.

3. Experience from core XP practices

In this section we will detail the experience we have from the core XP practices. The available space does not allow us to go into details with all 12 core practices, so we have selected some that have interesting or surprising lessons.

Pair Programming Three of the student coaches performed a thorough study on the PT students' attitudes and experience from pair programming during the project [8]. They conclude with some advice on how to use pair programming in an educational situation, e.g.:

- The coach can recommend developers to pair in a certain way in order to spread competence and work efficiently. However, it is the developers themselves that ultimately should decide on who to pair with.
- Personality matching seems to play a more important role than competence matching for a pair to work well.
- The coach should strive for assuring that everyone on the team pairs with as many of the others in the team as possible. This is important from a learning perspective and team building. However, certain pairs might not work well socially, and in such cases they can pair less often and take on simpler tasks in order to not cause bottlenecks for the project.
- Sometimes the two developers in a pair come into a conflict on how the code should be developed. In this case, the coach can step in and resolve the conflict, or call on a stand up meeting for letting the team as a whole resolve the conflict.

Some groups established a pattern of almost fixed pairs, while others changed partner more often. One group even made it a virtue to mandate a change of partner after each task. There were major differences in programming experience, but in most cases that did not seem to cause problems. Sometimes the coach would have to split a couple that were in crisis with respect to solving a task to get in "new blood" – or to simply reassign the task to another pair.

Planning Game From the beginning many students were somewhat sceptical at estimating tasks without any prior experience. However, they took on the challenge and gained practical experience on how to estimate new tasks. Most of the groups continued to do estimates and planning right to the end, but some groups did, however, not bother to do estimates towards the end – "we'll just do tasks and see how far we get".

Some of the teams estimated in hours and others in relative size of stories. Of the 40 hours available (5 pairs for 8 hours) during a long lab session, one group consistently got 25-30 estimated hours of work done. Especially the first iteration served to show the students that things took longer than they had thought.

A total of 35 stories were created for all of the 6 iterations, and most teams completed around 28-30 stories. New stories were created before each iteration and on some occasions the customer changed his mind on priorities between stories, or changed and extended data formats. This was not planned beforehand, but we found it a nice realistic illustration of how customer requirements do change.

Test First Some groups did test first by the book and some groups almost did it. However, in other cases unit tests were written after the code had been written. In general the students had big problems in understanding how to write unit tests in a useful way. Often some small changes to the code would also require that some unit tests needed to be changed or rewritten because they were too specifically tied to the implementation. At other times there would be unit tests that worked at too high a level and therefore did not catch more subtle bugs. For the next instance of the course we will try to remedy this by giving more training on writing good unit tests.

Small Releases The students did three releases – one every two iterations. The first release was done to the customer and included installation and user manuals. The customer was overwhelmed by work in evaluating and commenting the 12 releases, so for the subsequent releases they had to release to a peer group to relieve the customer. An additional advantage of this was that the students were forced to see the release from the customer's point of view. For these releases they should also include source code and documentation, not just the executable and manuals. In many groups the first release went wrong, so they did a new "first" release after iteration three as well (plan to throw one away).

On-site Customer Since the students are fairly inexperienced programmers and in a learning situation, we wanted to have good control over the user stories. There should be a sufficient number of stories so that several pairs could work in parallel, and be reasonably simple to implement so that a pair of students had a chance of getting through each story in one iteration (one day of programming). To accomplish this we needed a customer with XP experience. We therefore settled on not bringing in any outside customer, instead one of us acted as the customer. We picked a product where the customer had deep domain knowledge due to his leisure interests (the Enduro MC sport) to make the product and requirements realistic. It was a realistic option that the products developed by the students could in fact be used for a real Enduro competition.

Since we had only one customer, all teams had to share him. The customer made short visits to each team during both the long lab sessions and planning meetings. However, for spontaneous questions and discussions he was less available, and the coach therefore often acted as a stand-in customer.

4. Experience from the added practices

In this section we describe how we have applied the added practices and our experiences from them in a teaching perspective.

First Iteration The First Iteration practice [9] says that in the beginning of a project it is very important to build up an executable skeleton of the system, forming an initial thin but complete system. The idea is to make sure early-on that the necessary infrastructure can be built and that subsequent development can proceed in small chunks. This idea is somewhat similar to the Elaboration phase in the Unified Process, at least according to the recent interpretations of it as of Craig Larman's "Agile UP" [10]. In XP, First Iteration serves the role of getting early feedback on the system architecture. If some architectural aspect of the system is not working, it is better to evolve the architecture early on before too much time has been invested in building functionality. For this reason, First Iteration is also called "Zero Feature Iteration".

Building a First Iteration requires experienced programmers and would have been very difficult for our novice students to do. We therefore applied First Iteration by letting the coaches build a tiny first iteration of the system. The PT students could then immediately start adding functionality to the existing system. To aid the coaches in this initial phase we suggested three possible architectures of increasing complexity and suggested that they should start with the simplest one and later evolve it to the more advanced ones, if needed.

On-Site Coach The importance of having a coach, in particular when starting out with XP the first time, has been stressed by many XP practitioners [7, 1, 9]. In a situation of learning or adopting a new set of practices it is important to do a serious job of actually applying the practices. It is all too easy to forget or simply dismiss a practice while concentrating on the actual development. The coach knows the practices, can explain them and motivate why they are important, and can also help the team to actually enforce the practices. Once the practices are mastered the individual is in the position of challenging them and adapting them. We think this is an important way of adopting a new methodology regardless of whether it happens to be XP or something else.

In the accelerated process that we are working with in the project it is important that the coach is always available and actively follows the activities of the team members. The coach needs special skills and training and we therefore came up with the idea of creating a course for third and fourth year students on coaching software teams. The coaching activity is the trainee part of the Coaching course that also covers theoretical aspects of these areas. A pair of students from this course serve as coaches, project leader, tracker, and chief architect for a team of students doing the XP project. Before each iteration we have a 2 hour meeting with the coaches to discuss their experience from the previous iteration and give instructions for the next one.

During the long lab sessions, the coach constantly keeps track of what the team members are doing, "stresses" them when that is needed, and "caresses" them when that is appropriate. An important goal for the coach is team building, to make sure that the team members communicate and collaborate for the common product.

The first time we gave the PT course we naturally had no students with XP experience to enrol on the Coaching course. In order to "bootstrap" the process, around half of the coaches were teachers and Ph.D. students and the rest were hand picked undergraduate students that we believed would be interested as well as do a good job. The student coaches more than fulfilled our expectations, not the least considering team building. In this first instance of the coaching course, we included some condensed XP training with literature studies and discussions as well as lab sessions. There is a lot to be said about the coaching role and the coaching course, but that will be the focus of a forthcoming paper.

Team-in-one-room Real XP projects are often set up so that all of the members share an open workspace where program development takes place [3]. We adopted this practice: program development takes place only at the long labs where all members of the team are present in the same lab room. We found this to be an extremely important practice.

First of all, the students can easily communicate so that everyone is aware of what is happening, and help from fellow students is always near at hand. For example, when one pair got stuck they could immediately get help from others on the team, switch tasks, switch pairs, etc., in order to more easily solve the problem at hand.

Secondly, being all in one room allowed the coach to easily spot any problems, be it a specific programming task, some pair not following the practices, or a situation when the coach could see that two pairs needed to communicate. On such occasions the coach would take a "time-out", i.e., gather the team for a short stand-up meeting to discuss the problem and find a solution. Rather than telling the developers exactly what to do, the coach would on such occasions ask the developers to come up with a solution. This way, the coach helps the developers to learn to help each other, and soon the developers would themselves call on stand-up meetings when needed.

Thirdly, being all in one room very strongly promotes team building. The teams were put together randomly so initially the students did not know each other well. However, due to all the interaction during the long labs, most of the teams soon developed a very strong social team spirit which again promoted further communication and awareness.

It may not always be easy to schedule full day labs for students who take several classes at the same time. However, since these are 2nd year students, most of their schedule is still fixed by mandatory courses, and it was therefore possible for us to negotiate a schedule that did not interfere with other courses. For scheduling reasons, one third of the teams did their long lab from 1-10 PM (rather than from 8AM-5PM). Scheduling was a bit of a problem for some of the student coaches, but this was handled by letting them coach in pairs, so that at least one coach was always present for each team.

Spike time In addition to program development, the developers need time to do individual work, e.g., to read and learn about various practical issues, to think about how to solve a particular task, or to do experimental programming with new solutions. We termed this "spike time". During each planning meeting, the team allocated this spike time in the way they thought best for the team as a whole, thereby providing a pool of additional resources. We gave the coaches some initial ideas for how to allocate the spike time, and after some iterations the following patterns emerged:

- Spiking for a task. In order to be able to program a particular task at the long lab, the students experiment with some key aspects, for example find out what Java libraries to use, and write or find some simple example code that can be used as a starting point later in the long lab.
- Reading/learning about tools. In some teams, a "CVS expert" was appointed whose job it was to use all his/her spike time for learning about CVS in order to help the team mates at the long lab. In other teams, all team members were allocated a couple of hours for experimenting with CVS. Similar spiking was done for other basic tools like JUnit and makefiles, and also for tools introduced during the project such as a refactoring tool for one team, and an acceptance testing tool for another team.
- Refactoring. After a couple of iterations many teams found the need for doing large refactorings of the code. This was difficult to do during the long labs since it affected and/or delayed many teams and produced many merging conflicts. Several teams adopted the policy of allocating spike time for such refactorings. In these cases, refactorings were usually done by a single pair.
- Code review and unit tests. Some teams found that they had too few tests, and used spike time for doing systematic review in order to find code with missing unit tests and to remedy that.

For each team an additional CVS repository was set up that included results from the spikes. This way, the developers could easily share their results with their team members. Not only code was checked in, but also short manuals and other material that the developers produced during their spike time. The general rule was to not check in to the regular repository during spike time, since changes there should only happen when all the team was present at the long labs. However, many teams developed the practice that certain tasks that were allocated to spike time, e.g., big refactorings and adding test code, could be checked after agreeing before-hand at the planning meeting.

The coach meetings (when all coaches met and discussed the previous and next iteration) allowed the coaches to share ideas for how to use the spike time and resulted in many new ideas that we had not been able to foresee. At the last iterations, there was less need for spike time because development had become very intense, and the developers needed more time for development rather than for spikes for new tools or new tasks. However, there was always the need for increased code quality, which motivated e.g. spike time for writing more test cases and refactoring.

Reflection The Agile Manifesto [11] lists reflection as one of the principles in order to follow an agile methodology: *"At regular intervals, the team reflects on how to become more effective, then tunes and adjusts its behaviour accordingly"*. In our XP project, there were several occasions when such reflection occurred spontaneously, e.g. at stand up meetings called on by the coach in order to discuss a particular practice, and at the planning meetings when the results of the previous iteration were discussed. On such occasions it was often decided to do a spike to avoid that a problem repeated itself.

In the next instance of the course we will introduce reflection as an explicit practice so that all teams make a habit of doing some reflection over their work practices at each planning meeting. It is our experience that the spontaneous reflection that occurred in some teams, greatly helped in team building, as well as improved the effectiveness of the team.

Documentation XP does not prescribe any specific documentation, but views the code as the most important (and always up-to-date) documentation. However, core XP can of course be extended with additional practices to cater for appropriate additional documentation. In our XP project, we let the customer write a user story demanding a technical documentation of the system, including an architectural description, build description, description over internal file formats, etc. This was very easy to motivate since the customer might like to take the finished source code and let another team develop it further at a future time.

Several teams also spontaneously developed additional internal documentation like instructions for how to do a release, story test descriptions, etc. Part of this documentation was developed during spike time.

5. The lessons

We have learned many things from running the PT course in this new format, and we summarise our most important lessons below.

Team-In-One-Room is fundamental

Of all the additional practices we introduced, the practice of having the whole team in one room was perhaps the most important of all. We have heard of other experiments in applying XP in education where the teams are just left to themselves to find a common time and place for programming, in which case it usually results in the team splitting into fixed pairs, splitting the stories between them and programming them at different times without much communication, learning, or reflection. In these cases they usually also get problems with collective code ownership and resort to code owning practices [12]. We believe Team-In-One-Room is a fundamental practice to apply in an educational setting, and that if it is not possible to schedule full day lab sessions like we did, splitting into a couple of half day lab sessions is better than splitting the team.

Coaching by older students

In novice teams there is a need for someone with a bit more experience who can take an overall perspective on both the product architecture and the team practices. We had very good experience from applying older students as coaches. This way the coaches had some authority both due to their general seniority and in that they were given special training in the coaching course, yet they were not too distant socially from the PT students which made it easy for them to build a good team spirit. The coaches also found it very stimulating to take on the needed responsibilities.

Underestimated difficulties for the students

During the course it became apparent to us that we had underestimated the difficulty of several practices.

- The "Test First" practice was much more difficult to explain and teach than we initially thought. There is a need for very clear examples on how to write tests, and we will try to include that in the next instance of the course.
- The "Simple Design" practice was also more difficult to teach than we expected. Some students misinterpreted "Do the simplest thing that can possibly work" to mean "Change as little as possible to incorporate a new feature", resulting in a bad design. Here, there is again need for many good examples (and maybe also anti-examples) and to follow up this better during the project.
- A related point is refactoring. Only one of the teams used a refactoring tool in the project, and then only on an experimental basis. This lack of tools had the effect that the students were very reluctant to do refactoring, which again had a bad effect on maintaining a simple design. For the next iteration of the course we hope to introduce a refactoring tool, e.g., by using the Eclipse environment [13], and to give them lab exercises so they gain some confidence and proficiency in using such tools. We expect this to have a major impact on the designs.
- Both the students and we underestimated their problems in putting together a release. Fortunately though, we had scheduled for three releases. Several students thought it would take around 15 minutes to produce a release, whereas in reality it

took up to half a day for a pair, and many of the first releases did not even work. After this experience many of the teams allocated a pair at the next iteration to put together a "release process", i.e. to build a checklist for how to put together a release and what things to check in order to be assured that it would work. Once that was in place, the release process went very smoothly for most teams and they could produce a new release in a matter of minutes.

Although we underestimated many difficulties and the students ran into many problems during their project, this is not necessarily a bad thing. On the contrary, we found it very valuable for the students to run into these problems so they could better appreciate their solutions. Due to the many iterations they got experience from both having problems and solving them which provides a good basis for learning. The preceding theory part of the course together with the coaching during the project did, however, provide the students with a reasonable background and framework so they did not run into all problems at once, but could feel that they did progress with each iteration.

Being a customer is much work

We underestimated how much work it is to be a customer. We needed a good amount of stories that were not too difficult and that could be done in parallel by several pairs. Due to the very short 1-day iterations the stories needed to be much smaller than for a real XP project. To accomplish this we broke down the larger stories into smaller tasks, although this is something that normally the team would do itself, and we also gave the teams directions for the initial architecture and possible ways of evolving the architecture. For the next instance of the course we plan to simply use the same product and stories as we had this year. As we get more experience with the course we might get bolder and bring in new products on the fly, and put more responsibilities on the coach like breaking down stories to tasks and giving them more responsibilities for coming up with the architecture.

XP might have positive effects for minority students

The high interaction and collaboration within an XP team, in particular when guided by a trained coach, might have positive effects for students in minority groups. At the computing engineering program, only around 10% of the students are women. Most women on the course had very positive experiences from the course, and anecdotal evidence points towards them more easily being able to take on active roles as compared to earlier courses.

6. Related work

There seem to be several experiments on including some of the XP practices into the undergraduate education, e.g. [14, 15, 16], as well as experiments with a more complete set of XP practices. Müller and Tichy [17] performed a study of two small 4th year student XP teams, focusing primarily on evaluating the XP practices. They confirm our observation that coaching is very important. Noll [18] provides some observations from initial experience on applying XP to student projects, confirming our experience that XP is an excellent aid in learning, due to its highly iterative nature, allowing students to make mistakes and learn from them. Both these studies also confirm our experience that the Test First practice is difficult to learn. Our study differs by being much larger in scope, both in the number of students and teams, and in the number of additional practices applied. Our study also differs in being focused on XP as an aid in learning software engineering concepts rather than finding out if XP as such is efficient or not.

Williams and Upchurch [19] provide some guidance on the use of the XP practices in an educational context. Most of their advice is in agreement with our experience. However, their advice on not using collective code ownership for novice students is in contrast to our findings. We found collective code ownership to be very important and not problematic at all. All our teams used CVS and were taught to synchronise frequently. In combination with the practice of keeping the whole team in one room, this is probably the reason for our success with collective code ownership. Some teams did initially not synchronise frequently, but the merge problems they then got made them understand how important this is.

7. Conclusions

When our course in introductory Software Engineering needed to be revised we set out to try to teach basic principles applicable on the team level and to use XP as the method. Other secondary goals of the course is to get the students more experienced as programmers, to better understand the problems of working in a team with others, interacting with a customer/user and to expose them to some new programming tools. The course was taught in full scale with 107 students with a background in fundamentals of programming, but no training in Software Engineering. It is followed by courses giving a more traditional software engineering perspective.

In contrast to earlier versions of the course we decided to take a larger responsibility for the management of the project part of the course, actually teaching a method, enforcing and supporting it during the project. For us it was a very interesting alternative to use XP as the method which we judged would suit this situation and would be a vehicle to expose the students to some fundamental software engineering principles and practices.

The result was very positive: we feel that the students have a good understanding for fundamental problems and techniques in software development in mid size teams including testing, inspection, interaction with user/customer, requirements, release process. They also understand how to work in an iterative method and were exposed to the problems of changing requirements. During the project they learned the problems of being many developers changing the same source and some mechanisms to handle these: configuration management, merge, short check-out times, refactoring and separated tasks. The students gave a very positive feedback after the course - it was at times very intense for them, but they report that they learned a lot and were very satisfied with the course.

Our experience is also that XP worked very well for this setting, introducing practices and techniques that could be motivated directly by the situation the students were facing. Having a blank table to start with we set out to use as much of XP practices as we found motivated, expecting that they would support each other. We did, however, have to do some amendments and additions due to the particular teaching situation. The most important additions we feel are to provide support for the architecture, having to do with rather inexperienced students, and thus providing a first iteration from the start and putting more of the responsibility for the software architecture on the coaches. We also broke up the work in smaller tasks than customary in order to have the students perform many iterations.

The format of the course needed to be adjusted to the use of the XP method and in particular we managed to schedule one full day each week for software development. We thus had the students in the same location for 8 hours and could use pair programming with changing partners. Only during this time was it allowed to develop production code. The set-up also was very important in order to build a team and to get all the participants to actually know each other well enough. Another unusual set-up was to use students of a second SE course as coaches for the teams. This allowed a much more intensive coaching than would have been possible using ordinary faculty resources, and provided a realistic setting for the coaches to learn practical aspects of architecture, team building, and leadership.

Acknowledgements
The development of the PT course and the coaching course has been a large collaborative effort by many people at the department. In particular, we would like to thank Torbjörn Ekman and Christian Andersson who came up with the initial idea of full day lab sessions, and for being very helpful in the implementation of the course.

8. References

[1] K. Auer, R. Miller, *Extreme Programming Applied*, Addison-Wesley, 2002.
[2] R. Jeffries, A. Anderson, C. Hendrickson, *Extreme Programming Installed*, Addison-Wesley, 2001.
[3] K. Beck, *Embracing Change with eXtreme Programming*, IEEE Computer, October 1999.
[4] K. Beck, E. Gamma, *JUnit Cookbook*, http://junit.sourceforge.net/doc/cookbook/cookbook.htm.
[5] W.C. Wake, *The Test Code Cycle in XP: Part 1, Model*, http://www.xp123.com/xplor/xp0002.
[6] W.A. Babich, *Software Configuration Management – Coordination for Team Productivity, Chapter 1*, Addison-Wesley, 1986.
[7] K. Beck, *Extreme Programming Explained: Embrace Change*, Addison-Wesley, 2000.
[8] M. Nyström, J. Rix, K. Wanhainen, *En studie om parprogrammering i praktiken* (in Swedish), http://www.cs.lth.se/Education/LTH/01.Dokt.XP/Djupstudier/NystromRixWanhainen.pdf.
[9] W.C. Wake, *Extreme Programming Explored*, Addison-Wesley, 2002.
[10] C. Larman, *Applying UML and Patterns: An Introduction to Object-Oriented Analysis and Design and the Unified Process* (2nd Edition), Prentice-Hall, 2001.
[11] *Manifesto for Agile Software Development*, http://agilemanifesto.org/.
[12] L. Bendix, G. Hedin, *Summary of the Subworkshop on Extreme Programming*, Nordic Journal of Computing, Vol. 9, No. 3, Fall 2002.
[13] *Eclipse Platform Technical Overview*, Object Technology International, Inc., http://www.eclipse.org/.
[14] O. L. Astrachan, R. C. Duvall, E. Wallingford: *Bringing Extreme Programming to the Classroom*, in Extreme Programming Perspectives, Addison-Wesley, 2003.
[15] M. Holcombe, M. Gheorghe, F. Macias: *Teaching XP for Real: Some Initial Observations and Plans*, in Extreme Programming Perspectives, Addison-Wesley, 2003.
[16] D. H. Johnson, J. Caristi: *Extreme Programming and the Software Design Course*, in Extreme Programming Perspectives, Addison-Wesley, 2003.
[17] M.M. Müller, W.F. Tichy, *Case Study: Extreme Programming in a University Environment*, in proceedings of ICSE 2001, Toronto, Canada, May 2001.
[18] J. Noll, *Some Observations of Extreme Programming for Student Projects*, position paper at the Workshop on Empirical Evaluation of Agile Processes, Chicago, Illinois, August 7, 2002.
[19] L. Williams, R. Upchurch, *Extreme programming for software engineering education?*, in proceedings of the 31st ASEE/IEEE Frontiers in Education Conference, Reno, Nevada, October 10-13, 2001.

eXtreme Programming at Universities – An Educational Perspective

Jean-Guy Schneider, Lorraine Johnston
Swinburne University of Technology
School of Information Technology
P.O. Box 218, Hawthorn, Victoria 3122, Australia
{jschneider,ljohnston}@swin.edu.au

Abstract

To address the problems of traditional software development, recent years have shown the introduction of more light-weight or "agile" development processes (eXtreme Programming being the most prominent one). These processes are intended to support early and quick production of working code by structuring the development into small release cycles and focus on continual interaction between developers and customers. As such software development processes become more popular, there is a growing demand from industry to introduce agile development practices in tertiary education.
This is not a straightforward task as the corresponding practices may run counter to educational goals or may not be adjusted easily to a learning environment. In this paper, we discuss some of these issues and reflect on the problems of teaching agile processes in tertiary education.

1. Introduction

Imagine translating a book from Chinese into English, and the book changes overnight, the paper and pencil change while you are writing. The accepted practices involved in Software Engineering (SE) seem to change almost as fast as this. Therefore we have tended to place too much reliance on traditional process models to "explain" to students the best way to engineer software. However, experience has shown that education in "traditional" software development practices, such as the water-fall approach, will not always endow students with the appropriate knowledge and understanding for the workplace.

We need therefore to question whether it might be appropriate to teach our students about more light-weight processes. From an academic point of view, we have to ask:

- Should we introduce the practices of agile development processes in tertiary education?
- If so, how should they be introduced to avoid contradicting our educational goals?

This paper considers issues with using eXtreme Programming to educate students in Software Engineering.

The rest of this paper is organized as follows: in Section 2, we briefly introduce the main principles and practices of eXtreme Programming. In Section 3, we further outline the background of our study and define educational objectives for Software Engineering courses at a tertiary institution. In Section 4, we evaluate the practices of eXtreme Programming with regards to the previously defined educational objectives. Based on these observations, we come up with a few recommendations for software engineering curricula in Section 5. We conclude this paper in Section 6 with a summary of the main observations and suggest issues for further investigation.

2. eXtreme Programming in a Nutshell

eXtreme Programming is a so-called *agile* software development methodology [4], conceived and developed to address the specific needs of software development conducted by small teams in the face of vague and changing requirements [1, 3, 8]. It is a *light-weight* methodology combining a set of existing software development practices in such a way that developers are freed from "unnecessary work" (e.g. extensive documentation) and can concentrate on the main purpose of software development: writing quality code. This is mainly achieved by a highly iterative and incremental process starting with a simple design that meets an initial set of requirements and is constantly evolved to add needed flexibility, removing unneeded complexity. In essence, it attempts to produce the "simplest possible solution" fulfilling current requirements. Furthermore, eXtreme Programming assumes there is always a customer on-site, enforces *pair programming* [1], and promotes automated testing as well as continuous integration.

0-7695-1877-X/03 $17.00 © 2003 IEEE

3. Educational Objectives

Software Engineering aims to support the building of software on time and within budget. While definitions of "Software Engineering" abound, there is a general consensus that it deals with the application of engineering processes to the development of large-scale systems. In such a development, typically no one person can carry all the details of the system in their heads, teamwork becomes a hallmark, and process issues need careful consideration.

In building an aircraft, one can specify the properties of the required product, design a solution, and test a small scale model in a wind tunnel to establish the suitability of some of the properties of the final system. In principle, this is simple for a tangible product like an aircraft. The very fact that software is intangible means that the only evidence of development is in the artifacts that are produced—code, specifications, reports, etc.

For software systems, the complexity grows with size, and alternative development techniques become necessary. The concept of scalability is often one that escapes young aficionados of software development. Similarly, it is a somewhat foreign idea that a complex system does not lend itself to a haphazard approach for development, and requires good management. Additionally, time and resource constraints usually limit the scope of the systems on which students can work. Therefore, the Software Engineering curricula must be carefully crafted so that students can learn about large-scale problems and solutions during the course of their study, in a situation where there is little opportunity to expose them to sufficiently large and complex systems.

3.1. Focusing the educational aims

The IEEE-CS and the ACM have jointly proposed a body of software engineering knowledge (SEEK) [13], as an appropriate basis for the education of software engineers. Each of the defined topic areas in SEEK is addressed briefly here, in terms of its relevance for young software engineers.

Fundamentals. The underpinnings of Software Engineering lie in Mathematics and in the foundations of Computing and Engineering. This includes the ability to deal with abstraction and to understand the concept of models. Most students would have little difficulty comprehending the reason for including these topics in an SE program.

Professional Practice. While one could debate exactly what "Professional Practice" should encompass, it is fair to say that students need to learn about the ethical and social aspects of their profession, as well as more business-oriented aspects such as contracting models.

Software Requirements. Empirically, we know that an inadequate consideration of the perspectives of all stakeholders leads to rework later on. Hence, it is important to consider all relevant viewpoints up front, including the perspectives of both the end-user and the client. Students frequently need reminding of the importance of these issues.

Software Construction. Students tend to regard this topic as the key part of software engineering endeavours.

Software Design. Small systems can usually be modified more easily than complex systems. Students need to understand at least the need for design documentation to communicate the design, and the need for capturing design rationale. Beyond that, there is an urgent need for more instruction in architecture and related issues such as component-based systems and the use of patterns. An area often not discussed is that of interaction design, and the resulting user interface. Omitting this from curricula promises to produce a generation of software engineers who do not understand that functionality is not everything in a software product. Given basic functionality, the marketplace differentiates on quality attributes such as task efficiency, learnability, ease of use, aesthetics, and engagement.

Software Verification and Validation. Without extensive exposure to larger systems and to the theory of testing, the perception of students is that verification and validation equate to testing, or even debugging. However, students need to learn about traditional approaches such as white- and black-box testing, test planning, and testing to see if the desired non-functional properties have been met. It is also important that new engineers develop skills with and understanding of, not only testing, but also other verification and validation techniques such as inspections.

Software Evolution. Most newly-graduated software engineers are likely to find themselves employed, not on developing new systems, but on maintaining existing systems. Therefore, they need analytical skills enabling them to identify where and what changes are needed. For this, they need a good understanding of the architecture of the system, as well as clear ideas on the role of regression testing.

Software Engineering Process. The concept of "Process" goes hand-in-hand with that of management. Without a strong framework of required activities, students tend to espouse, and indeed use, *ad hoc* work practices.

Software Quality. Quality is said to be noted in its absence, rather than in its presence. Unfortunately, it is often then too late to fix the problem. Therefore, students need a solid understanding of the techniques and methods that can help produce a quality product. However, there is the problem that the techniques for ensuring quality in a large-scale product often seem to be an overkill for the size of products students confront. It may sometimes be necessary to impose processes which are not entirely suitable, purely from the perspective of exposing students to large-scale techniques.

Software Engineering Management. Many undergraduate students have little experience of managing anything. Some are of the age and mind-set to rebel against authority, and it is difficult for them to suddenly have to consider how a project is managed. Additionally, they often have little experience in a workplace and are unaware of expected behavioural protocols. This can have implications for how they interact and organise a team-based project. Richardson [12] observed that teaching SE to undergraduates was a difficult proposition owing to (i) their lack of computing experience, (ii) their lack of academic maturity to deal with ambiguity and conflicts between reality and theory, and (iii) their underdeveloped interpersonal skills. Young people usually have very good memories, and trust in their own ability to recall information. In this context, it is often difficult to convince students about the value, let alone necessity, of software configuration management. In class, students tend to work on "toy" examples, and configuration management seems simply an unnecessary overhead.

Like any other engineering discipline, to be efficient in a production environment, tools as well as specific techniques and methods are needed. Students need motivation to learn to use the tools, but also need to understand both the rationale for their use and the principles on which they are built. It is good for them to be exposed to specific tools, but it is also important that they realise the range available. This becomes an issue of education for understanding and application of knowledge versus training to use a specific product, the latter being a non-extendable position.

3.2. Putting it together in a project

Isolated topics in software engineering only provide the basis on which to build an understanding of the development of large-scale systems. The real learning takes place when the topics are not seen as isolated entities, but are put together in a real project. That is, when students are required to interact with a real user to discover the client's real problems, the pieces start to fall into place. For example, why should one trace where the requirement originated? Or, later, why should a design decision be documented? As any parent knows, it is in the experience itself, that the best learning takes place. Most undergraduate software engineering programs have a final project to provide the capstone of the studies. In the discussion that follows, the context is that of a team-based, final year project.

4. eXtreme Programming and Education

As mentioned previously, eXtreme Programming (XP) has been conceived for software development conducted by small teams of a maximum of 12 to 15 team members [1]. As this is also the maximum number of students we would consider as useful for final year software engineering projects, using XP as the development process would certainly be a feasible approach.

Recent work has shown that despite its success, XP does not address some important issues of software development [17] or should not be used for larger-scale and/or safety-critical systems [4]. Although further investigation of the (non-)applicability of XP for real-world software projects is certainly an important issue, this is beyond the scope of this paper. In this section, the focus is on evaluating some of the practices used in XP with regards to the previously defined educational objectives (see Section 3), with a special focus on two-semester software projects.

eXtreme Metaphor. In [1] Beck says that XP is principally nothing new, but "takes a set of common sense principles and practices to extreme levels." Most of these principles and practices are fairly well-known, were part of other software development methodologies, and have been taught in the context of a variety of courses before.

Unfortunately, some of these principles have previously not reached the required level of acceptance with students, e.g. the importance of testing (i.e. writing test cases *before* writing code), the focus on producing *quality* software in the first place, and the importance of coding standards and configuration management. We noticed there is definitely a better acceptance and understanding of these practices when they are introduced in an XP-like context. The *eXtreme* metaphor is the main contributing factor here as practices previously considered as being tedious become trendy.

Pair Programming. Probably the most extensively investigated practice of XP is pair programming. Several encouraging experience reports have been published in both industrial and academic settings (e.g. see [1, 5, 7, 11, 18]). In particular, there is empirical evidence that a pair of developers working on one computer can produce better quality software faster than the pair working separately.

However, we argue that this observation only holds if pair programming is done in the "right" environment with appropriately trained people. XP assumes all developers have reasonable programming skills, are capable of working in pairs, and are willing to do so.

One of the authors adopted pair programming some years ago in a large class of first year computing students (app. 500 students). The goal was to improve programming skills as it was thought students would help each other learn by discussion. Inevitably, the stronger one of the pair did most of the work, the weaker one usually failed the later examination, and only where there were well-matched pairs was the goal reached. We also noted different personality types and/or genders had a significant impact on pair programming performance. Unfortunately, there is little evidence that researchers have considered this yet.

Educational systems seem to be primarily based on a scheme where good marks are most highly rewarded, and many students are uncomfortable leaving this framework. In an XP environment, however, an ego-less attitude is required as people have to favour team success over personal rewards and assist other team members improve their working skills. These issues require a level of maturity to accept.

Process and Discipline. Agile methodologies are considered to be light-weight and impose less process burden upon the developers, which are some of the reasons why they have become so popular. However, the practices of any agile methodology must be applied in a disciplined way for projects to succeed. The relevance of discipline in XP is captured by Smith [15]: "XP is not a free form, anything goes discipline—it focuses [...] on a particular aspect of software development and a way of delivering value, and is quite prescriptive about the way this is to be achieved."

It is in the nature of young university students that they are less likely to enjoy prescriptive development methods and prefer approaches which leave them more freedom to explore. Furthermore, experience has shown that they have the tendency to struggle if they have to work in a disciplined way over a longer period. The combination of these two observations leads to a situation quite accurately described by one of our colleagues as "students dislike process, but they like discipline even less." Hence there is a big risk that a light-weight development methodology such as XP cannot be successfully applied in an educational environment.

We therefore argue that a less flexible development process with more guidance is better suited to the educational environment than a process based on "less process, more discipline." The latter should only be applied if all participants have the necessary experience and maturity, and fully understand the consequences of choosing a light-weight development process. This was best summarized by another colleague: "XP is for professionals, not students."

Distribution and Availability. One of the main practices of XP (and most other agile development processes) is that the development team is co-located, preferably even in a single office. The physical arrangement of the office needs to facilitate, or even encourage, brainstorming, joint discussions, pair programming, etc. [1, pp. 78]. Furthermore, it is assumed all developers are on-site most of their work time.

Unfortunately, such an environment is fanciful in most universities. More often than not, laboratory space is a limited resource, and as many machines as possible are put into one room, making them very crowded and noisy. Joint working is therefore awkward and, unsurprisingly, students prefer working at home. Furthermore, as most students have part-time jobs and their timetables are relatively disjoint, it is often difficult to find suitable times for scheduling joint working sessions outside timetabled classes at all.

Hence, student software projects are probably more aligned with distributed projects than co-located ones. Thus, one of the main prerequisites for applying XP is not fulfilled and the benefits of a joint working environment are lost, in particular the *warm communication paths* [4]. As a result, stricter rules for documenting project activities have to be put in place and the whole process immediately becomes more heavy-weight. There are efforts to adapt XP practices to distributed work environments (e.g. a recent article by Kircher et al. [9]), but the necessary changes and the resulting consequences are not yet fully understood.

At our institution, we happily acquired a laboratory with a small number of workstations especially set up for the needs of two project teams. Interestingly, one team decided to do most of their design and coding there and scheduled their joint working sessions based on their respective timetables (mostly late afternoons or evenings). The other team's members, however, used the room infrequently, preferred to work at home, and for collaboration relied on phone calls or internet technology (instant messaging, email, online chat, etc.). They occasionally organized coding sessions at one of the students' homes. Encouragement of the second team to use the laboratory more seems to have failed because of ignorance of the benefits of joint working sessions. They reverted to "the way we have been working throughout the previous years of our studies."

On-site Client. A similar problem arises with regards to having an on-site customer. Considering that this is often wishful thinking even in industry projects, with students' timetables it is probably a fair assumption that being able to contact the client by email or phone during working hours is as "ideal" a situation as we can hope for.

We have noted on several projects that clients do not fully understand the benefits of regular developer-client interactions. They do not want to be "bothered" by giving feedback to all team members, and they often ask for a liaison person for interaction. Also, students are loathe to be continually contacting the client: "we do not want to bother our clients with small or trivial issues all the time."

As a result, students often spend quite some time in getting certain aspects of the system "perfect" and understandably get frustrated when they receive negative feedback on what they thought was completed work. The issue of not having feedback when needed is magnified by the problem of students working at home, alone and/or at night. Being able to talk to the client earlier and more freely would certainly help to rectify these kinds of problems.

Development Cycles. XP is a highly iterative and incremental development process with iterations taking one to two weeks and a new release coming out every month or two. In fact, short development cycles are crucial for successful projects [1, 3]. Each iteration is supposed to add functionality of a certain value to the customer. To achieve these kinds of development, XP assumes that developers can work exclusively on the project for 40 hours a week.

In an educational setting, we do not have the luxury of having students exclusively available for 40 hours project work each week; an average of 10 to 15 hours per week is much more likely. To gain the same amount of value added per iteration or release as in an ideal setting, we end up with iterations of four to six weeks and release cycles of six to eight months! Considering that student projects generally run over a period of one to two semesters, this is neither a practical nor an acceptable option. To keep the cycles short(er), one must reduce the scope of each cycle. However, it is doubtful whether any significant value can be added to the software with these kinds of cycles, and we end up with a situation which is not really acceptable, either.

Project Deliverables. The authors of the Agile Software Development Manifesto [2] claim that "running software is considered to be the most important deliverable" of a software project and "working software is the primary measure of progress." There are very good reasons why this applies to certain types of projects (and possibly not to others), but we must question the relevance in an educational context.

There is no doubt that having running software at some stage in a project is desirable and reflects progress. Additionally, it provides both satisfaction that meaningful work has been done and the necessary motivation to keep working. However, the lessons learned during a software project are at least as important as running software and must be considered as a kind of deliverable, too. Unfortunately, the desired learning can often only be achieved by making mistakes, analyzing the resulting problems, and rectifying them. This takes time, and during this period, there is no progress which can be measured in terms of working code.

Furthermore, we believe that code being the main deliverable sends the wrong message to students. If we consider the cooperative game principle of Cockburn [4, pp. 31], then code only addresses the first goal of the software development game (i.e. deliver useful, working software), but neglects the second goal (i.e. prepare for the next game). There are many kinds of (larger-scale) projects where more than just running code is required, e.g., re-engineering projects where extracting and documenting the design of an existing legacy system is a necessary step for any forward-engineering activity [6].

Finally, one cannot equitably assess a team of developers (either individually or as a group) on running software alone, as issues such as personal initiative, dedication to quality work etc. are not judged to the required level of accuracy. Other "products" of the development process are needed. The reader should note this does not only apply to educational contexts, but also to situations in industry where promotions are based on any such assessment schemes.

Perception. Students without the required level of maturity to fully understand what is important in software development and the consequences of certain practices, can be mislead by agile development practices as they only tend to see "what can be omitted." As an example, we organized a complementary lecture on agile software development (given by an expert in the field) to the final year software engineering students halfway through semester one of their two-semester project. In the following team meeting with one of the teams, a student commented that "we should have chosen XP as our development process; then it would not have been necessary to write a requirements specification." As it turned out, misconceptions in the requirements resulted in that team running into trouble in semester two.

It can be said that development processes such as XP certainly have their benefits and can have a positive impact in an educational context. However, there are important educational goals which are not met and, therefore, changes to the process have to be made in order to address these goals.

5. Recommendations

SE education aims to produce software engineers with the knowledge and skills to adapt their practices in an ever-changing environment. This is distinct from training them as experts in the techniques and processes which are currently most popular and being touted as "the way to go." While XP has many positive aspects, many of its tenets are not compatible with the real environment of most students.

Some of the difficulties lie with the prior educational experiences of students. There are problems when the student mindset prioritizes outcomes in the order (i) a pass in a course, (ii) a good grade in a course, (iii) the learning experience, and (iv) helping another student. A re-engineering of this mindset is necessary before the practices of XP can work well. The question of how to refocus the student experience is being considered by many educationalists, but clearly an early focus on teamwork and cooperation is important for SE studies. Instilling the concept of "ego-less working" at an early stage is a key element, the introduction of learning communities [16] another.

Location and scheduling problems are difficult to overcome in an academic environment. Leverage may possibly be found with additional research into distributed lightweight methods, and their application to educational situations. Currently the co-location issues are difficult to solve.

One way to present a large-scale project to students is to offer a team-based maintenance project, where extensions are needed. This has some overlap with the idea of the Real World Laboratory at Georgia Institute of Technology [14]. If the base system is sufficiently large and complex, many of the large-scale objectives can be met. Students must view the system at various levels of abstraction, and identify the location for change from the existing system artifacts. They must design and implement the changes, performing all the relevant levels of testing, and "plan" for future changes. Where there is little or no existing documentation, apart from in the code itself, students become very aware of how much planning for change went into the original product. They will more likely agree that running software alone should not be the criterion of a well-engineered product.

In academia, it is appropriate to place the primary emphasis on process, rather than product, which does not always delight the management-averse students. If the goal is to have students learn techniques suitable for large-scale development, then we must simulate at least the development of a complex system. It may be necessary to impose on their project work a regime which otherwise would not be the development process of choice for that system.

Rather than learn to apply only XP techniques, it is preferable that students are exposed to a set of techniques that help them manage a variety of projects (from small to large-scale), introduced the ideas in the context of the positive and negative issues associated with any process model, and given guidelines how to select a process model for the particular situation. The Crystal methodologies [4] is a process-kit which could be used for this purpose, the Rational Unified Process [10] another.

Education includes giving students a set of tools to craft a solution. Part of the collection of knowledge and skills needed by new engineers is the ability to tailor a process to suit their needs. Teaching students how to tailor their processes is likely to have a more beneficial effect than seeing a light-weight development process such as XP as the answer.

6. Conclusions

Agile development processes like XP are increasingly popular in industry. However, in tertiary institutions, there is little teaching experience of agile processes beyond pair programming. Further evaluation is needed to gain necessary insights. As discussed, some practices of XP can be used in a learning environment, others negate educational goals. Curriculum changes are needed so that students embrace a less self-centred philosophy than is currently the case. Consequently, we believe that eXtreme Programming as it stands does not lend itself for use in tertiary education.

References

[1] K. Beck. *Extreme Programming Explained: Embrace Change*. Addison-Wesley, 1999.

[2] K. Beck, M. Beedle, A. van Bennekum, A. Cockburn, W. Cunningham, M. Fowler, J. Grenning, J. Highsmith, A. Hunt, R. Jeffries, J. Kern, B. Marick, R. C. Martin, S. Mellor, K. Schwaber, J. Sutherland, and D. Thomas. Manifesto for Agile Software Development. Available at http://agilemanifesto.org/.

[3] K. Beck, M. Fowler, and J. Kohnke. *Planning Extreme Programming*. The XP Series. Addison-Wesley, 2000.

[4] A. Cockburn. *Agile Software Development*. Addison-Wesley, 2001.

[5] A. Cockburn and L. Williams. The Cost and Benefits of Pair Programming. In G. Succi and M. Marchesi, editors, *Extreme Programming Examined*, The XP Series. Addison-Wesley, May 2001.

[6] S. Demeyer, S. Ducasse, and O. Nierstrasz. *Object-Oriented Reengineering Patterns*. Morgan Kaufmann/dPunkt, 2002.

[7] M. Holcombe, M. Gheorghe, and F. Macias. Teaching XP for Real: some initial observations and plans. In *Proceedings of the Second International Conference on Extreme Programming and Flexible Processes in Software Engineering (XP2001)*, pages 14–17, Cagliari, Italy, May 2001.

[8] R. Jeffries, A. Anderson, and C. Hendrickson. *Extreme Programming Installed*. The XP Series. Addison-Wesley, 2000.

[9] M. Kircher, P. Jain, A. Corsaro, and D. Levine. Distributed eXtreme Programming. In *Proceedings of the Second International Conference on Extreme Programming and Flexible Processes in Software Engineering (XP2001)*, pages 66–71, Cagliari, Italy, May 2001.

[10] P. Kruchten. *The Rational Unified Process: An Introduction*. Object Technology Series. Addison-Wesley, Second edition, 2000.

[11] M. M. Müller and W. F. Tichy. Case study: Extreme programming in a university environment. In H. A. Müller, editor, *Proceedings ICSE 2001*, pages 537–544, Toronto, Canada, May 2001. IEEE Computer Society.

[12] W. E. Richardson. Undergraduate Software Engineering Education. In G. A. Ford, editor, *Proceedings of the Second SEI Conference on Software Engineering Education*, LNCS 327, pages 121–144, Fairfax, Virginia, Apr. 1988. Springer.

[13] Software Engineering Education Knowledge (SEEK). Second Draft, available at http://sites.computer.org/ccse/, Dec. 2002.

[14] D. M. Smith. Real World Laboratory. 3 semester project at Georgia Institute of Technology, refer to http://www.cc.gatech.edu/classes/RWL/Web.

[15] J. Smith. A Comparison of RUP and XP. White Paper, Rational Software Corporation, 2001.

[16] V. Tinto. Colleges as Communities: Taking Research on Student Persistence Seriously. *The Review of Higher Education*, 21(2):167–177, 1998.

[17] D. Turk, R. France, and B. Rumpe. Limitations of Agile Software Processes. In *Proceedings of the Third International Conference on Extreme Programming and Flexible Processes in Software Engineering (XP2002)*, pages 43–46, Alghero, Italy, May 2002.

[18] L. A. Williams and R. R. Kessler. The Effects of "Pair-Pressure" and "Pair-Learning" on Software Engineering Education. In S. A. Mengel and P. J. Knoke, editors, *Proceedings of the Thirteenth Conference on Software Engineering Education & Training*, pages 59–65. IEEE Computer Society, Mar. 2000.

Software Engineering Education and Training

Undergraduate Education

The Impact of Pair Programming on Student Performance, Perception and Persistence

Charlie McDowell and Linda Werner
Computer Science Department
University of California, Santa Cruz
{charlie,linda}@cs.ucsc.edu,

Heather E. Bullock and Julian Fernald
Psychology Department
University of California, Santa Cruz
{hbullock,jfernald}@cats.ucsc.edu

Abstract

This study examined the effectiveness of pair programming in four lecture sections of a large introductory programming course. We were particularly interested in assessing how the use of pair programming affects student performance and decisions to pursue computer science related majors. We found that students who used pair programming produced better programs, were more confident in their solutions, and enjoyed completing the assignments more than students who programmed alone. Moreover, pairing students were significantly more likely than non-pairing students to complete the course, and consequently to pass it. Among those who completed the course, pairers performed as well on the final exam as non-pairers, were significantly more likely to be registered as computer science related majors one year later, and to have taken subsequent programming courses. Our findings suggest that not only does pairing not compromise students' learning, but that it may enhance the quality of their programs and encourage them to pursue computer science degrees.

1. Introduction

In recent years, the growth of extreme programming (XP) has brought considerable attention to collaborative programming. Developed over a fifteen year period by Kent Beck and his colleagues, Ron Jeffries and Ward Cunningham[1], XP is a computer software development approach that credits much of its success to the use of pair programming by all programmers, regardless of experience[2]. The pair programming dimension of XP requires that teams of two programmers work simultaneously on the same design, algorithm, code, or test. Sitting shoulder to shoulder at one computer, one member of the pair is the "designated driver," actively creating code and controlling the keyboard and mouse. The "non-driver" constantly reviews the keyed data in order to identify tactical and strategic deficiencies, including erroneous syntax and logic, misspelling, and implementations that don't map to the design. After a designated period of time, the partners reverse roles. Code produced by only one partner is discarded, or reviewed collaboratively before it is integrated.

Computer science faculty are increasingly experimenting, either formally or informally, with pair programming in the classroom. All of the published studies to date indicate that pair programming has a positive impact on some aspect of student performance or enjoyment, while none have demonstrated that student learning is compromised[2-4]. Nevertheless, many instructors continue to require students to complete programming assignments independently. Presumably, continued reliance on solo programming in academic settings is rooted in instructor concern that one of the partners in a pair will not learn as much as they would if they completed the assignment alone. In the worst case, one member of the pair might do essentially all of the work. Although this would not be "pair programming," it is often difficult, if not impossible, to monitor how students actually spend their programming time and how closely they are following the pairing protocol.

Previously, we reported on preliminary data from two of the four introductory programming sections discussed in this paper[3]. We found that a greater percentage of students who were required to use pair programming made it to the final exam, and that among those who completed the course, pairing and non-pairing students performed equally well on the final exam. In this paper we report on course performance data from all four sections. We also present data about students' confidence in their programming solutions, and their enjoyment of, and satisfaction with the process, as well as subsequent course taking patterns and major declarations.

2. Method

The purpose of this study was to investigate the effects of pair programming on student performance and subsequent pursuit of computer science related degrees among both female and male college students. Participants were 555 students (413 men and 141 women[1]) who attempted an introductory computer programming course,

[1] Gender information was unavailable for one student.

0-7695-1877-X/03 $17.00 © 2003 IEEE

intended primarily for computer science, computer engineering, electrical engineering, and information systems management majors, at the University of California-Santa Cruz during the 2000-01 academic year.

Four sections of the course were offered during the year: one in the Fall quarter, two in Winter, and one during the Spring. One of the principle investigators of this study, Charlie McDowell, taught the Fall and Spring sections of the course. The two Winter sections were taught by UCSC faculty members not associated with this project.

Students enrolled in the Fall and Winter sections were required to complete all assignments using pair programming. Students in the Spring section, on the other hand, were required to complete programming assignments independently. On the first day of class students in the pairing sections were given a brief 15 to 20 minute description of pair programming and instructed to read Williams and Kessler's paper "All I Really Need to Know About Pair Programming I Learned in Kindergarten [5]." As an incentive to read the paper they were told that the first quiz might include a question about it.

Students in the pairing sections submitted a list of three names of potential partners, and partners were assigned based on these preferences. In nearly all instances, students were assigned a partner from their list. Those that stated no preference were randomly assigned a partner. Whenever possible students remained with the same partner throughout the quarter, however, due to schedule changes and drops, a small number of partner reassignments were necessary. As a result of hardships such as heavy work schedules or living far from campus seventeen students across the three pairing sections were permitted to program alone for various reasons. Data from these students was combined with the data from the students in the non-pairing section.

Although each student was assigned to one 90-minute lab time per week, most programming assignments were completed outside of scheduled lab time. The labs functioned primarily as teaching assistant office hours. There were no specific in-lab assignments and attendance was not mandatory.

Students in two of the three pairing classes and in the non-pairing class were required to submit five graded programming assignments. In the remaining pairing class students completed four graded assignments. In all four sections students were also encouraged to complete four additional practice programming assignments that did not contribute directly to their grade. Programming assignments were scored for functionality and readability. Along with each assignment students submitted a log indicating the amount of time they spent on the assignment (pairing students were asked to differentiate between time spent driving, reviewing, and alone), their level of confidence in their solution, how much they enjoyed working on the assignment, and how satisfied they were with the process.

Regardless of whether they completed assignments in pairs, all students took exams independently. The final exam assessed students' knowledge of programming concepts and their ability to write new code. Additionally, we collected information about students SAT scores, the courses they took over the following year, and their major declarations a year after taking the class.

3. Results

An important assumption of this study was that all four sections of the course were similar in terms of students' academic preparation to succeed. In order to test this assumption, one-way ANOVAs by course section on SAT math and verbal scores, and high school GPA (required of most freshmen applicants for admission to UCSC) and transfer GPA (required of all transfer students) were conducted. There were no significant differences between sections on SAT math scores, or on high school or transfer GPA. There was a significant main effect on SAT verbal scores $F(3, 465) = 5.05$, $p<.005$. Tukey follow-up tests revealed that the average SAT-V scores in one of the sections that required pairing was significantly lower than the two other pairing sections ($M = 521$ vs. $M = 559$ and $M = 573$), but not significantly different than the non-pairing section ($M = 547$). Combining the three pairing sections indicated that there was not a significant difference in SAT-V scores between all pairers and non-pairers ($M = 553$ and $M = 547$ respectively). Because the difference was only between pairing sections it seemed acceptable.

3.1. Completion and Pass Rates

Perhaps the most straightforward indicators of student success are completing the course and passing it. For the purpose of this study, we defined *completion* as taking the final exam, and *passing* as earning a "C" or above.

Table 1: Completion and pass rates

	Completion Rates for all Students	Pass Rates for all Students	Completer's Pass Rates
Pairers[2] (N=404)	90.8%	72.3%	79.6%
Non-pairers (N=148)	80.4%	62.8%	78.2%

A comparison of students who used pair programming with those who didn't indicated that pairers were significantly more likely to complete the course (90.8%)

[2] The pairing status of 3 students was unavailable.

than were non-pairers (80.4%), $\chi^2(1) = 11.21$, $p<.001$. Not surprisingly then, pairers were also more likely to pass the course (72.3% vs. 62.8%), $\chi^2(1) = 4.57$, $p < .05$. Among just those who took the final exam, the difference in pass rates between pairing (79.6%) and non-pairing students (78.2%) was not statistically significant (see Table 1).

Williams and Kessler have proposed "pair pressure" as a possible explanation for higher completion rates among paired versus unpaired students[6]. According to Williams and Kessler, students who work in pairs may be more likely to complete programming courses because of the shared responsibility that results from collaborative partnerships. As a consequence, paired students may remain in the class for the sake of their partner. Although this is a plausible explanation, it is not supported by these data. The fact that in our study there was no difference in pass rates between pairers who completed the course and non-pairers who completed the course suggests that it was not simply the case that pairers were more likely to "stick it out," but rather that a larger proportion of paired students were able to master enough of the course material to pass.

Overall the difference between women's and men's completion rates (85.8% and 89.1% respectively) was not statistically significant $\chi^2(1) = 1.10$, $p>.05$. An examination of the effects of pairing on women and men separately indicated that men who paired were significantly more likely to complete the course (91.7%) than men who did not pair (81.5%). On the other hand, there was not a significant difference in completion rates between women who paired and those who did not (88.1% vs. 79.5%). The fact that the 10% difference in completion rates between paired and unpaired men was statistically significant, while the 8% difference in completion rates between paired and unpaired women was not is probably best explained by the substantially smaller number of women (N = 141) than men (N = 413) in the programming classes.

3.2. Course Performance

In addition to completion and pass rates, we were interested in the effects of pairing on course performance. We measured two related, but distinct indicators of course mastery. The first, the quality of the programs that students produce was operationalized as student's normalized average score on the graded programming assignments. The second is the extent to which students are able to apply the concepts covered during the course. We used final exam scores, which all students took independently regardless of whether they paired or not, as the measure of the extent to which they had learned the material. For the following analyses we included only those students who completed the course, defined as taking the final exam (N=486).

Among students who completed the class, a two-way ANOVA (pair type X gender) indicated that those who paired produced significantly better programs (86.6%) than those who worked alone (68.1%), $F(1, 482) = 77.42$, $p<.001$. There was no significant gender difference in average programming scores (men's and women's scores were 81.9% and 82.5% respectively), nor was there an interaction between gender and pairing. In other words, pairing was associated with significantly higher scores for both women and men (see Table 2). A two-way (gender X partners' gender) ANOVA on pairer's programming scores indicated that neither pairers' gender nor their partner's gender was related to the quality of the programs they produced.

Table 2: Average programming scores

	Mean	Std. dev.
All pairers	86.6%	14.7
All non-pairers	68.1%	22.4
Paired women	86.9%	16.0
Unpaired women	70.1%	19.7
Paired men	86.5%	14.2
Unpaired men	67.3%	23.3

It may be that the reluctance of some computer science faculty to use pair programming in their classes is due to a concern that at least some students will "earn" grades that predominantly reflect their partner's work. It is possible, for example, that the pairing students in our study earned higher average programming scores simply because weaker students received scores that were primarily due to the work of the stronger student in the pair, thus artificially inflating the average programming scores of the pairers.

Elsewhere we have argued that the very process of working collaboratively enhances the quality of programs that pairs produce[3]. In that paper we compared the two sections of the introductory programming course that were taught by the same instructor, and for which assignments were intentionally designed to be equivalent. We found that the average score on programming assignments of all of the students in the pairing section was significantly higher than the average score of the top 50% (based on final exam scores) of the non-pairing section.

Nevertheless, it is important to understand the effects of pairing on individual student learning. Because all of the students in this study took the final exam independently, we considered final exam scores the best indication of the extent to which students had mastered the course material. A two-way (pairing X gender) ANOVA indicated that scores were not influenced by whether students paired, $F(1, 482) = .02$, $p>.05$. Pairers averaged 75.2% on the final compared with non-pairers' average of 74.4% (see Table 3). This finding strongly suggests that a student's ability to independently apply concepts to novel problems is not compromised by learning to program in pairs. Indeed, considering that a significantly greater percentage of the students who paired took the final, it seems that learning to program in pairs results in mastery for a greater percentage of students.

We did note a gender difference in final exam scores that approached, but did not reach significance, $F(1, 482) = 2.86$, $p = .09$. Men and women scored 76.2% and 71.4% respectively. Analysis of covariance (ANCOVA), using SAT math scores as a covariate ($F(1, 409) = .43$, $p = .51$.) indicated that the marginal gender difference we observed may be the result of differential preparation.

A two-way (gender X partner's gender) ANOVA on pairers exam scores only, revealed a significant main effect of gender on final exam scores, $F(1, 362) = 7.46$, $p < .01$. Men who paired averaged 76.7%, while women who paired averaged 70.8% (see Table 3). Again, this difference was not significant when math SAT scores were held constant, $F(1, 303) = 2.9$, $p > .05$. The gender of the partner was not related to performance on the final exam.

Table 3: Final exam scores

	Mean	Std. dev.	N
All pairers	75.2%	18.9	367
All non-pairers	74.4%	18.5	119
All men	76.2%	18.4	366
All women	71.4%	19.7	120
Paired men	76.7%	18.6	277
Paired women	70.8%	19.2	89

3.3. Confidence, satisfaction, and enjoyment

Table 4: Questions asked about each program

Confidence	On a scale from 0 (not at all confident) to 100 (very confident), how confident are you in your solution to this assignment?
Satisfaction (pairers only)	How satisfied are you with the way that you and your partner worked together on this assignment? (1=very dissatisfied, 7=very satisfied)
Satisfaction (non-pairers only)	How satisfied are you with how you spent your time on this assignment? (1=very dissatisfied, 7=very satisfied)
Enjoyment	How much did you enjoy working on this programming assignment? (1=not at all, 7=very much)

Of course the most important goal for students in any class is mastery of the material. This is certainly the case for introductory programming courses, where future success is dependent on a strong foundational knowledge. However, subjective experiences in introductory programming courses may also contribute to decisions about whether to pursue computer science related degrees. For this reason it is important to understand how the experience of pairing influences students' confidence in, enjoyment of, and satisfaction with their work. The specific questions students responded to in their logs are presented in Table 4.

3.3.1. Confidence in program solution

Overall, students who paired reported significantly higher confidence in their program solutions (89.4%) than students who worked independently (71.2%), $F(1,482) = 99.38$, $p < .001$, and men were significantly more confident (87.0%) than women (81.1%), $F(1,482) = 14.62$, $p < .001$. There was also a significant interaction between pairing and gender with regard to reported confidence. Simple effects follow-up tests of the interaction indicated that pairing resulted in more confidence for both women (86.8% vs. 63.0%), $F(1, 482) = 50.54$, $p < .001$ and men (90.3% vs. 74.6%), $F(1, 482) = 54.94$, $p < .001$. However, the 24% increase in confidence that pairing afforded women was even greater than the 15% confidence boost experienced by men who had the benefit of pairing (see Table 5). Partners' gender was unrelated to pairers' confidence levels.

Table 5: Confidence in solutions

	Mean	Std. dev.	N
All pairers	89.38	13.73	380
All non-pairers	71.21	23.95	106
All men	86.99	16.42	356
All women	81.11	21.57	130
Paired men	90.30	13.08	281
Unpaired men	74.61	16.42	75
Paired women	86.79	15.19	99
Unpaired women	62.97	28.29	31

3.3.2. Satisfaction with programming

Similarly, pairing students reported greater satisfaction ($M=5.95$) than non-pairing students ($M=4.58$), $F(1,475) = 118.05$, $p < .001$, and men reported greater satisfaction ($M=5.72$) than women ($M=5.45$), $F(1,475) = 4.56$, $p < .05$ (see Table 6). No interaction between pairing and gender was found. Because the question about satisfaction was not identical for the pairing and non-pairing students these results should be interpreted cautiously. We realized too late that we had asked the pairing students a question that was not appropriate for the non-pairers.

Table 6: Satisfaction (1=very dissatisfied, 7=very satisfied)

	Mean	Std. dev.	N
Pairers	5.95	.98	374
Non-pairers	4.58	1.28	105
Men	5.72	1.09	351
Women	5.45	1.40	128
Paired w/ a man	5.91	1.00	277
Paired w/ a woman	6.05	0.87	96

A partner by partner's gender ANOVA of pairers satisfaction revealed a marginal effect of partner's gender, $F(1,369)=3.84$, $p=.051$. Students that partnered with a woman were more satisfied with how they worked with their partner ($M=6.05$) than students that partnered with a man ($M=5.91$).

3.3.3. Enjoyment

A two-way (pairing X gender) ANOVA indicated that pairing students enjoyed working on programming assignments ($M=5.14$) more than non-pairing students ($M=4.69$), $F(1,482)=9.00$, $p<.005$. Overall women ($M=4.84$) and men ($M=5.11$) enjoyed the assignments equally well, $F(1,482)=2.69$, $p>.05$. However, among just the students who worked in pairs, men reported significantly higher enjoyment ($M=5.21$) than the women ($M=4.91$), $F(1,482)=6.42$, $p<.05$ (see Table 7) regardless of whether they partnered with a woman or a man.

Table 7: Enjoyment (1=very unenjoyable, 7=very enjoyable)

	Mean	Std. dev.	N
Pairers	5.14	1.14	380
Non-pairers	4.69	1.02	106
All men	5.11	1.11	356
All women	4.84	1.15	130
Paired men	5.21	1.13	280
Paired women	4.91	1.12	99

3.4. Persistence in computer science

In addition to being interested in the effects of programming on students' performance and subjective experiences with pairing, we were interested in the effect pairing might have on student persistence in computer science related majors. Specifically we wanted to know if using pairing as a learning tool for beginning programmers would influence subsequent computer programming course taking behavior, both in terms of attempts and pass rates, and students' decisions to major in computer science related fields.

Of course pursuing a computer science degree is dependent on success in the introductory course. For that reason we limited our analyses of persistence to the students who had successfully passed the class with a "C" or above. When interpreting these data it is important to keep in mind that nearly 10% more of the students who had paired in the introductory course successfully passed it. Because we followed students for one full academic year, our sub-sample was further limited to those who were still enrolled at UCSC three quarters after taking the course (N=321). Finally, although the introductory programming class is intended primarily for computer science majors, some students not intending to major in any of the computer science related fields also take the course. Most of the analyses below focus on those students who indicated on the first day of class an intention to pursue one of the computer science related majors offered at UCSC.

Among the students who were intending to pursue a computer science related major at the start of the introductory programming class, successfully passed the class with a "C" or better, and were still enrolled at UCSC a full year later (N=238; 187 men and 51 women), a significantly higher percentage of the students who had paired had gone on to attempt the subsequent programming course (Introduction to Data Structures) within a year (76.7%), than had the non-pairing students (62.2%), $\chi^2(1)=6.17$, $p<.05$. Separate analyses by gender of the effect of pairing on whether the subsequent course was attempted within a year revealed about an 18% difference between pairers and non-pairers for both women and men (73.8% of paired women vs. 55.6% of non-paired women, and 88.0% of paired men vs. 69.4% of unpaired men). The pairing effect was statistically significant for men, $\chi^2(1)=7.60$, $p<.01$, but not for women, $\chi^2(1)=1.19$, $p>.05$. The increase in the percentage of students associated with pairing appears to be quite similar for men and women. The fact that this difference was statistically significant for men but not women, again is most likely attributable to the relatively small number of women (51 compared to 186 men) in this study.

Among students that attempted the Data Structures course, there was no significant difference between pairers and non-pairers pass rates on their first attempt (see Table 8). That is, students who paired in the introductory programming course were more likely to attempt the subsequent programming class, and were just as likely to pass it as those who learned to program independently.

Among the students initially intending a computer science major, and who passed the introductory course and remained at UCSC for at least a year, the pairing students were also more likely to have declared a computer science related major 1 year after completing the introductory programming class, $\chi^2(1)$ =13.19, p <.001 This was the case for both women and men. Women who paired were more likely than women who worked independently to be in a computer science related major (59.5% vs. 22.2%), $\chi^2(1)$ =4.14, p <.05. Similarly pairing men were also more likely to have declared a computer science related major 1 year later than men who worked alone (74% vs. 47.2%), $\chi^2(1)$ =9.70, p <.005 (see Table 9).

Table 8: Attempted and passed data structures course

	Attempt Rates	Pass Rates (on 1st attempt) of Attempters
All pairers	76.7%	73.6%
All non-pairers	62.2%	72.4%
Paired women	73.8%	77.4%
Unpaired women	55.6%	66.0%
Paired men	88.0%	72.7%
Unpaired men	69.4%	75.0%

Interestingly, the same pattern of results was observed among all students who successfully completed the introductory programming course and were still enrolled at UCSC a year later, regardless of whether they had initially been planning to major in one of the computer science related majors. Pairers were significantly more likely to have declared a computer science related major than non-pairers, $\chi^2(1)$ =12.18, p <.001, and that was the case for both men, $\chi^2(1)$ =6.23, p <.05 and women, $\chi^2(1)$ =7.13, p <.01 (see Table 9 for percentages).

Table 9: Percentage of students declaring a computer science major 3 quarters after intro course

	Pairers	Non-pairers
Students intending CS majors	70.8%	42.2%
Women intending CS majors	59.5%	22.2%
Men intending CS majors	74.0%	47.2%
Students intending any major (including undeclared)	56.9%	33.8%
Women intending any major (including undeclared)	46.3%	11.1%
Men intending any major (including undeclared)	59.9%	41.1%

4. Conclusion

The results of this study provide some of the most compelling evidence to date of the effectiveness of pair programming as a pedagogical tool. It appears that pairing bolsters course completion and consequently course pass rates, and contributes to greater persistence in computer science related majors. Moreover, students who pair produce higher quality programs, are more confident in their work, and enjoy it more. We hope these findings will encourage instructors to use pair programming not only in their introductory courses, but also in their upper level courses.

The continued underrepresentation of women in computer science underscores the need for strategies that foster women's interest and promote their success[7]. Pair programming appears to be one such approach. That the benefits associated with pair programming extend to both men and women speaks to its broad-based appeal. As we continue to investigate the effects of this technique on attracting and retaining female students, parallel research investigating these phenomena in the workplace is also needed.

Acknowledgments

This work was funded by National Science Foundation grant EIA-0089989. Any opinions, findings, and conclusions or recommendations expressed in this paper are those of the authors and do not necessarily reflect the views of the National Science Foundation. We wish to thank undergraduate student Tristan Thomte and graduate students Wendy R. Williams, Wendy M. Limbert, Jennifer Bevan, and Brian Hanks for help with the data.

5. References

[1] Beck, K., *Extreme Programming Explained: Embrace Change*. 2000, Reading, Mass: Addison-Wesley.

[2] Williams, L., et al., *Strengthening the Case for Pair Programming*. IEEE Software, 2000. **17**(4): p. 19-25.

[3] McDowell, C., et al. *The Effects of Pair-Programming on Performance in an Introductory Programming Course*. in *33rd SIGCSE Technical Symposium on Computer Science Education*. 2002. Northern Kentucky: ACM Press.

[4] Nosek, J.T., *The Case for Collaborative Programming*. Communications of the ACM, 1998. **41**(3): p. 105-108.

[5] Williams, L.A. and R.R. Kessler, *All I Really Need to Know About Pair Programming I Learned in Kindergarten*. Communications of the ACM, 2000. **43**(5): p. 108-114.

[6] Williams, L.A. and R.R. Kessler. *The Effects of "Pair-Pressure" and "Pair-Learning" on Software Engineering Education*, in *Thirteenth Conference on Software Engineering Education and Training*. 2000. Austin Texas: IEEE Computer Soc.

[7] *Tech-Savvy Educating Girls in the New Computer Age Executive Summary*. 2000, American Association of University Women Education Foundation (available at http://www.aauw.org/2000/techsavvy.html).

Positive Experiences with an Open Project Assignment in an Introductory Programming Course

Guttorm Sindre[1,2], Steinar Line[1], Ottar V. Valvåg[1]
[1]*Dept. of Computer and Information Science, Norwegian University of Science and Technology (NTNU), Trondheim, Norway*
[2]*(visiting) Dept. of MSIS, U. Auckland, New Zealand*
{guttors, steinal, valvag}@idi.ntnu.no

Abstract

The course SIF8005 Object-Oriented Programming at the NTNU is in many respects taught in a quite traditional manner, with a well-known textbook, lectures in huge auditoria, and compulsory exercises that the students have to deliver to be allowed to sit a final written exam. The exercise part of the course is a mixture of individual exercises on a weekly basis, and a somewhat larger project to be done by groups of 4 students.

This paper particularly discusses the project, which has become a huge success after some notable changes were made for the 2001 offering of the course. Then the assignment profile was changed from one of fixed requirements set by staff to an open assignment, where each group made a computer game according to their own preferences. This change eliminated many of the problems present in earlier offerings and increased student inspiration.

1. Introduction

The course *SIF8005 Object-oriented Programming* is given to first year students (spring term) pursuing the degree Master of Technology at the Norwegian University of Science and Technology. It presupposes that the students have taken the course *SIF8001 Introduction to IT* in the initial autumn term (or that they have similar knowledge from elsewhere). Both these courses are one of four equal weight courses taken during their term.

SIF8001 is a broad top-down course covering many aspects of IT, including its organizational and societal implications, but for its practice part it includes the development of web pages with JSP scripts interfacing with a mySQL relational database. Hence, the students have done some simple programming before they enter SIF8005, being familiar with key concepts such as variables, method calls, branching and looping. Nevertheless, SIF8005 has many of the properties of an introductory programming course, as the amount of programming is quite limited in SIF8001. Moreover, although the language syntax is much the same, there is a paradigm shift from SIF8001 to SIF8005, in that code is no longer embedded as small fragments within HTML text but written as independent Java applications.

A large number of students take the course at each offering (711 spring 2002, 843 spring 2001), ranging from IT students for whom it is a core subject to students of several other engineering disciplines, where the course is wanted to ensure a wide platform of knowledge. Thus the student population is quite diverse, with varying levels of motivation and background knowledge.

The theory of the course is covered through a reading list (the 2000 run used [1] as its suggested textbook) with accompanying lectures in huge auditoria, plus colloquia in smaller rooms offered exclusively to bottom-end students who struggle with the course. To give the students practical exercise in programming, there are 7 weekly or bi-weekly exercises to be completed on an individual basis, followed by a larger project done in teams of 4 students, lasting for approximately 5 weeks (6 weeks of calendar time, but one week is lost due to Easter holidays).

The motivation for having both weekly exercises and a project, rather than only one or the other, is that they satisfy different pedagogical needs. The weekly / bi-weekly exercises, completed individually, are supposed to give each student a sufficient knowledge of key concepts and principles in programming. Each exercise focuses particularly on the topics dealt with in the lectures and reading material for the current or previous week, thus giving the students the opportunity to drill their practical understanding of the newly introduced concepts.

0-7695-1877-X/03 $17.00 © 2003 IEEE

The project trains the students' abilities to compose larger programs needing several classes and using all or most of the language concepts and features that the course covers. Moreover, it is supposed to stimulate their creative and collaborative abilities.

After some runs of the course, we have found it to be of key importance that the group project is preceded by a sufficient number of individual exercises. Otherwise, the poorest students will be unable to make a contribution in a project group and will hardly get started. At the same time, the project must be big enough to make sense as a group exercise. If it is too small, it will be hard to find a useful breakdown of the solution into modules that separate group members can implement, and then it is easier for the cleverest member of the group to develop the entire solution alone. Although a larger project does not prevent this from happening, it reduces the risk, justifying the effort of decomposing the task and integrating the code of different group members.

2. The Project before 2001

Up until 2000, the project assignment contained a set of detailed requirements set by the staff, informing the students what their program was supposed to do. All the student groups were given the same requirements, but a new project assignment was made for each new course offering, to prevent copying of old solutions. In many ways, this is an intuitive choice for a project in introductory programming. Requirements engineering is not a learning goal of such a course, so you do not want your students to spend a lot of time on that (e.g. interviewing real customers/users or staff posing as customers, or even clarifying by themselves requirements vaguely presented in the project assignment). With a huge number of students, it becomes impossible for staff to offer different project requirements for all the groups. Moreover, it becomes much easier to provide streamlined guidance if all are doing the same problem and thus running into the same difficulties.

On the other hand, a one-size-fits-all project with fixed requirements does embody a lot of problems, as clearly experienced at the NTNU up until 2000:

- Too little challenge for clever students, who would be able to finish more quickly working alone than having to collaborate with other poorer members of the group.
- Too hard for less clever students, who give up and do little or nothing (for instance leaving their share of work to other group members).
- Widespread copying of bigger or smaller parts of the solution between groups. While the teacher may officially prohibit this, it is very hard to enforce in practice. Since all groups are indeed supposed to come up with a program doing the same thing, in a fairly limited solution space, the existence of identical or near-identical code fragments may be a coincidence.
- Low inspiration. All groups are doing the same thing, the teacher's thing. So the students feel little ownership for their work.

Moreover, it is hard to define an assignment that makes a really useful program and is yet accomplishable for four freshmen in five weeks. The need for precise requirements easily tempts the teaching staff to choose quite abstract assignments, focusing on problems like mathematical computation, text formatting or parsing. The result was often that many students disliked the project, and learnt less from it than the time allotted should suggest.

The project was graded until 1998 (making up 50% of the grade, the exam the other 50%) but this was changed already for the 1999 offering. The reasons for this change were:

- Grading such a huge number of projects is costly and time-consuming, especially since Norwegian university regulations prohibit grading by staff alone, demanding an external censor.
- Some students got undeservingly good grades because of the project, as exam answers revealed that they could hardly program at all. Probably the nice project solution was done by other group members, or partly copied from other groups.

Hence, both with regards to fairness and teacher effort, it was found better to grade only the exam. The later offerings of the course have stuck to the practice of not grading the project and see no reason to change this.

3. The Project from 2001 onwards

Realizing that the previous offerings had not been optimal, three changes were made to the 2001 project:

- New principles for the grouping of the students.
- Computer games were the chosen product, instead of more boring tasks of previous years.
- The assignment was made open instead of the fixed requirements of previous years. So, each group could make their own choice of game, even invent a totally new one of their own liking.

The effects of these three changes will be discussed in the following subsections.

3.1. The new grouping paradigm

Previously, the grouping (teams of 4 students) had either been done randomly, or with an attempt to make all teams fairly equal in strength. So for instance, a group with two clever and two less clever students would be all right, a group with zero, one, three or four clever students less so. Selection could be based on grades from the preceding SIF8001, and/or on the students' own perceptions of their programming skills. The problem with this grouping paradigm, however, was that poor students often ended up taking little part in the project. And for the clever students it might be easier to volunteer to do all the work, rather than having to interface with, and try to fix, messy code written by a less clever group member. For the 2001 run, the grouping paradigm was thus changed:

- Preferably, all 4 members of a team should be at approximately the same skill level, e.g. four clever students, four average students, or four less clever students – or:
- Clever students could be grouped with less clever ones, given an up-front voluntary statement that they take on the duty of helping the less clever do their share of the work and learn from it, rather than just doing the work for them.

To achieve this grouping, students had to register for the project through a web form, answering questions about their perceived programming skills, ambition level for the course and project, and whether they would prefer to be in an equal level group or a group where the clever would partly have to teach the less clever.

Although not all preferences could be satisfied, the results of the new grouping paradigm seems to have been positive for students on all levels. There was hardly any quarreling within groups about the level of ambition for their projects. Four clever students could now challenge each other and learn from each other, as they might be good at different things. The less clever, teamed with other students on the same level, had to struggle together instead of simply leaving the work to other group members. Struggling together is much better than struggling alone, and you never feel as alone as if you are the single "stupid" student in a group otherwise consisting of whiz programmers.

3.2. Advantages of games

The switch to a game project may not be particularly original, as games or game inspired exercises have been used in programming courses for a long time. For instance, [2-7] all report success with game exercises. One obvious reason is that such exercises are more fun, thus motivating students more easily. Had this been the sole argument, though, the choice of game exercises could have been a reason for concern, turning education into entertainment [8]. However, there are also other arguments for games, as partly stated in [2-7]:

- Games are programs that the students may use and improve after the deadline, while most other exercise programs are delivered and then forgotten. Moreover, a game can proudly be shown off to friends and relatives – which is hardly the case for a program that computes π to 1000 decimals or unfancily administrates the simplified payrolls of a fictitious company.
- For games, the students themselves are plausible end-users and thus able to determine the quality of their programs, not only whether it "works" as required, but also in terms of usability. For a program that computes π or administrates a fictitious business, there is no one who really needs or wants the program, so its quality beyond output correctness cannot be appreciated.
- Games cover all kinds of topics that one may want to teach in a programming course, or even in a larger software engineering curriculum [9].
- Game development is useful for the students with regards to later jobs, as this is a huge and growing industry [10].

Of course, there are also arguments against:

- Game exercises may favour certain groups of students. One particular fear might be that games appeal more to boys than girls. But this seems to depend more on the kind of game [11], and hence one could just as well argue that there should be more focus on game development in education [10], to have more female game developers in the future.
- The students may spend too much time playing their games, neglecting more fruitful learning activities. Indeed, [12] indicates that game play may be negatively correlated with success in CS1, but the issue in that study seems to have been the playing of mass-market games, not self-developed games.

Anyway, with other success stories in mind, a switch to games for the project was something that one could feel pretty confident about.

3.3. Advantages of an open assignment

The third strategic change was, however, more original – and thus a braver leap. Instead of continuing with a project where detailed requirements were predefined by the teaching staff, a completely open project was proposed: *Make any kind of computer game* – each group could decide for itself. This is different from the game projects reported in [2-7], where the teachers gave precise requirements as to what game should be made. The only constraints currently given for the SIF8005 project teams are as follows:

- Must not break Norwegian law, neither in product nor development process (e.g., unlicensed gambling game, illegal pornographic content, plagiarism, theft, viruses...)
- Size of game > 125 LOC x # students in the team. The normal team size is 4, delivering a game of at least 500 LOC of Java, counted as the number of necessary semi-colons in the code. All these code lines must be self-written by the group.
- Each group member must have written > 100 LOC of the finally delivered product (to ensure that no one leaves the work to team-mates).
- The program shall be composed of several classes and use file i/o and interactive user input.
- It is allowed to reuse, e.g., library classes or code found on the net, as long as no copyright regulations are broken. However, this does not give the group any reduction of work, they still have to write 500 LOC themselves, and it must be clearly documented what is self-written and what is reused, from what source. It is not allowed to share code with other groups.

In addition there were some requirements on the process, demanding some intermediate deliverables:

1. *Outline*, due after approx. 1 week, containing a brief textual explanation of the game the group will develop, a UML class diagram for the suggested solution, and a progress and work-allocation plan for the rest of the project.
2. *Midway status report*, due after approx. 3 weeks. At this point they show their student assistant that they have written at least 60% of the code required. This to ensure that no one lags seriously behind.
3. *Final delivery*, including end report and a demo session where both teachers and other students can walk around looking at the various games.

For up front guidance, a memo on computer games is provided, classifying types of games and discussing what properties would generally make a game enjoyable to play. This note is particularly meant for students with little previous computer game experience. Also, there is a note providing hints on how to get maximum learning out of the project, and on group collaboration issues.

Of course, the teaching staff envisioned several risks with an open assignment:

- Guidance would become more difficult, due to the increased variety of programs, also increasing the variety of encountered problems.
- The staff would lose control over the coverage of topical learning goals. With a specific choice of game, one could ensure that, say, recursion had to be used, as in [2].
- Some groups might spend too much time pondering on what game to make, thus ending up with little time for design and programming.

However, the disadvantages were believed to be small compared to the gains:

- A huge reduction of the copying problem, because the various groups would now need different code. Also, if copying still were to happen, it would be much easier to detect and punish, as "coincidence" would no longer be a plausible excuse.
- More inspired students, due to an increased feeling of ownership for their work – making a game of their own choice rather than "the teacher's baby".
- Easier for each group to determine its own level of ambition. Some could invent brand new games, go for advanced graphics or AI reasoning, writing much more than 500 LOC if they wished. Others could start out with a simple adaptation of, say, a familiar dice game like Yatzy, make this work crudely, and then gradually extend their product while acquiring a sense of mastery.

The student response after the two game projects (2001 and 2002) has been overwhelmingly positive, with negative remarks only relating to details, whereas the previous projects were considered a drag by many. Indeed, it seems that the positive effects mentioned above all were realized, whereas the negative ones have not happened. Apparently, both clever and less clever students worked harder with this project than with previous ones. The clever were inspired to put in extra effort, the less clever did not feel that the requirements were beyond them (which caused many to simply give up and refrain to copying in previous runs).

It must be noted that the above gains are *impressions*, as a proper scientific evaluation of the learning outcomes of the course or project has not yet been undertaken. However, our impressions come from several sources that all support each other:

- Informal conversations with individual students, both during and after the course.
- Meetings with student dominated course evaluation groups. These collect input from all the students (e.g., in plenary classroom meetings, the teacher not present) and have 3-4 meetings with the teacher during the term. The assumption is that the group members as representatives, presenting

viewpoints that are not necessarily (or not only) their own, will dare to discuss the teaching more freely than the average individual student might. This increases the likelihood that important feedback on the course will reach the teacher.

- Input from our huge network of student assistants. These are themselves students, just a year or two ahead of those taking the course, employed part-time to provide programming lab assistance. The student assistants are those who get most closely in touch with the students as they help them with hands-on programming problems. Hence they also get a detailed picture of the students' attitudes and learning, what they master and what they struggle with. Since the student assistants took the course themselves just one or two years earlier, they also were quite capable of making comparisons between the new and old projects. The general opinion of the student assistants was that the new project assignment had worked far better.
- The exam results of 2001 also indicated that the students had a better learning experience than the year before.

The latter point does not mandate strong conclusions, however, as exam assignments are necessarily different from year to year, and the difference from 2000 to 2001 was even bigger than strictly required.

4. Discussion and Conclusions

4.1. Weaknesses

The absence of a proper scientific evaluation is of course a weakness of this paper. Although the various informal sources all support each other in concluding that the new kind of project was better, it would have been easier to make strong conclusions if some performance-based experiments or perception-based investigations (i.e., questionnaires investigating the students' own attitudes about the learning effects).

Such measures not taken, it is impossible to claim definite improvement in learning from 2000 to 2001, or that such improvement was due to the switch to an open project.

Still, all those who are involved in teaching the course have a firm impression that the new project was more motivating and rewarding for the students, and that this improved the learning in the course as a whole. With fixed exercise assignments, many courses in our university experience massive copying of exercise answers. This is effectively diminished by a project where each group make different requirements for their program. To write different fixed-requirements project assignments for +200 groups would be a too high burden for the teaching staff, so open assignments are the only way to do this. The open project also stimulates inventiveness and curiosity, allows for more flexibility in ambition levels, and increases the feeling of ownership to a higher extent than the closed game assignments reported in [2-7].

4.2. Ungraded, yet motivating

The project is not graded, only evaluated on a pass/fail basis. With students cynically motivated by achieving good grades, one might fear that they would do just the minimum, regardless of their skills. How are they motivated to do more?

First of all, the teaching staff stress that hard work *will* pay indirectly: A student who has improved his/her practical programming skills through the project is likely to perform better at the exam. To make this statement true, the exam assignments of 2001 onwards have been made more practical and realistic than earlier. Mainly, we have come up with four different kinds of questions:

- Program comprehension.
- Debugging.
- Programming within a given design, typically one method or one class, focusing on control structures, recursion and the like.
- Design and programming, i.e., given some requirements, solving the problem by choosing classes and writing code.

All the questions are exemplary rather than encyclopedic, and at least the three latter require practical programming skills that can, presumably, be trained better through project work than other activities. For instance, the debugging question presents a faulty program together with its requirements, and also shows the exact series of symptoms as on screen (e.g., error messages, wrong output). The students are then asked to pinpoint the fault and suggest how to correct it. Such questions are very hard to prepare for by reading the textbook, which contains little in the department of faulty programs or explanation of how to proceed when you get various error messages. But a lot of practical programming work would be likely to help. Then the student might have made similar faults in practice and learnt to deal with them.

Still, one might fear that the best students, who are already confident at getting a good grade, would just do the minimum in the project, and instead spend the time on other parallel courses where they are more worried about making a poor performance. But this does not seem to have happened. One possible explanation is that the clever students are carried away by the challenge and fun of the task. Another explanation could be the status associated with the final "JOscar" prize ceremony, where the best games are awarded in various categories. For instance there are prizes for best graphics, best sound effects, best new game plot, best adaptation of existing game, ... and of course the most prestigious of all: Best Game.

Although some students may be disappointed at not getting a certain prize, the general mood at the demo sessions and subsequent JOscar seems to be one of pride about their accomplishments, even for the students who have merely made something simple, perhaps struggling their way from an F to a D on the final exam.

Some teachers might feel that letting the students invent the requirements for their product is an abdication from teaching responsibility. But the better control that strictly defined requirements give may be illusory, for instance because of copying. Moreover, there are other arguments in favor of open assignments. One of the key differences between the development of bespoke software and packaged software is that the latter has no known customers before the first release, so the developers partly have to invent the requirements themselves [13]. This has largely been neglected in software engineering education, where mainstream methodology still focuses on the development of bespoke software, even if packaged software has surpassed it in aggregate global value. Hence, it could be quite in place to prepare the students for a future where they might also become inventors of packaged software, not only satisfying requirements specified by others.

The experiences reported in this paper suggest that SIF8005 should continue with its open project. A topic for further work could be to give the course and project a proper scientific evaluation by means of performance tests and/or questionnaires investigating student perceptions of their learning. This could also give ideas for further improvements of the teaching.

References

[1] R. Winder and G. Roberts, *Developing Java Software*, 2nd ed., Wiley, 2000.

[2]T. J. Feldman and J. D. Zelenski, "The Quest for Excellence in Designing CS1/CS2 Assignments", *Proc 27th SIGCSE Symposium in Computer Science Education,* Philadelphia, USA, February 1996.

[3] J. C. Adam, "Chance-It: An Object-Oriented Capstone Project for CS-1". *Proc 29th SIGCSE Symposium in Computer Science Education,* Atlanta, GA, February 1998.

[4] N. Faltin, "Designing Courseware on Algorithms for Active Learning with Virtual Board Games", *Proc. Conf on Integrating Technology into Computer Science Education (ITiCSE'99),* Cracow, Poland, June 1999.

[5] K. Becker, "Teaching with Games: The Minesweeper and Asteroids Experience", *The Journal of Computing in Small Colleges* 17(2): 22-32, December 2001.

[6] R. Moser, "A Fantasy Adventure Game as a Learning Environment: Why Learning to Program is so Difficult and What can be Done about it", *Proc Conf on Integrating Technology into Computer Science Education (ITiCSE'97),* Uppsala, Sweden, June 1997.

[7] C. Alphonce and P. Ventura. "Object-Orientation in CS1-CS2 by Design", *Proc 7th Annual Conference on Innovation and Technology in Computer Science Education (ITiCSE'02),* Aarhus, Denmark, June 2002.

[8] N. Postman, *Amusing Ourselves to Death.* Methuen Publishing, 1987.

[9] R. M. Jones, "Design and Implementation of Computer Games: A Capstone Course for Undergraduate Computer Science Education", *Proc. 31st SIGCSE Symposium in Computer Science Education,* Austin, TX, March 2000.

[10] C. M. Gorriz and C. Medina. "Engaging Girls with Computers through Software Games", *Communications of the ACM,* 43(1): 42, January 2000.

[11] E. Spertus, "Why Are There So Few Female Computer Scientists?", MIT Artificial Intelligence Laboratory Technical Report 1315, August 1991.

[12] B. C. Wilson and S. Shrock, "Contributing to Success in an Introductory Computer Science Course: A Study of Twelve Factors", *Proc 32nd SIGCSE Technical Symposium on Computer Science Education,* Charlotte, NC, February 2001.

[13] P. Sawyer, "Packaged Software: Challenges for RE", *Proc. 6th International Workshop on Requirements Engineering: Foundation for Software Quality (REFSQ'2000),* Stockholm, June 2000.

Some links in Norwegian.
Course web page: http://sif8005.idi.ntnu.no/
Games developed 2001: http://sif8005.idi.ntnu.no/prosjekt/spill/
2002: http://sif8005.idi.ntnu.no/prosjekt/levering/hentspill.php3

Problems and Programmers: An Educational Software Engineering Card Game

Alex Baker, Emily Oh Navarro, and André van der Hoek
Department of Information and Computer Science
University of California, Irvine
Irvine, CA 92697-3425 USA
abaker@uci.edu, emilyo@uci.edu, andre@ics.uci.edu

Abstract

Problems and Programmers is an educational card game that we have developed to help teach software engineering. It is based on the observation that students, in a typical software engineering course, gain little practical experience in issues regarding the software process. The underlying problem is time: any course faces the practical constraint of only being able to involve students in at most a few small software development projects. Problems and Programmers overcomes this limitation by providing a simulation of the software process. In playing the game, students become aware of not only general lessons, such as the fact that they must continuously make trade-offs among multiple potential next steps, but also specific issues such as the fact that inspections improve the quality of code but delay its delivery time. We describe game play of Problems and Programmers, discuss its underlying design, and report on the results of a small experiment in which twenty-eight students played the game.

1. Introduction

In surveying the state of software engineering education as reported in conferences [3, 13, 14] and special journal issues [1, 2, 4], it becomes clear that students gain remarkably little experience in exercising the software process. While the relevant theory certainly is taught in lectures, the practical side of most courses typically guides the students through a linear execution of the waterfall model.

The underlying problem is simple: class projects must be completed within the length of their course. Combined with the need for students to at least once exercise creating a set of project deliverables (e.g., requirements documents, design documents, test cases), little room is left to illustrate the many facets of the software process.

Industry has recognized this problem and over time has requested academia to better prepare its students for their future in the workplace [8, 9, 12, 16]. In response, many attempts have been undertaken to improve software engineering education. Some attempts involve basing an entire course on the latest software development approach, such as extreme programming [17] or PSP [5]. Other attempts involve intentionally applying a series of real-world complications during a class project, such as suddenly changing the requirements while design is in progress [10]. Unfortunately, none of these approaches addresses the core of the issue, and all suffer from being spot solutions that provide glimpses of at most a few difficulties.

As an initial investigation into the feasibility of a rather different approach, we have developed Problems and Programmers, an educational software engineering card game that simulates the software process. As a game-based simulation, Problems and Programmers provides students with an experience that is similar to a class project, but requires no deliverables to be built. It can therefore be played quickly and through repeated use illustrate many different aspects of the software process.

Problems and Programmers is built as a physical card game. Compared to computer-based simulations such as SESAM [11] and OSS [15], this has the distinct advantage of being easy and open to use. The complete game state is present on the table; the results of actions are immediately visible; and, because Problems and Programmers is set up as a competitive game, interactive games ensue in which students learn from each other.

To evaluate the educational value of Problems and Programmers, we conducted an experiment in which twenty-eight undergraduate students played the game. All of the students had already passed a sophomore-level software engineering class and, after playing, were asked to comment on the quality of the game and its value if it had been a standard part of that class. Results are encouraging: although some aspects of game play can certainly be improved, the overall reaction is that use of Problems and Programmers in a software engineering course would enhance students' understanding of the software process.

The remainder of this paper is structured as follows. In Section 2 we first discuss the main objectives of Problems and Programmers. We then discuss its design in Section 3. Section 4 introduces the details of game play. We present the results of our experimental study in Section 5, and conclude in Section 6 with an outlook at future work.

0-7695-1877-X/03 $17.00 © 2003 IEEE

2. Objectives

The first and foremost goal of Problems and Programmers is to enrich a student's understanding of the software process. To create this higher level of understanding, the game makes careful tradeoffs among faithfulness to reality, level of detail, usability, teaching objectives, and fun factors. Our choices in these tradeoffs were guided by the following high-level objectives.

- *The game should advocate proper use of software engineering techniques.* Moreover, it should discourage taking exorbitant risks or cutting corners. For example, while it is technically possible to skip design, this should generally lead to a loss in the game.
- *The game should illustrate both general and specific lessons concerning the software process.* General lessons concern such issues as the non-linearity of the software process and the need to make decisions that may have drastic consequences. Specific lessons include, among others, Brooks' Law [6] and the fact that the use of a configuration management system normally improves the overall development process.
- *The game should provide a student with clear feedback concerning their decisions.* Consider, for example, a student who rushes the implementation phase and at a later stage in the game loses some progress. The game must provide feedback and explain that the loss is due to the fact that hasty code development introduces a higher number of bugs than as compared to normal code development.
- *Game play should be easy and comparatively quick.* Without compromising the level of complexity that is needed to make each round of game play unique, a single game must neither be too difficult nor too long in order to maintain the interest of students and, thus, the game's value as an educational tool.
- *The game should encourage interaction among students.* It is well-known that collaborative learning has significant advantages [7]. Because some lessons in Problems and Programmers are not immediately visible and must be abstracted from repeated game play, interaction typically plays a critical role in uncovering these lessons.

Finally, we note that Problems and Programmers is explicitly meant to complement existing course materials in software engineering. Instead of replacing those materials, Problems and Programmers is best used in a role that builds upon the theory presented in lectures and in turn reinforces its lessons with actual experiences in subsequent (or parallel) project assignments.

3. Overall Design

Problems and Programmers is set up as a multiplayer game in which two or more players each attempt to be the first to complete a hypothetical software project. Different players usually take different strategies as determined by their own preferences and decisions, yet calibrated for the particular cards they draw. One player, for instance, may play cautiously by establishing solid requirements, carefully designing the system structure, and testing all code immediately. Another player may be more optimistic, only partially establish all requirements up front, rush the development of their code, and completely skip testing until integration time. In this scenario, the cautious player runs the risk of losing the game due to slow progress, whereas the optimistic player runs the risk of losing the game due to delays incurred by, for example, integration problems.

A distinct advantage of the competitive nature of Problems and Programmers is the fact that it encourages interaction. Because different players follow different strategies, more than one strategy is exposed per game. This allows players to not only evaluate their own strategy, but to also discuss and compare strategies followed by others. As a result, players learn from each other, which enhances the educational value of Problems and Programmers.

As shown in Figure 1, game play in Problems and Programmers follows the steps of the waterfall model. We considered incorporating other life cycle models, but two reasons prevent us from doing so. First, physically visualizing different life cycles creates non-uniform card layouts that are difficult to compare and interpret. Second, the need to establish different rules for different life cycles violates our objective of game play being easy. Players would be so burdened by the various rules as they apply in different situations, that they would lose the focus on actually understanding the software process and its issues.

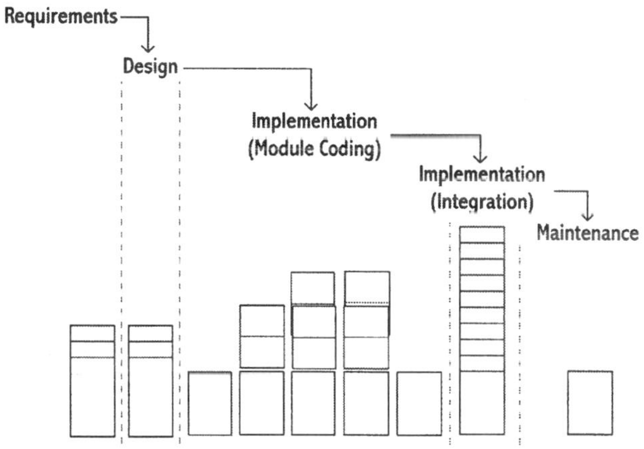

Figure 1. Different phases in Problems and Programmers.

By no means must players complete one phase of the waterfall before moving on to the next. Returning to previous phases in the life cycle is allowed (although it incurs a penalty to simulate the extra effort involved). As a result, players gain insight into two important, high-level lessons regarding the software process: it is not a linear sequence of actions and generally involves choosing among multiple viable alternatives as to what to do next.

The particular project to be completed is determined at the beginning of the game, when a single project card is drawn and placed in the middle amongst all players. As shown in Figure 2 with an example project card for a Payroll Controller system, a project card specifies a project in terms of its complexity, length, quality, and budget. The complexity and length are parameters defining the nature of the application to be developed. Complexity influences the amount of progress each player can make during the implementation phase (the higher the complexity, the less code each programmer can produce per turn) and length defines the size of the application to be developed as the number of code cards that must eventually be integrated to form the application.

The quality and budget represent other stakeholders in the process. Quality represents the customer's demands and defines the number of code cards that will be inspected for bugs. The player that is first in completing the integration process and succeeding in having all inspected code cards be bug free, wins the game. Finally, budget represents the development organization and constrains the project in how many programmers can be hired.

Together with the overall need to be the first to complete a project in order to win the game, a project card captures the typical tension that exists between time (need to win the game), quality (must pass the acceptance test inspections), and money (cannot exceed the budget). The game, thus, illustrates two more important lessons regarding the software process: it always involves multiple stakeholders and must balance multiple, conflicting goals at the same time.

Figure 2 shows three additional kinds of cards used in Problems and Programmers. First, programmer cards are used during the implementation phase. Each programmer is defined by a salary, skill, personality, and brief description. The salary defines the cost to the overall project of hiring a programmer; the sum of all programmer salaries may not exceed the project budget. The skill and personality of programmers define their behavior in terms of how productive they are in developing code and how cooperative they are within the organization, respectively. Finally, the particular values for salary, skill, and personality are explained with a brief textual description of the specific traits of the programmer.

Problem cards are at the heart of game play in Problems and Programmers. They, in fact, create many of the uncertainties that make winning the game difficult. Problem cards are drawn by one player and played upon another player. If that other player matches the condition on the problem card, they are penalized. The example problem card in Figure 2 illustrates this process. If played on a player who has more than one "unclear requirements" (e.g., a requirements card containing a problem that has not been resolved as of yet), that player must concede two code cards and one design card of their choice. Clearly, this particular problem card addresses the need to first establish unambiguous and clear requirements before code is developed. Many other problem cards exist that highlight all kinds of problems. Of note is that feedback is immediately present on the card: it explains the condition, names the problem, and describes the penalty.

Concept cards play the opposite role of problem cards: they represent benefits to a project. For example, the card shown in Figure 2 illustrates how a walkthrough helps to reduce unclear requirements or design. A few concepts will incur a cost. For example, one concept card increases the motivation of each programmer with a bonus, resulting in higher productivity. This card can only be played if its cost, $30K, can be absorbed by the project budget.

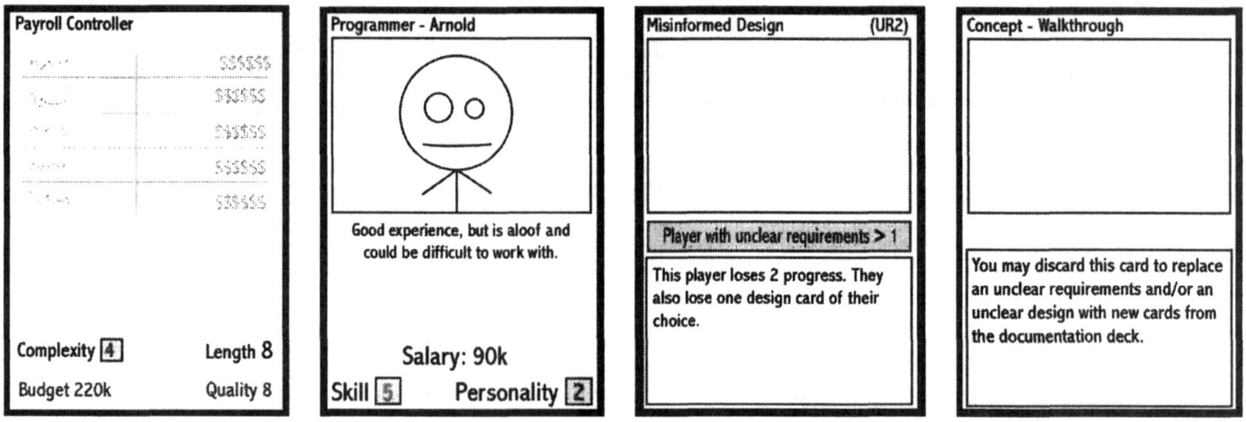

Figure 2. Examples of a project card, programmer card, problem card, and concept card.

4. Game Play

Game play in Problems and Programmers is straightforward. Each turn, a player takes the following six steps:

1. *Decide to move to the next phase of the life cycle, the previous phase, or remain in the current phase.*
2. *Allow each opponent the chance to play one problem card on them.*
3. *Draw cards.*
4. *Take actions, as allowed in the respective phase.*
5. *Play any programmer and concept cards.*
6. *Discard any extra cards.*

Play starts in the requirements phase, and ends when one player successfully completes their acceptance test.

Throughout the game, a player continues to draw cards at each turn that may include programmer, problem, and concept cards. These cards can be put into play after the normal actions have been taken, and effectively create a dynamic simulation in which different people slowly may take the upper hand at different stages of the game.

A small number of rules exist that govern "exceptional game states" (e.g., moving backwards to a previous phase in the life cycle; replacing one programmer with another; firing programmers that do not perform very well). Typically, certain negative consequences are associated with these actions that parallel the effects in the real world. Space limits us to further discuss these rules and the interested reader is referred to the web site of Problems and Programmers: *www.problemsandprogrammers.com*. Here, we focus on the actions that normally take place in each phase of the life cycle.

4.1 Requirements

Creating a requirements document constitutes the first phase of game play. Over a number of turns, a player must create a single column of requirements cards, the length of which simulates the size of the requirements document. Based on the project's complexity and length, a player must decide when the document is "complete" for their purposes. Some players will intentionally move on to the design phase rather quickly, others will take a more cautious approach and first build up a significantly sized requirements document.

Requirements cards are either clear or unclear. The presence of unclear requirements cards is problematic: certain problem cards trigger unwanted negative progress if too many requirements cards are unclear. Fortunately, players may forgo some or all of their creation of new requirements to rework existing unclear sections: at each turn a player may choose to draw two new requirements cards, draw one new and one replacement requirements card, or draw two replacement requirements cards.

4.2 Design

The design phase is played much like the requirements phase. Players create a—separate—stack for the design document, and at each turn can choose to add new cards, rework existing cards, or mix the two activities. Again, a player has to decide (based upon experience with repeated game play for projects with different complexities and sizes) upon the desired number of cards that will constitute a "good" design document for this project.

4.3 Implementation

Implementation is the most important phase in Problems and Programmers. Per turn, each programmer that a player has hired can take four different actions: program good code (cost equal to project complexity), program rush code (cost equal to project complexity divided by two), inspect code (cost one), and fix a bug (cost one or more). Total cost cannot exceed the skill-level of a programmer. A programmer of skill-level four working on a project of complexity two could choose to program two good code, one good code and two rush code, inspect four code cards, or any other combination totaling four or less.

Code is programmed by drawing code cards from the code deck and placing the cards face down in a column above the programmer. Good code is distinguished from rush code by the card color that is put at the top (blue and red, respectively). Inspection is not mandatory, but gives a player insight into their code quality by turning cards over and revealing whether the code has bugs. Three types of bugs exist: simple, normal, and nasty. Code containing a simple bug can be replaced with another code card when a player chooses to fix the bug. Of note is that the new code card is placed face down in the stack to simulate the fact that bug fixes can contain bugs themselves.

Normal bugs are fixed by swapping them, one-by-one, with the code cards above them until they are at the top of the column and can be gotten rid of like a simple bug. This process simulates that other code often must be modified as well if it builds on buggy code and emphasizes the importance of early bug detection and resolution.

Finally, nasty bugs are what they are called: they wipe out all progress above it in the column, and a player has to redevelop that code.

Inspecting code clearly has the benefit of uncovering bugs early in the process. Just like in the real world, however, improving code quality bears the cost of increased time-pressures that exist to get coding completed.

Note that when a player has reached the implementation phase, problem cards may be played upon that player. Some players may hold off on playing their problem cards until later in the process to wreak even more havoc (mimicking the fact that later changes typically are costlier).

4.4 Integration testing

During the integration phase, a player can take all of the code developed by a particular programmer and move it into the integrated code column. Code that is known to be buggy after inspection and code that has not yet been inspected can both be integrated, but doing so exposes the player to the risks described in the next section. Code is integrated programmer by programmer, illustrating trade-offs between having more programmers, which reduces the time needed to build the overall system, and fewer programmers, which makes integration quicker.

Note that once code has been integrated, problem cards no longer have an effect on it. Note also that a player does not have to wait until all programmers have finished coding in order to start the integration process.

4.5 Maintenance / acceptance testing

This is the final phase of the game and can only be entered after the length of the integrated code column equals or exceeds the length of the project. At that point, a player has to decide whether to continue integrating code or attempt to win the game. In the latter case, all integrated code is placed face down, shuffled, and a number of cards equaling the project quality (as stated on the project card) are pulled from the top of the pile. If no bugs appear, the player has won the game. If any bugs appear, however, the penalty is severe: all code cards must be placed above a single programmer of choice with the bugs that were discovered at the bottom of the column. Play continues: the bugs must be fixed, additional code can be inspected, and the player is once again vulnerable to problem cards.

5. Experiment

To evaluate Problems and Programmers, we conducted an experiment in which twenty-eight undergraduate students played the game. Teamed in pairs, each student was first introduced to the game, its objectives, and its mechanics of game play (30 minutes), then played twice against the other person (45 minutes per game), and was asked to fill out a questionnaire regarding their particular experiences (10 minutes). Our primary objective was not to observe or analyze the students' play, but rather to simply let them play and report on whether they considered the game helpful in learning about the software process.

To promote objectivity, the experiment was carried out independent of any particular software engineering course. Furthermore, while all students had passed the same software engineering course as background material (ICS 52, Introduction to Software Engineering), they did so in different quarters with different instructors. Finally, we randomly chose subjects from a full pool of applicants.

The questionnaire consisted of questions regarding the experience of playing the game and potential for the game to be used as a teaching aid. Two kinds of questions were asked: numerical score questions and open-ended questions. Table 1 presents the results for the numerical score questions, with 1 indicating a strongly negative answer and 5 indicating a strongly positive answer. Overall, the results are very encouraging. With the exception of question 4, which had an average score of only 2.6, all other questions indicate positive feedback with average values ranging from 3.3 (question 8) to 4.1 (question 1). Perhaps most indicative is the 3.7 average score for question 6, which is a clear vote of confidence in the game and its merits by the students who participated in the experiment.

Table 1. Questionnaire numerical scores.

Question	*1*	*2*	*3*	*4*	*5*
1. How enjoyable is it to play?			6	13	9
2. How difficult/easy is it to play?		3	10	12	3
3. How well does it reinforce knowledge?		6	9	6	6
4. How well does it teach new knowledge?	7	8	6	3	4
5. How well does it teach the software process?	1	4	8	12	3
6. Incorporate it as standard part of SE course?	1	6	3	12	6
7. As an optional part?	1	5	4	10	8
8. As a mandatory part?	1	6	8	11	2

Also informative were the answers given to the open-ended questions. Designed to present us with feedback to assist in further improving the game, questions focused on favorite and least-favorite parts, clarity, problematic parts, lessons learned, suggestions for improvement, and overall impressions. Again, results are encouraging: *"I learn that even though doing requirements and design take a lot of time, but if we don't do well on these parts of the project might actually take longer to finish!", "It reinforces the ideas taught in ICS 52 with a fun way to learn it.", "The game illustrates in 1 hour or 2 almost half of the material in ICS 52.", "I think I learned that having many programmers = more time in integrations.",* and *"Tells me WHY it is important to create quality code."* Most importantly, a significant number of respondents considered the competition aspects of the game enjoyable and helpful.

At the same time, the responses brought to light some issues with the game, e.g.: *"Requirements and design are boring.", "Add different life cycles.", "It was unclear the amount of time should be spent on requirements and design."* The majority of these comments were focused on the early phases of the game and we will take these and the other comments provided and examine whether we can improve the game accordingly. In particular, we intend to make the requirements and design phases more varied in order to introduce both more alternative strategies and more depth into the game.

6. Conclusions

Problems and Programmers represents a first attempt at using a physical card game for educating students in the many difficult issues inherent to the software process. While it certainly is not designed to teach the "right" answer to each particular situation (such an endeavor is impossible), repeatedly playing Problems and Programmers prepares a student for the breadth of issues they may face in their future careers, reinforces in a practical manner many of the theoretical lessons presented in lectures, and builds a student's understanding of their actions and role in the overall software development process.

Compared to existing automated simulations, our card-based simulation has the advantage of being highly visual, being easy and fun to play, engaging students in collaborative learning, and providing almost instantaneous feedback on the actions that students take. While we had to make some compromises to achieve this level of functionality and therefore were unable to include as many aspects of the software process as we would have liked, we believe the current incarnation of the game achieves a good balance among the objectives stated in Section 2.

The results of our experiments confirm our intuitions: students largely believe that use of the game in their software engineering class would have helped them in their studies. Our research, however, does not end here. First, we plan to actually use Problems and Programmers in our introductory software engineering class. Using an improved version based on the feedback received, we hope to further build our understanding of how the game helps in teaching the software process. Planned collaborations with three other institutions will provide us a broad sample size in this process. Second, we will develop an automated version of the game. Although losing the physical aspects of the game, automation facilitates easy distribution and allows us to build a version of the game that incorporates additional software engineering principles and life cycle models—the advantage being that the program, and not the player, enforces the rules of game play.

Acknowledgments

We thank the other members of our research group for their invaluable suggestions regarding the design and implementation of Problems and Programmers.

This research is supported by the National Science Foundation under Grant Number CCR-0093489. Effort also sponsored by the Defense Advanced Research Projects Agency, Rome Laboratory, Air Force Materiel Command, USAF under agreement numbers F30602-00-2-0599 and F30602-00-2-0607. The U.S. Government is authorized to reproduce and distribute reprints for governmental purposes notwithstanding any copyright annotation thereon. The views and conclusions contained herein are those of the authors and should not be interpreted as necessarily representing the official policies or endorsements, either expressed or implied, of the Defense Advanced Research Projects Agency, Rome Laboratory or the U.S. Government.

References

1. *IEEE Software, Special Issue on Educating Software Professionals.* Vol. 19 (5), September/October. 2002: IEEE.
2. *The Journal of Systems and Software.* Vol. 49. 1999: Elsevier Science Inc.
3. *Proceedings of the Fifteenth Conference on Software Engineering Education and Training.* 2002: IEEE.
4. Balci, O., *Annals of Software Engineering.* Vol. 6. 1998: Baltzer Science Publishers.
5. Borstler, J., et al., *Teaching PSP: Challenges and Lessons Learned.* IEEE Software, 2002. **19**(5): p. 42-48.
6. Brooks, F.P., *The Mythical Man-Month: Essays on Software Engineering.* 2 ed. 1995: Addison-Wesley. 336.
7. Bruffee, K.A., *Collaborative Learning: Higher Education, Interdependence, and the Authority of Knowledge.* 1983: John Hopkins University Press.
8. Callahan, D. and B. Pedigo, *Educating Experienced IT Professionals by Addressing Industry's Needs.* IEEE Software, 2002. **19**(5): p. 57-62.
9. Conn, R., *Developing Software Engineers at the C-130J Software Factory.* IEEE Software, 2002. **19**(5): p. 25-29.
10. Dawson, R., *Twenty Dirty Tricks to Train Software Engineers*, in *Proceedings of the 22nd International Conference on Software Engineering.* 2000, ACM. p. 209-218.
11. Drappa, A. and J. Ludewig, *Simulation in Software Engineering Training*, in *Proceedings of the 22nd International Conference on Software Engineering.* 2000, ACM. p. 199-208.
12. McMillan, W.W. and S. Rajaprabhakaran, *What Leading Practitioners Say Should Be Emphasized in Students' Software Engineering Projects*, in *Proceedings of the Twelfth Conference on Software Engineering Education and Training*, H. Saiedian, Editor. 1999, IEEE Computer Society. p. 177-185.
13. Mengel, S.A. and P.J. Knoke, *Proceedings of the Thirteenth Conference on Software Engineering Education & Training.* 2000: IEEE Computer Society.
14. Ramsey, D., P. Bourque, and R. Dupuis, *Proceedings of the Fourteenth Conference on Software Engineering Education and Training.* 2001: IEEE Computer Society.
15. Sharp, H. and P. Hall, *An Interactive Multimedia Software House Simulation for Postgraduate Software Engineers*, in *Proceedings of the 22nd International Conference on Software Engineering.* 2000, ACM. p. 688-691.
16. Shaw, M., *Software Engineering Education: A Roadmap*, in *The Future of Software Engineering*, A. Finkelstein, Editor. 2000, ACM. p. 373-380.
17. Shukla, A. and L. Williams, *Adapting Extreme Programming for a Core Software Engineering Course*, in *Proceedings of the Fifteenth Conference on Software Engineering Education and Training.* 2002, IEEE. p. 184-191.

Software Engineering Education and Training

Course Delivery and Evaluation

Evaluating Individual Contribution Toward Group Software Engineering Projects

Jane Huffman Hayes
University of Kentucky
hayes@cs.uky.edu

Timothy C. Lethbridge
University of Ottawa
tcl@site.uottawa.ca

Daniel Port
University of Southern California
dport@almaak.usc.edu

Abstract

It is widely acknowledged that group or team projects are a staple of undergraduate and graduate software engineering courses. Such projects provide students with experiences that better prepare them for their careers, so teamwork is often required or strongly encouraged by accreditation agencies. While there are a multitude of educational benefits of group projects, they also pose considerable challenge in fairly and accurately discerning individual contribution for evaluation purposes. Issues, approaches, and best practices for evaluating individual contribution are presented from the perspectives of the University of Kentucky, University of Ottawa, University of Southern California, and others.

The techniques utilized within a particular course generally are a mix of (1) the group mark is everybody's mark, (2) everybody reports what they personally did, (3) other group members report the relative contributions of other group members, (4) pop quizzes on project details, and (5) cross-validating with the results of individual work.

1. Introduction

Group or team projects are a staple of undergraduate and graduate software engineering courses. Such projects provide students with realistic experiences that better prepare them for their careers. This is so widely acknowledged as important that it is often required or strongly encouraged by accreditation agencies.

In this paper, we will look at some of the issues surrounding assessment of group work, since both instructors and students complain of the difficulties of doing this in a manner that is both fair and promotes educational objectives.

The authors of this paper come from several different universities each of which has a variety of courses involving group projects. The University of Kentucky requires group projects in the CS 499 Senior Design Project course and CS 616 Software Engineering course; the University of Ottawa assigns a group full-year capstone project (SEG 4000) [4] as well as group projects in several other courses; and the University of Southern California assigns group projects both in its one semester undergraduate software engineering course CS477 and its full year graduate level course CS577.

We note that although the project characteristics and grading criteria vary in each institution and course, the problems in grading group projects seem universal. Specifically, it is very difficult to objectively determine an individual student's contribution to a group project. Various approaches have been implemented with varying degrees of success.

The paper is organized as follows: Section 2 presents background information on group projects and challenges in evaluating these for grades, Section 3 presents approaches to grading individual effort, Section 4 presents grading practices that the three universities feel worked well, and Section 5 presents a summary and conclusions.

2. Background

In this section, we discuss the characteristics and benefits of group projects as well as the challenges of grading such projects.

2.1 Characteristics/benefits of group projects

The group project has become a staple of software engineering courses at the graduate and undergraduate level. Students are usually grouped into teams of three or more and are required to perform the entire software development lifecycle in one or more semesters. The project may be "real" with a customer and/or end user who will use the software product after its completion. Generally, the teams are required to prepare artifacts throughout the lifecycle, such as management plans, concept documents, requirement specifications, design specifications, test plans, etc. The end result of the project is often a documented software product. Milestone reviews may be held throughout the course to allow the instructor to determine progress. Also, an acceptance test may be required to assure successful completion of the project.

There are many benefits to group projects: They encourage students to learn to work in groups (stressing co-operation, teamwork, and negotiation); projects enable better learning by having students learn from each other, motivate each other, rely on each other, have to work at agreed-upon times, etc. Projects enable students to develop larger or more complex systems than would otherwise be possible, due to division of labor; projects also allow students to gain experience working as part of a team, as is normally the case in industry.

0-7695-1877-X/03 $17.00 © 2003 IEEE

Unfortunately, grading team projects is not an easy undertaking, and has many inherent challenges. Some of these, such as being fair, consistent and encouraging, apply to all forms of grading and are discussed in the next section. Group projects add additional challenges: the grading scheme must accurately reflect each individual's contribution to the overall project, and must reflect the difficulty of the project (if each group is allowed to select their own project). Also there may need to be a mechanism to account for situations where students drop out of groups or are 'fired.'

2.2 Existing literature

Literature on this topic has been relatively sparse; the following summarizes some relevant work.

The question of how to manage group projects has been studied in the field of education theory called "co-operative learning". This is discussed in some depth by Speck [7]; he covers grading group work, among other issues, but doesn't give many useful guidelines.

Johnson et al [3] propose several essential factors that must be present for effective co-operative learning in group projects: Firstly, there must be "positive interdependence" among the team members – i.e. the group members must benefit from each others' presence. Secondly, the group members must possess and use effective inter-personal skills. Thirdly, and of key relevance to this paper, the group members must hold each other *accountable* for their share of the work and analyze as a group how effectively they are co-operating.

Schultz [6] performed a survey in which he asked teams of students doing engineering projects what their greatest difficulties were with respect to teamwork. 31% of them cited "motivating slackers" as a concern; Schultz reports that many students felt "a lot of bitterness" around this issue.

The notion of accountability also appears in the work of Gates et al [2]. They focus on motivating students to contribute equally, so that the need for differentially evaluating their contributions is lessened. They suggest two strategies: First, students should maintain rough drafts of all work they contributed, including emails etc. The intent of this is to provide a body of evidence that students can use to back up their claim to having contributed effectively. Second, each group produces a statement describing what each person did in detail. Each member of the team must then sign that they agree with the statements made by each member.

McKinney [5] has produced a well-referenced set of guidelines for improving the functioning of groups, and fostering fair and equal participation and evaluation. In a manner similar to Gates et al she suggests requiring students to prepare a systematic dossier of all their individual work, which they must use as a "ticket" permitting them to participate in group work. She also suggests assigning individual grades based on a combination of the group grade, an assessment of the individual's rough work, a "division of labor" report produced by the group, and peer ratings of the team members.

Layton and Ohland [17] found no gender effects but did find race effects when students rated their peers as part of group projects. In [18], they modified their peer-rating instrument and added additional related instruction. Using this approach, they found no race effects, but they did find gender effects, indicating that their new approach was only partially successful. Sims-Knight et al [19] examined the effect that an assessment-based continuous improvement process can have on team skills when team projects are undertaken in software engineering courses. They found that "self-assessments of both knowledge base and team process plus team training reading and exercises were not sufficient to promote improvement even in basic declarative knowledge."

A theme running through several of the above authors' work is that whatever strategy you use, it must be explained openly to the students and the students should be given a say in assessing the effectiveness of the strategy. The well-known book on college classroom teaching by Angelo and Cross [1] provides some techniques for doing this.

3. Approaches to grading individual effort

This section will discuss grading criteria, grading individual effort within groups, handling team breakdown, and evaluating project-grading methods. Instructors should be able to use this section to derive and evaluate their group grading schemes. The points made in this section have been synthesized from the literature as well as the experiences of educators at our universities.

3.1 Criteria for good grading schemes

Many of the criteria for grading have been touched upon in section 2; the grading scheme should:

- Be fair
- Be consistent
- Reflect achievement of educational objectives
- Provide good, understandable feedback
- Encourage students and avoid unnecessary discouragement
- Not contribute to grade inflation or deflation
- Be easy (as regards workload) on the grader
- Control grading volatility, sensitivity, and risks
- Be accurate and unbiased across a wide range of project types, and finally
- Discourage "risk managing" among students towards grading criteria (e.g. minimizing effort).

Let us examine some of these more closely. First, for the scheme to be fair and consistent means that grades accurately reflect differences in accomplishment from group to group and among members of a group. The grades must take into account appropriate information (particular presentations, reports, exams, etc.) so as not to unreasonably penalize or reward particular students or groups. For example, a grading scheme that rewarded only the results of a "final product demonstration" might unfairly benefit a group in which all the work was done by a single programming guru, especially if the other team members learned little and the resulting system was undocumented and unmaintainable.

There should be no numerical anomalies caused by a grading formula used; that is, an increase in skill or knowledge should map to an increase in grade. Note that anomalies can be caused by some kinds of "step functions" or strong non-linearities. The scheme should be designed so that it cannot be "manipulated" by students in any way to thwart fairness, e.g. colluding with other groups, skipping things that don't count, etc. The scheme should minimize opportunities for cheating and be as objective as possible, so as not to introduce grader bias or arbitrariness.

Designing a scheme to ensure that grades reflect achievement of educational objectives is challenging because sometimes it is hard to avoid rewarding mere volume of work or pure effort (assuming that actual knowledge and skills are the real educational objectives).

Providing good, understandable feedback implies that students and groups know what they have to do, why they obtained their particular grade, and what they can or have to do in the future.

Regarding discouragement, students may be given the opportunity to make up for some bad early results if they do well later. Also, a student who has trouble working in a group through no fault of his/her own should still be able to obtain a fair grade.

At the University of Southern California, we have found that it is both practical and fruitful to utilize our real-project, client-based CS577 course as a software engineering "laboratory" to carry out software engineering experiments and collect research data outside the course educational objectives. The activities range from observational studies such as of development processes and effort distributions [11] and point interventions such as perspective based reading techniques [12], to longitudinal studies and fundamental process changes such as use of COTS [13] or schedule as an independent variable [14]. As a result, the last three items listed above have become essential in ensuring the validity of the experimental data and results in addition to expanded emphasis on the previously listed criteria. The experiments often continue or are repeated from semester to semester. While some of the additional criteria are self evident, some elaboration is in order. There are a multitude of uncontrollable factors within software engineering project courses such as project size and scope, quality of client, organizational politics, technology changes, and so forth. Volatility and risks in these factors are natural in real word projects and thus we do not attempt to control them, which might invalidate our experiments. Our grading must, however, be robust in the face of these uncontrolled factors.

3.2 Techniques for grading individual contribution

There are numerous ways to approach evaluating individual contribution, some of which were touched on in Section 2. Some grading schemes follow:

1) The group mark is everybody's mark.
2) Everybody reports what they personally did, and separate marks are given to those components by the grader. As mentioned, McKinney [5] suggests that this can be done by using either a dossier of rough work or a division of labor report produced by team members.
3) Other group members report (confidentially or openly) the relative contributions of other group members to allow for an adjustment of the final grade.
4) Pop quizzes in class to ensure that students know the intimate details of the project.
5) Cross-validating with the results of individual work (possibly reducing the weight of group work for students who perform poorly on exams or individual assignments).

We will now examine some of these approaches. It appears that 1) is probably the simplest approach, and probably the most common. It certainly is easy on the grader. However, it may be the least fair approach and may discourage students who have a "poor" team. Scheme 2) is more work for the marker and is not normally possible to completely implement. Also, this scheme is somewhat prone to manipulation (unless a dossier is presented, students can protect their peers by lying about what they and others did). For scheme 3), one way to combine the grades would be to have each team member grade the other members of the team on a scale of 100 and the average of these scores could be used to adjust the final grade. In large groups, it might be wise to drop the highest and lowest grades assigned by peers to reduce opportunities for collusion.

We have had interesting experiences with these approaches at our three universities. As a variant of scheme 2), Jurek Jaromczyk of the University of Kentucky (UK) requires each student to prepare and update a web log weekly. He then monitors this web log to track progress. This requires more effort for the grader, but is hard for the student to manipulate.

Paul Piwowarski of UK also required each project to have a web page. Among other things, the page provides the weekly activity of the group and of individuals. This is monitored during the semester. Despite using this scheme, Piwowarski ended up giving the same project grade to all team members: It was the first time he had taught the course and he did not feel that he had enough justification and proof to give disparate grades.

Tony Baxter, also of UK, uses the pop quiz method (Scheme 4). This requires considerable effort on the part of the grader, because he or she must be knowledgeable enough and up to date enough on each team's project to be able to detect a student's ineptitude.

The University of Southern California uses a combination of these approaches. Grading scheme (1) is utilized within the four major milestone reviews (LCO, LCA, RLCA, IOC see [15]) of project artifacts (two per semester). For scheme (2), there is weekly reporting of individual effort and a heavily weighted final individual project critique that asks a comprehensive set of questions. The same individual project critique asks students to discuss management and staffing issues for which low performing team members are commonly accounted for as does the bi-weekly project progress reports. We also ask the students to assess their own individual contribution for which a significant number of points are either applied on behalf of the student or are in part redistributed to deserving teammates. Finally, the various grading results are cross-validated with each other and the individual effort due to homework, project review presentations, and quizzes. A particularly notable pattern we've identified is when a student submits a poorly detailed individual critique, void of any real content or even constructive criticism: of the course, instructors, or teammates. When the answers are "the project was good. I learned a lot," we suspect that such a student was not engaged with their team and likely not to have contributed fully. We look at the entire team's individual critiques which often will indicate a low-performing team member as the cause of project shortfalls. We would then validate further by considering the students individual effort. Generally there will be many missing or low-scoring marks, further validating that this student was not engaged with the project.

At the University of Ottawa, our standard approach in the capstone project [4] is based on scheme 1), with scheme 3) being applied in exceptional circumstances. In a second-year software engineering course requiring compulsory group work [9], we apply approach 5), increasing the weight of exams for any student whose exam grade drops below 66%; exams are weighted at 100% of the mark if the exam mark falls below 50%. One advantage of this is that it requires absolutely no extra work on the part of the faculty member. It reduces animosity against slackers since all group members know that slackers will often do poorly on exams. It is essential, however, that the project be 'standard' so that material learned doing the project can be examined.

The University of Southern California used a hybrid of schemes 1,2,3, and 5 and found that project reviews and individual critiques worked very well. Each project team prepares a structured 80-minute presentation for the "architecture review board" reviewing their project based on the lifecycle anchor points [15]. The rule is that each team member must present something and they are individually graded in regards to their preparation and presentation content. Underperforming team members are readily recognized as they are unable to present appropriate detail on their project and are unable to answer questions effectively. One of the particularly salient benefits of this approach is that it serves as an early warning and intervention process. Through direct feedback and experience of their position in relation to their teammates during the review, underperforming team members often become motivated to improve before falling in to a tailspin from which they cannot recover. As instructors, we can note early on students that may require additional guidance and can help their teams risk manage potential consequences of an underperforming team member. The individual critique serves as a final measure of how engaged a student was in their team and applied material from the course. As noted previously, underperformers are easily spotted as they tend to respond with vagueness and generalities or muddled details. By the time we note this in a student's critique, it is too late for that student to improve. A low score on a critique assures a lower grade in the course than the student's more fully engaged teammates and we use critique results as cross-validation in combination with their project review presentation scores for allocating their individual contribution points to teammates. When confronted with overwhelming evidence from poor scores on review presentations, critique, and (usually) homework, underperformers generally confess their lack of participation and are eager to provide restitution by sacrificing their individual contribution points.

We have found that it does not work well to directly ask students to evaluate their teammates (scheme 3) as students are reluctant to provide details or "rat out" their teammates. This is generally unnecessary, as noted earlier we have multiple other means of spotting underperformers. What we do instead is ask students to evaluate within their critique the impact of problems they encountered, including team personal. Rather than "name names" they are more comfortable and candid with describing hardships such as "we would have been able to implement all the high-priority requirements if all the team members performed to the expected level." This provides critical information needed to gauge how much of an underperforming students individual contribution points should be allocated to the rest of the team – that is, student evaluations of other students are best used in *assessing magnitude* and not *identification*.

The University of Kentucky used scheme 3) and found that it worked very well [16], though this is contrary to the experience at USC. It was used in several variations. In one variation, an evaluation instrument was used. The students evaluated themselves as well as each team member. This instrument was used in three different software engineering project courses with undergraduate students and graduate students. Each semester there was at least one team that felt that one or more team members were not "pulling their weight." In all but one instance, the instructor had to serve as an intermediary. In two incidences, the "idle" team member acknowledged that they were not doing their share and their grade was lowered appropriately. In one incidence, the "idle" team member "vanished" from class and did not complete any further assignments or exams and received an appropriately low grade. In one incidence, the "idle" member "kicked it into high gear" and earned the respect of the other team members by over-performing at the end of the project. This pattern is not what we should promote as instructors, but at least solves the unfairness problem.

Table 1. Grading criteria mapped to individual effort grading.

Grading Criterion	All same grade	Each reports own effort	Each evaluates self and others	Each reports in weekly Web log	Each reports in journal	Quiz in class	Project reviews	Individual effort analysis
Fair			X			X		X
Consistent	X					X		X
Reflect Educ. Objectives				X		X	X	
Provide feedback		X	X			X	X	
Encourage students		X					X	
No grade inflation				X				X
Easy on grader	X	X	X		X			

The above scheme seemed to work well in that students were not reluctant to comment on an "idle" member. However, the instructor worried that the scheme may also have encouraged team members to "gang up" on another member. The scheme also did not allow frequent monitoring of the teams as the forms were only turned in three times throughout the semester. This scheme might be improved by combining it with other schemes and variations, such as having the students e-mail such evaluations to the instructor weekly. This would require more work on the part of the instructor, though.

The instructor found that one aspect of the project assignment was very good at uncovering students who had not contributed much: the project demonstration. The instructor required all team members to participate in this demonstration in the instructor's office or student lab. The instructor had developed an "acceptance plan" and asked the team members to perform the tests and/or the instructor performed some tests. The instructor also asked each member questions about the project and asked for demonstration of certain features. The demonstrations often "rooted out" students who did not know much about their projects (at the very end of the project schedule, no less).

Variations on this scheme such as weekly web logs, periodic journals, and random quizzes were also used at UK. It was found that the weekly web log and quizzes worked well. The web log needs to be more formal though. In the future, UK plans to tell all group members to review the web log for accuracy (of all members' accounts) as it will affect their individual grades on the project. The quizzes also need to contain more detailed, team-specific project questions.

In Table 1, each of the above grading schemes has been mapped to the grading criteria discussed earlier. Note that no single scheme meets all the grading criteria. It seems clear that using a combination of these schemes is the best approach for achieving adequate criteria coverage. The grading schemes may be combined in a number of ways:

- A fixed percentage of each person's grade is based on scheme 2) or 3); the remainder on scheme 1), e.g. S1*0.9 + S3*0.1.
- The group grade, scheme 1), is "multiplied" by a factor from scheme 3), e.g. simply S1 * S3/100.
- A fixed number of grades are available to be distributed among all the group members. The members decide who gets what. For example, the instructor grades a project (using scheme 1) as 90%. For a 3-person group this means that there are 90 * 3 = 270 marks that the 3 students can distribute among themselves in whatever manner they agree on.

Whatever the grading scheme, we reiterate the following issue raised by other researchers in section 2.1: It is important that the syllabus and/or grading policy clearly spell out the instructors' intent. The University of Kentucky often uses this paragraph:

"Group Projects:

The group project for the course will require you to work together with other students in the class. You will be evaluated on your contribution to the group project and presentations of the project results. The instructor will make group assignments. Group members are not guaranteed to receive the same grade; evaluation of the group will be individualized to determine individual understanding, commitment, and mastery of the project goals. As part of the project, written reports will be required. Proper language usage is required."

3.3 Preparing for when bad things happen

Generally there are some warning signs when things are not going well within a team. One or more disgruntled students will call, e-mail, or visit an instructor. At this time, we believe that the instructor should encourage the students to work it out among themselves. If this fails, the instructor can serve as an intermediary and meet with the team.

Hong-Mei Chen at the University of Hawaii [8] approaches the problem very much like industry. Once a student is part of a team and is not pulling his/her weight, the team can "fire" them. The "fired" student can then try to get rehired by another team. If unsuccessful, the student will be given an individual project to work on. If the latter occurs, it becomes labor intensive for the instructor and grader. A variation on this is that fired members could be assigned a 0 or a failing grade.

4. Suggested best practices

Based on the findings above, we feel that there are several best practices that can be suggested.

- Allow team members to evaluate each other, but carefully and/or frequently monitor this to prevent the "mob" mentality or collusion.
- Use project demonstrations and/or quizzes to further test project knowledge.
- Require frequent generation and/or posting of individual effort information, or the maintenance of individual dossiers
- Cross-validate individual effort evaluations with group evaluations
- Have multiple individual grading methods (e.g. individual project critique and individual effort) to enable adjustments for individual contribution
- Whatever grading scheme you use, evaluate it using the criteria we listed in section 3.1

5. Summary and conclusions

In this paper we have discussed how software engineering course instructors can tackle problems associated with grading group projects. We first pointed out that group projects are an essential component of software engineering curricula: Students must practice collaborating with teammates since this is what they will be doing in their careers.

Whenever an instructor is designing a grading scheme, he or she should evaluate the scheme according to the criteria we presented in Section 3.1. Among these criteria are issues of fairness, consistency, encouraging students, and preventing various kinds of anomalies. The fairness issue is one of the most important since studies have shown that students feel bitterness about slackers.

In Section 3.2, we examined some techniques and grading schemes that can help instructors meet the criteria. The various mechanisms encourage accountability or permit individual contributions and knowledge to be properly assessed. We suggest combining several techniques.

6. References

[1] Angelo, T.A. and Cross, K.P., "Group Work Evaluations", in *Classroom assessment techniques: a handbook for college teachers*, Jossey-Bass Publishers, a Wiley company, 1993, pp. 349-351.

[2] Gates, A.Q.; Delgado, N.; Mondragon, O., "A structured approach for managing a practical software engineering course", 30th Frontiers in Education conf, IEEE, 2000, pp. T1C/21 -T1C/26

[3] Johnson, D. W., Johnson, R. T., and Smith, K. A. "Cooperative learning: Increasing college faculty instructional productivity", *ASHE-ERIC Higher Education Report* 20, 4, Graduate School of Education and Human Development, The George Washington University, 1991.

[4] Lethbridge, T. "SEG 4000: Rules for Projects", University of Ottawa, web page as of Sept. 2002, http://www.site.uottawa.ca/~tcl/seg4000/rules.html

[5] McKinney, K. "Tips for Grading Group Work", Illinois State University, web page as of Sept. 2002, www.cat.ilstu.edu/teaching_tips/handouts/ tipsgroupwork.shtml

[6] Schultz, T.W., "Students assessing teams", proc. 29th Frontiers in Education conf, IEEE, 1999, pp. 13B2/1 -13B2/3.

[7] Speck, B.W., "Pedagogical Support for Classroom Collaborative Writing Assignments", *ASHE-ERIC Higher Education Report*, 28, 6, Jossey-Bass, a Wiley Company, 2002, pp. 1-139

[8] Chen, H-M., web page http://www.cba.hawaii.edu /HMCHEN/home.htm

[9] Lethbridge, T.C., University of Ottawa, SEG 2100 course web page: http://www.lloseng.com/seg2100

[10] Individual Critique Guidelines for CS577a 2000 http://sunset.usc.edu/classes/cs577a_2002/IndividualCritiqe.html

[11] Boehm, B., Egyed, A., Kwan, J., Port, D., Shah, A., and Madachy, R., "Using the WinWin Spiral Model: A Case Study," Computer, July 1998, pp. 33-44.

[12] Shull, F.; Rus, I.; and Basili, V.R. "How Perspective-Based Reading Can Improve Requirements Inspections". IEEE Computer 33, 7 (July 2000), 73-79.

[13] Port, D., Bhuta, J., Yang, Y., Boehm, B., "Not All CBS Are Created Equally: COTS Intensive Project Types," Accepted to ICCBSS 2003.

[14] Boehm, B., Brown, W., "Mastering Rapid Delivery and Change with the SAIV Process Model", Proceedings, ESCOM 2001, April 2001

[15] Boehm, B. (1996), "Anchoring the Software Process," IEEE Software, July, pp. 73-82.

[16] Hayes, J. Huffman. "Energizing Software Engineering Education through Real-World Projects as Experimental Studies," in *Proceedings of the 15th Conference on Software Engineering Education and Training (CSEET)*, Covington, KY, February 2002.

[17] Ohland, M. W., Layton, R A.. "Comparing the Reliability of Two Peer Evaluation Instruments". Proceedings. ASEE Annual Conference & Exposition, St. Louis, MO, Jun. 2000.

[18] Layton, R. A., Ohland, M W., "Peer Ratings Revisited: Focus on Teamwork, Not Ability". In Proceedings. ASEE Annual Conference & Exposition, Charlotte, NC, June. 2001.

[19] Sims-Knight, J., Upchurch, R., Powers, T.A., Haden, S., and Topciu, R. "Teams in Software Engineering Education". Proceedings of Frontiers in Education 2002, November 6 – 9, 2002, Boston, MA, pp. S3G17 – S3G22.

7. Acknowledgments

We would like to thank Hong-Mei Chen of the University of Hawaii, Jurek Jaromczyk, Paul Piwowarski, and Tony Baxter of the University of Kentucky for their insights and contributions to this paper.

On The Supervision and Assessment Of Part-Time Postgraduate Software Engineering Projects

Andrew Simpson, Andrew Martin, Jeremy Gibbons, Jim Davies, and Steve McKeever
Software Engineering Programme
Wolfson Building, Parks Road, Oxford OX1 3QD, United Kingdom

Abstract

This paper describes existing practices in the supervision and assessment of projects undertaken by part-time, postgraduate students in Software Engineering. It considers this aspect of the learning experience, and the educational issues raised, in the context of existing literature—much of which is focussed upon the experience of full-time, undergraduate students. The importance of these issues will increase with the popularity of part-time study at a postgraduate level; the paper presents a set of guidelines for project supervision and assessment.

1. Introduction

In [25] a lack of Computer Science-specific literature concerning projects is noted. This has started to be addressed within the community. For example, the United Kingdom's Effective Projectwork in Computer Science (EPCoS) consortium [30, 17] and the collection of papers of [22] represent positive moves in this respect. Internationally, journals such as *Computer Science Education* have also published many articles on the subject.

A significant proportion of this literature, as one would expect, is primarily concerned with projects undertaken by full-time undergraduates. However, the literature does step outside the boundaries of the traditional 'design-build-report'-style project module: some projects are run with an industrial partner [1, 13, 23], while others involve international collaboration [7, 27].

No matter what form projects take, efforts should be directed towards evaluating their role in the Computer Science curriculum [11]. This is done in [17], where a collection of examples of good practice for various forms of computing project are presented: allocation methods, supervision techniques and assessment methods are detailed for industrial-based projects, taught MSc courses, and so on. Our specific concern—projects undertaken by part-time postgraduate Software Engineering students—is not represented there. This paper has been written in the spirit of that collection. We pay particular attention to the topics of intellectual property and confidentiality, as this is perhaps more of a concern for our students (and their employers) than it is for full-time undergraduate students.

The structure of the remainder of this paper is as follows. In Section 2 we describe the University of Oxford's Software Engineering Programme, and outline the context in which the projects undertaken by the Programme's students are supervised and assessed. In Section 3 we relate our experiences of supervising and assessing projects to the published literature. In particular, we consider the six themes identified in [17]: *allocation*, *supervision*, *assessment*, *reflection*, *team or group projects*, and *motivation*. In Section 4 we offer some guidelines for the supervision of part-time postgraduate Software Engineering projects that may be of benefit to similar programmes. Finally, we summarise the contribution of this paper, and indicate areas for future work.

2. Software Engineering at the University of Oxford

Both in the United Kingdom and in the United States there is, on the one hand, the need for a highly-skilled work force, and, on the other hand, there is a decline in public support for higher education [4]. In addition, as more young people enter higher education in the United Kingdom, the possession of a postgraduate degree is becoming a more significant factor in the job market—at the same time as the level of funding for postgraduate taught courses is being reduced. This pattern is being replicated worldwide.

In [15], several themes that characterise higher education's response to these problems are identified. Two of these themes—"a shift from faculty-centered to learner-centered institutions" and "lifelong learning"—are at the heart of the Software Engineering Programme at the University of Oxford, the philosophy of which echoes the sentiments of [33], in which a vision for software engineering education and training for the twenty-first century is outlined.

0-7695-1877-X/03 $17.00 © 2003 IEEE

There has also been a shift in higher education's mission to include three additional goals: providing knowledge to the workforce, retooling people for new careers, and catering to the need for mental simulation [2]. Universities are now being asked to consider what it means to be a graduate [20] and to debate the transferable skills that such graduates should possess [18].

The Software Engineering Programme at the University of Oxford[1] is a joint venture between Oxford University Computing Laboratory and the University's Department for Continuing Education, which has the aim of making the educational resources of the University of Oxford more accessible to a wider public. The Programme offers a number of short courses—which may be taken individually, combined to form short programmes of study, or used as credit towards a postgraduate qualification—that covers a wide range of software engineering topics.

At any one time, approximately 200 students are registered for a part-time qualification: either a Postgraduate Certificate, a Postgraduate Diploma, an MSc, or a doctorate in Software Engineering (although we do not concern ourselves with doctoral students in this paper). These students—many of whom come from overseas—attend intensive, one-week courses at the Programme's own teaching facility. The Programme currently has a core staff of eight: five university lecturers, supported by an administrative staff of three.

The Programme allows students to register initially for one of three qualifications: a Postgraduate Certificate, a Postgraduate Diploma, or an MSc. It is only for the latter of these that the completion of a project is required (although, in previous years, this was also a requirement for the Diploma). Students on the MSc undertake a project carrying about a quarter of the weight of the degree; the dissertation has a 20,000 word limit. The project typically involves application of techniques taught on the Programme to a real-world problem or product of the student's employer. The project is supervised by one of the Programme lecturers, and graded by two people: one of the Programme lecturers other than the supervisor, and one of a committee of three examiners.

As well as allowing students to move from registration for a lower qualification to a higher one, the Programme also allows students to move back down the ladder: many part-time students find themselves in the position of being unable to make sufficient time to undertake the research associated with a project or to write up their findings (or, for that matter, both)—even though they have completed (and passed) the required number of taught courses. It would be a pity for such students to leave the Programme without an award of any sort; hence, the possibility of transferring to a lower award.

In this mode of delivery, the Programme is relatively novel, though by no means unique. For example, the Safety Critical Systems Engineering and System Safety Engineering[2] courses run by the University of York are both organised in a similar way. The University of Kansas also offers a part-time MSc in Software Engineering aimed at students from industry.[3] In addition, as is noted in [16], some institutes have gone further and are offering the electronic delivery of such courses.

[1] www.softeng.ox.ac.uk

3. Software Engineering projects: theory and practice

In [14], it is argued that the Graduate Engineer must be capable of demonstrating practical competence in action. This is the fundamental basis for including projects in the Computer Science curriculum. Furthermore, it is a requirement for the Programme's accreditation by the British Computer Society (BCS) [4] that a project component be included in the MSc. However, we feel that the project aspect of our degree is significantly different to the traditional project aspect—in terms of, for example, its role in the curriculum, the demands on supervision, the nature of topics undertaken, and the nature of assessment. We discuss such issues in this section.

The role of project work In [3], the view that the role of project work can be unclear is presented: students enter it with expectations that are often based upon ill-defined preparation, resulting in a preoccupation with technical issues [32]; prospective research students may be exercised in areas that they might later pursue [31]; and so on. Such issues are of little relevance to our students, as the role of project work for them is very clear. They are now in a position to use, or evaluate, these techniques with respect to problems that they face within their working environment; this is the role played by project work within our Programme. However, there are—of course—exceptions. For example, a student who works on a test team for an industrial strength Java Virtual Machine implementation must be stretched in different ways.

Industry relevance In the United Kingdom, criticisms have been made of the preparedness of graduates for entering the 'real world': the Dearing Report [12] and the UK Engineering Council's SARTOR (Standards and Routes to Registration) Report [34] have both made this point forcefully in recent years. As a result, some admirable efforts have been made to make projects of full-time Computer Science students more relevant to industry. For example, [35] describes the use of 'University based industrial projects' to provide full-time students with the advantages of industrial contacts,

[2] www.cs.york.ac.uk/MSc/SCSE

[3] www.eecs.ku.edu

[4] www.bcs.org.uk

while [21] describes an MSc course involving a real client and a professional software project manager. Another example is described in [36], which reports on "classroom experiences in software engineering coursework where students are placed in an industrial environment and given a real customer, a real project, and held to commercial practices and accountability." Such efforts are not, of course, restricted to the United Kingdom. Other examples include [19], which describes experiences at Monash University, and [10], which details experiences at Uppsala University of project-oriented courses in which the courses are chosen to be similar to genuine industrial projects. The projects undertaken by our students are, by their very nature, relevant to industry. Indeed, the projects have the added bonus of determining the industrial relevance of the techniques and methods that they have been taught as part of the Programme: this is an extremely valuable means of validating the material taught. Our students, however, face slightly different problems here. For example, a company whose student has submitted a project that includes a detailed critique of their internal practices risks losing a lot if such sensitive information were to leak out.

Supervisor influence In [6], the view that "individual students' experience of project work will depend heavily on the attitudes and beliefs of their supervisor" is given. The projects undertaken by our students are very much work-oriented, and, therefore, the potential impact of supervisors' attitudes and beliefs is restricted—and, at times, restricted to workload planning.

Technical challenges Many full-time students, at the end of their course of study, may have to demonstrate a significant amount of technical competence simply to use the development environment that they have chosen. As far as most of our students are concerned, they demonstrate this every day of their working lives. Therefore, the challenges presented by completing a project as part of their course are different to those of full-time students: work and family pressures have a far greater impact than the technical challenges presented to them.

Learning objectives The learning objectives for project work can "encompass the exercise and development of a wide range of skills varying from generic personal transferable skills, such as communication and teamwork, to technical skills such as the ability to design, construct and deliver a system meeting stated requirements . . . The required deliverables should reflect and reinforce the learning objectives" [5]. The impact of the learning outcomes can be increased if the objectives are stated clearly and explicitly at the start of the project process—something that we endeavour to do.

Allocation As with undergraduate courses, the Software Engineering Programme allows a degree of choice with regards to the selection of MSc project topics. There are, however, two main aspects that determine this choice. First, the project is seen as a culmination of the students' course of study. As such, the project is expected to involve the application of some of the techniques learnt during their studies. The specific problem to be solved is the second aspect that determines choice—it is typically expected that the problem area will be one associated with the students' workplace. It follows that the 'assignment problem' identified in [9], which requires the "variation of a classical approach to the Assignment Problem" [29] is not a concern here.

Supervision Due to the very nature of the Programme's students, the form of supervision taken is unusual. Supervision meetings are more infrequent than is the case for full-time undergraduate students. This is mainly due to the fact that the Programme's students are not (typically) located in Oxford. There are, of course, extremes: one student may visit every couple of weeks; another may visit right at the start of their project work and never be seen again. When students do make the trip to see their supervisor, this means that such meetings are longer and—arguably—more productive than is the case for full-time students. Another result of this distance is that regular email contact is far more important than is the case for full-time students.

Assessment A number of authors have discussed the concept of assessment authenticity (see, for example, [28], [8], and [37]). As noted in [17], there are many forms of such assessment. The fundamental basis for assessment of projects submitted by Programme students is the level to which they have demonstrated skill at understanding and applying the techniques taught.

Reflection To quote [17], "reflection on experience underpins the process of successful learning and is essential to the success of education." Nowhere is this more true than in project work, where, typically, this is the main opportunity for such activity. Our students are at an advantage in this regard: because the project is the culmination of their course of study (and also because of the nature of the project being undertaken), the reflection process is more widespread: there is the opportunity for reflection on the benefits of the whole course, as well as on the project work undertaken.

Team or group projects The projects undertaken by our students are all individual projects: given that there is no set start or end date (or duration), that the students are geographically distributed, and some projects may involve commercially sensitive material, it cannot be otherwise. That is not to say, however, that we do not value the roles of team or group projects: the final module undertaken by all students prior to them starting on their project work is a compulsory module in which students work in groups to specify, design, implement, and test a system. In addition, some students report on work they have individually carried out within a team context in their place of work, with the other members of the team being unconnected with the Programme.

Motivation In [24], four particular points in the learning cycle at which motivation may be addressed are listed: it can be affected by their *interest* in their work; their perception of its *relevance*; their *expectation* that they will succeed; and their *satisfaction* in their achievement. This has a neat fit with the philosophy of the Software Engineering Programme and—in particular—the project work undertaken.

Planning As detailed in [17], work schedules stretching over weeks or months are new to most full-time students: they should be encouraged to produce a time plan to enable both the student and supervisor to monitor progress. Most part-time students *are* used to generating time plans: typically the drive to produce a time plan comes from the student rather than the supervisor.

4. Guidelines

In this section we present some guidelines (in the spirit of [17]) that can be employed with regards to part-time postgraduate Software Engineering projects.

Understand the student's subject area The process of choosing of subject area for a student's project is significantly different than it is when dealing with a full-time undergraduate Computer Science student. Full-time undergraduates choose their project topics for a variety of reasons: they are keen on the subject area and want to explore it further; they want to work with a particular member of staff; or maybe they are assigned a project by a 'project supremo'. Part-time postgraduate students go through a very different process in their choice of project area. Typically, they will want to extend or reanalyse something associated with their everyday work (indeed, the Software Engineering Programme at Oxford encourages this)—the choice then becomes very simple. The difference here is that there is unlikely to be a supervisor who is familiar with the project, working practice, or work place in which the project is to be embedded—thus, there is a learning curve for the supervisor as well as the student. This brings us to the second guideline.

Understand that the supervisor-student relationship is genuinely a two-way relationship The supervision of students who actually work in the industry results in a flow of information is genuinely two-way. For example, part-time students can be the source of potential (applied) research ideas for their supervisors. The relationship between part-time students and their supervisors is unlike that between full-time students and their supervisors. In the latter, there is nearly always a huge gulf in age, experience, status, and authority; with regards to the former, it is more of a relationship between peers, with each party bringing different contributions to the table.

Understand the pressures faced by the student Full-time students typically have time pressures with regards to project submission: increasingly such students have to finance their studies through part-time (and, in some cases, full-time) jobs. Part-time students also have time pressures, but of a slightly different variety. Full-time students (usually) have a set date by which they should submit their project; part-time students (again, usually) do not. Without a firm target, real life gets in the way and progress is slow: therefore a realistic work plan with plenty of slack and a fixed submission date are essential.

Be realistic with regards to assessment Part-time students are not immersed in an academic culture, day-in, day-out. They do not have easy access to the university library—although they can access Web resources easily; they do not have easy access to their supervisor—although email contact is easy to establish. Most part-time software engineering students cannot be expected to produce research-based projects; they cannot be expected to work with recent research results; they cannot be expected to work with a supervisor in his or her specialist area. They can, however, be expected to demonstrate, apply, and evaluate what they have learnt during the taught part of the course. This must be the basis for the assessment of such projects.

Provide both formative and summative feedback We have found that our students have a strong desire for summative feedback: they feel that they have invested a tremendous amount of time and energy into their project work, and wish to know on what basis the grade awarded to them was arrived at. However, formative feedback is also a vital part of the project process. The students have gone through a process of employing techniques taught during their study to genuine problems in their workplace: many of these students wish to carry on doing so, and to be able to exploit this new knowledge successfully. In this regard, a final bit of constructive advice can be valuable.

Confidentiality The very nature of the projects undertaken by our students means that the issue of confidentiality is of concern, and so there is a responsibility on the Programme to ensure that—for some projects—only approved individuals (such as, for example, the supervisor and examiners) may have access to the final project.

As students are encouraged to undertake projects which are directly connected with their work, the majority are under a duty of confidentiality to their employer, and most are well aware of this. As a result, projects are undertaken within the confines of a non-disclosure agreement. The Programme has a pro-forma agreement to which most companies are happy to give their consent. This covers discussion with lecturers and examiners, and allows the project to be kept on very restricted access in the library. This, of course, has a negative impact on the pool of previous projects that can be made available for current students to read.

Intellectual property The University's normal practice is to place the projects in a library after they have been examined, and the University claims intellectual property rights in (among other things) software developed *in the course of, or incidentally to* the student's studies, if it possesses commercial potential.

Intellectual property raises a wider range of issues. The University's statutes are so phrased in order to protect it against exploitation by others of ideas substantially developed by its staff. In the case of full-time students this may be a significant concern. Part-time students, by the nature of their studies, have less interaction with University staff, and are much less likely therefore to discover a valuable idea with their aid. The delineation of work related or incidental to their studies, and work undertaken for their employer is often impossible; the two are intertwined.

Most students appear unaware of such concerns—consent to the University statutes is a small matter when they register for a degree. For very few will it be remotely of interest, the majority of projects generating little by way of valuable (or directly-exploitable) intellectual property. For many, however, if the issue is raised it will generate concern, even if they fall into this group.

Of course, where the student is in employment, they will have already (probably) assigned intellectual property rights to their employer, and so at the point of registering for a degree are not able to give any such rights to the University.

It is frequently necessary to advise a student to construct their project in such a way as to avoid placing interesting and/or ground-breaking developments within the scope of the project. For example, one student is developing a framework to enable companies in a particular sector to construct e-commerce solutions with particular ease. Rather than describe this work as an MSc project, and gain credit for doing so, they find themselves writing instead a project describing an application of the framework, developed alongside it in order to validate and refine its definition. Another student has developed a tool which will substantially aid their company in maintenance and development of a class of product. This student might happily submit a description of that tool for their MSc without fear of the company's rights being damaged. These two examples represent extremes. The inequity between students due to their employment situation with regard to intellectual property is seldom great, and very seldom likely to affect the outcome of the student's degree. Very few MSc projects develop intellectual property of significant value; the situation is nevertheless far from satisfactory.

5. Summary

In [17] a collection of examples of good practice are produced to aid potential supervisors of various forms of Computing projects. Our specific concern—projects undertaken by part-time postgraduate Software Engineering students—is not represented there. As a consequence, this paper has been written in the spirit of that collection. We paid particular emphasis to intellectual property and confidentiality because it is of considerable relevance to the projects undertaken by our students.

The role of projects within Computing curricula is very much an accepted part of such degree programmes—mainly because it helps prepare students for life in the 'real world'. Although the benefits that come from including a project component as part of our degree are very different to those associated with full-time undergraduate projects, the benefits are very real—for both students and supervisors.

In [26] four stakeholders in project work are identified: academic staff, students (before the work), students (after the work), and employers. In this paper we have focussed on the views of one of these stakeholders—the academic staff. We shall focus on the views of the others in future papers. Furthermore, it may be that many of the themes identified in this paper are relevant to similar courses in other fields—this shall also be a subject for future work.

References

[1] C. Bergman. Senior design projects with industry. In *Proceedings of FIE'98*. IEEE, November 1998.

[2] H. Blustain, P. Goldstein, and G. Lozier. Assessing the new competitive landscape. In R. N. Katz and associates, editors, *Dancing With The Devil: Information Technology And The New Competition In Higher Education*, pages 51–72. Jossey-Bass inc., 1999.

[3] R. D. Boyle and M. A. C. Clark. Non-technical issues in undergraduate CS project work or what are we (all) here for? In M. Holcombe, A. Stratton, S. Fincher, and G. Griffiths, editors, *Projects in the Computing Curriculum: Proceedings of the Project '98 Workshop*, pages 117–128. Springer, 1998.

[4] D. W. Breneman, J. E. Finney, and B. M. Roherty. Shaping The Future: Higher Education Finances In The 1990s. San Jose: California Higher Education Policy Centre, 1997.

[5] P. Capon. Maximizing learning outcomes of computer science projects. *Computer Science Education*, 9(3):184–199, 1999.

[6] M. A. C. Clark and R. D. Boyle. A personal theory of teaching computing through final year projects. *Computer Science Education*, 9(3):200–214, 1999.

[7] T. Clear. A collaborative learning trial between New Zealand and Sweden using Lotus Notes Domino in teaching the concepts of human computer interaction. In *Proceedings of ACM Innovation and Technology in Computer Science Education*, 1999.

[8] A. Collins. Portfolios for science education: issues in purpose, structure and authenticity. *Science Education*, 76:451–463, 1992.

[9] R. Cooper and R. Welland. Computing science projects at the University of Glasgow. In M. Holcombe, A. Stratton, S. Fincher, and G. Griffiths, editors, *Projects in the Computing Curriculum: Proceedings of the Project '98 Workshop*, pages 169–183. Springer, 1998.

[10] M. Daniels and L. Asplund. Full scale industrial project work: a one semester course. In *IEEE Frontiers in Education, San Juan, Costa Rica*, November 1999.

[11] M. Daniels, A. Berglund, and M. Petre. Some thoughts on international projects in the undergraduate education. In *Project 99, EPCoS, Exeter, UK*, September 1999.

[12] Report Of The National Committee On Higher Education. HM Government, HM Stationary Office, 1997.

[13] D. Dekker. Issues when using company sponsored projects to provide a design experience for students. In *Proceedings of FIE'97*. IEEE, November 1997.

[14] P. J. Denning. Educating a new engineer. *Communications of the ACM*, 35(12):82–97, December 1992.

[15] J. J. Duderstadt. Can colleges and universities survive in the information age? In R. N. Katz and associates, editors, *Dancing With The Devil: Information Technology And The New Competition In Higher Education*, pages 1–26. Jossey-Bass inc., 1999.

[16] G. C. Farrington. The new technologies and the future of residential undergraduate education. In R. N. Katz and associates, editors, *Dancing With The Devil: Information Technology And The New Competition In Higher Education*, pages 73–94. Jossey-Bass inc., 1999.

[17] S. Fincher, M. Petre, and M. Clark, editors. *Computer Science Project Work: Principles and Pragmatics*. Springer, 2001.

[18] A. Griffin. Transferring learning in higher education: problems and possibilities. In R. Barnett, editor, *Academic Community: Discourse or Discord?* Jessica Kingsley, 1992.

[19] D. Hagan, S. Tucker, and J. Ceddia. Industrial experience projects: A balance of process and product. *Computer Science Education*, 9(3):215–229, 1999.

[20] HEQC. Assessment In Higher Education And The Role Of 'Graduateness'. Higher Education Quality Council, London, 1997.

[21] M. Holcombe and H. H. Lafferty. Using computer professionals for managing student software projects. In D. Bateman and T. Hopkins, editors, *Proceedings of the Conference on Developments in the Teaching of Computer Science*. University of Kent at Canterbury, 1992.

[22] M. Holcombe, A. Stratton, S. Fincher, and G. Griffiths, editors. *Projects in the Computing Curriculum: Proceedings of the Project '98 Workshop*. Springer, 1998.

[23] A. Jackson. An industry-centered capstone experience for aeronautical management technology students at Arizona State University. In *Proceedings of FIE'98*. IEEE, November 1998.

[24] J. M. Keller. Motivational design of instruction. In C. M. Reigeluth, editor, *Instructional-Design Theories and Models*. Lawrence Erlbaum Associates, 1983.

[25] M. Knudsen and T. Vinther, editors. *Project Work in University Studies*. Roskilde University, Denmark, September 1997.

[26] M. R. Luck. Undergraduate research projects — why bother? In *EPCoS workshop, Leeds, UK*, January 1998.

[27] T. Macek, B. Mannova, J. Kolar, and B. Williams. Global cooperation project in computer programming course. In *Proceedings of SIGCSE'99*. ACM Press, March 1999.

[28] R. Mitchell. What is 'authentic assessment'? Portfolio: The Newsletter of Arts PROPEL, Harvard University, December 1989.

[29] C. H. Papdimitrou and K. Sterglitz. *Combinatorial Optimization*. Prentice Hall, 1982.

[30] M. Petre and S. Fincher. Using other people's experience of project work: realising fitness for purpose. In M. Holcombe, A. Stratton, S. Fincher, and G. Griffiths, editors, *Projects in the Computing Curriculum: Proceedings of the Project '98 Workshop*, pages 19–30. Springer, 1998.

[31] S. Rowett. Experience of a student-led final year degree project. In M. Boyle, editor, *Student led Projects at the University of Leeds*. University of Leeds, 1995.

[32] J. Ryder and J. Leach. Research projects in the UG science course: students learning about science through enculturation. In G. Gibbs, editor, *Improving Student Learning Through Course Design*. Oxford Centre for Staff Learning and Development, 1997.

[33] H. Saiedian. Software engineering education and training for the next millennium. *Journal of Systems and Software*, 47(12), December 1999.

[34] Standards and routes to registration (SARTOR). Engineering Council, 1997.

[35] A. Stratton, M. Holcombe, and P. Croll. Improving the quality of software engineering courses through university based industrial projects. In M. Holcombe, A. Stratton, S. Fincher, and G. Griffiths, editors, *Projects in the Computing Curriculum: Proceedings of the Project '98 Workshop*, pages 47–69. Springer, 1998.

[36] J. B. Vaughn jr. Teaching industrial practices in an undergraduate software engineering course. *Computer Science Education*, 11(1):21–32, 2001.

[37] G. Wiggins. A true test: toward more authentic and equitable assessment. *Phi Delta Kappan*, pages 703–713, 1989.

Using a Web-Based Project Process Throughout the Software Engineering Curriculum

Donald J. Bagert
Rose-Hulman Institute of Technology
Don.Bagert@rose-hulman.edu

Susan A. Mengel
Texas Tech University
Susan.A.Mengel@coe.ttu.edu

Abstract

In order to facilitate the study and use of software process, which is essential to the education of future software professionals, a standard and tailorable project process has been developed over the last five years at Texas Tech University for use in both undergraduate and graduate curricula, with a total 12 courses involved. The process is entirely web-based, and includes a complete set of HTML document templates in order to facilitate the creation of project artifacts which are posted to the course web page. This method enhances communication between team members, including distance education students, and between the project team and client. The project process has received positive feedback from all stakeholders involved.

This paper discusses the benefits of the web-based project process, its relation to curriculum models, and plans for a more formal assessment of the process. The portability of process to other institutions is also discussed, with an example provided.

1. Introduction

Virtually all aspects of software engineering (SE) can be found within the software development process. Furthermore, the use of a standard software development process within a software organization has become increasingly common over the past 10-15 years. Therefore, not only is the study of software process essential to the education of a future software professional, but the use of a standard, tailorable process throughout a computer science and software engineering curriculum can be beneficial in understanding how such a process can be used in different ways within the same software organization.

The Department of Computer Science at Texas Tech University (TTU) has used such a strategy part of the development of its curriculum models. Between the Master of Science in Software Engineering (MSSE) and Bachelor of Science in Computer Science (BSCS) programs at Texas Tech, there are 12 semester-long courses that deal with software engineering, from fundamentals through advanced concepts. Five years ago, a standard software project process was developed that is now present throughout the software engineering aspects of the curriculum - including capstone courses on both the undergraduate and graduate level - as well as classes that are more lecture-oriented but require assignments that use the project process.

In addition, this software process is completely web-based. All project artifacts are posted to the course web page, which enhances communication between team members, some of which are taking the course itself through the Internet (the entire MSSE degree is offered via distance education). This also facilitates interaction with the project clients, who often work for companies located outside of the community where TTU is located.

This paper will provide some background concerning the use of project processes in software engineering curricula, the BSCS and MSSE curricula at Texas Tech, the objectives and outcomes of the web-based process, and a presentation of the details of the Texas Tech software process and document set. The relationship of the process to software curriculum models is also addressed, as well as an ongoing effort to port the process to the Rose-Hulman Institute of Technology. Finally, some plans for a more formal assessment of the project process is outlined.

2. Background

2.1. Software Engineering at Texas Tech

Table 1 contains the 12 software engineering courses currently offered at Texas Tech. Three undergraduate courses are required for the BSCS. *Software Engineering* is the standard introductory course. This is where the project process is first introduced to the students. A small project is done during the second half of the course in order to expose the students to working in a large team (15-20 people) using a project process. The introductory course is followed by a two-semester senior capstone project *Senior Project Design* and *Senior Project Implementation Laboratory*) usually with an external (non-university) client.

0-7695-1877-X/03 $17.00 © 2003 IEEE

Table 1. Software Engineering Courses at Texas Tech.

Course Name	Level	Required?	Prerequisites
Software Engineering (SE)	Undergraduate	Yes	Data Structures
Senior Project Design (SPD)	Undergraduate	Yes	SE, Algorithm Analysis
Senior Project Implementation Laboratory	Undergraduate	Yes	SPD
Software Specification and Design (SS&D)	Graduate	Yes	SE or equivalent
Software Project Management (SPM)	Graduate	Yes	SE or equivalent
Real-Time & Time-Sharing Systems	Graduate	No	SE or equivalent, Systems Programming
Software Quality Assurance & Testing	Graduate	No	SE or equivalent
Web-Based Software Systems	Graduate	No	SE or equivalent
Software Process Improvement	Graduate	Yes	SE or equivalent
Software Construction & Evolution (SC&E)	Graduate	Yes	SS&D, SPM
Software Studio I (SS1)	Graduate	Yes	SS&D, SPM
Software Studio II	Graduate	Yes	SS1

There are currently nine software engineering courses in the Master of Science in Software Engineering curriculum. (This curriculum was gradually expanded from three courses in 1989, with the Master's degree being approved in 1998.) A student in the MSSE program must take six of those courses, plus two of the other three, for a total of eight software engineering courses. (Students must also do a thesis or take four computer science courses and pass a written comprehensive exam, depending on whether they choose a thesis or a non-thesis option, respectively.) The undergraduate Software Engineering course – or its equivalent through work experience – is a prerequisite for the beginning-level MSSE graduate courses.

At the end of the graduate coursework, a two-semester software studio provides a graduate capstone experience similar to the undergraduate senior project sequence; however, the software studio focuses more on research-oriented projects, and provides more interaction between the project teams. The original inspiration (and name) for these courses came from the 1990 Software Engineering Institute (SEI) graduate curriculum model [1].

2.2. Adapting the SEI Tomayko Model

From 1991 to 1997, the introductory software engineering course (and its graduate equivalent) at Texas Tech used the "concept to delivery" format using large teams (where each team member has a specific project role, e.g. configuration manager) in a one-semester course adapted from a model developed by James Tomayko of the Software Engineering Institute (SEI) [9]. Then (as now) the intention of the development of this process was to have a single, tailorable methodology for all software engineering team projects at Texas Tech. However, this first attempt at the development of a project had two limitations. First, as a concept-to-delivery method it needed to be modified in order to handle ongoing projects that were developed over several semesters or years. Second, the development of the Tomayko model precluded the invention of the World Wide Web, so the materials would need to be adapted in order to be effectively used on the Web.

2.3. Other Project Processes

Where you see processes mentioned in the literature are usually in the context of capstone or process courses. Normally, such processes include what would be expected, such as planning, requirements, design, implementation, and software quality assurance. Sometimes, however, they may not include a pointer to the materials actually used in a course. This situation is changing, however, with some processes being given in textbook format for educators to use. For example, educators may make extensive use of Humphrey's Personal Software Process[SM] and Team Software Process[SM] [3,4] in a software engineering curriculum. These texts lead students into understanding how to use their own process for developing software and then extending that into team efforts.

Another process gaining popularity among educators is the Unified Software Development Process [6] due to its attachment to the Unified Modeling Language. This process takes the developer from use cases to implementation to testing. Some processes may be homegrown and available on the web, such as Real World Lab (RWL) in the College of Computing at Georgia Tech

[SM] Personal Software Process and Team Software Process are service marks of Carnegie Mellon University.

(http://www.cc.gatech.edu/classes/RWL/Web). This lab was initially developed by Melody Moore [7,8] and has since undergone evolution as well with each subsequent instructor. It takes the developer through planning, requirements, design, implementation, and testing.

2.4. Need for the Process across the Curriculum

The use of a particular process is up to the educators who define the curriculum. It is of more benefit to the students and educators to have a common process in every course just simply because of the confusion it would cause if each educator used a different process. Some courses, however, may not directly involve software development and may instead do something else, such as a tutorial or experimental study. A process across the curriculum should incorporate the ability to do such things.

3. The Project Process

3.1. Introduction to the Process

The Project Process supports several roles in a project: software manager, configuration manager, subcontract manager, requirements analyst, designer, programmer, software quality assurance analyst, trainer, and study analyst. It has document templates for weekly reporting of work, reviewing documents, assessing team member performance, plans, requirements, design, software manuals, training materials, studies, and web pages. It supports different courses working together on a development or other type of project. It allows the inclusion of expert mentors to guide students in their projects and clients who would like software development work done. It also discusses team responsibilities, the team grievance process, professionalism, and grading.

The content of the document templates are as streamlined as possible so that students do not have to get too bogged down in documentation and give as much guidance as possible so that students do not have to wonder about what goes into a document. All documents normally require a revision history and a "To Do List" for what is outstanding before the document is complete. For example, the requirements document focuses the student on the user's environment, the requirements needed based upon the IEEE Requirements Specification Standard [5], client materials, a to do list, a reference list, and a revision history. Due consideration was given to the rest of the IEEE Standards, but they can be quite large; i.e., more than what students can handle in one or two semesters. As an additional example, the design document contains sections on the approach, similar work, architecture, user interface, external interfaces, data, detailed design, and cross-referencing to the requirements.

3.2. Evolution of the Process and Document Set

The Project Process was first developed in the fall of 1998 and was initially based heavily upon Georgia Tech's Real World Lab. (However, unlike the RWL, the Texas Tech process was developed with an entire curriculum in mind.) At that time, the authors were not able to find materials from other sources and it seemed a good idea to build off of a successful course. It was also decided to follow the Real World Lab paradigm and post materials to the Web. This seemed to be the most economical and efficient way to allow all stakeholders viewing privileges of the projects and Project Process.

Initially, the document templates were fairly unstructured (which was like the RWL) but certainly not without guidance to allow students some freedom. However, it was discovered rather rapidly that students would make use of their freedom in ways that are counterproductive to getting projects done, such as spending an inordinate amount of time on formatting instead of solving the problem. The document template set, therefore, underwent changes to provide more structure and focus on problem solving. In addition, templates were added to support user analysis studies, subcontracts to work with other courses, and studies to perform experiments.

The current version of the Project Process at Texas Tech can be found at http://sework.cs.ttu.edu/proj.

3.3. Software Projects Developed

Several projects developed with the Project Process have reached successful fruition and have been deployed. Several of these successful projects have been for on-campus ("internal") clients, who seem to be the easiest to use since they are usually very eager to get their software developed and do not usually leave the university suddenly as industrial clients may. Some industrially sponsored projects have failed because the one industry contact left the company or the company was sold to another. Three examples on-campus projects that have either been developed or are in ongoing development are:

- Bridge – This tool enables a successful program in the TTU College of Engineering to track incoming engineering students throughout their first semesters to help them succeed in the engineering discipline.
- EdDoc (Education Doctor) - This tool can be used to determine whether a student interested in engineering would be well-suited to the field, and also provides information on the person's learning styles.
- QUICK Schedule - This tool automates course scheduling; a student states what courses are desired

and what time slots cannot be used for taking classes, and QUICK provides a trial schedule, using the university's current list of open class sections.

Off-campus ("external") clients have provided a wide-range of potential projects, including:

- The development of a software tool to track project activities within a software organization for CMMI[SM] assessment purposes.
- Enhancement of a software tool's object-oriented design and code generation features.
- Porting an existing web application from a Windows to a Macintosh platform.

3.4. Use of the Process in Different Courses

3.4.1. Capstone Courses. The two-semester Senior Project sequence uses a tailored and extended project process in order to include the following:

- Document and code inspections, as opposed to the reviews used in the standard process
- Some additional detail given to software testing by the project team
- More focus on grading the project artifacts both within the weekly reviews and after they are posted and under configuration control
- Several weeks are provided for acceptance testing by the client, which allows for a short maintenance cycle not (easily) possible in a one-semester course.

The software studio sequence also takes advantage of the extended timeframe in order to have more acceptance testing and some maintenance. However, the reviews from the standard process are used instead of inspections in order to take advantage of the interaction between the project teams during their time together in the "studio" setting.

3.4.2. Examples from Other Courses. The Software Engineering undergraduate course enables students to focus on the basics of planning, requirements, design, implementation, training, and software quality assurance. Other parts of the Project Process are not used. These students work with an outside client and either continue with a previous project or start a new one.

The Software Specification and Design course focuses on the use of modeling techniques for specification purposes, how to accomplish architectural design, and how to flow into detailed design. This class may write a training tutorial on a certain part of specification and/or design and also use the Project Process document templates for requirements and design. They may also do a study on comparing various requirements or design techniques.

The Software Project Management courses looks at the scheduling, budgeting, and management of a development project. The students in this course focus upon the planning documents in the Project Process and may do a training tutorial on how to manage a project from beginning to end.

The Software Construction and Evolution course allows for assignments which focus on the post-design end of the Project Process, including implementation, detailed testing, code inspections, and creating more than one increment of the software (i.e., an example of software evolution).

In the Software Process Improvement class, the project process used in the other software engineering courses plays a different role. In this course, different project model frameworks such CMM[R] and ISO 9001 for Software are used to discuss process-based software engineering, and the definition, assessment and improvement of the process using it. In this context, the project process for the Texas Tech software engineering courses can frequently be used in various examples. In some semesters, students have been divided into teams in order to assess the Project Process against one or more of the widely-used models.

4. Benefits of the Process

The objective of the Project Process was to provide a process which could be used throughout both undergraduate and graduate curricula for both effective project development and providing the student with a greater understanding of the software process. A set of expected outcomes was formulated, but a rigorous assessment plan was not initially formulated. About a year after the initiation of the project process, the outcomes were informally evaluated, with a summary of the evaluation results below.

- *Increased communication between stakeholders.* Greatly improved communication was immediately realized by both the client and the course instructor, and continues to the present time. Also, the degree of teamwork within the student project teams (and their reviewers) has gradually improved.
- *Platform independence for viewing the Project Process and most of the artifacts.* The Web/HTML format has meant that project information can be accessed from virtually any type of computer on the Internet. Also, if

[SM] CMMI is a service mark of Carnegie Mellon University.

[R] CMM is registered in the U.S. Patent and Trademark Office.

the application being developed is web-based, this accessibility extends to the product itself.

- *More effective monitoring by the instructor of student progress and the timeliness of submissions.* Monitoring the submission or updating of project artifacts through the project web page has been very effective, and has also made checking the actual times of submissions simple.
- *The ability to handle larger-scale projects.* The use of an incremental software development model has meant that projects can proceed at various stages over several semesters. For instance, the QUICK Schedule project has been in operation at Texas Tech for over three years (http://ednet.coe.ttu.edu/quick) and is under maintenance and enhancement during its fifth year of existence. The only negative aspect to the longer projects is that there are more potential projects than there are students available to develop them!
- *Better-documented and more reliable products* - The web format makes it much easier to submit, locate and review project artifacts. The improved documentation and review process has in turn led to better functionality in the final product.
- *Effecting tailoring of a single process for all software projects* - The online accessibility of the process has allowed it to be used in a variety of courses. However, a method for easily documenting a particular tailoring of the process is still needed.
- *Increased motivation among stakeholders* – Students are very appreciative of the templates which make their work clearer and as mentioned before, everyone has the opportunity to monitor progress making everyone more willing to participate.

The subsequent development of a formal outcomes assessment model is discussed in Section 7.

5. Relationship to Curriculum Models

Having a good project process throughout a software engineering sequence is important because virtually every course in such a sequence is likely to have a project which can take advantage it. For instance, the aforementioned SEI graduate curriculum model [1] recommended six required core courses, covering requirements, design, construction and maintenance, V&V, project management, and formal methods. These courses all have assignments that can use the project process. The model also contains a capstone software studio.

The *Guidelines for Software Engineering Education*, a product of the Working Group for Software Engineering Education and released in 1999 as an SEI Technical Report [2], has been the *de facto* source for an undergraduate curriculum model in recent years. Once again, all of the eight software engineering courses recommended in the *Guidelines'* SE curriculum (except for a one-hour first year seminar and a Professionalism and Ethics course) are likely to be implemented as having projects as a component.

A joint IEEE-CS/ACM committee is developing *Computing Curricula – Software Engineering* (CCSE), which is part of the IEEE-CS/ACM *Computing Curricula* project. The CCSE committee is developing recommendations for undergraduate software engineering education and curricula. As of this writing, the primary product of CCSE has been the second public draft of SEEK (Software Engineering Education Knowledge), which can be found at http://sites.computer.org/ccse. This draft contains ten Software Engineering Knowledge Areas (KAs), generally reflecting topics that have been seen in the undergraduate and graduate models listed above. Several units and topics (the two levels of subareas for each knowledge area) of the Process KA directly reflect topics covered through learning and using the Project Process at Texas Tech, including process definition, process infrastructure, and process tailoring.

6. Porting the Process – An Example

In mid-2002, a project was undertaken to port the Texas Tech Project Process to the Rose-Hulman Institute of Technology (RHIT), coinciding with the change of affiliation of one of the authors (Dr. Bagert) to that school. Rose-Hulman is on the quarter system of study (with ten-week terms), but almost all of its courses have virtually the same number of contact hours as a three-credit semester course in the U.S. The BSCS at Rose-Hulman currently contains four SE courses – a two-course introductory sequence in the winter and spring (second and third) terms of the junior (third) year, followed by a two-term capstone project sequence in the fall and winter (first and second) terms of the senior (fourth) year. It was therefore decided to begin implementation of the web-based Project Process with the first course available, which was the first half of the senior project. Two different faculty members (including Dr. Bagert) were each supervising some of the project teams. The process was later tailored for the SE introductory sequence.

The software engineering courses at Rose-Hulman are a good test for the project process, since traditionally the team sizes are small (≤ 5), with an agile/prototyping model used for software development (as opposed to the more traditional methods commonly employed at Texas Tech). This, and the fact that the process previously used for senior projects at RHIT was less document-intensive and not as structured overall, meant that the process and its templates met some initial resistance, despite the fact that it had already been tailored somewhat from the Texas

Tech version before being posted on the Web and introduced to the students. However, the initial difficulties are being addressed through individual students interacting with the instructor and through discussions during team meetings with their project supervisor, and it appears that there has been progress made in the acceptance and effective use of the process.

It is interesting to compare the work done using the Project Process to date by senior project students at Rose-Hulman as opposed to their counterparts at Texas Tech. At TTU, senior project students have already used the process at least once before, and are therefore somewhat more proficient in its use. A proposal has been made for a new Bachelor of Science in Software Engineering at Rose-Hulman which would have nine required SE courses, so that in future years, students taking the capstone course should be well-versed in the process.

The Rose-Hulman process is currently at www.cs.rose-hulman.edu/curriculum/project_process.html.

7. Conclusions and Future Directions

In order to facilitate the study of software process, which is essential to the education of future software professionals, a standard, tailorable and web-based process was developed at Texas Tech University for use in its 12 undergraduate and graduate software engineering courses. All project artifacts using this process are posted to the course web page, which enhances communication between team members (including distance education students) and between the project team and their client. This process has received positive feedback from all stakeholders. Recently, the process has been ported to another institution (Rose-Hulman) with a different framework for its software engineering courses; this will allow for a comparison and facilitate greater understanding of the process model.

A formal outcomes assessment model for the project process is being developed at Rose-Hulman. The Office of Assessment at RHIT is well-known, and for the last five years has hosted *Best Assessment Processes*, an annual symposium with speakers and attendees from several countries. The assessment model for the Project Process will include an assessment of the various stakeholders using archival data, surveys, interviews and focus groups. It would also be useful to collect data on use of the project process in for a variety of application domain areas, although this may require its use at more schools.

In general, the Project Process is a living artifact and will continue to change as students give more feedback and as automated tools become available that can be taught without distracting the students from the important concepts of a course, due to the long learning curve. The undergraduate software engineering course at Texas Tech may only be able to incorporate a few automated tools, such as planning and tracking, but later courses can begin to use more complex tools for design modeling and testing. There is some benefit in teaching software engineering without the "noise" of automation; it can focus students more on practicing the concepts rather than learning the tools. Eventually, students who are proficient at practicing the concepts should learn the tools to make their job easier and faster. A short-term improvement is to have a guidance matrix for customizing the process to a particular course, which would show the course examples used in the software engineering courses at Texas Tech as well as other plausible scenarios for use of the process.

8. References

[1] M.A. Ardis and G.A. Ford, *1989 SEI Report on Graduate Software Engineering Education*, Technical Report CMU/SEI-89-TR-2, Carnegie Mellon University, Pittsburgh PA, 1989.

[2] D. Bagert, T. Hilburn, G. Hislop, M. Lutz, M. McCracken, S. Mengel, *Guidelines for Software Engineering Education*, Version 1.0. Technical Report CMU/SEI-99-TR-032, Software Engineering Institute, Carnegie Mellon University, Pittsburgh PA, October 1999.

[3] W.S. Humphrey, *A Discipline for Software Engineering*, Reading, MA: Addison-Wesley, 1995.

[4] W.S. Humphrey, *Introduction to the Team Software Process*, Reading, MA: Addison-Wesley, 2000.

[5] *IEEE Recommended Practice for Software Requirements Specifications*, IEEE Std. 830-1998, New York, NY: IEEE, 1998.

[6] I. Jacobson, G. Booch, and J. Rumbaugh, *The Unified Software Development Process*, Reading, MA: Addison-Wesley, 1999.

[7] M. Moore and T. Brennan, "Process Improvement in the Classroom", R.L. Ibrahim, ed., Proceedings of Eighth Conference on Software Engineering Education, New York, NY: Springer-Verlag, 1995, pp. 123-130.

[8] M. Moore and C. Potts, "Learning by Doing: Goals and Experiences of Two Software Engineering Project Courses", J.L. Diaz-Herrera, ed., Proceedings of Seventh Conference on Software Engineering Education, New York, NY: Springer-Verlag, 1994, pp. 151-164.

[9] J.E. Tomayko, *Teaching a Project-Intensive Introduction to Software Engineering*, Technical Report SEI-SR-87-1, Software Engineering Institute, Carnegie Mellon University, Pittsburgh, PA, 1987.

Software Engineering Education and Training

Process and Methodology

Beyond the Personal Software Process: Metrics collection and analysis for the differently disciplined

Philip M. Johnson Hongbing Kou Joy Agustin Christopher Chan
Carleton Moore Jitender Miglani Shenyan Zhen William E.J. Doane
Collaborative Software Development Laboratory
Department of Information and Computer Sciences
University of Hawai'i
Honolulu, HI 96822
johnson@hawaii.edu

Abstract

Pedagogies such as the Personal Software Process (PSP) shift metrics definition, collection, and analysis from the organizational level to the individual level. While case study research indicates that the PSP can provide software engineering students with empirical support for improving estimation and quality assurance, there is little evidence that many students continue to use the PSP when no longer required to do so. Our research suggests that this "PSP adoption problem" may be due to two problems: the high overhead of PSP-style metrics collection and analysis, and the requirement that PSP users "context switch" between product development and process recording. This paper overviews our initial PSP experiences, our first attempt to solve the PSP adoption problem with the LEAP system, and our current approach called Hackystat. This approach fully automates both data collection and analysis, which eliminates overhead and context switching. However, Hackystat changes the kind of metrics data that is collected, and introduces new privacy-related adoption issues of its own.

1. Introduction

> It would be nice to have a tool to automatically gather the PSP data. Because judgment is involved in most personal process data, however, no such tool exists or is likely in the near future.
> —*A Discipline for Software Engineering*[4]

Until the mid-1990's, most software engineering metrics were designed for use at the organizational rather than the individual level. A best practice for organizational metrics programs is the Software Process Group, which takes responsibility for collection and analysis of metric data. Indeed, an important reason for these groups is to prevent the failure of the metrics program due to increased developer workload. For example, an industrial case study of code inspection found that adoption was facilitated by providing additional staff for metrics collection and analysis in order to "overcome [developer's] natural resistance to paperwork—a syndrome typical of most metrics programs" [12].

In 1995, Watts Humphrey authored *A Discipline for Software Engineering*, a ground-breaking text that adapted organizational-level software measurement and analysis techniques to the individual developer along with a one semester curriculum. These techniques are called the Personal Software Process (PSP)[1]. The primary goals of the PSP are to improve project estimation and quality assurance. These goals are pursued by collecting size, time, and defect data on an initial set of software projects and performing various analyses on it. For example, given the estimated size of a new system, a PSP analysis called PROBE provides an estimate of the time required based upon the relationship between time and size on prior projects.

The PSP incorporates two interesting conjectures. First, it conjectures that PSP-style collection and analysis of metric data by an individual can provide significant benefits to that individual. Second, it conjectures that these benefits are large enough that the developer will continue to use the PSP after leaving the classroom.

Over the past six years, case studies have tested the first conjecture by analysis of the student-collected PSP data [7, 9, 10, 5, 13]. These studies support the first conjecture,

[1]Personal Software Process and PSP are registered service marks of Carnegie Mellon University

0-7695-1877-X/03 $17.00 © 2003 IEEE

Characteristic	Generation 1 (manual PSP)	Generation 2 (Leap, PSP Studio, PSP Dashboard)	Generation 3 (Hackystat)
Collection overhead	High	Medium	None
Analysis overhead	High	Low	None
Context switching	Yes	Yes	No
Metrics changes	Simple	Software edits	Tool dependent
Adoption barriers	Overhead, Context-switching	Context-switching	Privacy, Sensor availability

Figure 1. Three generations of approaches to metrics for individuals

indicating that PSP data can support both project estimation and quality assurance. In addition, researchers from the Software Engineering Institute analyzed data submitted to them by instructors of 23 PSP classes, and concluded that the PSP improved the students' estimation accuracy and product quality [2].

To our knowledge, there is no published empirical research directly addressing the second conjecture, such as studies reporting the actual percentage of PSP students who continue to use it one, two, and three years after having taken the class. (Publications on PSP adoption generally consist of speculative guidelines and/or short-term data which do not address the second conjecture.) However, anecdotal evidence does not support the second conjecture. For example, a report on a workshop of PSP instructors reveals that in one course of 78 students, 72 of them "abandoned" the PSP because they felt "it would impose an excessively strict process on them and that the extra work would not pay off." None of the remaining six students reported any perceived process improvements [1]. Our experiences teaching the PSP are similar: despite classroom improvements in estimation and quality assurance, few if any students adopted PSP-specific concepts.

If the first conjecture is true but the second is false, then studying the PSP is similar to studying Latin: a task that advocates suggest you learn for its indirect benefits, rather than because you'll actually use it in your daily life. The workshop report echos this PSP-as-Latin viewpoint when it conjectures, "Even if students don't use the PSP again, improving and making them aware of their programming habits will help them in their future academic and professional careers."

This paper presents a perspective on our research and educational experiences for the past six years regarding metrics collection and analysis for individual developers. We began by teaching and using the PSP in its original form, but students found the overhead of metrics collection and analysis to be excessive. To address this issue, we next developed a comprehensive toolkit for PSP-style metrics collection and analysis called Leap [8, 6]. Despite the automated support, adoption was still low, and this led us to the discovery of another adoption barrier: the need for students to continuously "context switch" between product development and process recording. We have now implemented a new system called Hackystat and have deployed it in two software engineering classes. Hackystat completely automates both collection and analysis of metric data and thus addresses both the overhead and context switching barriers to adoption. The next section discusses this research trajectory in more detail.

2. Three generations of metrics for individuals

Looking back, we can divide our research on metrics for individuals into three generations. Figure 1 illustrates five distinguishing characteristics of these generations.

The first generation approach uses the PSP as originally described in *A Discipline for Software Engineering.* Users of the PSP create and print out forms in which they manually log effort, size, and defect information. Additional forms use this data to support project estimation and quality assurance. This approach creates substantial overhead due to form filling. For example, the PSP requires students to write down every compiler error that occurs during development. It also recommends that the developer keep a stopwatch by their desk in order to keep track of all interruptions. A benefit of using forms is that changing metrics simply involves editing the affected forms and/or creating new ones.

We began teaching the PSP in 1996, and had success similar to that reported in other case studies. Most of our students were able to estimate both the size and time of their final project with 90% or better accuracy, and one student achieved 100% yield on one project. (This means that the student eliminated all syntax and semantic errors from the system prior to the first compile of that system.) Despite the obvious discipline displayed by these students, followup

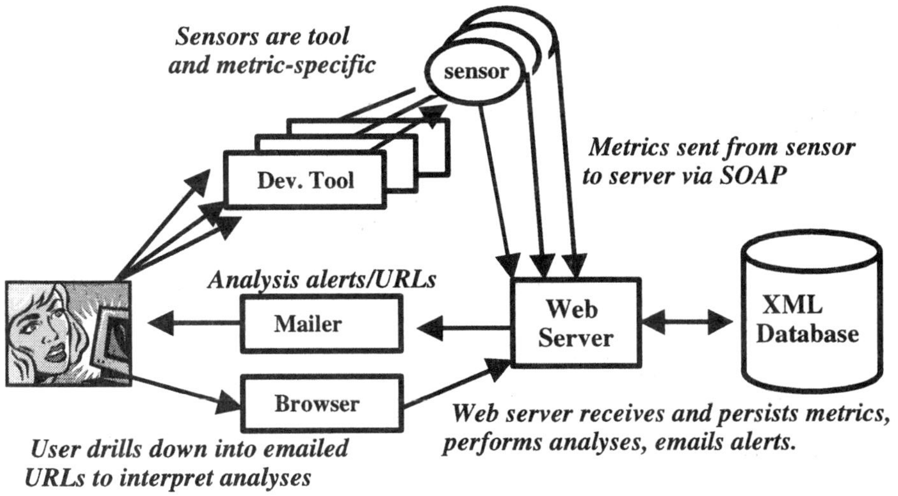

Figure 2. The basic Hackystat architecture and information flow

email indicated that none of them continued using the manual PSP after finishing the semester. We attributed this to the overhead involved in collection and analysis, and began the Leap research project in 1998 to pursue low overhead approaches to collection and analysis of individual software engineering metric data.

A second generation approach uses Leap or another automated tool for PSP-style metrics such as the PSP Studio [3] and PSP Dashboard [11]. These tools all have the same basic approach to user interaction: they display dialog boxes where the user records effort, size, and defect information. The tools also display various analyses when requested by the user. Second generation approaches do an excellent job of lowering the overhead associated with metrics analysis, and substantially reduce the overhead of metrics collection. However, metrics changes require changes to the software and are thus more complicated than in the first generation approach.

After teaching and using the Leap system we found that, similar to the manual PSP, developers can utilize their Leap historical data to substantially improve their project planning and quality assurance activities. Followup email indicated that adoption improved slightly: a handful of students continued to use Leap after the end of the semester, and a small number of industrial developers discovered the tool online and began using it. A few former students and developers continue to use at least some parts of Leap.

While "some adoption" is definitely an improvement over "no adoption", we were still surprised by the very low level of adoption of a toolkit that provided so much automated support. We then discovered that a major adoption barrier is the requirement that the user constantly switch back and forth between doing work and "telling the tool" what work is being done. Even if telling the tool is as simple and fast as pressing a button, this continual context switching is still too intrusive for many users who desire long periods of uninterrupted focus for efficient and effective development.

In May 2001, we began the Hackystat project, in which metrics are collected automatically by attaching sensors to development tools, metric data is sent by the sensors to a server, analyses over the gathered data are performed by a server, and alerts are emailed to the developer when triggered. With Hackystat, the overhead of metrics collection is effectively eliminated, developers never context switch between working and telling the tool that they're working, and analysis results can be provided in a "just in time" manner. While Hackystat successfully addresses the barriers to adoption identified in first and second generation approaches, it changes the nature of metric data that is collected, imposes requirements on development tools, and introduces new adoption issues. The remainder of the paper describes the system and our results in more detail.

3. An overview of Hackystat

Figure 2 shows the basic architecture of Hackystat and how information flows between the user and the system. Hackystat requires the development of client-side sensors that attach to development tools and that unobtrusively collect effort, size, defect, and other metrics regarding the user's development activities. Not every development tool is amenable to Hackystat instrumentation: Emacs is easy to integrate, Notepad is not.

The current system includes sensors for the Emacs and JBuilder IDEs, the Ant build system, and the JUnit testing tool. These sensors collect activity data (such as which file, if any, is under active modification by the developer at 30 second intervals), size data (such as the Chidamber-Kemerer object oriented metrics and non-comment source lines of Java code), and defect data (invocation of unit tests and their pass/fail status).

The developer begins using Hackystat by installing one or more sensors, and registering with a Hackystat server. During registration, the server sets up an account for the developer and sends her an email containing a randomly generated 12 character key that serves as her account password. This password prevents others from accessing her metric data or uploading their data to her account.

Once the developer has registered with a server and installed the sensors, she can return to her development activities. Metrics are collected by the sensors and sent unobtrusively to the server at regular intervals (if the developer is connected to the net) or cached locally for later sending (if the developer is working off line).

On the server side, analysis programs are run regularly over all of the metrics for each developer. A fundamental analysis is the abstraction of the raw metric data stream into a representation of the developer's activity at 5 minute intervals over the course of a day. We call this abstraction the "Daily Diary", and it is illustrated in Figure 3. This Daily Diary shows that the developer began work on Friday, June 21, 2002, at approximately 9:30am, and during the first five minutes of work the file that was edited most frequently was called Controller.java. The location of this file is also indicated along with its Chidamber-Kemerer metrics and size, computed from the .class file associated with the most recent compilation of this file in the developer workspace. Among other things, this Diary excerpt also shows that between 9:45am and 9:55am, the developer invoked 60 JUnit tests that passed, 1 that failed, and none that aborted due to exceptional conditions.

The Daily Diary is useful for visualizing and explaining Hackystat's representation of developer behavior, but is not intended as the "user interface" to the system. Instead, the Daily Diary representation serves as a basis for generating other analyses, such as: the amount of developer effort spent on a given module per day (or week, or month); the change in size of a module per day (or week, or month); the distribution of unit tests across a module, their invocation rate, and their success rate per day (or week, or month), the average number of new classes, methods, or lines of code written in a given module per day (or week, or month), and so forth.

Analysis results are available to each developer from their account home page on the web server, and can be retrieved manually to support, for example, project planning activities. However, a more interesting mechanism in Hackystat is the ability to define alerts, which are analyses that run periodically over developer data and that specify some sort of threshold value for the analysis. If the threshold is exceeded, the server sends an email to the developer indicating that an analysis has discovered data that may be of interest to the developer along with an URL to display more details about the data in question at the server.

One alert is called the "Complexity Threshold Alert", and it allows the developer to configure it to analyze the Chidamber-Kemerer metrics associated with each class she worked on during the previous seven days and trigger an email if the values of these metrics exceed developer-specified values. This enables the system to monitor the complexity of the classes that the developer works on and to send an email if they exceed the specified value.

Student usage creates an opportunity for specialized analyses and alerts. For example, analyses can help students see whether "last minute hacking" leads to more testing failures, less testing in general, and lower productivity. Alerts can help students monitor their usage and inform them when their effort falls below a certain level of consistency (such as at least one hour of effort at least 4 days a week).

Alerts provide a kind of "just-in-time" approach to metrics collection and analysis. The developer can effectively "forget about" metrics collection and analysis during her daily work, but the metrics will still be gathered and available to her when she has a need for them. Furthermore, the alert mechanism can make her aware of impending problems without her having to regularly "poll" her dataset looking for them.

4. Results

The Hackystat project began in early 2001, and the first operational release of the server and a small set of sensors occurred in July 2001. The server is written in Java and contains approximately 200 classes, 1000 methods, and 15,000 non-comment lines of code. Client-side, tool-specific code is much smaller: the JBuilder sensor code is approximately 200 lines of Java, and the Emacs sensor code is approximately 400 lines of Lisp. Hackystat is available without charge under an open source license and is available for download at http://csdl.ics.hawaii.edu/Tools/Hackystat. In addition, we maintain a public server running the latest release of Hackystat at http://hackystat.ics.hawaii.edu/.

Hackystat is currently being used by approximately 40 students in undergraduate and graduate software engineering classes at the University of Hawaii, as well as by one industry site. One user has development data for over 250 days spanning 15 months of usage. We will be gathering adoption data regarding the ongoing use of Hackystat throughout 2003.

Our research confirms the quote that begins this paper: we did not discover a means to automatically collect PSP-style effort, size, and defect data. On the other hand, our research shows that automatic collection of Hackystat-style

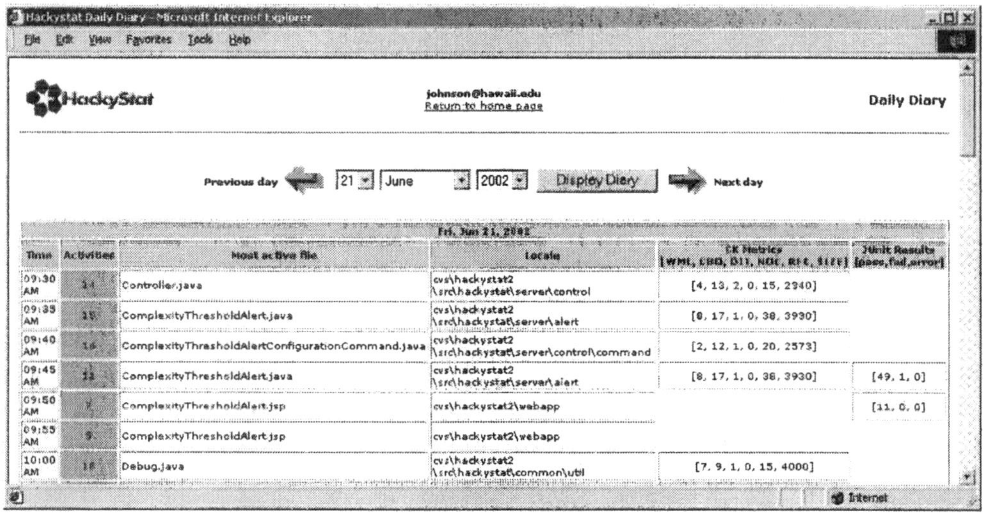

Figure 3. The Daily Diary: Developer metrics at five minute intervals.

effort, size, and defect data is indeed possible. It is instructive to compare and contrast the two approaches to these three metrics and its implications.

Effort. In the PSP, effort data (whether recorded by hand or using a tool) is always associated with a "project" and a "phase" of development. So, a developer might record that from 10:00am to 11:00am, she was working on Project "Timer1.2" in the phase "design". Although in theory this seems simple enough, in practice it incurs significant overhead to define unique "projects" for every development activity, determine the "phase" to be assigned, and record individual entries each time the developer switches to a different task or project. In addition, the PSP requires that you record "idle time", so every phone call or colleague's appearance at your door generates an additional recording activity.

In Hackystat, effort data is associated with active modification of a file, and has a fixed grain size of five minute increments. If the developer is not actively changing a file, then they are "idle". Instead of a "project", Hackystat has the concept of a "locale", which generally corresponds to a subdirectory (or package) hierarchy. There is currently no attempt to represent development "phase" in Hackystat.

While the PSP effort representation has the potential to be more accurate than Hackystat's, the reality is that the overhead and context switching required to conform to PSP effort collection makes it exceedingly costly to the developer. Hackystat effort data, on the other hand, is effectively "free". Another difference is in the application of effort data to planning and estimation. In the PSP, one plans using "projects" which are associated with various sizes and effort levels. In Hackystat, one can plan using "locales", which are also associated with various sizes and effort levels. However, one can also plan using simple "work week" data, which involves examining size and effort over a representative period of weeks.

Size. In the PSP, the developer invokes a source code analysis tool to collect size data at the end of project (and perhaps at the beginning, if the project is an incremental extension of an existing system). Size data consists of counts of classes, methods, and non-comment lines of code.

In Hackystat, similar size data is collected, but this data needs to be incrementally collected since there are no projects, much less defined start or end dates. This poses a problem, since the source code files parsed by the source code analysis tools are frequently syntactically incorrect while they are under active development. Hackystat solves this for Java by parsing the .class file associated with the most recent compilation of the source file. This enables Hackystat to provide size information such as the actual number of new methods added during a given day.

Defects. In the PSP, the developer must record every defect, including compilation defects, as well as the time it took to remove them, any other defects injected as a result of this defect, the phase in which the defect was injected into the product as well as the phase in which it was removed.

In Hackystat, pre-release defect data is automatically collected by attaching a sensor to a unit testing mechanism such as JUnit, and post-release defect data is automatically collected by attaching a sensor to a bug reporting system such as Bugzilla.

PSP defect collection supports a number of analyses not possible with Hackystat defect collection, such as the relationship between the cost of removal of a defect and the interval in phases between its injection and removal. On the other hand, PSP defect collection creates substantial developer overhead, and is quite sensitive to "collection fatigue". For example, if developers stop recording defects as conscientiously over time, then potentially incorrect and misleading analyses (such as a trend toward decreased defect density) can result. Hackystat defect collection is not susceptible to these problems, and does support activities such as complexity measurement validation (the development of models that predict post-release defect rates from pre-release complexity measures).

While Hackystat reduces barriers to adoption due to developer overhead, it creates a new adoption issue of its own: the specter of "Big Brother". As Figure 3 illustrates, Hackystat servers provide a fairly detailed log of developer activities, which may cause privacy concerns, particularly among professional developers who might worry about access to the data by management. We have taken several steps to address privacy. First, data access requires a password that should be known only to the developer who owns the data. Second, we maintain a public Hackystat server that allows developers to keep their data "off site" and thus unavailable to management. Third, a developer might alternatively decide to download the Hackystat server and run it locally so that all data is kept under their immediate control. We may investigate further measures, such as PGP encryption of data, if privacy issues are revealed to be a major barrier to adoption.

5. Conclusions and Future Directions

Our first conclusion is the need for further research on the issue of PSP adoption. While there now exists ample case study evidence that the PSP can provide software engineering benefits in a classroom setting, our own experience and other anecdotal evidence suggests that most developers abandon PSP practices after its use is no longer mandated.

Our second conclusion is that a significant barrier to adoption of metrics by individual developers occurs when there is the need to regularly "context switch" between product development and process recording. This indicates that second generation approaches that simply automate PSP-style effort, size, and defect collection might not be widely adopted.

Our third conclusion is that third generation approaches such as the Hackystat system present a promising means to eliminate the need for context switching by developers by automatic collection of metric data. However, the approach changes the nature of the data that is collected, and raises new adoption issues related to privacy. We hope that other researchers will download and evaluate Hackystat to explore these issues or be inspired to develop their own third (or fourth!) generation approach to metrics collection and analysis for individuals.

Hackystat is under active development, and we are currently developing sensors for Eclipse, Forte, and CVS. We are also beginning empirical studies regarding the construct validity of measures such as "Most Active File." Finally, we will be assessing the long-term adoption of Hackystat by following changes in usage patterns by students as they move on to other classes or professional work.

6. Acknowledgments

We gratefully acknowledge the hardworking and disciplined students from our current and prior software engineering courses. Support for this research was provided in part by grants CCR98-04010 and CCR02-34568 from the National Science Foundation.

References

[1] J. Borstler, D. Carrington, G. Hislop, S. Lisack, K. Olson, and L. Williams. Teaching PSP: Challenges and lessons learned. *IEEE Software*, 19(5), September 2002.

[2] W. Hayes and J. W. Over. The Personal Software Process (PSP): An empirical study of the impact of PSP on individual engineers. Technical Report CMU/SEI-97-TR-001, Software Engineering Institute, Pittsburgh, PA., 1997.

[3] J. Henry. Personal Software Process studio. http://www-cs.etsu.edu/softeng/psp/, 1997.

[4] W. S. Humphrey. *A Discipline for Software Engineering*. Addison-Wesley, January 1995.

[5] P. M. Johnson and A. M. Disney. The personal software process: A cautionary case study. *IEEE Software*, 15(6), November 1998.

[6] P. M. Johnson, C. A. Moore, J. A. Dane, and R. S. Brewer. Empirically guided software effort guesstimation. *IEEE Software*, 17(6), December 2000.

[7] S. Khajenoori and I. Hirmanpour. An experiential report on the implications of the Personal Software Process for software quality improvement. In *Proceedings of the Fifth International Conference on Software Quality*, pages 303–312, October 1995.

[8] C. A. Moore. Lessons learned from teaching reflective software engineering using the Leap toolkit. In *Proceedings of the 2000 International Conference on Software Engineering, Workshop on Software Engineering Education*, Limerick, Ireland, May 2000.

[9] M. Ramsey. Experiences teaching the Personal Software Process in academia and industry. In *Proceedings of the 1996 SEPG Conference*, 1996.

[10] B. Shostak. Adapting the Personal Software Process to industry. *Software Process Newsletter #5*, Winter 1996.

[11] D. Tuma. PSP dashboard. http://processdash.sourceforge.net/, 2000.

[12] E. F. Weller. Lessons learned from three years of inspection data. *IEEE Software*, pages 38–45, September 1993.

[13] L. A. Williams. *The Collaborative Software Process*. PhD thesis, University of Utah, 2000.

Teaching Contract Programming Concepts to Future Software Engineers

Donald F. Ross
Karlstad University, Department of Computer Science, 651 88 Karlstad, Sweden
Email: Donald.Ross@kau.se

Abstract

Current research in software engineering at Karlstad University is concentrated on non-formal software design methods with a focus on semantics. One goal is to produce methods, which may be applied in both industry and academia. In concrete terms, ideas from contract programming, including pre- and post-conditions have been introduced into the first year curriculum. This paper presents results taken from three surveys of the same group of first-year students during their second semester, in an attempt to ascertain how well the students have internalised these and other programming concepts. The results show that the majority of the students are aware of the concepts but are still at various stages of understanding. A good understanding of terminology emerges as one key area of focus for future courses. The results are a reasonable reflection of reality, given the limited time in which the students are expected to absorb these ideas, and provide feedback for further integration and development of the related programming courses.

1. Introduction

Teaching programming concepts and software engineering ideas to undergraduate students must take into account several factors including their age and experience, the limited number of introductory courses before the student is expected to program independently and the importance of good design techniques. Experience with increasing numbers of students in the last few years at Karlstad University, has shown that there must be greater integration between courses to provide the student with a clear programming philosophy. This in turn requires greater co-operation and awareness on the part of the teachers. At Karlstad University, we have been trying to achieve this through focussing on contract programming which provides (a) a conceptual tool for the student and (b) introduces semantic aspects of programming in addition to syntax and programming methods. This in turn has led to greater synergy between research and teaching in the department.

This paper presents results from a survey of first-year students taken at three different points in time in the second half of the same academic year. The goal of the survey is to measure to what extent the students have absorbed various programming concepts. The remaining sections are (2) background, (3) survey presentation, (4) the results and (5) conclusions and comments.

2. Background

Since 1997, research has been underway at the Department of Computer Science at Karlstad University into aspects of semantics in the design and writing of computer programs [1,2,3,4,5]. and has focussed on techniques based on contract programming using pre- and post-conditions [3], developed from the work of Meyer [8] and Kramer [7]. Similar ideas appear in [6]. The goal of this work is to establish and evaluate non-formal methods, which can be applied in both teaching and industrial contexts. This contract programming method [3] has been evaluated both in industrial projects [1,5,7] and in the academic environment [2,4]. In [4], the method was compared with a programming approach using exceptions, in a Java course using a project-based approach, with favourable reactions from both teachers and students. During their first year, the students typically are given an introductory programming course followed by one on program development and methodology (PUMA), in the second semester, where the ideas of contract programming and in particular pre- and post-conditions are introduced. The students then continue directly to a course in Data Structures and Algorithms (DSA), where the emphasis shifts from programming techniques to abstraction and where the students are assumed to have mastered the contract programming ideas sufficiently to be able to apply these ideas in the DSA course.

0-7695-1877-X/03 $17.00 © 2003 IEEE

3. The Survey

The academic year at Karlstad University consists of four teaching periods of 10 weeks each, periods 1 and 2 in the fall semester and 3 and 4 in the spring semester. The students completed the survey form at the beginning and end of the PUMA course in period 3 and at the end of the DSA course in period 4. By analysing the students' responses at these three points in time, indicators about the students' reaction to and internalisation of the contract programming method can be obtained.

In the first part of the form, students were asked to give textual replies to the four questions covering contract programming, pre- and post-conditions and the most important techniques that they had learnt so far. The second part comprised fifteen multiple-choice questions designed to see how the students reacted to various programming situations involving errors or what their views on more general programming aspects were. Selected replies are given below in section 4. In addition, the age and programming experience of each participating student was noted in order to estimate the general level of experience present in each group.

A common sub-group of 29 students participated in all three surveys. Comparison of the results from this sub-group with the result for the whole group in part 2 of each survey showed that the results reflected those for the group as a whole sufficiently to be used as indicators for the whole group.

4. Results

The total number of students that replied to each of the three surveys, was respectively 109, 63, and 64. Each table presents the results for surveys 1, 2, 3 on successive lines of the table.

4.1. Age and Programming Experience

The age and programming experience distributions of the sub-group of 29 students at the beginning of the survey are given in tables 1 and 2 respectively.

Table 1. Age (years)

20-24	25-29	>29
72%	22%	6%

Table 2. Programming experience (months)

0-11	12-23	24-35	36-47	>=48
57%	13%	17%	4%	9%

The group is mainly young, with little programming experience indicating that most students are starting from a similar level as regards programming.

4.2. Part 1 of the Survey

The students were asked to give textual replies to the questions below. The results were grouped into broad categories, which was necessarily a subjective grouping. The results for part 1 of the survey are based on information from all the students who participated.

Question 1: Give a brief description of what you think the term contract programming means. If you have no idea, you may write "do not know".

The percentage of students who replied "do not know" was respectively 74%, 5% and 11% and who did not reply 0%, 43%, 47%, for each of the three surveys. Of those who did reply, the answers were divided into two categories. The first category consisted of replies considered to be within the generally understood definitions of contract programming and the second category of other replies. This second category was further sub-divided into 3 areas.

a. legal interpretation - e.g. contract programming as an agreement between an employer and employee
b. time planning interpretation - e.g. that the programmer agreed to complete a program within a given time frame
c. organisational interpretation - e.g. that several programmers would be responsible for different parts of a program

These results are summarised in table 3.

Table 3. Part 1, question 1

contract	other	legal	time	org.
18%	82%	57%	11%	14%
73%	27%	15%	0%	12%
89%	11%	4%	0%	7%

Most of the students claim to have understood the idea of contract programming by the end of the PUMA course (73%) or the DSA course (89%).

Question 2: Give a brief description of what you think the terms pre- and post-conditions mean. If you have no idea, you may write "do not know".

The percentage of students who replied "do not know" was respectively 52%, 2% and 5% and who did not reply 0%, 71%, 75%, for each of the three surveys. The result was divided into "contract" and "other" as in part 1 question 1 and was (56%, 44%), (88%, 12%) and (77%, 23%) respectively for each survey, indicating that the majority of students who gave an opinion understand what is meant by pre- and post-conditions.

Question 3: Given a function, for example f(a), which returns a value, what should you do to ensure that the function is used correctly?

The percentage of students who replied "do not know" was respectively 56%, 14% and 0% and who did not reply 1%, 52%, 72%, for each of the three surveys. Again the result was divided into "contract" and "other" and was (45%, 55%), (71%, 29%) and (50% 50%) respectively for each survey.

Since neither contract programming nor pre- and post-conditions is mentioned explicitly in this question, the results may indicate that these ideas have not taken hold as strongly as the results to questions 1 and 2 might suggest.

Question 4: What do you think are the three most important techniques that you have so far learnt in your programming courses.

The number of different techniques mentioned in the three surveys was respectively 31, 21 and 25, and the total number of techniques mentioned 140, 143 and 140. The number of students naming 1, 2 or 3 techniques in each of the surveys, was respectively (16, 17, 30), (5, 9, 40) and (5, 8, 37).

A list of the "top ten" techniques named by the students is given in table 4 with the most frequently named techniques at the top of the table.

Table 4. Part 1 question 4 - top ten techniques

Survey 1	Survey 2	Survey 3
Functions	OO-prog.	Pre/post cond.
File management	Recursion	OO-prog.
JSP	Contract prog.	Recursion
Iteration	Pre/post cond.	Abstract thinking
Indentation	Modularity	Classes
Pointers	ADTs	Contract prog.
Call by value/ref	Linked lists	Pointers
Better prog'ing	Pointers	Modularity
Sorting	Structure	ADTs
Documentation	Classes	Linked lists

By the end of the PUMA course (survey 2), where contract programming techniques were introduced, the result reflects the emphasis placed on these techniques in that course. By the end of the DSA course (survey 3) where the emphasis is more on abstract thinking, the students are expected to apply previously acquired programming knowledge, in the laboratory exercises.

The result in table 4 appears promising and indicates that the students have realised the importance of the contract programming techniques for their development as programmers. The question of the degree to which the students understand the contract programming techniques is much more difficult to assess and is not answered by the questions in this section. Given the student age and experience profile, the results reflect what the students might reasonably be expected to absorb from two 10-week, 50% part-time programming courses.

4.3. Part 2 of the Survey

Part 2 of the survey was intended to find out how the students think about programming and programming techniques and how this thinking has been influenced by the course content of the introductory programming courses. The results presented in this section are a selection of those for the students who participated in all three surveys. There were 29 students in this group. There were 15 multiple-choice questions in this part. By its nature, multiple-choice surveys are restrictive and the answers here must be somewhat subjective. The questions arose from speculation about how the students themselves view ideas about programming, and to what extent the ideas in the courses have been internalised. As well as questions related to contract programming ideas, some more general questions have been included.

Three sets of measures are presented here: (1) **replies**, gives the percentage values for each question; (2) **trends**, the percentage values to the combination of replies to surveys 2 and 3. This indicator, is used to see how consistent the students were in their response or to what extent they changed their mind between the surveys. By summing the replies where the student gave the same reply in surveys 2 and 3, a third measure, a **consistency indicator** may be derived, showing to what extent the students have decided on particular programming techniques. For example, where a question has three choices, a, b or c, aa+bb+cc in the trends table is used to calculate the consistency indicator.

Contract programming is a technique for error handling based on error prevention rather than error detection and recovery. Many of the examples below involve some form of error detection and recovery representing techniques which the student may have learnt in the first programming course, with some alternatives being nearer to the ideas of pre- and post-conditions. Using a C/C++ pseudo-code, programming with pre- and post-conditions may be represented as

```
pre() ? f(x) : pre_fail();

pre() ? post(f(x)) ? OK() : post_fail() : pre_fail();
```

One question asked here is whether the students are beginning to use these pre- and post-condition ideas.

Question 1: Given a function, **void f(a),** *and a test function test(a) which returns true if parameter a is a legal value, which do you think is the best way to write code?*

```
a. if not test(a) print("Error - a"); else f(a);
b. if not test(a) print("Error - a"); f(a);
c. void function f(a) {
            if not test(a) print("Error - a");
            else <code for function a>;
            }
d. void function f(a) {
            if not test(a) print("Error - a");
            <code for function a>;
            }
```

Table 5. Part 2 question 1 - replies

a	b	c	d
48%	0%	30%	22%
63%	4%	22%	11%
78%	0%	15%	7%

Table 6. Part 2 question 1 - trends

aa	ac	ba	ca	cc	cd	da	dc
56%	7%	4%	11%	4%	7%	7%	4%

Consistency indicator - 60%

Since options (b) and (d) imply executing code after an error has been detected, it is encouraging to see that few students chose these options. Option (a) is the closest to a pre-condition style of programming and the result shows that most students favour this option.

Question 2: Given a function, int f(a), and a test function testf which returns true if the return value from f is a legal value, which do you think is the best way to write code?

```
a. int function f(a) {
      <code for function f>
        if not testf(return_value) return error_status;
        return return_value;
        }
b. int function f(a) {
      <code for function f>
        if not testf(return_value) return null;
        return return_value;
   }
c. value := f(a);  /* no test at all */
d. value := f(a);
   if not testf(value) print("Error - value");
```

Table 7. Part 2, question 2 - replies

a	b	c	d
32%	44%	0%	24%
40%	28%	8%	24%
44%	32%	4%	20%

Table 8. Part 2, question 2 - trends - %

aa	ab	ad	ba	bb	bd	ca	cc	da	db	dd
28	8	4	4	16	8	4	4	8	8	8

Consistency indicator - 56%

Here, option (d) is the closest to a post-condition style of programming but most students favour options (a) or (b). These combine returning a value or a status (or null value) which would seem to indicate that the student has not absorbed the idea of the function returning a correct value if the pre-condition is met.

Question 4: If function A calls function B, where does the responsibility lie for checking that the parameters to function B are correct?

a. 100% in function A
b. 100% in function B
c. shared between functions A and B

Table 9. Part 2, question 4 - replies

a	b	c
62%	14%	24%
86%	3%	10%
86%	0%	14%

Table 10. Part 2, question 4 - trends

aa	ac	ba	ca	cc
76%	10%	3%	7%	3%

Consistency indicator - 79%

A reasonable assumption here would be that in contract programming, the pre-condition includes a check on the parameters and the result here confirms this. A higher value for the consistency indicator and the result in question 1a also supports this conclusion. However the result in question 1c shows a number of students including the pre-condition within the function body, which is also reflected by taking the sum of 4b and 4c.

Question 8: Do you think that the user interface to a program should

a. *Check all possible input values and issue error messages*
b. *Only check those input values that appear in the specification and interrupt the program in case of an error*
c. *Only check certain unacceptable values and issue error messages*
d. *Assume that all input values are correct and not test at all*

Table 11. Part 2, question 8 - replies

a	b	c	d
48%	30%	22%	0%
74%	19%	4%	4%
67%	19%	15%	0%

Table 12. Part 2, question 8 - trends

aa	ab	ac	ba	bb	bc	cc	da
56%	11%	7%	7%	7%	4%	4%	4%

Consistency indicator - 67%

The user interface represents a level where the programmer has less control over the input than within the program at the function level so that it is encouraging to see that the majority favour option (a).

Question 10: When one writes a specification for a program, how is responsibility that the finished product will work shared?

a. *100% by the person writing the specification*
b. *100% by the person writing the program*
c. *50-50 between the author of the specification and the programmer*
d. *20-80 between the author of the specification and the programmer*
e. *80-20 between the author of the specification and the programmer*

Table 13. Part 2, question 10 - replies

a	b	c	d	e
0%	7%	56%	11%	26%
4%	4%	44%	30%	19%
0%	4%	33%	30%	33%

Table 14. Part 2, question 10 - trends - %

ae	bc	cb	cc	cd	ce	dc	dd	ec	ee
4	4	4	19	7	15	7	22	4	15

Consistency indicator - 56%

This question comes back to the idea of the specification as also representing a contract of sorts. Most students recognise that there is a degree of shared responsibility but opinion seems evenly divided as to the extent of that responsibility.

Question 13: What do you mean when you assert that a program works?

a. *That the program works under all possible conditions and seldom crashes*
b. *That the program corresponds to the specification 100%*
c. *That the program corresponds to the specification and includes a reasonable level of error handling*
d. *That the program works under all possible conditions and never crashes*
e. *That the program corresponds to the specification 100% and has been tested*

Table 15. Part 2, question 13 - replies

a	b	c	d	e
19%	7%	33%	7%	33%
4%	0%	48%	0%	48%
15%	30%	26%	0%	30%

Table 16. Part 2, question 13 - trends

ac	ca	cb	cc	ce	ea	eb	ee
4%	4%	15%	22%	7%	11%	15%	22%

Consistency indicator - 44%

This more general question is designed to ascertain how students view the concept of a working program. The results indicate that the students are realistic (13d) and set large store on the relationship of the program to the specification.

Question 15: If function A calls function B, where does the responsibility lie that the return value from function B is correct?

a. *100% in function A*
b. *100% in function B*
c. *Shared between function A and function B*

Table 17. Part 2, question 15 - replies

a	b	c
19%	56%	26%
11%	52%	37%
15%	48%	37%

Table 18. Part 2, question 14 - trends

aa	ac	bb	bc	ca	cb	cc
7%	4%	33%	19%	7%	15%	15%

Consistency indicator 55%

Opinion seems to be divided between options (b) and (c) with (c) perhaps indicating that the return value should be checked by a post-condition.

5. Conclusions and Comments

The goal of this survey has been to ascertain how well first-year students have absorbed ideas presented in the introductory courses and in particular those ideas from contract programming that are introduced in the second course on program development. This is part of an ongoing project to integrate research ideas into the undergraduate curriculum.

This kind of survey is necessarily somewhat subjective and the results should be treated as indicators. Part of the difficulty of teaching lies in seeing the world from a student perspective. This difficulty is akin to that of someone who can read trying to imagine how it would be not being able to read! This survey is an attempt to discover the students' view of programming and thus areas in the curriculum, which can be improved. In teaching the teacher knows what she means when presenting material but cannot know how the student perceives and understands the material without feedback. Such feedback often comes indirectly via lab exercises and answers to exam questions. In the latter case this is rather late to correct any misconceptions. With larger classes, it can be more difficult to obtain feedback and surveys are one method of doing so.

The results show, not surprisingly, that the students in the same group are at various stages of understanding. From part 1, the importance of terminology emerges and the need to increase the students' mastery of the terminology within this area. A similar observation is made in [9]. Evidence from other sources such as lab programs and answers to exam questions also indicates that this is an important area, which should be investigated further.

In part 1 question 4, the students' replies indicate that they are aware of which areas are important and that they perceive the areas of emphasis in each course. The results from part 2 indicate that the students are still in the process of absorbing these ideas. This is not unrealistic given that many have started as beginner programmers and have had a limited time, namely 2 part-time courses (50%, 10 weeks) in which to absorb these ideas.

One secondary effect within the department has been increased co-operation and discussion between teachers relating to the design, planning and integration of related courses, including a step-wise introduction of contract programming techniques. At Karlstad we teach three different programs in Computer Science and increased student numbers (90-120 students in some courses) have required greater integration between courses and an increased focus on teaching methods. Surveys such as this one provide input and feedback for ongoing planning discussions in our Teaching Forum as well as revealing areas such as terminology as focus for future discussions.

Future work must include a refinement of the survey to better focus on areas of interest such as contract programming techniques. An additional survey to cover a wider area of programming related techniques would be interesting in order to improve feedback from the students. This in turn will lead to better integration of the courses involved and a more student oriented approach.

References

[1] M. Blom, E. J. Nordby, A. Brunstrom, "An Experimental Evaluation of Programming by Contract", *Proceedings from the Ninth Annual IEEE International Conference and Workshop on the Engineering of Computer-Based Systems* (ECBS 2002), Lund, Sweden, 8-11 April 2002

[2] M. Blom, E. J. Nordby, A. Brunstrom, "Teaching Semantic Aspects of OO Programming", *Fifth Workshop on Pedagogies and Tools for Assimilating Object-Oriented Concepts*, OOPSLA 2001

[3] M. Blom, E. J. Nordby, A. Brunström. "Method description Semla - A Software Design Method with a Focus on Semantics" *Karlstad University Studies, 2000/25*, Karlstad University, Sweden May 2000.

[4] M. Blom, A. Brunström, E. J. Nordby. "A Software Engineering Course that Integrates Education and Research." Paper abstract, Proceedings from CSEET2000, 13th Conference on Software Engineering Education and Training. IEEE 2000, ISBN 0-7695-0421-3 , March 6-8, 2000, page 207

[5] M. Blom, E. J. Nordby, D. F. Ross, E. Jonsson. "Using Quality Criteria in Programming Industry: A Case Study." *Proceedings European Software Day*, Euromicro 98, Västerås, Sweden. August 1998.

[6] P. Bucci, T.J. Long, B.W. Weide, Do We Really Teach Abstraction? *Proceedings 32nd SIGCSE Technical Symposium on Computer Science Education,* ACM, 2001, pp26-30.

[7] R. Kramer, "iContract - the Java Design by Contract Tool", *Proceedings of TOOLS'98 Conference*, Santa Barbara, USA, 1998.

[8] B. Meyer, *Object Oriented Software Construction*, Prentice Hall 1988

[9] A. Robins, N. Rountree, J. Rountree, *My Program is correct but it doesn't run: A review of novice programming and a study of an introductory programming paper*, Technical Report OUCS-2001-06, University of Otago, New Zealand, 2001.

Empowering Software Engineers in Human-Centered Design

Ahmed Seffah and Alina Andreevskaia
Human-Centered Software Engineering Group
Department of Computer Science, Concordia University
Email: seffah@cs.concordia.ca

Abstract

Usability is about to become the quality measure of today's interactive software including Web sites, and mobile appliances. User-centered design approach emerges from this need for developing more usable products. However, interactive systems are still designed and tested by software and computer engineers unfamiliar with UCD and the related usability engineering techniques. While most software developers may have been exposed with basic concepts such as GUI design guidelines, few developers are able to understand the human/user-centered design (UCD) toolbox at a level that allows them to incorporate it into the software development lifecycle. This paper describes an approach for skilling developers and students enrolled in an engineering program in critical user-centered design techniques and tools. The proposed approach starts from the analysis of the usability and software engineer's work context, identifies critical UCD skills and then associates relevant learning resources with each of the identified skills. Our approach suggests a list of patterns for facilitating the integration the UCD skills into the software engineering lifecycle.

1. Motivation

Too often, human-centered engineering techniques remain the province of visionaries and a few enlightened software engineers, rather than the everyday practice of common software developers. One barrier to the wider practice of the human-centered design approach is that its structure and techniques are still relatively unknown, under-used, difficult to master, and essentially not well integrated in software development teams. While many developers may take a course on basic concepts of user interface design such as task analysis or heuristic evaluation, few of them have an understanding of the complete UCD toolbox at a level that allows them to incorporate it into the whole software development lifecycle.

Software engineers need a cost-effective educational framework to understand and master user-centered design in their own language and cultural context. They often don't understand why and how the usability and user problems should drive the development of the whole system they implement. They also argue that 'if users have a problem with the application they just have to consult the help system we provide. If the help system is also difficult to use, they take a look to the guided tour tutorial'. This approach has many consequences including an increase in the development and maintenance costs. Such situation stems mainly from the lack of means, i.e. the cultural barrier between usability practitioners and software engineers. This cultural obstacle should be a key topic in any course about user interface, usability and user-centered design.

Well-trained software engineers in UCD should have gained design skills in a multidisciplinary environment that involves end-users, requires the use of several methods, and handles the inconsistencies that can exist between these diverse methods. They should also develop an appreciation of the human-centered design approach including the importance and impact of usability as a quality factor as well as the difficulties and specificities of designing user interface. They should also know how to make a tradeoff in design decisions involving different dialogue types and input/output devices. An appropriate case study is also required to understand the resources available for design, to maximize the benefits and costs of developing user interface prototypes, as well as to evaluate system usability using different techniques. Finally, engineers building interactive systems must know the limits of their knowledge and in particular when and how to work with external human factor consultants, usability champions or teams. They should know the difficulty of measurement and the complexity of making decisions based on data gathered during tests. We should show how the principles underlying human-centered design philosophy could or should be applied to a large variety of

0-7695-1877-X/03 $17.00 © 2003 IEEE

user interfaces, including traditional GUI, Web applications, PDA and mobile applications.

To make UCD education more effective within a software engineering curriculum, current courses must be aligned with a new method of apprenticeship capable of empowering and sustaining self-learning in a team-oriented environment. Furthermore, this new approach must take into account software engineering students' background, skills, and interests. Dayton et al. [2] recommended apprenticeship with an experienced user interface designer as the best way for a programmer to learn HCI design on the job. Another idea is to establish several "usability advocates" within the company. Dayton and others suggested a 3-day user interface design workshop in which the project team works with end-users and conclude that this is a successful method of training developers. Such an idea is easily transferable to the academic setting by considering an industry case study.

2. Major steps in designing a skill-oriented course

The development of a skill-oriented course involved three stages, geared towards understanding what are UCD knowledge and techniques proposed and used by UCD experts, what skills software engineers need to become accomplished UCD practitioners, and what are learning resources that can cost-effectively address these skills. This approach was originally developed and validated in the PRISE project. PRISE — In French, *Programme de Réorientation des Ingénieurs Sans Emploi*; in English, A Curriculum for Retraining Unemployed Engineers — is a skill-oriented training program. PRISE was developed by the Computer Research Institute of Montreal (CRIM) in collaboration with the Quebec Ministry of Industry, Sciences, and Technologies, the Quebec Engineers Corporation, and several information technology and engineering companies in the Montreal area. The objective of the program was to retrain in software development more than 300 unemployed engineers in groups of 20 during 1999. For each group, the training duration was fixed at one year, alternating intensive skill-oriented training sessions in CRIM's continuing training center with practical work in companies participating in the program.

2.1. Identifying critical skills

In identifying the UCD skills, our first step was to analyze the varying contexts and software development teams in which usability engineers work. The next sub-step was to identify the skills that developers need to perform the different UI design activities. For this analysis, we used the following sources from both the HCI and software engineering education communities:

- University course evaluation forms completed by the students in the course we have been teaching during the last 8 years, including raw feedback from both software developers and students;
- The results of different surveys on the training practices in software development organizations, as well as on the relevance of software engineering and computer science education [8];
- The skill structures for software engineers [3]; [5];
- The results of different workshops and surveys dedicated to HCI education and/or curriculum development for computer science;
- An analysis we made of different courses including those based on the recommendations of ACM-SIGCHI curriculum (http://www.acm.org/sigchi/cdg) including the one that has been a source of inspiration for us [6];
- The classical textbooks and related booksites on HCI;
- The recent books on UCD have been also taken into account for validating the skills we identified;
- The software engineering body of knowledge, SWEBOK (www.swebok.org), was also a valuable source for understanding where exactly usability concerns and related UCD techniques and knowledge should be placed and integrated with existing software development knowledge to maximize the benefits gained from both.

We identified three groups of skills. The first group, *prerequisite skills*, is required for any student taking a course on UCD. These skills should be acquired prior to studying UCD, because subsequent learning depends on them:

1. Mastering the basic principles, foundations, and standards of software development methodologies
2. Having a considerable experience in using computers as well as good programming experience using rapid development tools and GUI builders

The second group, *specific skills*, assume a general understanding of the development lifecycle and provide the ability to perform key tasks during all phases of the UCD lifecycle as defined, for example in the ISO 13407 standard.

1. HCI design difficulties and challenges. Understanding UCD design as a multidisciplinary design field which has its difficulties and challenges
2. UCD philosophy. Mastering the human-centered design philosophy, its foundations, terminology, facts, principles and processes
3. Expert-based evaluation. Reviewing and evaluating, without users, early design concepts and low-fidelity prototypes including task models and scenarios

4. User characteristics, tasks, and UI requirements. Gathering, analyzing and specifying user characteristics, their tasks, their work environment and the usability/UI requirements
5. Screen layout and visual design. Choosing and designing screen layouts, information spaces, as well as visual metaphors and representations
6. Interaction design. Modeling and specifying the human-computer dialog, the system feedback and selecting the appropriate interaction styles and devices
7. Prototyping. Developing low, mid and high fidelity prototypes including mockups, storyboards, software and paper prototypes
8. User-based testing. Planning and conducting usability tests with end-users before, during and after the development and deployment
9. Patterns and guidelines. Gathering, disseminating and using users' experiences and best design practices via design patterns, guidelines and style guides
10. Wizards, help, online support systems. Developing user support resources including wizards, online help systems, training resources and electronic performance support systems
11. GUI design. Applying human-centered design techniques and tools to GUI and office desktop applications
12. Web design. Applying human-centered design techniques and tools to Web applications including Web sites, E.Commerce and Virtual Communities
13. Mobile applications design. Applying human-centered design techniques and tools to mobile and wireless applications including PDAs and wireless telephones

The third group, *generic skills*, is applicable to many UCD steps. These skills are also called "soft skills" [5]:

1. Integrating UI design and usability engineering techniques in the software development lifecycle and methods
2. Writing, formatting, and presenting technical documentation related to requirements, design and testing to a general audience
3. Conducting investigations and cost-benefit studies on software and usability tools and technologies
4. Communicating and working in a multidisciplinary team and in particular with clients, end-users and human factors engineers

These generic skills are also listed in ACM HCI curriculum as well as in the industry survey conducted by the Software Productivity Center (http://www.spc.ca/). We believe that by focusing on such skills, UCD educators can contribute significantly to overcoming this weakness in software engineering education in general. Software developers taking a course on UCD should learn how to involve and interact with end-users and stakeholders during the entire software development lifecycle.

Figure 1 shows a partial view of the skill map we defined. It defines the order in which the skills can be presented. This map is a directed graph where vertices correspond to skills and edges represent the order in which skills can be introduced. Some skills have to be presented in a predefined sequence that can't be altered (the corresponding arcs are solid); others can be introduced in more than one order (optional sequences are shown with dashed arrows). Each vertex of the skill graph has to be visited once and none can be visited more than once.

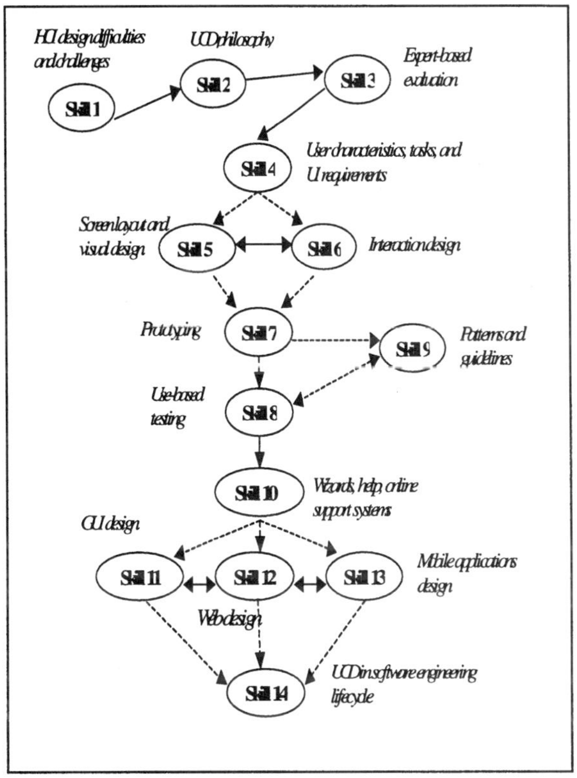

Figure 1. The UCD Skill Map.

2.2 Definition grid

The second step in our approach involved completing a *definition grid* for each identified skill. Each definition includes, among other things, the knowledge and concepts most often used by UCD experts and practitioners working in software development organizations. It should provide also a description of the main steps of the development process in which the skill is required. The performance criteria that we use to measure the quality of the work done by the usability expert should be also described. Table 1 presents a typical skill definition grid.

Table 1: A Sample Skill Definition Grid

Description of the skill / Concepts and knowledge / Major activities	Typical work situation / Constraints and standards / Performance criteria
Description of the skill Gathering, analyzing and specifying user characteristics, their tasks, their work environment and the usability/UI requirements **Concepts and knowledge** - Task analysis techniques including GOMS - Context of use, scenario, user archetypes - User, functional, user interface, usability requirements - Structured and unstructured interviews, focus groups, ethnographic studies, field observations, requirement reviews **Major activities** From the Usability Engineering Lifecycle [23] 1. Defining user characteristics including the mental models of their work processes and products 2. Analyzing of the users' current job and tasks 3. Describing the context of use including platform capabilities and constraints 4. Specifying the usability goals 5. Defining, eventually, a list of general design principles (style guides)	**Typical work situation** - Based on business requirement documentation - End users, stakeholders, usability expert, are directly involved **Constraints and standards that must be respected** - Consideration of the international standards and organization-specific procedures used for human-centered design **Performance criteria** - Appropriate use of requirements tools and techniques - Consideration of quality criteria including consistency, completeness, readability of requirements - Use of appropriate vocabulary and terminology - Respect of the procedures specified in international standards and/or company-specific procedures

2.3 Associating learning resources with skills

Finally, our approach associates a set of learning resources with each skill. From the learner's perspective, we should offer different types of resources that can be used to either achieve a greater understanding of a skill or to obtain further information about it. Furthermore problem solving–oriented resources should be available on the spot and just-in-time, and designed to help developers learn and execute major UCD activities. Examples and scaffolded examples [11], introduced as powerful tools for teaching object-oriented technology, are some of the avenues we investigated. In total we developed and selected from different sources 84 resources including six major case studies. Among these case studies, there is one that we developed recently and that presents a psychometric and heuristic evaluation for assessing CASE tools learnability and usability [7]. This case study is a good starting point in helping software engineers to realize the importance and impact of usability in their own context. It is also an excellent framework in which software organizations and engineers can learn and pick up from UCD and at the same time improve the usability-to-software engineers collaboration to manage the diversity of notations and tools they generally use.

We also designed a project that aims to be an integrative framework for providing skills to developers in user interface requirements, prototyping and usability testing. The project begins by getting to know the intended users, their tasks, and the context in which the system will be used. Only then, a task analysis and contextual inquiry is performed, followed by low-fidelity prototyping and rough usability studies, ending with a high-fidelity prototype that can be user tested more rigorously. Here again, Greenberg's and Sheiderman's courses have been a starting point for the development of our project [6].

3. Patterns as resources for encapsulating and transferring UCD knowledge to developers

In the area of user interfaces design, guidelines and usability patterns have been proposed as a medium to encapsulate user experiences and best design practices. It has been also reported that patterns are useful for a variety of reasons [4]. They are considered, by expert user interface designers, as a medium for transferring, by means of software development tools, the design knowledge of human factors and user interface designers to software engineers unfamiliar with usability engineering. Within our approach, we have been using three different categories of patterns:

- HCI (Human Computer Interface) patterns that are proven user experience solutions to a common usability problem. Different HCI pattern languages have been developed and are being used as an alternative/complementary design tool to guidelines [12].

- Usability patterns that describe human-centered design best practices. Such patterns, which are similar to process patterns [1], can be used as a Lingua Franca [4] in the sense that they have also the potential to support the whole design process.
  - Pedagogical patterns that implement effective learning and teaching strategies.

Many groups devoted themselves to the development of pattern languages for user interface design such as "Common Ground", "Experience", and "Amsterdam" play a major role in this field and wield significant influence [12]. For example, the convenient tool bar patters aims to help the user reach the most useful and frequently visited pages at any time throughout from any page. It can include home page, search, feedback, etc. This pattern can be used as a learning resource to master the two following skills 9 and 10 (see figure 1).

A Process pattern encapsulates good design practices shared among UCD practitioners. It describes UCD activities in the format of why, when, and how. For example, Building a Low-Fidelity Prototype patterns describe why and when a paper prototype can be used to validate user requirements. This pattern can be as a learning resource/strategy for illustrating skills 2 and 3.

Lilly and Manns [9] introduced the concept of pedagogical patterns as a promising way to teach object-oriented technology to traditional software developers. Pedagogical patterns play the same role in teaching and learning as design patterns play in software development. Specifically, a *pedagogical pattern* describes an abstract teaching approach from which contextualized training strategies can be generated, so that subsequent educators are not forced to start over when they design new courses and learning resources [9]. In our approach, we consider pedagogical patterns as the essence of learner-centered education in that they describe best practices for transmitting UCD skills to developers. Pedagogical patterns enable learners to build their understanding through a process of successive elaboration and integration. Pedagogical patterns should not only provide help in using learning resources or developing them, but also provide support for understanding UCD concepts and applying related methods by providing pedagogical examples and templates, assessing performance, and so on. For example, the DIRR (Design-Implement-Redesign-Reimplement) pattern described in Table 6 attempts to explain new concepts and methods based on legacy concepts (for instance, learning object-oriented fundamental concepts using structured software design methods).

Table 2: An example of a pedagogical pattern

Name	- Design-Implement-Redesign-Reimplement (DIRR) Pattern
Intent	- Explain new concepts and methods (e.g. UCD techniques) based on old concepts (e.g. Object-Oriented Methods).
Forces	- It is often hard to get students to make the paradigm shift from functional programming to object oriented programming. - The lecture-lab pedagogy provides a "concept" and "use" approach which can prevent the student from separating the "concept" from a specific "use".
Solution	- The DIRR pattern provides "relearning" methodology for reinforcing new concepts. - The students are asked to design and implement programming solutions using their current paradigm. - This is followed by a discussion of how the solution can be redesigned using concepts from the new paradigm. - Finally, the students reimplement their solution using the new paradigm concepts.
Applicability	- Use the Design-Implement-Redesign-Reimplement pattern to bridge the gap from an old paradigm to a new paradigm.
Resulting Context	- Provides students with first hand experience of both the "old way" and "new way" of developing solutions. - Students gain practical insight into how new concepts relate to their pre-established concepts. - Solving a problem more than one way often leads to deeper understanding of the concepts being addressed. - Questions arising from the students will tend to focus on the "why" things are done rather than on "how" they are done.

Another example of similar pattern to DIRR is New Pedagogy for New Paradigms pattern. It captures a good practice on how to teach something new to the students. The *DIRR* and *New Pedagogy for New Paradigms* patterns are very useful for bridging software and usability engineering concepts and practices. Another important category of pedagogical patterns includes those that can help a professor to develop, select and deliver learning resources. To a certain extent, these patterns are a professor's teaching experiences.

4. Validation and conclusion

The approach for developing and delivering a skill-oriented course on human-centered design presented in this paper is the result of 8 years of investigation. The first version of the skill map was developed between 1995 and 1999 when the first author was an adjunct professor at the University of Quebec at Montreal. He was mainly teaching a course on user interface design for both graduate and undergraduate computer science students. Between January 2000 and June 2002 at Concordia University, other colleagues and we have been using the skills, the learning resources and patterns in different courses. Some of our courses include the bachelor of electrical engineering, computer science, and software engineering, as well as the graduate diploma in computer science, the master of applied computer science and the graduate certificate in user interface design for software systems. The size of each of these classes was between 36 and 60 students. We also designed and offered an industry-oriented tutorial on UCD for software practitioners. In total, around 400 persons have been enrolled in our courses and tutorials during the four last years.

In the beginning of each class, we present our approach and the skill map to students. Based on their feedback, we define the order in which the skills should be presented. We also selected the main resources that we called required or mandatory resources from the large repository we developed. Of course, students have also a free access to all the other resources in the databases during the term. After each term, we always collected students' feedback using a questionnaire. Such evaluation has been used to refine the list of skills and to develop new learning resources and patterns. To facilitate the management, we also developed a Web site, called Human-centered Design for Software Engineers: Techniques, Tools and Applications. This Website provides a unique access to the learning resources, patterns, as well as to an extended list of readings and references including links to textbooks sites and well-known Websites on UCD engineering. Based on a usability test we conducted, a new version of this Website is under construction. At each step of the development of our course, we have been gathering and integrating in the course the students' feedback via structured and informal interviews. In one sentence, we applied the user and learner-centered design philosophy [10] to the development of the course itself including the definition of skills, patterns and resources. In observing and interviewing the different groups of students in our courses thus far, we discovered that we must develop more realistic case studies and examples. Pedagogical patterns need to be developed for evaluating the learner's evolution and performance, and others for the customization of the curriculum for different educational contexts and audiences.

We expect that nurturing continuous learning of UCD skills will be the most popular approach within the engineering educators community. We also expect they will be a major factor in educating the software workforce in developing more usable interactive systems. We are also revising and extending the list of resources and skills in the light of the recent published books on human-centered design and usability engineering.

5. References

[1] Ambler S.W., Process Patterns: Building Large-Scale Systems Using Object Technology, SIGS Books, Cambridge University Press, July 1998.

[2] Dayton, T., et al. (1993). Skills needed by user-centered design practitioners in real software development environments: Report on the CHI'92 workshop. SIGCHI Bulletin 25(3): 16-31.

[3] Denning, P.J., "Educating the New Engineers." Comm. ACM Vol. 35(12). December 1992, pp.88-97

[4] Erickson T., Lingua Franca for Design: Sacred Places and Pattern Languages, DIS 2000: Proceedings of Designing Interactive Systems, New York, August 17-19, 2000, ACM Press.

[5] European Informatics Skills Structure, Council of European Professional Informatics Societies, London, 1992, http://www.cepis.org.

[6] Greenberg, S., Teaching Human Computer Interaction to Programmers. ACM Interactions, 3(4), pp. 62-76, July-August 1996, ACM Press.

[7] Kline, R. A. Seffah, H. Javahery, M. Donayee and J. Rilling, Quantifying Developer Experiences via Heuristic and Psychometric Evaluation Symposium on Proceedings of 2002 IEEE Symposia on Human Centric Computing Languages and Environments (HCC 2002), Arlington, VA, September 3-6, 2002.

[8] Lethbridge, T., "A Survey of the Relevance of Computer Science and Software Engineering Education," Proc. 11th Conf. Software Eng. Education and Training, IEEE Computer Soc. Press, Los Alamitos, Calif., 1998, pp.56-66.

[9] Manns, M.L., "Pedagogical Patterns: Successes in Teaching Object Technology," ECOOP'96 Educator's Symposium. 1996.

[10] Norman, D. A. and Draper, S. W. (Eds.), User Centered System Design: New Perspectives on Human-Computer Interaction. Hillsdale, NJ: Erlbaum, 1986.

[11] Rosson B., and Carroll, J.M., Scaffolded examples for learning object-oriented design. Communications of the ACM. 39(4), May 1996, pp. 46-47.

[12] Tidwell J., "Common Ground: A Pattern Language for Human-Computer Interface Design," 1997, http://www.mit.edu/~jtidwell/common_ground.html

Invited Keynote Papers

The Grand Challenge of Trusted Components

Bertrand Meyer
ETH Zürich, Chair of Software Engineering
and Eiffel Software, Santa Barbara

se.inf.ethz.ch

Abstract

Reusable components equipped with strict guarantees of quality can help reestablish software development on a stronger footing, by taking advantage of the scaling effect of reuse to justify the extra effort of ensuring impeccable quality. This discussion examines work intended to help the concept of Trusted Component brings its full potential to the software industry, along two complementary directions: a "low road" leading to qualification of existing components, and a "high road" aimed at the production of components with fully proved correctness properties.

1 Overview

Progress in software engineering over the past four decades has undeniably had a beneficial effect on software quality. The advances fall short, however, of the kind of break-through that appear necessary to cope with the increasing demands on our software. The general idea developed in this article, reuse, is far from new; but the notion of *Trusted Component* brings in a critical concept: extreme attention to component quality. This is indeed the definition of the term:

> **Trusted Component**
> A Trusted Component is a reusable software element possessing specified and guaranteed property qualities.

(The term "trusted" as introduced in [14] appears destined to stay, but any confusion should be avoided with the notion of trust in secure computing. Although security properties will be part of the quality a component must provide, "trust" in Trusted Components extends to all other quality factors.)

2 Approaches to quality

The considerable existing literature on improving software quality advocates a variety of approaches, which one may classify along two orthogonal criteria: Management vs Technical; and A Priori vs A Posteriori.

The first division affects which of *process* and *product* is viewed as more important:

- Some authors consider that most serious software engineering problems are, in the end, *management* problems, and that technology is a secondary concern. Naturally they focus on process-oriented solutions: Capability Maturity Model, ISO certification, Six-Sigma, relationship of IT with the rest of the company, user awareness. As an example of this approach, the Standish Group's CHAOS reports [19], well-known for their large-scale analysis of software project failures, offer a recipe for project success consisting of ten "success factors" that are *all* non-technical: more user involvement, executive support, clear business objectives, experienced project manager, small milestones, firm basic requirements, competent staff, proper planning, ownership (complemented by "other"). This is an extreme variant of the management-first approach, not accounting for the report's own finding of a significant improvement in project success rates between 1994 and 1998. (It is not immediately evident why "user involvement" or "executive support" should have made major advances during that period; on the other hand, 1994 to 1998 was also the time when, at least in a partial form, object technology was spreading through the industry, a technology factor discounted by the list. The factors given are not even software-specific.) In less exclusive forms, books on software engineering economics [4] and "Peopleware" [6] emphasize non-technology factors. Frequently heard advice about the need for better education also falls in this category, even when the education is about technical topics. Yet another example is the systematic use of code inspections, whether for open source ("enough eyeballs") or in commercial settings.

By contrast, a large portion of the literature is devoted to technical solutions, from programming language features enhancing reliability (static typing, modular mechanisms...) to implementation support (garbage collection), testing techniques, formal development methods, design principles.

0-7695-1877-X/03 $17.00 © 2003 IEEE

The second division affects whether the techniques are applied to producing the software, or to assessing and correcting it once it exists:

- *A priori* techniques help avoid flaws in the first place; along ideas already cited, executive support and use of formal methods fall (from remote ends of the spectrum) into this category.
- *A posteriori* techniques apply when the software or at least some initial version already exists; they help identify and correct any deficiencies that may have escaped the a priori component of the quality effort.

Neither division is absolute: a technique such as configuration management spans the technology / management line; Design by Contract [10] [12] spans the a priori / a posteriori line. Most techniques, however, fit in one box of the following table showing some examples of the classification.

	Technical	*Management*
A priori	Design methods Object-oriented development Formal development	User involvement Executive support Better education for engineers and managers.
A posteriori	White-box testing Static analysis (e.g. PREfix) Proofs (of existing programs)	Testing and acceptance procedures

Figure 1: Varieties of quality advice — examples

Most of the ideas listed have a part to play in the search for software quality. As argued elsewhere [15], the field should avoid compartmentalization and the ever-present tendency to push various approaches as exclusive. There is no magical solution, and every little bit helps.

3 The limits of project-oriented techniques

Useful as they are, the solutions usually proposed tend to target individual projects. This seems unlikely to yield the breakthrough in quality and productivity that the field needs. So much new software gets produced every year — billions of lines — that a more efficient approach seems desirable. As to education, hordes of new developers enter the market every year; only a few of them will have had the benefit of a good software engineering education. It is unlikely for example that the reported 6 million Visual Basic developers are all trained computer scientists.

Education is of course necessary, but it's a never ending effort and we can hardly make the overall quality of software development dependent on its progress.

We can address the issue through Trusted Components. The availability of a large base of guaranteed-quality reusable elements would make application development less dedicated to producing software from the ground up, and hence less dependent on the individual skills of project developers; the focus would shift towards composition, combination, mix-and-match. This particularly applies to the huge amount of software being developed by non-computer-scientists. On such a large population, in whose concerns and jobs software is often only a part, our most earnest attempts at education can only have a limited effect. Our strongest lever is to give them impeccable components of ever broader scope, with a division of labor between component providers and component consumers.

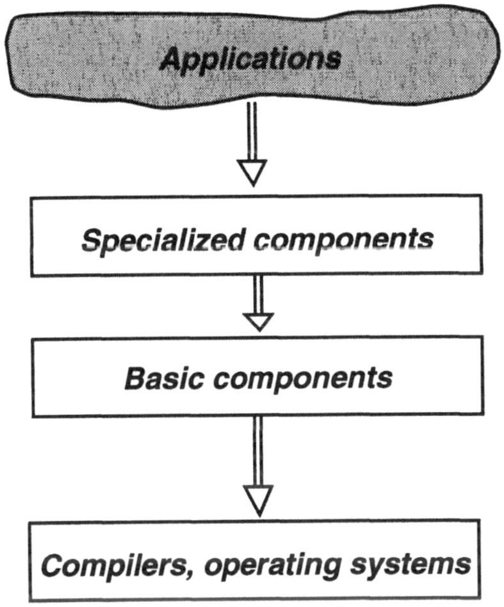

Figure 2: Levels of software and expertise

The application developers can still mess up when combining and extending components, but the more and better we give them the less this will happen. The division of labor suggested by figure 2 helps: an application expert may be best equipped to fight quality problems that depend on the specifics of the application, its users, its corporate environment; but to make sure that the infrastructure is right — to address typical software technology issues such as choice of data structures and algorithms, communication, synchronization, database optimization — it's more effective to rely on components put together by software professionals in these respective areas.

4 The case against quality

Dependence on programmer education is not the only obstacle to the potential effectiveness of the most widely cited approaches to improving software quality. An economic argument suggests that, applied to projects rather than components, they face a natural limit.

Considering the matter from an economic perspective is legitimate because quality, at least as perceived by project developers, their managers and the rest of an organization, has a cost. The theoretical argument that "Quality is free" because non-quality causes greater cost is of little interest to the project manager faced with looming deadlines and budget constraints. The practical question then becomes *how much* quality effort the project can afford. Every manager knows that a non-perfect but acceptable version on time is better than absolute perfection two years later, especially if the company has gone bust in the meantime for failing to release a product. There is a quality incentive, but it only leads to the acceptability point: the stage at which remaining deficiencies do not endanger its usefulness to the market. Beyond that point, most managers consider that further quality-enhancing measures yield a quickly diminishing return on investment.

This pragmatic view, which some have cited as one of the reasons behind Microsoft's success, is no longer the dirty secret of project management since Ed Yourdon gave it respectability under the name "Good Enough Software" [21].

> Although Yourdon has recently stated, citing Microsoft initiatives to address some security-related issues, that Good Enough may not be good enough any more in the post-September-11 climate, the overall industry attitude doesn't seem, at least so far, to have dramatically changed. (The hard economic times can have opposite effects on companies, some tempted to get rid of any non-core efforts such as quality initiatives, others realizing that improving quality is their best bet for survival.)

Good Enough Software is a global consequence of accumulating individual optima. The example of capitalism suggests we should strive, in human systems, for an equilibrium where the combination of individual strategies that each person considers optimal for his own purposes matches the global optimum that best benefits the group as a whole. The prevalence of the Good Enough approach indicates that in the software engineering field we have not reached such an equilibrium: the ideal for society is that all software should be as good as possible; but if I am a project manager the ideal for me is only to make my product good enough. In fact, by spending more money and time to make my product better than it strictly has to be for market acceptability, I am putting at risk the product, my company and my own career.

This is the culture that, in many places, has made "perfectionism" a dirty word for software development. The reasons are clear: programmer perfectionism can indeed be detrimental to key goals of management, chief among them timely delivery of an acceptable product. But that culture is unlikely to create the conditions from which to expect a breakthrough in software quality.

The same forces work against correcting instances of *non-quality*: bugs or, more generally, anything that could be done better. If someone points out a possible improvement to an application, and I am responsible for that application, then improving it is *my* job. Not surprisingly, my reaction may be to avoid fixing anything that's non-critical. That may indeed be my best personal survival strategy in the Darwinian world of industrial software development; but globally it's not good for the industry.

This clash between the optimization of individual strategies and the pursuit of the common good may be a stronger obstacle to software quality improvement than any technical limitation of current quality approaches such as the ones cited in section 2. Many known ideas and solutions — from better programming languages and advanced tools to formal methods — have the potential of ensuring better processes and products, and yet are not as widely used as they could; the various justifications for refusals to use them are often smokescreens for the real reason: that quality is only one the criteria, and improving it doesn't necessarily justify the cost.

If this hypothesis on how companies and projects react is correct, it puts a natural limit on the practical effect of any quality technique that entails any costs, as long as the technique is directed to individual *projects*. Major progress can only come from changing the economic incentives so that individual perfectionism is good not only for everyone else but for the individual as well. Basing software development on Trusted Components appears to do this:

- The component developers (producers) make quality components available to application developers (consumers), who can turn them to their advantage in building their applications.
- It is the common interest of the consumer and the producer that the components should be good, and that deficiencies should be fixed. Because the managerial and political framework is different, consumers' choices have a higher likelihood of being based on technical merit, since their goal is the success of their application, based on the components.
- If in the course of developing an application a consumer spots a deficiency in a component, the burden of correcting it falls on someone else. It is then in the consumer's interest to exert pressure to have the deficiency corrected; this is also in the producer's interest in a competitive situation.

As a result there appears to be, in this scenario, a better match between optimization of the common good and the combined optimization of individual goals.

5 Components and quality

The concept of Trusted Component is of course based on the idea of software reuse, long present in the software engineering literature. But arguing for Trusted Components is not just arguing for reuse.

Although reuse has often been advocated — at the same level as techniques such as those listed in section 2 — as one of the ways to improve quality, a reuse-based development process is not by itself a quality guarantee. The expected advantages come from the scaling-up effect, which lets new applications benefit, again and again, from a one-time investment; but reuse scales up everything, the bad as well as the good. The improper reuse of earlier software in the Ariane 5 maiden launch disaster has been widely cited as an illustration of the dangers [9].

Trusted Components are the combination of *reuse* with a special attention to the *quality* of the components being reused.

The quality standard for Trusted Components is far higher than what is commonly exercised on application software. To be more precise, the only area in which similar criteria apply (or should apply) is the construction of life-critical systems as in transportation and defense. There the analysis of costs and benefits justifies the extra effort. With Trusted Components, the justification comes not from the net impact of each software element by itself, but from its cumulated impact through the many applications that will reuse it.

This multiplicative effect of reuse also adds some personal and technical factors to the economic and political elements discussed so far. We should not underestimate the benefits of accepting and even encouraging developers' perfectionism. The common managerial perception that perfectionism is bad — because it delays the project and hence harms the company — fosters a general attitude of cynicism, detrimental to the morale of the best developers. With reusable components, the picture changes:

- It pays to improve the details; perfectionism is justified by the expected reuse effect. "Worse is better" [7] no longer has to hold.
- Conversely, *not* improving the details becomes dangerous. There is no "minor" flaw any more, since with the potential of widespread reuse for a component *any* deficiency has an increased likelihood that *some* client application will exercise it.

So as managers we can, without a bad conscience, let component developers exert their best creativity and pay attention to details.

Component development is one of the most exciting opportunities for a talented software developer. It's the opportunity to take the time to do things right, and let many consumers benefit.

Component development is also the place to try out the newest, most advanced techniques, before they find their way into ordinary application development. The development of reusable components is the Formula-1 of software engineering.

The term "component" has not been defined. As the reader may have guessed, this discussion doesn't restrict itself to the case of binary, directly deployable components as advocated by Szyperski [20]; rather, we accept a broad range of components that can extend from classes of object-oriented libraries (or even subroutines of numerical libraries) to very large-grain components, provided they meet specific criteria:

Definition: component

A component is a software element (modular unit) satisfying the following three conditions:

1• It can be used by other software elements, its "clients".

2• It possesses an official usage description, which is sufficient for a client author to use it.

3• It is not tied to any fixed set of clients.

Condition 1 distinguishes a component, meant to be used by other software, from a program, meant to be used by people or by non-software systems. A given software element may be usable both as a program and as a component, for example an application (say Excel) that is available to human users but can also be packaged into a COM object for use by software clients. Condition 2 brings in information hiding and the need for interface specification. Condition 3 excludes a software element that would useful only as part of a certain program or set of programs, and hence could take advantage of insider knowledge about the context of its use; a component should instead be part of a library and usable by any client that respects the interface conditions.

[16], part of discussions with Szyperski [3], has argued that what matters most is not the binary nature of components but information hiding and abstraction. Without again entering this debate we note that most of the present article applies equally to Szyperski's more specific view of components. For example, the lessons gained from the systematic development of the EiffelBase object-oriented library of fundamental data structures and algorithms, and the resulting principles as described in [11], seem largely to extend to components of other kinds; and more generally the principles of Design by Contract [10] [12] appear particularly relevant for components [2] [17].

6 High and low road

If Trusted Components are indeed one of the major hopes for a breakthrough in software quality, how do we go about establishing a base of high-quality components?

An examination of the state of the art in industry and research shows a great discrepancy between what's possible in both worlds:

- In industry, components have taken off in recent years, with great practical success, from object-oriented libraries (C++, Java, Eiffel) to ActiveX controls, COM objects, Enterprise Java Beans, .NET assemblies. These efforts could greatly benefit from a stronger quality focus and in particular from *component certification* applied to existing commercial components.

- In research, one of the great advances of the past decade has been the practical improvements to formal methods, and in particular to proof techniques, making it possible to produce sizable, realistic systems equipped with full proofs. Although it has not yet changed the generally negative image that "formal methods" convey to many people, this practical progress is undeniable. Applications so far have largely been focused on life-critical systems; the reasoning developed above suggests that components are another ideal application area, as the two notions of reuse and formal development seem destined for each other [13].

The gap, however, is huge. Choosing one of the directions to the exclusion of the other would mean ignoring either long-term prospects for major advances or the short-term needs of industry. This suggests defining two complementary paths for the progress of Trusted Components, a low and a high road:

- The *low road* starts from today's components, commercial or open-source. The extent of the quality guarantees we can achieve there is by nature limited; in particular, *proofs* are excluded in almost all cases, if only because the source code is generally not available in the commercial case, but more fundamentally because one of the lessons of formal methods is that one can't hope to prove software unless it has been produced with that goal in mind. Even if not accompanied with absolute guarantees, *certification* is still possible in this case; as we'll see next, we may hope to provide interesting if incomplete quality assessments.

- The *high road* is intended to lead to components with fully proved properties. The ambition of this goal implies that it's more long-term, and that its realization must start with relatively fine-grain (but practically critical) components such as library classes.

The efforts along both directions are different. An effective Trusted Components effort should be both realistic, following the low road for immediate benefits to industry interested in the quality of today's components, and ambitious, following the high road for the ultimate goal of fully proved components. The Trusted Components effort that we have started at ETH, with the aim of establishing a Component Certification Center, is intended to address both sets of issues.

7 Towards a Component Quality Model

One of the most important tasks on the "low road" is to define criteria against which to assess components. In other words we need a Component Quality Model, intended to assess products rather than (as the Capability Maturity Model) processes for obtaining these products.

A first framework for a Component Quality Model appears in figure 3. It divides properties of interest into five categories, the "ABCDE" of component quality (I am indebted for this terminology to Richard Walker of ANU in Canberra):

Acceptance A.1 Some reuse attested A.2 Producer reputation A.3 Published evaluations **Behavior** B.1 Examples B.2 Usage documentation B.3 Preconditioned B.4 Some postconditions B.5 Full postconditions B.6 Observable invariants **Constraints** C.1 Platform spec C.2 Ease of use C.3 Response time C.4 Memory occupation C.5 Bandwidth C.6 Availability C.7 Security	**Design** D.1 Precise dependency documentation D.2 Consistent API rules D.3 Strict design rules D.4 Extensive test cases D.5 Some proved properties D.6 Proofs of preconditions, post-conditions, invariants **Extension** E.1 Portable across platforms E.2 Mechanisms for addition E.3 Mechanisms for redefinition E.4 User action pluggability

Figure 3: Framework for a Component Quality Model (the ABCDE of Trusted Components)

The categories are largely orthogonal, as there is no single scale against which to assess components.

A, for Acceptance, is a non-technical dimension: a provider may claim a component is reusable, but it helps to have evidence of usage. This part of the classification addresses the natural question of a potential consumer: "Who else is reusing this?". A.1 to A.3 are a scale of evidence pointing to prior successful use of the component.

B, for behavior, addresses a key property of a good component: that it should be equipped with a precise list and individual specification of the functionalities it offers. Here too the levels make up a scale — a gradation towards better evidence of quality: at the minimum we expect examples of use, and probably (B.2) usage documentation. More precise specifications are desirable; for example it is dubious whether one can be comfortable with using a component unless it is equipped (B.3) with a precise specification of its *preconditions*, the conditions under which it will deliver a proper result. (Most commercial components, regrettably, don't include this in any precise way). The next two levels add more of the Design by Contract mechanisms: postconditions, providing either some or (more difficult) full specification of the outcome; invariants.

C, for constraints, covers performance considerations. Here we no longer have a scale, just a set of partly independent criteria, such as response time, security (protection against undesired use), bandwidth requirements, ease of use. Techniques of performance specification and enforcement are less developed than the techniques of behavior specification (the previous category), but the need is just as important.

D, for Design, a scale again, considers the *internal* perspective. What you want as a component consumer is a guarantee of the component's *external* properties — properties characterizing what it makes available to you — but any information on the principles and techniques that the component authors have used during development can reinforce your trust. At the very least you will want an indication of the component's dependencies on hardware and software elements [20]. The next few levels correspond to systematic design rules; our experience with EiffelBase, as documented in [11], has taught us that, beyond a few components, a library should follow strict and uniform rules for naming classes and their features, choosing arguments (operands and options), distinguishing between commands and queries (that is to say, staying away from side-effect-producing functions), uniform access. Knowledge that the library authors have followed a systematic policy of this kind is an important element to reassure component consumers. The last levels involve *proofs* and open up the "high road" of this discussion.

E, for Extension, addresses an important feature of software reuse: it's not only about reusing components as they are, but also (unlike reuse in the "hard" engineering disciplines, hard in the sense that their products are material and you can't just drive your fist into them) adapting a component to your specific needs. One aspect is portability: applicability to different platforms. For growing flexibility, you may have the possibility of adding your own mechanisms to the components; of redefining some existing components, as with inheritance in object-oriented development (under the guidance of contracts); and, the most flexible, the ability to plug in your own mechanisms, as with callbacks or higher-level versions of this notion.

This classification provides a first grid of criteria against which to assess components. The plan is, clearly, to develop it to the point where it can be used as a component certification standard.

8 The high road: proofs

The high road involves producing components with correctness proofs. It is in general meaningless to talk about "proving software": one can at best prove that the software satisfies specific properties. The phrase becomes legitimate, however, if we consider software elements that are already equipped with *correctness properties*; this is the case with the classes of Eiffel libraries which possess contracts. For this reason we are devoting our first efforts to this target, starting with the EiffelBase library which has the added interest of covering data structures and algorithms that are both often difficult to get right and constantly useful for everyday programming across essentially all application domains.

The contracts consist of preconditions, postconditions and class invariants, complemented (in the routine bodies) by loop variants and invariants, as well as "check" instructions. They have been present in EiffelBase and other libraries right from the start, but until now have been applied (even if the prospect of proofs was always latent) to other purposes [12]: as analysis and design aids, to get the software right; as support for readability; for documentation (the "contract form" is the official interface documentation of a class); as management aids (allowing managers to follow what's going on at a sufficiently high level of abstraction); for testing and debugging, through the run-time monitoring of contracts.

Thanks to theoretical and practical advances, it is now becoming possible to consider the contracts as properties — characterizing software abstractions and their implementations — to be proved mathematically. Beyond a certain level of complexity, manual proofs, tedious and error-prone, are not sufficient; we are working with proof tools such as Atelier B [1] [5] for this purpose. The challenges are numerous:

- Matching the usual top-down process of formal, proof-oriented development, usually applied to full systems, with the bottom-up style of component-based development and the needs of proving individual components.
- Developing appropriate modeling techniques for critical but tricky mechanisms such as pointers.
- Complementing the existing class contracts to arrive at full specification.
- Developing the appropriate proof techniques.
- Making sure these techniques are appropriate for mechanization, and feeding them into the proof engine.

As noted earlier, one can hardly hope to prove software that hasn't been built for this purpose. Even with the contract-rich style that exists throughout our libraries, we expect that the libraries themselves will have to be adapted to support proofs (apart from any correction of bugs uncovered during attempted proofs).

A number of ongoing papers [18] report on the progress we have achieved so far in these various directions.

We don't limit ourselves to proofs but also consider *tests* of contract-equipped components, using the contracts to guide test generation.

Many other groups are, of course, working on related issues.

The proofs we have studied so far apply to object-oriented library classes, only a part of the component story. We feel, however, that this is the right way to start the proof effort:

- These libraries, as noted, play a key role in everyday development. The ability to rest on a fully proved set of data structures and algorithms classes would be by itself a major boost to trust in software quality.
- The problems involved — such as extensive use of pointers — are difficult. The ability to solve them is an important prerequisite for proofs of other kinds of components, and a good testbench for proposed proof techniques.
- One of the conditions for performing proofs in any application domain is the existence of a *theory* for that domain. For business-oriented components, building such theories will take time. Data structures and algorithms have been researched for several decades and enjoy a wide body of theory, even if only a subset is useful for proofs.

We hope that this high-road approach, with its specific focus, will be an important complement to the more short-term approach of the low road, and that its relevance will continue to grow.

9 A grand challenge

Tony Hoare, in advocating a large-scale effort to produce a "verifying compiler", has listed a number of conditions [8] for a research goal to be a "grand challenge" that should mobilize a significant part of the community, on a key unsolved issue, for a decade or so, with ambitious goals that can in principle be attained, but not without special effort, resources and dedication. ("Send a human to the moon before the end of the decade".)

For software engineering, the major issue of yesterday and today, which pollutes everything we do, is our inability to produce industrial software, on a regular basis, with a quality level of which we can be proud. Approaches focused on single projects, however good individually, will not bring a solution.

Developing a base of guaranteed-quality components, and extensive techniques for qualifying reusable components, is one of the most exciting prospects for the software world today, perhaps the idea with the highest potential for changing things for real. It satisfies all of Hoare's criteria (arising from "*scientific curiosity about the nature and limits of the discipline*", being generally comprehensible, going beyond what's initially possible, calling for cooperation, necessitating collaboration of specialties etc.), currently with the exception of "*enthusiastic support from (almost) the entire research community, even those who do not participate*". I believe it deserves that enthusiastic support, and I hope this survey of issues, goals and approaches will help catalyze a collective effort to solve the Grand Challenge of Trusted Components.

References

[1] Jean-Raymond Abrial: *The B Book*, Cambridge University Press, 2002.

[2] Felix Bachmann, Len Bass, Charles Buhman, Santiago Comella-Dorda, Fred Long, John Robert, Robert Seacord, Kurt Wallnau: *Technical Concepts of Component-Based Software Engineering*, Software Engineering Institute, Carnegie-Mellon University, Pittsburgh (Pennsylvania), Report CMU/SEI-2000-TR-008, available at www.sei.cmu.edu/publications/documents/00.reports/00tr008.html; consulted September 2002.

[3] *Beyond Objects* column of *Software Development* magazine, articles by Bertrand Meyer and Clemens Szyperski, 1998-2000.

[4] Barry W. Boehm: *Software Engineering Economics*, Prentice Hall, 1981.

[5] ClearSy (name of company, no author listed): Web documents on Atelier B, www.atelierb.societe.com, consulted December 2002.

[6] Tom de Marco and Tim Lister: *Peopleware: Productive Projects and Teams*, 2nd edition. Dorset House Publishing, 1999.

[7] Richard Gabriel: *Is Worse really Better?*, in *JOOP (Journal of Object-Oriented Programming)*, Fall 1992.

[8] Tony Hoare: *Criteria for a Grand Challenge*, at www.cra.org/Activities/grand.challenges/hoare.pdf, consulted February 2003.

[9] Jean-Marc Jézéquel and Bertrand Meyer: *Put it in the Contract: The Lessons of Ariane*, in IEEE *Computer*, vol. 30, no. 7, pages 129-130, July 1997.

[10] Bertrand Meyer: *Applying "Design by Contract"*, in IEEE *Computer*, 25, 10, October 1992, pages 40. Also in *Object-Oriented Systems and Applications*, ed. David Rine, IEEE Computer Press, 1994.

[11] Bertrand Meyer: *Reusable Software: The Base Object-Oriented Libraries*, Prentice Hall, 1994.

[12] Bertrand Meyer: *Object-Oriented Software Construction, second edition*, Prentice Hall, 1997.

[13] Bertrand Meyer: *The next Software Breakthrough*, in IEEE *Computer*, vol. 30, no. 7, pages 113-114, July 1997, available at archive.eiffel.com/doc/manuals/technology/bmarticles/sd/contracts.html, consulted February 2003.

[14] Bertrand Meyer, Christine Mingins and Heinz Schmidt: *Providing Trusted Components to the Industry*, in IEEE *Computer*, vol. 31, no. 5, May 1998, pages 104-105.

[15] Bertrand Meyer: *Towards more reliable software: Every little bit counts*, in IEEE Computer, November 1999, pages 131-133, available at www.inf.ethz.ch/~meyer/publications/computer/reliable.pdf, consulted February 2003.

[16] Bertrand Meyer: *The Significance of Components*, in *Software Development*, November 1999, available at www.sdmagazine.com/documents/s=7207/sdm9911k/, consulted February 2003.

[17] Bertrand Meyer: *Contracts for Components*, in *Software Development*, July 2000, variant available at archive.eiffel.com/doc/manuals/technology/bmarticles/sd/contracts.html, consulted February 2003.

[18] Bertrand Meyer: articles on proving classes at www.inf.ethz.ch/~meyer/ongoing/references.

[19] Standish Group: CHAOS reports at www.standishgroup.com/, consulted November 2002.

[20] Clemens Szyperski: *Component Software: Beyond Object Oriented Programming*. Addison-Wesley, 1998.

[21] Ed Yourdon: *When Good-Enough Software is best*, IEEE *Software*, Vol. 12, no. 3, May 1995, pages 79-81.

Design by Contract is a trademark of Eiffel Software.

Must There Be So Few? Including Women in CS

J. McGrath Cohoon
University of Virginia
jmcohoon@virginia.edu

Abstract

Women's under-representation in academic computer science is described for the U.S. and internationally. Conditions that contribute to this situation are identified, and motivations for increasing women's participation in computer science are discussed. According to recent research in the U.S., effective interventions at the undergraduate level include: actively recruiting women, encouraging women to persist, and mentoring for the purpose of overcoming under-representation. The latter two practices are easily implemented.

1. Women are under-represented in CS.

Women's representation in many science, mathematics, and engineering disciplines historically has been low in the United States. Figure 1 illustrates data from the National Center for Educational Statistics [1] for several science, mathematics, and engineering (SME) disciplines. It shows that in 1970, women earned less than 40 percent of the bachelor's degrees in mathematics, biological sciences, physical sciences, engineering, and computer science. By 1985, women's representation had increased in all of these disciplines, especially computer science. And it continued to rise or remain close to 50 percent through the end of the century in every one of these disciplines, except computer science.

At the graduate level, women are fewer still, and this has an impact on their representation among faculty and in research positions. In the later half of the 1990s, women earned on average 16 percent of CS doctorates. Furthermore, CS retained women from the baccalaureate level through the doctorate at less than half the rate it retained men. Data obtained from the NSF WebCASAR online database [2] were used to approximate these retention rates by calculating doctoral degrees in 2000 relative to baccalaureate degrees ten years earlier. (Ten years is the average amount of time between the bachelor degree and the doctorate in CS.) The data showed that the number of CS doctorates awarded to women between

Figure 1.

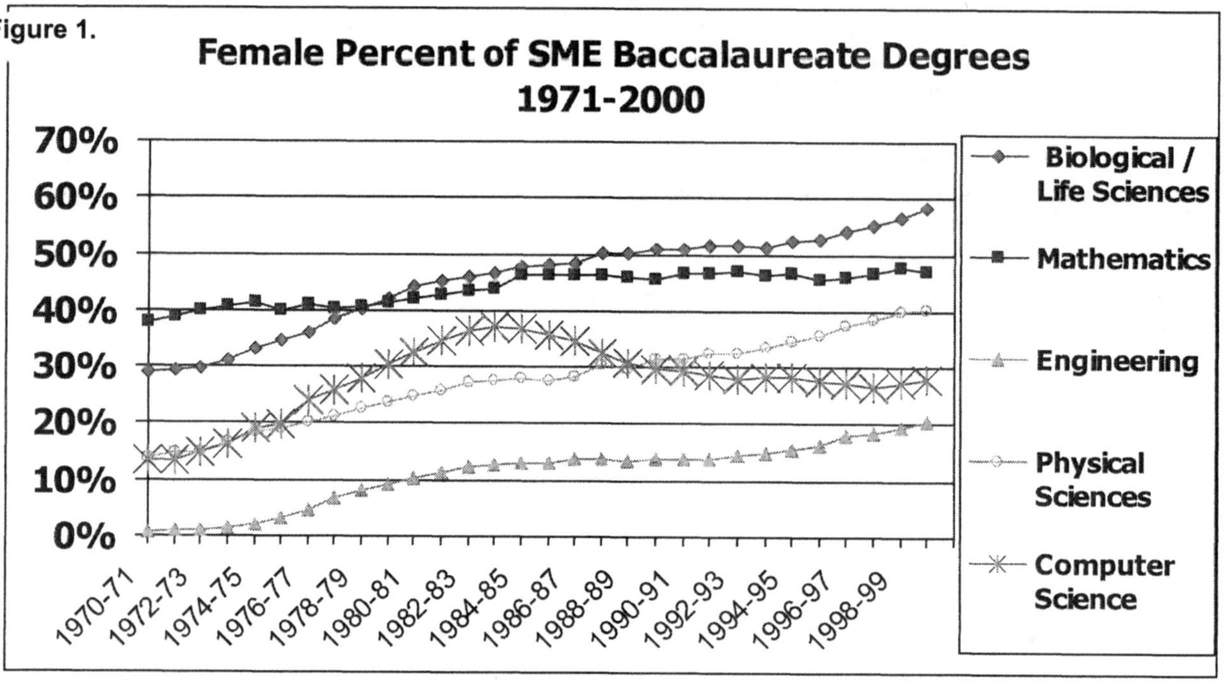

0-7695-1877-X/03 $17.00 © 2003 IEEE

Figure 2.

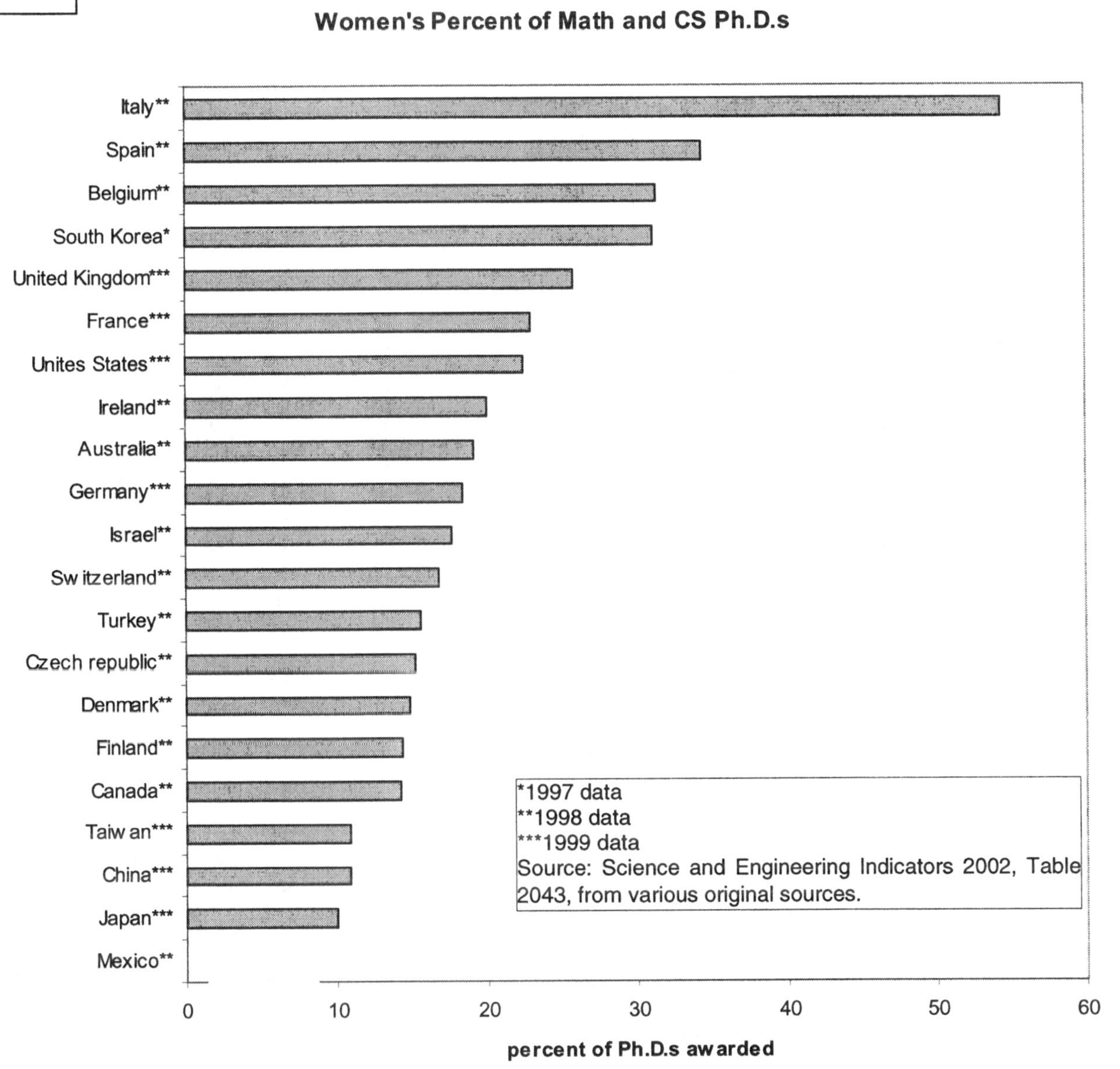

1995 and 2000 was on average 1.15 percent of the bachelor degrees awarded ten years earlier. For men, retention through the doctorate was on average 2.96 percent of bachelor degrees awarded ten years earlier. This gender difference in retention through the doctorate is about the same as that in mathematics where many more women than men stop before the doctorate to become teachers. However, the ratio of women's to men's rates is much smaller in CS than in the physical sciences where women's rates were well above half of men's.

In most industrialized countries, women appear to be a minority in computer science. Data comparing men's and women's CS education internationally showed that in 1995, men earned twice as many math and CS degrees as women earned in Canada, Germany, Ireland, Japan, Spain, and the U.S. (International data were only available with math and CS numbers combined.) Three times as many math and CS degrees went to men in Austria, New Zealand, Norway, and the UK. In Sweden, men were over-represented by a factor of four. Only in Italy did men and women earn close to the same number of math and CS degrees [3].

More recent international data that reports only on Ph.D.s is presented in Figure 2. These data affirm the considerable international variation in women's representation in math and CS, and that female computer scientists are still likely to be a minority in every country for which data were available, with the possible exception of Italy.

Figure 3.

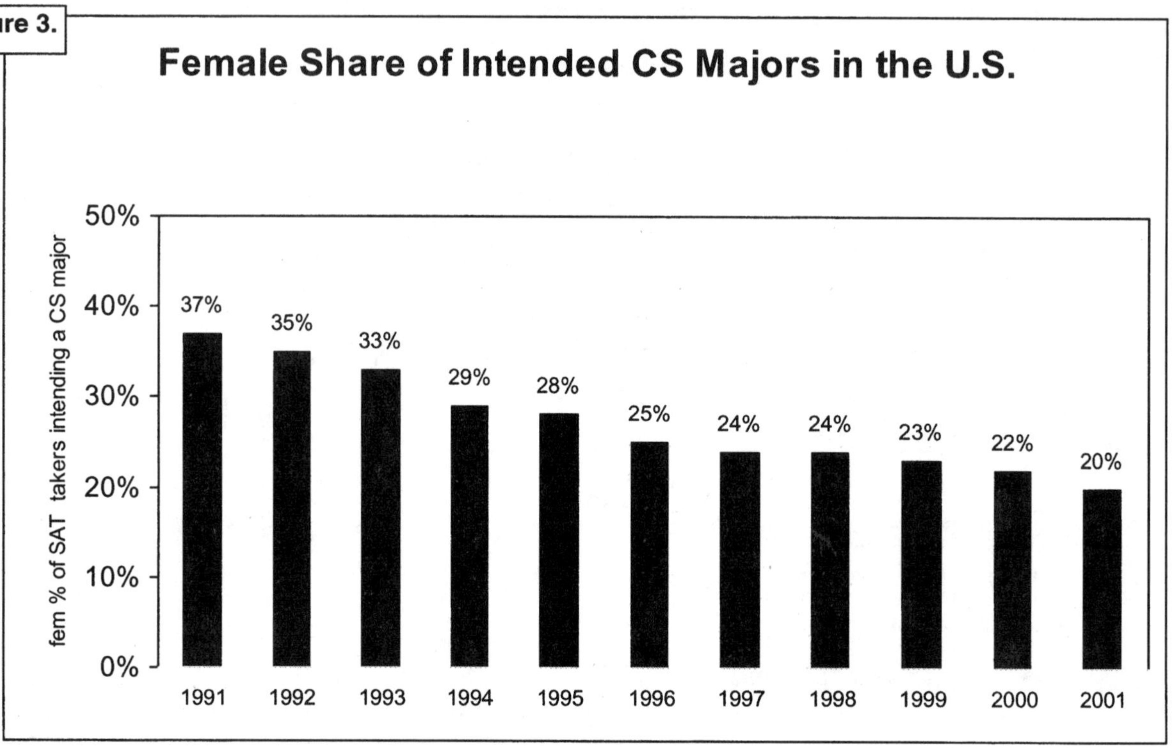

2. The situation in the U.S. is not likely to change soon.

Looking at U.S. high school seniors who intend to major in computer science, Figure 3 shows that women's portion of this group has been shrinking for years. Throughout a time when interest and demand for the CS major skyrocketed, women's numbers increased as well, but they comprised a smaller and smaller portion of the students interested in studying computer science in college. Thus, unless institutions of higher education attract women into the CS major, female representation is likely to continue declining at least for the next several years.

3. Conditions leading to women's under-representation

Why are there relatively few women in computer science? Some argue that it is simply a matter of preference, that women don't study computer science because they don't want to [4], or perhaps because they are unsuited due to lack of ability or preparation. However, Figure 1 showed that women's participation varies over time and across disciplines, and Figure 2 showed that it may also vary internationally, so it seems unlikely that some inherent female characteristic can fully account for women's under-representation. A better explanation can be found in the social conditions that channel men and women into disciplines and careers labeled appropriate for their gender.

3.1. Social context

Computing is widely viewed as a "male" activity. A striking example of this perspective was written in response to an online magazine article about the dearth of female computer scientists [5]. An anonymous computer consultant lumped programming with several other very stereotyped male behaviors when he wrote, "I guess life just isn't fair until women grow chest hair, spit, chew, bench press 250 pounds, and write a computer program." His expression was somewhat extreme, but the opinion that computing is a "guy thing" is not uncommon.

Parents and teachers communicate that computing is for guys when they provide opportunities for boys to enhance their computer skills, while failing to develop girls' interest. For example, it was observed in the 1980s that boys were much more likely than girls to attend computer camp [6], and a more recent observation of attendance at a Silicon Valley camp still showed a 5 to 1 ratio of male to female teenagers [7]. The early experience gained by boys gives them a head start on girls, who often develop their interest in computers at a later stage.

Media and popular culture reinforce the message through portrayals of computer scientists as geeks - young men who do nothing but live and breathe computers [8]. This image is common even among computer science majors at a leading institution. Although most of these students did not think they fit the image, they claimed that other CS majors did fit it [9].

The lack of encouragement and the unattractive image may explain why even the most mathematically able college women are more likely to major in the humanities than in a discipline like computer science [10]. Large numbers of well-prepared women in the U.S. choose to avoid computer science rather than take advantage of their ability and training.

This social context discourages girls from going into computer science, but it is not enough to keep them all away. My recent study of 210 mid- to large-sized undergraduate CS departments showed that in the average program, 25 percent of students enrolled were women.

3.2. Post-secondary education

The small number of women who overcome the pressures steering them away from CS is further diminished during the college years when women switch out of the major at higher rates than men switch [11]. As Figure 4 shows, many students who declare a CS major switch to some other major before earning their bachelor's degree. Fifteen percent of the men leave for a different major, and an even greater percentage - 21 percent - of the women leave. This gender gap in attrition rates, or "gendered attrition rate," shrinks women's representation to yet lower rates.

3.2.1. Gendered Attrition. College presents a new set of conditions that discourage women from staying in the CS major. These conditions are additional forms of the general lack of support present in society at large. Once they reach college, women in the CS major often lack the support from other students and faculty that could help them overcome the self-doubt that comes with acting in a way that does not fit gender stereotypes [12].

Students consider peer support to be essential for coping with the challenges of being a CS major. In focus groups that included 178 undergraduates in 16 departments, the most common coping strategy reported was calling on a classmate for help. For example, one student said, "If I didn't have people here that I could come to and say, 'What does this mean?' I don't think I would have stayed at all." Others agreed that students can be even more helpful than faculty. "You don't need a professor who's going to be like, 'Don't you know this information? Didn't I teach it to you last week?' You need a friend who says, 'Don't worry. Together we'll work at it, and we'll learn it.'" This kind of peer support was important to both male and female students, but women don't have the level of access to same-sex classmates that men have.

Being a small minority means that most of the peer support women do get must come from male classmates. This situation was comfortable for most of the women focus group participants. For example, many women explained that they had had mostly male friends for their entire lives, but this situation was not without consequences.

> "I've always, ever since I was tiny, had guys for friends. ... You know - I'm getting married; I can't seem to find any bridesmaids."
>
> Another woman in the focus group nodded in agreement. In her case, she added, "My brother's my maid of honor."

Apparently, these women were used to substituting available men to fill the roles of absent women.

However, even in CS, not all women were comfortable with relying on male classmates for support. For example, some women felt that when they didn't know anyone, it was easier to approach another woman

Figure 4.

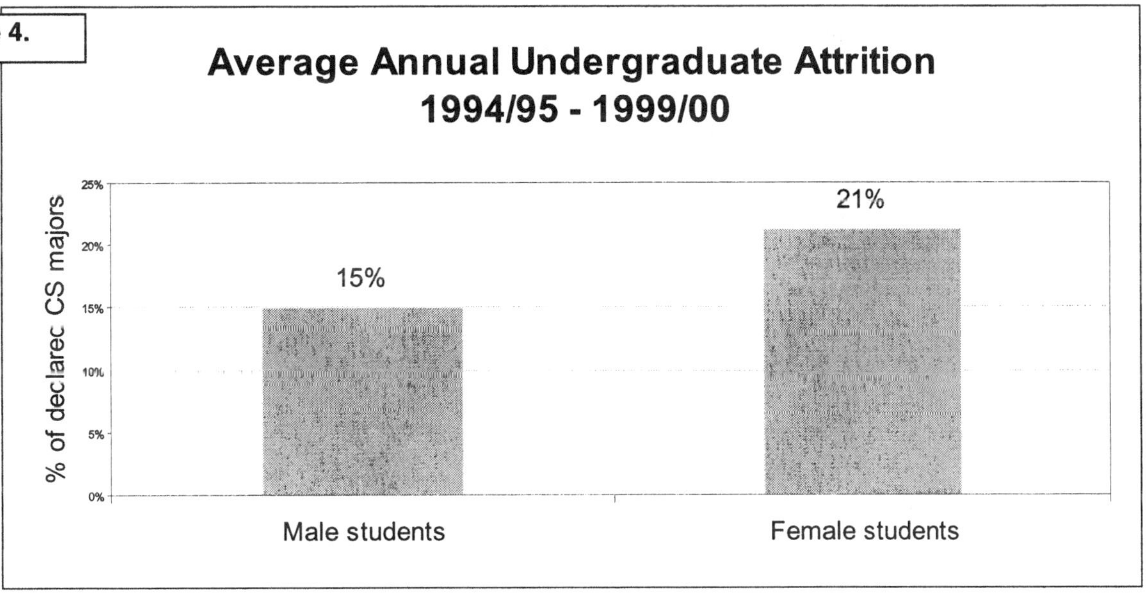

Figure 5.

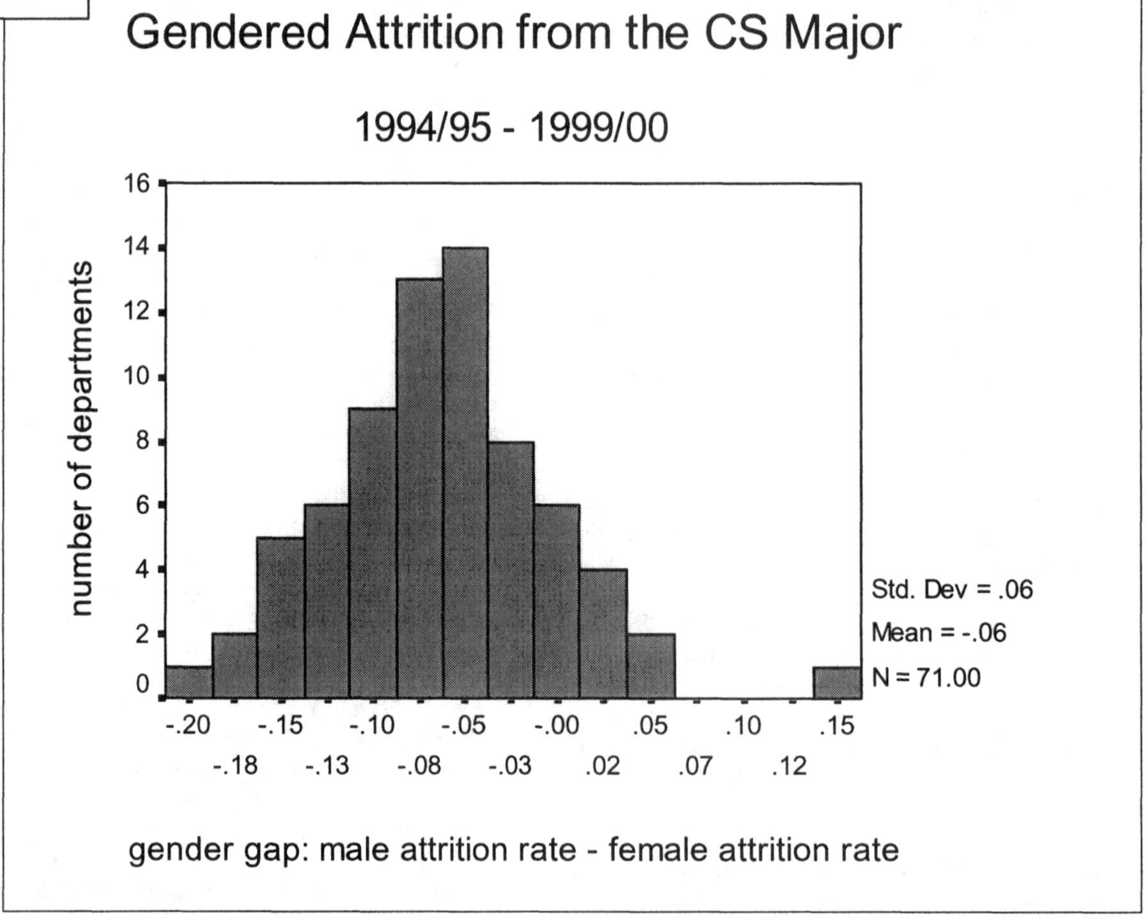

than to approach a man. Some women did not want to appear imperfect or inferior to a man. Another reason given for not asking a male classmate for help was that it could be misinterpreted as an indication of more than academic interest in him. For women such as these, who prefer to rely on other women, being in a minority is a disadvantage when they need help from another student.

Students also considered faculty support to be important for coping with the challenges of being a CS major. In the focus groups, students talked about friendly, available faculty who helped them succeed even when students doubted their own ability. The types of faculty support that had a statistically significant effect on shrinking the size of the gendered attrition rate were: encouraging students to persist and mentoring women to overcome their under-representation. An example of these faculty behaviors was offered by a student who reported,

> In the beginning I was having such a hard time with …the class itself and, for me, [this faculty member] was encouraging because she was, "Just keep at it. You can do it. We need more women in the field." (Laughter from other group participants.) And. Yeah. You're laughing, but it's true. It made me feel better. At least she's kind of acknowledging that hello, she's aware that I'm trying, and I'm not just stupid, and she thought I could do it.

In the face of her own self-doubt, this student relied on the confidence faculty had in her, and she persisted.

Evidence that women can be retained in the CS major at comparable rates to men comes from statistical analyses of faculty survey data together with measures of their departments' gendered attrition rates. Figure 5 illustrates the variation in departments' gendered attrition rates, demonstrating that under certain conditions women are retained at similar rates to men. Analyses of the relationship between departmental characteristics and gendered attrition rates show that the conditions associated with departments' having small gender gaps in their attrition rates were:

- Enroll enough women to offer same-sex peer support,
- Have faculty who encourage students to persist and who mentor women to overcome their under-representation.

Thus, when women are supported either by same-sex peers, or by faculty, they are able to persist at comparable rates to the men in their departments.

4. Why should we care?

Although some might argue that women's participation is of little concern to the discipline, computer scientists could have several reasons for wanting to increase women's representation in their field. These reasons include:

- Maintaining a supply of high-quality students to fill their classes, to populate their profession, and to teach future computer scientists;
- Offering the benefits that diverse viewpoints provide;
- Promoting gender equity.

According to the CRA Taulbee survey [13], the numbers of undergraduate students entering computer science in U.S. and Canadian institutions have declined in the past two years. Together with rising rates of migration from the major [14], these trends signal a change in CS enrollments. The tremendous growth programs experienced in the past is ending, and some programs may need to turn their attention to attracting and retaining students.

Even as enrollments decline, future workforce demands are expected to continue being strong despite the recent downturn in job opportunities. The U.S. Bureau of Labor Statistics predicts that seven of the top ten highest growth occupations in the next five years will be computer-related. A similar prediction of continued international demand for information technology professionals was made by Freeman and Aspray [15]. Thus, although it is unclear if the gap between supply and demand for computer professionals in the U.S. will ever reach the level it attained in the 1990s, the industry remains a driving force in modern economies. Meeting the need of this industry for qualified professionals can best be accomplished when nations facilitate the education of talented male *and* female students.

The supply of computer scientists prepared to teach future members of the profession fell between 1995 and 2000 as both Ph.D. production and the percentage of Ph.D. recipients accepting academic positions declined in the U.S. [16]. One action likely to reverse these trends would be to raise the proportion of women earning Ph.D.s in CS, because women are more likely than men to teach. Among currently employed U.S. computer and information scientists with doctorates, 44 to 50 percent of the women teach compared with about 30 percent of the men (calculated with data from 1997 and 1999 Scientist and Engineers Statistical Data [17])

In addition to supplying computer science with students, practitioners, and teachers, increasing women's representation would contribute their perspective to the content of the discipline. As the president of the National Academy of Engineering put it, "without diversity, we limit the set of life experiences that are applied, and as a result, we pay an opportunity cost – a cost in products not built, in designs not considered, in constraints not understood, and in processes not invented." [18]. As it has in biology, women's participation in computer science could broaden the set of problems that are addressed and solutions that are attempted, and it could add alternative interpretations of results.

Finally, computer scientists could be motivated by the desire for gender equity to increase women's representation in their discipline. Computer science offers many wonderful opportunities for creative and financially rewarding careers. Considering that women generally earn less than men and have less prestigious jobs, greater access to computing careers could improve this situation.

5. Opportunities for effective intervention in higher education

This research on CS departments in the U.S. showed that there are two actions institutions of higher education can take to keep interested women in the computer science major. They are encouraging and mentoring students. When faculty encourage students to persist, it makes a measurable difference in women's retention. Likewise, when faculty mentor women for the purpose of increasing their numbers in the discipline, it makes a measurable difference in women's retention. CS departments where these actions are common are more likely to retain their female students at rates comparable to their retention of male students.

One other action has a strong effect on increasing women's participation in CS – recruiting women. Carnegie Mellon University demonstrated that recruiting can be highly effective. They raised their proportion of women undergraduate CS majors from seven percent in 1995 to in 40 percent in 2000 [19] through a multi-faceted, research-based program that included outreach to high schools. Their results and the findings of the research reported here demonstrate that successful recruitment not only raises the number of women enrolled in college-level CS, but it has the extra benefit of gender-balanced retention rates.

6. Summary

Women are a minority in academic computer science at all levels and in most industrialized countries. However, the extent of their under-representation varies, demonstrating that certain conditions can hinder or promote women's participation. At the baccalaureate level, actively recruiting women, encouraging women to persist, and mentoring women to increase their representation are all effective strategies. These actions can help maintain the supply of high-quality students, practitioners, and teachers while offering the benefits of diversity and gender equity.

7. Author's Notes

This material is based upon work supported by the National Science Foundation under grant number EIA0089959. Any opinions, findings, and conclusions or recommendations expressed in this material are those of the authors and do not necessarily reflect the views of the National Science Foundation.

8. References

[1] National Center for Education Statistics, "Digest of Education Statistics, 2001," Institute of Education Sciences, U.S. Department of Education, Washington, DC 2002.

[2] WebCASPAR, "Online data compiled from IPEDS Completions Surveys," vol. 2003: National Science Foundation, 2003.

[3] M. Charles, K. Bradley, "Equal but Separate? A Cross-National Study of Sex Segregation in Higher Education," *American Sociological Review*, vol. 67, pp. 573-599, 2002.

[4] D. Gelernter, "Women and Science at Yale," in *Weekly Standard*, 1999.

[5] M. Seminario, "Is the "Nerd" Factor Keeping Women Out of High-Tech?," vol. 2001: ZDNet, 1998.

[6] R. D. Hess and I. T. Miura, "Gender Differences in Enrollment in Computer Camps and Classes," *Sex Roles*, vol. 13, pp. 193-203, 1985.

[7] P. Brutlag, J. Kim, C. K. Martin, J. Mizuno, J. Sheldon, "Stanford ACE Computer Camp Study," vol. 2003, 1998.

[8] S. Turkle, *The Second Self: Computers and the Human Spirit*. New York: Simon and Schuster, Inc., 1984.

[9] J. Margolis and A. Fisher, *Unlocking the Clubhouse: Women in Computing*. Cambridge: MIT Press, 2001.

[10] S. E. Turner and W. G. Bowen, "Choice of Major: The Changing (Unchanging) Gender Gap," *Industrial & Labor Relations Review*, vol. 52, pp. 289-313, 1999.

[11] J. M. Cohoon, "Toward Improving Female Retention in the Computer Science Major," *Communications of the ACM*, vol. 44, pp. 108-114, 2001.

[12] S. Beyer, "Gender Differences in the Accuracy of Self-Evaluations of Performance," *Journal of Personality and Social Psychology*, vol. 99, pp. 960-970, 1990.

[13] R. E. Bryant and , "2000-2001 Taulbee Survey Hope for More Balance in Supply and Demand," in *Computing Research News*, Vol. 14/No. 2 ed, 2002, pp. 4-11.

[14] J. M. Cohoon, "Migrating Out of Computer Science," in *Computing Research News*, Forthcoming, 2003.

[15] P. Freeman and W. Aspray, "The Supply of Information Technology Workers in the United States," ED459346, 1999 1999.

[16] J. McGrath Cohoon, R. Shwalb, and L. Chen, "Faculty Turnover in CS Departments," presented at SIGCSE Technical Symposium on Computer Science Education: Proceedings of the 34th technical symposium on computer science education, Reno Nevada, 2003.

[17] SESTAT: Division of Science Resources Statistics, "Employed U.S. scientists and engineers, by level and field of highest degree attained, sex, and primary/secondary work activity: 1997 and 1999," vol. 2003: National Science Foundation, 1997 and 1999.

[18] W. A. Wulf, "Testimony to the Commission on the Advancement of Women and Minorities in Science, Engineering, and Technology Development," in *National Academy of Engineering Committee on the Diversity of the Engineering Workforce*, 1999.

[19] L. Blum, "Women in Computer Science: The Carnegie Mellon Experience," Available online at http://www-2.cs.cmu.edu/~lblum/PAPERS/women_in_computer_science.pdf, 2001.

Invited Paper from the Awardees of the Most Influential Paper from ICSE'15

ViewPoints: meaningful relationships are difficult!

Bashar Nuseibeh
Department of Computing
The Open University
Walton Hall
Milton Keynes MK7 6AA, UK
B.A.Nuseibeh@open.ac.uk

Jeff Kramer
Department of Computing
Imperial College
180 Queen's Gate
London SW7 2BZ, UK
j.kramer@imperial.ac.uk

Anthony Finkelstein
Department of Computer Science
University College London
Gower Street
London WC1E 6BT, UK
a.finkelstein@cs.ucl.ac.uk

Abstract

The development of complex systems invariably involves many stakeholders who have different perspectives on the problem they are addressing, the system being developed, and the process by which it is being developed. The ViewPoints framework was devised to provide an organisational framework in which these different perspectives, and their relationships, could be explicitly represented and analysed. The framework acknowledges the inevitability of multiple inconsistent views, promotes separation of concerns, and encourages decentralised specification while providing support for integration through relationships and composition. In this paper, we reflect on the ViewPoints framework, current work, and future research directions.

1 Multi-Perspective Software Development

Any sizeable software development effort will involve a variety of stakeholders with different aspects of concern – or *perspectives* – that overlap, complement, or contradict each other. These stakeholders express their concerns using a variety of representations, and follow different processes to deploy those representations. This makes determining the relationships between different perspectives particularly difficult, yet crucial for checking consistency and managing inconsistency between those perspectives.

Such *multi-perspective software development* has motivated our research for over a decade. It embodies a number of characteristics that continue to lie at the heart of organising the software development activity. These characteristics include the need for separation of concerns during software development, the inevitability of having multiple inconsistent views of processes and products of software development, and the need to reason analytically over multiple views in order to understand the properties and consequences of a multi-perspective specification.

Much of this research has focused on requirements engineering (RE) activities within the software engineering life cycle. RE is prototypical of multi-perspective software development. Multiple stakeholders hold different views of the problems to be addressed, which in turn determine the different requirements of the system to be developed. These requirements are often inconsistent, but acceptably so, during some part of the RE process when requirements are still being elicited, negotiated, and prioritised.

This paper reflects briefly on the *ViewPoints framework* [10, 33], which we developed to organise and manage multi-perspective software development. The paper reviews the basic components of the framework, their *raison d'être*, and the way in which we have deployed them over the last ten years. The paper describes the use of explicit relationships between ViewPoints to manage multi-perspective software development, and reports on our most recent incarnation of the ViewPoints framework in the form of the xlinkit toolkit. The paper then speculates about the need for more meaningful relationships between multiple ViewPoints in order to reason more effectively about structured collections, or configurations, of such ViewPoints.

2 The ViewPoints Framework

The ViewPoints framework provided an infrastructure for capturing and organising software development knowledge. Our notion of a ViewPoint was of an object encapsulating cross-cutting and partial knowledge about notation, process, and domain of discourse, from the perspective of a particular stakeholder, or group of stakeholders, in the development process.

A system description – a specification – thus comprises a structured collection of loosely coupled, locally managed, distributable ViewPoints, with explicit relationships between them to represent their overlaps. These overlaps are the focal point for consistency checking between ViewPoints, and subsequent inconsistency management, should ViewPoint relationships be found not to hold.

2.1 Key principles

ViewPoints re-iterate a number of key, well-documented principles of software engineering, and surface a number of new ones.

Fundamentally, ViewPoints organise software development knowledge based on *separation of concerns.* A ViewPoint, expresses the concerns of a particular stakeholder, such as a development participant or a representative of an area of concern captured by that ViewPoint. Thus, a ViewPoint may represent an area of concern within a project, a product, or a process, or may simply present a particular

0-7695-1877-X/03 $17.00 © 2003 IEEE

perspective expressed in a particular notation. The choice of dimensions of concern along which to create ViewPoints may be the result of experience, the nature of the problem at hand, or simply organisational exigencies.

The next, but related, key principle is that of *heterogeneity of representations*. ViewPoints deliberately allow different perspectives to be represented using different notations, based on the observation that stakeholders will present their perspectives using different notations, depending on their preferences, needs, or circumstances. Of course, relating different perspectives will inevitably require some expression of the relationships between the different notations, and ViewPoints provide a framework for precisely such an expression.

Using the ViewPoints framework leads directly to the notion of distributable ViewPoints – that is, ViewPoints that can be distributed physically or logically. The key principle upon which this relies is *decentralisation* – the idea that the knowledge encapsulated within each ViewPoint is elicited locally, developed locally, and managed locally. Such decentralisation explicitly moves away from any notion of a monolithic system specification that can be checked or managed globally, towards collections of loosely coupled partial descriptions.

The consequence of heterogeneity, decentralisation, and partiality is that relationships between ViewPoints are crucial for achieving *integration* in its many forms. In the ViewPoints framework, integration is often methodological; that is, it is about meaningful linking of processes and notations in order to achieve *coordination* and *composition*, respectively [32]. Thus, methods may be *engineered* by relating different notations and prescribing when and how they are used. Also, methods may be *deployed*, leading to many ViewPoints linked by instantiations of relationships defined during method engineering.

Another consequence of a specification comprised of many different ViewPoints is the inevitable inconsistencies that arise between those ViewPoints. The approach adopted by the ViewPoints framework is one of *living with inconsistency*, in order to capture the diverse perspectives of stakeholders. Consistency is defined by *inter-ViewPoint rules* that express the (static semantic) relationships between ViewPoints [6, 34]. *Inconsistency management* is then the process of handling the potential plethora of rules and dealing with the ViewPoints when the desired relationships between them do not hold [7, 12, 35, 37].

2.2 Why ViewPoints are still relevant

The principles upon which ViewPoints are based continue to be relevant in the context of software development today. The aspect-oriented software development (AOSD) community has focused in recent years on precisely the kind of "cross-cutting" concerns investigated within the ViewPoints framework. This community has focused mostly on concerns in programming code, however, there is now increasing recognition that these concerns may also manifest themselves in requirements and designs, and so consideration of 'early aspects' may be necessary [4, 40].

The ViewPoints framework also provided an opportunity for method engineering – the customisation of methods by mixing notations [36], processes and guidelines for their deployment. During such method engineering, different types ("templates") of ViewPoints can be assembled together, and related, leading to multiple, heterogeneous ViewPoints when the methods are deployed (or in ViewPoints' terminology, when ViewPoint templates are instantiated). While method engineering as a research discipline, has not prospered it is in fact widely practiced. The Unified Modelling Language (UML) with its multiple, heterogeneous modelling notations, user-defined profiles, extension mechanisms, and variety of processes in which it is used, may be seen as an example of the move towards choosing the most appropriate method for the problem in hand [1]. Expressing and checking the relationships between the various models remains a challenge.

Decentralisation was at the heart of the ViewPoints framework. Many of the issues identified are of direct relevance for the provision of tool support to distributed software engineering teams working cooperatively and asynchronously [21, 30]. The consequences of supporting multiple views, namely, the need to live with and manage inconsistency between those views are of particular interest [3, 9, 15, 16].

2.3 A critical analysis

The software engineering community in general, and the RE community in particular, appear to have accepted the need to articulate and manage multiple views in the software development process. There are a variety of concerns along which these views may be separated, including aspects, actors, representation schemes, or processes. Dividing large monolithic specifications into many smaller partial specifications is one way of managing such specifications.

The ViewPoints framework articulated a research agenda in which the above ideas featured. It also, through cases studies and demonstrator tool support, presented a vision of multi-perspective software development in which methods can be engineered, many partial, inconsistent specifications created, and consistency relationships between them checked. The research agenda changed over time and assiduous reading of our papers will reveal different and, ironically, not wholly consistent variants of the framework.

What our early demonstrators did not achieve were truly heterogeneous representations. It is also fair to accuse our early work of providing a reference model without a plausible distributed implementation to support it.

Distribution has been largely addressed in our more recent

work on xlinkit, a toolkit for checking documents distributed on the web, described in the next section. Heterogeneity has posed somewhat more problems. The ViewPoints framework made great polemical play of heterogeneity. The coordinated use of multiple modelling notations is now common and widely accepted as the right approach to specification. It is not at all clear that our advocacy of heterogeneity in representing mappings between modelling representations and consistency relationships between models using multiple these notations was the right approach. Certainly, our later work [6, 12, 18, 27] has adopted a single meta-language for expressing the relationships between multiple views (as UML does in its adoption of a single meta-model and framework of constraints).

The single language is crucial for performing meaningful analytical reasoning. In much of our work we have adopted predicate logic as an underlying representation upon which to perform reasoning [12]. In some instances we found it necessary to adapt classical logic in order to perform reasoning in the presence of inconsistency [18]. In other cases, we used particular forms of classical logic in order to reason about the changing specifications [14, 41]. Most recently, in the context of xlinkit, we have based our techniques for repairing inconsistencies between specifications on first order predicate logic with some significant practical success [29].

3 xlinkit

xlinkit is a direct successor to much of the work on ViewPoints. It provides a partial realisation and a demonstration that many of the core ideas of the framework were sound. It has also, as implementations are wont to do, surfaced a wide range of new issues, to which we had paid scant attention in our earlier work.

xlinkit, a lightweight application service that provides rule-based link generation and checks the consistency of distributed web content. A full description can be found in [27, 28, 29] and online demonstrations, tutorials and other materials can be found at `http://www.xlinkit.com`.

The operation of xlinkit is quite simple. It is given a set of distributed XML resources and a set of potentially distributed rules that relate the content of those resources. The rules express consistency constraints across the resource types. xlinkit returns a set of XLinks, in the form of a linkbase, that support navigation between elements of the XML resources. Here XML is used as the common interchange language to overcome heterogeneity.

The xlinkit rule language is first-order logic (the concrete syntax being XML). The xlinkit 'check engine' provides a novel linking semantics to this language that returns hyperlinks between inconsistent elements instead of boolean values.

The hyperlinks provide very precise diagnostics that we believe are essential for inconsistency management. xlinkit has a reporting framework 'Pulitzer' that uses these diagnostics to provide informative reporting to resource, aka viewpoint, owners.

Recent work, reported at this conference, has concentrated on 'repair'. Using the rules, by static analysis, we can identify a set of repairs that can be used to restore consistency. These repairs, or at any rate a sensible subset of them, as determined by an appropriate authority, can be used in conjunction with our diagnostic reporting to support inconsistency management.

xlinkit leverages standard Internet technologies. It supports wide-scale document distribution and can support multiple deployment models. It has a strong formal foundation. We have completed a number of large-scale evaluations, including a study that checks UML models, Java code, EJB deployment information and UML profile information. This and similar studies give us confidence in xlinkit and demonstrate that we have gone some way towards making ViewPoints a reality. xlinkit is now being commercialised by Systemwire, a research spinout company.

Experience with xlinkit has brought home to us the challenges of scalability, in terms of the size of documents, the number of rules and the complexity of those rules. We have implemented an incremental checker, a distributed checker, smart caching using an XML repository and an ultra-high performance replicated checker. We have also devoted a large amount of effort to optimisation with a view to ensuring that checking and rechecking can be done on large document collections as and when necessary. Ensuring usability, good interfaces and meaningful error messages has also occupied much time. These are not peripheral issues, they have been essential in order to be able to complete the case studies, and attract the external users, that validate our work.

There is a substantial future research agenda for xlinkit. One of the key items on this agenda is the relationship between checking and workflow. The ViewPoints framework envisaged that checks would be triggered by the enaction of a process model. This process model would identify which checks should be applied when and the results of the checks could then be used to drive the process. This idea was first mooted in our work on Tool Assisted Requirements Analysis [TARA paper] and further explored in the context of Viewpoints in [21]. Our work on standards compliance is in much the same vein [8]. Cass & Osterweil [2] have been looking at doing process-centred checking in the context of xlinkit using Little-JIL as the process language. We are keen to do something similar, probably using a simple reactive approach that takes advantage of distributed event monitoring.

4 Final Viewpoints: current and future challenges

We have occupied ourselves with providing a framework for separation of concerns and have made some moderately successful attacks on the associated problems of integrity that result from this. We recognise however that this is only part of the story, "having divided to conquer, we must reunite to rule" [19]. Software development requires us to be able to perform rich reasoning and analysis across the multiple views.

While tools such as xlinkit help to establish links and check rules, it is still a far cry from the reasoning and analysis that we envisage should be supported. How can we make further progress in this regard?

An example of where this challenge is evident is in the relationship between requirements and software architectures, a hot topic in current software engineering research. In the 'twin peaks' model [17, 39] we outlined our view of the co-development of requirements and architectures. Obviously, we wish to separate the expression of requirements and the representation of the software architecture. On the other hand we know that many so-called non-functional requirements drive the identification of an appropriate architecture and, vice-versa, that architectural analysis informs requirements. Handling these relationships requires more than consistency checking, important though that is. We must be able to reason about properties of the systems that we expect to build based on an integration or composition of different ViewPoint specifications. We should also be able to identify incompleteness and to perform trade-off analysis between alternative development decisions.

Given our experience and interest in software architectures, we have also investigated support for reasoning across views by exploiting the common, underlying structure of the proposed software architecture. In particular, the architecture is used as the skeletal framework upon which to hang the aspects of interest [20, 24]. In contrast to the concept of a single source of information which supports multiple views, this approach provides for the elaboration of the common underlying structure or architecture with behaviour, performance, implementation, or other information. So far this work has been loosely based on the Darwin software architecture language [22] and the LTSA (Labelled Transition Systems Analyser) [23] for behaviour analysis and animation [25], and is being extended to include synthesis from scenarios [44] and performance analysis. However, here too the relationships are limited to the granularity supported by the components and interactions inherent in the architecture rather than to any deeper notions which may be at a finer granularity or orthogonal to the architecture.

It is clear that we still lack the means to express more diverse relationships in order to reason more effectively about structured collections, or configurations, of ViewPoints. A classic example is the kind of reasoning that is needed to trade-off usability against security. The relationships between two such system requirements are complicated by the variability or lack of precision in their expression. Thus, in order to express relationships between them, individual security and usability ViewPoints need to be better understood and articulated.

Finally, returning to our example of relating requirements and architectures, we are currently exploring ways of describing the multifaceted relationships that inevitably arise between problem and solution structures in software development. We are using Jackson's Problem Frames to map out shared phenomena between requirements, problem domains, and the (software) machine to be developed [17]. Thus, our problem frames not only bridge the gaps between problems and solutions, they are also an explicit representation of some quite complex relationships between different descriptions in the software development space. We have started to explore this kind of approach to better specify and analyse security requirements and to relate them to security threats [5]. The ViewPoints framework provides a generic means of expressing the relationships between descriptions in this context. However, our experience to date indicates that identifying, expressing, and reasoning about more meaningful relationships is hard!

Acknowledgements

The ViewPoints framework was inspired by the CORE method [26] and developed in collaboration with a number of colleagues and students over many years. Instrumental in the early conceptual work, particularly during his sabbatical at Imperial College in 1989, was Michael Goedicke [10]. Steve Easterbrook has also been, and continues to be, a key developer of the framework since completing his PhD at Imperial College in 1991 [6, 7, 37, 38]. George Spanoudakis contributed to the understanding of overlaps between ViewPoints [43] and Tony Hunter to the development of techniques for reasoning in the presence of inconsistency [12, 18]. Alessandra Russo performed some of the first major case studies applying ViewPoints to NASA requirements specifications [41], and has subsequently contributed significantly to the development of tools and techniques for reasoning about evolving ViewPoint specifications [14, 42]. Wolfgang Emmerich and Christian Nentwich have been partners in the development of xlinkit [27, 28, 29]. Early work on the bridge to ViewPoints was performed by Ernst Ellmer and Andrea Zisman.

We would like to acknowledge the financial support provided by the UK SERC and then EPSRC for over a decade through a series of projects (SEED, VOILA, MISE and VOICI). The work has also benefited from financial support of the European Union in the context of projects such as ESF, PROMOTER I/II and REX.

A number of related workshops [3, 9, 45] and journal special issues [13, 15, 16] contributed to the building of an active community in viewpoints and inconsistency management research.

This paper is a retrospective on the ICSE-15 (1993) [31] paper, which received the ICSE "Most Influential Paper" Award at ICSE-2003. The original paper was subsequently revised and expanded to appear in [34].

References

1. D. Avison and G Fitzgerald, "Where Now for Development Methodologies", *Communications of the ACM*, 46(1):79 -82, January 2003.
2. A. G. Cass and L. J. Osterweil, "Requirements-based design guidance: A process-centered consistency management approach", *Technical Report 2002-024, University of Massachusetts*, Department of Computer Science, March 2002.
3. M. Chechik and S. Easterbrook, eds., *ICSE-01 Workshop on Living with Inconsistency,* Toronto, Canada, May 2001.
4. S. Clarke, W. Harrison, H. Ossher, and P. Tarr, "Subject-Oriented Design: Towards Improved Alignment of Requirements, Design and Code", *Proceedings of OOPSLA-99*, November 1999.
5. R. Crook, D. Ince, L. Lin, and B. Nuseibeh, "Security Requirements Engineering: When Anti-requirements Hit the Fan", *Proceedings of IEEE International Requirements Engineering Conference (RE'02),* Essen, Germany, 9-13 September 2002.
6. S. Easterbrook, A. Finkelstein, J. Kramer and B. Nuseibeh, "Coordinating Distributed ViewPoints: The Anatomy of a Consistency Check", *International Journal on Concurrent Engineering: Research & Applications,* Special issue on conflict management, 2(3): 209-222, CERA Institute/Technomic Publishing Co. Inc, USA, 1994.
7. S. Easterbrook and B. Nuseibeh, "Using ViewPoints for Inconsistency Management", *Software Engineering Journal,* 11(1): 31-43, BCS/IEE Press, January 1996.
8. W. Emmerich, A. Finkelstein, C. Montangero, S. Antonelli, S. Armitage, and R. Stevens, "Managing Standards Compliance" *IEEE Transactions on Software Engineering,* 25(6):836-851, Nov/Dec. 1999.
9. M. Feather, S. Fickas, and J. Kramer, eds., *ICSE-97 Workshop on Living with Inconsistency,* Boston, USA, May 1997.
10. A. Finkelstein, J. Kramer, B. Nuseibeh, L. Finkelstein and M. Goedicke, "Viewpoints: A Framework for Multiple Perspectives in System Development," *International Journal of Software Engineering and Knowledge Engineering,* Special issue on 'Trends and Future Research Directions in SEE', World Scientific Publishing Company Ltd., 2(1): 31-57, March 1992.
11. A. Finkelstein and J. Kramer, "TARA: Tool Assisted Requirements Analysis", in *Conceptual Modelling, Databases & CASE: an integrated view of information systems development,* Loucopoulos, P. & Zicari, R. eds., 413-432, John Wiley, 1991.
12. A. Finkelstein, D. Gabbay, A. Hunter, J. Kramer and B. Nuseibeh, "Inconsistency Handling in Multi-Perspective Specifications", *Transactions on Software Engineering*, 20(8): 569-578, IEEE CS Press, August 1994.
13. A. Finkelstein and I. Sommerville, "The Viewpoints FAQ", *Software Engineering Journal,* (Special issue on viewpoints), 11(1):2-4, IEE/BCS, 1996.
14. A. Garcez. A. Russo, B. Nuseibeh, and J. Kramer, "Combining Abductive Reasoning and Inductive Learning to Evolve Requirements Specifications", *(to appear in) IEE Proceedings: Software,* 2003.
15. C. Ghezzi and B. Nuseibeh, eds, Special issue on Managing Inconsistency in Software Development, *IEEE Transactions on Software Engineering,* , 24(11):908-1001, November 1998.
16. C. Ghezzi and B. Nuseibeh, eds, Special issue on Managing Inconsistency in Software Development, *IEEE Transactions on Software Engineering,* 25(6):782-869, November/December 1999.
17. J. Hall, M. Jackson, R. Laney, B. Nuseibeh, and L. Rapanotti, "Relating Software Requirements and Architectures using Problem Frames", *Proceedings of IEEE International Requirements Engineering Conference (RE'02)*, Essen, Germany, 9-13 September 2002.
18. A. Hunter and B. Nuseibeh, "Managing Inconsistent Specifications: Reasoning, Analysis and Action", *Transactions on Software Engineering and Methodology,* ACM Press, October 1998.
19. M. Jackson, "Some Complexities in Computer-Based Systems and Their Implications for System Development", *Proceedings of International Conference on Computer Systems and Software Engineering (CompEuro '90)*, Tel-Aviv, 8-10th May 1990, 344-351, IEEE CS Press.
20. J. Kramer and J. Magee, "Exposing the Skeleton in the Coordination Closet", *Proceedings of Coordination Languages and Models, 2nd International Conference (COORDINATION '97),* Berlin, 1997, 18-31.
21. U. Leonhardt, A. Finkelstein, J. Kramer and B. Nuseibeh, "Decentralised Process Enactment in a Multi-Perspective Development Environment", *Proceedings of 17th International Conference on Software Engineering (ICSE-17)*, Seattle, Washington, USA, 24-28th April 1995, IEEE CS Press.

22. J. Magee, N. Dulay, S. Eisenbach, and J Kramer, "Specifying Distributed Software Architectures", *Proceedings of 5th European Software Engineering Conference (ESEC'95),* 137-153, Sitges, September 1995, LNCS 989, Springer-Verlag, 1995.
23. J. Magee, and J. Kramer, *Concurrency: State Models & Java Programs,* John Wiley & Sons, March 1999, 355 pages.
24. J. Magee, J. Kramer, and D. Giannakopoulou "Behaviour Analysis of Software Architectures", *First Working IFIP Conference on Software Architecture (WICSA1),* San Antonio, Texas, 22-24 February 1999, ed. Patrick Donohoe, (Kluwer Academic Pub.), 1999, 35-50.
25. J. Magee, N. Pryce, D. Giannakopoulou, and J. Kramer, "Graphical Animation of Behaviour Models", *Proceedings of 22nd IEEE/ACM Int. Conf. on Software Engineering (ICSE-2000),* Limerick, Ireland, June 2000, 499-508.
26. G. Mullery, "CORE - a method for controlled requirements expression", *Proceedings of 4th International Conference on Software Engineering (ICSE-4),* 126-135, IEEE CS Press, 1979.
27. C. Nentwich, W. Emmerich, and A. Finkelstein, "Static Consistency Checking for Distributed Specifications, *Proceedings of the 16th International Conference on Automated Software Engineering (ASE-01),* 115-124, Coronado Island, CA, IEEE Computer Society Press, November 2001.
28. C. Nentwich, L. Capra, W. Emmerich, and A. Finkelstein, "xlinkit: a Consistency Checking and Smart Link Generation Service", *ACM Transactions on Internet Technology,* 2(2): 151-185, May 2002.
29. C. Nentwich, W. Emmerich, and A. Finkelstein, "Consistency Management with Repair Actions", *Proceedings of the 25th International Conference on Software Engineering (ICSE-03),* Portland, Oregon, IEEE CS Press, May 2003.
30. B. Nuseibeh and A. Finkelstein, "ViewPoints: A Vehicle for Method and Tool Integration", *Proceedings of the 5th International Workshop on Computer-Aided Software Engineering (CASE '92),* 50-60, Montreal, Canada, 6-10th July 1992, IEEE CS Press.
31. B. Nuseibeh, J. Kramer and A. Finkelstein, "Expressing the Relationships Between Multiple Views in Requirements Specification", *Proceedings of the 15th International Conference on Software Engineering (ICSE-15),* 187-196, Baltimore, Maryland, USA, 17-21st May 1993, IEEE CS Press.
32. B. Nuseibeh, A. Finkelstein and J. Kramer, "Fine-Grain Process Modelling", *Proceedings of the 7th International Workshop on Software Specification and Design (IWSSD-7),* 42-46, Redondo Beach, California, USA, 6-7th December 1993, IEEE CS Press.
33. B. Nuseibeh, "A Multi-Perspective framework for Method Integration", *PhD Thesis,* Department of Computing, Imperial College, London, October 1994.
34. B. Nuseibeh, J. Kramer and A. Finkelstein, "A Framework for Expressing the Relationships Between Multiple Views in Requirements Specification", *Transactions on Software Engineering,* 20(10): 760-773, IEEE CS Press, October 1994.
35. B. Nuseibeh, "To Be And Not To Be: On Managing Inconsistency in Software Development", *Proceedings of 8th International Workshop on Software Specification and Design (IWSSD-8),* 164-169, Schloss Velen, Germany, 22-23 March 1996, IEEE CS Press.
36. B. Nuseibeh, A. Finkelstein and J. Kramer, "Method Engineering for Multi-Perspective Software Development", *Information and Software Technology Journal,* 38(4): 267-274, Elsevier Science B.V., April 1996.
37. B. Nuseibeh, S. Easterbrook and A. Russo, Leveraging Inconsistency in Software Development, *IEEE Computer*, 33(4):24-29, April 2000.
38. B. Nuseibeh, S. Easterbrook and A. Russo, Making Inconsistency Respectable in Software Development, *Journal of Systems and Software,* 58(2):171-180, September 2001, Elsevier Science Publishers.
39. B. Nuseibeh, "Weaving Together Requirements and Architecture", *IEEE Computer,* 34(3):115-117, March 2001.
40. A. Rashid, A. Moreira, J. Araujo, "Modularisation and Composition of Aspectual Requirements", *Proceedings of 2nd International Conference on Aspect-Oriented Software Development,* 17-21st March 2003, Boston, US.
41. A. Russo, B. Nuseibeh, and J. Kramer, "Restructuring Requirements Specifications", *IEE Proceedings: Software,* 146(1): 44-53, February 1999.
42. A. Russo, R. Miller, B. Nuseibeh, and J. Kramer, "An Abductive Approach for Analysing Event-Based Requirements Specifications", *Proceedings of 18th International Conference on Logic Programming (ICLP-02),* Copenhagen, Denmark, 29 July-1 August 2002.
43. G. Spanoudakis, A. Finkelstein, and D. Till, "Overlaps in Requirements Engineering", *Automated Software Engineering,* 6(2):171-198, April 1999.
44. S. Uchitel, J. Kramer, and J. Magee, "Synthesis of Behaviour Models from Scenarios", *IEEE Transactions on Software Engineering,* to appear 2003.
45. L. Vidal, A. Wolf, A. Finkelstein, G. Spanoudakis, *Joint proceedings of the second international software architecture workshop (ISAW-2) and international workshop on multiple perspectives in software development (Viewpoints '96),* San Francisco, USA, ACM SIGSOFT '96, 1996, ISBN:0-89791-867-3.

Invited Papers on the Frontiers of Software Practice

Component Technology - What, Where, and How?

Clemens Szyperski
Microsoft Corporation
research.microsoft.com/~cszypers/

Abstract

Software components, if used properly, offer many software engineering benefits. Yet, they also pose many original challenges starting from quality assurance and ranging to architectural embedding and composability. In addition, the recent movement towards services, as well as the established world of objects, causes many to wonder what purpose components might have.

This extended abstract summarizes the main points of my Frontiers of Software Practice (FOSP) talk at ICSE 2003. The topics covered aim to offer an end-to-end overview of what role components should play, where they should be used, and how this can be achieved. Some key open problems are also pointed out.

1. Why components?

1.1. Words ...

Composition is the act of applying a composition operator (that forms part of a composition model and theory) in a given context. *Components* are the subjects of composition. *Composites* (also called *assemblies*) are the results of composition. This about as much as can be said if we stay at the most abstract level.

To move to meaningful discussion and elaboration, we need to focus in on a particular domain of composition, leading to families of composition models and theories. In this paper, our focus is component software and components are thus *software components* [1,2]. To be sure: there are many component domains in the larger space of software engineering and software architecture. Most of them are not software components, in the sense used here, but that doesn't affect their value – merely their scope of applicability.

Hence, instead of listing technically motivated criteria that capture our domain of discourse, let's explore the ultimate reasons for what software components are meant to achieve. Then, we can work our way backwards and establish useful technical criteria.

1.2. Why components?

There are at least four 'tiers' of motivations for using software components. The oldest tier is along the lines of *Make and Buy*, grounded in the observation that many if not most organizations need to own some edge on top of acquired baseline products. Essentially, organizations need to strike a balance between the promised flexibility and competitive advantage of purpose-built software and the economic advantage of standard software. This is the space of traditional software reuse thinking and, often, it suffices to focus at the level of source components. *Source components* are components that are consumed at software development time and include architectural, design, and source code artifacts.

The second tier follows the line of reusing partial design and implementation fragments across multiple solutions or products. This is the space of software product lines and product line engineering. Often, it suffices to focus on *build-time components*, components that are consumed when building deliverable software out of multiple pieces. Like source components, build-time components do not

0-7695-1877-X/03 $17.00 © 2003 IEEE

necessarily survive the build process as identifiable parts of the deliverable. Traditional linkers are good examples of build-time tools that fuse their input into a single output.

The third tier assumes that components from multiple sources are integrated on site, that is, not as part of the software build process. Such customer-driven integration is typically called *deployment* and the matching components can be called *deployable components*. Deployable components are 'real' software components in the sense that they are units of deployment that, as such, remain identifiable. Deployment is usually distinguished from installation as being the last step allowing for detailed configuration or customization. Once deployed, a component can then be installed on many systems. A good example in this category is a web browser incorporating downloaded components into the functionality of an active web page. While the browser performs automatic installation, it is the web developer that deployed the component (and thus had an opportunity to customize and test it in the context of the particular web site).

The fourth tier is concerned with dynamic servicing, upgrading, extension, and integration of deployed systems. Varying degrees of redeployment and automatic install and uninstall serve this space. The desire grows to engineer solutions that – over their lifetime time – can deal with new and evolving contents, schemas, and services. This leads towards requirements to enter tier four; a tier that is mostly the realm of ongoing research.

1.3. Dynamic Upgrade and Extension

The most refined tier of applying software components, that of dynamic upgrading, extending, and integrating in running systems, is much at the cutting edge of current technology and understanding. Practical use of components today tends to end with the third tier: deployment of components. The most prominent example in this space are application servers (mostly J2EE/EJB and .NET/COM+).

Truly dynamic changes to solutions build on components are extremely challenging in terms of correctness, robustness, and efficiency of the resulting systems. However, even at tier three, most of the problems already surface. It cannot be assumed that an organization that deploys components is capable or willing to perform deep end-to-end integration tests. Even where such tests are performed (because, say, the solution in question is mission critical), it cannot be assumed that the deploying organization can do anything but outright reject the use of a third-party component that has serious problems. In particular, it cannot be expected that such components will be 'fixed' before deployment proceeds.

These observations lead to a quality assurance issue at the component supplier end: since components can be combined into an endless variety of compositions, there is no opportunity to perform any final integration tests at the component supplier's end. Component quality needs to be established in the absence of a closed-world assumption! In other words, component unit tests and other forms of quality assurance, such as verification of component properties, are of critical importance.

Truly dynamic contents and truly open sets of services cannot be handled by closed software. The resulting need to support tier four components grows as standards in the space of XML and web services lead to the broad availability of open contents and dynamically located service functionality. To cope with such situations, systems need to on-demand locate, install, and integrate components – or remotely use the dynamically discovered services.

A strong motivator to move into this technically difficult area is the desire to integrate across organizational boundaries. From enterprise application integration (EAI), to business-to-consumer and business-to-business (B2C and B2B) scenarios, to full peer-to-peer (P2P), it gets ever less likely that homogeneous schemas and protocols can be assumed.

1.4. Component maturity model

The multiple tiers of component concepts explored in the previous section, coupled with the observation that higher tiers require more refined competencies, lead to a simple *component maturity model*. (The familiarity of the resulting acronym is entirely coincidental.) In order of increasing organizational maturity requirements, the following levels can be distinguished:

1. *Maintainability*: modular solutions
2. *Internal reuse*: product lines
3.a.1 *Closed composition*: make and buy from closed pool of organizations
3.a.2 *Open composition*: make and buy from open market
3.b *Dynamic upgrade*
4. *Open and dynamic*

Somewhat depressingly, the state of the art of many software solutions doesn't even embrace modularity. Even advanced organizations are presently concerned with mostly level 2 issues.

Level 3 forks into two parallel options that, in combination, form level 4. The first fork opens solutions for third-party contributions – in two steps from select ('pooled') sources to open markets. The second fork opens solutions for dynamic upgrade. It is the combination of these two forks that leads to the most demanding forms of component use.

1.5. Compositional reasoning

To climb up the maturity ladder towards mastering systems that support open and dynamic composition, effective *compositional reasoning* at all levels is required. Compositional reasoning builds on modular reasoning: the ability to reason within confined scopes without needing to resort to any form of global inspection or analysis. In a proper compositional-reasoning framework, the results from modular reasoning 'survive' application of useful composition operators.

Some will say: 'Hey, it's just mathematics!' However, there is much room for future work. For instance, predictable assembly is a focus of current research: how can important assembly properties be predicted reliably, assuming just the known properties of components used and the known inference rules of a particular composition theory. Assembly properties of interest span the range of both functional and extra-functional properties.

2. What's a component?

2.1. What's a Software Component anyway?

The analysis of what it is that we would want from software components (sketched in the previous section), leads to a first approximation of what such components have to be. In particular, a software component has to be a *unit of deployment*. Furthermore, to enable dynamic scenarios, it has to also be a *unit of versioning and replacement*.

To be a unit of deployment, a software component has to be an executable deliverable for a (virtual) machine. To be machine executable, no human intervention should be required to turn the combination of a deployable component and a deployment descriptor into an installable component, ready for execution. This is because deployment is not a development activity and does not happen at the component supplier's site. While the deployment process does provide extra information (captured in a deployment descriptor), it shouldn't require a build environment or the presence of a developer.

To be a unit of replacement and versioning, it is important that a deployed software component remains invariant as it gets installed onto possibly many systems. That is, installed components should carry any *no observable state*. Therefore, software components live at the level of packages, modules, or classes, and not at the level of objects or distributed objects.

To fully explore the space of code and data, in their co-packaging in a component, it is useful to view software components as a collection of modules and resources. Modules contain immutable code (for instance, in the form of a set of classes). Resources contain immutable data (for instance, in the form of serialized objects). Immutable metadata can be contained in both modules (describing code) and in resources (describing data). In a deployed component (that is, an installable component), deployment information may have been folded into resources, modules, or both. For instance, some application server implementations meet requirements found in deployment descriptors by generating modified code from the code found in a deployable component.

2.2. What is Deployment?

Acquisition is the process of obtaining a software component; as discussed above, such a component arrives in deployable form. *Deployment* is the process of readying such a component for installation in a specific environment. The degrees of deployment freedom are typically captured in *deployment descriptors*, where deployment corresponds to filling in parameters of a deployment descriptor.

Installation is the process that follows deployment and that is often automated. Installation makes a component available on a particular host in a particular environment.

Loading is the process of enabling an installed component in a particular runtime context, such as a process. If a component carries definitions for 'static' (or 'global') variables, then these are instantiated as a side effect of loading. Finer-grained *instantiation* in the object-oriented sense follows loading and operates over parts of a loaded component (typically classes). Where instances have persistent state, such state is not carried by a software component, but needs to be mapped into a specific external store.

3. Components in Context

A software component:

- assumes architectural embedding;
- presents functionality via interfaces (these are called 'incoming' or provides-interfaces);
- has parametric dependencies via interfaces (called 'outgoing' or requires-interfaces);
- has static dependencies;
- targets specific component platform;
- requires other components; and
- requires per-instance context.

Of these, provides-interfaces are the traditional focus as they seem to capture the abstraction implemented by a component. Ignoring the others leads to implementations that cannot be composed. For example, classes do not compose in general.

To enable composition (and thus components that deserve their name), all significant dependencies and assumptions of a component's implementation also need to be captured.

Architectural embedding and various forms of dependencies are discussed in more detail in the following subsections. Per instance contexts are not discussed in this paper; this category includes the process hosting an instance and the container (or context) enclosing it.

3.1. Architectural embedding

Specifications (and implementations!) need to be grounded in a framework of common understanding. At the root is a common *ontology*, ensuring agreed upon terminology and domain concepts. Equally important are accepted conventions and best practice. In combination, these allow separate parties to communicate and (importantly) silently share a substantial context of assumptions.

Architecture contributes top-level factorings of quality responsibilities and reference models. Building on such reference models (or reference architecture), components can be designed that target specific niches. The result is that components do not fit into solutions by coincidence but by construction. Problems of component adaptation and impedance mismatch are reduced to exceptional situations. In other words, all good engineering minimizes the need for adapters.

(Note that 'glue code' is misnamed if it includes adaptation logic. Glue, in the real world, works only if applied to surfaces that already match each other closely. Gluing is not an adaptation but a composition technology.)

3.2. Parametric dependencies

To enable the use of components in many compositions, it is important that instance-level dependencies can be configured. A requires-interface is a means to this end: it states what an instance would need to function. In its simplest incarnation, a requires-interface is just the type of an instance variable. Setting that variable to refer to some other instance of appropriate type is then equivalent to *connecting* the two instances. Requires-interfaces lead to *parametric dependencies* because the dependency on the interface type does not imply the use of any particular (complete) implementation.

The concept of requires-interfaces can be generalized to *requires-types*. Exploring suitable type and composition systems is the subject of ongoing research. Examples include certain module systems, units, mixin layers, and parametric contracts.

Parametric dependencies are usually preferred over static component dependencies. However, not all static dependencies can be eliminated (following subsection). In addition, it is surprisingly possible to model parametric dependencies as a special case of static dependencies. The idea is to treat the type of the requires-interface as a regular type that is packaged as part of the metadata contained in some other component. In the limit case, all static type dependencies can be decoupled from implementation choices by only allowing static dependencies on pure metadata (pure types without any attached implementation).

Components that contain no implementation but only metadata are useful for reasons of reflection, dynamic composition, and so on.

3.3. Static dependencies

Static dependencies fall into three categories: dependencies on the component platform, dependencies on other components, and dependencies on the deployment context.

Dependencies on the *component platform* are ultimately unavoidable since it isn't practical to aim to parameterize everything. Examples of such dependencies include:

- the deployment format; required to even recognize a component as one – think JAR/EAR files or .NET assemblies;
- the (virtual) machine model – including the instruction set;
- mechanisms such as proof-carrying code for various forms of verification;
- ways to access well-known services – addressing the bootstrap problem (consider directory service);
- the supported *component model*: what is a component on this platform? What is the security model? Or that for authentication, trust, or certification?

Dependencies on other components serve many purposes. Ultimately, at least one such dependency per used component must exist somewhere or else that component would not even be loaded. (In highly configurable systems the single dependency might exist in a configuration file. However, in a pure model, that file would itself be the resource part of a component.)

An extreme form of static inter-component dependencies is a traditional Modula-2 or Ada style module system. Every module carries a list of static imports of other modules. There is no compositional freedom – each module is added in exactly one way.

At the other end is an extreme approach of no dependencies on other components at all. This could be called the game machine approach, since gaming machines (like Playstation, GameCube, or XBox) traditionally assume close to no software pre-installed on the machine and everything coming with the game. Such a game can be modeled as one (huge) component that has no dependencies on other components. The result is that no integration is provided above hardware primitives. If the hardware layer opens any communication channel, such as access to the Internet, then any component that carries a network stack can communicate with any other component that does so as well. This is an example of entirely parametric dependencies.

Dependencies on the *deployment context* are a per-instance concept. Each instance created by a component is placed in a context: an operating system process, a COM apartment, a COM+ context, an EJB container, a CLR AppDomains, and so on. Sometimes, deployment contexts are 'woven' into a component at (or before) deployment time or into instances. This corresponds to techniques used for static and dynamic aspect-oriented programming, respectively.

3.4. Atomic vs. composite components

Atomic components are created 'from first principles'. To make composition models generally useful, they need to provide for hierarchical composition means. Indeed, by simply treating composites as components again, hierarchical composition is a natural outcome.

A composite references the components over which it composes and typically adds modules or resources (or both) of its own that encapsulate the actual composition operator applications. That is, a module in a composite might contain the 'glue code' that instantiates and connects the components. Alternatively, a composite's resources could contain a serialized graph of instances that represent a composition prototype. Instantiating a composite amounts to executing its glue code or deserializing its prototype instance graph. (Since a composite is still just a collection of modules and resources, no extension of the general component characterization above is needed.)

It is important to understand that composites do *not* contain the components over which they compose. That is, all components exist in a flat universe. This is an important property, as it allows servicing of components without having to know all places where that component has been used. (A practically important example of servicing is the closing of a security hole.)

4. Naming, versioning, side-by-side

The technical process leading to software components is complex. The total number of components that may coexist in a system is huge. Component developers need to be able to name components without risking collisions with other developers. Components developers also need to be able to release new versions of their components; especially if they have been successful. Component deployers need to rely on strong component naming to ensure that the right components come into play. Component deployers also need to be able to affect versioning resolution to maintain robust configurations.

4.1. Making a component

The making of a component involves a large number of different inputs and typically involves a complex process and likely many individuals. (The latter is not true for fine-grained components. However, the former remains as fine-grained components are likely build in large sets, requiring significant build systems for economies of scale.)

Inputs into the build system delivering a deployable software component include:

- The collection of sources;
- all tools used, including compilers, transformers, generators, optimizers, linkers;
- referenced artifacts, such as other components listed as static dependencies;
- the build system itself, including the settings in the build environment.

4.2. Component versioning

Every input into the build process potentially affects the built component. That is obviously and intentionally the case for the sources. The impact of the build environment is easily underestimated. Only very careful build system setups or methods reduce this impact. For instance, search paths are a wide-spread evil. Referenced artifacts are expected to have an impact at the level of exposed metadata, but unless care is used, unexpected dependencies can sneak in. An example is the unintended propagation of compiler optimizations, such as offset calculations.

While it is generally understood that all involved tools have an impact, it is difficult to fully account for these dependencies. For instance, upgrading a compiler to a newer version can easily lead to different components, even if everything else is unchanged and even if the old and new compiler versions are provably equivalent. (The new component might have different performance or footprint characteristics.)

Thus, unless the resulting bits are one-for-one identical, it has to be assumed that a new version has been produced. This is a conservative rule, but moving to a more precise one requires great semantic care: Functional and extra-functional refinement need to be demonstrated, which is definitely hard in the general case.

4.3. Versioning and side-by-side

Version changes have transitive impact. Consider a component A that the makers of a component B used in its version 1. The makers of a component C used A as well, but in its version 2. A problem arises if another party is interested in using B and C in the same context. That is, if that latter party wishes to build a component D that depends on B and C, then loading D requires transitive loading of A – but in two different versions.

There are two fundamental strategies: either A is loaded only once (forcing B to roll forward to version 2 of A) or each version of A is loaded (forcing A and all its clients to tolerate the side-by-side existence of two versions in the same context).

In order to treat this situation soundly, components need to ship with an unambiguous name, which needs to include their version designation. Also, dependencies on other components need to be recorded explicitly, completely, and in a version-precise way. Finally, a component needs to indicate whether it can be loaded side-by-side in multiple versions or whether it should be rolled forward to the latest version available.

Then, as a design discipline, side-by-side components need to be factored from non-side-by-side ones. Deployed configurations need to allow for the coexistence of side-by-sideable versions and need to bind to the correct versions.

4.4. Side-by-side challenges

Fully supporting side-by-side installation of the majority of components promises the greatest degree of isolation and thus system robustness in the presence of component versioning. At the other end, in-place upgrading of components guarantees the occurrence of the phenomenon known as 'DLL hell'.

The problem with side-by-side support is its interference with cross-component integration. The degree of coupling between any two components determines how feasible side-by-side installations are. The most lightweight form of coupling is through shared pure types and contracts, the most heavyweight through dependencies on implementation detail.

To enable side-by-side integration for at least the most lightweight coupling, it is important to support at least the side-by-side existence of type versions and the simultaneous use of multiple versions of a type within a single component. For instance, if a class implements an interface in multiple versions, then the methods on those interfaces should not be 'folded' into a single implementation – a common mechanism in several popular object-oriented languages.

Enabling proper side-by-side coupling through other dependencies is increasingly harder. The case of side-by-side implementation inheritance is known to the surgeon general to lead to serious health risks.

5. What's a service?

Software services, especially in the specific shape of XML web services, are promising new levels of software integration and interoperability. Understanding how they relate to software components is critically important to benefit from the distinct properties of services without losing the separate advantages of components.

To put it simply, a service is an instantiated configured system that is run by a providing organization. That is, a service is fully grounded. Ultimately, it includes the power supply to the server machines as well as the organization that somehow manages to pay the power bill.

The service-providing organization installs, runs, maintains, and evolves hardware and software infrastructure and components. It provides physical and organizational means, including functions like client management, accounting, and so on.

5.1. Service-level agreements

Since a service is fully grounded and backed by a provider, it can be held to the standards of a service-level agreement (SLA) or a service contract. For instance, a service client signing such a contract with a provider might pay for the service, while the provider guarantees properties such as minimal up-time, performance, or capacity.

It is possible to abstract from the service instance to a suitable service type. At that level, services behave much like objects and service types like classes. External composition of services is just as limited as it is for objects and classes. However, the granularity is very different: viable services are much heavier than typical objects. Therefore, there is a trade-off between the strong guarantees and the limited composability that a service can offer.

Component properties, in contrast, are captured in technical contract between component and client implementers. Such contracts cannot offer service levels, but can (and should) offer parametric means to establish service levels when using a component to build a service. For example, while a component cannot guarantee performance or up-time, it can express its performance or redundancy needs relative to its parametric dependencies.

5.2. Contracts galore

Services, through the possible service-level agreements, offer per-use value in ways that components do not. It is thus justified (and common practice in other industries) to charge for services on a per-use or subscription basis. Such income offsets the real cost of providing a service, leading to plausible business models.

The offering of services under service-level agreements cannot be performed with absolute reliability. This is a standard aspect of any business and established mechanisms such as auditing and insurance can be used to mitigate the business risk.

The corresponding mechanisms in the component space are very different: components can be verified and certified to meet their specifications (contracts). In the ideal case of total verification, this is a once-and-for-all activity. Once published, a component remains an immutable artifact. Auditing a component, for example, is only meaningful when deployed into a full system, which makes it only a part of the larger activity of auditing a service.

6. Component specification and test

Compositions tend to exhibit a weakest link phenomenon: many compositions are as strong as the weakest component they compose over. Composites can be made stronger than that by applying error containing and handling mechanisms that ultimately rely on various forms of redundancy.

Even in the presence of such measures it is usually effective to aim for a higher reliability of the used components. Reliability of software is a curious notion: in a sense, a correct component is 100% reliable and a component that has the slightest defect is actually incorrect and thus 100% unreliable. In practice, defects do not show in all configurations and not under all load profiles. Therefore, reliability becomes an interesting measure, one asking for a careful foundation, though.

Instead of pursuing this thought further, the following subsections focus on ways to get components closer to correctness.

6.1. Component contracts

As explained earlier, interfaces play a crucial role in any world of components. Assuming that each interface has an attached specification (contract), there are two correlations over sets of interfaces that can be considered. Both turn out to be important in practice, though most approaches (including the one discussed in the following subsections) only focus on the former.

The first correlation is among all requires and provides-interfaces of a single component. One way to look at such a correlation is to view it as a set of invariants that couple model variables (specification variables) of the involved interfaces. For example, consider a component that has a provides-interface that delivers values that are the result of applying a transformation over values acquired through a requires-interface. The per-interface contract of the provides-interface should not mention the requires-interface (or its contract). Instead, it will contain a model variable referring to the abstract stream of incoming values. Likewise, the requires-interface introduces a model variable for the abstract stream of received values. The component-level invariant correlates the two by stating that these two model variables are always of equal value.

The second correlation is sort of dual to the first: it considers interfaces occurring on multiple components and how they need to be correlated to enable useful protocols. The only example known to the author of such inter-component interface correlations are Hans Jonkers' interaction specifications.

Such fine factoring of interfaces and their specifications is itself an interesting challenge. One way to even achieve at interfaces rather than classes is to use role-based modeling. That is, instead of following the path of entity-based or object-oriented modeling, roles are identified and fleshed out. Atomic roles lead to interfaces. Combined roles turn into multiply-derived interfaces that derive without adding any new features. The contracts of such combining interfaces are non-trivial as they correlate model variables introduced by the combined interfaces. (In a sense, such combining interfaces represent a third form of interface contract correlation.)

Once finely factored interfaces are identified, entities or objects that combine multiple interfaces can then be introduced in endless variations. However, the questions of how to specify contracts at this level, how to capture, validate, verify, or test remain.

6.2. One concrete approach: AsmL

There are many specification languages and approaches that support componentization to varying degrees. An example is the abstract state-machine language (AsmL) that is based on the theory of abstract state machines (formerly called evolving algebras). AsmL is being developed by the Foundations of Software Engineering (FSE) team at Microsoft Research in Redmond. The language definition, tutorials, and tools are freely available from their site: *http://research.microsoft.com/fse/*.

AsmL is used as an example here because it is now being used by some Microsoft product groups, leading to a practical refinement of the toolset. Nevertheless, AsmL is work in progress. Also, no claim is made that AsmL will ultimately be the one and only such tool and approach.

At the heart of ASM is the intention to capture operational semantics at a level of abstraction natural to the modeled process. Concretely, AsmL supports *executable model classes* and, inspired by the needs of component technology, *rich interfaces*. Originally targeting COM, the AsmL tools have been retargeted and extended such that AsmL is now a first-class CLR-hosted language. Rich interfaces combine all information required to generate full CLR interfaces with model-level specifications. Models can be a combination of declarative specifications (pre- and postconditions, assertions, invariants) and executable specifications (model programs). Atomic transactions, non-determinism, and mathematical types (such as sets, maps and sequences) help preventing overspecification: the single biggest danger when using operational semantics.

The connection between implementations and model specifications is established through abstraction functions. Test harnesses can use these functions to observe implementation state and test that it meets predicted model state. Declarative aspects of the specification can be injected into implementations to run-time check invariants, pre- and postconditions.

The overall emphasis of AsmL is on specification capture, validation, and implementation test, including automated test case generation. Clear opportunities for verification, checking, and correctness by construction (such as formal refinement) are present, but presently not exploited.

6.3. Example

Below is an example of a simple interface (*System.Collections.IEnumerator*, part of the .NET Framework).

```
interface IEnumerator
{
  object Current { get; }
  bool MoveNext ();
  void Reset ();
}
```

One possible informal specification is captured in the following paragraph:

> Initially, the enumerator is positioned before the first element in the collection. *Reset* also brings the enumerator back to this position. At this position, calling *Current* throws an exception. Therefore, you must call *MoveNext* to advance the enumerator to the first element of the collection before reading the value of *Current*. *Current* returns the same object until either *MoveNext* or *Reset* is called. *MoveNext* sets *Current* to the next element.

A formal AsmL specification of the same interface takes the following shape:

```
public interface IEnumerator
  public var visited as Set of Object
  public var unvisited as Set of Object
  public var current as Object
```

Here, *visited* is the set of elements 'handed out', *unvisited* is the rest of the elements, and *current* is a distinguished element. The specification of *Reset* is:

```
public Reset()
  ensure
    resulting current = null
  and
    resulting visited = {}
  and
    resulting unvisited = unvisited + visited
```

The clause *ensure* states a postcondition, where the modifier *resulting* refers to the after state of that variable and where the + operator denotes set union. A possible implementation of *Reset* might look like:

```
public class MyEnumerator:
System.Collections.IEnumerator
{
  private object[] myElements;
  private int myIndex = -1;
  ...
  public void Reset()
  {
    myIndex = 0;        // ERROR: should be -1
  }
  ...
}
```

6.4. *Abstraction Functions*

An abstraction function is now used to connect the *Reset* implementation to its specification. For example, it establishes that *current* is *null* if *myIndex* has the value -1 and that it has the value stored at *myElements*[*myIndex*] otherwise.

Since the range of abstraction functions covers AsmL types and since AsmL supports the full set of CLS and most of CTS types, it is possible to define abstraction functions in AsmL. (CLS and CTS are the common language specification and the common type system specification accompanying the CLR. The CTS is the union of all CLR-supported type concepts. The CLS is the CTS subset that is used to enable inter-language interoperability.)

Special so-called shadow fields in AsmL specifications grant access to private implementation fields. Here is the abstraction function for the model variable *unvisited*:

```
public property unvisited as Set of Object
  get
   return { myElements(i)
     | i in [myIndex+1..myElements.Length-1] }
```

6.5. *Test of Implementation*

Unit tests are performed simply by using the test subject in a number of test cases. There is no need to write a test oracle, since the specification can be evaluated to determine whether results are as specified or not. In the above running example, the following simple test (written in AsmL) will spot the error in *Reset*:

```
MyEnumerator e = new MyEnumerator();
while (e.MoveNext())
  Console.WriteLine("{0}", e.Current);

e.Reset();  // implementation error caught here
while (e.MoveNext())
  Console.WriteLine("{0}", e.Current);
```

6.6. *CIL Weaving on CLR*

The AsmL weaver is a tool that takes compiled AsmL and a compiled test subject and weaves them into a single CLR assembly. AsmL itself is implemented as a first-class CLR-hosted language. Thus, the weaver operates over two CLR assemblies, essentially merging condition checking code generated from the specification into the implementation code of the test subject. This approach enables the use of AsmL for specification and test of code implemented in any language hosted on the CLR.

7. Acknowledgements

I'd like to thank Mike Barnett, of the Microsoft Research FSE team, for providing the running AsmL example used in section 6.

8. References

Instead of providing a necessarily insufficient, incomplete, and in many ways unfair selection of references, I simply point to two recent books of mine that provide much deeper coverage and references.

[1] D.G. Messerschmitt and C. Szyperski, *Software Ecosystem – Understanding an Indispensable Industry and Technology*, MIT Press, 2003. (To appear.)

[2] C. Szyperski, *Component Software – Beyond Object-Oriented Programming*, second edition, Addison-Wesley, Harlow, England, 2002. (First edition, 1998.)

Patterns, Frameworks, and Middleware: Their Synergistic Relationships

Douglas C. Schmidt
douglas.c.schmidt@vanderbilt.edu
Electrical Engineering & Computer Science
Vanderbilt University
Nashville Tennessee, USA*

Frank Buschmann
Frank.Buschmann@mchp.siemens.de
Corporate Research
Siemens, AG
Munich, Germany

Abstract

The knowledge required to develop complex software has historically existed in programming folklore, the heads of experienced developers, or buried deep in the code. These locations are not ideal since the effort required to capture and evolve this knowledge is expensive, time-consuming, and error-prone. Many popular software modeling methods and tools address certain aspects of these problems by documenting how *a system is designed. However, they only support limited portions of software development and do not articulate* why *a system is designed in a particular way, which complicates subsequent software reuse and evolution.*

Patterns, frameworks, and middleware are increasingly popular techniques for addressing key aspects of the challenges outlined above. Patterns codify reusable design expertise that provides time-proven solutions to commonly occurring software problems that arise in particular contexts and domains. Frameworks provide both a reusable product-line architecture [1] – guided by patterns – for a family of related applications and an integrated set of collaborating components that implement concrete realizations of the architecture. Middleware is reusable software that leverages patterns and frameworks to bridge the gap between the functional requirements of applications and the underlying operating systems, network protocol stacks, and databases. This paper presents an overview of patterns, frameworks, and middleware, describes how these technologies complement each other to enhance reuse and productivity, and then illustrates how they have been applied successfully in practice to improve the reusability and quality of complex software systems.

1 Introduction

Emerging trends and challenges. Despite significant advances in computers, networks, programming languages, and software methodologies, developing quality applications on time and within budget remains hard. Some problems stem from the growing demands placed on software, such as requirements to provide predictable, reliable, scalable, and secure quality of service (QoS) simultaneously. Other problems stem from the propensity to rediscover and reinvent core software artifacts, such as programming languages, operating systems, networking protocols, and software component libraries. Moreover, the heterogeneity of hardware architectures, diversity of operating system (OS) and network platforms, and stiff global competition makes it increasingly infeasible to build high-quality software from scratch.

In today's time-to-market-driven environments, building quality software in cost-effective manner requires the *systematic reuse* of successful software models, designs, and implementations that have already been developed and tested. Unlike opportunistic reuse (in which developers simply cut and paste code from existing programs to create new ones), systematic reuse is an intentional and concerted effort to create and apply multiuse software artifacts throughout an organization. In a well-honed systematic reuse process, each new project leverages time-proven designs and implementations, mostly just adding new code that is specific to a particular application, and only refactoring existing software architectures and designs when they become inadequate to cover the evolving business cases and variability in the supported domains. Systematic reuse is essential to increase software productivity and quality by breaking the costly cycle of rediscovering, reinventing, and revalidating common software artifacts. Throughout the rest of the paper when we use the term "reuse" we therefore always mean "systematic reuse."

The skills required to develop, deploy, and support reusable software have traditionally been a "black art" practiced only by expert developers and architects. Moreover, these technical impediments to reuse are often exacerbated by a myriad of nontechnical impediments, such as organizational, economic, administrative, political, sociological, and psychological factors. It's therefore not surprising that significant levels of software reuse have been slow to materialize in many projects and

*This work was supported in part by DARPA, NSF, and Siemens.

0-7695-1877-X/03 $17.00 © 2003 IEEE

organizations.

Solution approach → Middleware, framework, and patterns. *Middleware* [2] is software that can significantly increase reuse by providing readily usable, standard solutions to common programming tasks, such as persistent storage, (de)marshaling, message buffering and queueing, request demultiplexing, and concurrency control. Developers who use middleware can therefore focus primarily on application-oriented topics, such as business logic, rather than wrestling with tedious and error-prone details associated with programming infrastructure software using lower-level OS APIs and mechanisms.

Over the past decade a number of middleware standards have emerged and matured. Some of these standards, such as the Common Object Request Broker Architecture (CORBA), are open systems sanctioned by international organizations, such as the Object Management Group (OMG). Other middleware standards, such as Java virtual machines, Jave 2 Enterprise Edition (J2EE), and .NET, have emerged from industry consortia and market leaders.

Crucial to the success of standard middleware are the *patterns* [3, 4, 5] and *frameworks* [6, 7] that reify the knowledge of how to develop and apply the middleware and applications that run atop it. Patterns support the reuse of design expertise by articulating the static and dynamic aspects of successful solutions to problems that arise when building software in a particular context. Frameworks are concrete realizations of groups of patterns that enable reuse of code by (1) capturing the common abstractions of an application domain – both their structure and mechanisms – while (2) yielding control of application-specific structure and behavior to application developers.

During the past decade a number of influential R&D efforts [4, 8, 5, 9, 10, 11, 12, 13] have focused on documenting patterns and developing frameworks that enable the effective development and reuse of middleware. As a result, middleware is now commonly developed using frameworks based on strategized composition and optimization patterns. These patterns and frameworks guide the integration and configuration of middleware that can meet the functional and QoS requirements of particular application domains more effectively than can realistically be developed manually from scratch in time-to-market driven environments.

The relationship between middleware, frameworks, and patterns is highly synergistic. For example, patterns help guide framework design and use, thereby reducing software development effort and training costs. In turn, frameworks can be used to develop middleware for product-line architectures [1], whose interfaces then provide application software with a simpler facade to access the powerful (and complex) internal component structure of the frameworks. Likewise, frameworks and patterns support the development of product-line architectures for specific application domains, such as warehouse management or hot rolling mill process automation [14], that apply particular types of middleware. A contribution of this paper is to illustrate by examples how these three technologies relate and complement each other.

Paper organization. The remainder of this paper is organized as follows: Section 2 presents an taxonomy of the layers of middleware; Sections 3 and 4 describe the key properties of frameworks and patterns, respectively; Section 5 then illustrates the synergies between all three technologies via a case study of how frameworks and patterns have been applied in practice to develop middleware for distributed real-time and embedded systems; Section 6 summarizes promising areas of future R&D; and Section 7 presents concluding remarks.

2 An Overview of Middleware

Some of the most successful techniques and tools devised to enhance the reuse of software center on middleware that helps manage the complexity and heterogeneity of distributed applications. This *distributed computing middleware* (henceforth referred to simply as *middleware*) provides reusable software that functionally bridges the gap between (1) end-to-end application functional requirements and (2) the lower-level operating systems, networking protocol stacks, databases, and hardware devices. Middleware provides reusable capabilities whose qualities are critical to help simplify and coordinate how application software is connected and how it interoperates.

Just as networking protocol stacks can be decomposed into multiple layers, such as the physical, data-link, network, transport, session, presentation, and application layers, so to can middleware be decomposed into the multiple layers [2] shown in Figure 1 and described in the remainder of this section.

Host infrastructure middleware encapsulates and enhances native OS mechanisms to create reusable event demultiplexing, interprocess communication, concurrency, and synchronization objects, such as reactors; acceptors, connectors, and service handlers; monitor objects; active objects; and service configurators [9, 10]. By encapsulating the peculiarities of particular operating systems, these reusable objects help eliminate many tedious, error-prone, and non-portable aspects of developing and maintaining application software via low-level OS programming APIs, such as Sockets or POSIX pthreads.

Common host infrastructure middleware includes the Sun Java Virtual Machine (JVM) and Microsoft's Common Language Runtime (CLR), which provide platform-independent ways of executing code by abstracting the differences between operating systems and CPU architectures. The ADAPTIVE Communication Environment (ACE) [9, 10] is portable

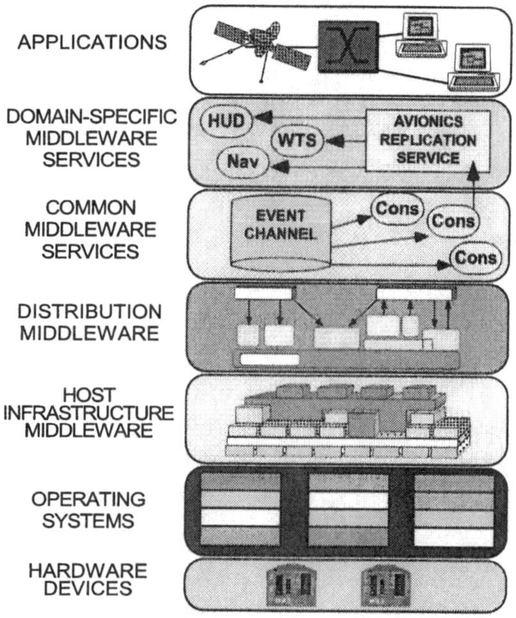

Figure 1: Middleware Layers in Context

C++ host infrastructure middleware that encapsulates native operating system capabilities, such as connection establishment, event demultiplexing, interprocess communication, (de)marshaling, dynamic configuration of application components, concurrency, and synchronization.

Distribution middleware defines higher-level distributed programming models whose reusable APIs and objects automate and extend the native OS mechanisms encapsulated by host infrastructure middleware. Distribution middleware enables clients to program applications by invoking operations on target objects without hard-coding dependencies on their location, programming language, OS platform, communication protocols and interconnects, and hardware.

At the heart of distribution middleware are request brokers, such as The OMG's Common Object Request Broker Architecture (CORBA) and Sun's Java Remote Method Invocation (RMI). The request brokers allow objects to interoperate across networks regardless of the platform on which they are deployed. SOAP is an emerging distribution middleware technology based on an XML-based protocol that allows applications to exchange structured and typed information on the Web using various Internet protocols, such as HTTP, SMTP, and MIME.

Common middleware services augment distribution middleware by defining higher-level domain-independent reusable services that allow application developers to concentrate on programming business logic, without the need to write the "plumbing" code required to develop distributed applications via lower-level middleware directly. For example, common middleware service providers bundle transactional behavior, security, and database connection pooling and threading into reusable components, so that application developers no longer need to write code that handles these tasks.

Whereas distribution middleware focuses largely on managing end-system resources in support of an object-oriented distributed programming model, common middleware services focus on allocating, scheduling, and coordinating various resources throughout a distributed system using a component programming and scripting model. Developers can reuse these component services to manage global resources and perform common distribution tasks that would otherwise be implemented in an *ad hoc* manner within each application. The form and content of these services will continue to evolve as the requirements on the applications being constructed expand.

Examples of common middleware services include the OMG's CORBA Common Object Services, such as event notification, logging, multimedia streaming, persistence, security, global time, real-time scheduling, fault tolerance, concurrency control, and transactions. Likewise, Sun's Enterprise Java Beans (EJB) technology and Microsoft's .NET allows developers to create n-tier distributed systems by linking a number of pre-built software service components without having to write much code manually.

Domain-specific middleware services are tailored to the requirements of particular domains, such as telecom, e-commerce, health care, process automation, or aerospace. Unlike the other three middleware layers discussed above that provide broadly reusable "horizontal" mechanisms and services, domain-specific middleware services are targeted at "vertical" markets and product-line architectures. Since they embody knowledge of a domain, moreover, reusable domain-specific middleware services have the most potential to increase the quality and decrease the cycle-time and effort required to develop particular types of application software.

An example of domain-specific middleware services includes the Siemens Medical Solutions Group has developed `syngo` (`www.syngo.com`), which is a product-line architecture that is both an integrated collection of domain-specific middleware services, as well as an open and dynamically extensible application server platform for medical imaging tasks and applications, including ultrasound, mammography, angiography, computer tomography, magnetic resonance, and nuclear medicine. The Boeing Bold Stroke [15, 16] product-line architecture is another example of domain-specific middleware. Bold Stroke uses COTS hardware and middleware to produce a non-proprietary, standards-based component architecture for military avionics mission computing capabilities, such as navigation, display management, sensor management and situational awareness, data link management, and weapons control.

As the products associated with the reusable middleware

layers summarized above have matured and become pervasive throughout the industry, the total amount of software that application developers must write has shrunk substantially. However, reduction in application developer effort also implies more work for middleware developers since they become responsible for an increasing number of software layers. While some believe that the techniques used to develop reusable middleware are simply implementation details, in practice these choices have a significant impact on other key middleware qualities, such as its affordability, extensibility, flexibility, portability, predictability, efficiency, reliability, scalability, and trustworthiness.

As a result, middleware developers must themselves apply more powerful reuse technologies to simplify the evolution of their software layers. Not surprisingly, frameworks and patterns are increasingly applied to improve the reusability and quality of both middleware and application software. The remainder of this paper presents overviews of frameworks and patterns and then shows how these technologies can be combined with middleware to enhance software reuse. It is important to note, however, that the reuse potential of frameworks and patterns is *not* limited to middleware!

3 Overview of Frameworks

As outlined in the previous section, in today's competitive, fast-paced computing industry, successful middleware and application software must possess (1) **affordability**, to ensure that the total ownership costs of software acquisition and evolution are not prohibitively high, (2) **extensibility**, to support successions of quick updates and additions to address new requirements and take advantage of emerging markets, (3) **flexibility**, to support a growing range of multimedia data types, traffic flows, and end-to-end QoS requirements, (4) **portability**, to reduce the effort required to support applications on heterogeneous OS platforms and compilers, (5) **predictability** and **efficiency**, to provide low latency to delay-sensitive real-time applications, high performance to bandwidth-intensive applications, and usability over low-bandwidth networks, such as wireless links, (6) **reliability**, to ensure that applications are robust and tolerant of faults, (7) **scalability**, to enable applications to handle large numbers of clients simultaneously, and (8) **trustworthiness**, to ensure integrity, confidentiality, and availability in distributed systems.

When software is developed monolithically, *i.e.*, as tightly coupled clumps of functionality that are not organized modularly or hierarchically, it is hard to achieve these qualities. *Frameworks* [6, 7] have emerged as a powerful technology for developing and reusing middleware and application software that possess the qualities listed above. Figure 2 illustrates the three characteristics of frameworks [17] described below that

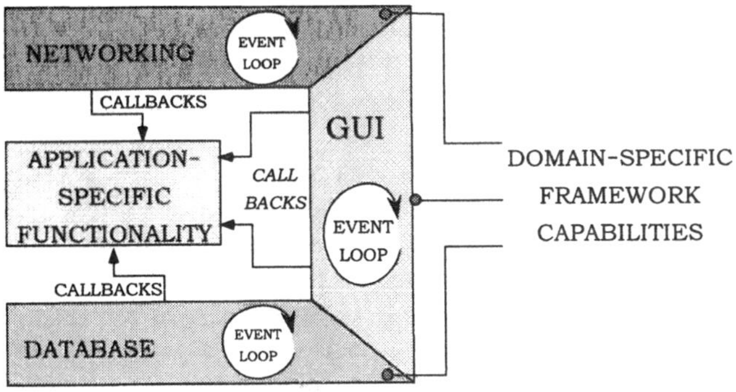

Figure 2: Relationships Between Framework Components

help them to achieve these qualities.[1]

- **A framework exhibits "inversion of control" at run time via callbacks** to component hook methods after the occurrence of an event, such as a mouse click or data arriving on a network connection. When an event occurs, the framework calls back to a virtual hook method in a pre-registered component, which then performs application-defined processing in response to the event. The virtual hook methods in the components decouple the application software from the reusable framework software, which makes it easier to extend and customize the applications as long as the interaction protocols and QoS properties are not violated.
- **A framework provides an integrated set of domain-specific structures and functionality.** Reuse of software depends largely on how well frameworks model the commonalities and variabilities [19] in application domains, such as business data processing, telecom call processing, graphical user interfaces, or real-time middleware. By leveraging the domain knowledge and prior efforts of experienced developers, frameworks embody common solutions to recurring application requirements and software design challenges that need not be recreated and revalidated for each new application.
- **A framework is a "semi-complete" application** that programmers can customize to form complete applications by extending reusable components in the framework. In particular, frameworks help abstract the canonical control flow of applications in a domain into product-line architectures and families of related components. At runtime, these components can collaborate to integrate customizable application-independent reusable code with customized application-defined code.

Since frameworks exhibit inversion of control, they can sim-

[1]While there are subtle technical distinctions between frameworks and components [18, 10], we subsume components into the discussion of frameworks below.

plify application design because the framework—rather than the application—runs the event loop to detect events, demultiplex events to event handlers, and dispatch hook methods on the handlers that process the events. Since frameworks reify the key roles and relationships of components in application domains, the amount of reusable code increases and the amount of code rewritten for each application decreases dramatically. Since a framework is a semi-complete application, it enables larger-scale reuse of software than can be achieved by reusing individual components or stand-alone functions.

Developers in certain domains have applied frameworks successfully for several decades. Early frameworks, such as MacApp, X-windows, and Interviews, originated in the domain of graphical user interfaces (GUIs). Java Swing and Microsoft Foundation Classes (MFC) are contemporary GUI frameworks that are widely used to create graphical applications on PC platforms. The broad adoption of reusable GUI frameworks has yielded many productivity and quality benefits for business and desktop applications.

Building upon their success in the GUI domain, frameworks are now being applied to many new and more complex domains [6, 7, 20]. For example, ACE and TAO described in Section 5.1 are frameworks for host infrastructure and distribution middleware, JBoss and BEA's WebLogic Server are component frameworks for application servers, and many recent R&D efforts, such as the Open Grid Service Infrastructure (OGSI), focus on frameworks for web services. There are also frameworks for specific application domains, such as SAP, and application frameworks for medical imaging systems, such as the Syngo platform. These frameworks are increasingly aligning with the layers of middleware standards and domain-specific product-line architectures discussed in Section 2.

4 Overview of Patterns

Developers of middleware and application software must address many challenges related to complex design and programming topics, such as persistence, data organization, connection management, service initialization, distribution, concurrency control, flow control, error handling, event loop integration, and dependability. Many of these challenges occur repeatedly in many applications and domains. Until the mid-1990's, the knowledge needed to resolve these challenges existed largely in programming folklore, the heads of expert researchers and developers, or buried deep in complex source code. These locations are not ideal because

- Discovering patterns from source code is expensive and time-consuming since it is hard to separate the essence of a design from its implementation details.
- If the insights and rationale of experienced designers are not documented, they will be lost over time and thus cannot be used to guide subsequent software evolution.
- Without guidance from earlier work, software developers must engineering complex systems from the ground up, rather than by reusing proven solutions.

Over the past decade, experienced software developers and architects have helped to address these problems by creating a body of literature that documents the following types of reusable knowledge:

- **Design patterns** [3], which provide a scheme for refining the elements of a software system and the relationships between them, and describe a common structure of communicating elements that solves a general design problem within a particular context.
- **Architectural patterns** [4], which express the fundamental, overall structural organization of software systems and provide a set of predefined subsystems, specify their responsibilities, and include guidelines for organizing the relationships between them.
- **Pattern languages** [21], which weave together a web of related patterns to define a vocabulary for talking about software development problems and provide a process for the orderly resolution of these problems.

Patterns help enhance reuse by capturing and reusing the static and dynamic structure and collaboration of key participants in software designs. They are particularly useful for documenting recurring micro-architectures, which are abstractions of software components that experienced developers apply to resolve common design and implementation problems. By studying and applying patterns and pattern languages, developers can often escape traps and pitfalls that have been avoided traditionally only via long and costly apprenticeships [22]. Patterns also raise the level of discourse in project design and programming activities, which helps improve team productivity and software quality.

Figure 3 illustrates the relationships amongst a pattern language [5] that addresses service access and configuration, event handling, interprocess communication, concurrency, and synchronization dimensions in various networked application domains, such as online financial services, remote process control, avionics mission computing, and telecommunications.[2] The relationships in this diagram reveal the following ways in which the patterns complement and complete each other in multiple ways to form a pattern language:

- Although each pattern is useful in isolation, the pattern language is even more powerful, because it integrates solutions to particular problems in important technical areas, such as event handling, connection management and

[2]Since it is beyond the scope of this paper to describe each pattern in detail, please see the references [5] for comprehensive coverage of these patterns.

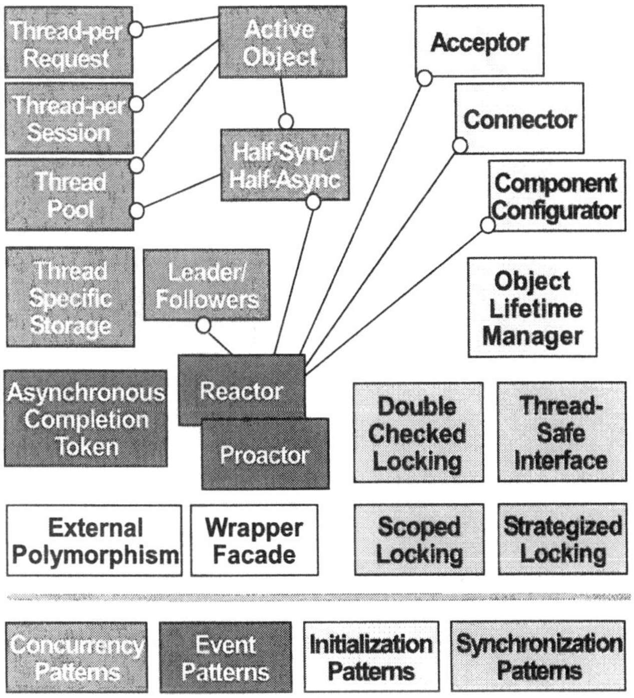

Figure 3: A Pattern Language for Network Programming

service access, concurrency models, and synchronization strategies. Each problem in these areas must be resolved coherently and consistently when developing concurrent and networked applications.

- The pattern language also exposes the interdependencies of these technical areas. For example, when selecting a particular event-handling pattern for a networked application, not all potentially-available concurrency patterns can be applied usefully.
- A pattern language describes an entire solution space for developing a particular type of system, system part, or system aspect – by offering alternative solutions to certain problems. A pattern language can therefore be applied many, many times without ever producing exactly the same architecture, design, or implementation. Yet each individual architecture, design, and implementation follows the same timeless, thus reusable, design knowledge embedded in each pattern language [23].

These three points become clear only when connecting patterns into a pattern language since each pattern in isolation only focuses on itself. In contrast, a pattern language-based design integrates the patterns consistently and synergistically by giving concrete and precise guidance in developing a specific (type of) system or system aspect. In particular, a pattern language conveys what are the key problems to be resolved, in what order should they be tackled, what alternatives exist for resolving a given problem, how are mutual dependencies between the problems handled, and how is each individual problem resolved effectively in the presence of its associated problems.

Many pattern languages exist today. Some support the creation of a specific types of software, such as the pattern languages for networked and concurrent computing [5] and enterprise application architectures [13]. Others pattern languages help to realize a certain part, subsystem, or large component of a software system. For instance, there is a pattern language for server components [12] that describes how to build well-structured server-side components. Yet other languages focus on a particular problem area of relevance in software, such as handling erroneous user input [24] and designing user-friendly interfaces to computer and information systems [25]. There are also pattern languages for good programming style and practice, such as Smalltalk best practice patterns [26], C++ reference accounting [27], and Java exception handling [28]. Section 6 describes other key areas where we expect future pattern languages will be published.

5 Illustrating the Synergies of Middleware, Frameworks, and Patterns

Sections 2–4 present overviews of middleware, frameworks, and patterns, emphasizing their particular contributions to software reuse. This section examines these technologies in terms of their relationships and synergies. To make the discussion tangible, we focus on The ACE ORB (TAO) [29] as a case study to illustrate how patterns and frameworks can help middleware developers build and evolve software by reducing the coupling between its components.

5.1 Overview of CORBA and TAO

CORBA Object Request Brokers (ORBs) [30] allow clients to invoke operations on distributed objects without concern for object location, programming language, OS platform, communication protocols and interconnects, and hardware. Figure 4 illustrates the components in the CORBA reference model, which collaborate to provide the portability, interoperability, and transparency mentioned above. The client stubs marshal client operations into General Inter-ORB Protocol (GIOP) requests that are transmitted to objects via the standard Internet Inter ORB Protocol (IIOP)[3] implemented in the ORB Core. The server ORB Core demultiplexes and receives these requests using one or more threads and passes them to the Object Adapter. The Object Adapter demultiplexes the requests to skeletons, which demarshal the requests and dispatch the

[3] IIOP is implemented atop TCP/IP.

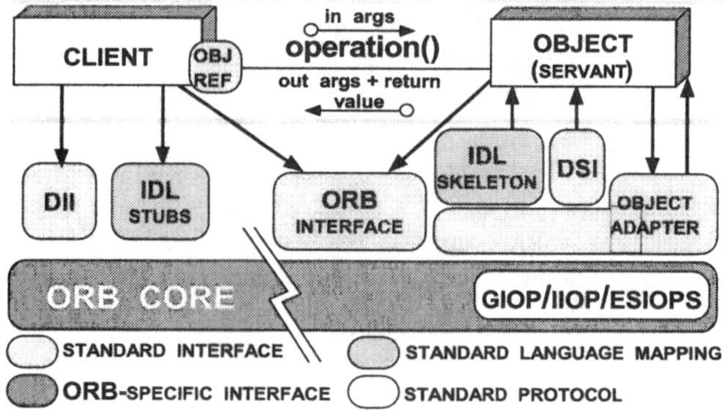

Figure 4: Components in the CORBA Reference Model

appropriate application-level servant method that implements the object's operation.

The ACE ORB (TAO) [29] is a high-performance, real-time implementation of the CORBA 3.0 specification [31] that supports the distribution middleware capabilities shown in Figure 4 and described in Section 2. TAO is targeted for applications with deterministic and statistical QoS requirements, as well as best effort requirements. As its name suggests, TAO is developed using the frameworks and components in the ACE host infrastructure middleware. ACE and TAO are open-source software that has evolved organically over the past decade. They are used in hundreds of production software systems in research labs and commercial projects, including avionics mission computing systems at Boeing, satellite communication systems at Lockheed and Raytheon, telecommunication systems at BBN, Cisco, Lucent, Motorola, Nortel, and Siemens, medical systems at GE, and online trading systems at Automated Trading Desk. Complete source code and documentation for ACE and TAO is available at `www.cs.wustl.edu/~schmidt/TAO/`.

5.2 Applying Patterns and Frameworks to TAO Middleware

The interfaces, protocols, and components shown in Figure 4 illustrate the primary capabilities provided by the CORBA reference architecture. As is often the case with architectural diagrams, however, it is not clear from this figure *how* the architecture behaves or *why* the architecture is designed the way it is. Naturally, a thorough understanding of these issues is essential to develop, configure, optimize, and evolve the reusable middleware effectively. To address these issues, we outline the key patterns and frameworks used by TAO's ORB Core to illustrate the synergies between these two reuse technologies in terms of improving the extensibility, maintainability, and performance of distribution middleware.

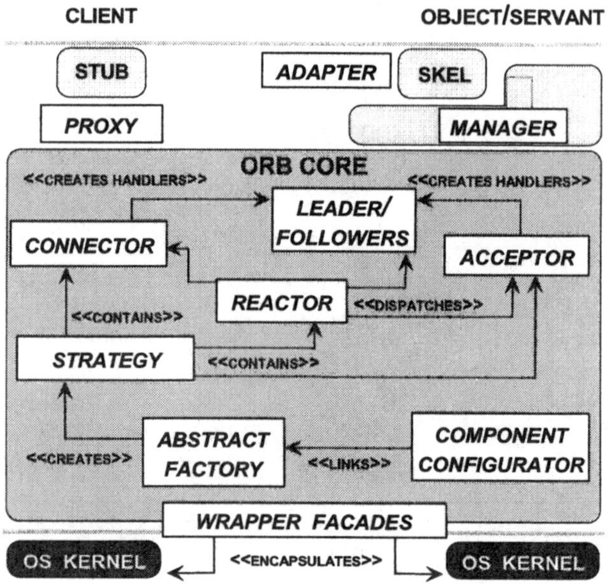

Figure 5: The Patterns Used in TAO

The key patterns used in the TAO ORB are shown in Figure 5 and described below:

- The **Wrapper Facade** pattern [5] simplifies the OS system programming interface by combining multiple related OS mechanisms, such as the socket API or POSIX threads, into cohesive OO abstractions. TAO uses this pattern to enhance its reuse by encapsulating the tedious, non-portable, and non-typesafe low-level OS system functions within C++ classes.
- The **Reactor** pattern [5] allows event-driven applications to react to events originating from a number of disparate sources, such as I/O handles, timers, and signals. TAO uses this pattern to dispatch ORB connection and I/O handlers in response to events that occur in the OS kernel.
- The **Acceptor-Connector** pattern [5] decouples the connection and initialization of cooperating peer services in a networked application from the processing they perform after being connected and initialized. TAO uses this pattern in its ORB Core to actively/passively establish connections and create I/O handlers that exchange GIOP messages independently of the underlying transports.
- The **Leader Followers** pattern [5] provides an efficient concurrency model where multiple threads take turns calling a synchronous event demultiplexer (such as `select()`) on sets of I/O handles to detect, demultiplex, dispatch, and process service requests that occur. TAO uses this pattern to improve its performance and predictability by reducing context switching, synchronization, and data allocation/movement overhead.
- The **Strategy** pattern [3] provides a means to select one of several candidate policies or algorithms and packaging

it with an object. This pattern is the foundation of TAO's extensible software architecture and makes it possible to configure custom ORB strategies for connection management, concurrency, and demultiplexing.

- The **Abstract Factory** pattern [3] provides a single component that builds related objects. TAO uses this pattern to create and consolidate its many strategy objects into a manageable number of abstract factories that can be reconfigured *en masse* into its ORB Core conveniently and consistently. TAO components use these factories to access related strategies without explicitly specifying their subclass name.
- The **Component Configurator** pattern [5] permits dynamic run-time configuration of abstract factories and strategies in an ORB [5]. TAO uses this pattern to dynamically link the abstract factories that produce custom ORB personalities, such as a high-throughput ORB, a predictable real-time ORB, or a small footprint ORB.
- The **Proxy** pattern [4, 3] defines a object (the proxy) that acts as surrogate for a (potentially remote) target object. TAO uses this pattern to perform the (de)marshaling operations defined by CORBA stubs.
- The **Adapter** pattern [3] allows objects to work together that have different interfaces. TAO uses this pattern in its object adapters and skeletons to integrate object implementations (servants) with the reusable ORB code. An object adapter also implements the **Manager** pattern [4] to control the lifecycle of the objects and servants it contains.

Knowing the patterns used in TAO is useful since it enables reuse of abstract design and architecture knowledge. However, reuse of patterns alone is insufficient since it does not directly yield flexible and efficient software. We therefore found it necessary to augment our study of patterns with the creation and use of the frameworks provided by ACE. These frameworks help developers of TAO middleware avoid costly reinvention of common software artifacts by refactoring recurring implementation roles. They also provide direct knowledge transfer by embodying patterns in a powerful toolkit that contains middleware domain experience and working code.

The primary ACE frameworks used in TAO's ORB Core are shown in Figure 6. Below, we describe each framework, outline which pattern(s) it implements, and discuss how it enhances reuse.

- The **Reactor** framework implements the Reactor and Leader/Followers patterns to facilitate a concurrency model where events indicating the ability to begin I/O operations. This framework enhances reuse in TAO by automating the detection, demultiplexing, and dispatching of *handlers* in response to I/O, timer, and signal events. The ACE Reactor drives the main event loop

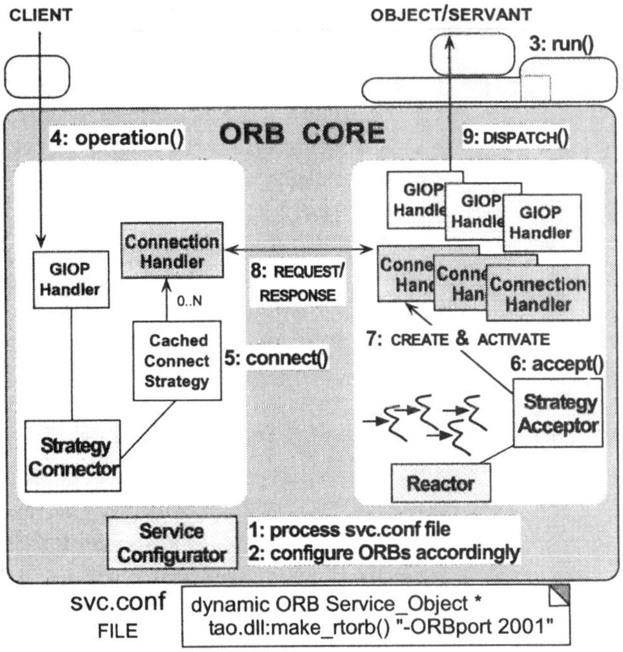

Figure 6: The ACE Frameworks Used in TAO

in TAO, which accepts connections and receives/sends client GIOP requests/responses via a pool of threads.

- The **Acceptor-Connector** framework leverages the Reactor framework and implements the Acceptor-Connector and Strategy patterns to decouple the active and passive initialization roles from application-defined service processing performed by communicating peer services after initialization is complete. This ACE framework enhances reuse by defining (1) *strategy connector* objects that automatically establish connections with servers and initialize handlers that transmit GIOP requests and (2) *strategy acceptor* objects that automatically accept connections from clients and initialize handlers that process GIOP requests from clients.

- The **Service Configurator** framework implements the Component Configurator pattern to support the flexible configuration of ORBs whose strategies can be determined and deployed at the appropriate time in the design cycle, *e.g.*, via the `svc.conf` configuration script at installation time and/or run time. This framework enhances reuse by enabling ORB abstract factories (and the strategies they embody) to be treated as interchangeable building blocks. Software with high availability requirements, such as online transaction processing or real-time industrial process automation, often require these flexible configuration capabilities.

The design of the ACE frameworks presented above is guided by many of the patterns shown in Figures 3 and 5. TAO uses these patterns and the ACE frameworks that reify them to develop an extensible ORB architecture. However, the patterns and frameworks described here are not limited to middleware. In fact, they have been applied in many other application domains, including telecom call processing [32] and switching [8], airplane flight control systems [15], multimedia videoconferencing [33], distributed interactive simulations [34], and enterprise business applications [20].

The patterns described above help to solve many common problems that arise when developing and using frameworks for middleware and applications. In the context of TAO, for example, a deep understanding of these patterns helps to

- **Preserve important design information** for developers who enhance and maintain the TAO middleware. Since scores of developers have worked on TAO over the past decade, this information would be lost if it was not documented, which would increase software entropy and decrease software maintainability and quality. The metrics reported in [35] quantify the extent to which knowledge of patterns helped to reduce the development and maintenance effort for TAO.
- **Guide design choices** for developers who are building new middleware and applications using TAO. The books in which the patterns outlined above appear document the common traps and pitfalls of developing middleware. This information helps TAO developers select suitable architectures, protocols, algorithms, and platform features without wasting time and effort (re)implementing solutions that have been shown to be inefficient or error prone.

5.3 Evaluating the Synergies Between Middleware, Frameworks, and Patterns

The short case study above illustrates how patterns and frameworks are both important techniques to achieve large-scale reuse by capturing successful software development strategies within a particular context, which in this case was distribution and host infrastructure middleware. All three of these technologies help to simplify the development, configuration, and optimization of software by codifying the accumulated expertise of developers who have successfully confronted similar problems before as follows:

- Frameworks codify this expertise in the form of reusable algorithms and component implementations.
- Patterns codify this expertise at a complementary level of reuse – recurring architectural design themes – which may be reused even when the algorithms or component implementations are not directly reusable.
- Middleware codifies this expertise in the form of interfaces and standard components that provide applications with a simpler facade to access the powerful (and complex) internal component structure of frameworks.

For example, as shown in our case study above, TAO middleware developers are more effective since the frameworks in ACE implement the core patterns associated with service access and configuration, event handling, interprocess communication, concurrency, and synchronization.

It is important to recognize that middleware, frameworks, and patterns are highly synergistic concepts, with none subordinate to the other [18]. Patterns can be characterized as more abstract descriptions of frameworks, which are often independent of a particular programming language, operating system, network, or database environment. Patterns have been used to document frameworks and middleware. Sophisticated middleware frameworks are concrete realizations of groups of dozens to hundreds of patterns. A framework also integrates various approaches to problems where there are no *a priori* context-independent and optimal solutions.

6 Future R&D Focus Areas

Over the past decade, R&D on patterns, frameworks, and middleware has focused largely on developing and refining the core concepts and infrastructure that can create the foundations for subsequent efforts [6, 7]. As a result of these advances, we expect the next generation of middleware will be developed using frameworks that consciously embody time-proven patterns. Patterns will also increasingly be used to document the form, content, and best practices of middleware and frameworks. Other key topics and domains that will benefit from the foundational work conducted thus far will include:

- **Distributed real-time and embedded systems**. An increasing number of patterns associated with middleware frameworks for concurrent and networked objects have been documented during the past five years [36, 5, 35]. A key next step is to document the patterns for distributed real-time and embedded (DRE) systems, which extends earlier work to focus on effective strategies and tactics for managing key QoS properties in DRE systems, including network bandwidth and latency, CPU speed, memory access time, and power levels. Since developing high-quality DRE systems is hard and remains somewhat of a "black art," relatively few reusable patterns [37, 38], frameworks [39], and middleware [29] exist for this domain today. We expect an increased focus on DRE systems in the future, however, due to the maturation of reusable object technology, together with the development tools, techniques, and processes that enable it to be applied successfully in the DRE domain.

- **Mobile systems**. Wireless networks are becoming pervasive and embedded devices are become smaller, lighter, and more capable. Thus, mobile systems will soon support many consumer communication and computing needs. Application areas for mobile systems include ubiquitous computing, mobile agents, personal assistants, position-dependent information provision, remote medical diagnostics and teleradiology, and home and office automation. In addition, Internet services, ranging from Web browsing to on-line banking, will be accessed from mobile systems. Mobile systems present many challenges, such as managing low and variable bandwidth and power, adapting to frequent disruptions in connectivity and service quality, diverging protocols, and maintaining cache consistency across disconnected network nodes. We expect that experienced developers of mobile systems will capture their expertise in the form of reusable pattern, frameworks, and middleware to help meet the growing demand for quality software in this area.
- **Adaptive QoS for COTS systems**. Distributed applications, such as streaming video, Internet telephony, and large-scale interactive simulation systems, have increasingly stringent QoS. To reduce development cycle-time and cost, these applications are increasingly being developed using multiple layers of COTS hardware, operating systems, and middleware components, such as those presented in Section 2. Historically, however, it has been hard to configure COTS-based systems that can simultaneously satisfy multiple QoS properties, such as security, timeliness, and fault tolerance [40]. As developers and integrators continue to master the complexities of providing end-to-end QoS guarantees, it is essential that they document the successful patterns and reify them in the form of reusable adaptive and reflective middleware frameworks [41] to help others configure, monitor, and control COTS-based distributed systems that possess a range of interdependent QoS properties.

7 Concluding Remarks

Application software has historically been developed largely from scratch. This development process has been applied many times in many companies, by many projects in parallel. Even worse, it has been applied by the same teams in a series of projects. Regrettably, this continuous rediscovery and reinvention of core concepts and code has kept costs unnecessarily high throughout the software development life cycle. This problem is exacerbated by the inherent diversity of today's hardware, operating systems, compilers, and communication platforms, which keep shifting the foundations of application software development.

In today's competitive, time-to-market-driven environments, it is increasingly infeasible to develop custom solutions manually from scratch. Such solutions are hard to customize and tune, because so much effort is spent just trying to make the software operational. Moreover, as requirements change over time, evolving custom software solutions becomes prohibitively expensive. End-users expect–or at least desire–software to be affordable, robust, efficient, and agile, which is hard to achieve without the solid architectural underpinnings achievable via systematic reuse.

The past decade has yielded significant progress in reuse of software in the form of the maturation of standard middleware, the documentation of patterns, and the development and adoption of frameworks. These software technologies provide the following general types of improvement for developing and evolving application software:

1. **Open standards**, which provide a portable and interoperable set of software artifacts, such as interoperable security, layered distributed resource management, and fault tolerance services. An increasingly important role is being played by open and/or standard COTS middleware frameworks that can be purchased or acquired via open-source means. COTS middleware frameworks are particularly important for organizations facing time-to-market pressures and limited software development resources.
2. **Strategic focus**, which elevates application developer focus beyond a preoccupation with low-level OS APIs. For example, the standard middleware artifacts outlined above help to direct the focus of developers toward higher-level software application architecture and design concerns. Without needing to worry as much about low-level details, developers can focus on more strategic, application-oriented concerns.
3. **Design reuse**, patterns are essential to guiding developers through the steps necessary to ensure successful creation and deployment of complex software systems. In particular, patterns enable developers to reuse higher-level software application designs, such as publisher/subscriber architectures, micro-kernels, and brokers [4]. These design artifacts represent some of the key strategic aspects of complex software. If they are understood and applied properly, the impact of many vexing complexities can be alleviated greatly.
4. **Implementation reuse**, which amortizes software life-cycle effort by leveraging previous development expertise and reifying implementations of key patterns [5, 3] into reusable middleware frameworks. In the future, most applications will be assembled by integrating and scripting domain-specific and common "pluggable" middleware service components, rather than being programmed entirely from scratch.

Despite their natural synergies, however, middleware, frameworks, and patterns are not silver bullets. They cannot, for example, absolve developers from responsibility for solving all complex concurrent and networked software analysis, design, implementation, validation, and optimization problems. Ultimately there is no substitute for human creativity, experience, discipline, diligence, and judgement. When used together properly, however, the technologies described in this paper help alleviate many inherent and accidental software complexities.

References

[1] P. Clements and L. Northrop, *Software Product Lines: Practices and Patterns*. Boston: Addison-Wesley, 2002.

[2] R. E. Schantz and D. C. Schmidt, "Middleware for Distributed Systems: Evolving the Common Structure for Network-centric Applications," in *Encyclopedia of Software Engineering* (J. Marciniak and G. Telecki, eds.), New York: Wiley & Sons, 2002.

[3] E. Gamma, R. Helm, R. Johnson, and J. Vlissides, *Design Patterns: Elements of Reusable Object-Oriented Software*. Reading, MA: Addison-Wesley, 1995.

[4] F. Buschmann, R. Meunier, H. Rohnert, P. Sommerlad, and M. Stal, *Pattern-Oriented Software Architecture—A System of Patterns*. New York: Wiley & Sons, 1996.

[5] D. C. Schmidt, M. Stal, H. Rohnert, and F. Buschmann, *Pattern-Oriented Software Architecture: Patterns for Concurrent and Networked Objects, Volume 2*. New York: Wiley & Sons, 2000.

[6] M. Fayad, R. Johnson, and D. C. Schmidt, eds., *Implementing Application Frameworks: Object-Oriented Frameworks at Work*. New York: Wiley & Sons, 1999.

[7] M. Fayad, R. Johnson, and D. C. Schmidt, eds., *Building Application Frameworks: Object-Oriented Foundations of Framework Design*. New York: Wiley & Sons, 1999.

[8] H. Hueni, R. Johnson, and R. Engel, "A Framework for Network Protocol Software," in *Proceedings of OOPSLA '95*, (Austin, TX), ACM, Oct. 1995.

[9] D. C. Schmidt and S. D. Huston, *C++ Network Programming, Volume 1: Mastering Complexity with ACE and Patterns*. Boston: Addison-Wesley, 2002.

[10] D. C. Schmidt and S. D. Huston, *C++ Network Programming, Volume 2: Systematic Reuse with ACE and Frameworks*. Reading, Massachusetts: Addison-Wesley, 2002.

[11] D. Alur, J. Crupi, and D. Malks, *Core J2EE Patterns: Best Practices and Design Strategies*. Prentice Hall, 2001.

[12] M. Volter, A. Schmid, and E.Wolff, *Server Component Patterns – Component Infrastructures illustrated with EJB*. New York: Wiley & Sons, 2002.

[13] M. Fowler, D. Rice, M. Foemmel, E. Hieatt, R. Mee, and R. Stafford, *Patterns of Enterprise Application Architecture*. Reading, Massachusetts: Addison-Wesley, 2002.

[14] F. Buschmann, A. Geisler, T. Heimke, and C. Schuderer, "Framework-Based Software Architectures for Process Automation Systems," in *Proceedings of the 9th IFAC Symposium on Automation in Mining, Mineral, and Metal Processing*, (Cologne, Germany), 1998.

[15] D. C. Sharp, "Reducing Avionics Software Cost Through Component Based Product Line Development," in *Proceedings of the 10th Annual Software Technology Conference*, Apr. 1998.

[16] B. S. Doerr and D. C. Sharp, "Freeing Product Line Architectures from Execution Dependencies," in *Proceedings of the 11th Annual Software Technology Conference*, Apr. 1999.

[17] R. Johnson and B. Foote, "Designing Reusable Classes," *Journal of Object-Oriented Programming*, vol. 1, pp. 22–35, June/July 1988.

[18] R. Johnson, "Frameworks = Patterns + Components," *Communications of the ACM*, vol. 40, Oct. 1997.

[19] J. Coplien, D. Hoffman, and D. Weiss, "Commonality and Variability in Software Engineering," *IEEE Software*, vol. 15, November/December 1998.

[20] M. Fayad and R. Johnson, eds., *Domain-Specific Application Frameworks: Frameworks Experience by Industry*. New York: Wiley & Sons, 1999.

[21] C. Alexander, S. Ishikawa, M. Silverstein, M. Jacobson, I. Fiksdahl-King, and S. Angel, *A Pattern Language*. New York, NY: Oxford University Press, 1977.

[22] J. O. Coplien and D. C. Schmidt, eds., *Pattern Languages of Program Design*. Reading, Massachusetts: Addison-Wesley, 1995.

[23] C. Alexander, *The Timeless Way of Building*. New York, NY: Oxford University Press, 1979.

[24] W. Cunningham, "The CHECKS Pattern Language of Information Integrity," in *Pattern Languages of Program Design* (J. O. Coplien and D. C. Schmidt, eds.), Reading, Massachusetts: Addison-Wesley, 1995.

[25] J. Borchers, *"A Pattern Approach To Interaction Design"*. New York: Wiley & Sons, 2001.

[26] K. Beck, *Smalltalk Best Practice Patterns*. Englewood Cliffs, NJ: Prentice-Hall, 1997.

[27] K. Henney, "C++ Patterns - Reference Accounting," in *Proceedings of the EuroPLoP 2002 conference*, (Irsee, Germany), July 2002.

[28] A. Haase, "Java Idioms: Exception Handling," in *Proceedings of the EuroPLoP 2003 conference*, (Irsee, Germany), July 2003.

[29] D. C. Schmidt, D. L. Levine, and S. Mungee, "The Design and Performance of Real-Time Object Request Brokers," *Computer Communications*, vol. 21, pp. 294–324, Apr. 1998.

[30] M. Henning and S. Vinoski, *Advanced CORBA Programming with C++*. Reading, MA: Addison-Wesley, 1999.

[31] Object Management Group, *The Common Object Request Broker: Architecture and Specification*, 3.0 ed., June 2002.

[32] G. Meszaros, "A Pattern Language for Improving the Capacity of Reactive Systems," in *Pattern Languages of Program Design* (J. O. Coplien, J. Vlissides, and N. Kerth, eds.), Reading, Massachusetts: Addison-Wesley, 1996.

[33] D. C. Schmidt, V. Kachroo, Y. Krishnamurthy, and F. Kuhns, "Applying QoS-enabled Distributed Object Computing Middleware to Next-generation Distributed Applications," *IEEE Communications Magazine*, vol. 38, pp. 112–123, Oct. 2000.

[34] R. Noseworthy, "IKE 2 – Implementing the Stateful Distributed Object Paradigm ," in *5th IEEE International Symposium on Object-Oriented Real-Time Distributed Computing (ISORC 2002)*, (Washington, DC), IEEE, Apr. 2002.

[35] D. C. Schmidt and C. Cleeland, "Applying Patterns to Develop Extensible ORB Middleware," *IEEE Communications Magazine*, vol. 37, Apr. 1999.

[36] D. Lea, *Concurrent Programming in Java: Design Principles and Patterns, Second Edition*. Boston: Addison-Wesley, 2000.

[37] D. Lea and J. Marlowe, "PSL: Protocols and Pragmatics for Open Systems," in *Proceedings of the* 9th *European Conference on Object-Oriented Programming*, (Aarhus, Denmark), ACM, Aug. 1995.

[38] J. Noble and C. Weir, *Small Memory Software: Patterns for Systems with Limited Memory*. Boston: Addison-Wesley, 2001.

[39] D. C. Schmidt, "R&D Advances in Middleware for Distributed, Real-time, and Embedded Systems," *Communications of the ACM special issue on Middleware*, vol. 45, pp. 43–48, June 2002.

[40] J. A. Zinky, D. E. Bakken, and R. Schantz, "Architectural Support for Quality of Service for CORBA Objects," *Theory and Practice of Object Systems*, vol. 3, no. 1, pp. 1–20, 1997.

[41] F. Kon, F. Costa, G. Blair, and R. H. Campbell, "The Case for Reflective Middleware," *Communications ACM*, vol. 45, pp. 33–38, June 2002.

Cybersecurity

Richard A. Kemmerer

Department of Computer Science
University of California Santa Barbara
kemm@cs.ucsb.edu

Abstract

As more business activities are being automated and an increasing number of computers are being used to store sensitive information, the need for secure computer systems becomes more apparent. This need is even more apparent as systems and applications are being distributed and accessed via an insecure network, such as the Internet. The Internet itself has become critical for governments, companies, financial institutions, and millions of everyday users. Networks of computers support a multitude of activities whose loss would all but cripple these organizations. As a consequence, cybersecurity issues have become national security issues. Protecting the Internet is a difficult task.

Cybersecurity can be obtained only through systematic development; it can not be achieved through haphazard seat-of-the-pants methods. Applying software engineering techniques to the problem is a step in the right direction. However, software engineers need to be aware of the risks and security issues associated with the design, development, and deployment of network-based software.

This paper introduces some known threats to cybersecurity, categorizes the threats, and analyzes protection mechanisms and techniques for countering the threats. Approaches to prevent, detect, and respond to cyber attacks are also discussed.

1. Introduction

In recent years, networks have evolved from a mere means of communication to a ubiquitous computational infrastructure. Networks have become larger, faster, and highly dynamic. The pervasive use of computer and network technologies in all walks of life has turned cybersecurity issues into national security issues.

1.1. How bad is it?

On September 11, 2001, the World Trade Center attack gave an example of how our lives can be affected by a single terrorist act. Within days of this physical attack, while the nation was still adjusting to the tragic loss of lives and property, an Internet worm cyber attack, called Nimda, spread nationwide in less than an hour and attacked 86,000 computers. This event raised our consciousness to how vulnerable to cyber attacks our systems are.

The latest Internet worm, called the Sapphire/Slammer SQL worm, is another example of how vulnerable systems on the Internet are and of how fast these worms can spread. According to preliminary analysis of the Sapphire worm performed by Silicon Defense and researchers at UC Berkeley [27] this was the fastest worm to date. It was able to spread worldwide in approximately 10 minutes, doubling in size every 8.5 seconds. According to their report, at its peak, which it reached just 3 minutes after its release, it "scanned the net at over 55 million IP addresses per second. It infected at least 75,000 victims and probably considerably more."

1.2. Why is it so bad?

Computers are everywhere. Almost everything that we do in our daily lives depends on computers and computer networks. The Internet has become a mission-critical infrastructure for governments, companies, and financial institutions. Computers and networks are used for controlling and managing manufacturing processes, water supplies, the electric power grid, air traffic control systems, and stock market systems, to mention a few. As a consequence, network attacks have started to impact the practical aspects of our lives.

Today's networks are very heterogeneous environments where highly critical software applications (e.g., the control system for a dam) run side-by-side with other non-critical network-based applications (e.g., a mail server). As a con-

0-7695-1877-X/03 $17.00 © 2003 IEEE

sequence, cyber attacks against apparently "non-critical" services may produce unforeseen side effects of devastating proportions.

The number, severity, sophistication, and cost of reported attacks is increasing [3]. Unfortunately, many attacks are not even detected; therefore, things are even worse than reported. That is, attackers are often able to hide their tracks by disabling logging facilities or modifying event logs, so their activity goes undetected.

The perpetrators of these attacks vary considerably. At the low end are *script kiddies*, who are usually unsophisticated users that download malicious software from hacker web sites and follow the posted instructions to execute an attack on some target. These attacks are often only annoyance attacks, but they can be more severe. At the next level are *hackers* who are trying to prove to their peers or to the world that they can compromise a specific system, such as a government web site. Next are *insiders*, who are legitimate users of a system that either access information that they should not have access to or damage the system or data because they are disgruntled. Insiders are often less knowledgeable then hackers, but they are often more dangerous because they have legal access to resources that the hackers need to access illegally. Next are organizational-level attacks. In this case, the organization's resources are used to get information illegally or to cause damage or deny access to other organizations to further the attacking organization's gain. These can be legitimate organizations, such as two companies bidding on the same contract where one wants to know the other's bid in order to make a better offer. They could also be criminal organizations that are committing fraud or some other illegal activity. At the highest level is the nation state that is trying to spy on or cause damage to another state. This level used to be called "national lab" attackers, because the attackers have a substantial amount of resources at their disposal, comparable to those that are available to researchers at a national lab, such as Los Alamos Laboratory or Lawrence Livermore Laboratory. After the September 11, 2001 terrorist attacks on the World Trade Center, the idea of nation state level cyber attacks being carried out by terrorists became a big concern.

In addition to the rising threat, as nation level attacks become more plausible, the vulnerabilities have also increased. One cause of this is that in addition to virtually every business being on the Internet, today most homes are also connected. This has become particularly true with the advent of relatively inexpensive DSL and cable connections. To make things worse, most home users do not know that their systems are vulnerable. They often say "I have nothing to hide," or "I don't care if someone else sees the information on my computer." Most of these users do not use a firewall, and they think that because their system came with an antivirus program they are protected. They often do not realize that virus programs need to be updated regularly. A big problem is that home users are not aware that their systems can serve as a jump off point for other attacks. In fact, many of the denial of service attacks use unsuspecting home computers as *zombies* to be awaken at a specific time to unwittingly accomplish a distributed denial of service.

Another reason that things are so bad is because, for the most part, computer security is reactive. That is, system administrators and security professionals are usually reacting to the latest attack. After they fix the vulnerability that allowed the attack, the attackers look for new vulnerabilities to exploit for new attacks. What is needed is a proactive approach.

Security is also expensive, both in dollars and in time taken from normal everyday tasks. As a result, security vulnerabilities often exist not because there is not a known fix, but because some administrator does not have the time to put in a patch to fix the problem.

Finally, there is not now, and never will be, a system with perfect security. That is, if functionality is a requirement, then there will always be security gaps. Security is a system attribute that must be traded off against user friendliness, efficiency, ease of use, and other desirable system properties.

The next section presents some basic security terminology and outlines some basic approaches to achieving secure systems. Section 3 presents eight principles to be followed when designing and implementing a secure system. Section 4 presents the twenty top vulnerabilities for Windows and Unix. Finally, Section 5 discusses how software engineering practice can help make systems more secure.

2. Background

In the early days of computing, when standalone systems were used by one user at a time, computer security consisted primarily of physical security. That is, the computer and its peripherals were locked in a secure area with a guard at the door that checked each user's identification before allowing them to enter the room.

As time sharing systems emerged in the mid to late 1960s and multiple jobs and users were able to run at the same time, controlling the access to the data on the system became a major point of concern. One solution that was used was to process classified data one level at a time and "sanitize" the system after the jobs from one level were run and before the jobs for the next level were run. This approach to computer security was known as *periods processing* because the jobs for each level were all run in their particular period of the day. This was an inefficient way to use the system, and an effort was made to find more efficient software solutions to the multilevel security problem.

Another effort that occurred in the mid to late 1970s was

the use of *tiger teams* to test the security of a system. These teams attempted to obtain unauthorized access to the system by exploiting design and implementation errors [21, 10]. The tiger team studies demonstrated the difficulty of providing secure software; virtually every system that was attacked by a tiger team was penetrated.

Before proceeding with more background, it is necessary to introduce some basic terminology. In the context of this paper, the term *computer security* means the protection of resources (including data and programs) from unauthorized disclosure, modification or destruction. In addition, the system resources must also be protected (i.e., access to system services should not be denied). These properties are usually referred to as confidentiality, integrity, and availability. More precisely, *confidentiality* ensures that sensitive information is not disclosed to unauthorized recipients; *integrity* ensures that data and programs are modified or destroyed only in a specified and authorized manner, and *availability* ensures that the resources of the system will be usable whenever they are needed by an authorized user.

The degree to which each of these three properties is needed varies from one application to another. For instance, the military is primarily interested in confidentiality. In contrast, the banking industry is primarily interested in integrity, and for the telephone industry availability is most important. This is not to say that any of these applications do not care about the other properties. For instance, the military would not want missile targets to be changed in an unauthorized manner, and they would like their battle plans to be available when needed. Thus, they are interested in integrity and availability too. The exact requirements that are needed for a particular system or application are expressed in the security policy for that system or application. A *security policy* defines what is and what is not allowed.

Cybersecurity consists largely of defensive methods used to detect and thwart would-be intruders. The principles of computer security thus arise from the kinds of threats intruders can impose. For instance, one general security stance is that "everything that is not permitted is prohibited." If this principle is enforced, then an intruder can not get access to some object just because the security administrator did not consider whether it should be restricted or not. Most members of the security community believe that if software were designed with more of an emphasis on security and if systems were configured properly, then there would be fewer security problems[1].

There are four general approaches to achieving a secure computing environment. They are the use of special procedures for working with the system, the inclusion of additional functions or mechanisms in the system, the use of assurance techniques to increase one's confidence in the security of the system, and the use of intrusion detection systems. Each of these is discussed in the following subsections.

[1] Other security principles are discussed in Section 3.

Some security requirements can either be achieved by requiring procedures to be followed or by using system mechanisms or functions to enforce the requirement. However, in some cases system users need to follow specific procedures in order to make security mechanisms effective. It is also possible to trade off assurance techniques for less mechanism. For instance, one can use assurance techniques, like formal proofs, to assure that the system can not get into a particular state; thus, alleviating the need for the software mechanism that would deal with that state.

2.1. Procedural Approaches

Procedural approaches prescribe the appropriate behavior for a user to follow when using a system. The periods processing approach for processing jobs at different security levels, which was presented above, is an example of a procedural solution to satisfy a security requirement.

User guidelines for the appropriate choice of strong passwords is the most prevalent example of using procedural approaches to achieve a security requirement. For example, to deter password guessing by a potential intruder one should choose a long password (at least eight characters) that is not obvious and not easily guessable (e.g., not a spouse's first name, a middle name, a login name, or any of these spelled backwards). Passwords should also use both upper and lower case letters, numerics and possibly special symbols. In addition, a password should not be written down, or, if it is, it should not be written in an obvious place. Furthermore, users should be trained to change their passwords at appropriate intervals. Many of these restrictions can be enforced by the system when a user chooses a new password.

Another example of a procedural approach is a set of rules for the appropriate handling of removable storage devices. Oftentimes data that is perfectly safe while in a protected system is compromised by an attacker getting access to removable storage, such as a dump tape, and analyzing it on an unrestricted system. For this reason most security conscious organizations have explicit rules for handling removable media, such as requiring them to be stored in an approved vault.

2.2. Function and Mechanism

Including additional functions or mechanisms in a computer system is another way of enhancing computer security. The mechanisms presented in this section are grouped into authentication mechanisms, access control, and inference control.

2.2.1 Authentication Mechanisms

Authentication mechanisms are used to assure that a particular user is who he/she claims to be. The first mechanism discussed is the *secure attention key*. This key, when hit by a user at a terminal, kills any process running at the terminal except the true system listener and thus guarantees a trusted path to the system. This will foil attempts at "spoofing," which is the process of fooling a user into believing that he/she is talking to the system, while instead the user is interacting with a malicious application. For instance, the spoofer may display what looks like the system login prompt on a terminal to make the terminal appear to be idle. Then when an unsuspecting user begins to use the terminal, the spoofer retrieves the login name and displays a new message asking for the user's password. After obtaining this information, the spoofer displays a message to try again, and the spoofer returns ownership of the terminal to the system. If a secure attention key is used, it is important that users make a habit of always hitting the key to begin a dialogue with the system. One way of ensuring this is for the system to only display the login prompt after the key is depressed. This is an example of procedures and mechanism working together to achieve a security property.

Most of the password guidelines that were discussed above as procedural approaches can be enforced by the system. For instance, the password program can require long passwords and it can check the password chosen against an online dictionary or against a list of obvious passwords. The login program can also inform the user when it is time to change passwords and not allow further logins if the password is not changed in time. Finally, the system can generate secure passwords for the users using a secure password generator.

The most sophisticated authentication devices are those that depend on a unique physiological or behavioral characteristic that can be examined and quantified for each user. When a user wants to be authenticated his/her characteristics are sampled, converted into a digital form, and compared to the previously stored sample characteristics for that user. The most common biometric devices are based on fingerprints, handprints, retina patterns, or facial characteristics. The most common behavioral devices use voice, signature, or keystroke characteristics. Most of these devices are used in a two-factor authentication system, such as with passwords.

2.2.2 Access Control

Assuming that by using authentication mechanisms and good password practice the system can guarantee that users are who they claim to be, the next step is to provide a means of limiting a user's access to only those files that policy determines should be accessed. These controls are referred to as *access control*. Different applications and systems have different security requirements, and these requirements are expressed in the *access control policy* for the application or system. Access control policies are enforced by the access control mechanisms.

There are two types of access control: *discretionary access control* (DAC) and *mandatory access control* (MAC). More precisely, for discretionary access control the owner of an object specifies what type of access the other users can have to the object. Thus, access is at the discretion of the owner. In contrast, for mandatory access control the system determines whether a user can access a resource based on the security attributes (e.g., labels or markings) of both the user and the object. Mandatory access control is often called non-discretionary access control.

One of the earliest forms of discretionary access control was the use of passwords for file access. That is, the owner selects a password for each file and distributes the password to those users to whom the owner wants to give access to the file. A major problem with this approach is that one user may pass a password on to another user without the consent of the owner of the file. A second major problem is that the owner cannot revoke access from one user without revoking access from all users and then selecting a new password for the file. A third problem with this approach is that the passwords tend to get embedded in other files and are vulnerable to browsing. The UNIX *owner/group/other* approach is another example of discretionary access control, because it is the owner of the file that sets the access rights.

To assure that all access control policies are enforced a means of mediating each access of an object by a subject is needed. The *reference monitor* [1] provides this mediation. A reference monitor is defined by three basic properties.

1. It must be tamperproof. That is, it should be isolated from modification by system entities.

2. It must always be invoked. That is, it must mediate every access.

3. It must be small enough to be subjected to analysis and tests, the completeness of which can be assured.

A *security kernel* is defined as the hardware and software that realize the reference monitor. The idea is to keep the security kernel small and to have it contain the security relevant parts of the system.

2.2.3 Inference Controls

The last class of security mechanisms discussed in this section is inference controls. These controls attempt to restrict database access to sensitive information about individuals while providing access to statistics about groups of individuals. The ideal is to have a statistical database that discloses no sensitive data.

As an example of the type of threat that is addressed by inference control mechanisms consider a database that contains enrollment and grade statistics for a university class. If Morgan is the only economics major in a particular class one could deduce Morgan's grade by retrieving the average grade for the course, the average grade of all non-economics majors in the class, and the number of students in the class.

Two approaches to solving the inference problem are to restrict queries that reveal certain types of statistics and to add "noise" to the results returned. To foil small and large query set attacks, such as the Morgan example above, a technique called *query-set-size control* is introduced. This forbids the release of any statistics pertaining to a group less than some predetermined size n or greater than N-n, where N is the total number of records in the database. Other techniques, restrict queries with more than some predetermined number of records in common or with too many attributes specified. The techniques that add noise to the statistical results usually return a rounded result or a result based on random sampling. For more information on these techniques see [7].

2.3. Assurance Techniques

The third approach to enhancing the security of a system is to subject the system to rigorous assurance techniques that will raise one's confidence that the system will perform as desired. Among these techniques are penetration analysis, formal specification and verification, and covert channel analysis. None of these methods guarantee a secure system. They only increase one's confidence in the security of the system.

2.3.1 Penetration Analysis

One approach to locating security flaws in computer systems is *penetration analysis*, This approach uses a collection of known flaws, generalizes these flaws, and tries to apply them to the system being analyzed. The tiger teams, discussed in Section 2, are an example of this approach.

Today tiger teams are usually called *red teams*, and red team/blue team experiments pit the red team attackers against the blue team defenders. The problem with the tiger team approach is that, like testing, "penetration teams prove the presence, not the absence of protection failures."

This observation has led to the use of *formal specification* and *verification techniques* to increase ones confidence in the reliability and security of a computer system.

2.3.2 Formal Verification

Formal verification demonstrates that an implementation is consistent with its requirements. This task is approached by decomposing it into a number of easier problems. The critical requirements, which are usually a natural language statement of what is desired, are first stated in precise mathematical terms. This is known as the *formal model* or *critical criteria* for the system. For example, the formal model for a secure system could be that information at one security level does not flow to another security level. Next, a high level formal specification of the system is stated. This specification gives a precise mathematical description of the behavior of the system omitting all implementation details, such as resource limitations. This is followed by a series of less abstract specifications each of which implements the next higher level specification, but with more detail. Finally, the system is coded in a high order language. This high order language implementation must be shown to be consistent with the original requirements.

The advent of the security kernel as a means of encapsulating all security relevant aspects of the system made formal verification feasible. That is, by developing kernel architectures that minimize the amount and complexity of software involved in security decisions and enforcement, the chance of successfully verifying that the system meets its security requirements is greatly increased. Because the remainder of the system is written using the facilities provided by the kernel, only the kernel code must be verified. Examples of work in this area are [24, 36, 33, 2]

Formal verification techniques have also been used for analyzing encryption protocols [17, 5, 30]. In this case, a formal specification is written for the different steps of the protocol, and a model checker is used to find a counter example.

2.3.3 Covert Channel Analysis

Secure computer systems use both mandatory and discretionary access controls to restrict the flow of information through legitimate communication channels, such as files, shared memory, and process signals. Unfortunately, in practice one finds that computer systems are built such that users are not limited to communicating only through the intended communication channels. As a result, a well-founded concern of security-conscious system designers is the potential exploitation of system storage locations and timing facilities to provide unforeseen communication channels to users. These illegitimate channels are known as covert storage channels and covert timing channels [20, 22, 26, 15, 16].

Covert channels signal information through system facilities not intended for data transfer, and they support this communication using methods not detected or regulated by the access control mechanisms. *Storage channels* transfer information using the manipulation of storage locations for their coding scheme. That is, the sending process alters some system attribute (e.g., a file lock or a device busy flag) and the receiving process monitors the alteration. For example, if two processes have only write access to a file, then the sending process could lock the file, and the receiving process could detect this change by attempting to write to the file. In this way, the receiver could interpret the file being locked as a one and it not being locked as a zero. *Timing channels* transfer information using the passing of time for their coding scheme; the sending process modulates the receiver's response time to detect a change in some shared entity.

Although there is concern that a user at a high security level may use a covert channel to signal information to a user at a lower level, the major threat from a covert channel is its potential to be exploited by a Trojan horse. A *Trojan horse* is a program that gives the appearance of providing normal functionality, but whose execution results in undesired side effects.

The severity of a covert channel threat has been traditionally measured in terms of the channel's bandwidth (i.e., the number of bits signaled per second). The higher the bandwidth, the greater the potential for serious compromise. An alarming possibility regarding covert channels is that as operating systems are ported to faster hardware architectures, the bandwidths of their covert channels may increase significantly. In fact, timing channels with estimated bandwidths in the megabits per second range have been demonstrated on symmetric multi-processing architectures [4].

2.4. Intrusion Detection

Significant progress has been made toward the improvement of computer system security. Unfortunately, the undeniable reality remains that all computers are vulnerable to compromise. Even the most secure systems built today are vulnerable to authorized users (insiders) who abuse their privileges. Given this reality, the need for user accountability is very important, both as a deterrent and for terminating abusive computer usage once it is discovered. In addition, the need to maintain a record of the transactions that have occurred on a system is crucial for performing damage assessment. In recognition of these needs and in recognition that security violations are a fact of life for computers, many systems implement a form of transaction record keeping called *audit collection*. The data collected is called an *audit log*. Additional systems and/or software are often required to generate the necessary audit data. For example, in order to produce audit records for Sun Microsystem's Solaris one needs to use the Basic Security Module (BSM) [34].

Although the audit logs normally contain enough information to determine that a computer abuse has occurred, the amount of data collected is so voluminous that manual audit data analysis is impractical. By introducing automated audit data analysis tools, referred to as *intrusion detection systems* (IDSs), security violations that might have once gone unnoticed can be identified. In addition, when intrusion detection is performed in real-time, the audit data can be used to track a user's behavior and to determine if the user's current actions represent a threat to security. If they do, the system can then preempt the user's actions.

Intrusion detection is not limited to processing audit records. More generally, intrusion detection is the process of analyzing information about the activities performed in a computer system or network, looking for evidence of malicious behavior. In addition to audit records produced by the operating system auditing facilities, the information may come in the form of log messages produced by different types of sensors and network devices, or in the form of raw network traffic obtained by eavesdropping a network segment. These data sources are used by intrusion detection systems in different ways, according to different paradigms.

There are two basic categories of intrusion detection approaches: *anomaly detection* and *misuse detection*. Anomaly detection relies on models of the intended behavior of users and applications and interprets deviations from this "normal" behavior as an attack [14, 8, 18, 9]. Misuse detection takes a complementary approach. Misuse detection systems contain a number of attack descriptions (or "signatures") that are matched against the stream of audit data looking for evidence that the modeled attack is occurring [12, 29, 28, 13]. Misuse and anomaly detection both have advantages and disadvantages. Misuse detection systems can perform focused analysis of the audit data and usually produce only a few false positives, which are erroneous detections. In contrast, the main disadvantage of misuse detection systems is that they can detect only those attacks that are known. That is, they can detect only attacks for which they have a defined signature. In contrast, the main advantage of anomaly detection systems is that they are able to detect previously unknown attacks. By defining what's normal, they make it possible to identify any variation, no matter whether it is part of the threat model or not. Unfortunately, the advantage of being able to detect previously unknown attacks is paid for in terms of a large number of false positives. Anomaly detection systems are also difficult to train when used in a very dynamic environment.

3. Principles for Designing Secure Systems

In a landmark paper in 1975 Saltzer and Schroeder introduced eight principles to be followed when designing secure systems [31]. Three decades later, these principles still apply. In this section we will only list the principles. The interested reader is directed to the original paper to get more details.

The eight principles are:

1. **Least privilege**: A user should only have the rights necessary to complete his/her task.
2. **Economy of mechanism**: The system must be sufficiently small and simple as to be verified and implemented.
3. **Complete mediation**: Every access to every object must be checked.
4. **Open design**: The system design should be open for scrutiny by the community.
5. **Separation of privilege**: Access to objects should depend on more than one condition being satisfied.
6. **Least common mechanism**: The amount of mechanism common to more than one user should be minimized.
7. **Psychological acceptability**: The user interface must be easy to use.
8. **Fail-safe defaults**: The default is a lack of access.

The next section presents the vulnerabilities that are most often exploited. If any of these vulnerabilities are the result of one or more of the secure design principles being violated, then the violation is illuminated.

4. Top 20 Vulnerabilities for 2002

Cyber attacks usually conform to a general multi-step process. The first step of this process is surveillance, which is the collection of information about a specific target network. Examples are ping scans and port scans to find out what hosts exist and what services are provided by each host. The second phase is the remote exploitation of vulnerabilities associated with the services that were identified during the first phase. When successful, this phase gives the attacker access to the system. After having obtained an entry point in a target system the attacker is now an insider, who has access to much more information. At this point, other attacks are launched from the compromised system. The goal is to either escalate the attacker's privileges or to extend the compromise to neighboring parts of the network, possibly by exploiting internal trust relationships.

The time between each of the steps of a multi-step attack may be seconds, or it may be days, or even months. That is, compromising the initial system may just be laying the foundation for attacks that will not occur until much later. This is the case in many denial of service attacks, where the slave (or zombie) systems are compromised, and then they may not be used for months until it is time for them to collectively perform the necessary steps to cause a denial of service.

Because the evidence of multi-step cyber attacks is scattered on many systems and may be separated by appreciable amounts of time, it is often difficult to correlate the various pieces of evidence to determine the "big picture." That is, identifying who the attackers are and what their goal is from what may at first appear to be unrelated events can be a challenging task. Therefore, much of the current intrusion detection research is focusing on the correlation and fusion of cyber alerts.

Although multi-step attacks can differ in terms of structure and timing, most of these attacks are based on only a few vulnerabilities. This is because attackers usually go for the "low-hanging fruit." That is, they try the easiest attacks first and only progress to the more difficult attacks when the easier ones fail. The SANS Institute, along with the FBI post a list of the ten most exploited Windows vulnerabilities and the ten most exploited Unix vulnerabilities [32]. These are the most common exploits, and fixing them will not guarantee a secure system. It will, however, remove the low-hanging fruits and cause the hackers to work harder to compromise your system.

The next two subsections present the top ten vulnerabilities for Windows and Unix, respectively. The material in these sections is a brief summary of what appears at the SANS/FBI Top Twenty site [32].

4.1. Windows Vulnerabilities

This section presents the ten top vulnerabilities for Windows systems.

- Internet Information Services (IIS): There are three basic vulnerabilities in IIS. They are the failure to handle unanticipated requests, buffer overflows, and insecure sample applications. The fact that unanticipated requests are a source of vulnerability is not surprising, since one of the first places where hackers or tiger teams usually look for security holes in a system is where the response to some action is undefined. If the system designers had followed the fail-safe defaults principle these vulnerabilities might not exist. The sample applications problem is an example of the trade off between being user friendly and being secure. These applications are provided to help the user become familiar with how to use the system. Unfortunately, they were written as pedagogical examples, and security was not one of the concerns. As a result, the example applications cannot withstand attacks.
- Microsoft Data Access Components (MDAC) – Remote Data Services: This flaw occurs only in the Re-

mote Data Services (RDS) component of older versions of MDAC. These older versions have a program flaw that allows a remote user to run applications locally with administrative privileges. This flaw is indicative of a general problem with keeping cyberspace secure: even though the flaw has been identified and a solution has existed for more than two years, there are many outdated or misconfigured systems that are still vulnerable.

- Microsoft SQL Server (MSSQL): The attacks that can be launched against the MSSQL server vary in severity from allowing remote users to obtain sensitive information, to modifying information in the database, to compromising the SQL server, and in some cases to compromising the host itself. The most commonly exercised vulnerability is that the administrative account is installed with a blank password. This violates the principle of fail-safe defaults. It is also likely a violation of the economy of mechanism principle and of the least privilege principle.

- NETBIOS – Unprotected Windows Networking Shares: Windows network shares are used to allow hosts to share files with each other. The problem is that these network shares are often misconfigured, which may allow an attacker to access critical system files and completely compromise the remote host that is sharing the files. It was the use of misconfigured file shares that enabled the Nimda worm to spread so quickly. This is an example of another violation of the principles that states that you should only share what is absolutely needed (least common mechanism).

- Anonymous Logon – Null Sessions: In Windows the null session is used to allow remote users to obtain information such as shares and user name from a host anonymously. The vulnerability occurs because the SYSTEM account, which is used for many critical systems operations, uses null sessions to obtain system information from other hosts. The SYSTEM account needs to do this, since it has no password. However, hackers can also use the null session to obtain sensitive information.

- LAN Manager Authentication – Weak LM Hashing: This is another example of the problems caused by using older systems; that is, the current windows environments no longer use LAN Managers. The problem with the LAN Manager (LM) is that LM passwords are stored locally, and the LM encryption scheme is very weak. Therefore, the passwords can be broken in a very short amount of time. To be more specific, LM passwords are 14 characters long. If they are longer they are truncated to 14, and if they are shorter they are padded with blanks. In addition, they are converted to all upper case characters and then split into two seven character parts. Therefore, the challenge is to crack two seven character all upper case passwords. There are many tools available on the Internet that could brute force LM passwords in a few hours [19].

- General Windows Authentication – Accounts with No Passwords or Weak Passwords: This is the typical problem of using either a bad password or no password at all. By compromising a password, an outsider becomes an insider. The attacker now has all of the privileges of the user whose password was compromised. The attacker can also get information to support a privilege escalation attempt or to compromise other neighbor machines more easily.

- Internet Explorer: Vulnerabilities exist on all versions of Microsoft Explorer. These vary in severity from allowing the attacker to obtain cookies, local files, or input data, to executing local programs and completely compromising the host running the browser. The vulnerabilities are usually based on web page spoofing, ActiveX controls, MIME-type misinterpretation and buffer overflows. Often they are the combination of more than one of these [25, 6].

- Remote Registry Access: The Windows Registry is a centralized hierarchical database that manages software, device configurations, and user settings. The problem is that the permissions and security settings are often not set correctly. As a result, attackers can remotely compromise the system by exploiting the improper settings. The fixes for this problem are to review the configuration of critical registry keys and set them appropriately. Access to the system registry must also be restricted. The real problem is that the Registry is too complex, which is likely also the reason that many of the registry keys were set wrong in the first place. This is a violation of the economy of mechanism principle.

- Windows Scripting Host: The problem with the Windows Scripting Host is that it allows any text file with a `.vbs` extension to be executed as a Visual Basic script when the text is displayed. This is the vulnerability used by many of the worms; in particular, the "I Love You" worm exploited this vulnerability. This is an example of user friendliness versus security. The solution to this problem is to turn off the Windows Scripting Host.

4.2. Unix Vulnerabilities

This section presents the ten top vulnerabilities for Unix systems.

- Remote Procedure Calls (RPC): Remote procedure calls allow a remote user to call procedures on another host and pass input and get results, just as if the procedure were local. The main exploits against the RPC services are accomplished by using buffer overflows. Since many of the procedures that are called remotely execute with root privileges, this allows the attacker to gain root privilege remotely.

- Apache Web Server: The main Apache web server problems are the result of running CGI scripts. Because the CGI scripts execute with the same privilege as the server, the scripts can be very dangerous. If the server is being run as root, the problem is even worse.

- Secure Shell (SSH): Secure Shell services are intended to be secure replacements for ftp, telnet, and the R-command programs, which are remote shell (`rsh`), remote copy (`rcp`), remote login (`rlogin`), and remote execution (`rexec`). SSH is often the only service that is made accessible through firewalls and other protection mechanisms. For this reason its implementation is under continuous scrutiny by the hacker community. Therefore, a vulnerability in SSH gives immediate access to a very large number of systems.

- Simple Network Management Protocol (SNMP): SNMP is one of the most popular protocols for monitoring and configuring remote TCP/IP-enabled devices. Management is accomplished by exchanging messages between the manager and the agent software running on the remote device. The messages are used to request information or configuration changes, respond to requests, enumerate SNMP objects, and send unsolicited alerts, called traps. The vulnerabilities identified are in the trap messages and the request handling, and they can result in denial-of-service conditions, format string vulnerabilities, and buffer overflows. Older SNMP versions also have a problem with their authentication mechanism. The mechanism depends on a "community string", and this string is often left unchanged from its default value, which is "public". This is another example of violating the fail-safe defaults principle.

- File Transfer Protocol (FTP): Some ftp servers allow anonymous access, which does not require a unique password, but even those with authenticated access have vulnerabilities. Some of the exploits allow root access and others allow user level command execution. Another vulnerability of the ftp service is that names and passwords are sent in the clear, so they can be captured by a network sniffer.

- R-Services – Trust Relationships: Trust relationships exist whenever there are entries in the `/etc/hosts.equiv` file, or in the `/.rhosts` file of a user. The first allows any remote user to use any of the R-commands from a host listed in the file, without having to provide a password. The second entry allows the user whose .rhosts file contains the remote host name to use the R-commands without having to provide a password. from any host listed in the file. This weakness allows a user cracking an account on one machine to execute R-commands to all other machines that have a trust relationship with the compromised account or with the host where the account was compromised. This is a violation of the complete mediation and least privilege principles. Another vulnerability of the R-services is that all information passed between an R-command client and an R-service are in the clear.

- Line Printer Daemon (LPD): The line printer daemon (lpd) is used to connect to a printer on a local machine or remotely through port 515. There are multiple programming flaws in several implementations of the lpd that allow buffer overflows that can result in root access to the printer server.

- Sendmail: Sendmail is the program that is used on most Unix systems to send and receive mail. The two main vulnerabilities of the sendmail program are buffer overflows and using an improperly configured machine to relay mail for spamming purposes. No new high severity Sendmail vulnerabilities have been identified for more than two years. However, there are many outdated or misconfigured systems that are still vulnerable.

- BIND/DNS: A Domain Name Service (DNS) allows one to retrieve a machine's IP address by presenting the name of the machine. BIND is the Berkeley Internet Name Domain package, which is the most popular DNS package. The main vulnerabilities of the BIND package are caused by implementation problems and bad configurations. This results in denial of service, buffer overflows, and wrong id to name mappings.

- General Unix Authentication – Accounts with No Passwords or Weak Passwords: This is the typical problem of either using a weak password or no password at all. By compromising a password an outsider becomes an insider. The attacker now has all of the privileges of the user whose password was compromised. The attacker can also get information to make a privilege escalation or to compromise other neighbor machines more easily.

4.3. Patches and Updates

The solution to fixing many of the vulnerabilities presented above is to apply patches provided by Microsoft, Sun Microsystems, Redhat, and others. In the case of Microsoft these patches come as Service Packs, Security Rollups, and Hotfixes. Automatic patches for Redhat Linux come from Redhat Update.

One of the problems with maintaining a secure system is that the administrator needs to be continuously applying patches to the system to keep up with the latest vulnerabilities. This takes time and energy. In addition, for large sites it may be necessary to continue using vulnerable software to meet operational or compatibility requirements [23]. The automatic patching facilities make this easier, but, unfortunately, they sometimes break the system.

5. How can Software Engineering Help?

Security needs to be proactive. That is, systems need to be designed and tested with security in mind right from the start. It can not be an add on or an afterthought. When designing a secure system, security is just one more desirable attribute for the system. It needs to be balanced with other desirable attributes, such as being user friendly and being efficient.

Secure systems should be built using good software engineering practices [35]. For instance, many of the known security breaches are the result of a vulnerability that was introduced when making an unplanned for change to the system. By planning for change and making secure systems extensible there are likely to be less problems introduced when changes need to be made to the system.

Testing is another area where more work is needed. Security testing is different from normal software testing. Normally, when testing a software system, the tester assumes that the user may only occasionally do something wrong. Therefore, some test cases with bad input values should be used. The majority of the test cases, however, will be for appropriate input values. In contrast, for security testing the tester assumes that the attacker is trying to do something wrong; therefore, the concentration should be on testing with unexpected input. For instance, buffer overflow attacks are the result of the user intentionally passing parameters that are larger than expected. As a result, the extra characters in the parameter overwrite the stack, often causing return addresses to be changed so that the program returns to the attacker's code rather than to where it was called. Security testing also takes a devious mind, for in order to do it right you need to anticipate what the attackers are likely to do.

Maintenance is also important. Most (or all) of the vulnerabilities presented in the previous section have patches. However, patching a system is often time-consuming and also may cause certain features to not work. Therefore, better tools for automatic configuration control and update are also needed.

There is also a need for software developers to be accountable for the systems they develop. That is, if a security breach occurs due to a programming flaw in a system implementation, then the software developer should be held liable for any losses that occur. One thing that may help in this area is the development of standards for developing secure software systems. The open source community has taken some initial steps in this direction with their Open-Source Security Testing Methodology Manual [11]. This is intended to set standards for performing Internet security testing.

Acknowledgments

Thanks to Giovanni Vigna for providing helpful comments on this paper.

This work was supported by the Army Research Office, under agreement DAAD19-01-1-0484. The U.S. Government is authorized to reproduce and distribute reprints for Governmental purposes notwithstanding any copyright annotation thereon.

The views and conclusions contained herein are those of the author and should not be interpreted as necessarily representing the official policies or endorsements, either expressed or implied, of the Army Research Office, or the U.S. Government.

References

[1] J. Anderson, et al. Computer Security Technology Planning Study. Technical Report ESD-TR-73-51, Deputy for Command and Management Systems, HQ Electronic Systems Division (AFSC), 1972. Vol. 1.

[2] W. Bevier. Kit: A study in operating system verification. *IEEE Transactions on Software Engineerin*, 15(11), November 1989.

[3] Cert coordination center statistics. `http://www.cert.org/stats/`, 2003.

[4] Minutes of the First Workshop on Covert Channel Analysis. IEEE Cipher, July 1990. Los Angeles, CA.

[5] Z. Dang and R. Kemmerer. Using the astral model checker to analyze mobile i. In *Proceedings of the International Conference on Software Engineering*, pages 132–141, May 1999.

[6] F. De Paoli, A. dos Santos, and R. Kemmerer. *Mobile Agents and Security*, volume 1419, chapter Web Browsers and Security, pages 235–256. Springer-Verlag, 1998.

[7] D. Denning. *Cryptography and Data Security*. Addison Wesley, Reading, Massachusetts, 1982.

[8] S. Forrest. A Sense of Self for UNIX Processes. In *Proceedings of the IEEE Symposium on Security and Privacy*, pages 120–128, Oakland, CA, May 1996.

[9] A. Ghosh, J. Wanken, and F. Charron. Detecting Anomalous and Unknown Intrusions Against Programs. In *Proceedings of the Annual Computer Security Application Conference (ACSAC'98)*, pages 259–267, Scottsdale, AZ, December 1998.

[10] B. Hebbard, et al. A Penetration Analysis of the Michigan Terminal System. *ACM Operating Systems Review*, 14(1), January 1980.

[11] P. Herzog. Open source security testing methodology manual. `http://www.isecom.org/projects/osstmm.htm`, February 2002.

[12] K. Ilgun, R. Kemmerer, and P. Porras. State Transition Analysis: A Rule-Based Intrusion Detection System. *IEEE Transactions on Software Engineering*, 21(3):181–199, March 1995.

[13] Internet Security Systems. *Introduction to RealSecure Version 3.0*, January 1999.

[14] H. Javitz and A. Valdes. The NIDES Statistical Component Description and Justification. Technical report, SRI International, Menlo Park, CA, March 1994.

[15] R. Kemmerer. Shared Resource Matrix Methodology: An Approach to Identifying Storage and Timing Channels. *ACM Transactions on Computer Systems*, 1(3), August 1983.

[16] R. Kemmerer. A practical approach to identifying storage and timing channels: Twenty years later. In *Proceedings of the Eighteenth Annual Computer Security Applications Conference*, Las Vegas, Nevada, December 2002.

[17] R. Kemmerer, C. Meadows, and J. Millen. Three systems for cryptographic protocol analysis. *Journal of Cryptography*, 7(2):79–130, 1994.

[18] C. Ko, M. Ruschitzka, and K. Levitt. Execution Monitoring of Security-Critical Programs in Distributed Systems: A Specification-based Approach. In *Proceedings of the 1997 IEEE Symposium on Security and Privacy*, pages 175–187, May 1997.

[19] `www.l0pht.com/l0phcrack`.

[20] B. Lampson. A Note on the Confinement Problem. *Communications of the ACM*, 16:613–615, October 1973.

[21] R. Linde. Operating System Penetration. In *Proceedings of the National Computer Conference*, volume 44, Montvale, N.J., 1975. AFIPS Press.

[22] S. Lipner. A Comment on the Confinement Problem. In *Proceedings of the Fifth Symposium on Operating Systems Principles*, The University of Texas at Austin, November 1975.

[23] R. Lippmann, S. Webster, and D. Stetson. The effect of identifying vulnerabilities and patching software on the utility of network intrusion detection. In A. Wespi, G. Vigna, and L. Deri, editors, *Proceedings of Recent Advances in Intrusion Detection*, pages 307–326. Springer, 2002.

[24] E. McCauley and P. Drognowski. KSOS: The Design of a Secure Operating System. In *Proceedings of the National Computer Conference*. AFIPS Press, June 1979.

[25] G. McGraw and E. Felten. *Java Security: Hostile Applets, Holes and Antidotes*. John Wiley and Sons, 1996.

[26] J. Millen. Security Kernel Validation in Practice. *Communications of the ACM*, 19:243–250, May 1976.

[27] D. Moore, V. Paxson, S. Savage, C. Shannon, S. Staniford, and N. Weaver. The spread of the sapphire/slammer worm. `http://www.silicondefense.com/research/sapphire/`, February 2003.

[28] NFR Security. *Overview of NFR Network Intrusion Detection System*, February 2001.

[29] M. Roesch. Snort - Lightweight Intrusion Detection for Networks. In *Proceedings of the USENIX LISA '99 Conference*, November 1999.

[30] P. Ryan, S. Schneider, M. Goldsmith, G. Lowe, and B. Roscoe. *Modelling and Analysis of Security Protocols*. Addison Wesley Professional, 2000.

[31] J. Saltzer and M. Schroeder. The protection of information in computer systems. *Proceedings of the IEEE*, 63(9):1278–1308, September 1975.

[32] Sans/fbi top 20 list. `http://www.sans.org/top20/`, 2002.

[33] J. Silverman. Reflections on the Verification of the Security of an Operating System Kernel. *Communications of the ACM*, 1983.

[34] Sun Microsystems, Inc. *Installing, Administering, and Using the Basic Security Module*. 2550 Garcia Ave., Mountain View, CA 94043, December 1991.

[35] J. Viega and G. McGraw. *Building Secure Software: How to Avoid Security Problems the Right Way*. Addison Wesley, October 2001.

[36] B. Walker, R. Kemmerer, and G. Popek. Specification and Verification of the UCLA Unix Security Kernel. *Communications of the ACM*, 23:118–131, 1980.

Panels

Panel: eXtreme Programming: Helpful or Harmful?

Hossein Saiedian
Electrical Engineering & Computer Science
University of Kansas, Lawrence, KS 66045, USA

Establishing a process for software development is a growing concern in industry. To alleviate the concerns, a relatively large number of proposals and models have been introduced since late 1980s, including CMM, SPICE, Unified Process, OPEN, as well as the more recent and emerging agile methodologies such as eXtreme Programming, SCRUM, Feature Driven Development (FDD), and Win-Win Spiral.

All of these models and methodologies define a set of 'best' practices, some of which, especially in the case of agile methodologies, are considered controversial and against the traditionally accepted 'best' practices. Nevertheless, agile methodologies have become very popular.

There are obviously some heated debates about which model or methodology is the most effective one. Among the emerging agile method ologies, eXtreme Programming has probably become most popular, thought many times project characteristics may determine which methodology, or sometimes, a combination of methodologies, to be used.

The concerns over the selection of the most effective methodology (or best practices) is also reflected in debates within the software engineering education circles. Here, the software engineering educators will have to decide which methodology is the right one for teaching the next generation of software engineers, or integrating into the software engineering education curricula. An excellent report [1] provides a brief review of several such methodologies as well as evaluative research and instructional issues related to agile methods and their potential impact.

This panel provides two opposing views vis-à-vis incorporating agile processes, and in particular eXtreme Programming, into software engineering education. The panel will be conducted slightly different from the traditional approaches. It will include normal paper presentations by the authors, followed by plenary debate.

The first paper (authored by Lars Benedix, Göel Hedin, and Boris Magnusson) presents an experience from using eXtreme Programming to teach software engineering concepts in an undergraduate course with over 100 students. The authors' experience is very positive. The second paper (authored by Jean-Guy Schneider and Lorraine Johnston) conclude that introducing an agile process such as eXtreme Programming in software engineering education is not a straightforward task and the corresponding practices may run counter to educational goals.

The paper presentations will serve as authors' position statements. Discussion and debate will follow.

References

[1] G. Hislop, M. Lutz, J. Naveda, W. McCracken, N. Mead, and L. Williams, Integrating Agile Practices into Software Engineering Courses, *Computer Science Education*, **12**(3):169–185, Swets & Zeitlinger, 2002.

Automotive Software Engineering

Manfred Broy
Institut für Informatik, Technische Universität München, D-80290 München, Germany
broy@in.tum.de

Abstract

Information technology has become the driving force of innovation in many areas of technology and also in cars. Embedded software controls the functions of cars, supports and assists the driver and realizes systems for information and entertainment. Software in automobiles is today one of the great challenges for software engineering. On modern cars we find all issues of software systems in a nutshell. It is a challenge for software and systems engineering.

1. Introduction

More than 98 % of all processors run in embedded systems. A modern car has up to 80 controllers that all have to be programmed. Over the years we observe an enormous increase of software in a car. In the near future software is expected to account for up to 10% of the overall cost of a car.

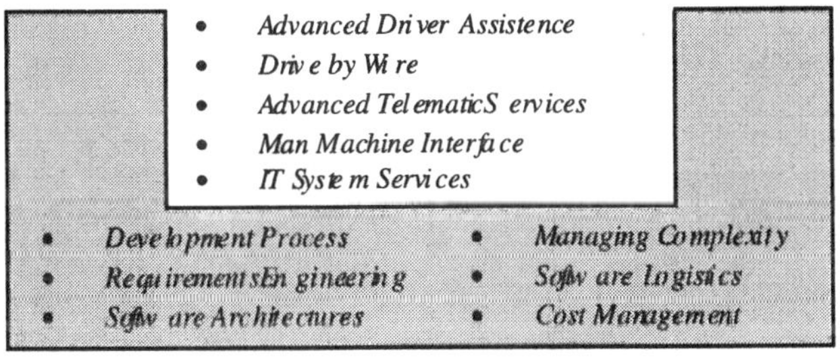

Fig. 1: Framework for Automotive SW-Engineering

Today, new functions in a car are mainly realized by software. Up to 90 % of innovations in cars are enabled by software. There are mainly two reasons for the rapid inclusion of new software in our cars: new functionalities as well as cheaper and better technical solutions substituting the realization of existing functionalities.

Fig. 1 outlines the software-based technical revolution in the car and the associated software engineering challenges.

2. The Technical Revolution

Car companies are traditionally in mechanical engineering. To some extent electrical engineering is present there, too. The embedded systems were traditionally realized based on control theory. Now within a few years digital technology and software became a driving force.

Software in Cars: The amount of software in a car is overwhelming. In current premium cars more than 60 MB of software is installed. Nearly all functions are controlled by software. Initially the software was mainly standalone, controlling a single functionality. Today software is connected, communicates over busses and by wireless techniques also to networks outside the car.

Advanced Driver Assistance: One field of innovation is driver assistance systems. They include functionalities such as adaptive cruise control with stop and go capabilities, lane keeping assistance, active front steering, stability control, brake assistance or parking assistance. More sophisticated solutions depend on the sensors and actuators available in a car and the options to supervise and control the driver's actions and attendance.

Drive by Wire: Drive by wire aims at the replacement of mechanical control devices by electronic ones. Examples are brake-by-wire or steer-by-wire. First solutions are on the road. To bring this technology into all cars has major advantages for the packaging, the costs, and advanced driver assistance. On the other hand difficult engineering problems have to be solved.

Advanced Telematics Services: More and more cars are connected by wireless technology to networks outside. This paves the road for many new functionalities such as traffic information, emergency calls, - remote maintenance and diagnostics, special driver information, road pricing, fleet management and much more.

Man Machine Interface: The man machine interface is changing in the car. The vast number of functions available calls for new solutions to avoid a flood of buttons and control lights. But it is not only the plain user interface – the question is how the many functions can be

0-7695-1877-X/03 $17.00 © 2003 IEEE

offered to a driver in a way that is transparent and useful.

IT System Services: An increasing software complexity needs sophisticated system monitoring and management services. Preserving system integrity after authorized software changes have to be addressed as well as dynamic aspects like power control, load balance, gateway functions, monitoring and logging services, etc.

3. Challenges

There are many challenges in automotive software engineering and in the organization of the development process.

Quality: Today the quality of software in the car is not as high as needed. Drive-by-wire solutions need a much higher reliability.

Supplier Management: A difficult issue is the fact that subparts of systems including software are manufactured by different suppliers and have to be integrated into the final product. This brings essential problems of requirements specification, interfaces, and system integration.

Portability and Reusability: Today most of the solutions are done in a rather proprietary way for each type of car again. Not much is reused. This cannot work in the future. The huge amount of software demands techniques for reuse and product lines.

Tools: The usage of tools for requirements engineering, modeling, simulation, prototyping, code generation, and verification (testing, model checking, deductional proof) is a must. Today the tools do not address the needs sufficiently nor do exist tool chains for a seamless development support.

Requirements Engineering: Due to much larger design spaces in software based systems, requirements engineering becomes much more important in automotive applications. Onc has to find out what the users really need and expect. In addition nonfunctional requirements get more complex. We have to deal with *functional requirements (logical requirements)* - properties of software related to its behavior, its offered services, and its performance, *nonfunctional and product requirements* - properties of software related to its representation and documentation as well as the way of its realization and distribution, and *process requirements* - properties of the software development process.

Software Architecture: So far digital systems in a car are often mainly structured in terms of hardware architecture. With software becoming dominant, the software architecture becomes essential. On the long run we need reference software architectures.

Managing Complexity: The software in cars has become large and complex. There are two main sources of complexity: the sheer size of the software and the complexity of the realized functions and the growing dependency.

Size of the Individual Functions: The size and complexity of the functions is growing. Today the light control, the locking management, the antiblocking systems or airbags become more sophisticated from generation to generations of cars.

Nonfunctional Requirements: For many applications in cars there are very different requirements concerning real-time behavior, reliability or startup behavior.. The idea to distinguish between critical and less critical functions is useful. Nevertheless noncritical functions are connected to critical ones and thus techniques for protection are needed. Drive by wire requires a higher reliability, in particular.

Functional Connectivity and Dependency: Today the functions in a car get more and more connected. Often this happens bottom up. As a result the hidden effects take place ("feature interactions") which make system integration a hard task. A top down approach to the architecture in cars is needed.

Software Logistics: Not only the development of software, also its role in the production process (how to download the software into the controllers in production) and the maintenance pose many problems. Cars will be in the field for a time span of 20 to 40 years. This calls for well-defined software logistics.

Software Maintenance: To maintain the software in the field includes many aspects such as version and configuration control, software update, error documentation, tracing and diagnosis.

Software Download: A critical issue is in particular the update of software in a car. It starts with the basic problem of the flash time and continues with more sophisticate questions of the compatibility of software versions.

Cost Management: So far the techniques for cost estimation and design to cost are highly insufficient. Although the software development and maintenance cost are now a considerable factor for a car, appropriate cost models do not exist.

4. Research Issues

There are many challenging research issues for automotive software.

Modeling: In practice, many methods for modeling and specification have been suggested (SA, SADT, SSADM, SDL, OMT, UML, ROOM, ...). But none of them addresses the needs of automotive software properly.

Reliability: To achieve the reliability that is required for innovative software solutions we have to extend and transfer results from formal methods in a pragmatic way to practice.

ACKNOWLEGEMENTS

Its is a pleasure to acknowledge helpful remarks Jan Romberg and from members in BMW CarIT, in particular Alexandre Saad and Ulrich Weinmann.

Panel: Empirical Validation—What, Why, When, and How

Robert J. Walker (Chair)
University of Calgary
Calgary, Canada
rwalker@cpsc.ucalgary.ca

Lionel C. Briand
Carleton University
Ottawa, Canada
briand@sce.carleton.ca

David Notkin
University of Washington
Seattle, USA
notkin@cs.washington.edu

Carolyn B. Seaman
University of Maryland, Baltimore County
Baltimore, USA
cseaman@umbc.edu

Walter F. Tichy
Universität Karlsruhe
Karlsruhe, Germany
tichy@ira.uka.de

All research requires validation, and where analytic solutions are not possible or not practical, empirical validation is necessary. Software engineering research covers a vast array of problems over which the level of maturity in our knowledge varies markedly.

Opinions as to the methodology to apply to SE research appear to be in disagreement, as a large variety of possibilities exist [7]. Tichy promotes quantitative, controlled, statistically-analyzable experimentation [6]. Kitchenham *et al.* recognize the value of "observational studies" in addition to formal experimentation [3], but emphasize industrial-context, quantitative evaluation, and statistics. Seaman promotes the value of qualitative evaluation [5]. Murphy *et al.* suggest that a different treatment is needed for emerging technologies than for more mature ones [4]. Briand *et al.* state that "each discipline needs to develop its own body of experience and strategies to answer its most pressing research questions" [1, p. 398].

Without some consensus, an SE researcher is faced with a difficult task of convincing their peers that their selected methodology is appropriate, let alone the details of their validation. This panel session strives to address these issues in order to determine where a consensus does and does not exist. Brief synopses of each panelist's thoughts follow.

Lionel C. Briand

Quantitative and qualitative evaluation are not really alternatives but are rather complementary. For example, when assessing the impact of a new technology in a controlled experiment, it may not be a good idea to assume that your research hypothesis is the unique reason for the results you observe. Questionnaires are commonly used to obtain qualitative but structured feedback from the experimental subjects for additional evidence of causation.

We need to study both current practices and new technologies. The former is needed to better understand what issues people are actually facing when developing and maintaining large software systems. The latter is needed to improve software quality and productivity.

Level of control is usually associated with internal and external validity. Fully controlled experiments usually take place in an artificial setting, for obvious practical reasons. In this case a very good internal validity is usually obtained (i.e., the treatment is likely to cause the effect) but external validity suffers from the fact that the setting may not reflect actual project conditions. When performing field studies, collecting data on actual projects and interviewing project participants, you then find yourself in the opposite situation.

In the end, when an important question arises regarding, for example, the evaluation of a new technology, both controlled experiments and field studies are necessary to build a credible body of evidence.

David Notkin

"Software engineering research is poorly evaluated and assessed" is a statement made by many in the community in print and perhaps more so in private. Although I believe that we have to make serious and significant improvements, I reject this statement as inaccurate and dangerous.

The statement is inaccurate because it makes assumptions that are not true; I address two of these assumptions. First, there is a strong implication that to get industrial adoption of a result, one must have empirical evidence for its utility. Empirical evidence may be material, and in some cases essential, but the general issue of technology transfer is extremely complicated. The Brooks–Sutherland Report [2] discussed how government, industry, and academic institutions play key roles in the development and transfer of influential technologies, with the process being an

0-7695-1877-X/03 $17.00 © 2003 IEEE

extremely dynamic one. Second, it generally appeals to "real science" as an example of what we should become. There are a number of reasons why this is inappropriate, not the least being an idealized but imprecise understanding of what research in these other fields looks like. Furthermore, the combination of heavily different environments (in terms of the kinds of software produced, the educational and experience backgrounds of the software engineers, etc.) with the uniquely rapid rate of change in our field makes the situation different from other "real science" fields.

The statement is dangerous because it encourages researchers to focus on problems that can evaluated in particular ways rather than on problems that need to be solved. We need to have strong demands about evaluation and assessment, but realize that one size does not fit all. Not all ideas nor claims are the same, and they should not generally be placed into pigeonholes. What is fundamentally important is for the claims to be appropriately justified: heavy claims demand heavy evaluation. Additionally, we need to have a sense of the lifetime of different ideas. Ideas in their early stages need to be given some room to grow, without overly restrictive expectations about their evaluation. More mature ideas need more mature evaluation.

Let's not strangle ourselves, and our chances of having an influence, by hiding behind a few specific approaches to evaluation of our work. Rather let's be demanding but flexible in this dimension.

Carolyn B. Seaman

One of the principles of empirical investigation in any field is triangulation. This is the premise that any stated finding should be supported by more than one piece of "evidence". Another way of saying this is that any data generated by an empirical study cannot be considered valid unless the same information has been generated from two different data sources, by using two different empirical methods, or by using two different measurement instruments.

Taking triangulation seriously in empirical studies of software engineering means that software engineering empirical researchers must broaden their repertoire of empirical methods. Qualitative research methods constitute a large body of well-defined, mature empirical methods that have not been fully employed in the study of software engineering. Qualitative research is empirical research in which the data is expressed textually or in images, rather than in quantifiable terms. Qualitative methods were originally developed principally for the study of human behavior, under the premise that such a subject is too complex to be captured adequately quantitatively. Thus, the qualitative approach allows the researcher to capture the full complexity of a phenomenon without having to abstract away important details that do not fit into a quantitative model.

Much of the complexity of many research questions in software engineering comes from the role of humans in the development and maintenance of software, and the fact that software itself is a product of human intellect. Thus, the use of qualitative methods in software engineering research provides a way to deal with the complexities of these questions, as well as providing excellent opportunities for triangulation, when used in conjunction with quantitative methods.

Walter F. Tichy

The quantity of empirical research in SE has increased dramatically. A sizeable proportion of papers in most major SE publications and conferences now presents empirical results. Now that quantity is up, quality must be improved as well. Some of the empirical work is unsatisfactory, for a variety of methodological reasons. I think reviewers have to be both more careful and more understanding: more careful in checking the validity of the results, and more understanding regarding what can be achieved in a single paper. There is no "silver bullet experiment" that will provide the final answer for a research question, nor can an empirical paper be rejected solely on the grounds of the results appearing "obvious" to the reviewer.

I think we should give up on correlating volume metrics (counting attributes of various documents in the life cycle) with cost estimates. Experiments have shown that the predictive power of volume metrics is poor and "tuning" them does not carry over from one project to another. Instead, we need to figure out better models of software development processes to achieve better estimates.

Besides metrics, there are many other pressing questions regarding the effectiveness of software tools and methods that can only be answered empirically.

References

[1] L. Briand et al. Empirical studies of object-oriented artifacts, methods, and processes. *Empiric. Softw. Eng.*, 4(4):387–404, 1999.

[2] F. P. Brooks, Jr., I. E. Sutherland, et al. *Evolving the High Performance Computing and Communications Initiative to Support the Nation's Information Infrastructure.* The National Academies Press, 1995.

[3] B. Kitchenham et al. Preliminary guidelines for empirical research in software engineering. *IEEE Trans. Softw. Eng.*, 28(8):721–734, 2002.

[4] G. Murphy, R. Walker, and E. Baniassad. Evaluating emerging software development techniques. *IEEE Trans. Softw. Eng.*, 25(4):438–455, 1999.

[5] C. Seaman. Qualitative methods in empirical studies of software engineering. *IEEE Trans. Softw. Eng.*, 25(4):557–572, 1999.

[6] W. Tichy. Should computer scientists experiment more? *Computer*, 31(5):32–40, 1998.

[7] M. Zelkowitz and D. Wallace. Experimental models for validating computer technology. *Computer*, 31(5):23–31, 1998.

Modularity in the New Millenium: A Panel Summary

Premkumar Devanbu, (*Panel Chair*)
Bob Balzer, Don Batory, Gregor Kiczales, John Launchbury, David Parnas, Peri Tarr (*Panelists*)

1 Introduction (Chair's Statement)

Parnas' seminal work [2] on *separation of concerns* in design has led to diverse innovations in programming language design, to support modularity. However, there has been a growing sentiment in many quarters that there are some concerns that stubbornly resist tidy confinement, when using established modularization mechanisms in programming languages. A diverse set of new approaches have emerged in response: aspects [1], monads [5], mixin layers [3], and multi-dimensional separation of concerns [4]. These approaches arose more or less independently of each other, and have (to varying degrees) developed technical maturity, real-world credibility and strong user bases. We are also now beginning to see strong scholarly comparisions of the intellectual foundations and practical utility of these different aproaches. This panel aims to support this trend.

In this panel, we bring together leading experts (Profs. Batory, Kiczales, and Launchbury, and Dr. Tarr) in these different areas. Each represents a particular perspective on how to evolve and adapt the old idea of modularization to deal with new challenges such as security, fault-tolerance, distribution, and auditing. In addition, we also have two pioneering researchers (Profs. Balzer and Parnas) to provide us with a historical perspective on the evolution (sic) of program modularization and evolution techniques.

Position statements of some of the panelists follow, presented in alphabetical order of their names:

2 Panel Statement: Don Batory

The future of software engineering lies in automation. Perhaps the most successful example of automated software engineering is relational query optimization (RQO). A query is specified in a declarative domain-specific language (SQL), mapped to an inefficient relational algebra expression, optimized by rewrite rules, and then an efficient query evaluation program is generated. RQO is also a great example of the holy grail problem of automatic programming transforming a declarative specification to an efficient program. Feature Oriented Programming (FOP) aims to generalize this powerful paradigm to other software domains. An FOP domain model is a set of operators that define an algebra. Each operator implements a feature that is characteristic of programs in that domain; compositions of these operators define a specific program. FOP is ideally suited for product-lines and program generators. AHEAD is both a model and tool suite for FOP that is based on step-wise refinement, the paradigm that builds complex applications from simple applications by progressively adding features. The AHEAD tool suite has been bootstrapped, where its 150+K LOC are being generated from simple, declarative specifications. Optimizations in our tool building process are now being introduced to make it like RQO.

3 "It's the cross-cutting": Gregor Kiczales

The idea of separation of concerns is not new; it is a basic element of modern thought.

We are however, constantly renewing our tools for separating, composing and otherwise operating on concerns throughout the lifecycle. We have seen several such evolutions, including the most recent major success, object-orientation.

The critical idea in aspect-oriented programming (AOP) is that no single decomposition can capture all the concerns in a complex system in a modular way. This incredibly simple idea is, in retrospect, nearly obvious. But until AOP we spent countless hours (days, weeks...) refactoring a system over-and-over trying to get a structure in which all concerns are modular. The frustration of working with single decompositions of complex systems led to the realization that choosing a nice structure for modularizing many concerns inherently means that some others cannot be modular, if they have to live within that primary structure. We call such concerns crosscutting, because they cut across the natural lines of the rest of the system.

The rapid uptake of AOP in industry is because developers find that adopting AOP tools like AspectJ is simple and natural their own experience helps them understand crosscutting concerns at a deep intuitive level.

4 Panel Statement: David Parnas

To a man with a hammer, everything looks like a nail. To a Computer Scientist, everything looks like a language design problem. Languages and compilers are, in their opinion, the only way to drive an idea into practice.

0-7695-1877-X/03 $17.00 © 2003 IEEE

My early work clearly treated modularisation as a design issue, not a language issue. A module was a work assignment, not a subroutine or other language element. Although some tools could make the job easier, no special tools were needed to use the principal, just discipline and skill.

When language designers caught on to the idea, they assumed that modules had to be subroutines, or collections of subroutines, and introduced unreasonable restrictions on the design. They also spread the false impression that the important thing was to learn the language; in truth, the important thing is to learn how to design and document.

We are still trying to undo the damage caused by the early treatment of modularity as a language issue and, sadly, we still try to do it by inventing languages and tools.

5 Panel Statement: Peri Tarr

Multi-dimensional separation of concerns (MDSOC) allows developers to encapsulate overlapping, interacting and crosscutting concerns, including features, aspects, variants, roles, business rules, components, frameworks, etc., simultaneously. One does not have to choose between, say, a data decomposition and a feature decomposition, since both can coexist, and each can be used when appropriate. All concerns are first-class components that can be integrated flexibly. MDSOC further supports developers by allowing concerns to be identified throughout the software lifecycle and relationships among concerns to be managed. MDSOC grew out of earlier work on subject-oriented programming. It retains the same style of composition, while adding the ability to extract concerns from existing software and maintain multiple decompositions simultaneously. The approach has been successful at feature-based development and integration, inserting probes, retrofitting and reusing design patterns, and unanticipated extension and adaptation, and has shown promise with creating and evolving product lines, extracting concerns from legacy software and reconciling different views and perspectives. Our first-generation tool, Hyper/J, was less successful at "uniform crosscutting," where common functionality is applied uniformly in multiple contexts, and did no semantic checking. AspectJ pointcuts, with their powerful patterns, address uniform crosscutting more effectively, and mixin layers provide semantic checking and predictability. In our current work on a new Concern Manipulation Environment (CME), we are introducing componentry to address these and other limitations. We have used Hyper/J to build a portion of the CME, and have identified many other places where the more powerful capabilities of the CME itself could be brought to bear.

6 Conclusion

This paper presents a brief summary of some of the panelist's positions. We hope that the contents will serve to encourage colleagues to attend the panel at the conference, and to stimulate further discussion.

References

[1] G. Kiczales, E. Hilsdale, J. Hugunin, M. Kersten, J. Palm, and W. G. Griswold. An overview of AspectJ. In *European Conference on Object Oriented Programming*, 2001.

[2] D. Parnas. The criteria to be used in decomposing systems into modules. *Communications of the ACM*, 14(1):221–227, 1972.

[3] Y. Smaragdakis and D. Batory. Implementing layered designs with mixin layers. In *European Conference on Object Oriented Programming*, 1998.

[4] P. L. Tarr, H. Ossher, W. H. Harrison, and S. M. S. Jr. N degrees of separation: Multi-dimensional separation of concerns. In *International Conference on Software Engineering*, 1999.

[5] P. Wadler. The essence of functional programming. In *Conference Record of the Nineteenth Annual ACM SIGPLAN-SIGACT Symposium on Principles of Programming Languages*, pages 1–14, Albequerque, New Mexico, 1992.

Mini-Tutorial

Writing Good Software Engineering Research Papers

Minitutorial

Mary Shaw
Carnegie Mellon University
mary.shaw@cs.cmu.edu

Abstract

Software engineering researchers solve problems of several different kinds. To do so, they produce several different kinds of results, and they should develop appropriate evidence to validate these results. They often report their research in conference papers. I analyzed the abstracts of research papers submitted to ICSE 2002 in order to identify the types of research reported in the submitted and accepted papers, and I observed the program committee discussions about which papers to accept. This report presents the research paradigms of the papers, common concerns of the program committee, and statistics on success rates. This information should help researchers design better research projects and write papers that present their results to best advantage.

Keywords: research design, research paradigms, validation, software profession, technical writing

1. Introduction

In software engineering, research papers are customary vehicles for reporting results to the research community. In a research paper, the author explains to an interested reader what he or she accomplished, and how the author accomplished it, and why the reader should care. A good research paper should answer a number of questions:

- ♦ What, precisely, was your contribution?
  - What question did you answer?
  - Why should the reader care?
  - What larger question does this address?
- ♦ What is your new result?
  - What new knowledge have you contributed that the reader can use elsewhere?
  - What previous work (yours or someone else's) do you build on? What do you provide a superior alternative to?
  - How is your result different from and better than this prior work?
  - What, precisely and in detail, is your new result?
- ♦ Why should the reader believe your result?
  - What standard should be used to evaluate your claim?
  - What concrete evidence shows that your result satisfies your claim?

If you answer these questions clearly, you'll probably communicate your result well. If in addition your result represents an interesting, sound, and significant contribution to our knowledge of software engineering, you'll have a good chance of getting it accepted for publication in a conference or journal.

Other fields of science and engineering have well-established research paradigms. For example, the experimental model of physics and the double-blind studies of medicines are understood, at least in broad outline, not only by the research community but also by the public at large. In addition to providing guidance for the design of research in a discipline, these paradigms establish the scope of scientific disciplines through a social and political process of "boundary setting" [5].

Software engineering, however, has not yet developed this sort of well-understood guidance. I previously [19, 20] discussed early steps toward such understanding, including a model of the way software engineering techniques mature [17, 18] and critiques of the lack of rigor in experimental software engineering [1, 22, 23, 24, 25]. Those discussions critique software engineering research reports against the standards of classical paradigms. The discussion here differs from those in that this discussion reports on the types of papers that are accepted in practices as good research reports. Another current activity, the Impact Project [7] seeks to trace the influence of software engineering research on practice. The discussion here focuses on the paradigms rather than the content of the research

This report examines how software engineers answer the questions above, with emphasis on the design of the research project and the organization of the report. Other sources (e.g., [4]) deal with specific issues of technical writing. Very concretely, the examples here come from the papers submitted to ICSE 2002 and the program committee review of those papers. These examples report research results in software engineering. Conferences often include other kinds of papers, including experience reports, materials on software engineering education, and opinion essays.

0-7695-1877-X/03 $17.00 © 2003 IEEE

2. What, precisely, was your contribution?

Before reporting what you did, explain what problem you set out to solve or what question you set out to answer —and why this is important.

2.1 What kinds of questions do software engineers investigate?

Generally speaking, software engineering researchers seek better ways to develop and evaluate software. Development includes all the synthetic activities that involve creating and modifying the software, including the code, design documents, documentation, etc. Evaluation includes all the analytic activities associated with predicting, determining, and estimating properties of the software systems, including both functionality and extra-functional properties such as performance or reliability.

Software engineering research answers questions about methods of development or analysis, about details of designing or evaluating a particular instance, about generalizations over whole classes of systems or techniques, or about exploratory issues concerning existence or feasibility. Table 1 lists the types of research questions that are asked by software engineering research papers and provides specific question templates.

Table 1. Types of software engineering research questions

Type of question	Examples
Method or means of development	How can we do/create/modify/evolve (or automate doing) X? What is a better way to do/create/modify/evolve X?
Method for analysis or evaluation	How can I evaluate the quality/correctness of X? How do I choose between X and Y?
Design, evaluation, or analysis of a particular instance	How good is Y? What is property X of artifact/method Y? What is a (better) design, implementation, maintenance, or adaptation for application X? How does X compare to Y? What is the current state of X / practice of Y?
Generalization or characterization	Given X, what will Y (necessarily) be? What, exactly, do we mean by X? What are its important characteristics? What is a good formal/empirical model for X? What are the varieties of X, how are they related?
Feasibility study or exploration	Does X even exist, and if so what is it like? Is it possible to accomplish X at all?

The first two types of research produce methods of development or of analysis that the authors investigated in one setting, but that can presumably be applied in other settings. The third type of research deals explicitly with some particular system, practice, design or other instance of a system or method; these may range from narratives about industrial practice to analytic comparisons of alternative designs. For this type of research the instance itself should have some broad appeal—an evaluation of Java is more likely to be accepted than a simple evaluation of the toy language you developed last summer. Generalizations or characterizations explicitly rise above the examples presented in the paper. Finally, papers that deal with an issue in a completely new way are sometimes treated differently from papers that improve on prior art, so "feasibility" is a separate category (though no such papers were submitted to ICSE 2002).

Newman's critical comparison of HCI and traditional engineering papers [12] found that the engineering papers were mostly incremental (improved model, improved technique), whereas many of the HCI papers broke new ground (observations preliminary to a model, brand new technique). One reasonable interpretation is that the traditional engineering disciplines are much more mature than HCI, and so the character of the research might reasonably differ [17, 18]. Also, it appears that different disciplines have different expectations about the "size" of a research result—the extent to which it builds on existing knowledge or opens new questions. In the case of ICSE, the kinds of questions that are of interest and the minimum interesting increment may differ from one area to another.

2.2 Which of these are most common?

The most common kind of ICSE paper reports an improved method or means of developing software that is, of designing, implementing, evolving, maintaining, or otherwise operating on the software system itself. Papers addressing these questions dominate both the submitted and the accepted papers. Also fairly common are papers about methods for reasoning about software systems, principally analysis of correctness (testing and verification). Analysis papers have a modest acceptance edge in this very selective conference.

Table 2 gives the distribution of submissions to ICSE 2002, based on reading the abstracts (not the full papers—but remember that the abstract tells a reader what to expect from the paper). For each type of research question, the table gives the number of papers submitted and accepted, the percentage of the total paper set of each kind, and the acceptance ratio within each type of question. Figures 1 and 2 show these counts and distributions.

Table 2. Types of research questions represented in ICSE 2002 submissions and acceptances

Type of question	Submitted	Accepted	Ratio Acc/Sub
Method or means of development	142(48%)	18 (42%)	(13%)
Method for analysis or evaluation	95 (32%)	19 (44%)	(20%)
Design, evaluation, or analysis of a particular instance	43 (14%)	5 (12%)	(12%)
Generalization or characterization	18 (6%)	1 (2%)	(6%)
Feasibility study or exploration	0 (0%)	0 (0 %)	(0%)
TOTAL	298(100.0%)	43 (100.0%)	(14%)

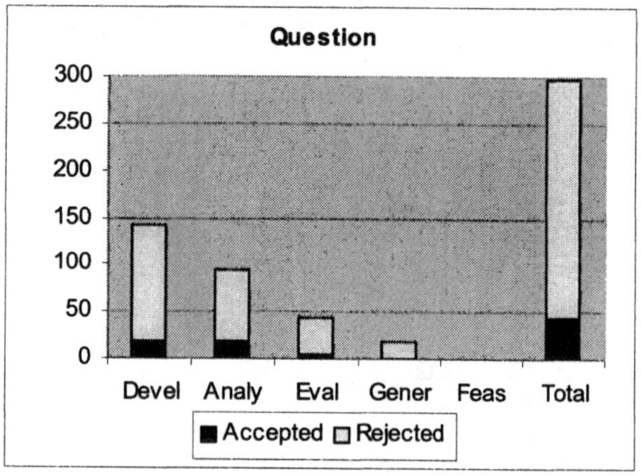

Figure 1. Counts of acceptances and rejections by type of research question

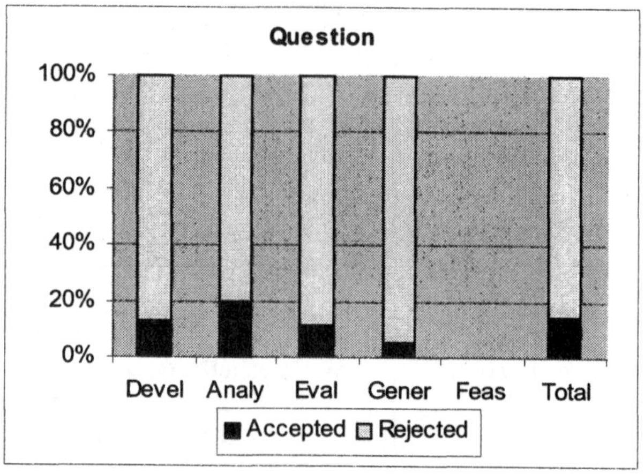

Figure 2. Distribution of acceptances and rejections by type of research question

2.3 What do program committees look for?

Acting on behalf of prospective readers, the program committee looks for a clear statement of the specific problem you solved—the question about software development you answered—and an explanation of how the answer will help solve an important software engineering problem. You'll devote most of your paper to describing your result, but you should begin by explaining what question you're answering and why the answer matters.

If the program committee has trouble figuring out whether you developed a new evaluation technique and demonstrated it on an example, or applied a technique you reported last year to a new real-world example, or evaluated the use of a well-established evaluation technique, you have not been clear.

3. What is your new result?

Explain precisely what you have contributed to the store of software engineering knowledge and how this is useful beyond your own project.

3.1 What kinds of results do software engineers produce?

The tangible contributions of software engineering research may be procedures or techniques for development or analysis; they may be models that generalize from specific examples, or they may be specific tools, solutions, or results about particular systems. Table 3 lists the types of research results that are reported in software engineering research papers and provides specific examples.

3.2 Which of these are most common?

By far the most common kind of ICSE paper reports a new procedure or technique for development or analysis. Models of various degrees of precision and formality were also common, with better success rates for quantitative than for qualitative models. Tools and notations were well represented, usually as auxiliary results in combination with a procedure or technique. Table 4 gives the distribution of submissions to ICSE 2002, based on reading the abstracts (but not the papers), followed by graphs of the counts and distributions in Figures 3 and 4.

Table 3. Types of software engineering research results	
Type of result	**Examples**
Procedure or technique	New or better way to do some task, such as design, implementation, maintenance, measurement, evaluation, selection from alternatives; includes techniques for implementation, representation, management, and analysis; a technique should be operational—not advice or guidelines, but a procedure
Qualitative or descriptive model	Structure or taxonomy for a problem area; architectural style, framework, or design pattern; non-formal domain analysis, well-grounded checklists, well-argued informal generalizations, guidance for integrating other results, well-organized interesting observations
Empirical model	Empirical predictive model based on observed data
Analytic model	Structural model that permits formal analysis or automatic manipulation
Tool or notation	Implemented tool that embodies a technique; formal language to support a technique or model (should have a calculus, semantics, or other basis for computing or doing inference)
Specific solution, prototype, answer, or judgment	Solution to application problem that shows application of SE principles – may be design, prototype, or full implementation; careful analysis of a system or its development, result of a specific analysis, evaluation, or comparison
Report	Interesting observations, rules of thumb, but not sufficiently general or systematic to rise to the level of a descriptive model.

Table 4. Types of research results represented in ICSE 2002 submissions and acceptances			
Type of result	**Submitted**	**Accepted**	**Ratio Acc/Sub**
Procedure or technique	152(44%)	28 (51%)	18%
Qualitative or descriptive model	50 (14%)	4 (7%)	8%
Empirical model	4 (1%)	1 (2%)	25%
Analytic model	48 (14%)	7 (13%)	15%
Tool or notation	49 (14%)	10 (18%)	20%
Specific solution, prototype, answer, or judgment	34 (10%)	5 (9%)	15%
Report	11 (3%)	0 (0%)	0%
TOTAL	348(100.0%)	55 (100.0%)	16%

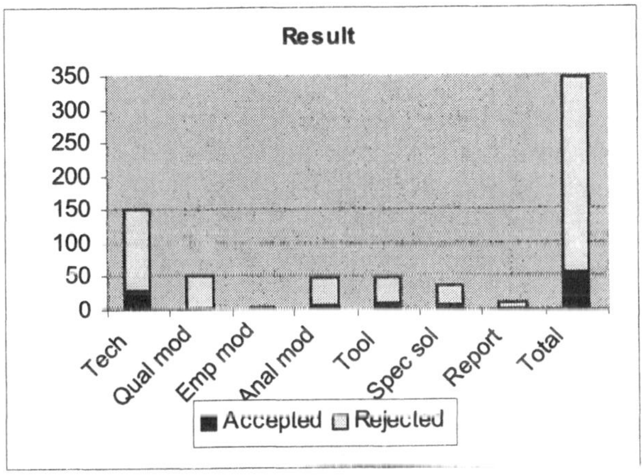

Figure 3. Counts of acceptances and rejections by type of result

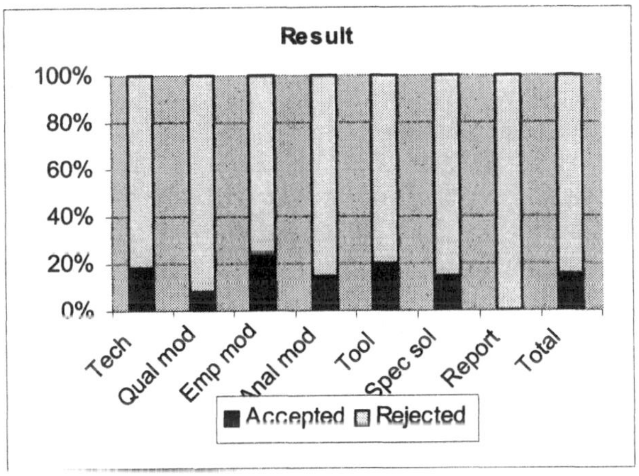

Figure 4. Distribution of acceptances and rejections by type of result

The number of results is larger than the number of papers because 50 papers included a supporting result, usually a tool or a qualitative model.

Research projects commonly produce results of several kinds. However, conferences, including ICSE, usually impose strict page limits. In most cases, this provides too little space to allow full development of more than one idea, perhaps with one or two supporting ideas. Many authors present the individual ideas in conference papers, and then synthesize them in a journal article that allows space to develop more complex relations among results.

3.3 What do program committees look for?

The program committee looks for interesting, novel, exciting results that significantly enhance our ability to develop and maintain software, to know the quality of the software we develop, to recognize general principles about software, or to analyze properties of software.

You should explain your result in such a way that someone else could use your ideas. Be sure to explain what's novel or original – is it the idea, the application of the idea, the implementation, the analysis, or what?

Define critical terms precisely. Use them consistently. The more formal or analytic the paper, the more important this is.

Here are some questions that the program committee may ask about your paper:

What, precisely, do you claim to contribute?

Does your result fully satisfy your claims? Are the definitions precise, and are terms used consistently?

Authors tend to have trouble in some specific situations. Here are some examples, with advice for staying out of trouble:

- *If your result ought to work on large systems*, explain why you believe it scales.
- *If you claim your method is "automatic"*, using it should not require human intervention. If it's automatic when it's operating but requires manual assistance to configure, say so. If it's automatic except for certain cases, say so, and say how often the exceptions occur.
- *If you claim your result is "distributed"*, it probably should not have a single central controller or server. If it does, explain what part of it is distributed and what part is not.
- *If you're proposing a new notation for an old problem*, explain why your notation is clearly superior to the old one.
- *If your paper is an "experience report"*, relating the use of a previously-reported tool or technique in a practical software project, be sure that you explain what idea the reader can take away from the paper to use in other settings. If that idea is increased confidence in the tool or technique, show how your experience should increase the reader's confidence for applications beyond the example of the paper.

What's new here?

The program committee wants to know what is novel or exciting, and why. What, specifically, is the contribution? What is the increment over earlier work by the same authors? by other authors? Is this a sufficient increment, given the usual standards of subdiscipline?

Above all, the program committee also wants to know what you actually contributed to our store of knowledge about software engineering. Sure, you wrote this tool and tried it out. But was your contribution the technique that is embedded in the tool, or was it making a tool that's more effective than other tools that implement the technique, or was it showing that the tool you described in a previous paper actually worked on a practical large-scale problem? It's better for you as the author to explain than for the program committee to guess. Be clear about your claim …

Awful	▼	• I completely and generally solved … (unless you actually did!)
Bad	▼	• I worked on galumphing. (or studied, investigated, sought, explored)
Poor	▼	• I worked on improving galumphing. (or contributed to, participated in, helped with)
Good	▲	• I showed the feasibility of composing blitzing with flitzing. • I significantly improved the accuracy of the standard detector. (or proved, demonstrated, created, established, found, developed)
Better	▲	• I automated the production of flitz tables from specifications. • With a novel application of the blivet transform, I achieved a 10% increase in speed and a 15% improvement in coverage over the standard method.

Use verbs that show results and achievement, not just effort and activity.

"***Try*** not. ***Do***, or ***do*** not. There is no ***try***." -- Yoda

What has been done before? How is your work different or better?

What existing technology does your research build on? What existing technology or prior research does your research provide a superior alternative to? What's new here compared to your own previous work? What alternatives have other researchers pursued, and how is your work different or better?

As in other areas of science and engineering, software engineering knowledge grows incrementally. Program committees are very interested in your interpretation of prior work in the area. They want to know how your work is related to the prior work, either by building on it or by providing an alternative. If you don't explain this, it's hard for the program committee to understand how you've added to our store of knowledge. You may also damage your credibility if the program committee can't tell whether you know about related work.

Explain the relation to other work clearly ...

Awful	▼	The galumphing problem has attracted much attention [3,8,10,18,26,32,37]
Bad	▼	Smith [36] and Jones [27] worked on galumphing.
Poor	▼	Smith [36] addressed galumphing by blitzing, whereas Jones [27] took a flitzing approach.
Good	▲	Smith's blitzing approach to galumphing [36] achieved 60% coverage [39]. Jones [27] achieved 80% by flitzing, but only for pointer-free cases [16].
Better	▲	Smith's blitzing approach to galumphing [36] achieved 60% coverage [39]. Jones [27] achieved 80% by flitzing, but only for pointer-free cases [16]. We modified the blitzing approach to use the kernel representation of flitzing and achieved 90% coverage while relaxing the restriction so that only cyclic data structures are prohibited.

What, precisely, is the result?

Explain what your result is and how it works. Be concrete and specific. Use examples.

If you introduce a new model, be clear about its power. How general is it? Is it based on empirical data, on a formal semantics, on mathematical principles? How formal is it—a qualitative model that provides design guidance may be as valuable as a mathematical model of some aspect of correctness, but they will have to satisfy different standards of proof. Will the model scale up to problems of size appropriate to its domain?

If you introduce a new metric, define it precisely. Does it measure what it purports to measure and do so better than the alternatives? Why?

If you introduce a new architectural style, design pattern, or similar design element, treat it as if it were a new generalization or model. How does it differ from the alternatives? In what way is it better? What real problem does it solve? Does it scale?

If your contribution is principally the synthesis or integration of other results or components, be clear about why the synthesis is itself a contribution. What is novel, exciting, or nonobvious about the integration? Did you generalize prior results? Did you find a better representation? Did your research improve the individual results or components as well as integrating them? A paper that simply reports on using numerous elements together is not enough, even if it's well-engineered. There must be an idea or lesson or model that the reader can take from the paper and apply to some other situation.

If your paper is chiefly a report on experience applying research results to a practical problem, say what the reader can learn from the experience. Are your conclusions strong and well-supported? Do you show comparative data and/or statistics? An anecdotal report on a single project is usually not enough. Also, if your report mixes additional innovation with validation through experience, avoid confusing your discussion of the innovation with your report on experience. After all, if you changed the result before you applied it, you're evaluating the changed result. And if you changed the result while you were applying it, you may have confounded the experiences with the two versions.

If a tool plays a featured role in your paper, what is the role of the tool? Does it simply support the main contribution, or is the tool itself a principal contribution, or is some aspect of the tool's use or implementation the main point? Can a reader apply the idea without the tool? If the tool is a central part of result, what is the technical innovation embedded in the tool or its implementation?

If a system implementation plays a featured role in your paper, what is the role of the implementation? Is the system sound? Does it do what you claim it does? What ideas does the system demonstrate?

- *If the implementation illustrates an architecture or design strategy*, what does it reveal about the architecture? What was the design rationale? What were the design tradeoffs? What can the reader apply to a different implementation?
- *If the implementation demonstrates an implementation technique*, how does it help the reader use the technique in another setting?
- *If the implementation demonstrates a capability or performance improvement*, what concrete evidence does it offer to support the claim?
- *If the system is itself the result*, in what way is it a contribution to knowledge? Does it, for example, show you can do something that no one has done before (especially if people doubted that this could be done)?

4. Why should the reader believe your result?

Show evidence that your result is valid—that it actually helps to solve the problem you set out to solve.

4.1. What kinds of validation do software engineers do?

Software engineers offer several kinds of evidence in support of their research results. It is essential to select a form of validation that is appropriate for the type of research result and the method used to obtain the result. As an obvious example, a formal model should be supported by rigorous derivation and proof, not by one or two simple examples. On the other hand, a simple example derived from a practical system may play a major role in validating a new type of development method. Table 5 lists the types of research validation that are used in software engineering research papers and provides specific examples. In this table, the examples are keyed to the type of result they apply to.

Table 5. Types of software engineering research validation

Type of validation	Examples
Analysis	I have analyzed my result and find it satisfactory through rigorous analysis, e.g. … For a formal model … rigorous derivation and proof For an empirical model … data on use in controlled situation For a controlled experiment … carefully designed experiment with statistically significant results
Evaluation	Given the stated criteria, my result... For a descriptive model … adequately describes phenomena of interest … For a qualitative model … accounts for the phenomena of interest… For an empirical model … is able to predict … because …, or … generates results that fit actual data … Includes feasibility studies, pilot projects
Experience	My result has been used on real examples by someone other than me, and the evidence of its correctness/usefulness/effectiveness is … For a qualitative model … narrative For an empirical model or tool … data, usually statistical, on practice For a notation or technique … comparison of systems in actual use
Example	Here's an example of how it works on For a technique or procedure …a "slice of life" example based on a real system … For a technique or procedure …a system that I have been developing … For a technique or procedure … a toy example, perhaps motivated by reality The "slice of life" example is most likely to be convincing, especially if accompanied by an explanation of why the simplified example retains the essence of the problem being solved. Toy or textbook examples often fail to provide persuasive validation, (except for standard examples used as model problems by the field).
Persuasion	I thought hard about this, and I believe passionately that ... For a technique … if you do it the following way, then … For a system … a system constructed like this would … For a model … this example shows how my idea works Validation purely by persuasion is rarely sufficient for a research paper. Note, though, that if the original question was about feasibility, a working system, even without analysis, can suffice
Blatant assertion	No serious attempt to evaluate result. This is highly unlikely to be acceptable

4.2 Which of these are most common?

Alas, well over a quarter of the ICSE 2002 abstracts give no indication of how the paper's results are validated, if at all. Even when the abstract mentions that the result was applied to an example, it was not always clear whether the example was a textbook example, or a report on use in the field, or something in between.

The most successful kinds of validation were based on analysis and real-world experience. Well-chosen examples were also successful. Persuasion was not persuasive, and narrative evaluation was only slightly more successful. Table 6 gives the distribution of submissions to ICSE 2002, based on reading the abstracts (but not the papers), followed by graphs of the counts and distributions. Figures 5 and 6 show these counts and distributions.

Table 6. Types of research validation represented in ICSE 2002 submissions and acceptances			
Type of validation	**Submitted**	**Accepted**	**Ratio Acc/Sub**
Analysis	48 (16%)	11 (26%)	23%
Evaluation	21 (7%)	1 (2%)	5%
Experience	34 (11%)	8 (19%)	24%
Example	82 (27%)	16 (37%)	20%
Some example, can't tell whether it's toy or actual use	6 (2%)	1 (2%)	17%
Persuasion	25 (8%)	0 (0.0%)	0%
No mention of validation in abstract	84 (28%)	6 (14%)	7%
TOTAL	300(100.0%)	43 (100.0%)	14%

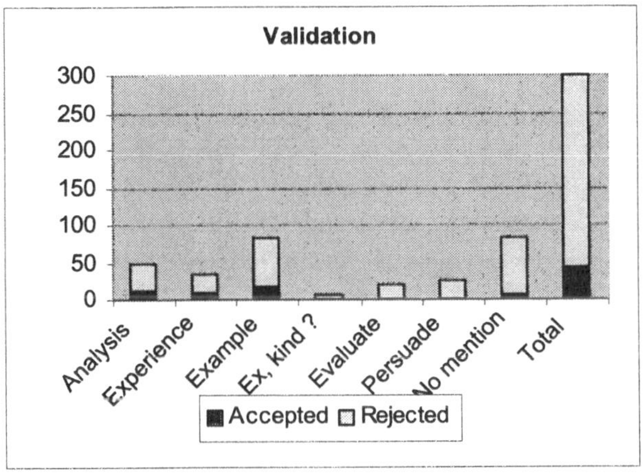

Figure 5. Counts of acceptances and rejections by type of validation

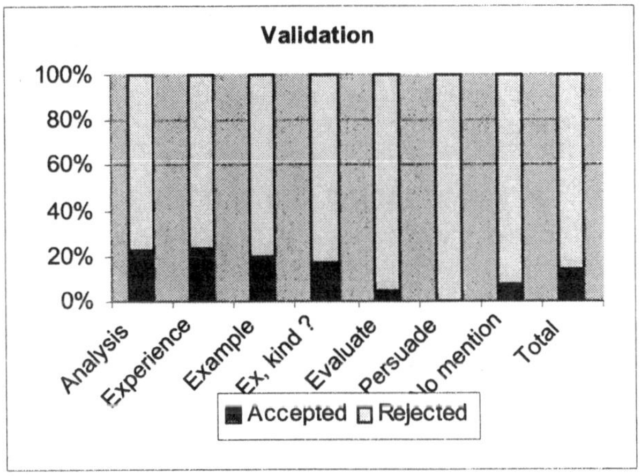

Figure 6. Distribution of acceptances and rejections by type of validation

4.3 What do program committees look for?

The program committee looks for solid evidence to support your result. It's not enough that your idea works for you, there must also be evidence that the idea or the technique will help someone else as well.

The statistics above show that analysis, actual experience in the field, and good use of realistic examples tend to be the most effective ways of showing why your result should be believed. Careful narrative, qualitative analysis can also work if the reasoning is sound.

Why should the reader believe your result?

Is the paper argued persuasively? What evidence is presented to support the claim? What kind of evidence is offered? Does it meet the usual standard of the subdiscipline?

Is the kind of evaluation you're doing described clearly and accurately? "Controlled experiment" requires more than data collection, and "case study" requires more than anecdotal discussion. Pilot studies that lay the groundwork for controlled experiments are often not publishable by themselves.

Is the validation related to the claim? If you're claiming performance improvement, validation should analyze performance, not ease of use or generality. And conversely.

Is this such an interesting, potentially powerful idea that it should get exposure despite a shortage of concrete evidence?

Authors tend to have trouble in some specific situations. Here are some examples, with advice for staying out of trouble:

- *If you claim to improve on prior art,* compare your result objectively to the prior art.
- *If you used an analysis technique,* follow the rules of that analysis technique. If the technique is not a common one in software engineering (e.g., meta-analysis, decision theory, user studies or other behavioral analyses), explain the technique and standards of proof, and be clear about your adherence to the technique.
- *If you offer practical experience as evidence for your result,* establish the effect your research has. If at all possible, compare similar situations with and without your result.

- *If you performed a controlled experiment,* explain the experimental design. What is the hypothesis? What is the treatment? What is being controlled? What data did you collect, and how did you analyze it? Are the results significant? What are the potentially confounding factors, and how are they handled? Do the conclusions follow rigorously from the experimental data?
- *If you performed an empirical study,* explain what you measured, how you analyzed it, and what you concluded. What data did you collect, and how? How is the analysis related to the goal of supporting your claim about the result? Do not confuse correlation with causality.
- *If you use a small example for explaining the result,* provide additional evidence of its practical use and scalability.

5. How do you combine the elements into a research strategy?

It is clear that not all combinations of a research question, a result, and a validation strategy lead to good research. Software engineering has not developed good general guidance on this question.

Tables 1, 3, and 5 define a 3-dimensional space. Some portions of that space are densely populated: One common paradigm is to find a better way to perform some software development or maintenance task, realize this in a concrete procedure supported by a tool, and evaluate the effectiveness of this procedure and tool by determining how its use affects some measure (e.g., error rates) of quality. Another common paradigm is to find a better way to evaluate a formalizable property of a software system, develop a formal model that supports inference, and to show that the new model allows formal analysis or proof of the properties of interest.

Clearly, the researcher does not have free choice to mix and match the techniques—validating the correctness of a formal model through field study is as inappropriate as attempting formal verification of a method based on good organization of rules of thumb.

Selecting a type of result that will answer a given question usually does not seem to present much difficulty, at least for researchers who think carefully about the choice. Blindly adopting the research paradigm someone used last year for a completely different problem is a different case, of course, and it can lead to serious misfits.

Choosing a good form of validation is much harder, and this is often a source of difficulty in completing a successful paper. Table 6 shows some common good matches. This does not, unfortunately, provide complete guidance.

When I advise PhD students on the validation section of their theses, I offer the following heuristic: Look carefully at the short statement of the result—the principal claim of the thesis. This often has two or three clauses (e.g., I found an efficient and complete method ..."); if so, each presents a separate validation problem. Ask of each clause whether it is a global statement ("always", "fully"), a qualified statement ("a 25% improvement", "for noncyclic structures..."), or an existential statement {"we found an instance of"). Global statements often require analytic validation, qualified statements can often be validated by evaluation or careful examination of experience, and existential statements can sometimes be validated by a single positive example. A frequent result of this discussion is that students restate the thesis claims to reflect more precisely what the theses actually achieve. If we have this discussion early enough in the thesis process, students think about planning the research with demonstrable claims in mind.

Concretely, Table 7 shows the combinations that were represented among the accepted papers at ICSE 2002, omitting the 7 for which the abstracts were unclear about validation:

Table 7. Paradigms of ICSE2002 acceptances

Question	Result	Validation	#
Devel method	Procedure	Analysis	2
Devel method	Procedure	Experience	3
Devel method	Procedure	Example	3
Devel method	Qual model	Experience	2
Devel method	Analytic model	Experience	2
Devel method	Notation or tool	Experience	1
Analysis method	Procedure	Analysis	5
Analysis method	Procedure	Evaluation	1
Analysis method	Procedure	Experience	2
Analysis method	Procedure	Example	6
Analysis method	Analytic model	Experience	1
Analysis method	Analytic model	Example	2
Analysis method	Tool	Analysis	1
Eval of instance	Specific analysis	Analysis	3
Eval of instance	Specific analysis	Example	2

6. Does the abstract matter?

The abstracts of papers submitted to ICSE convey a sense of the kinds of research submitted to the conference. Some abstracts were easier to read and (apparently) more informative than others. Many of the clearest abstracts had a common structure:

- Two or three sentences about the current state of the art, identifying a particular problem
- One or two sentences about what this paper contributes to improving the situation

- One or two sentences about the specific result of the paper and the main idea behind it
- A sentence about how the result is demonstrated or defended

Abstracts in roughly this format often explained clearly what readers could expect in the paper.

Acceptance rates were highest for papers whose abstracts indicate that analysis or experience provides evidence in support of the work. Decisions on papers were made on the basis of the whole papers, of course, not just the abstracts—but it is reasonable to assume that the abstracts reflect what's in the papers.

Whether you like it or not, people judge papers by their abstracts and read the abstract in order to decide whether to read the whole paper. It's important for the abstract to tell the story. Don't assume, though, that simply adding a sentence about analysis or experience to your abstract is sufficient; the paper must deliver what the abstract promises

7. Questions you might ask about this report

7.1. Is this a sure-fire recipe?

No, not at all. First, it's not a recipe. Second, not all software engineers share the same views of interesting and significant research. Even if your paper is clear about what you've done and what you can conclude, members of a program committee may not agree about how to interpret your result. These are usually honest technical disagreements, and committee members will try hard to understand what you have done. You can help by explaining your work clearly; this report should help you do that.

7.2 Is ICSE different from other conferences?

ICSE recognizes several distinct types of technical papers [6]. For 2002, they were published separately in the proceedings

Several other conferences offer "how to write a paper" advice:

In 1993, several OOPSLA program committee veterans gave a panel on "How to Get a Paper Accepted at OOPSLA" [9]. This updated the 1991 advice for the same conference [14]

SIGSOFT offers two essays on getting papers accepted, though neither was actually written for a software engineering audience. They are "How to Have Your Abstract Rejected" [26] (which focuses on theoretical papers) and "Advice to Authors of Extended Abstracts", which was written for PLDI. [16].

Rather older, Levin and Reddell, the 1983 SOSP (operating systems) program co-chairs offered advice on writing a good systems paper [11]. USENIX now provides this advice to its authors. Also in the systems vein, Partridge offers advice on "How to Increase the Chances Your Paper is Accepted at ACM SIGCOMM" [15].

SIGCHI offers a "Guide to Successful Papers Submission" that includes criteria for evaluation and discussion of common types of CHI results, together with how different evaluation criteria apply for different types of results [13]. A study [8] of regional factors that affect acceptance found regional differences in problems with novelty, significance, focus, and writing quality.

In 1993, the SIGGRAPH conference program chair wrote a discussion of the selection process, "How to Get Your SIGGRAPH Paper Rejected" [10]. The 2003 SIGGRAPH call for papers [21] has a description of the review process and a frequently-asked questions section with an extensive set of questions on "Getting a Paper Accepted".

7.3. What about this report itself?

People have asked me, "what would happen if you submitted this to ICSE?" Without venturing to predict what any given ICSE program committee would do, I note that as a research result or technical paper (a "finding" in Brooks' sense [3]) it falls short in a number of ways:

- There is no attempt to show that anyone else can apply the model. That is, there is no demonstration of inter-rater reliability, or for that matter even repeatability by the same rater.
- The model is not justified by any principled analysis, though fragments, such as the types of models that can serve as results, are principled. In defense of the model, Bowker and Starr [2] show that useful classifications blend principle and pragmatic descriptive power.
- Only one conference and one program committee is reflected here.
- The use of abstracts as proxies for full papers is suspect.
- There is little discussion of related work other than the essays about writing papers for other conferences. Although discussion of related work does appear in two complementary papers [19, 20], this report does not stand alone.

On the other hand, I believe that this report does meet Brooks' standard for "rules of thumb" (generalizations, signed by the author but perhaps incompletely supported by data, judged by usefulness and freshness), and I offer it in that sense.

8. Acknowledgements

This work depended critically on access to the entire body of submitted papers for the ICSE 2002 conference, which would not have been possible without the cooperation and encouragement of the ICSE 2002 program committee. The development of these ideas has also benefited from discussion with the ICSE 2002 program committee, with colleagues at Carnegie Mellon, and at open discussion sessions at FSE Conferences. The work has been supported by the A. J. Perlis Chair at Carnegie Mellon University.

9. References

1. Victor R. Basili. The experimental paradigm in software engineering. In *Experimental Software Engineering Issues: Critical Assessment and Future Directives*. Proc of Dagstuhl-Workshop, H. Dieter Rombach, Victor R. Basili, and Richard Selby (eds), published as *Lecture Notes in Computer Science #706*, Springer-Verlag 1993.
2. Geoffrey Bowker and Susan Leigh Star: *Sorting Things Out: Classification and Its Consequences*. MIT Press, 1999
3. Frederick P. Brooks, Jr. Grasping Reality Through Illusion—Interactive Graphics Serving Science. *Proc 1988 ACM SIGCHI Human Factors in Computer Systems Conf (CHI '88)* pp. 1-11.
4. Rebecca Burnett. *Technical Communication*. Thomson Heinle 2001.
5. Thomas F. Gieryn. *Cultural Boundaries of Science: Credibility on the line*. Univ of Chicago Press, 1999.
6. ICSE 2002 Program Committee. *Types of ICSE papers*. http://icse-conferences.org/2002/info/paperTypes.html
7. Impact Project. "Determining the impact of software engineering research upon practice. Panel summary, *Proc. 23rd International Conference on Software Engineering (ICSE 2001)*, 2001
8. Ellen Isaacs and John Tang. *Why don't more non-North-American papers get accepted to CHI?* http://acm.org/sigchi/bulletin/1996.1/isaacs.html
9. Ralph E. Johnson & panel. How to Get a Paper Accepted at OOPSLA. *Proc OOPSLA'93*, pp. 429-436, http://acm.org/sigplan/oopsla/oopsla96/how93.html
10. Jim Kajiya. How to Get Your SIGGRAPH Paper Rejected. Mirrored at http://www.cc.gatech.edu/student.services/phd/phd-advice/kajiya
11. Roy Levin and David D. Redell. How (and How Not) to Write a Good Systems Paper. *ACM SIGOPS Operating Systems Review*, Vol. 17, No. 3 (July, 1983), pages 35-40. http://ftp.digital.com/pub/DEC/SRC/other/SOSPadvice.txt
12. William Newman. A preliminary analysis of the products of HCI research, using pro forma abstracts. *Proc 1994 ACM SIGCHI Human Factors in Computer Systems Conf (CHI '94)*, pp.278-284.
13. William Newman et al. *Guide to Successful Papers Submission at CHI 2001*. http://acm.org/sigs/sigchi/chi2001/call/submissions/guide-papers.html
14. OOPSLA '91 Program Committee. How to get your paper accepted at OOPSLA. *Proc OOPSLA'91*, pp.359-363. http://acm.org/sigplan/oopsla/oopsla96/how91.html
15. Craig Partridge. How to Increase the Chances your Paper is Accepted at ACM SIGCOMM. http://www.acm.org/sigcomm/conference-misc/author-guide.html
16. William Pugh and PDLI 1991 Program Committee. *Advice to Authors of Extended Abstracts*. http://acm.org/sigsoft/conferences/pughadvice.html
17. Samuel Redwine, et al. *DoD Related Software Technology Requirements, Practices, and Prospects for the Future*. IDA Paper P-1788, June 1984.
18. S. Redwine & W. Riddle. Software technology maturation. *Proceedings of the Eighth International Conference on Software Engineering*, May 1985, pp. 189-200.
19. Mary Shaw. The coming-of-age of software architecture research. *Proc. 23rd Int'l Conf on Software Engineering (ICSE 2001)*, pp. 656-664a.
20. Mary Shaw. What makes good research in software engineering? Presented at ETAPS 02, appeared in Opinion Corner department, *Int'l Jour on Software Tools for Tech Transfer*, vol 4, DOI 10.1007/s10009-002-0083-4, June 2002.
21. SigGraph 2003 Call for Papers. http://www.siggraph.org/s2003/cfp/papers/index.html
22. W. F. Tichy, P. Lukowicz, L. Prechelt, & E. A. Heinz. "Experimental evaluation in computer science: A quantitative study." *Journal of Systems Software*, Vol. 28, No. 1, 1995, pp. 9-18.
23. Walter F. Tichy. "Should computer scientists experiment more? 16 reasons to avoid experimentation." *IEEE Computer*, Vol. 31, No. 5, May 1998
24. Marvin V. Zelkowitz and Delores Wallace. Experimental validation in software engineering. *Information and Software Technology*, Vol 39, no 11, 1997, pp. 735-744.
25. Marvin V. Zelkowitz and Delores Wallace. Experimental models for validating technology. *IEEE Computer*, Vol. 31, No. 5, 1998, pp.23-31.
26. Mary-Claire van Leunen and Richard Lipton. *How to have your abstract rejected*. http://acm.org/sigsoft/conferences/vanLeunenLipton.html

One- and Two-Day Tutorials

Practical Software Measurement

David N. Card
Software Productivity Consortium
card@software.org

Abstract

This tutorial provides a one-day overview of Practical Software Measurement (PSM). The measurement approach focuses on satisfying the information needs of project managers. Innovative elements of PSM include the measurement process model and the measurement information model. Rather than discussing specific numerical techniques in detail, this course emphasizes basic concepts.

1. Introduction

This tutorial provides an ***introduction*** to the basic concepts of software measurement for project management purposes including measurement planning, project estimation, feasibility analysis, and status monitoring. The specific objectives of the course are to:

- Describe a systematic approach to software measurement for project management purposes.
- Explain the relationship of this approach to other initiatives and approaches
- Introduce "standard" measurement information and process models

This tutorial is based on the book of the same name [1]. This book is an implementation guide for ISO/IEC Standard 15939 [2]. The standard defines two key concepts – the measurement information model and measurement process model. This course explains how those models can be instantiated to support project management decision-making. (ISO/IEC 15939 has been adopted as the basis for the Measurement and Analysis Process Area of the CMMI [3].)

2. Measurement Information Model

One of the goals of the standardization effort was define a consistent set of terminology for basic measurement concepts. The result was a structure that defines the relationships among information needs, several types of measures (i.e., indicators, derived measures, base measures), and measurable entities. This Measurement Information Model defines a generic measurement product. PSM further describes the type of product appropriate for project management. It defines seven categories of information needs. Information needs are similar to goals in the GQM approach [4]. However, they are more general (not limited to goals) and less open-ended (PSM provides potential solutions for the project manager).

3. Measurement Process Model

Regardless of the purpose for which measurement is conducted, several activities have to be undertaken to obtain meaningful measurement results. The Measurement Process Model defines four basic activities:

Plan Measurement – the activity in the process model concerned with understanding the information needs of the project and defining appropriate measures to satisfy them. It "designs" the desired measurement product.

Perform Measurement – the activity in the process model concerned with populating or executing the information model to produce the results necessary to support decision-making.

Evaluate Measurement – the activity in the process model concerned with evaluating the measures, themselves, as well as the measurement process.

Establish Measurement – the activity in the process model concerned with establishing and sustaining a measurement program within an organization.

0-7695-1877-X/03 $17.00 © 2003 IEEE

The first two activities are sometimes referred to as the "core" measurement process. The attached figure shows all major components of the measurement process model

4. Summary

PSM provides a systematic method of planning and performing software measurement and analysis. The PSM and ISO/IEC 15939 approach to software measurement is becoming increasingly widely accepted in industry around the world. However, these concepts may also be of interest to measurement researchers who desire to understand the context in which their ideas may be applied in practice. PSM and ISO/IEC 15939 provide a common language that may improve communication on software measurement issues between practitioners and researchers.

More information about PSM, including a list of qualified trainers, may be obtained at www.psmsc.com.

5. References

[1] J. McGarry, D. Card, et al., _Practical Software Measurement_, Addison Wesley, 2002.

[2] K. el Emam and D. Card (Editors), _ISO/IEC Standard 15939, Software Measurement Process_, International Organization for Standardization, 2002.

[3] CMMI Development Team, _Capability Maturity Model - Integrated Systems/Software Engineering_, Software Engineering Institute, 2002.

[4] V. Basili and D. Weiss, A Methodology for Collecting Valid Software Engineering Data, _IEEE Transactions on Software Engineering_, October 1984.

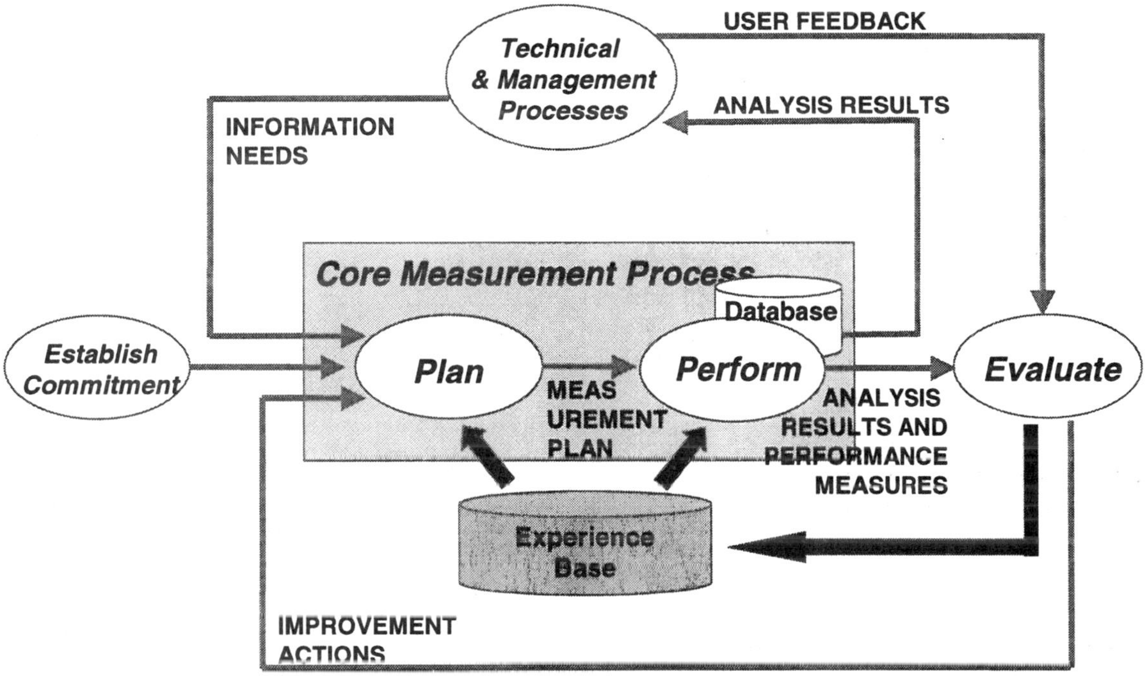

Documenting Software Architectures: Views and Beyond

Paul Clements*, David Garlan**, Reed Little*, Robert Nord*, Judith Stafford*
Carnegie Mellon University
Pittsburgh, Pennsylvania 15213 USA
{clements, little, rn, jas}@sei.cmu.edu, garlan@cs.cmu.edu

Software architecture has emerged as a foundational concept for the successful development of large, complex systems. Signs that the field is maturing to become an engineering discipline include textbooks on the subject; the work in repeatable design, exemplified by architectural styles and patterns; robust methods for evaluating software architectures; international conferences devoted to it; and recognition of architecture as a professional practice.

However, treatment of architecture to date has largely concentrated on its design, and to a lesser extent, its validation. But effectively *documenting* an architecture is as important as crafting it, because if the architecture is not understood (or worse, misunderstood) it cannot meet its goals as the unifying vision for system and software development.

Three years ago, researchers at the Software Engineering Institute and the Carnegie Mellon School of Computer Science set out to answer the question: "How should you document an architecture so that others can successfully use it, maintain it, and build a system from it?" The result of that work is an approach we loosely call "views and beyond." [1]

Modern software architecture practice embraces the concept of architectural *views*. A view is a representation of a set of system elements and relations associated with them. Modern systems are more than complex enough to make it difficult to grasp them all at once. Instead, we restrict our attention at any one moment to one (or a small number) of the software system's structures, which we represent as views.

Some authors prescribe a fixed set of views with which to engineer and communicate an architecture. Rational's Unified Process, for example, is based on Kruchten's 4+1 view approach to software [4]. The Siemens Four Views model [3] is another example. A recent trend, however, is to recognize that architects should produce whatever views are useful for the system at hand. IEEE 1471 exemplifies this philosophy; it holds that an architecture description consists of a set of views, each of which conforms to a *viewpoint*, which in turn is a realization of the concerns of one or more stakeholders.

This philosophy about views leads to the fundamental principle of the views-and-beyond approach:

> *Documenting an architecture is a matter of documenting the relevant views, and then adding documentation that applies to more than one view.*

This tutorial provides a practical and comprehensive approach to software architecture documentation that helps architects (a) understand what views are available with which to document an architecture and how each can be used in the system's lifecycle; (b) how to choose the set of views that will be most valuable to the architecture's community of stakeholders; (c) the information needed to document a view; and (d) the information needed to document information that applies across views. The tutorial presents the information in the context of prevailing prescriptive models for architecture, including the Rational Unified Process [4], Siemens Four Views [3], ANSI/IEEE-1471-2000 [2], and the UML. This tutorial is intended to help software architects and software lead designers whose job includes producing architectural documentation. The tutorial is also aimed at software technical managers whose job includes overseeing and managing the architecture documentation process, including the incorporation of stakeholder interests and needs.

Outline

The major topics of the tutorial include:

Principles of sound documentation. This lecture will cover seven fundamental principles that apply to all technical documentation, but especially to architecture documentation: (1) Write from the point of view of the reader; (2) Avoid unnecessary repetition; (3) Avoid ambiguity; (4) Use a standard organization; (5) Record rationale; (6) Keep documentation current but not too current; and (7) Review documentation for fitness of purpose.

* This author is with the Software Engineering Institute at Carnegie Mellon University.
** This author is with the School of Computer Science at Carnegie Mellon University.

0-7695-1877-X/03 $17.00 © 2003 IEEE

Viewtypes, styles, and views. The first principle for documenting software architectures is to document the relevant views and then document the information that applies beyond views. But what views are relevant? Rational's 4+1 approach prescribes one set; the Siemens Four Views approach prescribes another set. In order to choose the relevant views to document, the software architect must understand what views are available. Fundamentally, architects must think about the system in three ways:

(1) how the system is structured as a set of implementation units;

(2) how the system is structured as a set of elements that interact dynamically with each other at runtime; and

(3) how the software structures correspond to structures in the system's environment.

Views correspond to these informational categories, which we call *viewtypes*. Views in the *module viewtype* show elements that correspond to implementation units. Views in the *component-and-connector viewtype* show elements in execution. Views in the *allocation viewtype* show how the software relates to environmental entities. Within each viewtype, there are well-known patterns of design decisions (*styles*) that the architect can re-use. A style applied to a system is a *view*. This lecture establishes the important concepts of viewtype, style, and view, with examples.

The Style Zoo. This lecture will cover some of the styles commonly seen in each of the three viewtypes. Module styles covered include decomposition, layered, and generalization. Component-and-connector styles covered include shared-data, communicating-processes, client-server, and pipe-and-filter. Allocation styles covered include the implementation, work assignment, deployment. Each style is presented covering its elements and relations, what the style is useful for, what other styles are related (or often confused with), and some common ways to represent the style using formal and informal notations, especially the UML.

Advanced concepts. This lecture covers several advanced topics that a software architect must be comfortable with in order to produce a sound documentation package. These concepts include (1) refinement, the mechanism by which information is "chunked" into digestible units; (2) context diagrams, which show the relation of the software being documented to its environment; (3) combined views, which are a mechanism to convey different kinds of information in a single view in a disciplined, structured fashion; (4) variability, which is about showing how the architecture can vary at build-time or runtime; and (5) software interfaces, which covers how to document the interfaces to the architectural elements shown in the views.

Choosing the views. This lecture presents a simple 3-step procedure for choosing the relevant views. The procedure is stakeholder-based, using stakeholders (or stakeholder proxies) to determine the uses to which the documentation will be put, and the information best positioned to satisfy those uses. This ensures that the resulting documentation package will be one that the stakeholders find helpful and useful..

Building the documentation package. This lecture presents a seven-part template that architects can use to document views, and a 7-part template that architects can use to document the information beyond views.

Conclusions. This lecture maps the concepts and templates explored in this tutorial with well-known architectural prescriptions, including the 4+1 approach of the Rational Unified Process, the Siemens Four Views approach, and the ANSI/IEEE-1471-2000 recommended best practice for documenting architectures for software-intensive systems. The lecture concludes by re-capping the highlights of the tutorial, and asking for feedback.

References

[1] Clements, P., F. Bachmann, L. Bass, D. Garlan, J. Ivers, R. Little, R. Nord, J. Stafford. *Documenting Software Architectures: Views and Beyond*. Addison-Wesley, Boston, 2002.

[2] IEEE 2000. IEEE Product No.: SH94869-TBR: Recommended Practice for Architectural Description of Software-Intensive Systems. IEEE Standard No. 1471-2000. Available at http://shop.ieee.org/store/.

[3] Hofmeister, C., R. Nord, and D. Soni. *Applied Software Architecture*, Addison-Wesley, Boston, 2000.

[4] Kruchten, P. *The Rational Unified Process: An Introduction*, Second Edition. Addison-Wesley, Boston, 2001.

Computing Systems Dependability

John C. Knight
Department of Computer Science, University of Virginia
Charlottesville, VA 22904-4740
+1 434 982 2216
knight@cs.virginia.edu

1. Introduction

Computer systems provide us with a wide range of services upon which we have come to depend. Many computers are embedded in more complex devices that we use such as automobiles, aircraft, appliances, and medical devices. Others are part of sophisticated systems that provide us with a variety of important facilities such as financial services, telecommunications, transportation systems, and energy production and distribution networks. Engineering systems to be as dependable as we require them to be is a significant challenge and requires a variety of analysis and development techniques.

It is important that computer engineers, software engineers, project managers, and users understand the major elements of current technology in the field of dependability, yet this material tends to be unfamiliar to researchers and practitioners alike. Researchers are often concerned in one way or another with some aspect of what is mistakenly called software "reliability". All practitioners are concerned with the "reliability" of the software that they produce but researchers and practitioners tend not to understand fully the broader impact of their work. A lot of research, such as that on testing, is concerned directly with software dependability. Understanding dependability more fully allows researchers to be more effective. Similarly, practitioners can direct their efforts during development more effectively if they have a better understanding of dependability.

2. Concepts and Definitions

Many systems need to be *dependable*. The notion of dependability is broken down into six fundamental properties: (1) reliability; (2) availability; (3) safety; (4) confidentiality; (5) integrity; and (6) maintainability. Informally, it is expected that a dependable system will be operational when needed (availability), that the system will keep operating correctly while being used (reliability), that there will be no unauthorized disclosure (confidentiality) or modification (integrity) of information that the system is using, and that operation of the system will not be dangerous (safety). Precise definitions of these terms have been developed over a period of many years by a group of researchers led by J.C. Laprie [2].

It is important to note that security [1] is not included explicitly in this list. Rather, it is covered by the second, fourth and fifth items in the list. It is also important to note that some aspects of dependability are not completely intuitive. For example: (1) a communications system can be highly available but unreliable; (2) an aircraft system can have low availability but be safe; and (3) an information system can be reliable yet insecure.

The first step in developing a dependable computer system is to define the dependability requirements. As an example, consider an implantable heart pacemaker. Clearly, such a device has to be dependable because a pacemaker failure is obviously serious. A pacemaker does not have any requirement for security but has very strong requirements for safety and availability. The device does not necessarily have to be reliable (in the formal sense). If it failed just after one heartbeat but reset itself and resumed proper operation before the next one, there would probably be no damage.

Once the dependability requirements for a system have been determined, the next step is to determine the system hazards. *Hazards* are system states that could lead to undesirable outcomes which result from using a system. Hazards are not obvious, and determining the hazards for a given system is often a difficult and complex task. The primary danger in most medical systems, for example, is patient injury, and so any state in which a patient might be injured is a hazard. For a pacemaker, the most serious and obvious hazard is failure to pace the patient's heart when required. A second, much less obvious hazard would be to pace the heart when it was *not* required. Either could be fatal.

If a system were perfect and stayed that way, it would never fail to supply acceptable service, and there would be no concern for its performance. However, systems do fail, they do break as time passes, and in some cases, they contain defects in their basic design. Informally, a *failure* has occurred when a system no longer meets users expectations. The notion of failure is only relevant to what the system's users experience. This is an important concept

0-7695-1877-X/03 $17.00 © 2003 IEEE

because the failure of components within a system is both expected and possibly common. The trick to dependable design is to make sure that failed components within a system do not lead to system failure.

An *error* is a system state which, if nothing is done to prevent it, might lead to a system failure. Thus, for example, a system state in which various data elements are corrupted for some reason might well lead to a system failure unless the system detects and corrects the error. It is important to remember, therefore that *failure* is when an *error* reaches the service interface. Errors that do not reach the service interface are not relevant to the user because they do not impact the service provided.

A *fault* is the adjudged cause of an error. A defect in a piece of software that causes some of the system's data elements to become corrupted is a fault. Similarly, computer hardware that malfunctions is a fault, as is a break in a power or communications cable caused by corrosion.

There are two basic types of fault—*degradation* faults and *design* faults. Degradation faults arise over time, and a component that operates correctly for some period of time might stop doing so as a result of a degradation fault. The simplest example of a degradation fault is when the filament in a light bulb breaks. Degradation faults have to be expected, and, if such faults could lead to failure, the system has to be designed to operate acceptably after such faults have occurred. This concept is referred to as *fault tolerance*. Thus fault tolerance is a mechanism by which, in part, a system dependability property (such as availability) is achieved.

A design fault is something that is wrong with a system that has been there from the outset. It is not the result of a component wearing out. All software faults are design faults because software does not degenerate in the usual sense. Design faults can be *avoided* altogether by careful design processes, *removed* during development by correcting the design after some form of analysis reveals the fault, or tolerated during operation.

To build a pacemaker that meets typical dependability requirements, it is necessary to deal with a variety of both design and degradation faults. Such a device is very complex and contains a lot of software. Thus a wide range of design faults must be expected including design faults in the microprocessor's circuitry, in the wiring between discrete components, and in the software. Similarly, a wide range of degradation faults must be expected including gate failures in the microprocessor, battery failure, sensor failure, and wiring failures between discrete components.

3. Software's Role

Software is a key component in any computer system, and it has been a factor in many serious failures. Numerous problems arise because of the interaction between software engineering and systems engineering. In a system that employs fault tolerance, it is usually the case that software implements the fault tolerance designed to deal with hardware faults. In a pacemaker, for example, it is completely unacceptable for the device to cease operation if a sensor fails. Where the sensor is providing critical data about heart activity, it might be impossible to continue to provide full functionality without that sensor. The software must be written in such a case to diagnose the situation, record the details for subsequent analysis, and switch to a simple but safe emergency pacing algorithm.

The Achilles' heel of software development for most types of system is requirements specification. In the pacemaker example, it is necessary for the software specification to include full medical functionality, hardrware fault diagnosis, patient data recording, communication with external equipment, and emergency functionality. Specification of such systems is difficult and error prone.

A great deal of effort has been expended on the development of formal notations for specification and analysis with the goal of allowing complete, unambiguous and analyzable specifications to be built. There have been notable successes with this technology.

Verification is another major challenge in the development of software for most applications. Again, many techniques have been developed to facilitate verification including formal verification and model checking. Testing, however, remains the dominant approach to verification in practice. Testing also remains problematic. It is impossible to execute a sufficient number of tests to permit a statistical assessment of extreme dependability and so the results of almost any testing process are informal [3]. Running tests on many systems is difficult because test harnesses have to duplicate a complex operating environment.

4. Conclusion

Computer systems offer tremendous capabilities but making them dependable is a complex process. An elaborate interplay between techniques from systems engineering and software engineering has to be undertaken. Additional information can be obtained from textbooks such as those by Storey [5] and Leveson [4], from a variety of journals and conferences.

5. References

[1] Anderson, R., *Security Engineering: A Guide to Building Dependable Distributed Systems*, Wiley, 2001.

[2] Avizienis, Laprie, Randell, "Fundamental Concepts in System Dependability", *IARP / IEEE-RAS Workshop on Robot Dependability*, May 2001.

[3] Butler, R. and G. Finelli, "The infeasibility of experimental quantification of life-critical software reliability." IEEE Trans. on Software Engineering, 19(1):3--12, Jan. 1993.

[4] Leveson, N., Safeware: *System Safety and Computers*, Addison Wesley, 1995.

[5] Storey, N., *Safety-Critical Computer Systems*, Addison Wesley, 1996.

Goal-Oriented Requirements Engineering: From System Objectives to UML Models to Precise Software Specifications

Axel van Lamsweerde
Department of Computing Science, University of Louvain
B-1348 Louvain-la-Neuve (Belgium)
avl@info.ucl.ac.be

Abstract

This tutorial presents a comprehensive overview of state-of-the-art techniques for eliciting, modeling, specifying, analyzing and documenting high-quality system requirements.

1. Context and Motivation

Requirements engineering (RE) is the branch of systems engineering concerned with the elicitation of the objectives to be achieved by the system envisioned, the operationalization of such objectives into specifications of services and constraints, the assignment of responsibilities for the resulting requirements to agents such as humans, devices and software, and the evolution of such requirements over time and across system families. Getting adequate, consistent and complete requirements is difficult and critical. Recent surveys have confirmed the growing recognition of RE as an area of primary concern in software engineering research and practice.

State-of-the-art reports on RE usually remain at a fairly high level of coverage by discussing general principles and guidelines [6, 7, 12]. Recent textbooks on software modeling generally focus on modeling designs without much concern for where such models are coming from [1, 5].

The aim of this full-day tutorial is to fill this gap by presenting a systematic approach for engineering high-quality requirements. The approach covers the entire RE lifecycle and integrates state-of-the-art techniques for requirements elicitation, modeling, specification, analysis and assignment. We concentrate on the technical aspects of requirements engineering, with a strong emphasis on a constructive approach to requirements quality assurance.

In particular, we present a systematic *method* to elaborate complex system models, analyze them, and derive software specifications from them. The method, known as KAOS ("Keep All Objectives Satisfied"), has been developed and refined by the author and his group for about ten years of research and experience in real projects [3, 4, 8, 9, 10, 11].

2. Tutorial Structure

The tutorial addresses the entire requirements engineering lifecycle. It covers goal elicitation, domain analysis, system modeling, goal operationalization into requirements and assumptions, assignment of responsibilities among the software and the environment, software specification, and (lightweight) formal analysis.

The *first part* of the tutorial introduces some basic principles including the aim and scope of RE, the products and processes involved, the target qualities and frequent pitfalls, the critical role played by requirements in the software lifecycle, and so on. Key notions such as "requirement", "domain property", "environmental assumption", and "software specification" are precisely defined and related to each other.

The *second part* is devoted to system modeling in the specific context of engineering requirements. A multi-view framework is introduced that integrates the following submodels:

- AND/OR goal diagrams for the refinement and abstraction of functional and non-functional objectives in the current system and in the system-to-be,
- UML class diagrams for modeling conceptual objects concerned by the objectives in the two systems,
- context diagrams for modeling agents (such as humans, devices and software) in the system-to-be, their responsibilities and interfaces,
- UML use case diagrams for modeling software services that operationalize the functional goals assigned to software agents,
- UML sequence and state diagrams for requirements mining and behavior modeling.

We conclude this part by discussing mechanisms for integrating these multiple models and for modeling-in-the-large.

0-7695-1877-X/03 $17.00 © 2003 IEEE

The *third part* of the tutorial briefly presents lightweight techniques for precise specification of the goals, objects, agents and operations from these various models.

The *fourth part* reviews various techniques for RE-specific analysis including:

- semi-formal and formal techniques for goal refinement, responsibility assignment and goal operationalization;
- qualitative reasoning techniques for selecting among alternative system proposals (that is, alternative refinements of functional goals and alternative responsibility assignments to agents) based on the non-functional goals refined in the goal model;
- inductive reasoning techniques for mining goals from concrete, operational material such as scenarios,
- semi-formal and formal techniques for obstacle analysis, that is, the generation and resolution of abnormal behaviors of agents in the software or its environment in order to produce more complete requirements for robust, high assurance systems,
- semi-formal and formal techniques for managing conflicts between system goals, software requirements and environmental assumptions.

The *final part* of the tutorial puts all previous pieces together by presenting a constructive method for elaborating a full, robust and consistent system model and software specification through incremental integration of the goal, object, agent, and operation submodels.

3. Modalities

The presentation strongly relies on running examples from two completely different types of systems: an information system and a process control system. In addition, the method and associated tools are shown in action on a system simplified from a real project.

Material distributed to the participant includes slide handouts and chapters of a forthcoming book.

4. Conclusions

By the end of the tutorial attendants will have gained some deep insights on the specific problems raised during the requirements engineering process, have a good sense of the range of technical solutions to these problems, and have the practical ability to apply the various modeling notations, structuring mechanisms, specification constructs, analysis techniques and method steps introduced and illustrated at length.

5. Bibliography

[1] G. Booch, J. Rumbaugh and I. Jacobson, *The Unified Modeling Language User Guide*. Addison-Wesley, 1999.

[2] L. Chung, B. Nixon, E. Yu and J. Mylopoulos, *Non-functional requirements in software engineering*. Kluwer Academic, 2000.

[3] A. Dardenne, A. van Lamsweerde and S. Fickas, "Goal-Directed Requirements Acquisition", *Science of Computer Programming* Vol. 20, North Holland, 1993, pp. 3-50.

[4] R. Darimont and A. van Lamsweerde, "Formal Refinement Patterns for Goal-Driven Requirements Elaboration", *Proceedings FSE-4 - 4th ACM Symp. on the Foundations of Software Engineering*, Oct. 1996, pp. 179-190.

[5] D.F. D'Souza and A. C. Wills, *Objects, Components, and Frameworks with UML – The CATALYSIS Approach*. Addison Wesley, 1999.

[6] M. Jackson, *Software Requirements & Specifications - A Lexicon of Practice, Principles and Prejudices*. ACM Press, Addison-Wesley, 1995.

[7] G. Kotonya and I. Sommerville, *Requirements Engineering - Processes and Techniques*. Wiley, 1997.

[8] A. van Lamsweerde and E. Letier, "Handling Obstacles in Goal-Oriented Requirements Engineering", *IEEE Transactions on Software Engineering,* Special Issue on Exception Handling, Vol. 26 No. 10, October 2000, 978-1005.

[9] A. van Lamsweerde, R. Darimont and E. Letier, "Managing Conflicts in Goal-Driven Requirements Engineering", *IEEE Transactions on Software Engineering*, Special Issue on Managing Inconsistency in Software Development, November 1998.

[10] A. van Lamsweerde, "Requirements Engineering in the Year 00: A Research Perspective", Invited Paper for *ICSE'2000 - 22nd International Conference on Software Engineering*, Limerick, ACM Press, 2000, 5-19.

[11] E. Letier and A. van Lamsweerde, "Agent-Based Tactics for Goal-Oriented Requirements Elaboration", *Proc. ICSE'2002 - 24th International Conference on Software Engineering*, Orlando, May 2002.

[12] P. Loucopoulos and V. Karakostas, *System Requirements Engineering*. McGraw-Hill, 1995.

Usage-Centered Software Engineering: An Agile Approach to Integrating Users, User Interfaces, and Usability into Software Engineering Practice

Larry L. Constantine
University of technology, Sydney (Australia)
Constantine & Lockwood, Ltd.
lconstantine@foruse.com

Lucy A. D. Lockwood
Constantine & Lockwood, Ltd.
llockwood@foruse.com

Abstract

Usage-centered design is a systematic, model-driven approach to visual and interaction design with an established record of effectiveness in a wide variety of settings and areas of application. The tutorial introduces the models and methods of usage-centered design and explores the integration of usage-centered approaches into software engineering practice. Agile approaches to modeling will be emphasized, with the focus on use cases, which are central to usage-centered design and serve as a common thread throughout an integrated usage-centered software engineering process.

1. Introduction

In the final analysis, nearly all software is intended to serve the needs and support the interests of its human users, yet software engineering is often weakest when it comes to addressing the critical areas of user requirements, usability, user interfaces, and interaction design. Often these concerns are either minimized, ignored, or relegated to "other" disciplines as a responsibility outside the scope of software engineering. This tutorial shows how user requirements, usability, and user interface design can be made the very core of a successful software engineering process.

Usage-centered design [1, 2] is a systematic, model-driven approach to visual and interaction design for user interfaces in software and Web-based applications. On projects of widely varying scope and scale in a variety of application areas [2, 3, 4, 5, 6], usage-centered design has proved capable of delivering superior designs [7]. As the name suggests, usage-centered design differs from conventional user-centered approaches primarily in a shift of focus from users per se to usage, that is, to the tasks to be accomplished by users. This difference in emphasis is reflected in differing practices. Instead of trial-and-error design through repeated cycles of prototyping, user feedback, and usability testing, usage-centered design constructs robust and highly refined abstract models and more or less directly derives from these an initial design requiring only limited usability testing and minimal refinement.

Usage-centered design integrates readily with software engineering precisely because it is grounded in a strong engineering orientation and was developed from the outset to be compatible with object-oriented software engineering [9]. The very same extensions and refinements to well established models and techniques, such as actors and use cases [8, 9], that drive the user interface design can also be employed directly for software engineering [10].

2. Agile Methods and Usability

Extreme programming [11] and other of the emerging agile methods [12] represent an important new direction in software engineering and development. The emphasis in all the agile methods is on accelerated but highly disciplined development of high-quality software based on close coordination with customers or customer representatives and minimal analysis and design artifacts. As a body of practice, agile methods have a track record on usability and user interface design that is no better than traditional large-scale software engineering methods. However, the adaptability of both usage-centered design and the agile methods has made possible thgeir successful integration [4].

The tutorial will introduce the models and methods of usage-centered design with an emphasis on agile modeling and design techniques [2, 13, 14, 15], both for their inherent simplicity and for their advantages as a framework for hands-on learning. The integration of usage-centered approaches into software engineering practice will be considered, with special emphasis on task cases (or essential use cases) [8, 16], which are central to

0-7695-1877-X/03 $17.00 © 2003 IEEE

usage-centered design and serve as a common thread tying together the entire usage-centered software engineering process [8, 10].

A usage-centered task model differs from both use cases and ubiquitous scenarios in providing a much simpler and finer-grained representation of the elemental structure of work being accomplished by users. This simplicity and granularity enables more comprehensive modelling, facilitates validation of models, and promotes reuse of design elements and components in the software engineering process.

3. References

[1] Constantine, L. L., and Lockwood, L. A. D. *Software for Use: A Practical Guide to the Models and Methods of Usage-Centered Design.* Addison-Wesley, Reading, MA, 1999.

[2] Constantine, L. L., and Lockwood, L. A. D. "Usage-Centered Engineering for Web Applications. *IEEE Software, 19* (2), March/April. 2002.

[3] Anderson, J., Fleek, F., Garrity, K., and Drake, F. "Integrating Usability Techniques into Software Development. *IEEE Software, 18* (1), January/February, 2001.

[4] Patton, J. "Extreme design: Usage-Centered Design in XP and Agile Development." In L. Constantine (Ed.), *forUSE 2002: Proceedings of the First International Conference on Usage-Centered, Task-Centered, and Performance-Centered Design.* Ampersand Press, Rowley, MA, 2002.

[5] Strope, J. "Putting Usage-Centered Design to Work: Clinical Applications." In L. Constantine (Ed.), *forUSE 2002: Proceedings of the First International Conference on Usage-Centered, Task-Centered, and Performance-Centered Design.* Ampersand Press, Rowley, MA, 2002.

[6] Windl, H. "Designing a Winner: Creating STEP 7 Lite with Usage-Centered Design." In L. Constantine (Ed.), *forUSE 2002: Proceedings of the First International Conference on Usage-Centered, Task-Centered, and Performance-Centered Design.* Ampersand Press, Rowley, MA, 2002.

[7] Windl, H., and Constantine, L. "Performance-Centered Design: STEP 7 Lite." Winning submission, Performance-Centered Design 2001, http://foruse.com/pcd/

[8] Constantine, L. L., and Lockwood, L. A. D. "Structure and Style in Use Cases for User Interface Design." In M. van Harmelan (Ed.), *Object Modeling and User Interface Design.* Addison-Wesley, Boston, 2001.

[9] Jacobson, I., Christerson, M., Jonsson, P., and Övergaard, G. *Object-Oriented Software Engineering: A Use Case Driven Approach.* Addison-Wesley, Reading, MA, 1992.

[10] Biddle, R., Noble, J., and Tempero, E. "From Essential Use Cases TO Objects." In L. Constantine (Ed.), *forUSE 2002: Proceedings of the First International Conference on Usage-Centered, Task-Centered, and Performance-Centered Design.* Ampersand Press, Rowley, MA, 2002.

[11] Beck, K. *Extreme Programming Explained.* Addison-Wesley, Reading, MA, 2000.

[12] Cockburn, A. *Agile Software Development.* Addison-Wesley, Boston, 2002.

[13] Ambler, S. Agile Modeling: *Effective Practices for Extreme Programming and the Unified Process.* Wiley, New York, 2002.

[14] [Constantine, L. L. "Cutting Corners: Shortcuts in Model-Driven Web Design." *Software Development, 8* (2). Reprinted in L. Constantine (Ed.), *Beyond Chaos: The Expert Edge in Managing Software Development.* Addison-Wesley, Boston, 2001.

[15] Constantine, L. L. "Process Agility and Software Usability: Toward Lightweight Usage-Centered Design." *Information Age, 8* (2). Reprinted in L. Constantine (Ed.), *Beyond Chaos: The Expert Edge in Managing Software Development.* Addison-Wesley, Boston, 2001.

[16] Constantine, L. L. (1995) "Essential Modeling: Use Cases for User Interfaces," *interactions 2* (2).

Internet Security and Intrusion Detection

Richard A. Kemmerer and Giovanni Vigna
University of California, Santa Barbara
(kemm,vigna)@cs.ucsb.edu

1. The Internet Under Attack

In recent years, networks have evolved from a mere means of communication to a ubiquitous computational infrastructure. Networks have become larger, faster, and highly dynamic. In particular, the Internet, the world-wide TCP/IP network, has become a mission-critical infrastructure for governments, companies, and financial institutions. As a consequence, network attacks have started to impact practical aspects of our lives.

Today's networks are very heterogeneous environments where highly critical software applications (e.g., the control system for a dam) run side-by-side with other non-critical network-based applications (e.g., a mail server). As a consequence, network-based attacks against apparently "non-critical" services may produce unforeseen side effects of devastating proportions.

Software engineers should be aware of the risks and security issues associated with the design, development, and deployment of network-based software [14]. A first important step is to understand what the most common attack techniques that are used to violate the security of computer systems are [9]. The second step is to be informed about the current approaches to preventing such attacks [2]. The third step is to understand and deploy technologies that support the detection of network-based attacks [10].

The tutorial presents the principal attack techniques that are used in the Internet today and possible countermeasures. In particular, intrusion detection techniques are analyzed in detail. This tutorial mixes a practical character with a discussion of the current research in the field. Participants will learn how the security of networks is violated and how such violations can be detected and prevented.

2. The Internet Security Problem and Attack Techniques

Network-based attacks often conform to a general multi-step process. This process starts with the collection of information about a specific target network. This phase is followed by the remote exploitation of vulnerabilities that have been identified. After having obtained an entry point in a target system other attacks are launched from the compromised system. The goal is either to escalate privileges or to extend the compromise to neighboring parts of the network, possibly by exploiting internal trust relationships.

The tutorial presents the basic attack techniques used in each of the phases described above. After a brief introduction to the Internet and the TCP/IP protocol suite, the basic scanning techniques are presented. Then, both network-based and application-based attack techniques are discussed. Examples of multi-step network attacks are also presented.

3. Prevention Mechanisms and Techniques

The second part of the tutorial provides an overview of the technologies that are available today for securing network-based applications. After a brief introduction to the basic building blocks of security protocols [12], the most used network-level and transport-level security technologies are presented [13]. These technologies provide a way to protect the interaction between the distributed components of a network-based application. A complementary technique is the use of filtering systems, such as firewalls, that selectively block network access to selected services [3].

0-7695-1877-X/03 $17.00 © 2003 IEEE

4. Detection Mechanisms and Techniques

The third part of the tutorial is dedicated to intrusion detection [8]. Intrusion detection is the process of analyzing information about the activities performed in a computer system or network, looking for evidence of malicious behavior. The information may come in the form of audit records produced by the operating system auditing facilities, log messages produced by different types of sensors and network devices, or in the form of raw network traffic obtained by eavesdropping a network segment. These data sources are used by intrusion detection systems (IDSs) in different ways, according to different paradigms.

The tutorial covers the two basic categories of intrusion detection approaches: *anomaly detection* and *misuse detection*. Anomaly detection relies on models of the intended behavior of users and applications and interprets deviations from this "normal" behavior as an attack [4, 6]. Misuse detection takes a complementary approach. Misuse detection systems contain a number of attack descriptions (or "signatures") that are matched against the stream of audit data looking for evidence that the modeled attack is occurring [7, 11]. Misuse and anomaly detection both have advantages and disadvantages. Misuse detection systems can perform focused analysis of the audit data and usually produce only a few false positives, which are erroneous detections. The main disadvantage of misuse detection systems is that they can detect only those attacks that are known. That is, they can detect only attacks for which they have a defined signature. The main advantage of anomaly detection systems is that they are able to detect previously unknown attacks. By defining what's normal, they make it possible to identify any variation, no matter whether it is part of the threat model or not. The advantage of being able to detect previously unknown attacks is paid for in terms of a large number of false positives. Anomaly detection systems are also difficult to train when used in a very dynamic environment.

The tutorial presents the techniques in use today and the directions currently pursued by the research community in both the anomaly detection and misuse detection fields [1]. The challenges associated with evaluating intrusion detection systems, developing intrusion detection metrics, and performing alert correlation and fusion are also discussed. In particular, the speakers discuss their experience with designing, implementing, deploying, and evaluating a family of intrusion detection systems [15, 5, 16].

References

[1] R. Bace and P. Mell. Special Publication on Intrusion Detection Systems. Technical Report SP 800-31, National Institute of Standards and Technology, November 2001.

[2] M. Bishop. *Computer Security: Art and Science.* Addison-Wesley-Longman, December 2002.

[3] W. Cheswick and S. Bellovin. *Firewalls and Internet Security: Repelling the Wily Hacker.* Addison-Wesley, 1994.

[4] D. Denning. An Intrusion Detection Model. *IEEE Transactions on Software Engineering*, 13(2):222–232, Feb. 1987.

[5] S. Eckmann, G. Vigna, and R. Kemmerer. STATL: An Attack Language for State-based Intrusion Detection. *Journal of Computer Security*, 10(1/2):71–104, 2002.

[6] S. Forrest. A Sense of Self for UNIX Processes. In *Proceedings of the IEEE Symposium on Security and Privacy*, pages 120–128, Oakland, CA, May 1996.

[7] K. Ilgun, R. Kemmerer, and P. Porras. State Transition Analysis: A Rule-Based Intrusion Detection System. *IEEE Transactions on Software Engineering*, 21(3):181–199, March 1995.

[8] R. Kemmerer and G. Vigna. Intrusion Detection. *IEEE Computer*, 2002. Special publication on Security and Privacy.

[9] S. McClure, J. Scambray, and G. Kurtz. *Hacking Exposed: Network Security Secrets & Solutions.* Osborne/McGraw-Hill, third edition, 2001.

[10] S. Northcutt and J. Novak. *Network Intrusion Detection.* New Riders Publishing, third edition, August 2002.

[11] M. Roesch. Snort - Lightweight Intrusion Detection for Networks. In *Proceedings of the USENIX LISA '99 Conference*, November 1999.

[12] B. Schneier. *Applied Cryptography: Protocols, Algorithms, and Source Code in C.* John Wiley & Sons, second edition, October 1995.

[13] W. Stallings. *Network Security Essentials.* Prentice Hall, second edition, November 2002.

[14] J. Viega and G. McGraw. *Building Secure Software: How to Avoid Security Problems the Right Way.* Addison Wesley, October 2001.

[15] G. Vigna and R. Kemmerer. NetSTAT: A Network-based Intrusion Detection System. *Journal of Computer Security*, 7(1):37–71, 1999.

[16] G. Vigna, R. Kemmerer, and P. Blix. Designing a Web of Highly-Configurable Intrusion Detection Sensors. In W. Lee, L. Mè, and A. Wespi, editors, *Proceedings of the 4th International Symposiun on Recent Advances in Intrusion Detection (RAID 2001)*, volume 2212 of *LNCS*, pages 69–84, Davis, CA, October 2001. Springer-Verlag.

Pattern-Oriented Distributed System Architectures

Douglas C. Schmidt
douglas.c.schmidt@vanderbilt.edu
Electrical Engineering & Computer Science
Vanderbilt University
Nashville Tennessee, USA

Tutorial Overview

Developing software for distributed systems that effectively utilizes concurrency over high-speed, low-speed, and mobile networks is hard; developing high quality reusable distributed systems is even harder. The principles, methods, and skills required to develop reusable software cannot be learned by generalities. Instead, developers must learn through experience how reusable software components and frameworks can be designed, implemented, optimized, validated, maintained, and enhanced by applying good development practices and patterns.

This tutorial describes how to apply patterns and middleware frameworks to alleviate the complexity of developing software for distributed systems. These patterns and framework components have been used successfully by the presenter on production communication software projects at many commercial companies for telecommunication systems, network management for personal communication systems, electronic medical imaging systems, real-time avionics and aerospace systems, distributed interactive simulations, and automated stock trading.

The tutorial illustrates by example how to significantly simplify and enhance the development of communication software that effectively utilizes concurrency and distribution via the use of:

- **Object-oriented design techniques**, such as patterns, layered modularity, and data/control abstraction.
- **Object-oriented language features**, such as abstract classes, inheritance, dynamic binding, and parameterized types.
- **Middleware**, such as object-oriented frameworks for host infrastructure middleware (*e.g.*, JVMs and ACE) and distribution middleware (*e.g.* CORBA and J2EE).
- **Advanced operating system mechanisms**, such as event demultiplexing, multi-threading, multi-processing, synchronization, and dynamic linking.

The tutorial examines patterns and framework solutions abstracted from production systems in domains ranging from telecommunications, avionics, distributed electronic medical imaging systems, web servers, and real-time object request brokers to illustrate the key technical design and implementation issues. The material presented in this tutorial is based in part on the book "Pattern-Oriented Software Architecture: Patterns for Concurrent and Distributed Objects" [1], which is the second volume in the Pattern-Oriented Software Architecture (POSA) series [2].

References

[1] D. C. Schmidt, M. Stal, H. Rohnert, and F. Buschmann, *Pattern-Oriented Software Architecture: Patterns for Concurrent and Networked Objects, Volume 2.* New York: Wiley & Sons, 2000.

[2] F. Buschmann, R. Meunier, H. Rohnert, P. Sommerlad, and M. Stal, *Pattern-Oriented Software Architecture—A System of Patterns.* New York: Wiley & Sons, 1996.

0-7695-1877-X/03 $17.00 © 2003 IEEE

Industrial-Strength Software Product-Line Engineering

John Klein
Avaya CRM
kleinjr@avaya.com

Barry Price
Avaya CRM
rbprice@avaya.com

David Weiss
Avaya Labs
weiss@avaya.com

Abstract

Software product-line engineering is one of the few approaches to software engineering that shows promise of improving software productivity by factors of 5 to 10. There are still few examples of its successful application on a large scale, partly because of the complexity of initiating a product-line engineering project and the many factors that must be addressed for such a project to be successful.

This tutorial draws on experiences in introducing and sustaining product-line engineering in Lucent Technologies and in Avaya. The objective is to convey to participants the obstacles involved in transitioning to product line engineering and how to overcome such obstacles, particularly in large software development organizations. Participants will learn both technical and organizational aspects of the problem. Participants will leave the tutorial with many ideas on how to introduce product line engineering into an organization in a systematic way.

1. Introduction

Software product-line engineering is one of the few approaches to software engineering that shows promise of improving software productivity by factors of 5 to 10. There are still few examples of its successful application on a large scale partly because of the complexity of the problem of initiating a product-line engineering project and of the many factors that must be addressed for such a project to be successful. Practitioners and researchers alike are confronted with issues such as the following:

- How have others been able to succeed in creating and maintaining a software product-line?
- What approaches have been tried?
- How do I construct a convincing business case for product-line engineering?
- Whom do I have to convince?
- What key activities are needed to start a product-line engineering project and to make it successful?
- How do I recognize when my organization is ready to or needs to start product-line engineering?
- How do I measure the effectiveness of product-line engineering in my organization?
- How long will it take me to show some return?
- What does a product-line organization look like? How is it different from what my organization looks like now?
- What resources will I need?
- What training will my people need?

This one-day tutorial draws on experiences in introducing and sustaining product-line engineering in Lucent Technologies and in Avaya to answer such questions. Our objective is to convey to participants the obstacles involved in transitioning to product line engineering and how to overcome such obstacles, particularly in large software development organizations. Participants will learn both technical and organizational aspects of the problem. We expect them to leave the tutorial with many ideas on how they can start introducing product line engineering into an organization in a systematic way.

2. Case Study

Much of the experience we describe and the material we use comes from a large-scale product-line engineering project currently in progress in Avaya. We give participants an inside look at an organization that is transitioning into product-line engineering on a large scale. Success in such a project depends on both technical issues in creating and evolving a product-line, and organizational issues in transforming an organization to be compatible with the product-line engineering process. Participants will see the problems of applying product-line engineering from both the technical and organizational perspectives. They will be shown by example what events and actions must take place at what times to be successful in introducing product-line engineering.

0-7695-1877-X/03 $17.00 © 2003 IEEE

The case study for the product-line engineering project includes several constraints typical of large software development organizations. The project involved multi-million lines of code systems, large multi-site development teams, and a transition from legacy products. The case study organization faced the typical software development problems of time-to-market, product quality, competitive features and inflexible solution delivery.

These constraints and issues motivated the transition to product line engineering. The case study describes the business case, choices and steps taken by the product-line engineering champions to change the organization, product architecture, tools infrastructure and development processes. These changes involved challenges and risks before arriving at the expected benefits and measurable success of product-line engineering.

3. Theory and Industry Experiences

There is now a body of theory and industry practices around software product line engineering. The tutorial will provide clear definitions, an economic decision model, activities and alternative approaches, typical work products and roles needed in a product line engineering process.

The basic product line engineering steps of product scoping, domain analysis, commonality and variability analysis, domain and product implementation are explained. However, theory and practice often differ. We will review other industry experiences to provide examples and illustrate alternative approaches. The tutorial includes a reference list of industry resources, cases studies and university references.

5. Transition Steps

Changing an organization to product line engineering is a series of transitional steps. Starting with convincing the organization to adopt product line practices, and the critical first activities, the tutorial will walk through each activity. Examples are given of identifying key stakeholders and decision makers, and how to educate and align their concerns with the motivations for adopting Product Line Engineering.

The tutorial will review the relationship of product line architecture to the transition activities. A key learning is how to overcome organizational inertia to successfully bootstrap a product line engineering transition project.

4. Organizational Changes

One of the fundamental changes is establishing the organization and processes that support product line engineering. All business processes are affected, not just software development. Each part of the organization must identify the new practices, tools and processes needed. These will be reviewed across typical development and business organizations.

There are alternative organizational approaches with varying risks and benefits. Each organization has to identify the key measures for success. The organizational transition period must involve the sense of urgency and vision characteristic of good organizational change management to achieve product line engineering benefits. Even after institutionalization of product line engineering, organizational metrics and continuous improvement are required.

5. References

[1] P. Clements and L. Northrop, *Software Product Lines, Practices and Patterns*, Addison-Wesley, 2002.

[2] D. Weiss and C.T.R. Lai, *Software Product-Line Engineering: A Family-Based Software Development Process*, Addison-Wesley, Boston, 1999.

[3] D. Weiss and D. Hoffman, editors, *Software Fundamentals*, Addison-Wesley, Boston, 2002.

A Tutorial on Feature Oriented Programming and Product-Lines

Don Batory
Department of Computer Sciences
University of Texas at Austin
Austin, Texas, 78712 U.S.A.
batory@cs.utexas.edu

1 Abstract

Feature Oriented Programming (FOP) is a design methodology and tools for program synthesis. The goal is to specify a target program in terms of the features that it offers, and to synthesize an efficient program that meets these specifications. FOP has been used to develop ***product-lines*** in disparate domains, including compilers for extensible Java dialects [3], fire support simulators for the U.S. Army [5], high-performance network protocols [1], and program verification tools [14].

2 Overview

Specifying non-software products via features is common. Familiar examples are found at the Dell or Gateway web sites where HTML pages provide simple declarative ***domain-specific languages (DSLs)*** for specifying customized configurations of PCs (e.g., single or dual processor options, monitor options, disk options, etc.). A goal of FOP is to do the same for software products.

GenVoca is a simple, powerful, and algebraic model of FOP. It is based on ***step-wise refinement (SWR)***, a methodology for building software by progressively adding details. SWR was abandoned by practitioners decades ago because the increment of programming detail, called a ***refinement***, was so small (e.g., `x+1` ⇒ `inc(x)`) that hundreds or thousands of such refinements had to be composed to produce admittedly small programs. While the approach is fundamental and industrial infrastructures are being developed [7][13], GenVoca extends step-wise refinement by scaling refinements to a component or multi-class granularity, so that applications of significant complexity can be expressed by composing a few large-scale refinements called ***feature refinements.***

A feature refinement encapsulates the implementation of a feature. It is a modularization concept that is more general than traditional packages. In addition to encapsulating sets of complete classes, a feature refinement can also encapsulate fragments of multiple classes. Figure 1 depicts a package of three classes, `c1`—`c3`. Refinement `r1` ***cross-cuts*** these classes, i.e., it encapsulates fragments of `c1`—`c3`. The same holds for refinements `r2` and `r3`. Composing refinements `r1`—`r3` yields a package of fully-formed classes `c1`—`c3`. Because refinements reify levels of abstraction, feature refinements are often called ***layers*** — a name that is visually reinforced by the stratification of `c1`—`c3` in Figure 1. In general, feature refinements are modular, albeit unconventional, building blocks of programs.

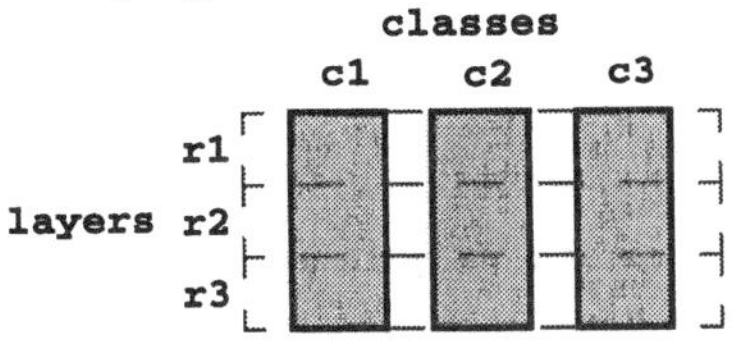

Figure 1. Classes and Refinements (Layers)

Aspect-Oriented Programming (AOP) is closely related to FOP. Both deal with modules that encapsulate cross cuts of multiple classes, and both can be expressed as large-scale refinements. The primary difference between AOP and FOP is emphasis. Aspects (as defined by AspectJ) deal with join-points and quantification.[1] Given an existing or legacy program, join-points and quantification allow a programmer to specify where "advice" code will be injected. In contrast, FOP defines refinements from a design perspective, namely, how do available algorithms and components fit together? The thought processes that are invoked by traditional OO design methodologies on which FOP relies, do *not* involve join-points and quantification. Thus, how one thinks about cross-cuts in AOP and FOP, how cross-cuts are specified, and the tools that are used can be quite different. FOP is closer in spirit to work on ***Multi-Dimensional Separation of Concerns (MDSC)***, where modularity is viewed in terms of multidimensional spaces of units, and hyperslices correspond to refinements [12].

GenVoca defines an architectural model for FOP. Programs are constants and feature refinements are functions. The names given to constants and functions correspond to the features that they implement. The following constants represent programs with different features:

```
f        // program with feature f
g        // program with feature g
```

1. A *join-point* is a element of a program (e.g., method call, exception handler, variable reference). A *point-cut* is a predicate that defines a set of join-points to which *advice* — before, after, or around code — can be added.

0-7695-1877-X/03 $17.00 © 2003 IEEE

A feature refinement is a function that takes a program as input and produces a feature-augmented program as output:

```
i(x)      // adds feature i to program x
j(x)      // adds feature j to program x
```

A multi-featured application is an ***equation*** that is a named expression. Different equations define a family or product-line of applications, such as:

```
app1 = i(f)       // app1 has features i and f
app2 = j(g)       // app2 has features j and g
app3 = i(j(f))    // app3 has features i, j, f
```

A GenVoca ***domain model*** is a set of constants and functions. It is an abstract way to specify building blocks of programs, but it also has significant advantages, some of which are described in the following paragraphs.

First, the constants and functions of a domain model — which is an algebra[2] — can be implemented with many different technologies, ranging from simple objects and templates to sophisticated metaprograms and program transformation systems.

Second, equational representations of programs are very powerful. For example, a function represents both a feature *and* its implementation. There can be different functions with different implementations of the *same* feature:

```
k1(x)    // adds k with implementation1 to x
k2(x)    // adds k with implementation2 to x
```

When an application requires the use of feature `k`, it is a problem of *equation optimization* to determine which implementation of `k` is best (e.g., provides the best performance). It is possible to automatically design software (i.e., produce an equation that optimizes some criteria) given a set of declarative constraints for a target application. An example of this kind of automated reasoning — historically called ***automatic programming*** — is [4].

Third, although GenVoca constants and functions seem untyped, typing constraints do exist as design rules. *Design rules* capture semantic constraints that govern legal compositions. It is common that the selection of a feature will disable or enable the selection of other features. There are simple and automatic algorithms for validating compositions of features (e.g., equations) in FOP [11][2][9].

Fourth, FOP need not be limited to the synthesis of source code. There are many other non-code artifacts (such as UML models, makefiles, grammars) that can be given equational representations, and be derived and generated just like source code [6]. Equations and refinements provide a simple and powerful way to abstractly represent the generation of all kinds of artifacts.

Fifth, equational representations of programs scale naturally to ***product-families*** — suites of different but integrated programs (e.g., MS Office). Techniques have been developed and demonstrated for building ***product-lines of product-families***; the key idea is that features can impact or cross-cut multiple programs and product-families have equational representations.

3 References

[1] D. Batory and S. O'Malley, "The Design and Implementation of Hierarchical Software Systems with Reusable Components", *ACM TOSEM*, October 1992.

[2] D. Batory and B. Geraci, "Validating Compositions and Subjectivity and GenVoca Generators", *IEEE TSE* Feb. 1997.

[3] D. Batory, B. Lofaso, and Y. Smaragdakis, "JTS: A Tool Suite for Building GenVoca Generators", *ICSR* 1998.

[4] D. Batory, G. Chen, E. Robertson, and T. Wang, "Design Wizards and Visual Programming Environments for GenVoca Generators", *IEEE TSE* May 2000.

[5] D. Batory, C. Johnson, B. MacDonald, and D. von Heeder, "Achieving Extensibility Through Product-Lines and Domain-Specific Languages", ACM TOSEM, April 2002.

[6] D. Batory, J.N. Sarvela, and A. Rauschmayer, "Scaling Step-Wise Refinement". *International Conference on Software Engineering (ICSE) 2003.*

[7] I. Baxter, "Design Maintenance Systems", *CACM* Apr. 1992.

[8] K. Czarnecki and U.W. Eisenecker, "Components and Generative Programming", *ACM SIGSOFT* 1999.

[9] K. Czarnecki, T. Bednasch, P. Unger, and U. Eisenecker, "Generative Programming for Embedded Software: An Industrial Experience Report", GPCE 2002.

[10] G. Kiczales, J. Lamping, A. Mendhekar, C. Maeda, C. Lopes, J. Loingtier, and J. Irwin, "Aspect-Oriented Programming", *ECOOP 97*, 220-242.

[11] D. Perry, "The Logic of Propagation in The Inscape Environment", *ACM SIGSOFT* 1989.

[12] H. Ossher and P. Tarr. "Using Multi-Dimensional Separation of Concerns to (Re)Shape Evolving Software." CACM 44(10): 43-50, *October 2001.*

[13] C. Simonyi, "The Death of Computer Languages, the Birth of Intentional Programming", *NATO Science Committee Conference*, 1995.

[14] R.E.K. Stirewalt and L.K. Dillon, "A Component-Based Approach to Building Formal Analysis Tools, *ICSE 2001.*

2. Relational algebra is a set of operators, whose compositions define a domain of query evaluation programs. An FOP domain model is also an algebra whose constants and functions (i.e., operators) are composed to define a domain of programs that can be synthesized.

Tutorial H2:
An Overview of UML 2.0

Bran Selic
Rational Software Canada
bselic@rational.com

Abstract

This half-day tutorial covers the salient aspects of the first major revision of the Unified Modeling Language, UML 2.0. It includes background information on what drove the requirements and the design rationale—from the point of view of one of its primary designers. The overall structure of UML 2.0 is described followed by a more detailed description of the most prominent new modeling features illustrated with many examples. The ability of UML 2.0 to deal with the needs of model-driven development methods is also covered.

1. Introduction

The Unified Modeling Language (UML) was launched in 1995 and adopted as an industry standard by the Object Management Group in 1997 [9]. Since then, it has been adopted widely by industry and academia. As experience with UML grew and the problems of software modeling better understood, new requirements for UML emerged, and a request for proposal for a major revision of the existing standard was issued in the year 2000 [2] [3] [4] [5]. The requirements called for increased precision, greater clarity of the specification, and new modeling capabilities.

A major challenge posed to the drafting team was to avoid the treacherous "language bloat" syndrome, whereby numerous new features are added to a language to the point of unwieldiness. The result is a language that has only a small number of new features compared to its predecessor, but which is characterized by a much greater clarity and precision. This makes it suitable for a *model-driven* approach to software development as specified by the recent Model-Driven Architecture (MDA) initiative launched by the OMG.

2. Major topics covered

The major topics covered in this tutorial include:

- A review of the lessons learned from the application and study of the original UML standard
- The overall structure and design philosophy of UML 2.0
- Modeling capabilities for modeling high-level software structures such as those required for architectural specifications
- New modeling capabilities for describing complex behavior of objects and groupings of objects
- The application of UML 2.0 in model-driven software development methods based on executable models and the use of automatic code generation.

3. Tutorial outline

1. Introduction

Since UML is a modeling language, we first examine the role that modeling plays in any engineering endeavor and identify the essential properties of good models. This is followed by a discussion on how these general principles apply in the case of software. In particular, we identify the aspects that are unique to software models—both advantages and disadvantages.

2. An overview and critique of UML 1.x

This is a critical review of the first-generation UML including the design philosophy behind it and the structure of its definition. Special focus is given to the major shortcomings identified in practical usage.

3. Requirements for UML 2.0

The requirements for the first revision are covered in this section. This includes a discussion of the MDA (Model-Driven Architecture) initiative launched by the OMG and which is expected to provide the technical setting for the application of UML 2.0.

0-7695-1877-X/03 $17.00 © 2003 IEEE

4. An overview of UML 2.0

This is a top-level view of the proposed major revision of UML: the overall design rationale, the structure of the specification, and a list of salient new features. The conceptual infrastructure supporting the UML modeling concepts is explained.

5. Architectural modeling facilities

This is a review of what is probably the most prominent new capability in UML: the ability to render essential software structures used in architectural descriptions. Most of the conceptual input for this came from various architectural description languages such as Acme [1] and UML-RT [8].

6. The dynamic semantics of UML and the modeling of behavior

This part covers the essentials of the relationship between structure and behavior and the model of causality that underlies all behavioral modeling in UML.

7. Modeling of object interactions

This covers some major new capabilities for representing complex object interaction sequences. Such sequences can be reused and also composed into hierarchies allowing very complex behaviors to be specified.

8. Modeling complex activities and actions

Activity modeling in UML 2.0 is based on a completely new conceptual foundation—which allows modeling of much more complicated activity sequences than before.

9. New state machine capabilities

The statechart formalism of UML has been enhanced with new modularization capabilities allowing states to act as encapsulation contexts or state machines to be reused in multiple contexts.

10. Other new capabilities

This is a brief review of some the less prominent new modeling capabilities, such as information flows, as well changes made to some of the existing capabilities, such as profiles.

11. UML 2.0 and model-driven development

This topic covers how UML 2.0 matches against the requirements for model-driven software development methods like MDA. These are methods in which the primary artifacts and focus of development are models, expressed using a modeling language such as UML, rather than programs (the latter are generated using mostly automatic techniques).

12. Concluding remarks

The material covered is summarized and an outline given of the possible future directions in the field. The tutorial concludes with an open discussion.

4. Tutorial presenter

Bran Selic is Principal Engineer at Rational Software. He has over 30 years of experience with industrial real-time systems in telecommunications, aerospace, and robotics. He is the principal author of a popular textbook on the use of the object paradigm in real-time applications [7] and was one of the members of the core team responsible for defining the UML standard within the OMG. In addition, he is a primary contributor to the real-time UML profile, which was recently adopted by the OMG for use in embedded, real-time, and other resource-sensitive applications. At present, he is a member of a multi-enterprise team working on the first major revision of UML (version 2.0) and is one of the chairs of that team. Mr. Selic has lectured extensively on these topics and is a frequent invited speaker at various technical and scientific conferences. He is also a member of the editorial board of several technical publications, and adjunct professor at Carleton University. He is based in Kanata, Ontario, Canada.

5. References

[1] D. Garlan, et al., "ACME: Architectural Description of Component-Based Systems," in G. Leavens and M. Sitarman (eds.), *Foundations of Component-Based Systems,* Cambridge University Press, pp. 47-68. 2000.

[2] Object Management Group, The, "UML 2.0 infrastructure RFP," OMG document no. ad/00-09-01. Available at: http://cgi.omg.org/docs/ad/00-09-01.pdf. September 2000.

[3] Object Management Group, The, "UML 2.0 superstructure RFP," OMG document no. ad/00-09-02. Available at: http://cgi.omg.org/docs/ad/00-09-02.pdf. September 2000.

[4] Object Management Group, The, "UML 2.0 OCL RFP," OMG document no. ad/00-09-03. Available at: http://cgi.omg.org/docs/ad/00-09-03.pdf. September 2000.

[5] Object Management Group, The, "UML 2.0 diagram interchange RFP," OMG document no. ad/00-09-04. Available at: http://cgi.omg.org/docs/ad/00-09-04.pdf. September 2000.

[6] Object Management Group, The, "Model-Driven Architecture," OMG document no. ormsc/2001-07-01. Available at: : http://cgi.omg.org/docs/ormsc/01-07-01.pdf . July 2001.

[7] B. Selic, et al., *Real-Time Object-Oriented Modeling*, John Wiley & Sons, New York, 1994.

[8] B. Selic and J. Rumbaugh. *Using UML for modeling complex real-time systems.* April 1998. White paper available at: http://www.rational.com/products/whitepapers/442.jsp.

[9] J. Rumbaugh, et al., *The Unified Modeling Language Reference Manual*, Addison-Wesley-Longman, Reading, Mass., 1998.

Designing Software Architectures for Usability

Jan Bosch
University of Groningen
Department of Computing Science
NL9700 AV Groningen
The Netherlands
Jan.Bosch@cs.rug.nl

Natalia Juristo
Technical University of Madrid
Computing Science School
28660 Boadilla del Monte. Madrid
Spain
natalia@fi.upm.es

Abstract

Usability is increasingly recognized as a quality attribute that one has to design for. The conventional alternative is to measure usability on a finished system and improve it. The disadvantage of this approach is, obviously, that the cost associated with implementing usability improvements in a fully implemented system are typically very high and prohibit improvements with architectural impact. In this tutorial, we present the insights gained, techniques developed and lessons learned in the EU-IST project STATUS (SofTware Architectures That supports USability). These include a forward-engineering perspective on usability, a technique for specifying usability requirements, a method for assessing software architectures for usability and, finally, for improving software architectures for usability. The topics are extensively illustrated by examples and experiences from many industrial cases.

1. Introduction

Software architecture has, during the last decade, become an area of intense research in the software engineering community. Considerable progress has been made in developing the technological and methodological basis for "engineering" architectural design. Its relevance is due to the fact that the software architecture represents the first mapping from requirements to computational components.

The increased importance of software architecture is based on two aspects [1]. First, in the first design decisions the most fundamental structure and ideas of the system are captured, which are also the most difficult to change at a later stage. Second, the software architecture constrains the quality attributes of the system. Consequently, bad architectural design decisions may make it impossible for the system to satisfy its quality requirements. From this, we can conclude that software architectures need to be explicitly designed for their quality attributes. This requires that software architects are able to assess software architectures for relevant quality attributes and understand the consequences of design decisions for these quality attributes.

Several quality attribute classifications agree on the importance of considering usability as a quality attribute [3]. Most quality attributes focus on characteristics that are desirable from the point of view of the software development organisation. Usability, on the other side, is a quality attribute perceived directly by the client/user. One definition of usability is quality in use [4].

Fundamentally, usability reflects how easy the system is to learn and use, how productively users will be able to work and how much support users need. A system's usability deals not only with the user interface, it also relates closely to the software's overall structure. In order to understand the depth and scope of the usability of a system it is useful to make a distinction between the visible part of the user interface (buttons, pull-down menus, check-boxes, background colour, etc.) and the interaction part of the system. By interaction we mean the coordination of information exchange between the user and the system. This interaction must be carefully designed and must be considered not just when designing the visible part of the user interface, but also when designing the rest of the system [5].

Since usability can be viewed as a quality attribute of a system, similar to other quality attributes such as performance, reliability and modifiability. We should, therefore, design software architectures for usability as we design for other quality attributes [2]. This requires techniques to assess for usability and to improve the support for usability in software architecture.

The partners of the EU-IST STATUS research project, have developed and continue to develop techniques and methodological support to the forward-engineering of

0-7695-1877-X/03 $17.00 © 2003 IEEE

usability in software architectures. The tutorial presents the results and discusses design for usability in the context of generic software architecture design.

2. Outline

The aim of this tutorial is to present the insights gained, techniques developed and lessons learned in the EU-IST project STATUS (SofTware Architectures That supports Usability). These include a forward-engineering perspective on usability, a technique for specifying usability requirements, a method for assessing software architectures for usability and, finally, for improving software architectures for usability.

The tutorial contains the following parts:

- Software Architecture Design: An Overview
  - o definition of software architecture
  - o moving from project-centric to architecture-centric software engineering
  - o QASAR software architecture design method

- Introduction to Usability
  - o concept of usability
  - o Human-Computer Interaction perspective
  - o usability attributes and properties

- Designing Software Architectures for Usability: An Overview
  - o relation between usability and software architecture
  - o iterative architecture assessment and improvement

- Specifying Usability Requirements
  - o defining and relevance of context, usability stakeholders and tasks
  - o specifying and balancing usability properties
  - o complete, selected and abstract usability scenario profiles

- Assessing Software Architectures for Usability
  - o expert-based assessment
  - o design-decision based assessment
  - o use-case map based assessment
  - o integrated usability assessment

- Improving Software Architectures for Usability
  - o usability patterns
  - o selecting design solutions

- Case studies: examples and experiences

- Concluding remarks

3. Acknowledgements

The authors wish to thank the partners of the STATUS EU-IST project, i.e. Alberto de Andrés, Manuel Montejo, Rafael Pous and Silvia Sánchez from the Information Highway Group, Xavier Ferré and Ana María Moreno from the University of Madrid, Eelke Folmer and Jilles Van Gurp from the University of Groningen, Robert Chatley, Jeff Kramer and Jeff Magee from Imperial College London and Manolis Chrysostalis, George Marks and Dimitris Tsirikos from LogicDIS.

4. References

[1] Jan Bosch, *Design and Use of Software Architectures: Adopting and Evolving a Product Line Approach,* Pearson Education (Addison-Wesley & ACM Press), ISBN 0-201-67494-7, May 2000.

[2] Eelke Folmer and Jan Bosch, Architecting for Usability: A Survey, Accepted for the *Journal of Systems and Software*, December 2002.

[3] IEEE. *IEEE Std 1061: Standard for a Software Quality Metrics Methodology*. IEEE, 1998.

[4] ISO/IEC. *ISO/IEC 14598-1, Software Product Evaluation: General Overview*. ISO/IEC, 1999.

[5] X. Ferré, N. Juristo, H. Windl, L. Constantine. Usability Basics for Software Developers. *IEEE Software*. Vol. 18, N. 1. pp. 22-30. January 2001.

Quality of Service Engineering with UML, .NET, and CORBA

Torben Weis, Andreas Ulbrich, Kurt Geihs
TU Berlin, iVS, Einsteinufer 17, 10587 Berlin, Germany
{weis,ulbi,geihs}@ivs.tu-berlin.de

Abstract

The concern for non-functional properties of software components and distributed applications has increased significantly in recent years. Non-functional properties are often subsumed under the term Quality of Service (QoS). It refers to quality aspects of a software component or service such as real-time response guarantees, availability and fault-tolerance, the degree of data consistency, the precision of some computation, or the level of security. Consequently, the specification and implementation of QoS mechanisms has become an important concern in the engineering of distributed applications. In this tutorial the attendees will learn how non-functional requirements can be engineered in a systematic way into applications on top of distribution platforms such as CORBA and .NET. The tutorial focuses on two major subjects areas: (1) Specification of QoS properties and (2) implementation of QoS mechanisms in middleware. We present a comprehensive, model-driven approach. It starts with a platform-independent model (PIM) in UML that captures the application QoS requirements. This model is mapped by a tool to a platform-specific model (PSM) tailored for a specific middleware, which is extended with the corresponding QoS mechanisms. Finally, the PSM is translated to code. Participants in this tutorial will get a thorough understanding of general QoS requirements, QoS modeling alternatives and QoS mechanism integration in respect to popular distributed object middleware. Furthermore, we will discuss the pros and cons of CORBA and .NET for QoS engineering. A tool will be demonstrated that eases substantially the modeling stages and the code generation.

1. Motivation

The concern for non-functional properties of software components and distributed applications has increased significantly in recent years. Users and managers demand guaranteed quality properties for software products, and software developers face non-functional requirements that they need to pay attention to in the design and implementation of distributed software systems. The objective of this half-day tutorial is to teach the attendees guidelines on how to handle non-functional properties (QoS) in distributed systems throughout the entire software development life-cycle.

QoS-enabled middleware platforms support the development of QoS-aware applications. However, middleware can not completely shield applications from the implications of QoS. Therefore, QoS provision affects the application design, too. Hence, the tutorial consists of two sessions. The first session focuses on the design of QoS-aware applications while the second session concentrates on middleware QoS issues. Thus, we aim at the conceptual foundations as well as the implementation implications. A new UML modeling tool [3] and our .NET QoS extension [2] are used during the workshop to illustrate the material. The tools will be available for download after the tutorial.

2. Part I: Modeling QoS with UML

There is a large gap in complexity between QoS specification and QoS realization. Furthermore, different QoS-enabled middleware platforms demand special considerations by the designer. Hence, a model-driven approach [1] can simplify the design and development. Application designers can start with a platform independent model (PIM) that captures QoS properties independently of a concrete realization [4]. A model transformation automatically maps the platform independent model to a platform (middleware and implementation language) specific model (PSM).

The advantage of this approach is two fold. First, the gap in complexity can be bridged (at least partially) by a tool that simplifies the development and captures expert knowledge in the model transformation process. Second, the platform independent model can be much clearer since it is not affected by realization details.

The platform independent model presented in the tutorial builds on the proposed UML2 component model since the UML 1.4 component model has several weaknesses. Most notably, the concepts of ports and connectors are missing.

The presented approach provides means to specify QoS

properties for tasks. This concept is much more powerful then attaching QoS properties to single methods only. Especially in large distributed enterprise applications the performance or availability of a single method invocation is not that interesting. The important question is whether a certain task can be finished or how long the processing of the task will take. Our approach uses the improved hierarchical message sequence charts (HMSC) to model such tasks and their QoS properties.

We have developed a new CASE-tool that supports these new modeling techniques. Furthermore, the tool supports model transformation. Such transformations are simple scripts that can be adapted by users to customize the transformation process.

3. Part II: QoS in Object Middleware

QoS provisioning happens at application and at middleware level. Current standard middleware platforms such as CORBA or .NET do not provide generic QoS support. Hence, they have to be extended.

Some CORBA ORBs have built-in extensions for special QoS categories such as real-time or fault tolerance. In contrast, .NET Remoting is a new middleware platform that is part of Microsoft's .NET SDK. .NET does not feature built-in QoS support and its default use of SOAP and HTTP for message transmission has been considered to be a major drawback for performance oriented applications. However, due to the inherent modularity and component-orientation of .NET, its transport mechanisms can be simply exchanged by more efficient ones. Together with the advanced features of the .NET runtime it is a viable candidate for QoS support.

Our research on the CORBA compliant MICO ORB has shown that QoS-enabling a CORBA ORB usually requires changes to the ORB's implementation. Such ORBs usually introduce an extended IDL or some aspect language to specify QoS properties. New languages or language extensions increase the learning curve.

That is not the case for .NET. DotQoS [2] - our QoS extension for .NET - is built on top of a standard .NET SDK and does not require changes to the implementation of .NET. Furthermore, DotQoS does not require any IDL or aspect language for specifying QoS properties. This is possible due to .NET's support of meta-data, reflection and communication channels. Meta-data can be used to enrich the source code with information about required QoS-properties. Using reflection DotQoS can determine at runtime which QoS mechanisms have to be used for a method invocation. Finally, .NET Remoting allows controlling almost every detail of a remote method invocation by inserting new or replacing existing message handlers in the communication channel.

4. Outline

1. *Introduction*
   The tutorial starts with an introduction to the QoS terminology and highlights the difficulties in building QoS-aware applications. Then we motivate the usage of a model-driven approach in the realm of QoS-aware applications.

2. *QoS Specification*
   An UML extension is presented that supports QoS specification in a platform independent application design. The usage of this extension is illustrated with examples. Finally, a brief tool demonstration shows how such QoS-aware models can be created conveniently and how to transform them to standard UML models.

3. *QoS Implementation*
   QoS must be supported by the middleware platform, too. This section discusses how .NET and CORBA can be enhanced with QoS support. The architecture and extensibility of .NET Remoting and CORBA are analyzed and differences discussed. We illustrate how to utilize the advanced features of .NET for QoS provisioning, negotiation and monitoring by means of our DotQoS middleware.

4. *Conclusions and Final Discussion*
   We summarize the tutorial material and comment briefly about future directions of the field. An open discussion concludes the tutorial.

5. Who Should Attend

The tutorial aims at software engineers, architects and developers who are concerned with innovative software projects and explicit quality requirements. Participants will learn how to approach the engineering of non-functional properties into software, how to model and refine such properties, and what it takes to realize such properties systematically with popular middleware architectures.

References

[1] OMG. Model-Driven Architecture, http://www.omg.org/mda, 2003.

[2] A. Ulbrich and T. Weis. www.dotqos.org, 2003.

[3] T. Weis. www.kase-tool.org, 2003.

[4] T. Weis, C. Becker, K. Geihs, and N. Plouzeau. A UML Metamodel for Contract Aware Components. *Springer LNCS*, 2185, 2001.

Workshops

Report on the ICSE 2003 Doctoral Symposium

BACKGROUND ON THE SYMPOSIUM

The ICSE Doctoral Symposium is a forum for Ph.D. students to publicly discuss their research goals, methods, and results prior to completion of their doctorates. The Symposium aims to provide useful guidance for completion of the dissertation research and initiation of a research career. The Symposium and ICSE also provide an opportunity for student participants to interact with established researchers and others in the wider software engineering community.

The Symposium itself is a day-long session usually held prior to the opening of the main ICSE meeting. A half dozen experienced software-engineering faculty members are present, comprising the Symposium Committee. Each student gives a formal presentation, which is then discussed by the Committee and by other students in attendance. The atmosphere is supportive and non-threatening. (Well, we try hard.)

Students who participate in the Doctoral Symposium should be at least six months away from completion of their dissertations, but must have settled on a research area or dissertation topic.

Each prospective student participant submits a package of materials for consideration by the Symposium Committee. The Committee selects participants using the following criteria:

1. The potential quality of the research and its relevance to software engineering.

2. The stage of the research. The Committee will select students across a range of research stages.

3. Diversity of background, research topic, and approach.

Participants accepted to present their work at the Symposium are given complementary admission to the Symposium and to the regular ICSE sessions.

Applicants who are not accepted to present their work are nonetheless encouraged to attend the Symposium and participate in the discussions. If they attend they are given a brief time to describe their research.

THE 2003 SYMPOSIUM

We received 25 applications, of which eight were selected for presentation. Two others would have been selected except that the students were so close to completion and under such obviously good supervision that the Committee decided they would hardly benefit from the Symposium. They were invited to attend as a model for others, and except for presentation, were treated as successful applicants. Two additional applications were received late, but these were treated as unsuccessful applications without examining them.

THE SUCCESSFUL APPLICANTS

Each successful applicant was asked to write a 300-word abstract of her/his dissertation research, which appear (unedited) below, in the order they were received. The first two (short) abstracts are from the two applicants who were judged too close to completion to benefit from the Symposium.

A SEMANTICS-BASED APPROACH FOR MAPPING SPECIFICATION NOTATIONS TO ANALYSIS TOOLS

Jianwei Niu
jniu@uwaterloo.ca
University of Waterloo
Advisors: Joanne M. Atlee, Nancy A. Day

We propose an approach for automatically mapping model-based notations to analysis tools using the notations' semantics. We formally define an operational semantics template for model-based notations.

A FRAMEWORK FOR FAULT LOCALIZATION

Manos Renieris
er@cs.brown.edu
Brown University
Advisor: Steve Reiss

0-7695-1877-X/03 $17.00 © 2003 IEEE

A framework will be built and evaluated for automated fault localization, based on the separation of spectra (run abstractions) and models (ways of combining them).

RISK MANAGEMENT IN AGILE PROCESSES

Anne Fuller
University of Wollongong
annef@uow.edu.au
Advisor:Peter Croll
Expected completion:December, 2004

The various methods classified as "Agile" share a number of features aimed at meeting the needs of today's software projects. However, despite their reported successes, there is some concern that Agile Processes (APs) lack the discipline to allow them to be more widely utilized. This research aims to show how APs in general address risk by providing a mapping between a model unifying the defining elements common to all APs and the common risk elements identified in the Software Engineering Institute's Taxonomy of Risk.

APs adhere to a set of principles rather than follow a common process, thus the model developed it is not itself process oriented. Rather it illustrates the essential components of an AP and attempts to show that being "agile" is a specific combination of practices.

Sixteen elements typifying an AP have been identified and are represented as one piece of a complete jigsaw. The jigsaw symbolism was chosen firstly it is an allegory for the way many traditionalists view APs: they have all the pieces, but can't put them together to see the overall picture. Secondly, if any one of the pieces is missing then the agile picture is incomplete. Thirdly, each piece has a unique shape illustrating that, while each AP has their own methods, provided the method fulfills the requirement of the particular element i.e. has the same overall shape, then it fits into the picture. This also implies that any piece can be replaced with a piece (or pieces) with the same outline. Lastly, the game metaphor is common in APs, e.g. eXtreme Programming (XP)'s planning game.

Future work will produce finer grained models specific to the methods applicable to XP and Dynamic Systems Development Method, APs with substantial records of successful industrial application, which will then be mapped to software risk elements.

TOOL SUPPORT FOR DISTRIBUTED PAIR PROGRAMMING

Brian F. Hanks
University of California, Santa Cruz
brianh@soe.ucsc.edu
Advisor: Charlie McDowell
Expected completion: June, 2004

Pair programming transforms what has traditionally been a solitary activity into a cooperative effort. In pair programming, two software developers share a single computer monitor and keyboard. The two developers alternate roles as 'driver' and 'navigator', with the driver entering software design, code, and test cases while the navigator offers advice, suggests corrections, and assists with design decisions.

Previous research suggests that pair programming provides significant benefits. Pairs produce software with fewer errors, have more confidence in their work, and report increased job satisfaction. Other researchers have found that having students pair in an introductory programming course resulted in a greater percentage of students completing the course, and in greater student retention in computer-related majors. Students who paired also produced higher quality solutions than those who did not.

A major drawback with pair programming is the collocation requirement. This prevents pair programming from being used on software projects with geographically distributed teams. Some students also find the collocation requirement burdensome. Eliminating the collocation requirement would allow the benefits of pair programming to be shared by a larger community of software developers.

I am investigating tool support for distributed pairing. I have enhanced the open source VNC screen sharing application to support distributed pairing, emphasizing three aspects: gesturing, floor control, and data collection.

I plan to experiment with the tool in an introductory programming class. Student volunteers randomly assigned to two groups will alternate traditional or distributed pairing. I will analyze data collected by the tool, student grades and student survey responses.

I hypothesize that:

1. There will be no difference in program grades earned by students in the two groups.

2. There will be no difference in the amount of time taken by the two groups.

3. Students in both groups will be equally confident in their solutions.

ADVANCES IN COMBINATORIAL INTERACTION TESTING

Myra B. Cohen
University of Auckland, New Zealand
myra@cs.auckland.ac.nz

Advisors: Peter B. Gibbons, Warwick B. Mugridge
Expected completion: December, 2003

Software is becoming increasingly complex in terms of components and their interactions. Traditional methods of testing are useful when searching for errors caused by unmatched requirements. However, component based development creates additional challenges for integration testing. The problem space grows rapidly when searching for unexpected interactions. For this reason, new tools and methods are needed. Our research examines one method that decreases the cost of integration testing. It reduces the size of test suites while guaranteeing a certain level of interaction coverage. It combines ideas from combinatorial design, computational search, statistical design of experiments and software engineering.

There are two distinct areas of active research on combinatorial designs for software testing. The mathematics community is focusing on building smaller designs of higher interaction strength using algebraic constructions and heuristic search. The software testing community is developing greedy search algorithms that build these in a more flexible environment, one that more closely matches real testing needs. Our research attempts to bridge this gap and develop methods which blend mathematical and software engineering techniques.

We have used simulated annealing to build optimal covering arrays for test suites and have made initial comparisons of this algorithm with several published greedy algorithms. In addition we have compared these with known algebraic constructions. Our program accepts seeded test cases, and exclusions. We have extended the idea of a covering array by proposing the variable strength array, which allows for multiple strengths of coverage in one test suite. We are developing a mathematical model for describing these and techniques for constructing them.

Lastly we are examining methods which allow us to build larger sized arrays from smaller ones as a prototype for combining computational and algebraic techniques in an integrated fashion.

BLACK-BOX TESTING OF GREY-BOX BEHAVIOR IN OBJECT-ORIENTED SYSTEMS

Benjamin Tyler
Ohio State University
`tyler@cis.ohio-state.edu`
Advisor: Neelam Soundarajan
Expected completion: May, 2004

The mechanisms of polymorphism and dynamic dispatch give object-orientation much of its power, and are essential for the proper functioning of many application frameworks. In such frameworks, the critical control-flow aspects that are common to all applications to be built on the framework are encoded in polymorphic template methods. In turn, application developers specialize the behavior appropriate to their individual needs by redefining the hook methods that the template methods invoke, while inheriting the template methods themselves from the framework.

How can we be sure that the resulting application will behave appropriately? We could deduce its precise behavior if we had the source code of the original framework–but this is often not the case. Furthermore, standard black-box specifications are inadequate for describing the behaviors of template methods because they lack the necessary information, specifically the pattern of hook method calls, which is critical in deducing the application's precise behavior.

The first major goal of my Ph.D. research is to develop new types of grey-box specifications that will provide needed control-flow information to users. This will allow developers to safely build applications on top of frameworks, while vendors will not have to reveal proprietary source code. I will also explore other practical uses for grey-box specifications, such as in event driven and distributed systems, where crucial information about sequences of interactions can be provided using such specifications.

A second major goal of my work is to develop ways we can *test* the behavior of framework-based systems. Here again, the lack of access to source code makes it problematic when testing against grey-box specifications since internal method calls are usually not directly observable from the outside. I have developed a novel way that exploits polymorphism to overcome this problem, and have implemented a prototype testing tool based on this approach.

EVALUATING SOFTWARE ARCHITECTURES FOR STABILITY

Rami Bahsoon
University College London (UCL)
`r.bahsoon@cs.ucl.ac.uk`
Supervisor: Wolfgang Emmerich
Expected completion: April, 2004

Architectural stability refers to the extent a software architecture is flexible to endure evolutionary changes in stakeholders' requirements and the environment, while leaving the architecture intact.

Architectural stability adds value to the software system and to the enterprise owning the architecture. The added value is attributed to flexibility and the options that flexibility creates over the evolutionary periods of the software system. The added value is strategic in essence and may not be immediate. It takes the form of (i) accumulated savings through enduring the change without 'breaking' the architecture; (ii) supporting reuse and enhancing the opportunities for strategic 'growth' (e.g. regarding an architecture as an asset and instantiating the asset to support new market products); and (iii) giving the enterprise a competitive advantage by banking the stable architecture like any other capitalized asset.

Approaches to evaluating software architectures for stability can be retrospective or predictive. Both approaches assume that the software architecture's primary goal is to guide the system's evolution. Retrospective evaluation looks at successive releases of the software system to analyse how smoothly the evolution has taken place. Predictive evaluation examines a set of likely changes and the extent the architecture can endure these changes. We take a predictive approach to evaluation. We use a value-based reasoning and exploit options theory to predict architectural stability. Specifically, we derive a predictive model from the Black & Scholes option pricing theory. Given likely evolutionary change(s), the model values the flexibility of an architecture to endure the likely change(s) and unlock future growth opportunities- as a way to make the value of stability tangible.

We will empirically evaluate the applicability of the approach and the effectiveness of the predictive model in an industrial setting.

PROPERTY ELICITATION AND SPECIFICATION PROCESS (PROSPEC)

Oscar A. Mondragon
University of Texas at El Paso
oscar@cs.utep.edu
Advisor: Dr. Ann Q. Gates
Expected completion: August, 2003

Formal verification techniques have been used for two decades to detect errors not captured with other verification approaches; however, they have not been widely adopted. The difficulty of writing and validating formal specifications are two reasons often cited. In particular, the high level of mathematical sophistication required makes the process hard, error prone, and inaccessible to practitioners.

To provide an intuitive method that assist users, domain experts, and developers in the elicitation, specification, validation, and verification of software system properties, the Property Specification System (Prospec) is being introduced. Prospec defines an elicitation process, generates formal specifications in Future Interval Logic (FIL), and provides a mapping from a subset of FIL formulas to the Meta Event Definition Language to assist in run-time verification. The elicitation process is built upon taxonomy of composite propositions and the Specification Pattern System (SPS). The composite proposition taxonomy categorizes and defines the relations of multiple propositions. highlighting the subtleties associated with the structure of sequential, concurrent, and non-deterministic behavior. The taxonomy extends SPS and provides graphical abstractions, including symbols, timeline diagrams, and Petri nets, to assist in the elicitation, specification, and validation of properties.

The proposed work will result in a tool that guides the user in the elicitation and specification process by presenting the user with visual representations of the properties being specified and prompts the user with options to helps him/her make explicit decisions about behavior of properties with multiple conditions. The significance of the work is that it will facilitate elicitation of complex system properties from domain experts and customers early in the requirements process. The automated generation of formal specifications reduces the introduction of syntactic and semantic errors. More importantly, the resulting specifications can be used in a variety of analysis and verification tools.

CROSS-CUTTING ADAPTATION OF DISTRIBUTED HETEROGENEOUS SYSTEMS

Eric Wohlstadter
University of California, Davis
wohlstad@ucdavis.edu
Advisor: Premkumar Devanbu
Expected completion: July 2004

Distributed heterogeneous software is particularly hard to adapt for deployment in disparate execution environments. This is because software on dissimilar hosts must cooperate to enable adaptations across an entire system. We are investigating the use of an adaptation service to coordinate cross-host services transparently to standard program components. An adaptation service is made up of client and server side components called adaplets. The functionality of adaplets is described in an IDL. Adaplets can be implemented by 3rd-party developers and later deployed on distributed applications.

Sometimes distribution forces applications to manage more details than are present in local computations. Information about security, distributed transaction propagation, or real-time scheduling must be shared between components deployed across the network. Cooperation should be possible even though the implementations may be in different programming languages or on different OS's. Modifying the interfaces of components to handle such concerns decreases modularization by forcing the component implementation to handle several types of functionality: not only application-related functions, but also functions related to security, transactions etc. Current middleware solutions only offer a fixed set of services. However, hand tailoring adaptations that are not offered directly by middleware tangles the implementation of several requirements and destroys program modularity. Furthermore, implementations are no longer usable when environmental conditions change.

We propose to develop a methodology and implementation techniques for the design and development of crosscutting adaptations to distributed heterogeneous software components. The overall designs should be general enough to be applicable for a wide range of implementation languages/platforms. However, support for cooperation between adaptations on heterogeneous systems must be provided. Thus, adaptations to manage concerns that span hosts will need to be coordinated. We believe transparent deployment of adaptations onto existing applications will make it more practical to evolve implementations to new usage scenarios.

A CUSTOMIZABLE SOURCE PROJECTION FRAMEWORK

Stoney Jackson
University of California, Davis
jacksoni@cs.ucdavis.edu
Advisor: Premkumar T. Devanbu
Expected Completion: June 2004

Source-code visualizations help programmers understand programs by visually encoding software related information in the textual representation of source-code. Many modern integrated development environments include source-code visualizations such as syntax highlighting and auto- indentation. However, currently, these visualizations are typically hand-tooled and rigid, allowing visual presentation of a fixed set of data using a fixed visual mapping; for each new kind of data and new kind of mapping, we must custom-build a new visualization tool. Thus, visualizations are not easily tailored to suit a particular maintenance task, to an individual's viewing preferences or visual handicaps (such as color blindness), or to take advantage of a new and interesting combination of program related data.

We propose a novel Source Projection Framework for simplifying the construction and reconfiguration of a variety of source-code visualizations. The literature contains no description of a framework for constructing interactive text-based software visualizations from multiple datasets. To guide our development and evaluation of such a framework, we identify several requirements. Among them, the framework must allow for a wide range of program related data to be visualized, provide an extensible set of visual attributes for encoding data, integrate with different visual environments and editors, allow programmers to customize their visualizations to suit their needs, and be retargetable to different programming languages. We also hope to unify within a single framework such (previously) disparate visualization techniques as Fisheyes and Seesoft.

We have built a prototype of our framework. At its core, visual encoders map datasets to visual attributes based on a high-level specification language. Visual encoders are reusable across different datasets, as datasets are required to be represented as a mapping between 0 to 1 values and abstract-syntax-tree nodes. While not meeting all of our design requirements, our prototype provides a proof of concept and identifies future design challenges.

DOCTORAL SYMPOSIUM COMMITTEE

Co-chairs:
Dick Hamlet (Portland State)
Mary Lou Soffa (Univ of Pittsburgh)

Committee:
Steve Easterbrook (Toronto)
Mary Jean Harrold (Georgia Tech)
David Notkin (Univ of Washington)
Kevin Ryan (Univ of Limerick)
André van der Hoek (UC Irvine)

–Edited by Dick Hamlet, Portland State University
hamlet@cs.pdx.edu.

New Software Engineering Faculty Symposium (NSEFS 03)

Leon J. Osterweil

University of Massachusetts, Amherst
Computer Science Department
Amherst, MA 01003
1-413-545-2186
ljo@cs.umass.edu

SUMMARY

The challenge of becoming a new Assistant Professor at a research university is one that most people accept with enthusiasm and energy, but also with some trepidation. One's tenure track appointment is a signal accomplishment and the culmination of many years of hard work. But, simultaneously, it signals the start of another round of hard work and challenges that are new and often unfamiliar. Among these new challenges are establishing an independent research program, learning how to teach, learning how to mentor, and deciding how to balance career and personal life. For a new software engineering faculty member there are additional challenges such as obtaining financial support, supervising the development of software systems, and dealing with skeptical faculty colleagues from other disciplines.

The purpose of NSEFS 03 is to help new software engineering faculty members to feel more comfortable and confident in dealing with these many challenges. NSEFS 03 will feature presentations by leading academic software engineering researchers who will provide advice and guidance based upon their personal experiences and insights into the contemporary academic software engineering community. There will also be ample time for informal and small group interactions with the presenters and other attendees.

NSEFS 03 is designed to be a service to those who are within two years of (either before or after) their initial tenure track academic appointment, although the symposium may be of significant interest and value to others.

0-7695-1877-X/03 $17.00 © 2003 IEEE

PROGRAM

What Every Young Software Engineering Faculty Member Needs to Know

9:00	Welcome, Introductions, Overview of the Day (Lee Osterweil)
9:30	Mapping out a Research Agenda (Barbara Ryder)
10:00	Publication Strategies (Carlo Ghezzi)
10:30	BREAK
11:00	Networking (Lori Clarke)
11:30	Teaching and Mentoring Students (to be announced)
12:15	LUNCH Obtaining Research Funding (breakout groups by nationality) Carlo Ghezzi, Jeff Kramer, Dieter Rombach, Dick Taylor
1:45	How to get Tenure (Lee Osterweil)
2:15	Time Allocation: Balancing Research, Teaching, and Service (Jeff Kramer)
2:45	How to Have a Life as Well as a Career--and Why! (Vic Basili)
3:15	BREAK
3:45	A view from the trenches -- Panel of successful young faculty members Gregg Rothermel, Bashar Nuseibeh, others to be announced
4:30	Summary and final advice

SE Pioneers Symposium

The First 25 Years – The Next 25 Years: On Doing Work of Lasting Value

Stuart R. Faulk
Computer and Information Science
University of Oregon
Eugene, Oregon 97403 USA
+1 541 346 1350
faulk@cs.uoregon.edu

Lawrence G. Votta
Mailstop UMPK18-216, Room 2482
18 Network Circle
Menlo Park, CA 94025
+1 650 786 7514
larry.votta@Sun.Com

ABSTRACT
The Pioneers' Symposium provides a forum in which Software Engineering's next generation of researchers, faculty, and practitioners have the opportunity to interact with and learn from some of the field's pioneering thinkers. The invited speakers are individuals whose works are not only seminal, but have demonstrated enduring value to both the research and development communities. Attendees will have the opportunity to understand and discuss the speakers' views on 1) what software engineering professionals should know, 2) thinking critically about the field, and 2) what it takes to do work of lasting value.

MOTIVATION
In spite of the fact that Software Engineering is a young field, we observe that many of the lessons of history are being lost on those now entering the profession. Software Engineering education, whether in the university classroom or on the job, tends to eschew older (seminal) works in favor of newer publications and the most recent trends. Whether this is because we assume that the newer material subsumes the old or because our "high-tech" industry is enamored of the new, the result is that many younger members of the community are entering software engineering professions as researchers, educators, and developers with little exposure to the field's foundational works.

The result is often a lack of perspective on the field - in particular, the genesis, origin, and evolution of software engineering's fundamental conceptual structures. Without the perspective of history, progress is not easily gauged, previous mistakes avoided, or well-founded research goals defined. Common manifestations of this lack of perspective that we have observed in both academics and industry include:

- *Inability to apply basic principles*: both students and professional software developers often do not know how to effectively apply fundamental software engineering principles (e.g., abstraction, modularization, information hiding) to achieve the critical properties desired of their programs (e.g., maintainability, reusability, safety).
- *Re-inventing the wheel*: researchers constantly re-invent and re-investigate old concepts in new guises without realizing that they are plowing infertile ground. The results add little, if anything, to the body of knowledge.
- *Repeating past errors*: we have accumulated a vast array of experiences in how **not** to develop software. Nonetheless, developers continue to apply processes, models, and methods (or lack thereof) that have consistent track records of failure. Similarly, researchers continue to put forward ideas and approaches long since debunked in practice.
- *Lack of critical judgment*: we often have difficulty distinguishing sound, well-founded approaches from those comprising more hype than substance. We waste time and effort on concepts of marginal and transient value.

The software engineering community seems to be revisiting the lesson that: those who will not learn the lessons of history are doomed to repeat them.

PURPOSE
The purpose of Pioneers Symposium is to provide a forum in which Software Engineer's next generation can share in the accumulated wisdom of some of the field's preeminent contributors.

Speakers will present their views on what software engineers really need to know, how to think critically about our own or other people's work, and what it takes to make substantive contributions to Software Engineering's body of knowledge. Topic covered will include the speaker's views on:

- What principles and concepts every software engineering professional should master – i.e., the key ideas that educators should teach and students should learn.
- How to examine prevailing assumptions (particularly our own) and think critically about the work in the field.
- What it takes to do meaningful research and to make enduring contributions to the field's body of knowledge.

0-7695-1877-X/03 $17.00 © 2003 IEEE

The Symposium will provide the opportunity both to hear the speakers' views and to interact with them in group and individual discussions.

THE SPEAKERS

The Symposium's speakers are representative of the field's intellectual pioneers whose work and whose research approach are worth emulating. An intellectual pioneer is distinguished not just for opening up new avenues of thought, but also for blazing a trail that serves as an example for others to follow. The invited speakers are each pioneers in this sense. They have not only made seminal contributions to the field, but those contributions have proven the test of time. In particular:

- Each has made one or more seminal contributions to Software Engineering's field of knowledge that remains important to read and understand today.
- Each has significantly influenced the direction of software engineering research in one or more areas that are currently active.
- Each has significantly influenced current software development practices in industry.

In short, each has made contributions of enduring value to both research and practice. In addition to their credentials as "pioneers," the speakers have been chosen to cover key areas in the field. They include:

Barry Boehm - Software Economics

Victor Basili - Empirical Methods

Michael Jackson - Software Process

Nancy Leveson - Software Safety

David Parnas – Software Design, Education

AUDIENCE

The Pioneers Symposium is primarily targeted to graduate students, new faculty, and young software engineering professionals interested in 1) gaining a better perspective on their field, 2) getting a better understanding of what they should know to do superior work in their chosen field and 3) understanding how to direct their research to produce results of lasting value. Software Engineering graduate students are particularly urged to attend.

ACKNOWLEDGEMENTS

The Software Engineering Pioneers Symposium has been made possible by generous grants from:

Sun Microsystems

National Science Foundation

Software Engineering for Large-Scale Multi-Agent Systems – SELMAS'2003

Carlos Lucena José Alberto Sardinha
Alessandro Garcia
Departamento de Informática – TecComm Group
Pontifícia Universidade Católica do Rio de Janeiro - Brazil
{lucena,sardinha,afgarcia}@inf.puc-rio.br

Jaelson Castro
Centro de Informática
Universidade Federal de Pernambuco - Brazil
jbc@cin.ufpe.br

Alexander Romanovsky
School of Computing Science
University of Newcastle upon Tyne - UK
alexander.romanovsky@ncl.ac.uk

Paulo Alencar Donald Cowan
School of Computer Science
University of Waterloo – Canada1
{palencar, dcowan}@csg.uwaterloo.ca

Abstract

Objects and agents are abstractions that exhibit points of similarity, but the development of multi-agent systems (MASs) poses other challenges to Software Engineering since software agents are inherently more complex entities. In addition, a large MAS needs to satisfy multiple stringent requirements such as reliability, trustability, security, interoperability, scalability, reusability, and maintainability. This workshop brings together researchers and practitioners to discuss the current state of the art and the future research directions in software engineering for large-scale MASs. A particular interest is to understand those issues in the agent technology that make it difficult and/or improve the production of complex distributed systems.

1. Motivation

Advances in networking technology have revitalized the investigation of the agent technology as a promising paradigm to engineer complex distributed software systems. Nowadays, the agent technology has been applied in a wide range of application domains, including e-commerce, human-computer interfaces, telecommunications, and concurrent engineering. In general, software agents are viewed as complex objects with an attitude. Like objects, agents provide a specific set of services for their users. In fact, objects and agents exhibit points of similarity, but the development of multi-agent systems (MASs) poses other challenges to Software Engineering since software agents are inherently more complex abstractions.

A single software agent is driven by goals, knowledge, and a number of behavioral properties such as autonomy, adaptation, interaction, collaboration, learning and mobility. While these features introduce additional complexity to the different phases of the software process, there are many techniques for dealing with individual agents or systems built using only few agents. Unfortunately, existing software engineering approaches are still unable to cope with the complexity of large MASs. It is because software engineering for MASs is still in its infancy. MAS features are now being applied to the development of large industrial software systems. Such systems involve hundreds, perhaps thousands of agents, and there is a pressing need for software engineering techniques that allow their complexity to be effectively managed, and principled methods are also required to guide the process of MAS development. Without adequate development techniques and methods, such systems will not be sufficiently dependable, trustable, extensible, difficult to comprehend, and their components will not be reusable.

The complexity associated with large MASs is not straightforward and involves numerous facets and dimensions. When a huge number of agents interact over heterogeneous environments, various phenomena occur which are not as to easy to explain as the behavior of few agents in a closed environment. As the multiple software agents become highly collaborative, new problems appear. It makes their coordination and management more difficult and increases the probability of manifestation of heterogeneous exceptional situations, security holes, privacy violations, unexpected global effects, and so on. Moreover, since users and software engineers delegate more autonomy to their MASs, and put more trust in their results, new concerns arise in real-life applications. Commercial success for MAS applications will require scalable solutions based on software engineering approaches in order to enable reuse and effective deployment. However, many existing agent-oriented solutions are far from ideal; in practice, the systems are often built in an ad-hoc manner and are error-prone, not scalable, not dynamic, and are not generally applicable to large-scale MAS.

2. Goals

This workshop follows up on the success of the 1st Workshop on Software Engineering for Large-Scale Multi-Agent Systems (SELMAS'02), held in Orlando, USA, May 19, 2002, as part of the ICSE'02. The 1st SELMAS workshop was very successful due to the high quality of the submissions, the active participation of the audience, the exceptional profile of the panelists, and the edition of a Springer book publishing extended workshop papers. The goal of this workshop is to bring together

0-7695-1877-X/03 $17.00 © 2003 IEEE

researchers and practitioners from both approaches to discuss the current state of the art and the future research directions in software engineering for large-scale MASs. Particular interests of this workshop are:

- Investigate the overlap and integration of agent-oriented software engineering and agent-based software engineering;
- Understand those issues in the agent technology that difficult and/or improve the production of complex distributed systems;
- Provide a comprehensive overview of existing software engineering techniques and methods that may successfully be applied to deal with the complexity associated with realistic multi-agent software.

3. Program Committee

Alessandro Garcia (PUC-Rio – Brazil) – **Chair**
A. Romanovsky (Univ. Newcastle upon Tyne-UK) – **Chair**
Anand Tripathi (University of Minnesota - USA)
Andrea Omicini (University of Bologna - Italy)
Anna Perini (University of Trento - Italy)
Awais Rashid (Lancaster University - UK)
Brian Henderson-Sellers (University of Technology-Australia)
Bruno Schulze (LNCC - Brazil)
Carlos A. I. Fernandez (Politechnical University of Madrid-Spain)
Carlos Lucena (PUC-Rio – Brazil) – **Chair**
Catholijn Jonker (Vrije Univ. Amsterdam - The Netherlands)
Cecilia Rubira (UNICAMP - Brazil)
Dan Marinescu (Central Florida University - USA)
Donald Cowan (University of Waterloo - Canada) – **Chair**
Eric Yu (University of Toronto - Canada)
Evandro de Barros Costa (UFAL - Brazil)
Federico Bergenti (University of Parma, Italy)
Franco Zambonelli (Univ. of Modena and Reggio Emilia - Italy)
Gerd Wagner (Eindhonven Univ. Technology – The Netherlands)
Gerhard Weiss (Technical University of Munich - Germany)
Gustavo Rossi (Universidad Nacional de La Plata - Argentina)
Jean-Pierre Briot (Laboratoire d'Informatique Paris 6-France)
Jaelson Castro (UFPE – Brazil) – **Chair**
John Debenham (University of Technology - Australia)
José Alberto Sardinha (PUC-Rio – Brazil) – **Chair**
José Carlos Maldonado (USP S. Carlos - Brazil)
Julio Leite (PUC-Rio - Brazil)
Katia Sycara (Carnegie Mellon University - USA)
Liz Kendall (Monash University - Australia)
Luiz Cysneiros (York University - Canada)
Marco Mamei (University of Modena & Reggio Emilia - Italy)
Marcus Fontoura (IBM Almaden Research Center - USA)
Marie-Pierre Gervais(Laboratoire d'Informatique Paris - France)
Marie-Pierre Gleizes (Universite Paul Sabatier - Toulouse)
Markus Endler (PUC-Rio - Brazil)
Martin Fredriksson (Blekinge Institute of Technology - Sweden)
Martin Griss (HP Research Laboratory - USA)
Michael Huhns (University of South Carolina - USA)
Michael Stal (Siemens - Germany)
Michael Weiss (Carleton University - Canada)
Olivier Gutknecht (LIRMM - France)
Paolo Giorgini (University of Trento - Italy)
Paulo Alencar (University of Waterloo - Canada) – **Chair**
Robert Kessler (University of Utah - USA)
Rogério de Lemos (University of Kent - UK)
Ruy Milidiu (PUC-Rio - Brazil)
Tom Holvoet (Katholieke Universiteit Leuven - Belgium)
Tom Maibaum (King's College London - UK)
Van Parunak (Altarum Institute - USA)
Yannis Labrou (Fujitsu Laboratories of America - USA)

4. Workshop Activities

SELMAS'2003 is a two full-day event, structured around sessions of theme-oriented presentations. Following each session, the workshop participants will engage in structured discussions. Prior to the workshop, participants will be asked to read all papers in his/her session. The main purpose is to foster the exchange of ideas and information in an informal setting, but with some boundaries placed on topics and time to ensure that the workshop stays on schedule.

The format of the sessions combines presentations on submitted position papers, invited talks, and focused discussion groups. SELMAS'2003 provides an opportunity for exchanging information related to exciting new research and empirical results in areas including (but not limited to):

- Software engineering theories for large-scale MAS
- Comparative studies between MAS and OO systems
- Experiments and case studies with large MAS development
- Advanced separation of concerns in the context of MAS
- Design patterns, design principles, and architectural styles
- Frameworks and software architectures
- Reflective software architectures
- Coordination architectures, infrastructures, and tools
- Domain-specific languages for MAS
- Requirements engineering for MAS
- Software reliability engineering and MAS
- Exception handling and fault-tolerance techniques
- Mobility and security issues in large MAS
- Software engineering techniques for resource-bounded MAS
- MAS development and pervasive computing
- Verification and validation techniques for MAS
- Software development environments for real-life MAS
- Modeling of large MAS
- UML application to large-scale MAS
- Methodologies for agent-oriented analysis and design
- Testing and metrics for MAS

By assembling together a diverse set of people with expertise in this broad range of topics, we will motivate the creation of the milieu necessary to focus our attention on themes that integrate rather than differentiate our perspectives on software engineering for large-scale MAS. At the end of the workshop there will be a general discussion, including a brainstorming session about areas or topics of research that the participants perceived as important.

5. Workshop Outputs

All the results obtained by discussion will be summarized and published as a technical report and made electronically available in the workshop web site. The aim is to highlight outstanding issues that should form a part of the forthcoming research agenda. For further details, please visit our web site:

www.teccomm.les.inf.puc-rio.br/selmas2003

Fifth International Workshop on Economics-driven Software Engineering Research (EDSER-5) "The Search for Value in Engineering Decisions"

(www.edser.org)

Jyrki Kontio
Helsinki University of Technology
jyrki.kontio@hut.fi

Shawn Butler
Carnegie Mellon University
shawnb@cs.cmu.edu

Abstract

The series of EDSER workshops are a unique forum to discuss and advance the state-of-the-art research and practice in economics driven software engineering. The EDSER-5 will bring together leading researchers and practitioners to provide further understanding how economic and business considerations affect -- and should affect -- software engineering decisions.

1. Problem

Traditionally, the study of software engineering has been primarily a technical endeavor with minimal attention given to its economic context. Design and implementation methods are proposed based on technical merits without making adequate links to economic considerations. Students are taught decision-making skills in an exclusively technical context. This is in stark contrast to the reality of software engineering. Engineering seeks to create value relative to resources invested. Regardless of how an organization defines "value", software development essentially is an irreversible capital investment. Therefore, software should add value to the organization just as any other capital expenditure. As such, the costs of development should not outweigh the returns from the product to achieve a net benefit.

2. Scope

The EDSER-5 workshop aims at improving the state-of-the-art and state-of-the-practice in economics and business driven software engineering in order to ensure that the engineering decisions made during software development fully address the relevant economic and business issues. While these technical engineering decisions form the foundation of software engineering, these decisions should be guided by the objective of adding value to stakeholders.

3. Workshop

The workshop will give an up-to-date view of the recent research in this area and it will also act as a forum where practitioners exchange views with leading researchers. Earlier EDSER workshops have shown that software engineering research and practice is starting to benefit from cross-disciplinary exchange of ideas and experiences. These previous workshops identified a wealth of applications ranging from software process, quality, project management and contract management, reuse prototyping, rapid development, and security.

This year's two-day workshop will start with half a day discussion on economic software engineering curriculum development. Last year's EDSER-4 participants saw the need for educators to have access to educational material so that they can begin to integrate economic analytical techniques in software engineering curriculums.

The remainder of the workshop will be devoted to presentations and discussions from selected papers submitted from participants. The workshop is targeted both at researchers in economics driven software engineering, as well as to practitioners that want to follow and

0-7695-1877-X/03 $17.00 © 2003 IEEE

contribute to the state-of-the-art research in this area.

4. Steering Committee

Kevin Sullivan; University of Virginia, USA; sullivan@virginia.edu
Mary Shaw; Carnegie Mellon University, USA; mary.shaw@cs.cmu.edu
David Notkin; University of Washington, USA; notkin@cs.washington.edu
Warren Harrison; Portland State University, USA; warren@cs.pdx.edu
Hakan Erdogmus; National Research Council, Canada; Hakan.Erdogmus@nrc-cnrc.gc.ca
Barry Boehm; University of Southern California, USA; boehm@sunset.usc.edu

6th ICSE Workshop on Component-Based Software Engineering: Automated Reasoning and Prediction

Ivica Crnkovic,
Mälardalen University
Sweden
ivica.crnkovic@mdh.se,

Heinz Schmidt
Monash University
Australia
hws@monash.edu.au

Judith Stafford
Tufts University
USA
jas@cs.tufts.edu

Kurt Wallnau
Carnegie Mellon University
USA
kcw@sei.cmu.edu

ABSTRACT

Component-based technologies and processes have been deployed in many organizations and in many fields over the past several years. However, modeling, reasoning about, and predicting component and system properties remains challenging in theory and in practice. CBSE6 builds on previous workshops in the ICSE/CBSE series, and in 2003 is thematically centered on automated composition theories. Composition theories support reasoning about, and predicting, the runtime properties of assemblies of components. Automation is a practical necessity for applying composition theories in practice. Emphasis is placed in this workshop on composition theories that are well founded theoretically, are verifiable or falsifiable, automated by tools, and supported by practical evaluation.

Keywords

Composition, components, system analysis, quality attributes

1 INTRODUCTION

Component-based technologies are today in widespread use. Components offer model realism from chip architectures through embedded or telecommunication systems to enterprise-level or governmental workflows and services. The spreading of component-based technologies in conjunction with software architecture and product lines is increasingly connected with measurable gains in flexibility and productivity. However, modeling, reasoning about, and predicting component and system properties remains challenging in theory and in practice.

CBSE6 builds on previous workshops in the ICSE/CBSE series, this year thematically centered on automated composition theories. Composition theories support reasoning about, and predicting, the runtime properties of assemblies of components. Automation is a practical necessity for applying composition theories in practice. Emphasis is placed in this workshop on composition theories that are well founded theoretically, automated by tools, and/or supported by evaluation.

Empirical and formal theories of composition are of interest. Questions relating to composition theory and practice include:

- Which properties are of interest in a given domain, and how should these properties be modeled?
- What general and property-specific models are useful for reasoning about, and predicting system behavior?
- How can component and assembly properties be measured?
- How can measurements and predictions be validated?
- How can composition theories be conveyed in a useful way to component users—the application builder?

Resolving these issues requires collaborative work of researchers across several domains in software engineering, computer science and engineering disciplines. The primary goal of CBSE6 is to achieve better understanding of the state of the art in automated compositional reasoning and prediction. While emphasizing state of the art, the workshop also aims at bridging theory and practice.

2 WORKSHOP ORGANIZATION

All participants were required to submit a 5-page position paper. Accepted papers are posted online at the workshop homepage, www.sei.cmu.edu/pacc/CBSE6. In keeping with the tradition of the ICSE/CBSE series, the format of the workshop is kept informal, and emphasizes discussion, debate, and dynamic planning. The opening session begins with short presentations of position statements (5-10 minutes). The organizers then propose a nominal discussion agenda and objectives, based on submissions. Workshop participants then confirm or modify the agenda and objectives, as they deem fit. There is no pre-set formula, and it is expected that the participants will decide on the most effective means to have productive sessions.

0-7695-1877-X/03 $17.00 © 2003 IEEE

Workshop Organizers:

Ivica Crnkovic, Mälardalen University, Sweden

Heinz Schmidt, Monash University, Australia

Judith Stafford, Tufts University, USA

Kurt Wallnau, Software Engineering Institute, USA

Program Committee:

Judith Bishop, University of Pretoria, South Africa

Jan Bosch, University of Groningen, The Netherlands

Jacky Estublier, LSR-IMAG, France

Kathi Fisler, WPI, USA

Dimitra Giannakopoulou, NASA Ames, USA

Richard Hall, Imag/Lsr, France

Dick Hamlet, Portland State University, USA

George Heineman, WPI, USA

Paola Inverardi, University of L'Aquila, Italy

Shriram Krishnamurthi, Brown University, USA

Otto Preiss, ABB/CRC, Switzerland

Clemens Szyperski, Microsoft Research, USA

Dave Wile, Teknowledge, Corp., USA

Christian Zeidler, ABB Research, Germany

Bridging the Gaps Between Software Engineering and Human-Computer Interaction

Rick Kazman
Software Engineering Institute, Pittsburgh, PA and *University of Hawaii, Honolulu, HI*
kazman@sei.cmu.edu

Len Bass
Software Engineering Institute, Pittsburgh, PA
ljb@sei.cmu.edu

Jan Bosch
University of Groningen, Groningen, The Netherlands
Jan.Bosch@cs.rug.nl

Abstract

The First International Workshop on the Relationships between Software Engineering and Human-Computer Interaction was held on May 3-4, 2003 as part of the 2003 International Conference on Software Engineering, in Portland, OR, U.S.A. This workshop was motivated by a perception among researchers, practitioners, and educators that the fields of Human-Computer Interaction and Software Engineering were largely ignoring each other and that they needed to work together more closely and to understand each other better. This paper describes the motivation, goals, organization, and outputs of the workshop.

1. Motivation

Almost half of the software in systems being developed today and thirty-seven to fifty percent of efforts throughout the software life cycle are related to the system's user interface. For this reason problems and methods from the field of human-computer interaction (HCI) affect the overall process of software engineering (SE) tremendously, and vice versa.

Yet despite these powerful reasons to practice and apply effective SE and HCI methods there still exist major gaps of understanding both between suggested practice and how software is actually developed in industry. Similarly there exist major gaps of understanding between the best practices of each of the fields. The standard curricula for each field make little if any reference to the other field and certainly do not teach how to interact with the other field. There are major gaps of communication between HCI and SE: the architectures, processes, methods and vocabulary being used in each community are often foreign to the other community. As a result, product quality is not as high as it could be, and (avoidable) re-work is frequently necessary.

2. Goals

The theme of this workshop was to bring together educators, practitioners and academics in the two fields in an attempt to enumerate and understand these gaps of understanding and communication, with an eventual goal of proposing practical techniques—shared processes, shared architectures, shared notations, etc.—for bridging these gaps.

3. Participant Selection

Participants were invited to submit brief position papers (up to 8 pages) describing their views on the interactions, problems, and connections between SE and HCI and on any proposals that they had for improving these relationships in terms of research, practice, education, tools, methods and processes.

These papers were reviewed by the program committee. A maximum of 30 people were to be selected for participation in the workshop as a result of this process. 16 papers, of very high quality, were eventually accepted.

4. Program Committee

The program committee was drawn from an international community of experts in the areas of HCI and SE. It consisted of the following people:

Organizers:

- Len Bass (SEI/CMU, USA)
- Jan Bosch (U. of Groningen, The Netherlands)
- Rick Kazman (SEI/CMU and U. of Hawaii, USA)

Program Committee Members:

- Rémi Bastide (University of Toulouse 1, France)

0-7695-1877-X/03 $17.00 © 2003 IEEE

- Stéphane Chatty (CENA, France)
- Joëlle Coutaz (U. Of Grenoble, France)
- Nicholas Graham (Queens U., Canada).
- Morten Borup Harning (Dialogical ApS, Denmark)
- Bonnie John (HCII/CMU, USA)
- Natalia Juristo (U. Politecnica de Madrid, Spain)
- Jeffrey Kramer (Imperial College, UK)
- Jeffrey Magee (Imperial College, UK)
- Laurence Nigay (U. of Grenoble, France)
- Philippe Palanque (Université de Toulouse 1, France)
- Fabio Paternò (CNUCE-CNR, Italy)
- Greg Phillips (Royal Military College, Canada)
- Joerg Roth (U. of Hagen, Germany)
- Chris Roast (U. of Sheffield, UK)
- Helmut Stiegler (STI Consulting, Germany)
- Daniel Salber (CWI, The Netherlands)
- Claus Unger (U. of Hagen, Germany)
- Leon Watts (U. of Manchester, UK)

5. Workshop Structure and Activities

Participation in the workshop was based on invitation. Invitations were extended to the authors of submitted position papers, all of which were presented during the course of the two days. A few other invitations were extended to individuals who expressed an interest in the learning more about the workshop topic, but who did not feel qualified to present a position.

All papers were distributed to the participants before the workshop started. The papers were grouped into panels and each presented paper was discussed by the other panel members and, of course, by the other members of the workshop.

During the first day, participants proposed issues to be discussed at the end of the day. During the second day in the morning we broke into working sub-groups and discussed the issues. In the afternoon we once again met in plenary to discuss our findings.

6. Workshop Outputs

The workshop led to a list of issues discussed, conclusions reached, disagreements identified, topics to be researched further, and an agenda for both research and advocacy.

All papers, commentaries, and discussion summaries were made available electronically at the workshop website at `http://www.se-hci.org/bridging/` soon after the workshop.

The parent site, `http://www.se-hci.org` is the home page of IFIP Working Group 2.7/13.4. It exists, in part, to be a repository that highlights research and outstanding issues in areas that bridge the concerns of human-computer interaction and software engineering.

ICSE Workshop on

Software Variability Management

Peter Knauber
University of
Applied Sciences Mannheim
Windeckstraße 110
D-68163 Mannheim, Germany
(+49) 621 – 292 6153
P.Knauber@fh-mannheim.de

Jan Bosch
University of Groningen
Department of Mathematics and Computing Science
PO Box 800
NL9700 AV Groningen, The Netherlands
(+31) 50 3633941
Jan.Bosch@cs.rug.nl

Abstract

Software Variability, Variability Management, Software Customization, Software Adaptation, Software Configuration

Abstract

During recent years, the amount of variability that has to be supported by a software artifact is growing considerably and its management is developing as a main challenge during development, usage, and evolution of software artifacts. Successful management of variability in software artifacts leads to better customizable software products that are in turn likely to result in higher market success.

The aim of this workshop is to study software variability management both from a 'problems' and from a 'solutions' perspective by bringing together people from industrial practice and from applied research in academia to present and discuss their respective experience.

Issues to be addressed include, but are not limited to, technological, process, and organizational aspects as well as notation, assessment, design, and evolution aspects.

1. Motivation

In a variety of approaches to software development, software artifacts are used in multiple contexts or for various purposes. The differences lead to so-called variation points in the software artifact. Software variability is the ability of a software system or artefact to be changed, customized or configured for use in a particular context. A high degree of variability allows the use of software in a broader range of contexts, i.e., the software is more reusable. Variability can be viewed as consisting of two dimensions, i.e. space and time.

The space dimension is concerned with the use of software in multiple contexts, e.g. multiple products in a software product family. The time dimension is concerned with the ability of software to support evolution and changing requirements in its various contexts.

During recent years, the amount of variability that has to be supported by a software artifact is growing considerably and its management is developing as a main technical challenge during development, usage, and evolution of software artifacts.

So far, variability management is recognized as a crosscutting concept in software engineering that has a key role in various areas but that is poorly understood as an issue in its own right. In different facets, variability management is part of many recent development approaches, including, but not limited to, object-oriented frameworks, design pattern, domain-oriented languages, generative programming, generic components, domain and requirements analysis, and software product families (also referred to as software product lines).

Successful management of variability in software artifacts leads to better customizable software products that are in turn likely to result in higher market success: in the information systems domain, the products are more easily adaptable to the needs of different user groups; in the embedded systems domain, the software can be more easily configured to work with different hardware and environmental constraints.

2. Goal of the Workshop

Management of software variability has been discussed in sessions of previous conferences and workshops, but

0-7695-1877-X/03 $17.00 © 2003 IEEE

only as one issue among others. Dedicating a full day workshop to variability will attract more people working on that topic and thus provide a better basis for achieving new and important results. By co-locating this workshop with the International Conference on Software Engineering (ICSE), the premier software engineering conference it can be expected to bring together people from industrial practice and from applied research in academia to present and discuss their respective experience with variability in software engineering. This mixture of industrial and research people will help to feed the results back into industrial practice and to set practically relevant research goals for the academic community.

Topics that are addressed during the workshop can be organized around designing, using and evolving for variability.

Design of variability is concerned with modeling the required variation and the provided variation points, assessing the provided variation against the required variation, selection of variability mechanisms, variability of quality attributes and managing dependencies between variation points.

During the use of variability several topics are of relevance. These include management of variability and variation points, feature-driven and automated configuration, run-time (re-) configuration and third party variants.

After their initial design and use, variation points evolve over time. Examples of typical evolution include changing the variation point binding time, changing variant addition time, adding and removing variation points to software artifacts and evolving quality attribute variability.

During the workshop, the issues surrounding the aforementioned topics and the techniques addressing these issues are the main topic of interest.

3. Workshop Format

The aim of the workshop is to study software variability management both from a 'problems' and from a 'solutions' perspective. The first 'problem' part of the workshop is dedicated to identifying, classifying, and categorizing issues associated with software variability management for all phases in the lifecycle, as well as, in addition to technology, process and organizational aspects. Also issues associated with notation, assessment, design, and evolution will be discussed.

The 'solutions' part of the workshop intends to study existing techniques and methods for managing software variability as well as proposals by workshop participants. Both existing and proposed technology will be assessed from a technical consistency perspective and evaluated for industrial applicability and feasibility.

Being a workshop, the format consists of four sessions, where the morning sessions start with very brief presentations followed by plenary discussions. The first session after lunch is devoted to breakout groups that focus on particular topics. During the last session, the results of the breakout groups are presented and integrated.

4. Publication of the Results of the Workshop

The organizers intend to publish the best papers of the workshop in form of a publicly available report. In addition, all accepted workshop papers will be available from the workshop website.

5. Workshop Organization

Chairs

- Peter Knauber, Mannheim University of Applied Sciences, Germany
- Jan Bosch, University of Groningen, The Netherlands

Organizers

- Gert Florijn, SERC, The Netherlands
- Danny Greefhorst, IBM Global Services, The Netherlands
- Kai Koskimies, Tampere University of Technology, Finland
- Henk Obbink, Philips Research, The Netherlands
- Klaus Pohl, University of Essen, Germany
- Paul Sorenson, University of Alberta, Edmonton, Canada

Information and Questions

For more information, contact the workshop chairs Peter Knauber (P.Knauber@fh-mannheim.de) or Jan Bosch (Jan.Bosch@cs.rug.nl)

ICSE 2003 Workshop on Software Architectures for Dependable Systems

Rogério de Lemos
University of Kent at Canterbury
Canterbury, CT2 7NF, UK
r.delemos@ukc.ac.uk

Cristina Gacek Alexander Romanovsky
University of Newcastle upon Tyne
Newcastle upon Tyne, NE1 7RU, UK
{cristina.gacek, alexander.romanovsky}@ncl.ac.uk

Abstract

This workshop summary gives a brief overview of a one-day workshop on "Software Architectures for Dependable Systems" held in conjunctions with ICSE 2003.

1. Statement

Architectural representations of systems have shown to be effective in assisting the understanding of broader system concerns by abstracting away from details of the system. The dependability of systems is defined as the reliance that can justifiably be placed on the service the system delivers. Dependability has become an important aspect of computer systems since everyday life increasingly depends on software. Although there is a large body of research in dependability, architectural level reasoning about dependability is only just emerging as an important theme in software engineering. This is due to the fact that dependability concerns are usually left until too late in the process of development. In addition, the complexity of emerging applications and the trend of building trustworthy systems from existing, untrustworthy components are urging dependability concerns be considered at the architectural level. Hence the questions that the software architecture and dependability communities are currently facing:

- What are the architectural principles involved in building dependable systems?
- How should these architectures be evaluated?

By bringing together researchers from both the software architectures and the dependability communities, this workshop will make contributions from dependability more visible within the software engineering community and vice-versa, thus helping to build strong collaboration possibilities among the participants. The workshop will provide software engineers with systematic and disciplined approaches to building dependable systems, as well as allow further dissemination of the state-of-the-art methods and techniques.

2. Objectives and Topics

The aim of the workshop is to bring together the communities of software architectures and dependability to discuss the state of research and practice when dealing with dependability issues at the architecture level, and to jointly formulate an agenda for future research in this emerging area. We are interested in submissions from both industry and academia on all topics related to software architectures for dependable systems. These include, but are not limited to:

- dependability modeling in software architectures;
- verification and validation of dependable software architectures;
- adaptable architectures for achieving dependability;
- architectural support for self-healing and self-repairing systems;
- run-time checks of dependable architectural model;
- dependability evaluation in software architectures;
- architectural patterns for dependable systems;
- exception handling in software architectures;
- redundancy and diversity at the level of architectures;
- dependable architectures and implementation.

During ICSE 2002 we organized the first workshop in the series (http://www.cs.ukc.ac.uk/wads/) [1][2], which was a success, and we are now editing a LNCS volume combining the state-of-the-art articles in the area; the core of this volume are papers based on the best workshop presentations.

3. Workshop Organizers

Rogério de Lemos
University of Kent at Canterbury, UK

Cristina Gacek
University of Newcastle upon Tyne, UK

Alexander Romanovsky
University of Newcastle upon Tyne, UK

0-7695-1877-X/03 $17.00 © 2003 IEEE

4. Program Committee

Jean Arlat (France)
Andrea Bondavalli (Italy)
Jan Bosch (The Netherlands)
David Garlan (USA)
Paola Inverardi (Italy)
Valerie Issarny (France)
Philip Koopman (USA)
Nicole Levy (France)
Neno Medvidovic (USA)
Dewayne E. Perry (USA)
Debra Richardson (USA)
Cecília Rubira (Brazil)
William Scherlis (USA)
Francis Tam (Finland)
Kishor S. Trivedi (USA)
Frank van der Linden (The Netherlands)
Paulo Veríssimo (Portugal).

5. Information about Workshop

More information about the workshop including its program and electronic version of the papers to be presented can be found on the workshop web page: http://www.cs.ukc.ac.uk/wads/.

References

Second Workshop on Scenarios and State Machines: Models, Algorithms, and Tools

Alexander Egyed *Teknowledge Corporation* *aeyged@acm.org*	Martin Glinz *University of Zurich* *glinz@ifi.unizh.ch*	Ingolf Krüger *UC San Diego* *ikrueger@ucsd.edu*
Tarja Systä *Tampere University of Technology* *tsysta@cs.tut.fi*	Sebastian Uchitel *Imperial College London* *s.uchitel@doc.ic.ac.uk*	Albert Zündorf. *University of Braunschweig* *zuendorf@ips.cs.tu-bs.de*

1. Introduction

Following the success of the "First Workshop on Scenarios and State Machines: Models, Algorithms, and Tools" held at ICSE 2002 in Orlando [1], this workshop aims at bringing together researchers and practitioners to build a shared understanding on the relation between scenarios and state machines and to gain insight into techniques and tools that may leverage the combination of these approaches to enhance our means for behavior modeling.

2. Background and Motivation

Behavior modeling plays an important role in the engineering of software-based systems; it is the basis for systematic approaches to requirements capture, specification, design, simulation, code generation, testing, and verification. A range of notations, techniques and tools supporting behavior modeling for these development tasks exists.

Two complementary approaches for modeling behavior have proven useful in practice: state- and scenario-based modeling. UML [3] statechart diagrams have become popular as a description technique for the intended behavior of class instances in object-oriented systems. State-based formalisms are also widely used for modeling distributed and real-time systems; the corresponding models can be rigorously analyzed using model checking techniques – this is a particular advantage of state based modeling.

Practitioners also use scenario-based notations and tools extensively; here, the focus of concern shifts from the complete behavior specification for individual components or objects to the (partial) specification of component collaboration. Use cases, interaction and sequence diagrams play an important role in scenario-based requirements elicitation. The International Telecommunication Union's Message Sequence Chart Standard [2] defines a scenario-notation for detailed specification of telecommunication system behavior.

The use of state machines and scenarios, however, is not limited to capturing intended system behavior; reverse engineering techniques use them extensively to capture the behavior of existing sub-systems.

Although there has been much research on both scenarios and state machines the relation between them has yet to be fully understood and, more importantly, exploited. The complementary nature of scenarios and state-machines suggests several avenues for combining the strengths of both modeling approaches. Scenarios can, for instance, be viewed as partial descriptions that are generalized through state machine specifications. Alternatively, scenarios can be thought to provide collaboration views while state machines stress local/component views. Finally, scenarios can be seen as use case realizations that aid in recognizing the operations and associations of classes and in specifying the behavior of objects as state machines. Scenarios can also be viewed as the source of test cases, used to validate an implementation.

3. Topics of Interest

In this second workshop on this topic we aim at discussing areas of research and tools that exploit the benefits of scenario- and state-machine-based techniques. Areas of interest include, but are not limited to:

- Models and notations (requirements for different application areas, shortcomings in current notations, new suggestions for models or notations, categorizations).
- Algorithms (e.g., synthesis, verification, simulations).

0-7695-1877-X/03 $17.00 © 2003 IEEE

- Tools (tool support for the issues above, different application areas).

4. Workshop Organization

A call for papers was widely distributed and made available at http://www.doc.ic.ac.uk/~su2/SCESM/CS/. Prospective participants were requested to submit a position paper of up to five pages. In order to focus contributions and provide a common basis for discussion, we encouraged participants to make use of the case study material provided by NASA Ames, available at http://www.doc.ic.ac.uk/~su2/SCESM/CS/. The material has been used in earlier studies and reported in the First Workshop on Scenarios and State Machines: Models, Algorithms, and Tools [4]. However, the use of the case study was not mandatory. Authors were allowed to use their own examples or focus on specific or related aspects of the case study.

The program committee reviewed submissions. Each submission was reviewed by at least three different program committee members. The program committee selected the position papers based on relevance, soundness and novelty.

The workshop is open and will have a maximum number of 30 participants; however, priority registration shall be given to those with accepted papers.

The workshop will be divided into sessions. The opening session will include a keynote by Prof. David Harel. Topics of the working sessions will be determined based on the distribution of accepted position papers. Each session will cluster three short presentations (10 min.) where authors will have an opportunity to present the main ideas of their position papers. The presentations shall serve as an opening statement of the session, after which there will be at least half an hour reserved for in-depth discussion of the presentations, related issues, and the implications for future research.

5. Workshop Organisers

Francis Bordeleau, University of Carleton, Canada.

Alexander Egyed, Teknowledge Corporation, USA.

Martin Glinz, University of Zurich, Switzerland.

Jeff Kramer, Imperial College London, UK.

Ingolf Krüger, UC San Diego, USA.

Axel van Lamsweerde, University of Louvain, Belgium.

Stefan Leue, University of Freiburg, Germany.

Wilhelm Schäfer, University of Paderborn, Germany.

Tarja Systä, Tampere University of Technology, Finland.

Sebastian Uchitel, Imperial College London, UK.

Jon Whittle, NASA Ames, USA.

Albert Zündorf, University of Braunschweig, Germany.

6. Reviewers

In addition to the workshop organizers, the following people participated in the reviewing process: Jean-Pierre Corriveau, Ira Diethelm, Leif Geiger, Thomas Maier, Toby McClean, Silvio Meier, Christian Seybold, and Yong Xia.

7. References

[1] *First ICSE Workshop on Scenarios and State Machines: model, algorithms and tools (SCESM'02)*, http://www.cs.tut.fi/~tsysta/ICSE/Main.html, 2002.

[2] ITU-TS, *Message Sequence Charts*, Recommendation Z.120, Geneva, 1996.

[3] OMG, *The Unified Modeling Language*, http://www.omg.org, 2003.

[4] J. Whittle and J. Schumann, "Statechart Synthesis from Scenarios: an Air Traffic Control Case Study" *in proceedings of the ICSE 2002 Workshop on Scenarios and State Machines: Models, Algorithms and Tools*, Orlando, 2002.

The 3rd Workshop on Open Source Software Engineering

Joseph Feller
University College Cork
Cork, Ireland
jfeller@afis.ucc.ie

Brian Fitzgerald
University of Limerick
Limerick, Ireland
bf@ul.ie

Scott Hissam
Software Engineering Institute
Pennsylvania, USA
shissam@sei.cmu.edu

Karim Lakhani
MIT Sloan School of Management
Boston Consulting Group
Massachusetts, USA
karim.lakhani@sloan.mit.edu

Abstract

Building on the success of "Making Sense of the Bazaar" and "Meeting Challenges and Surviving Success" – the 1st and 2nd Workshops on Open Source Software Engineering (ICSE 2001 and ICSE 2002) – this workshop ("Taking Stock of the Bazaar") brings together researchers and practitioners for the purpose of discussing the diverse array of techniques – as well as supporting tools and social/organizational contexts – which can be observed in the domain of open source software.

1. Introduction

Over the past five years, a substantial and diverse research literature on open source software (OSS) has emerged, including collections of peer-reviewed papers [e.g. 2,3,4], book length studies [e.g. 1], technical reports [e.g. 5] and virtual research communities [e.g. 6].

Despite the constantly growing body of research on OSS, our knowledge of the open source family of software engineering processes is far from complete, a point raised repeatedly by the participants of the first two workshops in this series. To address this knowledge gap, the 3rd workshop will facilitate the informed discussion of the key tools, techniques and contexts which can be observed in OSS development communities. Participants will be encouraged to address the processes which are involved in critical activities such as requirements gathering, analysis and design, leadership and decision making; coordination and collaboration; configuration management; testing and quality assurance; release management; debugging; documentation and support; translation and localization, etc.

2. Workshop Themes

The discussions will be organized around three key themes:

1. OSS tool kits and their use in addressing both general and OSS-specific software engineering challenges.
2. Techniques (both successful and not) utilized at any stage in the software engineering life-cycle within OSS projects.
3. Social and organizational structures that support the effective and efficient use of these tools and techniques.

3. Workshop Format

The 3rd Workshop on Open Source Software Engineering is an open, one-day workshop, with a maximum number of 40 participants. Accepted position papers will be published both in the workshop proceedings and on the workshop website at http://opensource.ucc.ie/icse2003. Authors of accepted papers will be given priority for workshop registration.

The workshop will include four mini-presentations, delivered by selected participants, and four open discussion sessions. As was the case for the first two workshops in this series, there will be a post-workshop debriefing following the close of the workshop day.

4. Organizing Committee

- Joseph Feller, PhD (Chair) – Business Information Systems, University College Cork, Ireland.
- Brian Fitzgerald, PhD – Frederick A. Krehbiel II Chair in Innovation in Global Business & Technology, Computer Science and Information Systems, University of Limerick, Ireland.
- Scott A. Hissam – Software Engineering Institute, Carnegie Mellon University, PA, USA.
- Karim R. Lakhani – MIT Sloan School of Management, and The Boston Consulting Group, MA, USA.

5. References

[1] Feller, J., Fitzgerald, B. *Understanding Open Source Software Development*. Addison-Wesley, London, UK, 2002.

[2] Feller, J., Fitzgerald, B. and van der Hoek, A. (eds) Special Issue on Open Source Software Engineering, *IEE Proceedings—Software*. Vol. 49, No. 1. 2002.

[3] Fitzgerald, B. and Feller, J.(eds) Special Issue on Open Source Software, Vol. 1. *Information Systems Journal*. Vol. 11, No. 4. 2001.

[4] Fitzgerald, B. and Feller, J.(eds) Special Issue on Open Source Software, Vol. 2. *Information Systems Journal*. Vol. 12, No. 1. 2002.

[5] Hissam, S., Weinstock, C.B., Plakosh, D., and Asundi, J., *Perspectives on Open Source Software*. CMU/SEI-2001-TR-019, Software Engineering Institute, Pittsburgh, PA, November, 2001.

[6] Lakhani, K. MIT Free/Open Source Research Community. http://opensource.mit.edu/.

ICSE 2003 Workshop on Software Engineering for High Assurance Systems: Synergies between Process, Product, and Profiling (SEHAS 2003)

M. S. Feather A. P. Nikora
Jet Propulsion Laboratory
California Inst. of Technology
martin.s.feather@jpl.nasa.gov
allen.p.nikora@jpl.nasa.gov

C. L. Heitmeyer
Ctr., High Assur. Computer Syst.
Naval Research Laboratory
heitmeyer@itd.nrl.navy.mil

N. R. Mead
Software Engineering Inst.
Carnegie Mellon Univ.
nrm@sei.cmu.edu

Abstract

A critical issue in software engineering is how to construct high assurance software systems, *i.e., software systems where compelling evidence is required that the system delivers its services in a manner satisfying critical properties, such as safety and security. This two-day ICSE workshop, the third in a series of workshops on high assurance systems, will provide a forum for researchers and practitioners to exchange ideas and experiences relevant to the development of software for aerospace systems, medical systems, systems controlling nuclear power plants, and other critical systems. Participants of the SEHAS 2003 workshop will explore the opportunities for, and benefits of, synergies between three important themes—product, process, and profiling—each theme reflecting an important aspect of software development for high assurance systems.*

1. Introduction

One of the most important challenges in software engineering is to develop mathematically well-founded, user-friendly methods for constructing *high assurance software systems*, software systems where compelling evidence is required that the system delivers its services in a manner satisfying certain critical properties. Among these properties are *security properties* (the system prevents unauthorized disclosure, modification and access to sensitive information), *safety properties* (the system prevents unintended events that could result in death, injury, illness, or property damage), *survivability properties* (the system continues to fulfill its mission despite malicious attacks, accidents, or failures), *fault-tolerance properties* (the system guarantees a certain quality of service despite faults, such as hardware, workload, or environmental anomalies), and *real-time properties* (the system delivers its outputs within specified time intervals). Examples of high assurance systems include control systems for nuclear plants, life-critical medical systems, aerospace systems, and weapons systems.

SEHAS 2003 is the third in a series of workshops on the topic of high assurance systems. The first workshop, a three-day workshop on High Assurance Computing held in 1995 and sponsored jointly by the Office of Naval Research and the Defense Advanced Research Projects Agency, formulated a research agenda [12]. The second workshop, RHAS '02, a one-day workshop held in conjunction with the 2002 IEEE International Requirements Engineering Conference, explored the requirements of high assurance systems [7]. Like the two earlier workshops, SEHAS 2003 will provide a forum for researchers and practitioners to exchange ideas and experiences relevant to the development of high assurance systems.

2. Workshop Themes

Participants of SEHAS 2003 will explore the opportunities for, and benefits of, synergies between three important themes, each reflecting an important aspect of high assurance software development. The themes are product, process, and profiling. Each theme has a strong computer science community underpinning it, with various workshops and conferences in which ideas are advanced.

- **Product.** This theme uses the system requirements and the structure of software artifacts to develop high confidence in the quality of the system as a whole by analyzing its specification, its individual parts, and how the system parts are combined. Useful techniques for developing confidence in the system and its implementation include formal specification and formal analysis [5, 6], fault tree and attack tree analysis [8, 10, 13], and measurements of software structure as predictors of faults [17].

0-7695-1877-X/03 $17.00 © 2003 IEEE

- **Process.** This theme views software as an artifact that is manufactured, and hence the manufacturing process itself is the focus; see, e.g., [9]. Studies of overall process improvement exist; for example, [11] relates software defects, productivity, development cycle time and effort estimation to process ratings akin to the Software Engineering Institute's Capability Maturity Model. Processes such as inspections, peer reviews, and tests may be used to improve the quality of software as it progresses through the development process [4, 1]. A particularly important challenge is deciding how to best invest limited resources so as to emerge with a high assurance software product [2].
- **Profiling.** This theme derives metrics from the development time activities and artifacts to yield insight into the progress of the development effort. For example, error detection and repair rates during testing may be used to predict the software's reliability or the number of remaining errors. See, e.g., [3, 14, 15, 16, 17].

3. Workshop Format and Goals

The workshop, which will be held on May 9–10, 2003, will consist of presentations and discussions. Participants will be selected on the basis of a position paper. To keep the workshop focused, participation is limited to 30 attendees. The major goals of SEHAS 2003 are to find synergies between the themes, to find topics where crossover work can lead to advances that might otherwise go unexplored, and to identify opportunities and needs for synergistic work. The opportunities will emerge from understanding different research areas relevant to high assurance systems and how collaborative research can provide methods and techniques for constructing high assurance software. The needs will emerge from an understanding of the practical aspects of limited resources, the need for prediction (e.g., of costs and required effort), etc.

4. For More Information

For a list of attendees and an electronic copy of the proceedings and presentations at SEHAS 2003, see `http://www.sei.cmu.edu/community/sehas-workshop/`. For a summary of the 1995 workshop on High Assurance Computing and three workshop reports, see `http://chacs.nrl.navy.mil/HighAssurWkshp/reports.html`. For an electronic copy of the accepted papers and presentations at RHAS '02, see `http://www.sei.cmu.edu/community/rhas-workshop/proceedings.html`.

References

[1] S. Biffl, B. Freimut, and O. Laitenberger. Investigating the cost-effectiveness of reinspections in software development. In *Proc. Internat. Conference on Software Engineering*, pages 155–164, 2001.

[2] M. S. Feather, B. Sigal, S. Cornford, and P. Hutchinson. Incorporating cost-benefit analysis into software assurance planning. In *Proc. IEEE/NASA 26th Software Engineering Workshop*, pages 62–68, Greenbelt, MD, Oct. 2001.

[3] S. Gokhale and K. Trivedi. Reliability prediction and sensitivity analysis based on software architecture. In *Proc. 13th Internat. Symposium on Software Reliability Engineering*, pages 64–75, Annapolis, MD, 2002.

[4] T. Graves, M. Harrold, J. Kim, A. Porter, and G. Rothermel. An empirical study of regression test selection techniques. In *Proc. Internat. Conference on Software Engineering*, pages 267–273, 1998.

[5] C. Heitmeyer, R. Jeffords, and B. Labaw. Automated consistency checking of requirements specifications. *ACM Trans. Software Eng. and Methodology*, 5(3):231–261, 1996.

[6] C. Heitmeyer, J. Kirby, B. Labaw, M. Archer, and R. Bharadwaj. Using abstraction and model checking to detect safety violations in requirements specifications. *IEEE Trans. on Software Engineering*, 24(11):927–948, 1998.

[7] C. Heitmeyer and N. Mead, editors. *RHAS '02: Internat. Workshop on Requirements for High Assurance Systems*, Essen, Germany, Sept. 2002. Software Engineering Inst., Pittsburgh, PA.

[8] N. Leveson. *Safeware: System Safety and Computers*. Addison-Wesley, Reading, MA, 1995.

[9] R. C. Linger, H. F. Lipson, J. McHugh, and N. Mead. Life-cycle models for survivable systems. Technical Report CMU/SEI-2002-TR-026, Software Engineering Inst., Pittsburgh, PA, Oct. 2002.

[10] R. Lutz and R. Woodhouse. Requirements analysis using forward and backward search. *Annals of Software Engineering*, 3:459–475, 1997.

[11] F. McGarry, S. Burke, and B. Decker. Measuring the impacts individual process maturity attributes have on software products. In *Proc. 5th Internat. Software Metrics Symposium*, pages 52–60, Greenbelt, MD, 1998.

[12] J. McLean and C. Heitmeyer. High assurance computer systems: A research agenda. In *Proc. America in the Age of Information, National Science and Technology Council Committee on Information and Communications Forum*, Bethesda, MD, 1995.

[13] A. P. Moore, R. J. Ellison, and R. C. Linger. Attack modeling for information security and survivability. Technical Report CMU/SEI-2001-TN-001, Software Engineering Inst., Pittsburgh, PA, Mar. 2001.

[14] A. Nikora and J. Munson. Determining fault insertion rates for evolving software systems. In *Proc. 9th Internat. Symposium on Software Reliability Engineering*, pages 127–136, Paderborn, Germany, 1998.

[15] N. F. Schneidewind. Software metrics model for integrating quality control and prediction. In *Proc. 8th Internat. Symposium on Software Reliability Engineering*, pages 402–415, Albuquerque, NM, 1997.

[16] N. F. Schneidewind. Investigation of the risk to software reliability and maintainability of requirements changes. In *Proc. 8th Internat. Conference on Software Maintenance,*, pages 127–136, Florence, Italy, 2001.

[17] S. M. Yacoub and H. H. Ammar. A methodology for architecture-level reliability risk analysis. *IEEE Trans. on Software Engineering*, 28(6):529–547, 2002.

3rd International Workshop on Adoption-centric Software Engineering ACSE 2003

http://www.acse2003.cs.uvic.ca

Robert Balzer,[1] Jens Jahnke,[2] Marin Litoiu,[3] Hausi A. Müller,[2]
Dennis B. Smith,[4] Margaret-Anne Storey,[2] Scott R. Tilley,[5] Ken Wong[6]
[1]*Teknowledge Corporation, USA;* [2]*University of Victoria, Canada*
[3]*IBM Canada Ltd., Canada;* [4]*Carnegie Mellon Software Engineering Institute, USA*
[5]*Florida Institute of Technology, USA;* [6]*University of Alberta, Canada;*
balzer@teknowledge.com, jens@cs.uvic.ca, marin@ca.ibm.com, hausi@cs.uvic.ca, dbs@sei.cmu.edu, mstorey@cs.uvic.ca, stilley@cs.fit.edu, kenw@cs.ualberta.ca

Abstract

The key objective of this workshop is to explore innovative approaches to the adoption of software engineering tools and practices—in particular by embedding them in extensions of Commercial Off-The-Shelf (COTS) software products and/or middleware technologies. The workshop aims to advance the understanding and evaluation of adoption of software engineering tools and practices by bringing together researchers and practitioners who investigate novel solutions to software engineering adoption issues.

1. Workshop theme and goals

Understanding adoption of software engineering tools and practices is critical for the software and information technology sectors, which are continually challenged to increase their productivity. Recent advances in effective standards and interfaces for tool extension and customization have opened new research avenues, which allow software engineering tools and technologies to be incorporated into commonly used Commercial Off-The-Shelf (COTS) products and middleware platforms and adopted as extensions of those COTS products.

The key objective of this workshop is to explore approaches where software engineering tools and practices are implemented as extension of COTS software products and middleware technologies that work in conjunction with software engineering tools as well as mined components. The workshop aims to advance the understanding and evaluation of adoption of software engineering tools and practices.

Research tools in software engineering often fail to be adopted and deployed in industry. Important barriers to adopting these tools include the user's lack of familiarity with these tools, their mismatch with the users' cognitive models, their lack of interface maturity, their limited scalability, their limited support for complex work products of software development, their poor interoperability, and their limited support for the realities of system documentation engineering. Developing and deploying innovative research tools and ideas as extensions to modern, commonly used platforms may ease these barriers.

2. How can the workshop advance software engineering research in practice?

One key problem in software engineering research is the integration of research tools into industrial software development processes. Tools developed by the software engineering research community often remain orphans due to adoption problems since research tools are rarely built for an industrial setting. Developing effective techniques and strategies to overcome this problem is timely and will have great value to the software and information technology sectors. Injecting more of the leading-edge software engineering research results into industrial practice has a potentially significant impact on the production of quality software. Thus, this research addresses three diverse markets: the software developers, who need to understand and document existing software systems, the researchers, who want to inject and validate their research tools in industrial development processes, and the tool users, who want to leverage their personal work environment in software engineering tools.

3. Background and related work

The notion of building software systems from existing building blocks, components, or parts has been around since the Sixties. Communities, such as Software Reuse,

0-7695-1877-X/03 $17.00 © 2003 IEEE

Commercial-of-the Shelf Components (COTS), or CBSE (Component-Based Software Engineering) have investigated many approaches and developed effective solutions to this problem. Their approaches differ in many aspects, including the granularity, genericity, or wrapping of the components. The goal of ACSE is to take a significant step back and approach this perennial problem from a radically different perspective. The idea is to select the host components according to a variety of *adoption criteria*.

Shaw observed that systems, such as interactive graphics applications, devote less than 10% of their code to the overt function of the system and more than 90% to the user interface [1]. Reiss leveraged FrameMaker, a COTS editor, for all editing aspects in his Desert software development environment [2]. Sullivan, Knight and Coppit use the term Package-Oriented Programming (POP) to support tasks, such as document embedding and scripting [3, 5]. The Software Bookshelf, built on top of Netscape, exploits the familiar Web interface [4].

In several recent conference keynotes, Balzer has advocated that software engineering researchers should exploit large COTS products for building software engineering tools rather than constructing stand-alone tools [7, 9]. Egyed and Balzer proposed an integration-architecture for COTS products, which provides access and visibility into the document information contained within a COTS tool [6]. The information that is shared with external tools allows users to track user actions and provide analysis and automation services for the user within the COTS tool. For example, they exploited this architecture to add semantics to PowerPoint diagrams and Word documents and to build defenses against malicious e-mail attachments.

The mandate of the Technology Transition Practices (TPP) group at Software Engineering Institute (SEI) is to identify, develop, promote, and apply *practices* that result in more rapid, affordable, and sustained transition of innovative software engineering technologies [10].

The hypothesis of the ACRE project [8] is that developers will more likely adopt tools that leverage the *cognitive support* and *interoperability mechanisms* of tools they use daily and know intimately (e.g., Lotus Notes, Office XP, or StarOffice). To increase their productivity, developers accumulate sripts, macros, and shortcuts in their personal work environment. Reusing such hard-won and treasured cognitive support features is a central idea of this project.

Beyond user-to-tool compatibility concerns of cognitive support, there must also be tool-to-tool compatibility. Towards this end, interoperability mechanisms for data, control, and presentation integration are critical factors to tool adoption. Recently developed middleware standards and technologies can offer unprecedented possibilities to seamlessly integrate new research tools into existing, familiar environments.

Since it is difficult to evaluate tool adoption in the course of a research project, ACRE concentrates on investigating how to leverage cognitive support and interoperability mechanisms from COTS products for software exploration and visualization tools.

4. References

[1] M. Shaw, "Prospects for an Engineering Discipline of Software," *IEEE Software*, 7(6):15-24, Nov. 1990.

[2] S.P. Reiss, "Simplifying Data Integration: The Design of the Desert Software Development Environment," *Proc. 18th IEEE/ACM Int. Conf. on Software Engineering,* Berlin, Germany, pp. 398-407, March 1996.

[3] K.J. Sullivan and J.C. Knight, "Experience Assessing an Architectural Approach to Large-Scale, Systematic Reuse," *Proc. 18th IEEE/ACM Int. Conf. on Software Engineering,* Berlin, Germany, pp. 220-229, March 1996.

[4] P. Finnigan, R. Holt, I. Kalas, S. Kerr, K. Kontogiannis, H. Müller, J. Mylopoulos, S. Perelgut, M. Stanley, and K. Wong, "The Software Bookshelf," *IBM Systems Journal,* Vol. 36, No. 4, pp. 564-593, Nov. 1997

[5] D. Coppit and K.J. Sullivan, "Multiple Mass-Market Applications as Components. *Proc. 22nd IEEE/ACM Int. Conf. on Software Engineering*, Limerick, Ireland, pp. 273-82, June 2000.

[6] A. Egyed and R. Balzer, "Unfriendly COTS Integration: Instrumentation and Interfaces for Improved Plugability," *Proc. 16th IEEE Int. Conf. on Automated Software Engineering (ASE 2001),* San Diego, USA, pp. 223-231, Nov. 2001.

[7] R. Balzer, "Tolerating Inconsistency Revisited," *Proc. 23rd IEEE/ACM Int. Conf. on Software Engineering (ICSE 2001),* Toronto, Canada, p. 665, May 2001.

[8] H.A. Müller, M.-A. Storey and K. Wong, "Leveraging Cognitive Support and Modern Platforms for Adoption-Centric Reverse Engineering (ACRE)," CSER Research Proposal, Nov. 2001. www.acse.cs.uvic.ca

[9] R. Balzer, "Living with COTS," 24th IEEE/ACM Int. Conf. on Software Engineering (ICSE 2002), Orlando, USA, p. 5, May 2002 and 2nd Int. Conf. on COTS-Based Software Systems, Ottawa, Canada, Feb 2003.

[10] Technology Transition Practices (TPP) Group, Software Engineering Inst., 2002. www.sei.cmu.edu/ttp/

ICSE Workshop on Remote Analysis and Measurement of Software Systems (RAMSS)

Alessandro Orso
College of Computing
Georgia Institute of Technology
801 Atlantic Drive
Atlanta, GA 30332
+1-404-385-2066
orso@cc.gatech.edu

Adam Porter
Department of Computer Science
University of Maryland
A.V. Williams Building
College Park, MD 20742
+1-301-405-2702
aporter@cs.umd.edu

Abstract

The goal of this workshop is to bring together researchers and practitioners interested in exploring how the characteristics of today's area of computing (e.g., high connectivity, substantial computing power for the average user, higher demand for and expectation of frequent software updates) can be leveraged to improve software quality and performance.

1 Introduction

Software engineering technologies—like many other things—are "a product of their generation." They are developed at a certain point in time and embody technical assumptions that seem reasonable at that time. If those assumptions lose their validity, then the technologies built on top of them may become less effective or may miss newly created opportunities. In the last years, we have witnessed a fundamental shift in the area of computing. Decades ago, there were relatively few software systems, running on a limited number of mostly disconnected computers, and available to a small set of users. With the PC revolution, the number of software systems and computers has increased exponentially. Moreover, the continuous growth of the Internet has dramatically increased the connectivity of computing devices, opening the way to new development paradigms, such as the open-source model, shortening the development process, and leading to the development of systems that are increasingly distributed and heterogeneous in nature.

Although these changes are raising new issues for software engineers, they also represent new opportunities that, if suitably exploited, may provide solutions to both new and existing problems and help improving the quality of software systems. Consider, for example, software quality assurance tasks such as testing and analysis. With rare exceptions, these activities are performed in-house, on developer platforms, using developer-provided inputs, and at great cost. Consequently, the expensive results obtained are often not representative of how the software will actually perform in the field, and software products are released with missing functionality, errors, incompatibilities with the running environment, security holes, or inferior usability. This situation is especially problematic in the case of systems that must function in many environments and with a number of variable configurations. To adequately address these problems, software engineers could benefit from shifting a considerable portion of testing and analysis tasks to actual user environments, so leveraging fielded resources and using real data.

Even though there are examples of techniques that perform some analysis of deployed systems, software engineers have been mostly resistant to explore this direction, under the assumption that it was technically and logistically infeasible at acceptably low costs. If this assumption were true ten or fifteen years ago, it may not be true anymore today. By considering the huge number of users as potential analyzers and testers and their interconnected computers as a virtual peta-op machine, software engineers can leverage this enormous computational power, human resources, and availability of real data for continuously improving the quality of software systems.

2 Theme and Goals

The theme of the workshop is to discuss how the paradigm shift from a few users operating in a mostly disconnected environment to a huge number of users operating in a highly connected environment is affecting software engineering disciplines in general, and quality assurance activities in particular.

The goal of the workshop is to identify ways of exploiting the opportunities brought about by the dramatic growth

0-7695-1877-X/03 $17.00 © 2003 IEEE

of the number of users of software systems, and the continuously increasing connectivity of software and hardware systems. More precisely, the workshop aims at gathering researchers and practitioners that are willing to (1) discuss what these new problems are and, most importantly, what new opportunities flow and challenges flow from them, (2) identify meaningful research directions in this area, and (3) investigate such research directions in the next years.

3 Areas of Interest

Areas of interest include, but are not limited to:

- Continuous, lightweight monitoring of deployed systems
- Detection and diagnosis of problems and failures in deployed systems
- Evolution, optimization, or adaptation of systems based on data-driven feedback from the field
- Dynamic analysis and profiling of web-based and distributed systems
- Identification of user profiles based on real usage data
- Dynamically analysis of deployed systems by combining data computed in-house and in-the-field
- Dynamic modification of deployed programs, such as adaptation, instrumentation, and updating
- Data mining and visualization of feedback-data from the field

4 Organization

The workshop is designed to be open and to last one day. Interested participants are invited to submit position papers to be reviewed by the workshop program committee. and accepted or rejected based on its relevance to the workshop topic and on its quality.

All accepted workshop position papers will be used to identify discussion topics and will be distributed electronically by publication on the workshop web page before the workshop, so as to facilitate the discussion.

Planned workshop activities include short presentations in a plenary session and follow-up discussions, possibly in breakout sessions. We will limit the time devoted to presentations, so as to foster dialog and interaction among the participants.

5 Organizing Committee

Program Co-chairs

- Alessandro Orso – Georgia Institute of Technology (USA)
- Adam Porter – University of Maryland (USA)

Program Committee

- Sebastian Elbaum – University of Nebraska (USA)
- Mary Jean Harrold – Georgia Institute of Technology (USA)
- Jeff Hollingsworth – University of Maryland (USA)
- David Notkin – University of Washington (USA)
- David Redmiles – University of California, Irvine (USA)
- Doug Schmidt – University of California, Irvine (USA)
- Michal Young – University of Oregon (USA)

6 Additional Information

Additional information about the workshop, including its program, the list of participants, and an electronic version of the accepted position papers will be available on the workshop web page:
`http://measure.cc.gt.atl.ga.us/ramss/`.

Addressing the Challenges of Software Industry Globalization: The Workshop on Global Software Development

Daniela Damian
University of Victoria, BC, Canada
danielad@cs.uvic.ca

Filippo Lanubile
University of Bari, Italy
lanubile@di.uniba.it

Heather L. Oppenheimer
Lucent Technologies, NJ, USA
hoppenheimer@lucent.com

Abstract

The goal of this workshop is to provide an opportunity for researchers and industry practitioners to explore both the state-of-the art and the state-of-the-practice in global software development (GSD).

Increased globalization of software development creates software engineering challenges due to the impact of temporal, geographical and cultural differences, and requires development of techniques and technologies to address these issues. The workshop will foster interaction between practitioners and researchers and help grow a community of interest in this area. Practitioners experiencing challenges in GSD will share their concerns and successful solutions and learn from research about current investigations. Researchers addressing GSD will gain a better understanding of the key issues facing practitioners and share their work in progress with others in the field.

1. Workshop description

This workshop is a continuation of the last five ICSE workshops on the same topic (1998-2002; [1-5]). Last year [5], after changing the title from the technology-focused "Software Engineering over the Internet" to the more general "Global Software Development", we observed increased participation by practitioners and more fruitful discussions between industry and academia. The report summarizing the workshop [5] discusses the challenges of engineering software in geographically distributed settings and indicates that further research needs to equally address issues of technical and social nature in global software development.

Global software development has been and continues to be a phenomenon fueled by factors such as access to a large and specialized labor pool, reduction in development costs, global presence and proximity to the customers. While we are witnessing reports of successful global teams, research reveals that distance contributes to heightened complexity in organizational processes. Primarily, processes of communication, coordination and control are affected by distance, with direct consequences on how software is defined, constructed, tested and delivered to customers, as well as how its development is managed. Further, cultural issues are possibly a most confusing and interesting feature of global teams. Members with diverse attitudes towards hierarchy, time management and risk avoidance come to work together in cross-functional teams.

These are only some of the factors that bring challenges to managing software projects developed in geographically distributed structures. Understanding the intricacies of this complex phenomenon is critical in framing research directions that aim at improving global software development practice. There is a need for tools and techniques that not only improve development processes but also address organizational and social issues in global software development. The previous workshops represented one more step in identifying and understanding issues in the complex phenomenon of global software development. In particular, the empirical evidence and discussions during the workshop last year indicate that technology is only a small part of enabling effective global teams; there is a strong need to address the study and practice of global software development from a multidisciplinary perspective, in which issues of social nature are as important as those of technical nature.

In this workshop we intend to continue fostering fruitful interactions between industry practitioners and researchers and help grow a community of interest in this area. Industry practitioners experiencing challenges in GSD will be encouraged to share their own solutions and learn from research about current investigations in this area. Researchers addressing GSD will have the opportunity to gain a better understanding of the key issues facing industry practitioners and share their work in progress with others in the field.

2. Workshop themes

The workshop solicits papers on topics that include, but are not limited to:

0-7695-1877-X/03 $17.00 © 2003 IEEE

- Empirical evaluations of effectiveness of global software projects
- Technologies & tools for distributed development environments
- Software engineering methodologies & processes for GSD
- Communication, collaboration, and knowledge management in distributed organizations

3. Workshop format

This workshop will focus on identifying issues of Global Software Development, sharing solutions, and brainstorming new approaches to those issues. The workshop is open to all participants interested in the topic; position papers or technical papers, though encouraged, are not required for attendance.

The "issues" part of the workshop will be dedicated to identifying, classifying, and categorizing Global Software Development issues that have been raised in previous literature, described in the position papers, and gathered during GSD 2002. To help focus the afternoon discussion, we will create some GSD scenarios that typify key issues. Throughout the workshop, participants can propose additional issues to be discussed at the end of the day.

The "solutions" part of the workshop will study existing techniques and methods for Global Software development. Selected authors of accepted technical papers will deliver very short presentations on their technological solutions or methodological approaches. Both existing and proposed technology will be assessed from a technical consistency perspective and evaluated for industrial applicability and feasibility. We will encourage each technical presenter to discuss how his or her ideas address or relate to the problems illustrated in the scenarios. The presentations will include a small amount of time for audience discussion of each set of presentations, hopefully allowing the group both to better understand the ideas and to relate them to other presentations and to the workshop themes.

The final part of the workshop will be a plenary discussion aimed at finding synergies between solutions, where crossover work can lead to advances that might otherwise go unexplored, and identifying opportunities for further work. At the end of the day, we will integrate and present the results of the discussion. The workshop will lead to a list of issues discussed, solutions proposed, conclusions reached, disagreements identified, and topics to be researched further.

All accepted papers will be published in both the workshop proceedings and on the workshop website at: http://gsd2003.cs.uvic.ca

4. About the organizers

Daniela Damian is an Assistant Professor at the University of Victoria, BC, Canada. She is a Killam Scholar in Canada and the recipient of the Best Paper Award at the International Conference on Requirements Engineering 2000. Daniela was the primary contact and co-organizer of the Workshop on Global Software Development (2002) and acted as a Member of Program Committee of the Australian Workshop on Requirements Engineering, 2000, 2001 and 2002, as well as the Time-Constrained Requirements Engineering Workshop at the Int'l Conf. on Requirements Engineering '02.

Filippo Lanubile is an Associate Professor at the University of Bari, Italy. While at University of Maryland (1995-1997) he was a recipient of the NASA Group Achievement Award (1996). On 2002, he was a program committee member for the Workshop on Global Software Development and the Workshop on Cooperative Support for Distributed Software Engineering Processes. In the last years he was also a member of the program committees of METRICS and ICSM. In 1997, he organized the Int. Workshop on Empirical Studies of Software Maintenance.

Heather Oppenheimer is a Distinguished Member of Technical Staff at Bell Laboratories, USA with 17 years of industry experience in software engineering. She has managed groups responsible for system test, process & quality engineering, and internet & collaborative development environments as well as all other aspects of the development life cycle. She currently leads a corporate software best practices initiative, develops and instructs internal courses in software architecture for systems engineers and for managers of development teams and leads software architecture reviews and project management audits throughout the Lucent Technologies global organization. She was a program committee member for the Workshop on Global Software Development (2002).

References

[1]. First Workshop on "Software Engineering over the Internet", online proceedings: http://sern.ucalgary.ca/~maurer/ICSE98WS/ICSE98WS.html

[2]. Second Workshop on "Software Engineering over the Internet", online proceedings: http://sern.ucalgary.ca/~maurer/ICSE98WS/ICSE99WS.html

[3]. Third Workshop on "Software Engineering over the Internet", online proceedings: http://sern.ucalgary.ca/~maurer/ICSE98WS/ICSE2000WS.html

[4]. Fourth Workshop on "Software Engineering over the Internet", online proceedings: http://sern.ucalgary.ca/~maurer/ICSE98WS/ICSE2001WS.html

[5]. International Workshop on Global Software Development, online proceedings at: http://www.cis.ohio-state.edu/~nsridhar/ICSE02/GSD

ICSE Workshop on Dynamic Analysis (WODA 2003)

Jonathan E. Cook
Department of Computer Science
New Mexico State University
Las Cruces, NM 88003 USA
jcook@cs.nmsu.edu

Michael D. Ernst
MIT Lab for Computer Science
Massachusetts Institute of Technology
Cambridge, MA 02139 USA
mernst@lcs.mit.edu

Abstract

Dynamic analysis of software systems has long proven to be a practical approach to gain understanding of the operational behavior of the system. This workshop will bring together researchers in the field of dynamic analysis to discuss the breadth of the field, order the field along logical dimensions, expose common issues and approaches, and stimulate synergistic collaborations among the participants.

1. Introduction

Dynamic analysis is a term that captures all the many techniques that attempt to reason about the observed dynamic behavior of systems [1]. Some examples of proven and common dynamic analysis techniques include assertion checking, memory allocation monitors, and profilers. Dynamic analysis techniques have a proven track record of being useful and practical across the software engineering field.

Dynamic analysis includes both offline techniques that might take intensive compute time and operate on a trace or some other captured representation of the system's behavior, and runtime techniques that operate while the system is producing its behavior. Some techniques may combine these two approaches, performing preliminary runtime data reduction computations for later offline, compute-intensive analyses. The thread that binds analyses under the dynamic analysis title is the use of observed behavior of the system in the analyses.

2. Workshop topic areas

Throughout the various dynamic analysis techniques run common themes and common needs, some of which are: instrumentation; data collection, description, and management; behavior descriptions; uncertainty; partial information; and reasoning with partial models. Issues that the workshop may cover in these areas are detailed below.

2.1. Data collection and management

In order to reason about the behavior of a system, some mechanism must exist to observe the behavior of the system and either collect those observations for later processing or reason about them in real time. Thus, dynamic analysis begins and depends on instrumentation and data collection techniques. Instrumentation carries with it the potential to modify the behavior of the system, and heavyweight instrumentation can produce incredible amounts of data very quickly, enough to overwhelm even today's storage capacities and processor speeds. Thus, adaptive and specialized instrumentation mechanisms are still needed for effective broad-based data analysis capabilities, and optimized algorithms for handling large amounts of data in real-time will need developed.

2.2. Data description

Virtually all data collected as observations of an executing system can be characterized as *events*. Methods which analyze program behavior within the context and knowledge of their implementation language may have events that correspond to expression evaluation, assignment, condition testing, function or method calls, and other language constructs. These events relate to each other both sequentially and hierarchically, within the language's grammar constraints. Other analysis methods may only look at a distributed system's messages on the network, which relate to each other according to some protocol model, but not hierarchically.

However, different dynamic analysis methods can require different levels of richness in their event data, and some reduction methods may aggregate the event data into other non-event forms. Common data descriptions and sharing methods still need developed.

2.3. Relationship to testing

Dynamic analysis shares a unique relation to testing, in that it generally works best when used with observed behaviors of the system that capture a representative sample of the whole domain of possible behavior. Testing techniques often aim to provide exactly that sample, in the most efficient manner possible. Testing can benefit from dynamic analysis in that not only can the output of the system be verified, but the observed intermediate behaviors can also be verified, providing more confidence in the system without requiring more testing. Thus, testing research and dynamic analysis research can benefit from each other.

2.4. Symbolic versus probabilistic reasoning

Dynamic analysis techniques can be split between symbolic and theoretically exact reasoning, and statistical and probabilistic reasoning. The former category produces exact, justifiable results over its input, similar to static analysis techniques but only over the observed behaviors. The latter attempts to characterize its results in terms of what is statistically likely to happen, or how probable some aspect of the behavior is. While not exact, these approaches can offer large data reduction and computation reduction benefits. Each approach offers its own unique contributions to system understanding.

2.5. Incorporating reasoning over models

In addition to data analysis, many dynamic analysis methods attempt to understand the behavior within the context of a model of the system. This might be in the form of hard-coded rules (e.g., array bounds checking, memory allocation monitors), or might be derived from static analysis of the system (e.g., path coverage testing). In either case, reasoning in the presence of either a partial model or partial behavioral information is needed. A partial model might be used because only one aspect of the system is being investigated, or it is too expensive to construct a complete model. Partial behavioral information might be used because it is too expensive or impossible to collect full information. Whether working with full or partial models or information, efficient algorithms for dynamic analysis are important, and results from the static analysis research field can often be leveraged.

3. Workshop scope and format

This workshop will focus on achieving a consensus among the participants as to the structure of the field, the important research directions this field should take, inputs needed from other research domains, and outputs that could benefit other research domains. It will cover a topical spectrum from enabling technologies; framework and common tool support; event type definition, classification, and specification; symbolic and theoretically exact reasoning techniques; statistical and probabilistic reasoning techniques; research foundations; relationships to static analysis; relationships to testing; and other potential topics.

Selected authors from those with accepted position papers will be asked to present their position as an opening for a discussion period over one of the subtopics. Focus in the workshop will be on discussion and the illumination of needed directions for future research and on recognizing potential collaborations.

4. Workshop output

This workshop will result in participants having new ideas for future research, identifying new potential collaborations, and creating a better general understanding of the scope and structure of the field of dynamic analysis. All accepted position papers will be available on the Web at

http://www.cs.nmsu.edu/~jcook/woda2003/

and the workshop will produce a report to be printed in the ACM Software Engineering Notes.

Acknowledgements

This work was supported in part by the National Science Foundation under grants EIA-9810732 and EIA-0220590. The content of the information does not necessarily reflect the position or the policy of the Government and no official endorsement should be inferred.

References

[1] T. Ball. The Concept of Dynamic Analysis. In *Proceedings of the Seventh European Software Engineering Conference / Seventh ACM SIGSOFT Symposium on the Foundations of Software Engineering*, pages 216–234. Springer-Verlag, Sept. 1999.

Second International Workshop on From SofTware Requirements to Architectures (STRAW'03)

Daniel M. Berry
School of Computer Science
University of Waterloo
Waterloo, ON N2L 3G1, Canada
dberry@uwaterloo.ca

Rick Kazman
Software Engineering Institute
Carnegie Mellon University
Pittsburgh, PA 15213, USA
kazman@sei.cmu.edu

Roel Wieringa
Department of Computer Science
University of Twente
7500 AW Enschede, the Netherlands
roelw@cs.utwente.nl

http://se.uwaterloo.ca/~straw03/

Abstract

The Second International Workshop on From SofTware Requirements to Architectures (STRAW'03) was held in Portland, Oregon, USA on 9 May 2003 just after the Twenty-Fifth International Conference on Software Engineering (ICSE'03). This brief paper outlines the motivation, goals, and organization of the workshop

1. Motivation

Over the past 10 years, software requirements engineering and software architecture have been the topic of fastly growing research disciplines.

Requirements engineering has seen the advent of

- goal-oriented approaches,
- scenario-based requirements engineering,
- sociology- and linguistics-based techniques, and
- formal techniques

for identifying and specifying requirements.

Architecture design has seen the advent of

- patterns research,
- architectural style research,
- attribute-based architecture design,
- architecture description languages,
- component-based approaches, and
- product-line architectures.

There is a clear relationship between requirements engineering and architecture design. However, for the most part, the two disciplines have evolved independently from each other, and promising areas of mutual interest remain to be explored. For example, an important type of design research consists of relating classes of problems to classes of solutions. In software engineering, there are interesting connections between software problem patterns and software solution patterns. Recent research in problem frames could therefore be extended by including architecture patterns and investigating relationships between the two kinds of patterns.

The patterns paradigm may be extended by including the wider business context, consisting of business processes, actors, and strategies. In this wider context, the problem is one of alignment of software architecture with business architecture. Here, domain knowledge may be codified using reference architectures.

A third area of potential fruitful interaction is that of component-based development. Assembling components into a system requires an architecture that mediates between the system requirements and the requirements on the components. More generally, when we extend our view from

0-7695-1877-X/03 $17.00 © 2003 IEEE

a single system to a hierarchy of systems, the interplay between requirements and architectures is a central guiding principle in system design.

2. Goal

The goal of the workshop was to bring together researchers from the requirements engineering and architecture communities to exchange views and results that are of mutual interest, and to discuss topics for further research. Topics of interest included, but were not limited to, the following list.

- Deriving architecture descriptions in concert with requirements specification
- Attribute-based architecture design
- Tracing architectural decisions to requirements
- Evolving architectures and requirements
- Alignment between software architecture and business architecture
- Relating architecture patterns to requirements patterns
- Reference architectures
- Reuse of requirements and architectures
- Systems engineering approaches
- Formal foundations of the requirements–architecture relationship
- Requirements and architecture specification languages
- Tools and environments for requirements engineers and software architects

3. Participant Selection

A maximum of 30 participants were selected on the basis of the submitted material. Papers were reviewed by a program committee in terms of their relevance to the aims of the workshop and technical content.

4. Program Committee

- Daniel Berry (co-chair), Canada
- Jaelson Castro, Brazil
- Anthony Finkelstein, UK
- Jaap Gordijn, Netherlands
- Carlo Ghezzi, Italy
- Rick Kazman (co-chair), USA
- Manuel Kolp, Belgium
- Jeff Kramer, UK
- Axel van Lamsweerde, Belgium
- Jeff Magee, UK
- John Mylopoulos, Canada
- Bashar Nuseibeh, UK
- Dewayne Perry, USA
- Roel Wieringa (co-chair), Netherlands

5. Workshop Structure and Activities

The workshop was closed. Participation was based upon the submitted papers, the best of which were presented. All papers were distributed to the participants before the workshop started. Each presented paper was assigned an opponent, who presented a brief counterpoint to the paper. During the day, participants proposed issues to be discussed at the end of the day. The workshop led to a list of issues discussed, conclusions reached, disagreements identified, and topics to be researched further.

6. Workshop Outputs

All papers, counterpoints, and discussion summaries were made available electronically at the workshop website at `http://se.uwaterloo.ca/~straw03/` soon after the workshop. The site aims to highlight outstanding issues that should be the focus of future research in the area.

Research Demonstrations

Research Demonstrations and Posters

Bruce Schafer
Industry Affairs Dept.
Engineering & Computer Science
Oregon University System
Portland, OR 97006 (USA)
schaferb@capital.ous.edu

Mauro Pezzè
Dipartimento di Informatica,
Sistemistica e Comunicazione
Università degli Studi di Milano Bicocca
Milano, 20122 (Italy)
pezze@disco.unimib.it

Automation plays an important role in software engineering. The transition from research breakthroughs to usable tools is neither linear nor easy, and requires a fortunate combination of many elements difficult to identify and merge. In this hard transition process, research prototypes are an important step. They allow researchers to early experience ideas and results on real case studies, and to learn both difficulties in applying new theoretical results and limitations of the theory; and enable practitioners, who can see beyond the frontiers of current state of practice, to identify new technology for improving the software development process and spot advances applicable in the near future.

With this spirit the ICSE conferences promote the presentation and demonstration of research prototypes. The *Research Demonstration* program hosts prototypes that implement late-breaking results that successfully moved to mature technology advances, and allows to perceive the practical applicability and limitations of research results. The *Poster* program hosts preliminary ideas that cannot be effectively demonstrated yet, but may represent the seeds of future advances. The fecund industrial reality of Portland encouraged the submissions of many proposals for demonstrating research prototypes and posting promising preliminary ideas. We had the privilege of reviewing many interesting proposals and selecting a set of exciting research demonstrations and posters.

Those who were unable to attend all the demonstrations or see all the posters, or simply want more information will find such information on the conference web site, including links to many of the authors' web sites, on the ICSE Conferences web site (www.icse-conferences.org) following the link to ICSE 2003.

ICSE 2003 hosted fourteen demonstrations of research prototypes that covered several aspects of software engineering ranging from software verification, to support of different software development phases, to applications of new technologies to specific domains.
Technology for enhancing software verification has been demonstrated by:

- David Chays and Yuetang Deng from the Polytechnic University of New York, who demonstrated *Agenda*, a tool for testing relational database applications;
- Steve Easterbrook, Marsha Chechik, Benet Devereux, Arie Gurfinkel, Albert Lai, Victor Petrovykh, Anya Tafliovich and Christopher Thompson-Walsh from the University of Toronto, who demonstrated χ*Chek*, a model checker for multi-valued reasoning;
- Reishi Yokomori, Takashi Ishio, Tetsuo Yamamoto, Makoto Matsushita, Shinji Kusumoto, and Katsuro Inoue from Osaka University and the Japan Science and Technology Corporation, who demonstrated the *Java Program Analysis Projects in Osaka University* that includes *ADAS*, a tool for aspect-based slicing for supporting debugging of JAVA programs, and *SPARS-J*, a system for searching use relations among components;
- Martin Robillard and Gail Murphy from the University of British Columbia, who demonstrated *FEAT*, a tool for locating, describing, and analyzing concerns in source code;
- Steven Reiss, from Brown University, who demonstrated *JIVE*, a tool for visualizing Java in action.

Tools for supporting different software development phases have been demonstrated by:

- Wang, Hassan, Guedem, Abdelmoez, Goseva-Popstojanova, and Ammar from West Virginia University, who demonstrated a tool for architectural level risk assessment based on UML specifications;
- Stan Jarzabek from the National University of Singapore, who demonstrated *XVCL*, a tool for supporting configuration management of product lines;

0-7695-1877-X/03 $17.00 © 2003 IEEE

- Jonathan Maletic, from Kent State University, who demonstrated *Source Viewer 3D (sv3D)*, a tool for software visualization;

- Keith Chan, Zhi Cong Leo Liang, Amir Michail, Minh Hoai Nguyen, and Nicholas Seow from the University of New South Wales, who demonstrated *DRT*, a tool for design recovery of interactive graphical applications;

- Frank Padberg from the University of Karlsruhe, who demonstrated a tool for simulating software process scheduling;

- Steve Reiss, Christina Kennedy, Tom Wooldridge, and Shriram Krishnamurthi from Brown University, who demonstrated *CLIME*, an environment for checking consistency among different artifacts

- Christian Seybold, Martin Glinz, Silvio Meier, and Nancy Merlot-Schett from the University of Zürich, who demonstrated a tool for handling space management for aspect visualization;

- Jeffry Russell and Margarida Jacome from the University of Texas at Austin, who demonstrated *Embedded Architect*, a tool for early performance evaluation of embedded software.

An interesting application of agent technology to the marine environment domain has been demonstrated by Martin Fredriksson and Rune Gustavsson from the Blekinge Institute of Technology.

ICSE 2003 hosted also eight poster presentations. Five posters addressed the problem of software verification and analysis:

- Shimon Rura and Barbara Lerner from Williams College presented new ideas for static semantic checking;

- Nassar, Rabie, Shereshevsky, Gradetsky, Ammar, Yu, Bogazzi, Mili from West Virginia University and the New Jersey Institute of Technology presented new ideas for error propagation analysis using UML architecture specifications;

- Nilay Oza, Tracy Hall, and Austen Rainer from the University of Hertfordshire discussed the role of trust in software outsourcing;

- Sampsa Fabritius, Raimondas Lencevicius, Edu Metz, and Alexander Ran from the Nokia Research Center presented new ideas for estimating software schedulability for varied processor frequencies;

- Scott McMaster from the University of Maryland presented new ideas for applying dynamic execution trace data to test case minimization.

Three posters addressed specific application domains:

- Wu Guoqing, Shu Fengdi, and Yang Jie from Wuhan University addressed embedded real time systems illustrating a new requirements engineering environment for such systems;

- Yan Liu, Shiping Chen, Ian Gorton, and Alan Fekete from the University of Sydney addressed component based systems presenting a new methodology for predicting the performance of such systems;

- Johannes Martin fro Johannes Gutenberg-Universität Mainz addressed legacy systems, presenting a framework for reengineering and migrating legacy information systems.

Acknowledgments

We would like to thank all authors who submitted their work for research demonstration and poster presentation. Without their excellent contributions, the work of the Research Demonstrations and Posters Committee would have been tedious and we would not have been able to prepare such a great research demonstration and poster program. We express our gratitude to the members of the Committee, Luciano Baresi, Stuart Faulk, Eric Frohlick, Andrea Savigni, and Andy Schürr, who gave an excellent support in reviewing the many proposals.

Demonstration of AGENDA Tool Set for Testing Relational Database Applications

David Chays
Yuetang Deng
Polytechnic University *
6 Metrotech Center
Brooklyn, NY 11201
{dchays,ytdeng}@cis.poly.edu

Abstract

Database systems play an important role in nearly every modern organization, yet relatively little research effort has focused on how to test them. AGENDA, A (test) GENErator for Database Applications, is a research prototype tool set for testing DB application programs. In testing such applications, the states of the database before and after execution play an important role, along with the user's input and system output. AGENDA components populate the database, generate inputs, and check aspects of the correctness of output and new DB state.

Keywords

database, software testing, test data

1. Introduction

A database application program can be viewed as an attempt to implement a function, just like programs developed using traditional paradigms. However, considered in this way, the input and output spaces include the database states as well as the explicit input and output parameters of the application. This has substantial impact on the notion of what a test case is, how to generate test cases, and how to check the results produced by running the test cases. Furthermore, DB application programs are usually written in a semi-declarative language, such as SQL, or a combination of an imperative language and a declarative language, such as a C program with embedded SQL, rather than using a purely imperative language. Most existing program-based software testing techniques are designed explicitly for imperative languages, and therefore are not directly applicable to the DB application programs of interest here.

2. AGENDA Tool Set

Our goal is to assist the database application developer or tester in a usable, useful way. AGENDA consists of five interacting components that operate with guidance from the tester. Design and implementation details of each component are provided in [2]. Our approach leverages the fact that the database schema is described formally in the Data Definition Language of SQL, in order to ensure that the data we generate satisfies the integrity constraints, and allows the user to provide additional information to guide the generation. We want to automate the testing process as much as possible, but not at the expense of usability. We don't want to burden users with having to describe their data and/or applications in yet another language, as is required by existing approaches.

AGENDA generates data that are known to satisfy the constraints and then populates the DB with it. Furthermore, the data is selected in such a way as to include situations that the tester believes are likely to expose faults in the application or are likely to occur in practice, to assure that such scenarios are correctly treated. In order to insure that the data are consistent, AGENDA takes advantage of the database schema, which describes the domains, the relations, and the constraints the database designer has explicitly specified. This information is expressed in a formal language, SQL's Data Definition Language (DDL), which makes it possible to automate much of the testing process.

To address the issues detailed in [1], we have developed a tool set, AGENDA, to help test database applications. The AGENDA architecture is shown in Figure 1. AGENDA

* Supported in part by NSF Grants CCR-9870270 and CCR-9988354, AT&T Labs, and the New York State Office of Science, Technology, and Academic Research.

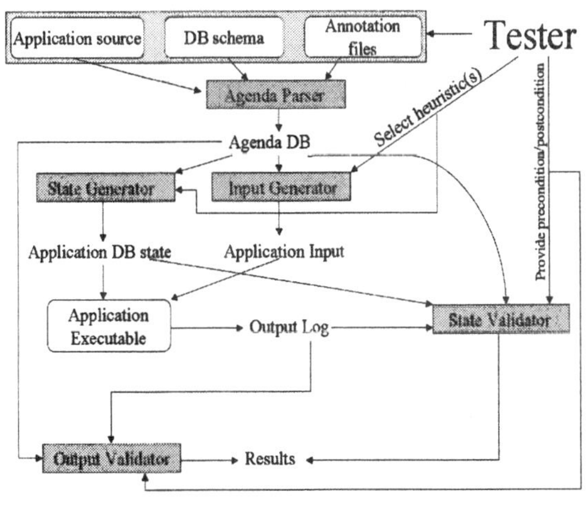

Figure 1. Architecture of the AGENDA tool set

takes as input the database schema of the database on which the application runs; the application source code; and "annotation files", containing some suggested values for attributes. The user interactively selects test heuristics and provides information about expected behavior of test cases. Using this information, AGENDA populates the database, generates inputs to the application, executes the application on those inputs and checks some aspects of correctness of the resulting database state and the application output.

The approach is loosely based on the Category-Partition method [3]: the user supplies suggested values for attributes, partitioned into groups, which we call *data groups*. This data is provided in the annotation files. The tool then produces meaningful combinations of these values in order to fill database tables and provide input parameters to the application program. Data groups are used to distinguish values that are expected to result in different application behavior, e.g. different categories of employees.

Using these data groups and guided by heuristics selected by the tester, AGENDA produces a collection of *test templates* representing abstract test cases. The tester then provides information about the expected behavior of the application on tests represented by each template.

In order to control the explosion in the number of test templates and to force the generation of particular kinds of templates, the tester selects heuristics. Available heuristics include one to favor "boundary values", heuristics to force the inclusion of NULL values where doing so is not precluded by not-NULL constraints, heuristics to force the inclusion of duplicate values where so doing is not precluded by uniqueness constraints, and heuristics to force the inclusion of values from all data groups.

Finally, AGENDA instantiates the templates with specific test values, executes the test cases and checks that the outputs and new database state are consistent with the expected behavior indicated by the tester.

The first component (*Agenda Parser*) extracts relevant information from the application's database schema, the application queries, and tester-supplied annotation files, and makes this information available to the other four components.

The second component (*State Generator*) uses the database schema along with information from the tester's annotation files, and populates the database tables with data satisfying the integrity constraints. Heuristics, listed above and detailed in [2], are used to guide the generation of both the application DB state and inputs.

The third component (*Input Generator*) generates input data to be supplied to the application. The data are created by using information that is generated by the Agenda Parser and State Generator components, along with information derived from parsing the SQL statements in the application program and information that is useful for checking the test results.

The fourth component (*State Validator*) investigates how the state of the application DB changes during execution of a test. The State Validator automatically logs the changes in the application tables and semi-automatically checks the state change.

The fifth component (*Output Validator*) is similar to the State Validator tool. When the application query is a `select` statement, it is handled by the Output Validator; otherwise, it is handled by the State Validator. The Output Validator captures the application's outputs and checks them against the query preconditions and postconditions that have been generated by the tool or supplied by the tester.

We believe that database application testing contains three levels: the query level, the transaction level, and the transaction concurrency level [2]. Currently, our system operates on the query level. Ongoing work involves adding more features to our existing system on the query level, and extending our tool set to the transaction level and transaction concurrency level.

References

[1] D. Chays, S. Dan, P. G. Frankl, F. I. Vokolos, and E. J. Weyuker. A framework for testing database applications. *Proceedings of the 2000 International Symposium on Software Testing and Analysis*, pages 147–157, Aug. 2000.

[2] D. Chays, Y. Deng, P. G. Frankl, S. Dan, F. I. Vokolos, and E. J. Weyuker. Agenda: A test generator for relational database applications. Technical Report TR-CIS-2002-04, Department of Computer Science, Polytechnic University, 2002.

[3] T. J. Ostrand and M. J. Balcer. The category-partition method for specifying and generating functional tests. *Commun. ACM*, 31(6):676–686, June 1988.

χChek: A Model Checker for Multi-Valued Reasoning

Steve Easterbrook, Marsha Chechik, Benet Devereux, Arie Gurfinkel, Albert Lai, Victor Petrovykh, Anya Tafliovich and Christopher Thompson-Walsh
Department of Computer Science
University of Toronto, Toronto, Canada M5S 3H5
xchek@cs.toronto.edu

This paper describes our multi-valued symbolic model-checker χChek. χChek is a generalization of an existing symbolic model-checking algorithm for a multi-valued extension of the temporal logic CTL. Multi-valued model-checking supports reasoning with values other than just TRUE and FALSE.

Multi-valued logics are useful in software engineering because they support explicit modeling of uncertainty, disagreement, and relative desirability or priority. For example, 3-valued logics have been used for interpreting results of static analysis with abstraction [5, 10], and for analyzing partial models [1]. The intermediate value of the logic is used to denote missing information. 4-valued logics have been used to model disagreements that arise when models drawn from different sources are composed [6]. The four values represent the four possible ways of combining the two classical values of the source models.

Our model checker generalizes these approaches — it works for the class of multi-valued logics whose logical values form a finite distributive lattice, and where there is a suitably defined negation operator that preserves De Morgan laws and involution ($\neg\neg a = a$). Such structures are called *quasi-boolean algebras* [9]. Classical logic, as well as the 3- and 4-valued logics described in the literature, are examples of quasi-boolean algebras. In [3], we describe the properties of these logics. For tractability, we restrict ourselves to logics with a finite number of values.

Examples of these logics are shown in Figure 1. 1(a) is classical 2-valued logic. 1(b) is a 3-valued logic suitable for representing partial models. 1(c) is the 4-valued logic describe above. Note that its lattice is the product of two 2-valued lattices. 1(d) is the product of two 3-valued lattices, and is suitable for composing two *partial* models allowing both disagreement *and* missing information.

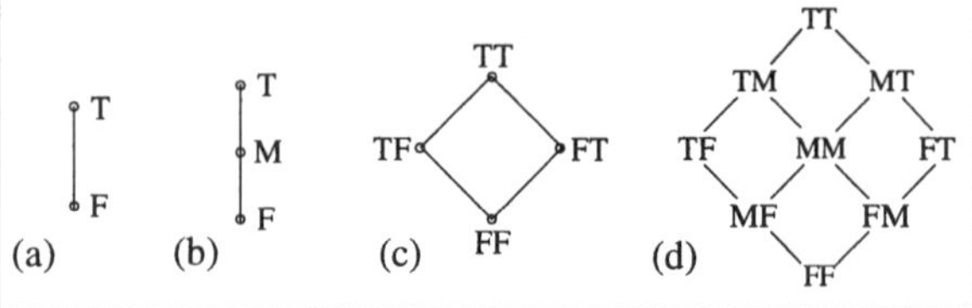

Figure 1. Some example lattices.

Implementation

χChek is implemented in Java, and provides support for both model-checking with fairness and the generation of counter-examples (or witnesses). The tool consists of three components: (1) the model-checking engine itself (χChek); (2) a counter-example generator (KEG); (3) a web-based front-end for interactive exploration and visualization of counter-examples (KegVis).

χChek receives a χKripke structure (a multi-valued generalization of a Kripke structure) K and a χCTL formula φ, and produces a value of φ at every state of K. The modular implementation of χChek allows it to support a wide variety of specification languages for χKripke structures. Currently, these structures can be specified either explicitly, as directed graphs in XML, or as compositions of modules expressed in an SMV-like notation.

The analysis is performed using different decision diagrams: MDDs and MBTDDs implemented as a custom decision diagram package [4], as well as BDDs and ADDs using the standard CUDD library. The complexity of model-checking of a χCTL formula φ, under the assumption that all operations on decision diagrams take constant time, is $O(|S| \times |\varphi|)$, where S is the state space of the model [7].

[3] presents a more detailed description of the architecture of χChek. The tool itself can be downloaded from http://www.cs.toronto.edu/fm.

Applications

Multi-valued model-checking has a number of potential applications in software engineering.

The intermediate values of the logic can represent incomplete information (or uncertainty). Such applications typically use a 3-valued logic. A 3-valued model can be

0-7695-1877-X/03 $17.00 © 2003 IEEE

interpreted as a compact representation for a set of *completions* [1], where a completion is generated by replacing each M value in the model by either T or F. If a property is T (respectively, F) in a partial model, then it is T (F) in all completions. If a property is M in a partial model, then it takes different values in different completions; the missing information affects the property. Thus, χChek can determine if a property holds, even though the model is incomplete. We can also use this approach to reduce the size of classical model-checking problems by creating (partial) abstractions of models that have large state-spaces. The approach can be generalized to logics with more than 3 values, to distinguish levels of uncertainty for the incomplete information, but we have not yet explored such applications.

The intermediate values of the logic can represent disagreement. Such applications typically use product lattices. A model based on a product lattice can be interpreted as a compact representation for a set of models (or *views*), where the views may disagree on the values of some transitions or propositions. For example, a 4-valued model based on the lattice of Figure 1(c) can be formed by merging information from two 2-valued views. Where the views disagree on the value of a transition or proposition, it will take the value TF or FT. If a property is TT (respectively, FF) in each individual view, then it will be TT (FF) in the merged model. If a property is FT or TF in the merged model, then the disagreement affects the property. χChek can check properties that cannot be expressed in the individual views, because the properties combine vocabulary of several views or refer to interactions between different views. We are exploring this approach for the feature interaction problem in telephony [6], and as a tool to support stakeholder negotiations in requirements engineering.

The intermediate values of the logic can represent relative desirability (or criticality). Such applications typically use chain lattices (total orders). A model based on a chain lattice can be interpreted as a compact representation for a set of partial *layers*, where each successive layer specifies values for transitions left unspecified by previous layers. For example, a model based on a 4-valued chain lattice can be used to represent a system with two levels of criticality. Transitions labeled T and F represent core functionality—transitions that must (or must not) occur. Transitions labeled with other values represent optional functionality. If a property is T (respectively, F) in this model, then it is true (false) in just the core layer, irrespective of behaviors at the optional layer. We are exploring this approach for reasoning about requirements prioritization and survivable systems. χChek allows us to check which properties are supported by which layer, without having to maintain separate models of the individual layers.

Elements of our quasi-boolean algebras need not be interpreted as logical values. Consider the *query-checking* problem [2] for which the inputs are a (classical) model and a temporal logic query (TLQ). A TLQ is a temporal logic formula with placeholders for some subformulas, e.g., $AG?$. A query-checker finds the strongest set of assignments of propositional formulas for each placeholder, such that replacing each placeholder with any assignment chosen from its set gives a temporal logic formula that holds in the model. Thus, query-checking can be used to discover invariants, guards, and postconditions of (sets of) transitions in the model. The query checking problem can be formulated as a multi-valued model checking problem, where the elements of the lattices are sets of propositional formulas ordered by set inclusion [8].

Acknowledgements: *Financial support was provided by NSERC and CITO.*

References

[1] G. Bruns and P. Godefroid. "Generalized Model Checking: Reasoning about Partial State Spaces". In C. Palamidessi, editor, *Proc. 11th Int. Conf. on Concurrency Theory (CONCUR'00)*, volume 1877 of *LNCS*, pp 168–182, University Park, PA, USA, Aug 2000. Springer.

[2] W. Chan. "Temporal-Logic Queries". In E. Emerson and A. Sistla, editors, *Proc. 12th Conf. on Computer Aided Verification (CAV'00)*, volume 1855 of *LNCS*, pp 450–463, Chicago, IL, USA, July 2000. Springer.

[3] M. Chechik, B. Devereux, S. Easterbrook, and A. Gurfinkel. "Multi-Valued Symbolic Model-Checking". *ACM Trans. on Software Engineering and Methodology*, Jan 2003. (Accepted for publication).

[4] M. Chechik, B. Devereux, S. Easterbrook, A. Lai, and V. Petrovykh. "Efficient Multiple-Valued Model-Checking Using Lattice Representations". In *Proc. 12th Int. Conf. on Concurrency Theory (CONCUR'01)*, volume 2154 of *LNCS*, pp 451–465, Aalborg, Denmark, Aug 2001. Springer.

[5] M. Chechik and W. Ding. "Lightweight Reasoning about Program Correctness". *Information Systems Frontiers*, 4(4), Nov 2002.

[6] S. Easterbrook and M. Chechik. "A Framework for Multi-Valued Reasoning over Inconsistent Viewpoints". In *Proc. Int. Conf. on Software Engineering (ICSE'01)*, pp 411–420, Toronto, Canada, May 2001. IEEE CS Press.

[7] A. Gurfinkel. "Multi-Valued Symbolic Model-Checking: Fairness, Counter-Examples, Running Time". Master's thesis, U. of Toronto, Dept. of Computer Science, Oct 2002.

[8] A. Gurfinkel, B. Devereux, and M. Chechik. "Model Exploration with Temporal Logic Query Checking". In *Proc. SIGSOFT Conf. on Foundations of Software Engineering (FSE'02)*, pp 139–148, Charleston, SC, Nov 2002.

[9] H. Rasiowa. *An Algebraic Approach to Non-Classical Logics. Studies in Logic and the Foundations of Mathematics.* Amsterdam: North-Holland, 1978.

[10] M. Sagiv, T. Reps, and R. Wilhelm. "Parametric Shape Analysis via 3-Valued Logic". In *Proc. 26th Annual ACM Symp. on Principles of Programming Languages*, pp 105–118, New York, NY, 1999.

Trustworthy and sustainable operations in marine environments

Martin Fredriksson and Rune Gustavsson
Societies of Computation Laboratory
Blekinge Institute of Technology
Box 520, Ronneby, Sweden.
martin.fredriksson@bth.se and rune.gustavsson@bth.se

Abstract

In order to address challenges and opportunities of engineering information systems for network-centric warfare, we have developed a prototype for trustworthy and sustainable operations in marine environments (TWOSOME). The system developed addressed qualities such as information fusion, target acquisition, and self-organization in open computational systems; comprised of distributed services. As such, the system prototype executes on a service-oriented layered architecture for communicating entities (SOLACE) and, furthermore, different perspectives of the prototype are visualized by means of a distributed interaction system for complex entity relation networks (DISCERN).

1. Introduction

The exercise of engineering software systems for network-centric warfare [1] boils down to one issue in particular – *sustainable behavior in open computational systems* [2]. A key aspect of the domain is automated management of unforeseen system events and dynamics. In open computational systems, new entities can enter and leave a physical environment at will. Computational or not, entities in such environments observe and interact with each other and such behavior is the origin of unpredictable events occurring. In order to make explicit a separation of concerns in engineering and sustaining qualities in such systems, we introduce a layered perspective involving the dimensions of *environment*, *fabric*, *system*, and *domain*.

In practice, we support this layered perspective by means of a platform for system articulation and construction (SOLACE[1]) and a tool for system observation and instrumentation (DISCERN[2]).

In order to identify requirements of the platforms and tools involved, we have investigated a prototype for trustworthy and sustainable operations in marine environments (TWOSOME[3]) as a joint effort between Blekinge Institute of Technology and Kockums. At the core of this prototype is the development of a multi-agent system, where interacting and coordinated entities come together in a physical setting; in order to perform a particular assignment under dynamic and hostile conditions. From a methodological perspective, we have focused this investigation and prototype development on *online engineering* of open computational systems. Specifically, we consider the involved systems to be of such a complex nature that the traditional approach of software engineering to analyze, design, implement, and deploy some particular system is no longer applicable. Instead, we argue that systems have to be continuously articulated, constructed, observed, and instrumented in an ongoing online process of adaptation.

2. Scenario

The prototype involves two interrelated aspects — attacker and defender — focused on creating and removing physical threats at some particular environment location. In essence, this state of affairs renders itself as a game of deception where one party continuously tries to outsmart the other by means of information fusion, coordination, and reasoning. If an entity at any point in time should fail to fulfill either one of these capabilities the game is lost.

An attacker — a smart mine — is deployed in the environment and set to detonate whenever the presence of a particular vessel is identified in its surroundings. Correspondingly, we assign three coordinated defenders — autonomous vessels emanating acoustic and magnetic signatures — the role of sweeping different environment locations and, consequently, aim at removing potential

[1] www.soclab.bth.se/practices/solace.html
[2] www.soclab.bth.se/practices/discern.html
[3] www.soclab.bth.se/systems/twosome.html

0-7695-1877-X/03 $17.00 © 2003 IEEE

attackers by means of making mines detonate in a harmless way. The goal of a team of defenders is to outsmart the mine by means of providing fake signatures of real vessels. In practice, according to the overall system quality of sustainability, this exercise involves the continuous adaptation and reconfiguration of roles and resources. In the particular case of TWOSOME, we identify the following roles and resources.

- *Sensor* — the sole purpose of sensor entities is to acquire information concerning their surrounding environment and pass it forward in an appropriate format to those entities that are dependent on such information in order to fulfill their particular goals, e.g., an operations center.

- *Operations centre* — an operations center gathers intelligence and is responsible for the overall safety of some physical environment. In practice, we can achieve this role by means of continuously delegating orders, based upon newly acquired intelligence, to other entities under the operation centre's control.

- *Defender* — a defender emanates different acoustic and magnetic signatures in order to exhibit characteristics similar to those of general naval vessel properties, e.g., propeller cavitations and engine acoustics. In doing so, the defense vessel has the ability to trigger the detonation mechanisms of artifacts such as mines. A team of defenders can, by means of coordination technology, form combinations of complex signatures as well provide for self-organization.

- *Transporter* — in the present scenario, we use multi-purpose vessels, e.g., a corvette class vessel, to transport a group of defenders from one location to another and subsequently delegate a defense order to the transported entities upon arrival.

- *Attacker* — we make the role of an attacker operational by means of a mine. The sole purpose of this mine is to detonate when it identifies certain acoustic and magnetic signatures — corresponding to targeted vessel types — in its surrounding environment.

In the particular case of TWOSOME, an attacker (an active mine) is created somewhere in the physical environment and thereby triggers observations by two different sensors. We forward this information to an operations centre that sends out a transporter carrying a number of defenders, i.e., autonomous vessels emanating deceiving acoustic and magnetic signatures. At some particular location, estimated by the operations centre and based on the information given by its sensors, the transporter deploys the defenders and travels back to its origin. It is at this point that we can start to understand the opportunities and challenges with trustworthy and sustainable operations in marine environments.

Each defender has the capability to navigate and cooperate with other defense vessels and thereby provide a potential attacker with more or less complex and deceiving vessel signatures. That is, a team of defenders can produce a complex vessel signature that is very difficult to distinguish from that produced by the actual vessel class threatened by an attacker. However, the coordinated structure of this efficient number of defenders is also very sensitive to perturbations in the surrounding environment.

Since the quality of the coordinated team of defenders corresponds to their effectiveness in deceiving some potential attacker — making it detonate and thereby removing the threat — it is essential that each defender produce an appropriate complex signature at the appropriate location. In order to do so, each entity must be able to observe and instrument its current context with respect to the given mission. For example, if we downgrade a particular defender's service of producing some specific signature or completely remove it, we have to reorganize the whole team. However, by means of self-organization, the team of defenders is capable of reconfiguring and reusing its currently available services and resources in order to provide for a particular complex signature at all times.

3. References

[1] D. Alberts, J. Garstka, R. Hayes, and D. Signori (2001) *Understanding Information Age Warfare*. CCRP Publication Series.

[2] M. Fredriksson, R. Gustavsson, and A. Ricci (2003) Sustainable coordination. In M. Klusch, S. Bergamaschi, P. Edwards, and P. Petta (eds.) *Intelligent information agents: The AgentLink perspective*. Lecture notes in artificial intelligence, vol. 2586. Springer Verlag. (to appear)

Architectural Level Risk Assessment Tool Based on UML Specifications [1]

T.Wang, A. Hassan, A. Guedem, W. Abdelmoez,
K. Goseva-Popstojanova, H. Ammar
Lane Department of Computer Science and Electrical Engineering,
West Virginia University, Morgantown, WV26506-6109
{twang, hassan, guedem, rabie, katerina, ammar}@csee.wvu.edu

Abstract

Recent evidences indicate that most faults in software systems are found in only a few of a system's components [1]. The early identification of these components allows an organization to focus on defect detection activities on high risk components, for example by optimally allocating testing resources [2], or redesigning components that are likely to cause field failures. This paper presents a prototype tool called Architecture-level Risk Assessment Tool (ARAT) based on the risk assessment methodology presented in [3]. The ARAT provides risk assessment based on measures obtained from Unified Modeling Language (UML) artifacts [4]. This tool can be used in the design phase of the software development process. It estimates dynamic metrics [5] and automatically analyzes the quality of the architecture to produce architectural-level software risk assessment [3].

1. Introduction

There is an increasing need for a tool that can be used to track the quality of software products during the software design phase. Some of the proposed tools get static metrics from source code [6], but source code metrics are affected by the programming language and programming style. When calculating the metrics from architectural descriptions such as UML, we achieve independency of languages and human factors [7]. Other metrics tools [8] only produce static metrics to describe the model with a limited capability to accurately represent the dynamic behavior of the architecture. We developed a tool for risk assessment at the architectural level, ARAT, that produces the dynamic metrics from UML diagrams. Using the methodology proposed in [3], ARAT estimates risk factor of a software system in hieratical fashion. This paper is organized as follow. Section 2 presents an overview of the tool structure. Section 3 provides some examples of the outputs from the tool. Finally, Section 4 concludes the paper.

2. Structure of the tool

The UML use case model of the tool is shown in Figure 1. The tool consists of six main use cases as follows.

Estimate dynamic metrics

Based on cyclomatic complexity [10], the ARAT computes the dynamic complexity [5] of the UML state charts as a dynamic complexity metric. It also computes dynamic coupling between components based on the message exchange between components in the sequence diagram [5].

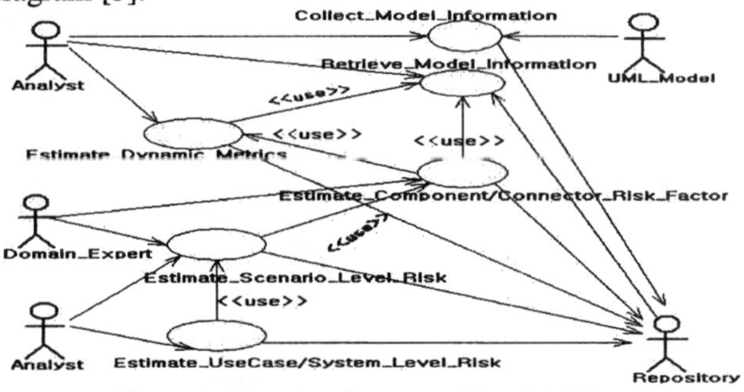

Figure 1. Use case diagram of the ARAT tool

Collect model information

Using a commercial tool Rose Real Time [9] as a front end for our tool we transform the visual UML model to a textual format data. We use Rose Script to transform UML diagrams to textual data.

Estimate component / connector risk factor

Based on the definition of risk [11], we calculate risk factors of each component (connector) in the architecture as

[1] This work is funded in part by grants to West Virginia University Research Corp. from the National Science Foundation Information Technology Research (ITR) Program grant number CCR-0082574, and from the NASA Office of Safety and Mission Assurance (OSMA) Software Assurance Research Program (SARP) managed through the NASA Independent Verification and Validation (IV&V) Facility, Fairmont, West Virginia.

a product of the dynamic complexity (coupling) and the severity level of a failure. The severity level of a failure of component/connector is estimated using FMEA [12].

Estimate scenario risk factor

The tool automatically constructs the Markov chain that represents the control flow graph of the active components and connectors in a specific scenario based on the textual representation of the UML sequence diagrams. The scenario risk factor for each severity level is computed using this Markov chain and the estimated values of component/connector risk factors [3].

Estimate use case and overall system risk factors.

The risk factors of each scenario in a specific use case are aggregated to calculate the use case risk factor [3]. Using the risk factor for each use case, the tool calculates the overall system risk factor [3].

3. Illustration of the tool outputs

Due to a space limitation we only illustrate some of the output results provided by the ARAT. These results are for the pacemaker [12] which is an implanted device that assists cardiac functions of the heart when the underlying pathologies make the intrinsic heartbeats low. Pacemaker is an example of a critical real-time application because the failure of the software operation of the device can cause loss of a patient's life. Figure 3 presents the identification of the critical components in the pacemaker example provided by ARAT. Thus, the components that have high risk factors with catastrophic severity in multiple scenarios are the most critical components that would require more careful development and/or more testing effort.

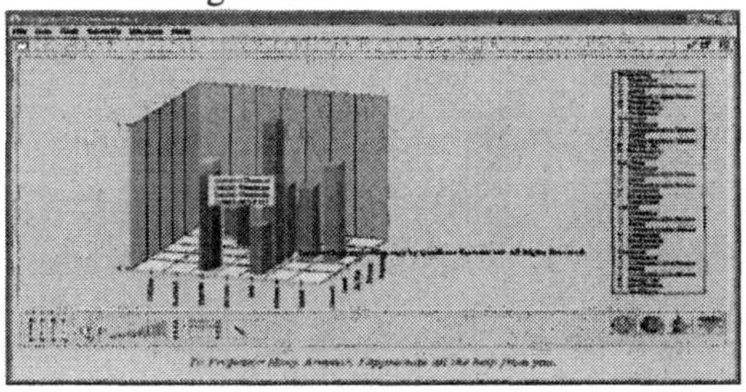

Figure 3. Identification of critical components

The distribution of the overall system risk factor among severity classes is presented in Figure 4. We see that the overall system risk factor is mostly distributed among marginal and catastrophic severity classes, which confirms that this is a high risk system.

4. Conclusion and future work

In this paper, we present ARAT, a tool for architectural level risk assessment based on UML specifications. The tool enables early assessment of risk and hence makes it possible for the analyst to identify critical components/connectors and scenarios/use cases early in the software lifecycle. The output of the tool can guide the allocation of development and testing effort based on critical use cases, scenarios, components, and connectors. Our future plan is to further extend the tool so that it computes static metrics, as well as to collect, store and analyze data which is used for interpretation of quality metrics, even though the result maybe not as sensitive and complete as dynamic metrics for early risk assessment. In addition, we plan to integrate the hazard analysis methodology into our tool to allow automatic and precise estimation of the severity level for each architectural element.

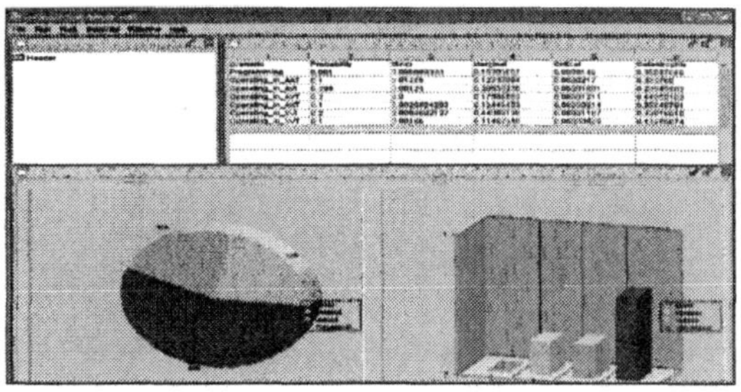

Figure 4. Distribution of the overall system risk factor

5. References

[1] N. Fenton, N. Ohlsson, "Quantitative Analysis of Faults and Failures in a Complex Software System", *IEEE Trans. Software Engineering*, Vol. 26, No. 8, pp. 797 -814, 2000.

[2] W. Harrison, "Using Software Metrics to Allocate Testing Resources", *Journal of Management Information Systems*, Vol. 4, No. 4, 1988, pp. 93-105.

[3] K. Goseva-Popstojanova , A. Hassan, A. Guedem, W. Abdelmoez, D. Nassar, H. Ammar, A. Mili, "Architectural-Level Risk Analysis using UML", submitted for publication.

[4] J. Rumbaugh, I. Jacobson, G. Booach, *The Unified Modeling Language Reference Manual*, Addison-Wesley, 1999.

[5] A. Hassan, W. M. Abdelmoez, R. M. Elnaggar, H. H. Ammar, "An Approach to Measure the Quality of Software Designs from UML Specifications," *7th International Conference Information Systems, Analysis and Synthesis*, 2001, Vol.IV, pp.559-564.

[6] M. Stojanovic, K. El-Emam, "ES1: A tool for collecting object-oriented design metrics", *NRC/ERB-1087*, May 2001.

[7] M. Hitz, K. Neuhold, "A Framework for Product Analysis", OOPSLA *1998 Workshop on Model Engineering*, Methods and Tools Interaction with CDIF, 1998.

[8] L. Nenonen, J. Gustafsson, J. Paakki A. Inkeri Verkamo, "Measuring object - oriented software architectures from UML diagrams", Proc. *4th International ECOOP Workshop on Quantitative Approaches in Object-Oriented Software Engineering*, 2000, pp. 87-100.

[9] UML Language Resource Center: Unified Modeling anguage, Standard Software Notation, http://www.rational.com.

[10] T. McCabe, "A Complexity Metrics", *IEEE Trans. Software Engineering*, Vol.2, No.4, 1976, pp 308-320.

[11] H. Ammar, T. Nikzadeh, J. Dugan, "A Methodology for Risk Assessment of Functional Specification of Software Systems Using Coherent Petri Nets", *Proc. 4th Inernationall Software Metrics Symposium*, 1997, pp. 108-117.

[12] S. Yacoub, H. Ammar, "A Methodology for Architectural-Level Reliability Risk Analysis," *IEEE Trans. Software Engineering*, Vol. 28, No. 6, 2002, pp.529-547.

XVCL: XML-based Variant Configuration Language

Stan Jarzabek[1], Paul Bassett[2], Hongyu Zhang[1] and Weishan Zhang[1]

[1]*Department of Computer Science*
School of Computing
National University of Singapore
Lower Kent Ridge Road, Singapore 117543
{stan, zhanghy, zhangws}@comp.nus.edu.sg

[2]*Canadian Information Processing Society*
National
2800 Skymark Ave., Suite 402
Mississauga, Ontario, Canada L4W 5A6
pbassett@cips.ca

1. An overview of XVCL

XVCL (XML-based Variant Configuration Language) is a meta-programming technique and tool that provides effective reuse mechanisms [2]. XVCL is an open source software (http://fxvcl.sourceforge.net) developed at the National University of Singapore. Being a modern and versatile version of Bassett's frames [1], a technology that has achieved substantial gains in industry, the underlying principles of the XVCL have been thoroughly tested in practice. Unlike original frames, XVCL blends with contemporary programming paradigms and complements other design techniques. XVCL uses "composition with adaptation" rules to generate a specific program from generic, reusable meta-components. Program generation rules are 100% transparent to a programmer, who retains full control over fine-tuning the generated code. Despite its simplicity, XVCL can effectively manage a wide range of program variants from a compact base of meta-components, structured for effective reuse.

Variants arise naturally in software reuse and evolution, in particular, if you deal with software product lines that encompass a family of similar systems. This is exactly the context in which we have developed and applied XVCL. Suppose you have a software product that you want to run on different platforms or hardware devices. Or you deliver versions of the same product to a number of customers and these product versions differ in some functional or non-functional requirements. XVCL allows you to configure product variants from a common core of generic, adaptable and reusable meta-components. And you can apply the same XVCL concepts and mechanisms to manage variants in a range of product line assets such as software architecture, program code, test cases, technical and user-level program documentation or requirement specifications.

XVCL includes a methodology and a tool – the XVCL processor. The XVCL methodology tells you how to discover the structure of the solution for your application domain and for the types of variants you want to address. The XVCL processor automates the routine yet error-prone program construction tasks, allowing you to focus on what is novel about your problem domains, requiring your creativity.

2. How does XVCL work?

XVCL works on the principle of constructing custom systems by composing generic, reusable meta-components, after possible adaptations. Adaptations of a meta-component take place at designated variation points marked by XVCL commands. This "composition with adaptation" process turns meta-components into concrete components of the custom system we wish to build.

To facilitate effective reuse, you split your program into generic, reusable and adaptable meta-components. A meta-component is an XML file with program code (written in any programming language), instrumented with XVCL commands for ease of change and evolution. XVCL commands, designed as XML tags, allow the composition of the meta-components, selection of pre-defined options based on certain conditions, etc. Meta-variables and expressions provide a powerful parameterization mechanism. Values of meta-variables are propagated across meta-components and variable scoping rules enhance genericity and reuse.

You organize meta-components into a layered hierarchy called an x-framework. Meta-components at lower-levels are building blocks for the higher-level meta-components - XVCL processor composes higher level meta-components from lower-level meta-components, after applying possible adaptations to them. An x-framework forms a base of reusable assets, such as a product line architecture, from which you build custom systems.

The XVCL processor traverses an x-framework, executes XVCL commands embedded in visited meta-components and generates custom code.

3. Applications and benefits of XVCL

Applications of XVCL include design of reusable program components, implementing product line architectures, design of compact, non-redundant,

0-7695-1877-X/03 $17.00 © 2003 IEEE

therefore, easy to maintain programs, and managing variants in multiple versions of software documents and models. We envision many other applications in software and non-software domains.

XVCL is based on Bassett's frame technology [1]. Frames have been applied in industry to manage variants and evolve multi-million-line, COBOL-based, information systems. While designing a frame architecture is not trivial, subsequent productivity gains are substantial. An independent analysis showed that frames can reduce large software project costs by over 84% and their times-to-market by 70%, when compared to industry norms (refer to QSM report in [1]). By reusing skillfully structured frame architectures, you need to focus on only the 5%-15% of a program solution that is unique; the other 85%-95% is reused. These gains are due to the flexibility of the resulting architectures and their evolvability over time.

Our XVCL is extensible and, of course, free of COBOL heritage. We applied XVCL to design product line architectures for component-based systems written in Java, and using RMI, J2EE or CORBA for component communication. We designed Facility Reservation System (FRS) and Computer Aided Dispatch system (CAD) product line architectures [3,4]. An FRS helps in the reservation of facilities (such as tutorial rooms, hotel rooms, lecture theaters) and specific equipment. Different organizations such as universities, hotels, hospitals and companies, have different physical facilities and arrangements for their reservation. The similarities and differences among FRSes yield a product line. We started by selecting common and variant functional requirements to be implemented in the FRS product line architecture. Our FRSes were built as EJB™ components, organized into a 3-tier architecture. We used XVCL to create generic, reusable meta-components from which we could generate custom runtime EJB components that met functional variants for a specific FRS we wish to build.

Computer Aided Dispatch systems (CAD for short) are used by police, fire and rescue and other similar organizations to dispatch resources (e.g., police cars) to handle incidents[1]. CAD systems are distributed over the Internet, with components dedicated to different roles (indicated in Figure 1) running on different computers. At the basic operational level, all CAD systems are similar - they support the dispatch of units to handle incidents. However, the specific context of the operation (such as police or fire & rescue) results in many variations on the basic operational scheme. We addressed CAD variants related to functional requirements, component distribution, platforms and reliability. For example, in some CAD systems Call Taker and Dispatcher roles may be played by two different people and in others - by the same person. This variant has impact on system functions, user interface and component distribution.

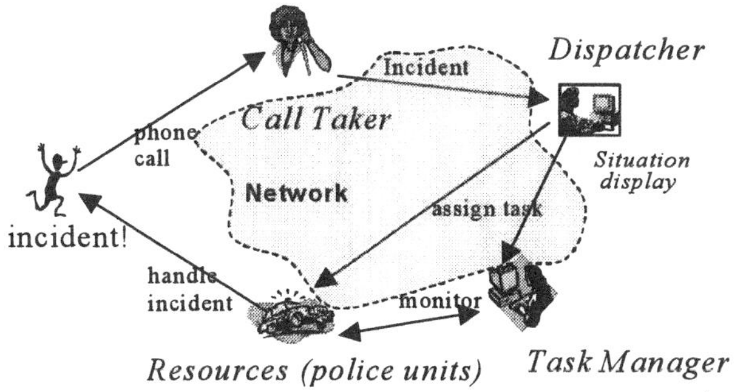

Figure 1. Highlight of a CAD system for police

We applied XVCL to manage variants in UML software models documenting FRS and CAD product lines [5]. In yet another project, we managed evolution of the City Guide System product line with XVCL.

XVCL is also effective in improving program maintenance. It is a well-known fact that redundant code obstructs program understanding and maintenance. Yet, programs are often polluted by redundant code. We analyzed a recently released Java Buffer library, JDK 1.4 Merlin and found many redundancies – the same or very similar code fragments recurring in may places. With XVCL, we generated the same Buffer library classes from compact, non-redundant meta-components whose size, in LOC, is just 40% of the original library. We posted the detailed results of this analysis at: http://www.comp.nus.edu.sg/labs/software/xvcl/buffer.html.

We envision many other applications in software and non-software domains, as we can apply XVCL to any domain that can be represented as a collection of textual documents.

References

[1] Bassett, P., *Framing software reuse - lessons from real world*, Yourdon Press, Prentice Hall, 1997

[2] Wong, T.W., Jarzabek, S., Myat Swe, S., Shen, R. and Zhang, H., "XML Implementation of Frame Processor," *Proc. ACM Symposium on Software Reusability, SSR'01*, Toronto, Canada, May 2001, pp. 164-172

[3] Jarzabek, S. and Seviora, R., "Engineering components for ease of customization and evolution," *IEE Proceedings - Software*, Vol. 147, No. 6, December 2000, pp. 237-248, a special issue on Component-based Software Engineering

[4] Cheong, Y.C. and Jarzabek, S., "Frame-based Method for Customizing Generic Software Architectures," *Proc. Symposium on Software Reusability, SSR'99*, Los Angeles, May 1999, pp. 103-112

[5] Jarzabek, S. and Zhang, H., "XML-based Method and Tool for Handling Variant Requirements in Domain Models", *Proc. of 5th IEEE International Symposium on Requirements Engineering, RE'01*, IEEE Press, August 2001, Toronto, Canada, pp. 166-173

[1] Project funded by Singapore National Science and Technology Board and Canadian Ministry of Energy, Science and Technology, involving National University of Singapore, Singapore Engineering Software Pte Ltd, University of Waterloo and Netron, Inc. (Toronto).

Source Viewer 3D (sv3D) – A Framework for Software Visualization

Jonathan I. Maletic, Andrian Marcus, Louis Feng
Department of Computer Science
Kent State University
Kent Ohio 44242
jmaletic@cs.kent.edu, amarcus@cs.kent.edu, lfeng@cs.kent.edu

Abstract

Source Viewer 3D is a software visualization framework that uses a 3D metaphor to represent software system and analysis data. The 3D representation is based on the SeeSoft pixel metaphor. It extends the original metaphor by rendering the visualization in a 3D space. New, object-based manipulation methods and simultaneous alternative mappings are available to the user.

1. Description

Source Viewer 3D (sv3D) is a software visualization framework that builds on the SeeSoft [1, 2] metaphor. It brings a number of enhancements and extensions over SeeSoft-type representations. In particular it creates 3D renderings of the raw data and various artifacts of the software system and their attributes can be mapped to the 3D metaphors at different abstraction levels. It implements improved, object-based user interactions, is independent of the analysis tool, and it accepts a simple and flexible input in XML format. The output of numerous analysis tools can be easily translated to sv3D input format and the design and implementation of our system is extensible.

SeeSoft-like tools have a variety of uses in assisting the user solving software engineering and comprehension tasks. sv3D can be used for all these tasks such as: fault localization [4], visualization of execution traces [6], source code browsing [3], impact analysis, evolution, complexity, and slicing [1], etc. In addition, by allowing visualization of additional information (via 3D), sv3D can be used for solving other more complex tasks. For example, in the case of Tarantula [4], using height instead of brightness would improve the visualization and make the user's task easier.

Most software engineering tasks during maintenance and evolution require understanding of various elements of the software system and also of data resulted from analysis. The main features of sv3D, namely, advanced user interactions and usage of the 3D space for visualization directly support the user in achieving a better understanding of analysis data. This process, in turn, directly supports a variety of tasks.

2. Support for User Interaction

We focus here on the types of user tasks and interactions that are supported by sv3D. While this is not directly related to solving/visualizing specific software engineering tasks it is prerequisite for a software visualization tool.

One of the strongest features of sv3D is its *overview* features. The underlying 2D visualization construct used in designing the poly cylinder containers is the pixel bar chart [5], which generalizes the concept used by SeeSoft. Thus sv3D can show large amounts of source code in one view just as the SeeSoft metaphor. Figure 1 shows a 3D overview of a small system with 30 C++ source code files and approximately 4000 lines of code. Each file is mapped to one container. Each container is made up of a number of poly cylinders. Each poly cylinder represents a line of source code. In this simple example shading (color) is used to represent the type of control structure a statement is in and the height is used to represent the nesting level. On top of each container the name of the associated file is visible. When manipulating a container in the 3D space, the name of the file always faces the camera.

sv3D supports *zooming* and *panning* at variable speeds. This is especially important because the visualization space can be quite large. Each container in the visualization can be manipulated individually (rotate, scale, translate). The user can also zoom in and out on the entire space. Files can be brought into a closer view and manipulated for a better camera angle.

At this point sv3D directly supports a number of *filtering* methods. Un-interesting units can be filtered through their attributes or by direct manipulation. Transparency is used to deal with both occlusion and filtering. The user can chose various degrees of transparency on each class of cylinder, based on their attributes (color, shape, or texture). With semi-transparency the global context is preserved and heuristic information is retained. Elevation can also be used to filter out un-interesting units by lifting them into separate levels.

Currently our emphasis with regard to *details-on-demand* is for simplicity. It is important to be able to support user interaction, therefore performance is

0-7695-1877-X/03 $17.00 © 2003 IEEE

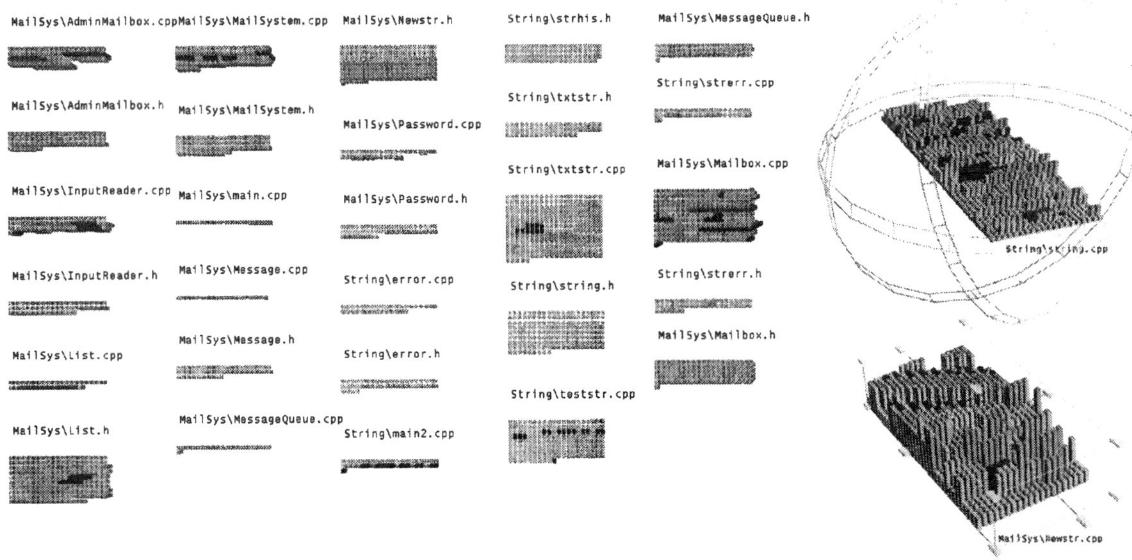

Figure 1. Overview in the 3D space of the mailing system. Color represents control structure and height represents nesting level. Two files have active manipulators (handle box for scaling on the left and track ball for rotating on the right). For a color view see www.sdml.cs.kent.edu

important. Two types of 3D manipulators (i.e., track ball and handle box) are available to the user to interact with the visualization. An information panel displays the data values on selected items.

The *relationships* between items are shown through the elements of the visualization that do not directly support representation of quantitative data (such as shape, texture, and position). The other elements (such as color and height) can also be used to show relationships. The 3D space allows arranging the containers in any place. We are investigating ways to use links between the 3D containers and arrange them in a graph layout.

The user can take snapshots of the current view to track a *history*. The current view is described by a scene graph, which is composed by the attributes of the camera and all 3D objects. These snapshots of the scene graph can be saved and reviewed. A sequence of such snapshots can be played, thus representing a path within the visualization. More than that, we intend to build into sv3D change tracking based on individual users.

3. Current and Future Work

sv3D is implemented in C++ and uses Qt for the user interfaces and Open Inventor for 3D rendering. See www.sdml.cs.kent.edu for additional information and downloads.

In the future versions of sv3D, position of the cylinder within a container can represent another type of information (or dimension). We need to define these visual attributes very carefully to ensure their usefulness. Containers in the 3D space can possibly be connected by edges to form a 3D graph. This will allow representation of hierarchical data and also diagrammatic visualizations (e.g., UML class diagrams). A number of user experiments to evaluate this system are being planned.

This work was supported in part by grants from the Office of Naval Research N00014-00-1-0769 and the National Science Foundation CCR-02-04175.

4. References

[1] Ball, T. and Eick, S., "Software Visualization in the Large", *Computer*, vol. 29, no. 4, April 1996, pp. 33-43.

[2] Eick, S., Steffen, J. L., and Summer, E. E., "Seesoft - A Tool For Visualizing Line Oriented Software Statistics", *IEEE TSE*, vol. 18, no. 11, November 1992, pp. 957-968.

[3] Griswold, W. G., Yuan, J. J., and Kato, Y., "Exploiting the Map Metaphor in a Tool for Software Evolution", in Proceedings of ICSE'01, Toronto, 2001, pp. 265-274.

[4] Jones, J. A., Harrold, M. J., and Stasko, J. T., "Visualization for Fault Localization", in Proceedings of ICSE 2001 Workshop on Software Visualization, Toronto, 2001, pp. 71-75.

[5] Keim, D. A., Hao, M. C., Dayal, U., and Hsu, M., "Pixel bar charts: a visualization technique for very large multi-attribute data sets", *Information Visualization*, vol. 1, no. 1, March 2002, pp. 20-34.

[6] Reiss, S. P., "Bee/Hive: A Software Visualization Back End", in Proceedings of ICSE 2001 Workshop on Software Visualization, Toronto, 2001, pp. 44-48.

DRT: A Tool for Design Recovery of Interactive Graphical Applications

http://www.cse.unsw.edu.au/~drt

Keith Chan, Annie Chen, Zhi Cong Leo Liang, Amir Michail, Minh Hoai Nguyen, Nicholas Seow
School of Computer Science and Engineering
University of New South Wales, Sydney, Australia, 2052
{kchan,anniec,leozc,amichail,mhng237,nickseow}@cse.unsw.edu.au

Abstract

Nowadays, the majority of productivity applications are interactive *and* graphical *in nature. In this demonstration, we explore the possibility of taking advantage of these two characteristics in a design recovery tool. Specifically, the fact that an application is interactive means that we can identify distinct execution bursts corresponding closely to "actions" performed by the user. The fact that the application is graphical means that we can describe those actions visually from a fragment of the application display itself. Combining these two ideas, we obtain an explicit mapping from high-level actions performed by a user (similar to use case scenarios/specification fragments) to their low-level implementation. This mapping can be used for design recovery of interactive graphical applications. We demonstrate our approach using LyX, a scientific word processor.*

1 Introduction

Almost all productivity applications in use today are *interactive* and *graphical* in nature. By interactive, we mean that the application takes user input (key presses, mouse clicks, etc.) and gives back an immediate response, then awaits for further input, and so on. This contrasts with older batch applications that simply take an input and terminate with the output. By graphical, we mean that the application shows its results in a graphical manner as with a word processor or web browser say. Graphical applications typically have a graphical user interface (GUI) incorporating menus and dialog boxes to facilitate interaction.

In this formal demonstration, we show a way to take advantage of these two characteristics – namely, the interactive and graphical natures of applications – in a design recovery tool. These two characteristics allow us to identify the key actions that are performed by the user in a demonstration of the application, much like use case scenarios, as well as the implementations of those actions. One can then search/browse a database of such actions and their implementations to understand the design of an application.

Intuitively speaking, an application that is interactive allows us to more easily identify actions performed by a user. Specifically, we can look for an "execution burst" that occurs when the user invokes an action. Moreover, the fact that the application is graphical gives us a way to describe the actions identified in this manner. Namely, we can describe an action by using a screenshot of the application display before and after the action is performed.

To illustrate our approach, we have built a tool, named DRT (for Design Recovery Tool), that works with most C/C++ X Window System applications irrespective of the GUI framework used. We shall demonstrate DRT using the scientific word processor LyX 1.2.1. LyX is a rather substantial X Window System application consisting of about 154,000 lines of C++ code.

Our approach is applicable to interactive graphical applications written in an event-driven programming style with alternation between user-initiated events and application responses. Most productivity software including word processors and spreadsheets is of this form. However, certain applications such as flight simulators and games are not, since the application proceeds even while the user is idle.

2 Searching and Browsing Actions

Given a collection of actions — done by others perhaps — it is possible to search/browse those actions to better understand the design of an application. Such an understanding can then be used to perform some maintenance task.

To search an action collection, one can use a *dynamic query*, which involves actually performing an action on a running application. In particular, we would run LyX under DRT and perform an action to see other similar actions

0-7695-1877-X/03 $17.00 © 2003 IEEE

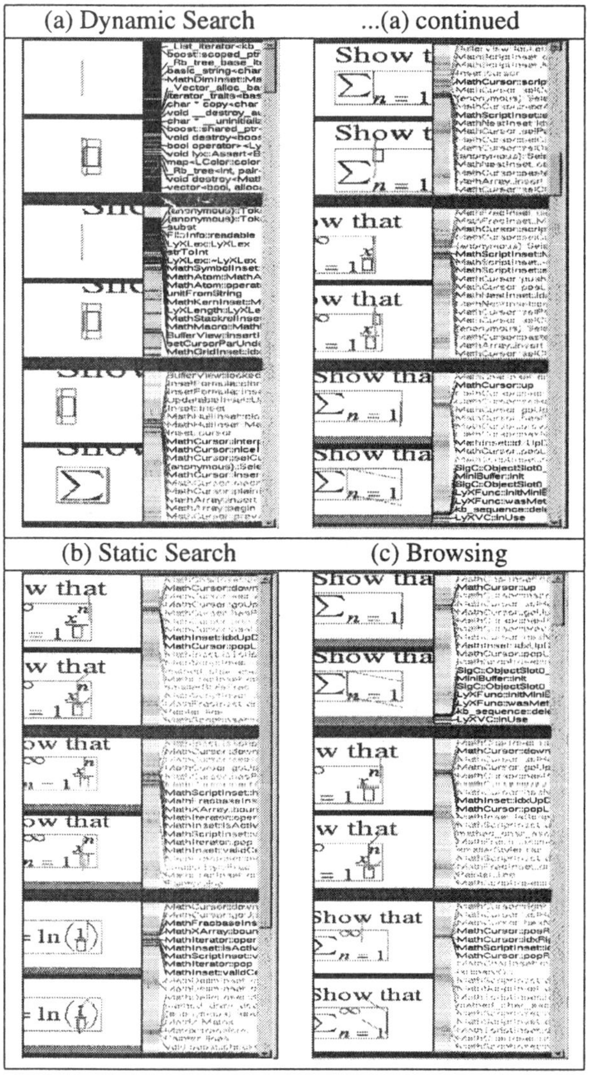

Figure 1. Searching/browsing LyX actions.

already in the action collection. Figure 1, (a) shows such a dynamic query where the user has entered math mode to use the formula editor. The query action is shown at the top followed by similar actions below ranked by similarity to the query action. By looking at the results of this dynamic query, we immediately see typical interactions with the formula editor described visually along with key functions responsible for implementing those interactions.

It is also possible to search by keyword (as with the "cursor down" query yielding the results in Figure 1, (b)) and to browse similar actions (as demonstrated by clicking on the last action in Figure 1, (a), which yields the results in the list of similar actions in Figure 1, (c)).

3 Related Work[1]

There has been related research done on selective tracing of atomic units of activity. For example, the drive-by analysis approach employed in the Jinsight tool [2] allows users to define their own notions of execution "burst" by specifying triggers, filters, requested threads, and burst ending criteria. Jinsight returns dynamic information from the burst only, thus allowing users to prune potentially very large amounts of trace data to only those items of interest. We also have a notion of an execution burst in the DRT tool, but we predefine it to automatically capture bursts that correspond closely to the user's notion of an action in an interactive graphical application. While Jinsight does share the generic idea of an execution burst with DRT, it does not take advantage of either the interactive or graphical aspects of applications to automatically find or describe such bursts.

However, there is an interaction-driven tool, LeNDI, for reverse engineering legacy interfaces [1, 3] that identifies the text screens encountered while an application is used and ways (e..g, keyboard input) for getting from one text screen to another. Such information can be helpful in migrating text-based legacy interfaces to newer platforms (e.g., GUIs or the web) or perhaps wrapping them for interaction with other systems. While it may seem that LeNDI is similar to DRT in the way it automatically extracts screens and transitions between them, LeNDI actually makes no connections to the corresponding burst code. The authors acknowledge that LeNDI does not shed much light on the application code [3]: "Clearly, if the end goal is to extend or modify the system functionality by modifying its current code, then such interaction-based understanding is insufficient because it provides only a model of the user tasks that the system supports and it completely ignores low-level design decisions such as data structures and algorithms."

References

[1] M. El-Ramly, P. Iglinski, E. Stroulia, P. Sorenson, and B. Matichuk. Modeling the system-user dialog using interaction traces. In *8th Working Conference on Reverse Engineering*, pages 208–217, 2001.

[2] W. D. Pauw, N. Mitchell, M. Robillard, G. Sevitsky, and H. Srinivan. Drive-by analysis of running programs. In *Proceedings for of ICSE 2001 Workshop on Software Visualization*, pages 17–22, 2001.

[3] E. Stroulia, M. El-Ramly, L. Kong, P. Sorenson, and B. Matichuk. Reverse engineering legacy interfaces: An interaction-driven approach. In *6th Working Conference on Reverse Engineering*, pages 292–301, 1999.

[1] For more related work, see our ICSE 2003 paper "Design Recovery of Interactive Graphical Applications" by Chan et al.

A Software Process Scheduling Simulator

Frank Padberg
Fakultät für Informatik
Universität Karlsruhe, Germany
padberg@ira.uka.de

1 Introduction

To cut development cost and meet tight deadlines in short staffed software projects, managers must optimize the project schedule. Scheduling a software project is extremely difficult, though, because the time needed to complete a software development activity is hard to estimate. Often, the completion of a task is delayed because of unanticipated rework caused by feedback between activities in the process.

In this research demo, we show how to use *process simulation* to support software project managers in scheduling. We present a discrete-time simulator tailored to software projects which explicitly takes a scheduling strategy as input. The simulator makes it easy to experiment with different scheduling strategies. It provides quick feedback about the impact that a particular strategy is likely to have on the progress and completion time of a project. A manager can compare different strategies and choose the strategy which he thinks is best for the next project's setting. In addition, a single step mode of the simulator allows a manager to view the dynamics of a project in detail.

The simulator is an implementation of the probabilistic scheduling model for software projects which we have presented earlier [6, 8]. The scheduling model describes the software process at a high level of abstraction: teams work on software components. Classical process phases such as coding or testing are not modeled explicitly. Still, the model captures much of the dynamics of software projects, representing varying staff skill levels, rework caused by design changes, component coupling, and changing task assignments.

Process simulation is an important technique to evaluate the impact of proposed process changes [5]. In particular, system dynamics simulations have been around for years, some of them addressing the problem of project staffing [1, 2]. By modeling individual teams and components as well as explicit task assignments, our model is much more fine-grained than system dynamics models. In addition, the particular way in which our model describes feedback between activities is novel in both software engineering and operations research [3, 7, 9].

2 Simulator

The simulator is written in the ModL language of the general-purpose simulation tool EXTEND [4]. The input data for the simulator are: the *base probabilities,* the *dependency degrees,* and the *scheduling strategy.*

For each team and component, there is a set of base probabilities which specify how likely it is that the team will need a prescribed amount of time to finish the component, report a high-level design problem, or finish reworking the component after a design change. In practice, the base probabilities must be computed from empirical data collected during previous projects.

The dependency degrees are a probabilistic measure for the strength of the coupling between the components and must be computed from the high-level design of the software. The stronger the coupling is the more likely it is that design changes which originate in one component will propagate to other components, thus leading to rework in these components.

The scheduling strategy (policy) specifies for each possible state of the project which team must work on which component. The scheduling strategy is implemented as a separate block in the simulator; thus, the strategy can be easily replaced. The state of the project includes the development time spent on each component so far, the project duration up to this point, the amount of rework left for each component, and the current task assignment. Plotters can be easily attached to the simulator to trace project state variables during the simulation.

Since the scheduling model is probabilistic, events will occur only with a certain probability at a particular point in time during the project. When the scheduling

0-7695-1877-X/03 $17.00 © 2003 IEEE

strategy is fixed, the simulator determines which step the project will take next by "throwing a dice". For example, some component might be finished in the next simulation step, or a design problem might get detected. The dice behaves according to the input probability distributions, taking into account the current state of the project.

Similarly, if a design change occurs in the project the simulator determines the set of those components which are affected by the change by throwing another dice which behaves according to the dependency degrees. This way, in each simulation run one possible full path of the project is simulated.

3 Example

As an example, we use the simulator to study the performance of different *list policies* for a small sample project. A list policy prescribes an order in which the components must be worked on; the next team to finish must work on the next component in the list. Since the completion time for an activity is subject to chance in the simulation, the actual schedule of the project depends on the progress of the project. List policies keep all teams busy during the whole project, which reflects management practice.

The sample project consists of four components and two teams. The base probabilities for the example are chosen in such a way that: team Two has a lower productivity than team One; components A and B have a similar complexity; components C and D require much more effort than components A and B. The dependency degrees are chosen to reflect that components C and D are strongly coupled.

In the sample project, using list policy ABCD will initially assign component A to team One and component B to team Two. Whichever team finishes its task first will work on component C. Finally, the next team to finish will work on component D.

We have implemented list scheduling as a single block where the list to be used is configurable. We ran 500 project simulations for each of the 24 possible list policies and observed the project completion time for each run. TABLE 1 shows the mean project completion time for each list policy.

The scheduling strategy has a significant impact on the completion time of the sample project. On average, list policy DCBA is best and CBAD is worst. List policy DCBA yields a schedule which on average is about 17 percent shorter than for CBAD.

From the histogram for the project completion time of each policy one can see that the *risk* for missing a tight deadline (say, 26) is much higher for CBAD than for DCBA. FIGURE 1 shows the histogram for policy

Table 1. Mean completion times for the sample project under different scheduling strategies.

policy	mean	policy	mean	policy	mean
ABCD	30.2	BCAD	30.1	CDAB	27.0
ABDC	26.4	BCDA	26.1	CDBA	26.9
ACBD	30.3	BDAC	27.8	DABC	29.5
ACDB	26.5	BDCA	26.6	DACB	26.2
ADBC	27.8	CABD	30.9	DBAC	29.4
ADCB	27.2	CADB	28.4	DBCA	26.9
BACD	29.1	CBAD	**31.2**	DCAB	26.4
BADC	27.2	CBDA	29.2	DCBA	**25.7**

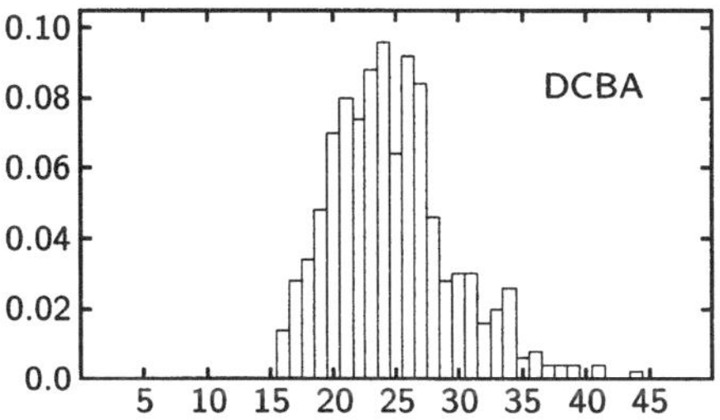

Figure 1. Histogram of the simulated project completion times for policy DCBA.

DCBA. Using the full simulation traces, it is possible to give a detailed analysis of the performance of the different policies by studying the actual task assignments and the rework in the simulated projects, see [8].

References

1. Abdel-Hamid, Madnick: *Software Project Dynamics*. Prentice Hall, 1991
2. Collofello e.a.: "A System Dynamics Simulator for Staffing Policies Decision Support", Annual Hawaii International Conference on System Sciences 31 (1998) 103–111
3. Derniame, Ali Kaba, Wastell: *Software Process: Principles, Methodology, and Technology*. Lecture Notes in Computer Science 1500, Springer 1999
4. EXTEND, http://www.imaginethatinc.com/
5. Kellner, Madachy, Raffo: "Software Process Simulation Modeling: Why? What? How?", Journal of Systems and Software 46 (1999) 91–105
6. Padberg: "Scheduling Software Projects to Minimize the Development Time and Cost with a Given Staff", Asia-Pacific Software Engineering Conference APSEC 8 (2001) 187–194
7. Padberg: "A Stochastic Scheduling Model for Software Projects", Dagstuhl Seminar on Scheduling in Computer and Manufacturing Systems, June 2002, Dagstuhl Report No. 343
8. Padberg: "Using Process Simulation to Compare Scheduling Strategies for Software Projects", Asia-Pacific Software Engineering Conference APSEC 9 (2002) 581–590
9. Weglarz: *Project Scheduling. Recent Models, Algorithms, and Applications*. Kluwer, 1999

CLIME: An Environment for Constrained Evolution

Demonstration Description

Steven P. Reiss, Christina M. Kennedy, Tom Wooldridge, Shriram Krishnamurthi
Department of Computer Science
Brown University
Providence, RI 02912
{spr,cmkenned,twooldri,sk}@cs.brown.edu

Abstract

We are building a software development environment that uses constraints to ensure the consistency of the different artifacts associated with software. This approach to software development makes the environment responsible for detecting most inconsistencies between software design, specifications, documentation, source code, and test cases. The environment provides facilities to ensure that these various dimensions remain consistent as the software is written and evolves. The environment works with the wide variety of artifacts typically associated with a large software system. It handles both the static and dynamic aspects of software. Moreover, it works incrementally so that consistency information is readily available to the developer as the system changes. The demonstration will show this environment and its capabilities.

1. Introduction

Software is multidimensional. Software systems consist of a wide variety of artifacts such as specifications, design diagrams and descriptions, source code, test cases, and documentation. Each of these dimensions describes only a limited part of the software — the actual system is properly the combination of all the artifacts.

Software evolution is the process whereby software changes to meet changing requirements, systems, or user needs. A major problem with software today is that the different artifacts of a software system tend to evolve at different rates. The result is that developers learn not to trust and thus not to use anything other than the source code, making software less reliable and much more difficult to understand and evolve.

We are in the process of developing a software development environment that addresses these issues using a constraint-based mechanism. The environment defines and analyzes the consistency of constraints on the software system, including ones that span different dimensions.

This environment provides several capabilities. First, it automatically extracts relevant information from each of the software artifacts. Second, the environment stores and maintains this information in a database, doing incremental updates automatically as the software changes. Third, the environment uses this information along with a description of the types of constraints to be generated to build the complete set of constraints for the software system. Fourth, it uses the information in the database to incrementally test the validity of these constraints. Finally, it provides facilities for presenting the results of these tests to the developers so that they may take steps to resolve inconsistencies.

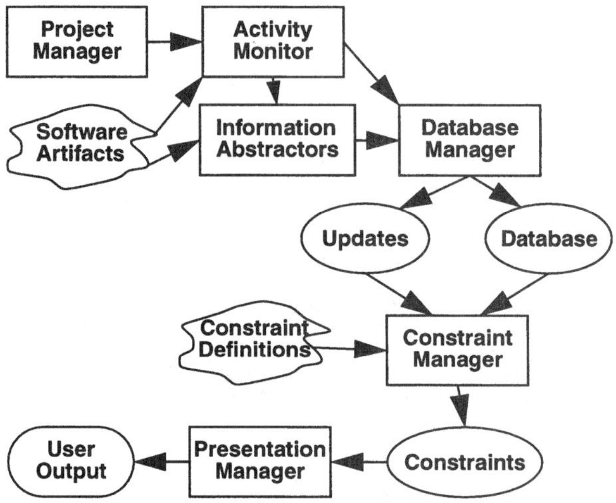

FIGURE 1. The architecture of the environment.

2. Environment Architecture

The overall environment consists of the components shown in Figure 1[1]. The components can be broken into two parts: the first part manages extracting the necessary information from the source artifacts while the second part uses this information to find, update, and display information about the constraints.

The *Project Manager* determines what files are part of the current project. This information is used by the *Activity Monitor* which determines when the files change, and then uses appropriate *Information Abstractors* to get relevant data about the corresponding software artifacts. This information is passed to the *Database Manager* which first determines what has actually changed and then updates the database according to those changes. We currently handle

1. Reiss, Steven P. "Constraining Software Evolution", *Proc. Intl. Conf. on Software Maintenance*, October, 2002, pp. 162-171.

0-7695-1877-X/03 $17.00 © 2003 IEEE

source files, UML diagrams, style rules, design patterns, semantic information, test cases, and history information in this first part of the system.

The *Constraint Manager* is based on metaconstraints of the form $\forall(x \in S)\varphi(x)\Theta(x)$. Here S is a relation in the database and x represents a tuple of that relation, φ(x) indicates the conditions under which the constraint is applicable, and Θ(x) is a qualified predicate the specifies the conditions the constraint must meet. It is passed the set of items that change in the database by the database manager, and uses the metaconstraints to generate appropriate SQL queries to create, update, and check the set of constraints that should be imposed on the system. This is done incrementally and can generally be done in background as the system changes.

Finally, the set of constraints are displayed to the user though the *Presentation Manager.* This tool gives the user the option of prioritizing the constraints and organizing the constraints as well as providing an understanding of what each constraint means and to what it applies.

3. Consistency Checking

The above architecture can be used to check a broad range of consistency conditions among software artifacts. The current conditions that are checked include:

- Constraints from UML class diagrams on the source code that indicate that every class has a corresponding source class, that every interface matches a source interface, that class and interface generalizations match the actual class hierarchy, that UML operations correspond to methods, that UML attributes correspond to fields, and that UML associations are reflected in the source.
- Constraints from the source code on UML class diagrams that ensure that all public classes and interfaces appear in the UML model, that all generalizations among public classes and interfaces are reflected by UML generalizations, that public methods and fields of public classes are reflected in the UML, and the associations based on fields are reported in the UML.
- The sequence of calls in a UML interaction diagram is realizable by the code.
- Constraints from test cases on the source code that ensure that a test case that covers a particular method has been run since the method was last modified.
- Constraints from documentation on the source code that ensure that any specification of parameters, see also links, and throws clauses correspond to the current source code.
- Constraints from the source code on documentation that ensure that all public methods of public classes or interfaces are documented.
- Naming conventions for classes, interfaces, methods, fields, local variables and constants.
- Pattern constraints for the Facade and Singleton patterns.
- Language usage conventions including the fact the all parameters not starting with an underscore are actually used, that all fields are read and written at least once, that all methods are called at least once, and that data fields are either private or protected.
- Test consistency checking that ensure that all procedures are covered by at least one test case which has been run since the procedure was last changed.
- Dynamic specifications of class usage such as Java Iterators must always call *hasNext* before calling *next* and files that are opened must be closed.
- Configuration management checking to ensure that all files that are checked in through CVS have a corresponding log message.

4. Experience

We have been using our constraint-based environment both on itself and for a small set of development projects, mainly to validate that the underlying systems work and that the approach is a viable one.

The system is currently used in its own development (40,000 lines of Java plus about 250,000 lines of external Java libraries). Our experience has been that we did not even notice when the updates were occurring. Moreover, periodic checks of the violated constraints showed them to be accurate and helpful in finding potential (or in some cases real) problems with the system. This experiment also validated our approach to incremental update of both the abstraction information and the constraints.

Finally, we ran experiments to see how and whether the approach can scale to larger systems. Specifically, we defined a project for the SOOT package for Java code analysis and optimization and generated the set of abstraction information and constraints. SOOT has approximately 200,000 lines of Java source The generated database here is about 140Mb in size and has about 15,000 constraints. While the initial setup of this database took about an hour, incremental updates have been extremely fast, i.e. well under a minute.

5. Demonstration

We will demonstrate various aspects of the system. The demonstration will take the viewer through the definition of a constraint through to seeing where and how the constraint is violated in the system. In doing this we will show how the system does incremental constraint analysis and how it is able to pinpoint the source of violations.

The demonstration will show both static and dynamic constraints, show our modified test coverage tool, and illustrate how both the standalone and the Eclipse-based user interface can be used.

Finally, the demonstration will illustrate the performance of the environment both in terms of setting up the initial set of constraints and for doing incremental update of that set.

JIVE: Visualizing Java in Action

Demonstration Description

Steven P. Reiss
Department of Computer Science
Brown University
Providence, RI 02912-1910
401-863-7641, FAX: 401-863-7657
spr@cs.brown.edu

Abstract

Dynamic software visualization should provide a programmer with insights as to what the program is doing. Most current dynamic visualizations either use program traces to show information about prior runs, slow the program down substantially, show only minimal information, or force the programmer to indicate when to turn visualizations on or off. We have developed a dynamic Java visualizer that provides a view of a program in action with low enough overhead that it can be used almost all the time by programmers to understand what their program is doing while it is doing it.

1. Introduction

Software visualization has not been particularly successful for program understanding. Visualizations that look at the static aspects of a software system are only able to provide limited insights and say nothing about the important and more complex dynamic behavior of the system. Dynamic visualizations have been expensive to use because they require the programmer to run the program in an environment that produces the appropriate trace data, generally slowing program execution by an order of magnitude or worse. The result is that programmers generally don't bother using visualizations even if they would be helpful.

We wanted to provide a dynamic visualization environment that could actually be used for real running programs. Such an environment would provide programmers with the information they needed to understand what their program was doing as it was doing it. The environment had to be simple to use, had to minimize the overhead involved with the visualization, had to work with arbitrary programs, and had to provide immediate feedback to the programmer. Moreover, the resultant system had to be not only informative but also entertaining — we wanted programers to use visualization just because it was fun.

A system meeting these requirements would provide a first step toward making visualizations both useful and used. Moreover, it would demonstrate that software visualization could be an everyday thing rather than something only to be used when problems were so severe that nothing else worked.

2. Getting Java Trace Data

The key to a successful real-time dynamic visualization system is obtaining appropriate trace data with minimal overhead.

Rather than attempt to show everything that the program was doing, we break the execution into intervals and then display a summary of what the program did during each interval. This let us cut down substantially on the amount of data that had to be conveyed from the application to the visualization tool and made sense since the visualization tool would have to report summary information in any case.

The information we provide for each interval includes:

- What classes were executing.
- The number of calls to or within each class.
- The number of synchronization calls for each class.
- What was being allocated.
- What was being deallocated.
- What threads are in the program.
- The state of each thread.
- The number of blocks caused by each thread.

This information is obtained by patching the user's program and associated libraries and system files using IBM's JikesBT byte code package.

The patching is kept to a minimum by dividing the application's classes into three categories. Detailed classes are those directly in the user's code. For these we provide information that considers all methods and details any nested classes for separate visualization. Library classes, on the other hand, are grouped into packages and we only generate events for the initial entry into the library. Finally, classes that are neither detailed nor library are treated at an intermediate level of granularity where nested classes are merged with their parent and we only consider public methods.

3. Box Display Visualization

Once the data is available, we needed to have a visualization for the data. In particular we wanted a visualization that could show a large number of objects (e.g. all the relevant classes and packages or all the application's threads) and several pieces of information about each object (e.g.

0-7695-1877-X/03 $17.00 © 2003 IEEE

for a class, the number of entries, the number of synchronization calls, the number of allocations, and the number of allocations by methods in this class; for a thread, the time spent in each of the possible states) in a small display area. We also needed something that was simple and fast since we wanted the visualization to run in real time.

We settled on what we call a box display. Here each class or thread is represented as a box on the display. Within the box we can display one or more colored rectangles. The various statistics can be reflected visually in the vertical and horizontal sizes of the colored display, in the color (hue, saturation and intensity as separate items) of the displayed region, or through textures where the density of the texture is used to represent the corresponding statistic.

For the class display, we typically display five simultaneous values. First, the height of the rectangle is used to indicate the number of calls. Second the width of the rectangle is used to represent the number of allocations by methods of the class. Third, the hue of the rectangle is used to represent the number of allocations of objects of the given class. Fourth, the saturation of the rectangle is used as a binary indicator as to whether the class was used at all during the interval. Finally, the brightness of the box is used to represent the number of synchronization events on objects of this class.

For threads, we create a stack of color rectangles inside each box. Here we vary the height of each rectangle based on the percent of time within the interval the thread is in the corresponding state and the width of each rectangle as the percent of time in this state represented by the given thread. The hue then is used to denote the actual thread state and saturation is used to indicate the number of blocks on this thread.

All of these parameters can be changed dynamically by the user through a dialog box. Moreover, the user can choose, for each of the count statistics, whether to use a linear or a log scale.

4. Running the Visualizer

The actual visualization window is divided into two panes as shown in Figure 1. The left half of the figure show class and package usage information while the right half shows the thread data.

Figure 1 shows the visualizer on an application that uses Java's Swing package. Here one can see the state of the various threads in the application and Swing, see what is being allocated (red), seeing what is doing the allocations (the wide rectangles), see what is actively running. In addition, one can quickly detect which threads are running (green for normal, yellow for synchronized), and what the remaining threads are waiting or blocking for.

The dynamic visualizer works in two different modes. It defaults to showing the current execution as it is happening. Alternatively, the visualizer can be used as a browser over the execution, either as it is happening, or more commonly, after the fact. The scroll bar on the bottom of the window is used to let the user scroll over time for the execution. The display updates dynamically as the user scrolls. This facility is useful for going back and viewing transient events and getting a better understanding of the application's execution. The dynamic display also can be viewed either incrementally or by looking at totals.

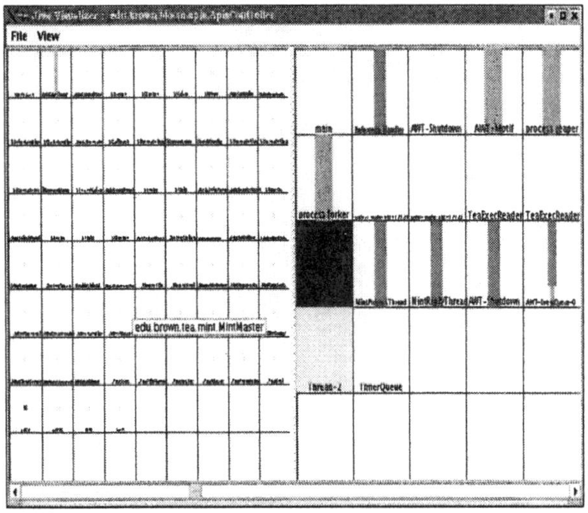

FIGURE 1. Dynamic view of a Java program using Swing.

5. Experience

While not perfect, our efforts show that dynamic visualization of real applications is possible and may be practical as a default way of running the application. The program runs with a slowdown of a factor typically between 2 and 3 depending on the structure of the application. Given the wide performance range of today's machines, this seems to be quite acceptable.

We have used the visualization tool on a wide variety of Java programs ranging from simple student programs, to complex single threaded applications (a static checker), to user-interface based applications, to a multithreaded web crawler. We have found that it provides useful information and that watching it makes one think more about what the application is actually doing. For example, we have noted that the visualization makes it obvious when the application goes through various phases. Each phase has its own distinctive set of active nodes, it is easy to tell the phases apart, and the phase transitions are obvious.

6. Demonstration

We will demonstrate the various capabilities of this system. The demonstration would involve running a variety of applications and viewing and interpreting the displays as the systems were running. During the demonstration we would illustrate how the system can be used effectively for software understanding and would illustrate its various features and capabilities.

FEAT
A Tool for Locating, Describing, and Analyzing Concerns in Source Code

Martin P. Robillard and Gail C. Murphy
University of British Columbia
Department of Computer Science
201-2366 Main Mall, Vancouver, BC
Canada, V6T 1Z4
{mrobilla,murphy}@cs.ubc.ca

1 Introduction

Developers working on existing programs repeatedly have to address concerns, or aspects, that are not well modularized in the source code comprising a system. In such cases, a developer has to first locate the implementation of the concern in the source code comprising the system, and then document the concern sufficiently to be able to understand it and perform the actual change task.

Several approaches are available to help software developers locate and manage scattered concern code. Lexical searching tools, such as grep [1], code browsers, such as the Smalltalk integrated development environment [3], cross-reference databases, such as CIA [2], and slicers [9], can each help a developer identify relevant points in the code and can help elicit the relationships between the different parts of a program. Alternatively, a developer may be able to leverage the identification of the change from a previous modification using version differencing in a source code repository. All of these tools produce a similar result: the developer is presented with the lines of source code contributing to the concern in the system. This ad hoc, source code-intensive representation of concerns is difficult to use as the basis for reasoning about and analyzing concerns for the purpose of software evolution.

To address the problem of effectively capturing knowledge about the implementation of a concern in source code, we have investigated the possibility of describing concerns as a graphs of relations between program elements. We have named this representation Concern Graph [7, 8]. We have developed a tool, called FEAT [6], to support building and analyzing Concern Graphs. Specifically, FEAT supports locating, describing, and analyzing the code implementing a one or more concerns in a Java system.

2 The FEAT Tool

FEAT is developed as a plugin for the Eclipse Platform [5], an integrated software development environment with a plugin architecture supporting the addition of functionality (Figure 1, last page).

With the FEAT plugin activated, users of Eclipse can use the integrated development environment as usual, to browse and modify code, perform searches, etc. However, if a user desires to create a concern representation, the FEAT Perspective can be activated and a concern representation created. At this point, a *concern* in FEAT is simply a named container for a fragment of a program which is of interest to a user. Any class, method, or field in a project can then be moved to the FEAT Perspective.

Elements in the FEAT Perspective can be analyzed for their dependencies to other elements in the source code. Any element or relations of interest to a user can be stored as part of a concern. The source code corresponding to any element or relation can also be viewed in code viewer (bottom window).

Concerns descriptions can be used to systematically analyze the code for a concern, or to compare two different concern descriptions. In both cases, FEAT automatically detects relations between elements in concerns, and presents the relations visually to the users.

The architecture of FEAT consists in three components: a *model* component providing operation on concerns and ensuring the consistency of the concern description, an Java bytecode *analyzer* component, built on top of IBM's Jikes Bytecode Toolkit [4], which provides relations between different elements in a program, and a *GUI* component which ties the tool into the Eclipse Platform.

We have successfully used an earlier prototype of the FEAT tool to locate, describe, and analyze concerns for the purpose of software evolution in 4 academic case stud-

0-7695-1877-X/03 $17.00 © 2003 IEEE

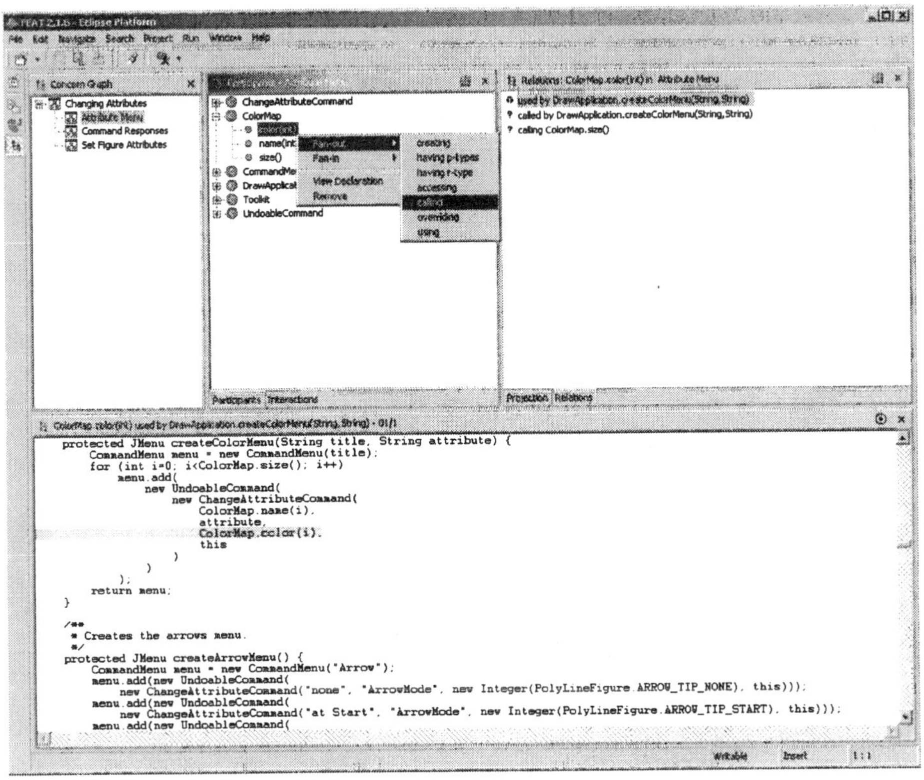

Figure 1. The FEAT tool.

ies [8], including a scalability study involving a large industrial code base. The current version of the tool is presently being used in a new series of user studies.

3 Description of the Demonstration

The demonstration will consist in performing part of a change task on a Java program with the help of FEAT. First, we will use FEAT to locate and analyze a set of concerns relevant to the change task. Specifically, we will show how, by visually navigating structural program dependencies through the tool's graphical interface, we can rapidly locate the code implementing a concern, and store the result as an abstract representation consisting of building blocks that are easy to manipulate and query. We will then show how the representation of the sample concern supported by FEAT can be used to investigate the relationships between the captured concern and the base code, between the different parts of the concern itself, and between different concern representations. Finally, we will show how FEAT can be used to keep track of the actual source code implementing the concern.

References

[1] A. V. Aho. Pattern matching in strings. In R. V. Book, editor, *Formal Language Theory: Perspectives and Open Problems*, pages 325–347, New York, 1980. Academic Press.

[2] Y.-F. Chen, M. Y. Nishimoto, and C. Ramamoorthy. The C information abstraction system. *IEEE Transactions on Software Engineering*, 16(3):325–334, March 1990.

[3] A. Goldberg. *Smalltalk-80: The Interactive Programming Environment*. Addison-Wesley, 1984.

[4] The Jikes bytecode toolkit. IBM, March 2000. http://www.alphaworks.ibm.com/tech/jikesbt.

[5] Object Technology International, Inc. Eclipse platform technical overview. White Paper, July 2001.

[6] M. P. Robillard. The FEAT Eclipse Plugin: A tool for locating, describing, and analyzing concerns in source code. http://www.cs.ubc.ca/~mrobilla/feat2.

[7] M. P. Robillard and G. C. Murphy. Capturing concern descriptions during program navigation. Position paper for the OOPSLA 2002 Workshop on Tool Support for Aspect oriented Software Development, November 2002.

[8] M. P. Robillard and G. C. Murphy. Concern Graphs: Finding and describing concerns using structural program dependencies. In *Proceedings of the 24th International Conference on Software Engineering*, May 2002.

[9] M. Weiser. Program slicing. *IEEE Transactions on Software Engineering*, 10(4):352–357, July 1984.

Embedded Architect: A Tool for Early Performance Evaluation of Embedded Software

Jeffry T Russell, Margarida F Jacome
Department of Electrical and Computer Engineering
University of Texas at Austin
Austin, TX 78712 USA
jeffry@mail.utexas.edu, jacome@ece.utexas.edu

Abstract

Embedded Architect is a design automation tool that embodies a static performance evaluation technique to support early, architecture-level design space exploration for component-based embedded systems. A static control flow characterization, called an evaluation scenario, is specified based on an incremental refinement of software source code, from which a pseudo-trace of operations is generated. In combination with architecture mapping and several component parameters, a software performance metric is estimated.

The novel contribution is the implementation of a tool that automates specification of an evaluation scenario, which sets the context for a rapid performance evaluation of distinct candidate architectures.

1. Introduction

The Embedded Architect design automation tool supports design space exploration for component-based, embedded systems. Specifically, it assists an experienced designer in the specification of control paths from software source code, which serve as the context for a performance evaluation. Embedded Architect targets architecture-level design of a class of embedded systems for which performance is a figure of merit, as opposed to real-time embedded systems for which performance constraints must be satisfied for proper system operation.

A performance analysis involving real time constraints requires an examination of all functional paths. In contrast, for the class of embedded systems contemplated, the designer faces the challenge of identifying characteristic functional paths to serve as the context for a performance evaluation, called *evaluation scenarios*. Our previous work proposed a performance evaluation technique based on the evaluation scenario to support a rapid, comparative assessment of embedded system architectures [3].

Component-based designs are beneficial in terms of shorter development cycles, reduced cost, and improved maintainability [2][4]. A component-based embedded system favors an architecture consisting of predefined subsystems, "packaged" as components, rather than custom specified subsystems. Hardware components such as CPUs or memories provide structural resources, and software components provide pure functionality.

For component-based embedded systems, the need to identify a subset of functionality for a performance evaluation is motivated by two primary issues. First, due to economy of scale, components often package functionality that goes unused in a final design [1]. Second, only a small subset of the useful functionality is considered for a performance evaluation. This is because components used in real designs have a functional description that is very complex, mostly arising from error checking, exception handling, initialization, or other "housekeeping" details. A "typical case" control flow through the specification serves as the basis for a performance evaluation.

The Embedded Architect tool demonstrates an implementation of our research into early, architecture-level design automation for component-based embedded systems. The novel contribution is automation of the evaluation scenario specification introduced in [3].

2. Approach

The evaluation scenario is interactively defined by identifying control flows in the system functionality that correspond to a representative system behavior; a challenging task that is assisted by an extended form of structural analysis that can be applied simultaneously to software and hardware components. An estimated trace is statically generated, and pertinent architecture features are used to estimate the execution time of this pseudo-trace.

2.1 Architecture Model

An *architecture* is an abstract representation of a design that is a configuration of subsystems, organized into two topologies. The *functional architecture* specifies a set of concurrent, sequential processes using subsystems to specify functionality and connections to indicate flow of control. The functional subsystems are specified with an imperative source code language that is predominantly software, but also includes hardware. The underlying formalism used to analyze software is a control flow graph (CFG) of primitive *operations*.

The *structural architecture* consists of subsystems that support execution of operations and connections that represent communication paths. Operations from the functional architecture are *mapped* to execution and storage resources in the structural architecture.

0-7695-1877-X/03 $17.00 © 2003 IEEE

A *component* is hardware or software whose specification is fixed, though possibly parameterized. A component represents some portion of an architecture, ranging from a single subsystem to a frozen portion of the configuration consisting of several subsystems and connections.

2.2 Design Space Exploration

Design space exploration (DSE) research can be classified as addressing aspects of representation, estimation, and exploration algorithms. As shown to the right, a DSE framework generates candidate architectures using a library of components. Each candidate is evaluated based on a set of metrics that may guide future architecture generation. Our Embedded Architect tool supports an evaluator in an existing framework by providing a rapid estimate of a performance metric.

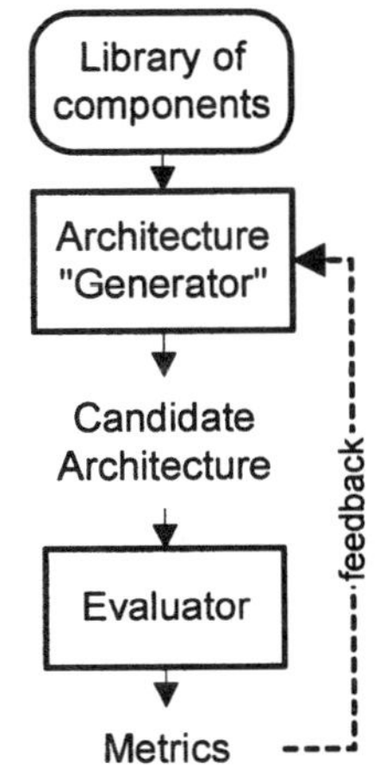

Figure 1. DSE flow

2.3 Scenario Specification

Intuitively, an evaluation scenario corresponds to a walk through the collection of CFGs that expresses the functional architecture. The flow to specify a scenario is shown in Figure 2, which begins with a set of CFGs to analyze and the start/end nodes of the scenario. To define a scenario, the designer needs to constrain all control operation predicates. An initial pruning cycle analyzes the control dependences between the start and end nodes and extracts predicate constraints. This begins an automatic cycle in which constraints are applied, nodes are pruned from the CFG, and data flow facts are propagated.

If the data flow fact propagation results in new constraints on any control operations, then subsequent automatic cycles continue until no new constraints are found. If there are any control operations left to constrain, a manual constraint cycle begins in which the designer provides a constraint. Using this constraint, more automatic constraint cycles are attempted, continuing until all predicates are constrained.

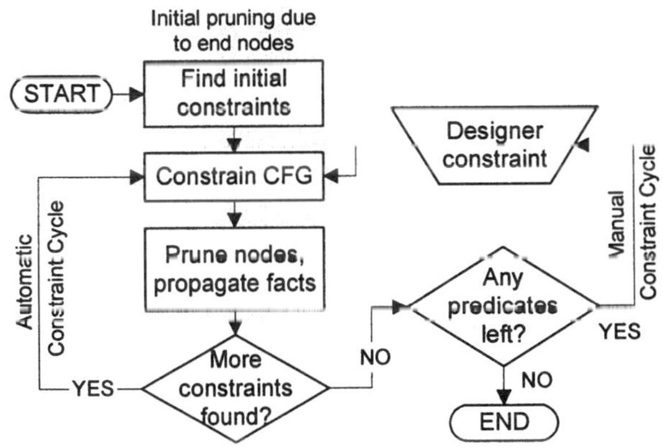

Figure 2. Flow to specify evaluation scenario.

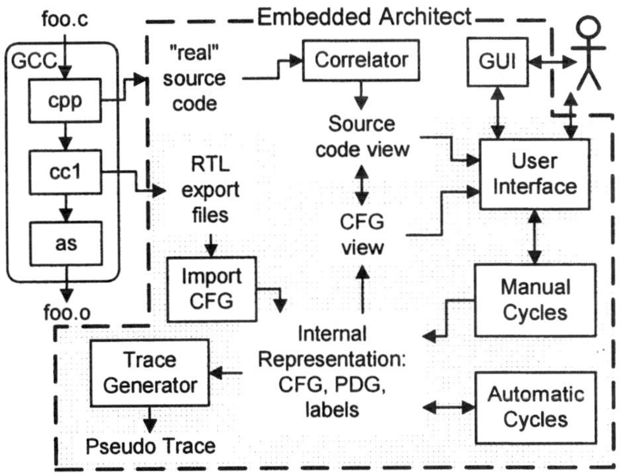

Figure 3. Embedded Architect implementation.

3. Implementation of Embedded Architect

An overview of the tool is shown in Figure 3. To provide for a comparison of performance estimates to code executing on real hardware, the starting point is the gcc compiler, as it can produce production quality code for a variety of processor architectures. The compiler was instrumented to export a CFG, which is imported into Embedded Architect. The dashed line represents Embedded Architect, and the shaded portion indicates the focus of the research prototype.

4. Future Work

Embedded Architect analyzes a candidate architecture and eventually leads to a performance estimate. In addition to comparing the fidelity of the estimates, the efficacy of the scenario specification is demonstrated based on the number of control operation nodes eliminated due to pruning (more is better), the number of constraints found automatically from propagation of data flow facts (more is better), and the number of manual constraints supplied by the designer (fewer is better).

5. References

[1] V. Basili, B. Boehm, COTS-Based Systems Top 10 List, *Computer*, v 34, n 5, May 2001, pp 91-93

[2] U. Rastofer, F. Bellosa, Component-based software engineering for distributed embedded real-time systems, *IEEE Proc.-Software*, v 148, n 3, June 2001

[3] J. Russell, M. Jacome, Scenario-Based Software Characterization as a Contingency to Traditional Program Profiling, *CASES '02*, Grenoble, France, Oct. 2002

[4] M. Sparling, Lessons learned through six years of component-based development, *Comm. ACM*, v43, n10, Oct 2000

An Effective Layout Adaptation Technique for a Graphical Modeling Tool

Christian Seybold, Martin Glinz, Silvio Meier, Nancy Merlo-Schett
Institut für Informatik
Universität Zürich
CH-8057 Zurich, Switzerland
{seybold | glinz | smeier | schett}@ifi.unizh.ch

Abstract

Editing graphic models always entails layout problems. Inserting and deleting items requires tedious manual work for shifting existing items and rearranging the diagram layout. Hence, techniques that automatically expand a diagram when space is required for insertion and contract it when free space becomes avaliable are highly desirable.

Existing layout generation algorithms are no good solution for that problem: they may completely rearrange a diagram after an editing operation, while users want to preserve the overall visual appearance of a diagram.

We have developed a technique which automatically expands or contracts a diagram layout when items are inserted or removed while preserving its overall shape, i.e. the positions of the items relative to each other. Our technique has been implemented in a prototype tool. We are using it not just for simplifying editing, but primarily for implementing an aspect-oriented visualization concept.

1. Introduction

With conventional graphical modeling tools, editing a diagram always entails layout problems. When inserting an element into an existing diagram, the space required for the new element has to be created manually by shifting existing elements of the diagram apart. On the other hand, removing elements from a diagram yields empty space. Compacting the resulting diagram again has to be done manually.

Alternatively, automatic layout generation algorithms could be employed. However, applying such algorithms can result in a complete rearrangement of the diagram layout, thus destroying the so-called secondary notation, i.e. the positioning of the diagram elements relative to each other. As the secondary notation bears important clues for remembering and comprehending the meaning of a diagram, users typically want to preserve the secondary notation when modifying a diagram.

We have developed a layout adaptation technique which automatically expands or contracts a diagram layout when elements are inserted or removed while preserving the secondary notation.

Such a technique is not only convenient for inserting or deleting elements. It is a key prerequisite for implementing aspect-oriented visualization techniques. Assume a diagram that visualizes some basic elements of a model. When we want to display a particular aspect, the elements representing this aspect have to be woven (i.e. inserted) into the diagram. On the other hand, when hiding an aspect from a diagram, all elements belonging to this aspect have to be removed and the resulting diagram has to be compacted.

We use this adaptation technique in a tool for visualizing models written in ADORA [1]. ADORA is a modeling language which—in contrast to UML—integrates all modeling aspects (structure, behavior...) into one coherent model. To prevent the user being drowned in a flood of information, ADORA employs an aspect-oriented visualization concept: starting from a base view displaying a hierarchy of objects only, a structure aspect, a behavior aspect, etc. can be woven into the base view, resulting in a structure view, a behavior view, etc. Any combinations of aspects are possible.

2. An example

As an example, we describe the process of hiding aspects from an ADORA model of a heating control system. Fig. 1 shows a base view combined with the structure, behavior and user aspects. In Fig. 2, the latter two aspects have been hidden. Hiding these aspects means that the scenario *Manage Local Room Temperature* (represented as an oval) and all states and state transitions (represented as rectangles with rounded corners and as arrows, respectively) have to be removed from the diagram. Please note how the tool has automatically compacted the resulting diagram while preserving the secondary notation, i.e. the positions of the remaining objects relative to each other.

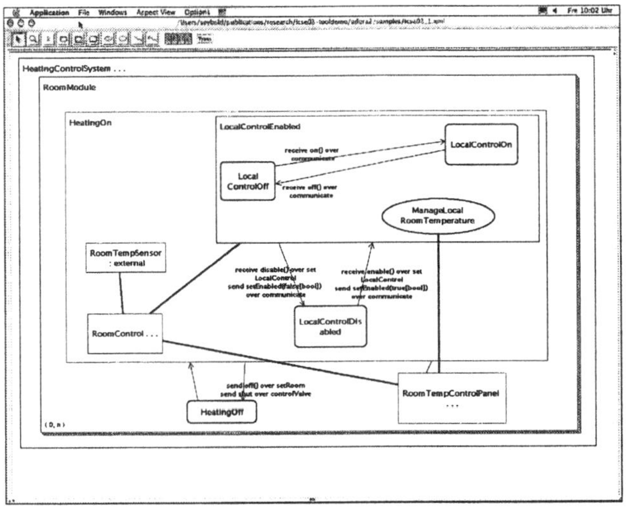

Figure 1. Base view woven with structure, user interaction and behavior aspects.

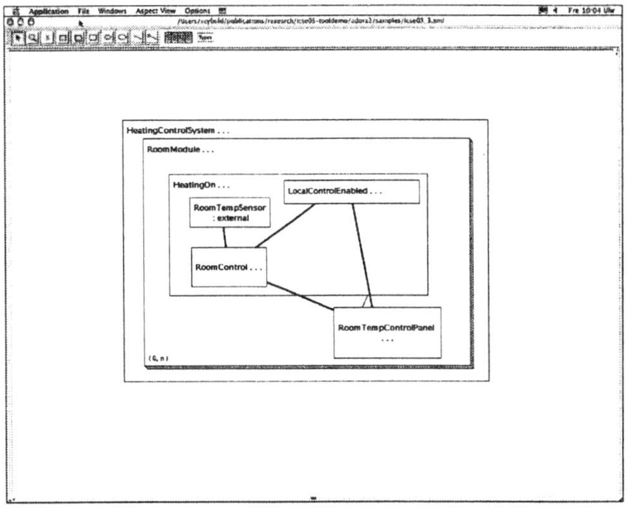

Figure 2. Contracted diagram after hiding the user interaction and behavior aspects.

3. Layout adaptation algorithm

In this section we sketch our algorithm. The details may be found in [4]. Below we describe the algorithm for compacting a diagram after removing items.

For simplicity, we consider removing a single object X and assume that all diagram items are rectangles. As we support a hierarchical modeling language, X is always embedded in a parent object P (root is of no interest here). Graphically spoken, P is a container for all its child objects, including X. Now let Z be the smallest bounding box containing all child objects of P before—and Z' after—X was removed. The idea is to keep the four horizontal and vertical distances from Z and Z' to the corresponding sides of P invariant. The algorithm works in four basic steps:

1. Shrink object X concentrically to a rectangle of zero size.
2. Shift all objects within P radially towards the center about half the size X was. Stop shifting objects when a minimum distance between them is reached (thus we avoid touching or overlapping objects). Their new positions define Z'.
3. Adjust the shape of P to the difference between Z and Z'.
4. Recursively apply the first three steps as long as P changes and in turn is contained in another parent object.

For expanding a diagram prior to inserting an item into it, we apply these steps in the same order, but in the reverse way (expanding instead of shrinking). Obviously, we can generalize this algorithm such that it handles removing or inserting a set of items with arbitrary convex shapes.

4. Conclusions

Achievements. We have developed an algorithmic technique that automatically adapts the layout of a diagram when elements are inserted or removed while preserving the secondary notation of the diagram (i.e. the relative positions of the elements). Our technique makes diagram editing considerably more comfortable for the user. Furthermore, it makes aspect-oriented visualization feasible for interactive tools. We consider this to be our main achievement.

Related work. We are not aware of any other modeling tool using similar techniques. Work has been done by others on automatic layout generation under constraints, where constraints can be used to specify structure-preserving layout adaptation [2], or on preserving a generated structure when solving overlappings [3].

State of work. The work reported here is part of a more general effort for developing a novel visualization concept for hierarchically structured models. Previously, we have developed context-preserving zooming algorithms for such models. All algorithms have been implemented and tested in our prototype tool for ADORA. We plan to fine-tune the algorithms and to conduct a validation study.

References

[1] M. Glinz, S. Berner, and S. Joos. Object-oriented modeling with ADORA. *Information Systems*, 27(6):425–444, 2002.

[2] W. H. Graf and S. Neurohr. Constraint-based layout in visual program design. In *Proceedings of the 11th International IEEE Symposium on Visual Languages (VL'95)*, 1995.

[3] W. Lai and P. Eades. Removing edge-node intersections in drawings of graphs. *Information Processing Letters*, 81:105–110, 2002.

[4] M. Marty. Analyse und Erweiterung von Algorithmen zur logischen Navigation in ADORA-Modellen [Analysis and extension of algorithms for logical navigation in ADORA models (in German)]. Diploma Thesis, University of Zurich, 2002.

Java Program Analysis Projects in Osaka University: Aspect-Based Slicing System ADAS and Ranked-Component Search System SPARS-J

Reishi Yokomori †, Takashi Ishio †, Tetsuo Yamamoto ††,
Makoto Matsushita †, Shinji Kusumoto † and Katsuro Inoue †
† Graduate School of Information Science and Technology, Osaka University
1-3 Machikaneyama, Toyonaka, Osaka 560-8531, Japan
†† Japan Science and Technology Corporation, 4-1-8, Honmachi,
Kawaguchi, Saitama 332-8531, Japan
{yokomori, t-isio, t-yamamt, matusita, kusumoto, inoue}@ist.osaka-u.ac.jp

Abstract

In our research demonstration, we show two development support systems for Java programs. One is an Aspect-oriented Dynamic Analysis and Slice calculation system named ADAS, and another is a Software Product archiving, Analyzing, and Retrieving System for Java named SPARS-J.

1. Introduction

In our research demonstration, we will show two types of development support systems for Java programs. The one is a slicing system for Java programs named ADAS(Aspect-oriented Dynamic Analysis and Slice calculation system), and another is a retrieval system for Java components named SPARS-J(Software Product archiving, Analyzing, and Retrieving System for Java). ADAS supports debugging tasks for Java programs based on program slicing technique, and SPARS-J provides a retrieval result with the evaluation value based on actual use relations among components.

2 Aspect-oriented Dynamic Analysis and Slice Calculation System: ADAS

ADAS is a tool, which aids debugging tasks based on program slicing technique.

Program slicing has been proposed to localize faults efficiently in the program[7]. By definition, slicing is a technique which extracts all statements that possibly affect some set of variables in the program. The set of all extracted statements is called a slice.

We have been extended the program slicing to DC slicing, using dynamic data dependence information to calculate accurate slices with lightweight costs [6].

In process of DC slice calculation, it is an important issue how to analyze dynamic data dependence. In the past research, such function have not been encapsulated in a single module. Actually, the function was implemented as a pre-processor which inserts analysis operations in the target program code, or as a customized Java Virtual Machine (JVM). But these approaches are hard to implement and to maintain. We have applied Aspect-Oriented Programming (AOP) to collect dynamic information. Since collection of dynamic information affects over all target program, this functionality becomes a typical crosscutting concern, which is modularized as an aspect in AOP [4].

ADAS is a DC slicing tool for Java. This system consists of three subsystems, the Dynamic Information Analyzer subsystem, the PDG (*Program Dependence Graph*) Constructor subsystem and the Slice Calculation subsystem.

The Dynamic Information Analyzer subsystem is implemented as an aspect. A programmer debugging a Java program adds this aspect to the target program and compiles all sources using AspectJ[1]. When the programmer executes the target program with a test case input, the added aspect collects runtime information, such as field data dependence, method polymorphism resolution and exception handling, and outputs the result to a file. AOP approach is independent of JVM features, and we prefer this approach for usability and adaptability. Since the module of the dynamic analysis is written as an aspect, a programmer can easily extend the analysis aspect using inheritance mechanism of AspectJ and add the analysis aspect to the file list to be compiled. Recent IDEs, support to manage configuration of the files.

0-7695-1877-X/03 $17.00 © 2003 IEEE

The PDG Constructor subsystem reads information from the file and analyze Java source files to construct a PDG, a directed graph whose nodes represent statements in the source program, and whose edges denote dependence relations (data dependence or control dependence) between statements[5].

The Slice Calculation subsystem provides a graphical user interface. A source code viewer shows source code and slice criterions contained in the file. When a programmer selects a slice criterion, the system calculates the slice and indicates it in the viewer.

3. SPARS-J : Software Product Archiving, Analyzing, and Retrieving System for Java

SPARS-J is a retrieval system for Java components. It would be easily imagined that similar programs have been developed independently in different locations of the world or in different times in the history, without sharing knowledge of other programs. It is considered that a well-organized collection of programs or program components will improve productivity of the development and quality of the developed software products.

SPARS-J might be considered as a Google-like[2] system for software engineers. In this system, various Java source programs are collected, and they are stored in a component archive. Those components are ranked by the evaluation values (called Component Ranks[3]), which are determined by their use relations. A component searcher who wants to know about a definition or a usage of a component will give queries by keywords to SPARS-J. These queries are analyzed and the matched results are listed by the Component Ranks. By the Component Ranks, we consider that components with high reusability can be found effectively.

SPARS-J consists of two subsystems, Constructing Databases subsystem and Searching Components subsystem.

In Constructing Databases subsystem, a database for component search is built from Java source code files. Collected various Java source programs are analyzed syntactically and stored in the archive with information, such as all the appearance words, use class names and the metrics in each component. The appearance words are indexed to make a reverse dictionary for retrieval. The use class names are analyzed to determine use-relations between components. The metrics are used for measurement of a similarity between components. In software development process, we can imagine that a component may be reused with minor changes, by not simple copying. In order to calculate these components as one group, this subsystem measures similarity between components. As an example of a metric value, we use LOC, cyclomatic complexity, and so on. Similar components are packed into one group, and use relations associated to those components are also merged. All components(groups) are ranked by the evaluation values called Component Ranks, which are determined by their use relations, and the Component Rank of each component is also stored in the archive.

On the other hand, Searching Components subsystem provides a retrieval function for user. Basically, this subsystem performs component retrieval from all the appearing words including comments in source code files. However, a user can request to perform an advanced search according to the purpose of the user. For example, this subsystem can remove the components with which keywords appear only in its comment from a result, or extract the only components with which keywords appears in the definition of a class or a method, or extract only the use example.

A query specified by a user is analyzed and decomposed into a set of keywords. For each keyword, this subsystem checks the component with which the keyword appears by referring to reverse dictionary. A result is ordered by the Component Ranks, the user receives the result through the browser with the information of each components and a part of its code. Furthermore, the user may click the results to get detailed information on the search components, or may add keywords to perform further retrieval. In this way, the user can effectively find a component that is used most frequently and has high reusability.

References

[1] AspectJ Team, "The AspectJ Programming Guide", http://aspectj.org/doc/dist/progguide/

[2] google, http://www.google.com/

[3] K. Inoue et al.: "Component Rank: Relative Significance Rank for Software Component Search", to be appeared in Proceedings of ICSE 2003, Portland, Oregon, 2003.

[4] G. Kiczales et al.: "Aspect Oriented Programming", Proceedings of ECOOP, vol.1241 of LNCS, pp.220-242(1997).

[5] K. J. Ottenstein and L. M. Ottenstein: "The program dependence graph in a software development environment", Proceedings of SESPSDE, pp.177–184, Pittsburgh, Pennsylvania, April (1984).

[6] T. Takada et al.:"Dependence-Cache Slicing: A Program Slicing Method Using Lightweight Dynamic Information", Proceedings of IWPC2002, pp.169-177, Paris, France, June (2002).

[7] M. Weiser: "Program slicing", IEEE Transactions on Software Engineering, SE-10(4):352-357(1984).

Author Index